SOCIOLOGY
Your Compass for a New World

Third Canadian Edition

Robert J. Brym
University of Toronto

John Lie
University of California, Berkeley

Steven Rytina
McGill University

D1259952

NELSON / EDUCATION

NELSON / EDUCATION

Sociology: Your Compass for a New World, Third Canadian Edition
by Robert J. Brym, John Lie, and Steven Rytina

Associate Vice President, Editorial Director:
Evelyn Veitch

Editor-in-Chief:
Anne Williams

Executive Editor:
Laura Macleod

Senior Marketing Manager:
David Tonen

Developmental Editors:
Lily Kalcevich, Liisa Kelly

Photo Researcher and Permissions Coordinator:
Melody Tolson

Senior Content Production Manager:
Natalia Denesiuk Harris

Copy Editor:
Lisa Berland

Proofreader:
Dawn Hunter

Indexer:
Jin Tan

Production Coordinator:
Ferial Suleman

Design Director:
Ken Phipps

Managing Designer:
Franca Amore

Interior Design Modifications:
Peter Papayanakis

Cover Design:
Wil Bache, Peter Papayanakis

Cover Image:
Dusan Zidar/Shutterstock

Compositor:
Integra

Printer:
Transcontinental

COPYRIGHT © 2010, 2007 by Nelson Education Ltd.

Adapted from Robert J. Brym and John Lie, *Sociology: Your Compass for a New World*, Third Edition, published by Wadsworth, a division of Cengage Learning Inc. Copyright ©2007 by Wadsworth/ Cengage Learning.

Printed and bound in Canada
2 3 4 5 13 12 11 10

For more information contact Nelson Education Ltd., 1120 Birchmount Road, Toronto, Ontario, M1K 5G4. Or you can visit our Internet site at http://www.nelson.com

Statistics Canada information is used with the permission of Statistics Canada. Users are forbidden to copy this material and/or redisseminate the data, in an original or modified form, for commercial purposes, without the expressed permissions of Statistics Canada. Information on the availability of the wide range of data from Statistics Canada can be obtained from Statistics Canada's Regional Offices, its World Wide Web site at <http://www.statcan.ca>, and its toll-free access number 1-800-263-1136.

ALL RIGHTS RESERVED. No part of this work covered by the copyright herein may be reproduced, transcribed, or used in any form or by any means—graphic, electronic, or mechanical, including photocopying, recording, taping, Web distribution, or information storage and retrieval systems— without the written permission of the publisher.

For permission to use material from this text or product, submit all requests online at www.cengage.com/permissions. Further questions about permissions can be emailed to permissionrequest@cengage.com

Every effort has been made to trace ownership of all copyrighted material and to secure permission from copyright holders. In the event of any question arising as to the use of any material, we will be pleased to make the necessary corrections in future printings.

Library and Archives Canada Cataloguing in Publication Data

Brym, Robert J., 1951–
   Sociology : your compass for a new world / Robert J. Brym, John Lie, Steven Rytina.— 3rd Canadian ed.

Includes bibliographical references and index.
ISBN 978-0-17-650062-7

   1. Sociology—Textbooks. I. Lie, John II. Rytina, Steven III. Title.

HM586.B795 2009   301
C2008-907770-9

ISBN-13: 978-0-17-650062-7
ISBN-10: 0-17-650062-6

Dedication

Many authors seem to be afflicted with stoic family members who gladly allow them to spend endless hours buried in their work. I suffer no such misfortune. The members of my family have demanded that I focus on what really matters in life. I think that focus has made this a better book. I am deeply grateful to Rhonda Lenton, Shira Brym, Talia Lenton-Brym, and Ariella Lenton-Brym. I dedicate this book to them with thanks and love.

Robert J. Brym

For Charis Thompson, Thomas Cussins, Jessica Cussins, and Charlotte Lie, with thanks and love.

John Lie

For Lucia Benaquisto, with love and gratitude.

Steven Rytina

Robert J. Brym (pronounced "brim") was born in Saint John, New Brunswick, studied sociology in Canada and Israel, and received his Ph.D. from the University of Toronto, where he is now on faculty and where he especially enjoys teaching introductory sociology. He won the 2007 Northrop Frye Award for excellence in teaching and research, and in 2008 he became a Fellow of the Royal Society of Canada. His work has been translated into half a dozen languages. Bob's research focuses on the social bases of politics and social movements in Canada, Russia, and the Middle East. His major books include *Intellectuals and Politics* (London: Allen & Unwin, 1980); *From Culture to Power: The Sociology of English Canada,* with Bonnie Fox (Toronto: Oxford University Press, 1989); *The Jews of Moscow, Kiev, and Minsk,* with Rozalina Ryvkina (New York: New York University Press, 1994); and *Sociology as a Life or Death Issue* (Toronto: Nelson, 2008). He served as editor of *The Canadian Review of Sociology and Anthropology* (1986–89), *Current Sociology* (1993–97), and *East European Jewish Affairs* (2001–2005). He is now heading a research project on collective and state violence in Israel and Palestine, the first results of which have been published in *Social Forces, Political Science Quarterly,* and *The Canadian Journal of Sociology. Sociology: Your Compass for a New World* has been published in Canadian, American, Brazilian, and Australian editions.

John Lie (pronounced "lee") was born in South Korea, grew up in Japan and Hawaii, and attended Harvard University. Currently the Dean of International and Area Studies and the Class of 1959 Professor of Sociology at the University of California, Berkeley, he has taught at the University of Hawaii at Manoa, the University of Illinois at Urbana-Champaign, and Harvard University in the United States, as well as universities in Japan, South Korea, Taiwan, and New Zealand. His main research interests are comparative macrosociology and comparative race and ethnic relations. John's major publications include *Blue Dreams: Korean Americans and the Los Angeles Riots* (Cambridge, MA: Harvard University Press, 1998), *Multiethnic Japan* (Cambridge, MA: Harvard University Press, 2001), and *Modern Peoplehood* (Cambridge, MA: Harvard University Press, 2004). He has taught introductory sociology classes ranging in size from 3 to more than 700 students in several countries and hopes this book will stimulate your sociological imagination.

Steven Rytina (pronounced "rye-TEEN-a") was born in Pennsylvania, mostly grew up in Michigan, and completed his Ph.D. at the University of Michigan. From there, he took up positions at the State University of New York at Albany, and at Harvard University, where he and John Lie enjoyed many stimulating conversations and Friday night volleyball games. In 1989, he joined the sociology department at McGill University where he teaches today. His research interests are injustice and stratification, informed by a taste for formal models of scale and complexity. Representative publications include *Encounters with Unjust Authority,* with William Gamson and Bruce Fireman (Homewood, IL: Dorsey Press, 1982); "Scaling in Intergenerational Continuity of Occupation: Is Occupational Inheritance Ascriptive After All?" *American Journal of Sociology* (97, 6: 1992), pp. 1658–88; and "Is Occupational Mobility Declining in the United States?" *American Journal of Sociology* (78, 4: 2000), pp. 1227–76. He began teaching introductory sociology as a teaching assistant at Michigan. In 1995, he took over the course at McGill, where enrolment ranges as high as 350, as a change of pace from serving as the Associate Dean of his faculty. He found he enjoyed it so much that he continues to this day.

Brief Contents

Contents

A Compass for a New World

> It was the best of times, it was the worst of times, it was the age of wisdom, it was the age of foolishness, it was the epoch of belief, it was the epoch of incredulity, it was the season of Light, it was the season of Darkness, it was the spring of hope, it was the winter of despair, we had everything before us, we had nothing before us, we were all going direct to Heaven, we were all going direct the other way—in short, the period was so far like the present period, that some of its noisiest authorities insisted on its being received, for good or for evil, in the superlative degree of comparison only.
>
> – Charles Dickens, *A Tale of Two Cities* (2002 [1859])

Dickens refers to the end of the eighteenth century, yet he offers a prophetic description of the times in which we live. We, too, set sail at the dawn of an age of superlatives, an age of uncertainty.

The Soviet Union was formally dissolved on December 21, 1991. On that day we learned that even a seemingly vast superpower can collapse and splinter almost overnight. One of the world's leading historians wrote that the twentieth century ended with the fall of the USSR, ushering in a new century of mounting indeterminacy (Hobsbawm, 1994). As if to prove the point, scientists announced on June 26, 2000, that they had finished sequencing the human genome, beginning a new era of scientific breakthroughs. Yet shortly after, the United Nations forecast that 85 million people will die of AIDS by 2020, convincing us (if we had not already been convinced) that, despite remarkable medical advances, the plague is still with us. Then, on September 11, 2001, terrorists attacked the World Trade Center in New York and the Pentagon in Washington, D.C., killing about 3000 people. We saw the world's mood and its political and economic outlook buoyant one day, uncertain the next.

The world is an unpredictable place. It is especially disorienting for students just entering adulthood. We wrote this book to show undergraduates that sociology can help them make sense of their lives, however uncertain they may appear to be. We hope it will serve as their sociological compass in the new world they are entering as young adults. Moreover, we show that sociology can be a liberating practical activity, not just an abstract intellectual exercise. By revealing the opportunities and constraints we face, sociology can help us navigate our lives, teaching us who we are and what we can become in this particular social and historical context. We cannot know what the future will bring, but we can at least know the choices we confront and the likely consequences of our actions. From this point of view, sociology can help us create the best possible future. That has always been sociology's principal justification, and so it should be today.

Unique Features

We have tried to keep sociology's main purpose and relevance front and centre in this book. As a result, *Sociology: Your Compass for a New World* differs from other major introductory sociology textbooks in five ways:

1. ***Drawing connections between one's self and the social world.*** To varying degrees, all introductory sociology textbooks try to show students how their personal experiences are connected to the larger social world. However, we employ two devices to make these connections clearer than in other textbooks. First, we illustrate key sociological ideas by using fresh examples that resonate deeply with student interests and experiences. For

example, we conclude our discussion of culture by showing how radical subcultures often become commercialized, focusing on the development of rap and heavy metal music. We examine the causes and consequences of glamorizing thin bodies in advertising. To demonstrate how functionalists study religion, we discuss the Stanley Cup finals. To illustrate the use of two- and three-variable tables, we study data on the number of sex partners people had in the past year. To characterize contemporary processes of urbanization, we consider the growth of theme parks. To demonstrate the reach of globalization processes, we trace the use of English slang among Japanese teenagers. To portray various aspects of the mass media, we investigate the growth of the World Wide Web and its convergence with television. We think these examples speak directly to today's students about important sociological ideas in terms they understand, thus making the connection between self and society clear.

We also developed several pedagogical features to draw the connection between students' experiences and the larger social world. "Where Do You Fit In?" is a question we ask in every chapter. In this feature, we repeatedly challenge students to consider how and why their own lives conform to, or deviate from, various patterns of social relations and actions. "It's Your Choice" is a feature of most chapters that sets out public policy alternatives on a range of pressing social issues. It teaches students that sociology can be a matter of the most urgent practical importance. Students also learn they can have a say in the development of public policy. "Sociology at the Movies" takes a universal and popular element of contemporary culture and renders it sociologically relevant. We provide brief reviews of movies, most of them recent releases, and highlight the sociological insights they contain.

"It's Your Choice" teaches students that sociology can have urgent practical importance—and that they can have a say in the development of public policy.

"Where Do You Fit In?" challenges students to consider how and why their own lives conform to various patterns of social relations and actions.

Students will be intrigued by **"Sociology at the Movies"**—this look at sociological insights that can be gleaned from current (and some classic) films demonstrates sociology's vitality and relevance to their lives.

2. **What to think versus how to think.** All textbooks teach students *what* to think about a subject and *how* to think about it from a particular disciplinary perspective. In our judgment, however, introductory sociology textbooks usually place too much stress on the "what" and not enough on the "how." The result: They sometimes read more like encyclopedias than enticements to look at the world in a new way. We have tipped the balance in the other direction. To be sure, *Sociology: Your Compass for a New World* contains definitions and literature reviews. It features standard pedagogical aids, such as a list of chapter aims at the beginning of each chapter and a "Summary," a list of "Key Terms," a set of "Questions to Consider," and a list of "Web Resources" at the end of each chapter. However, we devote more space than other authors to showing how sociologists think. We typically relate an anecdote to highlight an issue's importance, present contending interpretations of the issue, and then

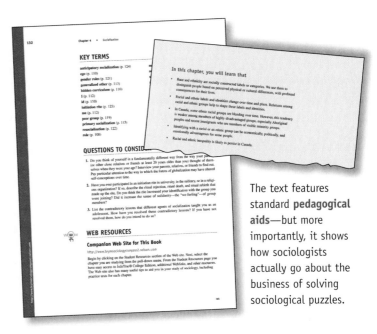

The text features standard **pedagogical aids**—but more importantly, it shows how sociologists actually go about the business of solving sociological puzzles.

adduce data to judge the merits of the various interpretations. We do not just refer to tables and graphs but also analyze them When evidence warrants, we reject theories and endorse others. Thus, many sections of the book read more like a simplified journal article than an encyclopedia. If all this sounds like a "lite" version of what sociologists do professionally, then we have achieved our aim: to present a less antiseptic, more realistic, and therefore intrinsically exciting account of how sociologists practise their craft. Said differently, one of the strengths of this book is that it does not present sociology as a set of immutable truths carved in stone tablets. Instead, it shows how sociologists actually go about the business of solving sociological puzzles.

3. **Objectivity versus subjectivity.** Sociologists since Max Weber have understood that sociologists—indeed, all scientists—are members of society whose thinking and research are influenced by the social and historical context in which they work. Yet introductory sociology textbooks present a stylized and not very sociological view of the research process. They tend to emphasize sociology's objectivity and the hypothetico-deductive method of reasoning, for the most part ignoring the more subjective factors that go into the research mix (Lynch and Bogen, 1997). We think this emphasis is a pedagogical error. In our own teaching, we have found that drawing the connection between objectivity and subjectivity in sociological research makes the discipline more appealing to students. It shows how research issues are connected to the lives of real flesh-and-blood women and men, and how sociology is related to students' existential concerns. Therefore, in each chapter of *Sociology: Your Compass for a New World*, we feature a "Personal Anecdote" that explains how certain sociological issues first arose in our own minds. We also place the ideas of important sociological figures in social and historical context. We show how sociological methodologies serve as a reality check, but we also make it clear that socially grounded personal concerns often lead sociologists to decide which aspects of reality are worth checking on in the first place. We believe *Sociology: Your Compass for a New World* is unique in presenting a realistic and balanced account of the role of objectivity and subjectivity in the research process.

Personal Anecdotes, like Robert Brym's "How to Spark a Riot," show how sociological issues first arose in the minds of the authors. Here, Brym's high-school experience with injustice and protest led to a lifelong interest in why people act (or don't act) to change society.

The **"Global Perspective"** feature in each chapter reinforces the importance of diversity and globalization themes for students.

"Technology Bytes" emphasizes the benefits and disadvantages of science and technology.

4. ***Diversity and a global perspective.*** It is gratifying to see how much less parochial introductory sociology textbooks are today than they were two decades ago. Contemporary textbooks highlight gender and race issues. They broaden the student's understanding of the world by comparing Canada with other societies. They show how global processes affect local issues and how local issues affect global processes. *Sociology: Your Compass for a New World* is no different in this regard. We have made diversity and globalization prominent themes of this book. We incorporate a "Global Perspective" feature in each chapter. We make frequent and effective use of cross-national comparisons between Canada and countries as diverse as India and Sweden. And we remain sensitive to gender and race issues throughout. This has been easy for us because we are members of racial and ethnic minority groups. We are multilingual. We have lived in other countries for extended periods. And we have published widely on countries other than Canada. As you will see in the following pages, our backgrounds have enabled us to bring greater depth to issues of diversity and globalization than other textbooks.

5. ***Currency.*** Every book bears the imprint of its time. It is significant, therefore, that the first editions of most major North American introductory sociology textbooks were published about 20 years ago. In 1990, not many more than 10 percent of Canadians owned personal computers. The World Wide Web did not exist. Genetic engineering was in its infancy. The USSR was a major world power. *Sociology: Your Compass for a New World* is one of the first North American introductory sociology textbooks of the twenty-first century, and it is the most up to date. This is reflected in the currency of our illustrations and references. For instance, we do not just recommend a few websites at the end of each chapter, as is typical in other introductory sociology textbooks. Instead, Web resources form an integral part of this book; fully one-sixth of our citations are websites. The currency of this book is also reflected in our "Technology Bytes" feature, which emphasizes the benefits and disadvantages of science and technology as they apply to each of sociology's major sub-fields. It is reflected in the fact that we devote entire chapters to "The Mass Media" and "Technology and the Global Environment." And it is reflected in the book's theoretical structure.

It made sense in the 1980s to simplify the sociological universe for introductory students by claiming that three main theoretical perspectives (functionalism, symbolic interactionism, and conflict theory) pervade all areas of the discipline. By now, however, that approach is no longer adequate. Functionalism is less influential than it once was. Feminism is an important theoretical perspective in its own right. Conflict theory and symbolic interactionism have become internally differentiated. For example, there is no longer a single conflict theory of politics but at least three important variants. Highly influential new theoretical perspectives, such as postmodernism and social constructionism, have emerged, and not all of them fit neatly into the old categories. *Sociology: Your Compass for a New World* incorporates not just the latest research findings in sociology but also recent theoretical innovations that are given insufficient attention in other major textbooks.

New in the Third Canadian Edition

We have been gratified and moved by the positive response to the first and second Canadian editions of this book. At the same time, we benefited from the constructive criticisms generously offered by numerous readers and reviewers.

Sociology: Your Compass for a New World, Third Canadian Edition, is a response to many of their suggestions. The main innovations in this edition include the following:

- Throughout, we incorporated data from the 2006 Census of Canada published as of May 1, 2008, to keep the book as up-to-date as possible. We also added new research findings where appropriate.
- "Sociology at the Movies" was one of the most popular features of earlier editions among both faculty members and students. Building on this popularity, we wrote nine new movie reviews, all of which teach students to see the movies and the society in which they live from a fresh, sociological perspective.
- For the convenience of students, we placed all definitions in the margins, bolded defined terms in the index, and posted a cumulative glossary on the book's website.

Ancillaries

A full range of high-quality ancillaries has been prepared to help instructors and students get the most out of *Sociology: Your Compass for a New World.*

Supplements for Instructors

- ***Instructor's Manual.*** The Instructor's Manual contains lecture outlines, supplemental lecture material, suggested activities for students, and Internet and InfoTrac® College Edition exercises. In addition, the manual reviews Nelson's "Think Outside the Book" video series and includes discussion questions to be used with each component. Edit and augment the Instructor's Manual (Word files) with your own notes and handouts.
- ***Microsoft PowerPoint® series.*** The PowerPoint series that accompanies the book clearly outlines each chapter of the text and reproduces all of the textbook's figures and tables. Instructors can access supplementary graphics that allow them to develop themes introduced in the text.
- ***NETA Test Bank.*** In most college and university courses, a large percentage of student assessment is based on multiple-choice testing. But many instructors use multiple-choice reluctantly, believing that it is a methodology best used for testing what a student *remembers* rather than what she or he has *learned.* Furthermore, the quality of publisher-supplied test banks can vary.

  Nelson Education Ltd. believes that a good quality multiple-choice test bank can test not just what students remember, but *higher-level thinking* skills as well. Recognizing the importance of multiple-choice testing in today's classroom, Nelson has created the Nelson Education Testing Advantage program (NETA) to ensure the high quality of our test banks.

  The test bank for *Sociology: Your Compass for a New World,* Third Canadian Edition, was developed under the Nelson Education Testing Advantage. NETA was created in partnership with David DiBattista, a 3M National Teaching Fellow and professor of psychology at Brock University. NETA ensures that test-bank authors have had training in two areas: developing clear multiple-choice test questions while avoiding common errors in construction, and creating multiple-choice test questions that "get beyond remembering" to assess higher-level thinking.

  The outcome of NETA development is that as you select multiple-choice questions from your Nelson test bank for inclusion in tests, you can easily identify whether items are memory-based or require your students to engage in higher-level thinking. By making your selections appropriately, you can construct tests that contain the proportion of recall and higher-level questions that reflects your personal instructional goals.

  All NETA test banks include David DiBattista's guide for instructors, "Multiple Choice Tests: Getting Beyond Remembering." This guide has been designed to assist you in using Nelson test banks to achieve your desired outcomes in the classroom.
- ***Instructor's Resource CD.*** ISBN 978-0-17-647442-3. This all-in-one resource includes each of the essential items listed above.

- ***InfoTrac® College Edition.*** Ignite discussions or augment your lectures with the latest developments in sociology and societal change. Create your own course reader by selecting articles or by using the search keywords provided at the end of each chapter. *InfoTrac® College Edition* (available with this text) gives you and your students four months of free access to an easy-to-use online database of reliable, full-length articles (not abstracts) from hundreds of top academic journals and popular sources. Among the journals available twenty-four hours a day, seven days a week are the *Canadian Review of Sociology and Anthropology,* the *Canadian Journal of Sociology, Canadian Ethnic Studies, Public Policy,* the *American Journal of Sociology, Social Forces, Social Research,* and *Sociology.* Contact your Nelson representative for more information. *InfoTrac® College Edition* is available only to North American college and university students. Journals are subject to change.

Classroom Presentation Tools for the Instructor

- **JoinIn™ on TurningPoint®.** Transform your lecture into an interactive student experience with JoinIn. Combined with your choice of keypad systems, JoinIn turns your Microsoft PowerPoint slides into audience response software. With a click on a hand-held device, students can respond to multiple-choice questions, short polls, interactive exercises, and peer-review questions. You can also take attendance, check student comprehension of concepts, collect student demographics to better assess student needs, and even administer quizzes. In addition, there are interactive text-specific slide sets that you can modify and merge with any of your own PowerPoint lecture slides. This tool is available to qualified adopters at http://www.turningtechnologies.com/groupresponsesystemsupport/downloads.cfm.
- ***Think Outside the Book: The Nelson Sociology Video Collection.*** This set of video segments, each 5 to 30 minutes in length, was created to stimulate discussion of topics raised in sociology. Produced in conjunction with Face to Face Media (Vancouver), the Jesuit Communication Project (Toronto), and the National Film Board of Canada, the selections have been edited to optimize their impact in the classroom. Many of the selections are taken from films that have won national and international awards.

Supplements for Students

- CengageNOW™

    http://hed.nelson.com

    This online diagnostic tool identifies each student's unique needs with a pretest that generates a personalized study plan for each chapter, helping students focus on concepts they're having the most difficulty mastering. Students then take a posttest to measure their understanding of the material. An instructor gradebook is available to track and monitor student progress.
- ***Society in Question,*** Fifth Edition, by Robert J. Brym, provides balanced coverage of the approaches and methods in current sociology as well as unique and surprising perspectives on many major sociological topics. All readings have been chosen for their ability to speak directly to contemporary Canadian students about how sociology can enable them to make sense of their lives in a rapidly changing world.
- ***Footprints: Introdyctory Readings in Sociology,*** Eleventh Edition, by Leonard Cargan and Jeanne H. Ballantine, is an anthology of sociological studies that provides a link between theoretical sociology and everyday life. This book offers classical, contemporary, popular, and multicultural articles in each chapter to show students a wide range of perspectives. Articles address today's most important and relevant social issues, such as violence, welfare reform, technology globalization, and terrorism. Each article is preceded by a short introductory essay, a serial of guideline questions, and a list of glossary terms found in the article, thus grounding the student's reading experience in a solid sociological framework.

- *Sociology as a Life or Death Issue,* First Canadian Edition, was written by Robert J. Brym. In a series of beautifully written essays on hip-hop culture, Palestinian suicide bombers, and the plight of hurricane victims in the Caribbean region and on the coast of the Gulf of Mexico, Robert Brym introduces sociology by analyzing the social causes of death. In doing so, he reveals the powerful social forces that help to determine who lives and who dies, and demonstrates the promise of a well-informed sociological understanding of the world. This brief and inexpensive volume is an eye-opener, an inspiration, and a guide for students of sociology and for anyone with an inquiring mind and hopes for a better world for future generations.
- **Website to accompany** *Sociology: Your Compass for a New World*
  http://www.compass3e.nelson.com
  Companion Web Site. In terms of substance, visual appeal, and interactivity, the book's website contains an unusually rich collection of materials. All of the materials on the site are closely tied to themes introduced in the text. For each chapter of the book, the site features three online tests, one online research project, one interactive exercise, and four carefully chosen Web links. A separate set of online tests is provided for each of the interactive exercises. In addition, the site contains more than 100 lectures and interviews on a wide variety of sociological topics, many of them featuring leading sociologists. Students hear the lectures and interviews using the free RealPlayer™ plug-in. A "Research Centre" offers students easy access to a full range of official statistics. Instructors can download the Instructor's Manual and the Microsoft® PowerPoint® series directly from the site.

Acknowledgments

Anyone who has gone sailing knows that when you embark on a long voyage you need more than a compass. Among other things, you need a helm operator blessed with a strong sense of direction and an intimate knowledge of likely dangers. You need crew members who know all the ropes and can use them to keep things intact and in their proper place. And you need sturdy hands to raise and lower the sails. On the voyage to complete the third Canadian edition of this book, the crew demonstrated all these skills. We are especially grateful to our acquisitions editor, Cara Yarzab, who saw this book's promise from the outset, understood clearly the direction we had to take to develop its potential, and on several occassions steered us clear of threatening shoals. We are also deeply indebted to the following crew members:

Lily Kalcevich and Liisa Kelly, developmental editors
Natalia Denesiuk Harris, senior content production manager
David Tonen, senior marketing manager
Lisa Berland, copy editor
Dawn Hunter, proofreader
Melody Tolson, permissions coordinator and photo researcher

Also, we would like to thank the following reviewers:

Ron McGivern	Thompson Rivers University
Laurie Forbes	Lakehead University
Daniel Popowich	Mohawk College
Juergen Dankwort	Kwantlen Polytechnic University

Robert J. Brym

John Lie

Steven Rytina

Foundations

CHAPTER

1

A Sociological Compass

In this chapter, you will learn that

- The causes of human behaviour lie mostly in the patterns of social relations that surround and permeate us.

- Sociology is the systematic study of human behaviour in the social context.

- Sociologists examine the connection between social relations and personal troubles.

- Sociologists are often motivated to do research by the desire to improve people's lives. At the same time, sociologists use scientific methods to test their ideas.

- Sociology originated during the Industrial Revolution. The founders of sociology diagnosed the massive social transformations of their day. They also suggested ways of overcoming the social problems created by the Industrial Revolution.

- Today's Postindustrial Revolution similarly challenges us. Sociology clarifies the scope, direction, and significance of social change. It also suggests ways of dealing with the social problems created by the Postindustrial Revolution.

- At the personal level, sociology can help to clarify the opportunities and constraints we all face. It suggests what each of us can become in today's social and historical context.

INTRODUCTION

Why You Need a Compass for a New World

PERSONAL ANECDOTE

"When I was a child, a cleaning lady came to our house twice a month," Robert Brym recalls. "Her name was Lena White, and she was what we then called an 'Indian.' I was fond of Lena because she possessed two apparently magical powers. First, she could let the ash at the end of her cigarette grow five centimetres before it fell off. I sometimes used to play where Lena was working just to see how long she could scrub, vacuum, climb the stepladder, and chatter before the ash made its inevitable descent to the floor. Second, Lena could tell stories. My mother would serve us lunch at the kitchen table. During dessert, as we sipped tea with milk, Lena would spin tales about Gluskap, the Creator of the world.

"I liked Gluskap because he was mischievous and enormously powerful. He fought giants, drove away monsters, taught people how to hunt and farm, and named the stars. But he also got into trouble and learned from his mistakes. For example, one day the wind was blowing so hard Gluskap couldn't paddle his canoe into the bay to hunt ducks. So he found the source of the wind: the flapping wings of the Wind Eagle. He then tricked the Wind Eagle into getting stuck in a crevice where he could flap no more. Now Gluskap could go hunting. However, the air soon grew so hot he found it difficult to breathe. The water became dirty and began to smell bad, and there was so much foam on it he found it hard to paddle. When he complained to his grandmother, she explained that the wind was needed to cool the air, wash the earth, and move the waters to keep them clean. And so Gluskap freed the Wind Eagle and the winds returned to the earth. Gluskap decided it was better to wait for good weather and then go duck hunting, rather than to conquer the winds.

"Like the tale of the Wind Eagle, many of the Gluskap stories Lena told me were about the need for harmony among humans and between humans and nature. You can imagine my surprise, therefore, when I got to school and learned about the European exploration of what was called the New World. My teachers taught me all about the glories of the *conquest* of nature—and of other people. I learned that in the New World, a Native population perhaps a hundredth as large as Europe's occupied a territory more than four times larger. I was taught that the New World was unimaginably rich in resources. European rulers saw that by controlling it they could increase their power and importance. Christians recognized new possibilities for spreading their religion. Explorers discerned fresh opportunities for rewarding adventures. A wave of excitement swelled as word spread of the New World's vast potential and challenges. I, too, became excited as I heard stories of conquest quite unlike the tales of Gluskap. Of course, I learned little about the violence required to conquer the New World."

In the 1950s I was caught between thrilling stories of conquest and reflective stories that questioned the wisdom of conquest. Today, I think many people are in a similar position. On the one hand, we feel like the European explorers because we, too, have reached the frontiers of a New World. Like them, we are full of anticipation. Our New World is one of instant long-distance communication, global economies and cultures, weakening nation-states, and technological advances that often make the daily news seem like reports from a distant planet. In a fundamental way, the world is not the same place it was just 50 years ago. Orbiting telescopes that peer to the fringes of the universe, human genetic code laid bare like a road map, fibre optic cable that carries a trillion bits of information per second, and spacecraft that transport robots to Mars help to make this a New World.

On the other hand, we understand that not all is hope and bright horizons. Our anticipation is mixed with dread. Gluskap stories make more sense than ever. Scientific breakthroughs are announced almost daily, but the global environment has never been in worse shape and AIDS is now the leading cause of death in Africa. Marriages and nations unexpectedly break up and then reconstitute themselves in new and unanticipated forms. We celebrate the advances made by women and minority groups only to find that some people oppose their progress, sometimes violently. Waves of people migrate between continents, establishing cooperation but also conflict between previously separated groups. New technologies make work more interesting and creative for some, offering unprecedented opportunities to become rich and famous. They also make jobs more onerous and routine for others. The standard of living goes up for many people but stagnates for many more.

Amid all this contradictory news, good and bad, uncertainty about the future prevails. That is why my colleagues and I wrote this book. We set out to show undergraduates that sociology can help them make sense of their lives, however uncertain they may appear to be. Five hundred years ago, the early European explorers of North and South America set themselves the task of mapping the contours of the New World. We set ourselves a similar task here. Their frontiers were physical; ours are social. Their maps were geographical; ours are sociological. But in terms of functionality, our maps are much like theirs. All maps allow us to find our place in the world and see ourselves in the context of larger forces. *Sociological* maps, as the famous American sociologist C. Wright Mills wrote, allow us to "grasp the interplay of [people] and society, of biography and history" (Mills, 1959: 4). This book, then, shows you how to draw sociological maps so you can see your place in the world, figure out how to navigate through it, and perhaps discover how to improve it. It is your sociological compass.

We emphasize that sociology can be a liberating practical activity, not just an abstract intellectual exercise. By revealing the opportunities and constraints you face, sociology can help teach you who you are and what you can become in today's social and historical context. We cannot know what the future will bring, but we can at least know the choices we confront and the likely consequences of our actions. From this point of view, sociology can help us create the best possible future. That has always been sociology's principal justification, and so it should be today.

The Goals of This Chapter

This chapter has three goals:

1. The first goal is to illustrate the power of sociology to dispel foggy assumptions and help us see the operation of the social world more clearly. To that end, we examine a phenomenon that at first glance appears to be solely the outcome of breakdowns in *individual* functioning: suicide. We show that, in fact, *social* relations powerfully influence suicide rates. This exercise introduces you to what is unique about the sociological perspective.

2. The chapter's second goal is to show that, from its origins, sociological research has been motivated by a desire to improve the social world. Thus, sociology is not just a dry, academic exercise but also a means of charting a better course for society. At the same time, however, sociologists use scientific methods to test their ideas, thus increasing the validity of the results. We illustrate these points by briefly analyzing the work of the founders of the discipline.

3. The chapter's third goal is to suggest that sociology can help you come to grips with your century, just as it helped the founders of sociology deal with theirs. Today we are witnessing massive and disorienting social changes. As was the case a hundred years ago, sociologists now try to understand social phenomena and suggest credible ways of improving society. By promising to make sociology relevant to you, this chapter is an open invitation to participate in sociology's challenge.

Before showing how sociology can help you understand and improve your world, we briefly examine the problem of suicide. That examination will help illustrate how the sociological perspective can clarify and sometimes overturn common-sense beliefs.

THE SOCIOLOGICAL PERSPECTIVE

Analyzing suicide sociologically tests the claim that sociology takes a unique, surprising, and enlightening perspective on social events. After all, suicide appears to be a supremely antisocial and non-social act. First, it is condemned by nearly everyone in society. Second, it is typically committed in private, far from the public's intrusive glare. Third, it is comparatively rare: In 2004, there were about 11 suicides for every 100 000 people in Canada (compared with the world average of about 16 suicides per 100 000 people; see Figure 1.1). And, finally, when you think about why people commit such acts, you are likely to focus on their individual states of mind rather than on the state of society. In other words, we are usually interested in the aspects of specific individuals' lives that caused them to become depressed or angry enough to do something as awful as killing themselves. We do not usually think about the patterns of social relations that might encourage or inhibit such actions in general. If sociology can reveal the hidden social causes of such an apparently non-social and antisocial phenomenon, there must be something to it!

Alex Colville's *Pacific* (1967)

The Sociological Explanation of Suicide

At the end of the nineteenth century, Émile Durkheim (1951 [1897]) demonstrated that suicide is more than just an individual act of desperation that results from a psychological disorder, as was commonly believed at the time. Suicide rates, Durkheim showed, are strongly influenced by social forces.

Durkheim made his case by examining the association between rates of suicide and rates of psychological disorder for different groups. The idea that psychological disorder causes suicide is supported, he reasoned, only if suicide rates tend to be high where rates of psychological disorder are high, and

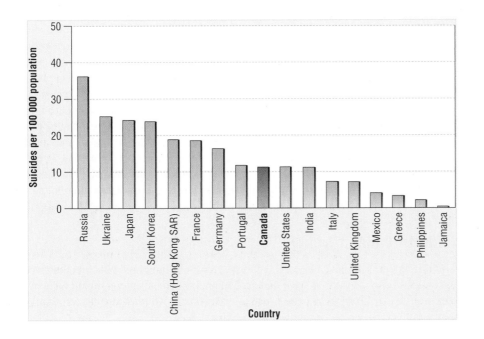

FIGURE 1.1
Suicide Rates, Selected Countries, circa 2004

Source: Rates were calculated based on data from World Health Organization, 2007, "Suicide Rates per 100,000 by Country, Year, and Sex (Table), Most Recent Year Available as of 2007." Retrieved January 3, 2008 (http://www.who.int/mental_health/prevention/suicide_rates/en/index.html).

FIGURE 1.2

Durkheim's Theory of Suicide

Durkheim argued that the suicide rate declines and then rises as social solidarity increases.

Durkheim called suicide in high-solidarity settings *altruistic*. Soldiers knowingly giving up their lives to protect comrades commit altruistic suicide. Suicide in low-solidarity settings is *egoistic* or *anomic*. *Egoistic suicide* results from the poor integration of people into society because of weak social ties to others. Someone who is unemployed is more likely to commit suicide than someone who is employed because the unemployed person has weaker social ties. *Anomic suicide* occurs when vague norms govern behaviour. The rate of anomic suicide is likely to be high among people living in a society lacking a widely shared code of morality.

Social solidarity refers to (1) the degree to which group members share beliefs and values, and (2) the intensity and frequency of their interaction.

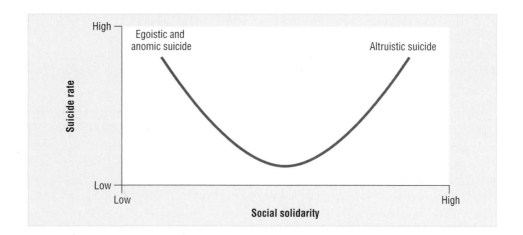

low where rates of psychological disorder are low. But his analysis of European government statistics, hospital records, and other sources revealed nothing of the kind. He discovered, for example, that there were slightly more women than men in insane asylums, but there were four male suicides for every female suicide. Jews had the highest rate of psychological disorder among the major religious groups in France, but they also had the lowest suicide rate. Psychological disorders occurred most frequently when a person reached maturity, but suicide rates increased steadily with age.

Clearly, suicide rates and rates of psychological disorder did not vary directly. In fact, they often appeared to vary inversely. Why? Durkheim argued that suicide rates varied as a result of differences in the degree of **social solidarity** in different categories of the population. According to Durkheim, the more beliefs and values a group's members share, and the more frequently and intensely they interact, the more social solidarity the group has. In turn, the more social solidarity a group has, the more firmly anchored individuals are to the social world and the less likely they are to take their own life if adversity strikes. In other words, Durkheim expected high-solidarity groups to have lower suicide rates than low-solidarity groups did—at least up to a certain point (see Figure 1.2).

To support his argument, Durkheim showed that married adults are half as likely as unmarried adults are to commit suicide. That is because marriage creates social ties and a kind of moral cement that bind the individual to society. Similarly, he argued that women are less likely to commit suicide than men are because women are more involved in the intimate social relations of family life. Jews, Durkheim wrote, are less likely to commit suicide than Christians are because centuries of persecution have turned them into a group that is more defensive and tightly knit. And the elderly are more prone than the young and the middle-aged are to take their own lives in the face of misfortune, because they are most likely to live alone, to have lost a spouse or partner, and to lack a job and a wide network of friends. In general, Durkheim wrote, "suicide varies with the degree of integration of the social groups of which the individual forms a part" (Durkheim, 1951 [1897]: 209). Of course, his generalization tells us nothing about why any particular individual may take his or her life. That explanation is the province of psychology. But it does tell us that a person's likelihood of committing suicide decreases with the degree to which he or she is anchored in society. And it says something surprising and uniquely sociological about how and why the suicide rate varies across groups.

Suicide in Canada Today

Durkheim's theory is not just a historical curiosity; it sheds light on the factors that account for variations in suicide rates today. Consider Figure 1.3, which shows suicide rates by age and sex in Canada. Comparing rates for men and women, we immediately see that, as in

Durkheim's France, men are about four times as likely as women are to commit suicide. In other respects, however, the Canadian data differ from the French data of more than a century ago. For example, when Durkheim wrote, suicide was extremely rare among youth. In Canada today, it is much more common, having increased substantially since the 1960s.

Although the rate of youth suicide was low in Durkheim's France, his theory of social solidarity helps us understand why it has risen in Canada. In brief, shared moral principles and strong social ties have eroded since the early 1960s, especially for Canada's youth. Consider the following facts:

Strong social bonds decrease the probability that a person will commit suicide if adversity strikes.

- Church, synagogue, mosque, and temple attendance is down, particularly among young people. Well over half of Canadians attended religious services weekly in the 1960s. Today the figure is below one-third and is only 15 percent for people born after 1960.
- Unemployment is up, again especially for youth. Thus, the unemployment rate was around 3 percent for most of the 1960s. It rose steadily to about 10 percent for most of the 1990s and reached 13.4 percent in 1994. Since then, the unemployment rate has declined, but it remains nearly twice as high for Canadians under the age of 25 as it is for Canadians above the age of 24 (in 2006, 11.6 percent compared with 6.3 percent).
- The rate of divorce has increased sixfold since the early 1960s. Births outside marriage are also much more common than they used to be. As a result, children are more often brought up in single-parent families now than in the past. This suggests that they enjoy less frequent and intimate social interaction with parents and less adult supervision.

In sum, the figures cited above suggest that the level of social solidarity is now lower than it was just a few decades ago, especially for young people. Less firmly rooted in society, and less likely to share moral standards, young people in Canada today are more likely than they were four decades ago to take their own lives if they happen to find themselves in a deep personal crisis (see also Box 1.1 on page 8).

FIGURE 1.3
Suicide Rates by Age and Sex, Canada, 2004

Sources: Statistics Canada, 2008, CANSIM, Table 102-0540. "Deaths by Cause, Chapter XX: External Causes of Morbidity and Mortality (V01 to Y89), Age, Group and Sex, Canada, Annual (Number) (44814 series)." Retrieved January 3, 2008 (http://www.statcan.ca/english/freepub/84F0209XIE/2003000/related.htm; Estimates of Population (2001 Census and Administrative Data), by Age Group and Sex, Canada, Provinces and Territories, Health Regions (June 2005 Boundaries) and Peer Groups, Annually (Number)." Retrieved January 3, 2008 (http://dc1.chass.utoronto.ca.myaccess.library.utnoronto.ca/cgi-bin/cansimdim).

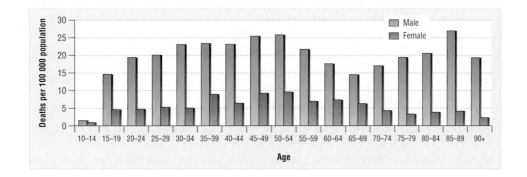

BOX 1.1
It's Your Choice

Suicide and the Innu of Labrador

The Canadians with the highest suicide rate are Aboriginal peoples. For example, the suicide rate of Aboriginal youth is five to six times as high as the national average and for Inuit youth it is 11 times as high. Suicide is the single greatest cause of injury-related deaths for Aboriginal people (Health Canada, 2004). Among Canada's Aboriginal peoples, the Innu of Labrador have the highest suicide rate. They are, in fact, the most suicide-prone people in the world. Among the Innu, the suicide rate is nearly 13 times as high as for all Canadians (Rogan, 2001; Samson, Wilson, and Mazower, 1999).

Durkheim's theory of suicide helps explain the Innu people's tragic propensity to commit suicide. Over the past half-century, the Innu's traditional norms and values have been destroyed. Moreover, the Innu have been prevented from participating in stable and meaningful patterns of social interaction. In other words, social solidarity among the Innu has been cut to an abysmally low level.

How did this happen? Historically, the Innu were a nomadic people who relied on hunting and trapping for their livelihood. In the mid-1950s, however, shortly after Newfoundland and Labrador became part of Canada, the provincial and federal governments were eager to gain more control of traditional Innu land so as to encourage economic development. Government officials felt that if new roads, mines, lumbering operations, hydroelectric projects, and low-level flight-training facilities for NATO air forces were to be built, the Innu would have to be concentrated in settlements. Furthermore, government officials believed that, to function in these new settlements, the Innu would have to learn practical and

cultural skills associated with a modern industrial society. As a result, governments put tremendous pressure on the Innu to give up their traditional way of life and settle in such places as Davis Inlet and Sheshatshui, the two communities where about 85 percent of the Innu now reside.[1]

In the new communities, Canadian laws, schools, and churches strongly discouraged the Innu from hunting, practising their religion, and raising their children in the traditional way. For example, Canadian hunting regulations limited Innu access to their age-old livelihood. Priests are known to have beaten children who missed church or school to go hunting, thus introducing interpersonal violence into a culture that formerly knew none. Teachers transmitted North American and European skills and culture, often denigrating Innu practices. In effect, Canadian authorities staged an assault on Innu culture as a whole. At the same time, few alternative jobs existed in the new communities. Most Innu wound up living in despair and on welfare. In the

absence of work, and lacking the stabilizing influence of their traditional culture, a people long known for nonviolence and their cooperative spirit became victims of widespread family breakdown, sexual abuse, drunkenness, and alcohol-related illness. Today in Sheshatshui, at least 20 percent of the children regularly get high by sniffing gasoline. In Davis Inlet, the figure is nearly 60 percent.

What is to be done about the tragedy of the Innu people? A study conducted in 1984 showed that a movement among the Innu to return to the land and their traditional hunting practices for up to seven months a year led to a dramatic improvement in their health. They lived a vigorous outdoor life. Alcohol abuse stopped. Diet improved. Their emotional and social environment stabilized and became meaningful. Suicide was unknown (Samson, Wilson, and Mazower, 1999: 25).

Unfortunately, a big political obstacle stands in the way of the Innu returning to their traditional lifestyle on a wide scale. Simply put, the governments of Canada and New-foundland and Labrador will not allow it. A widespread Innu return to the land conflicts with government and private economic development plans. For instance, the Lower Churchill Falls hydroelectric project (the second-biggest hydroelectric project in the world) and the Voisey's Bay nickel mine (the world's biggest deposit of nickel) are located in the middle of traditional Innu hunting and burial grounds. The Innu are vigor-ously attempting to regain control of their land and what happens to it. They also want to be able to decide *on their own* when and how to use Canadian health services, training facilities, and the like. Whether some compromise can be worked out between government and private plans for economic development and the continuity of the Innu people is unclear. What is clear is that, as a Canadian citizen, the outcome is partly your choice.

From Personal Troubles to Social Structures

You have known for a long time that you live in a society. But until now, you may not have fully appreciated that society also lives in you. That is, patterns of social relations affect your innermost thoughts and feelings, influence your actions, and thus help shape who you are. As we have seen, one such pattern of social relations is the level of social solidarity characteristic of the various groups to which you belong.

Sociologists call relatively stable patterns of social relations **social structures.** One of the sociologist's main tasks is to identify and explain the connection between people's personal troubles and the social structures in which people are embedded. This is harder work than it may seem at first. In everyday life, we usually see things mainly from our own point of view. Our experiences seem unique to each of us. If we think about them at all, social structures may appear remote and impersonal. To see how social structures influence us, we require sociological training.

An important step in broadening our sociological awareness involves recognizing that three levels of social structure surround and permeate us. Think of these structures as concentric circles radiating out from you:

1. **Microstructures** are patterns of intimate social relations. They are formed during face-to-face interaction. Families, friendship circles, and work associations are all examples of microstructures.

   Understanding the operation of microstructures can be useful. Let's say you are looking for a job. You might think you would do best to ask as many close friends and rel-atives as possible for leads and contacts. However, sociological research shows that people you know well are likely to know many of the same people. After asking a couple of close connections for help landing a job, you would therefore do best to ask more remote acquaintances for leads and contacts. People to whom you are *weakly* connected (and who are weakly connected among themselves) are more likely to know *different* groups of people. Therefore, they will give you more information about job possibilities and ensure that word about your job search spreads farther. You are more likely to find a job faster if you understand "the strength of weak ties" in microstructural settings (Granovetter, 1973).

2. **Macrostructures** are patterns of social relations that lie outside and above your circle of intimates and acquaintances.[2] Macrostructures include class relations, bureaucracies, and **patriarchy,** the traditional system of economic and political inequality between women and men in most societies (see Chapter 11, Sexuality and Gender).

   Understanding the operation of macrostructures can also be useful. Consider, for example, one aspect of patriarchy. In our society, most married women who work full-time in the paid labour force are responsible for more housework, child care, and care for the elderly than their husbands are. Governments and businesses support this arrangement insofar as they provide little assistance to families in the form of nurs-eries, after-school programs for children, seniors' homes, and so forth. Yet an aspect of patriarchy—the unequal division of work in the household—is a major source of

Social structures are relatively stable patterns of social relations.

Microstructures are the patterns of relatively intimate social relations formed during face-to-face interaction. Families, friendship circles, and work associations are all examples of microstructures.

Macrostructures are overar-ching patterns of social relations that lie outside and above your circle of intimates and acquaintances. Macrostructures include classes, bureaucracies, and power systems, such as patriarchy.

Patriarchy is the traditional system of economic and political inequality between women and men.

dissatisfaction within marriages, especially in families that cannot afford to buy these services privately. Thus, sociological research shows that when spouses share domestic responsibilities equally, they are happier with their marriages and less likely to divorce (Hochschild with Machung, 1989). When a marriage is in danger of dissolving, it is common for partners to blame themselves and each other for their troubles. However, it should now be clear that forces other than incompatible personalities often put stress on families. Understanding how the macrostructure of patriarchy crops up in everyday life, and doing something to change that structure, can thus help people lead happier lives.

3. The third level of society that surrounds and permeates us comprises **global structures.** International organizations, patterns of worldwide travel and communication, and economic relations between countries are examples of global structures. Global structures are increasingly important as inexpensive travel and communication allow all parts of the world to become interconnected culturally, economically, and politically.

Understanding the operation of global structures can be useful, too. For instance, many people are concerned about the world's poor. They donate money to charities to help with famine and disaster relief. Some people also approve of the Canadian government giving aid to poor countries. However, many of these same people do not appreciate that charity and foreign aid alone do not seem able to end world poverty. That is because charity and foreign aid have been unable to overcome the structure of social relations among countries that have created and now sustain global inequality.

Let us linger on this point for a moment. As we will see in Chapter 9 (Globalization, Inequality, and Development), Britain, France, and other imperial powers locked some countries into poverty when they colonized them between the seventeenth and nineteenth centuries. In the twentieth century, the poor (or "developing") countries borrowed money from these same rich countries and Western banks to pay for airports, roads, harbours, sanitation systems, basic health care, and so forth. Today, poor countries pay far more to rich countries and Western banks in interest on those loans than they receive in aid and charity. In recent years, foreign aid to the world's developing countries has been only one-seventh the amount that the developing countries pay to Western banks in loan interest (United Nations, 2004a: 201). Thus, it seems that relying exclusively on foreign aid and charity can do little to help solve the problem of world poverty. Understanding how the global structure of international relations created and helps maintain global inequality suggests new policy priorities for helping the world's poor. One such priority might involve campaigning for the cancellation of foreign debt in compensation for past injustices. Some Canadian and British government officials have been promoting this policy for the past few years.

As these examples illustrate, personal problems are connected to social structures at the micro-, macro-, and global levels. Whether the personal problem involves finding a job, keeping a marriage intact, or figuring out a way to act justly to end world poverty, social-structural considerations broaden our understanding of the problem and suggest appropriate courses of action.

The Sociological Imagination

Half a century ago, C. Wright Mills (1959) called the ability to see the connection between personal troubles and social structures the **sociological imagination**. He emphasized the difficulty of developing this quality of mind (see Box 1.2). His language is sexist by today's standards but his argument is as true and inspiring today as it was in the 1950s:

> When a society becomes industrialized, a peasant becomes a worker; a feudal lord is liquidated or becomes a businessman. When classes rise or fall, a man is employed or unemployed; when the rate of investment goes up or down, a man takes new heart or goes broke. When war happens, an insurance salesman becomes a rocket launcher; a store clerk, a radar man; a wife

GLOBAL PERSPECTIVE

Global structures are patterns of social relations that lie outside and above the national level. They include international organizations, patterns of worldwide travel and communication, and the economic relations between countries.

The sociological imagination is the quality of mind that enables a person to see the connection between personal troubles and social structures.

lives alone; a child grows up without a father. Neither the life of an individual nor the history of a society can be understood without understanding both.

Yet men do not usually define the troubles they endure in terms of historical change. . . . The well-being they enjoy, they do not usually impute to the big ups and downs of the society in which they live. Seldom aware of the intricate connection between the patterns of their own lives and the course of world history, ordinary men do not usually know what this connection means for the kind of men they are becoming and for the kind of history-making in which they might take part. They do not possess the quality of mind essential to grasp the interplay of men and society, of biography and history, of self and world. They cannot cope with

BOX 1.2
Sociology at the Movies

TAKE   ROLL

Minority Report (2002)

The year is 2054 and the place is Washington, D.C. John Anderton (played by Tom Cruise) is a police officer who uses the latest technologies to apprehend murderers *before* they commit their crimes. This remarkable feat is possible because scientists have nearly perfected the use of "Pre-Cogs"—or, at least, so it seems. The Pre-Cog system consists of three psychics whose brains are wired together and who are sedated so they can develop a collective vision about impending murders. Together with powerful computers, the Pre-Cogs are apparently helping to create a crime-free society.

All is well until one of the psychics' visions shows Anderton himself murdering a stranger in less than 36 hours. Suddenly, Anderton is on the run from his own men. Desperate to figure out if the Pre-Cog system is somehow mistaken, he breaks into the system, unwires one of the psychics, and discovers that they do not always agree about what the future will bring. Sometimes there is a "minority report." Sometimes the minority report is correct. Sometimes people are arrested even though they never would have broken the law. The authorities have concealed this system flaw and allowed the arrest of potentially innocent people in their zeal to create a crime-free society.

In *Minority Report*, John Anderton (Tom Cruise) works with "Pre-Cogs" to track down criminals before they commit their crimes. When he discovers a flaw in the system, he realizes the future is not entirely fixed and that, within limits, he can change it. His insight holds an important sociological lesson for us.

And so Anderton comes to realize that not everything is predetermined—that, in his words, "It's not the future if you stop it." And stop it he does. Herein lies an important sociological lesson. Many people believe two contradictory ideas with equal conviction. First, they believe they are perfectly free to do whatever they want. Second, they believe the "system" (or "society") is so

big and powerful they are unable to do anything to change it. Neither idea is accurate. As we emphasize throughout this book, social structures exert powerful influences on our behaviour; we are not perfectly free. Nonetheless, it is possible to change many aspects of society; we are not wholly predetermined either. As you will learn, changing social structures is possible under certain specifiable circumstances, with the aid of specialized knowledge and often through great individual and collective effort.

Understanding the social constraints and possibilities for freedom that envelop us requires an active sociological imagination. The sociological imagination urges us to connect our biography with history and social structure—to make sense of our lives against a larger historical and social background and to act in light of our understanding. Have you ever tried to put events in your own life in the context of history and social structure? Did the exercise help you make sense of your life? Did it in any way lead to a life more worth living? Is the sociological imagination a worthy goal?

Although movies are just entertainment to many people, they often achieve by different means what the sociological imagination aims for. Therefore, in each chapter of this book, we make the connection between a movie and a topic of sociological importance.

their personal troubles in such a way as to control the structural transformations that usually lie behind them.

What they need . . . is a quality of mind that will help them to [see] . . . what is going on in the world and . . . what may be happening within themselves. It is this quality . . . that . . . may be called the sociological imagination. (Mills, 1959: 3–4)

These words were penned in 1959, making "the sociological imagination" a recent addition to the human repertoire. True, in ancient and medieval times, some philosophers wrote about society. However, their thinking was not sociological. They believed God and nature controlled society. They spent much of their time sketching blueprints for the ideal society and urging people to follow those blueprints. They relied on speculation rather than on evidence to reach conclusions about how society works (see Figure 1.4).

Origins of the Sociological Imagination

The sociological imagination was born when three modern revolutions pushed people to think about society in an entirely new way:

1. The **Scientific Revolution** began about 1550. It encouraged the view that sound conclusions about the workings of society must be based on solid evidence, not just on speculation. People often link the Scientific Revolution to specific ideas, such as Newton's laws of motion and Copernicus's theory that the earth revolves around the sun. However, science is less a collection of ideas than a method of inquiry. For instance, in 1609 Galileo pointed his newly invented telescope at the heavens, made

---

The **Scientific Revolution** began about 1550. It encouraged the view that sound conclusions about the workings of society must be based on solid evidence, not just on speculation.

FIGURE 1.4

The European View of the World, about 1600

In Shakespeare's time, most educated Europeans pictured a universe in which God ultimately determines everything. Thus, in this early-seventeenth-century engraving, a chain extends from God's hand to the hand of a woman representing Nature; she in turn holds a chain extending to the "ape of Nature," representing humankind. This suggests that God and his intermediary, Nature, shape all human actions. Notice also that the engraving places humans at the centre of the universe, suggesting that God created the universe chiefly for human benefit. Finally, note that the engraving arranges all the elements of the universe—angels, heavenly objects, humans, animals, vegetables, minerals—in a hierarchy. It suggests that higher elements, such as the stars and the planets, influence lower elements, such as the fate of humans.

Source: Robert Fludd, *Ultriusque Cosmi Maioris Scilicet et Minoris Metaphysica, Physica Atqve Technica Historia.* 1617–19. (Oppenheim, Germany. Johan-Thedori de Bry.) By permission of Houghton Library, Harvard University.

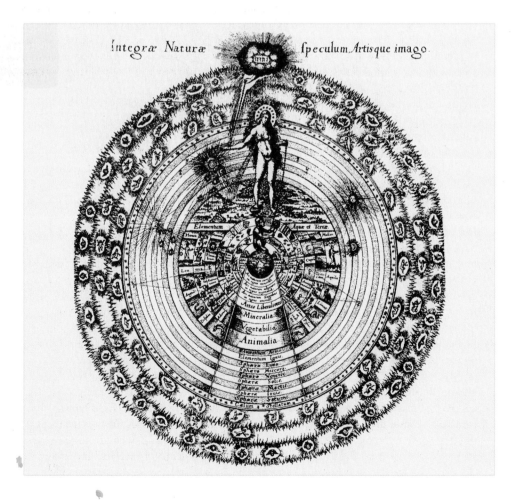

some careful observations, and showed that his observations fit Copernicus's theory. This is the core of the scientific method: using evidence to make a case for a particular point of view. By the mid-seventeenth century, some philosophers, such as Descartes in France and Hobbes in England, were calling for a science of society. When sociology emerged as a distinct discipline in the nineteenth century, commitment to the scientific method was one firm pillar of the sociological imagination.

2. The **Democratic Revolution** began about 1750. It suggested that people are responsible for organizing society and that human intervention can therefore solve social problems. Four hundred years ago, most Europeans thought otherwise. For them, God ordained the social order. The American Revolution (1775–83) and the French Revolution (1789–99) helped to undermine that idea. These democratic political upheavals showed that society could experience massive change in a short period. They proved that people could replace unsatisfactory rulers. They suggested that *people* control society. The implications for social thought were profound. For if it were possible to change society by human intervention, then a science of society could play a big role. The new science could help people find ways of overcoming social problems, improving the welfare of citizens and effectively reaching given goals. Much of the justification for sociology as a science arose out of the democratic revolutions that shook Europe and North America.

3. The **Industrial Revolution** began about 1780. It created a host of new and serious social problems that attracted the attention of social thinkers. As a result of the growth of industry, masses of people moved from countryside to city, worked agonizingly long hours in crowded and dangerous mines and factories, lost faith in their religions, confronted faceless bureaucracies, and reacted to the filth and poverty of their existence by means of strikes, crime, revolutions, and wars. Scholars had never seen a sociological laboratory like this. The Scientific Revolution suggested that a science of society was possible. The Democratic Revolution suggested that people could intervene to improve society. The Industrial Revolution presented social thinkers with a host of pressing social problems crying out for a solution. They responded by giving birth to the sociological imagination.

The Scientific Revolution began in Europe around 1550. Scientists proposed new theories about the structure of the universe and developed new methods to collect evidence so they could test those theories. Shown here is an astrolabe used by Copernicus to solve problems relating to the position of the sun, the planets, and the stars.

The Democratic Revolution began about 1750. It suggested that people are responsible for organizing society and that human intervention can therefore solve social problems.

The Industrial Revolution, often regarded as the most important event in world history since the development of agriculture and cities, refers to the rapid economic transformation that began in Britain in the 1780s. It involved the large-scale application of science and technology to industrial processes, the creation of factories, and the formation of a working class.

THEORY, RESEARCH, AND VALUES

French social thinker Auguste Comte (1798–1857) coined the term *sociology* in 1838 (Thompson, 1975). Comte tried to place the study of society on scientific foundations. He said he wanted to understand the social world as it was, not as he or anyone else imagined it should be. Yet there was a tension in his work: Although Comte was eager to adopt the scientific method in the study of society, he was a conservative thinker, motivated by strong opposition to rapid change in French society. This was evident in his writings. When he moved from his small, conservative hometown to Paris, Comte witnessed the democratic forces unleashed by the French Revolution, the early industrialization of society, and the rapid growth of cities. What he saw shocked and saddened him. Rapid social change was destroying much of what he valued, especially respect for traditional authority. He therefore urged slow change and the preservation of all that was traditional in social life. Thus, scientific methods of research *and* a vision of the ideal society were evident in sociology at its origins.

Although he praised the value of scientific methods, Comte never conducted any research. Neither did the second founder of sociology, British social theorist Herbert Spencer (1820–1903). However, Spencer believed that he had discovered scientific laws governing the operation of society. Strongly influenced by Charles Darwin's theory of evolution, he thought societies comprised interdependent parts, just as biological organisms did. These interdependent parts included families, governments, and the economy. According to Spencer, societies evolve in the same way as biological species do:

Eugene Delacroix's *Liberty Leading the People, July 28, 1830*. The democratic forces unleashed by the French Revolution suggested that people are responsible for organizing society and that human intervention can therefore solve social problems. As such, democracy was a foundation stone of sociology.

Individuals struggle to survive and the fittest succeed in this struggle; the least fit die before they can bear offspring. This allows societies to evolve from "barbaric" to "civilized." Deep social inequalities exist in society, but that is just as it should be if societies are to evolve, Spencer suggested (Spencer, 1975 [1897–1906]).

Spencer's ideas, which came to be known as "social Darwinism," were popular for a time in North America and Great Britain. Wealthy industrialists, like the oil baron John D. Rockefeller, found much to admire in a doctrine that justified social inequality and trumpeted the superiority of the wealthy and the powerful. Today, few sociologists think that societies are like biological systems. We have a better understanding of the complex economic, political, military, religious, and other forces that cause social change. We know that people can take things into their own hands and change their social environment in ways that no other species can. Spencer remains of interest because he was among the first social thinkers to assert that society operates according to scientific laws—and because his vision of the ideal society nonetheless showed through his writings.

To varying degrees, we see the same tension between belief in the importance of science and a vision of the ideal society in the work of the three giants in the early history of

Diego Rivera's *Detroit Industry, North Wall* (1932–33). Fresco (detail). Copyright 1997. The Detroit Institute of Arts. The first Industrial Revolution began in the late eighteenth century. The so-called Second Industrial Revolution began in the early twentieth century. Wealthy entrepreneurs formed large companies. Steel became a basic industrial material. Oil and electricity fuelled much industrial production. At the same time, Henry Ford's assembly lines and other mass-production technologies transformed the workplace.

sociology: Karl Marx (1818–83), Émile Durkheim (1858–1917), and Max Weber (pronounced VAY-ber; 1864–1920). The lives of these three men spanned just over a century. They witnessed various phases of Europe's wrenching transition to industrial capitalism. They wanted to explain the great transformation of Europe and suggest ways of improving people's lives. Like Comte and Spencer, they were committed to the scientific method of research. They actually adopted scientific research methods in their work. However, they also wanted to chart a better course for their societies. The ideas they developed are not just diagnostic tools from which we can still learn but, like many sociological ideas, are also prescriptions for combating social ills.

The tension between analysis and ideal, diagnosis and prescription, is evident throughout sociology. This becomes clear if we distinguish three important terms: theories, research, and values.

Theory

Sociological ideas are usually expressed in the form of theories. **Theories** are tentative explanations of some aspect of social life. They state how and why certain facts are related. For example, in his theory of suicide, Durkheim related facts about suicide rates to facts about social solidarity. This enabled him to explain suicide as a function of social solidarity. In our broad definition, even a hunch qualifies as a theory if it suggests how and why certain facts are related. As Albert Einstein wrote, "The whole of science is nothing more than a refinement of everyday thinking" (Einstein, 1954: 270).

Theories are tentative explanations of some aspect of social life that state how and why certain facts are related.

Research

After sociologists formulate theories, they can conduct research. **Research** is the process of carefully observing social reality, often to "test" a theory or assess its validity. For example, Durkheim collected suicide statistics from various government agencies to see whether the data supported or contradicted his theory. Because research can call the validity of a theory into question, theories are only *tentative* explanations. We discuss the research process in detail in Chapter 2, How Sociologists Do Research.

Research is the process of carefully observing reality to assess the validity of a theory.

Values

Before sociologists can formulate a theory, they must make certain judgments. For example, they must decide which problems are worth studying. They must make certain assumptions about how the parts of society fit together. If they are going to recommend ways of improving the operation of some aspect of society, they must even have an opinion about what the ideal society should look like. As we will soon see, these issues are shaped largely by sociologists' values. **Values** are ideas about what is right and wrong. Inevitably, values help sociologists formulate and favour certain theories over others (Edel, 1965; Kuhn, 1970 [1962]). As such, sociological theories may be modified and even rejected because of research, but they are often motivated by sociologists' values.

Values are ideas about what is right and wrong.

Durkheim, Marx, and Weber stood close to the origins of the major theoretical traditions in sociology: functionalism, conflict theory, and symbolic interactionism. A fourth theoretical tradition, feminism, has arisen in recent decades to correct some deficiencies in the three long-established traditions. It will become clear as you read this book that many more theories exist in addition to these four. However, because these four traditions have been especially influential in the development of sociology, we present a thumbnail sketch of each one.

SOCIOLOGICAL THEORY AND THEORISTS

Functionalism

Durkheim

Durkheim's theory of suicide is an early example of what sociologists now call **functionalism.** Functionalist theories incorporate these four features:

Functionalism stresses that human behaviour is governed by relatively stable social structures. It underlines how social structures maintain or undermine social stability. It emphasizes that social structures are based mainly on shared values or preferences. And it suggests that re-establishing equilibrium can best solve most social problems.

1. They stress that human behaviour is governed by relatively stable patterns of social relations or social structures. For example, Durkheim emphasized how suicide rates are influenced by patterns of social solidarity. Usually the social structures analyzed by functionalists are macrostructures.

2. Functionalist theories show how social structures maintain or undermine social stability. For example, Durkheim analyzed how the growth of industries and cities in nineteenth-century Europe lowered the level of social solidarity and contributed to social instability, one result of which was a higher suicide rate.

3. Functionalist theories emphasize that social structures are based mainly on shared values or preferences. Thus, when Durkheim wrote about social solidarity, he sometimes meant the frequency and intensity of social interaction, but more often he thought of social solidarity as a sort of moral cement that binds people together.

4. Functionalism suggests that re-establishing equilibrium can best solve most social problems. Thus, Durkheim said that social stability could be restored in late-nineteenth-century Europe by creating new associations of employers and workers that would lower workers' expectations about what they could get out of life. If, said Durkheim, more people could agree on wanting less, social solidarity would rise and there would be fewer strikes, fewer suicides, and so on. Functionalism, then, was a conservative response to widespread social unrest in late-nineteenth-century France. A more liberal or radical response would have been to argue that if people are expressing discontent because they are getting less out of life than they expect, discontent can be lowered by figuring out ways for them to get more out of life.

S. D. Clark (1910–2003) received his Ph.D. from the University of Toronto. He became the first chair of the Department of Sociology at that institution. Born in Lloydminster, Alberta, he is especially well known for his studies of Canadian social development as a process of dis-organization and reorganization on a series of economic frontiers (Clark, 1968). The influence of functionalism on his work is apparent in his emphasis on the way society re-establishes equilibrium after experiencing disruptions caused by economic change.

Functionalism in North America

Although functionalist thinking influenced North American sociology at the end of the nineteenth century, it was only during the continent's greatest economic crisis ever, the Great Depression of 1929–39, that functionalism took deep root here (Russett, 1966). With a quarter of the paid labour force unemployed and labour unrest rising, it is not entirely surprising that sociologists with a conservative frame of mind were attracted to a theory that focused on how social equilibrium could be restored. Functionalist theory remained popular for about 30 years. It experienced a minor revival in the early 1990s but never regained the dominance it had enjoyed from the 1930s to the early 1960s.

Harvard sociologist Talcott Parsons was the foremost North American proponent of functionalism. Parsons is best known for identifying how various institutions must work to ensure the smooth operation of society as a whole. He argued that society is well integrated and in equilibrium when the family successfully raises new generations, the military successfully defends society against external threats, schools are able to teach students the skills and values they need to function as productive adults, and religions create a shared moral code among the people (Parsons, 1951).

Parsons was criticized for exaggerating the degree to which members of society share common values and social institutions contribute to social harmony. This led North America's other leading functionalist, Robert Merton, to propose that social structures may have different consequences for different groups of people. Merton noted that some of those consequences may be disruptive or **dysfunctional** (Merton, 1968 [1949]). Moreover, said Merton, although some functions are **manifest** (visible and intended), others are **latent** (unintended and less obvious). For instance, a manifest function of schools is to transmit skills from one generation to the next. A latent function of schools is to encourage the development of a separate youth culture that often conflicts with parents' values (Coleman, 1961; Hersch, 1998).

Similarly, to anticipate an argument we make below, the manifest function of clothing is to keep people warm in cool weather and cool in warm weather. Yet clothing may be fashionable or unfashionable. The particular style of clothing we adopt may indicate whom we want to associate with and whom we want to exclude from our social circle. What we wear may thus express the position we occupy in society, how we think of ourselves, and how we want to present ourselves to others. These are all latent functions of clothing.

Conflict Theory

The second major theoretical tradition in sociology emphasizes the centrality of conflict in social life. **Conflict theory** incorporates these features:

- It generally focuses on large macrolevel structures, such as "class relations" or patterns of domination, submission, and struggle between people of high and low standing.
- Conflict theory shows how major patterns of inequality in society produce social stability in some circumstances and social change in others.
- Conflict theory stresses how members of privileged groups try to maintain their advantages while subordinate groups struggle to increase theirs. From this point of view, social conditions at a given time are the expression of an ongoing power struggle between privileged and subordinate groups.
- Conflict theory typically leads to the suggestion that eliminating privilege will lower the level of conflict and increase total human welfare.

Marx

Conflict theory originated in the work of German social thinker Karl Marx. A generation before Durkheim, Marx observed the destitution and discontent produced by the Industrial Revolution and proposed a sweeping argument about the way societies develop (Marx, 1904 [1859]; Marx and Engels, 1972 [1848]). Marx's theory was radically different from Durkheim's. **Class conflict**, the struggle between classes to resist and overcome the opposition of other classes, lies at the centre of his ideas.

Marx argued that owners of industry are eager to improve the way work is organized and to adopt new tools, machines, and production methods. These innovations allow them to produce more efficiently, earn higher profits, and drive inefficient competitors out of business. However, the drive for profits also causes capitalists to concentrate workers in larger and larger establishments, keep wages as low as possible, and invest as little as possible in improving working conditions. Thus, said Marx, a large and growing class of poor workers opposes a small and shrinking class of wealthy owners.

Marx believed that workers would ultimately become aware of belonging to the same exploited class. He called this awareness "class consciousness." He believed working-class consciousness would encourage the growth of trade unions and labour parties. According to Marx, these organizations would eventually seek to end private ownership of property, replacing it with a "communist" society: a system in which there is no private property and everyone shares property and wealth.

Weber

Although some of Marx's ideas have been usefully adapted to the study of contemporary society, his predictions about the inevitable collapse of capitalism have been questioned. Max Weber, a German sociologist who wrote his major works a generation after Marx, was among the first to find flaws in Marx's argument (Weber, 1946). Weber noted the rapid

Dysfunctional consequences are effects of social structures that create social instability.

Manifest functions are visible and intended effects of social structures.

Latent functions are invisible and unintended effects of social structures.

Conflict theory generally focuses on large macrolevel structures and shows how major patterns of inequality in society produce social stability in some circumstances and social change in others.

Class conflict is the struggle between classes to resist and overcome the opposition of other classes.

John Porter (1921–79) was
Canada's premier sociologist in
the 1960s and 1970s. Born in
Vancouver, he received his Ph.D.
from the London School of
Economics. He spent his
academic career at Carleton
University in Ottawa, serving
as chair of the Department of
Sociology and Anthropology,
dean of Arts and Science, and
vice-president. His major work,
The Vertical Mosaic (1965), is
a study of class and power in
Canada. Firmly rooted in
conflict theory, it influenced
a generation of Canadian
sociologists in their studies on
social inequality, elite groups,
French–English relations, and
Canadian–American relations.

**The Protestant ethic is the
belief that religious doubts
can be reduced, and a state
of grace ensured, if people
work diligently and live
ascetically. According to
Weber, the Protestant work
ethic had the unintended
effect of increasing savings
and investment and thus
stimulating capitalist growth.**

growth of the service sector of the economy, with its many non-manual workers and
professionals. He argued that many members of these occupational groups stabilize society
because they enjoy higher status and income than manual workers employed in
manufacturing. In addition, Weber showed that class conflict is not the only driving force of
history. In his view, politics and religion are also important sources of historical change (see
below). Other writers pointed out that Marx did not understand how investing in technology
would make it possible for workers to toil fewer hours under less oppressive conditions. Nor
did he foresee that higher wages, better working conditions, and welfare state benefits would
pacify manual workers. Thus, we see that Weber and other sociologists called into question
many of the particulars of Marx's theory.

Conflict Theory in North America

Conflict theory had some advocates in North America before the 1960s. Most noteworthy is
C. Wright Mills, who laid the foundations for modern conflict theory in the 1950s. Mills
conducted pioneering research on American politics and class structure. One of his most
important books is *The Power Elite,* a study of the several hundred men who occupied the
"command posts" of the American economy, military, and government. He argued that
power is highly concentrated in American society, which is therefore less of a democracy
than we are often led to believe (Mills, 1956).

Exceptions like Mills notwithstanding, conflict theory did not really take hold in North
America until the 1960s, a decade that was rocked by growing labour unrest, Quebec
separatism, anti-Vietnam War protests, the rise of the black power movement, and the first
stirrings of feminism. Strikes, demonstrations, and riots were almost daily occurrences in the
1960s and early 1970s, and therefore many sociologists of that era thought conflict among
classes, nations, races, and generations was the very essence of society. Many of today's
leading sociologists attended graduate school in the 1960s and 1970s and were strongly
influenced by the spirit of the times. As you will see throughout this book, they have made
important contributions to conflict theory during their professional careers.

Symbolic Interactionism

Weber, Mead, and Goffman

We noted above that Weber criticized Marx's interpretation of the development of
capitalism. Among other things, Weber argued that early capitalist development was caused
not just by favourable economic circumstances but that certain *religious* beliefs also
facilitated robust capitalist growth (Weber 1958 [1904–05]). In particular, sixteenth- and
seventeenth-century Protestants believed their religious doubts could be reduced and a state
of grace ensured if they worked diligently and lived modestly. Weber called this belief
the **Protestant ethic.** He believed it had an unintended effect: People who adhered to the
Protestant ethic saved and invested more money than others did. Thus, capitalism developed
most robustly where the Protestant ethic took hold. In much of his research, Weber emphasized the importance of empathetically understanding people's motives and the meanings
they attach to things to gain a clear sense of the significance of their actions. He called this
aspect of his approach to sociological research the method of *Verstehen* (which means
"understanding" in German).

The idea that subjective meanings and motives must be analyzed in any complete
sociological analysis was only one of Weber's contributions to early sociological theory.
Weber was also an important conflict theorist, as you will learn in later chapters. It is enough
to note here that his emphasis on subjective meanings found rich soil in the United States in
the late nineteenth and early twentieth centuries because his ideas resonated deeply with the
individualism of American culture. A century ago, people widely believed that individual
talent and initiative could allow anyone to achieve just about anything in that land of
opportunity. Small wonder then that much of early American sociology focused on the
individual or, more precisely, on the connection between the individual and the larger

society. This was certainly a focus of sociologists at the University of Chicago, the most influential Department of Sociology in the country before World War II. For example, the University of Chicago's George Herbert Mead (1863–1931) was the driving force behind the study of how the individual's sense of self is formed in the course of interaction with other people. We discuss his contribution in Chapter 4, Socialization. Here, we note only that the work of Mead and his colleagues gave birth to symbolic interactionism, a distinctively American theoretical tradition that continues to be a major force in sociology today.

Functionalist and conflict theories assume that people's group memberships—whether they are rich or poor, male or female, black or white—influence their behaviour. This can sometimes make people seem like balls on a pool table: They get knocked around and cannot choose their own destinies. We know from our everyday experience, however, that people are not like that. We often make choices, sometimes difficult ones. We sometimes change our minds. Moreover, two people with similar group memberships may react differently to similar social circumstances because they interpret those circumstances differently.

Recognizing these issues, some sociologists focus on the subjective side of social life. They work in the symbolic interactionist tradition, a school of thought that was given its name by sociologist Herbert Blumer (1900–86), Mead's student at the University of Chicago. **Symbolic interactionism** incorporates these features:

- Symbolic interactionism's focus on interpersonal communication in microlevel social settings distinguishes it from both functionalist and conflict theories.
- Symbolic interactionism emphasizes that social life is possible only because people attach meanings to things. It follows that an adequate explanation of social behaviour requires understanding the subjective meanings people associate with their social circumstances.
- Symbolic interactionism stresses that people help to create their social circumstances and do not merely react to them. For example, Canadian sociologist Erving Goffman (1922–82), one of the most influential symbolic interactionists, analyzed the many ways people present themselves to others in everyday life so as to appear in the best possible light. Goffman compared social interaction to a carefully staged play, complete with front stage, backstage, defined roles, and a wide range of props. In this play, a person's age, gender, race, and other characteristics may help to shape his or her actions, but there is much room for individual creativity as well (Goffman, 1959).
- By focusing on the subjective meanings people create in small social settings, symbolic interactionists sometimes validate unpopular and unofficial viewpoints. This increases our understanding and tolerance of people who may be different from us.

To understand symbolic interactionism better, let us briefly return to the problem of suicide. If a police officer discovers a dead person at the wheel of a car that has run into a tree, it may be difficult to establish whether the death was an accident or suicide. Interviewing friends and relatives to discover the driver's state of mind just before the crash may help rule out the possibility of suicide. As this example illustrates, understanding the intention or motive of the actor is critical to understanding the meaning of a social action and explaining it. A state of mind must be interpreted, usually by a coroner, before a dead body becomes a suicide statistic (Douglas, 1967).

For surviving family and friends, suicide is always painful and sometimes embarrassing. Insurance policies often deny payments to beneficiaries in the case of suicide. As a result, coroners are inclined to classify deaths as accidental whenever such an interpretation is plausible. Being human, they want to minimize a family's suffering after such a horrible event. Sociologists therefore believe that official suicide rates are about one-third lower than actual suicide rates.

Social Constructionism

One variant of symbolic interactionism that has become especially popular in recent years is **social constructionism**. Social constructionists argue that when people interact, they typically assume things are naturally or innately what they seem to be. However, apparently natural or innate features of life are often sustained by *social* processes that vary historically and

Erving Goffman (1922–82) was born in Mannville, Alberta. He studied sociology and anthropology at the University of Toronto. He completed his Ph.D. at the University of Chicago and pursued his academic career at the University of California, Berkeley, and the University of Pennsylvania. Goffman developed an international reputation for his "dramaturgical" approach to symbolic interactionism.

Symbolic interactionism focuses on interaction in microlevel social settings and emphasizes that an adequate explanation of social behaviour requires understanding the subjective meanings people attach to their social circumstances.

Social constructionism argues that apparently natural or innate features of life are often sustained by social processes that vary historically and culturally.

Margrit Eichler (1942–) was born in Berlin, Germany. She took her Ph.D. at Duke University in the United States before beginning her academic career in Canada. She served as chair of the Department of Sociology at the Ontario Institute for Studies in Education and became head of the Women's Studies Program at the University of Toronto. She is internationally known for her work on feminist methodology (Eichler, 1987). Her work on family policy in Canada has influenced students, professional sociologists, and policymakers for two decades (Eichler, 1988a).

Feminist theory claims that patriarchy is at least as important as class inequality in determining a person's opportunities in life. It holds that male domination and female subordination are determined not by biological necessity but by structures of power and social convention. It examines the operation of patriarchy in both micro and macro settings. And it contends that existing patterns of gender inequality can and should be changed for the benefit of all members of society.

culturally. For example, many people assume differences in the way women and men behave are the result of their different biological makeup. In contrast, social constructionists show that many of the presumably natural differences between women and men depend on the way power is distributed between them and the degree to which certain ideas about women and men are widely shared (see Chapter 11, Sexuality and Gender; Berger and Luckmann, 1966). People usually do such a good job of building natural-seeming social realities in their everyday interactions that they do not notice the materials used in the construction process. Social constructionists identify those materials and analyze how they are pieced together.

In sum, the study of the subjective side of social life helps us get beyond the official picture, deepening our understanding of how society works and supplementing the insights gained from macrolevel analysis. By stressing the importance and validity of subjective meanings, symbolic interactionists increase tolerance for minority and deviant viewpoints. By stressing how subjective meanings vary historically and culturally, social constructionists show that many seemingly natural features of social life actually require painstaking acts of social creation.

Feminist Theory

Few women figured prominently in the early history of sociology. The strict demands placed on them by the nineteenth-century family and the lack of opportunity in the larger society prevented most women from earning a higher education and making major contributions to the discipline. Women who made their mark on sociology in its early years tended to have unusual biographies. Some of these exceptional people introduced gender issues that were largely ignored by Marx, Durkheim, Weber, Mead, and other early sociologists. Appreciation for the sociological contribution of these pioneering women has grown in recent years because concern with gender issues has come to form a substantial part of the modern sociological enterprise.

Martineau and Addams

Harriet Martineau (1802–76) is often called the first female sociologist. Born in England to a prosperous family, she never married. She was able to support herself comfortably from her journalistic writings. Martineau translated Comte into English, and she wrote one of the first books on research methods. She undertook critical studies of slavery, factory laws, and gender inequality. She was a leading advocate of voting rights for women, higher education for women, and gender equality in the family. As such, Martineau was one of the first feminists (Yates, 1985).

In the United States in the early twentieth century, a few women from wealthy families attended university, received training as sociologists, and wanted to become professors of sociology, but they were denied faculty appointments. Typically, they turned to social activism and social work instead. A case in point is Jane Addams (1860–1935). Addams was co-founder of Hull House, a shelter for the destitute in Chicago's slums, and she spent a lifetime fighting for social reform. She also provided a research platform for sociologists from the University of Chicago, who often visited Hull House to interview its clients. In recognition of her efforts, Addams received the ultimate award in 1931—the Nobel Peace Prize.

Modern Feminism

Despite its early stirrings, feminist thinking had little impact on sociology until the mid-1960s, when the rise of the modern women's movement drew attention to the many remaining inequalities between women and men. Because of feminist theory's major influence on sociology, it may fairly be regarded as sociology's fourth major theoretical tradition. Modern feminism has several variants (see Chapter 11, Sexuality and Gender). However, the various strands of **feminist theory** share the following features:

- Feminist theory focuses on various aspects of patriarchy, the system of male domination in society. Patriarchy, feminists contend, is as important as class inequality, if not more so, in determining a person's opportunities in life.

- Feminist theory holds that male domination and female subordination are determined not by biological necessity but by structures of power and social convention. From their point of view, women are subordinate to men only because men enjoy more legal, economic, political, and cultural rights.
- Feminist theory examines the operation of patriarchy in both microlevel and macrolevel settings.
- Feminist theory contends that existing patterns of gender inequality can and should be changed for the benefit of all members of society. The main sources of gender inequality include differences in the way boys and girls are reared; barriers to equal opportunity in education, paid work, and politics; and the unequal division of domestic responsibilities between women and men.

Summing Up

The theoretical traditions outlined above are summarized in Table 1.1 (see also Figure 1.5 on page 22). As you will see in the following pages, sociologists have applied them to all of the discipline's branches. They have elaborated and refined each of them. Some sociologists work exclusively within one tradition. Others conduct research that borrows from more than one tradition. But all sociologists are deeply indebted to the founders of the discipline.

To illustrate how much farther we are able to see using theory as our guide, we now consider how the four traditions outlined above improve our understanding of an aspect of social life familiar to everyone: the world of fashion.

Theoretical Tradition	Main Level of Analysis	Main Focus	Main Question	Image of Ideal Society
Functionalism	Macro	Values	How do the institutions of society contribute to social stability?	A state of equilibrium
Conflict theory	Macro	Class inequality	How do privileged groups seek to maintain their advantages and subordinate groups seek to increase theirs, often causing social change in the process?	The elimination of privilege, especially class privilege
Symbolic interactionism	Micro	Meaning	How do individuals communicate so as to make their social settings meaningful?	Respect for the validity of minority views
Feminist theory	Micro and macro	Patriarchy	Which social structures and interaction processes maintain male dominance and female subordination?	The elimination of gender inequality

TABLE 1.1
The Main Theoretical Traditions in Sociology

FIGURE 1.5

A Sociological Timeline of Some Major Figures in the Development of Sociological Theory, 1820–1960

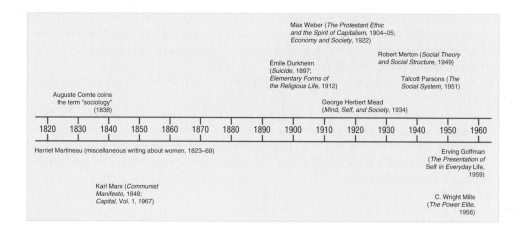

APPLYING THE FOUR THEORETICAL PERSPECTIVES: THE PROBLEM OF FASHION

> "Oh. Two weeks ago I saw Cameron Diaz at Fred Segal and I talked her out of buying this truly heinous angora sweater. Whoever said orange is the new pink is seriously disturbed."
> — Elle Woods (Reese Witherspoon) in *Legally Blonde* (2001)

In December 2002 the *Wall Street Journal* announced that Grunge might be back (Tkacik, 2002). Since 1998, one of the main fashion trends among white, middle-class, preteen and young teenage girls was the Britney Spears look: bare midriffs, highlighted hair, wide belts, glitter purses, big wedge shoes, and Skechers "energy" sneakers. But in 2002 a new pop star, Avril Lavigne, was rising in the pop charts. Nominated for a 2003 Grammy Award in the Best New Artist category, the 17-year-old skater-punk from Napanee in eastern Ontario (2001 population: 15 132; Statistics Canada, 2002d) affected a shaggy, unkempt look. She sported worn-out T-shirts, 1970s-style plaid Western shirts with snaps, low-rise blue jeans, baggy pants, undershirts, ties, backpacks, chain wallets, and, for shoes, Converse Chuck Taylors. The style was similar to the Grunge look of the early 1990s, when Nirvana and Pearl Jam were the big stars on MTV and Kurt Cobain was king of the music world.

Why in late 2002 were the glamorous trends of the pop era giving way in one market segment to "neo-Grunge"? Why, in general, do fashion shifts take place? Sociological theory has interesting things to say on this subject (Davis, 1992).

Until the 1960s, the standard sociological approach to explaining the ebb and flow of fashion trends was *functionalist.* In the functionalist view, fashion trends worked like this: Every season, exclusive fashion houses in Paris and, to a lesser extent, Milan, New York, and

Britney Spears versus Avril Lavigne

London, would show new styles. Some of the new styles would catch on among the exclusive clientele of Chanel, Dior, Givenchy, and other big-name designers. The main appeal of wearing expensive, new fashions was that wealthy clients could distinguish themselves from people who were less well off. Thus, fashion performed an important social function. By allowing people of different rank to distinguish themselves from one another, fashion helped to preserve the ordered layering of society into classes. ("It is an interesting question," wrote nineteenth-century American writer Henry David Thoreau in *Walden,* "how far [people] would retain their relative rank if they were divested of their clothes.") By the twentieth century, thanks to technological advances in clothes manufacturing, it didn't take long for inexpensive knockoffs to reach the market and trickle down to the lower classes. New styles then had to be introduced frequently so that fashion could continue to perform its function of helping to maintain an orderly class system. Hence the ebb and flow of fashion.

The functionalist theory was a fairly accurate account of the way fashion trends worked until the 1960s. Then, fashion became more democratic. Paris, Milan, New York, and London are still hugely important fashion centres today. However, new fashion trends are increasingly initiated by lower classes, minority groups, and people who spurn high fashion altogether. Napanee is, after all, pretty far from Paris, and today big-name designers are more likely to be influenced by the inner-city styles of hip-hop than vice versa. Avril Lavigne became the new face of Chanel in 2006, suggesting that new fashions no longer just trickle down from upper classes and a few high-fashion centres. Upper classes are nearly as likely to adopt lower-class fashion trends that emanate from just about anywhere. As a result, the functionalist theory no longer provides a satisfying explanation of fashion cycles.

Some sociologists have turned to conflict theory as an alternative view of the fashion world. Conflict theorists typically view fashion cycles as a means by which industry owners make big profits. Owners introduce new styles and render old styles unfashionable because they make more money when many people are encouraged to buy new clothes often. At the same time, conflict theorists think fashion keeps people distracted from the many social, economic, and political problems that might otherwise incite them to express dissatisfaction with the existing social order and even rebel against it. Conflict theorists, like functionalists, thus believe that fashion helps to maintain social stability. Unlike functionalists, however, they argue that social stability bestows advantages on industrial owners at the expense of non-owners.

Conflict theorists have a point. Fashion *is* a big and profitable business. Owners *do* introduce new styles to make more money. They have, for example, created the Color Marketing Group (known to insiders as the "Color Mafia"), a committee that meets regularly to help change the international palette of colour preferences for consumer products. According to one committee member, the Color Mafia makes sure that "the mass media, . . . fashion magazines and catalogs, home shopping shows, and big clothing chains all present the same options" (Mundell, 1993).

Yet the Color Mafia and other influential elements of the fashion industry are not all-powerful. Remember what Elle Woods said after she convinced Cameron Diaz not to buy that heinous angora sweater: "Whoever said orange is the new pink is seriously disturbed." Like many consumers, Elle Woods *rejected* the advice of the fashion industry. And, in fact, some of the fashion trends initiated by industry owners flop, one of the biggest being the introduction of the midi-dress (with a hemline midway between knee and ankle) in the mid-1970s. Despite a huge ad campaign, most women simply would not buy it.

This points to one of the main problems with the conflict interpretation: It incorrectly makes it seem as if fashion decisions are dictated from above. Reality is more complicated. Fashion decisions are made partly by consumers. This idea can best be understood by thinking of clothing as a form of *symbolic interaction,* a sort of wordless "language" that allows us to tell others who we are and to learn who they are.

If clothes speak, sociologist Fred Davis has perhaps done the most in recent years to help us see how we can decipher what they say (Davis, 1992). According to Davis, a person's identity is always a work in progress. True, we develop a sense of self as we mature. We come to think of ourselves as members of one or more families, occupations, communities, classes, ethnic and racial groups, and countries. We develop patterns of behaviour and belief associated with each of these social categories. Nonetheless, social categories change over time, and so do we as we move through them and as we age. As a result, our identities are always in flux. We often become anxious or insecure about who we are. Clothes help us express our shifting identities. For example, clothes can convey whether you are "straight," sexually available, athletic, conservative, and much else, thus telling others how you want them to see you and the kinds of people with whom you want to associate. At some point you may become less conservative, sexually available, and so on. Your clothing style is likely to change accordingly. (Of course, the messages you try to send are subject to interpretation and may be misunderstood.) For its part, the fashion industry feeds on the ambiguities within us, investing much effort in trying to discern which new styles might capture current needs for self-expression.

For example, capitalizing on the need for young girls' self-expression in the late 1990s, Britney Spears hit a chord. Feminist interpretations of the meaning and significance of Britney Spears are especially interesting in this respect because they focus on the gender aspects of fashion.

Traditionally, feminists have thought of fashion as a form of patriarchy, a means by which male dominance is maintained. They have argued that fashion is mainly a female preoccupation. It takes a lot of time and money to choose, buy, and clean clothes. Fashionable clothing is often impractical and uncomfortable, and some of it is even unhealthy. Modern fashion's focus on youth, slenderness, and eroticism diminishes women by turning them into sexual objects, say some feminists. Britney Spears is of interest to traditional feminists because she supposedly helps to lower the age at which girls fall under male domination.

In recent years, this traditional feminist view has given way to a feminist interpretation that is more compatible with symbolic interactionism ("Why Britney Spears Matters," 2001). Some feminists now applaud the "girl power" movement that crystallized in 1996 with the release of the Spice Girls' hit single "Wannabe." These feminists regard Britney Spears as part of that movement. In their judgment, Spears's music, dance routines, and dress style express a self-assuredness and assertiveness that resonate with the less submissive and more independent role that girls are now carving out for themselves. With her kicks, her shadow boxing, and her songs like the 2000 single "Stronger," Spears speaks for the *empowerment* of young women. Quite apart from her musical and dancing talent, then, some feminists think many young girls are wild about Britney Spears because she helps them express their own social and sexual power. Of course, not all young girls agree. Some, like Avril Lavigne, find Spears "phony" and too much of a "showgirl." They seek "more authentic" ways of asserting their identity through fashion (Pascual, 2002). Still, the symbolic interactionist and feminist interpretations of fashion help us see more clearly the ambiguities of identity that underlie the rise of new fashion trends.

Our analysis of fashion shows that each of the four theoretical perspectives—functionalism, conflict theory, symbolic interactionism, and feminist theory—can clarify different aspects of a sociological problem. This does not mean that each perspective always has equal validity. Often, the interpretations that derive from different theoretical perspectives are incompatible. They offer *competing* interpretations of the same social reality. It is then necessary to do research to determine which perspective works best for the case at hand. Nonetheless, all four theoretical perspectives usefully illuminate some aspects of the social world. We therefore refer to them often in this textbook.

A SOCIOLOGICAL COMPASS

Our summary of the major theoretical perspectives in sociology suggests that the founders of the discipline developed their ideas in an attempt to solve the great sociological puzzle of their time—the causes and consequences of the Industrial Revolution. This raises two interesting questions. What are the great sociological puzzles of *our* time? How are today's sociologists responding to the challenges presented by the social settings in which *we* live? We devote the rest of this book to answering these questions in depth. In the remainder of this chapter, we outline what you can expect to learn from this book.

It would be wrong to suggest that the research of tens of thousands of sociologists around the world is animated by just a few key issues. Viewed up close, sociology today is a heterogeneous enterprise enlivened by hundreds of theoretical debates, some focused on small issues relevant to particular fields and geographical areas, others focused on big issues that seek to characterize the entire historical era for humanity as a whole.

Among the big issues, two stand out. Perhaps the greatest sociological puzzles of our time are the causes and consequences of the Postindustrial Revolution and globalization. The **Postindustrial Revolution** is the technology-driven shift from manufacturing to service industries—the shift from employment in factories to employment in offices—and the consequences of that shift for nearly all human activities (Bell, 1973; Toffler, 1990). For example, as a result of the Postindustrial Revolution, non-manual occupations now outnumber manual occupations, and women have been drawn into the system of higher education and the paid labour force in large numbers. The shift to service industries has transformed the way we work and study, our standard of living, the way we form families, and much else.

Globalization is the process by which formerly separate economies, states, and cultures become tied together and people become increasingly aware of their growing interdependence (Giddens, 1990: 64; Guillén, 2001). Especially in recent decades, rapid increases in the volume of international trade, travel, and communication have broken down the isolation and independence of most countries and people. Also contributing to globalization is the growth of many institutions that bind corporations, companies, and cultures together. These processes have caused people to depend more than ever on people in other countries for products, services, ideas, and even a sense of identity.

Sociologists agree that globalization and postindustrialism promise many exciting opportunities to enhance the quality of life and increase human freedom. However, they also see many social-structural barriers to the realization of that promise. We can summarize both the promise and the barriers by drawing a compass—a sociological compass (see Figure 1.6). Each axis of the compass contrasts a promise with the barriers to its realization. The vertical axis contrasts the promise of equality of opportunity with the barrier of inequality of opportunity. The horizontal axis contrasts the promise of individual freedom with the barrier of constraint on that freedom. Let us consider these axes in more detail because much of our discussion in the following chapters turns on them.

The Postindustrial Revolution refers to the technology-driven shift from manufacturing to service industries and the consequences of that shift for virtually all human activities.

Globalization is the process by which formerly separate economies, states, and cultures become tied together and people becoming increasingly aware of their growing interdependence.

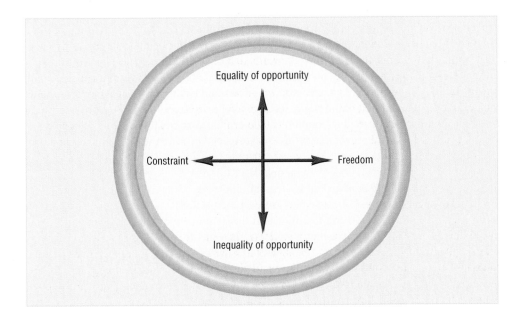

FIGURE 1.6
A Sociological Compass

Equality versus Inequality of Opportunity

Optimists forecast that postindustrialism will provide more opportunities for people to find creative, interesting, challenging, and rewarding work. In addition, the postindustrial era will generate more "equality of opportunity," that is, better chances for *all* people to get an education, influence government policy, and find good jobs.

You will find evidence to support these claims in this book. For example, we show that the average standard of living and the number of good jobs are increasing in postindustrial societies, such as Canada. Women are making rapid strides in the economy, the education system, and other institutions. Postindustrial societies like Canada are characterized by a decline in discrimination against members of minority groups, while democracy is spreading throughout the world. Desperately poor people form a declining percentage of the world's population.

Yet, as you read this book, it will also become clear that all these seemingly happy stories have a dark underside. For example, it turns out that the number of routine jobs with low pay and few benefits is growing faster than the number of creative, high-paying jobs. An enormous opportunity gulf still separates women from men. Racism and discrimination are still a part of our world. Our health care system is in crisis just as our population is aging rapidly and most in need of health care. Many of the world's new democracies are only superficially democratic, while Canadians and citizens of other postindustrial societies are increasingly cynical about the ability of their political systems to respond to their needs. Many people are looking for alternative forms of political expression. The *absolute* number of desperately poor people in the world continues to grow, as does the gap between rich and poor nations. Many people attribute the world's most serious problems to globalization. They have formed organizations and movements—some of them violent—to oppose it. In short, equality of opportunity is an undeniably attractive ideal, but it is unclear whether it is the inevitable outcome of a globalized, postindustrial society.

Freedom versus Constraint

Growing freedom is also evident—but within limits. In an earlier era, most people retained their religious, ethnic, racial, and sexual identities for a lifetime, even if they were not particularly comfortable with them. They often remained in social relationships that made them unhappy. One of the major themes of *Sociology: Your Compass for a New World* is that many people are now freer to construct their identities and form social relationships in ways that suit them. To a greater degree than ever before, it is possible to *choose* who you want to be, with whom you want to associate, and how you want to associate with them. The postindustrial and global era frees people from traditional constraints by encouraging virtually instant global communication, international migration, greater acceptance of sexual diversity and a variety of family forms, the growth of ethnically and racially diverse cities, and so forth. For instance, in the past people often stayed in marriages even if they were dissatisfied with them. Families often involved a father working in the paid labour force and a mother keeping house and raising children without pay. Today, people are freer to end unhappy marriages and create family structures that are more suited to their individual needs.

Again, however, we must face the less rosy aspects of postindustrialism and globalization. In many of the following chapters, we point out how increased freedom is experienced only within certain limits and how social diversity is limited by a strong push to conformity in some spheres of life. For example, we can choose a far wider variety of consumer products than ever before, but consumerism itself increasingly seems a compulsory way of life. Moreover, it is a way of life that threatens the natural environment. Meanwhile, some new technologies, such as surveillance cameras, cause us to modify our behaviour and act in more conformist ways. Large, impersonal bureaucracies and standardized products and services dehumanize both staff and customers. The tastes and the profit motive of vast media conglomerates, most of them American-owned, govern most of our cultural consumption and arguably threaten the survival of distinctive national cultures. Powerful interests are trying to shore up the traditional nuclear family even though it does not suit some people. As these examples show, the push to uniformity counters the trend toward growing social diversity. Postindustrialism and globalization may make us freer in some ways, but they also place new constraints on us.

WHY SOCIOLOGY?

Our overview of themes in *Sociology: Your Compass for a New World* drives home a point made by Anthony Giddens, renowned British sociologist and adviser to former British Prime Minister Tony Blair. According to Giddens, we live in an era "suspended between extraordinary opportunity . . . and global catastrophe" (Giddens, 1990: 166). A whole range of environmental issues; profound inequalities in the wealth of nations and of classes; religious, racial, and ethnic violence; and unsolved problems in the relations between women and men continue to profoundly affect the quality of our everyday lives.

Despair and apathy are possible responses to these complex issues, but they are not responses that humans favour. If it were our nature to give up hope, we would still be sitting around half-naked in the mud outside a cave.

People are more inclined to look for ways of improving their lives, and this period of human history is full of opportunities to do so. We have, for example, advanced to the point where, for the first time, we have the means to feed and educate everyone in the world. Similarly, it now seems possible to erode some of the inequalities that have always been the major source of human conflict.

Careers in Sociology

Sociology offers useful advice on how to achieve the goals of equality and freedom because it is more than just an intellectual exercise. Sociology is an applied science with practical, everyday uses in the realms of teaching and public policy, and the creation of laws and regulations by organizations and governments (see Box 1.3 on page 28). That is because sociologists are trained not just to see what is, but also to see what is possible.

WHERE DO YOU FIT IN?

Students often ask: "Can I get a good job with a sociology degree?" "Exactly what kind of work could I do with a major in sociology?" "Aren't all the good jobs these days in technical areas and the natural sciences?" To answer these questions—and to help you decide whether it makes sense for you to major in sociology or another social science—consider the following data on the employment of Canadians with degrees in sociology and related fields.

A study based on 1988 data found that a higher percentage of Canadian sociology graduates were employed full-time than were graduates in the other social sciences (Guppy and Hedley, 1993). A study based mainly on 1996 data (Allen, 1999) showed that, in Canada,

- the unemployment rate among social science graduates was lower than among graduates in math, physics, engineering, agriculture, and biology.
- between 1991 and 1996, there were more new jobs for people with social science degrees than for people with degrees in other fields.
- although women earned less than men in all fields in 1996, the discrepancy between men's and women's income was smallest among social science graduates.

On the basis of these findings, it seems that sociology degrees promise more employment security for both men and women, and less income discrimination against women, than do other degrees. It also seems that the postindustrial economy requires more new employees with a social science background than new employees with a background in some technical and scientific fields.

Tens of thousands of Canadians have a B.A. in sociology. A sociology B.A. improves a person's understanding of the diverse social conditions affecting men and women; people with different sexual orientations; and people from different countries, regions, classes, races, and ethnic groups. Therefore, people with a B.A. in sociology tend to be attracted to

BOX 1.3
Social Policy: What Do You Think?

Are Corporate Scandals a Problem of Individual Ethics or Social Policy?

In 2002 the Sloan School of Management at the Massachusetts Institute of Technology conducted a survey of 600 graduates as part of its 50th anniversary observance. Sixty percent of survey respondents said that honesty, integrity, and ethics are the main characteristics of a good corporate leader. Most alumni felt that living a moral professional life is more important than pulling in large paycheques and generous perquisites.

Unfortunately, the behaviour of North American executives sometimes fails to reflect high ethical standards. In 2002, for example, investigators uncovered the biggest corporate scandals ever to rock the United States. Things got so bad that Andy Grove, a founder of Intel, said he was "embarrassed and ashamed" to be a corporate executive in America today (quoted in Hochberg, 2002), and the Wall Street investment firm of Charles Schwab ran a highly defensive television ad claiming to be "almost the opposite of a Wall Street firm." What brought about such astonishing statements was that several corporate giants, including Enron, WorldCom, Tyco, Global Crossings, and Adelphia Communications, were shown to have engaged in accounting fraud to make their earnings appear higher than they actually were. This practice kept their stock prices artificially high—until investigators made public what was going on, at which time their stock prices took a nosedive. Ordinary stockholders lost hundreds of billions of dollars. Many company

employees lost their pensions (because they had been encouraged or compelled to place their retirement funds in company stock) and their jobs (because their companies soon filed for bankruptcy). In contrast, accounting fraud greatly benefited senior executives. They had received stock options as part of their compensation package. If you own stock options, you can buy company stock whenever you want at a fixed low price, even if the market price for the stock is much higher. Senior executives typically exercised their stock options *before* the stocks crashed, netting them billions of dollars in profit.

Canada has not been immune to unethical behaviour in the highest corporate ranks. For example, thousands of ordinary Canadians lost billions of dollars, including substantial pension savings, when senior executives of telecommunications giant Nortel grossly overstated the company's profitability and prospects, earned huge bonuses on the basis of false accounting, and then watched the stock slide from a high of $124.50 in July 2000 to 64 cents in October 2002. Several senior executives lost their jobs, but they were not prosecuted and they all kept their ill-gotten gains. In 2004, a group of Canadian investors launched a class-action lawsuit against newspaper baron Conrad Black and other executives of Hollinger International for $4 billion in damages. The suit claimed market losses may have been caused by controversies involving Black's management and allegations that he and associates quietly pocketed $400 million to which they were not entitled. (Black was eventually found guilty in an American court of fraud and

obstruction of justice and was sentenced to a 6-1/2-year jail term.)

Can we rely on individual morality or ethics to show senior executives how to behave responsibly, that is, in the long-term interest of their companies and society as a whole? Ethics courses have been taught at all business schools for years but, as the dean of one business school noted, these courses can't "turn sinners into saints. . . . If a company does a lot of crazy stuff but its share price continues to rise, a lot of people will look the other way and not really care whether senior management is behaving ethically or not" (quoted in Goll, 2002).

Because individual ethics often seem weak in the face of greed, some observers have suggested that new public policies, that is, laws and regulations passed by organizations and governments, are required to regulate executive compensation. For example, some people think the practice of granting stock options to senior executives should be outlawed, stiff jail terms should be imposed on anyone who engages in accounting fraud, and strong legal protection should be offered to anyone who "blows the whistle" on executive wrongdoing.

Sociology helps us see what may appear to be personal issues in the larger context of public policy. Even our tendency to act ethically or unethically is shaped in part by public policy—or the lack of it. Therefore, we review a public policy debate in each chapter of this book. It is good exercise for the sociological imagination, and it will help you gain more control over the forces that shape your life.

jobs requiring good "people skills" and jobs involved in managing and promoting social change (see Table 1.2).

People with a B.A. in sociology often go on to take graduate and professional degrees in other fields, including law, urban planning, industrial relations, social work, and public

Government

Community affairs officer
Urban/regional planner
Legislative aide
Affirmative action/
employment equity
worker
Foreign service officer
Human rights officer
Personnel coordinator

Research

Social research specialist
Consumer researcher
Data analyst
Market researcher
Survey researcher
Census officer/analyst
Demographer/population
analyst
Systems analyst

Community Affairs

Occupational/career
counsellor
Homeless/housing worker

Public health/hospital
administrator
Child development
technician
Public administration
assistant
Social assistance advocate
Resident planning aide
Group home worker
Rehabilitation program
worker
Rural health outreach
worker
Housing coordinator
Fundraising director/
assistant
Caseworker/aide
Community organizer
Youth outreach worker

Corrections

Corrections officer
Criminology assistant
Police officer
Rehabilitation counsellor
Criminal investigator
Juvenile court worker
Parole officer

Teaching

College/university
placement worker
Public health educator
Teacher
Admissions counsellor

Business

Market analyst
Project manager
Sales representative
Real estate agent
Journalist
Public relations officer
Actuary
Insurance agent
Human resources manager
Production manager
Labour relations officer
Administrative assistant
Quality control manager
Merchandiser/purchaser
Computer analyst
Data entry manager
Publishing officer
Advertising officer
Sales manager

TABLE 1.2

Jobs Commonly Held by
Canadians with Degrees
in Sociology

Source: Neil Guppy and R. Alan
Hedley. (1993). *Opportunities in
Sociology* (Montreal: Canadian
Sociology and Anthropology
Association). Reprinted with
permission of the Canadian
Sociology and Anthropology
Association.

policy. Most people with a graduate degree in sociology teach and conduct research in universities, with research being a more important component of the job in larger and more prestigious institutions. But many sociologists do not teach. Instead, they conduct research and give policy advice in a wide range of settings outside the system of higher education. In many federal government agencies, for example, sociologists are employed as researchers and policy consultants. Sociologists also conduct research and policy analysis in trade unions, non-governmental organizations, and professional and public interest associations. In the private sector, you can find sociologists practising their craft in firms specializing in public opinion polling, management consulting, market research, standardized testing, and evaluation research, which assesses the impact of particular policies and programs before or after they go into effect.

One way to see the benefits of a sociological education is to compile a list of some of the famous practical idealists who studied sociology in university. That list includes several former heads of state, among them President Fernando Cardoso of Brazil, President Tomas Masaryk of Czechoslovakia, Prime Minister Edward Seaga of Jamaica, and President Ronald Reagan of the United States. The former vice-president of the Liberal Party of Canada and president and vice-chancellor of York University in Toronto, Lorna Marsden, is a sociologist. Anthony Giddens, former director of the London School of Economics and adviser to former British Prime Minister Tony Blair, also holds a doctorate in sociology. So do Martin Goldfarb, chairman, president, and CEO of Goldfarb Consultants International, and Donna Dasko, senior vice-president of Environics; they head two of Canada's leading public opinion firms with offices and affiliates around the world. Alex Himelfarb, former clerk of the Privy Council and secretary to the Cabinet in Ottawa, and now the Canadian ambassador to Italy, holds a sociology Ph.D. too. British Columbia native Steve Nash of the Phoenix Suns is widely considered the best team player in professional basketball today, and his agent claims he is "the most color-blind person I've ever known" (Robbins, 2005). Arguably, Nash's sociology degree contributes to his team-building ability and his performance on the court by helping him to better understand the importance of groups and diverse social conditions in shaping human behaviour.

In sum, although sociology does not offer easy solutions to the question of how the goal of improving society may be accomplished, it does provide a useful way of understanding our current predicament and seeing possible ways of dealing with it, of leading us a little farther away from the mud outside the cave. You sampled sociology's ability to tie personal troubles to social-structural issues when we discussed suicide. You reviewed the major theoretical perspectives that enable sociologists to connect the personal with the social-structural. When we outlined the half-fulfilled promises of postindustrialism and globalization, you saw sociology's ability to provide an understanding of where we are and where we can go.

We frankly admit that the questions we raise in this book are tough to answer. Sharp controversy surrounds them all. However, we are sure that if you try to grapple with them, you will enhance your understanding of your society's, and your own, possibilities. In brief, sociology can help you figure out where you fit into society and how you can make society fit you.

NOTES

1. At the end of 2002, the Innu began to be relocated at government expense to new homes in Natuashish, a modern village carved out of the wilderness 15 kilometres west of Davis Inlet. By 2005, it was clear that modern dwellings alone were unable to solve the complex social problems of the Innu, which merely reproduced themselves in Natuashish.

2. Some sociologists also distinguish *mesostructures,* social relations that link microstructures and macrostructures. See Chapter 6, Networks, Groups, Bureaucracies, and Societies.

SUMMARY

1. What does the sociological study of suicide tell us about society and about sociology?
   Durkheim noted that suicide is an apparently non-social and antisocial action that people often, but unsuccessfully, try to explain psychologically. He showed that suicide rates are influenced by the level of social solidarity of the groups to which people belong. This theory suggests that a distinctively *social* realm influences all human behaviour.

2. What is the sociological perspective?
   The sociological perspective analyzes the connection between personal troubles and three levels of social structure: microstructures, macrostructures, and global structures.

3. How are values, theories, and research related?
   Values are ideas about what is right and wrong. Values often motivate sociologists to define which problems are worth studying and to make initial assumptions about how to explain sociological phenomena. A theory is a tentative explanation of some aspect of social life. It states how and why specific facts are connected. Research is the process of carefully observing social reality to test the validity of a theory. Sociological theories may be modified and even rejected through research, and those theories are often motivated by sociologists' values.

4. **What are the major theoretical traditions in sociology?**
   Sociology has four major theoretical traditions. Functionalism analyzes how social order is supported by macrostructures. The conflict approach analyzes how social inequality is maintained and challenged. Symbolic interactionism analyzes how meaning is created when people communicate in microlevel settings. Feminist theories focus on the social sources of patriarchy in both macrolevel and microlevel settings.

5. **What were the main influences on the rise of sociology?**
   The rise of sociology was stimulated by the Scientific, Industrial, and Democratic Revolutions. The Scientific Revolution encouraged the view that sound conclusions about the workings of society must be based on solid evidence, not just on speculation. The Democratic Revolution suggested that people are responsible for organizing society and that human intervention can therefore solve social problems. The Industrial Revolution created a host of new and serious social problems that attracted the attention of many social thinkers.

6. **What are the main influences on sociology today and what are the main interests of sociology?**
   The Postindustrial Revolution is the technology-driven shift from manufacturing to service industries. Globalization is the process by which formerly separate economies, states, and cultures become tied together and people become increasingly aware of their growing interdependence. The causes and consequences of postindustrialism and globalization form the great sociological puzzles of our time. The tensions between equality and inequality of opportunity, and between freedom and constraint, are among the chief interests of sociology today.

KEY TERMS

class conflict (p. 17)

conflict theory (p. 17)

Democratic Revolution (p. 13)

dysfunctional consequences (p. 17)

feminist theory (p. 20)

functionalism (p. 16)

global structures (p. 10)

globalization (p. 25)

Industrial Revolution (p. 13)

latent functions (p. 17)

macrostructures (p. 9)

manifest functions (p. 17)

microstructures (p. 9)

patriarchy (p. 9)

Postindustrial Revolution (p. 25)

Protestant ethic (p. 18)

research (p. 15)

Scientific Revolution (p. 12)

social constructionism (p. 19)

social solidarity (p. 6)

social structures (p. 9)

sociological imagination (p. 10)

symbolic interactionism (p. 19)

theories (p. 15)

values (p. 15)

QUESTIONS TO CONSIDER

1. What is the difference between objectivity and subjectivity? What roles do objectivity and subjectivity play in sociology?

2. What does Durkheim mean by "social solidarity"? How does he apply the term to the study of suicide? Comparing Canada 100 years ago with Canada today, how and why do you think the level of social solidarity has changed? What accounts for the change?

What are some consequences of the change? Has the level of social solidarity changed more for some groups than for others? If so, why and with what consequences?

3. Do you think Canadians have more or less freedom and equality of opportunity now than they did 100 years ago? Do you think we will have more or less freedom and equality of opportunity in 100 years than we do today? Justify your argument.

WEB RESOURCES

Companion Website for This Book

http://www.compass3e.nelson.com

Begin by clicking on the Student Resources section of the website. Next, select the chapter you are studying from the pull-down menu. From the Student Resources page you have easy access to InfoTrac® College Edition, additional Weblinks, and other resources. The website also has many useful tips to aid you in your study of sociology, including practice tests for each chapter.

InfoTrac® Search Terms

These search terms are provided to assist you in beginning to conduct research on this topic by visiting http://www.infotrac-college.com:

conflict theory
feminism
functionalism
social structure
suicide
symbolic interactionism

Recommended Websites

For an inspiring essay on the practice of the sociological craft by one of North America's leading sociologists, see Gary T. Marx, "Of Methods and Manners for Aspiring Sociologists: 37 Moral Imperatives," on the World Wide Web at http://web.mit.edu/gtmarx/www/37moral.html.

SocioWeb is a comprehensive guide to sociological resources on the World Wide Web at http://www.socioweb.com.

The Canadian Sociological Association (CSA) is the professional organization of Canadian sociologists. Visit the CSA website at http://www.csaa.ca.

CengageNOW™

http://hed.nelson.com

This online diagnostic tool identifies each student's unique needs with a Pretest that generates a personalized Study Plan for each chapter, helping students focus on concepts they're having the most difficulty mastering. Students then take a Posttest after reading the chapter to measure their understanding of the material. An Instructor Gradebook is available to track and monitor student progress.

How Sociologists Do Research

In this chapter, you will learn that

- Scientific ideas differ from common sense and other forms of knowledge. Scientific ideas are assessed in the clear light of systematically collected evidence and public scrutiny.

- Sociological research depends not just on the rigorous testing of ideas but also on creative insight. Thus, the objective and subjective phases of inquiry are both important in good research.

- The main methods of collecting sociological data include experiments, surveys, systematic observations of natural social settings, and the analysis of existing documents and official statistics.

- Each data collection method has characteristic strengths and weaknesses. Each method is appropriate for different kinds of research problems.

SCIENCE AND EXPERIENCE

PERSONAL
ANECDOTE

OTTFFSSENT

"Okay, Mr. Smarty Pants, see if you can figure this one out." That's how Robert Brym's 11-year-old daughter, Talia, greeted him one day when she came home from school. "I wrote some letters of the alphabet on this sheet of paper. They form a pattern. Take a look at the letters and tell me the pattern."

Robert took the sheet of paper from Talia and smiled confidently. "Like most North Americans, I'd had a lot of experience with this sort of puzzle," says Robert. "For example, most IQ and SAT tests ask you to find patterns in sequences of letters, and you learn certain ways of solving these problems. One of the most common methods is to see if the 'distance' between adjoining letters stays the same or varies predictably. For example, in the sequence ADGJ, there are two missing letters between each adjoining pair. Insert the missing letters and you get the first 10 letters of the alphabet: A(BC)D(EF)G(HI)J.

"This time, however, I was stumped. On the sheet of paper Talia had written the letters OTTFFSSENT. I tried to use the distance method to solve the problem. Nothing worked. After 10 minutes of head scratching, I gave up."

"The answer's easy," Talia said, clearly pleased at her father's failure. "Spell out the numbers 1 to 10. The first letter of each word—<u>o</u>ne, <u>t</u>wo, <u>t</u>hree, and so forth—spells OTTFFSSENT. Looks like you're not as smart as you thought. See ya." And with that she bounced off to her room.

"Later that day, it dawned on me that Talia had taught me more than just a puzzle. She had shown me that experience sometimes prevents people from seeing things. My experience with solving letter puzzles by using certain set methods kept me from solving the unusual problem of OTTFFSSENT." Said differently, reality (in this case, a pattern of letters) is not just a thing "out there" we can learn to perceive "objectively." As social scientists have appreciated for more than a century, *experience* helps determine how we perceive reality, including what patterns we see and whether we are able to see patterns at all (Hughes, 1967: 16).

The fact that experience filters perceptions is the single biggest problem for sociological research. In sociological research, the filtering occurs in four stages (see Figure 2.1). First, as noted in Chapter 1, A Sociological Compass, the real-life experiences and passions of sociologists motivate much research. That is, our *values* often help us decide which problems are worth investigating. These values may reflect the typical outlook of our class, race, gender, region, historical period, and so on. Second, our values lead us to formulate and adopt favoured *theories* for interpreting and explaining those problems. Third, sociologists' interpretations are influenced by *previous research,* which we consult to find out what we already know about a subject. And fourth, the *methods* we use to gather data mould our perceptions. The shape of our tools often helps determine which bits of reality we dig up.

FIGURE 2.1
How Research Filters
Perception

Values → Theories → Previous research → Methods → "Reality"

Given that values, theories, previous research, and research methods filter our perceptions, you are right to conclude that we can never perceive society in a pure or objective form.[1] What we can do is use techniques of data collection that minimize bias. We can also clearly and publicly describe the filters that influence our perceptions. Doing so enables us to eliminate obvious sources of bias. It also helps others see biases we miss and try to correct for them. The end result is a more accurate perception of reality than is possible by relying exclusively on blind prejudice or common sense.

It is thus clear that a healthy tension pervades all sociological scholarship. On the one hand, researchers generally try to be objective in order to perceive reality as clearly as possible. They follow the rules of the scientific method and design data collection techniques to minimize bias. On the other hand, the values and passions that grow out of personal experience are important sources of creativity. As Max Weber said, we choose to study "only those segments of reality which have become significant to us because of their value-relevance" (Weber, 1964 [1949]: 76). So objectivity and subjectivity each play an important role in science, including sociology. Oversimplifying a little, we can say that although objectivity is a reality check, subjectivity leads us to define which aspects of reality are worth checking on in the first place.

Most of this chapter is about the reality check. It explores how sociologists try to adhere to the rules of the scientific method. We first contrast scientific and unscientific thinking. We next discuss the steps involved in the sociological research process. We then describe the main methods of gathering sociological data and the decisions that have to be made during the research process. Finally, we return to the role of subjectivity in research.

Scientific versus Unscientific Thinking

In science, seeing is believing. In everyday life, believing is seeing. In other words, in everyday life our biases easily influence our observations. This often leads us to draw incorrect conclusions about what we see. In contrast, scientists, including sociologists, develop ways of collecting, observing, and thinking about evidence that minimize their chance of drawing biased conclusions.

On what basis do you decide statements are true in everyday life? Below we describe 10 types of unscientific thinking (Babbie, 2000). As you read about each one, ask yourself how frequently you think unscientifically. If you often think unscientifically, use this chapter to help you develop more objective ways of thinking.

WHERE DO YOU FIT IN?

1. "Chicken soup helps get rid of a cold. *It worked for my grandparents, and it works for me.*" This statement represents knowledge based on *tradition*. Although some traditional knowledge is valid (sugar will rot your teeth), some is not (masturbation will not blind you). Science is required to separate valid from invalid knowledge.

2. "Weak magnets can be used to heal many illnesses. *I read all about it in the newspaper.*" This statement represents knowledge based on *authority*. We often think something is true because we read it in an authoritative source or hear it from an expert. But authoritative sources and experts can be wrong. For example, nineteenth-century Western physicians commonly bled their patients with leeches to draw "poisons" from their bodies. This often did more harm than good. As this example suggests, scientists should always question authority to arrive at more valid knowledge.

3. "The car that hit the cyclist was dark brown. I was going for a walk last night when *I saw the accident.*" This statement represents knowledge based on *casual observation*. Unfortunately, we are usually pretty careless observers. That is why good lawyers can often trip up eyewitnesses in courtrooms. Eyewitnesses are rarely certain about what they saw. In general, uncertainty can be reduced by observing in a conscious and deliberate manner and by recording observations. That is just what scientists do.

4. "If you work hard, you can get ahead. *I know because several of my parents' friends started off poor but are now comfortably middle class.*" This statement represents knowledge based on *overgeneralization*. For instance, if you know a few people who started off poor, worked

Perhaps the first major advance in modern medicine took place when doctors stopped using unproven interventions in their treatment of patients. One such intervention involved bleeding patients, shown here in a medieval drawing.

hard, and became rich you may think any poor person can become rich if he or she works hard enough. You may not know about the more numerous poor people who work hard and remain poor or about the rich people who never worked hard. Scientists, however, sample cases that are representative of entire populations. This enables them to avoid overgeneralization. They also avoid overgeneralization by repeating research, which ensures that they do not draw conclusions from an unusual set of research findings.

5. "I'm right because *I can't think of any contrary cases*." This statement represents knowledge based on *selective observation*. Sometimes we unconsciously ignore evidence that challenges our firmly held beliefs. Thus, you may actually know some people who work hard but remain poor. However, to maintain your belief that hard work results in wealth, you may keep them out of mind. The scientific requirement that evidence be drawn from representative samples of the population minimizes bias arising from selective observation.

6. "Mr. Smith is poor even though he works hard, but that's because he has a disability. People with disabilities are the only *exception to the rule* that if you work hard you can get ahead." This statement represents knowledge based on *qualification*. Qualifications or "exceptions to the rule" are often made in everyday life, and they are in science, too. The difference is that in everyday life, qualifications are easily accepted as valid, while in scientific inquiry they are treated as statements that must be carefully examined in the light of evidence.

7. "The Toronto Blue Jays won 50 percent of their baseball games over the last three months but 65 percent of the games they played on Thursdays. *Because it happened so often before,* I bet they'll win next Thursday." This statement represents knowledge based on *illogical reasoning*. In everyday life, we may expect the recurrence of events without reasonable cause, ignoring the fact that rare sequences of events occur just by chance. For example, it is possible for you to flip a coin 10 times and have it come up heads each time. On average, this will happen once every 1024 times you flip a coin 10 times. In the absence of any apparent reason for this happening, it is merely coincidental. It is illogical to believe otherwise. Scientists refrain from illogical reasoning. They also use statistical techniques to distinguish between events that are probably due to chance and those that are not.

8. "*I just can't be wrong*." This statement represents knowledge based on *ego-defence*. Even scientists may be passionately committed to the conclusions they reach in their research because they have invested much time, energy, and money in them. It is other scientists—more accurately, the whole institution of science, with its commitment to publishing research results and critically scrutinizing findings—that put strict limits on ego-defence in scientific understanding.

9. "*The matter is settled once and for all*." This statement represents knowledge based on the *premature closure of inquiry*. This way of thinking involves deciding that all the relevant evidence has been gathered on a particular subject. Science, however, is committed to the idea that all theories are only temporarily true. Matters are never settled.

10. "*There must be supernatural forces at work here*." This statement represents knowledge based on *mystification*. When we can find no rational explanation for a phenomenon, we may attribute it to forces that cannot be observed or fully understood. Although such forces may exist, scientists remain skeptical. They are committed to discovering observable causes of observable effects.

CONDUCTING RESEARCH

The Research Cycle

Sociological research seeks to overcome the kind of unscientific thinking described above. It is a cyclical process that involves six steps (Figure 2.2).

First, the sociologist must *formulate a research question*. A research question must be stated so it can be answered by systematically collecting and analyzing sociological data.

Even Albert Einstein, often hailed as the most intelligent person of the twentieth century, sometimes ignored evidence in favour of pet theories. However, the social institution of science, which makes ideas public and subjects them to careful scrutiny, often overcomes such bias.

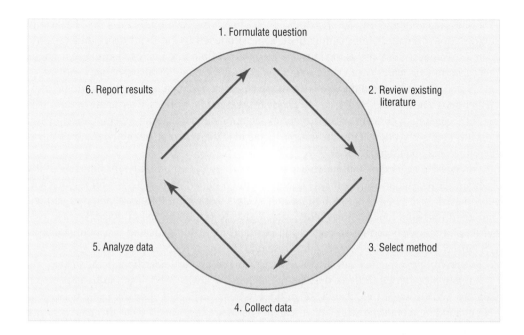

FIGURE 2.2
The Research Cycle

Sociological research cannot determine whether God exists or what the best political system is. Answers to such questions require faith more than evidence. Sociological research can determine why some people are more religious than others are and which political systems create more opportunities for higher education. Answers to such questions require evidence more than faith.

Second, the sociologist must *review the existing research literature.* Researchers must elaborate their research questions in light of what other sociologists have already debated and discovered. Why? Because reading the relevant sociological literature stimulates researchers' sociological imagination, allows them to refine their initial questions, and prevents duplication of effort.

Selecting a research method is the third step in the research cycle. As we will see in detail below, each data collection method has strengths and weaknesses. Each method is therefore best suited to studying a different kind of problem. When choosing a method, we must keep these strengths and weaknesses in mind. (In the ideal but, unfortunately, infrequent case, several methods are used simultaneously to study the same problem. This can overcome the drawbacks of any single method and increase confidence in the findings.)

Carol Wainio's *We Can Be Certain* (1982). Research involves taking the plunge from speculation to testing ideas against evidence.

The fourth stage of the research cycle involves *collecting data* by observing subjects, interviewing them, reading documents produced by or about them, and so forth. Many researchers think this is the most exciting stage of the research cycle because it brings them face to face with the puzzling sociological reality that so fascinates them.

Other researchers find the fifth step of the research cycle, *analyzing the data,* the most challenging. During data analysis you can learn things that nobody ever knew before. It is the time when data confirm some of your expectations and confound others, requiring you to think creatively about familiar issues, reconsider the relevant theoretical and research literature, and abandon pet ideas.

Of course, research is not much use to the sociological community, the subjects of the research, or the wider society if researchers do not *publish the results* in a report, a scientific journal, or a book. That is the research cycle's sixth step. Publication serves another important function, too. It allows other sociologists to scrutinize and criticize the research. On that basis, errors can be corrected and new and more sophisticated research questions can be formulated for the next round of research. In this sense, the practice of science is a social activity governed by rules defined and enforced by the scientific community.

It would be wrong to think that the research cycle always begins at the first stage and then proceeds to stage two, then to stage three, and so forth. The research cycle is a useful way of thinking about the stages of research—an ideal, if you will—but the exact starting point and progression of research varies from one project to the next. For example, sometimes research begins with a personal puzzle, sometimes with alternative interpretations of observations collected in a project, and sometimes with a skeptical perspective on the research literature.

Ethical Considerations

Throughout the research cycle, researchers must be mindful of the need to *respect their subjects' rights,* which means, in the first instance, that researchers must do their subjects no harm. This is the right to safety. People must have the right to decide whether they can be studied and, if so, in what way. Second, research subjects must have the right to decide whether their attitudes and behaviours may be revealed to the public and, if so, in what way. This is the right to privacy. Third, researchers cannot use data in a way that allows them to be traced to a particular subject. This is the subject's right to confidentiality. Fourth, subjects must be told how the information they supply will be used. They must also be allowed to judge the degree of personal risk involved in answering questions. This is the right to informed consent.

Ethical issues arise not only in the treatment of subjects but also in the treatment of research results. For example, plagiarism is a concern in academic life, especially among students, who write research papers and give them to professors for evaluation. A 2003 study found that 38 percent of college students admitted to committing "cut and paste" plagiarism when writing essays, up from just 10 percent in 2000 (Edmundson, 2003). Ready-made essays are also widely available for purchase.

Increased plagiarism is a consequence of the spread of the web and the growing view that everything on it is public and therefore does not have to be cited. That view is wrong. The Code of Ethics of the American Sociological Association states that we must "explicitly identify, credit, and reference the author" when we make any use of another person's written work, "whether it is published, unpublished, or electronically available" (American Sociological Association, 1999: 16).

Making such ethical standards better known can help remedy the problem of plagiarism. So can better policing. Powerful web-based applications are now available that help university and college instructors determine whether essays are plagiarized in whole or in part (visit http://www.turnitin.com). Perhaps the most effective remedy, however, is for instructors to ensure that what they teach really matters to their students. If they do, students won't be as inclined to plagiarize because they will regard essay writing as a process of personal discovery. You can't cut, paste, or buy enlightenment (Edmundson, 2003).

Bearing in mind our thumbnail sketch of the research cycle, we devote the rest of this chapter mainly to exploring its fourth and fifth stage, the gathering and analyzing of evidence. In this context we describe each of sociology's major research methods. These methods include participant observation, experiments, surveys, and the examination of existing documents and official statistics. We begin by describing participant observation research and related research methods.

THE MAIN METHODS OF SOCIOLOGY

Field Methods: From Detached Observation to "Going Native"

Eikoku News Digest published a column in the late 1990s by a supposed expert observer of English social life. It advised Japanese residents of England how to act English. One column informed readers that once they hear the words "You must come round for dinner!" they will have been accepted into English social life and must therefore know how to behave appropriately. The column advised readers to obey the following dinner party rules:

1. Arrive 20 minutes late because in England dinner always takes 20 minutes longer to prepare than expected.
2. Don't compliment the décor because in England everyone else's taste in décor is considered dreadful.
3. Bring a cheap wine because the English can't taste the difference.
4. Praise the food by saying "mmmm." The larger the number of "m"s, the greater the compliment.
5. After the meal, don't say it was good. "If someone asks how your dinner was, do not praise the food in detail. They will deduce that the conversation was boring. . . . And do not talk about the interesting conversation you had. They will assume that the food was particularly unpleasant." ("Going Native: Dinner Parties," 2003)

This advice was almost certainly meant as a joke. However, its absurdity serves to caution all students of social life about the dangers of drawing conclusions based on casual observation. By observing others casually, we can easily get things terribly wrong.

Some sociologists undertake **field research**, or research based on the observation of people in their natural settings. The field researcher goes wherever people meet. Settings investigated by field researchers include hospital intensive care units, the Yukon International Storytelling Festival, white teenage heavy-metal gangs, the studio audience of a daytime TV talk show, the gay community, the alternative hard rock scene, ethnic slums, and the rave subculture (Chambliss, 1996; Cruikshank, 1997; Gaines, 1990; Grindstaff, 1997; Humphreys, 1975; Schippers, 2002; Whyte, 1981 [1943]; Wilson, 2002). When they arrive in the field, however, researchers come prepared with strategies to avoid getting things terribly wrong.

One such strategy is *detached observation*. This approach involves classifying and counting the behaviour of interest according to a predetermined scheme. For example, a sociologist wanted to know more about how gender segregation originates. He observed children of different ages playing in summer camps and daycare centres in Canada and Poland. He recorded the gender composition of play groups, the ages at which children started playing in gender-segregated groups, and the kinds of play activities that became gender segregated (Richer, 1990). Similarly, two sociologists wanted to know more about why some American college students don't participate in class discussions. They sat in on classes and recorded the number of students who participated, the number of times they spoke, and the gender of the instructor and of the students who spoke (Karp and Yoels, 1976). In both research projects, the sociologists were interested in knowing how young people express gender in everyday behaviour, and they knew what to look for before they entered the field.

Field research is research based on the observation of people in their natural settings.

Two main problems confound direct observation. First, the presence of the researcher may itself affect the behaviour of the people being observed. Sociologists sometimes call this problem the *Hawthorne effect* because researchers at the Western Electric Company's Hawthorne factory in the 1930s claimed to find that workers' productivity increased no matter how they changed their work environment. Productivity increased, they said, just because the researchers were paying attention to the workers.[2] Similarly, some students may participate less in classroom discussion if researchers come in and start taking notes; the presence of the researchers may be intimidating. The second problem with direction observation is that the *meaning* of the observed behaviour may remain obscure to the researcher. The twitch of an eye may be an involuntary muscle contraction, an indication of a secret being kept, a sexual come-on, a parody of someone else twitching an eye, and so on. We cannot know what it means simply by observing the eye twitch.

To understand what an eye twitch (or any other behaviour) means we must be able to see it in its social context and from the point of view of the people we are observing. Anthropologists and a growing number of sociologists spend months or even years living with a people so they can learn their language, values, mannerisms—their entire culture— and develop an intimate understanding of their behaviour. This sort of research is called **ethnographic** when it describes the entire way of life of a people (*ethnos* means "nation" or "people" in Greek; Burawoy et al., 2000; Geertz, 1973; Gille and Riain, 2002).

In rare cases, ethnographic researchers have "gone native," actually giving up their research role and becoming members of the group they are studying. Going native is of no value to the sociological community because it does not result in the publication of new findings. However, going native is worth mentioning because it is the opposite of detached observation. Usually, field researchers employ techniques for collecting data between the two extremes of detached observation and going native. The field method they employ most often is participant observation.

Participant Observation

Sociologists engage in **participant observation** when they attempt to observe a social milieu objectively *and* take part in the activities of the people they are studying (Lofland and Lofland, 1995). By participating in the lives of their subjects, researchers are able to see the world from their subjects' point of view. This method allows them to achieve a deep and sympathetic understanding of people's beliefs, values, and motives. In addition, participant observation requires that sociologists step back and observe their subjects' milieu from an outsider's point of view. This helps them see their subjects more objectively. In participant-observation research, then, there is a tension between the goals of subjectivity and objectivity. As you will see, however, this is a healthy tension that enhances our understanding of many social settings.

The Professional Fence

A well-known example of participant-observation research is Carl B. Klockars's analysis of the professional "fence," a person who buys and sells stolen goods (Klockars, 1974). Among other things, Klockars wanted to understand how criminals can knowingly hurt people and live with the guilt. Are criminals capable of this because they are "sick" or unfeeling? Klockars came to a different conclusion by examining the case of Vincent Swaggi (a pseudonym).

Swaggi buys cheap stolen goods from thieves and then sells them in his store for a handsome profit. His buying is private and patently criminal. His selling is public and, to his customers, it appears to be legal. Consequently, Swaggi faces the moral dilemma shared by all criminals to varying degrees. He has to reconcile the very different moral codes of the two worlds he straddles, cancelling out any feelings of guilt he derives from conventional morality.

"The way I look at it, I'm a businessman," says Swaggi. "Sure I buy hot stuff, but I never stole nothing in my life. Some driver brings me a couple of cartons, though, I ain't gonna turn him away. If I don't buy it, somebody else will. So what's the difference? I might as

The **ethnographic** researcher spends months or even years living with a people to learn their language, values, mannerisms—their entire culture—and develop an intimate understanding of their behaviour.

Participant observation involves carefully observing people's face-to-face interactions and participating in their lives over a long period of time, thus achieving a deep and sympathetic understanding of what motivates them to act in the way they do.

well make money with him instead of somebody else." Swaggi thus denies responsibility for his actions. He also claims his actions never hurt anyone:

> Did you see the paper yesterday? You figure it out. Last year I musta had $25,000 wortha merchandise from Sears. In this city last year they could'a called it Sears, Roebuck, and Swaggi. Just yesterday I read where Sears just had the biggest year in history, made more money than ever before. Now if I had that much of Sears's stuff can you imagine how much they musta lost all told? Millions, must be millions. And they still had their biggest year ever. . . . You think they end up losing when they get clipped? Don't you believe it. They're no different from anybody else. If they don't get it back by takin' it off their taxes, they get it back from insurance. Who knows, maybe they do both.

And if he has done a few bad things in his life, then, says Swaggi, so has everyone else. Besides, he's also done a lot of good. In fact, he believes his virtuous acts more than compensate for the skeletons in his closet. Consider, for example, how he managed to protect one of his suppliers and get him a promotion at the same time:

> I had this guy bringin' me radios. Nice little clock radios, sold for $34.95. He worked in the warehouse. Two a day he'd bring me, an' I'd give him fifteen for the both of 'em. Well, after a while he told me his boss was gettin' suspicious 'cause inventory showed a big shortage. . . . So I ask him if anybody else is takin' much stuff. He says a couple of guys do. I tell him to lay off for a while an' the next time he sees one of the other guys take somethin' to tip off the boss. They'll fire the guy an' clear up the shortage. Well he did an' you know what happened? They made my man assistant shipper. Now once a month I get a carton delivered right to my store with my name on it. Clock radios, percolators, waffle irons, anything I want fifty off wholesale. (quoted in Klockars, 1974: 135–61)

Lessons in Method

Without Klockars's research, we might think that all criminals are able to live with their guilt only because they are pathological or lack empathy for their fellow human beings. But thanks partly to Klockars's research, we know better. We understand that criminals are able to avoid feeling guilty about their actions and get on with their work because they weave a blanket of rationalizations over their criminal activities. These justifications make their illegal activities appear morally acceptable and normal, at least to the criminals themselves. We understand this aspect of criminal activity better because Klockars spent 15 months befriending Swaggi and closely observing him on the job. He interviewed Swaggi for a total of about 400 hours, taking detailed "field notes" most of the time. He then wrote up his descriptions, quotations, and insights in a book that is now considered a minor classic in the sociology of crime and deviance.

Why is observation *and* participation necessary in participant-observation research? Because sociological insight is sharpest when researchers stand both inside and outside the lives of their subjects. Said differently, we see more clearly when we move back and forth between inside and outside.

By immersing themselves in their subjects' world, by learning their language and their culture in depth, insiders are able to experience the world just as their subjects do. Subjectivity can, however, go too far. After all, "natives" are rarely able to see their cultures with much objectivity and inmates of prisons and mental institutions do not have access to official information about themselves. It is only by regularly standing apart and observing their subjects from the point of view of outsiders that researchers can raise analytical issues and see things their subjects are blind to or are forbidden from seeing.

Objectivity can also go too far. Observers who try to attain complete objectivity will often not be able to make correct inferences about their subjects' behaviour. That is because they cannot fully understand the way their subjects experience the world and cannot ask them about their experiences. Instead, observers who seek complete objectivity must rely only on their own experiences to impute meaning to a social setting. Yet the meaning a situation holds for observers may differ from the meaning it holds for their subjects.

In short, opting for pure observation or pure participation compromises the researcher's ability to see the world sociologically. Instead, participant observation requires the researcher to keep walking a tightrope between the two extremes of objectivity and subjectivity.

It is often difficult for participant-observers to gain access to the groups they want to study. They must first win the confidence of their subjects, who must feel at ease in the presence of the researcher before they behave naturally. *Reactivity* occurs when the researcher's presence influences the subjects' behaviour (Webb, Campbell, Schwartz, and Sechrest, 1966). Reaching a state of non-reactivity requires patience and delicacy on the researcher's part. It took Klockars several months to meet and interview about 60 imprisoned thieves before one of them felt comfortable enough to recommend that he contact Swaggi. Klockars had to demonstrate genuine interest in the thieves' activities and convince them he was no threat to them before they opened up to him. Often, sociologists can minimize reactivity by gaining access to a group in stages. At first, researchers may simply attend a group meeting. After a time, they may start to attend more regularly. Then, when their faces are more familiar, they may strike up a conversation with some of the friendlier group members. Only later will they begin to explain their true motivation for attending.

Klockars and Swaggi are both white men. Their similarity made communication between them easier. In contrast, race, gender, class, and age differences sometimes make it difficult, and occasionally impossible, for some researchers to study some groups. We can scarcely imagine a sociologist nearing retirement conducting participant-observation research on youth gangs or a black sociologist using this research method to study skinheads. Nonetheless, in many participant-observation studies, the big social differences between sociologists and their subjects were overcome and resulted in excellent research (e.g., Liebow, 1967; Stack, 1974).

Most participant-observation studies begin as **exploratory research**, which means researchers at first have only a vague sense of what they are looking for and perhaps no sense at all of what they will discover in the course of their study. They are equipped only with some hunches based on their own experience and their reading of the relevant research literature. They try, however, to treat these hunches as hypotheses. **Hypotheses** are unverified but testable statements about the phenomena that interest researchers. As they immerse themselves in the life of their subjects, their observations constitute sociological data that allow them to reject, accept, or modify their initial hypotheses. Indeed, researchers often purposely seek out observations that enable them to determine the validity and scope of their hypotheses. ("From previous research I know seniors are generally more religious than young people, and that seems to be true in this community, too. But does religiosity vary among people of the same age who are rich, middle class, working class, and poor? If so, why? If not, why not?") Purposively choosing observations results in the creation of a grounded theory. A **grounded theory** is an explanation of a phenomenon based not on mere speculation but on the controlled scrutiny of subjects (Glaser and Straus, 1967).

Methodological Problems

Measurement

The great advantage of participant observation is that it lets researchers get "inside the minds" of their subjects and discover their view of the world in its full complexity. It is an especially valuable technique when little is known about the group or phenomenon under investigation and the sociologist is interested in constructing a theory about it. But participant observation has drawbacks too. To understand these problems, we must say a few words about measurement in sociology.

When researchers think about the social world, they use mental constructs or concepts, such as "race," "class," "gender," and so forth. Concepts that can have more than one value are called **variables**. Height and wealth are variables. Perhaps less obviously, affection and perceived beauty are, too. Just as a person can be 160 centimetres or 190 centimetres tall, rich or poor, someone can be passionately in love with, or indifferent to, the girl next

Exploratory research is an attempt to describe, understand, and develop a theory about a social phenomenon in the absence of, or with little, previous research on the subject.

Hypotheses are unverified but testable statements about the relationship between two or more variables.

A grounded theory is an explanation of a phenomenon based not on mere speculation but on the controlled scrutiny of subjects.

A variable is a concept that can take on more than one value.

door on the grounds that she is beautiful or plain. In each case, we know we are dealing with a variable because height, wealth, affection, and perceived beauty can take different values.

Once researchers identify the variables that interest them, they must decide which real-world observations correspond to each variable. Should "class," for example, be measured by determining people's annual income? Or should it be measured by determining their accumulated wealth, or years of formal education, or some combination of these or other indicators of rank? Deciding which observations to link to which variables is known as **operationalization**.

Sociological variables can sometimes be measured by casual observation. It is usually easy to tell whether someone is a man or a woman, and participant-observers can learn a great deal more about their subjects through extended discussion and careful observation. When researchers find out how much money their subjects earn, how satisfied they are with their marriages, whether they have ever been the victims of a criminal act, and so forth, they are measuring the values of the sociological variables embedded in their hypotheses.

Researchers must establish criteria for assigning values to variables. At exactly what level of annual income can someone be considered "upper class"? What are the precise characteristics of settlements that allow them to be characterized as "urban"? What features of a person permit us to say she is a "leader"? Answers to such questions all involve measurement decisions.

Reliability, Validity, Generalizability, and Causality

In a given research project, participant-observers usually work alone and usually investigate only one group or one type of group. Thus, when we read their research results, we must be convinced of three things if we are to accept their findings. We must be confident that another researcher would interpret things in the same way. We must be confident that their interpretations are accurate. And we must be confident that the findings extend beyond the single case examined. Let us examine each of these points in turn (see Figure 2.3 on page 44):

1. *Would another researcher interpret or measure things in the same way?* This is the problem of **reliability.** If a measurement procedure repeatedly yields consistent results, we consider it reliable. However, in the case of participant observation, there is usually only one person doing the measuring in only one setting. Therefore, we have no way of knowing whether repeating the procedures would yield consistent results.

2. *Are the researcher's interpretations accurate?* This is the problem of **validity**, the problem of whether confirmation of the measures can be found in the real world. If a measurement procedure measures what it is supposed to measure, then it is valid. All valid measures are reliable. However, not all reliable measures are valid. Measuring a person's shoe with a ruler may give us a reliable indicator of that person's shoe size. That is because the ruler repeatedly yields the same results. However, regardless of consistency, shoe size as measured by a ruler is a totally invalid measure of a person's annual income. Similarly, you may think you are measuring annual income by asking people how much they earn. Another interviewer at another time may get exactly the same result when posing the same question. But, despite such reliability, respondents may understate their true income. (A respondent is a person who answers the researcher's questions.) Our measure of annual income may therefore lack validity. Perfectly consistent measures may, in other words, have little truth-value.

   Participant-observers have every right to feel they are on solid ground when it comes to the question of validity. If anyone can tell whether respondents are understating their true income, surely it is someone who has spent months or even years getting to know everything about their lifestyle. Still, doubts may creep in if the criteria used by the participant-observers to assess the validity of their measures are all *internal* to the settings they are investigating. Our confidence in the validity of researchers' measures increases if we are able to use *external* validation criteria. Consider age.

Operationalization is the procedure by which researchers establish criteria for assigning values to variables.

Reliability is the degree to which a measurement procedure yields consistent results.

Validity is the degree to which a measure actually measures what it is intended to measure.

FIGURE 2.3

Measurement as Target Practice: Validity, Reliability, and Generalizability Compared

Validity, reliability, and generalizability can be explained by drawing an analogy between measuring a variable and firing at a bull's-eye. In case 1, above, shots (measures) are far apart (not reliable) and far from the bull's-eye (not valid). In case 2, shots are close to each other (reliable) but far from the bull's-eye (not valid). In case 3, shots are close to the bull's-eye (valid) and close to each other (reliable). In case 4, we use a second target. Our shots are again close to each other (reliable) and close to the bull's-eye (valid). Because our measures were valid and reliable for both the targets in cases 3 and 4, we conclude our results are generalizable.

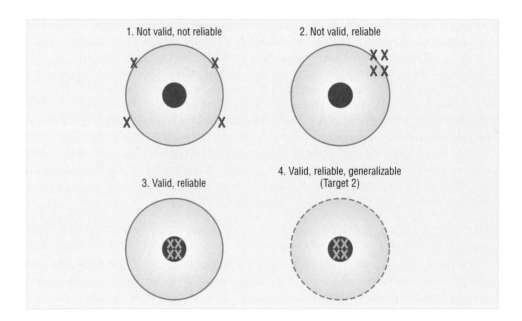

Generalizability exists when research findings apply beyond the specific case examined.

Causality involves the analysis of causes and their effects.

Asking people their age is one way to determine how old they are. The problem with this measure is that people tend to exaggerate their age when they are young and understate it when they are old. A more valid way to determine people's age is to ask them about their year of birth. Year of birth is generally reported more accurately than responses to the question "How old are you?" It is therefore a more valid measure of age. A still more valid measure of age can be found in the "year of birth" entry on people's birth certificates. The point is that validity increases if we have some external check on our measure of age.

3. *Do the research findings apply beyond the specific case examined?* This is the problem of **generalizability**, and it is one of the most serious problems faced by participant-observation studies. Klockars, for example, studied just one professional fence in depth. Can we safely conclude his findings are relevant to all professional fences? Do we dare apply his insights to all criminals? Are we foolhardy if we generalize his conclusions to nearly all of us on the grounds that most of us commit deviant acts at one time or another and must deal with feelings of guilt? None of this is clear from Klockars's research. Nor are questions of generalizability clearly answered by many participant-observation studies, since they are usually studies of single cases.

Related to the issue of generalizability is that of **causality**, the analysis of causes and their effects. Information on how widely or narrowly a research finding applies can help us establish the causes of a social phenomenon. For instance, we might want to know how gender, race, class, parental supervision, police surveillance, and other factors shape the type and rate of juvenile delinquency. If so, we require information on types and rates of criminal activity among teenagers who have a variety of social characteristics and are in a variety of social settings. A participant-observation study of crime is unlikely to provide that sort of information. It is more likely to clarify the process by which a specific group of people in a single setting learns to become criminal. Indeed, researchers who conduct participant-observation studies tend not to think in somewhat mechanical, cause-and-effect terms at all. They prefer instead to view their subjects as engaged in a fluid process of social interaction. As a result, participant-observation is not the preferred method for discovering the general causes of social phenomena.

In sum, participant observation has both strengths and weaknesses. It is especially useful in exploratory research, constructing grounded theory, creating internally valid measures, and developing a sympathetic understanding of the way people see the world. It is often deficient when it comes to establishing reliability, generalizability, and causality. As you will soon learn, these are precisely the strengths of surveys and experiments. Only a small percentage of sociologists conduct experiments. Nonetheless, experiments are important because they set certain standards that other more popular methods try to match. We can show this by discussing experiments concerning the effects of television on real-world violence.

Experiments

In the mid-1960s, about 15 years after the introduction of commercial TV in North America, rates of violent crime began to increase dramatically. Some people were not surprised. The first generation of North American children exposed to high levels of TV violence virtually from birth had reached their mid-teens. TV violence, some commentators said, legitimized violence in the real world, making it seem increasingly normal and acceptable. As a result, they concluded, North American teenagers in the 1960s and subsequent decades were more likely than pre-1960s teens to commit violent acts.

Social scientists soon started investigating the connection between TV and real-world violence by using experimental methods. An **experiment** is a carefully controlled artificial situation that allows researchers to isolate hypothesized causes and measure their effects precisely (Campbell and Stanley, 1963). It uses a special procedure called **randomization** to create two similar groups. Randomization involves assigning individuals to the two groups by chance processes. It then introduces the hypothesized cause to only one of the groups. By comparing the state of the two groups before and after only one of the groups has been exposed to the hypothesized cause, an experiment can determine whether the presumed cause has the predicted effect.

Here is how an experiment on the effects of TV violence on aggressive behaviour might work:

1. *Selection of subjects.* Researchers advertise in local newspapers for parents willing to allow their children to act as research subjects. Fifty children are selected for the experiment.

2. *Random assignment of subjects to experimental and control groups.* At random, each child draws a number from 1 to 50 from a box. The researchers assign children who draw odd numbers to the **experimental group**. This is the group that will be exposed to a violent TV program during the experiment. They assign children who draw even numbers to the **control group**. This is the group that will not be exposed to a violent TV program during the experiment.

   Note that randomization and repetition make the experimental and control groups similar. By assigning subjects to the two groups by using a chance process, and repeating the experiment many times, researchers ensure that the experimental and control groups are likely to have the same proportion of boys and girls, members of different races, children highly motivated to participate in the study, and so forth. Random assignment eliminates bias by allowing a chance process and only a chance process to decide which group each child is assigned to.

3. *Measurement of dependent variable in experimental and control groups.* The researchers put small groups of children in a room and give them toys to play with. They observe the children through a one-way mirror, rating each child in terms of the aggressiveness of his or her play. This is the child's pretest score on the dependent variable, aggressive behaviour. The **dependent variable** is the effect in any cause-and-effect relationship.

4. *Introduction of independent variable to experimental group.* The researchers show children in the experimental group an hour-long TV show in which many violent and aggressive acts take place. They do not show the film to children in the control

Aggressive behaviour among children is common, from siblings fighting to bullying in the schoolyard. Since the inception of home TV in the 1950s, social scientists have sought to develop research designs capable of examining the causal effects, if any, of viewing violence on television.

An experiment **is a carefully controlled artificial situation that allows researchers to isolate hypothesized causes and measure their effects precisely.**

Random **means "by chance"— for example, having an equal and nonzero probability of being sampled.**
Randomization **involves assigning individuals to groups by chance processes.**

An experimental group **in an experiment is the group that is exposed to the independent variable.**

A control group **in an experiment is the group that is not exposed to the independent variable.**

A dependent variable **is the presumed effect in a cause-and-effect relationship.**

An independent variable is the presumed cause in a cause-and-effect relationship.

group. In this experiment, the violent TV show is the independent variable. The **independent variable** is the presumed cause in any cause-and-effect relationship.

5. *Remeasurement of dependent variable in experimental and control groups.* Immediately after the children see the TV show, the researchers again observe the children in both groups at play. Each child's play is given a second aggressiveness rating—the posttest score.

6. *Assessment of experimental effect.* Posttest minus pretest scores are calculated for both the experimental and the control groups. If the posttest minus pretest score for the experimental group is significantly greater than the posttest minus pretest score for the control group, the researchers conclude the independent variable (watching violent TV) has a significant effect on the dependent variable (aggressive behaviour). This conclusion is warranted because the introduction of the independent variable is the only difference between the experimental and control groups.

Experiments on Television Violence

Experiments allow researchers to isolate the single cause of theoretical interest and measure its effect with high reliability, that is, consistently from one experiment to the next. Yet many sociologists argue that experiments are highly artificial situations. They believe that removing people from their natural social settings lowers the validity of experimental results, that is, the degree to which they measure what they are actually supposed to measure. Thus, many experiments show that exposure to media violence has a short-term effect on violent behaviour in young children, especially boys. However, the results of experiments are mixed when it comes to assessing longer-term effects, especially on older children and teenagers (Anderson and Bushman, 2002; Browne and Hamilton-Giachritsis, 2005; Freedman, 2002).

To understand why experiments on the effects of media violence may lack validity, consider that, in the real world, violent behaviour usually means attempting to harm another person physically. Shouting or kicking a toy is not the same thing. In fact, such acts may enable children to relieve frustrations in a fantasy world, lowering their chance of acting violently in the real world. Moreover, in a laboratory situation, aggressive behaviour may be encouraged because it is legitimized. Simply showing a violent TV program may suggest to subjects how the experimenter expects them to behave. Nor is aggressive behaviour punished or controlled in the laboratory setting as it is in the real world. If a boy watching a violent TV show stands up and delivers a karate kick to his brother, a parent or other caregiver is likely to take action to prevent a recurrence. This reaction usually teaches the boy not to engage in aggressive behaviour. In the lab, the lack of disciplinary control may facilitate unrealistically high levels of aggression (Felson, 1996).

Field and Natural Experiments

In an effort to overcome the validity problems noted above and still retain many of the benefits of experimental design, some sociologists have conducted experiments in natural settings. In such experiments, researchers forgo strict randomization of subjects. Instead, they compare groups that are already quite similar. They either introduce the independent variable themselves (this is called a *field experiment*) or observe what happens when the independent variable is introduced to one of the groups in the normal course of social life (this is called a *natural experiment*).

Some field experiments on media effects compare boys in institutionalized settings, such as boarding schools. The researchers expose half the boys to violent TV programming. Measures of aggressiveness taken before and after the introduction of violent programming allow researchers to calculate its effect on behaviour. One re-analysis of 28 such studies yielded mixed results. Although 16 of the field experiments (57 percent) suggested that subjects engage in more aggression following exposure to violent films, 12 (43 percent) did not (Wood, Wong, and Chachere, 1991).

Natural experiments have compared rates of aggressive behaviour in Canadian and other towns with and without TV service, but their results are inconclusive. They are also muddied by the fact that there are substantial differences among the towns apart from the presence or absence of TV service. It is therefore unclear whether differences in child aggressiveness are due to media effects.

Because of the validity problems noted above, it has not been convincingly demonstrated that TV violence generally encourages violent behaviour. The sociological consensus is that TV violence probably affects only a very small percentage of viewers. Some young people—those who are weakly connected to family, school, community, and peers—seem susceptible to translating media violence into violent behaviour. Lack of social support allows their personal problems to become greatly magnified—and if guns are readily available, these youth are prone to using violent media messages as models for their own behaviour. In contrast, for the overwhelming majority of young people, violence in the mass media is just a source of entertainment and a fantasy outlet for emotional issues, not a template for action (Anderson, 2003; Felson, 1996; Harding, Fox, and Mehta, 2002; Sullivan, 2002).

Surveys

Sampling

Surveys are part of the fabric of everyday life in North America. You see surveys in action when the CBC conducts a poll to discover the percentage of Canadians who approve of the prime minister's performance, when someone phones to ask about your taste in breakfast cereal, and when the late advice columnist Ann Landers asked her readers, "If you had to do it over again, would you have children?" In every **survey**, people are asked questions about their knowledge, attitudes, or behaviour, either in a face-to-face or telephone interview or in a paper-and-pencil format.

Remarkably, Ann Landers found that fully 70 percent of respondents would not have had children if they could make the choice again. She ran a shocking headline saying so. Should we have confidence in her finding? Hardly. As the letters from her readers indicated, many of the people who answered her question were angry with their children. All 10 000 respondents felt at least strongly enough about the issue to take the trouble to mail in their replies at their own expense. Like all survey researchers, Ann Landers wanted to study part of a group—a **sample**—in order to learn about the whole group—the **population** (in this case, all North American parents). The trouble is, she got replies from a *voluntary response sample,* a group of people who chose *themselves* in response to a general appeal. People who choose themselves are unlikely to be representative of the population of interest. In contrast, a *representative sample* is a group of people chosen so their characteristics closely match those of the population of interest. The difference in the quality of knowledge we can derive from the two types of samples cannot be overstated. Thus, a few months after Ann Landers

In a survey, people are asked questions about their knowledge, attitudes, or behaviour, either in a face-to-face or telephone interview or in a paper-and-pencil format.

A sample is the part of the population of research interest that is selected for analysis.

A population is the entire group about which the researcher wants to generalize.

Researchers collect information using surveys by asking people in a representative sample a set of identical questions. People interviewed on a downtown street corner do *not* constitute a representative sample of Canadian adults; the sample does not include people who live outside the urban core, it underestimates the number of seniors and people with disabilities, it does not take into account regional diversity, and so forth.

conducted her poll, a scientific survey based on a representative sample found that 91 percent of North American parents *would* have children again (Moore, 1995: 178).

How can survey researchers draw a representative sample? You might think that setting yourself up in a public place, such as a shopping mall, and asking willing passersby to answer some questions would work. However, this sort of *convenience sample,* which chooses the people who are easiest to reach, is also highly unlikely to be representative. People who go to malls are richer than average. Moreover, a larger proportion of homemakers, retired people, and teenagers visit malls than can be found in the Canadian population as a whole. Convenience samples are almost always unrepresentative.

To draw a representative sample, respondents cannot select themselves, as in the Ann Landers case. Nor can the researcher choose respondents, as in the mall example. Instead, respondents must be chosen at random, and an individual's chance of being chosen must be known and greater than zero. A sample with these characteristics is known as a **probability sample**.

In a probability sample, the units have a known and nonzero chance of being selected.

To draw a probability sample, you first need a *sampling frame.* This is a list of all the people in the population of interest. You also need a randomizing method. This is a way of ensuring every person in the sampling frame has a known and nonzero chance of being selected.

Up-to-date membership lists of organizations are useful sampling frames if you want to survey members of organizations. But if you want to investigate, say, the religious beliefs of Canadians, then the membership lists of places of worship are inadequate; many Canadians do not belong to such institutions. In such cases, you might turn to another frequently used sampling frame, the telephone directory. The telephone directory is now available for the entire country on CD-ROM. However, even the telephone directory lacks the names and addresses of some poor and homeless people (who do not have phones) and some rich people (who have unlisted phone numbers). Computer programs are available that dial residential phone numbers at random, including unlisted numbers. However, that still excludes about 1.3 percent of Canadian households from any survey that relies on the telephone directory as a sampling frame.

Homelessness is increasingly a focus of public policy. But public support may not be adequate if the homeless are not counted properly in the census. Statistics Canada first included a count of the homeless in the 2001 census. However, because the count is based on information about the use of shelters and soup kitchens, combined with an attempt at street counts, these numbers are estimates.

As the example of the telephone directory shows, few sampling frames are perfect. Even the largest and most expensive survey in Canada, the census, misses an estimated 2 percent of the population. Researchers believe that much of the undercounted population is composed of specific and identifiable groups, thus introducing sampling bias (see the section called "Analysis of Existing Documents and Official Statistics" later in this chapter). Nevertheless, researchers maximize the accuracy of their generalizations by using the least-biased sampling frames available and adjusting their analyses and conclusions to take account of known sampling bias.

Once a sampling frame has been chosen or created, individuals must be selected by a chance process. One way to do this is by picking, say, the 10th person on your list and then every 20th (or 30th or 100th) person after that, depending on how many people you need in your sample. A second method is to assign the number 1 to the first person in the sampling frame, the number 2 to the next person, and so on. Then you create a separate list of random numbers by using a computer or consulting a table of random numbers, which you can find at the back of almost any elementary statistics book or online. Your list of random numbers should have the same number of entries as the number of people you want in your sample. The individuals whose assigned numbers correspond to the list of random numbers are the people in your sample.

Sample Size and Statistical Significance

How many respondents do you need in a sample? That depends on how much inaccuracy you are willing to tolerate. Large samples give more precise results than small samples do. For most sociological purposes, however, a random sample of 1500 people will give acceptably accurate results, even if the population of interest is the entire adult population of Canada. More precisely, if you draw 20 random samples of 1500 individuals each, 19 of them will provide estimates that will be accurate within 2.5 percent of actual population values. Imagine, for example, that 50 percent of the people in a random sample of 1500 respondents say they support the Liberal Party. We can be reasonably confident that only 1 in 20 random samples of that size will not yield results between 47.5 percent and 52.5 percent. When we read that a finding is statistically significant, it usually means we can expect similar findings in 19 out of 20 samples of the same size. Said differently, researchers in the social sciences are generally prepared to tolerate a 5 percent chance that the characteristics of a population are different from the characteristics of their sample (1/20 = 5 percent). If the survey showed that 52 percent of the respondents support the Liberals and 48 percent support the Conservatives, the appropriate conclusion is *not* that the Liberals are in the lead. Instead, you should conclude that there is no detectable difference in support for the two parties given the 2.5 percent margin of error in the survey (see Figure 2.4).

In sum, probability sampling enables us to conduct surveys that permit us to generalize from a part (the sample) to the whole (the population) within known margins of error. Now let us consider the validity of survey data.

Survey Questions and Validity

We can conduct a survey in three main ways. Sometimes, a *self-administered questionnaire* is used. For example, a form containing questions and permitted responses can be mailed to the respondent and returned to the researcher through the mail system. The main advantage of this method is that it is relatively inexpensive. It also has drawbacks. For one thing, it sometimes results in unacceptably low *response rates*. The response rate is the number of people who answer the questionnaire divided by the number of people asked to do so, expressed as a percentage. Moreover, if you use mail questionnaires, an interviewer is not present to explain problematic questions and response options to the respondent. *Face-to-face interviews* are therefore generally preferred over mail questionnaires. In this type of survey, questions and allowable responses are presented to the respondent by the interviewer during a meeting. However, training interviewers and sending them around to conduct interviews is very expensive. That is why *telephone interviews* have become increasingly popular over the past two or three decades. They can elicit relatively high response rates and are relatively inexpensive to administer.

Questionnaires can contain two types of questions. A *closed-ended question* provides the respondent with a list of permitted answers. Each answer is given a numerical code so the data can later be easily input into a computer for statistical analysis. *Open-ended questions* allow respondents to answer questions in their own words. They are particularly useful in exploratory research, where the researcher does not have enough knowledge to create a meaningful and complete list of possible answers. Open-ended questions are more time-consuming to analyze than closed-ended questions are, although computer programs for analyzing text make the task easier.

Researchers want the answers elicited by surveys to be valid, to actually measure what they are supposed to. To maximize validity, researchers must guard against several dangers. We have already considered one threat to validity in survey research: *undercounting* some categories of the population because of an imperfect sampling frame.

FIGURE 2.4

The Margin of Error in a Sample

In a sample of 1500 people, 48 percent of the respondents support the Conservatives and 50 percent support the Liberals. However, because the 2.5 percent margins of error overlap, we cannot be sure whether support for the two parties differs in the population. To conclude that support for the two parties differs in the population, the margins of error must not overlap.

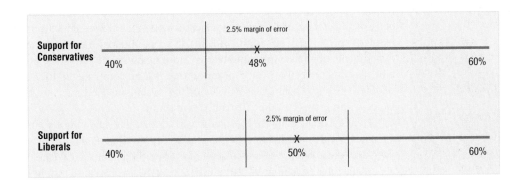

**TECHNOLOGY
BYTES**

Survey researchers who put their questionnaires on the World Wide Web confront a new variant of the problem of undercounting. Below each question they list allowable responses. Beside each allowable response they place a clickable box. They ask people who visit the website containing the questionnaire to read the questions and click the appropriate boxes to indicate their responses. Respondents' answers are automatically stored in a computerized database as soon as they click. For non-web surveys, data entry clerks must be hired to enter questionnaire responses into a computer. This expensive step is eliminated with web surveys. Web surveys also save the cost of postage and interviewers. However, the people who respond to web surveys select themselves in much the same fashion as the respondents to Ann Landers's parenthood question. Moreover, to answer a web survey, you have to have access to a computer connected to the Internet. A sample drawn from Internet users would not be representative of the Canadian population as a whole, let alone the population of a less-developed country where Internet access is rare. In 2000, 42 percent of Canadians had never used the Internet and another 10 percent used it rarely. The 52 percent of Canadians in this category tend to be seniors, have low incomes, and have no postsecondary education (Crompton, Ellison, and Stevenson, 2002). So although a web survey of Internet users might have validity, a web survey of the general population would likely give invalid results because of the unrepresentative nature of the sample on which it is based.

Other threats to validity in survey research aside from undercounting exist. Even if an individual is contacted about a survey, he or she may refuse to participate. This threat to validity is known as *non-response*. If non-respondents differ from respondents in ways that are relevant to the research topic, the conclusions drawn from the survey may be in jeopardy. For instance, some alcoholics may not want to participate in a survey on alcohol consumption because they regard the topic as sensitive. If so, a measure of the rate of alcohol consumption taken from the sample would not be an accurate reflection of the rate of alcohol consumption in the population. Actual alcohol consumption in the population would be higher than the rate in the sample.

Survey researchers pay careful attention to non-response. They try to discover whether non-respondents differ systematically from respondents so they can take this into account before drawing conclusions from their sample. They also take special measures to ensure that the response rate remains acceptably high—generally, around 70 percent or more of people contacted. Proven tactics ensure a high response rate. Researchers can notify potential respondents about the survey in advance. They can remind them to complete and mail in survey forms. They can have universities and other prestigious institutions sponsor the survey. They can stress the practical and scientific value of the research. And they can give people small rewards, such as a lottery ticket or a toonie, for participating.

If respondents do not answer questions accurately, a third threat to validity is present: *response bias*. The survey may focus on sensitive, unpopular, or illegal behaviour. As a result, some respondents may not be willing to answer questions frankly. The interviewer's attitude, gender, or race may suggest that some responses are preferred. This can elicit biased responses. Some of these problems can be overcome by carefully selecting and training interviewers and closely supervising their work. Response bias on questions about sensitive, unpopular, or illegal behaviour can be minimized by having such questions answered in private (Smith, 1992).

Fourth, validity may be compromised by *wording effects*. That is, the way questions are phrased or ordered can influence and invalidate responses. Experienced survey researchers have turned questionnaire construction into a respected craft. Increasingly, they refine the lessons learned from experience with evidence from field experiments. These experiments divide samples into two or more randomly chosen subsamples. Different question wording or ordering is then administered to the people in each subsample so that wording effects can be measured. Detected problems can then be resolved in future research.

Both experience and field experiments suggest that survey questions must be specific and simple. They should be expressed in plain, everyday language. They should be phrased neutrally, never leading the respondent to a particular answer and never using inflammatory terms. Because people's memories are often faulty, questions are more likely to elicit valid responses if they focus on important, singular, current events rather than on less salient, multiple, past events. Breaking these rules lowers the validity of survey findings (Converse and Presser, 1986; Ornstein, 1998).

Causality

In 1991, Erin Brockovich was down and out. She was a twice-divorced mother of three small children, and she had no university education. She had recently been seriously injured in a traffic accident, and she was unable to find work. She hired a law firm to argue her case but the $25 000 settlement covered only a fraction of her debts.[3]

Then came a turning point in Brockovich's life. She convinced the law firm that had settled her car accident case to hire her as a filing clerk at $1800 a month. Soon after she began working for the firm, Brockovich came across some medical records that piqued her curiosity. Her boss let her look into the matter. Brockovich's dogged investigation eventually established that a giant power utility had allowed a toxic chemical to leak into the groundwater of a nearby town, ruining the health of more than 600 residents. Although she was not a lawyer and had no formal education even as a law clerk or a paralegal, Brockovich spearheaded a court case that resulted in the largest legal settlement in North American history. In 1996, the power utility was ordered to pay $500 million to the victims. Brockovich herself received $3 million for her efforts. In 2000, these events were dramatized in the hit movie *Erin Brockovich,* starring Julia Roberts in the title role. The movie was nominated for five Academy Awards and Roberts won the best actress award for her portrayal of Brockovich (Ellis, 2002).

Erin Brockovich's story is unusual for two reasons. First, crimes committed by big corporations are rarely prosecuted successfully, and even successful prosecutions typically result in modest settlements (see Chapter 7, Deviance and Crime). Second, unemployed divorced women with small children and no university education rarely compete successfully against big-time lawyers, regardless of how bright and energetic they may be. Because of a lack of education and the demands of family, the cards are stacked too heavily against them (see Chapter 11, Sexuality and Gender). But what if we even out the playing field? What if we compare men and women who are more alike? What if we compare, say, male and female lawyers? Are male lawyers generally more successful? And if so, why? These are the questions sociologists Fiona Kay and John Hagan (1998) set out to answer in a survey of Ontario lawyers.[4]

Kay and Hagan analyzed self-administered questionnaires completed by a representative sample of 905 lawyers. The respondents had all been called to the Ontario

Erin Brockovich (2000) raises the question of why successful prosecutions of corporate crime are so rare. It also raises the question of why bright, energetic men often earn more than equally bright, energetic women.

bar between 1975 and 1990, remained in practice in 1990, and had begun practice on a partnership track.

Partnership is a measure of success in legal practice. Achieving the rank of partner means that a lawyer is one of the owners of his or her firm. Partnership enhances the lawyer's earnings and opens additional opportunities for career advancement. Kay and Hagan found that 46 percent of the men in their sample were partners, compared with just 25 percent of the women. That is, they found an **association** between gender and promotion. In general, an association exists between two variables if the value of one variable (in this case, partner versus non-partner) changes with the value of the other (in this case, male versus female).

Why were men substantially more likely to become partners than women were? One explanation for why some people have more successful careers focuses on their "human capital," that is, the investments they make in their occupation. In this view, a person's success comes from improving his or her education, work experience, and work skills. If women devote more attention than men do to domestic labour and raising children, while men devote more attention to upgrading their education, work experience, and work skills, men will be more successful in their careers than women are (Becker, 1991).

We can test human capital theory by comparing male and female lawyers who have invested *equally* in human capital. Our confidence in human capital theory would *increase* if female lawyers who have invested as much in human capital as male lawyers have were as likely as male lawyers to become partners. Our confidence in human capital theory would *decrease* if male lawyers were more successful than female lawyers even when women and men made identical investments in their careers.

How can we measure investment in human capital? The number of years since graduation from law school is one measure, because it indicates years of job experience. A second measure is the number of years spent in law practice. If a person takes time off work to have children and raise them, that person will have less work experience. Significantly, when Kay and Hagan compared male and female lawyers with equal years of job experience and time since graduation, they found that men were still more likely to become partners than women were. Their findings thus decrease our confidence in human capital theory. That is because gender differences in success persist even when investment in human capital is the same for women and men.

Kay and Hagan (1998: 729) propose an alternative explanation for the greater career success of men: "[W]omen must display greater career commitment than men to receive the same, or even smaller, rewards." Their data support this argument. For example, Kay and Hagan's survey data show that women's career prospects improve if they are eager to engage in various "extracurricular" activities that enhance the reputation of their firms and attract clients. Such activities include being honoured by a professional organization, receiving public recognition for their work, and serving as a member of the bench in the Law Society of Upper Canada. Men's career prospects are unaffected by these activities. This illustrates that, to advance to the level of partner, women must display greater career commitment than men do.

In the course of developing an explanation for the association between gender and promotion, Kay and Hagan performed a causal analysis. They had to satisfy four conditions to establish causality. Since these four conditions must be satisfied in *any* causal analysis, they are worth considering at length.

First, Kay and Hagan had to be confident that the independent variable occurred before the dependent variable. This is the *time order* criterion. Time order is straightforward in the relationship between gender and promotion. Chronologically, gender precedes promotion.

Second, Kay and Hagan had to establish the existence of a correlation between the independent and dependent variables. This is the *association* criterion. We saw that 46 percent of men and 25 percent of women received promotions to partners. The association is not perfect. A perfect association would see 100 percent of men versus 0 percent of women receiving promotion. But clearly the partnership experiences of women and men differ substantially. If the difference between the percentages were 3 percent rather than 21 percent $(46 - 25 = 21)$, we might be tempted to say that the difference is very small and probably due to chance fluctuation, that is, the individuals who happened to be included in the sample. However, a 21 percent difference establishes a sizable association between gender and partnership.

An association exists between two variables if the value of one variable changes with the value of the other.

Men are usually more successful in the legal profession than women. By comparing male and female lawyers with similar levels of job experience, sociologists Fiona Kay and John Hagan (1998) found that female lawyers have to be more committed to their jobs than male lawyers are to be as successful.

Third, Kay and Hagan had to show that the effect resulted from the cause and not from some other factor. This is the *spuriousness* criterion. It may be that an association between independent and dependent variables is erroneous since the association may be due to the effect of a third variable. For instance, in Scandinavia there is an association between storks and babies. The more storks in a region, the higher the birth rate. Does this mean that storks bring babies? Of course not. Rural regions have more storks *and* more babies than urban regions do. If you look at rural regions only, there is no association at all between storks and the birth rate. The same holds true if you look at urban regions only. "Region" accounts for the association between storks and babies. It is a control variable. Statistical control removes the effect of a third variable (in this case, region) from an association (in this case, between storks and babies). Statistical **control** shows how the third variable influences the original association. Because in this case controlling for region makes the original association disappear, we say that the association between storks and babies is a **spurious association**. In general, spuriousness exists between an independent and a dependent variable when the introduction of a causally prior control variable makes the initial association disappear.

Similarly, Kay and Hagan wanted to see whether the association between gender and promotion was spurious. To find out, they examined the effect of human capital on the association. They found that human capital had no effect on the association. That is, men were still more likely to be promoted than women even when comparing women and men who had made equal investments in human capital. Unlike the association between storks and babies after controlling for region, the association between gender and promotion after controlling for human capital remained strong. This suggests that in Kay and Hagan's research, the control variable (human capital) is *not* responsible for the original association (between gender and promotion).

Fourth, Kay and Hagan had to demonstrate the existence of a mechanism or process linking the cause and the effect. This is the *rationale* criterion. Their rationale for the link between gender and promotion was the variable "work commitment." When Kay and Hagan controlled for work commitment, the association between gender and promotion disappeared. They found that if women displayed more work commitment than men did, they were as likely as men to be promoted. This is similar to the storks and babies example with region controlled. Just as region accounted for the association between storks and babies, work commitment accounted for the association between gender and promotion. Kay and Hagan's causal reasoning is illustrated in Figure 2.5 on page 54.

Control in statistics refers to removing the influence of one or more variables on the association between an independent and a dependent variable.

A **spurious association** exists between an independent variable and a dependent variable when the introduction of a causally prior control variable makes the initial association disappear.

FIGURE 2.5

Establishing Causality by Testing an Association for Spuriousness

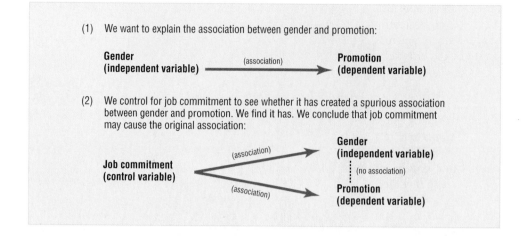

(1) We want to explain the association between gender and promotion:

Gender
(independent variable) —— (association) ——▶ Promotion
(dependent variable)

(2) We control for job commitment to see whether it has created a spurious association between gender and promotion. We find it has. We conclude that job commitment may cause the original association:

Job commitment
(control variable)

(association) ——▶ Gender
(independent variable)

⋮ (no association)

(association) ——▶ Promotion
(dependent variable)

Analysis of survey data involves more than just testing for spurious associations. Many interesting and unexpected things can happen when a two-variable association is elaborated by controlling for a third variable (Hirschi and Selvin, 1972). The original association may remain unchanged. It may strengthen. It may weaken. It may disappear or weaken in only some categories of the control variable. It may even change direction entirely. Data analysis is therefore full of surprises, and accounting for the outcomes of statistical control requires a lot of creative theoretical thinking.

Reading Tables

A survey is not an ideal instrument for conducting exploratory research. It cannot provide the kind of deep and sympathetic understanding we gain from participant observation. However, surveys do produce results from which we can confidently generalize. If properly crafted, they provide valid measures of many sociologically important variables. Because they allow the same questions to be asked repeatedly, surveys enable researchers to establish the reliability of measures with relative ease. And, finally, as we have just seen, survey data are useful for discovering relationships among variables, including cause-and-effect relationships.

One of the most useful tools for analyzing survey data is the contingency table. A **contingency table** is a cross-classification of cases by at least two variables that allows you to see how, if at all, the variables are associated. To understand this definition better, consider Table 2.1, taken from a nationwide Canadian poll. One survey question was worded as follows: "As you may know, we have a number of genetically engineered or genetically modified foods in our food system. Do you strongly approve, somewhat approve, somewhat disapprove, or strongly disapprove of 'genetically engineered' or 'genetically modified' food?" Table 2.1 shows the results on this question for women and men. To simplify our analysis we combined the two categories of approval to form one category. We did the same for the two categories of disapproval. The table shows the number and percentage of Canadian women and men who approve and disapprove of genetically modified food. It allows us to see whether gender affects attitudes toward genetically modified food.

Note that gender, the independent variable (the presumed cause) is arrayed across the top of the table. Attitude toward genetically modified food (the presumed effect) is

A contingency table is a cross-classification of cases by at least two variables that allows you to see how, if at all, the variables are associated.

TABLE 2.1

Attitude toward Genetically Modified Food by Sex, Canada

Source: Environics Research Group, 1999.

| | Sex of Respondent | | |
Attitude to GM Food	Male	Female	Row Totals
Approve	468 (49.5%)	295 (32.5%)	763 (41.2%)
Disapprove	478 (50.5%)	612 (67.5%)	1090 (58.8%)
Column totals	946 (100.0%)	907 (100.0%)	1853 (100.0%)

arrayed along the side of the table. The table consists of four core cells, one defined by the cross-classification of approval and men, another by the cross-classification of approval and women, a third by the cross-classification of disapproval and men, and the fourth by the cross-classification of disapproval and women.

Although 2049 people were interviewed in the survey, 196 did not answer the question. All 1853 who responded can be assigned to cells of the table based on their characteristics. For example, men who approved of genetically modified food are assigned to the top left core cell. Women who disapproved are placed in the lower right core cell.

Do women and men differ in their attitude toward genetically modified food? Does the difference between the values of the independent variable produce a difference between the values of the dependent variable? Table 2.1 shows that 468 men and 295 women approved of genetically modified food. However, the absolute number of men and women in these cells tells us little because more men than women may have been interviewed. An easy way to take this into account is to convert the absolute numbers to percentages. Effectively, this asks: For every one hundred men, how many approved of genetically modified food? For every one hundred women, how many approved of genetically modified food?

The percentages are in parentheses in the table: 49.5 percent of men approved of genetically modified food ($468/946 \times 100 = 49.5$). The comparable figure for women is 32.5 percent. The independent variable (men versus women) produces a 17 percent difference in the approval of genetically modified food ($49.5 - 32.5 = 17$).

One reason for this difference might be that men are more politically conservative or right wing than women are (Everitt, 1998; Howell and Day, 2000). A simple way to measure political preferences is to ask people which federal political party they would vote for "if an election were held today." In our analysis we have combined the Conservative Party with the Alliance/Reform Party on the political right, kept the Liberal Party as a centrist party on its own, and combined the NDP and the Bloc Québécois on the political left.

The analysis becomes more complex with three variables in the analysis. In Table 2.2 you will quickly notice that we effectively have a sub-table for men (on the left) and another sub-table for women (on the right). As well, since some respondents did not state a party preference, we have only 1503 people in this table.

Are there differences in levels of approval of genetically modified food among people who have different political party preferences? Yes and no. For men, those who support parties on the right or in the centre tend to approve of genetically engineered food by a small margin (52.7 percent and 54.8 percent, respectively). However, men who favour parties on the left are not as approving (36.1 percent). So, yes, for men party preference does make a difference in approval levels. For women, there are virtually no differences by party preference. Only about a third of women approve of genetically modified foods, and approval does not differ by party preference.

So we see that contingency tables are effective tools for causal analysis. They enable us to see whether an association exists between two variables and to examine the effects of control variables on the original association.

Sex of Respondent	Male			Female		
Political Preference	**Right**	**Centre**	**Left**	**Right**	**Centre**	**Left**
Attitude to GM Food						
Approve	149 (52.7%)	207 (54.8%)	48 (36.1%)	57 (31.7%)	123 (34.1%)	55 (32.7%)
Disapprove	134 (47.3%)	171 (45.2%)	85 (63.9%)	123 (68.3%)	238 (65.9%)	113 (67.3%)
Column totals	283 (100.0%)	378 (100.0%)	133 (100.0%)	180 (100.0%)	361 (100.0%)	168 (100.0%)

TABLE 2.2

Attitude toward Genetically Modified Food by Sex, Controlling for Political Preference, Canada

Source: Environics Research Group, 1999.

Analysis of Existing Documents and Official Statistics

Apart from participant observation, experiments, and surveys, there is a fourth important sociological research method: the *analysis of existing documents and official statistics.* What do existing documents and official statistics have in common? They are created by people other than the researcher for purposes other than sociological research.

The three types of existing documents that sociologists have mined most widely and deeply are diaries, newspapers, and published historical works. For example, one of the early classics of American sociology, a study of Polish immigrants, is based on a close reading of immigrants' diaries and letters (Thomas and Znaniecki, 1958 [1918–20]). In recent decades, sociologists have made outstanding contributions to the study of political protest by systematically classifying nineteenth- and early-twentieth-century French, Italian, and British newspaper accounts of strikes and demonstrations (Tilly, Tilly, and Tilly, 1975).

In recent decades, sociologists have tried to discover the conditions that led some countries to dictatorship and others to democracy, some to economic development and others to underdevelopment, some to becoming thoroughly globalized and others to remaining less tied to global social processes. In trying to answer such broad questions, sociologists have had to rely on published histories as their main source of data. No other method would allow the breadth of coverage and depth of analysis required for such comparative and historical work. For example, Barrington Moore (1967) spent a decade reading the histories of Britain, France, Russia, Germany, China, India, and other countries to figure out the social origins of dictatorship and democracy in the modern world. Immanuel Wallerstein (1974–89) canvassed the history of virtually the entire world to make sense of why some countries became industrialized while others remain undeveloped. What distinguishes this type of research from purely historical work is the kind of questions posed by the researchers. Moore and Wallerstein asked the same kind of big, theoretical questions (and used the same kinds of research methods) as Marx and Weber did. They have inspired a generation of younger sociologists to adopt a similar approach. Comparative-historical research is therefore one of the growth areas of the discipline.

Census data, police crime reports, and records of key life events are perhaps the most frequently used sources of official statistics. Canadian censuses have been conducted regularly since 1871. The modern census tallies the number of Canadian residents and classifies them by place of residence, race, ethnic origin, occupation, age, and hundreds of other variables (see Box 2.1). Statistics Canada publishes an annual Uniform Crime Reporting (UCR) Survey that reports the number of crimes in Canada and classifies them by location and type of crime, age and sex of offenders and victims, and other variables. It also regularly publishes an *Annual Compendium of Vital Statistics* that reports births, deaths, marriages, and divorces by sex, age, and so forth.

BOX 2.1
It's Your Choice

Who Should Be Counted in the Canadian Census?

It may seem odd to say so, but the census is a political document. Often seen as little more than a dry, scientific compilation of numbers, of interest mainly to bureaucrats and bean-counters, the census is actually a record of the political interests and power struggles that

have shaped Canadian history (Brym, 2009; Curtis, 2001). In particular, the census has always counted certain kinds of people and excluded others. By rendering some people and groups "invisible" it profoundly influences social policy.

The census excluded some people right from the beginning. Jean Talon completed New France's first census in

1666. The count: 3215 French settlers. Talon did not count the much larger population of Aboriginal peoples, did not even try to estimate their number and socioeconomic characteristics. That is because the first "Canadian" census was not a neutral tally of all residents of New France but a means of providing information that could be used to help wrest control of the territory from the Aboriginal peoples and establish a stable and prosperous French colony. Talon needed the numbers to rationalize the taxation of the French colonists, to further their economic development, to organize new colonization efforts, and, by implication, to interfere with, and even destroy, the livelihoods and lives of the Native population. The fact that Aboriginal peoples were not counted only added to the sense that they did not matter. In this respect, the first census added to the mythology that New France was empty, virgin territory, just waiting for European colonists to exploit its riches. Could there be a more political purpose?

That was the seventeenth century. You might think that the tendency of the census to exclude some kinds of people is ancient history. If so, you would be wrong. The census still undercounts Aboriginal peoples. Members of several reserves and settlements refuse to participate in the census as an act of political protest. They simply do not recognize the authority of the federal government. In addition, the census undercounts homeless people, who by definition have no fixed address. Still other Canadians refuse to participate in the census because they regard it as an invasion of their privacy.

Apart from undercounting certain types of individuals, the census renders certain *characteristics* of individuals invisible and denies the existence of certain *groups*. Consider the following:

- Until 1981, the census required every Canadian to specify one and only one ethnic or cultural origin.

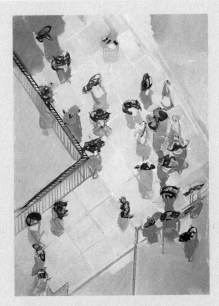

The census has always counted certain kinds of people and excluded others. By rendering some people and groups "invisible" it profoundly influences social policy. Shown here is Tom Campbell's *Above the Street* (1995).

A person born to a Ukrainian-Canadian mother and an Italian-Canadian father may have felt attached to Ukrainian, Italian, *and* Canadian cultures. But such multiple ethnic attachments were not recognized by the census. People who felt they were of mixed heritage were counted as individuals in the census, but their multiple ethnic attachments were rendered invisible.

- Remarkably, it was only in 1996 that the census listed "Canadian" as a possible response to the ethnic question. Suddenly, "Canadian" became the most frequently chosen ethnic origin in the country. At midnight between May 13 and 14, 1996, Canada "lost" millions of

citizens who had formerly specified European, Asian, African, and other ancestries, and gained millions of "Canadians." Before the 1990s, the census made the Canadian ethnic group invisible.

- Until recently the census let people say they were from Jamaica or China but it did not allow them to identify themselves as members of a "visible minority." The recognition of the diverse *racial* origins of Canadians is something quite new.
- Some people lived common-law before 1981. However, the 1981 census was the first to ask people if they were living common-law.
- Women did most of the country's domestic labour before 1996 (as they do today), but only in 1996 did the census recognize unpaid domestic labour by asking questions about it.

People who perform domestic labour, people living common-law, members of visible minorities, members of the Canadian ethnic group, and people who identify with more than one ethnic group have been slighted by the Canadian census until recently. Homeless people and Aboriginal peoples still are. This matters because government programs and government funding are based on census counts. If some types of people are undercounted, what negative implications might this have for them? Can you think of types of people other than those listed above who are rendered invisible by the Canadian census? Should they be counted, too? As a Canadian citizen, it's your choice.

Existing documents and official statistics have four main advantages over other types of data. First, they can save the researcher time and money because they are usually available at no cost in libraries or on the World Wide Web. (See the Web Resources at the end of the chapter for useful websites containing official statistics.) Second, official statistics usually cover entire populations and are collected using rigorous and uniform methods, thus yielding high-quality data. Third, existing documents and official statistics are especially useful for historical analysis. The analysis of data from these sources is the only sociological method that does not require live subjects. Fourth, since the method does not require live subjects, reactivity is not a problem; the researcher's presence does not influence the subjects' behaviour.[5]

However, existing documents and official statistics share one big disadvantage. These data sources are not created with the researchers' needs in mind. They often contain biases that reflect the interests of the individuals and organizations that created them. Therefore, they may be less than ideal for research purposes and must always be treated cautiously.

To illustrate the potential bias of official statistics, consider how researchers compare the well-being of Canadians and people living in other countries. They sometimes use a measure called gross domestic product per capita (GDPpc). GDPpc is the total dollar value of goods and services produced in a country in a year divided by the number of people in the country. It is a convenient measure because all governments regularly publish GDPpc figures.

Most researchers are aware of a flaw in GDPpc, however. The cost of living varies from one country to the next. A dollar can buy you a cup of coffee in many Canadian restaurants but that same cup of coffee will cost you $6 in a Japanese restaurant. GDPpc looks at how many dollars you have, not at what the dollars can buy. Therefore, governments started publishing an official statistic called purchasing power parity (PPP). It takes the cost of goods and services in each country into account.

Significantly, however, both PPP and GDPpc ignore two serious problems. First, it is possible for GDPpc and PPP to go up while most people in a society become worse off. The richest people may earn all the newly created wealth while the incomes of most people fall. Any measure of well-being that ignores the *distribution* of well-being in society is biased toward measuring the well-being of the well-to-do. Second, in some countries the gap in well-being between women and men is greater than in others. A country like Kuwait ranks quite high on GDPpc and PPP. However, women benefit far less than men do from that country's prosperity. A measure of well-being that ignores the gender gap is biased toward measuring the well-being of men.

This story has a happy ending. Realizing the biases in official statistics, such as GDPpc and PPP, social scientists at the United Nations created two new measures of well-being in the mid-1990s. First, the human development index (HDI) combines PPP with a measure of average life expectancy and average level of education. The reasoning of the UN social scientists is that people living in countries that distribute well-being more equitably will live longer and be better educated. Second, the gender empowerment measure (GEM) combines the percentage of parliamentary seats, good jobs, and earned income controlled by women.

Table 2.3 lists the countries ranked first through fifth on all four measures of well-being we have mentioned. As you can see, the list of the top five countries differs for each measure. There is no "best" measure. Each measure has its own bias, and researchers have to be sensitive to these biases, as they must whenever they use official statistics.

GLOBAL PERSPECTIVE

TABLE 2.3

Rank of Countries by Four Measures of Well-Being, 2007

Sources: United Nations, 2007, *Human Development Report 2007/2008,* New York. Retrieved January 3, 2008 (http://hdr.undp.org/en/media/hdr_20072008_en_complete.pdf), pp. 229, 330; International Monetary Fund, 2007, "Select Countries." Retrieved January 3, 2008 (http://www.imf.org/external/pubs/ft/weo/2007/02/weodata/weoselco.aspx?g=2001&sg=All+countries).

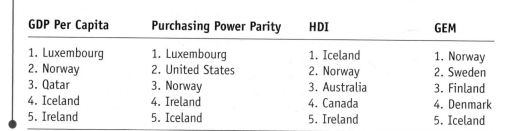

GDP Per Capita	Purchasing Power Parity	HDI	GEM
1. Luxembourg	1. Luxembourg	1. Iceland	1. Norway
2. Norway	2. United States	2. Norway	2. Sweden
3. Qatar	3. Norway	3. Australia	3. Finland
4. Iceland	4. Ireland	4. Canada	4. Denmark
5. Ireland	5. Iceland	5. Ireland	5. Iceland

THE IMPORTANCE OF BEING SUBJECTIVE

In the following chapters, we show how participant observation, experiments, surveys, and the analysis of existing documents and official statistics are used in sociological research. You are well equipped for the journey. By now you should have a pretty good idea of the basic methodological issues that confront any sociological research project. You should also understand the strengths and weaknesses of some of the most widely used data collection techniques (Table 2.4).

Our synopsis of sociology's "reality check" should not obscure the fact that sociological research questions often spring from real-life experiences and the pressing concerns of the day. But before sociological analysis, we rarely see things as they are. We see them as *we* are. Then, a sort of waltz begins. Subjectivity leads; objectivity follows. When the dance is finished, we see things more accurately (see Box 2.2).

TABLE 2.4

Strengths and Weaknesses of Four Research Methods

Method	Strengths	Weaknesses
Participant observation	Allows researchers to get "inside" the minds of their subjects and discover their worldview; useful for exploratory research and the discovery of grounded theory; high internal validity	Low reliability; low external validity; low generalizability; not very useful for establishing cause-and-effect relationships
Experiments	High reliability; excellent for establishing cause-and-effect relationship	Low validity for many sociology problems (field and natural experiments somewhat better)
Surveys	Good reliability; useful for establishing cause-and-effect relationships; good generalizability	Some problems with validity (but techniques exist for boosting validity)
Analysis of existing documents and official statistics	Often inexpensive and easy to obtain, provides good coverage; useful for historical analysis; non-reactive	Often contains biases reflecting the interests of their creators and not the interests of the researcher

BOX 2.2
Sociology at the Movies

TAKE   **ROLL**

Kinsey (2004)

In early-twentieth-century New Jersey, Alfred Kinsey's father sermonized that the telephone and the automobile were the devil's work. In his opinion, these conveniences increased interaction between young men and women, thereby promoting impure thoughts, petting, and all manner of sexual perversions.

Not surprisingly, the adolescent Alfred rejected his father's Puritanism and petty tyranny. He escaped to Harvard to study biology and zoology. He devoted 20 years to collecting and analyzing 100 000 specimens of the gall wasp, but underneath his mania for counting, classifying, and marvelling at natural diversity, his rebellion against sexual repression and imposed sexual uniformity never ended.

In the 1930s, now a full professor of zoology at Indiana University,

Kinsey began to investigate human sexual behaviour with the same fervour he had formerly invested in the gall wasp. Between 1938 and 1963, he and his associates conducted 18 216 in-depth interviews that formed the basis of two best-selling volumes on human sexual behaviour that astounded the North American public and put Kinsey on the cover of *Time* (Kinsey, Pomeroy, and Martin, 1948; Kinsey, Pomeroy, Martin, and Gebhard, 1953). In an era when masturbation, contraception, and premarital sex were widely considered sins, Kinsey's work sparked a revolution in attitudes toward sex by showing that even far more scandalous practices— extramarital affairs, homosexuality, and so forth—were commonplace. For many North Americans, his findings were liberating. For others, they were filthy lies that threatened to undermine the moral fibre of the nation. Both reactions, and the life of the man who caused them, are portrayed in *Kinsey* (2004), starring Liam Neeson in the title role.

Equipped with the information in this chapter, you can appreciate that Kinsey's methods were primitive and biased by modern sociological standards (Ericksen, 1998). We single out four main problems:

1. *Sampling.* Kinsey relied on what we today call a "convenience sample" of respondents. He and his colleagues interviewed accessible volunteers rather than a randomized and representative sample of the American population. About one-third of Kinsey's respondents had a known "sexual bias." They were prostitutes, members of secretive homosexual communities, patients in mental hospitals, residents of homes for unwed mothers, and the like. Two-thirds of these people were convicted felons. Five percent were male prostitutes. But even if we eliminate respondents with a

Liam Neeson as Alfred Kinsey

sexual bias, we do not have a representative sample. For example, 84 percent of the men without a sexual bias went to college. Most of them were from the Midwest, especially Indiana (Gebhard and Johnson, 1979). In Kinsey's defence, scientific sampling was in its infancy when he did his research. Still, we are obliged to conclude that it is difficult to generalize from Kinsey's work because his sample is unrepresentative.

2. *Questionnaire design.* Kinsey required that his interviewers memorize long questionnaires including 350 or more questions. He encouraged them to adapt the wording and ordering of the questions to suit the "level" of the respondent and the natural flow of conversation that emerged during the interview. Yet much research now shows that even subtle changes in question wording and ordering can produce sharply different results. A question about frequency of masturbation per month yields means between 4 and 15 depending on how the question is phrased (Bradburn and

Sudman, 1979). To avoid such problems, modern researchers prefer standardized questions. They also prefer questionnaires considerably briefer than Kinsey's because asking 350 questions can take hours and often results in "respondent fatigue," a desire on the part of respondents to offer quick and easy answers (as opposed to considered, truthful responses) so they can end the interview as quickly as possible.

3. *Interviewing.* People are generally reluctant to discuss sex with strangers, and Kinsey and his associates have often been praised for making their respondents feel at ease talking about the most intimate details of their personal life. Yet to establish rapport with respondents, Kinsey and his colleagues did not remain neutral. They expressed empathy with the pains and frustrations many respondents expressed, often reassuring them that their sexual histories were normal and decent. Today, researchers frown on any departure from neutrality in the interview situation because it may influence respondents to answer

questions in a less than truthful way. The reassurance and empathy expressed by Kinsey and his associates may have led some respondents to offer exaggerated reports of their behaviour.

4. *Data analysis.* It is unclear how Kinsey decided whether the effect of one variable on another was significant. He rarely used statistical tests for this purpose. He never introduced control variables to see if observed associations between variables were spurious. Moreover, he saw no problem in lumping together data collected over decades. Yet between 1938, when Kinsey started collecting data, and 1953, the year in which his second book was published, North America experienced unprecedented social change fuelled by economic depression and boom, war and peace. Sexual attitudes and behaviour undoubtedly changed, and we may wonder whether it is meaningful to analyze respondents from the late 1930s and the early 1950s together.

Since Kinsey, researchers have conducted more than 750 scientific surveys of the sexual behaviour of North Americans. Today, using modern research methods, we are able to describe and explain sexual behaviour more accurately and insightfully than did Kinsey and his pioneering colleagues. We know that many of the details of Kinsey's writings are suspect. But we also know that despite the serious methodological problems summarized above, his basic finding is accurate. The sexual behaviour of North Americans is highly diverse. As Kinsey says in the movie, "Variation is the only reality."

Herein, too, lies an important lesson about the relationship between subjectivity and objectivity in research. Clearly, Kinsey's biography and his passions helped to shape his innovative scientific agenda. There is nothing unusual in that; all good scientists are passionate about their work, and their research agendas are often rooted in their biographies. Like Kinsey, they try to be objective, but even if they fail, they can rely on the scientific community to uncover biases and discover the imaginative and valid core of every good theory. Without human emotions grounded in our subjectivity, there could never be a quest for truth; without research methods that improve our objectivity, there could never be a science.

Feminism provides a prime example of this process. Here is a *political* movement of people and ideas that, over the past 40 years, has helped shape the sociological *research* agenda. The division of labour in the household, violence against women, the effects of child-rearing responsibilities on women's careers, the social barriers to women's participation in politics and the armed forces, and many other related concerns were sociological "non-issues" before the rise of the modern feminist movement. Sociologists did not study these problems. Effectively, they did not exist for the sociological community (although they did, of course, exist for women). But subjectivity led. Feminism as a political movement brought these and many other concerns to the attention of the Canadian public. Objectivity followed. Large parts of the sociological community began doing rigorous research on feminist-inspired issues and greatly refined our knowledge of them.

The entire sociological perspective began to shift as a growing number of scholars abandoned gender-biased research (Eichler, 1988b; Tavris, 1992). Thus, approaching sociological problems from an exclusively male perspective is now less common than it used to be. For instance, it is less likely in 2009 than in 1969 that a sociologist would study work but ignore unpaid housework as one type of labour. Similarly, sociologists now frown on using data on one gender to draw conclusions about all people. As these advances in sociological thinking show, and as has often been the case in the history of the discipline, objective sociological knowledge has been enhanced as a result of subjective experiences. And so the waltz continues. As in *Alice in Wonderland,* the question now is, "Will you, won't you, will you, won't you, will you join the dance?"

APPENDIX

Four Statistics You Should Know

In this book we sometimes report the results of sociological research in statistical form. You need to know four basic statistics to understand this material:

1. The *mean* (or arithmetic average). Imagine we know the height and annual income of the first nine people who entered your sociology classroom today. The height and income data are arranged in Table 2.5. From Table 2.5 you can calculate the mean by summing the values for each student or *case* and dividing by the number of cases. For example, the nine students are a total of 1547 centimetres (609 in.) tall. Dividing 1547 by 9, we get the mean height—172 centimetres (67.7 in.).

2. The *median*. The mean can be deceiving when some cases have exceptionally high or low values. For example, in Table 2.5, the mean income is $37 667, but because one lucky fellow has an income of $200 000, the mean is higher than the income of seven of the nine students. It is therefore a poor measure of the centre of the income distribution. The median is a better measure. If you order the data from the lowest to the highest income, the median is the value of the case at the midpoint. The median income in our example is $15 000. Four students earn more than that; four earn less. (Note: If you have an even number of cases, the midpoint is the average of the middle two values.)

3. *Correlation*. We have seen how valuable contingency tables are for analyzing relationships among variables. However, for variables that can assume many values, such as height and income, contingency tables become impracticably large. In such cases, sociologists prefer to analyze relationships among variables by using *scatterplots*. Markers in the body of the graph indicate the score of each case on both the independent and the dependent variables. The pattern formed by the markers is inspected visually and through the use of statistics. The strength of the association between the two variables is measured by a statistic called the *correlation coefficient* (signified as *r*). The value of *r* can vary from −1.0 to 1.0. If the markers are scattered around a straight, upward-sloping trend line, *r* takes a positive value. A positive *r* suggests that, as the value of one variable increases, so does the value of the other (see Figure 2.6, scatterplot 1). If the markers are scattered around a straight, downward-sloping trend line, *r* takes a negative value. A negative *r* suggests that, as the value of one variable increases, the value of the other decreases (see Figure 2.6, scatterplot 2). Whether positive or negative, the magnitude (or absolute value) of *r* decreases the more widely scattered the markers are from the line. If the degree of scatter is very high, *r* = 0; that is, there is no association between the variables (see Figure 2.6,

TABLE 2.5

The Height and Annual Income of Nine Students

Student	Height (in cm and in.)	Income ($000)
1	170 (67)	5
2	165 (65)	8
3	152 (60)	9
4	163 (64)	12
5	183 (72)	40
6	173 (68)	15
7	178 (70)	20
8	175 (69)	30
9	188 (74)	200

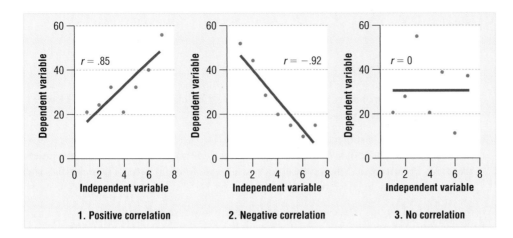

FIGURE 2.6
Correlation

scatterplot 3). However, a low *r* or an *r* of zero may derive from a relationship between the two variables that does not look like a straight line. It may look like a curve. As a result, it is always necessary to inspect scatterplots visually and not just rely on statistics like *r* to interpret the data.

4. A *rate* lets you compare the values of a variable among groups of different size. For example, let's say 1000 women got married last year in a city of 100 000 people and 2000 women got married in a city of 300 000 people. If you want to compare the likelihood of women getting married in the two cities, you have to divide the number of women who got married in each city by the total number of women in each city. Since 1000/100 000 = 0.01, or 1 percent, and 2000/300 000 = 0.00666, or 0.67 percent, we can say that the *rate* of women marrying is higher in the first city even though fewer women got married there last year. Note that rates are often expressed in percentages. In general, dividing the number of times an event occurs (e.g., a woman getting married) by the total number of people to whom the event could occur in principle (e.g., the number of women in a city) will give you the rate at which an event occurs.

NOTES

1. Some scholars think it is possible to examine data without any preconceived notions and then formulate theories on the basis of this examination. However, they seem to form a small minority (Medawar, 1996: 12–32).

2. Subsequent analysis questioned the existence of a productivity effect in the Hawthorne study (Franke and Kaul, 1978). However, the general principle derived from the Hawthorne study—that social science researchers can influence their subjects—is now widely accepted (Webb et al., 1966).

3. Throughout, we convert U.S. dollars to Canadian dollars.

4. For clarity, we simplify Kay and Hagan's analysis.

5. When researchers finish analyzing survey data, they typically deposit computer-readable files of the data in an archive. This allows other researchers to conduct secondary analyses of survey data years later. Such data are widely used. They are not collected by government departments, but they have all the advantages of official statistics listed above, although they are based on samples rather than on populations. The largest social science data archive includes Canadian data and is housed at the University of Michigan's Inter-university Consortium for Political and Social Research (ICPSR). The ICPSR website, at http://www.icpsr.umich.edu, allows visitors to conduct elementary data analyses online.

SUMMARY

1. **What is the aim of science and how is it achieved?**
   The aim of science is to arrive at knowledge that is less subjective than other ways of knowing. A degree of objectivity is achieved by testing ideas against systematically collected data and leaving research open to public scrutiny.

2. **Does science have a subjective side?**
   It does. The subjective side of the research enterprise is no less important than the objective side. Creativity and the motivation to study new problems from new perspectives arise from individual passions and interests.

3. **What methodological issues must be addressed in any research project?**
   To maximize the scientific value of a research project, researchers must address issues of reliability (consistency in measurement), validity (precision in measurement), generalizability (the applicability of findings beyond the case studied), and causality (cause-and-effect relations among variables).

4. **What is participant observation?**
   Participant observation is one of the main sociological methods. It involves carefully observing people's face-to-face interactions and participating in their lives over a long period. Participant observation is particularly useful for doing exploratory research, constructing grounded theory, and validating measures on the basis of internal criteria. Issues of external validity, reliability, generalizability, and causality make participant observation less useful for other research purposes.

5. **What is an experiment?**
   An experiment is a carefully controlled artificial situation that allows researchers to isolate hypothesized causes and measure their effects by randomizing the allocation of subjects to experimental and control groups and exposing only the experimental group to an independent variable. Experiments get high marks for reliability and analysis of causality, but validity issues make them less than ideal for many research purposes.

6. **What is a survey?**
   In a survey, people are asked questions about their knowledge, attitudes, or behaviour, either in a face-to-face interview, telephone interview, or paper-and-pencil format. Surveys rank high on reliability and validity as long as researchers train interviewers well, phrase questions carefully, and take special measures to ensure high response rates. Generalizability is achieved through probability sampling, statistical control, and the analysis of causality by means of data manipulation.

7. **What are the advantages and disadvantages of using official documents and official statistics as sources of sociological data?**
   Existing documents and official statistics are inexpensive and convenient sources of high-quality data. However, they must be used cautiously because they often reflect the biases of the individuals or organizations that created them.

KEY TERMS

association (p. 52)

causality (p. 44)

contingency table (p. 54)

control (p. 53)

control group (p. 45)

dependent variable (p. 45)

ethnographic (p. 40)

experiment (p. 45)

experimental group (p. 45)

exploratory research (p. 42)

field research (p. 39)

generalizability (p. 44)

grounded theory (p. 42)   **randomization** (p. 45)

hypotheses (p. 42)   **reliability** (p. 43)

independent variable (p. 46)   **sample** (p. 47)

operationalization (p. 43)   **spurious association** (p. 53)

participant observation (p. 40)   **survey** (p. 47)

population (p. 47)   **validity** (p. 43)

probability sample (p. 48)   **variable** (p. 42)

QUESTIONS TO CONSIDER

1. What is the connection between objectivity and subjectivity in sociological research?

2. What criteria do sociologists apply to select one method of data collection over another?

3. What are the methodological strengths and weaknesses of various methods of data collection?

WEB RESOURCES

Companion Website for This Book

http://www.compass3e.nelson.com

Begin by clicking on the Student Resources section of the website. Next, select the chapter you are studying from the pull-down menu. From the Student Resources page you have easy access to InfoTrac® College Edition, additional Weblinks, and other resources. The website also has many useful tips to aid you in your study of sociology, including practice tests for each chapter.

InfoTrac® Search Terms

These search terms are provided to assist you in beginning to conduct research on this topic by visiting http://www.infotrac-college.com:

census
historical sociology
participant observation
sociological survey
sociology experiment

Recommended Websites

Bill Trochim at Cornell University has put together a comprehensive and impressive sociological research methods course at http://www.socialresearchmethods.net/kb.

For a comprehensive listing of websites devoted to qualitative research, go to http://www.nova.edu/ssss/QR/web.html.

"Statistics Every Writer Should Know" is an exceptionally clear presentation of basic statistics at http://www.robertniles.com/stats.

The World Wide Web contains many rich sources of official statistics. In preparing this book we relied heavily on data from the websites of Statistics Canada, http://www.statcan.ca, and the United Nations, http://www.un.org.

http://www.compass3e.nelson.com

CengageNOW™

http://hed.nelson.com

This online diagnostic tool identifies each student's unique needs with a Pretest that generates a personalized Study Plan for each chapter, helping students focus on concepts they're having the most difficulty mastering. Students then take a Posttest after reading the chapter to measure their understanding of the material. An Instructor Gradebook is available to track and monitor student progress.

PART 2

Basic Social Processes

CHAPTER

3

Culture

In this chapter, you will learn that

- Culture is the sum of shared ideas, practices, and material objects that people create to adapt to, and thrive in, their environments.

- Humans have thrived in their environments because of their unique ability to think abstractly, cooperate with one another, and make tools.

- Although sociologists recognize that biology sets broad human limits and potentials, most sociologists do not believe that specific human behaviours and social arrangements are biologically determined.

- In some respects, the development of culture makes people freer. For example, culture has become more diversified and consensus has declined in many areas of life, allowing people more choice in how they live.

- In other respects, the development of culture puts limits on who we can become. For example, the culture of buying consumer goods has become a virtually compulsory pastime. Increasingly, therefore, people define themselves by the goods they purchase.

CULTURE AS PROBLEM SOLVING

If you follow or participate in sports, you probably know that many athletes perform little rituals before each game. Canadian hockey legend Wayne Gretzky never got his hair cut while playing on the road because the last time he did, his team lost. He always put his equipment on in the same order: left shin pad, left stocking, right shin pad, right stocking, pants, left skate, right skate, shoulder pads, left elbow pad, right elbow pad, and finally, jersey—with the right side tucked into his pants. During warm-up, he would always shoot his first puck far to the right of the goal. When he went back to the dressing room, he would drink a Diet Coke, a glass of ice water, a Gatorade, and another Diet Coke—in that order. Former goalie Patrick Roy juggled a puck between periods and bounced it on the ground. "Then I put it in a special place where no one will find it and make off with it, otherwise . . . so the legend goes, bad luck could befall the culprit and he would suddenly turn into an alligator" ("Mad about Hockey: Superstitions," 2002). Meanwhile, during his days in the NHL, Bruce Gardiner dipped his hockey stick in a toilet before taking to the ice (Arace, 2000).

The superstitious practices of athletes make some people chuckle. But these rituals put athletes at ease. Like soldiers going off to battle, undergraduate students about to write final exams, and other people in high-stress situations, athletes invent practices to help them stop worrying and focus on the job at hand. Some wear a lucky piece of jewellery or item of clothing. Others say special words or a quick prayer. Still others cross themselves. And then there are those who engage in more elaborate rituals. For example, two sociologists interviewed 300 university students about their superstitious practices before final exams. One student felt she would do well only if she ate a sausage and two eggs sunny-side up on the morning of each exam. She had to place the sausage vertically on the left side of her plate and the eggs to the right of the sausage so they formed the "100" percent she was aiming for (Albas and Albas, 1989). Of course, the ritual had a more direct influence on her cholesterol level than on her grades. Yet indirectly it may have had the desired effect. To the degree it helped relieve her anxiety and relax her, she may have done better on her exams.

When some people say "culture," they are referring to opera, ballet, art, and fine literature. For sociologists, however, this definition is too narrow. Sociologists define **culture** broadly as all the ideas, practices, and material objects that people create to deal with real-life problems. For example, when the university student invented the ritual of preparing for exams by eating sausage and eggs arranged just so, she was creating culture in the sociological sense. This practice helped the student deal with the real-life problem of high anxiety. Sociologists call opera, ballet, art, and similar activities **high culture**. They distinguish high culture from **popular culture** or **mass culture**. Although popular or mass culture is consumed by all classes, high culture tends to be consumed mainly by upper classes.

Similarly, tools help people solve the problem of how to plant crops and build houses. Religion helps people face the problem of death and how to give meaning to life. Tools and religion are also elements of culture because they, too, help people solve real-life problems. Note, however, that religion, technology, and many other elements of culture differ from the superstitious practices of athletes and undergraduates in one important respect. Superstitions are often unique to the individuals who create them. In contrast, religion and technology are widely shared. They are even passed from one generation to the next. How does cultural sharing take place? By means of communication and learning. Thus, shared culture is *socially* transmitted. We conclude that culture comprises the socially transmitted ideas, practices, and material objects that enable people to adapt to, and thrive in, their environments.

Culture is the sum of practices, languages, symbols, beliefs, values, ideologies, and material objects that people create to deal with real-life problems. Cultures enable people to adapt to, and thrive in, their environments.

High culture is culture consumed mainly by upper classes (opera, ballet, etc.).

Popular culture (or **mass culture**) is culture consumed by all classes.

The Origins of Culture

You can appreciate the importance of culture for human survival by considering the predicament of early humans about 100 000 years ago. They lived in harsh natural environments. They had poor physical endowments, being slower runners and weaker fighters than many other animals. Yet, despite these disadvantages, they survived. More than that, they

Abstraction is the capacity to create general ideas or ways of thinking that are not linked to particular instances.

Symbols are things that carry a particular meaning, including the components of language, mathematical notations, and signs. Symbols allow us to classify experience and generalize from it.

Cooperation is the capacity to create a complex social life by establishing generally accepted ways of doing things and ideas about what is right and wrong.

Norms are generally accepted ways of doing things.

Values are ideas about what is right and wrong.

Production is the human capacity to make and use tools. It improves our ability to take what we want from nature.

Material culture comprises the tools and techniques that enable people to get tasks accomplished.

Non-material culture is composed of symbols, norms, and other intangible elements.

By cooperating, people are able to accomplish things that no person could possibly do alone.

prospered and came to dominate nature. This was possible largely because they were the smartest creatures around. Their sophisticated brains enabled them to create cultural survival kits of enormous complexity and flexibility. These cultural survival kits contained three main tools. Each tool was a uniquely human talent. Each gave rise to a different element of culture.

The first tool in the human cultural survival kit is **abstraction**, the ability to create general ideas or ways of thinking. **Symbols**, for example, are ideas that carry meaning. Languages and mathematical signs are sets of symbols. They allow us to classify experiences and generalize from them. For instance, we recognize that we can sit on many objects but that only some of them have four legs, a back, and space for one person. We distinguish the latter from other objects by giving them a name: chairs. By the time most babies reach the end of their first year, they have heard the word "chair" often and understand that it refers to a certain class of objects.

Cooperation is the second tool in the human cultural survival kit. It is the capacity to create a complex social life by establishing **norms**, or generally accepted ways of doing things, and **values**, or ideas about what is right and wrong, good and bad, beautiful and ugly. For example, family members cooperate to raise children, and in the process, they develop and apply norms and values about which child-rearing practices are appropriate and desirable. Note, however, that different times and places give rise to different norms and values. In our society today, parents might ground children for swearing, but in pioneer times, parents would typically "beat the devil out of them." As this example suggests, by analyzing how people cooperate and produce norms and values, we can learn much about what distinguishes one culture from another.

Production is the third main tool in the human cultural survival kit. It involves making and using tools and techniques that improve our ability to take what we want from nature. Such tools and techniques are known as **material culture** because they are tangible, whereas symbols, norms, values, and other elements of **non-material culture** are intangible. All animals take from nature to subsist, and apes may sometimes use rocks to break other objects, or walking sticks to steady themselves as they cross fast-flowing streams. But only humans are intelligent and agile enough to manufacture tools and use them to produce everything from food to satellites. In this sense, production is a uniquely human activity.

Table 3.1 lists each of the human capacities we have discussed and illustrates their cultural offshoots in the field of medicine. As in medicine, so in all fields of human activity: abstraction, cooperation, and production give rise to specific kinds of ideas, norms, and elements of material culture that help us deal with real-life problems.

TABLE 3.1
The Building Blocks of Culture

Source: Adapted from Bierstedt (1963).

The human capacity for...	Abstraction	Cooperation	Production
Gives rise to these elements of culture	↓ **Ideas**	↓ **Norms and values**	↓ **Material culture**
In medicine, for example...	*Theories* are developed about how a certain drug might cure a disease.	*Experiments* are conducted to test whether the drug works as expected.	*Treatments* are developed on the basis of the experimental results.

Three Types of Norms: Folkways, Mores, and Taboos

If a man walks down a busy street wearing nothing on the top half of his body, he is violating a **folkway**. If he walks down the street wearing nothing on the bottom half of his body, he is violating a **more** (the Latin word for "custom," pronounced MOR-ay). Folkways are norms that specify social *preferences*. Mores are norms that specify social *requirements*. People are usually punished when they violate norms, but the punishment is usually minor if the norm is a folkway. Some onlookers will raise their eyebrows at the shirtless man. Others will shake their head in disapproval. In contrast, the punishment for walking down the street without pants is bound to be moderately harsh. Someone is bound to call the police, probably sooner than later (Sumner, 1940 [1907]). The strongest and most central norms, however, are **taboos**. When someone violates a taboo, it causes revulsion in the community, and punishment is severe. Incest is one of the most widespread taboos.

Folkways are the least important norms and they evoke the least severe punishment.

Mores (pronounced MOR-ays) are core norms that most people believe are essential for the survival of their group or their society.

Taboos are among the strongest norms. When someone violates a taboo it causes revulsion in the community and punishment is severe.

CULTURE AND BIOLOGY

"Nature, Mr. Allnut, is what we are put in this world to rise above."
— Rose Sayer (Katharine Hepburn) in *The African Queen* (1951)

The Evolution of Human Behaviour

We have seen how the human capacity for abstraction, cooperation, and production enables us to create culture and makes us distinctively human. This capacity is built on a solid biological foundation. Biology, as every sociologist recognizes, sets broad human limits and potentials, including the potential to create culture.

However, some students of human behaviour who are trained as biologists go a step further. Practitioners of what originated as sociobiology and is now commonly known as evolutionary psychology claim that genes—chemical units that carry traits from parents to children—account not just for physical characteristics but also for specific behaviours and social practices (Pinker, 2002; Tooby and Cosmides, 1992; Wilson, 1975). This kind of argument has become increasingly popular since the early 1970s. Most sociologists disagree with it, however. Let us therefore devote a few paragraphs to its misconceptions (see also Chapter 11, Sexuality and Gender).

Evolutionary psychology's starting point is Charles Darwin's theory of evolution. Darwin (1859) observed wide variations in the physical characteristics of members of each species. For example, some deer can run quickly. Others run slowly. The colouring of some frogs lets them blend perfectly into their surroundings. The colouring of other frogs does not camouflage them as well. Some tigers are more ferocious than others are. Because of such variations, some members of each species—the quicker deer, the better-camouflaged frog, the more ferocious tiger—are more likely to survive. In general, the species members that are best adapted to their environments (or "fittest") are most likely to live long enough to have offspring. Therefore, concluded Darwin, the species characteristics that endure are those that increase the survival chances of the species.

Male Promiscuity, Female Fidelity, and Other Myths

Contemporary evolutionary psychologists make similar arguments about human behaviour and social arrangements. Typically, *they first identify a supposedly universal human behavioural trait*. For example, they claim that men are more likely than women are to want many sexual partners.

They next offer an explanation as to why this behaviour increases survial chances. Thus to continue with our example, they account for supposedly universal male promiscuity and female fidelity as follows. Every time a man ejaculates, he produces hundreds of millions of sperm. In contrast, a woman typically releases only one egg per month between puberty and menopause when she is not pregnant. Evolutionary psychologists claim that because of these sex differences, men and women develop different strategies to increase the chance they will reproduce their genes. Because a woman produces few eggs, she improves her chance of reproducing her genes if she has a mate who stays around to help and protect her during those few occasions when she is pregnant, gives birth, and nurses a small infant. Because a man's sperm is so plentiful, he improves his chance of reproducing his genes if he tries to impregnate as many women as possible. In short, women's desire for a single mate and men's desire for many sexual partners is simply the way men and women play out the game of survival of the fittest. Even male rapists, writes one evolutionary psychologist, may just be "doing the best they can to maximize their [reproductive] fitness" (Barash, 1981: 55).

The final part of the evolutionary psychologists' argument is that the behaviour in question cannot easily be changed. The characteristics that maximize the survival chances of a species supposedly are encoded or "hardwired" in our genes. It follows that what exists is necessary.

Most sociologists and many biologists and psychologists are critical of the reasoning of evolutionary psychologists (Gould and Lewontin, 1979; Lewontin, 1991; Schwartz, 1999). In the first place, *some behaviours discussed by evolutionary psychologists are not universal and some are not even that common.* Consider male promiscuity. Is it true that men are promiscuous and women are not? We lack Canadian data on the subject, but a respected American survey conducted in 2002 tells a different story. According to the survey, only a minority of adult American men (21 percent) claimed they had more than one sex partner in the previous year (see Table 3.2). The figure for adult American women was significantly lower (10 percent). However, if we consider married adults only, the figures fall to 5 percent for men and 1 percent for women, a much smaller difference (see Table 3.3). Apparently, certain *social* arrangements, such as the institution of marriage, account in substantial measure for variation in male promiscuity. There is no *universal* propensity to male promiscuity.

Still, 11 percent more men than women said they had had more than one sex partner in the year preceding the survey. Among unmarried people, the male–female difference was 14 percent. Researchers have identified two main reasons for the difference (McConaghy, 1999: 311–14). First, men seem to be somewhat more likely than women are to have sexual relations with members of their own sex, and men who do so are more likely to have many sex partners than women who do so.[1] This finding contradicts the evolutionary psychologists' argument, which ties male promiscuity to male reproductive strategies. Second, men apparently tend to exaggerate how many sexual partners they have when asked about this subject in surveys because our culture puts a premium on male sexual performance. This, too, is bad news for the evolutionary

TABLE 3.2

Number of Sex Partners by Respondent's Sex, United States, 2002 (in percent)

Number of Sex Partners	Respondent's Sex	
	Male	Female
0 or 1	79	90
More than 1	21	10
Total	100	100
N	1004	1233

Source: From National Opinion Research Center, 2004, *General Social Survey, 1972–2002* (Chicago: University of Chicago), machine-readable file. Reprinted with permission.

TABLE 3.3

Number of Sex Partners by Respondent's Sex, United States, 2002, Married Respondents Only (in percent)

Number of Sex Partners	Respondent's Sex	
	Male	Female
0 or 1	95	99
More than 1	5	1
Total	100	100
N	499	534

Source: From National Opinion Research Center, 2004, *General Social Survey, 1972–2002* (Chicago: University of Chicago), machine-readable file. Reprinted with permission.

psychologists, who would like us to believe that men are actually and naturally promiscuous, not influenced by cultural standards to simply say they are.

In general, then, the evolutionary psychologists' claim about male promiscuity and female fidelity is false. So are many of their other claims about so-called behavioural constants or universals.

The second big problem with evolutionary psychology is that nobody has ever verified that specific behaviours and social arrangements are associated with specific genes (for an exception, see the discussion of language below). Therefore, when it comes to supporting their key argument, evolutionary psychologists have little to stand on apart from a fragile string of maybes and possibilities: "[W]e *may* have to open our minds and admit the *possibility* that our need to maximize our [reproductive] fitness *may* be whispering somewhere deep within us and that, *know it or not*, most of the time we are heeding these whisperings" (Barash, 1981: 31; our emphasis). Maybe. Then again, maybe not.

Finally, even if researchers eventually discover an association between particular genes and particular behaviours, it would be wrong to conclude that variations among people are due just to their genes (see Figure 3.1). As one of the world's leading biologists writes, "variations among individuals within species are a unique consequence of both genes *and environment* in a constant interaction . . . [and] random variation in growth and division of cells during development" (Lewontin, 1991: 26–7; our emphasis). Genes *never* develop without environmental influence. The genes of a human embryo, for example, are profoundly affected by whether the mother consumes the recommended daily dosage of calcium or nearly overdoses daily on crack cocaine. And what the mother consumes is, in turn, determined by many social factors. Even if someone inherits a mutant cancer gene, the chance of developing cancer is strongly influenced by diet, exercise, tobacco consumption, and factors associated with occupational and environmental pollution.[2] It follows that the pattern of your life is not entirely hardwired by your genes. Changes in social environment do produce physical and, to an even greater degree, behavioural change. However, to figure out the effects of the social environment on human behaviour, we have to abandon the premises of evolutionary psychology and develop specifically sociological skills for analyzing the effects of social structure and culture.

FIGURE 3.1

A Genetic Misconception

When scientists announced they had finished sequencing the human genome on June 26, 2000, some people thought all human characteristics could be read from the human genetic "map." They cannot. The functions of most genes are still unknown. Moreover, because genes mutate randomly and interact with environmental (including social) conditions, the correspondence between genetic function and behavioural outcome is highly uncertain.

Source: *National Post,* 2000.

The Problem of Language

Is Language Innate or Learned?

One important field in which biological thinking has been influential in recent years is the study of language. A language is a system of symbols strung together to communicate thought. Equipped with language, we can share understandings, pass experience and knowledge from one generation to the next, and make plans for the future. In short, language allows culture to develop. Consequently, sociologists commonly think of language as a cultural invention that distinguishes humans from other animals.

Yet Montreal-born MIT cognitive scientist Steven Pinker, a leading figure in the biological onslaught, says culture has little to do with our acquisition of language. In his view, "people know how to talk in more or less the sense that spiders know how to spin webs" (Pinker, 1994: 18). Language, says Pinker, is an "instinct."

Pinker bases his radical claim on the observation that most people can easily create and understand sentences that have never been uttered before. We even invent countless new words (including the word *countless,* which was invented by Shakespeare). We normally develop this facility quickly and without formal instruction at an early age. This suggests that people have a sort of innate recipe or grammar for combining words in patterned ways. He supports his case by discussing cases of young children with different language backgrounds who were brought together in settings as diverse as Hawaiian sugar plantations in the 1890s and Nicaraguan schools for the deaf in the 1970s and who spontaneously created their own language system and grammatical rules.

If children are inclined to create grammars spontaneously at a young age, we can also point to seats of language in the brain; damage to certain parts of the brain impairs the ability to speak although intelligence is unaffected. Moreover, scientists have identified a gene that may help wire these seats of language into place. A few otherwise healthy children fail to develop language skills. They find it hard to articulate words and they make a variety of grammatical errors when they speak. If these language disorders cannot be attributed to other causes, they are diagnosed as specific language impairment (SLI). Recently it was discovered that a mutation of a gene known as FOXP2 is associated with SLI (Pinker, 2001). Only when the gene is normal do children acquire complex language skills at an early age. From these and similar observations, Pinker concludes that language is not so much learned as it is grown. Should we believe him?

The Social Roots of Language

From a sociological point of view, there is nothing problematic about the argument that we are biologically prewired to acquire language and create grammatical speech patterns. What is sociologically interesting, however, is how the social environment gives these predispositions form. We know, for example, that young children go through periods of rapid development, and if they do not interact symbolically with others during these critical periods, their language skills remain permanently impaired (Sternberg, 1998: 312). This suggests that our biological potential must be unlocked by the social environment to be fully realized. Language must be learned. The environment is, in fact, such a powerful influence on language acquisition that even a mutated FOXP2 gene doesn't seal one's linguistic fate. As York University's Stuart Shanker notes, up to half of children with SLI recover fully with intensive language therapy (Shanker, 2002).

In an obvious sense, all language is learned even though our potential for learning and the structure of what we can learn is rooted in biology. Our use of language depends on which language communities we are part of. You say tomāto and I say tomăto, but Luigi says *pomodoro* and Shoshanna says *agvaniya.* But what exactly is the relationship among our use of language, the way we think, and our social environment? We now turn to just that question.

The Sapir-Whorf Thesis and Its Critics

In the 1930s, linguists Edward Sapir and Benjamin Lee Whorf first proposed that experience, thought, and language interact in what came to be known as the Sapir-Whorf thesis. The Sapir-Whorf thesis holds that we experience certain things in our environment and form concepts about those things (path 1→2 in Figure 3.2). We then develop language to express our concepts (path 2→3). Finally, language itself influences how we see the world (path 3→1).

Whorf saw speech patterns as "interpretations of experience" (path 1→2→3; Whorf, 1956: 137). This seems uncontroversial. The Garo of Burma, a rice-growing people, distinguish many types of rice. Nomadic Arabs have more than 20 different words for camel (Sternberg, 1998: 305). Verbal distinctions among types of rice and camels are necessary for different groups of people because these objects are important in their environment. As a matter of necessity, they distinguish among many different types of what we may regard as "the same" object.[3] Similarly, terms that apparently refer to the same things or people may change to reflect a changing reality. For example, a committee used to be headed by a *chairman*. When women entered the paid labour force in large numbers in the 1960s and some of them became committee heads, the term changed to *chairperson* or simply *chair*. In such cases, we see clearly how the environment or experience influences language.

It is equally uncontroversial to say that people must think before they can speak (path 2→3). Anyone who has struggled for just the right word or rewritten a sentence to phrase a thought more precisely knows this.

The controversial part of the Sapir-Whorf thesis is path 3→1. In what sense does language *in and of itself* influence the way we experience the world? In the first wave of studies based on the Sapir-Whorf thesis, researchers focused on whether speakers of different languages perceive colour in different ways. By the 1970s, they concluded that they did not. People who speak different languages may have a different number of basic colour terms, but everyone with normal vision is able to see the full visible spectrum. There are two words for blue in Russian and only one in English, but this does not mean that English speakers are somehow handicapped in their ability to distinguish shades of blue.

In the 1980s and 1990s, researchers found some effects of language on perception. For example, the German word for *key* is masculine while the Spanish word for *key* is feminine. When German and Spanish speakers are asked to describe keys, German speakers tend to use words like "hard," "heavy," and "jagged" while Spanish speakers use such words as "lovely," "shiny," and "shaped." Apparently, the gender of the noun in and of itself influences how people see the thing to which the noun refers (Minkel, 2002). Still, the degree to which language itself influences thought is a matter of controversy. Some men use terms like *fox, babe, bitch, ho,* and *doll* to refer to women. These terms are deeply offensive to many people. They certainly reflect and reinforce underlying inequalities between women and men. Some people assert that these terms *in and of themselves* influence people to think of

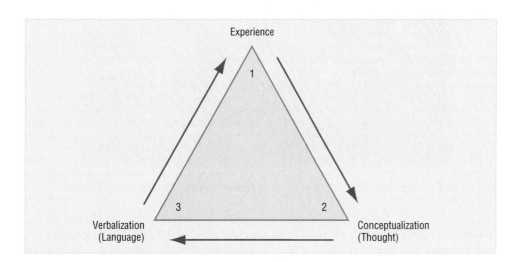

FIGURE 3.2
The Sapir-Whorf Thesis

women simply as sexual objects, but social scientists have yet to demonstrate the degree to which they do so.

We conclude that biological thinking about culture has both benefits and dangers. On the one hand, biology helps us see more clearly the broad limits and potentials of human creativity. On the other hand, some scholars have managed to get themselves trapped in a biological straitjacket. They fail to appreciate how the social environment unlocks biological potentials and how it creates enormous variation in the cultural expression of those potentials. Analyzing culture in all its variety and showing how cultural variations are related to variations in social structure are jobs for the sociologist. In the rest of this chapter, we show how sociologists go about these jobs. We begin by first considering how it is possible to observe culture in a relatively unbiased fashion.

Culture and Ethnocentrism: A Functionalist Analysis of Culture

Despite its central importance in human life, culture is often invisible. That is, people tend to take their own culture for granted; it usually seems so sensible and natural they rarely think about it (see Box 3.1). In contrast, people are often startled when confronted by cultures other than their own. The ideas, norms, and techniques of other cultures frequently seem odd, irrational, and even inferior.

Ethnocentrism is the tendency for a person to judge other cultures exclusively by the standards of his or her own.

Judging another culture exclusively by the standards of our own is known as **ethnocentrism** (Box 3.1). Ethnocentrism impairs sociological analysis. This can be illustrated by a practice that seems bizarre to many Westerners: cow worship among Hindu peasants in India.

BOX 3.1
Sociology at the Movies
TAKE   ROLL

Borat: Cultural Learnings of America for Make Benefit Glorious Nation of Kazakhstan (2006)

Borat is a journalist from Kazakhstan who visits the United States so he can learn about American culture and return home with useful lessons. The movie's humour turns on the apparent differences between Borat's culture and that of his audience and the people he meets. His values, beliefs, and norms seem deeply offensive to the Americans he encounters. Since Borat is capable of seeing the world only from his own cultural viewpoint, the movie at one level is a story of ethnocentrism gone mad.

The joke is apparent from the get-go. Many DVDs let you choose to hear the dialogue in English, French,

Borat Sagdiyev (Sacha Baron Cohen) and Azamat Bagatov (Ken Davitian) in *Borat*

or Spanish. The *Borat* DVD appears to give you the additional options of hearing the dialogue in Russian or Hebrew. However, when you select

"Hebrew," you hear the repeated warning, "Jew in vocinity, Jew in vocinity," while the screen flashes the following messages: "You have been trapped, Jew!" "Keep your claws where they can be seen." "Do not attempt to shift your shape."

We soon discover that Kazakhs are not just anti-Semites. They are racists, homophobes, and sexists too. At its Toronto Film Festival debut, Borat (played by Sacha Baron Cohen) sat with a horse in a cart pulled by four women dressed as peasants. As Borat explained in an interview, in Kazakhstan the highest being is God. Next comes man, followed by the horse, the snake, "the little crawly thing," and, finally, woman.

Borat directs many of our biggest laughs against Americans. At one point he secures the agreement of a rodeo organizer in Salem, Virginia, to let him sing the national anthem before the show begins. Borat first makes a little speech: "My name Borat, I come from Kazakhstan. Can I say first, we support your war of terror. [applause and cheers] May we show our support to our boys in Iraq. [applause and cheers] May U S and A kill every single terrorist! [applause and cheers] May George Bush drink the blood of every single man, woman, and child of Iraq! [applause and cheers] May you destroy their country so that for the next 1000 years not even a single lizard will survive in their desert! [applause and cheers]" After thus demonstrating the inhumanity of his audience, Borat sings the Kazakh national anthem in English to the tune of the United States national anthem:

Kazakhstan is the greatest country in the world.
All other countries are run by little girls.
Kazakhstan is number one exporter of potassium.
Other Central Asian countries have inferior potassium.
Kazakhstan is the greatest country in the world.
All other countries is the home of the gays.

To the suggestion that another country exceeds the United States in glory, the audience responds with jeers and boos that grow so loud, one fears for Borat's life. In this and other scenes, the movie forces us to conclude that American culture is as biased in its own way as Kazakh culture allegedly is.

Is *Borat* just one long prejudiced rant against Jews, Americans, Kazakhs, blacks, gays, women, and so on? Some people think so. But that opinion is not credible for two reasons. First, it is inconsistent with who Sacha Baron Cohen is. He is a well-educated liberal who completed a degree in history at Cambridge and wrote his thesis on the civil rights movement in the United States. And he is a Jew who strongly identifies with his ethnic heritage. (One of the movie's biggest and largely unappreciated jokes is that Borat speaks mostly Hebrew to his sidekick, Azamat Bagatov [Ken Davitian]).

Borat certainly is one long and very funny rant, but the real objects of its satire are the world's racists, sexists, anti-Semites, and homophobes, regardless of their race, creed, or national origin. The deeper message of *Borat* is anything but ethnocentric: respect for human dignity is a value that rises above all cultures, and people who think otherwise deserve to be laughed at.

Does *Borat* help you see the prejudices of other people more clearly? Does *Borat* help you see your own prejudices more clearly? Borat talks and acts like a bigot from the opening title to the closing credits. Do you think that the expression of bigotry is inherently offensive and should always be avoided? Or do you believe that the satirical expression of bigotry can usefully reveal hidden prejudices?

Hindu peasants refuse to slaughter cattle and eat beef because, for them, the cow is a religious symbol of life. Pinup calendars throughout rural India portray beautiful women with the bodies of fat, white cows, milk jetting out of each teat. Cows are permitted to wander the streets, defecate on the sidewalks, and stop to chew their cud in busy intersections and on railroad tracks, causing traffic to come to a complete halt. In Madras, police stations maintain fields where stray cows that have fallen ill can graze and be nursed back to health. The government even runs old-age homes for cows where dry and decrepit cattle are kept free of charge. All this seems utterly inscrutable to most Westerners, for it takes place amid poverty and hunger that could presumably be alleviated if only the peasants would slaughter their "useless" cattle for food instead of squandering scarce resources feeding and protecting them.

According to anthropologist Marvin Harris, however, ethnocentrism misleads many Western observers (Harris, 1974: 3–32). Cow worship, it turns out, is an economically rational practice in rural India. For one thing, Indian peasants cannot afford tractors, so cows are needed to give birth to oxen, which are in high demand for plowing. For another, the cows produce hundreds of millions of kilograms of recoverable manure, about half of which

Many Westerners find the Indian practice of cow worship bizarre. However, cow worship performs a number of useful economic functions and is in that sense entirely rational. By viewing cow worship exclusively as an outsider (or, for that matter, exclusively as an insider), we fail to see its rational core.

is used as fertilizer and half as a cooking fuel. With oil, coal, and wood in short supply, and with the peasants unable to afford chemical fertilizers, cow dung is, well, a godsend. What is more, cows in India don't cost much to maintain since they eat mostly food that is not fit for human consumption. And they represent an important source of protein and a livelihood for members of low-ranking castes, who have the right to dispose of the bodies of dead cattle. These "untouchables" eat beef and form the workforce of India's large leather-craft industry. The protection of cows by means of cow worship is thus a perfectly sensible and highly efficient economic practice. It only seems irrational when judged by the standards of Western agribusiness.

Harris's analysis of cow worship in rural India is interesting for two reasons. First, it illustrates how functionalist theory can illuminate otherwise mysterious social practices. Harris uncovers a range of latent functions performed by cow worship, thus showing how a particular social practice has unintended and unobvious consequences that make social order possible. Second, we can draw an important lesson about ethnocentrism from Harris's analysis. If you refrain from taking your own culture for granted and judging other cultures by the standards of your own, you will have taken an important first step toward developing a sociological understanding of culture.

CULTURE AS FREEDOM

Culture has two faces. First, culture provides us with an opportunity to exercise our *freedom*. We create elements of culture in our everyday life to solve practical problems and express our needs, hopes, joys, and fears.

However, creating culture is just like any other act of construction in that we need raw materials to get the job done. The raw materials for the culture we create consist of cultural elements that either existed before we were born or are created by other people after our birth. We may put these elements together in ways that produce something genuinely new. But there is no other well to drink from, so existing culture puts limits on what we can think and do. In that sense, culture *constrains* us. This is culture's second face. In the rest of this chapter we take a close look at both faces of culture.

Cultural Production and Symbolic Interactionism

Until the 1960s, many sociologists argued that culture is a "reflection" of society. Using the language introduced in Chapter 2, we can say they regarded culture as a dependent variable. Harris's analysis of rural Indians certainly fits that mould. In Harris's view, the social necessity of protecting cows gave rise to the cultural belief that cows are holy.

In recent decades, the symbolic interactionist tradition that we introduced in Chapter 1 has influenced many sociologists of culture. Symbolic interactionists, you will recall, are inclined to regard culture as an *independent* variable. In their view, people do not accept culture passively; we are not empty vessels into which society pours a defined assortment of beliefs, symbols, and values. Instead, we actively produce and interpret culture, creatively fashioning it and attaching meaning to it in accordance with our diverse needs (Hall, 1980; Hoggart, 1958; Thompson, 1968). This line of thought gave rise to the field of cultural studies, which overlaps the sociology of culture (Griswold, 1992; Long, 1997; Spillman, 2002).

The idea that people actively produce and interpret culture implies that, to a degree, we are at liberty to choose how culture influences us. Let us linger a moment on the question of why we enjoy more such freedom today than ever before.

Cultural Diversity

Part of the reason we are increasingly able to choose how culture influences us is that there is more to choose from. Like many societies in the world, Canada is undergoing rapid cultural diversification because of a rising number of immigrants and change in their countries of origin. Immigrants made up 19.8 percent of Canada's population in 2006, the highest proportion since 1931 (Statistics Canada, 2007b). Moreover, since the 1960s, traditional, European sources of immigrants have become far less important than Caribbean and especially Asian sources. Statistics Canada therefore projects that nearly 20 percent of Canada's population will consist of members of "visible minorities" by 2016 (Statistics Canada, 1998a: 75).

Canada continues to diversify culturally.

The cultural diversification of Canadian society is evident in all aspects of life, from the growing popularity of Latino and Brazilian music, through the increasing influence of Asian design in clothing and architecture, to the ever-broadening international assortment of foods consumed by most Canadians. Marriage between people of different ethnic groups is widespread, and interracial marriage is increasingly accepted (see Chapter 15, Families).

Multiculturalism

At the political level, cultural diversity has become a source of conflict. This disagreement is nowhere more evident than in the debates that have surfaced in recent years concerning curricula in the Canadian educational system.

Although each provincial and territorial government in Canada has jurisdiction over education, it was common until recent decades for schools across Canada to stress the common elements of our culture, history, and society. Students learned the historical importance of the "charter groups"—the English and the French—in Canada's history. School curricula typically neglected the contributions of non-whites and non-French or non-English to Canada's historical, literary, artistic, and scientific development. Moreover, students learned little about the less savoury aspects of Canadian history, including Canada's racist immigration policies that actively sought to preserve Canada's "English stock" by restricting or denying entry to certain groups (Chapter 10, Race and Ethnicity). In general, history books were written from the perspective of the victors, not the vanquished.

For the past few decades, some educators have argued that the experiences of women, Aboriginal peoples, members of visible minorities, and other disadvantaged groups must be incorporated into Canada's classrooms. In the words of one group of experts: "The purpose of schooling must be to 'empower' . . . [members of minority groups], to give them the ability to participate fully in struggles, large and small, to gain respect, dignity and power" (Gaskell, McLaren, and Novogrodsky, 1995: 105). Such advocates of multiculturalism suggest we must bring our educational system in line with Canada's status as the first officially multicultural society in the world. In 1971, the Canadian government declared that Canada, while officially bilingual, had no "official" culture—that is, none of the distinguishable cultures in Canada takes precedence over the others. With the passage of the Canadian Multiculturalism Act in 1988, the federal government confirmed its commitment to the recognition of all Canadians "as full and equal participants in Canadian society." In short, multiculturalists argue that, to the extent that existing curricula are biased in both what is included and what is excluded, our schools are failing to provide students with the type of education a country truly devoted to multiculturalism demands.

Most critics of multiculturalism in education do not argue against teaching cultural diversity. What they fear is that multicultural education is being taken too far (Bissoondath, 2002; Fekete, 1994; Glazer, 1997; Schlesinger, 1991; Stotsky, 1999). Specifically, they say multiculturalism has three negative consequences:

1. Critics believe that multicultural education hurts students who are members of minority groups by forcing them to spend too much time on non-core subjects. To get ahead in the world, they say, students need to be skilled in English, French, and math. By taking time away from these subjects, multicultural education impedes the success of minority group members in the work world. Multiculturalists counter that students who are members of minority groups develop pride and self-esteem from a curriculum that stresses cultural diversity. They argue that this helps students get ahead in the work world.

2. Critics also believe that multicultural education causes political disunity and results in more interethnic and interracial conflict. Therefore, they want curricula to stress the common elements of the national experience and highlight Europe's contribution to our

culture. Multiculturalists reply that political unity and interethnic and interracial harmony simply maintain inequality in Canadian society. Conflict, they say, while unfortunate, is often necessary to achieve equality between majority and minority groups.

3. Critics complain that multiculturalism encourages the growth of **cultural relativism**. Cultural relativism is the opposite of ethnocentrism. It is the belief that all cultures and all cultural practices have equal value. The trouble with this view is that some cultures oppose the most deeply held values of most Canadians. Other cultures promote practices that most Canadians consider inhumane. Should we respect racist and anti-democratic cultures, such as the apartheid regime that existed in South Africa from 1948 until 1992? What about female circumcision, still widely practised in some parts of Africa (see Box 3.2 on page 82)? Or the Australian aborigine practice of driving spears through the limbs of criminals (Garkawe, 1995)? Critics argue that to the degree it promotes cultural relativism, a truly multicultural system of education might encourage respect for practices that are abhorrent to most Canadians. Multiculturalists reply that cultural relativism need not be taken to such an extreme. *Moderate* cultural relativism encourages tolerance, and it should be promoted.

Clearly, multiculturalism in education is a complex and emotional issue that requires much additional research and debate. It is worth pondering here, however, because it says something important about the state of Canadian culture today and, more generally, about how world culture has developed since our remote ancestors lived in tribes. In general, as we will now see, cultures tend to become more heterogeneous over time, with important consequences for everyday life.

The Rights Revolution: A Conflict Analysis of Culture

Underlying cultural diversification is what Canadian political philosopher Michael Ignatieff (2000) calls the **rights revolution**, the process by which socially excluded groups have struggled to win equal rights under the law and in practice. After the outburst of nationalism, racism, and genocidal behaviour among the combatants in World War II, the United Nations proclaimed the Universal Declaration of Human Rights in 1948. Its preamble reads in part:

> Whereas recognition of the inherent dignity and of the equal and inalienable rights of all members of the human family is the foundation of freedom, justice and peace in the world. . . . Now, therefore, The General Assembly proclaims this Universal Declaration of Human Rights as a common standard of achievement for all peoples and all nations, to the end that every individual and every organ of society, keeping this Declaration constantly in mind, shall strive by teaching and education to promote respect for these rights and freedoms and by progressive measures, national and international, to secure their universal and effective recognition and observance. (United Nations, 1998a)

Fanned by such sentiment, the rights revolution was in full swing by the 1960s. Today, women's rights, the rights of members of minority groups, gay and lesbian rights, the rights of people with special needs, constitutional rights, and language rights are key parts of our political discourse. Through the rights revolution, democracy has been widened and deepened (Chapter 14, Politics). The rights revolution is by no means finished. Many categories of people are still discriminated against socially, politically, and economically. However, in much of the world all categories of people now participate more fully than ever before in the life of their societies.

The rights revolution raises some difficult issues. For example, some members of groups that have suffered extraordinarily high levels of discrimination historically, such as Aboriginal Canadians, have demanded reparations in the form of money, symbolic gestures, land, and political autonomy (Chapter 10, Race and Ethnicity). Much controversy surrounds the extent of the obligation of current citizens to compensate for past injustices.

Cultural relativism is the belief that all cultures have equal value.

The rights revolution is the process by which socially excluded groups struggled to win equal rights under the law and in practice beginning in the second half of the twentieth century.

BOX 3.2
It's Your Choice

Female Genital Mutilation

The World Health Organization defines female genital mutilation as "all procedures involving partial or total removal of the external female genitalia or other injury to the female genital organs whether for cultural or other nontherapeutic reasons" (World Health Organization, 2001). Elderly women who lack medical training usually perform these procedures.

Female genital mutilation results in pain, humiliation, psychological trauma, and loss of sexual pleasure. In the short term it is associated with infection, shock, injury to neighbouring organs, and severe bleeding. In the long term it is associated with infertility, chronic infections in the urinary tract and reproductive system, increased susceptibility to hepatitis B and HIV/AIDS, and more.

Although frequently associated with Islam, female genital mutilation is rare in many predominantly Muslim countries. It is a social custom, not a religious practice. It is nearly universal in Somalia, Djibouti, and Egypt, and common in other parts of Africa. More than 132 million women and girls have undergone female genital mutilation. About two million girls are at risk of undergoing it every year (Ahmad, 2000; World Health Organization, 2001).

Female genital mutilation is typically performed as a rite of passage on girls between the ages of 4 and 14. In some cultures, people think it enhances female fertility. Furthermore, they commonly assume that women are naturally "unclean" and "masculine" inasmuch as they possess a "vestige" of the "male" sex organ, the clitoris. From this point of view, women who have not experienced genital mutilation are more likely to demonstrate "masculine" levels of sexual interest and activity. They are less likely to remain virgins before marriage and faithful within it. Accordingly, some people think female genital mutilation lessens or eradicates sexual arousal in women.

One reaction to female genital mutilation is from a human rights perspective. In this view, the practice is simply one manifestation of gender-based oppression and the violence that women experience universally. Adopting this perspective, the United Nations has defined female genital mutilation as a form of violence against women. This perspective is also reflected in a growing number of international, regional, and national agreements that commit governments to preventing female genital mutilation, assisting women at risk of undergoing it, and punishing people who commit it. For example, female genital mutilation is illegal in Canada (Hussein, 1995; Scott, 2000). Moreover, section 273.3 of the Criminal Code prohibits anyone from removing children who are ordinarily resident in Canada and subjecting them to female genital mutilation.

Proponents of a second perspective on female genital mutilation are cultural relativists. They regard the human rights perspective as ethnocentric. The cultural relativists view interventions that interfere with the practice as little more than neo-imperialist attacks on African cultures. From their point of view, all talk of "universal human rights" denies cultural sovereignty to less powerful peoples. Moreover, opposition to female genital mutilation undermines tolerance and multiculturalism while reinforcing racist attitudes. Accordingly, cultural relativists argue that we should affirm the right of other cultures to practise female genital mutilation even if we regard it as destructive, senseless, oppressive, and abhorrent. We should respect the fact that other cultures regard female genital mutilation as meaningful and as serving useful functions.

Which of these perspectives do you find more compelling? Do you believe that certain principles of human decency transcend the particulars of any culture? If so, what are those principles? If you do not believe in the existence of any universal principles of human decency, then does anything go? Would you agree that, say, genocide is acceptable if most people in a society favour it? Or are there limits to your cultural relativism? In a world where supposedly universal principles often clash with the principles of particular cultures, where do you draw the line? It's your choice.

Such problems notwithstanding, the rights revolution is here to stay and it affects our culture profoundly. Specifically, the rights revolution fragments Canadian culture by (1) legitimizing the grievances of groups that were formerly excluded from full social participation and (2) renewing their pride in their identity and heritage. Our history books, our literature, our music, our use of languages, our very sense of what it means to be Canadian have diversified culturally. White, male, heterosexual property owners of north European origin are still disproportionately influential in Canada, but our culture is no longer dominated by them in the way that it was just four decades ago.

From Diversity to Globalization

In preliterate or tribal societies, cultural beliefs and practices are virtually the same for all group members. For example, many tribal societies organize **rites of passage**. These cultural ceremonies mark the transition from one stage of life to another (e.g., coming-of-age ceremonies) or from life to death (e.g., funerals). These religious rituals involve elaborate body painting, carefully orchestrated chants and movements, and so forth. They are conducted in public. No variation from prescribed practice is allowed. Culture is homogeneous (Durkheim, 1976 [1915]).

In contrast, preindustrial Western Europe and North America were rocked by artistic, religious, scientific, and political forces that fragmented culture. The Renaissance, the Protestant Reformation, the Scientific Revolution, the French and American revolutions— between the fourteenth and eighteenth centuries, all these movements involved people questioning old ways of seeing and doing things. Science placed skepticism about established authority at the very heart of its method. Political revolution proved there was nothing ordained about who should rule and how they should do so. Religious dissent ensured that the Catholic Church would no longer be the supreme interpreter of God's will in the eyes of all Christians. Authority and truth became divided as never before.

Cultural fragmentation picked up steam during industrialization as the variety of occupational roles grew and new political and intellectual movements crystallized. Its pace is quickening again today in the postindustrial era as a result of globalization. Globalization is the process by which formerly separate economies, states, and cultures are tied together and people become aware of their growing interdependence.

One of the most important roots of globalization is the expansion of international trade and investment. Even the most patriotic of Canadians has probably dined at least once at McDonald's—and even a business as "American" as McDonald's now reaps 60 percent of its profits from outside the United States. Indeed, McDonald's international operations are expected to grow at four times the rate of its U.S. outlets (Commins, 1997). At the same time, members of different ethnic and racial groups are migrating and coming into sustained contact with one another. A growing number of people date, court, and marry across religious, ethnic, and racial lines. Influential transnational organizations, such as the International Monetary Fund, the World Bank, the European Union, Greenpeace, and Amnesty International, are multiplying. Relatively inexpensive international travel and communication make contacts among people from diverse cultures routine. The mass media make Vin Diesel and *Survivor* nearly as well known in Warsaw as in Winnipeg. MTV brings rock music to the world via MTV Canada, MTV Latino, MTV Brazil, MTV Europe, MTV Asia, MTV Japan,

Rites of passage are cultural ceremonies that mark the transition from one stage of life to another (e.g., baptisms, confirmations, weddings) or from life to death (funerals).

The idea of globalization first gained prominence in marketing strategies in the 1970s. In the 1980s, such companies as Coca-Cola and McDonald's expanded into non-Western countries to find new markets. Today, Kellogg's markets products in more than 160 countries. Basmati Flakes cereal was first produced by the Kellogg's plant in Tajola, India, in 1992.

MTV Mandarin, and MTV India (Hanke, 1998). Globalization, in short, destroys political, economic, and cultural isolation, bringing people together in what Canadian media analyst Marshall McLuhan (1964) called a "global village." As a result of globalization, people are less obliged to accept the culture into which they are born and freer to combine elements of culture from a wide variety of historical periods and geographical settings. Globalization is a schoolboy in New Delhi, India, listening to Bob Marley on his MP3 player as he rushes to slip into his Levis, wolf down a bowl of Kellogg's Basmati Flakes, and say goodbye to his parents in Hindi because he's late for his English-language school.

The Globalization of English

A good indicator of the influence and extent of globalization is the spread of English. In 1600, English was the mother tongue of between four million and seven million people. Not even all people in England spoke it. Today, more than one billion people speak English worldwide, more than half as a second language. With the exception of the many varieties of Chinese, English is the most widespread language on earth.[4] More than half the world's technical and scientific periodicals are written in English. English is the official language of the Olympics, of the Miss Universe contest, of navigation in the air and on the seas, and of the World Council of Churches (Figure 3.3).

English is dominant because Britain and the United States have been the world's most powerful and influential countries—economically, militarily, and culturally—for more than 200 years. (Someone once defined *language* as a dialect backed up by an army.) In recent decades, the global spread of capitalism, the popularity of Hollywood movies and American TV shows, and the widespread access to instant communication via telephone and the Internet have increased the reach of the English language. There are now more speakers of excellent English in India than in Britain, and when a construction company jointly owned by German, French, and Italian interests undertakes a building project in Spain, the language of business is English (McCrum, Cran, and MacNeil, 1992).

Because of the rise of English (as well as the influence of French, Spanish, and the languages of a few other colonizing nations), several thousand languages around the world are being eliminated. These endangered languages are spoken by the tribes of Papua New Guinea; the native peoples of the Americas; the national and tribal minorities of Asia, Africa, and Oceania; and marginalized European peoples, such as the Irish and the Basques. The estimated 5000 to 6000 languages spoken in the world today will be reduced to between 1000 and 3000 in a century. Much of the culture of a people—its prayers, humour, conversational styles, technical vocabulary, myths, and so on—is expressed through language. Therefore, the loss of language amounts to the disappearance of tradition and perhaps even

FIGURE 3.3

English as Official or Majority Language

Sources: United Nations Educational, Scientific, and Cultural Organization, 2001; Central Intelligence Agency, 2002.

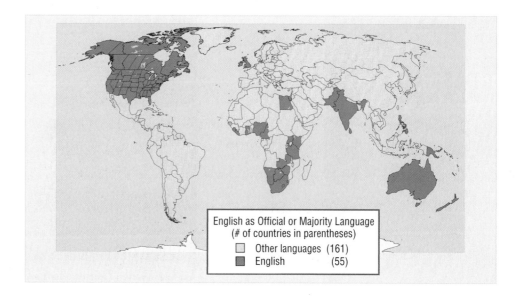

English as Official or Majority Language
(# of countries in parentheses)
☐ Other languages (161)
■ English   (55)

identity. These are often replaced by the traditions and identity of the colonial power, with television playing an important role in the transformation (Woodbury, 2003).

Still, major languages other than English are holding their own and even pushing back the English onslaught in some areas. Consider the pie charts in Figure 3.4, which show how language use on the Internet changed from June 2001 to June 2007. In this six-year period, English usage dropped nearly 14 percent, while Chinese usage jumped more than 7 percent and Spanish usage grew more than 3 percent. These figures suggest that globalization does not necessarily involve the homogenization of culture—an important theme that we will take up again in Chapter 9 (Globalization, Inequality, and Development).

Aspects of Postmodernism

Some sociologists think so much cultural fragmentation and reconfiguration has taken place in the last few decades that a new term is needed to characterize the culture of our times: **postmodernism**. Scholars often characterize the last half of the nineteenth century and the first half of the twentieth century as the era of modernity. During this hundred-year period, belief in the inevitability of progress, respect for authority, and consensus around core values characterized much of Western culture. In contrast, postmodern culture involves an eclectic mix of elements from different times and places, the erosion of authority, and the decline of consensus around core values. Let us consider each of these aspects of postmodernism in turn.

An eclectic mix of elements from different times and places. In the postmodern era, it is easier to create personalized belief systems and practices by blending facets of different cultures and historical periods. Consider religion. The great majority of Canadians say they believe in God and continue to identify themselves as Christians. But increasing numbers identify themselves as adherents of non-Christian religions (6.4 percent of the total in 2001) or as having "no religion" (16.5 percent in 2001; Statistics Canada 2005i; Chapter 16, Religion). In addition, Canadians are increasingly willing to feast off of a religious smorgasbord that combines a conventional menu with a wide assortment of less conventional beliefs and practices, including astrology, tarot, New Age mysticism, psychic phenomena, and communication with the dead (Bibby, 1987: 233; Bibby, 2001: 195; Table 3.4). In the words of one journalist: "In an age when we trust ourselves to assemble our own investment portfolios and cancer therapies, why not our religious beliefs?" (Creedon, 1998). Many people now draw on religions much like consumers shop in a mall. Meanwhile, churches, synagogues, and other religious institutions have diversified their services to appeal to the spiritual, leisure, and social needs of religious consumers and retain their loyalties in the competitive market for congregants and parishioners (Finke and Stark, 1992).

The mix-and-match approach we see when it comes to religion is evident in virtually all spheres of culture. Purists may scoff at this sort of cultural blending. However, it probably

Postmodernism is characterized by an eclectic mix of cultural elements and the erosion of consensus.

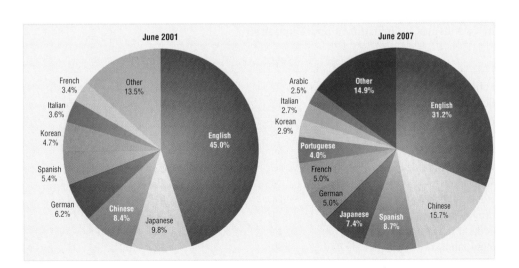

FIGURE 3.4

Internet Usage by Language Group, June 2001 and June 2007

Sources: Global Reach, 2001, 2004; Internet World Stats, 2007; Internet World Statistics, 2007, "Internet World Users by Language." Retrieved December 17, 2007 (http://www.internetworldstats.com/stats7.htm).

TABLE 3.4

Religious Beliefs across
Generations, Canada, 2000
(in percent)

Source: Bibby, 2001: 252.

Conventional Beliefs	Teens	Young Adults	Adults	Parents	Grandparents
God exists	73	78	81	81	85
God or a higher power cares about you	68	71	73	72	77
Jesus was the divine son of God	65	68	72	71	77
Life after death	78	72	68	69	64
Have felt the presence of God/higher power	36	42	47	47	51
Less Conventional Beliefs					
Near-death experiences	76	76	68	71	57
ESP	59	67	66	70	59
Personally experienced precognition	63	68	58	61	46
Can have contact with the spirit world	43	57	45	48	30
Astrology	57	36	34	34	31

has an important positive social consequence. It seems likely that people who engage in cultural blending are usually more tolerant and appreciative of ethnic, racial, and religious groups other than their own.

The erosion of authority. Half a century ago, Canadians were more likely than they are today to defer to authority in the family, schools, politics, medicine, and so forth. As the social bases of authority and truth have multiplied, however, we are more likely to challenge authority. Authorities once widely respected, including parents, physicians, and politicians, have come to be held in lower regard by many people. In the 1950s, Robert Young played the firm, wise, and always-present father in the TV hit series *Father Knows Best.* Fifty years later, Homer Simpson plays a fool in *The Simpsons.* Compared with their counterparts in 2000, Canadian teenagers in the 1980s were more likely to express confidence in our police, politicians, court system, and religious organizations (Bibby, 2001: 193). Today, both young and old Canadians are likely to be critical of social institutions, including those, such as religious organizations, that previously enjoyed special veneration (see Table 3.5). The rise of

TABLE 3.5

Confidence in Institutions
across Generations, Canada,
2000

Source: Adapted from Bibby,
2001: 245.

Percentage Indicating Have "A Great Deal" or "Quite a Bit" of Confidence, by Institution and Generation

	Teens	Adults
Police	62	67
Schools	63	47
Newspapers	60	41
Radio	48	41
Major business	48	37
Religious organizations	40	33
Television	44	29
Music industry	54	27
Provincial government	41	26
Federal government	41	24
Movie industry	60	22

Homer Simpson and the decline of confidence in government both reflect the erosion of traditional authority (Nevitte, 1996).

The decline of consensus around core values. Half a century ago, people's values remained quite stable over the course of their adult lives and many values were widely accepted. Today, value shifts are more rapid and consensus has broken down on many issues. For example, in the middle of the twentieth century, the great majority of adults remained loyal to one political party from one election to the next. However, specific issues and personalities have increasingly eclipsed party loyalty as the driving forces of Canadian politics (Clarke, Jenson, LeDuc, and Pammett, 1996; Nie, Verba, and Petrocik, 1979). Today, people are more likely to vote for different political parties in succeeding elections than they were in 1950.

We may also illustrate the decline of consensus by considering the fate of big historical projects. For most of the past 200 years, consensus throughout the world was built around big historical projects. Various political and social movements convinced people they could take history into their own hands and create a glorious future just by signing up. German Nazism was a big historical project. Its followers expected the Reich to enjoy 1000 years of power. Communism was an even bigger big historical project, mobilizing hundreds of millions of people for a future that promised to end inequality and injustice for all time. However, the biggest and most successful big historical project was not so much a social movement as a powerful idea—the belief that progress is inevitable, that life will always improve, mainly because of the spread of democracy and scientific innovation.

The twentieth century was unkind to big historical projects. Russian communism lasted 74 years. German Nazism endured a mere 12. And the idea of progress fell on hard times as 100 million soldiers and civilians died in wars; the forward march of democracy took wrong turns into fascism, communism, and regimes based on religious fanaticism; and pollution from urbanization and industrialization threatened the planet. In the postmodern era, more and more people recognize that apparent progress, including scientific advances, often has negative consequences (Scott, 1998). As the poet E. E. Cummings once wrote, "nothing recedes like progress."

Postmodernism has many parents, teachers, politicians, religious leaders, and not a few university professors worried. Given the eclectic mixing of cultural elements from different times and places, the erosion of authority, and the decline of consensus around core values, how can we make binding decisions? How can we govern? How can we teach children and adolescents the difference between right and wrong? How can we transmit accepted literary

A hallmark of postmodernism is the combining of cultural elements from different times and places. For example, the "Michael Lee-Chin crystal" that was added to the Royal Ontario Museum created a postmodern nightmare in the eyes of some critics.

tastes and artistic standards from one generation to the next? These are the kinds of issues that plague people in positions of authority today.

Although their concerns are legitimate, many authorities seem not to have considered the other side of the coin. The postmodern condition, as we have described it above, empowers ordinary people and makes them more responsible for their own fate. It frees people to adopt religious, ethnic, and other identities they are comfortable with, as opposed to identities imposed on them by others. It makes them more tolerant of difference. That is no small matter in a world torn by group conflict. And the postmodern attitude encourages healthy skepticism about rosy and naive scientific and political promises.

Canada: The First Postmodern Culture?

Until the mid-1960s, the image of Canadians among most sociologists was that of a stodgy people: peaceful, conservative, respectful of authority, and therefore quite unlike our American cousins.

According to conventional wisdom, the United States was born in open rebellion against the British motherland. Its Western frontier was lawless. Vast opportunities for striking it rich bred a spirit of individualism. Thus, American culture became an anti-authoritarian culture.

Canada developed differently according to the conventional view. It became an independent country not through a revolutionary upheaval but in a gradual, evolutionary manner. The North-West Mounted Police and two hierarchical churches (Roman Catholic and Anglican) established themselves on the Western frontier *before* the era of mass settlement, allowing for the creation of an orderly society rather than a Wild West. Beginning with the Hudson's Bay Company, large corporations quickly came to dominate the Canadian economy, hampering individualism and the entrepreneurial spirit. Thus, Canadian culture became a culture of deference to authority. That, at least, was the common view until the 1960s (Lipset, 1963).

Although the contrast between deferential Canadian culture and anti-authoritarian American culture may have had some validity 40 years ago, it is an inaccurate characterization today (Adams, 1997: 62–95). As we have seen, the questioning of authority spread throughout the Western world beginning in the 1960s. Nowhere, however, did it spread as quickly and thoroughly as in Canada. Canadians used to express more confidence in big business than Americans did, but surveys now show the opposite. Canadians used to be more religious than Americans, but that is no longer the case. Fewer Canadians (in percentage terms) say they believe in God and fewer attend weekly religious services. Confidence in government has eroded more quickly in Canada than in the United States. Americans are more patriotic than Canadians, according more respect to the state. Finally, Americans are more likely than Canadians to regard the traditional nuclear family as the ideal family form and to think of deviations from tradition—same-sex couples, single-parent families, cohabitation without marriage—as the source of a whole range of social problems. Thus, whether sociologists examine attitudes toward the family, the state, the government, religion, or big business, they now find that Americans are more deferential to traditional institutional authority than Canadians are.

Because Canadians are less deferential to traditional institutional authority than Americans are, some commentators say that Canadians lack a distinct culture. For example, American patriotism sparks awareness of great national accomplishments in art, war, sports, science, and, indeed, all fields of human endeavour. Anthems, rituals, myths, and celebrations commemorate these accomplishments and give Americans a keen sense of who they are and how they differ from non-Americans. Not surprisingly, therefore, a larger percentage of Americans than Canadians think of themselves in unhyphenated terms—as "Americans" plain and simple rather than, say, Italian-Americans. In Canada, a larger percentage of the population thinks of itself in hyphenated terms; compared with the Americans, our identity is qualified, even tentative.

Does this mean that Canadians lack a distinct national culture? Hardly. It means that, while American culture is characterized by a relatively high degree of deference to dominant institutions, Canadian culture is characterized by a relatively high degree of tolerance and respect for diversity. We are more likely than Americans are to favour gender equality, accept gay and lesbian relationships, encourage bilingualism and multiculturalism, and accept the right of Aboriginals to political autonomy. Characteristically, a large international survey by a condom manufacturer found that Americans have sex more often than anyone else, but Canadians are most likely to say that the pleasure of their partner is very important. As public opinion pollster Michael Adams (1997: 171) writes:

> Twenty-five years of public-opinion polling in Canada has taught me a seemingly paradoxical truth. Canadians feel *strongly* about their *weak* attachments to Canada, its political institutions and their fellow citizens. In other words, they feel strongly about the right to live in a society that allows its citizens to be detached from ideology and critical of organizations, and not to feel obliged to be jingoistic or sentimentally patriotic. Canadians' *lack* of nationalism is, in many ways, a distinguishing feature of the country.

In short, Canadian culture *is* distinctive, and its chief distinction may be that it qualifies us as the first thoroughly postmodern society.

CULTURE AS CONSTRAINT

We noted above that culture has two faces. One we labelled freedom, the other constraint. Diversity, globalization, the rights revolution, and postmodernism are all aspects of the new freedoms that culture allows us today. We now examine several aspects of culture that act as constraining forces on our lives.

Rationalization

One of the most powerful social forces constraining our freedom is **rationalization**, Max Weber's term for (1) the application of the most efficient means to achieve given goals and (2) the unintended, negative consequences of doing so. Weber claimed that rationality of means has crept into all spheres of life, leading to unintended consequences that constrain and dehumanize us.

Weber believed that the rationalization process is exemplified by bureaucracies—large, impersonal organizations comprising many clearly defined positions arranged in a hierarchy (Chapter 6, Networks, Groups, Bureaucracies, and Societies). Modern bureaucracies, Weber said, are increasingly influential organizations. The factory, the government office, the military, the system of higher education, and the institutions of science are all bureaucratically organized. Yet bureaucracies are made up of officials who are not elected. Consequently, they concentrate power and threaten democracy. Moreover, bureaucracies discourage officeholders from considering what the goals of their organization ought to be. Bureaucrats are asked only to determine the best way of achieving the goals defined by their superiors. Officeholders thus lose their spontaneity, their inventiveness, and all opportunity to act heroically. It is "horrible to think," wrote Weber, "that the world could one day be filled with nothing but those little cogs, little men clinging to little jobs and striving towards bigger ones . . ." (quoted in Mayer, 1944: 127).

McDonaldization

Sociologist George Ritzer argues that, just as the modern bureaucracy epitomized the rationalization process for Weber at the turn of the twentieth century, the McDonald's restaurant is the epitome of rationalization today (Ritzer, 1993, 1996). Instead of adapting institutions to the needs of people, says Ritzer, people must increasingly adapt

Rationalization is the application of the most efficient means to achieve given goals and the unintended, negative consequences of doing so.

Reprinted here are the Chinese characters for "listening" *(t'ing)* in traditional Chinese script (left) and simplified, modern script (right). Each character comprises several word-symbols. In classical script, listening is depicted as a process involving the eyes, the ears, and the heart. It implies that listening demands the utmost empathy and involves the whole person. In contrast, modern script depicts listening as something that merely involves one person speaking and the other "weighing" speech. Modern Chinese script has been rationalized. Has empathy been lost in the process?

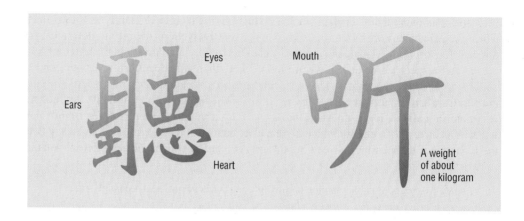

Ears — 聽 — Eyes — Heart

听 — Mouth — A weight of about one kilogram

to the needs of "McDonaldization." We are dehumanized in the process (Leidner, 1993; Reiter, 1991).

Ritzer shows that McDonald's has lunch down to a science. The meat and vegetables used to prepare your meal must meet minimum standards of quality and freshness. Each food item contains identical ingredients. Each portion is carefully weighed and cooked according to a uniform and precisely timed process. McDonald's executives have carefully thought through every aspect of your meal. They have turned its preparation into a model of rationality. With the goal of making profits, they have optimized food preparation to make it as fast and as cheap as possible.

Unfortunately, however, the rationalization of food dehumanizes both staff and customers. For instance, meals are prepared by nonunionized, uniformed workers who receive minimum wage. They must execute their tasks quickly and within specific time limits. To boost sales, they must smile as they recite fixed scripts ("Would you like some fries with your burger?"). Nearly half of all McDonald's employees are so dissatisfied with their work they quit after a year or less. To deal with this problem, McDonald's is now field testing vending machines that will be used to replace staff and boost sales. Anyone for an e-burger?

Meanwhile, customers are expected to spend as little time as possible eating the food—hence the drive-through window, chairs designed to be comfortable for only about 20 minutes, and small express outlets in subways and department stores where customers eat standing up or on the run. Customers are also expected to eat unhealthy food. A Big Mac, small fries, medium Coke, and apple pie can provide up to 67 percent of your recommended daily calorie intake and 88 percent of your recommended daily fat intake (calculated from McDonald's Corporation, 1999). That is why physicians and nutritionists regularly decry the popularity of fast food.

"McDonaldization" is a global phenomenon, as this busy McDonald's restaurant in Beijing, China, suggests.

Nonetheless, powerful forces make the Big Mac popular. On the demand side, fast food fits the rushed lifestyle of many individuals and families in the more affluent countries of the world and the growing middle class in the developing countries. On the supply side, people can make big profits by turning meal preparation into a mass production industry. Motivated by these forces, rationality of means (turning lunch into a science) results in irrationality of ends (dehumanizing staff and customers).

The Rationalization of Time

Rationalization is also evident in the way we have allowed the clock to determine the pace of daily life. This story begins nearly 700 years ago in Germany, when an upsurge in demand for textiles caused loom owners to look for ways of increasing productivity. They imposed longer hours on loom workers and installed a new technology—mechanical clocks—to signal the beginning of the workday, the timing of meals, and quitting time.

Workers were accustomed to enjoying many holidays and a fairly flexible and vague work schedule regulated only approximately by the seasons and the rising and setting of the sun. The regimentation imposed by the work clocks made their lives harder. They staged uprisings to silence the clocks—but to no avail. City officials sided with the employers and imposed fines for ignoring the work clocks. Harsher penalties, including death, were imposed on anyone trying to use the clocks' bells to signal a revolt (Thompson, 1967).

Now, nearly 700 years later, many people are, in effect, slaves of the work clock. This is especially true of urban North American couples who are employed full-time in the paid labour force and have preteen children. For them, life often seems an endless round of waking up at 6:30 a.m.; getting everyone washed and dressed; preparing the kids' lunches; getting them out the door in time for the school bus or the car pool; driving to work through rush-hour traffic; facing the speedup at work that resulted from the recent downsizing; driving back home through rush-hour traffic; preparing dinner; taking the kids to their soccer game; returning home to clean up the dishes and help with homework; getting the kids washed, brushed, and into bed; and (if they haven't brought some office work home) grabbing an hour of TV before collapsing, exhausted, for 6.5 hours of sleep before the story repeats itself. Life is less hectic for residents of small towns, unmarried people, couples without small children, retirees, and the unemployed. But the lives of most people are so packed with activities that time must be carefully regulated, each moment precisely parcelled out so that we may tick off item after item from an ever-growing list of tasks that need to be completed on schedule (Schor, 1992).

After centuries of conditioning, it is unusual for people to rebel against the clock in the town square any more. In fact, we now wear a watch on our wrist without giving it a second thought; we have accepted and internalized the regime of the work clock. Allowing clocks to precisely regulate our activities seems the most natural thing in the world—which is a sign that the work clock is, in fact, a product of culture that constrains our behaviour without most of us noticing.

Is the precise regulation of time rational? It certainly is rational as a means of ensuring the goal of efficiency. Minding the clock maximizes how much work you do in a day. The regulation of time makes it possible for trains to run on schedule and university classes to begin punctually. But is minding the clock rational as an end in itself? For many people, it is not. They complain that the precise regulation of time is out of hand. Life has simply become too hectic for many people to enjoy. In this sense, a *rational means* (the work clock) has been applied to a *given goal* (maximizing work) but has led to an *irrational end* (a hectic life).

As the examples of McDonald's and the work clock show, rationalization enables us to do just about everything more efficiently but at a steep cost. Because it is so widespread, rationalization is one of the most constraining aspects of culture today. In Weber's view, it makes life in the modern world akin to living inside an "iron cage."

TECHNOLOGY
BYTES

Have we come to depend too heavily on the work clock? Harold Lloyd in *Safety Last* (1923).

**WHERE DO
YOU FIT IN?**

**Consumerism is the tendency
to define ourselves in terms
of the goods we purchase.**

Consumerism

The second constraining aspect of culture we examine is consumerism. **Consumerism** is the tendency to define ourselves in terms of the goods and services we purchase.

Recent innovations in advertising take full advantage of our tendency to define ourselves in terms of the goods we purchase. For example, when channel surfing and the use of TiVo spread, advertisers realized they had a problem on their hands. Viewers started skipping TV ads that cost millions of dollars and untold hours of creative effort to produce. As a result, advertisers had to think up new ways of drawing products to the attention of consumers. One idea they hit on was paying to place their products in TV shows and movies. They realized that when Brad Pitt or some other big star drinks a can of Coke or lights up a Marlboro, members of the audience tend to associate the product with the star. Wanting to be like the star, they are increasingly likely to buy the product. In the slick 2003 movie *The Italian Job,* starring Mark Wahlberg and Charlize Theron, a small fleet of high-performance Mini Coopers plays a key role in the big heist. As expected, sales of the Mini Coopers skyrocketed soon after the film was released. The product became part of who we are or who we want to be.

Because advertising stimulates sales, there is a tendency for business to spend more on advertising over time. Because advertising is widespread, most people unquestioningly accept it as part of their lives. In fact, many people have *become* ads. When your father was a child and quickly threw on a shirt, allowing a label to hang out, your grandmother might have admonished him to "tuck in that label." In contrast, many people today proudly display consumer labels as marks of status and identity. Advertisers teach us to associate the words "Gucci" and "Nike" with different kinds of people, and when people display these labels on their clothes they are telling us something about the kind of people they are. Advertising becomes us.

Where do you fit in? If you don't display labels on your clothes, what does your reluctance to do so tell people about who you are? If you do display labels on your clothes, which ones are they? What do the labels tell others about who you are? Do your friends display clothing labels similar to yours? What about people you dislike? Do you think it is reasonable to conclude that clothing labels are cultural artifacts that increase the solidarity of social groups and segregate them from other groups?

The rationalization process, when applied to the production of goods and services, enables us to produce more efficiently, to have more of just about everything than our parents did. But it is consumerism, the tendency to define ourselves in terms of the goods we purchase, that ensures all the goods we produce will be bought. Of course, we have a lot of choice. We can select from dozens of styles of running shoes, cars, toothpaste, and

What is being sold here: the clothes or the attitude?

all the rest. We can also choose to buy items that help define us as members of a particular **subculture**, adherents of a set of distinctive values, norms, and practices within a larger culture. But regardless of individual tastes and inclinations, nearly all of us have one thing in common: We tend to be good consumers. We are motivated by advertising, which is based on the accurate insight that people will likely be considered cultural outcasts if they fail to conform to stylish trends. By creating those trends, advertisers push us to buy even if we must incur large debts to do so (Schor, 1999). That is why North Americans' "shop-till-you-drop" lifestyle prompted French sociologist Jean Baudrillard to remark pointedly that even what is best in North America is compulsory (Baudrillard, 1988). And it is why we say that consumerism, like rationalization, acts as a powerful constraint on our lives.

A **subculture** is a set of distinctive values, norms, and practices within a larger culture.

From Counterculture to Subculture

In concluding our discussion of culture as a constraining force, we note that consumerism is remarkably effective at taming countercultures. **Countercultures** are subversive subcultures. They oppose dominant values and seek to replace them. The hippies of the 1960s formed a counterculture and so do environmentalists today.

Countercultures are subversive subcultures.

Countercultures rarely pose a serious threat to social stability. Most often, the system of social control, of rewards and punishments, keeps countercultures at bay. In our society, consumerism acts as a social control mechanism that normally prevents countercultures from disrupting the social order. It does that by transforming deviations from mainstream culture into means of making money and by enticing rebels to become entrepreneurs (Frank and Weiland, 1997). Two examples from popular music help illustrate the point:

- Ozzy Osbourne was an important figure in the counterculture that grew up around heavy metal music beginning in the late 1960s. He and his band, Black Sabbath, inspired Metallica, KISS, Judas Priest, Marilyn Manson, and others to play loud, nihilistic music; reject conventional morality; embrace death and violence; and foment youthful rebellion and parental panic. In 1982, he bit the head off a bat during a performance and later urinated on the Alamo. He was given rabies shots for the former and arrested for the latter. Around the same time, Tipper Gore, wife of the future presidential candidate, formed the Parents Music Resource Center (PMRC) to fight against violence and sex in the lyrics of popular music. Osbourne was one of the PMRC's principal targets. The Prince of Darkness, as he was often called, was about as rebellious a figure as one could imagine in 1982.

   Flash forward 20 years. In 2002, Osbourne became the star of a popular TV show. MTV placed a dozen cameras in his Beverly Hills mansion, and every week viewers got to see everything going on in the Osbourne household for half an hour. According to *USA Today,* Osbourne was "a lot like anyone's adorable dad. Shuffles a bit. Forgets things. Worries about the garbage. Snores on the couch while the TV blares. Walks the dog" (Gundersen, Keveney, and Oldenburg, 2002: 1A). Rosie O'Donnell said to Ozzy's wife, Sharon, "What I love most about [your show] is not only the relationship you have with Ozzy—and you obviously adore each other—but the honesty with which you relate to your children. The love is so evident between all of you. It's heartwarming" (Gundersen, Keveney, and Oldenburg, 2002: 2A). Sharon and Ozzy were invited to dinner at the White House in 2002. *The Osbournes,* it seems, was a comfort to many people. It proved that heavy metal's frightening rejection of mainstream culture in the 1970s and 1980s was just a passing phase and that the nuclear family remained intact. Ozzy Osbourne was thus transformed from the embodiment of rebellion against society to a family man, a small industry, and a conservative media icon.

- The development of hip-hop also illustrates the commercialization and taming of rebellion (Brym, 2008b). Originating in the poverty and despair of inner-city American ghettos in the 1970s, hip-hop gave rise to a highly political counterculture. Early hip-hop artists glorified the mean streets of the inner city and held the police, the mass media, and other pillars of

Ozzy Osbourne (holding plaque)
en famille

In March 2005, a sidewalk gun battle broke out near a hip-hop radio station in New York City between the entourages of rap stars The Game and 50 Cent. Four years earlier, on the same street corner, a similar incident occurred between followers of Lil' Kim and of Capone. In both gunfights, the rap stars' followers discharged many rounds at close range but damage was minor. It seems reasonable to conclude that the gunfights were really for show. Rap stars are multimillionaire members of the music elite, but the gunfights confer "the illusion of their authenticity as desperate outlaws" (Hajdu, 2005). The shootouts are properly seen as low-risk investments by savvy businesspeople.

Cartoon by Jonathan Twingley, *New York Times*, March 10, 2005.

white society in contempt, blaming them for arbitrary arrests, the political suppression of black activists, and the spreading of lies about African Americans. However, by the time Public Enemy became a hit in the late 1980s, MTV had aired its first regular program devoted to hip-hop, and much of hip-hop's audience was composed of white, middle-class youth. Hip-hop artists were quick to see the potential of commercialization. Soon Wu-Tang

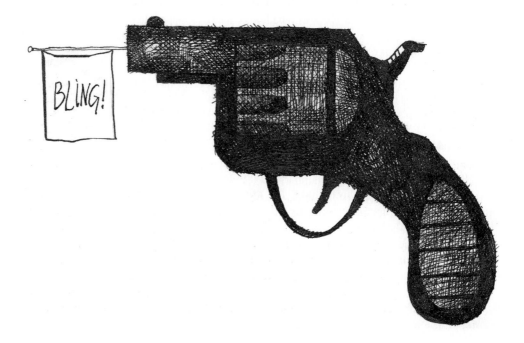

BLING!

Clan had its own line of clothes and Versace was marketing clothing influenced by ghetto styles. Puff Daddy reminded his audience in his 1999 CD *Forever*: "N—— get money, that's simply the plan." According to *Forbes* magazine, he has become one of the 40 richest men under 40 in the United States. By 2005, he had his own line of popular clothing, Sean John, and renamed himself Diddy. No less than heavy metal, hip-hop's radicalism gave way to the lures of commerce.

The fate of heavy metal and hip-hop is testimony to the capacity of consumerism to change countercultures into mere subcultures, thus constraining dissent and rebellion. They are compelling illustrations of culture's second face.

NOTES

1. There were too few respondents in the 2002 General Social Survey to be able to draw this conclusion with confidence, so we base it on cumulative data from 1988 to 2002 (*n* = 13 981). In this period, 9.1 percent of men with more than one sex partner had sexual relations with other men, while 7.7 percent of women with more than one sex partner had sexual relations with other women.

2. Some cancers are more heritable than others, but even the most heritable cancers seem to be much more strongly influenced by environmental than by genetic factors (Fearon, 1997; Hoover, 2000; Kevles, 1999; Lichtenstein et al., 2000; Remennick, 1998).

3. Whorf wrote that Inuit have seven words for different types of snow but the claim is misleading. Inuktitut has no single word for snow—or bear or people or fish—simply because the language combines adjectives and nouns into new terms. It is this grammatical feature of Inuktitut that allows separate words for "snow on the ground," "water-soaked snow," "snowbank around the house," and even "snow that has been peed on." Meanwhile, in English, too, we have many words for types of snow: sleet, hail, powder, slush, hardpack, flurry, and so on (Crucefix, 2003; Minkel, 2002).

4. Concern over the possible erosion of the French language led, in part, to the 1969 passage of Canada's Official Languages Act and the 1977 passage of the Charter of the French Language (Bill 101) in Quebec, which established French as the only official language of education, work, and the public sector in that province.

SUMMARY

1. What are the main components of culture and what is culture's main function?
   Culture comprises various types of ideas (such as symbols, language, values, and beliefs), norms of behaviour, and material objects. The ability to create symbols, cooperate, and make tools has enabled humans to thrive in their environments.

2. What role does biology, as opposed to culture, play in shaping specific human behaviours and social arrangements?
   Biology sets broad *limits* and *potentials* on human behaviour and social arrangements. However, most of the *variation* in human behaviour and social arrangements is due to social forces. The roles of biology and culture are illustrated by the development of language skills. We are biologically prewired to acquire language and create grammatical speech patterns. However, the social environment gives form to these predispositions. We know, for example, that people can never acquire language proficiency unless they are exposed to language in the first years of life. Moreover, our use of language is shaped by the language community or communities to which we belong.

3. What is the ideal vantage point for analyzing a culture?

We can see the contours of culture most sharply if we are neither too deeply immersed in it nor too much removed from it. Understanding culture requires refraining from taking your own culture for granted and judging other cultures by the standards of your own.

4. What does it mean to say that culture has "two faces"?

First, culture provides us with increasing opportunities to exercise our freedom in some respects. The rights revolution, multiculturalism, globalization, and postmodernism reflect this tendency. Second, culture constrains us in other respects, putting limits on what we can become. The growth of rationalization and the spread of consumerism reflect this tendency.

5. What is the multiculturalism debate?

Advocates of multiculturalism want school and postsecondary curricula to reflect the country's growing ethnic and racial diversity. They also want school and postsecondary curricula to stress that all cultures have equal value. They believe that multicultural education will promote self-esteem and economic success among members of racial minorities. Critics fear that multiculturalism results in declining educational standards. They believe that multicultural education causes political disunity and interethnic and interracial conflict. They argue that it promotes an extreme form of cultural relativism.

6. What is the "rights revolution"?

The rights revolution is the process by which socially excluded groups have struggled to win equal rights under the law and in practice. In full swing by the 1960s, the rights revolution involves the promotion of women's rights, the rights of members of minority groups, gay and lesbian rights, the rights of people with special needs, constitutional rights, and language rights. The rights revolution fragments culture by legitimizing the grievances of groups that were formerly excluded from full social participation and renewing their pride in their identity and heritage.

7. What does the "globalization" of culture involve?

The globalization of culture has resulted from the growth of international trade and investment, ethnic and racial migration, influential transnational organizations, and inexpensive travel and communication.

8. What is postmodernism?

Postmodernism involves an eclectic mixing of elements from different times and places, the decline of authority, and the erosion of consensus around core values.

9. What is rationalization?

Rationalization involves the application of the most efficient means to achieve given goals and the unintended, negative consequences of doing so. Rationalization is evident in the increasingly regulated use of time and in many other areas of social life.

10. What is consumerism?

Consumerism is the tendency to define ourselves in terms of the goods we purchase. Excessive consumption puts limits on who we can become, constrains our capacity to dissent from mainstream culture, and degrades the natural environment.

KEY TERMS

abstraction (p. 70)

consumerism (p. 92)

cooperation (p. 70)

countercultures (p. 93)

cultural relativism (p. 81)

culture (p. 69)

ethnocentrism (p. 76)

folkways (p. 71)

high culture (p. 69)

mass culture (p. 69)

material culture (p. 70)

mores (p. 71)

non-material culture (p. 70)

norms (p. 70)

popular culture (p. 69)

postmodernism (p. 85)

production (p. 70)

rationalization (p. 89)

rights revolution (p. 81)

rites of passage (p. 83)

subculture (p. 93)

symbols (p. 70)

taboos (p. 71)

values (p. 70)

QUESTIONS TO CONSIDER

1. We imbibe culture but we also create it. What elements of culture have you created? Under what conditions were you prompted to do so? Was your cultural contribution strictly personal or was it shared with others? Why?

2. Select a subcultural practice that seems odd, inexplicable, or irrational to you. By interviewing members of the subcultural group and reading about them, explain how the subcultural practice you chose makes sense to members of the subcultural group.

3. Do you think the freedoms afforded by postmodern culture outweigh the constraints it places on us? Why or why not?

WEB RESOURCES

Companion Website for This Book

http://www.compass3e.nelson.com

Begin by clicking on the Student Resources section of the website. Next, select the chapter you are studying from the pull-down menu. From the Student Resources page you have easy access to InfoTrac® College Edition, additional Weblinks, and other resources. The website also has many useful tips to aid you in your study of sociology, including practice tests for each chapter.

InfoTrac® Search Terms

These search terms are provided to assist you in beginning to conduct research on this topic by visiting http://www.infotrac-college.com:

consumerism

culture

globalization

multiculturalism

postmodernism

rationalization

Recommended Websites

Bernard Barber, "Jihad vs. McWorld," on the World Wide Web at http://www.theatlantic.com/doc/199203/barber, is a brief, masterful analysis of the forces that are simultaneously making world culture more homogeneous and more heterogeneous. The article was originally published in *The Atlantic Monthly* (March 1992). For the full story, see Bernard Barber, *Jihad vs. McWorld: How Globalism and Tribalism Are Reshaping the World* (New York: Ballantine Books, 1996).

http://www.compass3e.nelson.com

Adbusters is an organization devoted to analyzing and criticizing consumer culture. Its provocative website is at http://www.adbusters.org.

Sarah Zupko's Cultural Studies Center is our favourite site on the sociology of popular culture. Visit it at http://euphrates.wpunj.edu/faculty/wagnerk/webagogy/zupko.htm.

The Resource Center for Cyberculture Studies is devoted to studying emerging cultures on the World Wide Web. Its website is at http://rccs.usfca.edu.

CengageNOW™

http://hed.nelson.com

This online diagnostic tool identifies each student's unique needs with a Pretest that generates a personalized Study Plan for each chapter, helping students focus on concepts they're having the most difficulty mastering. Students then take a Posttest after reading the chapter to measure their understanding of the material. An Instructor Gradebook is available to track and monitor student progress.

Socialization

In this chapter, you will learn that

- The view that social interaction unleashes human abilities is supported by studies showing that children raised in isolation do not develop normal language and other social skills.

- Although the socializing influence of the family decreased in the twentieth century, the influence of schools, peer groups, and the mass media increased.

- People's identities change faster, more often, and more completely than they did just a couple of decades ago; the self has become more plastic.

- The main socializing institutions often teach children and adolescents contradictory lessons, making socialization a more confusing and stressful process than it used to be.

- Declining parental supervision and guidance, increasing assumption of adult responsibilities by youth, and declining participation in extracurricular activities are transforming the character of childhood and adolescence today.

SOCIAL ISOLATION AND THE CRYSTALLIZATION OF SELF-IDENTITY

One day in 1800, a 10- or 11-year-old boy walked out of the woods in southern France. He was filthy, naked, unable to speak, and had not been toilet trained. After being taken by the police to a local orphanage, he repeatedly tried to escape and refused to wear clothes. No parent ever claimed him. He became known as "the wild boy of Aveyron." A thorough medical examination found no major physical or mental abnormalities. Why, then, did the boy seem more animal than human? Because, until he walked out of the woods, he had been raised in isolation from other human beings (Shattuck, 1980).

Similar horrifying reports lead to the same conclusion. Occasionally a child is found locked in an attic or a cellar, where he or she saw another person for only short periods each day to receive food. Like the wild boy of Aveyron, such children rarely develop normally. Typically, they remain disinterested in games. They cannot form intimate social relationships with other people. They develop only the most basic language skills.

Some of these children may suffer from congenitally subnormal intelligence. It is uncertain how much and what type of social contact they had before they were discovered. Some may have been abused. Therefore, their condition may not be due only to social isolation. However, these examples do at least suggest that the ability to learn culture and become human is only a potential. To be actualized, **socialization** must unleash this human potential. Socialization is the process by which people learn their culture. They do so by (1) entering and disengaging from a succession of roles and (2) becoming aware of themselves as they interact with others. A **role** is the behaviour expected of a person occupying a particular position in society.

Convincing evidence of the importance of socialization in unleashing human potential comes from a study conducted by René Spitz (1945, 1962). Spitz compared children who were being raised in an orphanage with children who were being raised in a prison nursing home. Both institutions were hygienic and provided good food and medical care. However,

SAVAGE OF AVEYRON.

while their mothers cared for the babies in the nursing home, just 6 nurses cared for the 45 orphans. The orphans, therefore, had much less contact with other people. Moreover, from their cribs, the nursing home infants could taste a slice of society. They saw other babies playing and receiving care. They saw mothers, doctors, and nurses talking, cleaning, serving food, and providing medical treatment. In contrast, it was established practice in the orphanage to hang sheets from the cribs to prevent the infants from seeing the activities of the institution. Depriving the infants of social stimuli for most of the day apparently made them less demanding.

Social deprivation had other effects, too. Because of the different patterns of child care in the two institutions, by the age of 9 to 12 months the orphans were more susceptible to infections and had a higher death rate than the babies in the nursing home had. By the time they were two to three years old, all the children from the nursing home were walking and talking, compared with fewer than 8 percent of the

Socialization is the process by which people learn their culture—including norms, values, and roles—and become aware of themselves as they interact with others.

A **role** is the behaviour expected of a person occupying a particular position in society.

In the 1960s, researchers Harry and Margaret Harlow placed baby rhesus monkeys in various conditions of isolation to witness and study the animals' reactions. Among other things, they discovered that baby monkeys raised with an artificial mother made of wire mesh, a wooden head, and the nipple of a feeding tube for a breast were later unable to interact normally with other monkeys. However, when the artificial mother was covered with a soft terry cloth, the infant monkeys clung to it in comfort and later exhibited less emotional distress. Infant monkeys preferred the cloth mother even when it had less milk than the wire mother did. The Harlows concluded that emotional development requires affectionate cradling.

orphans. Normal children begin to play with their own genitals by the end of their first year. Spitz found that the orphans began this sort of play only in their fourth year. He took this as a sign that they might have an impaired sexual life when they reached maturity. This had happened to rhesus monkeys raised in isolation. Spitz's natural experiment thus amounts to quite compelling evidence for the importance of childhood socialization in making us fully human. Without childhood socialization, most of our human potential remains undeveloped.

The formation of a sense of self continues in adolescence, a particularly turbulent period of rapid self-development. Many people can remember experiences from their youth that helped crystallize their self-identity. Do you? Robert Brym clearly recalls one such defining moment.

"I can date precisely the pivot of my adolescence," says Robert. "I was in grade 10. It was December 16. At 4 p.m. I was a nobody and knew it. Half an hour later, I was walking home from school, delighting in the slight sting of snowflakes melting on my upturned face, knowing I had been swept up in a sea change.

"About 200 students had sat impatiently in the auditorium that last day of school before the winter vacation. We were waiting for Mr. Garrod, the English teacher who headed the school's drama program, to announce the cast of *West Side Story*. I was hoping for a small speaking part and was not surprised when Mr. Garrod failed to read my name as a chorus member. However, as the list of remaining characters grew shorter, I became despondent. Soon only the leads remained. I knew that an unknown kid in grade 10 couldn't possibly be asked to play Tony, the male lead. Leads were almost always reserved for more experienced grade 12 students.

"Then came the thunderclap. 'Tony,' said Mr. Garrod, 'will be played by Robert Brym.'

"'Who's Robert Brym?' whispered a girl two rows ahead of me. Her friend merely shrugged in reply. If she had asked *me* that question, I might have responded similarly. Like nearly all 15-year-olds, I was deeply involved in the process of figuring out exactly who I was. I had little idea of what I was good at. I was insecure about my social status. I wasn't sure what I believed in. In short, I was a typical teenager. I had only a vaguely defined sense of self.

"A sociologist once wrote that 'the central growth process in adolescence is to define the self through the clarification of experience and to establish self-esteem' (Friedenberg, 1959: 190). From this point of view, playing Tony in *West Side Story* turned out to be the

PERSONAL
ANECDOTE

first section of a bridge that led me from adolescence to adulthood. Playing Tony raised my social status in the eyes of my classmates, made me more self-confident, taught me I could be good at something, helped me to begin discovering parts of myself I hadn't known before, and showed me that I could act rather than merely be acted upon. In short, it was through my involvement in the play (and, subsequently, in many other plays throughout high school) that I began to develop a clear sense of who I am."

The crystallization of self-identity during adolescence is just one episode in a life-long process of socialization. To paint a picture of the socialization process in its entirety, we must first review the main theories of how a sense of self develops during early childhood. We then discuss the operation and relative influence of society's main socializing institutions or "agents of socialization": families, schools, peer groups, and the mass media. In these settings, we learn, among other things, how to control our impulses, think of ourselves as members of different groups, value certain ideals, and perform various roles. You will see that these institutions do not always work hand in hand to produce happy, well-adjusted adults. They often give mixed messages and are often at odds with one another. That is, they teach children and adolescents different and even contradictory lessons. You will also see that although recent developments give us more freedom to decide who we are, they can make socialization more disorienting than ever before. In the concluding section of this chapter, we examine how decreasing supervision and guidance by adult family members, increasing assumption of adult responsibilities by youth, and declining participation in extracurricular activities are changing the nature of childhood and adolescence today. Some analysts even say that childhood and adolescence are vanishing before our eyes. Thus, the main theme of this chapter is that the development of self-identity is often a difficult and stressful process—and it is becoming more so.

It is during childhood that the contours of the self are first formed. We therefore begin by discussing the most important social-scientific theories of how the self originates in the first years of life.

THEORIES OF CHILDHOOD SOCIALIZATION

Freud

Socialization begins soon after birth. Infants cry out, driven by elemental needs, and are gratified by food, comfort, and affection. Because their needs are usually satisfied immediately, they do not at first seem able to distinguish themselves from their main caregivers, usually their mothers. However, social interaction soon enables infants to begin developing a self-image or sense of **self**—a set of ideas and attitudes about who they are as independent beings.

Sigmund Freud proposed the first social-scientific interpretation of the process by which the self emerges (Freud, 1962 [1930], 1973 [1915–17]). Freud was the Austrian founder of psychoanalysis. He referred to the part of the self that demands immediate gratification as the **id**. According to Freud, a self-image begins to emerge as soon as the id's demands are denied. For example, at a certain point, parents usually decide not to feed and comfort a baby every time it wakes up in the middle of the night. The parents' refusal at first incites howls of protest. Eventually, however, the baby learns certain practical lessons from the experience—to eat more before going to bed, sleep for longer periods, and put itself back to sleep if it wakes up. Equally important, the baby begins to sense that its needs differ from those of its parents, that it has an existence independent of others, and that it must somehow balance its needs with the realities of life.

Because of many such lessons in self-control, including toilet training, the child eventually develops a sense of what constitutes appropriate behaviour and a moral sense of right and wrong. Soon a personal conscience or, to use Freud's term, a **superego**, crystallizes. The superego is a repository of cultural standards. In addition, the child develops a third

The **self** consists of your ideas and attitudes about who you are.

The **id**, according to Freud, is the part of the self that demands immediate gratification.

The **superego**, according to Freud, is a part of the self that acts as a repository of cultural standards.

component of the self, the **ego**. According to Freud, the ego is a psychological mechanism that, in well-adjusted individuals, balances the conflicting needs of the pleasure-seeking id and the restraining superego (Figure 4.1).

In Freud's view, the emergence of the superego is a painful and frustrating process. In fact, said Freud, to get on with our daily lives we have to repress memories of denying the id immediate gratification. Repression involves storing traumatic memories in a part of the self that we are not normally aware of: the **unconscious**. Repressed memories influence emotions and actions even after they are stored away. Particularly painful instances of childhood repression may cause psychological problems of various sorts later in life, requiring therapy to correct. However, some repression is the cost of civilization. As Freud said, we cannot live in an orderly society unless we deny the id (Freud, 1962 [1930]).

Researchers have called into question many of the specifics of Freud's argument. Three criticisms stand out:

1. *The connections between early childhood development and adult personality are more complex than Freud assumed.* Freud wrote that when the ego fails to balance the needs of the id and the superego, individuals develop personality disorders. Typically, he said, this occurs if a young child is raised in an overly repressive atmosphere. To avoid later psychiatric problems, Freud and his followers recommended raising young children in a relaxed and permissive environment. Such an environment is characterized by prolonged breastfeeding, nursing on demand, gradual weaning, lenient and late bladder and bowel training, frequent mothering, freedom from restraint and punishment, and so forth. However, sociological research reveals no connection between these aspects of early childhood training and the development of well-adjusted adults (Sewell, 1958). One group of researchers who were influenced by Freud's theories tracked people from infancy to age 32 and made *incorrect* predictions about personality development in two-thirds of the cases. They "had failed to anticipate that depth, complexity, problem-solving abilities, and maturity might derive from painful [childhood] experiences" (Coontz, 1992: 228).

2. *Many sociologists criticize Freud for gender bias in his analysis of male and female sexuality.* Freud argued that psychologically normal women are immature and dependent on men because they envy the male sexual organ. Women who are mature and independent he classified as abnormal. We discuss this fallacy in detail in Chapter 11, Sexuality and Gender.

3. *Sociologists often criticize Freud for neglecting socialization after childhood.* Freud believed that the human personality is fixed by about the age of five. However, sociologists have shown that socialization continues throughout the life course. We devote much of this chapter to exploring socialization after early childhood.

Sigmund Freud (1856–1939) was the founder of psychoanalysis. Many issues have been raised about the specifics of his theories. Nevertheless, his main sociological contribution was his insistence that the self emerges during early social interaction and that early childhood experience exerts a lasting impact on personality development.

The ego, according to Freud, is a psychological mechanism that balances the conflicting needs of the pleasure-seeking id and the restraining superego.

The unconscious, according to Freud, is the part of the self that contains repressed memories we are not normally aware of.

FIGURE 4.1
The Components of the Well-Adjusted Self According to Freud

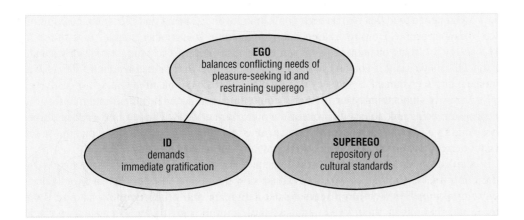

Despite the shortcomings listed above, the sociological implications of Freud's theory are profound. His main sociological contribution was his insistence that the self emerges during early social interaction and that early childhood experience exerts a lasting impact on personality development. As we will now see, North American sociologists and social psychologists took these ideas in a still more sociological direction.

Cooley's Symbolic Interactionism

More than a century ago, sociologist Charles Horton Cooley introduced the idea of the "looking-glass self," making him a founder of the symbolic interactionist tradition and an early contributor to the sociological study of socialization. Cooley observed that when we interact with others, they gesture and react to us. This allows us to imagine how we appear to them. We then judge how others evaluate us. Finally, from these judgments we develop a self-concept or a set of feelings and ideas about who we are. In other words, our feelings about who we are depend largely on how we see ourselves evaluated by others. Just as we see our physical body reflected in a mirror, so we see our social selves reflected in people's gestures and reactions to us (Cooley, 1902).

The implications of Cooley's argument are intriguing. Consider, for example, that the way other people judge us helps determine whether we develop a positive or negative self-concept. Among other things, having a negative self-concept is associated with low achievement in school and postsecondary institutions (Hamachek, 1995). Some students' poor performance in school may be partly a result of teachers evaluating them negatively, perhaps because of the students' class or race. Similarly, the way others evaluate us helps determine the size of the discrepancy between our self-concept and the person we would like to be. To compensate for a large discrepancy between actual and ideal self-concepts, some people may engage in compulsive buying sprees or out-of-control collecting or binge gift giving. Young women seem to be more prone to such behaviour than other categories of the population. This behaviour may reflect the difficulty many young women have of achieving the ideals of body weight and body shape that are promoted by the mass media (Benson, 2000). Cooley's notion of the looking-glass self was introduced more than a century ago. These examples highlight its contemporary relevance.

Mead

George Herbert Mead (1934) took up and developed the idea of the looking-glass self. Like Freud, Mead noted that a subjective and impulsive aspect of the self is present from birth. Mead called it simply the **I**. Again, like Freud, Mead argued that a repository of culturally approved standards emerges as part of the self during social interaction. Mead called this objective, social component of the self the **me**. However, while Freud focused on the denial of the id's impulses as the mechanism that generates the self's objective side, Mead drew attention to the unique human capacity to "take the role of the other" as the source of the me.

Mead understood that human communication involves seeing yourself from the point of view of other people. How, for example, do you interpret your mother's smile? Does it mean "I love you," "I find you humorous," or something else entirely? According to Mead, you can know the answer only if you use your imagination to take your mother's point of view for a moment and see yourself as she sees you. In other words, you must see yourself objectively, as a "me," to understand your mother's communicative act. All human communication depends on being able to take the role of the other, wrote Mead. The self thus emerges from people using symbols, such as words and gestures, to communicate. It follows that the "me" is not present from birth. It emerges only gradually during social interaction.

Unlike Freud, Mead did not think that the emergence of the self was traumatic. On the contrary, he thought it was fun. Mead saw the self as developing in four stages of role-taking. First, children learn to use language and other symbols by *imitating* important people in their lives, such as their mother and father. Mead called such

The **I**, according to Mead, is the subjective and impulsive aspect of the self that is present from birth.

The **me**, according to Mead, is the objective component of the self that emerges as people communicate symbolically and learn to take the role of the other.

people **significant others**. Second, children pretend to *be* other people. That is, they use their imaginations to role-play in games, such as "house," "school," and doctor." Third, by the time they reach the age of about seven, children learn to play complex games requiring that they simultaneously take the role of *several* other people. In baseball, for example, the infielders have to be aware of the expectations of everyone in the infield. A shortstop may catch a line drive. If she wants to make a double play, she must be aware almost instantly that a runner is trying to reach second base and that the person playing second expects her to throw there. If she hesitates, she probably cannot execute the double play. Once a child

Much socialization takes place informally, with the participants unaware they are being socialized. These girls are learning gender roles as they shop at the mall.

Significant others are people who play important roles in the early socialization experiences of children.

can think in this complex way, she can begin the fourth stage in the development of the self. This involves taking the role of what Mead called the **generalized other**. Years of experience may teach an individual that other people, employing the cultural standards of their society, usually regard her as funny or temperamental or intelligent. A person's image of these cultural standards and how they are applied to her is what Mead meant by the generalized other.

The generalized other, according to Mead, is a person's image of cultural standards and how they apply to him or her.

Piaget

Since Mead, psychologists have continued to study childhood socialization. For example, they have identified the stages in which thinking and moral skills develop from infancy to the late teenage years. Let us briefly consider some of their most important contributions.

The Swiss psychologist Jean Piaget divided the development of thinking (or "cognitive") skills during childhood into four stages (Piaget and Inhelder, 1969). In the first two years of life, he wrote, children explore the world only through their five senses. Piaget called this the "sensorimotor" stage of cognitive development. At this point in their lives, they cannot think using symbols.

According to Piaget, children begin to think symbolically between the ages of two and seven, which he called the "preoperational" stage of cognitive development. Language and imagination blossom during these years. However, children at this age are still unable to think abstractly. Piaget illustrated this lack of ability by asking a series of five- and six-year-olds to inspect two identical glasses of coloured water. He then asked them whether the glasses contained the same amount of coloured water. All the children said the glasses contained the same amount. Next, the children watched Piaget pour the water from one glass into a wide, low beaker and the water from the second glass into a narrow, tall beaker. Obviously, the water level was higher in the second beaker although the volume of water was the same in both containers. Piaget then asked each child whether the two beakers contained the same amount of water. Nearly all the children said that the second beaker contained more water. Clearly, the abstract concept of volume had no meaning for them.

In contrast, most seven- or eight-year-old children understood that the volume of water was the same in both beakers, despite the different water levels. This suggests that abstract thinking begins at about the age of seven. Between the ages of 7 and 11, children are able to see the connections between causes and effects in their environment. Piaget called this the "concrete operational" stage of cognitive development. Finally, by about the age of 12, children develop the ability to think more abstractly and critically. This behaviour marks the beginning of what Piaget called the "formal operational" stage of cognitive development.

Kohlberg

Lawrence Kohlberg, an American social psychologist, took Piaget's ideas in a somewhat different direction. He showed how children's *moral* reasoning—their ability to judge right from wrong—also passes through developmental stages (Kohlberg, 1981). Kohlberg argued that young children distinguish right from wrong based only on whether something gratifies their immediate needs. At this stage of moral growth, which Kohlberg labelled the "preconventional" stage, what is "right" is simply what satisfies the young child. For example, from the point of view of a two-year-old, it is entirely appropriate to grab a cookie from a playmate and eat it. An abstract moral concept like theft has no meaning for the very young child.

Teenagers, in contrast, begin to think about right and wrong in terms of whether specific actions please their parents and teachers and are consistent with cultural norms. This phase is the "conventional" stage of moral growth in Kohlberg's terminology. At this stage, a child understands that theft is a proscribed act and that getting caught stealing will result in punishment.

Some people never advance beyond conventional morality. Others, however, develop the capacity to think abstractly and critically about moral principles. This phase is Kohlberg's "postconventional" stage of moral development. At this stage, a person may ponder the meaning of such abstract terms as freedom, justice, and equality. They may question whether the laws of society or the actions of their parents, teachers, or other authorities conform to lofty moral principles. For instance, a 19-year-old who believes the settlement of Europeans in North America involved the theft of land from Aboriginal peoples is thinking in postconventional moral terms. Such an adolescent is applying abstract moral principles independently and is not merely accepting them as interpreted by authorities.

Vygotsky

Modern psychology has done much to reveal the cognitive and moral dimensions of childhood development. However, from a sociological point of view, the main problem with this body of research is that it minimizes the extent to which society shapes the way we think. Thus, most psychologists assume that people pass through the same stages of mental development and think in similar ways, regardless of the structure of their society and their position in it. Many sociologists disagree with these assumptions.

A few psychologists do, too. Belarusian psychologist Lev Vygotsky and American educational psychologist Carol Gilligan offer the most sociological approaches to thinking about cognitive and moral development, respectively. For Vygotsky, ways of thinking are determined not so much by innate factors as they are by the nature of the social institutions in which individuals grow up.

Consider, for example, the contrast between ancient China and Greece. In part because of complex irrigation needs, the rice agriculture of ancient southern China required substantial cooperation among neighbours. It had to be centrally organized in an elaborate hierarchy within a large state. Harmony and social order were therefore central to ancient Chinese life. Ancient Chinese thinking, in turn, tended to stress the importance of mutual social obligation and consensus rather than debate. Ancient Chinese philosophies focused on the way in which wholes, not analytical categories, caused processes and events. In contrast, the hills and seashores of ancient Greece were suited more to small-scale herding and fishing than to large-scale, centrally organized agriculture. Ancient Greek society was less socially complex than that of ancient China. It was more politically decentralized, and it gave its citizens more personal freedom. As a result, ancient Greek thinking stressed personal agency. Debate was an integral part of politics. Philosophies tended to be analytical, which means, among other things, that processes and events were viewed as the result of discrete categories rather than of whole systems. Markedly different civilizations grew up on these different cognitive foundations; ways of thinking depended less on innate characteristics than on the structure of society (Cole, 1995; Nisbett, Peng, Choi, and Norenzayan, 2001; Vygotsky, 1987).

Gilligan and Gender Differences

One of the best-known examples of how social position affects socialization comes from the research of Carol Gilligan. Gilligan demonstrated that sociological factors help explain differences in the sense of self that boys and girls usually develop. Parents and teachers tend to pass on different cultural standards to boys and girls. Such adult authorities usually define the ideal woman as eager to please and therefore non-assertive. Most girls learn this lesson as they mature. The fact that girls encounter more male teachers and fewer female teachers and other authority figures as they grow up reinforces the lesson. Gilligan found that girls therefore suffer a decline in self-esteem between the ages of 5 and 18 whereas boys do not. (Brown and Gilligan, 1992; Gilligan, 1982; Gilligan, Lyons, and Hanmer, 1990). Subsequent research failed to find a decline in the self-esteem of teenage girls, although it did find that boys tend to score somewhat higher than girls on self-esteem (Kling, Hyde, Showers, and Buswell, 1999).

Influenced more by the approaches of Vygotsky and Gilligan than by Piaget and Kohlberg, we now assess the contribution of various agents of socialization to the development of the self. These agents of socialization include families, schools, peer groups, and the mass media. We emphasize differences in socialization between societies, social groups, and historical periods. Our approach to socialization, therefore, is rigorously sociological.

AGENTS OF SOCIALIZATION

Families

Freud and Mead understood well that the family is the most important agent of **primary socialization**, the process of mastering the basic skills required to function in society during childhood. They argued that, for most babies, the family is the world. This fact is as true today as it was a hundred years ago. The family is well suited to providing the kind of careful, intimate attention required for primary socialization. The family is a small group. Its members are in frequent face-to-face contact. Child abuse and neglect exist, but most parents love their children and are therefore highly motivated to care for them. These characteristics make most families ideal, even today, for teaching small children everything from language to their place in the world.

The family into which we are born also exerts an *enduring* influence over the course of our entire lives. Consider the long-term effect of the family's religious atmosphere, for instance. Research shows that the main way religious groups grow is by recruiting and retaining children whose parents already belong to the group (Bibby, 2001: 115). Parents are the key source of their children's religious identification throughout life. Even Canadians who say they have abandoned the religious faith of their parents—or claim to have no religious identification—typically readopt the religious identities of their parents when they participate in rites of passage, such as marriage and baptism (Bibby, 2001: 200). Clearly, the religious atmosphere of the family into which a person is born exerts a strong influence on his or her religious practice as an adult.

Despite the continuing importance of the family in socialization, things have changed since Freud and Mead wrote their important works in the early twentieth century. They did not foresee how the relative influence of various socialization agents would alter during the

In her research, Carol Gilligan attributed differences in the moral development of boys and girls to the different cultural standards parents and teachers pass on to them. By emphasizing that moral development is socially differentiated and does not follow universal rules, Gilligan has made a major sociological contribution to our understanding of childhood development.

Primary socialization is the process of acquiring the basic skills needed to function in society during childhood. Primary socialization usually takes place in a family.

The family is still an important agent of socialization, although its importance has declined since the early twentieth century.

Secondary socialization is socialization outside the family after childhood.

The hidden curriculum in school involves teaching obedience to authority and conformity to cultural norms.

next century. The influence of some socialization agents increased, while the influence of others—especially the family—declined.

The socialization function of the family was more pronounced a century ago, partly because adult family members were more readily available for child care than they are today. As industry grew, families left farming for city work in factories and offices. Especially after the 1950s, many women had to work outside the home for a wage to maintain an adequate standard of living for their families. Fathers, for the most part, did not compensate by spending more time with their children. In fact, because divorce rates have increased, and many fathers have less contact with their children after divorce, children may see less of their fathers on average now than they did a century ago. As a result of these developments, child care—and therefore child socialization—became a big social problem in the twentieth century (Figure 4.2).

Schools

For children over the age of five, the child-care problem was partly resolved by the growth of the public school system, which was increasingly responsible for **secondary socialization**, or socialization outside the family after childhood. Industry needed better-trained and educated employees. Therefore, by the early twentieth century every province had prescribed minimum and maximum ages between which a child had to attend school. Today, more than two-thirds of Canadians over the age of 14 have completed high school and Canadians are among the most highly educated people in the world.

Class, Race, and Conflict Theory

Instructing students in academic and vocational subjects is just one part of the school's job. In addition, a **hidden curriculum** teaches students what will be expected of them in the larger society once they graduate. The hidden curriculum teaches them how to be conventionally "good citizens." Most parents approve of this instruction. According to one survey conducted in several highly industrialized countries, the capacity of schools to socialize students is more important to the public than all academic subjects except mathematics (Galper, 1998).

What is the content of the hidden curriculum? In the family, children tend to be evaluated on the basis of personal and emotional criteria. As students, however, they are led to believe that they are evaluated solely on the basis of their performance on impersonal, standardized tests. They are told that similar criteria will be used to evaluate them in the work world. The lesson is, of course, only partly true. As you will see in Chapters 8 (Social

FIGURE 4.2

The Proportion of Children Aged Six Months to Five Years Old in Child Care, 1994–1995 to 2002–2003

Source: Adapted from Statistics Canada, 2005,"Child Care 1994/95 and 2000/01," *The Daily*, Catalogue 11-001. February 7. Retrieved March 14, 2006 (http://www.statcan.ca/Daily/English/050207/d050207b.htm); and Bushnik, Tracy, 2006, "Child Care in Canada," Ottawa: Statistics Canada, p. 10. Retrieved January 4, 2008 (http://www.statcan.ca/english/research/89-599-MIE/89-599-MIE2006003.pdf).

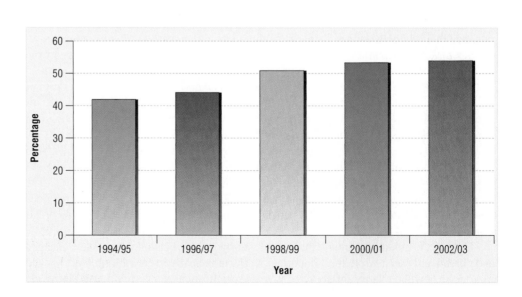

Stratification: Canadian and Global Perspectives), 10 (Race and Ethnicity), 11 (Sexuality and Gender), and 17 (Education), it is not just performance but also class, gender, sexual orientation, and racial criteria that help determine success in school and in the work world. But the accuracy of the lesson is not the issue here. The important point is that the hidden curriculum has done its job if it convinces students that they are judged on the basis of performance alone. Similarly, a successful hidden curriculum teaches students punctuality, respect for authority, the importance of competition in leading to excellent performance, and other conformist behaviours and beliefs that are expected of good citizens, conventionally defined.

The idea of the hidden curriculum was first proposed by conflict theorists, who, you will recall, see an ongoing struggle between privileged and disadvantaged groups whenever they probe beneath the surface of social life (Willis, 1984 [1977]). From the point of view of conflict theory, some poor students and some students who are members of racial minority groups accept the hidden curriculum, thereby learning to act like conventionally good citizens. Other such students reject the hidden curriculum, consequently doing poorly in school and eventually entering the work world near the bottom of the socioeconomic hierarchy. In either case, the hidden curriculum helps sustain the overall structure of society, with its privileges and disadvantages.

The Self-Fulfilling Prophecy

Why do some poor students and some students who are members of racial minority groups reject the hidden curriculum in whole or in part? Their experience, and the experience of their friends, peers, and family members, may make them skeptical about the ability of school to open job opportunities for them. As a result, they rebel against the authority of the school. Expected to be polite and studious, they openly violate rules and neglect their work.

Believing that school does not lead to economic success can act as a **self-fulfilling prophecy**, which is an expectation that helps cause what it predicts. W. I. Thomas and Dorothy Swaine Thomas had a similar idea in stating what became known as the **Thomas theorem**: "Situations we define as real become real in their consequences" (Thomas, 1966 [1931]: 301). For example, believing that school won't help you get ahead may cause you to do poorly in school, and performing poorly makes it more likely you will wind up near the bottom of the class structure (Willis, 1984 [1977]).

A self-fulfilling prophecy is an expectation that helps bring about what it predicts.

The Thomas theorem states, "Situations we define as real become real in their consequences."

Learning disciplined work habits is an important part of the socialization that takes place in schools.

Teachers, for their part, can also develop expectations that turn into self-fulfilling prophecies. In one famous study, two researchers informed teachers in a primary school that they were going to administer a special test to the pupils to predict intellectual "blooming." In fact, the test was just a standard IQ test. After the test, they told teachers which students they could expect to become high achievers and which they could expect to become low achievers. In fact, the researchers assigned pupils to the two groups at random. At the end of the year, the researchers repeated the IQ test. They found that the students singled out as high achievers scored significantly higher than those singled out as low achievers. Since the only difference between the two groups of students was that teachers expected one group to do well and the other to do poorly, the researchers concluded that teachers' expectations alone influenced students' performance (Rosenthal and Jacobson, 1968). The clear implication of this research is that if a teacher believes that poor children or children from minority groups are likely to do poorly in school, chances are they will.

Peer Groups

A person's **peer group** comprises people who are about the same age and of similar status as the individual. The peer group acts as an agent of socialization.

Status refers to a recognized social position an individual can occupy.

A second socialization agent whose importance increased in the twentieth century is the **peer group**. Peer groups consist of individuals who are not necessarily friends but who are about the same age and of similar status. (**Status** refers to a recognized social position an individual can occupy.) Peer groups help children and adolescents separate from their families and develop independent sources of identity. They are especially influential over such lifestyle issues as appearance, social activities, and dating. In fact, from middle childhood through adolescence, the peer group is often the dominant socializing agent.

As you probably learned from your own experience, conflict often erupts between the values promoted by the family and those promoted by the adolescent peer group. Adolescent peer groups are controlled by youth, and through them young people begin to develop their own identities. They do this by rejecting some parental values, experimenting with new elements of culture, and engaging in various forms of rebellious behaviour, including the consumption of alcohol, cigarettes, and drugs. In contrast, families are controlled by parents. They represent the values of childhood. Under these circumstances, such issues as hair and dress styles; music; curfews; tobacco, drug, and alcohol use; and political views are likely to become points of conflict between the generations.

We should not, however, overstate the significance of adolescent–parent conflict. First, the conflict is usually temporary. Once adolescents mature, the family exerts a more enduring influence on many important issues. Research shows that families have more influence than peer groups over the educational aspirations and the political, social, and religious preferences of adolescents and university students (Bibby, 2001: 55; Davies and Kandel, 1981; Milem, 1998).

A second reason that we should not exaggerate the extent of adolescent–parent discord is that peer groups are not just sources of conflict. They also help *integrate* young people into the larger society. A study of preadolescent children in a small North American city illustrates the point. Over eight years, sociologists Patricia and Peter Adler conducted in-depth interviews with school children between the ages of 8 and 11. They lived in a well-to-do community comprising about 80 000 whites and 10 000 racial minority group members (Adler and Adler, 1998). In each school they visited, they found a system of cliques arranged in a strict hierarchy, much like the arrangement of classes and racial groups in adult society. In schools with a substantial number of visible minority students, cliques were divided by race. Visible minority cliques were usually less popular than white cliques. In all schools, the most popular boys were highly successful in competitive and aggressive achievement-oriented activities, especially athletics. The most popular girls came from well-to-do and permissive families. One of the main bases of their popularity was that they had the means and the opportunity to participate in the most interesting social activities, ranging from skiing to late-night parties. Physical attractiveness was also an important basis of girls' popularity. Thus, elementary-school peer groups prepared these youngsters for the class and racial inequalities of the adult world and the gender-specific criteria that would often be used to evaluate them as adults, such as competitiveness in the case of boys and attractiveness in the case of girls. (For more on gender socialization, see the discussion of the mass media below and Chapter 11, Sexuality and Gender.) What we learn from this research is that peer groups function not only to help adolescents form an independent identity by separating them from their families but also to teach them how to adapt to the ways of the larger society.

The Mass Media

Like the school and the peer group, the mass media have become increasingly important socializing agents in the twenty-first century. The mass media include television, radio, movies, videos, CDs, audiotapes, the Internet, newspapers, magazines, and books.

The fastest-growing mass medium is the Internet. Worldwide, the number of Internet users jumped to more than 1.2 billion in 2007 from just 4 million in 1996 (Figure 4.3). Still, TV viewing consumes more of the average Canadian's free time than any other mass medium or, for that matter, any other activity (Table 4.1). In 1999, 99 percent of Canadians owned at least one colour television set (Statistics Canada, 2001d). A Statistics Canada survey shows that watching TV is Canadians' most time-consuming free-time activity. Although 9 out of 10 Canadians read newspapers on a regular basis, 8 out of 10 read magazines, and 7 out of 10 have read at least one book in the previous year (Vanier Institute of the Family, 2000: 168), free time typically becomes prime time. On average, Canadian men and women spend more time each day watching television than socializing in homes or other settings, playing sports, or enjoying a meal at a restaurant (*Canadian Global Almanac 2000*, 1999: 75). On average, Canadians spend more than 20 hours a week watching television (Statistics Canada, 2001d). Heavy users of TV are concentrated among socially disadvantaged groups, and that trend is intensifying over time (Hao, 1994; Robinson and Bianchi, 1997).

Self-Socialization

Children and adolescents use the mass media for entertainment and stimulation. The mass media also help young people cope with anger, anxiety, and unhappiness. Finally, the cultural materials provided by the mass media help young people construct their identities—for example, by emulating the appearance and behaviour of appealing movie stars, rock idols, and sports heroes. In performing these functions, the mass media offer youth much choice. Many Canadians have access to scores of radio stations and TV channels, hundreds of magazines, thousands of CD titles, hundreds of thousands of books, and millions of websites. Most of us can gain access to hip-hop, heavy metal, or Haydn

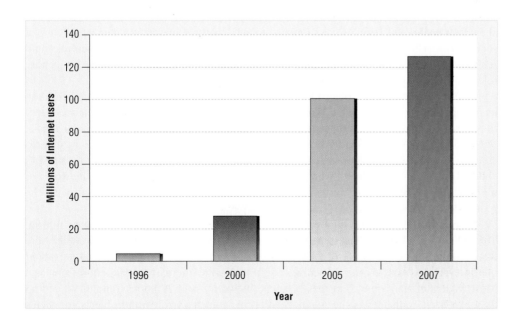

FIGURE 4.3

Number of Internet Users Worldwide, in Millions, 1996–2007

Source: "Face of the Web," 2000; and Internet Usage Statistics, 2008, "World Internet Usage and Population Statistics." Retrieved January 4, 2008 (http://www.internetworldstats.com/stats.htm).

TABLE 4.1

How Canadians Spend Their Free Time, Hours per Day, by Gender, 2005

Source: Statistics Canada, 2005, "Overview of the Time Use of Canadians." Retrieved January 4, 2008 (http://www.statcan.ca/english/freepub/12F0080XIE/12F0080XIE2006001.pdf).

Activity	Hours per Day	
	Men	**Women**
Paid work	9.1	7.9
Household work	3.1	4.3
Civic and voluntary activities	2.4	2.4
Education activities	6.1	5.7
Personal activities (sleep, meals, etc.)	10.5	10.8
Socializing	3.0	2.9
Passive leisure (TV, reading, etc.)	3.3	3.1
Live entertainment events	3.0	2.9
Active leisure	2.7	2.1

Note: Figures represent averages over a seven-day week for Canadians over the age of 15 who participated in the activities indicated. Total hours per day are greater than 24 because people may engage in several activities simultaneously (e.g., household work and watching TV, or socializing and attending live entertainment events) and because individuals who participated in one event (e.g., passive leisure) may not participate in others (e.g., paid work).

Self-socialization involves choosing socialization influences from the wide variety of mass media offerings.

with equal ease. Thus, although adolescents have little choice over how they are socialized by their family and their school, the very proliferation of the mass media gives them more say over which media messages will influence them. To a degree, the mass media allow adolescents to engage in what sociologist Jeffrey Jensen Arnett (1995) calls **self-socialization**, or choosing socialization influences from the wide variety of mass media offerings.

Gender Roles, the Mass Media, and the Feminist Approach to Socialization

A gender role is the set of behaviours associated with widely shared expectations about how males and females are supposed to act.

Although people are to some extent free to choose socialization influences from the mass media, they choose some influences more often than others. Specifically, they tend to choose influences that are more pervasive, fit existing cultural standards, and are made especially appealing by those who control the mass media. We can illustrate this by considering how feminist sociologists analyze gender roles. **Gender roles** are widely shared expectations about how males and females are supposed to act. They are of special interest to feminist sociologists, who claim that people are not born knowing how to express masculinity and femininity in conventional ways. Instead, say feminist sociologists, people *learn* gender roles, partly through the mass media.

The social construction of gender roles by the mass media begins when small children learn that only a kiss from Snow White's Prince Charming will save her from eternal sleep. It continues in magazines, romance novels, television, advertisements, and popular music. For example, most music videos, especially hip-hop videos produced by men, tend to demean women. Male hip-hop artists often portray themselves as pimps, refer to women as "bitches" and "hos," and depict women as sex objects whose chief virtue is (in the words of the Black Eyed Peas) their "humps." It is the men who drive the Mercedes and wear the bling; the scantily clad women gyrate for men's pleasure.

Another, older market segment finds gender roles reinforced by romance fiction. Toronto's Harlequin Enterprises, the world's largest publisher of romance fiction, sells more than 200 million books a year in 23 languages and more than 100 national markets. About one in every six mass-market paperbacks sold in North America is a Harlequin romance. Most readers of Harlequin romances consume between 3 and 20 books a month. A central theme in these romances is the transformation of women's bodies into objects for men's

Harlequin romance books

pleasure. In the typical Harlequin romance, men are expected to be the sexual aggressors. They are typically more experienced and promiscuous than women. Women are expected to desire love before intimacy. They are assumed to be sexually passive, giving only subtle cues to indicate their interest in male overtures. Supposedly lacking the urgent sex drive that pre-occupies men, women are often held accountable for moral standards and contraception (e.Harlequin.com, 2002; Grescoe, 1996; Jensen, 1984).

People do not passively accept such messages about appropriate gender roles. They often interpret them in unique ways and sometimes resist them. For example, Erykah Badu, Missy "Misdemeanor" Elliott, and Lauryn Hill have done much to change the stereotypes of black women in music videos (see Chapter 18, The Mass Media). For the most part, however, people try to develop skills that will help them perform gender roles in a conventional way (Eagley and Wood, 1999: 412–13). Of course, conventions change. It is important to note in this regard that what children learn about femininity and masculinity today is less sexist than what they learned just a few generations ago. For example, comparing *Cinderella* and *Snow White* with *Mulan,* we see immediately that children going to Disney movies today are sometimes presented with more assertive and heroic female role models than the passive heroines of the 1930s and 1940s. However, the amount of change in gender socialization should not be exaggerated. *Cinderella* and *Snow White* are still popular movies. Moreover, for every *Mulan* there is a *Little Mermaid,* a movie that simply modernizes old themes about female passivity and male conquest. In the end, the Little Mermaid's salvation comes through her marriage. The vast majority of heroic, gutsy, smart, and enterprising leads in nearly all children's movies are still boys (Douglas, 1994: 296–97).

As the learning of gender roles through the mass media suggests, then, not all media influences are created equal. We may be free to choose which media messages influence us, but most people are inclined to choose the messages that are most widespread, most closely aligned with existing cultural standards, and made most enticing by the mass media. In the case of gender roles, these messages are those that support conventional expectations about how males and females are supposed to act.

Resocialization and Total Institutions

In concluding our discussion of socialization agents, we must underline the importance of **resocialization** in contributing to the lifelong process of social learning. Resocialization takes place when powerful socializing agents deliberately cause rapid change in people's values, roles, and self-conception, sometimes against their will.

Resocialization occurs when powerful socializing agents deliberately cause rapid change in a person's values, roles, and self-conception, sometimes against a person's will.

Not all initiation rites or rites of passage involve resocialization, in which powerful socializing agents deliberately cause rapid change in people's values, roles, and self-conception, sometimes against their will. Some rites of passage are a normal part of primary and secondary socialization and merely signify the transition from one status to another. Here, a family celebrates the first communion of a young boy.

An **initiation rite** is a ritual that signifies the transition of the individual from one group to another and ensures his or her loyalty to the new group.

Total institutions are settings in which people are isolated from the larger society and under the strict control and constant supervision of a specialized staff.

You can see resocialization at work in the ceremonies that are staged when someone joins a fraternity, a sorority, the Canadian Armed Forces, or a religious order. Such a ceremony, or **initiation rite**, signifies the transition of the individual from one group to another and ensures his or her loyalty to the new group. Initiation rites require new recruits to abandon old self-perceptions and assume new identities. Often they comprise a three-stage ceremony involving (1) separation from the old status and identity (ritual rejection), (2) degradation, disorientation, and stress (ritual death), and (3) acceptance of the new group culture and status (ritual rebirth).

Much resocialization takes place in what Erving Goffman (1961) called **total institutions**. Total institutions are settings in which people are isolated from the larger society and under the strict control and constant supervision of a specialized staff. Asylums and prisons are examples of total institutions. Because of the "pressure cooker" atmosphere in such institutions, resocialization in total institutions is often rapid and thorough, even in the absence of initiation rites.

A famous failed experiment, fictionalized in the 2000 German film *Das Experiment,* illustrates the immense resocializing capacity of total institutions (Haney, Banks, and Zimbardo, 1973; Zimbardo, 1972). In the early 1970s, a group of researchers created their own mock prison. They paid about two dozen male volunteers to act as guards and inmates. The volunteers were mature, emotionally stable, intelligent university students from middle-class homes in the United States and Canada. None had a criminal record. By the flip of a coin, half the volunteers were designated prisoners, the other half guards. The guards made up their own rules for maintaining law and order in the mock prison. The prisoners were picked up by city police officers in a squad car, searched, handcuffed, fingerprinted, booked at the police station, and taken blindfolded to the mock prison. At the mock prison, each prisoner was stripped, deloused, put into a uniform, given a number, and placed in a cell with two other inmates.

To better understand what it means to be a prisoner or a prison guard, the researchers wanted to observe and record social interaction in the mock prison for two weeks. However, they were forced to end the experiment abruptly after only six days because what they witnessed frightened them. In less than a week, the prisoners and prison guards could no longer tell the difference between the roles they were playing and their "real" selves. Much of the socialization these young men had undergone over a period of about 20 years was quickly suspended.

About a third of the guards began to treat the prisoners like despicable animals, taking pleasure in cruelty. Even the guards who were regarded by the prisoners as tough but fair stopped short of interfering in the tyrannical and arbitrary use of power by the most sadistic guards.

All the prisoners became servile and dehumanized, thinking only about survival, escape, and their growing hatred of the guards. Had they been thinking as university students, they could have walked out of the experiment at any time. Some of the prisoners did, in fact, beg for parole. However, by the fifth day of the experiment they were so programmed to think of themselves as prisoners that they returned docilely to their cells when their request for parole was denied.

The Palo Alto experiment suggests that your sense of self and the roles you play are not as fixed as you may think. Radically alter your social setting and, like the university students in the experiment, your self-conception and patterned behaviour are also likely to change. Such change is most evident among people undergoing resocialization in total institutions. However, the sociological eye is able to observe the flexibility of the self in all social settings, including those that greet the individual in adult life.

ADULT SOCIALIZATION THROUGH THE LIFE COURSE

Although we form our basic personality and sense of identity early in life, socialization continues in adulthood. Adult socialization is necessary for four main reasons (Mortimer and Simmons, 1978: 425–27):

1. *Adult roles are often discontinuous.* That is, contradictory expectations are associated with earlier and later roles. For instance, we socialize children to be non-responsible, submissive, and asexual, whereas we expect adults to be responsible, assertive, and

sexually active. Similarly, we expect adults to be independent and productive whereas we expect retired people to be more dependent and less productive. We need adult socialization to overcome these role discontinuities. People must learn what others expect of them in their new adult roles.

2. *Some adult roles are largely invisible.* Adult roles are often hidden to people too young to perform them. For example, children have a very limited knowledge of what it means to be married and only a vague sense of what specific occupational roles involve. Adult socialization is required to overcome such role invisibility.

3. *Some adult roles are unpredictable.* People know about the role changes mentioned above before they occur. To help us learn a predictable new role, we typically engage in **anticipatory socialization**, which involves taking on the norms and behaviours of the role to which we aspire. For instance, 10-year-olds who are fans of the TV program *Friends* engage in anticipatory socialization insofar as the program teaches them what it can be like to be single and in their 20s. However, in adult life many events cause unpredictable role change. They include falling in love and marrying someone from a different ethnic, racial, or religious group; separation and divorce; the sudden death of a spouse; job loss and long-term unemployment; forced international migration; and the transition from peace to war. Unpredictable role changes caused by such events require adult socialization.

4. *Adult roles change as we mature.* Forces outside the individual shape the three types of role change just listed. The fourth and final role change that demands adult socialization is mainly the result of inner developmental processes. For example, as children and parents mature, family roles change. When people reach middle age, they may grow more aware of their eventual demise and begin to question their way of life. Hence the so-called midlife crisis. These kinds of role changes also demand adult socialization.

In the process of learning life's final role—that of the terminally ill person—we can see all four reasons for adult socialization operating. The role of the terminally ill person is characterized by *discontinuity* in the sense that we expect retired people to find new ways of enjoying life yet, at some point, we expect them to prepare for imminent death. Learning to accept death requires socialization. *Invisibility* characterizes the role of the terminally ill person because our culture makes a great effort to deny death and keep us at a distance from it. We celebrate youth in movies and in advertising. We typically use technology to prolong life even when we know death is imminent. We have no holiday like the Mexican Day of the Dead, which helps young people learn to accept death. We normally consign terminally ill people to die apart from us, in a hospital and not at home, as is common in less industrialized societies. The fact that the role of the terminally ill person is thus rendered largely invisible makes socialization for dying necessary. Finally, although we may think of death as an inevitable part of the course of life, discovering the imminence of death is always a surprise. Learning the role of the terminally ill person thus requires socialization because it combines *maturation* and *unpredictability*.

The simultaneous operation of role discontinuity, invisibility, maturation, and unpredictability makes the role of the terminally ill person hard to learn. Research shows, however, that people are more likely to accept the role if they receive an unambiguous prognosis. In addition, acceptance is greater when primary caregivers (family, friends, physicians) encourage terminally ill people to accept that treatment will no longer help and that they should focus on the alleviation of pain and suffering. Finally, people are more likely to learn the role of the terminally ill person if their physicians lack affiliation with a teaching hospital. Physicians associated with a teaching hospital are more likely to be involved in research on how to prolong life and are therefore reluctant to encourage death (Prigerson, 1992). In short, role clarity, encouragement of role acceptance by significant others, and social distance from people who thwart role learning are associated with acceptance of the role of the terminally ill person. Indeed, these factors are associated with the successful learning of all adult roles. They help overcome all four of the difficulties of adult socialization discussed previously.

American Private Lynndie England became infamous when photographs were made public showing her and other American soldiers abusing Iraqi prisoners in obvious contravention of international law. "She's never been in trouble. She's not the person that the photographs point her out to be," said her childhood friend Destiny Gloin (quoted in "Woman Soldier," 2004). Ms. Gloin was undoubtedly right. Private England at Abu Ghraib prison was not the Lynndie England from high school. As in the Palo Alto prison experiment, she was transformed by a structure of power and a culture of intimidation that made the prisoners seem subhuman.

Anticipatory socialization involves taking on the norms and behaviours of the role to which we aspire.

Adult Socialization and the Flexible Self

Older sociology textbooks acknowledge that the development of the self is a lifelong process. They note that when young adults enter a profession and get married, they must learn new occupational and family roles. If they marry someone from an ethnic, racial, or religious group other than their own, they are likely to adopt new cultural values or at least modify old ones. Retirement and old age present an entirely new set of challenges. Giving up a job, seeing children leave home and start their own families, losing a spouse and close friends—all these changes later in life require people to think of themselves in new ways, to redefine who they are.

In our judgment, however, older treatments of adult socialization underestimate the plasticity or flexibility of the self (Mortimer and Simmons, 1978). We believe that, today, people's identities change faster, more often, and more completely than they did just a couple of decades ago.

One important factor contributing to the growing flexibility of the self is globalization. As we saw in Chapter 3, Culture, people are now less obliged to accept the culture into which they are born. Because of globalization, they are freer to combine elements of culture from a wide variety of historical periods and geographical settings.

A second factor that increases our freedom to design our selves is our growing ability to fashion new bodies from old. People have always defined themselves partly in terms of their bodies; your self-conception is influenced by whether you're a man or a woman, tall or short, healthy or ill, conventionally good looking or plain. But our bodies used to be fixed by nature. People could do nothing to change the fact that they were born with certain features and grew older at a certain rate.

Now, however, thanks largely to various technological innovations, you can change your body, and therefore your self-conception, radically and virtually at will—if, that is, you can afford it. Consider these examples:

TECHNOLOGY BYTES

- Bodybuilding, aerobic exercise, and weight-reduction regimes are more popular than ever.
- Sex-change operations, while infrequent, are no longer a rarity.
- Plastic surgery allows people to buy new breasts, noses, lips, eyelids, and hair—and to remove unwanted fat, skin, and hair from various parts of their bodies. In 2005, 10.5 million North Americans had cosmetic surgery (American Society of Plastic Surgeons, 2006). Although the vast majority of people who undergo cosmetic surgery are women, the number of men opting for cosmetic surgery has doubled in the past two decades. Men account for between one-quarter and one-third of Canadians seeking to redesign their appearance (Chisholm, 1996). One in three Canadians undergoing cosmetic surgery each year is a repeat customer (CBC News, 2001; Nelson and Robinson, 2002: 144–45).
- The use of collagen, Botox, and other non-surgical procedures to remove facial wrinkles is increasingly common. In fact, a growing number of plastic surgeons are organizing Botox parties—sort of like Tupperware parties but with needles. At a typical Botox party, a plastic surgeon invites about 10 clients to an evening of champagne, chocolate truffles, Brie, and botulinum toxin type A. When injected in the face at a cost of about $300 per injection, the toxin relaxes muscles and erases signs of aging for a few months.
- Organ transplants are routine. At any given time, about 3000 Canadians are waiting for a replacement organ (Health Canada, 1999a). There is a brisk illegal international trade in human hearts, lungs, kidneys, livers, and eyes that enables well-to-do people to enhance and extend their lives (Rothman, 1998).
- In 2002 Kevin Warwick, a professor of cybernetics in the United Kingdom, became the first cyborg (part man, part computer) when he had a computer chip implanted in his wrist and connected to about 100 neurons. A wire runs under the skin up his arm to a point just below his elbow, where a junction box allows data from his neurons to be

transmitted wirelessly to a computer. He plans on implanting a similar device in his wife. Through an Internet connection, they will each be able to feel what the other feels in his or her arm. Warwick predicts that before 2020 more sophisticated implants will allow a primitive form of telepathy (Akin, 2002).

- As if all this were not enough to change how people think of themselves, Dr. Robert J. White, a medicine professor in Cleveland, has performed the first whole-body transplant. He removed the head of a rhesus monkey and connected it by tubes and sutures to the trunk of another monkey. The new entity lived and gained consciousness, although it was paralyzed below the neck because there is no way yet to connect the millions of neurons bridging the brain and the spinal column. Could the same operation be done on a human? No problem, says White. Because the human body is larger and we know more about human anatomy than monkey anatomy, the operation would in fact be simpler than it is on monkeys. And, notes White, because research on spinal regeneration is advancing rapidly, it is only a matter of time before it will be possible to create a fully functional human out of one person's head and another's body (ABC Evening News, 1998; Browne, 1998). We used to think of our selves as congruent with our bodies but the two have now become disjointed. As a result, the formerly simple question, "Who are you?" has grown complex.

As these examples illustrate, technology has introduced many new opportunities for changing one's self-conception in recent decades.

Identity and the Internet

Further complicating the process of identity formation today is the growth of the Internet and its audiovisual component, the World Wide Web. In the 1980s and early 1990s most observers believed that social interaction by means of computer would involve only the exchange of information between individuals. It turns out they were wrong. Computer-assisted social interaction can profoundly affect how people think of themselves (Brym and Lenton, 2001; Dibbell, 1993; Haythornthwaite and Wellman, 2002; Wellman, Salaff, Dimitrova, Garton, Gulia, and Haythornthwaite, 1996).

Internet users interact socially by exchanging text, images, and sound via e-mail; messaging services; such as MSN Messenger; Internet phone; videoconferencing; computer-assisted work groups; Facebook; and online dating services. In the process, they form **virtual communities**. Virtual communities are associations of people, scattered across the country or the planet, who communicate via computer and modem about subjects of common interest.

Some virtual communities are short-lived and loosely structured in the sense that they have few formal rules and people quickly drift in and out of them. Chat groups are typical of this genre. Other virtual communities are more enduring and structured. For example, discussion groups cater to people's interest in specialized subjects, such as Latino culture, BMWs, dating, or white-water canoeing. Still other virtual communities are highly structured, with many formal rules and relatively stable membership. For example, MUDs (multiple-user dimensions), such as Second Life, are computer programs that allow people to role-play and engage in a sort of collective fantasy. These programs define the aims and rules of the virtual community and the objects and spaces it contains. Users around the world log on to the MUD from their computers and define their character—their identity—any way they want. They interact with other users by exchanging text messages or by having their "avatars" (graphical representations) act and speak for them.

Because virtual communities allow interaction using concealed identities, people are free to assume new identities and encouraged to discover parts of themselves they were formerly unaware of. In virtual communities, shy people can become bold, normally assertive people can become voyeurs, old people can become young, straight people can become gay, and women can become men (Turkle, 1995). Experience on the Internet thus reinforces our

A **virtual community** is an association of people, scattered across the country, continent, or planet, who communicate via computer and modem about a subject of common interest.

main point. In recent decades, the self has become increasingly flexible, and people are freer than ever to shape their selves as they choose.

However, this freedom comes at a cost, particularly for young people. In concluding this chapter, we consider some of the socialization challenges Canadian youth face today. To set the stage for this discussion, we first examine the emergence of "childhood" and "adolescence" as categories of social thought and experience some 400 years ago.

DILEMMAS OF CHILDHOOD AND ADOLESCENT SOCIALIZATION

The Emergence of Childhood and Adolescence

In preindustrial societies, children were thought of as small adults. From a young age, they were expected to conform as much as possible to the norms of the adult world, largely because they were put to work as soon as they could contribute to the welfare of their families. Often, this meant doing chores by the age of 5 and working full-time by the age of 10 or 12. Marriage, and thus the achievement of full adulthood, was common by the age of 15 or 16.

Children in Europe and North America fit this pattern until the late seventeenth century, when the idea of childhood as a distinct stage of life emerged. At that time, the feeling grew among well-to-do Europeans and North Americans that boys should be permitted to play games and receive an education that would allow them to develop the emotional, physical, and intellectual skills they would need as adults. Girls continued to be treated as "little women" (the title of Louisa May Alcott's 1869 novel) until the nineteenth century. Most working-class boys did not enjoy much of a childhood until the twentieth century. Thus, it is only in the last century that the idea of childhood as a distinct and prolonged period of life became universal in the West (Ariès, 1962 [1960]).

The idea of childhood emerged when and where it did because of social necessity and social possibility. Prolonged childhood was *necessary* in societies that required better-educated adults to do increasingly complex work. That is because childhood gave young people a chance to prepare for adult life. Prolonged childhood was *possible* in societies where improved hygiene and nutrition allowed most people to live more than 35 years, the average life span in Europe in the early seventeenth century. In other words, before the late seventeenth century, most people did not live long enough to permit the luxury of childhood. Moreover, there was no social need for a period of extended training and development before the comparatively simple demands of adulthood were thrust upon young people.

In general, wealthier and more complex societies whose populations enjoy a long average life expectancy stretch out the pre-adult period of life. For example, we saw that in Europe in 1600, most people reached mature adulthood by the age of about 16. In contrast, in such countries as Canada today, most people are considered to reach mature adulthood only around the age of 30, by which time they have completed their formal education, married, and "settled down." Once teenagers were relieved of adult responsibilities, a new term had to be coined to describe the teenage years: *adolescence*. Subsequently, the term *young adulthood* entered popular usage as an increasingly large number of people in their late teens and twenties delayed marriage to attend university (Box 4.1).

Although these new terms describing the stages of life were firmly entrenched in North America by the middle of the twentieth century, some of the categories of the population they were meant to describe soon began to change dramatically. Somewhat excitedly, a number of analysts began to write about the "disappearance" of childhood and adolescence altogether (Friedenberg, 1959; Postman, 1982). Although undoubtedly overstating their case, these social scientists identified some of the social forces responsible for the changing character of childhood and adolescence in recent decades. We examine these social forces in the concluding section of this chapter.

BOX 4.1
Sociology at the Movies

TAKE   ROLL

Wedding Crashers (2005)

John Beckwith (Owen Wilson) and Jeremy Grey (Vince Vaughn) are 30-something partners in a divorce mediation firm. Neither is married because they believe that, as Jeremy says during one particularly heated mediation, "The real enemy here is the institution of marriage. It's not realistic. It's crazy."

So what do these handsome, single, professional men do for excitement come spring? They crash weddings, party till dawn, and bed the unsuspecting beauties who fall for their fast talk and scripted charm.

Early in the movie, John expresses misgivings:

John (Owen Wilson; left) and Jeremy (Vince Vaughn) in *Wedding Crashers*

John: You ever think we're being a little—I don't want to say sleazy, because that's not the right word—but a little irresponsible? I mean . . .

Jeremy: No. One day you'll look back on all this and laugh, and say we were young and stupid. Coupla dumb kids, runnin' around . . .

John: We're not that young.

Indeed they're not, which is why John's reflective moment raises an important sociological issue posed by a host of recent movies. *Wedding Crashers, The 40 Year-Old Virgin* (2005), *Failure to Launch* (2006), and *Clerks II* (2006) all raise the question of how it came about that people old enough to be considered adults just a couple of generations ago now seem stuck between adolescence and adulthood. They aren't married. Some of them live with their parents. They may still be in school. And some of them lack steady, well-paying, full-time jobs. Sometimes called "kippers" (kids in parents' pockets, eroding retirement savings), they represent a growing category of young adults who are often a big worry to their elders.

Between 1981 and 2001, the percentage of Canadians between the ages of 25 and 34 living with their parents doubled—rising from 12 percent to 24 percent for the 25–29 age cohort and from 5 percent to 11 percent for the 30–34 age cohort (Beaupré, Turcotte, and Milan, 2007). One reason for this phenomenon is economic. In the first few decades after World War II, housing and education costs were low, and the number of years people had to spend in school to get a steady, well-paying job was modest. Today, housing and education costs are high, and young people must typically spend more years in school before starting their careers. As a result, many young people continue to live in their parents' home into their 20s and 30s as a matter of economic necessity.

Such economic factors undoubtedly affect working- and middle-class families more than upper-middle- and upper-class families. For the latter, a change in child-rearing practices seems to account in part for the reluctance of some young adults to leave home. Many

well educated and well-to-do parents seem to be raising children who are simply too dependent. They are reluctant to insist that their children get part-time jobs when they are in their mid-teens, and they neglect to teach them the importance of saving money by always giving them as much money as they want. They provide too much assistance with schoolwork (either by themselves or by hiring tutors), and they organize too many extracurricular activities for their children, thus not giving them enough space to figure out their interests for themselves.

In *Wedding Crashers,* John and Jeremy finally seem able to break the mould when Jeremy marries Gloria Cleary (Isla Fisher) and John commits to her sister Claire (St. Thomas, Ontario's Rachel McAdams). But as the happy foursome drive away, they get the bright idea of posing as a folk-singing quartet from Utah and crashing a wedding for the great Japanese food that is bound to be served. It seems that their parents' worries are far from over.

WHERE DO YOU FIT IN?

Problems of Childhood and Adolescent Socialization Today

When you were between the ages of 10 and 17, how often were you at home or with friends but without adult supervision? How often did you have to prepare your own meals or take care of a younger sibling while your parent or parents were at work? How many hours a week did you spend cleaning house? How many hours a week did you have to work at a part-time job to earn spending money and save for university? How many hours a week did you spend on extracurricular activities associated with your school? on TV viewing and other mass media use? If you were like most Canadian preteens and teenagers from working- and middle-class families, many of your waking hours outside of school were spent without adult supervision or assuming substantial adult responsibilities, such as those listed above. You are unlikely to have spent much time on extracurricular activities associated with your school but quite a lot of time viewing TV and using other mass media.

Declining adult supervision and guidance, increasing mass media and peer group influence, and the increasing assumption of substantial adult responsibilities to the neglect of extracurricular activities have done much to change the socialization patterns of Canadian youth over the past 40 years or so. Let us consider each of these developments in turn.

- *Declining adult supervision and guidance.* In a six-year, in-depth study of adolescence, Patricia Hersch wrote that "in all societies since the beginning of time, adolescents have learned to become adults by observing, imitating and interacting with grown-ups around them" (Hersch, 1998: 20). However, in contemporary North America, notes Hersch, adults are increasingly absent from the lives of adolescents. Why? According to Hersch, "society has left its children behind as the cost of progress in the workplace" (p. 19). What she means is that more adults are working longer hours outside the home. Consequently, they have less time to spend with their children than they used to. We examine some reasons for the increasing demands of paid work in Chapter 13 (Work and the Economy). Here, we stress a major consequence for youth: Young people, especially those from working- and middle-class families, are increasingly left alone to socialize themselves and build their own community. This community sometimes revolves around high-risk behaviour. To be sure, more is involved in high-risk behaviour than socialization patterns (see Box 4.2). However, it is not coincidental in this connection that girls are less likely to engage in juvenile crime than are boys. That is partly because parents tend to supervise and socialize their sons and daughters differently (Hagan, Simpson, and Gillis, 1987). Parents typically exert more control over girls, supervising them more closely and socializing them to avoid risk. This research finding suggests that many of the teenage behaviours commonly regarded as problematic result from declining adult guidance and supervision.
- *Increasing media influence.* Declining adult supervision and guidance also leaves North American youth more susceptible to the influence of the mass media and peer groups. As one parent put it, "When they hit the teen years it is as if they can't be children anymore. The outside world has invaded the school environment" (quoted in Hersch, 1998: 111). In an earlier era, family, school, church, and community usually taught young people more or less consistent beliefs and values. Now, however, the mass media offer a wide variety of cultural messages, many of which differ from each other and from those taught in school and at home. The result for many adolescents is confusion (Arnett, 1995). Should the 10-year-old girl dress modestly or in a sexually provocative fashion? Should the 14-year-old boy devote more time to attending church, synagogue, temple, or mosque—or to playing electric guitar in the garage? Should you "just say no" to drugs? The mass media and peer groups often pull young people in different directions from the school and the family, leaving them uncertain about what constitutes appropriate behaviour and making the job of growing up more stressful than it used to be.
- *Declining extracurricular activities and increasing adult responsibilities.* As the opening anecdote about Robert Brym's involvement in high-school drama illustrates, extracurricular activities are important for adolescent personality development. That is,

BOX 4.2
It's Your Choice

Socialization versus Gun Control

On April 29, 1999, Columbine High School in Littleton, Colorado, was the scene of a mass shooting by two students. The students murdered 13 people (12 fellow students and 1 teacher) and then turned their guns on themselves.

After the massacre at Columbine High School, newspapers, magazines, Internet chat rooms, and radio and television talk shows were abuzz with the problem of teenage violence. "What is to be done?" people asked. One solution that seems obvious to many Canadians is to limit the availability of firearms. Their reasoning is simple: All advanced industrial societies except the United States sharply restrict gun ownership, and only the United States has a serious problem with teenagers shooting one another. Of course, other countries have problems with extreme teenage violence—even Canada. Just eight days after the shooting rampage at Columbine, a 15-year-old boy in Taber, Alberta, gunned down one teen and wounded another in a school hallway. In 2005, authorities at Saint John High School in New Brunswick uncovered a plot to copy the Columbine massacre. The fact remains, however, that in countries where guns are less readily available, such as Canada, Australia, Britain, and Japan, teenage violence only very rarely leads to mass killings. According to a Canadian government report, the annual rate of homicide using firearms per 100 000 people is 2.2 in Canada, 1.8 in Australia, 1.2 in Japan, 1.3 in Britain—and 9.3 in the United States (Department of Justice, Canada, 1995).

Students from W. R. Myers High School in Taber, Alberta, console one another following a memorial service for slain student Jason Lang. Are acts of violence committed by teenagers best understood as the result of faulty socialization, inadequate controls on firearms, or some combination of both?

In the United States, however, most political discussions about teenage violence focus on the problem of socialization, not on gun control. Soon after the Columbine tragedy, for example, the U.S. House of Representatives passed a juvenile crime bill. It cast blame on the entertainment industry, especially Hollywood movies, and the decline of "family values." Tom DeLay, a Republican congressman from Texas, worried: "We place our children in daycare centers where they learn their socialization skills . . . under the law of the jungle . . ." (quoted in Lazare, 1999: 58). In other words, according to these American politicians, teenage massacres result from poor childhood socialization, the corrupting influence of Hollywood movies, and declining family values.

Some politicians want to reintroduce Christianity into public schools to help overcome this presumed decay. DeLay thus reported an e-mail message he received. It read: "'Dear God, why didn't you stop the shootings at Columbine?' And God writes, 'Dear student, I would have, but I wasn't allowed in school'" (quoted in Lazare, 1999: 57–58). One consequence of the Littleton massacre was not a gun control bill but a bill to display the Ten Commandments in public schools.

What do you think? Is the problem of students shooting each other a problem of socialization, lack of gun control, or a combination of both? In answering this question, think about the situation in Canada as well as other countries and refer back to the discussion of media influence in Chapter 2, How Sociologists Do Research.

they provide opportunities for students to develop concrete skills and thereby make sense of the world and their place in it. In schools today, academic subjects are too often presented as disconnected bits of knowledge that lack relevance to the student's life. Drama, music, and athletics programs are often better at giving students a framework within which they can develop a strong sense of self, for they are concrete activities with clearly defined rules. By training and playing hard on a hockey team, mastering a string or a band instrument, or acting in plays, you can learn something about your physical, emotional, and social capabilities and limitations, about what you are made of, and about what you can and cannot do. These are just the sorts of activities adolescents require for healthy self-development.

However, if you're like most young Canadians today, you spent fewer hours per week on extracurricular activities associated with school than your parents did when they went to school. Educators estimate that only about a quarter of today's high-school students take part in sports, drama, music, and so forth (Hersch, 1998). Many of them are simply too busy with homework, household chores, child-care responsibilities, and part-time jobs to enjoy the benefits of school activities outside the classroom. One survey found that half of Canadian teenagers are working at jobs for an average of 15 hours a week (Bibby, 2001: 35).

Some analysts wonder whether the assumption of so many adult responsibilities, the lack of extracurricular activities, declining adult supervision and guidance, and increasing mass media and peer group influence are causing childhood and adolescence to disappear. As early as 1959, one sociologist spoke of "the vanishing adolescent" in North American society (Friedenberg, 1959). More recently, another commentator remarked: "I think that we who were small in the early sixties were perhaps the last generation . . . who actually had a childhood, in the . . . sense of . . . a space distinct in roles and customs from the world of adults, oriented around children's own needs and culture rather than around the needs and culture of adults" (Wolf, 1997: 13; see also Postman, 1982). Childhood and adolescence became universal categories of social thought and experience in the twentieth century. Under the impact of the social forces discussed above, however, the experience and meaning of childhood and adolescence now seem to be changing radically.

SUMMARY

1. **Why is social interaction necessary?**
   Studies show that children raised in isolation do not develop normally. This finding supports the view that social interaction unleashes human potential.

2. **What are the major theories of childhood socialization?**
   Freud called the part of the self that demands immediate gratification the id. He argued that a self-image begins to emerge when the id's demands are denied. Because of many lessons in self-control, a child eventually develops a sense of what constitutes appropriate behaviour, a moral sense of right and wrong, and a personal conscience or superego. The superego is a repository of cultural standards. A third component of the self, the ego, develops to balance the demands of the id and superego.

   Like Freud, Mead noted that an impulsive aspect of the self is present from birth. He called it the I. Developing Cooley's idea of the looking-glass self, Mead also argued that a repository of culturally approved standards emerges as part of the self during social interaction. Mead called it the me. However, Mead drew attention to the unique human capacity to "take the role of the other" as the source of the me. People develop, he wrote, by first imitating and pretending to be their significant others, then learning to play complex games that require understanding several roles simultaneously, and finally developing a sense of cultural standards and how they apply.

   Since the early twentieth century, Piaget and Kohlberg have contributed to our understanding of cognitive and moral socialization, but Vygotsky and Gilligan have done more to underline the social conditions that account for variations in cognitive and moral development. Specifically, their work suggests that gender and economic and political structures shape socialization patterns.

3. How has the influence of various social agents changed over the past century?
Over the past century, the increasing socializing influence of schools, peer groups, and the mass media was matched by the decreasing socializing influence of the family.

4. Why is adult socialization necessary?
Adult socialization is necessary because roles change. Specifically, roles mature and are often discontinuous, invisible, and unpredictable.

5. In what sense is the self more flexible than it used to be?
People's self-conceptions are subject to more flux now than they were even a few decades ago. Cultural globalization, medical advances, and computer-assisted communication are among the factors that have made the self more plastic.

6. What social forces have caused and are causing change in the character and experience of childhood and adolescence?
Childhood as a distinct stage of life emerged for well-to-do boys in the late seventeenth century when life expectancy started to increase and boys had to be trained for more complex work tasks. Girls were treated as "little women" until the nineteenth century, and most working-class boys first experienced childhood only in the twentieth century. Once teenagers were relieved of adult responsibilities, the term "adolescence" was coined to describe the teenage years. Subsequently, the term "young adulthood" entered popular usage as an increasingly large number of people in their late teens and 20s delayed marriage to attend postsecondary schools.

Today, decreasing parental supervision and guidance, the increasing assumption of substantial adult responsibilities by children and adolescents, declining participation in extracurricular activities, and increased mass media and peer group influence are causing changes in the character and experience of childhood and adolescence. According to some analysts, childhood and adolescence as they were known in the first half of the twentieth century are disappearing.

KEY TERMS

anticipatory socialization (p. 115)

ego (p. 103)

gender role (p. 112)

generalized other (p. 105)

hidden curriculum (p. 108)

I (p. 104)

id (p. 102)

initiation rite (p. 114)

me (p. 104)

peer group (p. 110)

primary socialization (p. 107)

resocialization (p. 113)

role (p. 100)

secondary socialization (p. 108)

self (p. 102)

self-fulfilling prophecy (p. 109)

self-socialization (p. 112)

significant others (p. 105)

socialization (p. 100)

status (p. 110)

superego (p. 102)

Thomas theorem (p. 109)

total institutions (p. 114)

unconscious (p. 103)

virtual community (p. 117)

QUESTIONS TO CONSIDER

1. Do you think of yourself in a fundamentally different way from the way your parents (or other close relatives or friends at least 20 years older than you) thought of themselves when they were your age? Interview your parents, relatives, or friends to find out.

Pay particular attention to the way in which the forces of globalization may have altered self-conceptions over time.

2. Have you ever participated in an initiation rite in university, in the military, or in a religious organization? If so, describe the ritual rejection, ritual death, and ritual rebirth that made up the rite. Do you think the rite increased your identification with the group you were joining? Did it increase the sense of solidarity—the "we-feeling"—of group members?

3. List the contradictory lessons that different agents of socialization taught you as an adolescent. How have you resolved these contradictory lessons? If you have not resolved them, how do you intend to do so?

WEB RESOURCES

Companion Website for This Book

http://www.compass3e.nelson.com

Begin by clicking on the Student Resources section of the website. Next, select the chapter you are studying from the pull-down menu. From the Student Resources page you have easy access to InfoTrac® College Edition, additional Weblinks, and other resources. The website also has many useful tips to aid you in your study of sociology, including practice tests for each chapter.

InfoTrac® Search Terms

These search terms are provided to assist you in beginning to conduct research on this topic by visiting http://www.infotrac-college.com:

hidden curriculum
initiation rite
peer group
primary socialization
secondary socialization

Recommended Websites

For an online simulation, slide show, and discussion questions on the prison experiment discussed in the text, visit http://www.prisonexp.org.

For the socialization experiences that characterize different generations, go to a major search engine on the web, such as Yahoo at http://www.yahoo.com, and search for *teenagers, generation X, baby boomers, seniors,* and so on.

Initiation rites (or rites of passage) are conveniently summarized in the online version of the *Encarta* encyclopedia. Go to the Encarta search engine at http://encarta.msn.com and search for *rites of passage.*

CengageNOW™

http://hed.nelson.com

This online diagnostic tool identifies each student's unique needs with a Pretest that generates a personalized Study Plan for each chapter, helping students focus on concepts they're having the most difficulty mastering. Students then take a Posttest after reading the chapter to measure their understanding of the material. An Instructor Gradebook is available to track and monitor student progress.

CHAPTER

5

Social Interaction

In this chapter, you will learn that

- Social interaction involves people communicating face to face, acting and reacting in relation to each other. The character of every social interaction depends on people's distinct positions in the interaction (statuses), their standards of conduct (norms), and their sets of expected behaviours (roles).

- Humour, fear, anger, grief, disgust, love, jealousy, and other emotions colour social interactions. However, emotions are not as natural, spontaneous, authentic, and uncontrollable as we commonly believe. Various aspects of social structure influence the texture of our emotional life.

- Nonverbal means of communication, including facial expressions, gestures, body language, and status cues, are as important as language in social interaction.

- People interact mainly out of fear, envy, or trust. Domination, competition, and cooperation give rise to these three emotions.

- Sociological theories focus on six aspects of social interaction: (1) the way people exchange valued resources; (2) the way they maximize gains and minimize losses; (3) the way they interpret, negotiate, and modify norms, roles, and statuses; (4) the way they manage the impressions they give to others; (5) the way preexisting norms influence social interaction; and (6) the way status hierarchies influence social interaction.

WHAT IS SOCIAL INTERACTION?

In the early decades of the twentieth century, the service personnel on ocean liners and trains were mostly men. When some commercial airlines first started operating in the 1910s and 1920s, hiring cabin boys and stewards therefore seemed the natural thing to do.

Things began to change a little in the 1930s and even more by the early 1950s. The government tightly regulated the airline industry at the time. It decided where and when planes could fly and how much they could charge passengers. On transatlantic flights, the government even decided the allowable amount of passenger legroom and the number and types of courses that constituted a meal. This regulation made all the airlines pretty much identical. How then could one airline stand out from the others and thereby win more business? The airlines came up with a creative answer. In the 1950s, they started hiring large numbers of women as stewardesses (known today by the gender-neutral term "flight attendants"). The airlines outdid one another in training and marketing stewardesses as glamorous sex objects, using them to lure the still largely male clientele to fly with them as opposed to their competitors.

The plan required the establishment of a new form of **social interaction**, the creation of a novel way for people to communicate face to face or via computer, acting and reacting in relation to each other. As is generally the case, this social interaction was structured around specific statuses, roles, and norms.

The Structure of Social Interaction

Status

In everyday speech, *status* means "prestige," but when sociologists say **status** they mean a recognized social position that an individual can occupy. Flight attendants and passengers occupy distinct statuses. Note that each person occupies many statuses. Thus, an individual may be a flight attendant, a wife, and a mother at the same time. Sociologists call the entire ensemble of statuses occupied by an individual a **status set**. If a status is involuntary, it is an **ascribed status**. If it is voluntary, it is an **achieved status**. "Daughter" is an ascribed status, "flight attendant" an achieved status. Some statuses matter more than others for a person's identity. A person's **master status** is the status that is most influential in shaping his or her life at a given time.

Roles

Social interaction also requires **roles**, or sets of expected behaviours. Whereas people *occupy* statuses, they *perform* roles. For example, people who occupy the status of flight attendant have to play several roles—that of in-flight server, in-flight safety expert, and so on. In the role of server, flight attendants are expected to deliver snacks to passengers in a friendly way, while in the role of safety expert they are expected to act efficiently to ensure that passengers come to no harm. Expectations define the role. The entire cluster of roles attached to a single status is called a **role set** (Figure 5.1).

Norms

Finally, social interaction requires **norms**, or generally accepted ways of doing things. Norms may be prescriptive or proscriptive. *Prescriptive* norms suggest what a person is expected to do while performing a particular role. *Proscriptive* norms suggest what a person is expected *not* to do while performing a particular role. Norms often change over time. At one point in time, some norms are universal, whereas others differ from situation to situation and from role to role.

Social interaction involves people communicating face to face or via computer and acting and reacting in relation to other people. It is structured around norms, role, and statuses.

Status refers to a recognized social position an individual can occupy.

A **status set** is the entire ensemble of statuses occupied by an individual.

An **ascribed status** is an involuntary status.

An **achieved status** is a voluntary status.

A person's **master status** is his or her overriding public identity. It is the status that is most influential in shaping that person's life at a given time.

Roles are sets of expected behaviours.

A **role set** is a cluster of roles attached to a single status.

Norms are generally accepted ways of doing things.

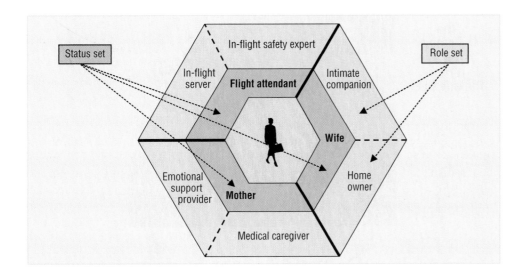

FIGURE 5.1
Role Set and Status Set

A person occupies several recognized positions or statuses at the same time—for example, mother, wife, and flight attendant. All of these statuses together form a status set. Each status is composed of several sets of expected behaviours or roles—for example, a wife is expected to act as an intimate companion to her husband and to assume certain legal responsibilities as co-owner of a house. In Figure 5.1, dashed lines separate roles and solid lines separate statuses.

Case Study: Stewardesses and Their Clientele

Let us consider these three elements of social interaction in the context of the evolution of the stewardess's job.

The Changing Role of the Stewardess

In 1930, Boeing Air Transport hired Ellen Church, the world's first stewardess (United Airlines, 2003). Trained as a nurse, she wore her white uniform on all flights, which says something about the nature of her role. Flying was much more dangerous than it is today. Although Ellen Church served coffee and sandwiches, her main role was to reassure apprehensive flyers they were in safe hands in the event of an emergency requiring medical attention (though we can imagine that seeing a uniformed nurse walking around might have had the opposite effect on some passengers). With the introduction of pressurized cabins and other safety features, nurse's uniforms gave way to tailored suits. However, the real revolution in the role of stewardess was signalled by the first of a series of radical uniform changes in 1965. An advertising executive persuaded now defunct Braniff International Airways to hire a leading fashion designer to redesign its stewardesses' uniforms (see the chapter-opening photo). The new op-art pastels and hemlines 15 centimetres (6 inches) above the knee were a sensation. Everyone wanted to fly Braniff. Braniff stock rose from $24 to $120 per share.

Soon all the airlines were in on the act. Advertising reflected the new expectations surrounding the stewardess's role. "Does your wife know you're flying with us?" one Braniff ad teased. A National Airlines ad used this blunt come on: "I'm Linda. Fly me." Pan Am's radio commercials asked: "How do you like your stewardesses?" Continental, which painted its planes with splashes of gold and whose stewardesses wore gold-coloured uniforms, advertised itself as "The Proud Bird with the Golden Tail" and later emphasized "we really move our tail for you." Movies and books solidified the stewardess's new role as sex object. The 1965 movie *Boeing, Boeing* featured Tony Curtis juggling three stewardess girlfriends on different flight schedules. *Coffee, Tea or Me,* a novel published in 1967, advertised itself as an exposé of the stewardess's life behind the scenes, "the uninhibited memoirs of two airline stewardesses" according to the book jacket. It was translated into 12 languages and sold three million copies (Handy, 2002).

The Enforcement of Norms

The airlines specified and enforced many norms pertaining to the stewardess's role. The expectations of passengers helped to reinforce those norms. For example, until 1968 stewardesses had to be single. Until 1970 they could not be pregnant. They had to be attractive, have a good smile, and achieve certain standards on IQ and other psychological tests. In 1954, American Airlines imposed a mandatory retirement age of 32 that became the industry standard. Stewardesses had to have a certain "look": slim, wholesome, and not too

Tony Curtis, Dany Saval (left), and Thelma Ritter (right) in *Boeing, Boeing* (1965).

buxom. They were assigned an ideal weight based on their height and figure. Preflight weigh-ins ensured they did not deviate from the ideal. All stewardesses had to wear girdles and supervisors did a routine "girdle check" by flicking an index finger against a buttock. Weight and height standards were not abolished until 1982 (Lehoczky, 2003). Then there was the question of "personality." Stewardesses were expected to be charming and solicitous at all times. They also had to at least appear "available" to the clientele.

Role Conflict and Role Strain

Role conflict occurs when two or more statuses held at the same time place contradictory role demands on a person. Today's female flight attendants experience role conflict to the degree that working in the airline industry requires frequent absences from home whereas being a mother and a wife requires spending considerable time at home. In contrast, in the 1950s and 1960s role conflict was minimal. Back then, sick children and demanding husbands could hardly interfere with the performance of the stewardess role because the airlines did not allow stewardesses to be mothers or wives. Conversely, the demands and expectations placed on the stewardess in the 1960s maximized role strain. **Role strain** occurs when incompatible role demands are placed on a person in a single status. For instance, constantly having to be suggestive while also politely warding off unwanted, impolite, and even crude overtures made the stewardess role a lot more stressful than it appeared in the ads (see Figure 5.2).

Change in Status

From the 1950s to the late 1970s or early 1980s, the role of stewardess was certainly glamorous. Dating a stewardess was not that different from dating an actress, and people often stared enviously at stewardesses marching proudly through an airport terminal on their way to a presumably exotic location, sporting the latest fashions and hairstyles. However, the pay was anything but glamorous. Top pay for a starting stewardess in 1960 was just over $24 000 in 2002 dollars. Stewardesses typically had to live four or five to an apartment and, as one stewardess said, "if you wanted to eat you had to find a boyfriend real quick" (quoted in Handy, 2002: 220). Moreover, working conditions were far from ideal. One stewardess described her job to *Newsweek* in 1968 as "food under your fingernails, sore feet, complaints and insults" (quoted in Handy, 2002: 220).

In the past couple of decades, the status of the stewardess (the position of the stewardess in relation to others) has changed. In the era of shoe searches, deep discount no-frills service, and packaged peanut snacks, little of the glamour remains. However, in the 1960s and 1970s stewardesses won changes in rules regarding marriage, pregnancy, retirement, and the hiring

Role conflict occurs when two or more statuses held at the same time place contradictory role demands on a person.

Role strain occurs when incompatible role demands are placed on a person in a single status.

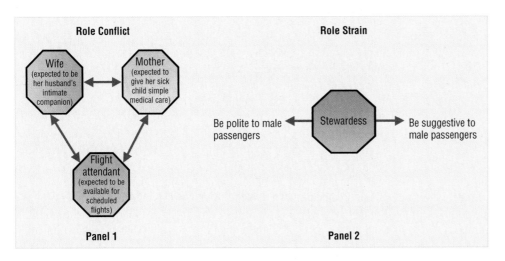

FIGURE 5.2
Role Conflict and Role Strain

(Panel 1): Role conflict takes place when different role demands are placed on a person by two or more statuses held at the same time. How might a flight attendant experience role conflict because of the contradictory demands of the statuses diagrammed in the figure?

(Panel 2): Role strain occurs when incompatible role demands are placed on a person in a single status. Why was the status of stewardess in the 1960s and 1970s high in role strain?

of men. Stewardesses, once considered sex objects, became flight attendants, and what often used to be a two-year stint leading to marriage became a career.

What Shapes Social Interaction?

Such norms, roles, and statuses as those just illustrated are the building blocks of all face-to-face communication. Whenever people communicate face to face, these building blocks structure their interaction. This argument may be hard to swallow because it runs counter to common sense. After all, we typically think of our interactions as outcomes of our emotional states. For example, we interact differently with people depending on whether they love us, make us angry, or make us laugh. More precisely, we usually think of emotions as deeply personal states of mind that are evoked involuntarily and result in uncontrollable action. We all know that nobody loves, gets angry, or laughs in quite the same way as anyone else; and literature and the movies are full of stories about how love, anger, and laughter often seem to happen by chance and easily spill outside the boundaries of our control. So can we truthfully say that norms, roles, and statuses shape our interactions? We answer this question in the affirmative in the next section. As you will see, our emotions are not as unique, involuntary, and uncontrollable as we are often led to believe. Underlying the turbulence of emotional life is a measure of order and predictability governed by sociological principles.

Just as building blocks need cement to hold them together, norms, roles, and statuses require a sort of "social cement" to prevent them from falling apart and to turn them into a durable social structure. What is the nature of the cement that holds the building blocks of social life together? Asked differently, exactly how is social interaction maintained? This is the most fundamental sociological question we can ask, for it is really a question about how social structures and society as a whole are at all possible. There are three main ways of maintaining social interaction and thereby cementing social structures and society as a whole: by means of domination, competition, and cooperation. In this chapter's second section, we investigate each of these modes of interaction in detail. First, however, we turn to the problem of emotions, beginning with laughter and humour.

THE SOCIOLOGY OF EMOTIONS

Laughter and Humour

> Every joke is a tiny revolution.
> — George Orwell

Robert Provine (2000) and his research assistants eavesdropped on 1200 conversations of people laughing in public places, such as, shopping malls. When they heard someone laughing, they recorded who laughed (the speaker, the listener, or both) and the gender of the speaker and the listener. To simplify things, they eavesdropped only on two-person groups, or *dyads*.

Provine found that in general, speakers laugh more often than listeners do (79.8 percent vs. 54.7 percent of incidents; percentages do not total 100 percent because the speaker, the audience, or both may laugh during an incident). Moreover, interesting patterns emerged when Provine considered the gender of the speaker and the listener. Women, it turns out, laugh more than men in everyday conversations. The biggest discrepancy in laughing occurs when the speaker is a woman and the listener is a man. In such cases, women laugh more than twice as often as men do (88.1 percent vs. 38.9 percent). However, even when a man speaks and a woman listens, the woman is more likely to laugh than the man is (71 percent vs. 66 percent). In contrast, men get more laughs from their audiences than women do. Not surprisingly in light of this finding, only about 6 percent of standup comics in North America are women.

Some people might think Provine's findings confirm the stereotype of the giggling female. Others might interpret his data as confirming the view that when dealing with men, women have more to laugh at. A sociologist, however, would notice that the gender distribution of laughter fits a more general pattern. In social situations where people of different statuses interact, laughter is unevenly distributed across the status hierarchy. People with higher status get more laughs and people with lower status laugh more, which is perhaps why class clowns are nearly always boys. It is also why a classic sociological study of laughter among staff members in a psychiatric hospital discovered "downward humour" (Coser, 1960). At a series of staff meetings, the psychiatrists averaged 7.5 witticisms, the residents averaged 5.5, and the paramedics averaged a mere 0.7. Moreover, the psychiatrists most often made the residents the target of their humour whereas the residents and the paramedics targeted the patients or themselves. Laughter in everyday life, it turns out, is not as spontaneous as we may think. It is often a signal of dominance or subservience.

Much social interaction takes place among status equals—among members of the same national or racial group, for example. If status equals enjoy a privileged position in the larger society, they often direct their humour at perceived social inferiors. Canadians tell "Newfie" jokes. White Americans of Northern European origin make jokes about "Polacks" and blacks. The English laugh about the Irish and, more recently, the Welsh. The French howl at the Belgians. And the Russians make jokes about the impoverished and oppressed Chukchi people of northern Siberia. ("When a Chukchi man comes back from hunting, first he wants his supper on the table. Then he wants to make love to his wife. Then he wants to take off his skis.") Similarly, when people point out that the only good thing about having Alzheimer's disease is that you can hide your own Easter eggs, they are making a joke about a socially marginal and powerless group. This sort of joke is appropriately called a putdown. It has the effect of excluding outsiders, making you feel superior, and reinforcing group norms and the status hierarchy itself.

"Ain't nothing more horrifying than a bunch of poor white people," Chris Rock once quipped. "They blame n—— for everything. . . . 'Space shuttle blew up! Them damn n——, that's what it was!" Chris Rock is, of course, an African American, a member of a group that is disadvantaged in American society. Disadvantaged people often laugh at the privileged majority, but not always. Nation of Islam leader Louis Farrakhan organized the Million Man March in Washington, D.C., in 1996 as a celebration of black solidarity and pride. One of the speakers at the march was Marion Barry, the black mayor of Washington, D.C., who had been arrested on cocaine charges six years earlier. Here is what Chris Rock had to say about the incident in front of a black Washington audience: "Marion Barry at the Million Man March. You know what that means? That means even at our finest hour, we had a crackhead onstage!" (Farley, 1998). When members of disadvantaged groups are not laughing at the privileged majority, they are typically laughing at themselves.

People sometimes direct humour against government. Some scholars argue that the more repressive a government and the less free its mass media, the more widespread antigovernment jokes are (Davies, 1998). For instance, under communism in the Soviet

Union (1917–91), telling antigovernment jokes became a favourite pastime. (Q: We always hear that communism is on the horizon. What is communism? A: Communism is a society free from exploitation, a happy future where nobody lives in want. Q: Then what is a horizon? A: A horizon is an imaginary line that keeps moving further away as we get closer.) Sometimes, humour merely has a political edge, "political" here being understood broadly as having to do with the distribution of power and privilege in society. (During the 2000 U.S. presidential campaign, George W. Bush attended an $800-a-plate fundraiser and came up with one of his funniest lines ever: "This is an impressive crowd—the haves and the have-mores. Some people call you the elites; I call you my base.") And sometimes, humour seems to have no political content at all; one would be hard pressed to discern the political significance of a chicken crossing a road to get to the other side. Yet in a sense all jokes, even those about chickens crossing the road, are "little revolutions," as George Orwell once remarked, for all jokes invert or pervert reality. They suddenly and briefly let us see beyond the serious, taken-for-granted world. Analyzed sociologically, jokes even enable us to see the structure of society that lies just beneath our laughter (Zijderveld, 1983).

Members of disadvantaged groups often poke fun at themselves. That is how Chris Rock gets many of his laughs.

Emotion Management

> My marriage ceremony was chaos, unreal, completely different than I imagined it would be. . . . My sister didn't help me get dressed or flatter me, and no one in the dressing room helped until I asked. I was depressed. I wanted to be so happy on our wedding day. I never ever dreamed how anyone could cry at their wedding. . . . [Then] from down the long aisle we looked at each other's eyes. His love for me changed my whole being from that point. When we joined arms I was relieved. The tension was gone. From then on, it was beautiful.
>
> I was in the sixth grade at the time my grandfather died. I remember being called to the office of the school where my mother was on the phone from New York (I was in California). She told me what had happened and all I said was, "Oh." I went back to class and a friend asked me what had happened and I said, "Nothing." I remember wanting very much just to cry and tell everyone what had happened. But a boy doesn't cry in the sixth grade for fear of being called a sissy. So I just went along as if nothing happened while deep down inside I was very sad and full of tears. (quoted in Hochschild, 1983: 59–60, 67)

Some scholars think that emotions are like the common cold. In both cases, an external disturbance causes a reaction that we experience involuntarily. The external disturbance may involve exposure to a particular virus that causes us to catch cold or exposure to a grizzly bear attack that causes us to experience fear. In either case, we cannot control our body's patterned response. Emotions, like colds, just happen to us (Thoits, 1989: 319).

The trouble with this argument is that we can and often do control our emotions. Emotions do not just happen to us; we manage them. If a grizzly bear attacks you in the woods, you can run as fast as your legs will carry you or you can calm yourself, lie down, play dead, and silently pray for the best. You are more likely to survive the grizzly bear attack if you control your emotions and follow the second strategy.[1] You will also temper your fear with a new emotion: hope (see Figure 5.3 on page 132).

When we manage our emotions, we tend to follow certain cultural "scripts," like the culturally transmitted knowledge that lying down and playing dead gives you a better chance of surviving a grizzly bear attack. That is, we usually know the culturally designated emotional response to a particular external stimulus and we try to respond appropriately. If we don't succeed in achieving the culturally appropriate emotional response, we are likely to feel guilty, disappointed, or (as in the case of the grizzly bear attack) something much worse.

The reminiscences quoted at the beginning of this section illustrate typical emotional response processes. In the first case, the bride knew she was not experiencing her wedding

FIGURE 5.3

How We Get Emotional

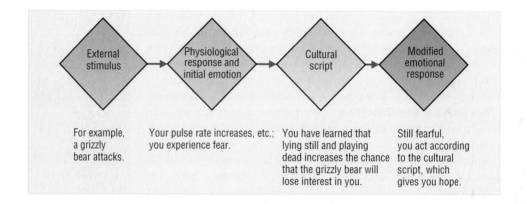

External stimulus

For example, a grizzly bear attacks.

Physiological response and initial emotion

Your pulse rate increases, etc.; you experience fear.

Cultural script

You have learned that lying still and playing dead increases the chance that the grizzly bear will lose interest in you.

Modified emotional response

Still fearful, you act according to the cultural script, which gives you hope.

day the way she was supposed to, that is, the way her culture defined as appropriate. So by an act of will she locked eyes with the groom and pulled herself out of her depression. In the second case, the schoolboy entirely repressed his grief over his grandfather's death so as not to appear as a "sissy" in front of his classmates. As these examples suggest, emotions pervade all social interaction but they are not, as we commonly believe, spontaneous and uncontrollable reactions to external stimuli. Rather, the norms of our culture and the expectations of the people around us pattern our emotions.

Sociologist Arlie Russell Hochschild is one of the leading figures in the study of **emotion management**. In fact, she coined the term. She argues that emotion management involves people obeying "feeling rules" and responding appropriately to the situations in which they find themselves (Hochschild, 1979, 1983). So, for example, people talk about the "right" to feel angry and they acknowledge that they "should" have mourned a relative's death more deeply. We have conventional expectations not only about what we should feel but also about how much we should feel, how long we should feel it, and with whom we should share our feelings. Moreover, feeling rules vary from one category of the population to the next. For example, Hochschild claims that "women, Protestants, and middle-class people cultivate the habit of suppressing their own feelings more than men, Catholics, and lower-class people do" (Hochschild, 1983: 57). This variation exists because our culture invites women to focus more on feeling than on action and men to focus more on action than on feeling. Similarly, Protestantism invites people to participate in an inner dialogue with God whereas the Catholic Church offers sacrament and confession, which allow and even encourage the expression of feeling. Finally, more middle-class than lower-class people are employed in service occupations in which the management of emotions is an important part of the job. Hence they are more adept at suppressing their own feelings.

Emotion management involves people obeying "feeling rules" and responding appropriately to the situations in which they find themselves.

Emotion labour is emotion management that many people do as part of their job and for which they are paid.

A Catholic priest taking confession

Emotion Labour

Hochschild distinguishes emotion management (which everyone does in their personal life) from **emotion labour** (which many people do as part of their job and for which they are paid). For example, teachers, sales clerks, nurses, and flight attendants must be experts in emotion labour. They spend a considerable part of their work time dealing with other people's misbehaviour, anger, rudeness, and unreasonable demands. They spend another part of their work time in what is essentially promotional and public relations work on behalf of the organizations that employ them. In all these tasks, they carefully manage their own emotions while trying to render their clientele happy and orderly. Hochschild estimates that in the United States, nearly half the jobs women do and one-fifth of the jobs men do involve substantial amounts of emotion labour.

Across occupations, different types of emotion labour are required. According to Hochschild, the flight attendant and the bill collector represent two extremes. If an appropriate motto for the flight attendant is "please, placate, and promote," the bill collector's motto might be "control, coerce, and collect." Flight attendants seek to smooth ruffled feathers, ensure comfort and safety, and encourage passengers to fly the same airline on their next trip. But as Hochschild found when she studied a debt collection office, bill collectors seek to get debtors riled up, ensure their discomfort, and intimidate them to the point where they pay what they owe. As the head of the office once shouted to his employees, "I don't care if it's Christmas or what goddamn holiday! You tell those people to get that money in!" Or on another occasion, "Can't you get madder than *that*? Create alarm!" (quoted in Hochschild, 1983: 141, 146).

Notwithstanding this variation, all jobs requiring emotion labour have in common the fact that "they allow the employer, through training and supervision, to exercise a degree of control over the emotional activities of employees" (Hochschild, 1983: 147). Moreover, as the focus of the economy shifts from the production of goods to the production of services, the market for emotion labour grows. More and more people are selected, trained, and paid for their skills in emotion labour. Emotion labour becomes a commodity that employers buy in much the same way as a furniture manufacturer buys fabric to upholster chairs. The emotional life of workers—or at least the way they openly express their feelings—is increasingly governed by the organizations for which they work and is therefore less and less spontaneous and authentic.

Emotions in Historical Perspective

Social structure impinges on emotional experiences in many ways. As we have seen, status hierarchies influence patterns of laughter. Cultural scripts and the expectations of others influence the way we manage our emotions in our personal lives. The growth of the economy's service sector requires more emotion labour, turns it into a commodity, and decreases the ability of people to experience emotions spontaneously and authentically. In these and other ways, the common-sense view of emotions as unique, spontaneous, uncontrollable, authentic, natural, and perhaps even rooted in biology proves to be misguided.

We can glean additional evidence of the impact of society on our emotional life from historical studies. It turns out that feeling rules take different forms under different social conditions, which vary historically. Three examples from the social history of emotions help illustrate the point:

- *Grief.* Among other factors, the crude death rate (the annual number of deaths per 1000 people in a population) helps determine our experience of grief (Lofland, 1985). In Europe as late as 1600, life expectancy was only 35 years. Many infants died at birth or in their first year of life. Infectious diseases decimated populations. The medical profession was in its infancy. The risk of losing family members, especially babies, was thus much greater than today. One result of this situation was that people invested less emotionally in their children than we typically do. Their grief response to the death of children was shorter and less intense than ours is; the mourning period was briefer and people became less distraught. As health conditions improved and the infant mortality rate fell over the years, emotional investment in children increased. It intensified especially in the nineteenth century when women starting having fewer babies on average as a result of industrialization (see Chapter 20, Population and Urbanization). As emotional investment in children increased, grief response to children's deaths intensified and lasted longer.
- *Anger.* Industrialization and the growth of competitive markets in nineteenth-century North America and Europe turned the family into an emotional haven from a world increasingly perceived as heartless (see Chapter 15, Families). In keeping with the enhanced emotional function of the family, anger control, particularly by women, became increasingly important for the establishment of a harmonious household. The early twentieth century witnessed mounting labour unrest and the growth of the service sector. Avoiding anger thus

Manners in Europe during the Middle Ages were disgusting by our standards today.

became an important labour relations goal. This trend influenced family life too. Child-rearing advice manuals increasingly stressed the importance of teaching children how to control their anger (Stearns and Stearns, 1985, 1986).

• *Disgust.* Manners in Europe in the Middle Ages were disgusting by our standards. Even the most refined aristocrats spat in public and belched shamelessly during banquets (with the King in attendance, no less). Members of high society did not flinch at scratching themselves and passing gas at the dinner table, where they ate with their hands and speared food with knives. What was acceptable then causes revulsion now because feeling rules have changed. Specifically, manners began to change with the emergence of the modern political state, especially after 1700. The modern political state raised armies and collected taxes, imposed languages, and required loyalty. All this coordination of effort necessitated more self-control on the part of the citizenry. Changes in standards of public conduct—signalled by the introduction of the fork, the nightdress, the handkerchief, the spittoon, and the chamber pot—accompanied the rise of the modern state. Good manners also served to define who had power and who lacked it. For example, there is nothing inherently well mannered about a father sitting at the head of the table carving the turkey and children waiting to speak until they are spoken to. These rules about the difference between good manners and improper behaviour were created to signify the distribution of power in the family by age and gender (Elias, 1994 [1939]; Scott, 1998).

We thus see that although emotions form an important part of all social interactions, they are neither universal nor constant. They have histories and deep sociological under-pinnings in statuses, roles, and norms. Bearing these important lessons in mind, we now turn to the second main task of this chapter, analyzing the "social cement" that binds together the building blocks of social life and turns them into durable social structures.

MODES OF SOCIAL INTERACTION

Interaction as Competition and Exchange

Have you ever been in a conversation where you couldn't get a word in edgewise? If you are like most people, this situation is bound to happen occasionally. The longer this kind of one-sided conversation persists, the more neglected you feel. You may make increasingly less subtle attempts to turn the conversation your way. But if you fail, you may decide to end the interaction altogether. If this experience repeats itself—if the person you are talking to consistently monopolizes conversations—you are likely to want to avoid getting into conversations with him or her in the future. Maintaining interaction (and maintaining a relationship) requires that both parties' need for attention is met.

Most people do not consistently try to monopolize conversations. If they did, there wouldn't be much talk in the world. In fact, turn-taking is one of the basic norms that govern conversations; people literally take turns talking to make conversation possible. Nonetheless, a remarkably large part of all conversations involves a subtle competition for attention. Consider the following snippet of dinner conversation:

John: "I'm feeling really starved."
Mary: "Oh, I just ate."
John: "Well, I'm feeling really starved."
Mary: "When was the last time you ate?"

Charles Derber recorded this conversation (Derber, 1979: 24). John starts by saying how hungry he is. The attention is on him. Mary replies that she is not hungry, and the attention shifts to her. John insists he is hungry, shifting attention back to him. Mary finally allows the conversation to focus on John by asking him when he last ate. John thus "wins" the competition for attention.

Derber recorded 1500 conversations in family homes, workplaces, restaurants, classrooms, dormitories, and therapy groups. He concluded that North Americans usually try to turn conversations toward themselves. They usually do so in ways that go unnoticed. Nonetheless, says Derber, the typical conversation is a covert competition for attention. In Derber's words (1979: 23), there exists

> a set of extremely common conversational practices which show an unresponsiveness to others' topics and involve turning them into one's own. Because of norms prohibiting blatantly egocentric behaviour, these practices are often exquisitely subtle. . . . Although conversationalists are free to introduce topics about themselves, they are expected to maintain an appearance of genuine interest in [topics] about others in a conversation. A delicate face-saving system requires that people refrain from openly disregarding others' concerns and keep expressions of disinterest from becoming visible.

You can observe the competition for attention yourself. Record a couple of minutes of conversation in your dorm, home, or workplace. Then play back the recording. Evaluate each statement in the conversation. Does the statement try to change who is the subject of the conversation? Or does it say something about the *other* conversationalists or ask them about what they said? How does not responding or merely saying "uh-huh" in response operate to shift attention? Are other conversational techniques especially effective in shifting attention? Who "wins" the conversation? What is the winner's gender, race, and class position? Is the winner popular or unpopular? Do you think a connection exists between the person's status in the group and his or her ability to win? You might even want to record yourself in conversation. Where do you fit in?

Derber is careful to point out that conversations are not winner-take-all competitions. Unless both people in a two-person conversation receive some attention, the interaction is likely to cease. As such, conversation typically involves the *exchange* of attention.

**WHERE DO
YOU FIT IN?**

Exchange and Rational Choice Theories

The idea that social interaction involves trade in attention and other valued resources is the central insight of **exchange theory** (Blau, 1964; Homans, 1961). Exchange theorists believe, as did the Beatles, that "in the end, the love you take is equal to the love you make." But not just love: social exchange theorists argue that all social relationships involve a literal give and take. From this point of view, when people interact, they exchange valued resources (including attention, pleasure, approval, prestige, information, and money) or punishments. With payoffs, relationships endure and can give rise to various organizational forms. Without payoffs, relationships end. Paradoxically, relationships

Exchange theory holds that social interaction involves trade in valued resources.

can also endure because *punishments* are exchanged. The classic case involves "tit-for-tat" violence, where one party to a conflict engages in violence, another party retaliates, the first party seeks revenge, and so on.

A variant of this approach is **rational choice theory** (Coleman, 1990; Hechter, 1987). Rational choice theory focuses less on the resources being exchanged than the way interacting people weigh the benefits and costs of interaction. According to rational choice theory, interacting people always try to maximize benefits and minimize costs. Businesspeople want to keep their expenses to a minimum so they can keep their profits as high as possible. Similarly, everyone wants to gain the most from their interactions—socially, emotionally, and economically—while paying the least.

Undoubtedly, we can explain many types of social interaction in terms of exchange and rational choice theories. However, some types of interaction cannot be explained in these terms. For example, people get little or nothing of value out of some relationships, yet they persist. Slaves remain slaves not because they are well paid or because they enjoy the work but because they are forced to do it. Some people remain in abusive relationships because their abusive partner keeps them socially isolated and psychologically dependent. They lack the resources needed to get out of the abusive relationship.

At the other extreme, people often act in ways they consider fair or just even if this does not maximize their personal gain (Frank, 1988; Gamson, Fireman, and Rytina, 1982). Some people even engage in altruistic or heroic acts from which they gain nothing. They do so even though altruism and heroism can sometimes place them at considerable risk. Consider a woman who hears a drowning man cry "help" and decides to risk her life to save him (Lewontin, 1991: 73–74). Some analysts assert that such a hero is willing to save the drowning man because she thinks the favour may be returned in the future. To us, this seems far-fetched. In the first place, the probability that today's rescuer will be drowning someday and that the man who is drowning today will be present to save her is close to zero. Second, a man who cannot swim well enough to save himself is just about the last person you would want to rescue you if the need arose. Third, heroes typically report they decide to act in an instant, before they have a chance to weigh any costs and benefits. Heroes respond to cries for help based on emotion (which, physiologists tell us, takes 1/125 of a second to register in the brain), not calculation (which takes seconds or even minutes).

When people behave fairly or altruistically, they are interacting with others based on *norms* they have learned—norms that say they should act justly and help people in need, even if substantial costs are attached. Such norms are for the most part ignored by exchange and rational choice theorists. Exchange and rational choice theorists assume that most of the norms governing social interaction are like the "norm of reciprocity." This norm states that you should try to do for others what they try to do for you, because if you do not, then others will stop doing things for you (Homans, 1950). But social life is richer than this narrow view suggests. Interaction is not all selfishness. One researcher found that first-year sociology and economics majors were equally "selfish," but by the time they graduated, the economics majors were much more likely than the sociology majors to consider "selfish" actions natural and normal (Frank, 1988). Clearly, what we learn has an impact on our norms and expectations regarding social interaction.

Moreover, as you will now see, we cannot assume what people want because norms (as well as roles and statuses) are not presented to us fully formed. Nor do we mechanically accept norms when they are presented to us. Instead, we constantly negotiate and modify norms—as well as roles and statuses—as we interact with others. We will now explore this theme by considering the ingenious ways in which people manage the impressions they give to others during social interaction.

Rational choice theory focuses on the way interacting people weigh the benefits and costs of interaction. According to rational choice theory, interacting people always try to maximize benefits and minimize costs.

Interaction as Symbolic

The best way of impressing [advisers] with your competence is asking questions you know the answer to. Because if they ever put it back on you, "Well what do you think?" then you can tell them what you think and you'd give a very intelligent answer because you knew it. You didn't ask it to find out information. You ask it to impress people.

— A third-year medical student

Soon after they enter medical school, students become adept at managing the impression they make on other people. As Jack Haas and William Shaffir (1987) show in their study of professional socialization at McMaster University's medical school in Hamilton, students adopt a new medical vocabulary and wear a white lab coat to set themselves apart from patients. They try to model their behaviour after that of doctors who have authority over them. They may ask questions to which they know the answers so that they can impress their teachers. When dealing with patients, they may hide their ignorance under medical jargon to maintain their authority. By engaging in these and related practices, medical students reduce the distance between their pre-medical-school selves and the role of doctor. By the time they finish medical school, they have reduced the distance so much that they no longer see any difference between who they are and the role of doctor. They come to take for granted a fact they once had to socially construct—the fact that they are doctors (Haas and Shaffir, 1987: 53–83).

Haas and Shaffir's study is an application of symbolic interactionism, a theoretical approach introduced in Chapter 1. Symbolic interactionists regard people as active, creative, and self-reflective. Whereas exchange theorists assume what people want, symbolic interactionists argue that people create meanings and desires in the course of social interaction. According to Herbert Blumer (1969), symbolic interactionism is based on three principles. First, "human beings act toward things on the basis of the meaning which these things have for them." Second, "the meaning of a thing" emerges from the process of social interaction. Third, "the use of meanings by the actors occurs through a process of interpretation" (Blumer, 1969: 2; see also Berger and Luckmann, 1966; Strauss, 1993).

Dramaturgical Analysis: Role-Playing

Although there are several distinct approaches to symbolic interactionism (Denzin, 1992), probably the most widely applied approach is **dramaturgical analysis**. As first developed by sociologist Erving Goffman (1959), dramaturgical analysis takes literally Shakespeare's line from *As You Like It*: "All the world's a stage and all the men and women merely players."

From Goffman's point of view, we are constantly engaged in role-playing. This is most evident when we are "front stage," that is, in public settings. Just as being front stage in a drama requires the use of props, set gestures, and memorized lines, so does acting in public space. A server in a restaurant, for example, must dress in a uniform, smile, and recite fixed lines. ("How are you? My name is Sam and I'm your server today. May I get you a drink before you order your meal?") When the server goes "backstage," he or she can relax from the front stage performance and discuss it with fellow actors ("Those kids at table six are driving me nuts!"). Thus, we often distinguish between our public roles and our "true" selves. Note, however, that even backstage we engage in role-playing and impression management. It's just that we are less likely to be aware of it. For instance, in the kitchen, a server may try to present herself in the best possible light to impress another server so that she can eventually ask him out. Thus, the implication of dramaturgical analysis is that there is no single self, just the ensemble of roles we play in various social contexts (see Box 5.1 on page 138). Servers in restaurants play many roles off the job. They play on basketball teams, sing in church choirs, and hang out with friends at shopping malls. Each role is governed by norms about what kinds of clothes to wear, what kind of conversation to engage in, and so on. We play on many front stages in everyday life.

We do not always do so enthusiastically. If a role is stressful, we may engage in role distancing. **Role distancing** involves giving the impression that we are just "going through the motions" but actually lack serious commitment to a role. Thus, when people think a role they are playing is embarrassing or beneath them, they typically want to give their peers the impression that the role is not their "true" self. My parents force me to sing in the church choir; I'm working at McDonald's just to earn a few extra dollars, but I'll be going back to college next semester; this old car I'm driving is just a loaner—these are the kinds of rationalizations people offers when distancing themselves from a role.

Dramaturgical analysis views social interaction as a sort of play in which people present themselves so that they appear in the best possible light.

Role distancing involves giving the impression that we are just "going through the motions" but actually lack serious commitment to a role.

BOX 5.1
Sociology at the Movies

TAKE   ROLL

Miss Congeniality (2000)

Scene: A New Jersey schoolyard in 1982. An eight-year-old schoolyard bully is picking a fight with another, smaller boy. Unexpectedly, a girl comes to the rescue, telling the bully to back off. The following dialogue ensues:

Bully: "If you weren't a girl I'd beat your face off."
Girl: "If you weren't a girl I'd beat your face off.'
Bully: "You calling me a girl?"
Girl: "You called me one."

Whereupon the bully takes a swing at the girl, which she neatly evades, and she proceeds to deck him. She then approaches the other boy and says sweetly:

Girl: "Forget those guys. They're just jealous. You're funny. You're smart. Girls like that."
Other Boy: "Well I don't like you. Now everyone thinks I need a girl to fight for me. You are a dork brain."

Girl punches other boy in nose. End of scene.

Almost predictably, the girl grows up to become a tough-talking and tomboyish undercover agent (played by Sandra Bullock) with a chronic boyfriend problem: She doesn't have one and can't get one. Little wonder. She snorts when she laughs. She clomps instead of walking. She is the very opposite of glamorous.

The plot thickens when Bullock's character is forced to take an undercover

Sandra Bullock in Miss Congeniality (2000)

assignment as a contestant in a beauty contest. Someone is plotting a terrorist act during the pageant and she has to find out who it is. First, however, she has to undergo a role change, something far deeper than a mere makeover. A beauty consultant (played by Michael Caine) teaches her how to walk like most women, wear makeup, and dress to kill. In her interaction with the other contestants, she begins to learn how to behave in a conventionally feminine way. She even becomes a finalist in the beauty pageant. In the end, she gets the bad guy, captures the heart of the handsome FBI agent (played by Benjamin Bratt), and wins the pageant's "Miss Congeniality" award. Her true self

emerges and everyone goes home happy.

This is not the first movie in which Sandra Bullock plays an unglamorous woman who undergoes such a transformation. In *While You Were Sleeping* (1995), she is a lonely Chicago subway toll collector who spends most of her time with her cat but eventually turns into a captivating woman who wins her Prince Charming. Nor does Sandra Bullock have a monopoly on this theme, which is at least as old as Cinderella. In Hollywood as in fairy tales, the emergence of the "true self" is often the resolution of the conflict that animates the story.

Life rarely comes in such neat packages. The sociological study of social interaction shows how we balance different selves in front stage and backstage performances, play many roles simultaneously, get pulled in different directions by role strain and role conflict, and distance ourselves from some of our roles. To make matters even more complex and dynamic, sociology underlines how we continually enter new stages, roles, conflicts, strains, and distancing manoeuvres as we mature. This social complexity makes our "true self" not a thing we discover once and for all time but a work in progress. The resolution of every conflict that animates our lives is temporary. *Miss Congeniality* is an entertaining escape from reality's messiness but a poor guide to life as we actually live it. For that we need sociology.

Ethnomethodology

Goffman's view of social interaction seems cynical. He portrays people as inauthentic, or constantly playing roles but never really being themselves. His mindset is not much different from that of Holden Caulfield, the antihero of J. D. Salinger's *The Catcher in the Rye*. To Holden Caulfield, all adults seem "phony," "hypocritical," and "fake," constantly pretending to be people they are not.

However discomforting Goffman's cynicism may be, we should not overlook his valuable sociological point: The stability of social life depends on our adherence to norms, roles, and statuses. If that adherence broke down, social life would become chaotic. Take something as simple as walking down a busy street. Hordes of pedestrians rush toward you yet rarely collide with you. Collision is avoided because of a norm that nobody actually teaches and few people are aware of but almost everyone follows. If someone blocks your way, you move to the right. When you move to the right and the person walking toward you moves to the right (which is your left), you avoid bumping into each other. Similarly, consider the norm of "civil inattention." When we pass people in public, we may establish momentary eye contact out of friendliness but we usually look away quickly. According to Goffman, such a gesture is a "ritual" of respect, a patterned and expected action that affirms our respect for strangers. Just imagine what would happen if you fixed your stare at a stranger for a few seconds longer than the norm. Rather than being seen as respectful, your intention might be viewed as rude, intrusive, or hostile. Thus, we would not even be able to walk down a street in peace were it not for the existence of certain unstated norms. These and many other norms, some explicit and some not, make an orderly social life possible (Goffman, 1963, 1971).

By emphasizing how we construct social reality in the course of interaction, symbolic interactionists downplay the importance of norms and understandings that *precede* any given interaction. **Ethnomethodology** tries to correct this shortcoming. Ethnomethodology is the study of the methods ordinary people use, often unconsciously, to make sense of what others do and say. Ethnomethodologists stress that everyday interactions could not take place without *preexisting* shared norms and understandings. The norm of moving to the right to avoid bumping into an oncoming pedestrian and the norm of civil inattention are both examples of preexisting shared norms and understandings.

> **Ethnomethodology is the study of how people make sense of what others do and say by adhering to preexisting norms.**

To illustrate the importance of preexisting shared norms and understandings, Harold Garfinkel conducted a series of experiments. In one such experiment he asked one of his students to interpret a casual greeting in an unexpected way (Garfinkel, 1967: 44):

> Acquaintance: [waving cheerily] How are you?
> Student: How am I in regard to what? My health, my finances, my schoolwork, my peace of mind, my . . .?
> Acquaintance: [red in the face and suddenly out of control] Look! I was just trying to be polite. Frankly, I don't give a damn how you are.

As this example shows, social interaction requires tacit agreement between the actors about what is normal and expected. Without shared norms and understandings, no sustained interaction can occur. People are likely to get upset and end an interaction when someone violates the assumptions underlying the stability and meaning of daily life.

Assuming the existence of shared norms and understandings, let us now inquire briefly into the way people communicate in face-to-face interaction. This issue may seem trivial. However, as you will soon see, having a conversation is actually a wonder of intricate complexity. Even today's most advanced supercomputer cannot conduct a natural-sounding conversation with a person (Kurzweil, 1999: 61, 91).

Verbal and Nonverbal Communication

Fifty years ago an article appeared in the British newspaper *News Chronicle,* trumpeting the invention of an electronic translating device at the University of London. According to the article, "[a]s fast as [a user] could type the words in, say, French, the equivalent in Hungarian or Russian would issue forth on the tape" (quoted in Silberman, 2000: 225). The report was an exaggeration, to put it mildly. It soon became a standing joke that if you ask a computer to translate "The spirit is willing, but the flesh is weak" into Russian, the output would read "The vodka is good, but the steak is lousy." Today, we are closer to high-quality machine translation than we were in the 1950s. However, a practical Universal Translator exists only on *Star Trek.*

The Social Context of Language

The main problem with computerized translation systems is that computers find it difficult to make sense of the *social and cultural context* in which language is used. The same words may mean different things in different settings, so computers, lacking contextual cues, routinely botch translations. For this reason metaphors are notoriously problematic for computers. The following machine translation, which contains both literal and metaphorical text, illustrates this point:

English original:

Babel Fish is a computerized translation system (at http://babelfish.yahoo.com) that is available on the World Wide Web. You can type a passage in a window and receive a nearly instant translation in one of twelve languages. Simple, literal language is translated fairly accurately. But when understanding requires an appreciation of social context, as most of our everyday speech does, the computer can quickly get you into a pickle. What a drag!

Machine translation from English to French:

Le poisson de Babel est un système de traduction automatisé qui est disponible sur le World Wide Web http://babelfish.yahoo.com. Vous pouvez taper un passage dans un Window et recevoir une traduction presque instantanée dans un de douze langages. Le langage simple et littéral est traduit assez exactement. Mais quand la compréhension exige une appréciation de contexte social, en tant que majeure partie de notre discours journalier, l'ordinateur peut rapidement vous entrer dans des conserves au vinaigre. Quelle drague!

Machine translation from French back to English:

The fish of Babel is an automated system of the translation that is available in the World Wide Web http://babelfish.yahoo.com. You can press a passage in a Window and receive an almost immediate translation in one of twelve languages. The simple, literal language is translated rather exactly. But when the understanding requires an esteem of the social context, like most of our daily speech, the computer can obtain to him in a brine quickly. One what friction!

Despite the complexity involved in accurate translation, human beings are much better at it than computers are. Why is this so? A hint comes from computers themselves. Machine translation works best when applications are restricted to a single social context—say, weather forecasting or oil exploration. In such cases, specialized vocabularies and meanings specific to the context of interest can be built into the program. Ambiguity is thus reduced and computers can "understand" the meaning of words well enough to translate them with reasonable accuracy. Similarly, humans must be able to reduce ambiguity and make sense of words to become good translators. They do so by learning the nuances of meaning in different cultural and social contexts over an extended time.

Mastery of one's own language happens the same way. People are able to understand one another not just because they are able to learn words—computers can do that well enough—but because they can learn the social and cultural contexts that give words meaning. The meaning of "Don't play with rough boys" would be ambiguous to a computer, but a five-year-old human would take just milliseconds to figure out that his mother isn't asking him to find smooth boys to play with (Miller, 2001). People are greatly assisted in the task of removing ambiguity from social and cultural contexts by *nonverbal* cues.

Let us linger for a moment on the question of how nonverbal cues enhance meaning. Sociologists, anthropologists, and psychologists have identified numerous nonverbal means of communication that establish context and meaning. The most important types of nonverbal communication involve the use of facial expressions, gestures, body language, and status cues.

Facial Expressions, Gestures, and Body Language

The April 2000 issue of *Cosmopolitan* magazine featured an article advising female readers on "how to reduce otherwise evolved men to drooling, panting fools." Basing his analysis on the work of several psychologists, the author of the article first urges readers to "[d]elete the old-school seductress image (smoky eyes, red lips, brazen stare) from your consciousness." Then, he writes, you must "[u]pload a new inner temptress who's equal parts good girl and wild child." This involves several steps, including the following:

1. Establish eye contact by playing sexual peek-a-boo. Gaze at him, look away, peek again, and so on. By interrupting the intensity of your gaze, you heighten his anticipation of the next glance. The trick is to hold his gaze long enough to rouse his interest yet briefly enough to make him want more. Three seconds of gazing followed by five seconds of looking away seems to be the ideal.

2. Sit down with your legs crossed to emphasize their shapeliness. Your toes should be pointed toward the man who interests you and should reach inside the one-metre (three-foot) "territorial bubble" that defines his personal space.

3. Speak quietly. The more softly you speak, the more intently he must listen. Speaking just above a whisper will grab his full attention and force him to remain fixed on you.

4. Invade his personal space and enter his "intimate zone" by finding an excuse to touch him. Picking a piece of lint off his jacket and then leaning in to tell him in a whisper what you've done ought to do the trick. Then you can tell him how much you like his cologne.

5. Raise your arm to flip your hair. The gesture subliminally beckons him forward.

6. Finally, smile—and when you do, tilt your head to reveal your neck because he'll find it exciting (Willardt, 2000).

If things progress, another article in the same issue of Cosmopolitan explains how you can read his body language to tell whether he is lying (Dutton, 2000).

Whatever we may think of the soundness of *Cosmopolitan*'s advice or the image of women and men it tries to reinforce, this example drives home the point that social interaction typically involves a complex mix of verbal and nonverbal messages. The face alone is capable of more than 1000 distinct expressions reflecting the whole range of human emotion. Arm movements, hand gestures, posture, and other aspects of body language send many more messages to an audience (Wood, 1999; see Figure 5.4 on page 142).

Despite the wide variety of facial expressions in the human repertoire, most researchers believed until recently that the facial expressions of six emotions are similar across cultures. These six emotions are happiness, sadness, anger, disgust, fear, and surprise (Ekman, 1978). A smile, it was believed, looks and means the same to advertising executives in Manhattan and members of an isolated tribe in Papua New Guinea. Researchers concluded that the facial expressions that express these basic emotions are reflexes rather than learned responses.

Since the mid-1990s, however, some researchers have questioned whether a universally recognized set of facial expressions reflects basic human emotions. Among other things, critics have argued that "facial expressions are not the readout of emotions but displays that serve social motives and are mostly determined by the presence of an audience" (Fernandez-Dols, Sanchez, Carrera, and Ruiz-Belda, 1997: 163). From this point of view, a smile will reflect pleasure if it serves a person's interest to present a smiling face to his or her audience. Conversely, a person may be motivated to conceal anxiety by smiling or to conceal pleasure by suppressing a smile.

Some people are better at deception than others. Most people find it hard to deceive others because facial expressions are hard to control. If you have ever tried to stop yourself from blushing you will know what we mean. Sensitive analysts of human affairs—not just sociologists trained in the fine points of symbolic interaction but also police detectives, lawyers, and other specialists in deception—can often see through phony performances. They know that a crooked smile, a smile that lasts too long, or a smile that fades too quickly may suggest that something fishy is going on beneath the superficial level of impression management. Still, smooth operators can fool experts. Moreover, experts can be mistaken. Crooked smiles and the like may be the result of innocent nervousness, not deception.

No gestures or body postures mean the same thing in all societies and all cultures. In our society, people point with an outstretched hand and an extended finger. However, people

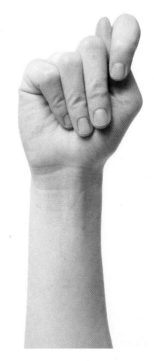

Like many hand gestures, the "fig" means different things in different times and places. We probably know it as a sign that adults make when they play with children and pretend "I've got your nose." But in ancient Rome, the fig was meant to convey good luck, in India it represents a threat, and in Russia, Turkey, and South Korea it means "screw you." It means "T" in the American Sign Language alphabet, but it had to be modified in the International Sign Language alphabet to avoid giving offence.

FIGURE 5.4
Body Language

Among other things, body language communicates the degree to which people conform to gender roles, or widely shared expectations about how males or females are supposed to act. In these photos, which postures suggest power and aggressiveness? Which suggest pleasant compliance? Which are "appropriate" to the gender of the person?

raised in other cultures tip their head or use their chin or eyes to point out something. We nod our heads "yes" and shake "no," but others nod "no" and shake "yes."

Finally, we must note that in all societies people communicate by manipulating the space that separates them from others (Hall, 1959, 1966). This point is well illustrated in our *Cosmopolitan* example, where women are urged to invade a man's "personal space" and "intimate zone" to arouse his interest. Sociologists commonly distinguish four zones that surround us. The size of these zones varies from one society to the next. In North America, an intimate zone extends about 45 centimetres (18 inches) from the body. It is restricted to people with whom we want sustained, intimate physical contact. A personal zone extends from about 45 centimetres (18 inches) to 1.2 metres (4 feet) away. It is reserved for friends and acquaintances. We tolerate only a little physical intimacy from such people. The social zone is situated in the area roughly 1.2 metres (4 feet) to 3.7 metres (12 feet) away from us. Apart from a handshake, no physical contact is permitted from people we restrict to this zone. The public zone starts around 3.7 metres (12 feet) from our bodies. It is used to distinguish a performer or a speaker from an audience.

Status Cues

Status cues are visual indicators of other people's social position.

Aside from facial expressions, gestures, and body language, a second type of nonverbal communication takes place by means of **status cues,** or visual indicators of other people's social position. Goffman (1959) observed that when individuals come into contact, they typically try to acquire information that will help them define the situation and make interaction easier. This goal is accomplished in part by attending to status cues. Elijah Anderson (1990) developed this idea by studying the way African Americans and European Americans interact on the street in two adjacent urban neighbourhoods. Members of both groups visually inspect strangers before concluding that they are not dangerous. They make assumptions about others on the basis of skin colour, age, gender, companions, clothing, jewellery, and the objects they carry with them. They evaluate the movements of strangers, the time of day, and other factors to establish how dangerous they might be. In general, children pass inspection easily. White women and white men are treated with greater caution, but not as much caution as African American women and African American men. Urban dwellers are most suspicious of African American male teenagers. People are most likely to interact verbally with individuals who are perceived as the safest.

Although status cues may be useful in helping people define the situation and thus greasing the wheels of social interaction, they also pose a social danger: Status cues can quickly degenerate into **stereotypes,** or rigid views of how members of various groups act regardless of whether individual group members really behave that way. Stereotypes create social barriers that impair interaction or prevent it altogether. For instance, some police officers routinely stop young black male drivers without cause to check for proper licensing, possession of illegal goods, and so on. In this case, a social cue has become a stereotype that guides police policy. Young black males, the great majority of whom never commit an illegal act, view this police practice as harassment. Racial stereotyping therefore helps to perpetuate the sometimes poor relations between the black community and law enforcement officials.

As these examples show, face-to-face interaction may at first glance appear to be straightforward and unproblematic. Most of the time it is. However, underlying the taken-for-granted surface of human communication is a wide range of cultural assumptions, unconscious understandings, and nonverbal cues that make interaction possible.

Power and Conflict Theories of Social Interaction

In our discussion of the social cement that binds statuses, roles, and norms together, we have made four main points:

1. One of the most important forces that cement social interaction is the competitive exchange of valued resources. People communicate to the degree that they get something valuable out of the interaction. Simultaneously, however, they must engage in a careful balancing act. If they compete too avidly and prevent others from getting much out of the social interaction, communication will break down. This is exchange and rational choice theory in a nutshell.

2. Nobody hands values, norms, roles, and statuses to us fully formed, nor do we accept them mechanically. We mould them to suit us as we interact with others. For example, we constantly engage in impression management so that others will see the roles we perform in the best possible light. This is a major argument of symbolic interactionism and its most popular variant, dramaturgical analysis.

3. Norms do not emerge entirely spontaneously during social interaction, either. In general form, they exist before any given interaction takes place. Indeed, sustained interaction would be impossible without preexisting shared understandings. This is the core argument of ethnomethodology.

4. Nonverbal mechanisms of communication greatly facilitate social interaction. These mechanisms include facial expressions, hand gestures, body language, and status cues.

We now want to highlight a final point that has been lurking in the background of our discussion. **Conflict theories of social interaction** emphasize that when people interact, their statuses are often arranged in a hierarchy. People on top enjoy more power than those on the bottom—that is, they are "in a position to carry out [their] own will despite resistance" (Weber, 1947: 152). In face-to-face communication, the degree of inequality strongly affects the character of social interaction between the interacting parties (Bourdieu, 1977 [1972]; Collins, 1982; Kemper, 1978, 1987; Molm, 1997).

We can clearly see how the distribution of power affects interaction by examining male–female interaction. Women are typically socialized to assume subordinate positions in

Stereotypes are rigid views of how members of various groups act, regardless of whether individual group members really behave that way.

Conflict theories of social interaction emphasize that when people interact, their statuses are often arranged in a hierarchy. Those on top enjoy more power than those on the bottom. The degree of inequality strongly affects the character of social interaction between the interacting parties.

life whereas men assume superordinate positions. As we saw in Chapter 4, Socialization, this distribution of power is evident in the way men usually learn to be aggressive and competitive and women learn to be cooperative and supportive (see also Chapter 11, Sexuality and Gender). Because of this learning, men often dominate conversations. Thus, conversation analyses conducted by Deborah Tannen show that men are more likely than women to engage in long monologues and interrupt when others are talking (Tannen, 1994a, 1994b; see Box 5.2). They are also less likely to ask for help or directions because doing so would imply a reduction in their authority. Much male–female conflict results from these differences. A stereotypical case is the lost male driver and the helpful female passenger. The female passenger, seeing that the male driver is lost, suggests that they stop and ask for directions. The male driver does not want to ask for directions because he thinks that would make him look incompetent. If both parties remain firm in their positions, an argument is bound to result.

Domination is a mode of interaction in which nearly all power is concentrated in the hands of people of similar status. Fear is the dominant emotion in systems of interaction based on domination.

Types of Interaction

To get a better grasp on the role of power in social interaction, let us consider two extreme cases and the case that lies at the midpoint between the extremes (Table 5.1). **Domination** represents one extreme type of interaction. In social interaction based on domination, nearly all power is concentrated in the hands of people of similar status, whereas people of different status enjoy

---

BOX 5.2
Social Policy: What Do You Think?

Allocating Time Fairly in Class Discussions

When John Lie was chair of the Department of Sociology at the University of Illinois (Urbana-Champaign), he often heard student complaints. Sometimes they were reasonable. Sometimes they were not. A particularly puzzling complaint came from a self-proclaimed feminist taking a women's studies class. She said, "The professor lets the male students talk in class. They don't seem to have done much of the reading, but the professor insists on letting them say something even when they don't really have anything to say." John later talked to the professor, who claimed she was only trying to let different opinions come out in class.

Policy debates often deal with important issues at the provincial or territorial, national, and international levels. However, they may revolve around everyday social interaction. For instance, as this chapter's discussion of Deborah Tannen's work suggests, gender differences in con-

versational styles have a big impact on gender inequality, and many professors use class participation to evaluate students. Your grade may depend in part on how often you speak up and whether you have something interesting to say. But Tannen's study suggests that men tend to speak up more often and more forcefully than women. Men are more likely to dominate classroom discussions. Therefore, does the evaluation of class participation in assigning grades unfairly penalize female students? If so, what policies can you recommend that might overcome the problem?

One possibility is to eliminate class participation as a criterion for student evaluation. However, most professors would object to this approach on the grounds that good discussions can demonstrate students' familiarity with course material, sharpen students' ability to reason logically, and enrich everyone's educational experience. A college or university lacking energetic discussion and debate would not be much of an educational institution.

A second option is to systematically encourage women to participate in classroom discussion. A third option is to allot equal time for women and men or to allot each student equal time. Criticisms of such an approach come readily to mind. Shouldn't time be allocated only to people who have done the reading and have something interesting to say? The woman who complained to John Lie made that point. Encouraging everyone to speak or forcing each student to speak for a certain number of minutes, even if they do not have something interesting to contribute, would probably be boring or frustrating for better-prepared students.

As you can see, the question of how time should be allocated in class discussions has no obvious solution. In general, the realm of interpersonal interaction and conversation is an extremely difficult area in which to impose rules and policies. So what should your professor do to ensure that class discussion time is allocated fairly?

| | **Mode of Cooperation** | | | |
Mode of Interaction	**Domination**	**Competition**	**Cooperation**	
Level of inequality	High	Medium	Low	
Characteristic emotion	Fear	Envy	Trust	
Efficiency	Low	Medium	High	

TABLE 5.1

Main Modes of Interaction

almost no power. Guards versus inmates in a concentration camp and landowners versus slaves on plantations in the antebellum South were engaged in social interaction based on domination. In extreme cases of domination, subordinates live in a state of near-constant fear.

The other extreme involves interaction based on **cooperation.** Here, power is more or less equally distributed between people of different status. Cooperative interaction is based on feelings of trust. As we will see in Chapter 15, Families, marriages are happier when spouses share housework and child care equitably. Perceived inequity breeds resentment and dissatisfaction. It harms intimacy. It increases the chance that people will have extramarital affairs and will divorce. In contrast, a high level of trust between spouses is associated with marital stability and enduring love (Wood, 1999).

Between the two extremes of interaction based on domination and interaction based on cooperation is interaction based on **competition.** In this mode of interaction, power is unequally distributed but the degree of inequality is less than in systems of domination. Most of the social interactions analyzed by exchange and rational choice theorists are of this type. If trust is the prototypical emotion of relationships based on cooperation, and fear is the characteristic emotion of subordinates involved in relationships based on domination, envy is an important emotion in competitive interaction.

Significantly, the mode of interaction in an organization strongly influences its efficiency or productivity, that is, its ability to achieve its goals at the least possible cost. Thus, African American slaves on plantations in the antebellum South and Jews in Nazi concentration camps were usually regarded as slow and inept workers by their masters (Collins, 1982: 66–69). This characterization was not just a matter of prejudice. Slavery *is* inefficient because, in the final analysis, fear of coercion is the only motivation for slaves to work. Yet as psychologists have known for more than half a century, punishment is a far less effective motivator than is reward (Skinner, 1953). Slaves hate the tedious and often backbreaking labour, they get little in exchange for it, and therefore they typically work with less than maximum effort.

In a competitive mode of interaction, subordinates receive more benefits, including prestige and money. Prestige and money are stronger motivators than the threat of coercion. Thus, if bosses pay workers reasonably well and treat them with respect, they will work more efficiently than slaves even if they do not particularly enjoy their work or identify with the goals of the company. Knowing that they can make more money by working harder and that their efforts are appreciated, workers will often put in extra effort (Collins, 1982: 63–65).

As Randall Collins and others have shown, however, the most efficient workers are those who enjoy their work and identify with their employer (Collins, 1982: 60–85; Lowe, 2000). Giving workers a bigger say in decision making, encouraging worker creativity, and ensuring that salaries and perks are not too highly skewed in favour of those on top all help to create high worker morale and foster a more cooperative work environment. Company picnics, baseball games, and, in Japan, the singing of company songs before the workday begins, all help workers feel they are in harmony with their employer and are playing on the same team. Similarly, although sales meetings and other conferences have an instrumental purpose (the discussion of sales strategies, new products, etc.), they also offer opportunities for friendly social interaction that increases workers' identification with their employer. When workers identify strongly with their employers, they will be willing to undergo self-sacrifice, take the initiative, and give their best creative effort, even without the prospect of increased material gain.

Table 5.2 (page 146) summarizes the theories of social interaction we have discussed.

Cooperation is a basis for social interaction in which power is more or less equally distributed between people of different status. The dominant emotion in cooperative interaction is trust.

Competition is a mode of interaction in which power is unequally distributed but the degree of inequality is less than in systems of domination. Envy is an important emotion in competitive interactions.

TABLE 5.2
Theories of Social Interaction

Theory	People maintain social relationships by . . .	Main Theorist(s)	Example(s)
Exchange theory	Exchanging valued resources and punishments	Homans, Blau	Interaction persists if I pay attention to you and you pay attention to me, or if I commit an act of violence against you and you retaliate.
Rational choice theory	Maximizing gains and minimizing losses	Coleman, Hechter	I weigh the costs and benefits of interacting with you. You do the same with me. If our calculations allow us to strike a deal that satisfies both of us, interaction persists.
Symbolic interactionism	Interpreting, negotiating, and modifying norms, roles, and statuses	Blumer, Denzin	I interpret your cry for help in light of what I have learned about the virtue of sacrifice for others, and so I help youeven though I don't benefit from my action and infact put myself at risk.
Dramaturgical analysis	Impression management	Goffman	When we interact as student and professor, it is as if we are acting in a play. We play roles defined by each other's expectations, and we use props, gestures, and set lines to cast ourselves in the best possible light.
Ethno-methodology	Conforming to preexisting norms	Garfinkel	When you say "Come here," I don't need to ask how many centimetres in front of you I should stand because norms preceding our interaction define how close I should stand.
Conflict theory	Complying with status hierarchies	Bourdieu, Collins	We are in love; a roughly equal distribution of power between us encourages us to experience trust and act cooperatively. We want jobs in a corporation; an unequal distribution of power in the corporate hierarchy influences us to experience envy and act competitively. We are slaves; a grossly unequally distribution of power on the plantation causes us to experience fear and work inefficiently.

Handwritten annotations:

- expanding of pwn and review

- calc used to see if both parties will bene(fit) from interaction

- acting in a play
- diff roles being played

- using norms that already exist to help you act in a certain situation

— competition
  └ job @ corp
    → envy
— coopertively
  └ marriage
— trust
— domination
  └ slaves
    → fear

FROM SMALL PROCESSES TO BIG STRUCTURES

At several points in this chapter we referred to norms, roles, and statuses as the "building blocks" of social life. These building blocks form the microstructures within which face-to-face interaction takes place. In concluding we add that sustained microlevel interaction often gives rise to higher-level structures—mesostructures, such as networks, groups, and organizations. In the next chapter, we examine these intermediate-level structures. Then, in Part 4 of this book, we show how these intermediate-level structures can form macrolevel structures known as *institutions*.

Society, it will emerge, fits together like a set of nested Russian dolls, with face-to-face interaction constituting the smallest doll in the set. Big structures set limits to the behaviour of small structures. However, it is within small structures that people interpret, negotiate, and modify their immediate social settings, thus giving big structures their dynamism and their life.

Society fits together like a set of nested Russian dolls, with face-to-face interaction constituting the smallest doll in the set.

NOTE

1. Standard advice for polar and black bear attacks is to yell and fight back.

SUMMARY

1. What is social interaction?
   Social interaction involves verbal and nonverbal communication between people acting and reacting to each other. It is ordered by norms, roles, and statuses.

2. Don't emotions govern all social interaction? Aren't emotions natural, spontaneous, and largely uncontrollable?
   Emotions do form an important part of all social interactions. However, they are less spontaneous and uncontrollable than we commonly believe. For example, your status in an interaction and in the larger society affects how much you laugh and what you laugh at. Similarly, people manage their emotions in personal life and at work according to "feeling rules" that reflect historically changing cultural standards and the demands of organizations.

3. In what sense is social interaction based on competition?
   When we interact socially, we exchange valued resources—everything from attention and pleasure to prestige and money. However, because people typically try to maximize their rewards and minimize their losses, social interaction may be seen as a competition for scarce resources.

4. Is competition the only basis of social interaction?
   No, it is not. People may interact cooperatively and altruistically because they have been socialized to do so. They may also maintain interaction based on domination. Thus, the three major modes of interaction—domination, competition, and cooperation—are based, respectively, on fear, envy, and trust.

5. How do symbolic interactionists analyze social interaction?
   Symbolic interactionists focus on how people create meaning in the course of social interaction and on how they negotiate and modify roles, statuses, and norms. Symbolic interactionism has several variants. For example, dramaturgical analysis is based on the idea that people play roles in their daily lives in much the same way as actors on stage do. When we are front stage, we act publicly, sometimes from ready-made scripts. Backstage, we relax from our public performances and allow what we regard as our

"true" selves to emerge (even though we engage in role performances backstage, too). We may distance ourselves from our roles when they embarrass us, but role-playing nonetheless pervades social interaction. Together with various norms of interaction, role-playing enables society to function. Ethnomethodology is another symbolic interactionist approach to social interaction. It analyzes the methods people use to make sense of what others do and say. It insists on the importance of preexisting shared norms and understandings in making everyday interaction possible.

6. Is all social interaction based on language?

No, it is not. Nonverbal communication, including socially defined facial expressions, gestures, body language, and status cues, is as important as verbal communication in conveying meaning.

7. Is domination the most efficient basis of social interaction?

Not usually. We might expect slaves to be highly efficient because they must do what their masters dictate. However, slaves typically expend minimal effort because they are rewarded poorly. Efficiency increases in competitive environments where rewards are linked to effort. It increases further in cooperative settings where status differences are low and people enjoy their work and identify with their organization.

KEY TERMS

achieved status (p. 126)

ascribed status (p. 126)

competition (p. 145)

conflict theories of social interaction (p. 143)

cooperation (p. 145)

domination (p. 144)

dramaturgical analysis (p. 137)

emotion labour (p. 132)

emotion management (p. 132)

ethnomethodology (p. 139)

exchange theory (p. 135)

master status (p. 126)

norms (p. 126)

rational choice theory (p. 136)

role conflict (p. 128)

role distancing (p. 137)

roles (p. 126)

role set (p. 126)

role strain (p. 128)

social interaction (p. 126)

status (p. 126)

status cues (p. 142)

status set (p. 126)

stereotypes (p. 143)

QUESTIONS TO CONSIDER

1. Draw up a list of your current and former girlfriends or boyfriends. Indicate the race, religion, age, and height of each person on the list. How similar or different are you from the people with whom you have chosen to be intimate? What does this list tell you about the social distribution of intimacy? Is love blind? What criteria other than race, religion, age, and height might affect the social distribution of intimacy?

2. Is it accurate to say that people always act selfishly to maximize their rewards and minimize their losses? Why or why not?

3. In what sense (if any) is it reasonable to claim that all of social life consists of role acting and that we have no "true self," just an ensemble of roles?

WEB RESOURCES

Companion Website for This Book

http://www.compass3e.nelson.com

Begin by clicking on the Student Resources section of the website. Next, select the chapter you are studying from the pull-down menu. From the Student Resources page you have easy access to InfoTrac® College Edition, additional Weblinks, and other resources. The website also has many useful tips to aid you in your study of sociology, including practice tests for each chapter.

InfoTrac® Search Terms

These search terms are provided to assist you in beginning to conduct research on this topic by visiting http://www.infotrac-college.com:

dramaturgical analysis
exchange theory
rational choice theory

Recommended Websites

If you need convincing that social interaction on the Internet can have deep emotional and sociological implications, read Julian Dibbell's "A Rape in Cyberspace," on the World Wide Web at http://www.juliandibbell.com/texts/bungle.html. This compelling article is especially valuable for showing how social structure emerges in virtual communities. Originally published in *The Village Voice* (December 21, 1993, 36–42).

For social interaction on the World Wide Web, visit The MUD Connector at http://www.mudconnect.com.

The Society for the Study of Symbolic Interaction is a professional organization of sociologists "interested in qualitative, especially interactionist, research." Visit their website at http://www.espach.salford.ac.uk/sssi/index.php.

CengageNOW™

http://hed.nelson.com

This online diagnostic tool identifies each student's unique needs with a Pretest that generates a personalized Study Plan for each chapter, helping students focus on concepts they're having the most difficulty mastering. Students then take a Posttest after reading the chapter to measure their understanding of the material. An Instructor Gradebook is available to track and monitor student progress.

CHAPTER

6

Networks, Groups, Bureaucracies, and Societies

In this chapter, you will learn that

- We commonly explain the way people act in terms of their interests and emotions. However, sometimes people act against their interests and suppress their emotions because various social collectives (groups, networks, bureaucracies, and societies) exert a powerful influence on what people do.

- We live in a surprisingly small world. Only a few social ties separate us from complete strangers.

- The patterns of social ties through which emotional and material resources flow form social networks. Information, communicable diseases, social support, and other resources typically spread through social networks.

- People who are bound together by interaction and a common identity form social groups. Groups impose conformity on members and draw boundary lines between those who belong and those who do not.

- Bureaucracies are large, impersonal organizations that operate with varying degrees of efficiency. Efficient bureaucracies keep hierarchy to a minimum, distribute decision making to all levels of the bureaucracy, and keep lines of communication open between different units of the bureaucracy.

- Societies are collectives of interacting people who share a culture and a territory. As societies evolve, the relationship of humans to nature changes, with consequences for population size, the permanence of settlements, the specialization of work tasks, labour productivity, and social inequality.

- Although our freedom is constrained by various social collectives, we can also use them to increase our freedom. Networks, groups, organizations, and entire societies can be mobilized for good or evil.

BEYOND INDIVIDUAL MOTIVES

**PERSONAL
ANECDOTE**

The Holocaust

In 1941, the large stone and glass train station was one of the proudest structures in Smolensk, a provincial capital of about 100 000 people on Russia's western border. Always bustling, it was especially busy on the morning of June 28: Besides the usual passengers and well-wishers, hundreds of Soviet Red Army soldiers were nervously talking, smoking, writing hurried letters to their loved ones, and sleeping fitfully on the station floor waiting for their train. Nazi troops had invaded the nearby city of Minsk in Belarus a couple of days before. The Soviet soldiers were being positioned to defend Russia against the inevitable German onslaught.

Robert Brym's father, then in his 20s, had been standing in line for nearly two hours to buy food when he noticed flares arching over the station. Within seconds, Stuka bombers, the pride of the German air force, swept down, releasing their bombs just before pulling out of their dive. Inside the station, shards of glass, blocks of stone, and mounds of earth fell indiscriminately on sleeping soldiers and nursing mothers alike. Everyone panicked. People trampled over one another to get out. In minutes, the train station was rubble.

Nearly two years earlier, Robert's father had managed to escape Poland when the Nazis invaded his hometown near Warsaw. Now, he was on the run again. By the time the Nazis occupied Smolensk a few weeks after their dive-bombers had destroyed its train station, Robert's father was deep in the Russian interior serving in a workers' battalion attached to the Soviet Red Army.

"My father was one of 300 000 Polish Jews who fled eastward into Russia before the Nazi genocide machine could reach them," says Robert. "The remaining three million Polish Jews were killed in various ways. Some died in battle. Many more, like my father's mother and younger siblings, were rounded up like diseased cattle and shot. However, most of Poland's Jews wound up in the concentration camps. Those deemed unfit were shipped to the gas chambers. Those declared able to work were turned into slaves until they could work no more. Then they, too, met their fate. A mere 9 percent of Poland's 3.3 million Jews survived World War II. The Nazi regime was responsible for the death of six million Jews in Europe (Burleigh, 2000).

"One question that always perplexed my father about the war was this: How was it possible for many thousands of ordinary Germans—products of what he regarded as the most advanced civilization on earth—to systematically murder millions of defenceless and innocent Jews, Roma ('Gypsies'), homosexuals, and people with mental disabilities in the death camps? To answer this question adequately, we must borrow ideas from the sociological study of networks, groups, and bureaucracies."

The Social Origins of Evil

How could ordinary German citizens commit the crime of the century? The conventional, non-sociological answer is that many Nazis were evil, sadistic, or deluded enough to think that Jews and other undesirables threatened the existence of the German people. Therefore, in the Nazi mind, the innocents had to be killed. This answer is given in the 1993 movie *Schindler's List* and in many other accounts.

Yet, it is far from the whole story. Sociologists emphasize three other factors:

1. **Norms of solidarity demand conformity.** When we form relationships with friends, lovers, spouses, teammates, and comrades-in-arms, we develop shared ideas or "norms of solidarity" about how we should behave toward them to sustain the relationships. Because these relationships are emotionally important to us, we sometimes pay more

German industrialist Oskar Schindler (Liam Neeson, centre) searches for his plant manager, Itzhak Stern, among a trainload of Polish Jews about to be deported to Auschwitz-Birkenau in *Schindler's List*. The movie turns the history of Nazism into a morality play, a struggle between good and evil forces. It does not probe into the sociological roots of good and evil.

attention to norms of solidarity than to the morality of our actions. For example, a study of Nazis who roamed the Polish countryside to shoot and kill Jews and other "enemies" of Nazi Germany found that the soldiers often did not hate the people they systematically slaughtered, nor did they have many qualms about their actions (Browning, 1992). They simply developed deep loyalty to one another. They felt they had to get their assigned job done or face letting down their comrades. Thus, they committed atrocities partly because they just wanted to maintain group morale, solidarity, and loyalty. They committed evil deeds not because they were extraordinarily bad but because they were quite ordinary— ordinary in the sense that they acted to sustain their friendship ties and to serve their group, just like most people. It is the power of norms of solidarity that helps us understand how soldiers are able to undertake many unpalatable actions. As one soldier says in the 2001 movie *Black Hawk Down*: "When I go home people will ask me, 'Hey, Hoot, why do you do it, man? Why? Are you some kinda war junkie?' I won't say a goddamn word. Why? They won't understand. They won't understand why we do it. They won't understand it's about the men next to you. And that's it. That's all it is."

The case of the Nazi regime may seem extreme, but other instances of going along with criminal behaviour uncover a similar dynamic at work. Why do people rarely report crimes committed by corporations? Employees may worry about being reprimanded or fired if they become whistleblowers, but they also worry about letting down their co-workers. Why do gang members engage in criminal acts? They may seek financial gain, but they also regard crime as a way of maintaining a close social bond with their fellow gang members (see Box 6.1).

A study of the small number of Polish Christians who helped save Jews during World War II helps clarify why some people violate group norms (Tec, 1986). The heroism of these Polish Christians was not correlated with their educational attainment, political orientation, religious background, or even attitudes toward Jews. In fact, some Polish Christians who helped save Jews were quite anti-Semitic. Instead, these Christian heroes were, for one reason or another, estranged or cut off from mainstream norms. Because they were poorly socialized into the norms of their society, they were freer not to conform and instead act in ways they believed were right. We could tell a roughly similar story about corporate whistleblowers or people who turn in their fellow gangmembers. They are disloyal from an insider's point of view but heroic from an outsider's viewpoint, often because they have been poorly socialized into the group's norms.

BOX 6.1
Social Policy: What Do You Think?

Group Loyalty or Betrayal?

Group cohesion led Nazi soldiers to commit genocide. Group loyalty led many ordinary German citizens to support them. Although the Nazis are an extreme case, ordinary people often face a stark choice between group loyalty and group betrayal.

Glen Ridge, New Jersey, is an affluent suburb of 7800 people: white, orderly, and leafy. It is the hometown of *the* all-American boy, Tom Cruise. It was also the site of a terrible rape case in 1989. A group of 13 teenage boys lured a sweet-natured young woman with an IQ of 49 and the mental age of a child in grade 2 into a basement. There, four of them raped her while three others looked on; six left when they realized what was going to happen. The rapists used a baseball bat and a broomstick. The boys were the most popular students in the local high school. They had everything going for them. They were every mother's dream, every father's pride. The young woman was not a stranger to them. Some of them had known her since she was five years old, when they had convinced her to lick the point of a ballpoint pen that had been coated in dog feces.

What possessed these boys to gang rape a helpless young woman? And how can we explain the subsequent actions of many of the leading citizens of Glen Ridge? It was weeks before anyone reported the rape to the police and years before the boys went to trial. At trial, many members of the community rallied behind the boys, blaming and ostracizing the rape victim. The courts eventually found three of the four young men guilty of first-degree rape, but they were allowed to go free for eight years while their cases were appealed and they finally received only light sentences in 1997. With good behaviour, two were expected to be released from jail in 1999 and one in 1998. Why did

members of the community refuse to believe the clear-cut evidence? What made them defend the rapists? Why were the boys let off so easily?

Bernard Lefkowitz (1997a) interviewed 250 key players and observers in the Glen Ridge Rape case. Ultimately, he indicted the *community* for the rape. He concluded that "[the rapists] adhered to a code of behaviour that mimicked, distorted, and exaggerated the values of the adult world around them," while "the citizens supported the boys because they didn't want to taint the town they treasured" (Lefkowitz, 1997a: 493). What were some of the community values the elders upheld and the boys aped?

- *The subordination of women.* All the boys grew up in families where men were the dominant personalities. Only one of them had a sister. Not a single woman occupied a position of authority in Glen Ridge High School. The boys classified their female classmates either as "little mothers" who fawned over them or as "bad girls" who were simply sexual objects.

- *Lack of compassion for the weak.* According to the minister of Glen Ridge Congregational Church, "[a]chievement was honored and respected almost to the point of pathology, whether it was the achievements of high school athletes or the achievements of corporate world conquerors." Adds Lefkowitz: "Compassion for the weak wasn't part of the curriculum" (Lefkowitz, 1997a: 130).

- *Tolerance of male misconduct.* The boys routinely engaged in delinquent acts, including one spectacular trashing of a house. However, their parents always paid damages, covered up the misdeeds, and rationalized them with phrases like "boys will be boys." Especially because they were town football

heroes, many people felt they could do no wrong.

- *Intense group loyalty.* "The guys prized their intimacy with each other far above what could be achieved with a girl," writes Lefkowitz (1997a: 146). The boys formed a tight clique, and team sports reinforced group solidarity. Under such circumstances, the probability of someone "ratting" on his friends was very low. In the end, of course, there was a "rat." His name was Charles Figueroa. He did not participate in the rape but he was an athlete, part of the jock clique, and therefore aware of what had happened. Significantly, he was one of the few black boys in the school, tolerated because of his athletic ability but never trusted because of his race and often called an—— by his teammates behind his back. This young man's family was highly intelligent and morally sensitive. He was the only one to have the courage to betray the group (Lefkowitz, 1997a, 1997b).

Lefkowitz presents a strong indictment of the community as a whole and the values it upheld. Beyond that, however, he raises the important question of where we ought to draw the line between group loyalty and group betrayal. Considering your own group loyalties, are there times when you regret not having spoken up? Are there times when you regret not having been more loyal? What is the difference between these two types of situations? Can you specify criteria for deciding when loyalty is required and when betrayal is the right thing to do? You may have to choose between group loyalty and betrayal on more than one occasion, so thinking about these criteria—and clearly understanding the values for which your group stands—will help you make a more informed choice.

2. *Structures of authority tend to render people obedient.* Most people find it difficult to disobey authorities because they fear ridicule, ostracism, and punishment. This was strikingly demonstrated in an experiment conducted by social psychologist Stanley Milgram (1974). Milgram informed his experimental subjects they were taking part in a study on punishment and learning. He brought each subject to a room where a man was strapped to a chair. An electrode was attached to the man's wrist. The experimental subject sat in front of a console. It contained 30 switches with labels ranging from "15 volts" to "450 volts" in 15-volt increments. Labels ranging from "slight shock" to "danger: severe shock" were pasted below the switches. The experimental subjects were told to administer a 15-volt shock for the man's first wrong answer and then increase the voltage each time he made an error. The man strapped in the chair was, in fact, an actor. He did not actually receive a shock. As the experimental subject increased the current, however, the actor began to writhe, shouting for mercy and begging to be released. If the experimental subjects grew reluctant to administer more current, Milgram assured them the man strapped in the chair would be fine and insisted that the success of the experiment depended on the subject's obedience. The subjects were, however, free to abort the experiment at any time. Remarkably, 71 percent of experimental subjects were prepared to administer shocks of 285 volts or more even though the switches at starting that level were labelled "intense shock," "extreme intensity shock," and "danger: severe shock" and despite the fact that the actor appeared to be in great distress at this level of current (see Figure 6.1).

Milgram's experiment teaches us that as soon as we are introduced to a structure of authority, we are inclined to obey those in power. This is the case even if the authority structure is new and highly artificial, even if we are free to walk away from it with no penalty, and even if we think that by remaining in its grip we are inflicting terrible pain on another human being. In this context, the actions and inactions of German citizens in World War II become more understandable if no more forgivable.

3. *Bureaucracies are highly effective structures of authority.* The Nazi genocide machine was effective because it was bureaucratically organized. As Max Weber (1978) defined the term, a **bureaucracy** is a large, impersonal organization comprising many clearly defined positions arranged in a hierarchy. A bureaucracy has a permanent, salaried staff of qualified experts and written goals, rules, and procedures. Staff members always try to find ways of running their organization more efficiently. *Efficiency* means achieving the bureaucracy's goals at the least cost. The goal of the Nazi genocide machine was to kill Jews and other undesirables. To achieve that goal with maximum efficiency, the job was broken into many small tasks. Most officials performed only one function, such as checking train schedules, organizing entertainment for camp guards, maintaining supplies of Zyklon B gas, and removing ashes from the crematoria. The full horror of what was happening eluded many officials or at least could be conveniently ignored as they concentrated on their jobs, most

---

A **bureaucracy** is a large, impersonal organization comprising many clearly defined positions arranged in a hierarchy. A bureaucracy has a permanent, salaried staff of qualified experts and written goals, rules, and procedures. Ideally, staff members always try to find ways of running the bureaucracy more efficiently.

FIGURE 6.1

Social Distance Increases Obedience to Authority

Milgram's experiment supports the view that separating people from the negative effects of their actions increases the likelihood of compliance. When the subject and actor were in the same room and the subject was told to force the actor's hand onto the electrode, 30 percent of subjects administered the maximum, 450-volt shock. When the subject and actor were merely in the same room, 40 percent of subjects administered the maximum shock. When the subject and actor were in different rooms but the subject could see and hear the actor, 62.5 percent of subjects administered the maximum shock. When subject and actor were in different rooms and the actor could be seen but not heard, 65 percent of subjects administered the maximum shock.

Source: Based on Milgram, 1974: 36. Bar graph based on information in Chapter 4, "Closeness of the Victim," from *Obedience to Authority* by Stanley Milgram. Copyright © 1974 by Stanley Milgram. Reprinted by permission of HarperCollins Publishers, Inc.

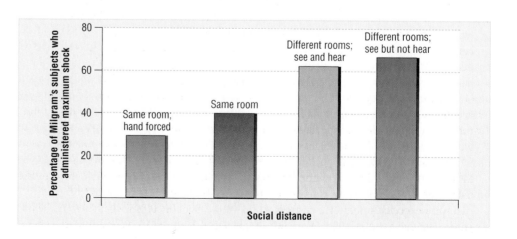

of them far removed from the gas chambers and death camps in occupied Poland. Many factors account for variations in Jewish victimization rates across Europe during World War II. One factor was bureaucratic organization. Not coincidentally, the proportion of Jews killed was highest not in the Nazi-controlled countries where the hatred of Jews was most intense (e.g., Romania), but in countries where the Nazi bureaucracy was best organized (e.g., Holland) (Bauman, 1991; Sofsky, 1997 [1993]).

In short, the sociological reply to the question posed by Robert's father is that it was not just blind hatred but the nature of groups and bureaucracies that made it possible for the Nazis to kill innocent people so ruthlessly.

We commonly think *individual* motives prompt our actions, and for good reason. As we saw in Chapter 5, Social Interaction, we often make rational calculations to maximize gains and minimize losses. In addition, our deeply held emotions partly govern our behaviour. However, this chapter asks you to make a conceptual leap beyond the individual motives that prompt us to act in certain ways. We ask you to consider the way four kinds of social *collectivities* shape our actions: networks, groups, bureaucratic organizations, and whole societies. The limitations of an analysis based exclusively on individual motives should be clear from our discussion of the social roots of evil. The advantages of considering how social collectivities affect us should become clear below. We begin by considering the nature and effects of social networks.

Dr. Jeffrey Wigand was one of the most famous whistle-blowers of the 1990s. Vice-president of research and development at Brown and Williams Tobacco Corp., Wigand was fired after he discovered that the company was adding ammonia and other chemicals to cigarettes to enhance nicotine absorption and speed up addiction. Despite threats and harassment, Wigand told all on the CBS public affairs program *60 Minutes*, ultimately leading to a US$368 billion suit against big tobacco for health-related damages. The story is the subject of the 1999 movie *The Insider*.

NETWORKS

It's a Small World

The Internet Movie Database (2003) contains information on the half-million actors who have ever performed in a commercially released movie. Although this number is large, you might be surprised to learn that, socially, they form a small world. We can demonstrate that by first selecting an actor who is not an especially big star—someone like Kevin Bacon. We can then use the Internet Movie Database to find out which other actors have ever been in a movie with him (University of Virginia, 2003). Acting in a movie with another actor constitutes a link. Two links tie 119 754 actors to Bacon. They have never been in a movie with Bacon but they have been in a movie with *another* actor who has been in a movie with him. Remarkably, more than 85 percent of the half-million actors in the database have one, two, or three links to Bacon. Nearly 99 percent of the half-million actors have four or fewer links to him. We conclude that although film acting stretches back more than a century and has involved people in many countries, the half-million people who have ever acted in films form a pretty small world.

What is true for the world of film actors turns out to be true for the rest of us, too. Jeffrey Travers and Stanley Milgram (1969) conducted a famous study in which they asked 300 randomly selected people in Nebraska and Kansas to mail a document to a complete stranger, a stockbroker in Boston. However, the people could not mail the document directly to the stockbroker. They had to mail it to a person they knew on a first-name basis who, in turn, could send it only to a person *he or she* knew on a first-name basis, and so forth. Travers and Milgram defined this passing of a letter from one person to another as a link or a "degree of separation." Most people thought it would take many degrees of separation, perhaps hundreds, to get the letter to the Boston stockbroker. Remarkably, however, the average number was about six. Following publication of the study, the idea became widespread that no more than six degrees of separation separate any two people in the United States.

You have probably said "It's a small world" more than once, and you are right. There are more than 33 million Canadians, of whom just a few hundred are your family members,

Among all actors who have ever performed in a movie, Kevin Bacon is the 1161st most central. That is, 1160 other actors have a smaller average number of ties to all other actors. Still, nearly a quarter of all people who have ever acted in a movie are separated from Bacon by just one or two links, and more than 85 percent are separated by fewer than four links.

A social network is a bounded set of individuals who are linked by the exchange of material or emotional resources. The patterns of exchange determine the boundaries of the network. Members exchange resources more frequently with one another than with non-members. They also think of themselves as network members. Social networks may be formal (defined in writing), but they are more often informal (defined only in practice).

friends, acquaintances, and work colleagues. Yet if you were asked to get in touch with a complete stranger on the other side of the country by using only personal ties—you contact a person you know on a first-name basis and that person contacts someone else whom he or she knows on a first-name basis, and so forth—it would take only about six contacts to reach the stranger. How is it possible that only about six links separate any of us from people we don't know on the other side of the country?

Network Analysis

The short sociological answer is that we are enmeshed in overlapping sets of social relations, or social networks. Although any particular individual may know a small number of people, his or her family members, friends, co-workers, and others know many more people who extend far beyond that individual's personal network. So, for example, the authors of this textbook are likely to be complete strangers to you. Yet your professor may know one of us or at least know someone who knows one of us. Probably no more than three links separate us from you. Put differently, although our personal networks are small, they lead quickly to much larger networks. We live in a small world because our social networks connect us to the larger world.

What is a social network? A **social network** is a bounded set of individuals linked by the exchange of material or emotional resources, everything from money to friendship. The patterns of exchange determine the boundaries of the network. Members exchange resources more frequently with one another than with non-members. They also think of themselves as network members. Social networks may be formal (defined in writing) or informal (defined only in practice). The people you know personally form the boundaries of your personal network. However, each of your network members is linked to other people. This is what connects you to people you have never met, creating a "small world" that extends far beyond your personal network.

The study of social networks is not restricted to ties among individuals (Berkowitz, 1982; Wasserman and Faust, 1994; Wellman and Berkowitz, 1997). The units of analysis or *nodes* in a network can be individuals, groups, organizations, and even countries. Thus, social network analysts have examined everything from intimate relationships between lovers to diplomatic relations among nations. For example, in Chapter 9, Globalization, Inequality, and Development, we show how patterns in the flow of international trade divide the world into three major trading blocs, with the United States, Germany, and Japan and China at the centre of each bloc. In Chapter 13, Work and the Economy, we show how corporate networks create alliances that are useful for exchanging information and influencing government. In both cases, our analysis of social networks teaches us something new and unexpected about the social bases of economic and political affairs.

Unlike organizations, most networks lack names and offices. There is a Boy Scouts of Canada but no North American Trading Bloc. In a sense, networks lie beneath the more visible collectivities of social life, but that makes them no less real or important. Some analysts claim we can gain only a partial sense of why certain things happen in the social world by focusing on highly visible collectivities. From their point of view, the whole story requires probing below the surface and examining the network level. The study of social networks clarifies a wide range of social phenomena, including how people find jobs, how information, innovations, and communicable diseases spread, and how some people exert influence over others. To illustrate further the value of network analysis, we now focus on each of these issues in turn.

Finding a Job

The old saying "It's not what you know but who you know" contains much sociological truth. For example, many bright and inquisitive students have passing thoughts about becoming a professor. What might transform that momentary interest into a lifelong career is often a mentor who encourages the student and provides him or her with useful advice, including introductions to other ambitious students, stimulating professors, great books, and graduate programs.

Parents can help their graduating children find jobs by getting them plugged into the right social networks. Here, in the 1968 movie *The Graduate,* a friend of the family advises Dustin Hoffman that the future lies in the plastics industry.

Many people learn about important events, ideas, and opportunities from their social networks. Friends and acquaintances often introduce you to everything from an interesting postsecondary course or a great restaurant to a satisfying occupation or a future spouse. Of course, social networks are not the only source of information, but they are highly significant.

Consider how people find jobs. Do you look in the "Help Wanted" section of your local newspaper, scan the Internet, or walk around certain areas of town looking for "Employee Wanted" signs? Although these strategies are common, people often learn about employment opportunities from other people. But what kind of people? According to Mark Granovetter (1973), you may have strong or weak ties to another person. You have strong ties to people who are close to you, such as family members and friends. You have weak ties to mere acquaintances, such as people you meet at parties and friends of friends. In his research, Granovetter found that weak ties are more important than strong ties in finding a job, which is contrary to common sense. You might reasonably assume that a mere acquaintance would not do much to help you find a job whereas a close friend or relative would make a lot more effort in this regard. However, by focusing on the flow of information in personal networks, Granovetter found something different. Mere acquaintances are more likely to provide useful information about employment opportunities than friends or family members are because people who are close to you typically share overlapping networks. Therefore, the information they can provide about job opportunities is often redundant. In contrast, mere acquaintances are likely to be connected to *diverse* networks. They can therefore provide information about many different job openings and make introductions to many different potential employers. Moreover, because people typically have more weak ties than strong ties, the sum of weak ties holds more information about job opportunities than the sum of strong ties. These features of personal networks allow Granovetter to conclude that the "strength of weak ties" lies in their diversity and abundance.

Urban Networks, Scientific Innovation, and the Spread of HIV/AIDS

We rely on social networks for a lot more than job information. Consider everyday life in the big city. We often think of big cities as cold and alienating places where few people know one another. In this view, urban acquaintanceships tend to be few and functionally specific; we know someone fleetingly as a bank teller or a server in a restaurant but not as a whole person. Even dating often involves a long series of brief encounters. In contrast, people often think of small towns as friendly, comfortable places where everyone knows everyone else (and everyone else's business). Indeed, some of the founders of sociology emphasized just this distinction. Notably, German sociologist Ferdinand Tönnies (1988 [1887]) contrasted "community" with "society." According to Tönnies, a community is marked by intimate and emotionally intense social ties, whereas a society is marked by impersonal relationships held together largely by self-interest. A big city is a prime example of a society in Tönnies's judgment.

Tönnies's view prevailed until network analysts started studying big city life in the 1970s. Where Tönnies saw only sparse, functionally specific ties, network analysts found elaborate social networks, some functionally specific and some not. For example, Barry Wellman and his colleagues studied personal networks in Toronto (Wellman, Carrington, and Hall, 1997). They found that each Torontonian has an average of about 400 social ties, including immediate and extended kin, neighbours, friends, and co-workers. These ties provide everything from emotional aid (e.g., visits after a personal tragedy) and financial support (e.g., small loans) to minor services (e.g., fixing a car) and information of the kind Granovetter studied. Strong ties that last a long time are typically restricted to immediate family members, a few close relatives and friends, and a close co-worker or two. Beyond that, however, people rely on a wide array of ties for different purposes at different times. Downtown residents sitting on their front porch on a summer evening, sipping soft drinks and chatting with neighbours as the kids play road hockey, may be less common than they were 50 years ago. However, the automobile, public transportation, the telephone, and the Internet help people stay in close touch with a wide range of contacts for a variety of purposes (Haythornthwaite and Wellman, 2002). Far from living in an impersonal and alienating world, Torontonians' lives are network-rich. Research conducted elsewhere in North America reveals much the same pattern of urban life.

One of the advantages of network analysis is its focus on people's actual social relationships rather than their abstract attributes, such as their age, gender, or occupation. This focus is useful for helping us understand many aspects of social life. For example, how does information spread? You might think that people with a particular set of occupational attributes, such as leading scientists in a particular field of study, first gain and then distribute information to other scientists in their field. At a crude level, this fact is true. However, new information does not diffuse evenly throughout a scientific community. Instead, it flows through networks of friends, co-researchers, and people who have studied together, only later spreading to the broader community (Rogers, 1995). Networks also shape scientific influence because scientists in a social network tend to share similar scientific beliefs and are thus more open to some influences than others are (Friedkin, 1998).

Another example of the usefulness of focusing on concrete social ties rather than on abstract attributes comes from the study of how communicable diseases spread. HIV/AIDS was widely considered a "gay" disease in the 1980s. HIV/AIDS spread rapidly in the gay community during that decade. However, network analysis helped to show that the characterization of HIV/AIDS as a "gay disease" was an oversimplification (Watts, 2003). The disease did not spread uniformly throughout the community. Rather, it spread along the friendship and acquaintanceship networks of people first exposed to it. Meanwhile, in India and parts of Africa, HIV/AIDS did not initially spread among gay men at all. Instead, it spread through a network of long-distance truck drivers and the prostitutes who catered to them. Again, concrete social networks—not abstract categories like "gay men" or "truck drivers"—track the spread of the disease.

The Building Blocks of Social Networks

Researchers often use mathematical models and computer programs to analyze social networks. However, no matter how sophisticated the mathematics or the software, network analysts begin from an understanding of the basic building blocks of social networks.

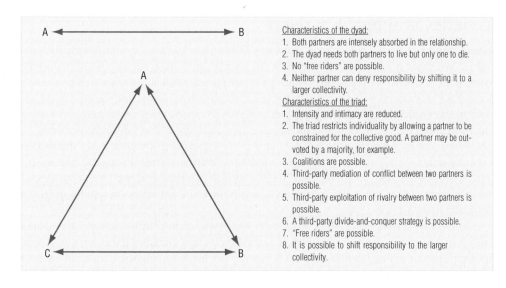

Characteristics of the dyad:
1. Both partners are intensely absorbed in the relationship.
2. The dyad needs both partners to live but only one to die.
3. No "free riders" are possible.
4. Neither partner can deny responsibility by shifting it to a larger collectivity.

Characteristics of the triad:
1. Intensity and intimacy are reduced.
2. The triad restricts individuality by allowing a partner to be constrained for the collective good. A partner may be out-voted by a majority, for example.
3. Coalitions are possible.
4. Third-party mediation of conflict between two partners is possible.
5. Third-party exploitation of rivalry between two partners is possible.
6. A third-party divide-and-conquer strategy is possible.
7. "Free riders" are possible.
8. It is possible to shift responsibility to the larger collectivity.

FIGURE 6.2
Dyad and Triad

The most elementary network form is the **dyad**, a social relationship between two nodes or social units (e.g., people, firms, organizations, countries, etc.). A **triad** is a social relationship among three nodes. The difference between a dyad and a triad may seem small. However, the social dynamics of these two elementary network forms are fundamentally different, as sociologist Georg Simmel showed early in the twentieth century (Simmel, 1950; see Figure 6.2).

In a dyadic relationship, such as a marriage, both partners tend to be intensely and intimately involved. Moreover, the dyad needs both partners to live—but to "die" it needs only one to opt out. A marriage, for example, can endure only if both partners are intensely involved; if one partner ceases active participation, the marriage is over in practice if not in law. The need for intense involvement on the part of both partners is also why a dyad can have no "free riders," or partners who benefit from the relationship without contributing to it. Finally, in a dyadic relationship, the partners must assume full responsibility for all that transpires. Neither partner can shift responsibility to some larger collectivity because no larger collectivity exists beyond the relationship between the two partners.

In contrast, when a third person (or other social unit) enters the picture, thereby creating a triad, relationships tend to be less intimate and intense. Equally significantly, the triad restricts individuality by allowing one partner to be constrained for the collective good. This situation occurs when a majority outvotes one partner. The existence of a triad also allows coalitions or factions to form. Furthermore, it allows one partner to mediate conflict between the other two, exploit rivalry between the other two, or encourage rivalry between the other two to achieve dominance. Thus, the introduction of a third partner makes possible a completely new set of social dynamics that are structurally impossible in a dyadic relationship.

A **dyad** is a social relationship between two nodes or social units (e.g., people, firms, organizations, countries).

A **triad** is a social relationship among three nodes or social units (e.g., people, firms, organizations, countries).

GROUPS

Love and Group Loyalty

Although intensity and intimacy characterize dyadic relationships, outside forces often destroy them. For instance, the star-crossed lovers in *Romeo and Juliet* are torn between their love for each other and their loyalty to the feuding Montague and Capulet families. In the end, Romeo and Juliet die, victims of the feud.

Love thwarted by conflicting group loyalty is the stuff of many tragic plays, novels, and movies. Most audiences have no problem grasping the fact that group loyalty is often more powerful than romantic love. However, why group loyalty holds such power over us is unclear. The sociological study of groups provides some useful answers.

Varieties of Group Experience

A social group comprises one or more networks of people who identify with one another and adhere to defined norms, roles, and statuses.

A social category comprises people who share a similar status but do not identify with one another.

In primary groups, norms, roles, and statuses are agreed on but are not put in writing. Social interaction leads to strong emotional ties. It extends over a long period, and involves a wide range of activities. It results in group members knowing one another well.

Social groups comprise one or more networks of people who identify with one another and adhere to defined norms, roles, and statuses. We usually distinguish social groups from **social categories**, people who share similar status but do not identify with one another. Coffee drinkers form a social category. They do not, however, typically share norms and identify with one another. In contrast, members of a group, such as a family, sports team, or college, are aware of shared membership. They identify with the collective and think of themselves as members.

Many kinds of social groups exist. However, sociologists make a basic distinction between primary and secondary groups. In **primary groups**, norms, roles, and statuses are agreed on but are not put in writing. Social interaction creates strong emotional ties. It extends over a long period and involves a wide range of activities. It results in group members knowing one another well. The family is the most important primary group.

Secondary groups are larger and more impersonal than primary groups. Compared with primary groups, social interaction in secondary groups creates weaker emotional ties. It extends over a shorter period and involves a narrow range of activities. It results in most group members having at most a passing acquaintance with one another. Your sociology class is an example of a secondary group.

Bearing these distinctions in mind, we can begin to explore the power of groups to ensure conformity.

Conformity and "Groupthink"

Television's first reality TV show was *Candid Camera*. On an early episode, an unsuspecting man waited for an elevator. When the elevator door opened, he found four people, all confederates of the show, facing the elevator's back wall. Seeing the four people with their backs to him, the man at first hesitated. He then tentatively entered the elevator. However, rather than turning around so he would face the door, he remained facing the back wall, just like the others. The scene was repeated several times. Men and women, black and white, all behaved the same way. Confronting unanimously bizarre behaviour, they chose conformity over common sense.

The main primary group is the family, which is an enduring, multifunctional social unit characterized by unwritten consensus concerning norms, roles and statuses, emotional intensity, and intimacy.

Conformity is an integral part of group life, and primary groups generate more pressure to conform than do secondary groups. Strong social ties create emotional intimacy. They also ensure that primary group members share similar attitudes, beliefs, and information. Beyond the family, friendship groups (or cliques) and gangs demonstrate these features. Group members tend to dress and act alike, speak the same "lingo," share the same likes and dislikes, and demand loyalty, especially in the face of external threat. Conformity ensures group cohesion.

A classic study of soldiers in World War II demonstrates the power of conformity to get people to face extreme danger. Samuel Stouffer and his colleagues (Stouffer, Suchman, DeVinney, Star, and Williams, 1949) showed that primary group cohesion was the main factor motivating soldiers to engage in combat. Rather than belief in a cause, such as upholding liberty or fighting the evils of Nazism, the feeling of camaraderie, loyalty, and solidarity with fellow soldiers supplied the principal motivation to face danger. As Brigadier General S. L. A. Marshall (1947: 160–61) famously wrote: "A man fights to help the man next to him. . . . Men do not fight for a cause but because they do not want to let their comrades down." As such, if you want to create a great military force, you need to promote group solidarity and identity. Hence the importance of wearing uniforms, singing anthems, displaying insignia, hoisting flags, conducting drills, training under duress, and instilling hatred of the enemy.

A famous experiment conducted by social psychologist Solomon Asch half a century ago also demonstrates how group pressure creates conformity (Asch, 1955). Asch assembled a group of seven men. One of them was the experimental subject; the other six were Asch's confederates. Asch showed the seven men a card with a line drawn on it. He then showed them a second card with three lines of varying length drawn on it (see Figure 6.3). One by one, he asked the confederates to judge which line on card 2 was the same length as the line on card 1. The answer was obvious. One line on card 2 was much shorter than the line on card 1. One line was much longer. One was exactly the same length. Yet, as instructed by Asch, all six confederates said that either the shorter or the longer line was the same length as the line on card 1. When it came time for the experimental subject to make his judgment, he typically overruled his own perception and agreed with the majority. Only 25 percent of Asch's experimental subjects consistently gave the right answer. Asch thus demonstrated how easily group pressure can overturn individual conviction and result in conformity.

Asch's work and subsequent research show that several factors affect the likelihood of conformity (Sternberg, 1998: 499–500). First, the likelihood of conformity increases as *group size* increases to three or four members. For groups larger than four, the likelihood of conformity generally does not increase. Second, as *group cohesiveness* increases, so does the likelihood of conformity. Where greater intimacy and sharing of values occur, group members are less likely to express dissent. Third, *social status* affects the likelihood of conformity. People with low status in a group (e.g., because of their gender or race) are less likely to dissent than people with high status. Fourth, *culture* matters. People in individual-istic societies, like Canada, tend to conform less than do people in collectivist societies, like China. Fifth, the *appearance of unanimity* affects the likelihood of conformity. Even one dissenting voice greatly increases the chance that others will dissent.

The power of groups to ensure conformity is often a valuable asset. Armies could not function without willingness to undergo personal sacrifice for the good of the group, nor could sports teams excel. However, being a good team player can have a downside because the consensus of a group can sometimes be misguided or dangerous. Dissent might save the group from making mistakes, but the pressure to conform despite individual misgivings—sometimes called **groupthink** (Janis, 1972)—can lead to disaster.

Great managers are able to encourage frank and open discussion, assess ideas based on their merit, develop a strategy that incorporates the best ideas voiced, and *then* create consensus on how to implement the ideas. Inadequate managers feel they know it all. They rationalize their plan of action, squelch dissent, and fail to examine alternatives. They create a group culture that inhibits people from expressing their misgivings and use the fact that people do not want to appear disloyal to *impose* consensus on the group. High-stress situations—a war room, an operating room—often do not allow a more democratic managerial style. Therefore, it is precisely in high-stress situations that the dangers of groupthink are greatest. Groupthink was at work in high-level meetings preceding the space shuttle *Columbia* disaster in 2003. Transcripts of those meetings show that the NASA official who ran shuttle management meetings, a non-engineer, believed from the outset that foam insulation debris could not damage the spacecraft. She dismissed the issue and cut off discussion when an engineer expressed his concerns. The others present quickly fell into line with the non-engineer running the meeting (Wald and Schwartz, 2003). A few days later, damage caused by foam insulation debris caused *Columbia* to break apart on reentry into Earth's atmosphere.

Secondary groups are larger and more impersonal than primary groups. Compared with primary groups, social interaction in secondary groups creates weaker emotional ties. It extends over a shorter period, and it involves a narrow range of activities. It results in most group members having at most a passing acquaintance with one another.

Groupthink is group pressure to conform despite individual misgivings.

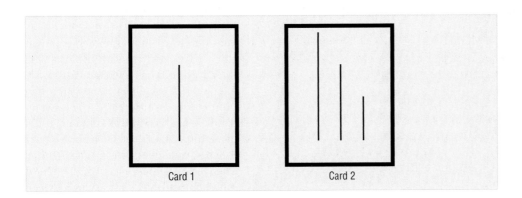

FIGURE 6.3
The Asch Experiment

Famous examples of how the lack of a single dissenting voice can result in tragedy come from two homicide cases that grabbed the world's attention. In 1964 in Queens, New York, 28-year-old Kitty Genovese parked her car after returning home from work. When she got out, a man grabbed and stabbed her. She screamed for help. For 35 minutes, at least 38 middle-class, law-abiding neighbours watched from darkened windows as the man repeatedly attacked Genovese and stabbed her 17 times. Finally, one neighbour called the police, but only after he had called a friend and asked what to do. Some of the neighbours later pleaded ignorance. Others said they thought it was just a lovers' quarrel or "some kids having fun." Still others admitted they did not want to get involved (Gado, 2003). A similar thing happened in 1993 near Liverpool, England. Two 10-year-old boys abducted 2-year-old James Bulger from a shopping mall. They took him on a long, aimless walk, torturing him along the way—dropping him on his head and kicking him in the ribs. Motorists and pedestrians saw the toddler crying, noticed his wounds, and even witnessed some of the violence. "A persuading kick" was the way one motorist later described the blow to the ribs (Scott, 2003). Nobody called the police. These cases illustrate "bystander apathy." As the number of bystanders increases, the likelihood of any one bystander helping another decreases because the greater the number of bystanders, the less responsibility any one individual feels. This behaviour shows that people usually take their cues for action from others and again demonstrates the power of groups over individuals. If no one else in a large collectivity responds, most people figure nothing is wrong.

Inclusion and Exclusion

In-group members are people who belong to a group.

Out-group members are people who are excluded from an in-group.

Natural or artificial boundaries—rivers, mountains, highways, railway tracks—typically separate groups or communities.

If a group exists, some people do not belong to it. Accordingly, sociologists distinguish **in-group** members (those who belong) from **out-group** members (those who do not). Members of an in-group typically draw a boundary separating themselves from members of the out-group, and they try to keep out-group members from crossing the line. Anyone who has gone to high school knows all about in-groups and out-groups. They have seen first-hand how race, class, athletic ability, academic talent, and physical attractiveness act as boundaries separating groups. Sadly, only in the movies can someone in a high school out-group get a chance to return to school as a young adult and use her savvy to become a member of the in-group (see *Never Been Kissed*, starring Drew Barrymore [1999]).

Why do group boundaries crystallize? One theory is that group boundaries emerge when people compete for scarce resources. For example, old immigrants may greet new immigrants with hostility if the latter are seen as competitors for scarce jobs (Levine and Campbell, 1972). Another theory is that group boundaries emerge when people are motivated to protect their self-esteem. From this point of view, drawing group boundaries allows people to increase their self-esteem by believing that out-groups have low status (Tajfel, 1981).

Both theories are supported by the classic experiment on prejudice, *The Robber's Cave Study* (Sherif, Harvey, White, Hood, and Sherif, 1988 [1961]). Researchers brought two groups of 11-year-old boys to a summer camp at Robber's Cave State Park in Oklahoma in 1954. The boys were strangers to one another and for about a week the two groups were kept apart. They swam, camped, and hiked. Each group chose a name for itself and the boys printed their group's name on their caps and T-shirts. Then the two groups met. A series of athletic competitions was set up between them. Soon, each group became highly antagonistic toward the other. Each group came to hold the other in low esteem. The boys ransacked cabins, started food fights, and stole various items from members of the other group. Thus, under competitive conditions, the boys drew group boundaries starkly and quickly.

The investigators next stopped the athletic competitions and created several apparent emergencies whose solution required cooperation between the two groups. One such emergency involved a leak in the pipe supplying water to the camp. The researchers assigned the boys to teams of members from *both* groups. Their job was to inspect the pipe and fix the leak. After engaging in several such cooperative ventures, the boys started playing together without fighting. Once cooperation replaced competition and the groups ceased to hold each other in low esteem, group boundaries melted away as quickly as they had formed. Significantly, the two groups were of equal status—the boys were all white, middle class, and 11 years old—and their contact involved face-to-face interaction in a setting where norms established by the investigators promoted a reduction of group prejudice. Social scientists today recognize that all these conditions must be in place before the boundaries between an in-group and an out-group fade away (Sternberg, 1998: 512).

Is it possible to imagine everyone in the world as a community? Why or why not? Under what conditions might it be possible?

The boundaries separating groups often seem unchangeable and even "natural." In general, however, dominant groups construct group boundaries in particular circumstances to further their goals (Barth, 1969; Tajfel, 1981). Consider Germans and Jews. By the early twentieth century, Jews were well integrated into German society. They were economically successful, culturally innovative, and politically influential, and many of them considered themselves more German than Jewish. In 1933, the year Hitler seized power, 44 percent of marriages involving at least one German Jew were marriages to a non-Jew. In addition, some German Jews converted before marrying non-Jewish Germans (Gordon, 1984). Yet, although the boundary separating Germans from Jews was quite weak, the Nazis chose to redraw and reinforce it. Defining a Jew as anyone who had at least one Jewish grandparent, the Nazis passed a series of anti-Jewish laws and, in the end, systematically slaughtered the Jews of Europe. The division between Germans and Jews was not "natural." It came into existence because of its perceived usefulness to a dominant group.

Groups and Social Imagination

So far, we have focused almost exclusively on face-to-face interaction in groups. However, people also interact with other group members in their imagination. Take reference groups, for example. A **reference group** comprises people against whom an individual evaluates his or her situation or conduct. Put differently, members of a reference group function as role models. The classic case of a reference group is Theodore Newcomb's (1943) study of college students although nearly all the students came from politically conservative families, they tended to become more liberal with every passing year. Twenty years later, they remained liberals. Newcomb argued that their liberalism grew because over time they came to identify less with their conservative parents (members of their primary group) and more with their liberal professors (their reference group). Interestingly, reference groups may influence us even though they represent a largely imaginary ideal. For example, the advertising industry promotes certain body ideals that many people try to emulate, although we all know that hardly anyone looks like a runway model or a Barbie doll (see Chapter 11, Sexuality and Gender and Chapter 12, Sociology of the Body: Disability, Aging, and Death).

A **reference group** comprises people against whom an individual evaluates his or her situation or conduct.

We should not exaggerate the influence of reference groups, however; despite their influence, most people continue to highly value the opinions of in-group members. Thus, professors did not influence the individual students that Newcomb studied one by one. Rather, groups of students came to admire and emulate the faculty reference group. Similarly, individual girls do not dream of looking like Barbie. Rather, groups of girls come to share the body ideal represented by the Barbie role model. Reference groups are important influences, but evidence gathered by social psychologists points to the preponderant power of in-groups in determining which reference groups matter to us (Wilder, 1990).

We have to exercise our imagination vigorously to participate in the group life of a society like ours, because much social life in a complex society involves belonging to secondary groups without knowing or interacting with most group members. For an individual to interact with any more than a small fraction of the 33 million people living in this country is impossible. Nonetheless, most Canadians feel a strong emotional bond to their fellow citizens. Similarly, think about the employees and students at your college or university. They know they belong to the same secondary group and many of them are probably loyal to it. Yet how many people at your school have you met? Probably no more than a small fraction of the total. One way to make sense of the paradox of intimacy despite distance is to think of your postsecondary institution or Canada as "imagined communities." They are imagined because you cannot possibly meet most members of the group and can only speculate about what they must be like. They are, nonetheless, communities because people believe strongly in their existence and importance (Anderson, 1991).

Formal organizations are secondary groups designed to achieve explicit objectives.

Many secondary groups are **formal organizations**, secondary groups designed to achieve explicit objectives. In complex societies like ours, the most common and influential formal organizations are bureaucracies. We now turn to an examination of these often frustrating but necessary organizational forms.

BUREAUCRACIES

Bureaucratic Inefficiency

At the beginning of this chapter, we noted that Weber regarded bureaucracies as the most efficient type of secondary group. This runs against the grain of common knowledge. In everyday speech, when someone says *bureaucracy,* people commonly think of bored clerks sitting in small cubicles spinning out endless trails of "red tape" that create needless waste and frustrate the goals of clients (Figure 6.4). The idea that bureaucracies are efficient may seem odd.

Real events often reinforce the common view. Consider, for instance, the case of the *Challenger* space shuttle, which exploded shortly after takeoff on January 28, 1986, killing all seven crew members. The weather was cold, and the flexible O-rings that were supposed to seal the sections of the booster rockets had become rigid, which allowed burning gas to leak. The burning gas triggered the explosion. Some engineers at the National Aeronautics and Space Administration (NASA) and at the company that manufactured the O-rings knew they would not function properly in cold weather. However, this information did not reach NASA's top bureaucrats:

> [The] rigid hierarchy that had arisen at NASA ... made communication between departments formal and not particularly effective. [In the huge bureaucracy,] most communication was done through memos and reports. Everything was meticulously documented, but critical details tended to get lost in the paperwork blizzard. The result was that the upper-level managers were kept informed about possible problems with the O-rings ... but they never truly understood the seriousness of the issue. (Pool, 1997: 257)

As this tragedy shows, then, bureaucratic inefficiencies can sometimes have tragic consequences. Indeed, some of the lessons of the 1986 disaster appear to have gone unheeded. As mentioned above, in 2003 the shuttle *Columbia* was destroyed on reentry into earth's atmosphere, again killing all seven astronauts on board. NASA Administrator Sean O'Keefe was roundly criticized for bureaucratic mismanagement. The critics demanded to know why O'Keefe had not received internal NASA e-mails that expressed safety concerns about damage caused by debris during takeoff. As U.S. Representative Anthony Weiner told O'Keefe: "I read this stuff before you did. That's crazy" (quoted in Stenger, 2003).

How can we square the reality of bureaucratic inefficiencies—even tragedies—with Weber's view that bureaucracies are the most efficient type of secondary group? The answer

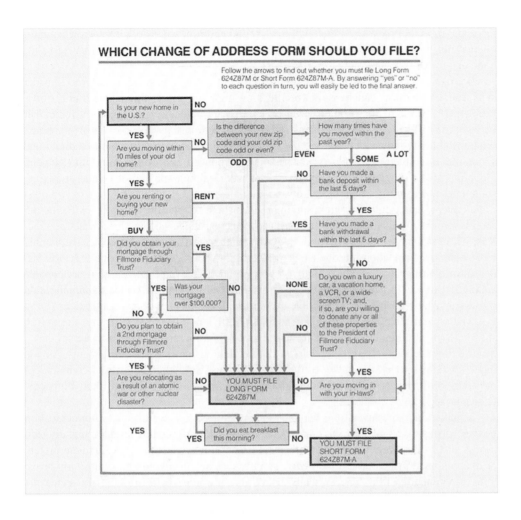

FIGURE 6.4
Red Tape

The 1980s Infocom game "Bureaucracy" satirized the conventional view of bureaucratic red tape.

Source: Infocom, 2003, "Bureaucracy." Retrieved March 14, 2003 (http:// infocom.elsewhere. org/gallery/ bureaucracy/ bureaucracy.html).

is twofold. First, we must recognize that when Weber wrote about the efficiency of bureaucracy, he was comparing it with older organizational forms. These operated on the basis of either traditional practice ("We do it this way because we've always done it this way") or the charisma of their leaders ("We do it this way because our chief inspires us to do it this way"). Compared with such "traditional" and "charismatic" organizations, bureaucracies *are* generally more efficient. Second, we must recognize that Weber thought bureaucracies could operate efficiently only in the ideal case. He wrote extensively about some of bureaucracy's less admirable aspects in the real world. In other words, he understood that reality is often messier than the ideal case. So should we. In reality, bureaucracies vary in efficiency. Therefore, rather than proclaiming bureaucracy efficient or inefficient, we should find out what makes bureaucracies work well or poorly. We can then apply this knowledge to improving the operation of bureaucracies.

Traditionally, sociologists have lodged four main criticisms against bureaucracies. First is the problem of **dehumanization**. Rather than treating clients and personnel as people with unique needs, bureaucracies sometimes treat clients as standard cases and personnel as cogs in a giant machine. This treatment frustrates clients and lowers worker morale. Second is the problem of **bureaucratic ritualism** (Merton, 1968 [1949]). Bureaucrats sometimes get so preoccupied with rules and regulations they make it difficult for the organization to fulfill its goals. Third is the problem of **oligarchy**, or "rule of the few" (Michels, 1949 [1911]). Some sociologists have argued that in all bureaucracies power tends to become increasingly concentrated in the hands of a few people at the top of the organizational pyramid. This tendency is particularly problematic in political organizations because it hinders democracy and renders leaders unaccountable to the public. Fourth is the problem of **bureaucratic inertia**. Bureaucracies are sometimes so

Dehumanization occurs when bureaucracies treat clients as standard cases and personnel as cogs in a giant machine. This treatment frustrates clients and lowers worker morale.

Bureaucratic ritualism involves bureaucrats becoming so preoccupied with rules and regulations that they make it difficult for the organization to fulfill its goals.

Oligarchy means "rule of the few." All bureaucracies have a supposed tendency for power to become increasingly concentrated in the hands of a few people at the top of the organizational pyramid.

Bureaucratic inertia refers to the tendency of large, rigid bureaucracies to continue their policies even when their clients' needs change.

large and rigid that they lose touch with reality and continue their policies even when their clients' needs change. Like the *Titanic,* they are so big that they find it difficult to shift course and steer clear of dangerous obstacles.

Two main factors underlie bureaucratic inefficiency: size and social structure. Consider size first. Something can be said for the view that bigger is almost inevitably more problematic. Some of the problems caused by size are evident even when you remember some of the differences between dyads and triads. When only two people are involved in a relationship, they may form a strong social bond. If they do, communication is direct and sometimes unproblematic. Once a third person is introduced, however, a secret may be kept, a coalition of two against one may crystallize, and jealousy may result. Thus, triads are sometimes more conflict ridden than dyads.

Problems can multiply in groups of more than three people. For example, as Figure 6.5 shows, only one dyadic relationship can exist between two people, whereas three dyadic relationships can exist among three people and six dyadic relationships among four people. The number of *potential* dyadic relationships increases exponentially with the number of people. Hence, 300 dyadic relationships are possible among 25 people and 1225 dyadic relationships are possible among 50 people. The possibility of clique formation, rivalries, conflict, and miscommunication rises as quickly as the number of possible dyadic social relationships in an organization.

The second factor underlying bureaucratic inefficiency is social structure. Figure 6.6 shows a typical bureaucratic structure. Note that it is a hierarchy. The bureaucracy has a head. Below the head are three divisions. Below the divisions are six departments. As you move up the hierarchy, the power of the staff increases. Note also the lines of communication that join the various bureaucratic units. Departments report only to their divisions. Divisions report only to the head.

Usually, the more levels in a bureaucratic structure, the more difficult communication becomes, because people have to communicate indirectly, through department and division heads, rather than directly with each other. Information may be lost, blocked, reinterpreted, or distorted as it moves up the hierarchy, or an excess of information may cause top levels to become engulfed in a "paperwork blizzard" that prevents them from clearly seeing the needs of the organization and its clients. Bureaucratic heads may have only a vague and imprecise idea of what is happening "on the ground" (Wilensky, 1967).

Consider also what happens when the lines of communication directly joining departments or divisions are weak or nonexistent. As the lines joining units in Figure 6.6 suggest, department A1 may have information that could help department B1 do its job better but may have to communicate that information indirectly through the division level. At the division level, the information may be lost, blocked, reinterpreted, or distorted. Thus, just as people who have authority may lack information, people who have information may lack the authority to act on it directly (Crozier, 1964 [1963]).

FIGURE 6.5

Number of Possible Dyadic Relationships by Number of People in Group

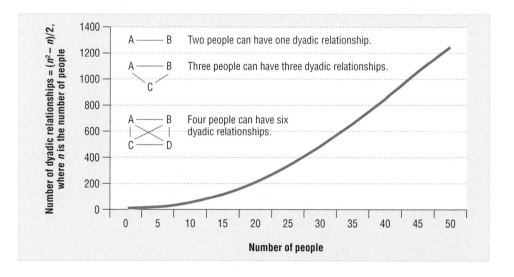

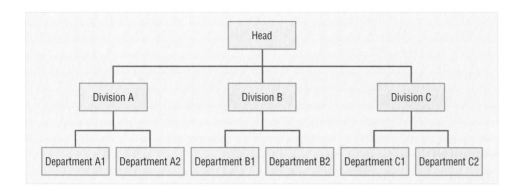

FIGURE 6.6
Bureaucratic Structure

Below we consider some ways of overcoming bureaucratic inefficiency. As you will see, these typically involve establishing patterns of social relations that flatten the bureaucratic hierarchy and cut across the sort of bureaucratic rigidities illustrated in Figure 6.6. As a useful prelude to this discussion, we first note some shortcomings of Weber's analysis of bureaucracy. Weber tended to ignore both bureaucracy's informal side and the role of leadership in influencing bureaucratic performance. Yet, as you will learn, it is precisely by paying attention to such issues that we can make bureaucracies more efficient.

Bureaucracy's Informal Side

Weber was concerned mainly with the formal structure or chain of command in a bureaucracy. He paid little attention to the social networks that underlie the chain of command.

Evidence for the existence of social networks and their importance in the operation of bureaucracies goes back to the 1930s. Officials at the Hawthorne plant of the Western Electric Company near Chicago wanted to see how various aspects of the work environment affected productivity. They sent social scientists in to investigate. Among other things, researchers found that workers in one section of the plant had established a norm for daily output. Workers who failed to meet the norm were helped by co-workers until their output increased. Workers who exceeded the norm were chided by co-workers until their productivity fell. Company officials and researchers previously had regarded employees merely as individuals who worked as hard or as little as they could in response to wage levels and work conditions. However, the Hawthorne study showed that employees are members of social networks that regulate output (Roethlisberger and Dickson, 1939).

In the 1970s, Rosabeth Moss Kanter conducted another landmark study of informal social relations in bureaucracies (Kanter, 1977). Kanter studied a corporation in which most women were sales agents. They were locked out of managerial positions. However, she did not find that the corporation discriminated against women as a matter of policy. She did find a male-only social network whose members shared gossip, went drinking, and told sexist jokes. The cost of being excluded from the network was high: To get good raises and promotions, a person had to be accepted as "one of the boys" and be sponsored by a male executive, which was impossible for women. Thus, despite a company policy that did not discriminate against women, an informal network of social relations ensured that the company discriminated against women in practice.

Despite their overt commitment to impersonality and written rules, bureaucracies rely profoundly on informal interaction to get the job done (Barnard, 1938; Blau, 1963). This fact is true even at

Informal interaction is common even in highly bureaucratic organizations. A water cooler, for example, can be a place for exchanging information and gossip, and even a place for decision making.

the highest levels. For example, executives usually decide important matters in face-to-face meetings, not in writing or via the phone. That is because people feel more comfortable in intimate settings, where they can get to know "the whole person." Meeting face to face, people can use their verbal and nonverbal interaction skills to gauge other people's trustworthiness. Socializing—talking over dinner, for example—is an important part of any business because the establishment of trust lies at the heart of all social interactions that require cooperation (Gambetta, 1988).

Leadership

Apart from overlooking the role of informal relations in the operation of bureaucracies, Weber also paid insufficient attention to the issue of leadership. Weber thought the formal structure of a bureaucracy largely determines how it operates. However, sociologists now realize that leadership style also has a big bearing on bureaucratic performance (Barnard, 1938; Ridgeway, 1983).

Research shows that the least effective leader is the one who allows subordinates to work things out largely on their own, with almost no direction from above. This is known as **laissez-faire leadership**, from the French expression "let them do." Note, however, that laissez-faire leadership can be effective under some circumstances. It works best when group members are highly experienced, trained, motivated, and educated, and when trust and confidence in group members are high. In such conditions, a strong leader is not really needed for the group to accomplish its goals. At the other extreme is **authoritarian leadership**. Authoritarian leaders demand strict compliance from subordinates. They are most effective in a crisis, such as a war or the emergency room of a hospital. They may earn grudging respect from subordinates for achieving the group's goals in the face of difficult circumstances, but they rarely win popularity contests. **Democratic leadership** offers more guidance than the laissez-faire variety but less control than the authoritarian type. Democratic leaders try to include all group members in the decision-making process, taking the best ideas from the group and moulding them into a strategy that all can identify with. Except for crisis situations, democratic leadership is usually the most effective leadership style.

In sum, contemporary researchers have modified Weber's characterization of bureaucracy in two main ways. First, they have stressed the importance of informal social networks in shaping bureaucratic operations. Second, they have shown that democratic leaders are most effective in non-crisis situations because they tend to widely distribute decision-making authority and rewards. As you will now see, these lessons are important when it comes to thinking about how to make bureaucracies more efficient.

Overcoming Bureaucratic Inefficiency

In the business world, large bureaucratic organizations sometimes find themselves unable to compete against smaller, innovative firms, particularly in industries that are changing quickly (Burns and Stalker, 1961). This situation occurs partly because innovative firms tend to have flatter and more democratic organizational structures, such as the network illustrated in Figure 6.7. Compare the flat network structure in Figure 6.7 with the traditional bureaucratic

Laissez-faire leadership allows subordinates to work things out largely on their own, with almost no direction from above. It is the least effective type of leadership.

Authoritarian leadership demands strict compliance from subordinates. Authoritarian leaders are most effective in a crisis, such as a war or the emergency room of a hospital.

Democratic leadership offers more guidance than the laissez-faire variety but less control than the authoritarian type. Democratic leaders try to include all group members in the decision-making process, taking the best ideas from the group and moulding them into a strategy with which all can identify. Outside crisis situations, democratic leadership is usually the most effective leadership style.

FIGURE 6.7
Network Structure

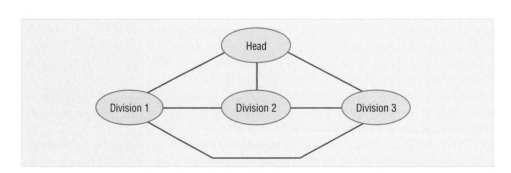

structure in Figure 6.6. Note that the network structure has fewer levels than the traditional bureaucratic structure. Moreover, in the network structure, lines of communication link all units. In the traditional bureaucratic structure, information flows only upward.

Much evidence suggests that flatter bureaucracies with decentralized decision making and multiple lines of communication produce more satisfied workers, happier clients, and bigger profits (Kanter, 1989). Some of this evidence comes from Sweden and Japan. Beginning in the early 1970s, such corporations as Volvo and Toyota were at the forefront of bureaucratic innovation in those countries. They began eliminating middle-management positions. They allowed worker participation in a variety of tasks related to their main functions. They delegated authority to autonomous teams of a dozen or so workers who were allowed to make many decisions themselves. They formed "quality circles" of workers to monitor and correct defects in products and services. As a result, product quality, worker morale, and profitability improved. Today, these ideas have spread well beyond the Swedish and Japanese automobile industry and are evident in such companies as General Motors, Ford, Boeing, and Caterpillar. In the 1980s and 1990s, companies outside the manufacturing sector introduced similar bureaucratic reforms, again with positive effects.

Organizational Environments

If flatter organizations are more efficient, why aren't all bureaucracies flatter? Mainly, say sociologists, because of the environment in which they operate. An **organizational environment** comprises a host of economic, political, and cultural factors that lie outside an organization and affect the way it works (Aldrich, 1979; Meyer and Scott, 1983). Some organizational environments are conducive to the formation of flatter, network-like bureaucracies. Others are not. We can illustrate the effects of organizational environments by discussing two cases that have attracted much attention in recent years: the United States and Japan.

In the 1970s, American business bureaucracies tended to be more hierarchical than their Japanese counterparts. This was one reason that worker dissatisfaction was high and labour productivity was low in the United States. In Japan, where corporate decision making was more decentralized, worker morale and productivity were high (Dore, 1983). Several aspects of the organizational environment help to explain Japanese–American differences in the 1970s:

- *Japanese workers were in a position to demand and achieve more decision-making authority than American workers were.* After World War II, the proportion of Japanese workers in unions increased whereas the proportion of American workers in unions declined (see Chapter 21, Collective Action and Social Movements). Unions gave Japanese workers more clout than their American counterparts enjoyed.
- *International competition encouraged bureaucratic efficiency in Japan.* Many big Japanese corporations matured in the highly competitive post–World War II international environment. Many big American corporations originated earlier, in an international environment with few competitors. Thus, Japanese corporations had a bigger incentive to develop more efficient organizational structures (Harrison, 1994).
- *The availability of external suppliers allowed Japanese firms to remain lean.* Many large American companies matured when external sources of supply were scarce. For example, when IBM entered the computer market in the 1950s, it had to produce all components internally because nobody else was making them. This situation led IBM to develop a large, hierarchical bureaucracy. In contrast, Japanese computer manufacturers could rely on many external suppliers in the 1970s. Therefore, they could develop flatter organizational structures (Podolny and Page, 1998).

Today, Japanese–American differences have substantially decreased because most big businesses in the United States have introduced Japanese-style bureaucratic reforms (Tsutsui, 1998). For instance, Silicon Valley, the centre of the American computer industry today, is full of companies that fit the "Japanese" organizational pattern. These companies

An organizational environment comprises a host of economic, political, and cultural forces that lie outside an organization and affect the way it works.

originated in the 1980s and 1990s, when external suppliers were abundant and international competitiveness was intense. In addition, American companies started to copy Japanese business structures because they saw them as successful (DiMaggio and Powell, 1983). We thus see how changes in the organizational environment help account for convergence between Japanese and American bureaucratic forms.

The experience of the United States over the past few decades holds out hope for increasing bureaucratic efficiency and the continued growth of employee autonomy and creativity at work. It does not mean, however, that bureaucracies in Japan and the United States will be alike in all respects in 20 or 50 or 100 years. The organizational environment is unpredictable, and sociologists are just beginning to understand its operation. It is therefore anyone's guess how far convergence will continue.

SOCIETIES

Societies are collectivities of interacting people who share a culture and a territory.

Networks, groups, and bureaucracies are embedded in **societies**, collectivities of interacting people who share a culture and a territory.[1] Like smaller collectivities, societies help shape human action. They influence the kind of work we do and how productively we work. They mould patterns of class, gender, racial, and ethnic inequality. They impinge on the way religious, family, and other institutions operate. They affect the way we govern and the way we think of ourselves.

Despite the pervasiveness of these influences, most people are blind to them. We tend to believe that we are free to do what we want. Yet the plain fact is that societies affect even our most personal and intimate choices. For example, deciding how many children to have is one of the most intensely private and emotional issues a woman must face. So why is it that tens of millions of women have decided in the space of just a few decades to have an average of two babies instead of six, or eight babies instead of four? Why do so many individuals make almost exactly the same private decision at almost precisely the same historical moment? The answer is that certain identifiable social conditions prompt them to reach the same conclusion, in this case to have fewer or more babies. And so it is with most decisions. Identifiable social conditions increase the chance that we will choose one course of action over another.

The relationship between people and nature is the most basic determinant of how societies are structured and therefore how people's choices are constrained. Accordingly, researchers have identified six stages of human evolution, each characterized by a shift in the relationship between people and nature. As we review each of these stages, note what happens to the human–nature relationship: With each successive stage, people are less at the mercy of nature and transform it more radically. The changing relationship between people and nature has huge implications for all aspects of social life. Let us identify these implications as we sketch the evolution of human society in bold strokes.

Foraging Societies

Foraging societies are societies in which people live by searching for wild plants and hunting wild animals. Such societies predominated until about 10 000 years ago. Inequality, the division of labour, productivity, and settlement size are very low in such societies.

Until about 10 000 years ago, all people lived in **foraging societies**. They lived by searching for wild plants and hunting wild animals (Lenski, Nolan, and Lenski, 1995; O'Neil, 2004; Sahlins, 1972). They were passively dependent on nature, taking whatever it made available and transforming it only slightly to meet their needs. They built simple tools, such as baskets, bows and arrows, spears, and digging sticks. They sometimes burned grasslands to encourage the growth of new vegetation and attract game, but they neither planted crops nor domesticated many animals.

Most foragers lived in temporary encampments, and when food was scarce they migrated to more bountiful regions. Harsh environments could support 3 people per 25 to 130 square kilometres (1 person per 10 to 50 square miles). Rich environments could support 25 to 80 people per square kilometre (10 to 30 people per square mile). Foraging communities or bands averaged about 25 to 30 people but could be as large as 100 people. *Aquatic foragers,* such as those on the western coast of North America, concentrated on fishing and hunting marine mammals. *Equestrian foragers,* such as the Great Plains Native peoples of North America, hunted large mammals from horseback. *Pedestrian foragers* engaged in diversified hunting and gathering on foot and could be found on all continents.

Until the middle of the twentieth century, most social scientists thought that foragers lived brief, grim lives. In their view, foragers were engaged in a desperate struggle for existence that was typically cut short by disease, starvation, pestilence, or some other force of nature. We now know that this characterization says more about the biases of early anthropologists than about the lives foragers actually lived. Consider the !Kung of the Kalahari Desert in southern Africa, who maintained their traditional way of life until the 1960s (Lee, 1979). Young !Kung did not fully join the workforce until they reached the age of 20. Adults worked only about 15 hours a week. Mainly because of disease, children faced a much smaller chance of surviving childhood than is the case in contemporary society, but about 10 percent of the !Kung were older than 60, the same percentage as Canadians in the early 1970s. It thus seems that the !Kung who survived childhood lived relatively long, secure, leisurely, healthy, and happy lives. They were not unique. The tall totem poles, ornate wood carvings, colourful masks, and elaborate clothing of the Kwakiutl on Vancouver Island serve as beautiful reminders that many foragers had the leisure time to invest considerable energy in ornamentation.

Equestrian foragers were hierarchical, male-dominated, and warlike, especially after they acquired rifles in the nineteenth century. However, the social structure of pedestrian foragers—the great majority of all foragers—was remarkably non-hierarchical. They shared what little wealth they had, and women and men enjoyed approximately equal status.

Pastoral and Horticultural Societies

Substantial social inequality became widespread about 10 000 years ago, when some bands began to domesticate various wild plants and animals, especially cattle, camels, pigs, goats, sheep, horses, and reindeer (Lenski, Nolan, and Lenski, 1995; O'Neil, 2004). By using hand tools to garden in highly fertile areas (**horticultural societies**) and herding animals in more arid areas (**pastoral societies**), people increased the food supply and made it more dependable. Nature could now support more people. Moreover, pastoral and horticultural societies enabled fewer people to specialize in producing food and more people to specialize in constructing tools and weapons, making clothing and jewellery, and trading valuable objects with other bands. Some families and bands accumulated more domesticated animals, cropland, and valued objects than others did. As a result, pastoral and horticultural societies developed a higher level of social inequality than was evident in most foraging societies.

As wealth accumulated, feuding and warfare grew, particularly among pastoralists. Men who controlled large herds of animals and conducted successful predatory raids acquired much prestige and power and came to be recognized as chiefs. Some chiefs formed large, fierce, mobile armies. The Mongols and the Zulus were horse pastoralists who conquered large parts of Asia and Africa, respectively.

Most pastoralists were nomadic, with migration patterns dictated by their animals' needs for food and water. Some pastoralists migrated regularly from the same cool highlands in the summer to the same warm lowland valleys in the winter and were able to establish villages in both locations. Horticulturalists often established permanent settlements beside

Horticultural societies are societies in which people domesticate plants and use simple hand tools to garden. Such societies first emerged about 10 000 years ago.

Pastoral societies are societies in which people domesticate cattle, camels, pigs, goats, sheep, horses, and reindeer. Such societies first emerged about 10 000 years ago.

Marine foragers had much leisure time to invest in ornamentation, suggesting that their lives were by no means a constant struggle for survival.

A medieval painting showing peasants harvesting outside the walls of their lord and master's castle. Why is it significant that the church is situated inside the walls?

Agricultural societies are societies in which plows and animal power are used to substantially increase food supply and dependability as compared with horticultural and pastoral societies. Agricultural societies first emerged about 5000 years ago.

Industrial societies are societies that use machines and fuel to greatly increase the supply and dependability of food and finished goods. The first such societies emerged about 230 years ago in Great Britain.

their croplands. These settlements might include several hundred people. However, the development of large permanent settlements, including the first cities, took place only with the development of intensive agriculture.

Agricultural Societies

Especially in the fertile river valleys of the Middle East, India, China, and South America, human populations flourished—so much so that, about 5000 years ago, they could no longer be sustained by pastoral and horticulture techniques. It was then that **agricultural societies** originated. The plow was invented to harness animal power for more intensive and efficient agricultural production. The plow allowed farmers to plant crops over much larger areas and dig below the topsoil, bringing nutrients to the surface and thus increasing yield (Lenski, Nolan, and Lenski, 1995; O'Neil, 2004).

Because the source of food was immobile, many people now built permanent settlements, and because people were now able to produce considerably more food than was necessary for their own subsistence, surpluses were sold in village markets. Some of these centres became towns and then cities, home to rulers, religious figures, soldiers, craft workers, and government officials. The population of some agricultural societies numbered in the millions.

The crystallization of the idea of private property was one of the most significant developments of the era. Among pedestrian foragers, there was no private ownership of land or water. Among horticulturalists, particular families might be recognized as having rights to some property, but only while they were using it. If the property was not in use, they were obliged to share it or give it to a family that needed it. In contrast, in societies that practised intensive agriculture, powerful individuals succeeded in having the idea of individual property rights legally recognized. It was now possible for people to buy land and water, to call them their own, and to transmit ownership to their offspring. People could now become rich and, through inheritance, make their children rich.

Ancient civilizations thus became rigidly divided into classes. Royalty surrounded itself with loyal landowners, protected itself with professional soldiers, and justified its rule with the help of priests, part of whose job was to convince ordinary peasants that the existing social order was God's will. Government officials collected taxes and religious officials collected tithes, thus enriching the upper classes with the peasantry's surplus production. In this era, inequality between women and men also reached its historical high point (Boulding, 1976).

Industrial Societies

Stimulated by international exploration, trade, and commerce, the Industrial Revolution began in Britain in the 1780s. A century later, it had spread to all of Western Europe, North America, Japan, and Russia. It involved the use of fuel—at first, water power and steam—to drive machines and thereby greatly increase productivity, the quantity of things that could be produced with a given amount of effort.

If you have ever read a Charles Dickens novel, such as *Oliver Twist,* you know that hellish working conditions and deep social inequalities characterized early **industrial societies**. Work in factories and mines became so productive that owners amassed previously unimaginable fortunes but ordinary labourers worked 16-hour days in dangerous conditions and earned barely enough to survive. They struggled for the right to form and join unions and expand the vote to all adult citizens, hoping to use union power and political influence to win improvements in the conditions of their existence. At the same time, new technologies and ways of organizing work made it possible to produce ever more goods at a lower cost per unit. This made it possible to meet many of the workers' demands and raise living standards for the entire population.

Increasingly, businesses required a literate, numerate, and highly trained workforce. To raise profits, they were eager to identify and hire the most talented people. They encouraged everyone to develop their talents and rewarded them for doing so by paying higher salaries. Even inequality between women and men began to decrease because of the demand for talent and women's struggles to enter the paid workforce on an equal footing with men. Why hire an incompetent man over a competent woman when you can profit more from the services of a capable employee? Put in this way, women's demands for equality made good business sense. For all these reasons, class and gender inequality declined as industrial societies matured.

Postindustrial Societies

In the early 1970s, sociologist Daniel Bell (1973) argued that industrial society was rapidly becoming a thing of the past. According to Bell, just as agriculture gave way to manufacturing as the driving force of the economy in the nineteenth century, so did manufacturing give way to service industries by the mid-twentieth century, resulting in the birth of **postindustrial societies.**

Even in pre-agricultural societies, a few individuals specialized in providing services rather than in producing goods. For example, a person considered adept at tending to the ill, forecasting the weather, or predicting the movement of animals might be relieved of hunting responsibilities to focus on these services. However, such jobs were rare because productivity was low. Nearly everyone had to do physical work for the tribe to survive. Even in early agricultural societies, it took 80 to 100 farmers to support one non-farmer (Hodson and Sullivan, 1995: 10). Only at the beginning of the nineteenth century in industrialized countries did productivity increase to the point where a quarter of the labour force could be employed in services. By 1960, all the highly industrialized countries had reached that threshold.

In postindustrial societies, women have been recruited to the service sector in disproportionately large numbers, and that has helped to ensure a gradual increase in equality between women and men in terms of education, income, and other indicators of rank (see Chapter 11, Sexuality and Gender). The picture with respect to inequality between classes is more complex. Most postindustrial societies, and especially the United States, have experienced large increases in class inequality. Other postindustrial societies, such as Canada, have not. At least one postindustrial society—France—had less inequality in 2000 than in 1977, bucking the broader trend (Smeeding, 2004). We discuss the reasons for these different patterns in Chapter 8, Social Stratification: Canadian and Global Perspectives.

Rapid change in the composition of the labour force during the final decades of the twentieth century was made possible by the computer. The computer automated many manufacturing and office procedures. It created jobs in the service sector as quickly as it eliminated them in manufacturing. The computer is to the service sector as the steam engine was to manufacturing, the plow was to intensive agriculture, domestication was to horticulture and pastoralism, and simple hand tools were to foraging.

Postindustrial societies are societies in which most workers are employed in the service sector and computers spur substantial increases in the division of labour and productivity. Shortly after World War II, the United States became the first postindustrial society.

Postnatural Societies

On February 28, 1953, two men walked into a pub in Cambridge, England, and offered drinks all around. "We have discovered the secret of life!" proclaimed one of the men. He was James Watson. With his colleague, Francis Crick, he had found the structure of deoxyribonucleic acid, or DNA, the chemical that makes up genes. During cell division, a single DNA molecule uncoils into two strands. New, identical molecules are formed from each strand. In this way, growth takes place and traits are passed from one generation to the next. It was one of the most important scientific discoveries ever (Watson, 1968).

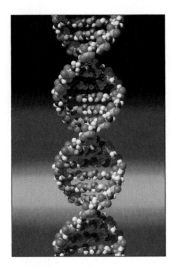

The DNA molecule

Recombinant DNA involves removing a segment of DNA from a gene or splicing together segments of DNA from different living things, thus effectively creating a new life form.

Postnatural societies are societies in which genetic engineering enables people to create new life forms. Although genetic engineering holds out much promise for improving productivity, feeding the poor, ridding the world of disease, and so on, social inequality could increase in postnatural societies unless people democratically decide on the acceptable risks of genetic engineering and the distribution of its benefits.

By the early 1970s, scientists were beginning to develop techniques for manipulating DNA (so-called **recombinant DNA**). Soon they could cut a segment out of a DNA strand and join the remaining sections together, or they could take a DNA strand and connect it to segments of DNA from another living thing. This meant that scientists could now create new life forms, a capability that had until then been restricted in the popular imagination to God alone. Enthusiasts proclaimed a "second genesis" as they began to speculate about the potential of the new technology to rid the world of hereditary disease; feed the hungry with higher-yield, disease-resistant farm products; and even create more intelligent, beautiful, and athletic children. For many millions of years, nature had selected the "fittest" living things for survival. Now it seemed possible for humans to speed up natural selection, thus escaping the whims of nature and creating a more perfect society under their control. The invention of recombinant DNA marked the onset of a new social era—what we prefer to call the era of **postnatural society** (Dyson, 1999; Watson, 2000).

We consider some of the perils of postnatural society in detail in this book's online chapter, Chapter 22, Technology and the Global Environment. Here we want only to emphasize that genetic engineering could easily result in increased social inequality. For example, the technology for creating more perfect babies will undoubtedly be expensive, so rich countries and rich people are more likely to benefit from it. Princeton University biologist Lee Silver and Nobel Prize–winning physicist Freeman Dyson go so far as to speculate that the ultimate result of genetic engineering will be several distinct human species. People who are in a position to take full advantage of genetic engineering will be better looking, more intelligent, less likely to suffer from disease, and more athletic. People who are not so fortunate will have to face nature's caprice in handing out talents and disadvantages, just as our foraging ancestors did (Brave, 2003). The main, and perhaps only, safeguard against such an outcome is true democracy, which would allow ordinary people to decide which risks are worth taking and how the benefits of genetic engineering should be distributed within and across populations (Häyry and Lehto, 1998).

FREEDOM AND CONSTRAINT IN SOCIAL LIFE

Throughout this chapter, we emphasized the capacity of networks, groups, bureaucracies, and societies to constrain human behaviour. As we have seen, such social collectivities can even encourage dangerously high levels of conformity, compel people to act against their better judgment, dominate people in a vice of organizational rigidities, and affect the level of social inequality in society.

We stressed the constraining aspect of social collectives because we wanted to counter the common-sense view that motives alone determine the way people act. Now, however, in conclusion, it would serve us well to remind you that people often have two options other than bowing to the will of their social collectivities: "exit" and "voice" (Hirschman, 1970). In some circumstances, they can leave the social collectivities to which they belong (exit). In other circumstances, they can struggle against the constraints their social collectivities seek to impose on them (voice). As French philosopher Jean-Paul Sartre once remarked, it is always possible to say no, even to the worst tyrant. Less dramatically but no less importantly, knowledge, including sociological knowledge, can increase the ability of people to resist the constraints imposed on them. Recall the Milgram experiment we discussed at the beginning of this chapter, in which subjects administered what they thought were painful shocks to people just because the experimenters told them to. When the experiment was replicated years later, many of the subjects refused to go along with the demands of the experimenters. Some invoked the example of the Nazis to justify their refusal to comply. Others mentioned Milgram's original experiment. Their knowledge, some of it perhaps gained in sociology courses, enabled them to resist unreasonable demands (Gamson, Fireman, and Rytina, 1982; Box 6.2).

Paradoxically, to succeed in challenging social collectivities, people must sometimes form a new social collectivity themselves. Half a century ago, Seymour Martin Lipset, Martin

BOX 6.2
Sociology at the Movies

TAKE | ROLL

Shake Hands with the Devil (2004)

Over a period of 100 days in 1994, the Hutus of Rwanda massacred 800 000 Tutsis—more than a tenth of Rwanda's population—with guns, machetes, hammers, and spears. Bodies were scattered everywhere, and the streets literally flowed with blood. The French trained and armed the Hutus in full knowledge of what would transpire. The Belgians knew too, and their 2000 troops could have done much to prevent it, but they withdrew their "peacekeepers" just before the massacre began. Canadian General Roméo Dallaire, who led a contingent of United Nations troops in Rwanda, reported to his bosses at the UN that he knew where the Hutu arms caches were located and requested permission to destroy them. Permission was denied. Most North Americans were busy watching the O. J. Simpson trial on TV and so barely noticed the genocide.

Dallaire and his 450 soldiers from Canada, Ghana, Tunisia, and Bangladesh nonetheless risked their lives to save an estimated 30 000 Rwandans in one of the twentieth century's great heroic acts. Like the Swedish World War II hero Raoul Wallenberg in Hungary, and Japanese consular official Chiune Sugihara in Lithuania, both of whom risked their lives to save thousands of Jews from the Nazis, Dallaire courageously swam against the stream of world apathy. *Shake Hands with the Devil,* which won the 2007 Emmy for best documentary, details Dallaire's actions, the heavy toll they took on his mental health, and his recovery from the trauma of 1994.

General Roméo Dallaire

Hutus and Tutsis had existed as somewhat distinct ethnic groups for centuries before 1994. The Hutus were mainly farmers and the Tutsis, mainly cattle herders. The Tutsis were the ruling minority yet they spoke the same language as the Hutus, shared the same religious beliefs, live side by side, and often intermarried. The two groups never came into serious conflict. When the Belgians colonized Rwanda in 1916, however, they made ethnic divisions far more rigid. Now one had to be a Tutsi to serve in an official capacity, and the Belgians started distinguishing Tutsis from Hutus by measuring the width of their noses; Tutsi noses, they arbitrarily proclaimed, were thinner. It as a preposterous policy (not least because half the population of

Rwanda is of mixed Hutu-Tutsi ancestry) and it served to sharply increase animosity between the two ethnic groups (Organization of African Unity, 2000: 10).

Before the Belgians decolonized Rwanda in 1962, they encouraged power sharing between the Tutsis and the Hutus but by then the damage had been done. The Tutsis objected to any loss of power and civil war broke out. Tutsi rebels fled to Uganda, and when Rwanda proclaimed independence, the Hutu majority took power. Then, in the early 1990s, descendants of the Tutsi rebels, backed by the United States and Britain, tried to overthrow the Hutu government, backed by France and Belgium. (Western interest in the region is high because it is rich in minerals; Rose, 2001.) The 1994 genocide erupted when the plane of the Hutu president was shot down, killing the president.

Although we know much about the origins of the 1994 Rwandan genocide, we know little about the conditions that create heroes. We do know that heroes are typically raised in an atmosphere of high moral principle and ethical standards of conduct. We know that they often demonstrate an independence of character and a willingness to defy authority and convention in the years preceding their heroic acts. Thus, while heroism sometimes requires a split-second decision, it is usually preceded by years of socialization that predispose the future hero to act compassionately even if doing so involves refusing to follow the herd (Franco and Zimbardo, 2006–07). As such, we have much to learn from the example of people like General Roméo Dallaire.

A. Trow, and James S. Coleman (1956) conducted a classic sociological study that made just this point. They investigated the remarkable case of the International Typographical Union—

remarkable because in the 1950s it was the outstanding exception to the tendency of trade union bureaucracies to turn into oligarchies, or organizations run by the few. The International Typographical Union remained democratic because the nature of printing as an occupation and an industry made the resources for democratic politics more widely available than is typical in trade unions. Strong local unions that valued their autonomy founded the international union. The local and regional markets typical of the printing industry at the time strengthened their autonomy. At the same time, strong factions in the union prevented any one faction from becoming dominant. Finally, robust social networks on the shop floor enabled ordinary printers to fight for their rights and resist the slide into oligarchy and dull obedience. What this case illustrates is the way people can form social collectivities to counteract other social collectives. Embedded in social relations, we can use them for good or evil.

NOTE

1. For "virtual societies" on the Internet, however, a shared territory is unnecessary.

SUMMARY

1. Do people act the way they do only because of their interests and emotions?
    People's motives are important determinants of their actions, but social collectivities also influence the way they behave. Because of the power of social collectivities, people sometimes act against their interests, values, and emotions.

2. Is it a small world?
    It is a small world. Most people interact repeatedly with a small circle of family members, friends, and co-workers. However, our personal networks overlap with other social networks, which is why only a few links separate us from complete strangers.

3. What is network analysis?
    Network analysis is the study of the concrete social relations linking people. By focusing on concrete ties, network analysts often come up with surprising results. For example, network analysis has demonstrated the strength of weak ties in job searches, explained patterns in the flow of information and communicable diseases, and demonstrated that a rich web of social affiliations underlies urban life.

4. What are groups?
    Groups are clusters of people who identity with one another. Primary groups involve intense, intimate, enduring relations; secondary groups involve less personal and intense ties; and reference groups are groups against which people measure their situation or conduct. Groups impose conformity on members and seek to exclude non-members.

5. Is bureaucracy just "red tape"? Is it possible to overcome bureaucratic inefficiency?
    Although bureaucracies often suffer from various forms of inefficiency, they are generally efficient compared with other organizational forms. Bureaucratic inefficiency increases with size and degree of hierarchy. By flattening bureaucratic structures, decentralizing decision-making authority, and opening lines of communication between bureaucratic units, efficiency can often be improved.

6. How accurate is Weber's analysis of bureaucracy?
    Social networks underlie the chain of command in all bureaucracies and affect their operation. Weber ignored this aspect of bureaucracy. He also downplayed the importance of leadership in the functioning of bureaucracy. However, research shows that democratic leadership improves the efficiency of bureaucratic operations in non-crisis

situations, authoritarian leadership works best in crises, and laissez-faire leadership is the least effective form of leadership in all situations.

7. What impact does the organizational environment have on bureaucracy?

The organizational environment influences the degree to which bureaucratic efficiency can be achieved. For example, bureaucracies are less hierarchical where workers are more powerful, competition with other bureaucracies is high, and external sources of supply are available.

8. How have societies evolved over the past 100 000 years?

Over the past 100 000 years, growing human domination of nature has increased the supply and dependability of food and finished goods, productivity, the division of labour, and the size and permanence of human settlements. Class and gender inequality increased until the nineteenth century and then began to decline. Class inequality began to increase in some societies in the last decades of the twentieth century and may continue to increase in the future.

In foraging societies, people lived by searching for wild plants and hunting wild animals. Horticultural and pastoral societies emerged about 10 000 years ago. In horticultural societies, people domesticated plants and used simple hand tools to garden. In pastoral societies, people domesticated cattle, camels, pigs, goats, sheep, horses, and reindeer. Agricultural societies first emerged about 5000 years ago. In such societies, people used plows and animal power to produce food. Great Britain was the first society to industrialize, beginning about 230 years ago. Industrial societies used machines and fuel to greatly increase the supply and dependability of food and finished goods. In postindustrial societies, most workers are employed in the service sector and computers spur substantial increases in the division of labour and productivity. Some societies may be said to have entered a postnatural phase in the early 1970s, when genetic engineering became possible. Genetic engineering enables people to create new life forms, holding out much promise for improving productivity, feeding the poor, ridding the world of disease, and so on, and much uncertainty as to whether these benefits will be equitably distributed.

9. What does the sociological analysis of networks, groups, bureaucracies, and societies tell us about the possibility of human freedom?

Networks, groups, bureaucracies, and societies influence and constrain everyone. However, people can also use these social collectivities to increase their freedom. In this sense, social collectivities are a source of both constraint and freedom.

KEY TERMS

agricultural societies (p. 172)

authoritarian leadership (p. 168)

bureaucracy (p. 154)

bureaucratic inertia (p. 165)

bureaucratic ritualism (p. 165)

dehumanization (p. 165)

democratic leadership (p. 168)

dyad (p. 159)

foraging societies (p. 170)

formal organizations (p. 164)

groupthink (p. 161)

horticultural societies (p. 171)

industrial societies (p. 172)

in-group (p. 162)

laissez-faire leadership (p. 168)

oligarchy (p. 165)

organizational environment (p. 169)

out-group (p. 162)

pastoral societies (p. 171)

postindustrial societies (p. 173)

postnatural societies (p. 174)

primary groups (p. 160)

recombinant DNA (p. 174)

reference group (p. 163)

secondary groups (p. 161)   social network (p. 156)

social category (p. 160)   societies (p. 170)

social group (p. 160)   triad (p. 159)

QUESTIONS TO CONSIDER

1. Would you have acted any differently from ordinary Germans if you had lived in Nazi Germany? Why or why not? What if you had been a member of a Nazi police battalion? Would you have been a traitor to your group? Why or why not?

2. If you were starting your own business, how would you organize it? Why? Base your answer on theories and research discussed in this chapter.

WEB RESOURCES

Companion Website for This Book

http://www.compass3e.nelson.com

Begin by clicking on the Student Resources section of the website. Next, select the chapter you are studying from the pull-down menu. From the Student Resources page you have easy access to InfoTrac® College Edition, additional Weblinks, and other resources. The website also has many useful tips to aid you in your study of sociology, including practice tests for each chapter.

InfoTrac® Search Terms

These search terms are provided to assist you in beginning to conduct research on this topic by visiting http://www.infotrac-college.com:

bureaucracy
rational choice theory
social network

Recommended Websites

An attempt to apply degrees of separation to the entire world via the Internet was conducted at Columbia University's Department of Sociology. You can see the results of the study at http://smallworld.columbia.edu/images/dodds2003pa.pdf.

Yahoo! sponsors many sociology discussion groups. To join, visit http://dir.groups. http://tech.dir.groups.yahoo.com/dir/Science/Social_Sciences/Sociology.

CengageNOW™

http://hed.nelson.com

This online diagnostic tool identifies each student's unique needs with a Pretest that generates a personalized Study Plan for each chapter, helping students focus on concepts they're having the most difficulty mastering. Students then take a Posttest after reading the chapter to measure their understanding of the material. An Instructor Gradebook is available to track and monitor student progress.

Inequality

CHAPTER

7

Deviance and Crime

In this chapter, you will learn that

- Deviance and crime vary among cultures, across history, and from one social context to another.

- Rather than being inherent in actions or the characteristics of individuals, deviance and crime are socially defined and constructed. The distribution of power is especially important in the social construction of deviance and crime.

- Following dramatic increases during the 1960s and 1970s, Canadian crime rates peaked in the early 1990s and have been falling steadily since then. The decline is due mainly to more effective policing, the declining number of young people in the population, and a booming economy throughout most of this period.

- Statistics show that a disproportionately large number of Aboriginal people are arrested, convicted, and imprisoned. Explanations for these statistics include the low social and economic standing of Aboriginal people, the commission of offences more likely to generate an official response from the criminal justice system, a decline in informal mechanisms of social control within Aboriginal communities, and racial discrimination in the criminal justice system.

- There are many theories of deviance and crime. Each theory illuminates a different aspect of the process by which people break rules and are labelled as deviants and criminals.

- As they do for deviance and crime, conceptions of appropriate punishment vary culturally and historically.

- Imprisonment is one of the main forms of punishment in industrial societies.

- Fear of crime may be subject to manipulation by commercial and political groups that benefit from it.

- Cost-effective and workable alternatives to currently predominant regimes of punishment exist.

CANADIAN ATTITUDES TOWARD CRIME

When Canadians between the ages of 18 and 49 sit down to watch TV in the evenings, they are more likely to choose crime or medical dramas than any other type of program—and medical dramas sometime weave criminal matters into their story lines (Table 7.1 on page 182). On this basis you might conclude that we are a society obsessed with crime. You would not be far off the mark. Canadians are often asked by pollsters to identify the top 10 social issues that concern them. Crime has been among the top three issues since the 1970s (Bibby, 1995: 94–95). National surveys routinely find that Canadians believe that crime in general, and violent crime in particular, is on the rise (Fedorowycz, 1999). Most Canadian adults and teenagers tell survey researchers that the courts are too soft on criminals, particularly young offenders, and that we should use the death penalty, at least in some cases (Besserer, 2002; Bibby, 1995, 2001: 45).

Why is there so much concern with crime in Canada and so much support for a get-tough approach? Since we commonly think of criminals as "the bad guys," we might be excused for thinking that Canada contains a disproportionately large number of bad people who have broken the law. For sociologists, however, this is an oversimplification for two reasons. First, the term *crime* simply indicates a technical violation of the criminal law. Knowing that someone has broken the law tells us little about his or her moral character and whether he or she is "good" or "bad." Consider, for example, that in the 1970s a popular CBC game show called *This Is the Law* took a tongue-in-cheek approach to the topic of crime. Each week on the show, panellists watched sketches in which crimes were being enacted. After the police had arrested the villain in the sketch, the panellists were asked to guess exactly what crime had been committed. The show's writers, it seemed, had no problem finding "ample examples of loony laws worldwide to keep the program stocked with fresh material and the panellists guessing" (Statistics Canada, 1998a: 508). One Canadian crime featured on this program was the "fraudulent practice of witchcraft," or fortune-telling. Another was a B.C. law that prohibited hairdressers in the province from advertising the price of haircuts.

Second, it would be useful to bear in mind that a list of famous people who have been labelled as criminals would include Socrates, Jesus, Martin Luther, Louis Riel, Mahatma Gandhi, Martin Luther King, Jr., and Nelson Mandela. For most people today, these historical figures are heroes. In contrast, people who planned and participated in the extermination of Jews, Roma (Gypsies), and homosexuals in Nazi Germany were acting in a way that was defined in Germany as law-abiding.

Most people would consider the actions taken by the Nazis in Germany, rather than the actions of Jesus or Martin Luther, to be deviant or criminal. That is because norms and laws have changed dramatically. Today, anyone who advocates or promotes genocide has committed a crime under Canadian law. Section 319 of the Criminal Code prohibits the wilful promotion of hatred against any identifiable group or "any section of the public distinguished by colour, race, sexual orientation, religion, or ethnic group." It also specifies that anyone doing so may be punished with a term of imprisonment of up to two years.

It is evident, then, that definitions of deviance and crime change over time and differ over place (Box 7.1 on page 182). For example, homosexuality used to be considered a crime and then a mental illness, but an increasing proportion of Canadians now recognize homosexuality as a legitimate sexual orientation (Mooney, Knox, Schacht, and Nelson, 2001). Similarly, acts that are right and heroic for some people are wrong and treacherous for others. If you ask any of the law enforcement officials and members of the Canadian Armed Forces who were brought in during the 1990 Oka crisis on the Kanesatake reserve in Quebec, they will almost certainly tell you that the Mohawk Warrior Society comprised common criminals whose actions led to the death of an officer of the Sûreté du Québec (Quebec Provincial Police). If you ask a member of the Mohawk Warrior Society or others who supported the Mohawks in their efforts, they will tell you that the blockade represented a peaceful attempt to direct

Nelson Mandela spent decades imprisoned in South Africa for activities designed to end apartheid. Today Mandela is hailed as a hero. He was awarded the Nobel Peace Prize in 1993 and served as the first democratically elected president of South Africa from 1994 to 1999.

TABLE 7.1

Canada's Top 10 Primetime TV Programs, September 17–October 14, 2007, Adults 18–49

Source: Throng, 2007.

Genre	Programs	Millions of Weekly Viewers
Crime	*CSI, CSI Miami, Prison Break*	2.8
Medical	*House, Grey's Anatomy*	2.8
Misc'l	*Heroes, Desperate Housewives*	2.1
Cartoon	*Family Guy, The Simpsons*	1.8
Reality	*Survivor: China*	1.3

national attention to a land dispute between the reserve and the municipality. Sociologists, however, will not jump to hasty conclusions. Instead, they will try to understand how social definitions, social relationships, and social conditions led to both the events and the labelling of the Warriors as criminal by the police, the military, and, later, the courts.

That is the approach to deviance and crime we take in this chapter. We first discuss how deviance and crime are socially defined. We then analyze crime patterns in Canada: who commits crimes and what accounts for changing crime rates over time. Next we assess the major theories of deviance and crime. Finally, we examine the social determinants of different types of punishment. We turn first to the social definition of deviance and crime.

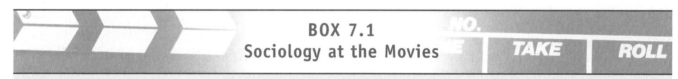

BOX 7.1
Sociology at the Movies

Paradise Now (2005)

Of all the social types who populate today's world, perhaps none is more difficult to understand than the suicide attacker. Many people in the West wonder: Who in their right mind would fly a plane into a building? What kind of person do you have to be to blow yourself up in a bus full of ordinary people or a mosque full of worshippers? Somehow, the terms "deviant" and "criminal" seem inadequate to describe such people; they are widely seen by people in the West as crazy fanatics who lack all conscience and humanity.

Paradise Now, nominated for an Oscar as best foreign-language film of 2005, demonstrates that the common Western view is ethnocentric. It sketches the social circumstances that shaped the lives of two suicide bombers, showing that they are a lot like us and that if we found ourselves in similar circumstances we might turn out to be a lot like them. The film is critical of suicide bombing, but it helps us understand what makes suicide bombers tick,

thereby enlightening us sociologically and politically.

Said (Kais Nashef) and Khaled (Ali Suliman) are ordinary 20-something garage mechanics and best friends. They live in the Palestinian city of Nablus, which, like the rest of the West Bank and the Gaza Strip, has been under Israeli military occupation their whole lives. As a result of the occupation, Said and Khaled have never been able to travel outside of the West Bank, they enjoy limited economic opportunities, they are bored stiff, and most importantly, they have been robbed of their dignity. Like all Palestinians, they want the Israelis out so they can establish an independent country of their own. But their demonstrations, their rock throwing, and their armed attacks have had no effect on the powerful Israeli military. Consequently, some time before the film begins, Said and Khaled volunteered to serve as weapons of last resort: suicide bombers.

A study of all 462 suicide bombers who attacked targets worldwide between 1980 and 2003 found not a single case of depression,

psychosis, past suicide attempts, or other such mental problems among them. The bombers were rarely poor and most often came from working- or middle-class families and were better educated than the populations from which they were recruited. Many of them were religious, but most of them, like Said and Khaled, were not. What they had in common was an ardent desire to liberate territory from what they regarded as foreign occupation or control (Pape, 2005). Said and Khaled are, then, quite typical suicide bombers: They are convinced by their powerlessness and their experience that they have no weapon other than suicide bombing that might help them achieve their aim of national liberation.

As *Paradise Now* opens, the two friends are informed that they have been selected for a suicide attack in 48 hours. Their mundane preparations are peppered with humour, errors, and everyday trivia that make Said and Khaled seem like very ordinary people. For example, in the middle of

Ali Suliman and Kais Nashef in *Paradise Now*

recording his "martyrdom tape" for TV broadcast, Khaled incongruously remembers to tell his mother, whom he knows will watch the tape, that he saw a bargain on water filters at a local merchant's store. But underlying such humanizing events is a tension that gives the movie its force. Said and Khaled are ambivalent about their mission, not just because they have misgivings about dying but because they feel guilty about its inhumanity to civilians and are unsure of its ultimate political utility.

In the end, only Said manages to go through with the attack, but not before we get the full story about his ambivalence. Suha (Lubna Azabal), the woman he loves, is the daughter of a famous martyr for the Palestinian cause, but she strongly opposes suicide bombing. Said listens intently when she argues that suicide bombing is contrary to the spirit of Islam, it kills innocent victims, and it accomplishes nothing because it invites retaliation in a never-ending cycle of violence. But more compelling are the forces pushing Said to carry out the attack. Thousands of Palestinians are paid, threatened, and blackmailed to serve as informants for the Israelis. Said's father was one of them. When he was caught, he was executed by Palestinian militants. Said has been deeply ashamed of his father's actions his whole life and angry with the Israelis for forcing his father to serve as a collaborator. His ultimate motivation for becoming a suicide bomber is retaliation against Israel for turning his father into an informant. Like most suicide bombers in the country, he is driven by the desire for revenge (Brym, 2007; Brym and Araj, 2006).

From whose point of view are suicide bombers deviant and criminal? From whose point of view are suicide bombers normal? Must you agree with the actions of suicide bombers to understand them? What would you do if you were in Said's position?

THE SOCIAL DEFINITION OF DEVIANCE AND CRIME

Types of Deviance and Crime

Deviance involves breaking a norm. If you were the only man in a university classroom full of women, you probably would not be considered deviant. However, if a man were to use a women's restroom, we would likely regard him as deviant. That is because deviance is not merely a departure from the statistical average, but rather a violation of an accepted rule of behaviour.

Many deviant acts go unnoticed or are considered so trivial they warrant no punishment. However, people who are observed committing more serious acts of deviance are typically punished, either informally or formally. **Informal punishment** is mild. It may involve raised eyebrows, gossip, ostracism, shaming, or stigmatization (Braithwaite, 1989). When people are **stigmatized**, they are negatively evaluated because of a marker that distinguishes them from others (Goffman, 1963). One of this book's authors, John Lie, was stigmatized as a young child and often bullied by elementary-school classmates because he had a Korean name in a Japanese school. "I was normal in other ways," says John. "I played the same sports and games; watched the same television shows; and looked, dressed, and acted like other Japanese students. However, my one

Deviance occurs when someone departs from a norm.

PERSONAL ANECDOTE

Informal punishment involves a mild sanction that is imposed during face-to-face interaction, not by the judicial system.

People who are stigmatized are negatively evaluated because of a marker that distinguishes them from others and this is labelled as socially unacceptable.

Formal punishment takes place when the judicial system penalizes someone for breaking a law.

deviation was enough to stigmatize me. It gave licence to some of my classmates to beat me up from time to time. I wondered at the time why no rules banned bullying and why no law existed against what I now call racial discrimination. If such a law did exist, my classmates would have been subject to formal punishment, which is more severe than informal punishment."

Formal punishment results from people breaking laws, which are norms stipulated and enforced by government bodies. For example, criminals may be formally punished by having to serve time in prison or perform community service.

Sociologist John Hagan (1994) usefully classifies various types of deviance and crime along three dimensions (see Figure 7.1). The first dimension is the *severity of the social response*. At one extreme, homicide and other very serious forms of deviance result in the most severe negative reactions, such as life imprisonment or capital punishment. At the other end of the spectrum, some people may do little more than express mild disapproval of slight deviations from a norm, such as wearing a nose ring.

The second dimension of deviance and crime is the *perceived harmfulness* of the deviant or criminal act. Although some deviant acts, such as sexual assault, are generally seen as very harmful, others, such as tattooing, are commonly regarded as harmless. Note that actual harmfulness is not the only issue here. *Perceived* harmfulness is. Coca-Cola got its name because, in the early part of this century, it contained a derivative of cocaine. Now cocaine is an illegal drug because people's perceptions of its harmfulness changed.

The third characteristic of deviance is the *degree of public agreement* about whether an act should be considered deviant. For example, people disagree about whether smoking marijuana should be considered a crime, especially as it may have therapeutic value in treating the pain and nausea associated with cancer. In contrast, virtually everyone agrees that murder is seriously deviant. Note, however, that even the social definition of murder varies over time and across cultures and societies. Thus, at the beginning of the twentieth century, Inuit communities sometimes allowed newborns to freeze to death. Life in the far north was precarious. Killing newborns was not considered a punishable offence if community members agreed that investing scarce resources in keeping the newborn alive could endanger everyone's well-being. Similarly, whether we classify the death of a miner as an accident or manslaughter depends on the kind of worker safety legislation in

FIGURE 7.1

Types of Deviance and Crime

Source: From *Crime and Disrepute* by John Hagan. Copyright © 1994 Pine Forge Press. Reprinted by permission of Sage Publications.

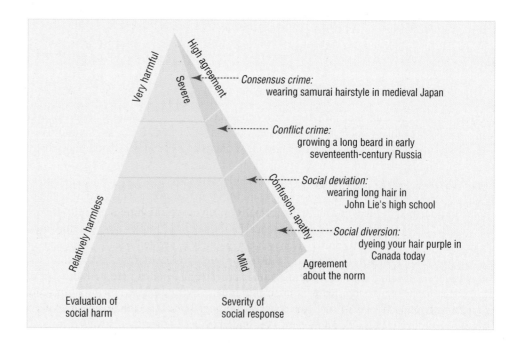

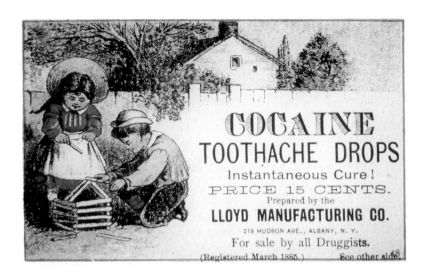

One of the determinants of the seriousness of a deviant act is its perceived harmfulness. Perceptions vary historically. For instance, until the early part of the twentieth century, cocaine was considered a medicine. It was an ingredient in Coca-Cola and toothache drops and in these forms was commonly given to children.

existence. Some societies have more stringent worker safety rules than others do, and deaths considered accidental in some societies are classified as criminal offences in others (McCormick, 1999). When organized sporting events include acts of violence that result in severe physical injury, it can be controversial whether a crime has occurred (see Box 7.2 on page 186). So we see that, even when it comes to consensus crimes, social definitions are variable.

As Figure 7.1 shows, Hagan's analysis allows us to classify four types of deviance and crime:

1. **Social diversions** are minor acts of deviance, such as participating in fads and fashions like dyeing your hair purple. People usually perceive such acts as harmless. They evoke, at most, a mild societal reaction, such as amusement or disdain, because many people are apathetic or unclear about whether social diversions are, in fact, deviant.

2. **Social deviations** are more serious acts. Large numbers of people agree these acts are deviant and somewhat harmful, and they are usually subject to institutional sanction. For example, John Lie's high school in Hawaii had a rule making long hair on boys a fairly serious deviation punishable by a humiliating public haircut.

3. **Conflict crimes** are deviant acts that the state defines as illegal but whose definition is controversial in the wider society. For instance, Tsar Peter the Great of Russia wanted to Westernize and modernize his empire, and he viewed long beards as a sign of backwardness. On September 1, 1698, he imposed a fine on beards in the form of a tax. Many Russians disagreed with his policy. Others agreed that growing long beards harmed Russia because it symbolized Russia's past rather than future. Because of this disagreement in the wider society about the harmfulness of the practice, wearing a long beard in late-seventeenth-century Russia can be classified as a conflict crime.

4. Finally, **consensus crimes** are widely recognized to be bad in themselves. There is little controversy over their seriousness. The great majority of people agree that such crimes should be met with severe punishment. For instance, in medieval Japan, hairstyle was an important expression of people's status. If you were a peasant and sported the hairstyle of the samurai (warrior caste), you could be arrested and even killed because you were seen to be calling the entire social order into question.

As these examples show, people's conceptions of deviance and crime vary substantially over time and between societies. Under some circumstances, an issue that seems quite trivial to us, such as hairstyle, can be a matter of life and death.

Social diversions are minor acts of deviance that are generally perceived as relatively harmless and that evoke, at most, a mild societal reaction, such as amusement or disdain.

Social deviations are non-criminal departures from norms that are nonetheless subject to official control. Some members of the public regard them as somewhat harmful while other members of the public do not.

Conflict crimes are illegal acts that many people consider harmful to society. However, other people think they are not very harmful. They are punishable by the state.

Consensus crimes are illegal acts that nearly all people agree are bad in themselves and harm society greatly. The state inflicts severe punishment for consensus crimes.

BOX 7.2
It's Your Choice

Violence and Hockey: Deviant, Criminal, or Normative?

On March 8, 2004, the NHL suspended Todd Bertuzzi of the Vancouver Canucks indefinitely for an on-ice assault whose repercussions echoed across the world of hockey. His victim was Steve Moore of the Colorado Avalanche.

Although fighting is hardly rare in the NHL, this was hardly a fight. The incident occurred in the third period with the Avalanche coasting atop an 8–2 lead. No collision was involved—afterward many described Bertuzzi's action as stalking. In the seconds leading up to the attack, Bertuzzi pursued Moore from one end of the rink to the other. When Moore tried to avoid Bertuzzi by turning his back and skating away, Bertuzzi grabbed the back of Moore's jersey. He then delivered a roundhouse sucker punch and followed through by using his 110-kilogram (245-pound) body to drive Moore face first into the ice.

As the crowd grew silent with awareness of what had happened, Moore lay in a pool of his own blood for several minutes until a stretcher arrived to carry him off.

A backdrop of previous run-ins was cited as precipitating circumstances. On February 16, 2004, Moore had knocked Canucks captain Markus Naslund unconscious with an open-ice shoulder hit to the head. Several Canucks players, including Bertuzzi, complained after the game about the absence of any penalty and one Canuck even spoke of a bounty being placed on Moore. However, in the immediate aftermath of Moore's injury, Canucks general manager Brian Burke said that the team was

Was Todd Bertuzzi's penalty adequate for his assault on Steve Moore?

thinking only of Moore's recovery. But he also insisted that "my player, Todd Bertuzzi, has my full backing." For his part, Naslund later criticized Moore and thereby offered some measure of support for Bertuzzi's actions. But relatively few people attempted to defend Bertuzzi's action in these or any other terms.

In contrast to the time Marty McSorley of the Boston Bruins injured Donald Bashear of the Vancouver Canucks with a stick to the head in a game in 2000, there was near-total silence from defenders of the NHL's custom of employing revenge and deterrence to try to maintain order on the ice. Even commentators like Don Cherry were critical of Bertuzzi's blind-side assault against someone trying to avoid a confrontation. Bertuzzi himself expressed remorse in the strongest terms at a tear-filled press conference two days later. "I just want to apologize for what happened

out there and I feel awful for what transpired," he said. "I'm relieved to hear that Steve's going to have a full recovery."

Unfortunately, Bertuzzi's prognosis proved overly optimistic. On August 8, 2005, when Bertuzzi was reinstated by the NHL, Moore was still unable to skate. Meanwhile, Bertuzzi's suspension had run for 17 months. He had lost more than US$500 000 in forfeited pay. (During the NHL lockout that took up much of that time, he was forbidden to play for money in Europe.) Moore never returned to the NHL.

Like McSorley before him, Bertuzzi was arrested to face assault charges in Vancouver. Eventually, he pleaded guilty to a charge of assault causing bodily harm, paid a fine of $500, and was sentenced to 80 hours of community service. The plea leaves him without a criminal record.

Do you think that Bertuzzi's penalty was adequate? Do you believe that athletes involved in contact sports should be treated differently under laws forbidding assault? Does this apply even in cases involving severe injury or death? Is this part of the risk that comes along with such sports and best left to sports administrators? Or should there be a crackdown on sports violence? Should more athletes be charged? Should coaches if they encourage such deeds? It's your choice.

Power and the Social Construction of Crime and Deviance

To truly understand deviance and crime, you have to study how people socially construct norms and laws. The school of sociological thought known as **social constructionism** emphasizes that various social problems, including crime, are *not* inherent in certain actions themselves. Instead, some people are in a position to create norms and pass laws that stigmatize other people. Therefore, we must study how norms and laws are created (or constructed) to understand why particular actions are defined as deviant or criminal in the first place.

Power is a crucial element in the social construction of deviance and crime. Power, you will recall from Chapter 5 (Social Interaction), is "the probability that one actor within a social relationship will be in a position to carry out his [or her] own will despite resistance" (Weber, 1947: 152). An "actor" may be an entire social group. Relatively powerful social groups are generally able to create norms and laws that suit their interests. Relatively powerless social groups are usually unable to do so.

The powerless, however, often struggle against stigmatization. If their power increases, they may succeed in their struggle. We can illustrate the importance of power in the social construction of crime and deviance by considering crimes against women and white-collar crime.

Social constructionism **argues that apparently natural or innate features of life are often sustained by social processes that vary historically and culturally. It emphasizes how some people are in a position to create norms and pass laws that define others as deviant or criminal.**

Transvestites dress in clothing generally considered appropriate to members of the opposite sex. Is transvestitism a social diversion, a social deviation, a conflict crime, or a consensus crime? Why?

Crimes against Women

We argued above that definitions of crime are usually constructed so as to bestow advantages on the more powerful members of society and disadvantages on the less powerful. As you will learn in detail in Chapter 11 (Sexuality and Gender), women are generally less powerful than men are in all social institutions. Has the law therefore been biased against women? We believe it has.

Until recently, many types of crimes against women were largely ignored in Canada and most other parts of the world. This was true even when the crime involved non-consensual sexual intercourse, an act that was defined under Canadian criminal law as *rape* before 1983 and is now considered a form of *sexual assault.* Admittedly, rapes involving strangers were sometimes severely punished. But so-called date rapes or acquaintance rapes involving a friend or an acquaintance were rarely prosecuted. And, until 1983, Canadian law viewed marital rape as a contradiction in terms, as if it were logically impossible for a married woman to be raped by her spouse. In her research, Susan Estrich (1987) found that law professors, judges, police officers, rapists, and even victims did not think date rape was "real rape." Similarly, judges, lawyers, and social scientists rarely discussed physical violence against women and sexual harassment until the 1970s. Governments did not collect data on the topic, and few social scientists showed any interest in what has now become a large and important area of study.

Today, the situation has improved. To be sure, as Diana Scully's (1990) study of convicted rapists shows, sexual assault is still associated with a low rate of prosecution. Rapists often hold women in contempt and do not regard sexual assault as a crime. Yet a series of changes to the criminal law in Canada emphasized that non-consensual sexual acts are sexual assaults. These new laws have helped raise people's awareness of date, acquaintance, and marital rape. Sexual assault is more often prosecuted now than it used to be. The same is true for other types of violence against women and for sexual harassment.

Why the change? In part, it is because women's position in the economy, the family, and other social institutions has improved over the past four decades. Women now have more autonomy in the family, earn more, and have more political influence. They also created a movement for women's rights that heightened concern about crimes disproportionately affecting them. For instance, until very recently, male sexual harassment of female workers was considered normal. Following Catharine MacKinnon's path-breaking work on the subject, however, feminists succeeded in changing the social definition of sexual harassment (MacKinnon, 1979). Sexual harassment is now considered a social deviation and, in some circumstances, a crime. Increased public awareness of the extent of sexual harassment has probably made it less common. We thus see how social definitions of crimes against women have changed with a shift in the distribution of power between women and men.

White-Collar Crime

White-collar crime refers to illegal acts "committed by a person of respectability and high social status in the course of his occupation" (Sutherland, 1949: 9). Such crimes include embezzlement, false advertising, tax evasion, insider stock trading, fraud, unfair labour practices, copyright infringement, and conspiracy to fix prices and restrain trade. Although some white-collar crimes hurt employers, many victimize employees or members of the public while bringing benefit to corporations or corporate insiders. Sociologists often contrast white-collar crimes with **street crimes**. The latter include arson, breaking and entering, robbery, assault, and other illegal acts. Although street crime is committed disproportionately by people from the lower classes, most white-collar crimes are open only to members of the middle or upper classes.

Many sociologists think white-collar crime is more costly to society than street crime is. Tax evasion alone has been estimated to cost Canadians $30 billion a year (Gabor, 1994). The Bre-X scandal, reputedly one of the world's largest stock frauds, cost investors $6 billion. In this case, the Calgary-based company's geologist sought to make a worthless mining property seem valuable by salting core samples with gold. After his actions became known, the market for Bre-X stock collapsed and the company's shares became worthless

White-collar crime refers to an illegal act committed by a respectable, high-status person in the course of his or her work.

Street crimes include arson, break and enter, assault, and other illegal acts disproportionately committed by people from lower classes.

(Hagan, 2000). Yet white-collar criminals, including corporations, are infrequently prosecuted. They are convicted even less often. White-collar crime is underreported. As Reiman (2003) argues, a culture that privileges profit-seeking makes many people unable to grasp the criminal content of frauds that financially ruin hundreds of families or safety violations that rob workers of health or even life. Yet these may be no less crimes—intentional violations of law in pursuit of selfish gain that unjustly harm others—than are the thefts and assaults that disproportionately concern police. Further, the police agencies most accessible to the public are not trained or equipped to process complaints about many white-collar crimes and instead generally restrict their attention to misdeeds open to all individuals, that is, to street crimes, and to disorderly conduct, drug offences, and the like. This narrowness of view ultimately extends to government statistical summaries, since estimates of rates and types of crimes are tabulated from forms filled out in police agencies (Statistics Canada, 2004a) where initial complaints are recorded. Complaints that are not recorded (or that are directed to different agencies) are thus invisible in the crime totals that are most widely reported and discussed.

White-collar crime results in few prosecutions and still fewer convictions for two main reasons. First, much white-collar crime takes place in private and is therefore difficult to detect. For example, corporations may illegally decide to fix prices and divide markets, but executives make the decisions in boardrooms and private clubs that are not generally subject to police surveillance. Second, corporations can afford legal experts, public relations firms, and advertising agencies that advise their clients on how to bend laws, build up their corporate image in the public mind, and influence lawmakers to pass laws "without teeth" (Blumberg, 1989; Clinard and Yeager, 1980; Hagan, 1989; Sherrill, 1997; Sutherland, 1949). Even when prosecutions are successful, the punishment is usually light (Snider, 1999).

Governments, too, commit serious crimes. However, it is difficult to punish political leaders (Chambliss, 1989). Authoritarian governments often call their critics *terrorists* and even torture people who are fighting for democracy, but such governments rarely have to account for their deeds (Herman and O'Sullivan, 1989). In defence, it is often argued that good motives excuse bad behaviour—that the end justifies the means. This claim is also commonly advanced in the case of so-called blue-collar crimes committed by police officers or agencies. For example, in the 1980s, the federal McDonald Commission of Inquiry into Certain Activities of the RCMP revealed that members of the RCMP had effectively put themselves above the law in their attempts to enforce the law. The end of law enforcement was seen to justify any means, including acts that, "if undertaken by any other citizen, would have resulted in substantial periods of incarceration" (Brannigan, 1984: 63). These acts were not minor wrongdoings but included such manifestly criminal conduct as arson, breaking and entering, theft, contravening the Post Office Act, kidnapping and forcible detention, and invasion of privacy. Nevertheless, when confronted with evidence of wide-scale and systemic wrongdoing by the RCMP, the Canadian government at the time showed a marked reluctance to treat these acts as crimes. As sociologist Augustine Brannigan (1984: 65) observed of the Canadian government's response to the findings of the McDonald Commission: "The opinion of the government seems to be that whatever the police need to do in order to do their job is *ipso facto* legal."

In sum, white-collar crime is underdetected, underprosecuted, and underconvicted because it is the crime of the powerful and the well-to-do. The social construction of crimes against women has changed over the past four decades, partly because women have become more powerful. In contrast, the social construction of white-collar crime has changed very little since 1970 because upper classes are no less powerful now than they were then.

Crime Rates

Some crimes are more common than others are, and rates of crime vary over place and time and among different social groups.

Before establishing these facts, however, we must say a word about crime statistics. Information on crime collected by the police is the main source of information on crime in Canada. Since 1962, Canada has used the Uniform Crime Reporting (UCR) Survey that was developed by Statistics Canada and the Canadian Association of Chiefs of Police. Under this system, information is collected from more than 400 municipal police departments across Canada on 91 detailed categories of crime. The information is then compiled and published each year with counts and rates per 100 000 population. Offences are grouped into major crime categories. For example, "crimes of violence" group together such acts as homicide, attempted homicide, assault, abduction, sexual assault, and robbery. "Property offences" include break and enter, theft of motor vehicles, possession of stolen goods, fraud, and so on. UCR data also provide information on the number of persons charged with different types of offences, with separate counts for adults and youths, males and females.

Drawbacks of Relying on Official Crime Statistics

Victimless crimes involve violations of the law in which no victim steps forward and is identified.

The crime statistics produced by the UCR survey have several shortcomings. First, much crime is not reported to the police. This is particularly true in relation to so-called **victimless crimes**, such as illegal gambling, the use of illegal drugs, and communicating for the purposes of prostitution. Although all these acts involve violations of the law, no complaining party steps forward and identifies himself or herself as a victim. In addition, many common or "level 1" assaults go unreported because the assailant is a friend or relative of the victim. Many victims of sexual assault are reluctant to report the crime because they are afraid they will be humiliated, not believed, or stigmatized. Moreover, authorities and the wider public decide which criminal acts to report and which to ignore. If, for instance, the authorities decide to crack down on drugs, more drug-related crimes will be counted, not because there are more drug-related crimes but because more drug criminals are apprehended. Changes in legislation, which either create new offences or amend existing offences, also influence the number of recorded offences. Recognizing these difficulties, students of crime often supplement official crime statistics with other sources of information.

In self-report surveys, respondents are asked to report their involvement in criminal activities, either as perpetrators or as victims.

Self-report surveys are especially useful. In such surveys, respondents are asked to report their involvement in criminal activities, either as perpetrators or as victims. Self-report data compensate for many of the problems associated with official statistics but are still subject to concealment as well as exaggeration. In general, self-report surveys report approximately the same rate of serious crime as official statistics but find two or three times the rate of less serious crimes. In consequence, *indirect measures* of crime are sometimes used as well. For instance, sales of syringes are a good index of the use of illegal intravenous drugs. Indirect measures are unavailable for many types of crime, however.

Self-report surveys are also useful because they show us that a majority of Canadians, young and old, have engaged in some type of "criminal" activity. As a result, the surveys remind us that committing an act in violation of the law does not always or automatically result in being officially labelled a criminal. The process of criminal labelling can be likened to a funnel (Figure 7.2).

To be officially identified as a criminal, an individual's law-violating behaviour must first be observed and felt to justify action. The behaviour must be reported to the police who, in turn, must respond to the incident, decide that it warrants further investigation, file a report, and make an arrest. Next, the accused person must appear at a preliminary hearing (an arraignment) and a trial. If the person does not plead guilty, there is always the possibility that he or she will not be convicted because his or her guilt has not been proven "beyond a reasonable doubt." At every stage, then, a person who has, in fact, violated the law, may nevertheless avoid official labelling as a criminal. Figure 7.2 makes it clear why generalizations based on samples of incarcerated offenders may not apply beyond inmate populations.

Victimization surveys are surveys in which people are asked whether they have been victims of crime.

In **victimization surveys**, people are asked whether they have been victims of crime. Here as well, however, responses are influenced by people's willingness and ability to discuss criminal experiences frankly. Although these types of surveys date back to the mid-1960s in the United States, no national victimization survey was done in Canada until 1988 (Fattah, 1991). For Statistics Canada's 1999 General Social Survey (GSS), 26 000 people aged 15 and older were interviewed by telephone and asked if they had been victimized by crime and, if so, where and when the crime had occurred and whether it had been reported to the police (Besserer, Brzozowski, Hendrick, Ogg, and Trainor, 1999). In addition, respondents were queried on their perceptions of the level of crime in their neighbourhood, their personal fear of crime, and their views on the criminal justice system (Tufts, 2000).

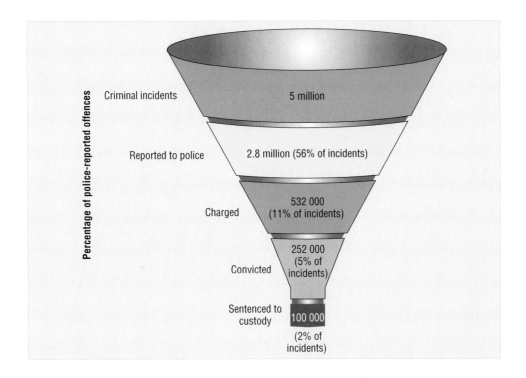

FIGURE 7.2
The Canadian Crime Funnel

Note: An offence is considered "actual" when a police investigation confirms that a criminal offence has occurred. An offence is "cleared" when police are satisfied that they have identified an offender. However, it may not be possible to lay a charge against an offender because he or she is dead, under age 12, is a youth (aged 12 to 17) whom police feel is better dealt with in another manner, has diplomatic immunity, is already in prison, and so on. If police lay a charge against an offender, the offence is "cleared by charge."

Sources: Adapted from Statistics Canada, 1997, "Youth Court Statistics 1995–96 Highlights," "Adult Criminal Court Statistics, 1995–96," and "Canadian Crime Statistics, 1996," *Juristat,* Catalogue 85-002, Vol. 17, No. 10; Vol. 17, No. 6; and Vol. 17, No. 8.

The International Crime Victim Survey (ICVS) collected victimization data using the same questionnaire simultaneously in many countries, including Canada, in 1989, 1992, 1996–97, and 2000 (Besserer, 2002). It examines householders' experiences with crime, policing, crime prevention, and feelings of being unsafe. This survey has found that, on average, 55 percent of victimization incidents are reported to police, with property crimes more likely to be reported than crimes against persons are. In part, this reflects the general requirement by insurance companies that individuals seeking compensation for property stolen or damaged as the result of a criminal act file a police report. Although victimization surveys provide detailed information about crime victims, they provide less reliable data about offenders.

What Official Crime Rates Show

Bearing these caveats in mind, what does the official record show? Most Canadians would be understandably alarmed to hear that, in 2006, nearly 2.7 million Criminal Code incidents (*excluding* traffic and drug incidents) were reported to Canadian police agencies. They might assume that these incidents were reflected in the dramatic crimes reported each day in newspaper headlines and on the nightly news. However, that is not the case— violent crimes are typically deemed the most newsworthy. In 2006, 43 percent of Criminal Code incidents involved property crimes, 12 percent involved violent crimes, and 45 percent involved other Criminal Code offences, primarily mischief and disturbing the peace. Although the crime rate was nearly three times higher in 2006 than in 1962, it has been falling since 1991 and is lower than at any time since 1978 (Silver, 2007: 3, 9, 10; Figure 7.3 on page 192).

In addition, the rates of many of the most serious crimes decreased or remained stable. For example, the homicide rate has been falling since the mid-1970s and stood at 1.85 per 100 000 in 2006. (To put this in perspective, although in 2006 there were 605 homicides in Canada, there were 921 in the state of New York, which has about 60 percent of Canada's population ("New York Crime Rates," 2007). Overall, the American homicide rate is about three times as high as Canada's, largely because guns are more widely available in the United States; Figure 7.4 on page 192). Rates of robbery, sexual assault, drug arrests, and property crime are also falling. How can we explain the good news?

FIGURE 7.3

Crime Rate, Canada, 1962–2006

Source: Silver, 2007.

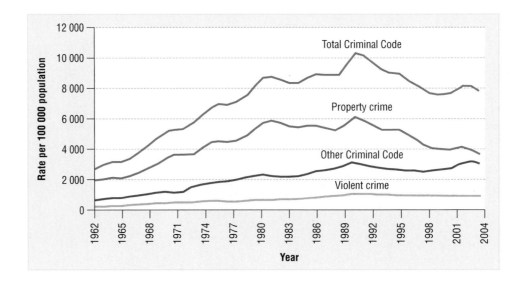

Explanations for Declining Crime Rates

Four explanations exist for the decline in Canadian crime rates. First, the "war against crime" is increasingly being fought by large numbers of well-trained soldiers: "Veritable armies of law enforcement and correctional officers have grown phenomenally since the 1960s, not only in manpower but in programs and technical sophistication" (Mohr and Spencer, 1999: 588). It has been suggested that recent declines in Canada's crime rate may reflect the introduction of community policing initiatives, enforcement efforts that target specific types of crime and attempt to reduce their incidence, the refinement of case-management methods, improvements in the field of forensics, and efforts directed toward crime prevention (Logan, 2001: 3).

Second, young men are most prone to street crime, but Canada is aging and the number of young people in the population has declined (see Figure 7.5). Although those between the ages of 15 and 24 have a high risk of offending, this high-risk age group has decreased in size by 6 percent since 1991 (see Figure 7.6; Logan, 2001: 3). Unlike the 1960s, when the baby boom generation (that is, those born between 1947 and 1966) came into their years of highest risk, the 1990s saw the products of the baby bust years (1967 to 1979). Simply put, "[t]here has been a smaller pool of people who are at the greatest risk with respect to criminal behaviour" (John Howard Society, 1999a: 2).

FIGURE 7.4

Gunshot Death Rate by Percentage of Households with Guns

Source: Ted R. Miller and Mark A. Cohen, 1997, "Cost of Gunshot and Cut/Stab Wounds in the United States with Some Canadian Comparisons," *Accident Analysis and Prevention*, Vol. 29, pp. 329–41. Reprinted with permission from Elsevier.

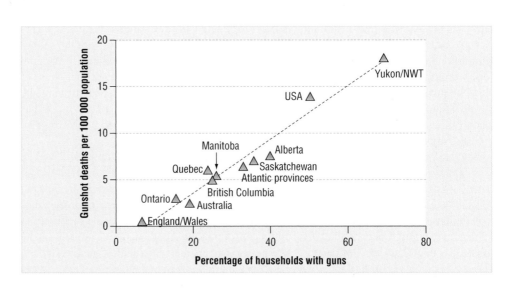

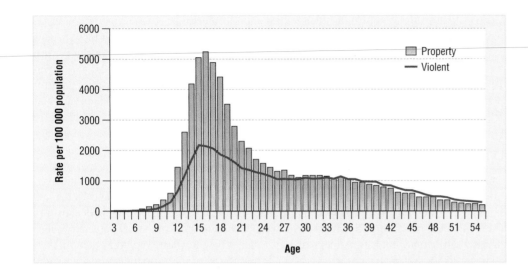

FIGURE 7.5
Persons Accused of Violent Crimes and Property Crime by Age, Canada, 2003

Source: Adapted from Statistics Canada, 2003, "Crime Statistics in Canada," *Juristat,* Catalogue 85-002, Vol. 24, No. 6.

Third, following a steep recession in 1990–91, the economy boomed and, except for a brief recession in 2001, grew every year between 1993 and 2009. Economic conditions may have favoured a decrease in crime. A 1993 Statistics Canada study concluded that the variable most strongly correlated with the crime rate was the male unemployment rate (John Howard Society, 1999b: 3). Adverse economic conditions in the 1980s may have further amplified the baby boom effect. Ouimet (2002) provided demographic evidence that the very large cohorts born in Canada during the 1960s had higher levels of criminal involvement because their initial efforts to gain legal employment were hampered by the unfavourable economic conditions of the early 1980s.

Finally, and more controversially, some American researchers argue that declining crime rates may be linked to the legalization of abortion (Donahue and Levitt, 2001). They observe that, in the United States, the crime rate started to decline 19 years after abortion was legalized in that country. They suggest that this drop occurred because, beginning in 1972 with the legalization of abortion, there were proportionately fewer unwanted children in the population. Unwanted children, they argue, are more prone to criminal behaviour than wanted children are because they tend to receive less parental supervision and guidance. In Canada, no comparable research has been conducted to date.

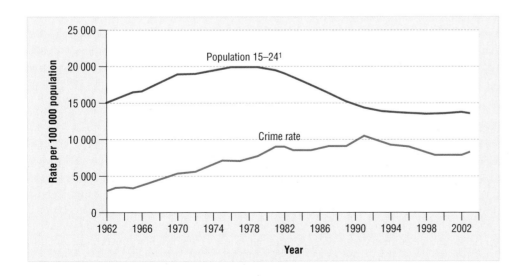

FIGURE 7.6
Crime Rate and Population Aged 15–24, Canada, 1962–2003

[1] *This line represents the number of 15-to 24-year olds expressed as a rate per 100 000 population and not the crime rate of this age group.*

Source: Adapted from Statistics Canada, 2003, "Crime Statistics in Canada," *Juristat,* Catalogue 85-002, Vol. 24, No. 6.

Social control **refers to methods of ensuring conformity.**

Note that we have not claimed that putting more people in prison and imposing tougher penalties for crime help to account for lower crime rates. We will explain why these actions generally do not result in lower crime rates later in the chapter, when we discuss **social control** (methods of ensuring conformity) and punishment. We will also probe one of the most fascinating questions raised by official statistics: If crime rates fell in the 1990s, what accounts for our increased enthusiasm for get-tough policies, our expanding prison population, and our widespread and growing fear of crime?

Criminal Profiles

Canadian adult criminal court statistics for 2003–04 indicate that 83 percent of cases involved a male accused.[1] Males accounted for 85 percent of crimes against a person and 78 percent of crimes against property. Women accounted for a significant percentage of offenders in only a small number of crimes: 45 percent of offences involving prostitution, 29 percent of those charged with fraud, and 27 percent of those charged with theft (including shoplifting; Thomas, 2004: 3). This pattern reappears for cases processed in the youth courts of Canada. In 2002–03, males accounted for 77 percent of youth court cases (Robinson, 2004: 3). However, with every passing year women compose a slightly bigger percentage of arrests (Hartnagel, 2000). This change is partly due to the fact that, in the course of socialization, traditional social controls and definitions of femininity are less often being imposed on women (see Chapter 11, Sexuality and Gender).

Most crime is committed by people who have not reached middle age. The 15- to 24-year-old age cohort is the most prone to criminal behaviour (see Figure 7.5). Although this age cohort represented merely 14 percent of the total Canadian population in 2003, it accounted for 45 percent of those charged with a property crime and 32 percent of those charged with a violent crime (Wallace, 2004: 3).

Race and Incarceration

Analysis of official statistics also reveals that race is a factor in who is arrested. Although Aboriginals represent 2 percent of the adult population in Canada, they are overrepresented as a proportion of those incarcerated in both federal and provincial or territorial institutions. In recent years, Aboriginals have consistently accounted for 15 percent to 18 percent of admissions to both provincial or territorial and federal sentenced custody (Johnson, 2004: 16; see Figure 7.7). The overrepresentation of Aboriginal people in Canada's prisons is particularly marked in the Prairie provinces (see Figure 7.8). Although they represent 10 percent of Saskatchewan's population, they accounted for 77 percent of the adults sentenced to custody in 2004–05. In Alberta, where Aboriginal people make up 4 percent of the population, they accounted for 38 percent of custodial sentences. Aboriginal people were a majority among those sentenced to custody in Nunavut, Northwest Territories, Yukon, Saskatchewan, and Manitoba (Beattie, 2006; see Figure 7.8).

In recent years, changes made by Parliament to the sentencing provisions of the Canadian Criminal Code have attempted to address the overrepresentation of Aboriginal people in Canada's inmate population. For example, section 718.2 specifies that "all available sanctions other than imprisonment that are reasonable in the circumstances should be considered for all offenders, *with particular attention to the circumstances of aboriginal offenders*" (emphasis added). Although being Aboriginal does not automatically result in a lesser sentence, the Supreme Court of Canada has urged judges, when sentencing an Aboriginal offender, to recognize the "broad systemic and background factors affecting Aboriginal people" (Lonmo, 2001: 8).

Nevertheless, Aboriginal Canadians continue to be overrepresented in the prison population. Compared with non-Aboriginal inmates, Aboriginal inmates are more likely to have had more extensive contact with both the criminal justice system and the correctional system, to have come from dysfunctional backgrounds, and to have served prison sentences for defaulting on court-ordered fines. Aboriginal women are particularly overrepresented in Canada's correctional institutions (La Prairie, 1996).

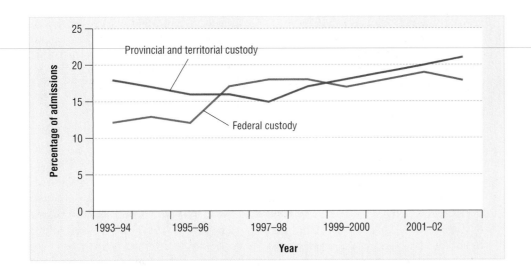

FIGURE 7.7

Aboriginal People as a Proportion of Total Admissions to Sentenced Custody, 1993–1994 to 2001–2002

Source: Adapted from Statistics Canada, 2004, "Adult Correctional Services in Canada, 2002/03," *Juristat,* Catalogue 85-002, Vol. 24, No. 10.

Several explanations for the overrepresentation of Aboriginal people in Canada's prisons can be found in the literature (Hartnagel, 2000). First, a disproportionately large number of Aboriginal people are poor. Although the great majority of poor people are law abiding, poverty and its handicaps are associated with elevated crime rates. Second, Aboriginal people commit crimes that are more detectable than are those committed by non-Aboriginal people. For example, as we have seen, "street crimes" are generally more detectable than "suite crimes" (white-collar offences), and they more often lead to prosecution and conviction. Third, the police, the courts, and other institutions may discriminate against Aboriginal people. As a result, Aboriginal people may be more likely to be apprehended, prosecuted, and convicted. Fourth, contact with Western culture has disrupted social life in many Aboriginal communities (see Chapter 10, Race and Ethnicity). This has led to a weakening of social control over community members. Some people think that certain "races" are *inherently* more law abiding than others, but they are able to hold such an opinion only by ignoring the powerful *social* forces that cause so many Aboriginal people to be incarcerated in Canada (Roberts and Gabor, 1990).

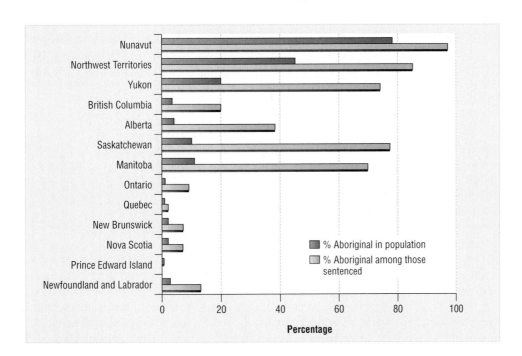

FIGURE 7.8

Aboriginal People as a Proportion of Adult Population of Those Sentenced to Custody, by Jurisdiction, Canada, 2004–2005

Source: Beattie, 2006: 16.

In the 1957 classic movie *12 Angry Men,* the character played by Henry Fonda (third from left) convinces the members of a jury to overcome their prejudices, examine the facts dispassionately, and allow a disadvantaged minority youth accused of murdering his father to go free. Does the problem of ethnic and racial bias still plague the criminal justice system?

EXPLAINING DEVIANCE AND CRIME

Lep: "I remember your li'l ass used to ride dirt bikes and skateboards, actin' crazy an' shit. Now you want to be a gangster, huh? You wanna hang with real muthaf—— and tear shit up, huh? Stand up, get your li'l ass up. How old is you now anyway?"

Kody: "Eleven, but I'll be twelve in November."

— quoted in Shakur, 1993: 8.

"Monster" Scott Kody eagerly joined the notorious gang the Crips in South Central Los Angeles in 1975 when he was in grade six. He was released from Folsom Prison on parole in 1988, at the age of 24. Until about three years before his release, he was one of the most ruthless gang leaders in Los Angeles and the California prison system. In 1985, however, he decided to reform. He adopted the name Sanyika Shakur, became a black nationalist, and began a crusade against gangs. Few people in his position have chosen that path. In Kody's heyday, about 30 000 gang members roamed Los Angeles County. Today, there are an estimated 85 000 (Winton, 2005).

What makes engaging in crime an attractive prospect? In general, why do deviance and crime occur at all? Sociologists have proposed dozens of explanations. However, we can group them into two basic types. **Motivational theories** identify the social factors that *drive* people to commit deviance and crime. **Constraint theories** identify the social factors that *impose* deviance and crime (or conventional behaviour) on people. Later we examine three examples of each type of theory. Before doing so, however, we want to stress that becoming a *habitual* deviant or criminal is a learning process that occurs in a social context. Motive and lack of constraint may ignite a single deviant or criminal act, but repeatedly engaging in that act requires the learning of a deviant or criminal role.

Becoming Deviant: The Case of Marijuana Users

Howard S. Becker, a giant in the sociological study of deviance, analyzed this learning process in a classic study of marijuana users (Becker, 1963: 41–58). In 1948 and 1949, Becker financed his Ph.D. studies at the University of Chicago by playing piano in local jazz

Motivational theories identify the social factors that drive people to commit deviant and criminal acts.

Constraint theories identify the social factors that impose deviance and crime (or conventional behaviour) on people.

bands. He used the opportunity to do participant-observation research, carefully observing his fellow musicians, informally interviewing them in depth, and writing up detailed field notes after performances. Becker observed and interviewed 50 jazz musicians who smoked marijuana.

Becker found that his fellow musicians had to pass through a three-stage learning process before becoming regular marijuana users. Failure to pass a stage meant failure to learn the deviant role and become a regular user. These are the three stages:

1. *Learning to smoke the drug in a way that produces real effects.* First-time marijuana smokers do not ordinarily get high. To do so, they must learn how to smoke the drug in a way that ensures a sufficient dosage to produce intoxicating effects (taking deep drags and holding their breath for a long time). This process takes practice, and some first-time users give up, typically claiming that marijuana has no effect on them or that people who claim otherwise are just fooling themselves. Others are more strongly encouraged by their peers to keep trying. If they persist, they are ready for stage two.

2. *Learning to recognize the effects and connect them with drug use.* Those who learn the proper smoking technique may not recognize that they are high or they may not connect the symptoms of being high with smoking the drug. They may get hungry, laugh uncontrollably, play the same song for hours on end, and yet still fail to realize that these are symptoms of intoxication. If so, they will stop using the drug. Becker found, however, that his fellow musicians typically asked experienced users how they knew whether they were high. Experienced users identified the symptoms of marijuana use and helped novices make the connection between what they were experiencing and smoking the drug. Once they made that connection, novices were ready to advance to stage three.

3. *Learning to enjoy the perceived sensations.* Smoking marijuana is not inherently pleasurable. Some users experience a frightening loss of self-control (paranoia). Others feel dizzy, uncomfortably thirsty, itchy, forgetful, or dangerously impaired in their ability to judge time and distance. If these negative sensations persist, marijuana use will cease. However, Becker found that experienced users typically helped novices redefine negative sensations as pleasurable. They taught novices to laugh at their impaired judgment, take special pleasure in quenching their deep thirst, and find deeper meaning in familiar music. If and only if novices learned to define the effects of smoking as pleasurable did they become habitual marijuana smokers.

So we see that becoming a regular marijuana user involves more than just motive and opportunity. In fact, learning any deviant or criminal role requires a social context like the one Becker describes. Experienced deviants or criminals must teach novices the "tricks of the trade." Bearing this fact in mind, we now examine the two main types of theories that seek to explain deviance and crime—those that ask what motivates people to break rules and those that ask how social constraints sometimes fail to prevent rules from getting broken.

Motivational Theories

Strain Theory

Durkheim argued that the absence of clear norms—a state of what he called "anomie"—can result in elevated rates of suicide and other forms of deviant behaviour (see Chapter 1, A Sociological Compass). Robert Merton's **strain theory**, summarized in Table 7.2 on page 198, extends Durkheim's insight (Merton, 1938). Merton argued that cultures often teach people to value material success. Just as often, however, societies do not provide enough legitimate opportunities for everyone to succeed. As a result, some people experience strain. Most of them will force themselves to adhere to social norms despite the strain (Merton called this *conformity*). The rest adapt in one of four ways. They may drop out of conventional society (*retreatism*). They may reject the goals of conventional society but continue to follow its rules (*ritualism*). They may protest against convention and support

Strain theory holds that people may turn to deviance when they experience strain. Strain results when a culture teaches people the value of material success and society fails to provide enough legitimate opportunities for everyone to succeed.

TABLE 7.2

Merton's Strain Theory of Deviance

Source: Adapted from Merton, 1938.

		Institutionalized Means		
		Accept	**Reject**	**Create New**
Cultural Goals	*Accept*	Conformity	Innovation	—
	Reject	Ritualism	Retreatism	—
	Create New	—	—	Rebellion

alternative values (*rebellion*). Or they may find alternative and illegitimate means of achieving their society's goals (*innovation*)—that is, they may become criminals. The "American Dream" of material success, as Merton referred to it, starkly contradicts the lack of opportunity available to poor youths. As a result, poor youths sometimes engage in illegal means of attaining socially approved-of goals.

Subcultural Theory

Subcultural theory argues that gangs are a collective adaptation to social conditions. Distinct norms and values that reject the legitimate world crystallize in gangs.

A second type of motivational theory, known as **subcultural theory**, emphasizes the importance of social groups. It suggests that deviant and criminal acts, including the formation of criminal gangs, are a *collective* adaptation to social conditions. Moreover, this collective adaptation involves the formation of a subculture with distinct norms and values. Members of this subculture reject the legitimate world that, they feel, has rejected them (Cohen, 1955).

The literature emphasizes three features of criminal subcultures. First, depending on the availability of different subcultures in their neighbourhoods, delinquent youths may turn to different types of crime. In some areas, delinquent youths are recruited by organized crime, such as the Mafia. In areas that lack organized crime networks, delinquent youths are more likely to create violent gangs. Thus, the relative availability of different subcultures influences the type of criminal activity to which a person turns (Cloward and Ohlin, 1960).

A second important feature of criminal subcultures is that their members typically spin out a whole series of rationalizations for their criminal activities. These justifications make their illegal activities appear morally acceptable and normal, at least to the members of the subculture. Typically, criminals deny personal responsibility for their actions ("What I did harmed nobody"). They condemn those who pass judgment on them ("I'm no worse than anyone else"). They claim their victims get what they deserve ("She had it coming to her"). And they appeal to higher loyalties, particularly to friends and family ("I had to do it because he dissed my gang"). The creation of such justifications and rationalizations enables criminals to clear their consciences and get on with the job. Sociologists call such rationalizations **techniques of neutralization** (Sykes and Matza, 1957; see also the case of the professional fence in Chapter 2, How Sociologists Do Research).

Techniques of neutralization are the rationalizations that deviants and criminals use to justify their activities. Techniques of neutralization make deviance and crime seem normal to deviants and criminals themselves.

Finally, although deviants may depart from mainstream culture in many ways, they are strict conformists when it comes to the norms of their own subculture. They tend to share the same beliefs, dress alike, eat similar food, and adopt the same mannerisms and speech patterns. Whether among professional thieves (Conwell, 1937) or young gang members (Short and Strodtbeck, 1965), deviance is strongly discouraged *within* the subculture. Paradoxically, deviant subcultures depend on internal conformity.

The main problem with strain and subcultural theories is that they exaggerate the connection between class and crime. Many self-report surveys find, at most, a weak tendency for criminals to come disproportionately from lower classes. Some self-report surveys report no such tendency at all, especially among young people and for less serious types of crime (Weis, 1987). A stronger correlation exists between *serious street crime* and class. Armed robbery and assault, for instance, are more common among people from lower classes. A stronger correlation also exists between *white-collar crime* and class. Middle- and upper-class people are most likely to commit white-collar crimes. Thus, generalizations about the relationship between class and crime must be qualified by taking into account the severity and type of crime (Braithwaite, 1981). Note also that official statistics usually exaggerate class differences because they are more accurate barometers of street crime than of suite crime. There is generally more police surveillance in lower-class neighbourhoods than in upper-class boardrooms.

Learning Theory

Apart from exaggerating the association between class and crime, strain and subcultural theories are problematic because they tell us nothing about which adaptation someone experiencing strain will choose. Even when criminal subcultures beckon ambitious adolescents who lack opportunities to succeed in life, only a minority join up. Most adolescents who experience strain and have the opportunity to join a gang reject the life of crime and become conformists and ritualists, to use Merton's terms. Why?

Edwin Sutherland (1939) addressed both the class problems and the choice problems 70 years ago by proposing a third motivational theory, which he called the theory of **differential association**. The theory of differential association is still one of the most influential ideas in the sociology of deviance and crime. In Sutherland's view, a person learns to favour one adaptation over another because of his or her life experiences or socialization. Specifically, everyone is exposed to both deviant and non-deviant values and behaviours as they grow up. If you happen to be exposed to more deviant than non-deviant experiences, chances increase that you will learn to become a deviant yourself. As the balance of your exposure tilts toward the deviant alternative, you are more likely to come to value a particular deviant lifestyle and consider it normal. Everything depends, then, on the exact mix of deviant and conformist influences a person faces. For example, a substantial body of participant-observation and survey research has failed to discover widespread cultural values prescribing crime and violence in the inner city of the United States (Sampson, 1997: 39). Most inner-city residents follow *conventional* norms, and that is one reason most inner-city adolescents do not learn to become gang members. Those who do become gang members tend to grow up in very specific situations and contexts that teach them the value of crime.

Significantly, the theory of differential association holds for people in all class positions. For instance, Sutherland applied the theory of differential association in his path-breaking research on white-collar crime. He noted that white-collar criminals, like their counterparts on the street, learn their skills from associates and share a culture that rewards rule-breaking and expresses contempt for the law (Sutherland, 1949).

Differential association theory holds that people learn to value deviant or non-deviant lifestyles depending on whether their social environment leads them to associate more with deviants or non-deviants.

In *The Sopranos,* having family members and friends in the Mafia predisposes a person to Mafia involvement—an illustration of the operation of the theory of differential association.

Constraint Theories

Motivational theories ask how some people are driven to break norms and laws. Constraint theories, in contrast, pay little or no attention to people's motivations. How are deviant and criminal "labels" imposed on some people? How do various forms of social control fail to impose conformity on them? How does the distribution of power in society shape deviance and crime? These are the kinds of questions posed by constraint theorists.

Labelling Theory

In 1995 in Saskatchewan, after a night of heavy drinking, two 20-year-old university students, Alex Ternowetsky and Steven Kummerfield, both white and middle class, picked up Pamela George, an Aboriginal single mother who occasionally worked as a prostitute, in downtown Regina. They drove the 28-year-old woman outside the city limits, demanded that she perform oral sex on them without pay, and then savagely beat her to death. Although originally charged with first-degree murder, a jury later found them guilty of the lesser charge of manslaughter. In a controversial move, Justice Ted Malone of the Saskatchewan Court of Queen's Bench instructed the jurors to consider that the two men had been drinking and that George was "indeed a prostitute." Members of the victim's family were appalled and Native leaders were outraged. Tone Cote of the Yorkton Tribal Council suggested the sentence was too lenient and would send the message that "[i]t's all right for little white boys to go out on the streets, get drunk and use that for an excuse to start hunting down our people."

In a variety of ways, this case, and the comments it raised, were eerily reminiscent of an earlier murder that had occurred in The Pas, Manitoba, in 1971. In that year, a 19-year-old Cree high-school student, Helen Betty Osborne, was abducted by four young white men from the main street in a practice known as "squaw hopping." Osborne was stabbed more than 50 times with a screwdriver when she resisted being raped and was left to bleed to death. For more than 16 years, no charges were laid against any of the youths, even though most people in the town probably knew about the youths' involvement in the murder (Griffiths and Yerbury, 1995: 394).

Labelling theory holds that deviance results not so much from the actions of the deviant as from the response of others, who label the rule breaker a deviant.

An important insight of **labelling theory** is that deviance results not just from the actions of the deviant but also from the responses of others, who define some actions as deviant and other actions as normal. As the above examples suggest, the term *deviant* or *criminal* is not automatic when a person engages in rule-violating behaviour. Some individuals escape being labelled as deviants despite having engaged in deviant behaviour. Others, however, who do not engage in deviant or criminal acts may find themselves wrongfully labelled as either deviant or criminal.

For example, if an adolescent misbehaves in high school a few times, teachers and the principal may punish him. However, his troubles really begin if the school authorities and the police label him as a delinquent or, more formally, as a young offender. Surveillance of his actions will increase. Actions that authorities would normally not notice or would define as of little consequence are more likely to be interpreted as proof that he, indeed, is a delinquent or criminal "type." He may be ostracized from non-deviant cliques in the school and eventually socialized into a deviant subculture. Over time, immersion in the deviant subculture may lead the adolescent to adopt "delinquent" as his **master status**, or overriding public identity. More easily than we may care to believe, what starts out as a few incidents of misbehaviour can amplify into a criminal career because of labelling (Matsueda, 1988, 1992).

A person's master status is his or her overriding public identity. It is the status that is most influential in shaping that person's life at a given time.

That labelling plays an important part in who is caught and who is charged with crime was demonstrated four decades ago by Aaron Cicourel (1968). Cicourel examined the tendency to label rule-breaking adolescents as juvenile delinquents if they came from families in which the parents were divorced. He found that police officers tended to use their discretionary powers to arrest adolescents from divorced families more often than adolescents from intact families who had committed similar delinquent acts. Judges, in turn, tended to give more severe sentences to adolescents from divorced families than to adolescents from intact families who were charged with similar delinquent acts. Sociologists and criminologists then collected data on the social characteristics of adolescents who were charged as juvenile delinquents, "proving" that children from divorced families were more likely to become juvenile delinquents. Their finding reinforced the beliefs of police officers and judges. Thus, the labelling process acted as a self-fulfilling prophecy.

Control Theory

All motivational theories assume that people are good and require special circumstances to make them bad. A popular type of constraint theory assumes that people are bad and require special circumstances to make them good. According to **control theory**, the rewards of deviance and crime are many. Proponents of this approach argue that nearly everyone wants fun, pleasure, excitement, and profit. Moreover, they say, if we could get away with it, most of us would commit deviant and criminal acts to acquire more of these valued things. For control theorists, the reason most of us don't engage in deviance and crime is that we are prevented from doing so. The reason deviants and criminals break norms and laws is that social controls are insufficient to ensure their conformity.

Travis Hirschi developed the control theory of crime (Gottfredson and Hirschi, 1990; Hirschi, 1969). He argued that adolescents are more prone to deviance and crime than adults are because they are incompletely socialized and therefore lack self-control. Adults and adolescents may both experience the impulse to break norms and laws, but adolescents are less likely to control that impulse. Hirschi went on to show that the adolescents who are most prone to delinquency are likely to lack four types of social control. They tend to have few social *attachments* to parents, teachers, and other respectable role models; few legitimate *opportunities* for education and a good job; few *involvements* in conventional institutions; and weak *beliefs* in traditional values and morality. Because of the lack of control stemming from these sources, they are relatively free to act on their deviant impulses.

Other sociologists have applied control theory to gender differences in crime. They have shown that girls are less likely to engage in delinquency than boys are because families typically exert more control over girls, supervising them more closely and socializing them to avoid risk (Hagan, Simpson, and Gillis, 1987; Peters, 1994). Sociologists have also applied control theory to different stages of life. Just as weak controls exercised by family and school are important in explaining why some adolescents engage in deviant or criminal acts, job and marital instability make it more likely that some adults will be unable to resist the temptations of deviance and crime (Sampson and Laub, 1993).

Labelling and control theories have little to say about why people regard certain kinds of activities as deviant or criminal in the first place. For the answer to that question, we must turn to conflict theory, a third type of constraint theory.

Conflict Theory

The day after Christmas in 1996, JonBenet Ramsey was found strangled to death in the basement of her parents' luxury home in Boulder, Colorado. The police found no footprints in the snow surrounding the house and no sign of forced entry. The investigators concluded that nobody had entered the house during the night when, according to the coroner, the murder took place. The police did find a ransom note saying that the child had been kidnapped. A linguistics expert from Vassar later compared the note with writing samples from the child's mother. In a 100-page report, the expert concluded that the child's mother was the author of the ransom note. It was also determined that all the materials used in the crime had been purchased by the mother. Finally, it was discovered that JonBenet had been sexually abused. Although by no means an open-and-shut case, enough evidence was available to cast a veil of suspicion over the parents. Yet, apparently because of the lofty position of the Ramsey family in their community, the police treated them in an extraordinary way.

On the first day of the investigation, the commander of the Boulder police detective division designated the Ramseys an "influential family" and ordered that they be treated as victims, not suspects (Oates, 1999: 32). The father was allowed to participate in the search for the child. In the process, he may have contaminated crucial evidence. The police also let

Control theory holds that the rewards of deviance and crime are ample. Therefore, nearly everyone would engage in deviance and crime if they could get away with it, and the degree to which people are prevented from violating norms and laws accounts for variations in the level of deviance and crime.

him leave the house unescorted for about an hour. This led to speculation that he might have disposed of incriminating evidence. Because the Ramseys are millionaires, they were able to hire accomplished lawyers who prevented the Boulder police from interviewing the family for four months and a public relations team that reinforced the idea that the Ramseys were victims. A grand jury decided on October 13, 1999, that nobody would be charged with the murder of JonBenet Ramsey.

Regardless of the innocence or guilt of the Ramseys, the way their case was handled adds to the view that the law applies differently to rich and poor. That is the perspective of **conflict theory**. In brief, conflict theorists maintain that the rich and powerful impose deviant and criminal labels on the less powerful members of society, particularly those who challenge the existing social order. Meanwhile, they are usually able to use their money and influence to escape punishment for their own misdeeds.

> The conflict theory of crime holds that deviance and crime arise out of the conflict between the powerful and the powerless.

Steven Spitzer (1980) conveniently summarizes this school of thought. He notes that capitalist societies are based on private ownership of property. Moreover, their smooth functioning depends on the availability of productive labour and respect for authority. When thieves steal, they challenge private property. Theft is therefore a crime. When so-called bag ladies and drug addicts drop out of conventional society, they are defined as deviant because their refusal to engage in productive labour undermines a pillar of capitalism. When young, politically volatile students or militant trade unionists strike or otherwise protest against authority, they, too, represent a threat to the social order and are defined as deviant or criminal.

Of course, says Spitzer, the rich and the powerful engage in deviant and criminal acts too. But, he adds, they tend to be dealt with more leniently. Industries can grievously harm people by damaging the environment, yet serious charges are rarely brought against the owners of industry. White-collar crimes are less severely punished than are street crimes, regardless of the relative harm they cause. Compare the crime of break and enter with fraud, for example. Fraud almost certainly costs society more than break and enter does. But breaking and entering is a street crime committed mainly by lower-class people, while fraud is a white-collar crime committed mainly by middle- and upper-class people. Not surprisingly, therefore, in Canada in 2000–01, 61 percent of convicted break and enter cases but just 35 percent of convicted fraud cases resulted in a prison sentence (Thomas, 2002: 9). Laws and norms may change along with shifts in the distribution of power in society. However, according to conflict theorists, definitions of deviance and crime, and also punishments for misdeeds, are always influenced by who's on top.

Many theories contribute to our understanding of the social causes of deviance and crime. Some forms of deviance and crime are better explained by one theory than by another. Different theories illuminate different aspects of the process by which people are motivated to break rules and be defined as rule breakers. Our overview should make it clear that no one theory is best. Instead, taking many theories into account allows us to develop a fully rounded appreciation of the complex processes surrounding the social construction of deviance and crime.

SOCIAL CONTROL AND PUNISHMENT

Trends in Social Control

No discussion of crime and deviance would be complete without considering in some depth the important issues of social control and punishment, for all societies seek to ensure that their members obey norms and laws. All societies impose sanctions on rule breakers. However, the *degree* of social control varies over time and from one society to the next. *Forms* of punishment also vary. Below we focus on how social control and punishment have changed historically.

Consider first the difference between preindustrial and industrial societies. Beginning in the late nineteenth century, many sociologists argued that preindustrial societies are characterized by strict social control and high conformity, while industrial societies are characterized by less stringent social control and low conformity (Tönnies, 1988 [1887]). Similar differences were said to characterize small communities versus cities. As an old German proverb says, "City air makes you free."

There is much truth in this point of view. Whether they are fans of opera or reggae, connoisseurs of fine wine or marijuana, city dwellers in industrial societies find it easier than do people in small preindustrial communities to belong to a group or subculture of their choice. In general, the more complex a society, the less likely many norms will be widely shared. In fact, in a highly complex society, such as Canada today, it is difficult to find an area of social life in which everyone is alike or in which one group can impose its norms on the rest of society without resistance.

Nonetheless, some sociologists believe that social control has intensified over time, at least in some ways. They recognize that individuality and deviance have increased but insist this has happened only within quite strict limits, beyond which it is now *more* difficult to move. In their view, many crucial aspects of life have become more regimented, not less.

Much of the regimentation of modern life is tied to the growth of capitalism and the state. Factories require strict labour regimes, with workers arriving and leaving at a fixed time and, in the interim, performing fixed tasks at a fixed pace. Workers initially rebelled against this regimentation since they were used to enjoying many holidays and a flexible and vague work schedule regulated only approximately by the seasons and the rising and setting of the sun. But they had little alternative as wage labour in industry overtook feudal arrangements in agriculture (Thompson, 1967). Meanwhile, institutions linked to the growth of the modern state—armies, police forces, public schools, health care systems, and various other bureaucracies—also demanded strict work regimes, curricula, and procedures. These institutions existed on a much smaller scale in preindustrial times or did not exist at all. Today they penetrate our lives and sustain strong norms of belief and conduct (Foucault, 1977).

In preindustrial societies, criminals who committed serious crimes were put to death, often in ways that seem cruel by today's standards. One method involved hanging the criminal with starving dogs.

Electronic technology makes it possible for authorities to exercise more effective social control than ever before. With millions of cameras mounted in public places and workplaces, some sociologists say we now live in a "surveillance society" (Lyon and Zureik, 1996). Cameras enable observers to see deviance and crime that would otherwise go undetected and take quick action to apprehend rule breakers. Moreover, when people are aware of the presence of cameras, they tend to alter their behaviour. For example, attentive shoplifters migrate to stores that lack electronic surveillance. On factory floors and in offices, workers display more conformity to management-imposed work norms. On campuses, students are inhibited from engaging in organized protests (Boal, 1998).

**TECHNOLOGY
BYTES**

Thanks to computers and satellites, intelligence services in Canada, the United States, Britain, Australia, and New Zealand now monitor all international telecommunications traffic, always on the lookout for threats. As easily as you can find the word *anomie* in your sociology essay by using the search function of your word processor, national security agencies can scan digitized telephone and e-mail traffic in many languages for key words and word patterns that suggest unfriendly activity (Omega Foundation, 1998). However, the system is also used to target sensitive business and economic secrets from Western Europe, and some people have expressed the fear that it could be used on ordinary citizens, robbing them of their privacy. Meanwhile, credit information on 95 percent of North American consumers is available for purchase, the better to tempt you with credit cards, marketing ploys, and junk mail. When you browse the Web, information about your browsing patterns is collected in the background by many of the sites you visit, again largely for marketing purposes. Most large companies monitor and record their employees' phone conversations and e-mail messages. These are all efforts to regulate behaviour, enforce conformity, and prevent deviance and crime more effectively by using the latest technologies (Garfinkel, 2000).

A major development in social control that accompanied industrialization was the rise of the prison. Today, prisons figure prominently in the control of criminals the world over. North Americans, however, have a particular affinity for the institution, as we will now see.

Roger Caron, who was 16 years old when he was first sentenced to prison for breaking and entering, has spent much of his life behind bars. His prison experiences turned him into a career criminal.

The Prison

In October 2001, a 63-year-old man suffering from Parkinson's disease and addicted to cocaine was arrested in Ottawa. A passerby had noticed that the man had a 32-gauge shotgun in his gym bag and notified the police. The man, who was charged with possession of a weapon, did not resist arrest. This fact was not, perhaps, surprising, for the man's knowledge of the Canadian criminal justice system was vast. Roger Caron, dubbed Mad Dog Caron by the press, had first been sentenced to prison at the age of 16 for breaking and entering. He had spent most of his adult life as an inept robber, going in and out of Eastern Canada's major prisons: Guelph, Kingston, Collins Bay, Millhaven, Stoney Mountain, St. Vincent de Paul, Dorchester, and an institution reserved for the criminally insane—Penetanguishene.

While incarcerated in the 1970s and after having already spent almost 20 years in prison, Caron wrote a chilling account of his life behind bars. He was still in prison when his book *Go-Boy!* was published in 1978. The book describes, in harrowing detail, the harshness of the prison experience—the violence, the intense hatreds that fester, the hard labour, the horrors of solitary confinement, the twisted, manipulative friendships formed within a prison setting, and the brutal use of corporal punishment. He describes the use of the "paddle"—"three leather straps with wooden handles, so thick and coarse as to barely sag. Each one was perforated with hundreds of tiny holes designed to trap and rip the flesh from the buttocks." He writes that when this form of punishment was first administered to him in 1955, "[w]hite searing pain exploded throughout my being and blood gushed from my lips as I struggled to stifle a scream. It was brutal and it was horrible" (Caron, 1979: 59; see also Farrell, n.d.).

Go-Boy! was honoured in 1978 with the Governor General's Award for literature and, in the years that followed, Caron wrote other books. However, he was unable to leave his past life totally. Following imprisonment for another botched robbery attempt, Caron was released from prison in 1998 and was still on parole at the time of his 2001 arrest. Regardless of the initial factors that caused Caron to turn to crime, it was his experiences in prison that turned him into a career criminal (CyberPress, 2001).

Caron's experience follows a pattern known to sociologists for a long time. Prisons are agents of socialization, and new inmates often become more serious offenders as they adapt to the culture of the most hardened, long-term prisoners (Wheeler, 1961).

Because prison often turns criminals into worse criminals, it is worth pondering the institution's origins, development, and current dilemmas. As societies industrialized, imprisonment became one of the most important forms of punishment for criminal behaviour (Garland, 1990; Morris and Rothman, 1995). In preindustrial societies, criminals were publicly humiliated, tortured, or put to death, depending on the severity of their transgressions. In the industrial era, depriving criminals of their freedom by putting them in prison seemed less harsh, more "civilized" (Durkheim, 1973 [1899–1900]).

Rationales for Incarceration

Some people still take a benign view of prisons, even seeing them as opportunities for *rehabilitation.* They believe that prisoners, while serving time, can be taught how to be productive citizens on release. In Canada, this rehabilitative ethos predominated from the 1950s to the early 1970s, when many prisons sought to reform criminals by offering them psychological counselling, drug therapy, skills training, education, and other programs that would help at least the less violent offenders reintegrate into society (McMahon, 1992: xvii).

Today, however, many Canadians scoff at the idea that prisons can rehabilitate criminals. We have adopted a much tougher line and politicians routinely campaign on promises of a get-tough approach to crime and to criminals. Some people see prison as a means of *deterrence*. In this view, people will be less inclined to commit crimes if they know they are likely to be caught and serve long and unpleasant prison terms. Others think of prisons as institutions of *revenge*. They believe that depriving criminals of their freedom and forcing them to live in poor conditions is fair retribution for their illegal acts. Still others see prisons as institutions of *incapacitation*. From this viewpoint, the chief function of the prison is simply to keep criminals out of society as long as possible to ensure they can do no more harm (Feeley and Simon, 1992; Simon, 1993; Zimring and Hawkins, 1995).

No matter which of these views predominates, one thing is clear. The Canadian public has demanded that more criminals be arrested and imprisoned, and it got what it wanted until 1994–95, when the incarceration rate started to decline gradually. In 2005, 107 of every 100 000 Canadians were in prison. Note, however, that although Canada's incarceration rate is higher than that of most West European countries, it is much lower than that of the United States, which had an incarceration rate of 737 in 2005 (Figure 7.9). The United States currently has far more people behind bars than any other country on earth—about 2.1 million.

Moral Panic

What accounts for our increased enthusiasm for get-tough policies? One answer is that the way in which the media report crime may exacerbate public fearfulness. An analysis of the ABC, NBC, and CBS nightly newscasts from 1990 through 1996 revealed that although coverage of crime ranked sixth from 1990 to 1992, it skyrocketed to first place after that with 7448 stories devoted to crime in a four-year period. Approximately 1 out of every 20 American network news stories over that period was about a murder, suggesting an unprecedented crime wave

WHERE DO
YOU FIT IN?

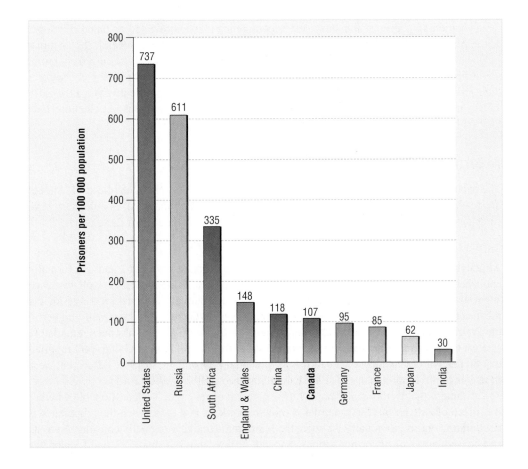

FIGURE 7.9

Number of Prisoners per 100 000 Population, Selected Countries, c. 2005

Source: The Sentencing Project, 2006.

(Kurtz, 1997). The massive presence of American programming in Canadian homes may encourage us to fuse and confuse the Canadian and American experience in relation to crime.

The National Media Archive examined 98 Canadian supper-hour TV newscasts that aired on three dates in 1997. *Chaos news*—news reports on crime, accidents, and natural disasters—accounted for 22 percent of Canadian TV news items. Canadian newscasts were more likely than American newscasts to feature news about government and "soft news" (e.g., general human-interest stories and stories about entertainment, the arts, and culture). In general, American stations were also much more likely to lead or begin their newscasts with a report on crime, accidents, disasters, or other forms of chaos. Nevertheless, to the extent we believe that the crimes that draw headlines are "typical" of crime in Canada, we may believe that the battle to win the "war against crime" requires the most punitive measures.

In short, media presentations of the crime problem may serve to promote a **moral panic**. That is, in response to lurid headlines that direct attention to the most notorious— and atypical—crimes and criminals, the public may prematurely conclude that all crime is violent and predatory, that all criminals are "dangerous," and that our current crime rate signals a grave threat to our society's well-being (Cohen, 1972; Goode and Ben-Yehuda, 1994). Are you part of the moral panic? Have you and your family taken special precautions to protect yourself from the "growing wave" of criminality? Even if you're not part of the moral panic, chances are you know someone who is. Therefore, to put things in perspective, you will need to recall an important fact from our discussion of recent trends in crime rates: According to official statistics, the moral panic is taking place during a period when major crime indexes are *falling*.

Why, then, the moral panic? Does anyone benefit from it? There may be several interested parties. First, the mass media benefit from moral panic because it allows them to rake in hefty profits. They publicize every major crime because crime draws big audiences, and big audiences mean more revenue from advertisers. After all, a front-page photograph of Karla Homolka or Paul Bernardo still generates newspaper sales more than a decade after their convictions—even if the story that accompanies it is abbreviated or banal. Fictional crime programs also draw tens of millions of viewers to their TVs. Second, the criminal justice system is a huge bureaucracy with thousands of employees. They benefit from moral panic because increased spending on crime prevention, control, and punishment secures their jobs and expands their turf. Third, the moral panic is useful politically. Since the early 1970s, many politicians have based entire careers on get-tough policies. At election time, they make combating crime a focal point of their campaign promises.

Alternative Forms of Punishment

The two most contentious issues concerning the punishment of criminals are these: (1) Should the death penalty be reintroduced to punish the most violent criminals? (2) Should alternative strategies be used? In concluding this chapter, we briefly consider each of these issues.

Capital Punishment

Although capital punishment has not been employed in Canada since 1962 and was formally abolished in this country in 1976, the state retains the right to bring it back. As well, evidence suggests that a majority of Canadians favour its reintroduction. Although support for the reinstatement of capital punishment is somewhat lower in Quebec and marginally higher in the Prairie provinces, on a national level, support for the death penalty has been remarkably consistent over time. Consider, for example, that in the fall of 1945, a Gallup poll reported that 80 percent of Canadians were in favour of capital punishment; in 1995, 82 percent were in favour of the death penalty in at least some instances (Bibby, 1995, 2001).

Although the death penalty ranks high as a form of revenge, it is questionable whether it is much of a deterrent. First, murder is often committed in a rage, when the perpetrator is not thinking entirely rationally. As such, the murderer is unlikely to coolly consider the costs and consequences of his or her actions. Second, critics point out that the United States has

A moral panic occurs when many people fervently believe that some form of deviance or crime poses a profound threat to society's well-being.

Intensive media coverage of the most notorious and violent crimes and criminals may lead to a heightened fear of crime and demands for tougher penalties. Karla Homolka, with her husband, Paul Bernardo, was responsible for the sexual assault and brutal murder of Tammy Homolka, Leslie Mahaffy, and Kristen French in the early 1990s.

a much higher murder rate than do Canada and Western European nations that do not practise capital punishment (Mooney et al., 2001: 131).

Moreover, we must remember that capital punishment, where it is actually practised, is hardly a matter of blind justice. This is particularly evident if we consider the racial distribution of people who are sentenced to death and executed in the United States. Murdering a white person in the United States is much more likely to result in a death sentence than is murdering a black person. For example, in Florida in the 1970s, an African American who killed a white person was 40 times as likely to receive the death penalty as an African American who killed another African American. Moreover, a white person who murders a black person is rarely sentenced to death, but a black person who murders a white person is one of the most likely to get the death penalty. Thus, of the 80 white people who murdered African Americans in Florida in the 1970s, not one was charged with a capital crime. In Texas, 1 was—out of 143 (Black, 1989; Haines, 1996; Tonry, 1995). Given this patent racial bias, we cannot view the death penalty as a justly administered punishment.

Sometimes people favour capital punishment because it saves money. They argue that killing someone outright costs less than keeping the person alive in prison for the rest of his or her life. However, after trials and appeals, a typical execution costs the taxpayer several times *more* than a 40-year stay in a maximum-security prison (Haines, 1996).

Finally, in assessing capital punishment, we must remember that mistakes are common. Nearly 40 percent of death sentences in the United States since 1977 have been overturned because of new evidence or mistrial (Haines, 1996). In Canada, the wrongful convictions of Donald Marshall, Guy Paul Morin, David Milgaard—and many others in recent times—for murders they did not commit should be sufficient to remind us that the wheels of justice do not always turn smoothly.

Alternative Strategies

In recent years, analysts have suggested two main reforms to our current prison regime. First, some analysts have argued that we should reconsider our stance on rehabilitation. Advocates of rehabilitation suggest that **recidivism rates**, or the extent to which convicted offenders commit another crime, can be reduced through such programs as educational and job training, individual and group therapy, substance abuse counselling, and behaviour modification. Second, they have argued that, whenever possible, we should attempt to *reduce* rather than increase the number of incarcerated offenders. Drawing on labelling theory, they suggest we pursue a policy of *radical non-intervention,* diverting offenders away from formal processing in the criminal justice system. Proponents of this idea say that at least part of the increase in crime we have witnessed in the past four decades is attributable to the introduction of new and broadened definitions of criminal conduct. They believe that charging and imprisoning more and more Canadians, especially youth, is unlikely to help these individuals develop prosocial behaviour. Accordingly, they advise us to seek alternative methods that divert adults and juveniles from formal criminal justice system processing.

Although alternative procedures vary across provinces and territories, their use generally arises after the police or Crown prosecutor recommends that an offender be considered suitable for "diversion." One example of an alternative measure is a victim–offender reconciliation program (VORP), in which victim and offender meet under controlled circumstances. The victim has an opportunity to describe the impact of the criminal event on himself or herself and the offender might, for example, be required to apologize and agree to compensate the victim financially. In 1998–99, some 33 173 youth cases were dealt with through alternative measures programs (Tufts, 2000: 10). These cases were more likely to involve male than female offenders. Young offenders selected for inclusion in these programs were usually over 15 years of age, and they generally completed the provisions of the agreements they made. Most cases referred for diversion involved theft under $5000 (e.g., shoplifting). This is not surprising, since to be recommended for diversion, the offence must be minor. As well, to be considered candidates for diversion, offenders must first acknowledge that they are guilty of the act they have been accused of committing.

Recidivism rates indicate the proportion of people re-arrested after an initial arrest.

In like fashion, proponents of *decarceration* recommend that such options as fines (the most commonly used penal sanction in Canada), probation, and community service become more widely used as alternatives to imprisonment. However, not everyone views this strategy as desirable. It has been argued that the increased use of community programs does not truly reduce the numbers of individuals subject to formal social control. Rather, such strategies may simply widen the net through the creation of more intensive, intrusive, and prolonged control mechanisms. These efforts might more accurately be labelled *transcarceration* than decarceration (Lowman, Menzies, and Palys, 1987). Noting such objections, some analysts suggest that we go further still and lobby for legislative reform that would *decriminalize* certain categories of conduct currently prohibited under Canadian criminal law, such as marijuana possession. This last suggestion serves to remind us, yet again, that crime and deviance are social constructs.

NOTE

1. Data are drawn from an analysis of adult criminal courts in eight provinces and territories; at the time that the analysis was conducted, data were unavailable for New Brunswick, Manitoba, British Columbia, the Northwest Territories, and Nunavut.

SUMMARY

1. What is deviance and how does it compare with crime?
   Deviance involves breaking a norm. Crime involves breaking a law. Both crime and deviance evoke societal reactions that help define the seriousness of the rule-breaking incident.

2. What determines the perceived seriousness of deviant and criminal acts?
   The seriousness of deviant and criminal acts depends on the severity of the societal response to them, their perceived harmfulness, and the degree of public agreement about whether they should be considered deviant or criminal.

3. What four broad classes of acts are ranked from lowest to highest on the three dimensions that determine seriousness?
   Acts that rank lowest on these three dimensions are called social diversions. Next come social deviations, and then come conflict crimes. Consensus crimes rank highest.

4. Are the definitions of crime and deviance fixed or variable?
   Definitions of deviance and crime are historically and culturally variable. They are socially defined and constructed. They are not inherent in actions or in the characteristics of individuals.

5. What enables some groups rather than others to define deviance and crime to best suit their interests?
   Power is a key element in defining deviance and crime. Powerful groups are generally able to create norms and laws that suit their interests. Less powerful groups are usually unable to do so.

6. What is an example of a change in the law brought about by the increasing power of a group and an example of relative immunity brought on by established power?
   The increasing power of women has led to greater recognition of crimes committed against them. However, no similar recognition has occurred in the prosecution of white-collar criminals because the distribution of power between classes has not changed much in recent decades.

7. What are the sources of statistics on how much crime occurs?
Crime statistics come from official sources, self-report surveys, and indirect measures. Each source has its strengths and weaknesses.

8. What trends in crime have occurred over the last several decades? What helps explain these trends?
The long crime wave that began its upswing in the early 1960s peaked and fell in the 1990s and, for nine years, decreased each year by an average of 3 percent. It has remained fairly stable since the 1990s. This stability stemmed, in part, from increased policing, a smaller proportion of young men in the population, and a booming economy.

9. How does race figure in crime and punishment?
Aboriginal people experience disproportionately high arrest, conviction, and incarceration rates. However, it would be inaccurate to conclude that race and crime are causally related. This finding may be a consequence of individual and institutional bias. Moreover, race and social class are closely related in that Aboriginal people are overrepresented in lower classes.

10. What are some major theories of deviance?
Theories of deviance include motivational theories (strain theory, subcultural theory, and learning theory) and constraint theories (labelling theory, control theory, and conflict theory). Different theories illuminate different aspects of the process by which people are motivated to break rules and become defined as rule breakers.

11. What is social control?
Social control is the effort exerted by all societies to ensure that their members obey norms and laws by imposing sanctions on rule breakers. The degree and form of social control vary historically and culturally.

12. Has social control weakened with the advent of industrialism?
Although some sociologists say that social control is weaker and deviance is greater in industrial societies than in preindustrial societies, other sociologists note that in some respects social control is greater in industrial societies.

13. What kind of societies use prisons for punishment? How has the rationale for using prisons for punishment shifted?
Modern industrial societies rely on prisons as an important form of punishment. Prisons now focus less on rehabilitation than on isolating and incapacitating inmates.

14. What is moral panic and where does it come from?
Moral panic occurs when many people fervently believe that some form of deviance or crime poses a profound threat to society's well-being. It may be set off when people are convinced that crime is rising and tougher measures against criminals are called for. However, such responses to crime may arise, in part, because of media presentations that focus attention on the most violent—and least representative—types of crime committed. A variety of commercial and political groups benefit from the moral panic over crime and therefore encourage it.

15. Does the death penalty effectively deter crime or serve justice?
Although the death penalty ranks high as a form of revenge, it is doubtful whether it acts as a serious deterrent. Moreover, where it exists, the death penalty is administered in a racially biased manner, does not save money, and sometimes results in tragic mistakes.

16. How should society respond to crime?
The question of how we should respond to crime results in many different suggestions. These range from the reintroduction of capital punishment to the suggestion that we decriminalize various types of conduct currently prohibited under Canadian law.

KEY TERMS

conflict crimes (p. 185)

conflict theory (p. 202)

consensus crimes (p. 185)

constraint theories (p. 196)

control theory (p. 201)

deviance (p. 183)

differential association (p. 199)

formal punishment (p. 184)

informal punishment (p. 184)

labelling theory (p. 200)

master status (p. 200)

moral panic (p. 206)

motivational theories (p. 196)

recidivism rate (p. 207)

self-report surveys (p. 190)

social constructionism (p. 187)

social control (p. 194)

social deviations (p. 185)

social diversion (p. 185)

stigma (p. 184)

strain theory (p. 197)

street crimes (p. 188)

subcultural theory (p. 198)

techniques of neutralization (p. 198)

victimization surveys (p. 190)

victimless crimes (p. 190)

white-collar crime (p. 188)

QUESTIONS TO CONSIDER

1. Has this chapter changed your view of criminals and the criminal justice system? If so, how? If not, why not?

2. Do you think different theories are useful in explaining different types of deviance and crime? Or do you think that one or two theories explain all types of deviance and crime while other theories are not very illuminating? Justify your answer by using logic and evidence.

3. Do TV crime shows and crime movies give a different picture of crime in Canada than this chapter provides? What are the major differences? Which picture do you think is more accurate? Why?

WEB RESOURCES

Companion Website for This Book

http://www.compass3e.nelson.com

Begin by clicking on the Student Resources section of the website. Next, select the chapter you are studying from the pull-down menu. From the Student Resources page you have easy access to InfoTrac® College Edition, additional Weblinks, and other resources. The website also has many useful tips to aid you in your study of sociology, including practice tests for each chapter.

InfoTrac® Search Terms

These search terms are provided to assist you in beginning to conduct research on this topic by visiting http://www.infotrac-college.com:

moral panic

prison

stigma
street crime
white-collar crime

Recommended Websites

For a measure of how widespread corruption is in the governments of every country in the world, visit http://transparency.org/cpi/2005/2005.10.18.cpi.en.html#cpi.

The Canadian Criminal Justice resource page at http://members.tripod.com/~BlueThingy/index.html contains many useful links.

The Sentencing Project provides cross-national data on rates of incarceration at http://www.sentencingproject.org/pdfs/1044.pdf.

CengageNOW™

http://hed.nelson.com

This online diagnostic tool identifies each student's unique needs with a Pretest that generates a personalized Study Plan for each chapter, helping students focus on concepts they're having the most difficulty mastering. Students then take a Posttest after reading the chapter to measure their understanding of the material. An Instructor Gradebook is available to track and monitor student progress.

CHAPTER

8

Social Stratification: Canadian and Global Perspectives

In this chapter, you will learn that

- Income is unequally distributed in Canada and government plays a small, but important, role in redistributing money to children and families who are poor.

- Income inequality in Canada is lower than in the United States but consistent with most other postindustrial societies.

- As societies develop, inequality at first increases. Then, after passing the early stage of industrialization, inequality in society declines. In the postindustrial stage of development, inequality begins to increase again in some countries.

- Most theories of social inequality focus on its economic roots.

- Prestige and power are important non-economic sources of inequality.

- Although some sociologists used to think that talent and hard work alone determine a person's position in the socioeconomic hierarchy, it is now clear that being a member of certain groups limits opportunities for success. In this sense, social structure shapes the distribution of inequality.

PATTERNS OF SOCIAL INEQUALITY

Shipwrecks and Inequality

Writers and filmmakers sometimes tell stories about shipwrecks and their survivors to make a point about social inequality. They use the shipwreck as literary device. It allows them to sweep away all traces of privilege and social convention. What remains are human beings stripped to their essentials, guinea pigs in an imaginary laboratory for the study of wealth and poverty, power and powerlessness, esteem and disrespect.

Daniel Defoe's *Robinson Crusoe,* first published in 1719, is a classic novel in this tradition. Defoe writes of an Englishman marooned on a deserted island. The man's strong will, hard work, and inventiveness turn the island into a thriving colony. Defoe was one of the first writers to portray the work ethic of capitalism favourably. He believed that people get rich if they possess the virtues of good businesspeople—and stay poor if they don't.

The 1974 Italian movie *Swept Away* tells almost exactly the opposite story. In the movie a beautiful woman, one of the idle rich, cruises in the Mediterranean. She treats the hard-working deckhands in a condescending and abrupt way. The deckhands do their jobs but seethe with resentment. Then comes a storm. The beautiful woman and one handsome deckhand are swept onto a deserted island. The deckhand asserts his masculine prowess on an initially unwilling and reluctant woman. The two survivors soon have passionate sex and fall in love.

All is well until their rescue. On returning to the mainland, the woman resumes her haughty ways. She turns her back on the deckhand; he becomes a common labourer again. Thus, the movie sends the audience four harsh messages, each contrasting with themes in Defoe's *Robinson Crusoe.* First, you do not have to work hard to be rich, because you can inherit wealth. Second, hard work does not always make you rich. Third, something about the structure of society causes inequality, for it is only on the deserted island, without society as we know it, that class inequality disappears. *Swept Away* also focuses attention on unequal power between the sexes. The two survivors are not equals; male privilege exerts itself in a context in which class differences have been obliterated. Here, then, is a fourth harsh message. Inequality has many interrelated dimensions, including class, sex, and race, and different contexts highlight different conditions of power and exploitation.

And then there is *Titanic,* a characteristically American take on the shipwreck-and-inequality theme. At one level, the movie shows that class differences are important. For example, in first class, living conditions are luxurious, while in third class, they are cramped. Indeed, on the *Titanic,* class divisions spell the difference between life and death. After the *Titanic* strikes an iceberg off the coast of Newfoundland, the ship's crew prevents second- and third-class passengers from entering the few available lifeboats. Priority goes to first-class passengers.

As the tragedy of the *Titanic* unfolds, however, a different theme emerges. Under some circumstances, we learn, class differences can be erased. In the movie, the sinking of the *Titanic* is the backdrop to a fictional love story about a wealthy young woman in first class and a working-class youth from the decks below. The sinking of the *Titanic* and the collapse of its elaborate class structure give the young lovers an opportunity to cross class divisions and profess devotion to each other. At another level, then, *Titanic* is an optimistic tale that holds out hope for a society in which class differences no longer matter, a society much like that of the "American Dream."

Robinson Crusoe, Swept Away, and *Titanic* raise many of the issues we address in this chapter. What are the sources of social inequality? Do determination, industry, and ingenuity shape the distribution of advantages and disadvantages in society, as the tale of *Robinson Crusoe* portrays? Or is *Swept Away* more accurate? Do certain patterns of social relations underlie and shape that distribution? Is *Titanic*'s first message of social class differences still valid? Does social inequality still have big consequences for the way we live? What about *Titanic*'s second message? Can people overcome or reduce inequality in society? If so, how?

To answer these questions, we first sketch the pattern of social inequality in Canada and around the world. We pay special attention to change over time. We then critically review the major theories of social inequality. We assess explanations for differences in inequality in the light of logic and evidence. Periodically, we take a step back and identify issues needing resolution before we can achieve a fuller understanding of social inequality, one of the fundamentally important aspects of social life.

Economic Inequality in Canada

The musical *Cabaret,* set in the 1930s, contains a song based on the saying "Money makes the world go round." In the 1980s, Madonna repeated the theme in her hit song, "Material Girl": "They can beg and they can plead/But they can't see the light (that's right)/'Cause the boy with the cold hard cash/Is always Mister Right" (Brown and Rans, 1984).

TECHNOLOGY BYTES

The idea that money is power is a perennial theme. Decade by decade, the saying "Everything has its price" becomes more and more accurate. Thus, the selling of blood, sperm, and ova is common in many countries. An international trade in the body parts of the living, and the dead, flourishes. These body parts are often used for education and research purposes. More controversial is the practice of purchasing human organs, in particular kidneys, for transplantation. In the typical supply and demand equation of modern commerce, as demand for available organs escalates, the supply of body parts expands. The global organ shortage "has encouraged the sale of organs, nowhere more conspicuously than in India. It has also stimulated the use of organs from executed prisoners, nowhere more systematically than in China. Thus, residents of Gulf States and other Asian countries frequently travel to India to obtain a kidney" (Rothman et al., 1997).

People selling body parts are almost invariably poor. People buying body parts are invariably rich. Though not a common practice, an increasing number of wealthy people travel to foreign countries with their own surgeons in tow in an attempt to prolong life through the purchase and use of body parts.

In North America, and especially in the United States, poor people are more likely than rich people are to suffer illnesses that could be alleviated by organ transplantation. However, they are less likely to be offered transplant opportunities (Wallich and Mukerjee, 1996). Especially in the United States, this is largely the result of the poor not having adequate private health insurance to cover transplantation expenses. However, it is also the case that the poor are more likely to be organ donors, even in Canada, because "the typical donor is still young and a victim of accidental or deliberate violence—which tends to strike the disadvantaged in disproportionate numbers" (Wallich and Mukerjee, 1996).

After weighing evidence and argument, an international report on organ trafficking "found no unarguable ethical principle that would justify a ban on the sale of organs" (Rothman et al., 1997). In particular, it notes that "a prohibition on sale might well cost would-be recipients their lives and infringe in important ways on the autonomy of would-be sellers" (Rothman et al., 1997). This latter point is particularly germane because it touches on a key debate about social inequality. From what perspective or standpoint can we make judgments about inequality and human misery? Who should make the choice between grinding poverty on the one hand and the sale of a kidney on the other? An easy response is to claim this is a false dichotomy. No one should have to make such a choice! Too easy. Such a response ignores all of human history, in which social inequality, the context of such a horrible choice, has existed always and everywhere.

Materialism, the attempt to satisfy needs by buying products or experiences, is a defining characteristic of modern society. Never have so many people, at least in the Western industrial world, been able to share so widely in material comforts (such as central heating, ample food, appropriate clothing, and so forth). Economic prosperity has made Canada one of the best countries in the world in which to live.

The growth of prosperity in the post–World War II Canadian economy is easy to illustrate. Figure 8.1 shows the growth in the average earnings of Canadian households.

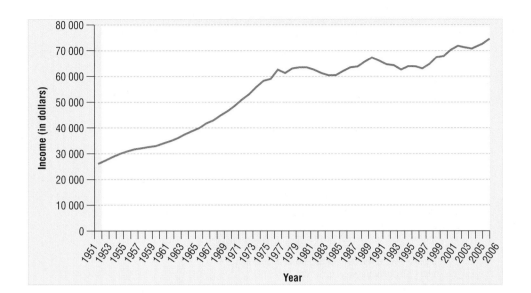

FIGURE 8.1
Average Income of Canadian
Families, 1951 to 2006
(in 2003 dollars)

Source: Adapted from various
documents from Statistics Canada
and from the Canadian Council on
Social Development.

In 2006, Canadian families earned an average income of more than $74 800. In the early 1950s, Canadian families earned less than $30 000 a year on average. Some of this increase may seem misleading since a soft drink that once cost a dime now costs a dollar. But the incomes in the graph are corrected for such inflation and still reveal a substantial increase.

The purchasing power of families rose because economic productivity was enhanced by improvements in workers' skills and by advances in the technologies used for production. Increases in family income, after adjusting for inflation, were most rapid from the end of World War II until the economic downturn that began around 1973.

Notice also from Figure 8.1 that the average earnings of Canadian families have increased at a slower rate recently. That is, the slope of the income line was flatter in the 1980s and 1990s than it was earlier. Recall, too, that the number of earners in a family increased over this recent interval as more women entered the paid labour force. Even so, the purchasing power of family earnings did not grow much. This difference has led to several recent public debates. Notably, the widespread demand for reduced taxes is, in part, a reaction to this relatively flat earnings trajectory. Despite working harder and longer, families' incomes have not grown proportionately. Coupled with this is the common awareness that the days of the single-breadwinner family of the 1950s and 1960s are past. Most families now have at least two earners, but the prospect of buying a house, and owning more of it than the bank does, is still a struggle.

Figure 8.1 simplifies reality because it is based on averages. Economic prosperity and the benefits of materialism are not equally shared. In your own experience you will have witnessed inequality when passing through skid row or the inner-city areas of many of our biggest communities. You may have seen the lineups for food banks or the poverty of some rural farmers. Here is a language and lifestyle of used clothes, of baloney and Spam, of fleas and roaches, of despair and depression. There is also a language of booze, illicit sex, welfare cheats, laziness, and cunning deceit. We will return to these contrasting descriptions later.

At the other end of the money spectrum is the luxury of our richest neighbourhoods, places you may have lived in or visited. This is the world of multimillion-dollar homes with indoor swimming pools and outdoor tennis courts, multi-car garages, and in-house security systems to deter those who might steal a piece of art. Here is a language and lifestyle of Gucci and Hugo Boss, of caviar and roast duckling, of coddled poodles and parakeets, of ambition and success. Here, too, is a different language, one of idle richness, of misbegotten inheritance, of greedy property owners, and of fraud and cunning deceit. This, too, is a contrast to which we will return (see Figure 8.2 on page 216).

The vast majority of us live between these two extremes. Many of us may have tasted both caviar and baloney, petted poodles and scratched fleas, but relatively few Canadians have

FIGURE 8.2

It's a Long Way to the Top: Canadian Income Inequality, 2004

Note: Drawn to scale.

Source: Data from Brian Murphy, Paul Roberts, and Michael Wolfson, 2007, *A Profile of High-Income Canadians, 1982–2004,* Statistics Canada. Retrieved May 1, 2008 (http://www. statcan.ca/english/research/75F0002 MIE/75F0002MIE2007006.pdf).

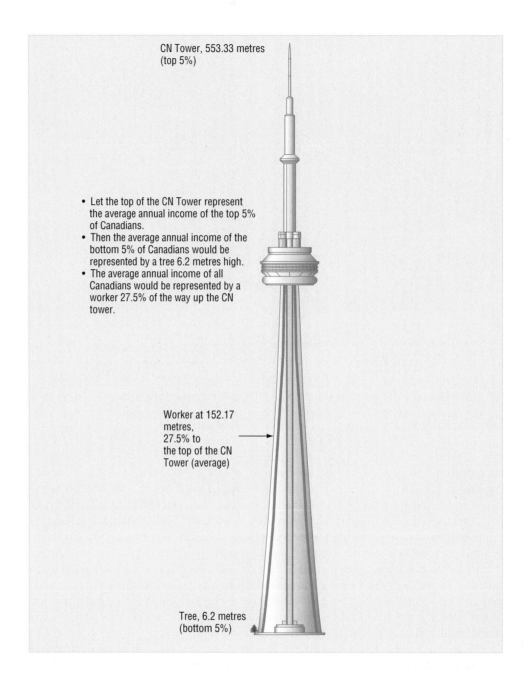

CN Tower, 553.33 metres (top 5%)

- Let the top of the CN Tower represent the average annual income of the top 5% of Canadians.
- Then the average annual income of the bottom 5% of Canadians would be represented by a tree 6.2 metres high.
- The average annual income of all Canadians would be represented by a worker 27.5% of the way up the CN tower.

Worker at 152.17 metres, 27.5% to the top of the CN Tower (average)

Tree, 6.2 metres (bottom 5%)

continuing experience with either abject poverty or substantial wealth. How do we measure inequality that falls between these two extremes? Not all families earn $74 800 per year, even though that is close to the average. How do we understand fluctuations or variations around this average, and, most important, how they have changed? Is economic inequality growing or shrinking?

Social scientists have come up with a simple yet powerful way to display patterns of inequality. Here is the method, by way of analogy. Step one: Among your classmates, think of how much money each person might have earned in the past three months. A few people with full-time, well-paying, steady jobs may have earned more than $5000. Put those people at the front of a line, the highest earner first. Others will have struggled to find consistent work or may have opted not to work. Put them at the back of the line, with the lowest earner at the very end of the line.

Now, step two: Add up how much everyone in the line has earned. Imagine you have 100 students in your lineup and in sum they earned $300 000.

The Thomsons, Canada's wealthiest family, ranked 10th on the *Forbes Magazine* list of the world's richest people in 2007. Their assets totalled $25.35 billion. Sir Kenneth Thomson, who died in June 2006, handed over the reins of the Thomson electronic media, publishing, and information services empire to his son, David. The Thomsons are an example of success through both hard work and family connections.

Step three: Divide the line into five equal groups, with 20 percent of your classmates in each group—technically, these groups are known as quintiles.

Step four: Add up how much the members of each of the five groups or quintiles earned. The group at the head of the line will have earned the most given how we constructed the line. Imagine that together the members of this group earned $120 000. The group at the back of the line will have earned the least. Imagine that they collectively earned $12 000. Final step: Calculate the percentage of money each group earned. The top quintile has 40 percent of the earnings ($120 000/$300 000 × 100), while the bottom quintile has only 4 percent. The remainder (56 percent) is shared by the other three quintiles.

The most unequal distribution would be if the top quintile held 100 percent of the money. The opposite, an equal distribution, would result if each quintile held 20 percent of the money. This concept of the share of income held by each quintile is frequently used to investigate income inequality in Canada and elsewhere. It is an easy idea to visualize, and by looking at how the share of income changes over time, it allows researchers to determine whether inequality is growing or shrinking.

Figure 8.3 on page 218 shows that for 2005, the most recent year for which data are available, the lowest quintile of income earners received 6.1 percent of market income (that is, income before taxes and government transfers), while the top quintile received 42.5 percent. Almost half of all income was held by 20 percent of individuals and families.

This level of inequality can be put into perspective in two ways. First, how does income inequality in Canada compare with income inequality in other countries? Among rich countries, income inequality is lowest in Sweden and highest in the United States. Canada stands between these two extremes.

We can also ask how income inequality has changed within Canada over time. Figure 8.3 shows that the distribution has changed little between 1951 and 2005. In 2005 the bottom quintile received 6.1 percent of total income (before income tax), while in 1951 the figure was exactly the same. At the top end, the richest quintile increased its share of total income slightly, from 41.1 percent to 42.5 percent. In the past few decades, income inequality has widened in most rich countries, but not by much in Canada (Förster and Pellizzari, 2000).

FIGURE 8.3

The Distribution of Total Market Income among Families, Canada, 1951 and 2005

Source: Dominion Bureau of Statistics, Statistics Canada Cat. 13-159, 2008. CANSIM Table 2020701. Retrieved May 1, 2008 (http://dc1.chass.utoronto.ca. myaccess.library.utoronto.ca/ chasscansim).

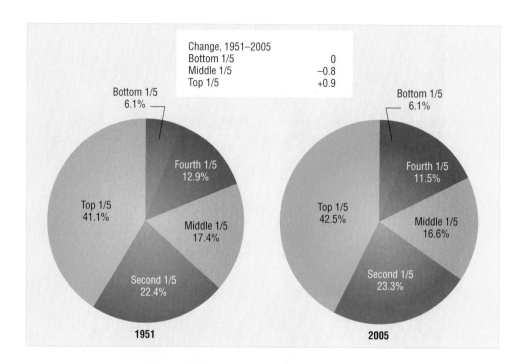

The incomes reported above and in Figure 8.3 are incomes Canadians receive before paying taxes. Given frequent reference to Canada as a "welfare state," you might imagine that after-tax income is distributed differently. The concept of a welfare state implies the image of Robin Hood, taking from the rich and giving to the poor. To what degree does the Canadian state act like Robin Hood?

As Table 8.1 illustrates, in 2005 the government redirected some income from the top quintile to the other quintiles. Compared with their pre-tax share of total income, the richest quintile of earners saw their income share decline by 2.9 percent. The after-tax income of all other quintiles rose modestly. Furthermore, since 1988 the redistributive effort of governments declined in Canada. Between 1988 and 2005, the share of after-tax income fell by 0.8 percent for the lowest quintile and rose by 2.8 percent for the richest quintile.

Explanations of Income Inequality

Why do some people fall into the highest quintile and others into the lowest quintile? What explains the distribution of income? The job a person holds plays a large role. Bank presidents are paid more than branch managers, who in turn make more than bank tellers do. Other jobs not only pay less well but also involve restricted hours of work or periods of unemployment. Thus, much about income inequality traces back to what kinds of work a person is able to obtain (see Table 8.2).

Some individuals earn unusually high salaries (and become famous) because they have natural talents at activities that are widely admired, in part because the activities are fulfilling recreations that many have attempted themselves. Jarome Iginla (hockey), Victoria Bertram

TABLE 8.1

Percentage Share of Pre-tax and After-Tax Income by Quintile for Families, 2005

Source: Adapted from Statistics Canada, CANSIM database, http://cansim2.statcan.ca, Table 202-0701.

Quintile	Total Pre-tax Income Share	Total After-Tax Income Share	Gain/Loss
Lowest quintile	6.1	7.0	+0.9
Second quintile	11.5	12.6	+1.1
Third quintile	16.6	17.4	+0.8
Fourth quintile	23.3	23.4	+0.1
Highest quintile	42.5	39.6	-2.9

Occupation	Median Annual Income
Judges, lawyers and Quebec notaries	99 305
Specialist managers	80 027
Professional occupations in health	77 515
Professional occupations in natural and applied sciences	65 601
Mechanics	45 942
Construction trades	35 639
Clerical occupations	35 028
Secretaries	32 505
Labourers in processing, manufacturing, and utilities	31 538
Retail salespersons and sales clerks	27 225
Child care and home support workers	21 980
Cashiers	17 758
Occupations in food and beverage service	16 654

TABLE 8.2

Median Annual Income, Full-Time Workers, Selected Occupations, Canada, 2005

Sources: Statistics Canada, 2008, "Median Earnings and Employment for Full-Year, Full-Time Earners, All Occupations, Both Sexes, for Canada, Provinces and Territories—20% Sample Data." Retrieved May 1, 2008 (http://www12.statcan.ca/english/census06/data/highlights/earnings/Table801.cfm?Lang=E&T=801&GH=4&SC=1&SO=99&O=A); Statistics Canada, 2008, "Earnings and Incomes of Canadian over the Past Quarter Century, 2006 Census." Retrieved May 1, 2008 (http://www12.statcan.ca/english/census06/analysis/income/pdf/97-563-XIE2006001.pdf).

(ballet), Ben Heppner (opera), Lorie Kane (golf), Shania Twain (popular music), and Mike Weir (golf) are Canadians whose success on the world stage has provided them with substantial earnings. Although sheer talent or genetic gifts surely play a part, close examination of lives blessed by extraordinary success often reveals unusual determination and hard work.

Although talent and effort matter, rewards follow only when these are refined into particular skills. But who gets to develop which skills depends on access to learning environments. Many skills are relative: People can only develop to the level of those to whom they are exposed. Tennis is a good example: Full development of skills requires exposure to stiff competition. Many skills require recognition and encouragement for development.

The ability to lend guidance or assistance is often scarce and unequally accessible. Most people begin the journey toward adult employment within a family circle and are certain to be exposed to whatever is prevalent there. The more fortunate acquire a vocabulary and outlooks consistent with highly rewarded employment, while the less fortunate must unlearn and relearn if they are to catch up. It is somewhat easier to understand and learn what our parents know and somewhat harder to learn about things they did not experience. Thus, when individuals begin to participate in formal education, what they encounter varies in compatibility with earlier experience, mostly gained with family members.

Success at formal schooling is the key to acquiring economically valued skills. Since the Industrial Revolution, an ever-growing proportion of jobs have required formal schooling in ever-greater amounts. For the vast majority of income earners, it is their ability to communicate persuasively, think critically, reason logically, and work creatively that affects the occupations they hold and the incomes they receive. Natural talent and effort are important ingredients in this process, to be sure, but education matters a lot.

The importance of education as a determinant of occupation and income continues to increase (Baer, 1999). As the Canadian occupational structure moves further away from its traditional resource-based foundation to a more mature knowledge-driven economy, the importance of education will continue to grow.

Although educational opportunities have expanded enormously, in nearly all developed economies, including Canada, the chances of advancing in educational systems has consistently remained higher for people born into families that are relatively more educated (Breen and Goldthorpe, 1997). Individuals must supply talent and effort to accumulate **human capital** (useful knowledge and skills) but rates of success also depend on the human capital their families accumulated in previous generations.

Human capital is the sum of useful skills and knowledge that an individual possesses.

Human Capital Theory

Human capital theory stresses the increasing centrality of education as a factor affecting economic success. If physical capital is understood as investment in industrial plants and equipment, human capital is investment in education and training. In a manner analogous to the way productivity increases by upgrading manufacturing plants and introducing new technology, productivity gains can also result from investment in the skills and abilities of people. Knowledge-intensive jobs (that is, jobs requiring advanced skills) are increasingly numerous in Canada. Better-educated workers are more skilled and productive in these jobs because they have made investments in acquiring the research skills and knowledge base essential to the new economy (Betcherman and Lowe, 1997).

Much evidence supports a human capital interpretation of the link between schooling and incomes (Baer, 1999). However, this is not a complete explanation for why people earn what they earn. In Chapter 2 (How Sociologists Do Research), we discussed the work of Kay and Hagan (1998). We saw that in the legal profession almost everyone makes the same human capital investment. Everyone acquires a law degree, yet economic rewards vary even for people with the same experience and type of legal practice.

Part of the reason that people with the same amount of human capital may receive different economic rewards is that they possess different amounts of social capital. **Social capital** refers to people's networks or connections. Individuals are more likely to succeed if they have strong bonds of trust, cooperation, mutual respect, and obligation with well-positioned individuals or families. Knowing the right people, and having strong links to them, helps in attaining opportunities (Coleman, 1988).

A related version of this argument is captured in the notion of **cultural capital** as proposed by the French sociologist Pierre Bourdieu (Bourdieu and Passeron, 1990). Bourdieu focuses on taste and aesthetics—*savoir-faire.* Cultural capital emphasizes a set of social skills people have, their ability to impress others, to use language and images effectively, and to influence and persuade people. Although the notion of social capital stresses your networks and connections with others, the idea of cultural capital emphasizes your impression-management skills, your ability to influence others. In different ways, both concepts emphasize being part of the right "social club."

What both concepts also have in common is the idea that families higher in the social hierarchy enjoy more capital of all types. Connections and culture help you find a good job. Hiring new recruits, then, depends on the talent, effort, and skills that people bring to the interview, but it also depends on the connections and culture that people have. Indeed, culture and connections often influence who gets an interview.

In summary, natural talent and effort are important, and are especially significant in becoming a paid performer who excels at activities that many try (e.g., hockey player or popular singer). For most Canadians, level of education (or developed skill) is a critical factor in finding continuous, well-paying employment. In addition, social or cultural capital is consequential for many in finding economic success. Explaining an individual's position in the income hierarchy depends on several factors, but the four themes or perspectives outlined in Figure 8.4 are crucial.

Income versus Wealth

How long would it take you to spend a million dollars? If you spent $1000 a day, it would take you nearly three years. How long would it take you to spend a *billion* dollars? If you spent $2500 a day, you couldn't spend the entire sum in a lifetime—at that rate of spending, a billion dollars would last for more than 1000 years. (This scenario assumes you do not invest the money; if you invested it sensibly, you could not exhaust a billion dollars by spending $10 000 a day.) Thus, a billion dollars is an almost unimaginably large sum of

Social capital refers to the networks or connections that individuals possess.

Cultural capital is the stock of learning and skills that increases the chance of securing a superior job.

FIGURE 8.4

Explanations for Income Inequality

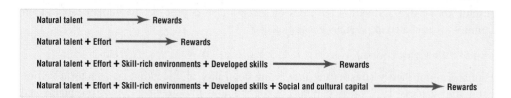

money. Yet between 2004 and 2007, the estimated fortune of Canada's richest person, David Thomson, increased 17 percent, from $21.67 billion to $25.35 billion. In contrast, the annual income of a full-time worker earning the Ontario minimum wage in 2005 was $15 596. Just the *increase* in Thomson's wealth between 2004 and 2007 was equal to the total annual income of 196 717 minimum-wage earners! We list the 10 richest Canadians in Table 8.3.

What are the sources of the fortunes listed in Table 8.3? For some names on the list (Thomson, Irving, Weston), inheritance is a critical factor. These are family dynasties—families that John Porter (1965) and Wallace Clement (1975) called members of the "Canadian corporate elite" back in the 1960s and '70s. Other people on the top-10 list had merely well-to-do or solid middle-class parents. None rose from rags to riches. On the whole, Table 8.3 suggests a mix of family fortune, business acumen, and opportunism as key determinants of wealth.

Only a very few families acquire the great wealth of major business enterprises. But most families own assets and these add up to greater or lesser family wealth. For most adults, assets include a car (minus the car loan) and some appliances, furniture, and savings (minus the credit card balance). Somewhat wealthier families also have equity in a house (the market value minus the mortgage). More fortunate families are able to accumulate other assets, such as stocks and bonds, retirement savings, and vacation homes. Figure 8.5 on page 222 shows the distribution of wealth among Canadian families in 1984, 1999, and 2005. The families are divided into quintiles. Notice that the bottom 40 percent of families own almost no assets. In fact, the bottom 20 percent owe more than they own. Notice also that the assets owned by the bottom 40 percent of families shrank in the 21 years covered by the graph. The assets owned by the top 60 percent of families grew, and by far the biggest increase in wealth was experienced by the top quintile; its median net worth grew by almost two-thirds between 1984 and 2005.

Wealth inequality is thus increasing rapidly in Canada—but not as much as in the United States, where 62 percent of the increase in national wealth in the 1990s went to the richest 1 percent of Americans and fully 99 percent of the increase went to the richest 20 percent. The United States surpasses all other highly industrialized countries in wealth inequality. Between 50 percent and 80 percent of the net worth of American families derives from transfers and bequests, usually from parents (Hacker, 1997; Keister, 2000; Keister and Moller, 2000; Levy, 1998; Spilerman, 2000; Wolff, 1996).

Individual or Family	Estimated Wealth	Assets and Notes
Thomson family	$25.35 billion	Information distribution; Thomson-Reuters, Woodbridge Co. Ltd.
Ted Rogers	$7.6 billion	Communications; entertainment; Rogers Communications Inc.
Galen Weston	$7.27 billion	Food; groceries; retail; real estate; Holt Renfrew; George Weston Ltd.; Loblaw Cos. Ltd.; President's Choice; Zehrs; Connors Seafood
Paul Desmarais, Sr.	$5.64 billion	Financial services; media; broadcasting; oil; Power Corp. of Canada
Irving family	$5.3 billion	Oil; forestry products; building supply stores; media; frozen foods; transportation; Irving Oil; JD Irving Ltd
James Pattison	$4.52 billion	Auto sales; food; media; forest products; export services; financial services; Jim Pattison Group
Jeff Skoll	$4.48 billion	Internet; film production; eBay
Michael Lazaridis	$4.36 billion	Communications; Research in Motion
James Balsillie	$4.09 billion	Communications; Research in Motion
Bernard Sherman	$3.61 billion	Pharmaceuticals; Apotex Group

TABLE 8.3

Ten Wealthiest Canadians, 2007

Source: Reprinted with permission from *Canadian Business*, 2007 (http://www.canadianbusiness.com/after_hours/article.jsp?content=20071131_198701_198701).

FIGURE 8.5

Median Net Worth of
Canadian Families, 1984,
1999, and 2005

Note: To make the three surveys
comparable, the following items are
not included: employer-sponsored
pension plans, contents of the home,
collectibles and valuables, annuities,
and registered retirement income
funds. If it were possible to include
these items, wealth inequalities
would be greater than shown. Net
worth for the lowest quintile in
1984 was 0. Calculating the
percentage decline for this quintile
would require dividing by zero,
which of course is not possible.
Accordingly, for the lowest quintile,
we show the decline in net worth in
dollars rather than as a percentage.

Source: René Morisette and Xuelin
Zhang, 2006, "Revisiting Wealth
Inequality," *Pespectives* (Statistics
Canada). Retrieved May 1, 2008
(http://www.statcan.ca/english/free
pub/75-001-XIE/11206/art-1.pdf).

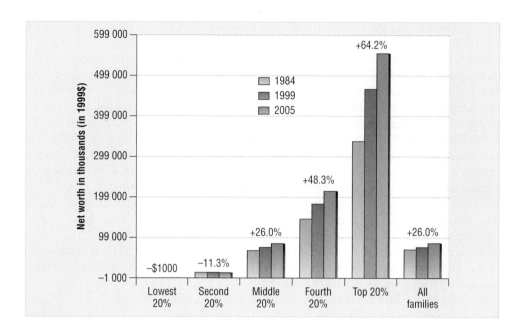

Note that only a modest correlation exists between income and wealth. Some wealthy
people have low annual incomes and some people with high annual incomes have little
accumulated wealth. As such, annual income may not be the best measure of a person's well-
being. Policies that seek to redistribute income from the wealthy to the poor, such as income-
tax laws, may not get at the root of economic inequality because income redistribution has little
effect on the distribution of wealth (Conley, 1999; Oliver and Shapiro, 1995).

Income and Poverty

At the other extreme of the income distribution are the homeless. In recent decades the
number of people with "no fixed address" has increased considerably. We do not know how
many Canadians are homeless. Yet in cities across the country, people sleep under bridges,
in back alleys, behind dumpsters, and in thickets in public parks. They do so night after
night, month after month.

Homelessness is one manifestation of poverty. Exactly how many Canadians are poor is a
matter of intense debate. Poverty lacks an agreed definition. A first disagreement occurs around
whether poverty should be defined in absolute or relative terms. An absolute definition of
poverty focuses on bare essentials, suggesting that poor families have resources inadequate to
acquire the basic necessities of life (e.g., food, shelter, clothing). Agreement on "bare essentials"
depends on values and judgments (Sarlo, 2001). What is essential varies from time to time, place
to place, and group to group. Many of our ancestors lived without indoor plumbing, and some
Canadians still do, but most people would define indoor plumbing as essential. A family could
survive on a steady diet of cod and potatoes, but most would define such a family as poor.

What constitutes bare essentials depends on social context. Again, most Canadians
would agree that the poverty experienced in Angola or Haiti or Ethiopia is not what
should be used to define poverty in Canada. That is because most people think of poverty
in relation to the social and economic context in which people live. Central heating is a
necessity in Canada's cold climate but not in Ethiopia or Haiti.

A relative poverty line also has drawbacks. Two questions are central:Relative to what?
How relative? Whether poverty ought to be defined narrowly, in terms of economic measures (e.g., income), or more broadly, with respect to community standards (e.g., safety of
working conditions, environmental quality, housing stock), illustrates this second area of
disagreement. Most definitions tend to be narrow, focusing primarily on income. But even
if a relative poverty line is defined narrowly, how relative ought it to be? one-third of average
income? one-half? some other fraction?

Yet another disagreement plagues any definition. Should poverty be defined on the basis of income or on the basis of consumption? Since "bare essentials" is a core idea in any definition of poverty, it makes good sense to ask about, and measure, poverty as the cost of purchasing bare essentials. Deprivation occurs when a family cannot acquire the essentials, not necessarily when income is too low. Income and consumption are correlated, of course, but people with high net wealth can live off their savings even with low income.

In one sense, the definition of poverty means little to a homeless man sleeping on top of a hot air vent. The immediate experience of poverty by families in remote coastal communities, by single parents in the urban core, and by farmers on the Prairies is unaffected by whether poverty is defined absolutely or relatively, narrowly or broadly, by income or by consumption. However, the definition of poverty is consequential for these people, because social policies are enacted, or not enacted, based on levels and trends in poverty. Definitions matter.

Social policy has a profound impact on the distribution of opportunities and rewards in Canada. Politics can reshape the distribution of income and the system of inequality by changing the laws governing people's right to own property. Witness First Nations land claims. Politicians can also alter patterns of inequality by entitling people to various welfare benefits and by redistributing income through tax policies. When politicians de-emphasize poverty, legislative efforts to maintain or expand welfare benefits and redistribute income are less likely. A definition of poverty showing fewer poor Canadians implies little need for government action. Conversely, for politicians and political parties supporting the poor, a definition of poverty showing a growing proportion of poor people is beneficial to their cause.

In addition to poverty definitions having political consequences, they are important research tools for the sociologist. A democratic society depends on the full participation of all citizens—everyone has the right to vote, anyone can run for political office, and the voice of everyone should influence political choices. As the National Council of Welfare (1999a: 4) argues, the proportion of Canadians who are poor is "one measure of how well our democracy is working." Can someone without a permanent home, someone in a family with bare cupboards, or someone with hand-me-down clothes participate fully in our national affairs?

Unlike some other countries, such as the United States, Canada does not have an official definition of poverty. Indeed, Statistics Canada argues that there is no internationally accepted definition of poverty and that any definition is arbitrary. Therefore, it does not attempt to estimate the number of Canadians who are poor. Instead, Statistics Canada reports what it calls a **low-income cutoff**. The low-income cutoff "represents an income threshold where a family is likely to spend 20% more of its income on food, shelter, and clothing than the average family" (Statistics Canada, 1999b). The threshold is reported for seven different family sizes and for five sizes of community since straitened circumstances depend on the number of people in your family and the place you live. Most advocates for the poor interpret these thresholds, shown for 2006 in Table 8.4 on page 224, as poverty lines. For example, in Canada's cities with a population of half a million or more, a family of four with an income of $33 221 or less after government transfer payments, such as GST credits and the Canada Child Tax Benefit, would be considered poor.

In recent decades, the prevalence of low income among Canadians peaked at 15.7 percent in 1996, declined to 11.6 percent in 2002, and rose to 15.3 percent in 2005. One difficulty in interpreting such overall rates, however, is that the risk of low income is different for different types of families. As Figure 8.6 on page 224 indicates, families without any earners are at especially high risk, especially if they are female lone-parent families; more than 81 percent of the latter are in the low-income category.

The rates reported in Table 8.4 are for the proportion of families living in low income at a given time. However, many families move in and out of poverty, most commonly because of unemployment, reduced work hours, and episodes of poor health. As Figure 8.7 indicates, larger proportions of families and individuals go through one or more spells of low income over

Low-income cutoff is Statistic Canada's term for the income threshold below which a family devotes a larger share of its income to the necessities of food, shelter, and clothing than an average family would, likely resulting in straitened circumstances.

Population of Community of Residence

TABLE 8.4

Low-Income Cutoffs after
Taxes and Including
Government Transfers, 2006

Source: Canadian Council on Social
Development, 2007, "Stats and
Facts." Retrieved May 1, 2008
(http://www.ccsd.ca/factsheets/
economic_security/poverty/
lico_06.htm).

* Includes cities with a population
between 15 000 and 30 000 and
small urban areas (fewer than
15 000)

Family Size	500 000+	100 000– 499 999	30 000– 99 999	Fewer than 30 000*	Rural
1	$17 570	$14 859	$14 674	$13 154	$11 494
2	$21 384	$18 085	$17 860	$16 010	$13 989
3	$26 628	$22 519	$22 239	$19 934	$17 420
4	$33 221	$28 095	$27 745	$24 871	$21 731
5	$37 828	$31 992	$31 594	$28 321	$24 746
6	$41 953	$35 480	$35 039	$31 409	$27 444
7+	$46 077	$38 967	$38 483	$34 496	$30 142

several years. For example, more than 3 out of 10 Canadian children lived in a low-income family for at least part of the time during the five years summarized by Figure 8.7.

Myths about the Poor

We noted earlier the contrasting images that are sometimes constructed to portray the poor. Are people poor because they are lazy drunks, or are they poor despite working hard? Such imagery leads many people to differentiate between the "deserving" and the "undeserving" poor. Research conducted in the past few decades continues to show that many popular images about the poor are inaccurate.

Myth 1: People are poor because they don't want to work. In most poor families at least one family member works. In 2001, 64 percent of poor families with heads of household under age 65 had one family member working at least part of the year. The National Council of Welfare (2004: 101) estimates that 271 000 unattached people were poor in 2001 even though they worked between 49 and 52 weeks. They compose 26 percent of all poor, unattached people under age 65. Some 85 000 families were poor, even when husbands and wives together worked for 103 or more weeks during the year (National Council of Welfare, 2004: 100). They compose 10 percent of all poor families with heads under 65. Although a good job is one of the best forms of insurance against living in poverty, having a job is not a perfect insulator. In part, that is because individuals working at a minimum wage of $8 per

FIGURE 8.6

Low-Income Rates for
Different Family Types,
Canada, 2005

Source: Statistics Canada, 2008,
"Earnings and Incomes of Canadians
over the Past Quarter Century, 2006
Census." Retrieved May 1, 2008
(http://www12.statcan.ca/english/
census06/analysis/income/pdf/
97-563-XIE2006001.pdf).

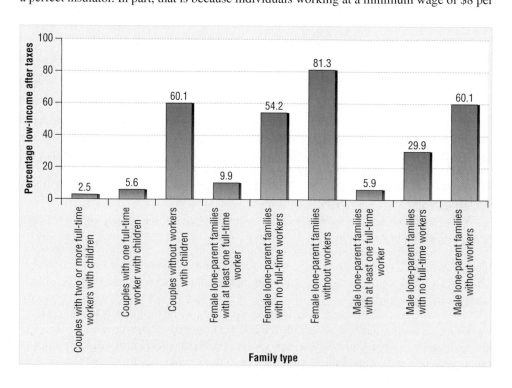

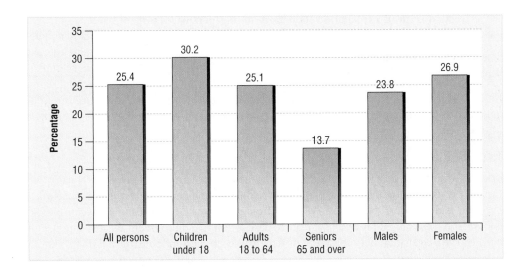

FIGURE 8.7

Persons Experiencing Low Income at Least One Year between 1996 and 2001

Source: Adapted from Statistics Canada, 2005, "Income in Canada, 2003," Catalogue 75-202, p. 123. Retreived at (http://www.statcan.ca/english/freepub/75-202-XIE/75-202-XIE2003000.pdf May 13, 2007)

hour have average annual incomes of $11 977, which is below the low-income cutoff for single individuals (National Council of Welfare, 2004: 105).

Myth 2: The overwhelming majority of poor people are immigrants. Individuals and family heads who are immigrants and who arrived in Canada before 1980 generally experience poverty at *lower* rates than native-born Canadians do (National Council of Welfare, 2004: 57). Higher poverty rates are evident among more recent immigrants who are less well established, but recent immigrants represent a fraction of all poor people.

Myth 3: The welfare rolls are crammed with young people who ought to be earning a living. In 1997 the National Council of Welfare (1998a) reported that only about 4 percent of welfare recipients were under the age of 20, and only 16 percent were under 25. Among single parents on welfare, only 3 percent were under the age of 20.

Myth 4: Most poor people are trapped in poverty. One in three people with a low income in 2002 had moved beyond it by 2003. Of the 25.4 percent of Canadians who experienced one or more years of low income (see Figure 8.7), only slightly more than one in eight of these (3.4 percent) lived in poverty for all six years. On average, those who experienced low income for at least one year spent 2.8 years or about one-half the total period in poverty (Statistics Canada, 2004d: 124). Thus, poverty for many is a result of family finances that are unstable; they slip into and out of difficult circumstances.

Explaining Poverty

Why are some Canadians poor? At one level, because poverty is a social construction—who is poor depends on the definition—the explanations focus on definitions. This explanation highlights the politics of poverty, in which levels and trends can be simply a consequence of definition. If we accept that some Canadians are poor, although granting that the number will vary depending on definition, then there is a second level of explanation. Here the question is, "Why are some people and families poor and others not?" Answers to this question vary from individual-level to structural explanations.

Individual-level explanations focus on the attributes of people who are poor, asking how these people differ from people who are not poor. This type of explanation focuses on causes that lie "within the person." Someone is poor, on this logic, because of a personal attribute, such as low intelligence or behaviour abnormality.

Some evidence suggests that individual attributes do explain a small amount of poverty. For example, we know that people who have physical disabilities or schizophrenia have a higher risk of living in poverty than others do. However, not all people with disabilities or with schizophrenia live in poverty, and the vast majority of people living in poverty have neither disabilities nor schizophrenia. On balance, this type of evidence teaches us that poverty is, for the most part, not a consequence of individual attributes, even though these are important in some cases.

A related form of explanation focuses more on the attitudes of individuals—not on attributes that are inherited, but on attributes or stigmas that are acquired. A social-psychological type of explanation emphasizes low self-esteem, lack of achievement motivation, and an inability to delay gratification. On this logic, poverty is perpetuated because poor families employ inadequate child-rearing practices that enhance bad attitudes. A related version of this argument stresses a "culture of poverty," a way of thinking and acting shared by poor families. This culture reinforces and perpetuates itself through poor upbringing and ill-formed personalities.

This type of reasoning is often dismissed by sociologists as "blaming the victim." You are poor, on this reasoning, because you have a poor work ethic, shoddy morals, no aspirations, no discipline, no fortitude, and so forth. Various objections undermine this type of explanation. First, there is a cause-and-effect, or chicken-and-egg, problem. People who are poor may develop "bad attitudes," but these may result from poverty and not be causes of poverty. The culture of poverty might provide an adequate description for some circumstances, but it is not an adequate explanation in general. Put differently, descriptions of poverty stressing a culture of depression, lack of hope, and fatalism may be accurate, but these effects of poverty ought not to be confused with the causes of poverty. Second, many people who are poor do work, are religious, don't smoke or drink, and so on. Therefore, evidence that supports explanations founded on personal deficits is often lacking.

Another form of explanation, one with greater currency in sociology, stresses the social organization of society, or subsystems in society, as explanations of poverty. The organization of our economy, for example, affects poverty. Capitalist economies feature cyclical booms and busts, periods of low unemployment and high profits followed by high unemployment and low profits. When unemployment rates rise, so do the numbers of families forced to live on reduced earnings, which for many means living in poverty. The right of employers to refuse to renew work contracts is an accepted part of our economic system. The reductions in income that result can hardly be attributed to changes in individual motivation. Low-wage jobs are also a part of the economy and some people in low-skill, nonunionized, part-year jobs will not earn enough to escape poverty. As Krahn and Lowe (1998: 405) summarize the situation, "a weak work ethic and a lack of effort" are seldom the explanation for individual poverty; "more often the problem is one of not enough good jobs."

Other analysts stress social policy as a factor affecting poverty levels. For example, as noted above, if you received the minimum hourly wage while working full time, full year, you would still be poor, especially if you had children to support. In this sense minimum-wage legislation is a social policy that creates a group of working poor. The social world is not quite so simple, of course, and if minimum wages were to rise, so too might the level of unemployment because some employers might not be able to afford to pay higher wages. Debate over these issues continues, but the point is that our social policies affect the well-being of people, and understanding the consequences of policies is critical.

The system of tax collection and tax allocation illustrates another way that social policies affect poverty. A progressive taxation system is one in which a greater proportion of income is paid in tax as incomes rise. For example, those who earn $100 000 pay a larger percentage of their income as tax than do those who earn $50 000. In Canada, although our income tax system is progressive, the overall tax system is relatively neutral. Most Canadian families pay about the same percentage of their total income in tax. This occurs because two interrelated factors undermine the "Robin Hood" effect of progressive income taxes. First, other taxes, such as GST and fuel taxes, are flat or neutral. They are not based on the income of the taxpayer. And since lower-income families typically spend higher proportions of their income on consumption, such taxes are somewhat regressive in impact. Second, those who earn more are able to shelter much of their income from taxation (e.g., in registered education saving plans, in registered retirement savings plans, through capital gains tax exemptions, and so forth). The net effect, as we saw above, is a system that does little to actually redistribute income and therefore relatively little to erode poverty.

Finally, other sociologists would stress ways of thinking, or ideological perspectives, as explanations for poverty. Negative images of various groups lead to an undervaluing of the ways of life of some people, such as First Nations and people with disabilities. Discrimination follows from this undervaluing, and discrimination seriously effects poverty. Undervaluing of talents and identities leads to less success in finding jobs. Even when employment is found, the work is often unsteady and low paying.

Is poverty an inevitable feature of society? It may be, at least to the extent that inequality is known to exist in all societies. However, the extent of poverty in Canada could be reduced if we chose to follow the examples of Western European nations. Many countries in Western Europe have poverty rates well below Canada's. That is because many European governments have established job-training and child-care programs that allow poor people to take jobs with livable wages and benefits. This is, however, a political choice. Many Canadians argue that providing welfare benefits dampens the work ethic and perpetuates poverty (see Box 8.1). Although the Western European evidence does not support that view, the political will does not currently exist in Canada to change our social policies to alleviate poverty.

BOX 8.1
It's Your Choice

Income Redistribution and Taxation

The idea of rugged individualism implies that our personal fortunes ought to rest on our own shoulders. "To each according to his or her abilities" is often held up as a supreme principle. Those who work hard, who persevere, who make wise decisions—those individuals supposedly deserve rewards, like Robinson Crusoe. By implication, those who are lazy and unwise deserve less.

A contrasting idea, the idea of collective responsibility, implies that as members of a community, we ought to look out for one another. In this view, "to each according to his or her need" ought to be a supreme principle. Those who have should share. The interests of the many should come before the riches of a few.

Few Canadians support either of these extreme ideas, but examples of each principle are easy to find. The unequal distribution of income in Canada and the high salaries of the presidents of large corporations are consistent with the theme of rugged individualism. Government support for postsecondary education and health care illustrates the theme of collective responsibility. Both of these themes represent contrasting social policies, one focused on the supremacy of individual rights, the other emphasizing collective responsibility and the common good.

How much tax revenue should governments collect, and should they redistribute that revenue in ways that benefit lower income groups? Should governments act like Robin Hood and transfer some tax money to the poor? Should governments support hospitals and schools with tax dollars, or should individual families pay directly for medical care and education? These are questions of social policy.

Here are some of the arguments for and against income redistribution, arguments that are fundamental to some of the major political debates in many countries in recent years. What choices would you make if you and your colleagues could run the government for a few years?

Against Redistribution

1. Taking from the rich and giving to the poor decreases the motivation for people in both groups to work hard.

2. The cost of redistribution is high. Taking from one group and giving to another requires some agency first to collect money and then to allocate it.

3. Some individuals and families will cheat and deceive. Some will hide or misrepresent their earnings, either to pay less in tax or to receive more through welfare. Redistribution promotes both tax cheats and welfare frauds.

For Redistribution

1. A society with a reasonable degree of equality is a better place to live in than a society with heightened levels of inequality.

2. An extra dollar to a poor family is more helpful than an extra dollar to a rich family.

3. Improving the material well-being of a poor family through benevolence enhances the social well-being of a rich family.

4. Aid to poorer families reduces the risk of crime and political conflict since poorer families are thereby less likely to seek illegal means of earning income or to unite in protest over living conditions.

In sum, sociological explanations look not to the personal qualities of the poor but to the organization of society as a way of explaining why some people are poor and why poverty persists. Notice, too, that the solutions to poverty vary depending on the approach. One solution is to define the problem in a way that minimizes poverty. Another solution looks to change poor people's skills through job-training and job-search programs for adults and compensatory education programs for children so they are better able to find well-paying work. Still another set of solutions looks at the organization of society and asks whether we could change the way we do things so as to benefit the poor. This would involve altering the tax system, encouraging the creation of good jobs, reducing discrimination, and the like.

International Differences

Global Inequality

Despite growing income inequality in recent years and a large low-income population, Canada is one of the richest countries in the world. Angola is a world apart. Angola is an African country of 13.3 million people. More than 650 000 of its citizens were killed in a civil war that raged between 1975 and 2002. Angola is one of the poorest nations on earth.

Most Angolans live in houses made of cardboard, tin, and cement blocks. Few houses have running water. Average income is about $7800 a year. Life expectancy is 38 years. More than half the population is unemployed or underemployed, and the poverty rate is 70 percent (Central Intelligence Agency, 2008). Adding to the misery of Angola's citizens are the millions of landmines scattered throughout the countryside, regularly killing and maiming innocent passersby. About 85 percent of the population survives on subsistence agriculture.

However, multinational companies, such as Exxon and Chevron, drill for oil in Angola. Oil exports account for 85 percent of GDP. In the coastal capital of Luanda, an enclave of North Americans who work for Exxon and Chevron live in gated, heavily guarded communities that contain luxury homes, tennis courts, swimming pools, house cleaners, and SUVs. Here, side by side in the city of Luanda, is a microcosm of the chasm separating rich from poor in the world.

Global inequality refers to differences in the economic ranking of countries.

Cross-national variations in internal stratification are differences among countries in their stratification systems.

Some countries, such as Canada, are rich. Others, such as Angola, are poor. When sociologists study such differences between countries, they are studying **global inequality**. However, it is possible for country A and country B to be equally rich while inside country A, the gap between rich and poor is greater than inside country B. When sociologists compare such differences, they are studying **cross-national variations in internal stratification**.

The United States, Canada, Japan, Australia, and a dozen or so Western European countries, including Germany, France, and the United Kingdom, are the world's richest postindustrial societies. The world's poorest countries cover much of Africa, South America, and Asia. Inequality between rich and poor countries is staggering. Nearly a fifth of the world's

Inequality on a global scale. *Left*: An Angolan boy, a victim of a landmine, hops home in Luanda. *Right*: Children relax at home in Luanda's North American enclave, built by Exxon for its supervisors and executives and their families.

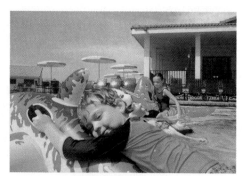

Country and Overall Rank	Life Expectancy (years)	Adult Literacy (percent)	School Enrolment Ratio	GDP per Capita ($US)
1. Norway	78.9	99.0	98	36 600
2. Sweden	80	99.0	100	26 050
3. Australia	79.1	99.0	100	28 260
4. Canada	79.3	99.0	95	29 480
5. Netherlands	78.3	99.0	99	29 100
173. Burundi	40.8	50.4	33	630
174. Mali	48.5	19	26	930
175. Burkina Faso	45.8	12.8	22	1 100
176. Niger	46	17.1	19	800
177. Sierra Leone	34.3	36	45	520
Least developed countries	64.6	76.7	60	4 054
High-income OECD (mature industrialized) countries	78.3	99	93	29 000

TABLE 8.5

United Nations Indicators of Human Development, 2004

Note: The United Nations publishes an annual index that combines four indicators of human development: life expectancy, adult literacy, school enrolment rates, and GDP per capita. The table lists the five highest-ranked countries, the five lowest-ranked, the value on each indicator for these countries, and some comparisons across the economic regions of the world.

Source: From United Nations, 2004, "Country Tables," *Human Development Report 2004*. Retrieved from http://hdr.undp.org/statistics/data/index_countries.cfm. Reprinted with permission. The United Nations is the author of the original material.

population lacks adequate shelter, and more than a fifth lacks safe water. About a third of the world's people are without electricity, and more than two-fifths lack adequate sanitation. In Canada, life expectancy is 79 years, annual income per person is more than $36 000, and inflation is about 3 percent (United Nations, 2004a; see Table 8.5). Canada has one of the highest enrolment rates in the world for postsecondary education but in many African countries, such as Angola, fewer than 50 percent of children are enrolled in primary schools. People living in poor countries are also more likely than people are in rich countries to experience extreme suffering on a mass scale. For example, because of political turmoil in many poor countries, tens of millions of people have been driven from their homes by force in recent years (Hampton, 1998). There are still about 27 million slaves in Mozambique, Sudan, and other African countries (Bales, 1999).

We devote much of Chapter 9 (Globalization, Inequality, and Development) to analyzing the causes, dimensions, and consequences of global inequality. You will learn that much of the wealth of the rich countries has been gained at the expense of the poor countries. We also discuss possible ways of dealing with this most vexing of social issues. For the moment, having merely noted the existence of the problem, we focus on the second type of international difference: cross-national variations in internal stratification.

Internal Stratification

Levels of global inequality aside, how does internal stratification differ from one country to the next? We can answer this question by first examining the **Gini index**, named after the Italian economist who invented it. The Gini index is a measure of income inequality. Its value ranges from zero to one. A Gini index of zero indicates that every household (or every income recipient) in the country earns exactly the same amount of money. At the opposite pole, a Gini index of one indicates that a single household earns the entire national income. These are theoretical extremes. In the real world, nearly all societies have Gini indices between 0.2 and 0.6.

Figure 8.8 on page 230 shows the Gini index for eight countries using the most recent international income data available. Of the eight countries, Sweden has the lowest Gini index (0.25) while Canada is around the middle at 0.331. The countries with the highest level of inequality include Russia (0.4), China (0.44), and the United States (0.45). Figure 8.8 suggests that among wealthy, postindustrial societies, income inequality in Canada is about average. Figure 8.8 also indicates that higher inequality and higher poverty rates tend to occur together.

The Gini index is a measure of income inequality. Its value ranges from zero (which means that every household earns exactly the same amount of money) to one (which means that all income is earned by a single household).

FIGURE 8.8

Household Income Inequality and Low Income, Selected Countries, 1995–2004

Note: Poverty data are not available for China.

Source: From Timothy M. Smeeding, 2004, "Public Policy and Economic Inequality: The United States in Comparative Perspective," Working Paper No. 367 (Maxwell School of Citizenship and Public Affairs, Syracuse University, NY). Retrieved June 24, 2006 (http://www.lisproject.org/publications/LISwps367.pdf). Reprinted with permission.

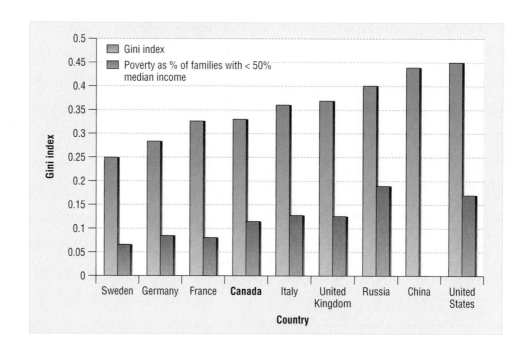

GLOBAL PERSPECTIVE

Development and Internal Stratification

What accounts for cross-national differences in internal stratification, such as those described in the previous section? Later in this chapter, you will learn that *political factors* explain some of the differences. For the moment, however, we focus on how *socioeconomic development* affects internal stratification.

You will recall from Chapter 6 (Networks, Groups, Bureaucracies, and Societies) that over the course of human history, as societies became richer and more complex, the level of social inequality first increased, then tapered off, and then began to decline (Lenski, 1966; Lenski, Nolan, and Lenski, 1995; see Figure 8.9). What follows is a recap.

Foraging Societies

For the first 90 000 years of human existence, people lived in nomadic bands of fewer than 100 people. To survive, they hunted wild animals and foraged for wild edible plants. Some foragers and hunters were undoubtedly more skilled than others were, but they did not hoard food. Instead, they shared food to ensure the survival of all band members. They produced little or nothing above what they required for subsistence. There were no rich and no poor.

FIGURE 8.9

Inequality and Development

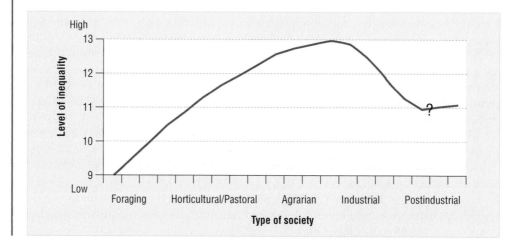

Horticultural and Pastoral Societies

About 10 000 years ago, people established the first agricultural settlements. These settlements were based on horticulture (the use of small hand tools to cultivate plants) and pastoralism (the domestication of animals). These technological innovations enabled people to produce wealth, a surplus above what they needed for subsistence. A small number of villagers controlled the surplus. Thus, significant **social stratification** emerged.

Agrarian Societies

About 5000 years ago, people developed plow agriculture. By attaching oxen and other large animals to plows, farmers could increase the amount they produced. Again thanks to technological innovation, surpluses grew. With more wealth came still sharper social stratification.

Agrarian societies developed religious beliefs justifying steeper inequality. People came to believe that kings and queens ruled by "divine right." They viewed large landowners as "lords." Moreover, if you were born a peasant, you and your children were likely to remain peasants. If you were born a lord, you and your children were likely to remain lords. In the vocabulary of modern sociology, we say that stratification in agrarian societies was based more on **ascription** than **achievement**. That is, a person's position in the stratification system was determined more by the features he or she was born with ("ascribed characteristics") than his or her accomplishments ("achieved characteristics"). Another way of saying this is that little **social mobility** took place.

A nearly purely ascriptive society existed in agrarian India. Society was divided into **castes**, four main groups and many subgroups arranged in a rigid hierarchy. Being born into a particular caste meant you had to work in the distinctive occupations reserved for that caste and marry someone from the same or an adjoining caste. The Hindu religion strictly reinforced the system (Srinivas, 1952). For example, Hinduism explained people's place in the caste system by their deeds in a previous life. If you were good, you were presumably rewarded by being born into a higher caste in your next life. If you were bad, you were presumably punished by being born into a lower caste. Belief in the sanctity of caste regulated even the most mundane aspects of life. Thus, someone from the lowest caste could dig a well for a member of the highest caste, but once the well was dug, the well digger could not so much as cast his shadow on the well. If he did, the well was considered polluted and upper-caste people were forbidden to drink from it.

Caste systems have existed in industrial times. For example, the system of **apartheid** existed in South Africa from 1948 until 1992. The white minority enjoyed the best jobs and other privileges, and they consigned the large black majority to menial jobs. Apartheid also prevented marriage between blacks and whites and erected separate public facilities for members of the two races. Asians and people of "mixed race" enjoyed privileges between these two extremes. However, apartheid was an exception. For the most part, industrialism causes a *decline* in inequality.

Industrial Societies

At first, the Industrial Revolution that began in the late eighteenth century did little to lower the level of social stratification. But improvements in the technology and social organization of manufacturing allowed people to produce more goods at a lower cost per unit, making a rise in living standards possible. Business leaders realized they could profit most by identifying, training, and hiring the most talented people, and they offered higher wages to recruit them. Workers used union power and growing political influence to win improvements in working conditions. As a result, social mobility became more widespread than ever before. Stratification declined as industrial societies developed.

Postindustrial Societies

Since the 1970s, social inequality has increased in nearly all postindustrial societies. Among rich countries, the United States exhibited the most social inequality in the 1970s, and since

Social stratification refers to the way in which society is organized in layers or strata.

An **ascription**-based stratification system is one in which the allocation of rank depends on characteristics a person is born with.

An **achievement**-based stratification system is one in which the allocation of rank depends on a person's accomplishments.

Social mobility refers to movement up or down the stratification system.

A **caste** system is an almost pure ascription-based stratification system in which occupations and marriage partners are assigned on the basis of caste membership.

Apartheid was a caste system based on race that existed in South Africa from 1948 to 1992. It consigned the large black majority to menial jobs, prevented marriage between blacks and whites, and erected separate public facilities for members of the two races. Asians and people of mixed race enjoyed privileges between these two extremes.

then inequality has grown faster in the United States than in any other rich country. The concentration of wealth in the hands of the wealthiest 1 percent of Americans is higher today than anytime in the past 100 years. The gap between rich and poor is bigger today than it has been for at least 50 years.

Technological factors are partly responsible for the trend toward growing inequality in most postindustrial countries. Many high-tech jobs have been created at the top of the stratification system over the past few decades. These jobs pay well. At the same time new technologies have made many jobs routine. Routine jobs require little training, and they pay poorly. Because the number of routine jobs is growing more quickly than the number of jobs at the top of the stratification system, the overall effect of technology today is to increase the level of inequality in most postindustrial societies. One reason for the especially high level of inequality in the United States is that it has proportionately more low-wage jobs than any other rich country does.

A second factor responsible for the growing trend toward social inequality is government policy. Through tax and social welfare policies, governments are able to prevent big income transfers to the rich. Among the rich postindustrial societies, however, only the French government has intervened to *lower* the level of inequality since the 1970s. The government that has done least to moderate the growth of inequality is that of the United States (Centre for Economic Policy Research, 2002; Smeeding, 2004).

These, then, are the basic patterns and trends in the history of social stratification. Bearing these descriptions in mind, we now examine how sociologists have explained social stratification. We begin with Karl Marx, who formulated the first major sociological theory of stratification 150 years ago (Marx and Engels, 1972 [1848]; Marx, 1904 [1859]).

THEORIES OF STRATIFICATION

Conflict Perspectives

Marx

In medieval Western Europe, peasants worked small plots of land owned by landlords. Peasants were legally obliged to give their landlords a set part of the harvest and to continue working for them under any circumstance. In turn, landlords were required to protect peasants from marauders. They were also obliged to open their storehouses and feed the peasants if crops failed. This arrangement was known as **feudalism**.

According to Marx, by the late fifteenth century, several forces were beginning to undermine feudalism. Most important was the growth of exploration and trade, which increased the demand for many goods and services in commerce, navigation, and industry. By the seventeenth and eighteenth centuries, some urban craftspeople and merchants had opened small manufacturing enterprises and saved enough capital to expand production. However, they faced a big problem: To increase profits they needed more workers. Yet the biggest potential source of workers—the peasantry—was legally bound to the land. Thus, feudalism had to wither if agricultural peasants were to become industrial workers. In Scotland, for example, enterprising landowners recognized they could make more money raising sheep and selling wool than by having their peasants till the soil. So they turned their cropland into pastures, forcing peasants off the land and into the cities. The former peasants had no choice but to take jobs as urban workers.

In Marx's view, relations between workers and industrialists first encouraged rapid technological change and economic growth. After all, industrial owners wanted to adopt new tools, machines, and production methods so they could produce more efficiently and earn higher profits. But this had unforeseen consequences. In the first place, some owners, driven out of business by more efficient competitors, were forced to become members of the working class. Together with former peasants pouring into the cities from

Feudalism was a legal arrangement in preindustrial Europe that bound peasants to the land and obliged them to give their landlords a set part of the harvest. In exchange, landlords were required to protect peasants from marauders and open their storehouses to feed the peasants if crops failed.

the countryside, this caused the working class to grow. Second, the drive for profits motivated owners to concentrate workers in larger and larger factories, keep wages as low as possible, and invest as little as possible in improving working conditions. Thus, as the ownership class grew richer and smaller, the working class grew larger and more impoverished.

Marx felt that workers would ultimately become aware of their exploitation. Their sense of **class consciousness** would, he wrote, encourage the growth of unions and workers' political parties. These organizations would eventually try to create a communist system in which there would be no private wealth. Instead, under communism, everyone would share wealth, said Marx.

We must note several points about Marx's theory. First, according to Marx, a person's **class** is determined by the source of his or her income, or, to use Marx's term, by a person's "relationship to the means of production." For example, members of the capitalist class (or **bourgeoisie**) own the means of production, including factories, tools, and land. However, they do not do any physical labour. They are thus in a position to earn profits. In contrast, members of the working class (or **proletariat**) do physical labour. However, they do not own means of production. They are thus in a position to earn wages. It is the source of income, not the amount, that distinguishes classes in Marx's view.

A second noteworthy point about Marx's theory is that it recognizes more than two classes in any society. For example, Marx discussed the **petite bourgeoisie**. This is a class of small-scale capitalists who own means of production but employ only a few workers or none at all. This situation forces them to do physical work themselves. In Marx's view, however, members of the petty bourgeoisie are bound to disappear as capitalism develops because they are economically inefficient. Just two great classes characterize every economic era, said Marx: landlords and serfs during feudalism, bourgeoisie and proletariat during capitalism.

Finally, it is important to note that some of Marx's predictions about the development of capitalism turned out to be wrong. Nevertheless, Marx's ideas about social stratification have stimulated thinking and research on social stratification even today, as you will see below.

A Critique of Marx

Marx's ideas strongly influenced the development of sociological conflict theory (see Chapter 1, A Sociological Compass). Today, however, more than 125 years after Marx's death, it is generally agreed that Marx did not accurately foresee some aspects of capitalist development:

- Industrial societies did not polarize into two opposed classes engaged in bitter conflict. Instead, a large and heterogeneous middle class of "white-collar" workers emerged. Some of them are non-manual employees. Others are professionals. Many of them enjoy higher income and status than manual workers. With a bigger stake in capitalism than propertyless manual workers, non-manual employees and professionals have generally acted as a stabilizing force in society. To take account of these changes, some neo-Marxists recognize *two* main divisions in the social relations of work. Although owners control the assets of the business and determine its purpose, in today's large industrial organizations they cannot immediately supervise or direct the work of every employee. This is especially the case when a company is owned by a great many people, as it is in many major corporations today. Therefore, a class of supervisors has arisen. This class, sometimes called the "new middle class" to illustrate its recency and its intermediate position, is defined by relations of authority and supervision. New middle-class workers take direction from owners and are responsible for coordinating and directing the work of other employees. Sociologists Wallace Clement and John Myles (1994) provide an excellent application of this new way of thinking about class in their comparative analysis of the Canadian, American, and Scandinavian class structures.

Class consciousness **refers to being aware of membership in a class.**

Class, **in Marx's sense of the term, is determined by a person's relationship to the means of production. In Weber's usage, class is determined by a person's "market situation."**

The bourgeoisie **in Marx's usage are owners of the means of production, including factories, tools, and land. They do not do any physical labour. Their income derives from profits.**

The proletariat, **in Marx's usage, is the working class. Members of the proletariat do physical labour but do not own means of production. They are thus in a position to earn wages.**

The petite bourgeoisie, **in Marx's usage, is the class of small-scale capitalists who own means of production but employ only a few workers or none at all, forcing them to do physical work themselves.**

- Marx correctly argued that investment in technology makes it possible for capitalists to earn high profits. However, he did not expect investment in technology also to make it possible for workers to earn higher wages and toil fewer hours under less oppressive conditions. Yet that is just what happened. Their improved living standard tended to pacify workers, as did the availability of various welfare state benefits, such as employment insurance.

- Communism took root not where industry was most highly developed, as Marx predicted, but in semi-industrialized countries, such as Russia in 1917 and China in 1948. Moreover, instead of evolving into classless societies, new forms of privilege emerged under communism. For example, in communist Russia, income was more equal than in the West. However, membership in the Communist Party, and particularly membership in the so-called *nomenklatura,* a select group of professional state managers, brought special privileges. These included exclusive access to stores where they could purchase scarce Western goods at nominal prices, luxurious country homes, free trips abroad, and so forth. According to a Russian quip from the 1970s, "Under capitalism, one class exploits the other, but under communism it's the other way around."

Weber

Writing in the early twentieth century, Max Weber foretold most of these developments. For example, he did not think communism would create classlessness. He also understood the profound significance of the growth of the middle class. As a result, Weber developed an approach to social stratification much different from Marx's.

Weber, like Marx, saw classes as economic categories (Weber, 1946: 180–95). However, he did not think a single criterion—ownership versus non-ownership of property—determines class position. Class position, wrote Weber, is determined by a person's "market situation," including the possession of goods, opportunities for income, level of education, and degree of technical skill. From this point of view, there are four main classes according to Weber: large property owners, small property owners, propertyless but relatively highly educated and well-paid employees, and propertyless manual workers. Thus, white-collar employees and professionals emerge as a large class in Weber's scheme.

If Weber broadened Marx's idea of class, he also recognized that two types of groups other than class have a bearing on the way a society is stratified: status groups and parties.

Status groups differ from one another in the prestige or social honour they enjoy and in their style of life. Consider members of a particular minority ethnic community who have recently immigrated. They may earn relatively high income but endure relatively low prestige. The longer-established members of the majority ethnic community may look down on them as vulgar "new rich." If their cultural practices differ from those of the majority ethnic group, their style of life may also become a subject of scorn. Thus, the position of the minority ethnic group in the social hierarchy does not derive just from its economic position but also from the esteem in which it is held.

In Weber's usage, **parties** are not just political groups but, more generally, organizations that seek to impose their will on others. Control over parties, especially large bureaucratic organizations, does not depend just on wealth or another class criterion. One can head a military, scientific, or other bureaucracy without being rich, just as one can be rich and still have to endure low prestige.

So we see why Weber argued that to draw an accurate picture of a society's stratification system, we must analyze classes, status groups, and parties as somewhat independent bases of social inequality. But to what degree are they independent of one another? Weber said that the importance of status groups as a basis of stratification is greatest in pre-capitalist societies. Under capitalism, classes and parties (especially bureaucracies) become the main bases of stratification.

Although sociologists dissect inequalities into abstract schemes, the underlying differences exist quite apart from abstractions that theorists propose. For many people, the most tangible reality of class is how it sorts people into different neighbourhoods. There is no exact rule involved and various ranking criteria blend into a complex synthesis. Because the rule is inexact, people act on it without even agreeing on what, if anything, to call it.

Status groups differ from one another in terms of the prestige or social honour they enjoy and also in terms of their style of life.

Parties, in Weber's usage, are organizations that seek to impose their will on others.

PERSONAL ANECDOTE

For example, Steven Rytina recalls: "When I was in elementary school, my family lived in a small coal-mining city. You could see the city's sharp stratification as your glance swept from the mine-owners' mansions on the hill to the shacks down by the river.

"One day when I was about 10, I was playing with some friends in what we knew as 'Perk's meadow.' One of my friends was over by the road when, for no apparent reason, a group of about a half-dozen boys came up and starting hitting him.

"We rushed over to help and they ran away. Who were they? We recognized only one of them. He lived about a half-block away but he never played in our ball games even though his house was closer to the field than were many of ours. We hardly knew him. Still, someone knew where he lived and so we ran over and barged into his house. But he wasn't there, so we retreated to the meadow and mobilized. We piled up a barrier of brush, collected apples and sticks for ammunition, and got the word out to the neighbourhoods up the hill.

"Over three days, larger and larger bodies of boys assembled from up-the-hill and from down-the-hill and met in the middle at Perk's meadow. There was lots of shouting, a little jostling, and bushels of apples thrown. On the final day, there were 30 or 40 on each side. By then, the fracas attracted the attention of some adults who put a quick end to it.

"It was only much later that I asked myself why people on both sides assumed that there were two sides and only two sides, and that boys would come, as they did, once they were told about the initial incident. (That no one invited girls was, in that time and place, not a puzzle.) Years later, the answer crystallized. The street that formed the boundary along Perk's meadow marked an abrupt transition. On the immediate up-hill side were the houses of the president of the local bank and the owner of the lumber mill. Almost without exception, families up the hill were business owners or professionals who belonged to the country club and enjoyed other privileges. Those on the down-hill side did not share in those privileges and the friendships they fostered. What both sides at Perk's meadow assumed, correctly even though nobody ever spoke of it directly, was that this class division existed and that their loyalty was to one and against the other. We were only kids, but the cleavages in the adult world were faithfully reflected in our little universe. We had no vocabulary to describe such differences and therefore no insight into why our loyalties (and living standards) turned so sharply on what our fathers did for a living. But everyone involved converged toward a common response as if this was somehow built into the very nature of things."

Functionalism

Marx and Weber were Germans who wrote their major works between the 1840s and the 1910s. Inevitably, their theories bear the stamp of the age in which they wrote. The next major developments in the field occurred in the United States in the mid-twentieth century. Just as inevitably, these innovations were coloured by the optimism, dynamism, and prejudices of that time and place.

Consider first in this connection the **functional theory of stratification**, proposed by Kingsley Davis and Wilbert Moore at the end of World War II (Davis and Moore, 1945). Davis and Moore observed that jobs differ in importance. A judge's work, for example, contributes more to society than the work of a janitor. This presents a problem: How can people be motivated to undergo the long training they need to serve as judges, physicians, engineers, and so forth? Higher education is expensive. You earn little money while training. Long and hard study rather than pleasure seeking is essential. Clearly, an incentive is needed to motivate the most talented people to train for the most important jobs. The incentives, said Davis and Moore, are money and prestige. More precisely, social stratification is necessary (or "functional") because the prospect of high rewards motivates people to undergo the sacrifices needed to get a higher education. Without substantial inequality, they conclude, the most talented people would have no incentive to become judges, physicians, and so forth.

Although the functional theory of stratification may at first seem plausible, we can conduct what Max Weber called a "thought experiment" to uncover one of its chief flaws. Imagine a society with just two classes of people—physicians and farmers. The farmers

> The **functional theory of stratification** argues that (1) some jobs are more important than others are, (2) people must make sacrifices to train for important jobs, and (3) inequality is required to motivate people to undergo these sacrifices.

According to the functional theory of stratification, "important" jobs require more training than "less important" jobs. The promise of big salaries motivates people to undergo that training. Therefore, the functionalists conclude, social stratification is necessary. As the text makes clear, however, one of the problems with the functional theory of stratification is that it is difficult to establish which jobs are important, especially when we take a historical perspective.

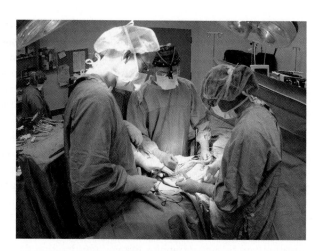

grow food. The physicians tend the ill. Then, one day, a rare and deadly virus strikes. The virus has the odd property of attacking only physicians. Within weeks, there are no more doctors in our imaginary society. As a result, the farmers are much worse off. Cures and treatments for their ailments are no long available. Soon the average farmer lives fewer years than his or her predecessors did. The society is less well off, though it survives.

Now imagine the reverse. Again we have a society comprising only physicians and farmers. Again a rare and lethal virus strikes. This time, however, the virus has the odd property of attacking only farmers. Within weeks, the physicians' stores of food are depleted. After a few more weeks, the physicians start dying of starvation. The physicians who try to become farmers catch the new virus and expire. Within months, there is no more society. Who, then, does the more important work, physicians or farmers? Our thought experiment suggests that farmers do, for without them society cannot exist.

From a historical point of view, we can say that *none* of the jobs regarded by Davis and Moore as "important" would exist without the physical labour done by people in "unimportant" jobs. To sustain the witch doctor in a tribal society, hunters and gatherers had to produce enough for their own subsistence plus a surplus to feed, clothe, and house the witch doctor. To sustain the royal court in an agrarian society, serfs had to produce enough for their own subsistence plus a surplus to support the royal family. By using taxes, tithes, and force, government and religious authorities have taken surpluses from ordinary working people for thousands of years. Among other things, these surpluses were used to establish the first institutions of higher learning in the thirteenth century. Out of these, modern universities developed.

The question of which occupations are most important is thus not clear-cut. To be sure, physicians earn a lot more money than farmers do today and they also enjoy a lot more prestige. But that is not because their work is more important in any objective sense of the word. (On the question of why physicians and other professionals earn more than non-professionals do, see Chapter 17, Education).

Other problems with the functional theory of stratification have been noted (Tumin, 1953). We mention two of the most important. First, the functional theory of stratification stresses how inequality helps society discover talent. However, it ignores the pool of talent lying undiscovered because of inequality. Bright and energetic adolescents may be forced to drop out of high school to help support themselves and their families. Capable and industrious high-school graduates may be forced to forgo a postsecondary education because they can't afford it. Inequality may encourage the discovery of talent but only among those who can afford to take advantage of the opportunities available to them. For the rest, inequality prevents talent from being discovered.

Second, the functional theory of stratification fails to examine how advantages are passed from generation to generation. Like Robinson Crusoe, the functional theory correctly emphasizes that talent and hard work often result in high material rewards. However, it is also the case that inheritance allows parents to transfer wealth to children regardless of their talent. For example, glancing back at Table 8.3, we see that many of the largest personal fortunes in Canada were inherited. Other examples strengthen the point. The McCain brothers are rich Canadians not because of their talent (although they surely have talent) but principally because their father gave them a food-processing empire.

Even rich people who do not inherit large fortunes often start near the top of the stratification system. Bill Gates, for example, is one of the richest people in the world. He did not inherit his fortune. However, his father was a partner in one of the most successful law firms in Seattle. Gates himself went to the most exclusive and expensive private schools in the city, followed by a stint at Harvard. In the late 1960s, his high school was one of the first in the world to boast a computer terminal connected to a nearby university mainframe. Gates's early fascination with computers dates from this period. Gates is without doubt a highly talented man, but surely the social advantages he was born with, and not just his talents, helped to elevate him to his present lofty status (Wallace and Erickson, 1992). An adequate theory of stratification must take inheritance into account, while recognizing how inequality prevents the discovery of talent.

Many of the ideas reviewed above emphasize the economic sources of inequality. However, as Weber correctly pointed out, inequality is not based on money alone. It is also based on prestige and power. We now turn to an examination of these non-economic sources of inequality.

NON-ECONOMIC DIMENSIONS OF INEQUALITY

Power

In November 1997, seven teenagers in Victoria, B.C.—six girls and a boy—attacked their schoolmate, 14-year-old Reena Virk, beating her unconscious and leaving her to drown. In March 2000, Hamed Nastoh, also 14, killed himself by jumping off the Pattullo Bridge between New Westminster and Surrey, B.C. Nine months later, 14-year-old Dawn-Marie Wesley of Mission, B.C., hanged herself in her bedroom with a dog leash. In April 2002, 14-year-old Emmet Fralick of Halifax shot and killed himself.

What do the cases of Virk, Nastoh, Wesley, and Fralick have in common? All four teenagers were bullied by their classmates. Three of them felt they had no recourse but to take their own lives. As Dawn-Marie Wesley wrote in her suicide note: "If I try to get help it will get worse. They are always looking for a new person to beat up and they are the toughest girls. If I ratted they would get suspended and there would be no stopping them. I love you all so much" (quoted in O'Malley and Ali, 2001).

Bullying was probably part of your upbringing, too. Recall your years in the schoolyard. Remember how some people had the power to "name," while others were forced to "wear" those names? "Four eyes," "fatty," and "spaz" were common names in many schools. If you had the misfortune of needing glasses, having a visible birthmark, or even having an unusual name, you might have been the victim of verbal abuse.

Why are so many children publicly shamed and humiliated? Because it makes those with the power to name feel superior and proud. The peer group is a place to "earn points" and win friends. To become one of the in-crowd, a child must commonly disparage outsiders. If a person is part of the out-crowd, he or she must commonly disparage members of the in-crowd as a defence aimed at maintaining self-esteem. Often it is cliques who do the mocking. Social class, ethnicity, grade level, and neighbourhood often define cliques.

Bullying is one form of power in action. Max Weber defined **power** as the ability of individuals or groups to get their own way, even in the face of resistance from others (Weber, 1947: 152). It would, however, be a mistake to think that power is an attribute that you either have or don't. That is because less powerful groups may organize and resist; and organization and resistance are themselves bases of power. Accordingly, less powerful groups may become more powerful when power holders seek to impose their will.

Power is ability to impose one's will on others.

Authority is legitimate, institutionalized power.

Sometimes, less powerful groups may even prevent power holders from achieving their aims. Power is therefore not an all-or-nothing attribute but a *social relationship,* the exercise of which may cause less-powerful people to become more powerful.

We must distinguish between power and authority. **Authority** rests on moral consent—I comply with your demands not because you force me to but because I believe they are legitimate. In this case, compliance occurs not because sanctions are or could be used, but because I agree your demands are valid. We agree that bringing a gun to school is inappropriate and that halting at stop signs is essential for safety. Most people obey these rules not out of fear of sanctions, but because they agree that they are sensible, legitimate practices.

It is also important to note that the use of power is often invisible. Powerful people often do not have to do anything to get their way because others understand that it would be futile to resist. Extremely powerful individuals or groups are even able to set agendas, frame issues, and shape ideas—to decide the topics that will be debated and how they will be debated. This enables them to exclude potentially contentious issues from debate. They may then win battles without having to fight them because others haven't even conceived of the need to raise certain issues or at least raise them in certain ways. This invisible use of power is less risky than allowing contentious issues to be put on an agenda, having less powerful individuals and groups organize and resist, and perhaps even having to use force to win an issue. The use of force is a sign of relative weakness.

Prestige and Taste

Let us now consider another non-economic dimension of social stratification: prestige or honour. Weber, you will recall, said status groups differ from one another in terms of their lifestyles and the honour in which they are held. Here we may add that members of status groups signal their rank by means of material and symbolic culture. That is, they seek to distinguish themselves from others by displays of "taste" in fashion, food, music, literature, manners, travel, and so forth.

The difference between *good taste, common taste,* and *bad taste* is not inherent in cultural objects themselves. Rather, cultural objects that are considered to be in the best taste are generally those that are least accessible.

To explain the connection between taste and accessibility, let us compare Bach's *The Well-Tempered Clavier* with Gershwin's *Rhapsody in Blue.* A survey by French sociologist Pierre Bourdieu showed different social groups prefer these two musical works (Bourdieu, 1984 [1979]: 17). Well-educated professionals, high-school teachers, professors, and artists prefer *The Well-Tempered Clavier.* Less well-educated clerks, secretaries,

The differences among *good taste, common taste,* and *bad taste* are not inherent in cultural objects themselves. Rather, cultural objects that are considered to be in the best taste are generally those that are least accessible. *Left:* Measha Brueggergosman. *Right:* Don Cherry.

and junior commercial and administrative executives favour *Rhapsody in Blue.* Why? The two works are certainly very different types of music. Gershwin evokes the jazzy dynamism of big-city America early in the twentieth century, Bach the almost mathematically ordered courtly life of early eighteenth-century Germany. But anyone would be hard-pressed to argue that *The Well-Tempered Clavier* is intrinsically superior music. Both are great art. Why then do more highly educated people prefer *The Well-Tempered Clavier* to *Rhapsody in Blue?* Because, according to Bourdieu, during their education they acquire specific cultural tastes associated with their social position. These tastes help to distinguish them from people in other social positions. Many of them come to regard lovers of Gershwin condescendingly, just as many lovers of Gershwin come to think of Bach enthusiasts as snobs. These distancing attitudes help the two status groups remain separate.

Bach is known for such musical innovations as counterpoint (playing two or more melodies simultaneously) and the fugue (in which instruments repeat the same melody with slight variations). His music is complex, and to really appreciate it a person may require some formal instruction. Many other elements of "high culture," such as opera and abstract art, are similarly inaccessible to most people because fully understanding them requires special education.

However, it is not just education that makes some cultural objects less accessible than others are. Purely financial considerations also enter the picture. A Mercedes costs four times more than a Ford, and a winter ski trip to Whistler can cost four times more than a week in a modest motel near the beach on Lake Erie or the Bay of Fundy. Of course, anyone can get from point A to point B quite comfortably in a Ford and have a perfectly enjoyable vacation in different places. Still, most people would prefer the Mercedes and Whistler, at least partly because they signal higher status. Access to tasteful cultural objects, then, is as much a matter of cost as of education.

Often, rich people engage in conspicuous displays of consumption, waste, and leisure not because they are necessary, useful, or pleasurable but simply to impress their peers and inferiors (Veblen, 1899). This display is evident if we consider how clothing acts as a sort of language that signals a person's status to others (Lurie, 1981).

For thousands of years, certain clothing styles have indicated rank. In ancient Egypt, only people in high positions were allowed to wear sandals. The ancient Greeks and Romans passed laws controlling the type, number, and colour of garments and the type of embroidery with which they could be trimmed. In medieval Europe, too, various aspects of dress were regulated to ensure that certain styles were specific to certain groups.

European laws governing the dress styles of different groups fell into disuse after about 1700, because a new method of control emerged as Europe became wealthier. From the eighteenth century on, the *cost* of clothing came to designate a person's rank. Expensive materials, styles that were difficult to care for, heavy jewellery, and superfluous trimmings became all the rage. It was not for comfort or utility that rich people wore elaborate powdered wigs, heavy damasked satins, the furs of rare animals, diamond tiaras, and patterned brocades and velvets. Such raiment was often hot, stiff, heavy, and itchy. They could scarcely move in many of these getups. And that was just their point—to prove not only that the wearer could afford enormous sums for handmade finery but also that he or she did not have to work to pay for them.

Today, we have different ways of using clothes to signal status. For instance, designer labels loudly proclaim the dollar value of garments. Another example: A great variety and quantity of clothing are required to maintain appearances. Thus, the well-to-do athletic type may have many different and expensive outfits that are "required" for jogging, hiking, cycling, aerobics, golf, tennis, and so forth. In fact, many people who really can't afford to obey the rules of conspicuous consumption, waste, and leisure feel compelled to do so anyway. As a result, they go into debt to maintain their wardrobes. Doing so helps them maintain prestige in the eyes of associates and strangers alike, even if their economic standing secretly falters.

SOCIAL MOBILITY

Mordecai Richler's *The Apprenticeship of Duddy Kravitz* (Richler, 1959) is one of the true classics of modern Canadian literature. Made into a 1974 film starring Richard Dreyfuss as Duddy, it is the story of a poor 18-year-old Jewish Montrealer in the mid-1940s desperately seeking to establish himself in the world. To that end, he waits on tables, smuggles drugs, drives a taxi, produces wedding and bar mitzvah films, and rents out pinball machines. He is an obnoxious charmer with relentless drive, a young man so fixed on making it that he is even willing to sacrifice his girlfriend and his only co-worker to achieve his goals. We cannot help but admire Duddy for his ambition and his artfulness even while being shocked by his guile and his single-mindedness.

Part of what makes *The Apprenticeship of Duddy Kravitz* universally appealing is that it could be a story about anyone on the make. It is not just some immigrants and their children who may start out as pushy little guys engaged in shady practices and unethical behaviour. As Richler reminds us in many places, some of the wealthiest establishment families in Canada and elsewhere started out in just this way. Duddy, then, is a universal symbol of "upward mobility"—and the compromises a person must sometimes make to achieve it (see Box 8.2).

Much of our discussion to this point has focused on how we describe inequality and how we explain its persistence. Now we take up a different, although related, set of questions. Is our position within the system of inequality fixed? To what extent, if at all, are we trapped in a disadvantaged social position or assured of maintaining an advantaged position? Canada is not a caste system. But at birth, do all people have the same freedom to gain wealth and fame? Are opportunities equally accessible to everyone?

Sociologists use the term *social mobility* to refer to the dynamics of the system of inequality and, in particular, to movement up and down the stratification system. If we think about inequality as either a hierarchy of more or less privileged positions or a set of higher and lower social classes, an important question is how much opportunity people have to change positions. Typically, change has been measured by using one of two benchmarks: your first position in the hierarchy (e.g., your first full-time job) or the position of your parents in the hierarchy. Comparing your first job to your current job is an examination of occupational or **intragenerational mobility**. Comparing the occupation(s) of parents to their children's current occupation is an examination of the inheritance of social position or **intergenerational mobility**.

Intragenerational mobility is social mobility that occurs within a single generation.

Intergenerational mobility is social mobility that occurs between generations.

Whichever benchmark is used, social mobility analysts are interested in the openness or fluidity of society. In open or fluid societies, there is greater equality of access to all positions in the hierarchy of inequality, both the low and the high. Regardless of your social origins, in more open societies you are more likely to rise or fall to a position that reflects your capabilities. In contrast, in closed or rigid societies, your social origins have major consequences for where you are located in the hierarchy of inequality. In such societies, poverty begets poverty, wealth begets wealth. In feudal Europe or in the Indian caste system, your birth determined your fate—you were a peasant or a lord based on the position of the family to which you were born.

More recently, societies have become more open in that your social origin does not completely determine your fate. Your chances in life are less dependent on the circumstances of your birth. Think about the changes in Canadian society over the last century. A mainly agrarian, resource-based economy has transformed into a modern, advanced postindustrial nation. We have experienced substantial growth in well-paying occupations in finance, marketing, management, and the professions. To what extent have people from all walks of life, from all economic backgrounds, been able to benefit from this transformation? This introduces a second, related theme to discussions of mobility—equality of opportunity.

As you can imagine from our earlier discussion, in the 1950s and 1960s proponents of the functional theory of stratification and human capital theory imagined that equality

BOX 8.2
Sociology at the Movies

TAKE   **ROLL**

Sweet Home Alabama (2002)

Sweet Home Alabama is a Cinderella story with a twist: The successful heroine from humble beginnings gets the handsome prince but is not sure he is truly what she wants.

In the seven years since Melanie Carmichael (Reese Witherspoon) left her small-town Alabama home, she has achieved impressive upward social mobility. Beginning as a daughter of the working class, she has become a world-famous fashion designer in New York City. As the film begins, the mayor's son is courting Melanie. Andrew (Patrick Dempsey) proposes to her in Tiffany's, the upscale jewellery store that symbolizes upper-class consumption in the popular imagination. She says yes, but before she can marry him she has to clear up a not-so-minor detail: she needs a divorce from Jake (Josh Lucas), the childhood sweetheart she left behind.

Most of the story unfolds back in rural Alabama, in a town where friends climb the local water tower to drink beer and watch the folks pass by below, where major social events include Civil War re-enactments and catfish festivals, and where special hospitality is shown by offering guests hot pickles "right out of the grease." Melanie finds herself caught between two classes and two subcultures, and the film follows her struggle to reconcile her conflicting

Josh Lucas and Reese Witherspoon in *Sweet Home Alabama* (2002)

identities. Her dilemma will require her to acknowledge and reconnect with her mother (Mary Kay Place), who lives in a trailer park, while standing up to her future mother-in-law, the mayor of New York City (Candice Bergen).

In the end, Melanie returns to Jake, while Andrew, briefly heart-broken, pleases his mother by marrying a woman of his own class. Melanie's homecoming does not, however, require that she return to life in a trailer park. She discovers that while she was in New York, Jake had transformed himself. The working-class "loser" built a successful business as a glass blower. This change allows Melanie to imagine an upwardly mobile future by Jake's side.

Sweet Home Alabama sends the message that people are happiest when they marry within their own subculture. That message is comforting because it helps the audience reconcile itself to two realities. First, although many people may want to "marry up," most people do not in fact succeed in doing so. We tend to marry within our own class—and within our own religion and ethnic and racial group (Kalmijn, 1998: 406–08). Second, marrying outside your subculture is likely to be unsettling insofar as it involves abandoning old norms, roles, and values, and learning new ones. It is therefore a relief to learn from *Sweet Home Alabama* that you're better off marrying within your own subculture, especially since you will probably wind up doing just that.

The message has an ideological problem, however. Staying put in your own subculture denies the dream of upward mobility. *Sweet Home Alabama* resolves the problem by holding out the promise of upward mobility without having to leave home, as it were. Melanie and the transformed Jake can enjoy the best of both worlds, moving up the social hierarchy together without forsaking the community and the subculture they cherish. *Sweet Home Alabama* achieves a happy ending by denying the often difficult process of adapting to a new subculture while experiencing social mobility.

of opportunity would pervade society. They argued that as more and more skilled jobs are created in the new economy, the best and the brightest must rise to the top to take those jobs and perform them diligently. We would then move from a society based on ascription to one based on achievement. In a system of inequality based on ascription, your family's station in life determines your own fortunes. Conversely, in a system based on achievement, your own talents and your own merit determine your lot in life. If you achieve good grades in school, your chance of acquiring a professional or managerial job rises.

Other sociologists, however, have cautioned that this scenario of high individual social mobility might not follow from the transformation of the economy. These theorists, focusing more on the reproduction of inequality, emphasized how advantaged families have long attempted to ensure that their offspring inherit their advantages (Collins, 1979).

On the world stage, Blossfeld and Shavit (1993) demonstrated that in 11 of 13 advanced industrial countries, little evidence supports the view that there is greater equality of opportunity in societies with expanding education systems (Sweden and the Netherlands are the two exceptions). In short, the openness or fluidity of the system of inequality did not increase over the last half of the twentieth century.

Richard Wanner (1999) has tested these ideas at the postsecondary level by using Canadian data. He set himself the task of testing the idea that "Canada's investment in educational expansion reduced the amount of ascription in educational attainment" (Wanner, 1999: 409). What he was asking was this: Has the growth of education—more high schools, more colleges and universities—benefited people from all social backgrounds equally?

Socioeconomic status (SES) combines income, education, and occupational prestige data in a single index of a person's position in the socioeconomic hierarchy.

If ascription is weaker now than in previous decades, then parents' **socioeconomic status (SES)**—an index combining income, education, and occupational prestige data—should now have less effect on a child's education. In simple terms, if in earlier decades the chances of children from poorer families going to university were small, these chances should have increased in more recent decades if ascription was weakening. As measures of socioeconomic background, Wanner used mother's and father's education and father's occupation. He tested his central question by using detailed information from a sample of 31 500 Canadians.

Wanner found that class-based ascription still operates strongly. Despite the fact that more Canadians are acquiring more years of schooling and more degrees than ever before, the long arm of family socioeconomic background continues to exert a strong hold on educational attainment. The link between family advantage and children's educational achievement has not weakened.

Explanations for how and why this occurs remain a matter of controversy (Davies, 1999). The school system has become increasingly differentiated. Many routes through high-school vocational programs and college diploma programs are taken by students from lower socioeconomic backgrounds. Students from higher socioeconomic backgrounds typically continue on to university. Also, new high-school programs have proliferated. These include storefront schools for "at-risk" students in poorer neighbourhoods, language-immersion streams, private schools, and enriched learning tracks. These types of schools tend to enrol students from different socioeconomic backgrounds.

More recently, data from the National Longitudinal Survey of Children and Youth has demonstrated socioeconomic differences in children's preparedness or readiness for school (Ross, Roberts, and Scott, 2000). Children from households with incomes below $20 000 are 4.5 times as likely to have delayed vocabulary development as are children from families with incomes at or more than $50 000. Not only are they themselves less ready for school learning, but because family incomes are similar in the same neighbourhood, these students also often find themselves in schools with others who are less well prepared (Hertzman, 2000). A recent international study has replicated these findings, showing that a family's socioeconomic status affects a student's reading literacy, in this case among 15-year-olds. Importantly, however, the effect of socioeconomic status was less pronounced in Canada than in other countries (OECD, 2001).

Sociologists have also distinguished "equality of opportunity" from "equality of condition" to emphasize this point. Although everyone might have the legal opportunity to go to school, not everyone is socially able to take advantage of the opportunity. Coming to kindergarten hungry or not having been in high-quality child care before age five has an effect on how well a child will begin his or her formal schooling career. Equality of opportunity focuses on chances of participation, while equality of condition focuses on chances of succeeding. By way of analogy, we may all be able to enter the race, but if you come with track shoes and good coaching and I come with boots and no coaching, your chances of winning are higher, assuming that we have equal athletic skills.

POLITICS AND THE PERCEPTION OF CLASS INEQUALITY

We expect you have had some strong reactions to our review of sociological theories and research on social stratification. You may therefore find it worthwhile to reflect more systematically on your own attitudes to social inequality. To start with, do you consider the family in which you grew up to have been lower class, working class, middle class, or upper class? Do you think the gaps between classes in Canadian society are big, moderate, or small? How strongly do you agree or disagree with the view that big gaps between classes are needed to motivate people to work hard and maintain national prosperity? How strongly do you agree or disagree with the view that inequality persists because it benefits the rich and the powerful? How strongly do you agree or disagree with the view that inequality persists because ordinary people don't join together to get rid of it? Answering these questions will help you clarify the way you perceive and evaluate the Canadian class structure and your place in it. If you take note of your answers, you can compare them with the responses of representative samples of Canadians, which we review below.

WHERE DO YOU FIT IN?

Surveys show that few Canadians have trouble placing themselves in the class structure when asked to do so. Most Canadians consider themselves to be middle class or working class. They also think that the gaps between classes are relatively large. But do Canadians think that these big gaps are needed to motivate people to work hard, thus increasing their own wealth and the wealth of the nation? Some Canadians think so, but most do not. A survey conducted in 18 countries, including Canada, asked more than 22 000 respondents if large differences in income are necessary for national prosperity. Canadians were among the most likely to disagree with that view (Pammett, 1997: 77).

So, Canadians know that they live in a class-divided society. They also tend to think that deep class divisions are not necessary for national prosperity. Why then do Canadians think inequality continues to exist? The 18-nation survey cited above sheds light on this issue. One of the survey questions asked respondents how strongly they agree or disagree with the view that "inequality continues because it benefits the rich and powerful." Most Canadians agreed with that statement. Only about a quarter of them disagreed with it in any way. Another question asked respondents how strongly they agree or disagree with the view that "inequality continues because ordinary people don't join together to get rid of it." Again, most Canadians agreed, with less than a third disagreeing in any way (Pammett, 1997: 77–78).

Despite widespread awareness of inequality and considerable dissatisfaction with it, most Canadians are opposed to the government playing an active role in reducing inequality. Most do not want government to provide citizens with a basic income. They tend to oppose government job-creation programs. They even resist the idea that government should reduce income differences through taxation (Pammett, 1997: 81). Most Canadians remain individualistic and self-reliant. On the whole, they persist in the belief that opportunities for mobility are abundant and that it is up to the individual to make something of those opportunities by means of talent and effort.

Significantly, however, all the attitudes summarized above vary by class position. For example, discontent with the level of inequality in Canadian society is stronger at the bottom of the stratification system than at the top. The belief that Canadian society is full of opportunities for upward mobility is stronger at the top of the class hierarchy than at the bottom. Considerably less opposition to the idea that government should reduce inequality exists as we move down the stratification system. This permits us to conclude that, if Canadians allow inequality to persist, it is because the balance of attitudes—and of power—favours continuity over change. We take up this important theme again in Chapter 14 (Politics), where we discuss the social roots of politics.

SUMMARY

1. **What is the difference between wealth and income? How are they distributed in Canada?**
   Wealth is assets minus liabilities. Income is the amount of money earned in a given period. Substantial inequality of both wealth and income exists in Canada but inequality of wealth is greater. Both types of inequality have increased over the past quarter of a century. Canada is less unequal than the United States in both regards, but Canada is more unequal in income than are several other wealthy societies.

2. **How does inequality change as societies develop?**
   Inequality increases as societies develop from the foraging to the early industrial stage. With increased industrialization, inequality declines. In the early stages of postindustrialism, inequality then increases in some countries (e.g., the United States) but not in others where governments take a more active role in redistributing income (e.g., France).

3. **What are the main differences between Marx's and Weber's theories of stratification?**
   Marx's theory of stratification distinguishes classes on the basis of their role in the productive process. It predicts inevitable conflict between bourgeoisie and proletariat and the birth of a communist system. Weber distinguished between classes on the basis of their "market relations." His model of stratification included four main classes. He argued that class consciousness may develop under some circumstances but is by no means inevitable. Weber also emphasized prestige and power as important non-economic sources of inequality.

4. **What is the functional theory of stratification?**
   Davis and Moore's functional theory of stratification argues that (1) some jobs are more important than others, (2) people have to make sacrifices to train for important jobs, and (3) inequality is required to motivate people to undergo these sacrifices. In this sense, stratification is "functional."

5. **Is stratification based only on economic criteria?**
   No. People often engage in conspicuous consumption, waste, and leisure to signal their position in the social hierarchy. Moreover, politics often influences the shape of stratification systems by changing the distribution of income, welfare entitlements, and property rights.

6. **How do Canadians view the class system?**
   Most Canadians are aware of the existence of the class system and their place in it. They believe that large inequalities are not necessary to achieve national prosperity. Most Canadians also believe that inequality persists because it serves the interests of the most advantaged members of society and because the disadvantaged do not join together to change things. However, most Canadians disapprove of government intervention to lower the level of inequality.

KEY TERMS

achievement (p. 231)

apartheid (p. 231)

ascription (p. 231)

authority (p. 238)

bourgeoisie (p. 233)

caste (p. 231)

class (p. 233)

class consciousness (p. 233)

cross-national variations in internal stratification (p. 228)

cultural capital (p. 220)

feudalism (p. 232)

functional theory of stratification (p. 235)

Gini index (p. 229)

global inequality (p. 228)

human capital (p. 219)

intergenerational mobility (p. 240)

intragenerational mobility (p. 240)

low-income cutoff (p. 223)

parties (p. 234)

petite bourgeoisie (p. 233)

power (p. 237)

proletariat (p. 233)

social capital (p. 220)

social mobility (p. 231)

social stratification (p. 231)

socioeconomic status (SES) (p. 242)

status groups (p. 234)

QUESTIONS TO CONSIDER

1. How do you think the Canadian and global stratification systems will change over the next 10 years? over the next 25 years? Why do you think these changes will occur?

2. Why do you think many Canadians oppose more government intervention to reduce the level of inequality in society? Before answering, think about the advantages that inequality brings to many people and the resources at their disposal for maintaining inequality.

3. Compare the number and quality of public facilities, such as playgrounds, public schools, and libraries, in various parts of your community. How is the distribution of public facilities related to the socioeconomic status of neighbourhoods? Why does this relationship exist?

4. Scientific advances in both microelectronics and biotechnology are significant features of this decade. How might these influence, and in turn be influenced by, inequality in contemporary Canada?

WEB RESOURCES

Companion Website for This Book

http://www.compass3e.nelson.com

Begin by clicking on the Student Resources section of the website. Next, select the chapter you are studying from the pull-down menu. From the Student Resources page you have easy access to InfoTrac® College Edition, additional Weblinks, and other resources. The website also has many useful tips to aid you in your study of sociology, including practice tests for each chapter.

InfoTrac® Search Terms

These search terms are provided to assist you in beginning to conduct research on this topic by visiting http://www.infotrac-college.com:

class

poverty

class consciousness

social mobility

global inequality

http://www.compass3e.nelson.com

Recommended Websites

For comprehensive income statistics about Canada, go to Statistics Canada at http://www.statcan.ca.

For financial information about Canada's publicly traded companies, go to the Toronto Stock Exchange at http://www.tsx.com.

For research on social and economic security, visit the Canadian Council on Social Development at http://www.ccsd.ca.

CengageNOW™

http://hed.nelson.com

This online diagnostic tool identifies each student's unique needs with a Pretest that generates a personalized Study Plan for each chapter, helping students focus on concepts they're having the most difficulty mastering. Students then take a Posttest after reading the chapter to measure their understanding of the material. An Instructor Gradebook is available to track and monitor student progress.

CHAPTER 9

Globalization, Inequality, and Development

In this chapter, you will learn that

- People and institutions across the planet are becoming increasingly aware of, and dependent on, one another. Sociologists call this tendency *globalization*.

- Globalization creates a world that is more homogeneous in some ways and more localized in others. Globalization also generates its own opposition.

- Globalization is a process that became highly significant along with the development of capitalism and world exploration about 500 years ago.

- Global inequality has increased tremendously since industrialization and is still increasing in some respects today.

- Global inequality has two competing explanations. One stresses how the deficiencies of some societies contribute to their own lack of economic growth. The other stresses how the history of social relations among countries enriched some nations at the expense of others.

- For identifiable reasons, some non-Western countries have successfully industrialized.

- Globalization has both benefits and disadvantages. Various reforms—especially more democratic participation in economic decision making—can increase the benefits.

INTRODUCTION

The Creation of a Global Village

Suppose you want to travel to Europe. You might check the Internet to buy an inexpensive plane ticket. You would then get your passport and perhaps buy a guidebook. Depending on the kind of person you are, you might spend a lot of time planning and preparing for the trip or you might just pack the basics—the passport, the ticket, a knapsack full of clothes, your credit card—and embark on an adventure.

How different things were just 25 years ago. Then, you probably would have gone to see a travel agent first, as most people did when they wanted airline tickets. Next, you would have had to make sure you had not only a valid passport but also visas for quite a few countries. Obtaining a visa was a tedious process. You had to drive to an embassy or a consulate or mail in your passport. Then you had to wait days or weeks to receive the visa. Today, fewer countries require visas.

The next step in organizing the European trip would involve withdrawing money from your bank account. ATMs were still rare. You had to stand in line at the bank before getting to a teller. Next, you had to take the with-drawn money to the office of a company that sold traveller's cheques because banks did not sell them. When you arrived in Europe, you needed to have local currency, which you could buy only from large banks and moneychangers. Few students had credit cards 25 years ago. Even if you were one of the lucky few, you could use it only in large stores and restaurants in large cities. If you ran out of cash and traveller's cheques, you were in big trouble. You could look for another Canadian tourist and try to convince him or her to take your personal cheque. Alternatively, you could go to a special telephone for international calls, phone home, and have money wired to a major bank for you. That was time consuming and expensive. Today, most people have credit cards and ATM cards. Even in small European towns, you can charge most of your shopping and restaurant bills on your credit card without using local currency. If you need local currency, you go to an ATM and withdraw money from your home bank account or charge it to your credit card; the ATM automatically converts your dollars to local currency.

Most European cities and towns today have many North American–style supermarkets. Speakers of English are also numerous, so social interaction with Europeans is easier. You would have to try hard to get very far from a McDonald's. It is also easy to receive news and entertainment from back home though the Internet. In contrast, each country you visited

Currency conversion, then and now

25 years ago would have featured a distinct shopping experience. English speakers were rarer. North American fast-food outlets were practically nonexistent. Apart from the *International Herald-Tribune,* which was available only in larger towns and cities, North American news was hard to come by. TV featured mostly local programming. You might see an American show now and then, but it would not be in English.

Clearly, the world seems a much smaller place today than it did 25 years ago. Some people go so far as to say that we have created a "global village." But what exactly does that mean? Is the creation of a global village uniformly beneficial? Or does it have a downside too? We now explore these questions in depth.

The Triumphs and Tragedies of Globalization

As suggested by our two imaginary trips to Europe, separated by a mere 25 years, people throughout the world are now linked together as never before (Table 9.1, and Figure 9.1 on page 250).

Consider these facts:

- International telecommunication has become easy and inexpensive. In 1930, a three-minute New York–London phone call cost more than $250[1] in today's dollars and only a minority of North Americans had telephones in their homes. In 2009, the same call costs as little as 15¢ and telephones, including cell phones, seem to be everywhere.
- Between 1982 and 2006, when the world's population increased by 41 percent, the number of international tourists increased by 205 percent.
- International trade and investment have increased rapidly. For example, from 1982 to 2006, worldwide investment across national borders ("foreign direct investment") increased by a remarkable 2114 percent.
- Many more international organizations and agreements now span the globe. In 1981, about 14 000 international organizations existed. By 2006, there were three-and-a-half times as many. Individual nation-states give up some of their independence when they join international organizations or sign international agreements. For example, when Canada, the United States, and Mexico entered the North American Free Trade Agreement (NAFTA) in 1994, they agreed that trade disputes would be settled by a three-country tribunal. The autonomy of nation-states has eroded somewhat with the creation of many such "transnational" bodies and treaties.
- The Internet did not exist in 1982, but in 2006 it comprised 439 million servers connecting more than one billion people from around the world through e-mail, file transfers, websites, and videoconferencing.

The benefits of the rapid movement of capital, commodities, culture, and people across national boundaries should be clear from comparing our imaginary trips to Europe today and 25 years ago. What was a struggle for a North American traveller 25 years ago is easy today. In this and many other ways, globalization has transformed and improved the way we live.

Yet not everyone is happy with globalization. Inequality between rich and poor countries remains staggering. In some respects, it is increasing. Arguably, rather than spreading the wealth, globalized industries and technologies may be turning the world into a more unequal

TABLE 9.1
Indicators of Globalization, 1982–2006

*1981

Sources: Internet Software Consortium, 2007; Union of International Associations, 2001, 2007; United Nations Conference on Trade and Development, 2007: xv; United Nations World Tourism Organization, 2007a, 2007b: 2.

	1982	2006	Percentage Change
International tourist arrivals (millions of people)	277	846	205
Foreign direct investment (billions of dollars)	59	1 306	2 114
Internet hosts (millions)	0	439	undefined
Number of international organizations	14 273*	58 859	312

FIGURE 9.1

Foreign Visitors per 100
Population, 1998

International tourism leads to the
sense that the world forms one
society. However, exposure to international tourism is higher in some
countries than in others. This map
shows the number of foreign visitors
who travelled to each country per
100 members of the local population.
Which countries are most exposed to
international tourism? Which countries are least exposed? What consequences might differential exposure
have for people's self-identity?

Source: United Nations, *World
Culture Report 2000—Cultural
Trade and Communications Trends:
International Tourism* at http://
www.unesco.org/culture/
worldreport/html_eng/stat2/table18.
pdf. Reprinted with permission. The
United Nations is the author of the
original material.

**Imperialism is the economic
domination of one country by
another.**

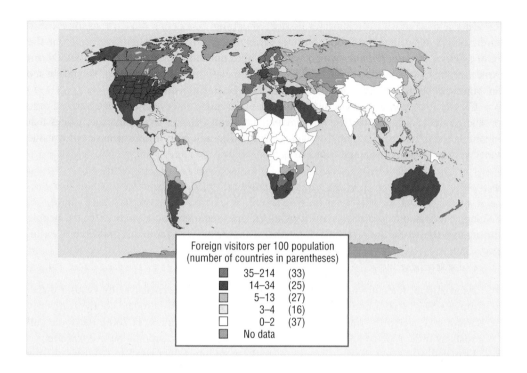

Foreign visitors per 100 population
(number of countries in parentheses)

▓	35–214	(33)
▓	14–34	(25)
▓	5–13	(27)
▢	3–4	(16)
▢	0–2	(37)
▓	No data	

place. Many people also oppose globalization because it may be hurting local cultures and the
natural environment. Some anti-globalization activists even suggest that globalization is a form
of **imperialism**, the economic domination of one country by another. From their point of view,
globalization puts the entire world under the control of powerful commercial interests.
Moreover, it contributes to the homogenization of the world, the cultural domination of less
powerful by more powerful countries. It is one thing, they say, for Indonesians and Italians to
have closer ties to North Americans, but is it desirable that they become *like* North Americans?

In the next section, we first explore what globalization is and how it affects our everyday
lives. To make the impact of globalization concrete, we trace the global movement of two
commodities familiar to everyone: money and athletic shoes. This exercise illuminates the
many ways in which far-flung individuals are bound together. Next, we consider the causes
of globalization, emphasizing the importance of political, economic, and technological factors. We then analyze whether globalization is forcing different parts of the world to become
alike. We also explore how the very process of globalization generates its own opposition.
Finally, we take a longer view and examine the roots of globalization historically.

The second task we set ourselves is to examine the nature and causes of global
inequality. We note that the gap between rich and poor countries is wide and that by some
measures it is getting wider. We then discuss the major theories that seek to explain global
inequality and conclude that poor countries are not doomed to remain poor. We close by considering what people can do to alleviate global inequality and poverty.

GLOBALIZATION

Globalization in Everyday Life

Has anyone ever asked you, "What's that got to do with the price of tea in China?" The question is of course rhetorical. The person who asked it was really saying that whatever you
were talking about is as *irrelevant* as the price of tea in China.

Yet globalization implies that the price of tea in China—and the condition of the rain
forest in Brazil, the outcome of the war in the Russian province of Chechnya, and the revival
of traditional Celtic dance in Ireland—actually do influence your life. Everything influences
everything else in a globalized world.

To explore this idea, Barbara Garson (2001) traced a small sum of money she invested in the Chase Manhattan Bank in the United States. Garson discovered that the bank almost immediately lent some of her money (along with additional money) to Caltex, a large U.S. corporation, for the construction of an oil refinery in Thailand. Initially, Thai officials opposed the refinery, mainly because Thai fishers and farmers believed the refinery would pollute and eventually destroy their livelihood and their villages. However, intensive lobbying by American politicians on behalf of Caltex eventually led Thai officials to relent and allow construction. Caltex secured the assistance of the politicians by using some of Garson's money for political party contributions. Caltex helped change the minds of Thai officials by using some of Garson's money for bribes. Some of Garson's money was used to help construct the oil refinery, which did contribute to the destruction of the natural environment and the displacement of farmers and fishers. Eventually, because of an economic downturn in Thailand, the refinery was shut down. When it closed, many Thai oil workers became unemployed.

In short, Garson learned that her small investment, together with many other small investments, had huge implications for people's everyday lives on the other side of the planet: "Wherever my money went, it changed the landscape and it changed lives," wrote Garson (2001: 319). Garson's money was caught up in the globalization of the world.

The difference between Garson and most of us is that we do not often appreciate that our actions have implications for people far away. Yet when we buy a commodity, we often tap into a **global commodity chain**, a worldwide "network of labour and production processes, whose end result is a finished commodity" (Hopkins and Wallerstein, 1986: 159).

A **global commodity chain** is a worldwide network of labour and production processes whose end result is a finished commodity.

We can better understand the web of global social relations by tracing the way one commodity—athletic shoes—binds consumers and producers in a global commodity chain. Until the 1970s, most sports shoes were manufactured in the United States. Today, corporations, such as Nike, produce all their shoes abroad. Manufacturing plants moved because governments eliminated many of the laws, regulations, and taxes that acted as barriers to foreign investment and trade. Consequently, Nike and other manufacturers started setting up overseas plants, where they could take advantage of low labour costs. The result was a new international division of labour. High-wage management, finance, design, and marketing services were concentrated in the United States and other advanced industrial countries, low-wage manufacturing in the less developed, industrializing countries (Fröbel, Heinrichs, and Kreye, 1980; see Chapter 13, Work and the Economy). Not just Nike but General Motors, General Electric, and many other large corporations closed some or all their plants in the United States and Canada (high-wage countries) and established factories in Mexico, Indonesia, and other developing economies.

The new international division of labour yielded high profits. For example, in the 1990s, "Nike spent $5.95 to make a pair of shoes in Indonesia, where workers were paid 14 cents an hour, then sold the shoes in the United States for between $49 and $125" (LaFeber, 1999: 126). Nike's Indonesian workers were not just poorly paid. They had to work as many as six hours a day overtime. Reports of beatings and sexual harassment by managers were common. When the workers tried to form a union to protect themselves, union organizers were fired and the military was brought in to restore order (LaFeber, 1999: 142). In 1976 Nike manufactured 70 million shoes in Indonesia but paid its 25 000 workers an average of just more than $2 a day. In the 1980s, Michael Jordan became a spokesperson for Nike and was paid a $20 million endorsement fee, more than the combined yearly wages of all the Indonesian workers who made the shoes (LaFeber, 1999: 107).

When someone buys a pair of Nike athletic shoes, they insert themselves in a global commodity chain. Of course, the buyer does not create the social relations that exploit Indonesian labour and enrich Michael Jordan. Still, it would be difficult to deny the buyer's part, however small, in helping those social relations persist.

Sociology makes us aware of the complex web of social relations and interactions in which we are embedded. The sociological imagination allows us to link our biography with history and social structure. Globalization extends the range of that linkage, connecting our biography with global history and global social structure. We live in a world where the price of tea in China is increasingly relevant to our lives.

The Sources of Globalization

Few people doubt the significance of globalization. Although social scientists disagree on its exact causes, most of them stress the importance of technology, politics, and economics.

Technology

Technological progress has made it possible to move things and information over long distances quickly and inexpensively. The introduction of commercial jets radically shortened the time necessary for international travel and its cost dropped dramatically after the 1950s. Similarly, various means of communication, such as telephone, fax, and e-mail, allow us to reach people around the globe inexpensively and almost instantly. Whether we think of international trade or international travel, technological progress is an important part of the story of globalization. Without modern technology, it is hard to imagine how globalization would be possible.

Politics

Globalization could not occur without advanced technology, but advanced technology by itself could never bring globalization about. Think of the contrast between North Korea and South Korea. Both countries are about the same distance from North America. You have probably heard of major South Korean companies, like Hyundai and Samsung, and may have met people from South Korea or other Korean Canadians. Yet unless you are an expert on North Korea, you will have had no contact with North Korea and its people. We have the same technological means to reach the two Koreas. Yet although we enjoy strong relations and intense interaction with South Korea, Canada did not extend diplomatic recognition to North Korea until 2001. As of 2008 Canada had not yet opened an embassy there. The reason is political. The South Korean government has been an ally of Canada since the Korean War in the early 1950s and has sought greater political, economic, and cultural integration with the outside world. North Korea, in an effort to preserve its authoritarian political system and communist economic system, has remained isolated from the rest of the world. As this example shows, politics is important in determining the level of globalization.

Economics

Finally, economics is an important source of globalization. As we saw in our discussion of global commodity chains and the new international division of labour, industrial capitalism is always seeking new markets, higher profits, and lower labour costs. Put differently, capitalist competition has been a major spur to international integration (Gilpin, 2001; Stopford and Strange, 1991).

Transnational corporations—also called multinational or international corporations— are the most important agents of globalization in the world today. They are different from traditional corporations in five ways (Gilpin, 2001; LaFeber, 1999):

Transnational corporations are large businesses that rely increasingly on foreign labour and foreign production; skills and advances in design, technology, and management; world markets; and massive advertising campaigns. They are increasingly autonomous from national governments.

1. Traditional corporations rely on domestic labour and domestic production. Transnational corporations depend increasingly on foreign labour and foreign production.
2. Traditional corporations extract natural resources or manufacture industrial goods. Transnational corporations increasingly emphasize skills and advances in design, technology, and management.
3. Traditional corporations sell to domestic markets. Transnational corporations depend increasingly on world markets.
4. Traditional corporations rely on established marketing and sales outlets. Transnational corporations depend increasingly on massive advertising campaigns.
5. Traditional corporations work with or under national governments. Transnational corporations are increasingly autonomous from national governments.

Technological, political, and economic factors do not work independently in leading to globalization. For example, governments often promote economic competition to help transnational corporations win global markets. Consider Philip Morris, the company that makes Marlboro cigarettes (Barnet and Cavanagh, 1994). Philip Morris introduced the

Marlboro brand in 1954. It soon became the best-selling cigarette in the United States, partly because of the success of an advertising campaign featuring the Marlboro Man. The Marlboro Man symbolized the rugged individualism of the American frontier, and he became one of the most widely recognized icons in American advertising. Philip Morris was the smallest of the country's six largest tobacco companies in 1954, but it rode on the popularity of the Marlboro Man to become the country's biggest tobacco company by the 1970s.

In the 1970s, the anti-smoking campaign began to have an impact, leading to slumping domestic sales. Philip Morris and other tobacco companies decided to pursue globalization as a way out of the doldrums. Economic competition and slick advertising alone did not win global markets for American cigarette makers, however. The tobacco companies needed political influence to make cigarettes one of the country's biggest and most profitable exports. To that end, the U.S. trade representative in the Reagan administration, Clayton Yeutter, worked energetically to dismantle trade barriers in Japan, Taiwan, South Korea, and other countries. He threatened legal action for breaking international trade law and said the United States would restrict Asian exports unless these countries allowed the sale of American cigarettes. Such actions were critically important in globalizing world trade in cigarettes. In 1986, the commercial counsellor of the U.S. Embassy in Seoul, South Korea, wrote to the public affairs manager of Philip Morris Asia as follows: "I want to emphasize that the embassy and the various U.S. government agencies in Washington will keep the interests of Philip Morris and the other American cigarette manufacturers in the forefront of our daily concerns" (quoted in Frankel, 1996). As the case of Philip Morris illustrates, economics and politics typically work hand in hand to globalize the world.

"I want to emphasize that the embassy and the various U.S. government agencies in Washington will keep the interests of Philip Morris and the other American cigarette manufacturers in the forefront of our daily concerns."

A World Like the United States?

We have seen that globalization links people around the world, often in ways that are not obvious. We have also seen that the sources of globalization lie in closely connected technological, economic, and political forces. Now let us consider one of the consequences of globalization, the degree to which globalization is homogenizing the world and, in particular, making the whole world look like the United States (see Figure 9.2).

FIGURE 9.2

The Size and Influence of the American Economy, 2000

This map will help you gauge the enormous importance of the United States in globalization because it emphasizes just how large the American economy is. The economy of each American state is as big as that of a whole country. Specifically, this map shows how the GDP of various countries compares with that of each state. For example, the GDP of California is equal to that of France, the GDP of New Jersey is equal to that of Russia, and the GDP of Texas is equal to that of Canada.

Source: From *The Globe and Mail*, March 8, 2003, p. F1. Reprinted with permission from *The Globe and Mail*.

Much impressionistic evidence supports the view that globalization homogenizes societies. Many economic and financial institutions around the world now operate in roughly the same way. For instance, transnational organizations, such as the World Bank and the International Monetary Fund, have imposed economic guidelines for developing countries that are similar to those governing advanced industrial countries. In the realm of politics, the United Nations (UN) engages in global governance, whereas Western ideas of democracy, representative government, and human rights have become international ideals (see Box 9.1). In the domain of culture, American icons circle the planet: supermarkets, basketball, Hollywood movies, Disney characters, Coca-Cola, MTV, CNN, McDonald's, and so on.

McDonaldization is a form of rationalization. It refers to the spread of the principles of fast-food restaurants, such as efficiency, predictability, and calculability, to all spheres of life.

Indeed, one common shorthand expression for the homogenizing effects of globalization is **McDonaldization.** George Ritzer (1996: 1) defines McDonaldization as "the process by which the principles of the fast-food restaurant are coming to dominate more and more sectors of American society as well as of the rest of the world." The idea of McDonaldization extends Weber's concept of rationalization, the application of the most efficient means to achieve given ends (see Chapter 3, Culture). Because of McDonaldization, says Ritzer, the values of efficiency, calculability, and predictability have spread from North America to the entire planet and from fast-food restaurants to virtually all spheres of life. As Ritzer shows, and as we noted in Chapter 3, McDonald's leaves nothing to chance. McDonald's is even field-testing self-service kiosks in which an automated machine cooks and bags French fries while a vertical grill takes patties from the freezer and grills them to your liking (Carpenter, 2003). Significantly, McDonald's now does most of its business outside the United States. You can find McDonald's restaurants in nearly every country in the world. McDonaldization has come to stand for the global spread of values associated with the United States and its business culture.

However, anyone familiar with symbolic interactionism should be immediately suspicious of sweeping claims about the homogenizing effects of globalization. After all, it is a central principle of symbolic interactionism that people create their social circumstances and do not merely react to them, that they negotiate their identities and do not easily settle for

BOX 9.1
Social Policy: What Do You Think?

Should the West Promote World Democracy?

"In starting and waging a war, it is not right that matters, but victory," said Adolf Hitler (quoted in "A Survey," 1998: 10). The same mindset rationalizes state brutality today, from the Serbian attack on Bosnia and Kosovo to the Indonesian war against East Timor. Cherished ideals, such as political democracy and human rights, are trampled on daily by dictatorships and military governments.

Opinions differ as to what Western governments should do about this situation. One influential argument is that of Samuel Huntington. He argues that Western nations should not be ethno-centric and impose Western values on people in other countries. If there are violations of democratic principles and human rights in these countries, they express in some way the indigenous values of those people. The West should not intervene to stop non-democratic forces and human rights abuses abroad.

Critics of Huntington argue that the ideals of democracy and human rights can be found in non-Western cultures, too. If we explore Asian or African traditions, for instance, we find "respect for the sacredness of life and for human dignity, tolerance of differences, and a desire for liberty, order, fairness and stability" (quoted in "A Survey," 1998: 10). Although Asian and African despots champion supposedly traditional values, people in Asia, Africa, and elsewhere struggle for democracy and human rights. For example, beginning in the mid-1970s, the Indonesian government tried to smother democracy in East Timor, but the East Timorese fought valiantly for democracy.

What do you think the role of the West should be? Should Western governments promote democracy and human rights? Or should they avoid what Huntington regards as ethnocentrism? Because foreign aid to authoritarian regimes may help non-democratic forces and thereby stifle human rights, should Western countries give foreign aid to such regimes?

identities imposed on them by others. Accordingly, some analysts find fault with the view that globalization is making the world a more homogeneous place based on North American values. They argue that people always interpret globalizing forces in terms of local conditions and traditions. Globalization, they say, may in fact sharpen some local differences. They have invented the term **glocalization** to describe the simultaneous homogenization of some aspects of life and the strengthening of some local differences under the impact of globalization (Shaw, 2000).

They note, for example, that McDonald's serves different foods in different countries (Watson, 1997). A burger at a Taiwanese McDonald's may be eaten with betel nuts. Vegetarian burgers are available at Indian McDonald's and kosher burgers are the norm at Israeli McDonald's. Dutch McDonald's serves the popular McKrocket, made of 100 percent beef ragout fried in batter. In Hawaii, McDonald's routinely serve Japanese ramen noodles with their burgers. McDonald's began to serve poutine in Quebec and the practice has spread across Canada to consumers undeterred by McDonald's nutrition guide, which lists a large serving as providing 130 percent of the recommended daily allowance for saturated fat (McDonald's, 2005). Although the Golden Arches may suggest that the world is becoming the same everywhere, once we go through them and sample the fare, we find much that is unique.

Those who see globalization merely as homogenization also ignore the **regionalization** of the world, the division of the world into different and often competing economic, political, and cultural areas. The argument here is that the institutional and cultural integration of countries often falls far short of covering the whole world. Figure 9.3 illustrates one aspect of regionalization. World trade is unevenly distributed across the planet and it is not dominated by just one country. Three main trade blocs exist—an Asian bloc dominated by Japan and, increasingly, China, a North American bloc dominated by the United States, and a European bloc dominated by Germany. These three trade blocs contain just over a fifth of the world's countries but account for more than three-quarters of world economic activity as measured by gross domestic product.[2] Most world trade takes place *within* each of these blocs. Each bloc competes against the others for a larger share of world trade. Politically, we can see regionalization in the growth of the European Union. Most Western European–bloc countries now share the same currency, the euro, and they coordinate economic, political, military, social, and cultural policies.

We conclude that globalization does not have a simple, one-way, and inevitable consequence. In fact, as you will now learn, its impact is often messy. Globalization has generated much criticism and opposition, unleashing a growing anti-globalization movement.

Glocalization is the simultaneous homogenization of some aspects of life and the strengthening of some local differences under the impact of globalization.

Regionalization is the division of the world into different and often competing economic, political, and cultural areas.

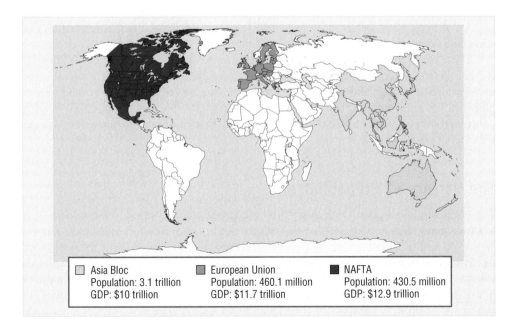

FIGURE 9.3
The Regionalization of World Trade

Source: York, 2006.

Asia Bloc	European Union	NAFTA
Population: 3.1 trillion	Population: 460.1 million	Population: 430.5 million
GDP: $10 trillion	GDP: $11.7 trillion	GDP: $12.9 trillion

Globalization and Its Discontents: Anti-globalization and Anti-Americanism

In 1996 political scientist Benjamin Barber published an important book titled *Jihad vs. McWorld.* Barber argued that globalization (the making of what he called "McWorld") was generating an anti-globalization reaction, which he called *jihad. Jihad* means "striving" or "struggle" in Arabic. Traditionally, Muslims use the term to mean perseverance in achieving a high moral standard. The term can also suggest the idea of a holy war against those who harm Muslims. In the latter sense, it represents an Islamic fundamentalist reaction to globalization. The most spectacular and devastating manifestations of fundamentalist Islamic *jihad* were the September 11, 2001, jet hijackings that led to the crash of an airliner in Pennsylvania and the destruction of the World Trade Center and part of the Pentagon. About 3000 people, 24 of them Canadians, lost their lives as a result of these attacks. The operatives of the al-Qaeda network sought to roll back the forces of globalization by attacking what they thought symbolized the global reach of godless American capitalism.

Islamic fundamentalism is the most far-reaching and violent of many reactions against globalization throughout the world. A less violent and less widespread reaction involved Mexican peasants in the southern state of Chiapas, who staged an armed rebellion against the Mexican government in the 1990s. The government provoked the peasants by turning over land, which was long regarded as communally owned, to commercial farmers so that they could increase their exports to the United States and Canada under the terms of NAFTA. The uprising involved violence and lasted several years.

Finally, we should mention the anti-globalization movement in the advanced industrial countries (Klein, 2000). In 1994 the governments of 134 countries set up the World Trade Organization (WTO) to encourage and referee global commerce. When the WTO met in Seattle in December 1999, some 40 000 union activists, environmentalists, supporters of worker and peasant movements in developing countries, and other opponents of transnational corporations staged protests that caused property damage and threatened to disrupt the proceedings. The police and the National Guard replied with concussion grenades, tear gas, rubber bullets, and mass arrests.

Subsequent meetings of the WTO and allied organizations in other countries met with the same sort of protest on the part of anti-globalization forces. These protests were, for the most part, nonviolent, often using street drama to make their point. For example, in spring 2001, 34 heads of government from North, Central, and South America and the Caribbean gathered in Quebec City to discuss the economic integration of the Americas and related matters. Among other tactics, protesters built large wooden catapults that sent volleys of miniature teddy bears at the riot police.

These examples illustrate that although globalization is far from universally welcome, the anti-globalization movement has many currents. Some are extremely violent, some nonviolent. Some reject only what they regard as the excesses of globalization, others reject globalization in its entirety. This complexity supports our view that globalization is not a simple process with predictable consequences. It is a multifaceted phenomenon, the outcome of which is unclear.

The History of Globalization

The extent of globalization since about 1980 is unprecedented in world history. Sociologist Martin Albrow therefore argues that the "global age" is only a few decades old (Albrow, 1997). He dates it from the spread of global awareness and skepticism about the benefits of modernization. However, Albrow and others are inclined to exaggerate the extent of globalization (Gilpin, 2001; Hirst and Thompson, 1999). The nation-state is still a major centre of power in the world. National borders remain important. Truly transnational corporations are rare; most companies concentrate their business in a single country. Most foreign trade occurs between advanced industrial countries and, as we have seen, within distinct regional groups of advanced industrial countries. Many developing countries are poorly integrated in the global economy. Most people in the world have little or no access to the advanced technologies that exemplify globalization, such as e-mail. Cultural differences remain substantial across the planet.

Furthermore, globalization is not as recent as Albrow would have us believe. Anthony Giddens (1990) argues that globalization is the result of industrialization and modernization, which picked up pace in the late nineteenth century. And, in fact, a strong case can be made that the world was highly globalized 100 or more years ago. In the late nineteenth century, people could move across national borders without passports. The extent of international trade and capital flow in the late twentieth century only restored the level achieved before World War I (1914–18; Hirst and Thompson, 1999).

World War I and the Great Depression (1929–39) undermined the globalization of the late nineteenth and early twentieth centuries. They incited racism, protectionism, and military build-up and led to Nazi and communist dictatorships that culminated in World War II (1939–45; Hobsbawm, 1994; James, 2001). International trade and investment plummeted between 1914 and 1945, and governments erected many new barriers to the free movement of people and ideas. A longer view of globalization suggests that globalization is not an inevitable and linear process. Periods of accelerated globalization—including our own—can end.

An even longer historical view leads to additional insight. Some sociologists, such as Roland Robertson (1992), note that globalization is as old as civilization itself and is in fact the *cause* of modernization rather than the other way around. Archaeological remains show that long-distance trade began 5000 years ago. People have been migrating across continents and even oceans for thousands of years. Alexander the Great conquered vast stretches of Europe, western Asia, and northern Africa, while Christianity and Islam spread far beyond their birthplace in the Middle East. All these forces contributed to globalization in Robertson's view.

So is globalization 30, 125, or 5000 years old, as Albrow, Giddens, and Robertson, respectively, suggest? The question has no correct answer. The answer depends on what we want globalization to mean. A short historical view—whether 125 or 30 years—misses the long-term developments that have brought the world's people closer to one another. Yet if we think of globalization as a 5000-year-old phenomenon, the definition and value of the term are diluted. After all, the price of tea in China was irrelevant 5000 years ago. Few people knew what tea was.

We prefer to take an intermediate position and think of globalization as a roughly 500-year-old phenomenon. We regard the establishment of colonies and the growth of capitalism as the main forces underlying globalization, and both **colonialism** and capitalism began about 500 years ago, symbolized by Columbus's voyage to the Americas. Colonialism is the direct political control of one country by another. As you will now see, the main advantage of thinking of globalization in this way is that it tells us much about the causes of development or industrialization and the growing gap between rich and poor countries and people. These topics will now be the focus of our attention.

Colonialism involves the control of developing societies by more developed, powerful societies.

DEVELOPMENT AND UNDERDEVELOPMENT

John Lie decided to study sociology because he was concerned about the poverty and dictatorships he had read about in books and observed during his travels in Asia and Latin America. "Initially," says John, "I thought I would major in economics. In my economics classes, I learned about the importance of birth-control programs to cap population growth, efforts to prevent the runaway growth of cities, and measures to spread Western knowledge, technology, and markets to people in less economically developed countries. My textbooks and professors assumed that if only the less developed countries

PERSONAL ANECDOTE

would become more like the West, their populations, cities, economies, and societies would experience stable growth. Otherwise, the developing countries were doomed to suffer the triple catastrophe of overpopulation, rapid urbanization, and economic underdevelopment.

"Equipped with this knowledge, I spent a summer in the Philippines working for an organization that offered farmers advice on how to promote economic growth. I assumed that, as in North America, farmers who owned large plots of land and used high technology would be more efficient and better off. Yet I found the most productive villages were those in which most farmers owned *small* plots of land. In such villages, there was little economic inequality. The women in these villages enjoyed low birth rates and the inhabitants were usually happier than were the inhabitants of villages in which there was more inequality.

"As I talked with the villagers, I came to realize that farmers who owned at least some of their own land had an incentive to work hard. The harder they worked, the more they earned. With a higher standard of living, they didn't need as many children to help them on the farm. In contrast, in villages with greater inequality, many farmers owned no land but leased it or worked as farm hands for wealthy landowners. They didn't earn more for working harder, so their productivity and their standard of living were low. They wanted to have more children to increase household income.

"Few Filipino farms could match the productivity of high-tech North American farms, because even large plots were small by North American standards. Much high-tech agricultural equipment would have been useless there. Imagine trying to use a harvesting machine in a plot not much larger than some suburban backyards.

"Thus, my Western assumptions turned out to be wrong. The Filipino farmers I met were knowledgeable and thoughtful about their needs and desires. When I started listening to them, I started understanding the real world of economic development. It was one of the most important sociological lessons I ever learned."

Let us begin our sociological discussion of economic development by examining trends in levels of global inequality. We then discuss two theories of development and underdevelopment, both of which seek to uncover the sources of inequality among nations. Next, we analyze some cases of successful development. Finally, we consider what we can do to alleviate global inequality in light of what we learn from these successful cases.

Levels and Trends in Global Inequality

We learned in Chapter 8 (Social Stratification: Canadian and Global Perspectives) that Canada is a highly stratified society. If we shift our attention from the national to the global level, we find an even more dramatic gap between rich and poor. In a Manhattan restaurant, pet owners can treat their cats to $100-a-plate birthday parties. In Cairo (Egypt) and Manila (the Philippines), garbage dumps are home to entire families who sustain themselves by picking through the refuse. People who travel outside the 20 or so highly industrialized countries of North America, Western Europe, Japan, and Australia often encounter scenes of unforgettable poverty and misery. The UN calls the level of inequality worldwide "grotesque" (United Nations, 2002: 19).

The average income of citizens in the highly industrialized countries far outstrips that of citizens in the developing societies. Yet because poor people live in rich countries and rich people live in poor countries, these averages fail to capture the extent of inequality between the richest of the rich and the poorest of the poor. It is perhaps more revealing to note that the richest 1 percent of the world's population earns as much income as the bottom 57 percent. The top 10 percent of U.S. income earners earn as much as the poorest 2 billion people in the world (United Nations, 2002). Of the world's 6.7 billion people, around 1 billion live on less than $1 a day, and 2.6 billion on less than $2 a day. Most desperately poor people are women, and racial and other minority groups often fare worse than their majority-group counterparts in the developing countries. The

A half-hour's drive from the centre of Manila, the capital of the Philippines, an estimated 70 000 Filipinos live on a 22-hectare (55-acre) mountain of rotting garbage, 45 metres (150 feet) high. It is infested with flies, rats, dogs, and disease. On a lucky day, residents can earn up to $5 retrieving scraps of metal and other valuables. On a rainy day, the mountain of garbage is especially treacherous. In July 2000 an avalanche buried 300 people alive. People who live on the mountain of garbage call it "The Promised Land."

citizens of the 20 or so rich, highly industrialized countries spend more on cosmetics or alcohol or ice cream or pet food than it would take to provide basic education, or water and sanitation, or basic health and nutrition for everyone in the world (Table 9.2).

Has global inequality increased or decreased over time? Figure 9.4 helps answer that question by focusing on gross domestic product (GDP) per person—the dollar value of goods and services produced in a year in each of the world's major regions divided by the number of people in that region. Between 1975 and 2005, the GDP gap between the 20 or so richest countries and the rest of the world grew enormously. GDP per person grew very slowly in the Arab countries and Latin America and the Caribbean. In sub-Saharan Africa, it actually fell.

Good/Service	Annual Cost (in US$ billion)
Basic education for everyone in the world	6
Cosmetics in the United States	8
Water and sanitation for everyone in the world	9
Ice cream in Europe	11
Reproductive health for all women in the world	12
Perfumes in Europe and the United States	12
Basic health and nutrition for everyone in the world	13
Pet foods in Europe and the United States	17
Business entertainment in Japan	35
Cigarettes in Europe	50
Alcoholic drinks in Europe	105
Narcotic drugs in the world	400
Military spending in the world	780

TABLE 9.2

Global Priorities: Annual Cost of Various Goods and Services (in US$ billion)

Note: Items in italics represent estimates of what they would cost to achieve. Other items represent estimated actual cost.

Source: United Nations, 1998b: 37.

FIGURE 9.4

Gross Domestic Product per Person, World Regions, 1975–2005 (in 2005 US$)

Source: United Nations, 2007: 280.

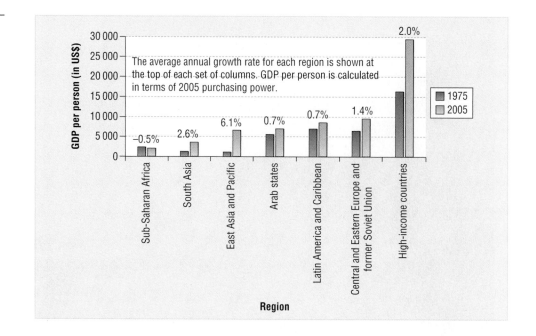

Table 9.3 focuses on individual rather than regional income. It shows that the share of world income going to the top 10 percent of individuals increased from 42.8 percent in 1820 to 53.4 percent in 1992. Over that same period, the share of world income going to the bottom 20 percent of individuals fell from 4.7 percent to just 2.2 percent. That trend has continued since 1992.

On the slightly brighter side, the actual number of people in the world living on less than $1 a day peaked in 1950 and then started declining. In percentage terms, the proportion of people living in extreme poverty fell from 83.9 percent in 1820 to 18 percent in 2004 (United Nations, 2007: 24). However, two regions are not benefiting from the decline in poverty. Between 1981 and 2001, the percentage of people in Latin America and the Caribbean earning less than $1 a day remained about 10 percent. In sub-Saharan Africa, the percentage of people earning less than $1 a day increased from 41.6 percent to 46.4 percent (Milanovic, 2005; Figure 9.5). These figures give little cause for joy.

Statistics never speak for themselves. We need theories to explain them. Let us now outline and critically assess the two main theories that seek to explain the origins and persistence of global inequality.

TABLE 9.3

Trends in Global Inequality, 1820–1992

Source: "Trends in Global Inequality, 1820–1992" from *Making Sense of Globalization: A Guide to the Economic Issues* (Centre for Economic Policy Research, London: 2002), p. 57.

	1820	1870	1910	1929	1950	1970	1992
Share of world income going to top 10%	42.8	47.6	50.9	49.8	51.3	50.8	53.5
Share of world income going to bottom 20%	4.7	3.8	3.0	2.9	2.4	2.2	2.2
Number of people living on $1 a day or less, adjusted for inflation (%)	83.9	75.4	65.6	56.3	54.8	35.6	23.7
Number of people living on $1 a day or less, adjusted for inflation (number)	887	954	1128	1150	1376	1305	1294

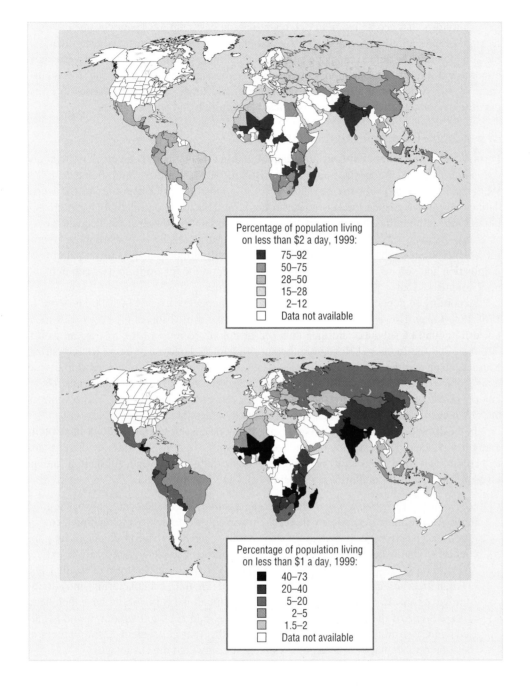

FIGURE 9.5

People Living on Less Than $2 and Less Than $1 a Day

Source: Poverty Mapping, 2005, "The Poverty Lines: Population Living with Less Than 2 Dollars and Less Than 1 Dollar a Day." Retrieved December 1, 2005 (http://www. povertymap.net/mapsgraphics/index .cfm?data_id=23417&theme).

Theories of Development and Underdevelopment

Modernization Theory: A Functionalist Approach

Two main sociological theories claim to explain global inequality. The first, **modernization theory**, is a variant of functionalism. According to modernization theory, global inequality results from various dysfunctional characteristics of poor societies themselves. Specifically, modernization theorists say the citizens of poor societies lack sufficient *capital* to invest in Western-style agriculture and industry. They lack rational, Western-style *business techniques* of marketing, accounting, sales, and finance. As a result, their productivity and profitability remain low. They lack stable, Western-style *governments* that could provide a secure framework for investment. Finally, they lack a Western *mentality*: values that stress the need for savings, investment, innovation, education, high achievement, and self-control in having children (Inkeles and Smith, 1976; Rostow, 1960). Societies characterized by these dysfunctions are

Modernization theory holds that economic underdevelopment results from poor countries lacking Western attributes. These attributes include Western values, business practices, levels of investment capital, and stable governments.

poor. It follows that people living in rich countries can best help their poor cousins by transferring Western culture and capital to them and eliminating the dysfunctions. Only then will the poor countries be able to cap population growth, stimulate democracy, and invigorate agricultural and industrial production. Government-to-government foreign aid can accomplish some of this. Much work also needs to be done to encourage Western businesses to invest directly in poor countries and to increase trade between rich and poor countries.

Dependency Theory: A Conflict Approach

Dependency theory views economic underdevelopment as the result of exploitative relations between rich and poor countries.

Proponents of **dependency theory**, a variant of conflict theory, have been quick to point out the chief flaw in modernization theory (Baran, 1957; Cardoso and Faletto, 1979; Wallerstein, 1974–89). For the past 500 years, the most powerful countries in the world deliberately impoverished the less powerful countries. Focusing on internal characteristics blames the victim rather than the perpetrator of the crime. It follows that an adequate theory of global inequality should not focus on the internal characteristics of poor countries themselves. Instead, it ought to follow the principles of conflict theory and focus on patterns of domination and submission—specifically, in this case, on the relationship between rich and poor countries. That is just what dependency theory does.

According to dependency theorists, less global inequality existed in 1500 and even in 1750 than today. However, beginning around 1500, the armed forces of the world's most powerful countries subdued and then annexed or colonized most of the rest of the world. Around 1780 the Industrial Revolution began. It enabled the Western European countries, Russia, Japan, and the United States to amass enormous wealth, which they used to extend their global reach. They forced their colonies to become a source of raw materials, cheap labour, investment opportunities, and markets for the conquering nations. The colonizers thereby prevented industrialization and locked the colonies into poverty.

In the decades following World War II, nearly all the colonies in the world became politically independent. However, the dependency theorists say that exploitation by direct political control was soon replaced by new means of achieving the same end: substantial foreign investment, support for authoritarian governments, and mounting debt.

- *Substantial foreign investment.* Many people assume that investment is always a good thing. According to dependency theorists, however, investment by multinational corporations has positive consequences for rich countries and negative consequences for poor countries. That is because investment in poor countries is typically used only to extract raw materials, create low-wage jobs, and siphon off wealth in the form of profits. The raw materials are used to create high-wage design, research, manufacturing, and administrative jobs back in the rich countries where multinational corporations have their head offices. Some of the manufactured goods are then sold back to the poor, unindustrialized countries for additional profit. Dependency theorists conclude that, for poor countries, the disadvantages of foreign investment far outweigh the advantages.
- *Support for authoritarian governments.* According to dependency theorists, multinational corporations and rich countries continued their exploitation of the poor countries in the postcolonial period by giving economic and military support to local authoritarian governments. These governments managed to keep their populations subdued most of the time. When that was not possible, Western governments sent in troops and military advisers, engaging in what became known as "gunboat diplomacy." The term itself was coined in colonial times. In 1839 the Chinese rebelled against the British importation of opium into China, and the British responded by sending a gunboat up the Yangtze River, starting the Opium War. The war resulted in Britain winning control of Hong Kong and access to five Chinese ports; what started as gunboat diplomacy ended as a rich feast for British traders. In the postcolonial period, the United States has been particularly active in using gunboat diplomacy in Central America. A classic case is Guatemala in the 1950s (LaFeber, 1993). In 1952 the democratic government of Guatemala began to redistribute land to impoverished peasants. Some of the land was owned by the United Fruit Company, a United States multinational corporation and the biggest landowner in

Guatemala. Two years later, the CIA backed a right-wing coup in Guatemala, preventing land reform and allowing the United Fruit Company to continue its highly profitable business as usual.

- *Mounting debt.* The governments of the poor countries struggled to create transportation infrastructures (airports, roads, harbours, etc.), build their education systems, and deliver safe water and at least the most basic health care to their people. To accomplish these tasks, they had to borrow money from Western banks and governments. Some rulers also squandered money on luxuries. So it came about that debt—and the interest payments that inevitably accompany debt—grew every year. By 1999 the poor countries owed the rich countries nearly 2.6 trillion dollars. That figure is 54 percent more than in 1992, allowing for inflation. At a 5 percent rate of interest, servicing that debt would cost $130 billion a year. These crushing interest payments leave governments of poor countries with too little money for development tasks. Foreign aid helps, but not much. Annual foreign aid to the world's developing countries is only about one-seventh the amount that the developing countries pay to Western banks in loan interest (United Nations, 2004a: 201).

Effects of Foreign Investment

Almost all sociologists agree that the dependency theorists are correct on one score. Since about 1500, Spain, Portugal, Holland, Britain, France, Italy, the United States, Japan, and Russia treated the world's poor with brutality to enrich themselves. They rationalized their actions by claiming they were bringing "civilization" to the "savages" and inventing other such stories, such as the notion of the Dutch colonizers in early-seventeenth-century Brazil that "there is no sin south of the equator." Colonialism did have a devastating economic and human impact on the poor countries of the world. In the postcolonial era, the debt burden has crippled the development efforts of many poor countries.

That said, a big question remains that research has not yet fully answered. Do foreign investment and liberalized trade policies have positive or negative effects today? Much hinges on the answer to this question. Modernization theorists want more foreign investment in poor countries and freer trade because they think that will promote economic growth and general well-being. They want trade and investment barriers to be dropped so free markets can bring prosperity to everyone. Dependency theorists oppose this strategy. They think foreign investment drains wealth out of poor countries. Therefore, they want the poor countries to revolt against the rich countries, throw up barriers to free trade and investment, and find their own paths to economic well-being.

Over the past couple of decades, researchers have carefully examined the effects of free trade and foreign investment. The results of their analyses depend partly on which variables they include in their analyses, which time periods they analyze, which countries they consider, and which statistical techniques they use (Bornschier and Chase-Dunn, 1985; Centre for Economic Policy Research, 2002; DeSoya and Oneal, 1999; Firebaugh and Beck, 1994; Weisbrot, Baker, Kraev, and Chen, 2001; Weisbrot and Baker, 2002). Not surprisingly, if you throw different countries, variables, time periods, and statistical techniques into the mix, you bake entirely different cakes. Yet a recent summary of research in this area cautiously reaches two conclusions (Centre for Economic Policy Research, 2002). First, in the 1980s and 1990s, but not in the 1960s and 1970s, openness to international trade and foreign investment generally seemed to have stimulated economic growth. Second, in most well-documented cases, openness to international trade and foreign investment also increased inequality. Few benefits of economic growth went to the neediest. This fact was true for China, Malaysia, Thailand, Chile, Colombia, and Mexico. Conversely, openness to international trade and foreign investment did not always increase inequality. No such increase took place in Taiwan and (with qualifications) Brazil and Indonesia.

In 1893 leaders of the British mission pose before taking over what became Rhodesia and is now Zimbabwe. To raise a volunteer army, every British trooper was offered about 23 square kilometres (9 square miles) of native land and 20 gold claims. The Matabele and Mashona peoples were subdued in a three-month war. Nine hundred farms and 10 000 gold claims were granted to the troopers and about 100 000 cattle were looted, leaving the native survivors without a livelihood. Forced labour was subsequently introduced by the British so that the natives could pay a £2 a year tax.

Note that the effect of free trade and foreign investment on highly developed countries is similarly diverse. In the 1980s and 1990s, the United States and the United Kingdom experienced increasing inequality as a result of openness, whereas Canada, France, and Germany did not. In the last two countries, government policies prevent inequality from growing.

These findings suggest that lumping all periods of history and all countries together when considering the effects of openness on economic growth and inequality is a mistake. After all, countries have different histories and different social structures. They may adopt a variety of economic policies that influence the effects of international trade and foreign direct investment in different ways. Consequently, international trade and foreign direct investment may have different effects in different times and places. Historical, social-structural, and policy factors matter greatly in determining how a particular country responds to international trade and foreign direct investment.

Core, Periphery, and Semiperiphery

Core capitalist countries are rich countries, such as the United States, Japan, and Germany, that are the major sources of capital and technology in the world.

The **peripheral capitalist countries** are former colonies that are poor and are major sources of raw materials and cheap labour.

The **semiperipheral capitalist countries**, such as South Korea, Taiwan, and Israel, consist of former colonies that are making considerable headway in their attempts to industrialize.

Immanuel Wallerstein (1974–89) proposes a variation on this theme. He argues that capitalist development has resulted in the creation of an integrated "world system" comprising three tiers. First are the **core capitalist countries** (the United States, Japan, and Germany), which are major sources of capital and technology. Second are the **peripheral capitalist countries** (the former colonies, such as Guatemala and Angola), which are major sources of raw materials and cheap labour. Third are the **semiperipheral capitalist countries** (such as South Korea, Taiwan, and Israel), consisting of former colonies that are making considerable headway in their attempts to become prosperous. To give just one dramatic illustration of this progress, South Korea and the African country of Ghana were among the poorest nations in the world in 1960. Ghana still is. But South Korea, the recipient of enormous foreign investment and aid, was nine times as wealthy as Ghana in 1997 (as measured by gross national product per capita; calculated from World Bank, 1999: 193). Comparing the unsuccessful peripheral countries with the more successful semiperipheral countries presents us with a useful natural experiment. The comparison suggests the circumstances that help some poor countries overcome the worst effects of colonialism.

The semiperipheral countries differ from the peripheral countries in four main ways (Kennedy, 1993: 193–227; Lie, 1998), which we outline below.

Type of Colonialism

Around the turn of the twentieth century, Taiwan and Korea became colonies of Japan. They remained so until 1945. However, in contrast to the European colonizers of Africa, Latin America, and other parts of Asia, the Japanese built up the economies of their colonies. They established transportation networks and communication systems. They built steel, chemical, and hydroelectric power plants. After Japanese colonialism ended, Taiwan and South Korea were thus at an advantage compared with Ghana, for example, at the time Britain gave up control of that country. South Korea and Taiwan could use the Japanese-built infrastructure and Japanese-trained personnel as springboards to development.

Geopolitical Position

Although the United States was the leading economic and military power in the world by the end of World War II, it began to feel its supremacy threatened in the late 1940s by the Soviet Union and China. Fearing that South Korea and Taiwan might fall to the communists, the United States poured unprecedented aid into both countries in the 1960s. It also gave them large, low-interest loans and opened its domestic market to Taiwanese and South Korean products. Because the United States saw Israel as a crucially important ally in the Middle East, it also received special economic assistance. Other countries with less strategic importance to the United States received less help in their drive to industrialize.

State Policy

A third factor that accounts for the relative success of some countries in their efforts to industrialize and become prosperous concerns state policies. As a legacy of colonialism, the Taiwanese and South Korean states were developed on the Japanese model. They kept workers' wages low, restricted trade union growth, and maintained quasi-military discipline in factories. Moreover, by placing high taxes on consumer goods, limiting the import of foreign goods, and preventing their citizens from investing abroad, they encouraged their citizens to put much of their money in the bank. This situation created a large pool of capital for industrial expansion. The South Korean and Taiwanese states also gave subsidies, training grants, and tariff protection to export-based industries from the 1960s onward. (Tariffs are taxes on foreign goods.) These policies did much to stimulate industrial growth. Finally, the Taiwanese and South Korean states invested heavily in basic education, health care, roads, and other public goods. A healthy and well-educated labour force combined with good transportation and communication systems laid solid foundations for economic growth.

Social Structure

Taiwan and South Korea are socially cohesive countries, which makes it easy for them to generate consensus around development policies. It also allows them to get their citizens to work hard, save a lot of money, and devote their energies to scientific education.

Social solidarity in Taiwan and South Korea is based partly on the sweeping land reform they conducted in the late 1940s and early 1950s. By redistributing land to small farmers, both countries eliminated the class of large landowners, who usually oppose industrialization. Land redistribution got rid of a major potential source of social conflict. In contrast, many countries in Latin America and Africa have not undergone land reform. The United States often intervened militarily in Latin America to prevent land reform because U.S. commercial interests profited handsomely from the existence of large plantations (LaFeber, 1993).

Seoul, capital of South Korea: South Korea is one of the semiperipheral countries that are making considerable headway in their attempts to become prosperous.

Another factor underlying social solidarity in Taiwan and South Korea is that both countries did not suffer from internal conflicts like those that wrack Africa south of the Sahara desert. British, French, and other Western European colonizers often drew the borders of African countries to keep antagonistic tribes living side by side in the same jurisdiction and often sought to foment tribal conflict. Keeping tribal tensions alive made it possible to play one tribe against another. That made it easier for imperial powers to rule. This policy led to much social and political conflict in postcolonial Africa. Today, the region suffers from frequent civil wars, coups, and uprisings. It is the most conflict-ridden area of the world. For example, the civil war in the Democratic Republic of the Congo from 1998 to 2003 resulted in millions of deaths, and renewed conflict in 2008 threatens the lives of many Congolese. This high level of internal conflict acts as a barrier to economic development in sub-Saharan Africa.

In sum, certain conditions seem to permit foreign investment to have positive economic effects. Postcolonial countries that enjoy a solid industrial infrastructure, strategic geopolitical importance, strong states with strong development policies, and socially cohesive populations are in the best position to join the ranks of the rich countries in the coming decades. We may expect countries that have *some* of these characteristics to experience some economic growth and increase in the well-being of their populations in the near future. Such countries include China, India, Chile, Thailand, Indonesia, Mexico, and Brazil. In contrast, African countries south of the Sahara are in the worst position of all. They have inherited the most damaging consequences of colonialism, and they enjoy few of the conditions that could help them escape the history that has been imposed on them.

Canada as a Semiperipheral Country

Many analysts regard Canada as a semiperipheral country that has managed to achieve prosperity despite its colonial past (Brym with Fox, 1989: 34–56; Laxer, 1989):

• The *type of colonialism* that Canada experienced is sometimes called "white settler colonialism." Like Australia, New Zealand, and the United States, Canada was settled by large numbers of Europeans who soon overwhelmed the Aboriginal population. They were determined to reproduce or improve the standard of living they enjoyed in the old country. Much of the wealth they produced was therefore reinvested locally. In contrast, when the European powers colonized Africa, they set up only small enclaves of white settlers. Their main aim was to exploit local resources and populations, sending nearly all of the wealth back to Europe.[3]

• Canada's *geopolitical position* has always been highly favourable to economic development. That is because it has served as a major supplier of raw materials and other goods to France, Great Britain, and the United States, and has fallen under the protective wing of each of these countries, all of which have viewed Canada as a staunch ally. For example, Canada played a disproportionately large role in World War II as a training ground, source of raw materials, and supplier of arms and soldiers to the Allies.

• Canada's *state policy* has sometimes acted to protect and stimulate the growth of Canadian industry, although admittedly not as consistently as the state policy of, say, South Korea. For example, the 1879 National Policy established a duty on imported manufactured goods. This sheltered the growth of Canadian industry, then in its infancy, by making foreign-made manufactured goods more expensive. Similarly, the 1965 Auto Pact required that foreign automobile companies wanting to sell cars in Canada duty-free manufacture cars in Canada and use a certain proportion of Canadian-made components. This stimulated the growth of an industry that, directly or indirectly, is now responsible for the employment of one-sixth of Ontario's labour force.

• Canada's *social structure* has arguably had fewer positive effects on economic development than is the case in such countries as South Korea and Taiwan. In Canada, the French–English conflict has drawn attention away from development policy. And although strong farmers' and workers' movements have pushed governments in other countries to attend closely to development issues, these movements have been relatively weak in Canada (Brym, 1992; Laxer, 1989). Canada is not a world centre of capital. Our manufacturing sector is proportionately smaller than those of Germany, the United States, and Japan. An unusually large percentage of our industry is foreign-owned. Still, Canada is one of the wealthiest countries in the world. Our semiperipheral status is clear.

NEOLIBERAL VERSUS DEMOCRATIC GLOBALIZATION

Globalization and Neoliberalism

For some political and economic leaders, the road sign that marks the path to prosperity reads "**neoliberal globalization**." Neoliberal globalization is a policy that promotes private control of industry; minimal government interference in the running of the economy; the removal of taxes, tariffs, and restrictive regulations that discourage the international buying and selling of goods and services; and the encouragement of foreign investment. Advocates of neoliberal globalization resemble the modernization theorists of a generation ago. They believe that if only the poor countries would emulate the successful habits of the rich countries, they would prosper as well.

Many social scientists are skeptical of this prescription. For example, Nobel Prize–winning economist and former chief economist of the World Bank Joseph E. Stiglitz (2002) argues that the World Bank and other international economic organizations often impose outdated policies on developing countries, putting them at a disadvantage in comparison with developed countries. In the African country of Mozambique, for example, foreign debt was 4.5 times the GNP in the mid-1990s. This means that the amount of money Mozambique owed to foreigners was four-and-a-half times more than the value of goods and services produced by all the people of Mozambique in a year. Facing an economic crisis, Mozambique sought relief from the World Bank and the International Monetary Fund (IMF). The response of the IMF was to argue that Mozambique's government-imposed minimum wage of less than $1 a day is "excessive." The IMF also recommended that Mozambique spend twice as much as its education budget and four times as much as its health budget on interest payments to service its foreign debt (Mittelman, 2000: 104). How such crippling policies might help the people of Mozambique is unclear.

Does historical precedent lead us to believe that neoliberalism works? To the contrary, with the exception of Great Britain, neoliberalism was *never* a successful development strategy in the early stages of industrialization. Germany, the United States, Japan, Sweden, and other rich countries became highly developed economically between the second half of the nineteenth century and the early twentieth century. South Korea, Taiwan, Singapore, and other semiperipheral countries became highly developed economically in the second half of the twentieth century. Today, China and, to a lesser degree, India are industrializing quickly. These countries did not pursue privatization, minimal government intervention in the economy, free trade, and foreign investment in the early stages of industrialization. Rather, the governments of these countries typically intervened to encourage industrialization. They protected infant industries behind tariff walls, invested public money heavily to promote national industries, and so forth. Today, China and India maintain among the highest barriers to international trade in the world (Chang, 2002; Gerschenkron, 1962; Laxer, 1989). Typically, it is only after industrial development is well under way and national industries can compete on the global market that countries begin to advocate neoliberal globalization to varying degrees. As one political economist writes, "The sensible ones liberalise in line with the growth of domestic capacities—they try to expose domestic producers to enough competition to make them more efficient, but not enough to kill them" (Wade in Wade and Wolf, 2002: 19). The exception that proves the rule is Great Britain, which needed less government involvement to industrialize because it was the first industrializer and had no international competitors. Even the United States, one of the most vocal advocates of

Neoliberal globalization **is a policy that promotes private control of industry; minimal government interference in the running of the economy; the removal of taxes, tariffs, and restrictive regulations that discourage the international buying and selling of goods and services; and the encouragement of foreign investment.**

neoliberal globalization today, invested a great deal of public money subsidizing industries and building infrastructure (roads, schools, ports, airports, electricity grids, etc.) in the late nineteenth and early twentieth centuries. It was an extremely protectionist country until the end of World War II. As late as 1930 the Smoot-Hawley Tariff Act raised tariffs on foreign goods 60 percent. Today, the United States still subsidizes large corporations in a variety of ways and maintains substantial tariffs on a whole range of foreign products, including agricultural goods, softwood lumber, and textiles. In this, the United States is little different from Japan, France, and other rich countries.

In sum, there is good reason to be skeptical about the benefits of neoliberal globalization for poor countries (Bourdieu, 1998a; Brennan, 2003). Yet, as you will now see, globalization can be reformed so that its economic and technological benefits are distributed more uniformly throughout the world.

Foreign Aid, Debt Cancellation, and Tariff Reduction

In the film *About Schmidt* (2002), Jack Nicholson plays Warren Schmidt, a former insurance executive. Retirement leaves Schmidt with little purpose in life. His wife dies. His adult daughter has little time or respect for him. He feels his existence lacks meaning. Then, while watching TV one night, Schmidt is moved to support a poor child in a developing country. He decides to send a monthly $27 cheque to sponsor a Tanzanian boy named Ndugu. He writes Ndugu long letters about his life. While Schmidt's world falls apart before our eyes, his sole meaningful human bond is with Ndugu. At the end of the movie, Schmidt cries as he looks at a picture Ndugu drew for him: an adult holding a child's hand.

WHERE DO
YOU FIT IN?

It does not take a Warren Schmidt to find meaning in helping the desperately poor. Many people contribute to charities that help developing countries in a variety of ways. Many more people contribute development aid indirectly through the taxes they pay to the federal government. Many Canadians think our contributions are generous. Do you? A 2002 survey found that while 71 percent of Canadians thought foreign aid important, only 51 percent favoured the government's announced plan of gradually increasing the total (Asia Pacific Foundation of Canada, 2002).

Was foreign aid by Canada already at a high level? The UN urges the world's 22 richest countries to contribute 0.7 percent of their GDP to development aid. (This goal was set at the urging of Canadian Prime Minister Lester Pearson in 1969.) In 2006, only 5 countries reached that goal: Sweden, Luxembourg, Norway, the Netherlands, and Denmark. Canada ranked sixteenth among the 22 rich nations at 0.29 percent. The United States ranked twenty-first at 0.18 percent, less than a fifth of Sweden's 1.02 percent. Only Greece, at 0.17 percent, performed worse than the United States (Organisation for Economic Co-operation and Development, 2007). In 2002, a World Bank official compared (1) the subsidies rich countries gave to farms and businesses within their borders with (2) the amount of development aid they gave developing countries. He concluded that "[t]he average cow [in a rich country] is supported by three times the level of income of a poor person in Africa" (quoted in Schuettler, 2002).

Since the United States is by far the world's richest country, it is the American contribution to foreign aid that potentially makes the greatest difference. But even if the United States quadrupled its foreign aid budget to meet UN guidelines, some foreign aid as presently delivered is not an effective way of helping the developing world. Foreign aid is often accompanied by high administrative and overhead costs. It is often given on condition that it is used to buy goods from donor countries that are not necessarily high-priority items for recipient countries. Food aid often has detrimental effects on poor countries. One expert writes: "As well as creating expensive [dependence on] nonindigenous cereals, and discouraging export-production of items like corn and rice in which the U.S.A. is expanding its own trade, [U.S. food aid] has frequently served as a major disincentive to the efforts of local farmers to grow food even for domestic consumption" (Hancock, 1989: 169). Some foreign aid organizations, such as Oxfam and Caritas Internationalis, waste little money on administration and overhead expenses because they are driven by high principles, pay their staffs low salaries, build partnerships with reputable local organizations, work with their partners to identify the most pressing needs of poor countries, and focus their efforts on meeting those needs (Ron, 2007). The efforts of such organizations remind us that foreign aid can be beneficial and that strict oversight is required to ensure that foreign aid is not wasted and that it is directed to truly helpful projects, such as improving irrigation and sanitation systems and helping people acquire better farming techniques. Increasing the amount of foreign aid and redesigning its delivery can thus help mitigate some of the excesses of neoliberal globalization.

So can debt cancellation. Many analysts argue that the world's rich countries and banks should simply write off the debt owed to them by the developing countries in recognition of historical injustices. They reason that the debt burden of the developing countries is so onerous that it prevents them from focusing on building up economic infrastructure, improving the health and education of their populations, and developing economic policies that can help them emerge from poverty. This proposal for blunting the worst effects of neoliberal globalization may be growing in popularity among politicians in the developed countries. For example, former Prime Minister Paul Martin, former British Prime Minister Tony Blair, and former U.S. President Bill Clinton, among others, support the idea. Former President George W. Bush and Prime Minister Stephen Harper support only limited versions of this proposal. It is widely expected that President Obama will favour it.

A third reform proposed in recent years involves the elimination or at least lowering of tariffs by the *rich* countries. Many of these tariffs prevent developing countries from exporting goods that could earn them money for investment in agriculture, industry, and infrastructure. Eliminating or lowering tariffs would require training some farmers in rich countries for new kinds of work, but it would stimulate economic growth in the developing countries. To date, however, there is little room for optimism in this regard. In 2002 a less developed country, like Mexico, gave its farmers an average subsidy of $1000 a year, while the United States gave its farmers an average subsidy of $16 000 a year. The comparable figures for Western Europe and Japan were $17 000 and $27 000, respectively. Talks to lower government subsidies to Western farmers broke down in 2003.

Democratic Globalization

The final reform we consider involves efforts to help spread democracy throughout the developing world. A large body of research shows that democracy lowers inequality and promotes economic growth (Pettersson, 2003; Sylwester, 2002; United Nations, 2002). Democracies have these effects for several reasons. They make it more difficult for elite groups to misuse their power and enhance their wealth and income at the expense of the less well-to-do. They increase political stability, thereby providing a better investment climate. Finally, because they encourage broad political participation, democracies tend to enact policies that are more responsive to people's needs and benefit a wide range of people from all social classes. For example, democratic governments are more inclined to take steps to avoid famines, protect the environment, build infrastructure, and ensure basic needs like education and health. These measures help create a population better suited to pursue economic growth.

Although democracy has spread in recent years, by 2002 only 80 countries with 55 percent of the world's population were considered fully democratic by one measure (United Nations, 2002: 2; see Chapter 14, Politics). For its part, the United States has supported as many anti-democratic as democratic regimes in the developing world. Especially between the end of World War II in 1945 and the collapse of the Soviet Union in 1991, the U.S. government gave military and financial aid to many anti-democratic regimes, often in the name of halting the spread of Soviet influence. These actions often generated unexpected and undesirable consequences, or what the Central Intelligence Agency (CIA) came to call "blowback" (Johnson, 2000). For example, in the 1980s the U.S. government supported Saddam Hussein when it considered Iraq's enemy, Iran, the greater threat to U.S. security interests. The United States also funded Osama bin Laden when he was fighting the Soviet Union in Afghanistan. Only a decade later, these so-called allies turned into the United States' worst enemies (Chomsky, 1991; Johnson, 2000; Kolko, 2002; Box 9.2).

In sum, we have outlined four reforms that could change the nature of neoliberal globalization and turn it into what we would like to call democratic globalization. These reforms include offering stronger support for democracy in the developing world, contributing more and better foreign aid, forgiving the debt owed by developing countries to the rich countries, and eliminating many of the tariffs that restrict exports from developing countries. These kinds of

---

BOX 9.2
Sociology at the Movies

Syriana (2005)

In the 1980s, the Cold War seemed to be a struggle between the "free world" led by the United States and the "evil empire" led by the Soviet Union. Back then, CIA agent Bob Barnes (George Clooney, nominated for a 2005 Oscar for best supporting actor) operated with confidence. He could tell his friends from his enemies. In the twenty-first century, he is not so sure. The high-tech CIA doesn't seem to need an experienced, multilingual agent like Barnes. And the knowledge and experience Barnes acquired during the Cold War can no longer help him figure out who the good guys and the bad guys are.

That is because there *are* no good guys in *Syriana*. The CIA orders a missile strike to eliminate an Arab prince who is pro-democracy but favours China over the United States in the competition for drilling rights. A poor Pakistani worker who loses his job when the Chinese take over the oil fields in the prince's country eventually becomes radicalized and participates in the suicide bombing of a major oil refinery. The young son of energy analyst Brian Woodman (Matt Damon) dies in a freak accident in the prince's swimming pool, and Woodman uses the accident as an opportunity to get a plum job with the prince. With the American government's knowledge, a Washington law firm finesses a legally questionable merger between two Texas oil companies.

George Clooney as CIA agent Bob Barnes in *Syriana* (2005)

The storylines that swirl through *Syriana* are so numerous and complex that it is almost impossible for the viewer to get the big picture. And that is precisely the aim of screenwriter and director Stephen Gaghan, whose work was nominated for an Oscar for best original screenplay of 2005. He wants *Syriana* to be as confusing as the real world of big oil. But he also wants to deliver a clear message: Oil corrupts everyone. As Danny D., adviser to the head of a Texas oil firm, says in the film:

Corruption? . . . We have laws about it precisely so we can get away with it. Corruption is our protection. Corruption is what keeps us safe and warm. Corruption is why you and I are here in the white-hot center of things instead of fighting each other for scraps of meat in the street. Corruption is how we win.

Gaghan also wrote the screenplay for *Traffic* (2000), a film about the war on drugs that won four Oscars, and he is on record as saying that *Syriana* is about addiction too—specifically, about the corrupting influence of the world's addiction to oil.

How are you addicted to oil? How does addiction to oil shape the Middle East policies of the United States and the West in general? What, if anything, should you do about your oil addiction and that of the West?

policies could plausibly help the developing world overcome the legacy of colonialism and join the ranks of the well-to-do. They would do much to ensure that the complex process we call globalization would benefit humanity as a whole.

NOTES

1. All dollar references are to U.S. currency unless otherwise indicated.

2. Gross national product (GNP) is the total dollar value of goods and services produced in a country in a year. It allocates goods and services based on the nationality of the owners. GDP is a similar measure, but it allocates goods and services based on the location of the owners. So, for example, goods and services produced overseas by foreign subsidiaries would be included in GNP but not in GDP.

3. From this point of view, South Africa and, to a lesser degree, Rhodesia (now Zimbabwe) represent intermediate cases between the rest of Africa on the one hand, and Canada, the United States, Australia, and New Zealand on the other.

SUMMARY

1. What is globalization and why is it taking place?
Globalization is the growing interdependence and mutual awareness of individuals and economic, political, and social institutions around the world. It is a response to many forces, some technological (e.g., the development of inexpensive means of rapid international communication), others economic (e.g., burgeoning international trade and investment), and still others political (e.g., the creation of transnational organizations that limit the sovereign powers of nation states).

2. What are the consequences of globalization?
Globalization has complex consequences, some of which are captured by the idea of "glocalization," which denotes the homogenization of some aspects of life and the simultaneous sharpening of some local differences. In addition, globalization evokes an anti-globalization reaction.

3. How long is the history of globalization?
Globalization has a long history. Its origins can be traced to the beginning of long-distance migration and trade. However, it was the beginning of European exploration and capitalism about 500 years ago that really spurred globalization.

4. What are the main trends in global inequality and poverty?
Global inequality and poverty are staggering and in some respects getting worse. The income gap between rich and poor countries and between rich and poor individuals has grown worldwide since the nineteenth century. In recent decades the number of desperately poor people has declined absolutely and in percentage terms worldwide, but it has increased in the less developed countries.

5. What are the main sociological theories of economic development?
Modernization theory argues that global inequality occurs as a result of some countries lacking sufficient capital, Western values, rational business practices, and stable governments. Dependency theory counters with the claim that global inequality results from the exploitative relationship between rich and poor countries. An important test of the two theories concerns the effect of foreign investment on economic growth, but research on this subject is equivocal. Apparently, historical, social-structural, and policy factors matter greatly in determining how a particular country responds to international trade and foreign direct investment.

6. What are the characteristics of formerly poor countries that emerged from poverty?
   The poor countries best able to emerge from poverty have a colonial past that left them with industrial infrastructures. They also enjoy a favourable geopolitical position. They implement strong, growth-oriented economic policies, and they have socially cohesive populations.

7. Can neoliberal globalization be reformed?
   Neoliberal globalization can be reformed so that the benefits of globalization are more evenly distributed throughout the world. Possible reforms include offering stronger support for democracy in the developing world, contributing more and better foreign aid, forgiving the debt owed by developing countries to the rich countries, and eliminating tariffs that restrict exports from developing countries.

KEY TERMS

colonialism (p. 257)

core capitalist countries (p. 264)

dependency theory (p. 262)

global commodity chain (p. 251)

glocalization (p. 255)

imperialism (p. 250)

McDonaldization (p. 254)

modernization theory (p. 261)

neoliberal globalization (p. 267)

peripheral capitalist countries (p. 264)

regionalization (p. 255)

semiperipheral capitalist countries (p. 264)

transnational corporations (p. 252)

QUESTIONS TO CONSIDER

1. How has globalization affected your life, family, and town? What would life be like in a place that has not been affected by globalization?

2. Think of a commodity you consume or use every day—bananas, coffee, shoes, cell phones, for example—and find out where and how it was manufactured, transported, and marketed. How does your consumption of the commodity tie you into a global commodity chain? How does your consumption of the commodity affect other people in other parts of the world in significant ways?

3. Should North Americans do anything to alleviate global poverty? Why or why not? If you think North Americans should be doing something to help end global poverty, then what should we do?

WEB RESOURCES

Companion Website for This Book

http://www.compass3e.nelson.com

Begin by clicking on the Student Resources section of the website. Next, select the chapter you are studying from the pull-down menu. From the Student Resources page you have easy access to InfoTrac® College Edition, additional Weblinks, and other resources. The website also has many useful tips to aid you in your study of sociology, including practice tests for each chapter.

InfoTrac® Search Terms

These search terms are provided to assist you in beginning to conduct research on this
topic by visiting http://www.infotrac-college.com:

dependency theory
modernization theory
globalization
world poverty

Recommended Websites

UN statisticians have created indicators of human development for every country. The
indicators for 2007–08 are available at http://hdr.undp.org/en/statistics.

Naomi Klein's *No Logo: Taking Aim at the Brand Bullies* (New York: HarperCollins,
2000) has been called the manifesto of the anti-globalization movement. For updates, visit
http://www.naomiklein.org/no-logo.

The World Bank has numerous reports and data on the state of the global economy as well
as on different nations at http://www.worldbank.org.

CengageNOW™

http://hed.nelson.com

This online diagnostic tool identifies each student's unique needs with a Pretest that
generates a personalized Study Plan for each chapter, helping students focus on concepts
they're having the most difficulty mastering. Students then take a Posttest after reading
the chapter to measure their understanding of the material. An Instructor Gradebook is
available to track and monitor student progress.

10

Race and Ethnicity

In this chapter, you will learn that

- Race and ethnicity are socially constructed labels or categories. We use them to distinguish people based on perceived physical or cultural differences, with profound consequences for their lives.

- Racial and ethnic labels and identities change over time and place. Relations among racial and ethnic groups help to shape these labels and identities.

- In Canada, some ethnic racial groups are blending over time. However, this tendency is weaker among members of highly disadvantaged groups, especially Aboriginal peoples and recent immigrants who are members of visible minority groups.

- Identifying with a racial or an ethnic group can be economically, politically, and emotionally advantageous for some people.

- Racial and ethnic inequality is likely to persist in Canada.

DEFINING RACE AND ETHNICITY

The Great Brain Robbery

About 150 years ago, Dr. Samuel George Morton of Philadelphia was the most distinguished scientist in North America. When he died in 1851, the *New York Tribune* wrote that "probably no scientific man in America enjoyed a higher reputation among scholars throughout the world, than Dr. Morton" (quoted in Gould, 1996: 81).

Among other things, Morton collected and measured human skulls. The skulls came from various times and places. Their original occupants were members of different races. Morton believed he could show that the bigger your brain, the smarter you were. To prove his point he packed BB-sized shot into a skull until it was full. Next he poured the shot from the skull into a graduated cylinder. He then recorded the volume of shot in the cylinder. Finally, he noted the race of the person from whom each skull came. This, he thought, allowed him to draw conclusions about the average brain size of different races.

As he expected, Morton found that the races ranking highest in the social hierarchy had the biggest brains, while those ranking lowest had the smallest brains. He claimed that the people with the biggest brains were whites of European origin. Next were Asians. Then came Native North Americans. The people at the bottom of the social hierarchy—and those with the smallest brains—were blacks.

Morton's research had profound sociological implications, for he claimed to show that the system of social inequality in North America and throughout the world had natural, biological roots. If, on average, members of some racial groups are rich and others poor, some highly educated and others illiterate, some powerful and others powerless, that was, said Morton, due to differences in brain size and mental capacity. Moreover, because he used science to show that Native North Americans and blacks *naturally* rested at the bottom of the social hierarchy, his ideas were used to justify two of the most oppressive forms of domination and injustice: colonization and slavery.

Despite claims of scientific objectivity, not a shred of evidence supported Morton's ideas. For example, in one of his three main studies, Morton measured the capacity of skulls robbed from Egyptian tombs. He found that the average volume of black people's skulls was 65.5 millilitres (4 cubic inches) smaller than the average volume of white people's skulls. This fact seemed to prove his case. Today, however, we know that three main issues compromise his findings:

1. Morton claimed to be able to distinguish the skulls of white and black people by the shapes of the skulls. However, even today archaeologists cannot precisely determine race by skull shape. As a result, it is unclear whether the skulls Morton identified as "Caucasian" belonged to white people and those he identified as "Negroid" or "Negro" belonged to black people.

2. Morton's skulls formed a small, unrepresentative sample. Morton based his conclusions on only 72 specimens—a very small number on which to base any generalization. Moreover, those 72 skulls are not representative of the skulls of white and black people in ancient Egypt or any other time and place. They were just the 72 skulls that Morton happened to have access to. For all we know, they were highly unusual.

3. Even if we ignore these first two problems, 71 percent of the skulls Morton identified as "Negroid" or "Negro" were women's, compared with only 48 percent of the skulls he identified as "Caucasian." Yet women's bodies are on average smaller than men's

bodies. To make a fair comparison, Morton would have had to ensure that the sex composition of the white and black skulls was identical. He did not. Instead, he biased his findings in favour of finding larger white skulls. When we compare Morton's black and white female skulls, the white skulls are only 32 millilitres (2 cubic inches) bigger. When we compare his black and white male skulls, the white skulls are 16 millilitres (1 cubic inch) *smaller* (Gould, 1996: 84, 91, 92).

Scientifically speaking, Morton's findings are meaningless. Yet they were influential for a long time. Some people still believe them. For example, in 1963 the author of an article about race in the *Encyclopedia Britannica,* the world's most authoritative general reference source, wrote that blacks have "a rather small brain in relation to their size" (Buxton, 1963: 864A). That claim was repeated in a controversial book written by a Canadian psychologist in the mid-1990s (Rushton, 1995). Yet there is no more evidence today than there was in 1850 that whites have bigger brains than blacks do.[1]

Race, Biology, and Society

Biological arguments about racial differences have grown more sophisticated over time. However, the scientific basis of these arguments is just as shaky now as it always was.

In medieval Europe, some aristocrats saw blue veins underneath their pale skin but could not see blue veins underneath the peasants' suntanned skin. They concluded that the two groups must be racially distinct. The aristocrats called themselves "blue bloods." They ignored the fact that the colour of blood from an aristocrat's wound was just as red as the blood from a peasant's wound.

About 80 years ago, some scholars expressed the belief that racial differences in average IQ scores were genetically based. Typically, in 1927, Canadian professor Peter Sandiford argued that Canada must institute selective immigration to ensure that only the best and the brightest arrived on our shores and that we kept out "misfits" and "defectives." He encouraged the recruitment of people of British, German, and Danish stock, and discouraged the recruitment of Polish people, Italians, and Greeks. Sandiford provided IQ test results supporting his selective immigration policy. He argued that his data showed the mental superiority of Northern Europeans compared with Eastern and Southern Europeans. However, his testing results also provided what he regarded as "profoundly disturbing" evidence. People of Japanese and Chinese ancestry had the highest intelligence scores—something he had not predicted. He dismissed this finding by asserting that a few clever Asians had apparently entered Canada. They were exceptions, he wrote, and should not detract from the "need" to keep Asians out of Canada too (McLaren, 1990).

In the nineteenth century, brain size was falsely held to be one of the main indicators of intellectual capacity. Average brain size was incorrectly said to vary by race. Researchers who were eager to prove the existence of such correlations are now widely regarded as practitioners of a racist quasi-science.

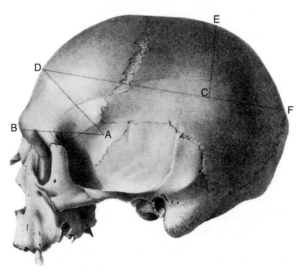

Similarly, in the United States, Jews scored below non-Jews on IQ tests in the 1920s. This was used as an argument against Jewish immigration. More recently, African Americans have on average scored below Euro-Americans on IQ tests. Some people say this justifies slashing budgets for schools in the inner city, where many African Americans live. Why invest good money in inner-city schooling, such people ask, if low IQ scores are rooted in biology and therefore fixed (Herrnstein and Murray, 1994)? However, the people who argued against Jewish immigration and better education for inner-city African Americans ignored two facts. First, Jewish IQ scores rose as Jews moved up the class hierarchy and could afford better education. Second, enriched educational facilities have routinely boosted the IQ scores of inner-city African-American children (Campbell and Ramey, 1994; Frank Porter Graham Child Development Center, 1999; Hancock, 1994; Steinberg, 1989). Much evidence shows that the social setting in which a person is raised and educated has a big impact on IQ. The claim that racial differences in IQ scores are biologically based is about as strong as evidence that aristocrats have blue blood (Cancio, Evans, and Maume, 1996; Fischer, Hout, Jankowski, Lucas, Swidler, and Voss, 1996; see Chapter 17, Education).[2]

If we cannot reasonably maintain that racial differences in average IQ scores are based in biology, what about differences in athletic prowess or other abilities? For example, some people insist that, for genetic reasons, black people are better than whites at singing and sports, and are more prone to crime. Is there any evidence to support these beliefs?

At first glance, the supporting evidence might seem strong. Consider sports. Aren't 65 percent of NBA players and 67 percent of NFL players black? Don't blacks of West African descent hold the 200 fastest 100-metre-dash times, all under 10 seconds? Don't North and East Africans regularly win 40 percent of the top international distance-running honours yet represent only a fraction of 1 percent of the world's population (Entine, 2000)? Although these facts are undeniable, the argument for the genetic basis of black athletic superiority begins to falter once we consider two additional points. First, no gene linked to general athletic superiority has yet been identified. Second, athletes of African descent do not perform unusually well in many sports, such as swimming, hockey, cycling, tennis, gymnastics, and soccer. The idea that people of African descent are in general superior athletes is simply untrue.

Sociologists have identified certain *social* conditions that lead to high levels of participation in sports (as well as entertainment and crime). These operate on all groups of people, whatever their race. Specifically, people who face widespread prejudice and discrimination often enter sports, entertainment, and crime in disproportionately large numbers for lack of other ways to improve their social and economic position. For these people, other avenues of upward mobility tend to be blocked. **Prejudice** is an attitude that judges a person on his or her group's real or imagined characteristics. **Discrimination** is unfair treatment of people because of their group membership (see Box 10.1 on page 278). For example, it was not until the 1950s that prejudice and discrimination against North American Jews began to decline appreciably. Until then, Jews played a prominent role in some professional sports. Thus, when the New York Knicks played their first game on November 1, 1946, beating the Toronto Huskies 68–66, the starting lineup for New York consisted of Ossie Schechtman, Stan Stutz, Jake Weber, Ralph Kaplowitz, and Leo "Ace" Gottlieb—an all-Jewish squad (National Basketball Association, 2000). Similarly, Koreans in Japan today are subject to much prejudice and discrimination. They often pursue careers in sports and entertainment. In contrast, Koreans in Canada face less prejudice and discrimination. Few of them become athletes and entertainers. Instead, they are often said to excel in engineering and science. As these examples suggest, then, social circumstances have a big impact on athletic and other forms of behaviour.

The idea that people of African descent are genetically superior to whites in athletic ability is the complement of the idea that they are genetically inferior to whites in intellectual ability. Both ideas reinforce black–white inequality.[3] For although there are just a few thousand professional athletes in North America, there are millions of pharmacists, graphic designers, lawyers, systems analysts, police officers, nurses, and people in other interesting occupations that offer steady employment and good pay. By promoting only the Jarome Iginlas and Donovan Baileys of the world as suitable role models for youth, the idea of "natural" black athletic superiority and intellectual inferiority in effect asks blacks to bet on a high-risk proposition—that they will make it in professional sports. At the same time, it deflects attention from a much safer bet—that they can achieve upward mobility through academic excellence (Doberman, 1997; Guppy and Davies, 1998).

An additional problem undermines the argument that genes determine the behaviour of racial groups. It is impossible to neatly distinguish races based on genetic differences.

Prejudice is an attitude that judges a person on his or her group's real or imagined characteristics.

Discrimination is unfair treatment of people because of their group membership.

BOX 10.1
Sociology at the Movies

TAKE   ROLL

Crash (2005)

Winner of three Oscars in 2005, including best picture, *Crash* is a story about Los Angelenos colliding into one another because of their racist assumptions and then, in some cases, learning that people who differ from them are as human as they are.

The movie mirrors the ethnic and racial complexities of Los Angeles by presenting many intersecting plot lines. Neighbours think an Iranian-American shopkeeper (Shaun Toub) is an Arab so they apparently feel little remorse when they loot his store. The shopkeeper thinks a Chicano locksmith (Michael Peña) is a gang member who will bring his homies in to rob him blind once he finishes the repair job. The locksmith is in fact a hardworking family man and an exemplary father. A black police officer (Don Cheadle) has an affair with his Latina partner (Jennifer Esposito) but keeps on insulting her by not remembering what country she was born in and stopping just one step short of saying "You people all look the same to me." Ryan, a white police officer (played by Matt Dillon, who was nominated

Christine (Thandie Newton; left) and Office John Ryan (Matt Dillon) in *Crash*

for an Oscar for best supporting actor), arbitrarily stops what he at first thinks is a white woman and a black man in an expensive car. He conducts a humiliating, overly thorough body search of the woman (who, he discovers, is actually a light-skinned African American) while her enraged husband looks on, unable to do anything because the police officer makes it clear what would happen if he tried. Later, we learn that Ryan is a compassionate man who is angry about his inability to help his dying father. Perversely, he expresses anger over his impotence by insulting blacks and making them feel power-

less. Yet he partly redeems himself when he risks his life to rescue a woman from a horrible car accident—realizing part way through the rescue that the victim is the same black woman he had earlier body-searched.

Some critics have complained that *Crash* exaggerates the extent of racism in the United States. After all, we don't often hear explicit racist comments in public. It seems to us, however, that these critics miss the point of the movie. The apparent intention of *Crash*—and in this it succeeds admirably—is to strip away all political correctness and tell us what people are thinking to themselves or saying to members of their own ethnic or racial group about members of other groups. In that sense it may be more realistic than what we hear in public. At the same time, *Crash* offers a measure of hope that things can be better. Ryan risks his life to save the woman even after realizing that she is black. He helps us appreciate that underlying our prejudices lies a deeper humanity.

Relatively consistent differences are observed only when people from distant locales, such as Norway versus Eastern Asia, are compared. Within continental landmasses, genetic contrasts are negligible for adjacent populations because migration and conquest bring about genetic mixing. Such mixing prevails whenever supposedly distinct groups have been in contact for more than a few generations. In North America, for instance, it was not uncommon for white male slave owners to rape black female slaves, who then gave birth to children of mixed race. Many Europeans had children with Aboriginal peoples in the eighteenth and nineteenth centuries. This fact undermines attempts to sort populations into distinct racial types. Many of today's supposed racial schemas, including the well-known "colour-code" contrasting red, yellow, brown, and white, are contrasts that derive from European seafarers' early encounters with groups then unfamiliar to them.

We know from the census that ethnic and racial intermarriage has been increasing in Canada at least since 1871. In the 2006 census, more than 41 percent of Canadians reported multiple ethnic or racial identities (Statistics Canada, 2008d). Usually, people who report multiple ethnic or racial identities have parents of different ethnic or racial origins

(Kalbach and Kalbach, 1998). A growing number of North Americans are similar to Tiger Woods. Woods claims he is of "Cablinasian" ancestry—part <u>Ca</u>ucasian, part <u>bl</u>ack, part Native American <u>In</u>dian, and part <u>Asian</u>. As these examples illustrate, the difference among *black, white, Asian,* and so forth, is often anything but clear-cut. In fact, some respected scholars believe we all belong to one human race, which originated in Africa (Cavalli-Sforza, Menozzi, and Piazza, 1994).

In modern times, humanity has experienced so much intermixing that race as a biological category has lost nearly all meaning. Some biologists and social scientists therefore suggest we drop the term "race" from the vocabulary of science. Most sociologists, however, continue to use the term "race." They do so because *perceptions* of race continue to affect the lives of most people profoundly. Everything from your wealth to your health is influenced by whether others see you as black, white, brown, or something else. Race as a *sociological* concept is thus an invaluable analytical tool. It refers to the existence of classification schemes that are widely understood and widely taken to be relevant. It is invaluable, however, only to the degree that people who use the term remember that it refers to *social significance* that is widely attached to physical differences (e.g., skin colour) rather than to biological differences that shape behaviour patterns.

Said differently, perceptions of racial difference are socially constructed and often arbitrary. The Irish and the Jews were regarded as "blacks" by some people a hundred years ago, and today some northern Italians still think of southern Italians from Sicily and Calabria as "blacks" (Gilman, 1991; Ignatiev, 1995; Roediger, 1991). During World War II, some people made arbitrary physical distinctions between Chinese allies and Japanese enemies that helped justify the Canadian policy of placing Japanese Canadians in internment camps. These examples show that racial distinctions are social constructs, not biological givens.

Finally, then, we can define **race** as a social construct used to distinguish people in terms of one or more physical markers. However, this definition raises an interesting question. If race is merely a social construct and not a useful biological term, why are perceptions of physical difference used to distinguish groups of people in the first place? Why, in other words, does race matter? Most sociologists believe that race matters because it allows social inequality to be created and perpetuated. The English who colonized Ireland, the Americans who went to Africa looking for slaves, and the Germans who used the Jews as a scapegoat to explain their deep economic and political troubles after World War I, all created systems of racial domination. (A **scapegoat** is a disadvantaged person or category of people that others blame for their own problems.) Once colonialism, slavery, and concentration camps were established, behavioural differences developed between subordinates and superordinates. For example, North American slaves and Jewish concentration camp inmates, with little motivating them to work hard except the ultimate threat of the master's whip, tended to do only the minimum work necessary to survive. Their masters noticed this tendency and characterized their subordinates as inherently slow and unreliable workers (Collins, 1982: 66–9). In this way, racial stereotypes are born. The stereotypes then embed themselves in literature, popular lore, journalism, and political debate, which reinforces racial inequalities (see Figure 10.1 on page 280). We thus see that race matters to the degree that it helps create and maintain systems of social inequality.

Athletic heroes, such as Donovan Bailey, are often held up as role models for black youth even though the chance of making it as an athlete is much less than the chance of getting a postsecondary education and succeeding as a professional. Racial stereotypes about black athletic prowess and intellectual inferiority are often reinforced through the idolization of sporting heroes.

Race is a social construct used to distinguish people in terms of one or more physical markers, usually with profound effects on their lives.

A scapegoat is a disadvantaged person or category of people that others blame for their own problems.

Ethnicity, Culture, and Social Structure

Race is to biology as ethnicity is to culture. A race is a socially defined category of people whose perceived *physical* markers are deemed significant. An **ethnic group** comprises people whose perceived *cultural* markers are deemed significant. Ethnic groups differ from one another in terms of language, religion, customs, values, ancestors,

FIGURE 10.1

The Vicious Circle of Racism

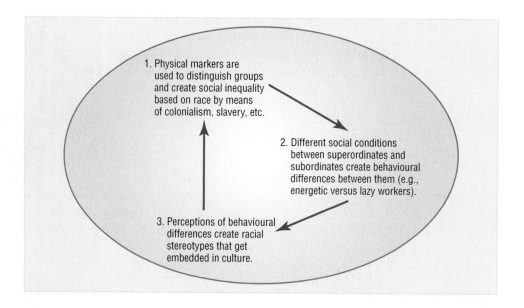

1. Physical markers are used to distinguish groups and create social inequality based on race by means of colonialism, slavery, etc.

2. Different social conditions between superordinates and subordinates create behavioural differences between them (e.g., energetic versus lazy workers).

3. Perceptions of behavioural differences create racial stereotypes that get embedded in culture.

An ethnic group comprises people whose perceived cultural markers are deemed socially significant. Ethnic groups differ from one another in terms of language, religion, customs, values, ancestors, and the like.

and the like. However, just as physical distinctions don't *cause* differences in the behaviour of various races, so cultural distinctions are often not by themselves the major source of differences in the behaviour of various ethnic groups. In other words, ethnic values and other elements of ethnic culture have less of an effect on the way people behave than we commonly believe. That is because *social structural* differences frequently underlie cultural differences.

An example will help drive home the point. People often praise Jews, Koreans, and other economically successful groups for their cultural values, including an emphasis on education, family, and hard work. People less commonly notice, however, that Canadian immigration policy has been highly selective. For the most part, the Jews and Koreans who arrived in Canada were literate, urbanized, and skilled. Some even came with financial assets (Brym, Shaffir, and Weinfeld, 1993; Li, 1995; Wong and Ng, 1998). They certainly confronted prejudice and discrimination but far less than that reserved for blacks and members of Canada's Aboriginal peoples. These *social-structural* conditions facilitated Jewish and Korean success. They gave members of these groups a firm basis on which to build and maintain a culture emphasizing education, family, and other middle-class virtues. In contrast, in the first decades of the twentieth century, black descendants of slaves and members of Canada's Aboriginal peoples were typically illiterate and unskilled, and they experienced more prejudice and discrimination than other ethnic or racial groups in Canada. These social-structural disadvantages—not their culture—made them less economically successful than Jews and Koreans on average.

In general, much Canadian research supports the argument that culture, in and of itself, is unimportant in determining the economic success of racial or ethnic groups. There *are* substantial differences in average annual income between some racial groups. For example, the average annual income of Aboriginal peoples is substantially below that of white Canadians. So is the average annual income of non-white immigrants. The point, however, is that these differences are due largely to such factors as how many years of education the average Aboriginal Canadian has and how many years the non-white immigrant has been in the country. There are practically no income differences between white Canadians and the Canadian-born children of non-white immigrants. A professor of law who happens to be an Aboriginal Canadian earns as much as a professor of law who happens to be white. The problem is that there are so few Aboriginal professors of law. Note, however, that the annual income of some categories of non-white immigrants, such as black men, remains below average even into the second generation because of persistent discrimination. We discuss this issue below.

Ethnic and Racial Stratification in Canada

As we saw in our brief comparison of Koreans and Jews with Aboriginal peoples, what matters in determining the economic success of an ethnic or racial group are the *resources* people possess, such as education, literacy, urbanity, and financial assets. We may now add that what also matters in determining economic success are the kinds of economic *opportunities* open to people. The latter point can be seen clearly if we compare Canada in the mid-twentieth century with Canada today.

In the middle of the twentieth century, Canada was a society sharply stratified along ethnic and racial lines. The people with the most power and privilege were of British origin. WASPs (white Anglo-Saxon Protestants) in particular controlled almost all the big corporations in the country and dominated politics. Immigrants who arrived later enjoyed less power and privilege. Even among them, big economic differences were evident, with European immigrants enjoying higher status than immigrants of Asian ancestry, for example.

John Porter, one of the founders of modern Canadian sociology, called mid-twentieth-century Canada an ethnically and racially stratified "vertical mosaic." He thought the retention of ethnic and racial culture was a big problem in Canada because it hampered the upward mobility of immigrants. In his view, the "Canadian value system" encouraged the retention of ethnic culture, making Canada a low-mobility society (Porter, 1965, 1979: 91).

By the 1970s, however, many Canadian sociologists, including Porter himself, had to qualify their view that ethnic and racial culture determines economic success or failure. Events upset their earlier assumptions. The Canadian economy grew quickly in the decades after World War II. Many members of ethnic and racial minority groups were economically successful despite ethnic and racial prejudice and discrimination. Economic differences among ethnic groups and, to a lesser degree, among racial groups diminished. Ethnic and racial diversity increased among the wealthy, politicians at all levels of government, and professional groups. Visible minority status, whether Asian, Caribbean, or Hispanic, had little bearing on educational, occupational, and income attainment in Canada, at least among the Canadian-born (Boyd, Goyder, Jones, McRoberts, Pineo, and Porter, 1985; Brym with Fox, 1989: 103–13; Guppy and Davies, 1998; Lian and Matthews, 1998; Nakhaie, 1997; Ogmundson and McLaughlin, 1992; Pendakur and Pendakur, 1998; Pineo and Porter, 1985; Reitz and Breton, 1994). The children of visible minority immigrants considered as a whole actually had above-average success in obtaining education (Boyd, 2002; see Table 10.1). Apparently, then, for the great majority of Canadians after World War II, ethnic and racial culture mattered less than the structure of mobility opportunities in determining economic success.

Beginning in the 1990s, recent immigrants who were members of visible minority groups were less successful economically than one would expect given their educational

TABLE 10.1

Percentage with Below-Average Canadian Income by Ethnic Identity and Place of Birth, Canada, 2001

Note: Data are for a random sample of 31 100 Canadian residents who gave a single ethnic origin in the 2001 census. Average individual annual income was $27 141. The income data were truncated at $200 000.

Source: Adapted from Statistics Canada, 2001 Census, Public-Use Microdata File, using http://dc1 .chass.utoronto.ca.myaccess.library .utoronto.ca/census/mainmicro.html (distributor). Computations and interpretation by Robert Brym.

	Born Abroad	Born in Canada
British	53	51
French	51	52
Other European	59	45
African	65	20
Arab	67	35
Other Asian	64	27
Caribbean	67	20
Other Latin, Central, and South American	55	34
Aboriginal	77	54
Canadian	62	50

and other resources (Kazemipur and Halli, 2001; Li, 2000). However, cultural values had little to do with this tendency. Canada experienced an unusually high rate of unemployment in the 1990s, hovering near 10 percent until late in the decade. This level of employment made it more difficult than in previous decades for recently arrived immigrants from visible minority groups to succeed economically, especially those who faced discrimination in the job market. In the early years of the twenty-first century, sociologists began focusing attention on how government policy could be restructured to better use the skills that immigrants from visible minority groups could bring to Canada (Reitz, 2007). This policy shift reinforces the idea that, in addition to the resources a person possesses, the structure of opportunities for economic advancement determines annual income and occupational and educational attainment. Ethnic or racial culture has little to do with it.

Canadian–American Differences

Immigrants face barriers to upward mobility, some more than others. In general, however, as one generation succeeds another, offspring diffuse more widely across the class structure. Sociologists have asked whether this pattern reflects Canada's official policy of **multiculturalism**, which emphasizes tolerance of ethnic and racial differences. Canada's multicultural policy is often seen as distinct from the United States' **melting pot** ideology, which values the disappearance of ethnic and racial difference.

Reitz and Breton (1994) reviewed a large body of evidence comparing the experience of immigrants in the two countries. They found that differences were usually minor and often contradicted claims about how Canada and the United States differ. For example, surveys show that Canadians are somewhat less likely than Americans to favour the retention of distinct immigrant cultures but somewhat more likely to accept people of different ethnicity as neighbours or co-workers. Canadians and Americans in roughly equal proportions disdain certain ethnic and racial groups in certain social settings. In both Canada and the United States, fluency in non-official languages falls rapidly with succeeding generations in the receiving country. In both countries, ethnic intermarriage rates are high. In both countries, foreign-born and first-generation immigrants remain relatively separated from the majority group and often face significant barriers to upward mobility, but their offspring face greatly diminished barriers. Thus, differences in ideology and official policy between the two countries appear to have little effect on creating different patterns in the retention of immigrant culture. In both countries, substantial cultural blending takes place between immigrants and natives within one or two generations after immigrants arrive.

In sum, we see that racial and ethnic inequality is more deeply rooted in social structure than in biology and culture. The biological and cultural aspects of race and ethnicity are secondary to their sociological character when it comes to explaining inequality. Moreover, the distinction between race and ethnicity is not as simple as the difference between biology and culture. As noted above for the Irish and the Jews, groups once socially defined as races may be later redefined as ethnicities, even though they do not change biologically. Social definitions, not biology and not culture, determine whether a group is viewed as a race or an ethnic group. The interesting question from a sociological point of view is why social definitions of race and ethnicity change. We now consider that issue.

RACE AND ETHNIC RELATIONS

Labels, Identity, and Symbolic Interaction

John Lie moved with his family from South Korea to Japan when he was a baby. He moved from Japan to Hawaii when he was 10 years old, and again from Hawaii to the American

Canada's multiculturalism policy emphasizes tolerance of ethnic and racial differences.

The melting pot ideology of the United States values the disappearance of ethnic and racial differences.

PERSONAL
ANECDOTE

mainland when he started university. The move to Hawaii and the move to the U.S. mainland changed the way John thought of himself in ethnic terms.

In Japan, Koreans form a minority group. Before 1945, when Korea was a colony of Japan, some Koreans were brought to Japan to work as miners and unskilled labourers. The Japanese thought the Koreans who lived there were beneath and outside Japanese society (Lie, 2001). Not surprisingly, then, Korean children in Japan, including John, were often teased and occasionally beaten by their Japanese schoolmates. "The beatings hurt," says John, "but the psychological trauma resulting from being socially excluded by my class-mates hurt more. In fact, although I initially thought I was Japanese like my classmates, my Korean identity was literally beaten into me.

"When my family immigrated to Hawaii, I was sure things would get worse. I expected Americans to be even meaner than the Japanese were. (By Americans, I thought only of white European-Americans.) Was I surprised when I discovered that most of my schoolmates were not white European-Americans, but people of Asian and mixed ancestry! Suddenly I was a member of a numerical majority. I was no longer teased or bullied. In fact, I found that students of Asian and non-European origin often singled out white European-Americans (called *haole* in Hawaiian) for abuse. We even had a 'beat up *haole* day' in school. Given my own experiences in Japan, I empathized somewhat with the white Americans. But I have to admit that I also felt a great sense of relief and an easing of the psychological trauma associated with being Korean in Japan.

"As the years passed, I finished public school in Hawaii. I then went to college in Massachusetts and got a job as a professor in Illinois. I associated with, and befriended, people from various racial and ethnic groups. My Korean origin became a less and less important factor in the way people treated me. There was simply less prejudice and discrim-ination against Koreans during my adulthood in the United States than in my early years in Japan. I now think of myself less as Japanese or Korean than as American. When I lived in Illinois, I sometimes thought of myself as a Midwesterner. Now that I have changed jobs and moved to California, my self-conception may shift again; my identity as an Asian American may strengthen given the large number of Asians who live in California. Clearly, my ethnic identity has changed over time in response to the significance others have attached to my Korean origin. I now understand what the French philosopher Jean-Paul Sartre meant when he wrote that "the anti-Semite creates the Jew" (Sartre, 1965 [1948]: 43).

The details of John Lie's life are unique. But experiencing a shift in racial or ethnic identity is common. Social contexts, and in particular the nature of the relations with members of other racial and ethnic groups, shape and continuously reshape a person's racial and ethnic identity. Change your social context and your racial and ethnic self-conception eventually changes too (Miles, 1989; Omi and Winant, 1986).

Consider Italian Canadians. Around 1900, Italian immigrants thought of themselves as people who came from a particular town or perhaps a particular province, such as Sicily or Calabria. They did not usually think of themselves as Italians. Italy had become a unified country only in 1861. A mere 40 years later, many Italian citizens still did not identify with their new Italian nationality. In both Canada and the United States, however, government officials and other residents identified the newcomers as Italians. The designation at first seemed odd to many of the new immigrants. Over time, however, it stuck. Immigrants from Italy started thinking of themselves as Italian Canadians because others defined them that way. A new ethnic identity was born (Yancey, Ericksen, and Leon, 1979).

As symbolic interactionists emphasize, the development of racial and ethnic labels, and ethnic and racial identities, is typically a process of negotiation. For example, members of a group may have a racial or an ethnic identity, but outsiders may impose a new label on them. Group members then reject, accept, or modify the label. The negotiation between outsiders and insiders eventually results in the crystallization of a new, more or less stable ethnic identity. If the social context changes again, the negotiation process begins anew.

One such case involves the labelling of the indigenous peoples of North America by European settlers. When Christopher Columbus landed in North America in 1492, he assumed he had reached India. He called the indigenous peoples *Indians* and the misnomer stuck—not only among European settlers but also among many indigenous peoples themselves. Indigenous peoples still identified themselves in tribal terms—as Mi'kmaq or Mohawk or Haida—but they typically thought of themselves collectively and *in opposition to European settlers* as Indians. A new identity was thus grafted onto tribal identities because indigenous peoples confronted a group that had the power to impose a name on them.

In time, however, an increasingly large number of indigenous people began to reject the term *Indian*. White settlers and their governments took land from the indigenous peoples and forced them onto reserves, causing resentment, anger, and solidarity to grow. Especially since the 1960s, indigenous North Americans have begun to fight back culturally and politically, asserting pride in their languages, art, and customs, and making legal claims to the land that had been taken from them. One aspect of their resistance involved questioning the use of the term *Indian*. In Canada, many of them preferred instead to be called Native Canadians, Indigenous Peoples, Aboriginal Canadians, or First Nations. These new terms, especially the last one, were all assertions of new-found pride. Today, many North Americans of European origin accept these new terms out of respect for indigenous North Americans and in recognition of their neglected rights. New, more or less stable ethnic identities have thus been negotiated as the power struggle between indigenous peoples and more recent settlers continues. As the social context changed, the negotiation of ethnic identities proceeded apace.

Ethnic and Racial Labels: Imposition versus Choice

The idea that race and ethnicity are socially constructed does not mean that everyone can always choose their racial or ethnic identity freely. There are wide variations over time and from one society to the next in the degree to which people can exercise such freedom of choice. Moreover, in a given society at a given time, different categories of people are more or less free to choose. To illustrate these variations, we next discuss the way in which the government of the former Soviet Union imposed ethnicity on the citizens of that country. We then contrast imposed ethnicity in the former Soviet Union with the relative freedom of ethnic choice in Canada. In the Canadian case, we also underline the social forces that make it easier to choose ethnicity than race.

State Imposition of Ethnicity in the Soviet Union

Until it formally dissolved in 1991, the Soviet Union was the biggest and one of the most powerful countries in the world (see Chapter 13, Work and the Economy, and Chapter 14, Politics). Stretching over 2 continents and 11 time zones, it comprised 15 republics—Russia, Ukraine, Kazakhstan, and so forth—with a combined population larger than that of the United States. In each republic, the largest ethnic group was the so-called titular ethnic group of that republic: Russians in Russia, Ukrainians in Ukraine, Kazakhs in Kazakhstan, and so forth.[4] More than 100 minority ethnic groups also lived in the republics. As Figure 10.2 shows, in some republics the combined number of minority ethnic group members was greater than that of the titular ethnic group.

The vast size and ethnic heterogeneity of the Soviet Union required that its leaders develop strategies to prevent the country from falling apart at the seams. One such strategy involved weakening the boundaries between the republics so "a new historical community, the Soviet people" could come into existence (Bromley, 1982 [1977]: 270). The creation of a countrywide educational system and curriculum, the spread of the Russian language, and the establishment of propaganda campaigns trumpeting remarkable national achievements helped create a sense of unity among many Soviet citizens.

A second strategy promoting national unity involved the creation of a system that allowed power and privilege to be shared among ethnic groups. This was accomplished administratively through the "internal passport" system. Beginning in the 1930s, Soviet governments issued identity papers or internal passports to all citizens at the age of 16. The fifth entry in each passport noted the bearer's ethnicity. Adolescents were obliged to adopt the ethnicity of their parents. Only if the parents were of different ethnic backgrounds could a 16-year-old choose the ethnicity of the mother or the father.

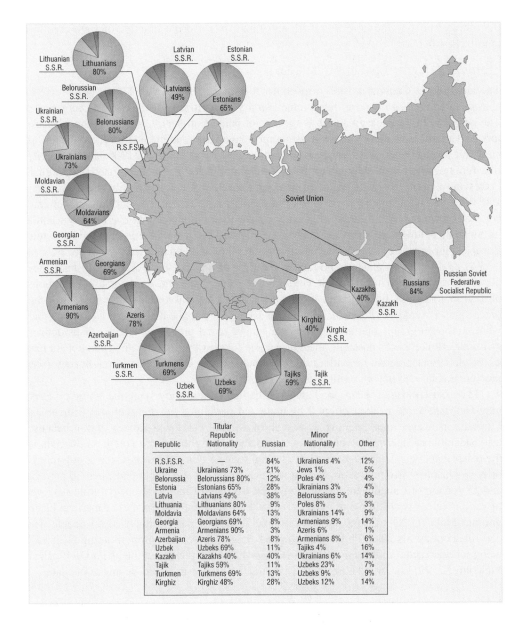

FIGURE 10.2

Ethnic Groups in the Soviet Union by Republic, 1979

Source: Perry-Castañeda Library Map Collection, 2000.

Republic	Titular Republic Nationality	Russian	Minor Nationality	Other
R.S.F.S.R.	—	84%	Ukrainians 4%	12%
Ukraine	Ukrainians 73%	21%	Jews 1%	5%
Belorussia	Belorussians 80%	12%	Poles 4%	4%
Estonia	Estonians 65%	28%	Ukrainians 3%	4%
Latvia	Latvians 49%	38%	Belorussians 5%	8%
Lithuania	Lithuanians 80%	9%	Poles 8%	3%
Moldavia	Moldavians 64%	13%	Ukrainians 14%	9%
Georgia	Georgians 69%	8%	Armenians 9%	14%
Armenia	Armenians 90%	3%	Azeris 6%	1%
Azerbaijan	Azeris 78%	8%	Armenians 8%	6%
Uzbek	Uzbeks 69%	11%	Tajiks 4%	16%
Kazakh	Kazakhs 40%	40%	Ukrainians 6%	14%
Tajik	Tajiks 59%	11%	Uzbeks 23%	7%
Turkmen	Turkmens 69%	13%	Uzbeks 9%	9%
Kirghiz	Kirghiz 48%	28%	Uzbeks 12%	14%

The internal passport system enabled officials to apply strict ethnic quotas in recruiting people to institutions of higher education, professional and administrative positions, and political posts. Ethnic quotas were even used to determine where people could reside. Thus, ethnicity became critically important in determining some of the most fundamental aspects of life. In particular, loyalty to the system was cultivated by granting advantages in education, occupation, and political influence to titular ethnic group members residing in their "home" republics. Of course, granting advantage to Ukrainians in the Ukraine and to Russians in Russia required imposing disadvantages on persons whose ethnic identity was mismatched with their place of residence. Members of non-titular groups were disadvantaged everywhere (Brym with Ryvkina, 1994: 6–16; Karklins, 1986; Zaslavsky and Brym, 1983).

Despite the goal of creating a new "Soviet People," imposing ethnic labels strongly tied to privilege reinforced ethnic identities. In 1991, when the Soviet Union disappeared, former Soviet citizens had no doubt as to whether they were Latvians, Georgians, or what have you because the ethnic classification in their internal passports had shaped opportunities for 60 years. Not until 1997 did the Russian government introduce internal passports that did not include the notorious fifth entry and thus end the practice of state-certified ethnic classification.

Ethnic and Racial Choice in Canada

The situation in Canada is vastly different from that of the Soviet Union before 1991. Canadians are freer to choose their ethnic identity than citizens of the Soviet Union were. The people with the most freedom to choose are white European Canadians whose ancestors arrived in Canada more than two generations ago. For example, identifying yourself as an Irish Canadian no longer has negative implications, as it did in, say, 1900. Then, in a city like Toronto, where a substantial number of Irish immigrants were concentrated, the English Protestant majority typically regarded working-class Irish Catholics as often drunk, inherently lazy, and born superstitious. This strong anti-Irish sentiment, which often erupted into conflict, meant the Irish found it difficult to escape their ethnic identity even if they wanted to. Since then, however, Irish Canadians have followed the path taken by many other white European groups. They have achieved upward mobility and blended with the majority.

As a result, Irish Canadians no longer find their identity imposed on them. Instead, they may *choose* whether to march in a St. Patrick's Day parade, enjoy the remarkable contributions of Irish authors to English-language literature and drama, and take pride in the athleticism and precision of Riverdance. For them, ethnicity is largely a *symbolic* matter, as it is for the other white European groups that have undergone similar social processes. Herbert Gans defines **symbolic ethnicity** as "a nostalgic allegiance to the culture of the immigrant generation, or that of the old country; a love for and a pride in a tradition that can be felt without having to be incorporated in everyday behavior" (Gans, 1991: 436).

In contrast, most African Canadians lack the freedom to enjoy symbolic ethnicity. They may well take pride in their cultural heritage and participate in such cultural festivals as Caribana. However, their identity as people of African descent is not an option because a considerable number of non-blacks are racists and impose the identity on them. **Racism** is the belief that a visible characteristic of a group, such as skin colour, indicates group inferiority and justifies discrimination. Recent surveys show that somewhere between 30 percent and 55 percent of Canadians (depending on the wording of the question) hold racist views of varying intensity (Henry et al., 2001: 147–51). In his autobiography, the American black militant Malcolm X poignantly noted how racial identity can be imposed on people. He described one of his black Ph.D. professors as "one of these ultra-proper-talking Negroes" who spoke and acted snobbishly. "Do you know what white racists call black Ph.D.s?" asked Malcolm X. "He said something like, 'I believe that I happen not to be aware of that . . .'

Symbolic ethnicity is a nostalgic allegiance to the culture of the immigrant generation, or that of the old country, that is not usually incorporated in everyday behaviour.

Racism is the belief that a visible characteristic of a group, such as skin colour, indicates group inferiority and justifies discrimination.

Many white Canadians lived in poor urban ghettos in the nineteenth and early twentieth centuries. However, a larger proportion of them experienced upward mobility than was the case for African Canadians in the late twentieth century. This photo shows a Manitoba tenement in 1912.

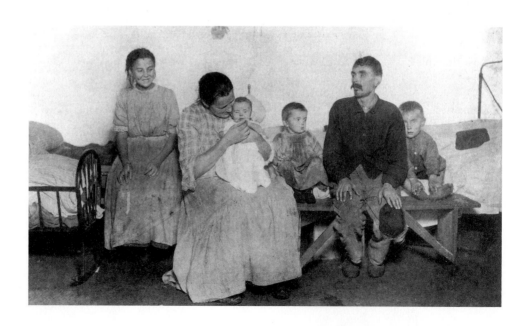

And I laid the word down on him, loud: 'N——!'" (X, 1965: 284). Malcolm X's point is that it doesn't matter to a racist whether a black person is a professor or a panhandler, a genius or a fool, a saint or a criminal. Where racism is common, racial identities are compulsory and at the forefront of self-identity.

As the contrast between Irish Canadians and African Canadians suggests, then, relations among racial and ethnic groups can take different forms. We now discuss several theories that explain why forms of racial and ethnic relations vary over time and from place to place.

THEORIES OF RACE AND ETHNIC RELATIONS

Ecological Theory

Nearly a century ago, Robert Park proposed an influential theory of how race and ethnic relations change over time (Park, 1950 [1914]). His ecological theory focuses on the struggle for territory. He distinguished five stages in the process by which conflict among ethnic and racial groups emerges and is resolved:

1. *Invasion.* One racial or ethnic group tries to move into the territory of another. The territory may be as large as a country or as small as a city neighbourhood.
2. *Resistance.* The established group tries to defend its territory and institutions against the intruding group by using legal means, violence, or both.
3. *Competition.* If the established group does not drive out the newcomers, the two groups begin to compete for scarce resources, including housing, jobs, public park space, and political positions.
4. *Accommodation and cooperation.* Over time, the two groups work out an understanding of what they should segregate, divide, and share. **Segregation** involves the spatial and institutional separation of racial or ethnic groups. For example, the two groups may segregate churches, heritage associations, and newspapers; divide political positions in proportion to the size of the groups; and share public parks equally.
5. *Assimilation.* **Assimilation** is the process by which a minority group blends into the majority population and eventually disappears as a distinct group. Park argued that assimilation is bound to occur as accommodation and cooperation allow trust and understanding to develop. Eventually, goodwill allows ethnic groups to fuse socially and culturally. Where there were formerly two or more groups, only one remains.

Park strongly influenced the first Canadian sociologists. Canada's first sociology department was established at McGill in 1922 by Carl Dawson, Park's student. Dawson regarded communities—groups of people who shared geographic locations—as the proper objects of sociological investigation. He investigated how community life is shaped by distinctive values and cultural practices and how community life shapes intergroup relations.

The co-author of Canada's first sociology textbook (Dawson and Gettys, 1929), Dawson, and his students, implemented Park's ideas by carrying out studies of Montreal neighbourhoods and their ethnically distinctive ways of life. They spent much time observing and talking to people, but they also compiled relevant census and other official data. Dawson received a large Rockefeller Foundation research grant and used part of it to study immigrant rural communities in the Canadian west. This study resulted in *Group Settlement: Ethnic Communities in Western Canada* (Dawson, 1936) and other important works.

Everett Hughes, another of Park's students, was recruited to McGill by Dawson. He drew on the same grant to complete the widely acclaimed *French Canada in Transition*

As Malcolm X noted, it doesn't matter to a racist whether a black person is a professor or a panhandler, a genius or a fool, a saint or a criminal. Where racism is common, racial identities are compulsory and at the forefront of self-identity.

Segregation involves the spatial and institutional separation of racial or ethnic groups.

Assimilation is the process by which a minority group blends into the majority population and eventually disappears as a distinct group.

(Hughes, 1943). Hughes applied Park's approach of combing direct observation with other kinds of data to study the relations between French and English in Drummondville, Quebec. At the time, the perception was widely shared that French Canada was somehow timeless and unchanging. Hughes showed otherwise by documenting increasing tension between French-speaking employees and English-speaking managers and owners.

Although Park's theory stimulated much other valuable research (e.g., Suttles, 1968), it eventually became apparent that it applies to some ethnic groups better than to others. In North America, it applies best to whites of European origin. As Park predicted, many whites of European origin stopped thinking of themselves as Italian Canadian or Irish Canadian or German Canadian after their families were in Canada for three or four generations. Today, they think of themselves just as Canadians (Boyd, 1999; Boyd and Norris, 2001), because, over time, they achieved rough equality with members of the majority group. In the process, they began to blend in with them. The story of the Irish is fairly typical. During the first half of the twentieth century, Irish Canadians experienced upward mobility. By the middle of the century they earned about as much as others of British origin did (the Scottish, the English, and the Welsh). The tapering off of working-class Irish immigration prevented the average status of the group from falling. As their status rose, Irish Canadians increasingly intermarried with members of other ethnic groups. Use of the Irish language, Gaelic, virtually disappeared. The Irish became less concentrated in particular cities and less segregated in certain neighbourhoods. Conflict with Canadians who were members of the majority group declined. With variations, a similar story may be told about Italian Canadians, German Canadians, and so forth.

However, the story does not apply to all Canadians. Park's theory resonates less well with the experiences of Aboriginal peoples, Québécois, African Canadians, and Asian Canadians in particular. For reasons we will now explore, some racial and ethnic groups seem stuck at Park's third and fourth stages (competition and accommodation/cooperation).

The Theory of Internal Colonialism

The main weakness of Park's theory is that it pays insufficient attention to the *social-structural* conditions that prevent some groups from assimilating. Robert Blauner examined one such condition: **internal colonialism** (Blauner, 1972; Hechter, 1974). Blauner's work is important because it stimulated the development of several theories that emphasize the social-structural (and especially class) roots of race and ethnicity.

Colonialism involves people from one country invading another country. In the process, the invaders change or destroy the native culture. They gain virtually complete control over the native population. They develop the racist belief that the native inhabitants are inherently inferior. And they confine natives to work considered demeaning. *Internal colonialism* involves much the same processes but within the boundaries of a single country. Internal colonialism prevents assimilation by segregating the colonized in terms of jobs, housing, and social contacts ranging from friendship to marriage. To varying degrees, Canada, the United States, Great Britain, Australia, France, Italy, Spain, Russia, and China have engaged in internal colonialism. In Canada, the main victims of internal colonialism are Aboriginal peoples, the Québécois, and people of African descent.

Canada's Aboriginal Peoples

The single word that best describes the treatment of Canada's Aboriginal peoples by European immigrants in the nineteenth century is *expulsion*. **Expulsion** is the forcible removal of a population from a territory claimed by another population.

Expulsion is dramatically illustrated by the plight of the Beothuk (pronounced bee-**aw**-thik), the Aboriginal inhabitants of what is today Newfoundland and Labrador. The Beothuk were Algonkian-speaking hunter-gatherers who probably numbered fewer than a thousand people at the time of European contact. In the sixteenth century, Europeans used Newfoundland and Labrador as a fishing port, returning to Europe each year after the fishing season. In the seventeenth century, year-round European settlement began. This caused a

Internal colonialism involves one race or ethnic group subjugating another in the same country. It prevents assimilation by segregating the subordinate group in terms of jobs, housing, and social contacts.

Expulsion is the forcible removal of a population from a territory claimed by another population.

revolution in the life of the Beothuk because the Europeans viewed them as a nuisance. They offered incentives to Mi'kmaq Indians from Nova Scotia to kill off the Beothuk. The Beothuk population declined and gradually withdrew from European contact.

As European settlement grew in the eighteenth century, the Beothuk were squeezed into the interior. There they competed for scarce resources with fur traders. Eventually the Beothuk were reduced to a small refugee population along the Exploits River system, living off the meagre resources of the Newfoundland and Labrador interior. The expulsion of the Beothuk from their traditional territories through European colonization led to the tribe's eventual extinction. Today, about all that remains of the Beothuk, aside from their tragic history and a few artifacts, is a statue outside the Newfoundland and Labrador provincial legislature.

The story of the Beothuk is an extreme case. However, *all* Aboriginal tribes had broadly similar experiences. In the eighteenth and nineteenth centuries, as the European settlers' fur trade gave way to the harvesting of timber, minerals, oil, and gas, Aboriginal peoples were shunted aside so the Canadian economy could grow. At the time, Europeans thought they were "assimilating" the Aboriginal peoples. The Indian Act spoke of the need to transform a hunting-gathering people into an agricultural labour force (Menzies, 1999). Sir John A. Macdonald, Canada's first prime minister, spoke of the need "to do away with the tribal system and assimilate the Indian people in all respects with the inhabitants of the Dominion, as speedily as they are fit to change" (quoted in Montgomery, 1965: 13). In contrast, many Aboriginal peoples understood the settlers' actions—the passage of the Indian Act, the establishment of the reserve system, the creation of residential schools, and so forth—less as an attempt to assimilate them than as an attempt to obliterate their heritage. It is in this sense that the government of Canada has been accused by some Aboriginal peoples of perpetuating cultural genocide (Cardinal, 1977). **Genocide** is the intentional extermination of an entire population defined as a "race" or a "people."

Adding insult to injury, early historical writing about Canada depicted Aboriginal peoples as either irrelevant or evil. Typically, in *The History of the Dominion of Canada,* a book widely used in Canadian schools at the turn of the twentieth century, only five pages were devoted to Aboriginal peoples (Clement, 1897). They are described as "cruel," "rude," "false," "crafty," "savages," and "ferocious villains" who plotted against the Europeans with "fiendish ingenuity" (see also Richardson, 1832; Roberts, 1915; and the overview by

Genocide is the intentional extermination of an entire population defined as a "race" or a "people."

The Canadian policy of assimilation: In its annual report of 1904, the Department of Indian Affairs published the photographs of Thomas Moore of the Regina Industrial School "before and after tuition." These images are "a cogent expression of what federal policy had been since Confederation and what it would remain for many decades. It was a policy of assimilation, a policy designed to move Aboriginal communities from their 'savage' state to that of 'civilization' and thus to make in Canada but one community—a non-Aboriginal one" (Milloy, 1999).

Francis, 1992). Canadian schoolbooks continued to portray Aboriginal peoples in pretty much this way until the mid-twentieth century.

So we see that, throughout North America, the confrontation with European culture undermined the way of life of the Aboriginal peoples. Because of internal colonialism and, in particular, expulsion from their traditional lands, Canada's Aboriginal peoples were prevented from practising their traditional ways and from assimilating into the larger society. Most of them languished on reservations and, in more recent times, in urban slums. There they experienced high rates of unemployment, poverty, ill health, and violence. The history of Canada's Aboriginal peoples raises in the most distressing way possible the issue of whether and in what form white society should take responsibility for past injustices, a subject to which we will return later.

The Québécois

Conquest is the forcible capture of land and the economic and political domination of its inhabitants.

A second form of internal colonialism involves not expulsion but **conquest,** the forcible capture of land and the economic and political domination of its inhabitants. For example, as part of their centuries-long struggle to control North America, the English conquered New France and its 60 000 settlers in 1759. The English thereby created a system of ethnic stratification that remained in place for more than 200 years and that turned out to be a major source of political conflict (McRoberts, 1988).

The British recognized that any attempt to impose their language, religion, laws, and institutions in the former French colony could result in unacceptably high levels of resistance and conflict. Therefore, they tried to accommodate farmers and the Catholic clergy by reinforcing their rights and privileges. The British believed this would win the allegiance of these two groups, who would in turn help build loyalty to Britain among the population as a whole. In contrast, the British undermined the rights and privileges of merchants engaged mainly in the fur trade. So while agriculture, religion, and politics remained the province of the French, the British took over virtually all large-scale commerce.

This pattern of ethnic stratification remained intact for two centuries. True, by 1950 most farmers had been transformed into urban, industrial workers. A contingent of Québécois had become physicians, lawyers, and members of the "new middle class" of administrators, technicians, scientists, and intellectuals. However, the upper reaches of the stratification system remained overwhelmingly populated by people of British origin. Social separation reinforced economic segregation. The French and the British tended to speak different languages, live in different towns and neighbourhoods, interact occasionally, befriend one another infrequently, and intermarry rarely. Characteristically, the novel that became emblematic of the social relations between French and English in Quebec is entitled *Two Solitudes* (MacLennan, 1945).

Apart from its rigid system of ethnic stratification, Quebec in the middle of the twentieth century was remarkable because of its undeveloped government services. Health, education, and welfare were largely controlled by the Catholic church. Government intervention in economic matters was almost unknown. Because of this political backwardness, members of Quebec's new middle class, together with blue-collar workers, began campaigning to modernize the provincial political system in the late 1940s. They pressed for more liberal labour laws that would recognize the right of all workers to form unions and strike. They wanted state control over education and a new curriculum that stressed the natural and social sciences rather than classical languages and catechism. They desired a government that would supply a wide range of social services to the population. They demanded that the state provide better infrastructure for economic development and help francophone entrepreneurs expand their businesses. The partial realization of these aims in the 1960s came to be known as the Quiet Revolution.

However, the modernization of the Quebec state failed to resolve four issues:

1. *The potential demographic decline of the Québécois.* By 1981, Québécois women were giving birth to fewer children on average than were women in any other province. In fact, they were having fewer than the 2.1 children that women must bear on average to ensure that the size of the population does not decline (Romaniuc, 1984: 14–18). Noticing this trend in the 1970s, many Québécois felt they were becoming an endangered species.

2. *The assimilation of immigrants into English culture.* Fears of demographic decline were reinforced by the preference of most new immigrants to have their children educated in English-language schools. Together with the falling birth rate, this development threatened to diminish the size—and therefore, potentially, the power—of Quebec's francophone population.

3. *Persistent ethnic stratification.* The Quiet Revolution helped create many thousands of jobs for highly educated francophones—but almost exclusively in the government bureaucracy, the educational system, and in new Crown corporations, such as Hydro-Québec. It became apparent in the 1970s that management positions in the private sector remained the preserve of English-origin Canadians.

4. *The continued use of English as the language of private industry.* English remained the language of choice in the private sector because the largest and technologically most advanced businesses were controlled by English Canadians and Americans. This situation was felt particularly keenly when the expansion of the state sector, and therefore the upward mobility of the francophone new middle class, slowed in the 1970s.

Because of the issues just listed, many Québécois felt that the survival and prosperity of their community required active state intervention in non-francophone institutions. For example, many Québécois came to believe that most shares of banks, trust companies, and insurance firms should be held in Quebec and that these financial institutions should be obliged to reinvest their profits in the province. They argued that the state should increase its role as economic planner and initiator of development and should forbid foreign ownership of cultural enterprises. Finally, the Québécois increasingly demanded compulsory French-language education for the children of most immigrants, obligatory use of French among private-sector managers, and French-only signs in public places. Most Québécois regarded these proposals as the only means by which their community could survive and attain equality with the English. Moreover, since the Quebec state did not have the legal authority to enact some of the proposed changes, they felt that the province ought to negotiate broader constitutional powers with the federal government. A large minority of Québécois went a step further. They became convinced that Quebec ought to become a politically sovereign nation, albeit a nation economically associated with Canada.

The pro-independence Parti Québécois won the provincial election in 1976. In 1980, it held a referendum to see whether Quebecers favoured "sovereignty-association." Nearly 60 percent voted no. A second referendum was held in 1995. This time, the forces opposed to sovereignty-association won by the narrowest of margins—about 1 percent. The Parti Québécois promises to hold additional referenda until it gets the result it wants. Thus, in the early twenty-first century, the economic, social, and cultural segregation of the Québécois from English Canada—a legacy of the conquest—meant Canada's future was still uncertain.

African Canadians

We have seen that internal colonialism, whether it is accomplished by means of expulsion or conquest, creates big barriers to assimilation that can endure for centuries. A third form of internal colonialism—slavery—creates similar barriers. **Slavery** is the ownership and control of people.

Slavery is the ownership and control of people.

By about 1800, 24 million Africans had been captured and placed on slave ships headed to North, Central, and South America. Because of violence, disease, and shipwreck, fewer than half survived the passage. Black slaves were bought and sold in Canada at least until the 1820s. Only in 1833, when the British government banned slavery throughout the British Empire, did the practice become illegal in Canada. Slavery was abolished in the United States 30 years later.

It is true that the extent of slavery in Canada paled in comparison with its widespread use in the United States, where tobacco and cotton production depended entirely on the work of dirt-cheap black labour. It is also true that for decades Canada served as the terminus of the "underground railway," a network of assistance that smuggled escaped slaves out of the United States to freedom in Canada. As Martin Luther King, leader of the American civil rights movement in the 1960s, said in 1967:

> Deep in our history of struggle for freedom Canada was the North Star. The Negro slave . . . knew that far to the north a land existed where a fugitive slave, if he survived the horrors of the journey, could find freedom. The legendary underground railroad started in the south and ended in Canada. . . . Our spirituals, now so widely admired around the world, were often codes. We sang of "heaven" that awaited us, and the slave masters listened in innocence, not realizing that we were not speaking of the hereafter. Heaven was the word for Canada and the Negro sang of the hope that his escape on the underground railroad would carry him there. One of our spirituals, "Follow the Drinking Gourd," in its disguised lyrics contained directions for escape. The gourd was the big dipper, and the North Star to which its handle pointed gave the celestial map that directed the flight to the Canadian border. (King, 1967: 1)

What King neglected to mention is that after the American Civil War (1861–65) the practice of encouraging black settlement in Canada was reversed. Government policy required the rejection of most immigration applications by black people. This policy reflected a deeply felt prejudice on the part of the Canadian population that persisted throughout the twentieth century (Goldstein, 1978; Sissing, 1996). Moreover, social relations between Canadians of African descent and the white European majority were anything but intimate and based on equality. Until the mid-twentieth century, African Canadians tended to do unskilled labour and be residentially and socially segregated—for example, in the Halifax community of Africville, established around 1850 by runaway American slaves (Clairmont and Magill, 1999).

Canadian immigration policy was liberalized in the 1960s. Racial and ethnic restrictions were removed. Immigrants were now admitted on the basis of their potential economic contribution to Canadian society (about 57 percent of all immigrants in 2004), their close family ties with Canadians (about 26 percent of the total), or their refugee status (about 14 percent of the total; Citizenship and Immigration Canada, 2004). As a result, Canada became a much more racially and ethnically diverse society (see Figure 10.3). Some 783 795 people living in Canada in 2006 were black (2.5 percent of the population; Statistics Canada, 2008f). Many new immigrants had completed postsecondary education abroad. Others attended colleges and universities in Canada. The social standing of Canada's black community thus improved significantly. Nonetheless, Canadians of African descent still tend to interact little with white Canadians of European descent, especially in their intimate relations, and they still tend to live in different neighbourhoods. Like the aftermath of expulsion and conquest, the aftermath of slavery—prejudice, discrimination, disadvantage, and segregation—continues to act as a barrier to assimilation.

Black Slave for Sale: Many distinguished persons were slave owners, including Peter Russell, who held positions in the executive and legislative councils and became administrator of Upper Canada.

TO BE SOLD,

A BLACK WOMAN, named PEGGY, aged about forty years ; and a Black boy her fon, named JUPITER, aged about fifteen years, both of them the property of the Subfcriber.

The Woman is a tolerable Cook and wafher woman and perfectly underftands making Soap and Candles.

The Boy is tall and ftrong of his age, and has been employed in Country bufinefs, but brought up principally as a Houfe Servant—They are each of them Servants for life. The Price for the Wowan is one hundred and fifty Dollars—for the Boy two hundred Dollars, payable in three years with Intereft from the day of Sale and to be properly fecured by Bond &c.— But one fourth lefs will be taken in ready Money.

PETER RUSSELL.

York, Feb. 10th 1806.

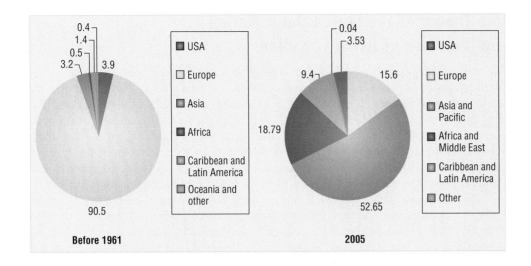

FIGURE 10.3

Immigrants by Place of Birth and Period of Immigration, Canada, Before 1961 and 2005 (in percent)

Sources: Adapted from Statistics Canada, 2003, "Canada's Ethnocultural Portrait: The Changing Mosaic, 2001 Census (Analysis series)," Catalogue 96F0030, January. Retrieved April 13, 2007 (http://www.statcan.ca/english/IPS/Data/96F003XIE2001008.htm); Citizenship and Immigration Canada, 2006, "Annual Report to Parliament on Immigration, 2006." Retrieved April 13, 2007 (http://www.cic.gc.ca/english/resources/publications/annual-report2006/index.asp).

WHERE DO YOU FIT IN?

You can easily judge for yourself the strength of social barriers between Canadians of different ethnic and racial backgrounds. You can also determine how this barrier has changed over time. Draw up a list of your five closest friends and note the ethnic or racial background of each one. Now ask one of your parents to do the same for *their* five closest friends. Finally, ask one of your grandparents to draw up a similar list. How racially and ethnically diverse is your friendship network? How do you explain its racial and ethnic diversity or lack of diversity? How racially and ethnically diverse is your friendship network compared with the friendship network of your parent and grandparent? How do you explain differences between generations? Now, instead of focusing on friends, perform the same exercise for your cousins and the cousins of your parent and grandparent. How racially and ethnically diverse is your kinship network? How diverse it is compared with the kinship network of your parent and grandparent? How do you explain differences among generations? Finally, compare the racial and ethnic diversity of friendship and kinship networks. For each generation (yours, your parent's, and your grandparent's), is the kinship or the friendship network more racially and ethnically diverse? Why? Where do you and your family fit into the web of racial and ethnic diversity that comprises Canadian society?

According to the 2006 census, the top 10 ethnic groups in Canada, other than British, French, and Canadian, include (in order of size) Canadians of German, Italian, Chinese, Aboriginal, Ukrainian, Dutch, Polish, East Indian, Russian, and Filipino origins.

The Theory of the Split Labour Market and the Case of Asian Canadians

The theory of the **split labour market** holds that where low-wage workers of one race and high-wage workers of another race compete for the same jobs, high-wage workers are likely to resent the presence of low-wage competitors and conflict is bound to result. Consequently, racist attitudes develop or are reinforced.

We have seen how the theory of internal colonialism explains the persistence of inequality and segregation between racial and ethnic groups. A second theory that focuses on the social-structural barriers to assimilation is the theory of the **split labour market**, first proposed by sociologist Edna Bonacich (1972). Bonacich's theory explains why racial identities are reinforced by certain labour market conditions. In brief, she argues that where low-wage workers of one race and high-wage workers of another race compete for the same jobs, high-wage workers are likely to resent the presence of low-wage competitors and conflict is bound to result. Consequently, racist attitudes develop or are reinforced.

This is certainly what happened during the early years of Asian immigration in Canada. Chinese, then Japanese, and later Sikhs were allowed into Canada from about the 1850s to the early 1920s for one reason: to provide scarce services and cheap labour in the booming West. Chinese-owned restaurants, grocery stores, laundries, and import businesses dotted the West and especially British Columbia by the early twentieth century (Li, 1998; Whitaker, 1987). Numerically more important, however, were the Asian labourers who worked in lumbering, mining, and railway construction. For example, 15 000 Chinese men were allowed into Canada to complete construction of the final and most difficult section of the Canadian Pacific Railway (CPR), which involved blasting tunnels and laying rail along dangerous Rocky Mountain passes. The Chinese were paid half the wages of white workers. It is said that they "worked like horses." It is also said that they "dropped like flies" due to exposure, disease, malnutrition, and explosions. Four Chinese workers died for every 1.6 kilometres (1 mile) of track laid.

Asian immigration in general was widely viewed as a threat to cherished British values and institutions, an evil to be endured only as long as absolutely necessary. Therefore, once the CPR was completed in 1885, the Chinese were no longer welcome in British Columbia. A prohibitively expensive "head tax" equal to two months' wages was placed on each Chinese immigrant. The tax was increased tenfold in 1903. In 1923, Chinese immigration was banned altogether. During the Great Depression, more than 28 000 Chinese were deported because of high unemployment, and Asian immigration did not resume on a large scale until the 1960s, when racial criteria were finally removed from Canadian immigration regulations.

Underlying European Canadian animosity against Asian immigration was a split labour market. The fact that Asian immigrants were willing to work for much lower wages than

Head tax certificate: In another example of legislated racism, immigrants from China were required by law to pay a "head tax" to enter Canada between 1885 and 1923. The tax began as a fee of $50 and rose to as high as $500.

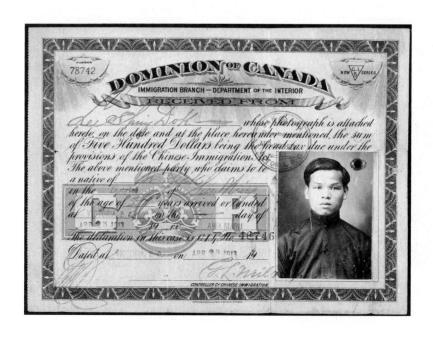

were European Canadians fuelled deep resentment among European Canadians, especially when the labour market was flooded with too many job seekers. European Canadians formed "exclusion leagues" to pressure the government to restrict Asian immigration, and on occasion they even staged anti-Asian riots. Such actions solidified racial identities among both the throwers and the victims of the bricks and made assimilation impossible (on the 1907 anti-Asian riots in Vancouver, see Chapter 21, Collective Action and Social Movements).

In sum, the theory of split labour markets, like the theory of internal colonialism, emphasizes the social-structural roots of race and ethnicity and helps overcome the main weakness of Park's ecological theory. The groups that have had the most trouble assimilating into the British values and institutions that dominate Canadian society are those that were subjected to expulsion from their native lands, conquest, slavery, and split labour markets. These circumstances left a legacy of racism that created social-structural impediments to assimilation—such impediments as forced segregation in low-status jobs and low-income neighbourhoods. By focusing on factors like these, we arrive at a more realistic picture of the state of race and ethnic relations in Canada than is afforded by ecological theory.

Some Advantages of Ethnicity

The theories of internal colonialism and split labour markets emphasize how social forces outside a racial or an ethnic group force its members together, preventing their assimilation into the dominant values and institutions of society. It focuses on the disadvantages of race and ethnicity. Moreover, it deals only with the most disadvantaged minorities. The theory has less to say about the internal conditions that promote group cohesion and in particular about the value of group membership. Nor does it help us to understand why some European Canadians, such as those of Greek or Polish or German origin, continue to participate in the life of their ethnic communities, even if their families have been in the country more than two or three generations.

A review of the sociological literature suggests that three main factors enhance the value of ethnic group membership for some white European Canadians who have lived in the country for many generations:

1. *Ethnic group membership can have economic advantages.* The economic advantages of ethnicity are most apparent for immigrants, who composed nearly 20 percent of the Canadian population in 2006 (see Figure 10.4 on page 296). Immigrants often lack extensive social contacts and fluency in English or French. Therefore, they commonly

Pier 21 is located at 1055 Marginal Road, Halifax. Many immigrants entered Canada at Pier 21. It opened its doors in 1928. As the era of ocean travel was coming to an end in March 1971, the Immigration Service left Pier 21. It is now Canada's Immigration Museum.

FIGURE 10.4

Foreign-Born as a Percentage of Canada's Population, 1901–2006

Sources: Adapted from Statistics Canada, "2001 Census: Analysis Series, Canada's Ethnocultural Portrait: The Changing Mosaic," Catalogue 96F0030XIE2001008. Retrieved January 21, 2003 (http://www12.statcan.ca/english/census01/products/analytic/companion/etoimm/canada.ctm); Statistics Canada, 2007, "Population by Immigrant Status and Period of Immigration, 2006 Counts, for Canada, Provinces and Territories— 20% Sample Data." Retrieved April 5, 2008 (http://www12.statcan.ca/english/census06/data/highlights/Immigration/Table403.cfm?Lang=E&T=403&GH=4&SC=1&S=99&O=A).

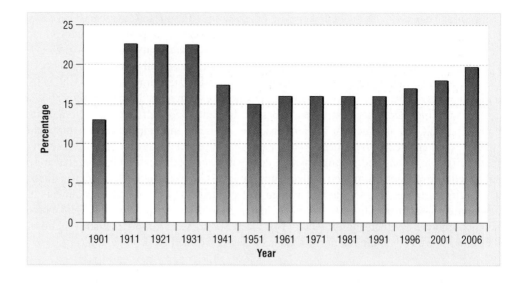

With the introduction of the point system in 1967, nationality and race were removed as selection criteria from the Immigration Act. Of the more than 250 000 people who came to Canada in 2005, more than 50 percent came from 10 source countries: China, India, Pakistan, the Philippines, Korea, the United States, Iran, Romania, Sri Lanka, and Britain.

rely on members of their ethnic group to help them find jobs and housing. In this way, immigrant communities become tightly knit. However, some economic advantages extend into the second generation and beyond. For example, community solidarity is an important resource for "ethnic entrepreneurs." These are businesspeople who operate largely within their ethnic community. They draw on their community for customers, suppliers, employees, and credit, and they may be linked economically to the homeland as importers and exporters. They often pass on their businesses to their children, who in turn can pass the businesses on to the next generation. In this way, strong economic incentives encourage some people to remain ethnic group members, even beyond the immigrant generation (Bonacich, 1973; Light, 1991; Portes and Manning, 1991).

2. *Ethnic group membership can be politically useful.* Consider, for instance, the way some Canadians reacted to the rise of separatism in Quebec in the 1960s. To bridge the growing divide between francophone Quebec and the rest of the country, the federal government under Pierre Trudeau's Liberals promoted a policy of bilingualism. French and English were made official languages. This meant that federal government services would be made available in both languages and instruction in French, including total immersion instruction, would be encouraged in English schools. Members of some ethnic groups, such as people of Ukrainian origin in Western Canada, felt neglected and alienated by this turn of events. They saw no reason for the French to be accorded special status and wanted a share of the resources available for promoting ethnic languages and cultures. As a result, the Trudeau government proclaimed a new policy of multiculturalism in 1971. Now federal funds became available for the promotion of Ukrainian and all other ethnic

cultures in Canada. This entire episode of Canadian ethnic history bolstered Western support for the Liberal Party (for less than a decade) and softened Western opposition to bilingualism. Moreover, it helped stimulate ethnic culture and ethnic identification throughout the country. We thus see that ethnicity can be a political tool for achieving increased access to resources. This is part of the reason for the persistence of ethnic identification for some white European Canadians whose families have lived in the country for many generations.

3. *Ethnic group membership tends to persist because of the emotional support it provides.* Like economic benefits, the emotional advantages of ethnicity are most apparent in immigrant communities. Speaking the ethnic language and sharing other elements of native culture are valuable sources of comfort in an alien environment. Even beyond the second generation, however, ethnic group membership can perform significant emotional functions. For example, some ethnic groups have experienced unusually high levels of prejudice and discrimination involving expulsion or attempted genocide. For people who belong to such groups, the resulting trauma is so severe it can be transmitted for several generations. In such cases, ethnic group membership offers security in a world still seen as hostile long after the threat of territorial loss or annihilation has disappeared (Bar-On, 1999). Another way in which ethnic group membership offers emotional support beyond the second generation is by providing a sense of rootedness. Especially in a highly mobile, urbanized, technological, and bureaucratic society, such as ours, ties to an ethnic community can be an important source of stability and security (Isajiw, 1978).

The three factors listed above make ethnic group membership useful to some Canadians whose families have been in the country for many generations. In fact, retaining ethnic ties beyond the second generation has never been easier. Inexpensive international communication and travel allow ethnic group members to maintain strong ties to their ancestral homeland in a way that was never possible in earlier times. Immigration used to involve cutting all or most ties to a person's country of origin. Travel by sea and air was expensive, long-distance telephone rates were prohibitive, and the occasional letter was about the only communication most immigrants had with relatives in the old country. Lack of communication encouraged assimilation in the newly adopted countries. Today, however, ties to the ancestral communities are often maintained in ways that sustain ethnic culture. For example, about 50 000 Jews have emigrated from the former Soviet Union to Canada since the early 1970s, settling mainly in Toronto. They frequently visit relatives in the former Soviet Union and Israel, speak with them on the phone, and use the Internet to exchange e-mail with them. They also receive Russian-language radio and TV broadcasts, act as conduits for foreign investment, and send money to relatives abroad (Brym, 2001; Brym with Ryvkina, 1994; Markowitz, 1993). This sort of intimate and ongoing connection with the motherland is typical of most recent immigrant communities in North America. Thanks to inexpensive international travel and communication, some ethnic groups have become **transnational communities** whose boundaries extend among countries. Characteristically, the Ticuani Potable Water Committee in Brooklyn has been raising money for the farming community of Ticuani in the Mixteca region of Mexico for decades. Its seal reads *"Por el Progreso de Ticuani: Los Ausentes Siempre Presentes. Ticuani y New York"* (translation: "For the Progress of Ticuani: The Absent Ones Always Present. Ticuani and New York"). The phrase "the absent ones always present" nicely captures the essence of transnational communities, whose growing number and vitality facilitate the retention of ethnic group membership beyond the second generation (Portes, 1996).

In sum, ethnicity remains a vibrant force in Canadian society for a variety of reasons. Even some white Canadians whose families settled in this country more than two generations ago have reason to identify with their ethnic group. Bearing this in mind, what is the likely future of race and ethnic relations in Canada? We conclude by offering some tentative answers to that question.

GLOBAL PERSPECTIVE

Transnational communities **are communities whose boundaries extend between or among countries.**

THE FUTURE OF RACE AND ETHNICITY IN CANADA

The world comprises more than 200 countries and more than 5000 ethnic and racial groups. As a result, no country is ethnically and racially homogeneous and in many countries, including Canada, the largest ethnic group forms less than half the population (see Table 10.2 and Figure 10.5). Of course, Canada's British roots remain important. Our parliamentary democracy is based on the British model. The Queen's representative, the governor general, is our titular head of state. We still celebrate May 24, Queen Victoria's birthday. And English is the country's predominant language, with more than 60 percent of Canadians

TABLE 10.2

Ethnic and Visible Minority Status of Canadians, 2006

Notes: * In reply to the ethnicity question on the census, people may specify one or more ethnicities. As a result, the number of ethnic responses is much larger than the number of Canadians.

** East Indian, Pakistani, Sri Lankan, etc.

*** Vietnamese, etc.

**** Arab, etc.

Source: Statistics Canada, 2008d, 2008f.

Ethnic Groups with Population 200,000+ (single and multiple responses*)	Percentage of Population	Number (millions)
Canadian	32.2	10.07
English	21.0	6.57
French	15.8	4.94
Scottish	15.1	4.72
Irish	13.9	4.35
German	10.2	3.18
Italian	4.6	1.45
Chinese	4.3	1.35
North American Indian	4.0	1.25
Ukrainian	3.9	1.21
Dutch	3.3	1.04
Polish	3.2	0.98
East Indian	3.1	0.96
Russian	1.6	0.50
Welsh	1.4	0.44
Filipino	1.4	0.44
Norwegian	1.4	0.43
Portuguese	1.3	0.41
Métis	1.3	0.41
Other British Isles	1.3	0.40
Swedish	1.1	0.33
Spanish	1.0	0.33
American	1.0	0.32
Hungarian	1.0	0.32
Jewish	1.0	0.32
Greek	0.7	0.24
Jamaican	0.7	0.23
Danish	0.6	0.20

Visible Minorities	Percentage of Population	Number (millions)
South Asian**	4.0	1.26
Chinese	3.9	1.22
Black	2.5	0.78
Filipino	1.3	0.41
Latin American	1.0	0.30
Southeast Asian***	0.8	0.24
Other****	2.7	0.89

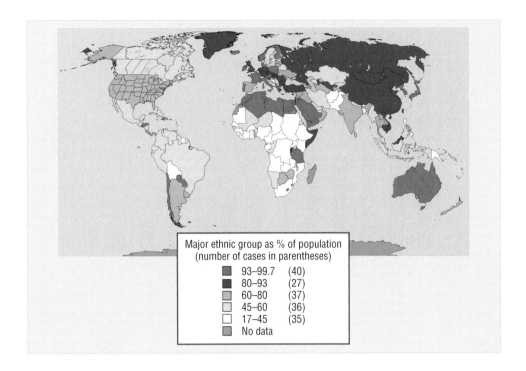

FIGURE 10.5

Percentage of Population Accounted for by Largest Ethnic Group

No country is ethnically homogeneous and in many countries the largest ethnic group forms less than half the population. Ethnic diversity has increased in recent years because of international migration. This map illustrates the world's ethnic diversity by showing the percentage of each country's population that is accounted for by the country's largest ethnic group. Which countries are most diverse? Which are least diverse? How might a country's level of ethnic diversity affect its population's self-identity? How ethnically diverse is Canada compared with other countries?

Sources: "Ethnic Groups," 2001; Central Intelligence Agency, 2001.

claiming it as their mother tongue. Nonetheless, Canada is a racially and ethnically heterogeneous society.

As racial and ethnic diversity has increased, Canadian ethnic and race relations have changed radically. Two hundred years ago, Canada was a society based on expulsion, conquest, slavery, and segregation. Today, we are a society based on segregation, pluralism, and assimilation, with **pluralism** being understood as the retention of racial and ethnic culture combined with equal access to basic social resources. Thus, on a scale of tolerance, Canada has come a long way in the past 200 years (see Figure 10.6).

In comparison with most other countries, too, Canada is a relatively tolerant land. In the late twentieth and early twenty-first centuries, racial and ethnic tensions in some parts of the world erupted into wars of secession and attempted genocide. Comparing Canada with such countries may seem to stack the deck in favour of concluding that Canada is a relatively tolerant society. However, even when we compare Canada with other rich, stable, postindustrial countries, our society seems relatively tolerant by most measures (see Figure 10.7 on page 300).

Pluralism is the retention of racial and ethnic culture combined with equal access to basic social resources.

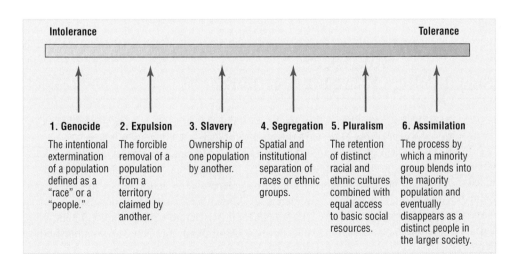

FIGURE 10.6

Six Degrees of Separation: Types of Ethnic and Racial Group Relations

Source: From KORNBLUM. *ACP SOCIOLOGY IN A CHANGING WORLD, 4E. ©1997 Wadsworth, a part of Cengage Learning, Inc. Reproduced by permission. www.cengage.com/permissions

FIGURE 10.7

Percentage Not Wanting Neighbour of a Different Race, Selected Countries, 2000

Source: World Values Survey. 2003. Machine readable data set. Ann Arbor MI: Inter-University Consortium for Political and Social Research. Reprinted with permission.

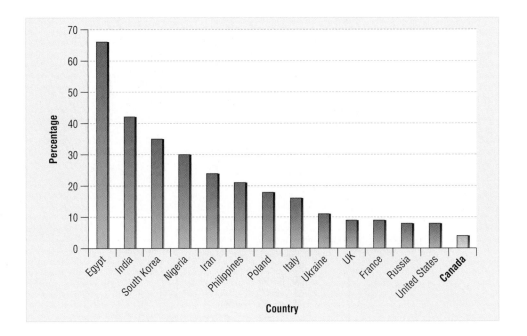

Because of such factors as intermarriage and immigration, the growth of tolerance in Canada is taking place in the context of increasing ethnic and racial diversity. Given continuing migration in the coming decades, Canada will become even more of a racial and ethnic mosaic than it is now (Pendakur, 2000). However, if present trends continue, the racial and ethnic mosaic will continue to be vertical. That is, some groups, especially Aboriginal peoples, will be disproportionately clustered at the bottom of the socioeconomic hierarchy. Unless dramatic changes occur, they will continue to enjoy less wealth, income, education, good housing, health care, and other social rewards than other Canadians do.

Political initiatives could decrease the verticality of the Canadian mosaic, speeding up the movement from segregation to pluralism and assimilation for the country's most disadvantaged groups. Such political initiatives include compensation for historical injustices (see Box 10.2), **affirmative action or employment equity** programs that encourage the hiring of qualified members of disadvantaged minority groups, government-subsidized job training and child care, improvements in public education, the creation of training courses designed to upgrade the credentials of foreign-trained professionals, and the shoring up of Canada's public health system. All these initiatives would most benefit disadvantaged Canadians, a disproportionately large number of whom are visible minority group immigrants and Aboriginal peoples.

Affirmative action or employment equity is a policy that gives preference to members of minority groups if equally qualified people are available for a position.

BOX 10.2
Social Policy: What Do You Think?

Should We Pay the Price of Past Wrongs?

July 28, 2001, was a hot, muggy day in Toronto, and Randall Robinson added to the heat with his fiery oration to the African Canadian Legal Clinic (ACLC). "We're owed at least $11 tril-

lion," he exhorted. "America must pay for slavery." The Harvard-educated Robinson was championing the cause of reparations for the descendants of American slaves—monetary compensation for past injustices. Americans of African descent, he argued, have been "bottom-stuck" since they were slaves.

Their disadvantaged position today, he argued, is the legacy of slavery.

Although slavery was abolished in Canada in 1833, Robinson's arguments were endorsed by the ACLC and other Canadian groups that are not of African descent. Japanese, Chinese, Aboriginal, and Jewish Canadians all had representatives and gave advice at the meeting of the ACLC in July 2001.

- *Japanese Canadians.* In 1942, three months after Japan attacked Pearl Harbor, the Canadian government invoked the War Measures Act. All people of Japanese origin residing within 160 kilometres (100 miles) of the Pacific Coast were removed from their homes. With about 24 hours' notice, almost 21 000 Japanese Canadians, 75 percent of them Canadian citizens, were moved to prisoner of war camps, work camps, and internment camps. Japanese Canadians sought and eventually received reparations for this historical injustice.
- *Chinese Canadians.* The descendants of many Chinese Canadians were forced to pay a highly discriminatory head tax between 1885 and 1903. Chinese Canadians received compensation for this mistreatment only in 2006.
- *Aboriginal peoples.* Many Aboriginal children were taken from their parents and placed in residential schools in the twentieth century. Many of them were physically and sexually abused in these schools. Aboriginal peoples also claim that much land was illegally taken from them. They, too, have sought and received a redress of grievances.
- *Jewish Canadians.* The Nazis enslaved and slaughtered European Jews by the millions during World War II. Jews were the first group to seek reparations (from the German government) for the historical injustices they suffered. Jewish Canadians have sought compensation from the Canadian government for refusing to allow a boatload of Jews fleeing Nazi Germany to land in Canada in 1939.

Other aggrieved groups who were apparently not represented at the meeting include Ukrainian and Croatian Canadians (some of whom were placed in internment camps during World War I), Italian and German Canadians (some of whom were placed in internment camps during World War II), and Sikh Canadians (a boatload of whom were refused entry in Vancouver in 1914).

In the past, what was past was past. The vanquished were vanquished and the powerful wrote the history books, taking no responsibility for what their ancestors had done. Today, things are different. Aggrieved groups in Canada and around the world are demanding reparations (Torpey, 2001). The recognition of fundamental human rights, signified first by the Human Rights Declaration of the United Nations in 1948, and the widespread delegitimization of racial and ethnic discrimination have provided fertile terrain for this historical turn. The mobilization of shame has triggered a revolutionary change in how some people and governments view past injustices.

What do you think about the reparations issue? Should *you* compensate African Canadians for slavery, Chinese Canadians for the head tax, Japanese Canadians for the internment camps, and Aboriginal peoples for residential schools and land? How responsible should *you* be for events that took place 50 or 200 years ago? In 1988 the Canadian government condemned the internment of Japanese Canadians during World War II, offered individual and community compensation to Japanese Canadians, and provided a $24 million endowment for the Canadian Race Relations Foundation. In 2005, $50 million in compensation was promised to Canadians of Chinese, Italian, Ukrainian, Croatian, German, Jewish, and Sikh origin. Also in 2005, an Agreement in Principle was reached to compensate former students of Aboriginal residential schools with $10 000 each plus $3000 for each year they spent in residence. Does this seem fair to you? What about the far larger demands of Aboriginal peoples for self-government and land rights given that they were pushed onto reserves to make way for exploration and resource development? Should Canada recognize its guilt and compensate those who have suffered? If not, why not? If so, should limits be placed on reparations? Why or why not?

NOTES

1. Controversy surrounds the terminology used throughout this chapter. Some scholars prefer to emphasize common descent and culture by using such terms as *African Canadian* and *Euro-Canadian* rather than *black* and *white*. However, terms that emphasize descent and culture can be ethnocentric. For example, there are millions of black immigrants from former British and French colonies in Europe. Therefore, *Euro-Canadian* does not accurately signify the white majority in Canada. Because there is no perfect set of terms to denote racial or ethnic communities, we use *white* and *Euro-Canadian*, as well as *black, African Canadian, and African American*.

2. Although sociologists commonly dispute a genetic basis of mean intelligence for races, evidence suggests that *individual* differences in intelligence are partly genetically

transmitted (Bouchard, Lykken, McGue, Segal, and Tellegen, 1990; Lewontin, 1991: 19–37; Scarr and Weinberg, 1978; Schiff and Lewontin, 1986).

3. The genetic argument also belittles the athletic activity itself by denying the role of training in developing athletic skills.

4. The Soviets termed these groups "nationalities."

SUMMARY

1. Is "race" a meaningful term?
Some biologists suggest that race is not a meaningful or useful term because the biological differences that distinguish races do not predict differences in social behaviour. However, sociologists retain the term because *perceptions* of racial difference have important consequences for people's lives. Whether a person is seen as belonging to one race or another affects that person's health, wealth, and many others aspects of life.

2. What is the difference between race and ethnicity?
A race is a category of people whose perceived *physical* markers are deemed socially significant. An ethnic group is a category of people whose perceived *cultural* markers are deemed socially significant. Just as physical distinctions do not cause differences in the behaviour of races, cultural distinctions are often not by themselves the major source of differences in the behaviour of various ethnic groups. *Social-structural* differences are typically the most important sources of differences in social behaviour.

3. What do sociologists mean by "the social construction of race and ethnicity"?
When sociologists speak of the social construction of race and ethnicity, they mean that race and ethnicity are not fixed and they are not inherent in people's biological makeup or cultural heritage. Rather, the way race and ethnicity are perceived and expressed depends on the history and character of race and ethnic relations in particular social contexts. These social contexts shape the way people formulate (or "construct") their perceptions and expressions of race and ethnicity. Thus, racial and ethnic labels and identities are variables. They change over time and place. For example, cordial group relations hasten the blending of labels and identities.

4. What is Robert Park's theory of race and ethnic relations?
Robert Park's ecological theory of race and ethnic relations focuses on the way racial and ethnic groups struggle for territory and eventually blend into one another. He divides this struggle into five stages: invasion, resistance, competition, accommodation and cooperation, and assimilation. The main problem with his theory is that some groups get "stuck" at stages 3 and 4, and Park offers no explanation for why this happens.

5. What are the main social-structural theories that supplement Park's theory?
The theory of internal colonialism and the theory of split labour markets usefully supplement Park's theory. The theory of internal colonialism highlights the way invaders change or destroy native culture, gaining virtually complete control over the native population, developing the racist belief that natives are inherently inferior, and confining natives to work they consider demeaning. Internal colonialism prevents assimilation by segregating the colonized in terms of jobs, housing, and social contacts ranging from friendship to marriage. The theory of the split labour market highlights the way low-wage workers of one race and high-wage workers of another race may compete for the same jobs. In such circumstances, high-wage workers are likely to resent the presence of low-wage competitors. Conflict is bound to result and racist attitudes are likely to develop or get reinforced.

6. Are racial and ethnic distinctions fading? Which groups are most resistant to change? Some ethnic groups are blending over time as members of society become more tolerant. However, this tendency is weak among members of highly disadvantaged groups, especially racial minorities. That is because such groups remain highly segregated in jobs, housing, and social contacts. To a considerable degree, this is a historical legacy of internal colonialism and split labour markets.

7. Aside from the historical legacy of internal colonialism and split labour markets, do other reasons exist for the persistence of racial and ethnic identity, even among some white Canadians of European origin whose ancestors came to this country generations ago? Identifying with a racial or an ethnic group can have economic, political, and emotional benefits. These benefits account for the persistence of ethnic identity in some white Canadian families of European origin, even after they have been in Canada for more than two generations. In addition, high levels of immigration renew racial and ethnic communities by providing them with new members who are familiar with ancestral languages, customs, and so forth.

8. What is the future of race and ethnicity in Canada? Racial and ethnic identities and inequalities are likely to persist in the near future. Affirmative action programs, more job training, improvements in public education, the creation of training courses designed to upgrade the credentials of foreign-trained professionals, and state-subsidized health care and child care would promote racial and ethnic equality.

KEY TERMS

affirmative action or employment equity (p. 300)

assimilation (p. 287)

conquest (p. 290)

discrimination (p. 277)

ethnic group (p. 280)

expulsion (p. 288)

genocide (p. 289)

internal colonialism (p. 288)

melting pot (p. 282)

multiculturalism (p. 282)

pluralism (p. 299)

prejudice (p. 277)

race (p. 279)

racism (p. 286)

scapegoat (p. 279)

segregation (p. 287)

slavery (p. 291)

split labour market (p. 294)

symbolic ethnicity (p. 286)

transnational communities (p. 297)

QUESTIONS TO CONSIDER

1. How do you identify yourself in terms of your race or ethnicity? Do conventional ethnic and racial categories, such as black, white, and Asian, fit your sense of who you are? If so, why? If not, why not?

2. Do you think racism is becoming a more serious problem in Canada and worldwide? Why or why not? How do trends in racism compare with trends in other forms of prejudice, such as sexism? What accounts for similarities and differences in these trends?

3. What are the costs and benefits of ethnic diversity in your university? Do you think it would be useful to adopt a policy of affirmative action or employment equity to make the student body and the faculty more ethically and racially diverse? Why or why not?

WEB RESOURCES

Companion Website for This Book

http://www.compass3e.nelson.com

Begin by clicking on the Student Resources section of the website. Next, select the chapter you are studying from the pull-down menu. From the Student Resources page you have easy access to InfoTrac® College Edition, additional Weblinks, and other resources. The website also has many useful tips to aid you in your study of sociology, including practice tests for each chapter.

InfoTrac® Search Terms

These search terms are provided to assist you in beginning to conduct research on this topic by visiting http://www.infotrac-college.com:

affirmative action
racism
assimilation
transnational community
discrimination

Recommended Websites

For information on the history and cultures of the people of Canada, visit Canadian Heritage at http://www.pch.gc.ca/index_e.cfm.

For a site that promotes cooperation between Aboriginal peoples and other Canadians, go to the Assembly of First Nations website at http://www.afn.ca.

To share the Japanese-Canadian experience, go to the site of the Japanese Canadian National Museum: http://www.jcnm.ca.

For issues relevant to Chinese Canadians, go to the Chinese Canadian National Council website, http://www.ccnc.ca.

For information about the United Nations human rights program, go to http://www.ohchr.org/EN.

CengageNOW™

http://hed.nelson.com

This online diagnostic tool identifies each student's unique needs with a Pretest that generates a personalized Study Plan for each chapter, helping students focus on concepts they're having the most difficulty mastering. Students then take a Posttest after reading the chapter to measure their understanding of the material. An Instructor Gradebook is available to track and monitor student progress.

CHAPTER

11

Sexuality and Gender

In this chapter, you will learn that

- Whereas biology determines sex, social structure and culture largely determine gender or the expression of culturally appropriate masculine and feminine roles.

- The social construction of gender is evident in the way parents treat babies, teachers treat pupils, and the mass media portray ideal body images.

- The social forces pushing people to assume conventionally masculine or feminine roles are compelling.

- The social forces pushing people toward heterosexuality operate with even greater force.

- The social distinction between men and women serves as an important basis of inequality in the family and the workplace.

- Male aggression against women is rooted in gender inequality.

SEX VERSUS GENDER

Is It a Boy or a Girl?

**TECHNOLOGY
BYTES**

**Intersexed infants are babies
born with ambiguous genitals
because of a hormone imbalance in the womb or some
other cause.**

On April 27, 1966, eight-month-old identical twin boys were brought to a hospital in Winnipeg to be circumcised. An electrical cauterizing needle—a device that seals blood vessels as it cuts—was used for the procedure. However, because of equipment malfunction or doctor error, the needle entirely burned off one baby's penis. The parents desperately sought medical advice. No matter whom they consulted, they were given the same prognosis. As one psychiatrist summed up the baby's future, "He will be unable to consummate marriage or have normal heterosexual relations; he will have to recognize that he is incomplete, physically defective, and that he must live apart" (quoted in Colapinto, 1997: 58).

One evening, more than half a year after the accident, the parents, now deeply depressed, were watching TV. They heard Dr. John Money, a psychologist from Johns Hopkins Hospital in Baltimore, say that he could *assign* babies a male or female identity. Money had been the driving force behind the creation of the world's first "sex change" clinic at Johns Hopkins. He was well known for his research on **intersexed** infants, babies born with ambiguous genitals because of a hormone imbalance in the womb or some other cause. It was Money's opinion that infants with "unfinished genitals" should be assigned a sex by surgery and hormone treatments, and reared in accordance with their newly assigned sex. According to Money, these strategies would lead to the child developing a self-identity consistent with its assigned sex.

The Winnipeg couple wrote to Dr. Money, who urged them to bring their child to Baltimore without delay. After consultation with various physicians and with Money, the parents agreed to have their son's sex reassigned. In anticipation of what would follow, the boy's parents stopped cutting his hair, dressed him in feminine clothes, and changed his name from Bruce to Brenda. Surgical castration was performed when the twin was 22 months old.

Early reports of the child's progress indicated success. In contrast to her biologically identical brother, Brenda was said to disdain cars, gas pumps, and tools. She was supposedly fascinated by dolls, a dollhouse, and a doll carriage. Brenda's mother reported that, at the age of four and a half, Brenda took pleasure in her feminine clothing: "[S]he is so feminine. I've never seen a little girl so neat and tidy . . . and yet my son is quite different. I can't wash his face for anything. . . . She is very proud of herself, when she puts on a new dress, or I set her hair" (quoted in Money and Ehrhardt, 1972: 11).

The "twins' case" generated worldwide attention. Textbooks in medicine and the social sciences were rewritten to incorporate Money's reports of the child's progress (Robertson, 1987: 316). But then, in March 1997, two researchers dropped a bombshell. A biologist from the University of Hawaii and a psychiatrist from the Canadian Ministry of Health unleashed a scientific scandal when they published an article showing that Bruce/Brenda had, in fact, struggled against his/her imposed girlhood from the start (Diamond and Sigmundson, 1999). Brenda insisted on urinating standing up, refused to undergo additional "feminizing" surgeries that had been planned, and, from age seven, daydreamed of her ideal future self "as a twenty-one-year-old male with a moustache, a sports car, and surrounded by admiring friends" (Colapinto, 2001: 93). She experienced academic failure and rejection and ridicule from her classmates, who dubbed her "Cavewoman." At age nine, Brenda had a nervous breakdown. At age 14, in a state of acute despair, she attempted suicide (Colapinto, 2001: 96, 262).

In 1980, Brenda learned the details of her sex reassignment from her father. At age 16, she decided to have her sex reassigned once more and to live as a man rather than as a woman. Advances in medical technology

David Reimer at about age 30.

made it possible for Brenda, who now adopted the name David, to have an artificial penis constructed. At age 25, David married a woman and adopted her three children, but that did not end his ordeal (Gorman, 1997). In May 2004, at the age of 38, David Reimer committed suicide.

Gender Identity and Gender Role

The story of Bruce/Brenda/David introduces the first big question of this chapter. What makes us male or female? Of course, part of the answer is biological. Your **sex** depends on whether you were born with distinct male or female genitals and a genetic program that released male or female hormones to stimulate the development of your reproductive system.

However, the case of Bruce/Brenda/David also shows that more is involved in becoming male or female than biological sex differences. Recalling his life as Brenda, David said, "[E]veryone is telling you that you're a girl. But you say to yourself, 'I don't *feel* like a girl.' You think girls are supposed to be delicate and *like* girl things—tea parties, things like that. But I like to *do* guy stuff. It doesn't match" (quoted in Colapinto, 1997: 66; our emphasis). As this quotation suggests, being male or female involves not just biology but also certain "masculine" and "feminine" feelings, attitudes, and behaviours. Accordingly, sociologists distinguish biological sex from sociological **gender**. A person's gender comprises the feelings, attitudes, and behaviours typically associated with being male or female. **Gender identity** is a person's identification with, or sense of belonging to, a particular sex—biologically, psychologically, and socially. When you behave according to widely shared expectations about how males or females are supposed to act, you adopt a **gender role**.

Contrary to first impressions, the case of Bruce/Brenda/David suggests that, unlike sex, gender is not determined just by biology. Research shows that babies first develop a vague sense of being a boy or a girl at about the age of one. They develop a full-blown sense of gender identity between the ages of two and three (Blum, 1997). We can therefore be confident that Bruce/Brenda/David already knew he was a boy when he was assigned a female gender identity at the age of 22 months. He had, after all, been raised as a boy by his parents and treated as a boy by his brother for almost two years. He had seen boys behaving differently from girls on TV and in storybooks. He had played with stereotypical boys' toys. After his gender reassignment, the constant presence of his twin brother reinforced those early lessons on how boys ought to behave. In short, baby Bruce's *social* learning of his gender identity was already far advanced by the time he had his sex-change operation. Many researchers believe that if gender reassignment occurs before the age of 18 months, it will usually be successful (Creighton and Mihto, 2001; Lightfoot-Klein, Chase, Hammond, and Goldman, 2000). However, once the social learning of gender takes hold, as with baby Bruce, it is apparently very difficult to undo, even by means of reconstructive surgery, hormones, and parental and professional pressure. The main lesson we draw from this story is not that biology is destiny but that the social learning of gender begins very early in life.

The first half of this chapter helps you to better understand what makes us male or female. We first outline two competing perspectives on gender differences. The first perspective argues that gender is inherent in our biological makeup and that society must reinforce those tendencies if it is to function smoothly. Functionalist theory is compatible with this argument. The second perspective argues that gender is constructed mainly by social influences and may be altered to benefit society's members. Conflict, feminist, and symbolic interactionist theories are compatible with the second perspective.

In our discussion we examine how people learn gender roles during socialization in the family and at school. We show how everyday social interactions and advertising reinforce gender roles. The imposition of relatively rigid gender roles consistent with patriarchy reduces options for both men and women, sometimes at substantial costs in personal fulfillment. We discuss how members of society enforce **heterosexuality**—the preference for members of the opposite sex as sexual partners. For reasons that are still poorly understood, some people

Your **sex** depends on whether you were born with distinct male or female genitals and a genetic program that released either male or female hormones to stimulate the development of your reproductive system.

Your **gender** is your sense of being male or female and your playing of masculine and feminine roles in ways defined as appropriate by your culture and society.

Gender identity is a person's identification with, or sense of belonging to, a particular sex—biologically, psychologically, and socially.

A **gender role** is the set of behaviours associated with widely shared expectations about how males and females are supposed to act.

Heterosexuality is the preference for members of the opposite sex as sexual partners.

resist and even reject the gender roles that are assigned to them based on their biological sex. When this occurs, negative sanctions are often applied to get them to conform or to punish them for their deviance. Members of society are often eager to use emotional and physical violence to enforce conventional gender roles.

The second half of the chapter examines one of the chief consequences of people learning conventional gender roles. Gender, as currently constructed, creates and maintains social inequality. We illustrate this in two ways. We investigate why gender is associated with an earnings gap between women and men in the paid labour force. We also show how gender inequality encourages sexual harassment and rape. In concluding our discussion of sexuality and gender, we discuss social policies that sociologists have recommended to decrease gender inequality and improve women's safety.

THEORIES OF GENDER

Essentialism is a school of thought that views gender differences as a reflection of biological differences between women and men.

Most arguments about the origins of gender differences in human behaviour adopt one of two perspectives. Some analysts see gender differences as a reflection of naturally evolved dispositions. Sociologists call this perspective **essentialism** because it views gender as part of the nature or "essence" of a person's biological makeup (Weeks, 2000). Other analysts see gender differences as a reflection of the different social positions occupied by women and men. Sociologists call this perspective *social constructionism* because it views gender as "constructed" by social structure and culture. Conflict, feminist, and symbolic interactionist theories focus on various aspects of the social construction of gender. We now summarize and criticize essentialism. We then turn to social constructionism.

Essentialism

Freud

Sigmund Freud (1977 [1905]) offered an early and influential essentialist explanation of male–female differences. He believed that differences in male and female anatomy account for the development of distinct masculine and feminine gender roles.

According to Freud, children around the age of three begin to pay attention to their genitals. As a young boy becomes preoccupied with his penis, he unconsciously develops a fantasy of sexually possessing the most conspicuous female in his life: his mother. Soon, he begins to resent his father because only his father is allowed to possess the mother sexually. Because he has seen his mother or another girl naked, the boy also develops anxiety that his father will castrate him for desiring his mother.[1] To resolve this fear, the boy represses his feelings for his mother. That is, he stores them in the unconscious part of his personality. In due course, repression allows him to begin identifying with his father. This leads to the development of a strong, independent masculine personality.

In contrast, the young girl begins to develop a feminine personality when she realizes she lacks a penis. According to Freud:

> [Girls] who notice the penis of a brother or playmate, strikingly visible and of large proportions, at once recognize it as the superior counterpart of their own small and inconspicuous organ, and from that time forward fall a victim to envy for the penis. . . . She has seen it and knows that she is without it and wants to have it. (quoted in Steinem, 1994: 50)

Because of her "penis envy," the young girl develops a sense of inferiority, according to Freud. She also grows angry with her mother, who, she naively thinks, is responsible for cutting off the penis she must have once had. She rejects her mother and develops an unconscious sexual desire for her father. Eventually, however, realizing she will never have a penis, the girl comes to identify with her mother. This is a way of vicariously acquiring her father's penis in Freud's view. In the "normal" development of a mature woman, the girl's wish to have a penis is transformed into a desire to have children. However, says Freud, since women are never able to resolve their penis envy completely, they are "naturally" immature and dependent on men. This dependence is evident from the "fact" that women can be fully sexually satisfied only by vaginally induced orgasms.[2] Thus, a host of gender differences in personality and behaviour follow from the anatomical sex differences that children first observe around the age of three.

Sociobiology and Evolutionary Psychology

For the past three decades, sociobiologists and evolutionary psychologists have offered a second essentialist theory. We introduced this theory in Chapter 3, Culture. According to sociobiologists and evolutionary psychologists, all humans instinctively try to ensure that their genes are passed on to future generations. However, men and women develop different strategies to achieve this goal. A woman has a bigger investment than a man does in ensuring the survival of any offspring because she produces only a small number of eggs during her reproductive life and, at most, can give birth to about 20 children. It is therefore in a woman's best interest to maintain primary responsibility for her genetic children and to find the best mate with whom to intermix her eggs. He is the man who can best help support the children after birth. In contrast, most men can produce as many as a billion sperm in a single ejaculation and this number can be replicated often (Saxton, 1990: 94–5). Thus, a man increases the chance his and only his genes will be passed on to future generations if he is promiscuous yet jealously possessive of his partners. Moreover, since men compete with other men for sexual access to women, men evolve competitive and aggressive dispositions that include physical violence (DeSteno and Salovey, 2001). Women, says one evolutionary psychologist, are greedy for money, while men want casual sex with women, treat women's bodies as their property, and react violently to women who incite male sexual jealousy. These are "universal features of our evolved selves" that presumably contribute to the survival of the human species (Buss, 2000). From the point of view of sociobiology and evolutionary psychology, then, gender differences in behaviour are based in biological differences between women and men.

Functionalism and Essentialism

Functionalists reinforce the essentialist viewpoint when they claim that traditional gender roles help to integrate society (Parsons, 1942). In the family, wrote Talcott Parsons, women traditionally specialize in raising children and managing the household. Men traditionally work in the paid labour force. Each generation learns to perform these complementary roles by means of gender role socialization.

For boys, noted Parsons, the essence of masculinity is a series of "instrumental" traits, such as rationality, self-assuredness, and competitiveness. For girls, the essence of femininity is a series of "expressive" traits, such as nurturance and sensitivity to others. Boys and girls first learn their respective gender traits in the family as they see their parents going about their daily routines. The larger society also promotes gender role conformity. It instills in men the fear that they won't be attractive to women if the men are too feminine, and it instills in women the fear that they won't be attractive to men if the women are too masculine. In the functionalist view, then, learning the essential features of femininity and masculinity integrates society and allows it to function properly.

A Critique of Essentialism from the Conflict and Feminist Perspectives

Conflict and feminist theorists disagree sharply with the essentialist account. They have lodged four main criticisms against it.

First, *essentialists ignore the historical and cultural variability of gender and sexuality.* Wide variations exist in what constitutes masculinity and femininity. Moreover, the level of gender inequality, the rate of male violence against women, the criteria used for mate

Definitions of *male* and *female* traits vary across societies. For example, the ceremonial dress of male Wodaabe nomads in Niger may appear "feminine" by conventional North American standards.

selection, and other gender differences that appear universal to the essentialists vary widely too. This variation deflates the idea that there are essential and universal behavioural differences between women and men. Three examples help illustrate the point:

1. In societies with low levels of gender inequality, the tendency decreases for women to stress the good provider role in selecting male partners, as does the tendency for men to stress women's domestic skills (Eagley and Wood, 1999).
2. When women become corporate lawyers or police officers or take other jobs that involve competition or threat, their production of the hormone testosterone is stimulated, causing them to act more aggressively. Aggressiveness is partly role-related (Blum, 1997: 158–88).
3. Literally hundreds of studies conducted mainly in North America show that women are developing traits that were traditionally considered masculine. Women have become considerably more assertive, competitive, independent, and analytical in the past few decades (Biegler, 1999; Duffy, Gunther, and Walters, 1997; Nowell and Hedges, 1998; Twenge, 1997).

As these examples show, gender differences are not constants and they are not inherent in men and women. They vary with social conditions.

The second problem with essentialism is that *it tends to generalize from the average, ignoring variations within gender groups.* On average, women and men do differ in some respects. For example, one of the best-documented gender differences is that men are, on average, more verbally and physically aggressive than women are. However, when essentialists say men are inherently more aggressive than women are, they make it seem as if that is true of all men and all women. As Figure 11.1 shows, it is not. When trained researchers measure verbal or physical aggressiveness, scores vary widely within gender groups. There is considerable overlap in aggressiveness between women and men. Thus, many women are more aggressive than the average man and many men are less aggressive than the average woman.

Third, *little or no evidence directly supports the essentialists' major claims.* Sociobiologists and evolutionary psychologists have not identified any of the genes that, they claim, cause male jealousy, female nurturance, the unequal division of labour between men and women, and so forth. Freudians have not collected any experimental or survey data

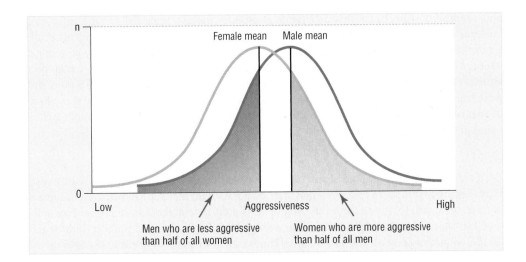

FIGURE 11.1

The Distribution of Aggressiveness among Men and Women

showing that boys are more independent than girls are because of their emotional reactions to the discovery of their sex organs.

Finally, *essentialists' explanations for gender differences ignore the role of power.* Essentialists assume that existing behaviour patterns help to ensure the survival of the species and the smooth functioning of society. However, as conflict and feminist theorists argue, essentialists generally ignore the fact that men are usually in a position of greater power and authority than women are.

Conflict theorists dating back to Marx's collaborator, Friedrich Engels, have located the root of male domination in class inequality (Engels, 1970 [1884]). According to Engels, men gained substantial power over women when preliterate societies were first able to produce more than the amount needed for their own subsistence. At that point, some men gained control over the economic surplus. They soon devised two means of ensuring that their offspring would inherit the surplus. First, they imposed the rule that only men could own property. Second, by means of socialization and force, they ensured that women remained sexually faithful to their husbands. As industrial capitalism developed, Engels wrote, male domination increased because industrial capitalism made men still wealthier and more powerful while it relegated women to subordinate, domestic roles.

Feminist theorists doubt that male domination is so closely linked to the development of industrial capitalism. For one thing, they note that gender inequality is greater in agrarian than in industrial capitalist societies. For another, male domination is evident in societies that call themselves socialist or communist. These observations lead many feminists to conclude that male domination is rooted less in industrial capitalism than in the patriarchal authority relations, family structures, and patterns of socialization and culture that exist in most societies (Lapidus, 1978: 7).

Despite this disagreement, conflict and feminist theorists concur that behavioural differences between women and men result less from any essential differences between them than from men being in a position to impose their interests over the interests of women. From the conflict and feminist viewpoints, functionalism, sociobiology, and evolutionary psychology can themselves be seen as examples of the exercise of male power, that is, as rationalizations for male domination and sexual aggression.

Social Constructionism and Symbolic Interactionism

Essentialism is the view that masculinity and femininity are inherent and universal traits of men and women, whether because of biological or social necessity or some combination of the two. In contrast, social constructionism is the view that *apparently* natural or innate features of life, such as gender, are actually sustained by *social* processes that vary historically

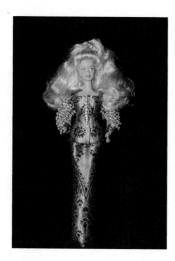

"Barbie was more than a doll to me. She was a way of living: the Ideal Woman."

and culturally. As such, conflict and feminist theories may be regarded as types of social constructionism. So may symbolic interactionism. Symbolic interactionists, you will recall, focus on the way people attach meaning to things in the course of their everyday communication. One of the things to which people attach meaning is what it means to be a man or a woman. We illustrate the symbolic interactionist approach by first considering how boys and girls learn masculine and feminine roles in the family and at school. We then show how gender roles are maintained in the course of everyday social interaction and through advertising in the mass media.

Gender Socialization

Barbie dolls have been around since 1959. Based on the creation of a German cartoonist, Barbie is the first modern doll modelled after an adult. (Lili, the German original, became a pornographic doll for men.) Some industry experts predicted mothers would never buy dolls with breasts for their little girls. Were *they* wrong! Mattel sells about 10 million Barbies and 20 million accompanying outfits annually. The Barbie trademark is worth US$1 billion.

What do girls learn when they play with Barbie? The author of a website devoted to Barbie undoubtedly speaks for millions when she writes, "Barbie was more than a doll to me. She was a way of living: the Ideal Woman. When I played with her, I could make her do and be ANYTHING I wanted. Never before or since have I found such an ideal method of living vicariously through anyone or anything. And I don't believe I am alone. I am certain that most people have, in fact, lived their dreams with Barbie as the role player" (Elliott, 1995; Nicolaiedis, 1998; Turkel, 1998).

One dream that Barbie stimulates among many girls concerns body image. After all, Barbie is a scale model of a woman with a 40-18-32 figure (Hamilton, 1996: 197). Researchers who compared Barbie's gravity-defying proportions with the actual proportions of several representative groups of adult women concluded that the probability of this body shape was less than 1 in 100 000 (Norton, Olds, Olive, and Dank, 1996). (Ken's body shape is far more realistic at 1 in 50.)

Nevertheless, for nearly half a century, Barbie has served as an identifiable symbol of stereotypical female beauty (Magro, 1997). Her pre-set Barbie Workout Scale registers a lithe 110 pounds (50 kilograms). The closets of her pink house are jammed with outfits. Bathrooms, gyms, and beauty parlours feature prominently among the Barbie sets available. Her quest for physical perfection seems largely geared to the benefit of Ken, her boyfriend (Nelson and Robinson, 2002: 131). When girls play with Barbie, they learn to want to be slim, blonde, shapely, and, implicitly, pleasing to men.

A comparable story, with competition and aggression as its theme, could be told about how boys' toys, such as GI Joe, teach stereotypical male roles. True, a movement to market more gender-neutral toys arose in the 1960s and 1970s. However, it has now been overtaken by the resumption of a strong tendency to market toys based on gender. As *The Wall Street Journal* pointed out, "gender-neutral is out, as more kids' marketers push single-sex products" (Bannon, 2000: B1). For example, in 2000, Toys "R" Us unveiled a new store design that included a store directory featuring Boy's World and Girl's World. The Boy's World section has action figures, sports collectibles, remote-controlled cars, Tonka trucks, boys' role-playing games, and walkie-talkies. The Girl's World section has Barbie dolls, baby dolls, collectible horses, play kitchens, housekeeping toys, girls' dress-up, jewellery, cosmetics, and bath and body products.

A movement to market more gender-neutral toys emerged in the 1960s and 1970s. However, it has now been overtaken by the resumption of a strong tendency to market toys based on gender.

Yet toys and the mass popular culture they represent are only part of the story of gender socialization and hardly its first or final chapter. Research shows that, from birth, infant boys and girls who are matched in length, weight, and general health are treated differently by parents—and by fathers in particular. Girls tend to be identified as delicate, weak, beautiful, and cute, boys as strong, alert, and well coordinated (Rubin, Provenzano, and Lurra, 1974). Recent attempts to update and extend this investigation found that although parents' gender-stereotyped perceptions of newborns have declined, especially among fathers, they have not disappeared entirely (Fagot, Rodgers, and Leinbach, 2000; Gauvain, Fagot, Leve, and Kavanagh, 2002; Karraker, Vogel, and Lake, 1995). When viewing videotape of a nine-month-old infant, adult experimental subjects tend to label its startled reaction to a stimulus as "anger" if the child has earlier been identified by the experimenters as a boy and as "fear" if it has earlier been identified as a girl, *whatever the infant's actual sex* (Condry and Condry, 1976; see also Martin, 1999).

Parents, and especially fathers, are more likely to encourage their sons to engage in boisterous and competitive play and discourage their daughters from doing likewise. In general, parents tend to encourage girls to engage in cooperative, role-playing games (Fagot, Rodgers, and Leinbach, 2000; Gauvain et al., 2002; Parke, 2001, 2002). These different play patterns lead to the heightened development of verbal and emotional skills among girls, and to more concern with winning and the establishment of hierarchy among boys (Tannen, 1990). Boys are more likely than girls are to be praised for assertiveness, and girls are more likely than boys are to be rewarded for compliance (Kerig, Cowan, and Cowan, 1993). Given this early socialization, it seems perfectly "natural" that boys' toys stress aggression, competition, spatial manipulation, and outdoor activities, while girls' toys stress nurturing, physical attractiveness, and indoor activities (Hughes, 1995). Still, what seems natural must be continuously socially reinforced. Presented with a choice between playing with a tool set and a dish set, preschool boys are about as likely to choose one as the other—unless the dish set is presented as a girl's toy and they think their fathers would view playing with it as "bad." Then, they tend to pick the tool set (Raag and Rackliff, 1998).

It would take someone who has spent very little time in the company of children to think they are passive objects of socialization. They are not. Parents, teachers, and other authority figures typically try to impose their ideas of appropriate gender behaviour on children, but children creatively interpret, negotiate, resist, and self-impose these ideas all the time. Gender, we might say, is something that is done, not just given (Messner, 2000; West and Zimmerman, 1987). This fact is nowhere more evident than in the way children play.

Gender Segregation and Interaction

Consider the grade 4 and 5 classroom that sociologist Barrie Thorne (1993) observed. The teacher periodically asked the children to choose their own desks. With the exception of one girl, they always segregated *themselves* by gender. The teacher then drew on this self-segregation in pitting the boys against the girls in spelling and math contests. These contests were marked by cross-gender antagonism and expression of within-gender solidarity. Similarly, when children played chasing games in the schoolyard, groups often *spontaneously* crystallized along gender lines. These games had special names, some of which, such as "chase and kiss," had clear sexual meanings. Provocation, physical contact, and avoidance were all sexually charged parts of the game.

Although Thorne found that contests, chasing games, and other activities often involved self-segregation of boys and girls, she observed many cases of boys and girls playing together. She also noticed quite a lot of "boundary crossing." Boundary crossing involves boys playing stereotypically girls' games and girls playing stereotypically boys' games. The most common form of boundary crossing involved girls who were skilled at specific sports that were central to the boys' world—such sports as soccer, baseball, and basketball. If girls demonstrated skill at these activities, boys often accepted them as participants. Finally, Thorne noticed occasions in which boys and girls interacted without strain and without strong gender identities coming to the fore. For instance, activities requiring cooperation, such as a group radio show or art project, lessened attention to gender. Another situation that lessened strain between boys and girls, causing gender to recede in importance, occurred when adults organized mixed-gender encounters in the classroom and in physical education periods. On such occasions, adults legitimized cross-gender contact. Mixed-gender interaction was also more common in less public and crowded settings. Thus, boys

In her research on schoolchildren, sociologist Barrie Thorne noticed quite a lot of "boundary crossing" between boys and girls. Most commonly, boys accepted girls as participants in soccer, baseball, and basketball games if the girls demonstrated skill at these sports.

and girls were more likely to play together in a relaxed way in the relative privacy of their neighbourhoods. In contrast, in the schoolyard, where they were under the close scrutiny of their peers, gender segregation and antagonism were more evident.

In sum, Thorne's research makes two important contributions to our understanding of gender socialization. First, children are actively engaged in the process of constructing gender roles. They are not merely passive recipients of adult demands. Second, although schoolchildren tend to segregate themselves by gender, boundaries between boys and girls are sometimes fluid and sometimes rigid, depending on social circumstances. In other words, the content of children's gendered activities is by no means fixed.

This is not to suggest that adults have no gender demands and expectations. They do, and their demands and expectations contribute importantly to gender socialization. For instance, many schoolteachers and guidance counsellors still expect boys to do better in the sciences and math and girls to achieve higher marks in English (Lips, 1999). Parents often reinforce these stereotypes in their evaluation of different activities (Eccles, Jacobs, and Harold, 1990). Although not all studies comparing mixed- and single-sex schools suggest that girls do much better in the latter, most do (Bornholt, 2001; Jackson and Smith, 2000). In single-sex schools, girls typically experience faster cognitive development; higher occupational aspirations and attainment; greater self-esteem and self-confidence; and more teacher attention, respect, and encouragement in the classroom. They also develop more egalitarian attitudes toward the role of women in society. Why? Because such schools place more emphasis on academic excellence and less on physical attractiveness and heterosexual popularity. They provide more successful same-sex role models. And they eliminate sex bias in teacher–student and student–student interaction since there are no boys around (Hesse-Biber and Carter, 2000: 99–100).

A **gender ideology** is a set of interrelated ideas about what constitutes appropriate masculine and feminine roles and behaviour.

Adolescents must usually start choosing courses in school by the age of 14 or 15. By then, their **gender ideologies** are well formed. Gender ideologies are sets of interrelated ideas about what constitutes appropriate masculine and feminine roles and behaviour. One aspect of gender ideology becomes especially important around grades 9 and 10: adolescents' ideas about whether, as adults, they will focus mainly on the home, paid work, or a combination of the two. Adolescents usually make course choices with gender ideologies in mind. Boys are strongly inclined to consider only their careers in making course choices. Most girls are inclined to consider both home responsibilities and careers, although a minority considers only home responsibilities and another minority considers only careers. Consequently, boys tend to choose career-oriented courses, particularly in math and science, more often than girls do. In college and university, the pattern is accentuated. In 2006 women accounted for just 17 percent of Canadian university students in architecture and engineering (see Chapter 17, Education).

Young women tend to choose courses that lead to lower-paying jobs because they expect to devote a large part of their lives to child rearing and housework (Eccles, Roeser, Wigfield, and Freedman-Doen, 1999). When a sample of Canadian undergraduates were asked to identify their preference, 53 percent of the women but only 6 percent of the men selected "graduation, full-time work, marriage, children, stop working at least until youngest child is in school, then pursue a full-time job" as their preferred lifestyle sequence (Schroeder, Blood, and Maluso, 1993).

These choices sharply restrict women's career opportunities and earnings in science and business. In 2000, 76.5 percent of people working full-year, full-time in the 10 lowest-paid occupations in Canada were women. The average earnings of women in these occupations was $19 459 (Department of Justice Canada, 2004). We examine the wage gap between women and men in depth in the second half of this chapter.

The Mass Media and Body Image

The social construction of gender does not stop at the school steps. Outside school, children, adolescents, and adults continue to negotiate gender roles as they interact with the mass media. If you systematically observe the roles played by women and men in television, movies, magazines, music videos, TV commercials, and print media advertisements, you will probably discover a pattern noted by sociologists since the 1970s. Women will more frequently be seen cleaning house, taking care of children, modelling clothes, and acting as objects of male desire (Signorielli, 1998). Men will more frequently be seen in aggressive, action-oriented, and authoritative roles. The effect of these messages on viewers is much the same as that of the Disney movies and Harlequin romances we discussed in Chapter 4, Socialization: They reinforce the normality of traditional gender roles.

Steven Rytina learned just how powerful the mass media's lessons about traditional gender roles are when he was in his 20s. For several years, he worked in a daycare facility for children between the age of four and six. "It was the 1970s," Steven recalls, "and a big concern was to not pass on traditional gender stereotypes. Since most of the kids were from families where mothers and fathers had earned or were earning professional degrees, this project was popular and seemed straightforward. We were conscientious about using gender-neutral language, our storybooks were carefully screened to make sure they didn't portray women and men in stereotypical feminine and masculine roles, and so forth. Many of the kids' parents told me that they were trying to instill the same gender-neutral messages at home as we were at daycare.

PERSONAL ANECDOTE

"But to our surprise and dismay, it didn't work. When the kids played, their fantasies were the opposite of what we hoped for. For example, without exception, it was the little boys who turned towels into capes and the little girls who acted out peril, helplessness, and gratitude to their brave protectors. Strongly traditional gender themes were not merely apparent but overwhelmingly dominant.

"Finding out why was as simple as asking. We learned that the kids watched a lot of TV. The fantasies of Disney and Warner Brothers were far more compelling to them than any book or any teacher telling stories. I expect that most of the kids I worked with eventually adopted gender attitudes nearer what we hoped for. However, every one of them was at first fully immersed in stereotypes that their teachers and parents professed to disdain. My daycare experience taught me that it is very difficult to prevent children from absorbing the gender messages that dominate the mass media."

People even try to shape their bodies after the images portrayed in the mass media. The human body has always served as a sort of personal billboard that advertises gender. However, the importance of body image to our self-definition has grown over the past century. Just listen to the difference in emphasis on the body in the diary resolutions of two typical white, middle-class North American girls, separated by a mere 90 years. From 1892: "Resolved, not to talk about myself or feelings. To think before speaking. To work seriously. To be self restrained in conversation and actions. Not to let my thoughts wander. To be dignified. Interest myself more in others." From 1982: "I will try to make myself better in any way I possibly can with the help of my budget and baby-sitting money. I will lose weight, get new lenses, already got new haircut, good makeup, new clothes and accessories" (quoted in Brumberg, 1997: xxi).

As body image became more important for self-definition during the twentieth century, the ideal body image became thinner, especially for women. For example, although Miss America beauty pageant winners became only a little taller between 1922 and 1999, they became much thinner (Curran, 2000). As one eating disorders expert observed, "Beauty pageants, like the rest of our media-driven culture, give young women in particular a message, over and over again, that it's exceedingly important to be thin to be considered successful and attractive" (quoted in Curran, 2000).[3]

Why did body image become more important to people's self-definition during the twentieth century? Why was slimness stressed? Part of the answer to both questions is that more North Americans grew overweight as their lifestyles became more sedentary. As they became

The "White Rock Girl," featured on the logo of the White Rock beverage company, dropped 15 pounds between 1894 (left) and 1947 (right).

The low-calorie and diet food industry promotes an ideal of slimness that is often impossible to attain and that generates widespread body dissatisfaction.

better educated, they also grew increasingly aware of the health problems associated with being overweight. The desire to slim down was, then, partly a reaction to bulking up. But that is not the whole story. The rake-thin models who populate modern ads are not promoting good health. They are promoting an extreme body shape that is virtually unattainable for most people (Tovee, Mason, Emery, McClusky, and Cohen-Tovee, 1997). They do so because it is good business. The fitness, diet, low-calorie food, and cosmetic surgery industries do billions of dollars of business a year in North America (Hesse-Biber, 1996). Bankrolled by these industries, advertising in the mass media blankets us with images of slim bodies and makes these body types appealing. Once people become convinced that they need to develop bodies like the ones they see in ads, many of them are really in trouble because these body images are impossible for most people to attain.

Survey data show just how widespread dissatisfaction with our bodies is and how important a role the mass media play in generating our discomfort. One survey of North American university graduates showed that 56 percent of women and 43 percent of men were dissatisfied with their overall appearance (Garner, 1997). Only 3 percent of the dissatisfied women, but 22 percent of the dissatisfied men, wanted to gain weight. This difference reflects the greater desire of men for muscular, stereotypically male physiques. Most of the dissatisfied men, and even more of the dissatisfied women (89 percent), wanted to lose weight. This finding reflects the general societal push toward slimness and its greater effect on women. According to the National Population Health Survey, even though Canadian women are almost five times more likely than Canadian men to be *underweight* (14 percent and 3 percent, respectively), they are more likely to report recent attempts to lose weight: "This desire to lose weight extended to many women who were already within the healthy weight range" (Health Canada, 1999a: 118).

Figure 11.2 reveals gender differences in body ideals in a different way. It compares North American women's and men's attitudes toward their stomachs. It also compares women's attitudes toward their breasts with men's attitudes toward their chests. It shows, first, that women are more concerned about their stomachs than men are about their own. Second, it shows that men are more concerned about their chests than women are about their breasts. Clearly, then, people's body ideals are influenced by their gender. Note also that Figure 11.2 shows trends over time. North Americans' anxiety about their bodies increased substantially between 1972 and 1997.

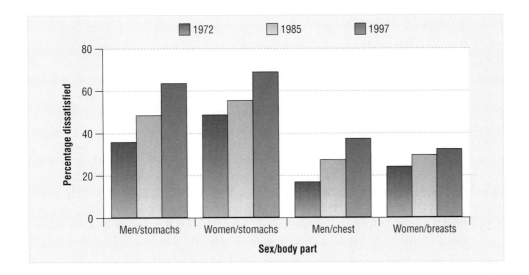

FIGURE 11.2

Body Dissatisfaction, North America, 1972–1997 (in percent, *n* = 4000)

Note: The *n* of 4000 refers to the 1997 survey only. The number of respondents in the earlier surveys was not given.

Source: From "The 1997 Body Image Results" by David M. Garner, *Psychology Today*, Vol. 30, No. 1, pp. 30–44. Reprinted from *Psychology Today Magazine*, copyright © (1997) Sussex Publishers, Inc.

Table 11.1 suggests that advertising is highly influential in creating anxiety and insecurity about appearance, and particularly about body weight. We see that nearly 30 percent of North American women compared themselves with the fashion models they saw in advertisements, felt insecure about their own appearance, and wanted to lose weight as a result. Among women who were dissatisfied with their appearance, the percentages were much larger, with about 45 percent making comparisons with fashion models and two-thirds feeling insecure and wanting to lose weight. It seems safe to conclude that fashion models stimulate body dissatisfaction among many North American women.

Body dissatisfaction, in turn, motivates many women to diet. Because of anxiety about their weight, 84 percent of North American women in the 1997 survey said they had dieted. The comparable figure for men was 54 percent. Just how important is it for people to achieve their weight goals? According to the survey, it's a life or death issue: 24 percent of women and 17 percent of men said they would willingly trade more than three years of their lives to achieve their weight goals.

Body dissatisfaction prompts some people to take dangerous and even life-threatening measures to reduce their size. In the 1997 survey, 50 percent of female smokers and 30 percent of male smokers said they smoked to control their weight. Other surveys suggest that between 1 percent and 5 percent of North American women suffer from anorexia nervosa (characterized by weight loss, excessive exercise, food aversion, distorted body image, and an intense and irrational fear of body fat and weight gain). About the same percentage of North American female university students suffer from bulimia, characterized by cycles of binge eating and purging (through self-induced vomiting or the use of laxatives, purgatives, or diuretics). For university men, the prevalence of bulimia is between 0.2 percent and 1.5 percent (Averett and Korenman, 1996: 305–06).

TABLE 11.1

The Influence of Fashion Models on Feelings about Appearance, North America (in percent; *n* = 4000)

Source: From "The 1997 Body Image Results" by David M. Garner, *Psychology Today*, Vol. 30, No. 1, pp. 30–44. Reprinted with permission from *Psychology Today Magazine*, copyright © (1997) Sussex Publishers, Inc.

	Men	Women	Extremely Dissatisfied Women
I always or often:			
Compare myself with models in magazines	12	27	43
Carefully study the shape of models	19	28	47
Very thin or muscular models make me:			
Feel insecure about my weight	15	29	67
Want to lose weight	18	30	67

Male–Female Interaction

The gender roles children learn in their families, at school, and through the mass media form the basis of their social interaction as adults. For instance, by playing team sports, boys tend to learn that social interaction is most often about competition, conflict, self-sufficiency, and hierarchical relationships (leaders versus the led). They understand the importance of taking centre stage and boasting about their talents (Messner, 1995). Because many of the most popular video games for boys exclude female characters (*Game Boy* wasn't named *Game Boy* for nothing!), use women as sex objects, or involve violence against women, they reinforce some of the most unsavoury lessons of traditional gender socialization (Dietz, 1998). However, by playing with dolls and baking sets, girls tend to learn that social interaction is most often about maintaining cordial relationships, avoiding conflict, and resolving differences of opinion through negotiation (Subrahmanyam and Greenfield, 1998). They are informed of the importance of giving advice and not promoting themselves or being bossy.[4]

Because of these early socialization patterns, misunderstandings between men and women are common. A stereotypical example: Harold is driving around lost. However, he refuses to ask for directions because doing so would amount to an admission of inadequacy and therefore a loss of status. Meanwhile, it seems perfectly "natural" to Sybil to want to share information, so she urges Harold to ask for directions. The result: conflict between Harold and Sybil (Tannen, 1990: 62).

Gender-specific interaction styles also have serious implications for who is heard and who gets credit at work. Here are some examples uncovered by Deborah Tannen's research (1994a: 132–59):

- A female office manager doesn't want to seem bossy or arrogant. She is eager to preserve consensus among her co-workers. So she spends a good deal of time soliciting their opinions before making an important decision. She asks questions, listens attentively, and offers suggestions. She then decides. But her boss perceives her approach as indecisive and incompetent. He wants to recruit leaders for upper-management positions, so he overlooks the woman and selects an assertive man for a senior job that just opened up.
- Male managers are inclined to say "I" in many situations where female managers are inclined to say "we"—as in "I'm hiring a new manager and I'm going to put him in charge of my marketing division" or "This is what I've come up with on the Lakehill deal." This sort of phrasing draws attention to personal accomplishments. In contrast, Tannen heard a female manager talking about what "we" had done, when in fact she had done all the work alone. This sort of phrasing camouflages women's accomplishments.

The contrasting interaction styles illustrated above can result in female managers not getting credit for competent performance. That may be part of the reason why women sometimes complain about a **glass ceiling**, a social barrier that makes it difficult for them to rise to the top level of management. As we will soon see, factors other than interaction styles, such as outright discrimination and women's generally greater commitment to family responsibilities, also support the glass ceiling. Yet gender differences in interaction styles seem to play an independent role in constraining women's career progress.

The glass ceiling is a social barrier that makes it difficult for women to rise to the top level of management.

Transgendered people break society's gender norms by defying the rigid distinction between male and female.

Transsexuals believe they were born with the "wrong" body. They identify with, and want to live fully as, members of the "opposite" sex.

HOMOSEXUALITY

The preceding discussion outlines some powerful social forces that push us to define ourselves as conventionally masculine or feminine in behaviour and appearance. For most people, gender socialization by the family, the school, and the mass media is compelling and is sustained by daily interactions. A minority of people, however, resists conventional gender roles.

Transgendered people defy society's gender norms and blur widely accepted gender roles (Cole, Denny, Eyler, and Samons, 2000: 151). About 1 in every 5000 to 10 000 people in North America is transgendered. Some transgendered people are **transsexuals**. Transsexuals are individuals who want to alter their gender by changing their appearance or resorting to medical intervention. Transsexuals believe they were born with the "wrong" body. They identify with, and want to live fully as, members of the "opposite" sex. They often take the lengthy and painful path to a sex change operation. About 1 in every 30 000 people in North America is a transsexual (Nolen, 1999). **Homosexuals** are people who prefer sexual partners of the same sex, and **bisexuals** are people who enjoy sexual partners of either sex. People usually call homosexual men *gay* and homosexual women *lesbians*. In 2000, about 6 percent of Torontonians identified themselves as homosexual or bisexual ("Homosexuality and Bisexuality," 2000). In 2003, 1.8 percent of Canadian men and 1.5 percent of Canadian women described themselves as homosexual or bisexual in response to surveys (Statistics Canada, 2004c). The most comprehensive survey of sexuality conducted in North America reports that an approximately comparable 2.8 percent of American men and 1.4 percent of American women pick homosexual or bisexual as self-descriptions. However, the American investigation also discovered that 10.1 percent of men and 8.6 percent of women think of themselves as homosexual or bisexual *or* have had some same-sex experience or desire (see Table 11.2; Laumann, Gagnon, Michael, and Michaels, 1994: 299). It seems likely that because of widespread animosity toward homosexuals, some people who have desired or engaged in same-sex acts do not identify themselves as gay, lesbian, or bisexual (Flowers and Buston, 2001; Herdt, 2001).

Homosexuality has existed in every society. Some societies, such as ancient Greece, have encouraged it. More frequently, however, homosexual acts have been forbidden (see Box 11.1 on page 320). In both the past and present, most laws prohibiting homosexual behaviour have targeted male rather than female homosexuality (Brown, 2000). Worldwide as of 2008, 7 countries mandated the death penalty for male and female homosexuality, while 76 countries and 6 other jurisdictions mandated imprisonment. Some 49 countries and 33 other jurisdictions had antidiscrimination laws on the books. Only 19 countries and 14 other jurisdictions legally recognized same-sex unions. A mere 5 countries (Belgium, Canada, the Netherlands, South Africa, and Spain) allowed same-sex marriage (International Lesbian and Gay Association, 2008).

Homosexuals were not identified as a distinct category of people until the 1860s, when the term *homosexuality* was coined. The term *lesbian* is of even more recent vintage.

We do not yet understand well why some individuals develop homosexual orientations. Some scientists believe that the cause of homosexuality is mainly genetic (Hamer, Copeland, Hu, Magnuson, Hu, and Pattatucci, 1993; Pillard and Bailey, 1998), others think it is chiefly hormonal, while still others point to life experiences during early childhood as the most important factor (Brannock and Chapman, 1990; Doell, 1995). The scientific consensus is that homosexuality "emerges for most people in early adolescence without any prior sexual experience . . . [it] is not changeable" (American Psychological Association, 1998). A study of homosexual men in the United States found that 90 percent believed they were born with their homosexual orientation and only 4 percent felt that environmental factors were the sole cause (Lever, 1994). Gallup poll findings also suggest that the general public increasingly believes that homosexuality is not so much a "preference" as an innate orientation (13 percent in 1977 compared with 34 percent in 1999; Gallup Organization, 2000). Beliefs about the causes of homosexuality are also related to people's attitudes

Homosexuals are people who prefer sexual partners of the same sex. People usually call homosexual men *gay* and homosexual women *lesbians*.

Bisexuals are people who enjoy sexual partners of both sexes.

	Men	Women
Identified themselves as homosexual or bisexual	2.8	1.4
Had sex with person of same sex in past 12 months	3.4	0.6
Had sex with person of same sex at least once since puberty	5.3	3.5
Felt desire for sex with person of same sex	7.7	7.5
Had some same-sex desire or experience or identified themselves as homosexual or bisexual	10.1	8.6

TABLE 11.2

Homosexuality in the United States (in percent; $n = 3432$)

Source: Michael, Gagnon, Laumann, and Kolata, 1994: 40.

BOX 11.1
Sociology at the Movies

TAKE   ROLL

Brokeback Mountain (2005)

It would not be an exaggeration to say that Westerns—often called "Cowboy and Indian" movies—shaped a generation of North Americans' expectations about gender and sexuality. John Wayne, Gary Cooper, Jimmy Stewart, and many others became role models for North American men and their idea of masculinity: silent but strong, gentle toward the weak (women and children) but ferocious toward the evil (often Aboriginals), community-minded but ultimately lone, rugged individualists. Even today, it's hard not to be stirred and engrossed by such classic Westerns as *The Man Who Shot Liberty Valance* and *High Noon*.

Jack (Jake Gyllenhaal; left) and Ennis (Heath Ledger) in *Brokeback Mountain*

Westerns, however, have not been a popular genre since the 1970s. The Civil Rights movement questioned the racial ideology of many Westerns, which presumed the superiority of the white race against the native populations. The movement against the War in Vietnam challenged the vision of the world as a place that ought to be pacified and ruled by whites. The feminist movement criticized the patriarchal masculine viewpoint of Westerns. The few Westerns since the 1970s have therefore deviated from classical Westerns, often parodying them.

Brokeback Mountain (2005), nominated for the 2005 best picture Oscar, traces the romantic love between two cowboys. They fall in love in the early 1960s, when both are 19 years old, long before they had heard of gay culture or

even the notion of homosexual identity. They lead seemingly conventional married lives. Yet they continue to love each other and carry on their affair for two decades, periodically telling their wives that they are going on fishing trips together but raising suspicions when they fail to bring any fish home. More than the passion, however, what the movie depicts is the high emotional cost of keeping one's sexual orientation and one's love a secret. Eventually, their marriages crumble, their social relationships suffer, and happiness and fulfillment prove elusive.

One of the reasons that Ennis (the late Heath Ledger, nominated for the 2005 best actor Oscar) cannot imagine the possibility of settling down with Jack (Jake Gyllenhaal,

nominated for the 2005 best supporting actor Oscar) is a childhood experience. His father took him to see two men who were beaten to death, two "tough old birds" who happened to be "shacked up together." Fear of expressing his homosexuality was thus instilled early on. (In fact, both men deny their homosexuality. After their first night together, Ennis says to Jack, "You know I ain't queer." To which Jack replies, "Me neither.") Jack and Ennis's affair ends when Jack is beaten to death by homophobic men. Three grisly murders of gay men, then, provide the tragic backdrop to *Brokeback Mountain*. How much have things changed since the 1960s, '70s, and '80s? Could *Brokeback Mountain* be set in 2009?

toward homosexuals. For example, one national poll reported that "those who believe homosexuals choose their sexual orientation are far less tolerant of gays and lesbians and more likely to conclude homosexuality should be illegal than those who think sexual orientation is not a matter of personal choice" (Rosin and Morin, 1999: 8).

In general, sociologists are less interested in the origins of homosexuality than in the way it is socially constructed, that is, in the wide variety of ways it is expressed and repressed (Plummer, 1995). It is important to note in this connection that homosexuality

Especially since the middle of the twentieth century, gays and lesbians have gone public with their lifestyles. They have organized demonstrations, parades, and political pressure groups to express their self-confidence and demand equal rights with the heterosexual majority. This has done much to legitimize homosexuality and sexual diversity in general.

has become less of a stigma over the past century. Two factors are chiefly responsible for this, one scientific, the other political. In the twentieth century, sexologists—psychologists and physicians who study sexual practices scientifically—first recognized and stressed the wide diversity of existing sexual practices. Alfred Kinsey was among the pioneers in this field. He and his colleagues interviewed thousands of men and women. In the 1940s, they concluded that homosexual practices were so widespread that homosexuality could hardly be considered an illness affecting a tiny minority (Kinsey, Pomeroy, and Martin, 1948; Kinsey et al., 1953; see also Box 2.2 in Chapter 2, How Sociologists Do Research).

Sexologists, then, provided a scientific rationale for belief in the normality of sexual diversity. However, it was sexual minorities themselves who provided the social and political energy needed to legitimize sexual diversity among an increasingly large section of the public. Especially since the middle of the twentieth century, gays and lesbians have built large communities and subcultures, particularly in major urban areas, such as Vancouver, Winnipeg, Toronto, and Montreal (Greenhill, 2001; Ingram, 2001). They have gone public with their lifestyles (Owen, 2001). They have organized demonstrations, parades, and political pressure groups to express their self-confidence and demand equal rights with the heterosexual majority (Goldie, 2001). This has done much to legitimize homosexuality and sexual diversity in general.

Yet opposition to people who don't conform to conventional gender roles remains strong at all stages of the life cycle. When you were a child, did you ever poke fun at a sturdily built girl who was good at sports by referring to her as a "dyke"? As an adolescent or a young adult, have you ever insulted a man by calling him a "fag"? If so, your behaviour was not unusual. Many children and adults believe that heterosexuality is superior to homosexuality and they are not embarrassed to say so. "That's so gay!" is commonly used as an expression of disapproval among teenagers.

Among adults, such opposition is just as strong. What is your attitude today toward transgendered people, transsexuals, and homosexuals? Do you, for example, think relations between adults of the same sex are always, or almost always, wrong? If so, you are again not that unusual. A national survey of Canadians conducted in 2000 found that almost one in three Canadians believed same-sex relations were "always wrong." Although discouraging to some people, this figure represents an increase in Canada's acceptance of homosexuality over the past three decades. In 1975, 63 percent of Canadians viewed homosexuality

WHERE DO YOU FIT IN?

in this disapproving way (*Maclean's*, 2002: 12). Another indication of changing sentiments is that in 2005 Parliament authorized marriage for same-sex couples, making Canada the world's fourth country to adopt such legislation (the Netherlands was first in 2001). Nonetheless, a 2005 survey showed that only 48 percent of Canadians favoured same-sex marriage (CBC News, 2005). Tolerance is advancing and is most widespread among young Canadians, but substantial hostility remains.

Antipathy to homosexuals is so strong among some people that they are prepared to back up their beliefs with force. A study of about 500 young adults in the San Francisco Bay area (one of the most sexually tolerant areas in North America) found that 1 in 10 admitted physically attacking or threatening people he or she believed were homosexuals. Twenty-four percent reported engaging in anti-gay name-calling. Among male respondents, 18 percent reported acting in a violent or threatening way and 32 percent reported name-calling. In addition, a third of those who had *not* engaged in anti-gay aggression said they would do so if a homosexual flirted with, or propositioned, them (Franklin, 1998; see also Bush and Sainz, 2001; Faulkner and Cranston, 1998).

The consequences of such attitudes can be devastating. For example, 14-year-old Christian Hernandez of Niagara Falls, Ontario, told his best friend that he was gay. "He told me he couldn't accept it," recalls Hernandez. "And he began to spread it around." For two years, Hernandez was teased and harassed almost daily. After school one day, a group of boys waited for him. Their leader told Hernandez that "he didn't accept faggots, that we brought AIDS into the world" and stabbed him in the neck with a knife. Hernandez required a week's hospitalization. When he told his parents what had happened, his father replied that he'd "rather have a dead son than a queer son" (Fisher, 1999).

Homophobic people are afraid of homosexuals.

Research suggests that some anti-gay crimes may result from repressed homosexual urges on the part of the aggressor (Adams, Wright, and Lohr, 1998). From this point of view, aggressors are **homophobic** or afraid of homosexuals because they cannot cope with their own, possibly subconscious, homosexual impulses. Their aggression is a way of acting out a denial of these impulses. Although this psychological explanation may account for some anti-gay violence, it seems inadequate when set alongside the finding that fully half of all young male adults admitted to some form of anti-gay aggression in the San Francisco study cited above. An analysis of the motivations of these San Franciscans showed that some of them did commit assaults to prove their toughness and heterosexuality. Others committed assaults just to alleviate boredom and have fun. Still others believed they were defending themselves from aggressive sexual propositions. A fourth group acted violently because they wanted to punish homosexuals for what they perceived as moral transgressions (Franklin, 1998). It seems clear, then, that anti-gay violence is not just a question of abnormal psychology but a broad cultural problem with several sources.

Anecdotal evidence suggests that opposition to anti-gay violence is also growing (see Box 11.2). The 1999 movie *Boys Don't Cry* also raised awareness of the problem of violence directed against sexual minorities. The movie, for which Hilary Swank won the Best Actress Oscar, tells the true story of Teena Brandon, a young woman with a sexual identity crisis. She wants a sex-change operation but can't afford one. So she decides to change her name to Brandon Teena and pass as a man. She soon develops an intimate relationship with a woman by the name of Lana Tisdel. When Lana's ex-boyfriend and his friend discover the truth about Teena, they beat, rape, and ultimately murder her. Teena's only transgression was that she wanted to be a man.

In sum, strong social and cultural forces lead us to distinguish men from women and heterosexuals from homosexuals. We learn these distinctions throughout the socialization process, and we continuously construct them anew in our daily interactions. Most people use positive and negative sanctions to ensure that others conform to conventional heterosexual gender roles. Some people resort to violence to enforce conformity and punish deviance.

Our discussion also suggests that the social construction of conventional gender roles helps create and maintain social inequality between women and men. In the remainder of this chapter, we examine the historical origins and some of the present-day consequences of gender inequality.

BOX 11.2
It's Your Choice

Hate Crime Law and Homophobia

On November 17, 2001, Aaron Webster, a 42-year-old gay man, was beaten to death in Vancouver. Tim Chisholm, Aaron's friend for 15 years, discovered Aaron's bloodied body, naked except for his hiking boots, in a parking lot in Stanley Park. Aaron had been bludgeoned with either a baseball bat or a pool cue by a group of three to four men. After phoning 911, Chisholm attempted CPR on his unconscious friend. It was no use. Aaron died in Chisholm's arms before help could arrive.

This brutal murder is believed to have been British Columbia's first fatal "gay bashing." At a memorial service for Webster that drew more than 1500 people, Vancouver Police Inspector Dave Jones identified Webster as the victim of "a hate crime, pure and simple" and pledged that the city's police department would "do everything in our power" to find the perpetrators and "bring them to justice" (Associated Press, 2001; Nagle, 2001).

One issue raised by Webster's death concerns the definition of hate crime (Wetzel, 2001). Hate crimes are criminal acts motivated by a victim's race, religion, or ethnicity. Under section 319 of the Canadian Criminal Code, the willful promotion of hatred against any identifiable group (that is, "any section of the public distinguished by colour, race, religion, or ethnic group") and the advocating of genocide are crimes punishable by up to two years' imprisonment. In 1999, following the gay bashing of a student in Fredericton, New Brunswick, then Justice Minister Anne McLellan announced that she would introduce amendments to protect lesbians and gays from hate crimes. She did not do so. Following Webster's murder, MP Svend Robinson introduced a Private Member's Bill that sought to include sexual orientation among the grounds protected by hate crimes legislation.

If hate motivates a crime, Canadian law requires that the perpetrator be punished more severely than otherwise. Under section 718.2 of the Criminal Code of Canada, "evidence that the offence was motivated by bias, prejudice or hate based on race, national or ethnic origin, language, colour, religion, sex, age, mental or physical disability, sexual orientation or any other similar factor" is to be considered an aggravating circumstance only in sentencing convicted offenders. For example, assaulting a person during an argument generally carries a lighter punishment than assaulting a person because he or she is gay or Jewish or black. However, despite this provision in law, "gay-bashers are often able to rely on the discredited 'homosexual panic' defence, claiming they were justified in committing murder because the victim 'came on' to them" (EGALE, 2001).

Do you think crimes motivated by the victim's sexual orientation are the same as crimes motivated by the victim's race, religion, or ethnicity? If so, why? If not, why not? Do you think crimes motivated by the perceived sexual orientation of the victim should be included in the legal definition of a hate crime? Why or why not?

GENDER INEQUALITY

The Origins of Gender Inequality

Contrary to what essentialists say, men have not always enjoyed much more power and authority than women have. Substantial inequality between women and men has existed for only about 6000 years. It was socially constructed. Three major socio-historical processes account for the growth of gender inequality.

Long-Distance Warfare and Conquest

The anthropological record suggests that women and men were about equal in status in nomadic hunting-and-gathering societies, the dominant form of society for 90 percent of human history. Rough gender equality was based on the fact that women produced a substantial amount of the band's food, up to 80 percent in some cases (see Chapter 15, Families). The archaeological record from "Old Europe" tells a similar story. Old Europe is a region stretching roughly from Poland in the north to the Mediterranean island of Crete in the south, and from Switzerland in the west to Bulgaria in the east (see Figure 11.3 on page 324). Between 7000 and 3500 BCE, men and women enjoyed approximately equal

FIGURE 11.3

Old Europe

Source: Gimbutas, 1982: 16.

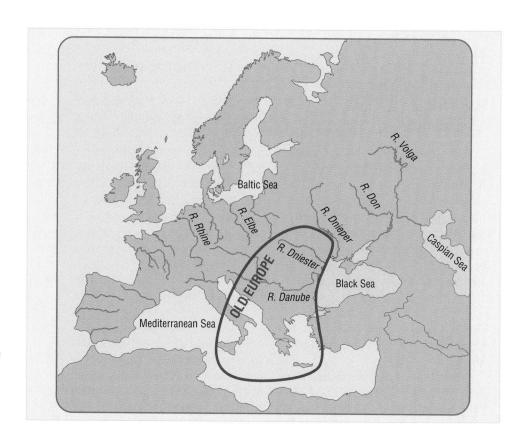

status throughout the region. In fact, the religions of the region gave primacy to fertility and creator goddesses. Kinship was traced through the mother's side of the family. Then, sometime between 4300 and 4200 BCE, all this began to change. Old Europe was invaded by successive waves of warring peoples from the Asiatic and European northeast (the Kurgans) and the deserts to the south (the Semites). Both the Kurgan and Semitic civilizations were based on a steeply hierarchical social structure in which men were dominant. Their religions gave primacy to male warrior gods. They acquired property and slaves by conquering other peoples and imposed their religions on the vanquished. They eliminated, or at least downgraded, goddesses as divine powers. God became a male who willed that men should rule women. Laws reinforced women's sexual, economic, and political subjugation to men. Traditional Judaism, Christianity, and Islam all embody ideas of male dominance, and they all derive from the tribes that conquered Old Europe in the fifth millennium BCE (Eisler, 1987; see also Lerner, 1986).

Plow Agriculture

Long-distance warfare and conquest catered to men's strengths and so greatly enhanced male power and authority. Large-scale farming using plows harnessed to animals had a similar effect. Plow agriculture originated in the Middle East around 5000 years ago. It required that strong adults remain in the fields all day for much of the year. It also reinforced the principle of private ownership of land. Since men were on average stronger than women were, and since women were restricted in their activities by pregnancy, childbirth, and nursing, plow agriculture made men more powerful socially. Thus, men owned land and ownership was passed from the father to the eldest son (Coontz and Henderson, 1986).

The Separation of Public and Private Spheres

In the agricultural era, economic production was organized around the household. Men may have worked apart from women in the fields but the fields were still part of the *family* farm. In contrast, during the early phase of industrialization, men's work moved out of the household and into the factory and the office. Most men became wage or salary workers. Some men assumed decision-making roles in economic and political institutions. Yet while men went public, women who could afford to do so remained in the domestic or private sphere. The idea soon developed that this was a natural division of labour. This idea persisted until the second half of the twentieth century, when a variety of social circumstances, ranging from the introduction of the birth control pill to women's demands for entry into higher education, finally allowed women to enter the public sphere in large numbers.

So we see that, according to social constructionists, gender inequality derives not from any inherent biological features of men and women but from three main socio-historical circumstances: the arrival of long-distance warfare and conquest, the development of plow agriculture, and the assignment of women to the domestic sphere and men to the public sphere during the early industrial era.

The Earnings Gap Today

After reading this brief historical overview, you might be inclined to dismiss gender inequality as a thing of the past. If so, your decision would be hasty. Gender inequality is evident if we focus on the earnings gap between men and women, one of the most important expressions of gender inequality today.

Canadian data on the earnings of women and men were first reported in 1967. At that time, the ratio of female to male earnings stood at around 58 percent. In 1992, it passed 70 percent and has fluctuated near that level since then (Figure 11.4).

Figure 11.5 on page 326 shows that women earn less than men do at every level of education. However, the wage gap between men and women varies among different categories. For example, Table 11.3 on page 327 illustrates the gender wage gap in the average earnings of people in the 10 highest-paying and 10 lowest-paying occupations in Canada. If the wage gap were due to universal gender differences, it would not vary across occupations. But it does vary considerably, suggesting that social conditions specific to given occupations account in part for the magnitude of the gender wage gap.

Four main factors contribute to the gender gap in earnings (Bianchi and Spain, 1996; England, 1992):

1. *Gender discrimination.* In February 1985, when Microsoft already employed about 1000 people, it hired its first two female executives. According to a well-placed source involved in the hiring, both women got their jobs because Microsoft was trying to win a U.S. Air Force contract. Under the government's guidelines, it didn't have enough women in top management positions to qualify. The source quotes then 29-year-old Bill

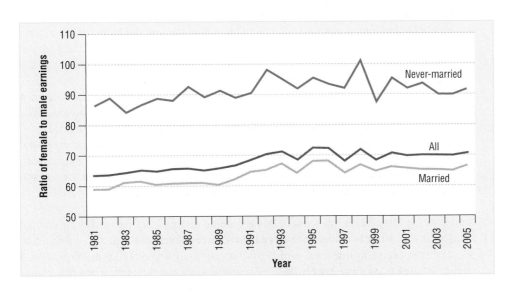

FIGURE 11.4

Ratio of Female to Male Earnings, Canada, 1980–2005

Source: Statistics Canada, 2008, CANSIM Table 2020104. Retrieved May 2, 2008 (http://dc1.chass. utoronto.ca.myaccess.library.utoronto. ca/cgi-bin/cansimdim/c2_ search Cansim.pl).

FIGURE 11.5

Hourly Wages by Educational Attainment for Men and Women, Canada, 2003

Source: Adapted from Statistics Canada, 2003, "The Canadian Labour Market at a Glance," Catalogue 71-222. Retrieved November 17, 2004 (http://www.statcan.ca/english/freepub/71-222-XIE/71-222-XIE2004000.htm).

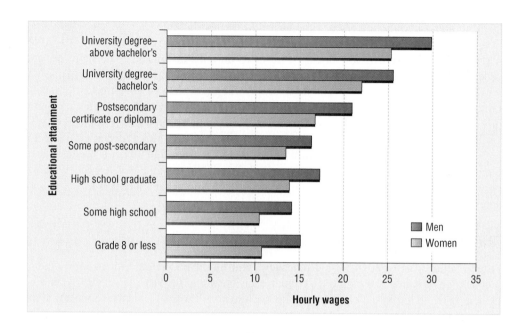

Gender discrimination **involves rewarding men and women differently for the same work.**

Gates, president of Microsoft, as saying: "Well, let's hire two women because we can pay them half as much as we will have to pay a man, and we can give them all this other 'crap' work to do because they are women" (quoted in Wallace and Erickson, 1992: 291). This incident is a clear illustration of **gender discrimination**, rewarding women and men differently for the same work. Discrimination on the basis of sex is against the law in Canada. Yet progress is slow; as noted earlier, the female–male earnings ratio has not improved since 1992. If the rate of improvement between 1980 and 2005 were to persist, women would not earn as much as men until 2118.

2. *Women tend to be concentrated in low-wage occupations and industries.* The second factor leading to lower earnings for women is that the programs they select in high school and afterwards tend to limit them to jobs in low-wage occupations and industries. The concentration of women in certain occupations and men in others is referred to as *occupational sex segregation.* Although women have made big strides since the 1970s, especially in managerial employment, they are still concentrated in lower-paying clerical and service occupations and underrepresented in higher-paying manual occupations (Table 11.4 on page 328). This is particularly true for women of colour, Aboriginal women, and women with disabilities (Chard, 2000: 229). In contrast to men in visible minority groups, who are concentrated in professional occupations and service jobs in higher proportions than Canadians are overall, women in visible minority groups are more likely than Canadian women as a whole to do manual labour. Similarly, working-age women with disabilities are less likely than working-age men with disabilities to be employed (Shain, 1995).

3. *Heavy domestic responsibilities reduce women's earnings.* In 2005, Canadian women who had never been married earned 91.7 cents for every dollar earned by men. The comparable figure for married women was 66.7 cents (see Figure 11.4). A substantial part of this 25-cent gap represents the economic cost to women of getting married and assuming disproportionately heavy domestic responsibilities. Of course, raising children can be one of the most emotionally satisfying experiences. That should not, however, blind us to the fact it is also work that decreases the time available for education, training, and paid work. Because women are disproportionately involved in child rearing, they suffer the brunt of this economic reality. They devote fewer hours to paid work than men do, experience more labour-force interruptions, and are more likely than men to take part-time jobs, which pay less per hour and offer fewer benefits than full-time work does (Waldfogel, 1997). Women also do considerably more housework

NEL

TABLE 11.3

Earnings of Men and of Women and Gender Composition in the Ten Best and Ten Worst Paid Occupations, Canada, 2000

Note: Only full-time, full-year workers are included.

Source: Adapted from Statistics Canada, Publication Profile of the Canadian Population by Age and Sex: Canada Ages, 2001 Census, Catalogue No. 96F0030XIE2001002.

Occupation	Number Employed	Average Earnings in $	Average Male Earnings in $	Average Female Earnings in $	Female Percentage in Occupation	F/M Earnings Percentage
Judges	1 825	142 518	146 008	131 663	24.4	90.2
Specialist physicians	12 480	141 597	160 833	98 383	30.8	61.2
Senior managers: Financial, communications carriers, and other business services	40 910	130 802	141 829	90 622	21.5	63.9
General practitioners and family physicians	22 040	122 463	133 789	96 958	30.8	72.5
Dentists	8 710	118 350	129 104	82 254	22.9	63.7
Senior managers: Goods production, utilities, transportation, and construction	44 630	115 623	120 914	75 267	11.6	62.2
Lawyers and Quebec notaries	47 290	103 287	114 894	77 451	31.0	67.4
Senior managers: Trade, broadcasting and other services, N.E.C.	37 690	101 176	108 527	67 161	17.8	61.8
Securities agents, investment dealers, and traders	17 765	98 919	124 290	55 299	36.8	44.5
Petroleum engineers	4 370	96 703	100 633	61 057	10.0	60.7
Babysitters, nannies, and parents' helpers	26 670	15 846	15 310	15 862	97.1	104.3
Food counter attendants, kitchen helpers, and related occupations	54 290	19 338	20 241	19 053	71.8	94.1
Food and beverage servers	54 660	18 319	22 671	17 030	77.1	75.1
Service station attendants	8 315	18 470	19 475	15 750	9.2	80.9
Bartenders	16 175	19 877	22 008	18 347	58.2	83.4
Cashiers	58 775	19 922	22 925	19 391	85	84.5
Harvesting labourers	2 215	20 158	21 971	18 246	48.8	83.0
Tailors, dressmakers, furriers, and milliners	13 425	20 499	27 690	18 882	81.6	68.2
Sewing machine operators	31 040	20 575	26 782	19 997	91.5	74.7
Ironing, pressing, and finishing occupations	3 860	20 663	23 041	19 319	63.9	83.8

TABLE 11.4

Percentage Female in Broad
Occupational Categories
in Canada, 1987, 1997,
and 2007

Source: Adapted from the Statistics
Canada, 2008, CANSIM Table 282-
0010. Retrieved May 2, 2008
(http://dc1.chass.utoronto.ca.
myaccess.library.utoronto.ca/cgi-bin/
cansimdim/c2_getArrayDim.pl).
Computations by Robert Brym.

Occupational Category	1987	1997	2007
	Percentage Females in Occupation		
Senior management	21.2	27.1	26.5
Other management	31.3	37.5	37.8
Professions in business and finance	38.6	47.8	50.6
Financial, secretarial, and administrative	83.2	85.1	82.9
Clerical	68.0	69.2	71.1
Scientists	20.0	20.0	22.1
Health professions (including nursing)	79.3	79.1	80.9
Social science, government, and religion	57.4	64.8	68.4
Teachers and professors	52.8	60.3	64.1
Artistic/literary/recreational	48.5	52.6	54.7
Sales and service	55.5	56.3	56.9
Trade and transport	5.2	6.1	6.9
Primary industry	19.6	20.7	20.0
Processing, manufacturing, utilities	33.2	31.9	31.2
All occupations	43.2	45.4	47.1

and elder care than men do (Sauve, 2002). Globally, women do between two-thirds and three-quarters of all unpaid child care, housework, and care for aging parents (Boyd, 1997: 55). Even when they work full-time in the paid labour force, women continue to shoulder a disproportionate share of domestic responsibilities (Chapter 15, Families).

4. *Finally, work done by women is commonly considered less valuable than work done by men because it is viewed as involving fewer skills.* Women tend to earn less than men do because the skills involved in their work are often undervalued (Figart and Lapidus, 1996; Sorenson, 1994). For example, kindergarten teachers (nearly all of whom are women) earn less than office machine repair technicians (nearly all of whom are men). It is, however, questionable whether it takes less training and skill to teach a young child the basics of counting and cooperation than it takes to get a photocopier to collate paper properly. As this example suggests, we apply somewhat arbitrary standards to reward different occupational roles. In our society, these standards systematically undervalue the kind of skills needed for jobs where women are concentrated.

We thus see that the gender gap in earnings is based on several *social* circumstances rather than on any inherent difference between women and men. This fact means that people can reduce the gender gap if they want to. Below, we discuss social policies that could create more equality between women and men. But first, to stress the urgency of such policies, we explain how the persistence of gender inequality encourages sexual harassment and rape.

Male Aggression against Women

Serious acts of aggression between men and women are common. The great majority are committed by men against women. For example, 6 percent of Canadian women under the age of 25 reported being sexually assaulted and 9 percent reported being stalked in 2004 alone (Johnson, 2006: 36).

Rape is one of the most violent forms of sexual assault. Although rapists have typically been regarded as deranged individuals, research on acquaintance rape—sexual assaults committed by someone the victim knows—demonstrates that normal men are capable of acts of coercive sex (Meyer, 1984; Senn, Desmarais, Veryberg, and Wood, 2000). One study found that more than 20 percent of female Canadian postsecondary students said they gave in to unwanted sexual intercourse because they were overwhelmed by a man's continued arguments and pressure, nearly 7 percent reported they had unwanted sexual intercourse because a man threatened or used some degree of physical force, and nearly 14 percent claimed that, while they were either intoxicated or under the influence of drugs, a man had attempted unwanted sexual intercourse (DeKeseredy and Kelly, 1993).

Another study found that half of first- and second-year university women reported unwanted attempts at intercourse by males of their acquaintance. In 83 percent of cases, they knew the man at least moderately well. One-third of these attempts were accompanied by "strong" physical force and another third by "mild" physical force. The women seemed constrained by traditional roles in their responses, which were largely passive and accepting; 37 percent did nothing. Only a minority gave a strong verbal response (26 percent) or a physical response (14 percent). Half the attacks succeeded; the stronger the victim's response, the less likely it was that the attempted rape was completed. None of the women reported the attack to the authorities and half talked to no one about it. The remainder told friends. Only 11 percent ended the relationship, whereas almost three-quarters either accepted or ignored the attack. Half continued to be friends (25 percent) or dating or sex partners (25 percent). Most blamed themselves at least partially (Murnen, Perot, and Byrne, 1989; Figure 11.6).

Why do men commit more frequent (and more harmful) acts of aggression against women than women commit against men? It is not because men on average are physically more powerful than women are. Greater physical power is more likely to be used to commit acts of aggression when norms justify male domination and men have much more *social* power than women do. When women and men are more equal socially, and norms justify gender equality, the rate of male aggression against women is lower. This is evident if we consider various types of aggressive interaction, including sexual assault and sexual harassment (see also the discussion of wife abuse in Chapter 15, Families).

Sexual Assault

Some people think rapists are men who suffer a psychological disorder that compels them to achieve immediate sexual gratification even if violence is required. Others think rape

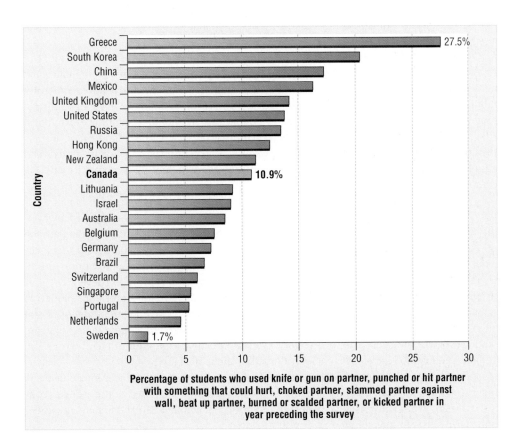

FIGURE 11.6

Percentage of University Students Who Severely Assaulted a Dating Partner in the Past Year, by Country, 2001–2005 (*n* = 6700)

Note: Some of the American data were collected in 1998.

Source: From International Dating Violence Study, tabulation courtesy of Murray A. Straus based on Emily M. Douglas and Murray A. Straus, (2006) "Assault and injury of dating partners by university students in 19 nations and its relation to corporal punishment experienced as a child," *European Journal of Criminology* 3: 293–318. Reprinted with permission.

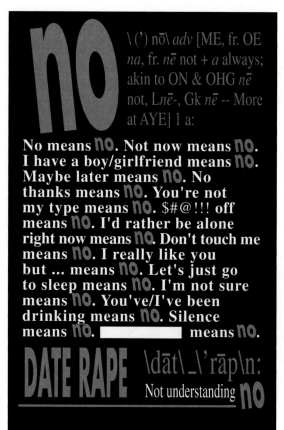

This poster suggests that men still need to be reminded that no means no.

occurs because of flawed communication. They believe some victims give mixed signals to their assailants by, for example, drinking too much and flirting with them.

Such explanations are not completely invalid. Interviews with victims and perpetrators show that some offenders do suffer from psychological disorders. Others misinterpret signals in what they regard as sexually ambiguous situations (Hannon, Hall, Kuntz, Laar, and Williams, 1995). But such cases account for only a small proportion of the total. Men who commit sexual assault are rarely mentally disturbed, and it is abundantly clear to most assailants that they are doing something their victims strongly oppose.

What then accounts for sexual assault being as common as it is? A sociological answer is suggested by the fact that sexual assault is sometimes not about sexual gratification at all. Some offenders cannot ejaculate or even achieve an erection. Significantly, however, all forms of sexual assault involve domination and humiliation as principal motives. It is not surprising, therefore, that some offenders were physically or sexually abused in their youth. They develop a deep need to feel powerful as psychological compensation for their early powerlessness. Others are men who, as children, saw their mothers as potentially hostile figures who needed to be controlled or as mere objects available for male gratification. They saw their fathers as emotionally cold and distant. Raised in such an atmosphere, rapists learn not to empathize with women. Instead, they learn to want to dominate them (Lisak, 1992).

Other social situations also increase the rate of sexual aggression. One such situation is war. In war, conquering male soldiers often feel justified in wanting to humiliate the vanquished, who are powerless to stop them. Rape is often used for this purpose, as was especially well documented in the ethnic wars that accompanied the breakup of Yugoslavia in the 1990s (Human Rights Watch, 1995).

The relationship between male dominance and sexual aggression is also evident in research on American fraternities. Many fraternities tend to emphasize male dominance and aggression as a central part of their culture. Sociologists who have interviewed fraternity members have shown that most fraternities try to recruit members who can reinforce a macho image and avoid any suggestion of effeminacy and homosexuality. Research also shows that fraternity houses that are especially prone to sexual assault tend to sponsor parties that treat women in a particularly degrading way. By emphasizing a very narrow and aggressive form of masculinity, some fraternities tend to facilitate sexual assault on campuses (Boswell and Spade, 1996).

Another social circumstance that increases the likelihood of sexual assault is participation in athletics. Of course, the overwhelming majority of athletes are not rapists. However, there are proportionately more rapists among men who participate in athletics than among non-athletes (Welch, 1997). That is because many sports embody a particular vision of masculinity in North American culture: competitive, aggressive, and domineering. By recruiting men who display these characteristics and by encouraging the development of these characteristics in athletes, sports can contribute to off-field aggression, including sexual aggression. Furthermore, among male athletes, there is a distinct hierarchy of sexual aggression. Male athletes who engage in contact sports are more prone to be rapists than are other athletes. There are proportionately even more rapists among athletes involved in collision and combative sports, notably football (Welch, 1997).

Sexual assault, we conclude, involves using sex to establish dominance. Its incidence is highest in situations where early socialization experiences predispose men to want to control women, where norms justify the domination of women, and where a big power imbalance between men and women exists.

Sexual Harassment

There are two types of sexual harassment. **Quid pro quo sexual harassment** takes place when sexual threats or bribery are made a condition of employment decisions. (The Latin phrase *quid pro quo* means "something for something.") **Hostile environment sexual harassment** involves sexual jokes, comments, and touching that interferes with work or creates a hostile work environment. Research suggests that relatively powerless women are the most likely to be sexually harassed. Specifically, women who are young, unmarried, and employed in non-professional jobs are most likely to become objects of sexual harassment, particularly if they are temporary workers, if the ratio of women to men in the workplace is low, and if the organizational culture of the workplace tolerates sexual harassment (Rogers and Henson, 1997; Welsh, 1999). However, female doctors (Schneider and Phillips, 1997) and lawyers (Rosenberg, Perlstadt, and Phillips, 1997) also report high rates of sexual harassment, in the first case by male patients and in the second by male colleagues.

Ultimately, male aggression against women, including sexual harassment and sexual assault, is encouraged by a lesson most of us still learn at home, in school, at work, through much of organized religion, and in the mass media—that it is natural and right for men to dominate women. Despite change, it is still more common for men to hold positions of power and authority, than for women to hold such positions. Along with this comes widespread willingness to tolerate or even encourage dominance in males and to discourage it in females. Daily patterns of gender domination, viewed as legitimate by most people, are built into our courtship, sexual, family, and work norms. As a result, aggressive behaviour by males against females typically encounters less notice, resistance, or sanctions than would similar behaviour by females toward males.

This does not mean that all men endorse the principle of male dominance, much less that all men are inclined to engage in sexual assault or other acts of aggression against women. Many men favour gender equality, and most men never abuse a woman (Messerschmidt, 1993). Yet the fact remains that many aspects of our culture legitimize male dominance, making it seem valid or proper. For example, pornography, jokes about "dumb blondes," and leering might seem harmless. At a subtler, sociological level, however, they are assertions of the appropriateness of women's submission to men. Such frequent and routine reinforcements of male superiority increase the likelihood that some men will consider it their right to assault women physically or sexually if the opportunity to do so exists or can be created. "Just kidding" has a cost. For instance, researchers have found that university men who enjoy sexist jokes are more likely than other university men to report engaging in acts of sexual aggression against women (Ryan and Kanjorski, 1998).

We conclude that male aggression against women and gender inequality are not separate issues. Gender inequality is the foundation of aggression against women. In concluding this chapter, we consider how gender inequality can be decreased in the coming decades. As we proceed, you should bear in mind that gender equality is not just a matter of justice. It is also a question of safety.

> **Quid pro quo sexual harassment** takes place when sexual threats or bribery are made a condition of employment decisions.

> **Hostile environment sexual harassment** involves sexual jokes, comments, and touching that interferes with work or creates an unfriendly work environment.

TOWARD 2118

The twentieth century witnessed growing equality between women and men in many countries. In Canada, the decline of the family farm made children less economically useful and more costly to raise. As a result, women started having fewer children. The industrialization of Canada, and then the growth of the economy's service sector, increased demand for women in the paid labour force (Figure 11.7 on page 332). This change gave them substantially more economic power and also encouraged them to have fewer children. The legalization and availability of contraception made it possible for women to exercise unprecedented control over their own bodies. The women's movement

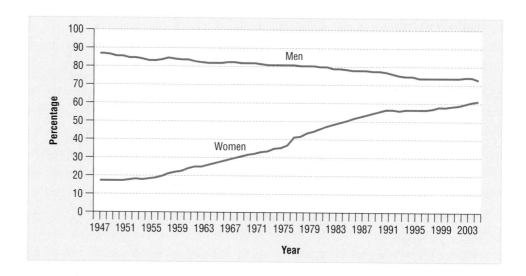

FIGURE 11.7

Percentage of Men and Women in Paid Labour Force, Canada, 1946–2007

Source: Adapted from Statistics Canada, 1983, "Historical Statistics of Canada," Catalogue 11-516, July 29, 1999, Series D160-174. Retrieved May 2, 2008 (http://www.statcan.ca/english/freepub/11-516-XIE/sectiond/sectiond.htm), and from the Statistics Canada CANSIM database, Table 282-0002, using E-STAT (distributor). Retrieved May 2, 2008 (http://estat.statcan.ca/cgiwin/CNSMCGI.EXE?CANSIMFILE-Estat\English\CII_1_E.htm); Statistics Canada, 2008, "Labour Force Indicators by Age Groups for Males, Participation Rate (2006), for Canada, Provinces and Territories—20% Sample Data." Retrieved May 2, 2008 (http://www12.statcan.ca/english/census06/data/highlights/Labour/Table601.cfm?SR=1).

GLOBAL PERSPECTIVE

FIGURE 11.8

Gender Empowerment Measure, Top 10 and Bottom 10 Countries, 2007

Note: Data are available for 93 countries.

Source: United Nations, 2007–2008, *Human Development Report 2007–2008*. Retrieved May 2, 2008 (http://hdrstats.undp.org/indicators/280.html). The United Nations is the author of the original material.

fought for, and won, increased rights for women on a number of economic, political, and legal fronts. All these forces brought about a massive cultural shift, a fundamental reorientation of thinking on the part of many Canadians about what women could and should do in society.

One indicator of the progress of women is the Gender Empowerment Measure (GEM). The GEM is computed by the United Nations. It takes into account women's share of seats in Parliament; women's share of administrative, managerial, professional, and technical jobs; and women's earning power. A score of 1.0 indicates equality with men on these three dimensions.

As Figure 11.8 shows, Norway, Sweden, Finland, and Denmark were the most gender-egalitarian countries in the world in 2007. They had GEM scores ranging from 0.910 to 0.875. On average, women in these countries are about 87 percent of the way to equality with men on these three dimensions. Canada ranked tenth in the world, with a GEM score of 0.820.

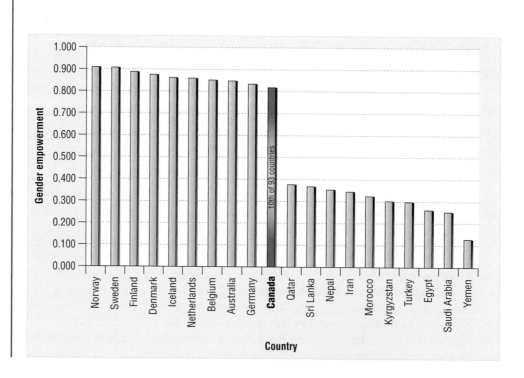

In general, there is more gender equality in rich than in poor countries. Thus, the top 11 countries shown in Figure 11.8 are all rich. This suggests that gender equality is a function of economic development. However, our analysis of the GEM data suggests that there are some exceptions to the general pattern. Gender equality is also a function of government policy. Thus, in some of the former communist countries of Eastern Europe—such as Slovakia (ranked at 26), Latvia (29), and the Czech Republic (30)—gender equality is *higher* than we would expect given their level of economic development. Meanwhile, in some of the Islamic countries, gender inequality is *lower* than we would expect given their level of economic development (e.g., Bahrain and Saudi Arabia). These anomalies exist because the former communist countries made gender equality a matter of public policy while many Islamic countries do just the opposite (Brym et al., 2005). To cite just one extreme case, in 1996 authorities in the Islamic country of Afghanistan made it illegal for girls to attend school and women to work in the paid labour force. (The situation has improved in some areas since the overthrow of the Taliban regime in 2001.)

The GEM figures suggest that Canadian women still have a considerable way to go before they achieve equality with men. We have seen, for example, that the gender gap in earnings is shrinking but will disappear only in 2118—and then only if it continues to diminish at the same rate as it did between 1980 and 2005. That is a big "if," because progress is never automatic.

Socializing children at home and in school to understand that women and men are equally adept at all jobs is important in motivating women to excel in non-traditional fields. Hiring more women to compensate for past discrimination in hiring, firing, promotion, and training is also important. However, without in any way minimizing the need for such initiatives, we should recognize that their impact will be muted if women continue to undertake disproportionate domestic responsibilities and if occupations containing a high concentration of women continue to be undervalued in monetary terms.

Two main policy initiatives will probably be required in the coming decades to bridge the gender gap in earnings. One is the development of a better child-care system. The other is the development of a policy of "equal pay for work of equal value." Let us consider both of these issues.

Child Care

High-quality, government-subsidized, affordable child care is widely available in most Western European countries but not yet in Canada (Chapter 15, Families). Sixty percent of children in the United Kingdom are in regulated child care as are 69 percent of children in France and 78 percent in Denmark. But a team from the Organisation for Economic Co-operation and Development (OECD) strongly faulted Canada's efforts as a patchwork that has been chronically underfunded. Only 20 percent of Canadian children under the age of seven are in regulated child care (OECD, 2004a: 7). As a result, many Canadian women with small children are either unable to work outside the home or able to work outside the home only on a part-time basis.

A universal system of daycare was proposed in Canada as early as 1970 but little was done at the federal level or in most provinces and territories. Quebec is an exception. In 1997 that province introduced a comprehensive family policy that attempts to integrate family benefits, paid parental leave, child care, and kindergarten. Its child-care component heralded universally available, affordable child care. A rapid expansion in the number of spaces occurred, although waiting lists grew as well. By 2004, 40 percent of the regulated daycare spaces available in Canada were in Quebec. Unfortunately, that was in part because no new spaces had been added outside Quebec in the preceding decade.

There is no lack of need. In 2001, 52 percent of Canadian preschoolers received some kind of care outside of the home, up from 42 percent just seven years earlier. But only 25 percent of these children were enrolled in daycare programs; a growing number were cared for by relatives: 14 percent, up from 8 percent in 1994 (Statistics Canada, 2005b).

In 2004, affordable, high-quality, regulated daycare was a central electoral promise of the victorious Liberal Party. By mid-2005, the beginnings of a national system began to take shape when the federal government reached child-care agreements with Saskatchewan, Manitoba, Ontario, and Newfoundland and Labrador. The system, had it taken root across the country, would potentially have paid for itself. One study estimated that a high-quality, affordable, universal system of child care and early child-care education would cost $7.9 billion, while the increased employment of mothers would be worth $6.2 billion and the improvement in child development would be worth $4.3 billion (Cleveland and Krashinsky, 1998). However, after his election in 2006, Prime Minister Stephen Harper scrapped the agreements in favour of taxable benefits of $1200 paid to parents for each child under age six. The amount and the targeting were widely criticized as failing to address what women who work for pay needed to support their families.

Equal Pay for Work of Equal Value

On paper, Canadian women have had the right to equal pay for the same jobs done by men since the 1950s. But although early laws proclaimed lofty goals, they failed to result in fair wages. Because of occupational sex segregation, few men and women were doing the same jobs, and "women's" jobs paid less than "men's" jobs.

In the 1980s, researchers found women earned less than men did partly because jobs in which women are concentrated are valued less than jobs in which men are concentrated. They therefore tried to establish gender-neutral standards by which they could judge the dollar value of work. These standards include such factors as the education and experience required to do a particular job and the level of responsibility, amount of stress, and working conditions associated with it. Researchers felt that, by using these criteria to compare jobs in which women and men are concentrated, they could identify pay inequities. The underpaid could then be compensated accordingly. In other words, women and men would receive **equal pay for work of equal value**, even if they did different jobs.

In the mid-1980s, some governments amended the law to state that women should be paid equally for work of equal value. Employers were now required to compare the rates of pay for women and men in dissimilar jobs that nevertheless involved the same skill, effort, responsibility, and working conditions. In 1985, Manitoba became the first Canadian province to demand that its public sector implement equal pay for work of equal value—or "pay equity," as it came to be called. Pay equity is now official policy in 10 of 13 Canadian jurisdictions (Alberta, Saskatchewan, and the Northwest Territories are the exceptions). However, provisions for pay equity vary widely. In some provinces they apply only to the public sector and even where they apply more broadly, such as in Ontario and Quebec, small businesses are exempt. In many cases it has been argued that there are no "male" jobs that can be reasonably compared to jobs in which women are segregated. In one case (Newfoundland and Labrador), the provincial government has argued it simply cannot afford a pay equity settlement. Enforcement mechanisms are meagre and employers have found various ways to argue that unequal wages do not signify discrimination based on sex. As a result, only about a fifth of female-dominated jobs have received pay equity adjustments (Moorcroft, 2005; Smeenk, 1993). Thus, while pay equity is undoubtedly a significant step toward achieving gender equality, inequity remains, as evidenced by the persistence of the wage gap between working men and working women.

The Women's Movement

Improvements in the social standing of women do not depend just on the sympathy of government and business leaders. Progress on this front has always depended in part on the strength of the organized women's movement. That is likely to be true in the future, too. In

Equal pay for work of equal value **refers to the equal dollar value of different jobs. It is established in gender-neutral terms by comparing jobs in terms of the education and experience needed to do them and the stress, responsibility, and working conditions associated with them.**

concluding this chapter, it is therefore fitting to consider the state of the women's movement and its prospects.

The first wave of the women's movement emerged during the late nineteenth century and lasted into the early 1920s. Its most important public achievements in Canada were the right to vote and the right (granted in 1929) to be considered *persons,* and not chattels (personal property), under Canadian law. In 1916, women in Alberta, Manitoba, and Saskatchewan were granted the right to vote in provincial elections. All the other provinces followed suit by 1925 except Quebec, which granted women the right to vote only in 1940. These rights were first granted to white women. Women from certain ethnic and racial groups did not receive the franchise until later (Nelson and Robinson, 2002).

In the mid-1960s, the second wave of the women's movement emerged. Second-wave feminists were inspired in part by the successes of the civil rights movement in the United States. They felt that women's concerns were largely ignored despite persistent and pervasive gender inequality. Like their counterparts more than a century earlier, they held demonstrations, lobbied politicians, and formed women's organizations to further their cause. They demanded equal rights with men in education and employment, the elimination of sexual violence, and control over their own reproduction. However, the second wave of the women's movement did not always or consistently recognize, include, or champion the needs of all Canadian women equally. It is only recently that the second wave of the women's movement has begun to respond positively to the claim that white, middle-class feminists have "denied, dismissed, and denigrated" the experiences of women of different races, abilities, and classes (Cassidy, Lord, and Mandell, 1998: 26).

There is considerable diversity in the modern feminist movement concerning ultimate goals. Three main streams can be distinguished (Tong, 1989):

1. *Liberal feminism* is the most popular current in the women's movement today. Its advocates believe that the main sources of women's subordination are learned gender roles and the denial of opportunities to women. Liberal feminists advocate nonsexist methods of socialization and education, more sharing of domestic tasks between women and men, and the extension to women of all the educational, employment, and political rights and privileges men enjoy.

2. *Socialist feminists* regard women's relationship to the economy as the main source of women's disadvantages. They believe that the traditional nuclear family emerged along with inequalities of wealth and that the economic and sexual oppression of women has its roots in capitalism. Socialist feminists also assert that the reforms proposed by liberal feminists are inadequate, because they can do little to help working-class women, who are too poor to take advantage of equal educational and work opportunities. Socialist feminists conclude that only the elimination of private property and the creation of economic equality can bring about an end to the oppression of all women.

3. *Radical feminists,* in turn, find the reforms proposed by liberals and the revolution proposed by socialists inadequate. Patriarchy—male domination and norms justifying that domination—is more deeply rooted than capitalism, say the radical feminists. After all, patriarchy predates capitalism. Moreover, it is just as evident in self-proclaimed communist societies as it is in capitalist societies. Radical feminists conclude that the very idea of gender must be changed to bring an end to male domination. Some radical feminists argue that new reproductive technologies, such as in vitro fertilization, are bound to be helpful in this regard because they can break the link between women's bodies and child bearing (see Chapter 15, Families). However, the revolution envisaged by radical feminists goes beyond the realm of reproduction to include all aspects of male sexual dominance. From their

The second wave of the women's movement started to grow in the mid-1960s. Members of the movement advocated equal rights with men in education and employment, the elimination of sexual violence, and control over their own reproduction.

point of view, pornography, sexual harassment, restrictive contraception, sexual assault, incest, sterilization, and physical assault must be eliminated for women to reconstruct their sexuality on their own terms.

This thumbnail sketch by no means exhausts the variety of streams of contemporary feminist thought. For example, since the mid-1980s, *anti-racist* and *post-modernist* feminists have criticized liberal, socialist, and radical feminists for generalizing from the experience of white women and failing to understand how women's lives are rooted in particular historical and racial experiences (hooks, 1984). These new currents have done much to extend the relevance of feminism to previously marginalized groups.

Partly because of the political and intellectual vigour of the women's movement, some feminist ideas have gained widespread acceptance in Canadian society over the past three decades. Most Canadians, men and women, agree or strongly agree that being able to have a paying job is either important or very important for women's personal happiness. About 7 of 10 Canadian men and women agree or strongly agree that both spouses should contribute to household income. However, these values appear to conflict with other attitudes and beliefs. For example, more than half of Canadians agree or strongly agree that preschool-age children are likely to suffer if both parents are employed. And around 45 percent of Canadians agree or strongly agree that a "job is alright, but what most women really want is a home and children" (Ghalam, 1997: 16). It appears that the tapestry of our social lives features interwoven threads of the new and the old.

NOTES

1. Freud called this set of emotions the *Oedipus complex* after the ancient Greek legend of Oedipus. Oedipus was abandoned as a child. When he became an adult he accidentally killed his father and unwittingly married his mother. Discovering his true relationship to his mother, he blinded himself and died in exile.

2. Freud called this set of emotions the *Electra complex* after the ancient Greek legend of Electra. Electra persuaded her brother to kill their mother and their mother's lover to avenge their father's murder. Incidentally, some sexologists call into question the existence of vaginal orgasm and stress the importance of clitoral stimulation (Masters, Johnson, and Kolodny, 1992, 1994). This viewpoint emerged around the same time as the modern feminist movement and as more and more people came to view sexuality not just as a means of reproduction but also as a means of enjoyment.

3. This message is borne out by research in the United States, Germany, and Britain that finds that upwardly mobile women "are much thinner than their counterparts who marry men of the same social class or lower" (Etcoff, 1999: 200–201).

4. Displaying direct aggression is more strongly associated with peer rejection for girls than for boys (Bukowski, Gauze, Hoza, and Newcomb, 1993). Also, compared with boys, girls demonstrate higher levels of indirect or relational aggression— acts designed to damage another's peer relationships or reputation (e.g., gossiping, spreading malicious rumours, exclusionary acts)—than boys do (Crick, 1997).

SUMMARY

1. Are sex and gender rooted in nature?

Sex refers to certain anatomical and hormonal features of a person, while gender refers to the culturally appropriate expression of masculinity and femininity. Sex is largely rooted in nature, although people can change their sex by undergoing a sex-change operation and hormone therapy. In contrast, social as well as biological forces strongly influence gender. Sociologists study the way social conditions affect the expression of masculinity and femininity.

2. What are some of the major social forces that channel people into performing culturally appropriate gender roles?

Various agents of socialization channel people into performing culturally approved gender roles. The family, the school, and the mass media are among the most important of these agents of socialization. Once the sex of children is known (or assumed), parents and teachers tend to treat boys and girls differently in terms of the kind of play, dress, and learning they encourage. The mass media reinforce the learning of masculine and feminine roles by making different characteristics seem desirable in boys and girls, men and women.

3. What is homosexuality and why does it exist?

Homosexuals are people who prefer sexual partners of the same sex. We do not yet well understand the causes of homosexuality—whether it is genetic, hormonal, psychological, or some combination of the three. We do know that homosexuality does not appear to be a choice and that it emerges for most people without prior sexual experience in early adolescence. Sociologists are, in any case, more interested in the way homosexuality is expressed and repressed. For example, they have studied how, in the twentieth century, scientific research and political movements made the open expression of homosexuality more acceptable. Sociologists have also studied the ways in which various aspects of society reinforce heterosexuality and treat homosexuality as a form of deviance subject to tight social control.

4. Aside from agents of socialization, are there other social forces that influence the expression of masculinity and femininity?

Yes. One of the most important non-socialization forces that influences the expression of masculinity and femininity is the level of social inequality between men and women. High levels of gender inequality encourage more traditional or conventional gender roles. There are fewer differences in gender roles where low levels of gender inequality prevail. Historically, high levels of gender inequality have been encouraged by far-ranging warfare and conquest, plow agriculture, and the separation of public and private spheres. Each of these changes enhanced male power and added a layer of what we now consider tradition to gender roles.

5. How does the existence of sharply defined gender roles influence men's and women's income?

The gender gap in earnings derives from outright discrimination against women, women's disproportionate domestic responsibilities, women's concentration in low-wage occupations and industries, and the undervaluation of work typically done by women.

6. What helps explain male aggression against women?

Male aggression against women is rooted in gender inequality. Thus, where women and men are more equal socially, and norms justify gender equality, the rate of male aggression against women is lower.

7. How might the gender gap in earnings be reduced or eliminated?

Among the major reforms that could help eliminate the gender gap in earnings and reduce the level and expression of gender inequality are (a) the development of an affordable, accessible system of high-quality daycare and (b) the remuneration of men and women on the basis of their work's actual worth.

KEY TERMS

bisexuals (p. 319)	**heterosexuality** (p. 307)
equal pay for work of equal value (p. 334)	**homophobic** (p. 322)
	homosexuals (p. 319)
essentialism (p. 308)	**hostile environment sexual harassment** (p. 331)
gender (p. 307)	
gender discrimination (p. 326)	**intersexed** (p. 306)
gender identity (p. 307)	**quid pro quo sexual harassment** (p. 331)
gender ideology (p. 314)	**sex** (p. 307)
gender role (p. 307)	**transgendered** (p. 318)
glass ceiling (p. 318)	**transsexuals** (p. 318)

QUESTIONS TO CONSIDER

1. By interviewing your family members and using your own memory, compare the gender division of labour in (a) the households in which your parents grew up and (b) the household(s) in which you grew up. Then, imagine the gender division of labour you would like to see in the household you hope to live in about 10 years from now. What accounts for change over time in the gender division of labour in these households? Do you think your hopes are realistic? Why or why not?

2. Systematically note the roles played by women and men on TV programs and ads one evening. Is there a gender division of labour on TV? If so, describe it.

3. Are you a feminist? If so, which of the types of feminism discussed in this chapter do you find most appealing? Why? If not, what do you find objectionable about feminism? In either case, what is the ideal form of gender relations in your opinion? Why do you think this form is ideal?

WEB RESOURCES

Companion Website for This Book

http://www.compass3e.nelson.com

Begin by clicking on the Student Resources section of the website. Next, select the chapter you are studying from the pull-down menu. From the Student Resources page you have easy access to InfoTrac® College Edition, additional Weblinks, and other resources. The website also has many useful tips to aid you in your study of sociology, including practice tests for each chapter.

InfoTrac® Search Terms

These search terms are provided to assist you in beginning to conduct research on this topic by visiting http://www.infotrac-college.com:
gender
glass ceiling
gender discrimination
sexual harassment
gender role

http://www.compass3e.nelson.com

Recommended Websites

For a useful discussion of women and work worldwide see the article "Women, Gender and Work: Part II" by Janneke Plantenga and Johan Hansen, available on the World Wide Web at www.ilo.org/public/english/revue/download/pdf/intro994.pdf.

To learn about the history of women and gender in Canada, go to the World History Archives page at http://www.hartford-hwp.com/archives/44/index-eb.html.

For information on gender roles and stereotyping in children's literature, see http://www.indiana.edu/~reading/ieo/bibs/childgen.html.

A variety of useful links about gender can be found at Gender.org.uk: http://www.gender.org.uk.

Visit the website of Status of Women Canada at http://www.swc-cfc.gc.ca.

For more on the United Nations Gender Empowerment Measure (GEM) discussed in the text, see http://hdr.undp.org/en/statistics/indices/gdi_gem.

CengageNOW™

http://hed.nelson.com

This online diagnostic tool identifies each student's unique needs with a Pretest that generates a personalized Study Plan for each chapter, helping students focus on concepts they're having the most difficulty mastering. Students then take a Posttest after reading the chapter to measure their understanding of the material. An Instructor Gradebook is available to track and monitor student progress.

CHAPTER

12

Sociology of the Body: Disability, Aging, and Death

In this chapter, you will learn that

- Seemingly "natural" features of the human body, such as height and weight, have social causes and consequences of far-reaching importance.

- Enhancing body image to conform to prevailing norms became especially important in urban, industrial societies.

- People have defined and dealt with disability in different ways in different times and places.

- Age is an important basis of social stratification. However, the correlation between age and the command of resources is far from perfect, and political conflicts shape the degree to which any given age cohort exercises resource control.

- Although prejudice and discrimination against older people are common in Canada, older people have wielded increasing political power in recent decades.

NIP/TUCK

"Tell me what you don't like about yourself." With these simple words, plastic surgeons Christian Troy and Sean McNamara begin each consultation in the popular TV series *Nip/Tuck*. At first, the words seem unremarkable. Why *wouldn't* we assume that prospective

cosmetic surgery patients are dissatisfied with their appearance? Yet once the words sink in, they shock us. They shock us, first, when we remember how widespread the incidence of body dissatisfaction is. About 1 percent of Canadian adults underwent cosmetic surgery and minimally invasive cosmetic procedures, such as Botox injections, in 2004, up roughly sevenfold over the preceding decade (estimated from American Society of Plastic Surgeons, 2005; International Society of Aesthetic Plastic Surgeons, 2005). Add to this number the many people who want cosmetic surgery but cannot afford it, and we can reasonably conclude that body dissatisfaction is not an individual idiosyncrasy but a mass social phenomenon. The plastic surgeons' words are shocking, too, because they point to dissatisfaction that is more than skin deep. Troy and McNamara don't ask prospective patients what they dislike about their bodies. They ask them what they dislike about their *selves*. Implicit in their question is the assumption that our bodies faithfully represent our selves, that weight, proportions, hairiness, and so forth, say something fundamentally important about a person's character. It is an assumption that most people share.

Embedded in the idea that our bodies reflect our selves is a sociological principle that is the main lesson of this chapter. The human body is not just a wonder of biology; it is also a sociological wonder (Turner, 1996). Its parts, its disabilities, its aging, and its death mean different things and have different consequences for different cultures, historical periods, and categories of people. For example, a person's height, weight, and attractiveness may seem to be facts of nature. Closer inspection reveals, however, that the standards by which we define a "normal" or "desirable" body vary historically. Moreover, a person's height, weight, and perceived attractiveness influence his or her annual income, health, likelihood of getting married, and much else. We explore the relationship between body characteristics and social status in the next section.

The relationship between the body and society is especially clear in the case of disability. The very definition of what constitutes a disability has varied over time and place. So have strategies for dealing with disabilities. In the following pages, we illustrate these variations. Among other things, we show that the dominant treatment tendency since the nineteenth century has involved the rehabilitation and integration of people with disabilities into "normal" society. Then, in the early twentieth century, some governments tried to eliminate people with disabilities altogether. Finally, in the late twentieth century, people with disabilities began to assert their dignity and normality. One consequence of this new attitude is a vigorous move toward self-help and the establishment of independent communities of people with disabilities.

In this chapter's final section, we turn to the problems of aging and death. We show that aging is not just a natural process of growth and decline. Age is one basis of social inequality. Thanks to improved social policy and medical advances, the social condition of the aged is much better than it was just four or five decades ago. However, older people face prejudice and discrimination. The systems for providing personal care and adequate pensions are in trouble. Poverty is a looming possibility for some and a bitter reality for others. We survey each of these issues and conclude by training our sociological eye on the ultimate social problems: dying and death.

SOCIETY AND THE HUMAN BODY

The Body and Social Status

Height

In an experiment, four people of the same height and roughly similar appearance were introduced to a group of students. The first person was introduced as a fellow undergraduate, the second as a graduate student, the third as an assistant professor, and the fourth as a professor. Members of the group were asked to rank the four people in terms of their height. Despite the fact that all four were of equal stature, the students estimated that the professor was the tallest, the assistant professor next tallest, then the graduate student, and finally the undergraduate. Apparently believing that physical stature reflects social stature, the students correlated social status with height ("Short Guys Finish Last," 1995–96).

Is this perception accurate? Do tall people really tend to enjoy high social status? And why are some people tall in the first place? We can begin to answer these questions by first acknowledging that genes are an important determinant of any particular individual's height. However, different *populations* are approximately the same genetically. A complex series of *social* factors determines the average height of any population, whether the population consists of members of a country, a class, a racial or an ethnic group, and so on. Moreover, a complex series of social consequences flow from differences in height.

Figure 12.1 shows some of the main social causes and consequences of height. For purposes of illustration, consider the impact of family income on stature. Average family income is the single most important determinant of the quality of a person's diet (especially protein consumption). Higher family income translates into a higher-quality diet. In turn, the quality of diet during childhood strongly influences a person's stature. Thus, Japanese men were on average five centimetres (two inches) taller at the end of the twentieth century than they were at mid-century (French, 2001). Norwegian men were on average nearly eight centimetres (three inches) taller in 1984 than in 1761 (Floud, Wachter, and Gregory, 1990). North American–born children of immigrants are taller than their parents who were born abroad (Roberts, 1995). In all these cases, the main cause of growing stature is the same: A higher standard of living led to an improved diet that allowed the human body to come closer to realizing its full growth potential. The correlation between per capita family income and average height across many countries is very strong ($r = 0.82$ or higher; Steckel, 1995: 1912).

As we might expect, within countries there is also a correlation between stature and class position. Class differences in height are smaller than they were centuries ago. Even today, however, members of upper classes are on average taller than members of middle classes, who are in turn taller than members of working classes are. The Scandinavian countries are the exceptions that prove the rule. There are no differences in stature between classes in Scandinavia. That is because class inequality is less pronounced in Sweden, Norway, and the rest of Scandinavia than anywhere else in the world (Floud, Wachter, and Gregory, 1990; Kingston, 1997).

FIGURE 12.1

Selected Social Causes and Consequences of Height in Human Populations

Source: Adapted from Steckel, 1995: 1908.

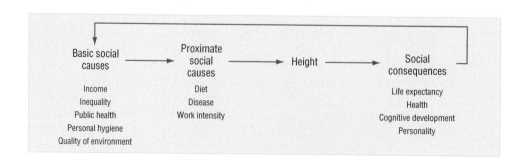

The *consequences* of stature are important too. Scrutiny of many sources, ranging from U.S. Army records since the Civil War to all Norwegian X-ray records from the 1950s, reveals that, on average, tall people live longer than others do. In only three of the United States presidential elections held over the past century did the shorter candidate win ("Short Guys Finish Last," 1995–96). Tall people also earn more than others earn and tend to reach the top of their profession more quickly (Kingston, 1997; McCulloch, 2003). One of the most through studies of the effect of height on income was recently conducted in Canada. Tom Perks (2005) found that an additional centimetre in height is associated with an additional $222 in annual income for men and an additional $57 for women. This means that over 10 years, a man who is 10 centimetres taller than another man but like him in all other relevant respects will earn $22 200 more on average. Remarkably, Perks also found that, in Canada, height has a bigger effect on income than whether one is an immigrant or a member of a visible minority group.

At least part of the reason that short people tend to be less successful in some ways than tall people are is that they experience subtle discrimination based on height. This argument may seem far-fetched. However, your own attitudes may help drive the point home. Is it important that you choose a spouse who is taller than you are? If you are a woman, there is a very good chance you will answer yes. Is it important that you choose a spouse who is shorter than you are? If you are a man, there is a very good chance you will answer yes. Why is this so? Practically speaking, it is unimportant whether the husband or the wife is taller. Yet the overwhelming majority of people believe that husbands should be taller than wives. They find it odd when a husband is shorter than his wife is or even when they are the same height. This attitude is widespread because, for most people, height is an indicator of status and most people believe that men should enjoy higher status than women do. You can extend this example to other kinds of relationships. Think about the leaders of your sports teams, friendship circles, college or university tutorials, families, and other groups to which you belong. Height will surely not be the only determinant of leadership, but you are likely to observe a tendency for leaders to be taller than followers are. This is so despite the fact that there is no practical reason that leaders need to be taller than followers are. Finally, consider where you sit in the status hierarchy based on height. Have you ever felt advantaged or disadvantaged because of your height? Where do you fit in?

WHERE DO YOU FIT IN?

Weight

What is true for height is also true for body weight. Body weight influences status because of the cultural expectations we associate with it. Thus, one study of more than 10 000 young adults found that overweight women tend to complete four fewer months of school than women who are not overweight. They are also 20 percent less likely to be married. An overweight woman's household is likely to earn nearly $8500 less per year than the household of a woman who is not overweight does. Overweight women are 10 percent more likely to live in poverty. The consequences of being overweight are less serious for men. Still, overweight men are 11 percent less likely to be married than men who are not overweight (Gortmaker et al., 1993; see also Averett and Korenman, 1996).

Interestingly, the negative effects of being overweight are evident even for women matched in terms of their social and economic backgrounds. This fact suggests the need to revise the simple, conventional view that poverty encourages obesity. It is certainly true that poor women have fewer opportunities and resources that would allow them to eat healthier diets, get more exercise, and bring down their weight. For example, if you live in a poor, high-crime neighbourhood, it is dangerous to go out for a speed walk and you may not be able to afford anything more nutritious than high-calorie fast food when you go out for a meal. However, the reverse is also true: Obesity in and of itself tends to make women poorer. This conclusion seems reasonable because, for women matched in terms of their social and economic backgrounds, being overweight still has negative effects on income. There is apparently a "reciprocal relationship" between obesity and social class, with each variable affecting the other (Gortmaker et al., 1993).

Rubens's *The Toilette of Venus* (1613). Venus, the Roman goddess of beauty, as depicted by Peter Paul Rubens four centuries ago. Would Venus need a tummy tuck and a membership in a diet club to be considered beautiful today?

In preindustrial societies, people generally favoured well-rounded physiques because they signified wealth and prestige. Not surprisingly, beautiful women as depicted by the great artists of the past tend to be on the heavy side from our contemporary perspective.

In contrast, in our society, being well rounded usually signifies undesirability. Being overweight in Canada has become a source of negative stereotyping and even outright discrimination. Many of us think of overweight people as less attractive, industrious, and disciplined than thin people.

The percentage of overweight people is big and growing in Canada. Consider the following facts (Statistics Canada, 2002b, 2002d; see Figure 12.3):

• In 2000–01, 15 percent of Canadian adults were obese, up from 13 percent in 1994–95 (see Figure 12.2 for the definition of obesity).
• Men accounted for two-thirds of the increase between 1994–95 and 2000–01.
• Obesity is increasing for all age–sex groups except women between the ages of 20 and 34, among whom the obesity rate fell 9 percent in the six-year period.
• Obesity increases with age.
• Obesity decreases with increasing class position (poor people are the most likely to be obese).

Thus, a large and expanding number of Canadians live with a stigma that affects their life chances.

Sociology of the Body

The Body and Society

Our discussion of height and weight should make it clear that our bodies are not just biologically but also socially defined. Let us now develop this point by considering how social forces influence the way we manipulate our body image. We then turn to an analysis of disability—how we define it and how people with and without disabilities deal with it.

In Canada and other highly developed countries, people tend to think they have rights over their own bodies. Typically, the feminist movement asserts the right of every woman

FIGURE 12.2

Percentage of Adults Who Are Obese, Selected Countries, 2003–2006

Note: Obese adults have a BMI of 30 or higher (BMI = weight in kilograms divided by the square of height in metres).

Source: World Health Organization, 2008, "Health Topic Page." Retrieved January 13, 2008 (http://www.who.int/infobase/report.aspx?rid=112&ind=BMI&goButton=Go).

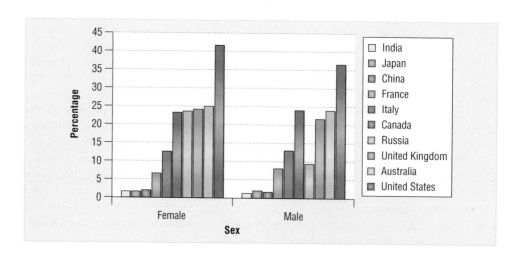

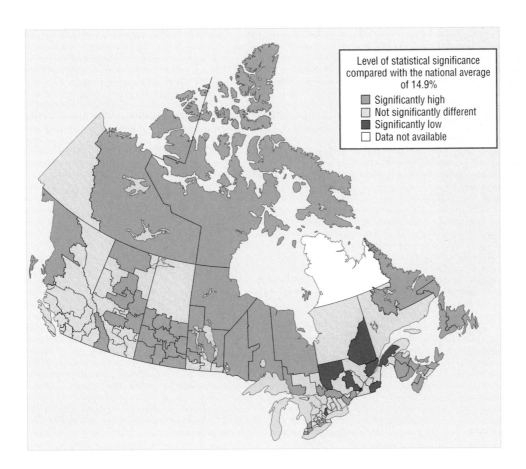

FIGURE 12.3
The Regional Distribution of Obesity in Canada, 2000–2001

Source: Adapted from Statistics Canada, 2005, "Health Indicators," Catalogue 82-221, No. 1. Retrieved May 27, 2008 (http://statcan.ca/ english/freepub/ 82-221-XIE/00502/pdf /1226m.pdf).

to control her own reproductive functions through birth control, for example (Gordon, 1990). Yet people have not always endorsed this view (and some Canadians still contest it). For instance, slaves' bodies were the property of their owners. In most slave societies, masters could use their slaves' bodies for anything they wanted, including hard labour and sex. Similarly, in deeply patriarchal societies, a husband effectively owned his wife's body. Because his wife's body was at his disposal, a husband could rape his wife with impunity.

Despite the widespread view that people have rights over their own bodies, most people do not treat their bodies in wildly idiosyncratic ways. Instead, norms of body practice influence us. Catholic priests are defined partly by sexual abstinence. Male Jews and Muslims are typically defined partly by circumcision. Many of the most important social distinctions—gender, race, age, tribe, and so forth—are "written" on the body by different styles of dress, jewellery, tattoos, cosmetics, and so forth. People have always attempted to affect their body shape and appearance, but they do so according to principles laid out by society.

For social, economic, and technological reasons, enhancing body image to conform to prevailing norms became especially important in urban, industrial societies:

- *Socially,* urbanized societies present people with many more opportunities to meet and interact with strangers. This increases the need for the kinds of status cues and impression management techniques that can make social interaction easier (see Chapter 5, Social Interaction). Manipulating body image helps grease the wheels of social interaction in complex societies by making it clear to strangers exactly who you are.
- *Economically,* industrialized societies enable people to afford body enhancement. For example, peasants in preindustrial societies had no access to relatively inexpensive, mass-produced clothing, something we take for granted.

Many of the most important social distinctions—gender, race, age, tribe, and so forth—are "written" on the body by different styles of dress, jewellery, tattoos, cosmetics, and so forth. People have always attempted to affect their body shape and appearance, but they do so according to principles laid out by society.

Impaired people are considered deficient in physical or mental capacity.

Disability is a physical or mental problem that keeps people from performing within the range of "normal" human activity.

Rehabilitation involves curing disabilities to the extent possible through medical and technological intervention; trying to improve the lives of people with disabilities by means of care, training, and education; and integrating people with disabilities into society.

• *Technologically,* we have created many new techniques for transfiguring the body. Consider something as basic as your teeth and gums. Until recently, the daily practice of brushing, much less of flossing, was uncommon. Two hundred years ago, a 40-year-old might boast a nice set of wooden dentures; poor people were often toothless and without false teeth. Today, dental hygiene, dentistry, and orthodontics allow many people to enjoy a set of straight, white teeth for a lifetime, with bridges, crowns, and implants indistinguishable from the real thing.

Thus, social, economic, and technological forces have transformed the way we manipulate our body image. As you will now see, they have also radically altered the way we deal with disability.

DISABILITY

The Social Construction of Disability

Pity the poor lefty, for centuries considered inferior. About 400 years ago, the Catholic Church declared left-handed people servants of the Devil and burned some of them at the stake. Then it forced lefties to become right-handed in school. In Japan as recently as the early twentieth century, left-handedness in a wife was grounds for divorce. Natives in Papua New Guinea don't let their left thumbs touch their beer mugs because they believe that would poison the beer. Maori women in New Zealand weave ceremonial cloth with the right hand because they believe that using the left desecrates the cloth. Some African tribes along the Niger River do not allow women to prepare food with the left hand for fear of being poisoned. Almost universally, people have considered left-handedness a disability, so much so that the sentiment has been embedded in many languages. In Russian, to do something *na levo* means to do it under the table or illegally, but literally it means "on the left." In English, the word *left* derives from an Old English word that means "weak" or "worthless." Also in English, *gauche* means "ill-mannered"—but the French from which it is derived means "left." (In contrast, *adroit* means "proper" in English—but the French from which it is derived means "to the right.") In Latin, "right" is *dexter* (as in the English *dextrous,* a desirable attribute) while "left" is *sinister,* which of course means "evil" in English. *Linkisch* is German for "leftish"—and "awkward."

To us, negative attitudes toward left-handedness seem like so much nonsense. We don't think of left-handed people—roughly 10 percent of the population—as **impaired** or deficient in physical or mental capacity. Nor do we think of them as having a **disability** or being incapable of performing within the range of "normal" human activity. The fact that so many people once thought otherwise suggests that definitions of disability are not based on self-evident biological realities. Instead, they vary socially and historically. Note also that some people, but not others, consider a 1.5-metre-tall (4-foot-tall) person to have a disability, and that most people must be convinced by advertising that erectile dysfunction in a 75-year-old man is a disability. These examples suggest that definitions of disability differ across societies and historical periods and that in any one time and place, people may disagree over these definitions.

Rehabilitation and Elimination

Modern Western approaches to disability emerged in the nineteenth century. All scientists and reformers of the time viewed disability as a self-evident biological reality. Some scientists and reformers sought the **rehabilitation** of those with disabilities. Rehabilitation involves curing disabilities to the extent possible through medical and technological intervention. It also involves trying to improve the lives of people with disabilities by means of care, training, and education. Finally, it involves integrating people with disabilities into "normal" society (Stiker, 1999 [1982]; Terry and Urla, 1995). The desire for rehabilitation motivated the establishment of schools for the blind, the widespread use of prosthetics, the construction of wheelchair-accessible buildings, and so forth. It also prompted the passage of laws that benefit those with disabilities by mandating accessibility to buildings, public transportation, and jobs. These laws have done much to help integrate people with disabilities into "normal" society.

Other scientists and reformers took a different tack. They sought to eliminate disability altogether by killing people who had a disability or sterilizing them and preventing them from having children. The Nazis adopted this approach in Germany beginning in 1933. They engineered the sterilization and killing of the mentally "deficient" and the physically "deviant," including the blind and the deaf (Proctor, 1988).

One of the ugliest chapters in our history involves the government-funded, forced sterilization of native North American women from the 1920s to the 1970s. The "disability" these women were alleged to have was that they were Aboriginal and were deemed by physicians to be having too many babies. Tubal ligations and hysterectomies were performed as a form of birth control on many thousands of native North Americans, some of them minors, without their informed consent. In two cases, doctors told 15-year-old girls they were having their tonsils out and then proceeded to remove their ovaries. Tremendous damage had been inflicted on the Native North American population by the time such practices were outlawed. According to one estimate, in 1982, when 15 percent of white North American women of childbearing age had been sterilized for various reasons, the figure for Native North American women was about 40 percent (DeFine, 1997; England, n.d.; Johansen, 1998; *The Sterilization*, 1996).

Ableism

Perhaps a tenth of the world's people identify themselves as having a disability or are characterized as such by others (Priestly, 2001). Because the human environment is structured largely around the norms of those without disabilities, people with them suffer many disadvantages. Their deprivations are still greater if they are seniors, women, or members of a lower class or a disadvantaged racial or ethnic group.

Specifically, people routinely stigmatize people with disabilities, negatively evaluating them because of a characteristic that supposedly sets them apart from others. People also routinely employ stereotypes when dealing with people with disabilities, expecting them to behave according to a rigid and often inaccurate view of how everyone with that disability acts. The resulting prejudice and discrimination against people with disabilities is called **ableism**. A historical example of ableism is the widespread belief among nineteenth-century Western educators that blind people are incapable of high-level or abstract thought. Because of this prejudice, the blind were systematically discouraged from pursuing intellectually challenging tasks and occupations. Similarly, an 1858 article in the *American Annals of the Deaf and Dumb* held that "the deaf and dumb are guided almost wholly by instinct and their animal passions. They have no more opportunity of cultivating the intellect and reasoning facilities than the savages of Patagonia or the North American Indians" (quoted in Groce, 1985: 102). Racists think of members of racial minorities as naturally and incurably inferior. Ableists think of people with disabilities in the same way. As the preceding quotation suggests, racists and ableists were often the same people.

Ableism involves more than active prejudice and discrimination. It also involves the largely unintended *neglect* of the conditions of people with disabilities. This point should be clear to anyone who has to get around in a wheelchair. Many buildings were constructed without the intention of discriminating against people in wheelchairs, yet they

The social environment turns an impairment into a disability. Architecture and urban planning that neglect some modes of mobility make life difficult for people who depend on wheelchairs.

Ableism is prejudice and discrimination against people who have disabilities.

are extremely inhospitable to them. Impairment becomes disability when the human environment is constructed largely on the basis of ableism. Ableism exists through both intention and neglect.

Challenging Ableism: The Normality of Disability

In 1927 science fiction writer H. G. Wells published a short story called "The Country of the Blind" (Wells, 1927). It provocatively reversed the old saying that "in the country of the blind, the one-eyed man is king." In the story, the protagonist, Nunez, survives an avalanche high in the Andes. When he revives in a mountain valley, he discovers he is on the outskirts of an isolated village whose members are all blind because of a disease that struck 14 generations earlier. For them, words like *see, look,* and *blind* have no meaning.

Because he can see, Nunez feels vastly superior to the villagers; he thinks he is their "Heaven-sent King and master." Over time, however, he realizes that his sight places him at a disadvantage vis-à-vis the villagers. Their senses of hearing and touch are more highly developed than his are, and they have designed their entire community for the benefit of people who cannot see. Nunez stumbles where his hosts move gracefully and he constantly rants about seeing—which only proves to his hosts that he is out of touch with reality. The head of the village concludes that Nunez is "an idiot. He has delusions; he can't do anything right." In this way, Nunez's vision becomes a disability. He visits a doctor who concludes there is only one thing to do. Nunez must be cured of his ailment. As the doctor says:

> Those queer things that are called eyes . . . are diseased . . . in such a way as to affect his brain. They are greatly distended, he has eyelashes, and his eyelids move, and consequently his brain is in a state of constant irritation and distraction. . . . I think I may say with reasonable certainty that, in order to cure him complete, all that we need to do is a simple and easy surgical operation—namely, to remove these irritant bodies.

Thus, Wells suggests that in the country of the blind, the man who sees must lose his vision or be regarded as a raving idiot.

Wells's tale is noteworthy because it makes blindness seem utterly normal. Its depiction of the normality of blindness comes close to the way many people with disabilities today think of their disabilities—not as a form of deviance but as a different form of normality. As one blind woman wrote: "If I were to list adjectives to describe myself, blind would be only one of many, and not necessarily the first in significance. My blindness is as intrinsically a part of me as the shape of my hands or my predilection for salty snacks. . . . The most valuable insight I can offer is this: blindness is normal to me" (Kleege, 1999: 4; Box 12.1).

The idea of the normality of disability has partly supplanted the rehabilitation ideal which, as we saw, originated in the nineteenth century. Reformers without disabilities led the rehabilitation movement. They represented and assisted people with disabilities, who participated little in efforts to improve the conditions of their existence. This situation began to change in the 1960s. Inspired by other social movements of the era, people with disabilities began to organize themselves (Campbell and Oliver, 1996; Shapiro, 1993). The founding of the Disabled Peoples International in 1981 and inclusion of the rights of those with disabilities in the United Nations Universal Declaration of Human Rights in 1985 signified the growth—and growing legitimacy—of the new movement globally. Since the 1980s, people with disabilities have begun to assert their autonomy and the "dignity of difference" (Charlton, 1998; Oliver, 1996). Rather than requesting help from others, they insist on self-help. Rather than seeing disability as a personal tragedy, they see it as a social problem. Rather than regarding themselves as deviant, they think of themselves as inhabiting a different but quite normal world.

The deaf community typifies the new challenge to ableism. Increasingly, deaf people share a "collective identity" with all other deaf people (Becker, 1980: 107). Members of the deaf community have a common language and culture, and they tend to marry other deaf people (Davis, 1995: 38). Rather than feeling humiliated by the seeming disadvantage of

BOX 12.1
Sociology at the Movies

TAKE ROLL

Shallow Hal (2001)

Hal is so shallow that when someone asks him if he would prefer a woman with one breast or half a brain, he replies: "How big is the breast?" His balding sidekick, Mauricio (who sprays on most of his hair), isn't any deeper. They are obnoxious men with below-average looks and sexist values, always on the make but with nothing to offer any woman with even half a brain. They are oblivious to their character flaws and that is what makes them so funny.

Then one day, Hal (played by Jack Black) gets trapped in an elevator with self-help guru Tony Robbins and everything changes. After a brief conversation, Robbins hypnotizes Hal and tells him to see only the inner beauty of women. Suddenly, Hal's "luck" with women improves. He meets Rosemary, an ex-Peace Corps volunteer who now works in a children's hospital. When Hal looks at her, she is an intelligent and generous soul from a wealthy family and she just happens to look like Gwyneth Paltrow. When *we* look at her, she is an intelligent and generous soul from a wealthy family and she just happens to weigh 135 kilograms (300 pounds). (Rosemary is played by Gwyneth Paltrow, alternately wearing and not wearing a fat suit.)

All is well until Mauricio (Jason Alexander) breaks the hypnotic spell. Hal then sees all of Rosemary's 135 kilograms and must make the decision of his life. Should he continue with his shallow ways or go for inner beauty? He makes the right choice, and in the end we see Rosemary carrying Hal to his car as they leave for a Peace Corps assignment.

The Farrelly brothers made this movie. They also made *Dumb and Dumber* (1994), a buddy movie about two guys with low IQs; *There's*

Gwyneth Paltrow and Jack Black in *Shallow Hal* (2001)

Something About Mary (1998), about a paraplegic suitor; and *Me, Myself, and Irene* (2000), about a schizophrenic police officer. Are the lives of the Farrelly brothers just one big sick joke? Have they devoted themselves to poking fun at people with disabilities? Quite the contrary. What is striking about their movies, and particularly *Shallow Hal,* is that they make us see the normality of disability. *Shallow Hal* is densely populated by people with disabilities and oddities who turn out to be just like everyone else. There is the little girl in Rosemary's hospital with horrific facial scars from third-degree burns; the cross-dressing receptionist at the fancy restaurant where Hal first sees Rosemary's true girth; Rosemary's former boyfriend, who suffers from chronic and highly visible psoriasis; Hal's best friend, Mauricio, who has a vestigial tail at the base of his spine; and, most important, Walt (Rene Kirby). Walt has a curvature of the spine so severe he must walk on all fours. However, he doesn't use a wheelchair. He skis, rides horses, cycles, and does acrobatics. He is a successful businessperson who sells

his software company to Microsoft for a fortune. He loves life and he loves women and he can laugh at himself. Consider this great pickup line, delivered at a nightclub: "Hey, Sally, I've got a leash. Would you like to take me for a walk?" To which Sally, greatly amused, replies, "Come on, boy." The male viewer may be excused for wondering why he could never come up with such a clever opener.

The point of all this is not just that people with disabilities are ordinary folk with all the problems, quirks, deficiencies, and virtues of everyone else—and a good deal more to contend with besides—but that many of us are odd for not being able to see their normality. The Farrelly brothers may be trying to tell us that the person with the biggest disability in *Shallow Hal* is Hal as we first meet him and that the people with the biggest disability in real life are all the "normal" people who think like him, equating difference with inferiority. Some audience members may think Rosemary is lucky for winning Hal, but in fact Hal is the one who really lucks out.

deafness, they take pride in their condition. Indeed, many people in the deaf community are eager to remain deaf even if medical treatment can "cure" them (Lane, 1992). As one deaf activist put it: "I'm happy with who I am . . . I don't want to be 'fixed.' . . . In our society everyone agrees that whites have an easier time than blacks. But do you think a black person would undergo operations to become white?" (quoted in Dolnick, 1993: 38).

AGING

Sociology of Aging

Disability affects some people. Aging affects us all. Many people think of aging as a natural process that inevitably thwarts our best attempts to delay death. Sociologists, however, see aging in a more complex light. For them, aging is also a process of socialization or learning new roles appropriate to different stages of life (see Chapter 4, Socialization). The sociological nature of aging is also evident in the fact that its significance varies from one society to the next. That is, different societies attach different meanings to the progression of life through its various stages. Menopause, for example, occurs in all mature women. In Canada, we often see it as a major life event. Thus, the old euphemism for menopause was the rather dramatic expression "change of life." In contrast, menopause is a relatively minor matter in Japan. Moreover, while menopausal Canadian women frequently suffer hot flashes, menopausal Japanese women tend to complain mainly about stiff shoulders (Lock, 1993). In many Western countries, complaining about stiff shoulders is a classic symptom of having just given birth. As this example shows, the stages of life are not just natural processes but events deeply rooted in society and culture. As we will see, the same holds for death.

Aging and the Life Course

All individuals pass through distinct stages of life, which, taken together, sociologists call the **life course**. These stages are often marked by **rites of passage** or rituals signifying the transition from one life stage to another (Fried and Fried, 1980). Baptism, confirmation, the bar mitzvah and bat mitzvah, high school graduation, college or university convocation, the wedding ceremony, and the funeral are among the best-known rites of passage in Canada. Rituals do not mark some transitions in the life course, however. For example, in Canada people often complain about the "terrible twos," when toddlers defy parental demands in their attempt to gain autonomy. Similarly, when some Canadian men reach the age of about 40, they experience a "midlife crisis," in which they attempt to defy the passage of time and regain their youth. (It never works.)

Some stages of the life course are established not just by norms but also by law. For example, most societies have laws that stipulate the minimum age for smoking tobacco, drinking alcohol, driving a vehicle, and voting. Most societies have a legal retirement age. Moreover, the duration of each stage of life differs from one society and historical period to the next. For example, there are no universal rules about when a person becomes an adult. In preindustrial societies, adulthood arrived soon after puberty. In Japan, a person becomes an adult at 20. In Canada, adulthood arrives at 18 (the legal voting age and the legal drinking age in some provinces) or 19 (the legal drinking age in other provinces). Until the 1970s, the legal voting age was 21 and the legal drinking age ranged between 18 and 21.

Even the number of life stages varies historically and across societies. For instance, childhood was a brief stage of development in medieval Europe (Ariès, 1962 [1960]). In contrast, childhood is a prolonged stage of development in rich societies today, and adolescence is a new phase of development that was virtually unknown just a few hundred years ago (Gillis, 1981). Increased life expectancy and the need for a highly educated labour force made childhood and adolescence possible and necessary. (**Life expectancy** is the average age at death of the members of a population.)

The **life course** refers to the distinct phases of life through which people pass. These stages vary from one society and historical period to another.

Rites of passage are cultural ceremonies that mark the transition from one stage of life to another (e.g., baptisms, confirmations, weddings) or from life to death (funerals).

Life expectancy is the average age at death of the members of a population.

Finally, although some life-course events are universal—birth, puberty, marriage, and death—not all cultures attach the same significance to them. Thus, ritual practices marking these events vary. For example, formal puberty rituals in many preindustrial societies are extremely important because they mark the transition to adult responsibilities. However, adult responsibilities do not immediately follow puberty in industrial and postindustrial societies because of the introduction of a prolonged period of childhood and adolescence. Therefore, formal puberty rituals are less important in such societies.

Age Cohort

As you pass through the life course, you learn new patterns of behaviour that are common to people about the same age as you are. Sociologically speaking, a category of people born in the same range of years is called an **age cohort**. For example, all Canadians born between 1980 and 1989 form an age cohort. **Age roles** are patterns of behaviour that we expect of people in different age cohorts. Age roles form an important part of our sense of self and others (Riley, Foner, and Waring, 1988). As we pass through the stages of the life course, we assume different age roles. To put it simply, a child is supposed to act like a child, an older person like an older person. We may find a 5-year-old dressed in a suit cute but look askance at a lone 50-year-old on a merry-go-round. "Act your age" is an expression that can be applied to people of all ages who do not conform to their age roles. Many age roles are informally known by character types, such as the "rebellious teenager" and "wise old woman." We formalize some age roles by law. For instance, the establishment of minimum ages for smoking, drinking, driving, and voting formalizes certain aspects of the adolescent and adult roles.

We find it natural that children in the same age cohort, such as preschoolers in a park, should play together or that people of similar age cluster together at parties. Conversely, many people find romance and marriage between people widely separated by age problematic and even repulsive.

Differences between age cohorts are sufficiently large in Canada that some sociologists regard youth culture as a distinct subculture. Adolescents and teenagers—divided though they may be by gender, class, race, and ethnicity—frequently share common interests in music, movies, and so forth (Allahar and Côté, 1994).

An age cohort is a category of people born in the same range of years.

Age roles are norms and expectations about the behaviour of people in different age cohorts.

A generation is an age group that has unique and formative historical experiences.

Generation

A **generation** is a special type of age cohort. Many people think of a generation as people born within a 15- to 30-year span. Sociologists, however, usually define generation more narrowly. From a sociological point of view, a generation comprises members of an age cohort who have unique and formative experiences during youth. Age cohorts are statistically convenient categories, but most members of a generation are conscious of belonging to a distinct age group. For example, "baby boomers" are North Americans who were born in the prosperous years from 1946 to 1964. Most of them came of age between the mid-1960s and the early 1970s. Common experiences that bind them include major historical events (the war in Vietnam, Trudeaumania, Canada's centenary, Expo '67) and popular music (the songs of the Beatles, the Rolling Stones, and the Guess Who). "Generation X" followed the baby boomers. Members of Generation X faced a period of slower economic growth and a job market glutted by the baby boomers. Consequently, many of them resented having to take so-called McJobs when they entered the labour force. Thus, Vancouver's Douglas Coupland, the novelist who invented the term Generation X, cuttingly defined a McJob as a "low pay, low-prestige, low-dignity, low-benefit, no-future job in the service sector. Frequently considered a satisfying career choice by people who have never held one" (Coupland, 1991: 5).

Tragedies can help to crystallize the feeling of being a member of a particular generation. For instance, when you are much older you will probably remember where you were when you heard about the attacks of September 11, 2001. Such memories may someday distinguish you from those who are too young to remember these tragic events. The outbreak of World War II may play a similar role in the memory of your grandparents.

Woodstock. A generation comprises members of an age cohort who have unique and formative experiences during their youth.

The crystallization of a generational "we-feeling" among youth is a quite recent phenomenon. The very ideas of youth and adolescence gained currency only in the nineteenth century because of increased life expectancy, extended schooling, and other factors. Middle-class youth culture often challenged tradition and convention (Gillis, 1981). It was marked by a sense of adventure and rebellion, especially against parents, that manifested itself in political liberalism and cultural radicalism.

Finally, we note that generations sometimes play a major role in history. Revolutionary movements, whether in politics or the arts, are sometimes led by members of a young generation who aggressively displace members of an older generation (Eisenstadt, 1956; Mannheim, 1952).

Aging and Inequality

Age Stratification

Age stratification is social inequality between age cohorts.

Age stratification refers to social inequality between age cohorts. It exists in all societies and we can observe it in everyday social interaction. For example, there is a clear status hierarchy in most high schools. On average, students in grade 12 enjoy higher status than those in grade 10 do, while students in grade 10 enjoy higher status than those in grade 9 do.

The very young are often at the bottom of the stratification system. Such age stratification is evident in rich countries today, where poverty is more widespread among children than among adults, and it was even more evident in preindustrial and early industrial societies. In some preindustrial societies, people occasionally killed infants so populations would not grow beyond the ability of the environment to support them. Facing poverty and famine, parents sometimes abandoned children. Many developing countries today are overflowing with orphans and street children. During the early stages of Western industrialization, adults brutally exploited children. The young chimney sweeps in *Mary Poppins* may look cute, but during the Industrial Revolution skinny "climbing boys" as young as four were valued in Britain because they could squeeze up crooked chimney flues no more than half a metre (a foot or two) in diameter 12 hours a day. Space was tight, so they worked naked, and they rubbed their elbows, knees, noses, and other protrusions raw against the soot, which was often hot. The first description of job-related cancer appeared in an article published in 1775. "Soot-wart," as it was then known, killed chimney sweeps as young as eight (Nuland, 1993: 202–05).

Gerontocracy

A gerontocracy is a society ruled by older people.

Some people believe that ancient China and other preindustrial societies were **gerontocracies**, or societies in which the oldest men ruled, earned the highest income, and enjoyed the most prestige. Even today, people in some industrialized countries pay more attention to age than North Americans do. In South Korean corporations, for instance, when a new manager starts work, everyone in the department who is older than the new manager may resign or be reassigned. Given the importance of age seniority in South Korea, it is considered difficult for a manager to hold authority over older employees. Older employees in turn find it demeaning to be managed by a younger boss (Lie, 1998).

Although some societies may approximate the gerontocratic model, its extent has been exaggerated. Powerful, wealthy, and prestigious leaders are often mature, but not the oldest, people in a society. Canada today is typical of most societies, past and present, in this regard. For example, median earned income for men gradually rises with age, reaching its peak at age 45, and then declines through later life (Guppy, Curtis, and Grabb, 1999: 249).

In general, true gerontocracy is rare. Like King Lear, seniors often give up power and become marginalized. Even in traditional societies that held seniors in high esteem, aging was not usually seen as an unambiguous good. After all, aging denotes physical and mental decline and the nearness of death. Ambivalence about aging—especially as people reach the oldest age cohorts—is a cultural universal. As one historian writes: "Youth has always and everywhere been preferred to old age. Since the dawn of history, old people have regretted [the loss of] their youth and young people have feared the onset of old age" (Minois, 1989 [1987]).

Just as true gerontocracy is uncommon, so is rule by youth. True, as noted previously, relatively young age cohorts sometimes supply most of a country's political leadership. This happened in revolutionary France in the late eighteenth century, revolutionary Russia in the early twentieth century, and revolutionary China in the mid-twentieth century. However, youthful ruling cadres may become gerontocracies in their own right, especially in non-democratic societies. This was the case with the Russian communist leadership in the 1980s and the Chinese communist leadership in the 1990s; the young generation that grabbed power half a century earlier still clung on as senility approached.

Theories of Age Stratification

The Functionalist View

How can we explain age stratification? *Functionalists* observe that in preindustrial societies, family, work, and community were tightly integrated (Parsons, 1942). People worked in and with their family, and the family was the lifeblood of the community. However, industrialization separated work from family. It also created distinct functions for different age cohorts. Thus, while traditional farming families lived and worked together on the farm, the heads of urban families work outside the home. Children worked for their parents in traditional farming families but in urban settings they attend schools. At the same time, industrialization raised the standard of living and created other conditions that led to increased life expectancy. The cohort of retired people thus grew. And so it came about that various age cohorts were differentiated in the course of industrialization.

At least in principle, social differentiation can exist without social stratification. But, according to the functionalists, age stratification did develop in this case because different age cohorts performed functions of differing value to society. For example, in preindustrial societies, older people were important as a storehouse of knowledge and wisdom. With industrialization, their function became less important and so their status declined. Age stratification, in the functionalist view, reflects the importance of each age cohort's current contribution to society, with children and seniors distinctly less important than adults employed in the paid labour force. Moreover, all societies follow much the same pattern. Their systems of age stratification "converge" under the force of industrialization.

Conflict Theory

Conflict theorists agree with the functionalists that the needs of industrialization generated distinct categories of youth and seniors. They disagree, however, on two points. First, they dispute that age stratification reflects the functional importance of different age cohorts (Gillis, 1981). Instead, they say, age stratification stems from competition and conflict. Young people may participate in a revolutionary overthrow and seize power. Seniors may organize politically to decrease their disadvantages and increase their advantages in life.

The second criticism lodged by conflict theorists concerns the problem of convergence. Conflict theorists suggest political struggles can make a big difference in how much age stratification exists in a society. We saw, for example, that child poverty is higher in the United States than in other rich countries. That is because in other rich countries, particularly in Continental Western Europe, successful working-class political parties have struggled to implement more generous child welfare measures and employment policies that lower the poverty level. This suggests that the fortunes of age cohorts are shaped by other forms of inequality, such as class stratification (Gillis, 1981; Graff, 1995). Power and wealth do not necessarily correlate perfectly with the roles the functionalists regard as more or less important. Competition and conflict may redistribute power and wealth between age cohorts.

Symbolic Interactionist Theory

Symbolic interactionists focus on the meanings people attach to age-based groups and age stratification. They stress that the way in which people understand aging is nearly always a matter of interpretation. Symbolic interactionists have done especially important research in community studies of seniors. They have also helped us to understand better the degree and nature of prejudice and discrimination against seniors. For example, one study examined how movies from the 1940s to the 1980s contributed to the negative stereotyping of older people, particularly women. Among other things, it found that young people were overrepresented numerically in the movies (as compared with their representation in the general population) and tended to be portrayed as leading active, vital lives. Older women were underrepresented numerically and tended to be portrayed as unattractive, unfriendly, and unintelligent (Brazzini, McIntosh, Smith, Cook, and Harris, 1997).

Seniors

Canada's population, along with that of many other rich countries around the world, is greying. In 1901, only 5 percent of Canada's population was 65 or older and the median age of Canadians was just 22.7 years (Novak, 1997). In contrast, according to the 2006 census, the median age was 39.5 years and 13.7 percent of the population was 65 or older (Statistics Canada, 2007a).

Another way of considering the greying of Canada is to examine **population pyramids**, graphs that show the percentage of the population in various age and sex cohorts (Figure 12.4 and Figure 12.5). In 1901, Canada's population pyramid looked very much like a true pyramid. The base of the pyramid was wide, indicating that most people were younger, and the top was small, suggesting a small senior population. By 2050, however,

Population pyramids are graphs that show the percentage of the population in various age and sex cohorts.

FIGURE 12.4

Population Pyramid, Canada, 1901

Source: McVey and Kalbach, 1995.

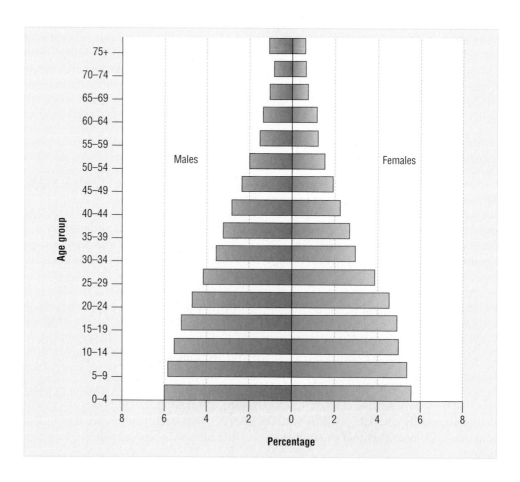

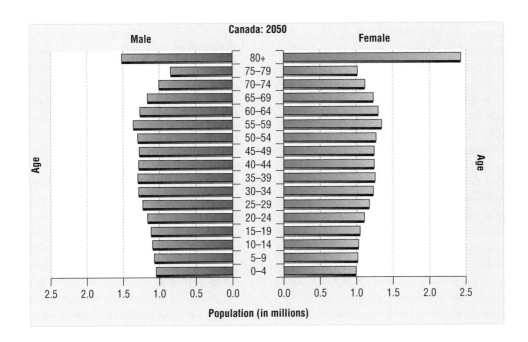

FIGURE 12.5
Population Pyramid, Canada, 2050 (projected)

Source: U.S. Census Bureau, International Database.

Canada's population pyramid will look more like a T, indicating roughly the same percentage of people in all age cohorts except the oldest, which will be much more numerous. This change in population composition has wide-ranging implications for our social security system, housing, education, employment, and health care.

The number of seniors in Canada has increased for three main reasons. First, about a third of Canada's citizens (approximately 10 million people) were born during the 20-year "baby boom" after World War II. During that period, Canadian families averaged four children, resulting in more baby boomers per capita than in the United States, Australia, and New Zealand (Nikiforuk, 1999). Second, life expectancy has increased as a result of improvements in medical care, sanitation, nutrition, and housing. Third, Canada's current low birth rate contributes to a higher percentage of older people.

Ageism and the Decline of Old Stereotypes

Especially in a society that puts a premium on vitality and youth, such as Canada's, being older is still a social stigma. **Ageism** is prejudice about, and discrimination against, older people. Ageism is evident, for example, when older men are stereotyped as "grumpy." Ageism affects women more than men. Thus, the same person who considers some older men "distinguished-looking" may disparage older women as "haggard" (Banner, 1992).

Often, however, seniors do not conform to the negative stereotypes applied to them, which is why the old stereotypes are in decline. In Canada, 65 is sometimes considered the age at which people become seniors since 65 is the age at which most Canadians become eligible to receive Old Age Security benefits. But just because someone is 65 or older does not mean he or she is decrepit and dependent. On the contrary, most people who retire from an active working life are far from being a tangle of health problems and a burden on society. This change is due to the medical advances of recent decades, the healthier lifestyles followed by many older people, and the improved financial status of seniors.

Contrary to stereotypes, the housing arrangements of older people are not usually desolate and depressing (Hochschild, 1973; Myerhoff, 1978). The likelihood that an individual will live in a special-care home increases with age, but in 2001 only about 5 percent of Canadian men and 9 percent of Canadian women over the age of 65 lived in such institutions. More than 7 out of 10 seniors lived with a spouse or alone, and fewer than 2 out of 10 lived with other relatives (Statistics Canada, n.d.). Moreover, although stereotypes depict seniors as burdens on their families, evidence shows that Canada's seniors contribute much to the lives of their

Ageism is prejudice and discrimination against older people.

The active life of many seniors today is a far cry from traditional stereotypes.

children, grandchildren, friends, neighbours, and communities (Vanier Institute of the Family, 2000: 172).

Many sociologists of aging refer to seniors who enjoy relatively good health—usually people between the ages of 65 and 74—as the "young old" (Neugarten, 1974; Laslett, 1991). The young old, as well as people in the 75–84 age cohort, are far from the stereotypes that used to be applied to seniors just a few decades ago. Close to 20 percent of Canada's older people may be living on low incomes, but more than 80 percent are reasonably well off or even well-to-do.

Consider these profiles of older Toronto-area women in 2006: Ruth Goldsmith, 76, enjoys financial stability. She exercises every morning (Aquafit, the treadmill, or yoga), meets friends for lunch, goes to the theatre and the symphony, travels to music festivals in Quebec, belongs to a book club, volunteers at the Older Women's Network, visits her sister in England annually, and is planning a trip to Israel. At 72, she learned how to use a computer. She dotes on her daughter and three grandchildren. Her friend, Margaret Hawthorn, 69, has a good pension from her years as a university librarian. She owns a car and a house and enjoys babysitting her grandson once a week. She also enjoys lawn bowling, swimming, and cycling, and has become fluent in Spanish. She travels extensively, sometimes off the beaten path; once she visited Baffin Island. She works for the NDP and is involved in a big garden restoration project. "I have to say that this is the best time—and I've had a reasonably good life," Hawthorn remarks. Nan Cooper, 67, has taken up painting in retirement and has rented an apartment in Italy so she can spend time visiting art galleries. Rosalie Brown, 73, loves dancing—square, ballroom, and line—and complains that she and her friend Margaret Hawthorn are so busy, they have to make appointments to see each other. "I feel I'm into maybe a bit too much," she says. She dates regularly and says it is as pleasurable as when she was younger. Or consider these high-profile appointments in 2006: 68-year-old Michael Wilson was appointed Canadian ambassador to the United States. Frank Iacobucci, also 68, was appointed chair of Torstar Corp. Purdy Crawford, 74, was appointed to lead the initiative to create a national securities regulator.

In a survey of 5000 older Canadians, two-thirds of respondents said they view retirement as an opportunity to start a new business and the same number said retirement freed them up to pursue a "dream job." Noticeably absent from this vibrant group are old people in rocking chairs eating cat food for supper (Galt, 2006; Kopun, 2006).

The "Old Old"

The situation is different for people 85 and older, whom sociologists refer to as the "old old." The rising number of old old concerns many people because the old old are most likely to suffer general physical decline and life-threatening diseases. Among seniors, the old old are also the most likely to face social isolation and poverty.

Significantly, the sex ratio (the number of men compared with the number of women) falls with age. In other words, because women live longer than men do on average, there are more women than men among seniors. This imbalance is most marked in the oldest age cohorts. Therefore, poverty and related problems among the oldest Canadians are in part a gender issue.

Economic inequality between older women and men is largely the result of women's lower earning power when they are younger. Women are entering the paid workforce in increasing numbers, but there are still more women than men who are homemakers and do not work for a wage. Therefore, fewer women than men receive employer pensions when they retire (Nelson and Robinson, 2002). Moreover, women who are in the paid labour force tend to earn less than men do. As a result, when they retire, their employer pensions are generally inferior. Consequently, the people most in need—older women—receive the fewest retirement benefits.

The Power and Wealth of Seniors

Since the 1960s, Canadian seniors have benefited from rising incomes. In 1951 seniors earned on average about half that of Canadians of working age but now the annual income of these two categories is close to the same (Statistics Canada, 1998b). Because of income security programs such as the Guaranteed Income Supplement, the Old Age Security pension, and the Spouse's Allowance, Canadian seniors do not have to rely on welfare any more frequently than people in the general population do. The poverty rate for seniors is about the same as the poverty rate for non-seniors (National Council of Welfare, 1998a).

One reason for the improved economic security of seniors is that they are well organized politically. Their voter participation rate is above average, and they are overrepresented among those who hold positions of political, economic, and religious power. Many groups seek to improve the status of seniors. One of the earliest and most radical groups in North America was the Gray Panthers, founded in 1970, with 50 000 to 70 000 members. Much larger is CARP, Canada's Association for the Fifty-Plus, with about 370 000 members. CARP is a nonprofit association that does not accept funding from any government body. It speaks out on a wide range of issues important to those over 50.

Seniors' activism may have led to a redistribution of resources away from young people. For example, while educational funding has declined, funding has increased for medical research related to diseases that disproportionately affect older people. This redistribution of resources has led to the growth of the belief in some rich countries that seniors are a burden on the economy and especially on the nation's youth. According to a study conducted by the Organisation for Economic Co-operation and Development (OECD), there is already "growing evidence of disaffection among the young in communities with larger proportions of wealthy retired people" (quoted in Peritz, 1999). In anticipation of government shortfalls, South Korea requires workers to save 35 percent of their income for retirement. In Japan,

BOX 12.2
It's Your Choice

A Social Security Crisis?

One of the greatest triumphs of public policy has been the development of the public health system, which has led to a substantial increase in life expectancy. Another major public policy achievement is social welfare, especially as it applies to seniors. The combination of social security, medicare, and other government programs goes a long way toward ensuring that seniors are not doomed to poverty and illness.

A longer and more secure life span is a wonderful thing. However, some scholars and policymakers worry that a major crisis is looming. Canada may not be able to afford government programs for seniors in the future, because of the expected retirement of baby boomers, those born in

the 20-year period after World War II. Many Canadians born in that period contribute to social security and other measures to support older people. As the baby boomers begin to retire from the active labour force, however, fewer Canadians will be contributing to government coffers.

Some scholars argue that economic growth and higher immigration could offset the expected decline in the active labour force. However, others argue that we need more concrete measures to deal with the expected crisis in government support for seniors. Some of the possible policy proposals include the following:

- increase national savings
- lower health care costs, especially the disproportionately higher burden of medical costs for seniors

- provide government support only to the truly needy, thereby eliminating or lowering social security and other federal benefits for the well-off

What do you think? Should Canadians worry about the expected crisis in social security and other government programs that support seniors? If you expect the potential crisis to erupt in your lifetime, what should you be doing now to avert the crisis? What are the advantages and disadvantages of each of the policy proposals listed above? What kind of lifestyle do you expect to lead when you are in your 60s, 70s, and 80s? Do you think you will be working full time, or will you be fully or partly retired? The policy proposals listed above are your choice.

government benefits can be cancelled if redistribution of tax money is needed to ensure "equity between the generations" (Peterson, 1997). Whether Canadians are prepared to tolerate such tax burdens and cutbacks is questionable (see Box 12.2).

DEATH AND DYING

It may seem odd to say so, but the ultimate social problem everyone must face is his or her own demise. Why are death and dying *social* problems and not just religious, philosophical, and medical issues?

For one thing, attitudes toward death vary widely across time and place. So do the settings within which death typically takes place. Although individuals have always dreaded death, in most traditional societies, such as Europe until early modern times, most people accepted it (Ariès, 1982). That is partly because most people apparently believed in life after death, whether in the form of a continuation of life in heaven or in cyclical rebirth. What also made death easier to accept is that the dying were not isolated from other people. They continued to interact with household members and neighbours, who offered them continuous emotional support. Finally, because the dying had previous experience giving emotional support to other dying people, they could more easily accept death as part of everyday life.

In contrast, in Canada today, dying and death tend to be separated from everyday life. Most terminally ill patients want to die peacefully and with dignity at home, surrounded by their loved ones. Yet about 80 percent of Canadians die in hospitals. Often, hospital deaths are sterile, noiseless, and lonely. Dying used to be public. It is now private. The frequent lack of social support makes dying a more frightening experience for many people (Elias, 1985 [1982]). In addition, our culture celebrates youth and denies death (Becker, 1973). We use diet, fashion, exercise, makeup, and surgery to prolong youth or at least the appearance of youth. This makes us less prepared for death than our ancestors were.

Our reluctance to accept death is evident from the many euphemisms we use as a means of distancing ourselves from it. People used to say that the dead had "entered the Pearly Gates" or had gone to "sing in God's heavenly choir." We are now more likely to say that the dead have "passed away" or "gone to meet their maker" in "a better place" or that they lie in "their final resting place." Sometimes we use humorous expressions as a distancing mechanism. We say that people have "croaked" or "kicked the bucket" or "cashed in their chips" or that they are now "pushing up daisies." These and other similar expressions allow us to separate ourselves symbolically from the horror of death.

Psychiatrist Elisabeth Kübler-Ross's analysis of the stages of dying also suggests how reluctant we are to accept death (Kübler-Ross, 1969). She based her analysis on interviews with patients who were told they have an incurable disease. At first, the patients went into *denial*, refusing to believe their death was imminent. Then they expressed *anger*, seeing their demise as unjust. *Negotiation* followed; they pled with God or with fate to delay their death. Then came *depression*, when they resigned themselves to their fate but became deeply despondent. Only then did the patients reach the stage of *acceptance*, when they put their affairs in order, expressed regret over not having done certain things when they had the chance, and perhaps spoke about going to Heaven.

Euthanasia

The reluctance of many Canadians to accept death is clearly evident in the debate over euthanasia, also known as mercy killing or assisted suicide (Rothman, 1991). Various medical technologies, including machines that are able to replace the functions of the heart and lungs, can prolong life beyond the point that was possible in the past. This raises the question of how to deal with people who are near death. In brief, is it humane or immoral to hasten the death of terminally ill patients?

Euthanasia is any "deliberate act undertaken by one person with the intention of ending the life of another person to relieve that person's suffering, where that act is the cause of death" (McTeer, 1999: 117). A narrower definition of euthanasia involves a doctor

Euthanasia (also known as mercy killing and assisted suicide) involves a doctor prescribing or administering medication or treatment that is intended to end a terminally ill patient's life.

TECHNOLOGY BYTES

prescribing or administering medication or treatment that is *intended* to end a terminally ill patient's life. This form of euthanasia is sometimes referred to as *active euthanasia* inasmuch as it involves the commission of an act. So-called *passive euthanasia* involves intentionally withholding a life-saving medical procedure.

In Canada, assisting suicide or intentional killing, even in an attempt to end suffering, is a crime. In addition, doctors are legally prevented from withholding or withdrawing life-sustaining procedures. They are also legally obliged to ensure that patients whom they believe to be suicidal are prevented from harming themselves. Nevertheless, the reality of modern medicine is that doctors do practise passive euthanasia; not all of them, but rare is the doctor that has not, at the request of the patient, the patient's family, or on his or her own accord, decided to discontinue life-support. Studies also show that many doctors have acquiesced to life-ending drug dosages in cases of advanced terminal illness (Duhaime, 1997).

According to a 2001 survey, many Canadians support a terminally ill person's right to die and believe that doctor-assisted suicide for terminally ill people should be legal. Just over three-quarters of Canadians believe that an individual who helps end the life of a loved one suffering from an incurable and extremely painful illness should not be prosecuted. However, almost 60 percent of Canadians oppose "mercy killing" by a parent of a child who has severe disabilities. Although 42 percent believe that access to euthanasia is necessary for those who are critically ill or have severe disabilities because current nursing-home and end-of-life care is inadequate, almost three-quarters agree that "if people with disabilities or those with chronic or terminal disease had access to adequate pain management and social services, there would be less demand for euthanasia" (Canada NewsWire, 2001).

Montreal physician Balfour Mount, who has been called Canada's father of palliative care, expressed a similar viewpoint. In the *Journal of the Royal College of Physicians and Surgeons of Canada,* Mount noted that "our courts voted against euthanasia by the narrowest of margins, while . . . our governments have failed to give adequate support to palliative care" ("Poor Palliative Care," 2001). Mount warns that unless more palliative care is provided, the "appeal of [euthanasia and assisted suicide] as a 'compassionate' alternative to overcrowded clinical services, inadequate fiscal resources, and increasing family caregiver burden is unlikely to lessen."

Euthanasia is bound to become a major political issue in coming decades as medical technologies for prolonging life improve, the number of older people increases, and the cost of medical care skyrockets. Some people will uphold extending the lives of terminally ill patients by all means possible as an ethical imperative. Others will regard it as immoral because it increases suffering and siphons scarce resources from other pressing medical needs.

Sue Rodriguez, who suffered from amyotrophic lateral sclerosis (ALS; also known as Lou Gehrig's disease), launched a legal battle for the right to have a doctor help her die. She argued that the section of the Criminal Code that makes assisted suicide a criminal offence violates three rights guaranteed to all Canadians under the Charter of Rights and Freedoms: the right to life, liberty, and security of the person; the right not to be discriminated against on the basis of disability; and the right not to be subjected to cruel and unusual punishment. The Supreme Court of British Columbia dismissed her application. In 1993, the Supreme Court of Canada, in a 5–4 decision, dismissed her appeal.

SUMMARY

1. The human body is a biological wonder. In what sense is it a sociological wonder too?
   The body's parts, its disabilities, its aging, and its death mean different things and have different consequences for different cultures, historical periods, and categories of people. The human body cannot be fully understood without appreciating its sociological dimension.

2. What is the connection between body type and social status?
   Because low status influences diet and other factors, it is associated with people of short stature and people who are overweight. In turn, people of short stature and people who are overweight tend to receive fewer social rewards because of their body type.

3. In what sense do people have rights over their own body?
   Most people believe they should and do have rights over their own body. Advances in medical technology and changing social norms encourage us to transform our bodies

through surgery, prosthesis, and other means. However, we do not treat our bodies in idiosyncratic ways. Norms of body practice influence the way we treat our bodies.

4. Are disabilities defined similarly everywhere and at all times? Have disabilities always been handled in the same way?
    No. The definition of disability varies over time and place. For example, some people used to consider left-handedness and being Aboriginal as disabilities, but we do not share that view. As far as treatment is concerned, we also see much variation. People with disabilities have traditionally suffered much prejudice and discrimination, but attempts were made from the nineteenth century on to integrate and rehabilitate them. Some governments sought to eliminate people with disabilities from society in the twentieth century. Recently, people with disabilities have begun to organize themselves, assert the normality of disability, and form communities of those with disabilities.

5. What is sociological about the aging process?
    People attach different meanings to aging in different societies and historical periods. Thus, the stages of life vary in number and significance across societies.

6. Is there a positive correlation between age and status?
    Although it is true that the young have been, and still are, disadvantaged in many ways, it is rarely true that the eldest people in society are the best off. In most societies, including Canada, people of middle age have the most power and economic clout.

7. What are the main approaches to age stratification?
    Functionalist theory emphasizes that industrialization led to the differentiation of age cohorts and the receipt of varying levels of reward by each age cohort based on its functional importance to society. This supposedly results in the convergence of age stratification systems in all industrialized societies. Conflict theory stresses the way competition and conflict can result in the redistribution of rewards between age cohorts and the divergence of age stratification systems. Symbolic interactionists focus not on these macrosociological issues but on the meanings people attach to different age cohorts.

8. How is Canada aging?
    Canada's population is aging rapidly. Between 1901 and 2001 the median age of Canadians increased from 22.7 to 37.6 years, while the proportion of Canadians 65 or older increased from 5 percent to 12.9 percent. The age–sex distribution looked like a pyramid in 1901 but by 2050 all but one age–sex cohorts will be about the same size; only people 80 and over will form a disproportionately large part of the population. As the population ages, the ratio of men to women falls.

9. How are seniors faring economically in Canada?
    Economically speaking, senior Canadians are faring reasonably well, partly because they have considerable political power. However, economic inequality exists between older women and men, largely because of women's lower earning power when they are younger; they have smaller pensions and fewer assets once they retire. A disproportionately large number of poor seniors are women, people living alone, people with disabilities, and people living in rural areas.

10. If seniors in Canada are doing reasonably well economically and politically, then does this mean that they don't face significant problems in our society?
    Older Canadians face much prejudice and discrimination based on age because our society values youth and vitality and because some people think that seniors command a disproportionately large share of societal resources at the expense of young people.

11. What is sociological about death and dying?
    Attitudes toward death vary widely across time and place, as do the settings within which death typically takes place. For example, many Canadians are reluctant to accept death, as is evident in the debate over euthanasia.

KEY TERMS

ableism (p. 347)

age cohort (p. 351)

age roles (p. 351)

age stratification (p. 352)

ageism (p. 355)

disability (p. 346)

euthanasia (p. 358)

generation (p. 351)

gerontocracy (p. 352)

impaired (p. 346)

life course (p. 350)

life expectancy (p. 350)

population pyramids (p. 354)

rehabilitation (p. 346)

rite of passage (p. 350)

QUESTIONS TO CONSIDER

1. If you do not use a wheelchair, borrow one and try to get around campus for a few hours. If you cannot borrow a wheelchair, imagine you are in one. Draw up an inventory of difficulties you face. How would the campus have to be redesigned to make access easier? Alternatively, if you are not overweight, borrow some big clothes and add padding to make you look overweight. Go shopping for a few hours and see if sales clerks and other shoppers treat you differently from the way you are normally treated. Record your observations.

2. What generation do you belong to? What is the age range of people in your generation? What are some of the defining historical events that have taken place in your generation? How strongly do you identify with your generation? Ask the same questions of someone of a different race, gender, or class. How do these variables influence the experience of a generation?

WEB RESOURCES

Companion Website for This Book

http://www.compass3e.nelson.com

Begin by clicking on the Student Resources section of the website. Next, select the chapter you are studying from the pull-down menu. From the Student Resources page you have easy access to InfoTrac® College Edition, additional Weblinks, and other resources. The website also has many useful tips to aid you in your study of sociology, including practice tests for each chapter.

InfoTrac® Search Terms

These search terms are provided to assist you in beginning to conduct research on this topic by visiting http://www.infotrac-college.com:

age discrimination

disability

euthanasia

Recommended Websites

Public health focuses on the connection between the physical and mental health of a population and the society and environment in which the population resides. The Public Health

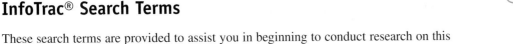

http://www.compass3e.nelson.com

Agency of Canada at http://www.publichealth.gc.ca provides an annual report on the state of public health in Canada, public health alerts, and a wide range of other information on public health in Canada.

Visit the website of CARP at http://www.fifty-plus.net to learn about the many issues faced by retirees and the individual and collective actions they are taking to deal with these issues. CARP's services include discounted mail-order drugs, investment opportunities, travel information, volunteer opportunities, and news updates on issues of concern to people 50 and older.

Michael Kearl maintains one of the most frequently visited websites on the sociology of death and dying at http://www.trinity.edu/~mkearl/death.html.

CengageNOW™

http://hed.nelson.com

This online diagnostic tool identifies each student's unique needs with a Pretest that generates a personalized Study Plan for each chapter, helping students focus on concepts they're having the most difficulty mastering. Students then take a Posttest after reading the chapter to measure their understanding of the material. An Instructor Gradebook is available to track and monitor student progress.

PART 4

Institutions

CHAPTER

13

Work and the Economy

In this chapter, you will learn that

- Three work-related revolutions—one in agriculture, one in manufacturing, and one in the provision of services—have profoundly altered the ways in which people earn a living and how societies are organized.

- In the past few decades, the number of "good" jobs has grown, but so too has the number of "bad" jobs.

- With varying degrees of success, people seek to control work through unions, professional organizations, corporations, and markets.

- The growth of large corporations and global markets has shaped the transformation of work in recent decades and will shape the choices you face as a member of the labour force and as a citizen.

THE PROMISE AND HISTORY OF WORK

Salvation or Curse?

The computerization of the office began in earnest about 20 years ago. Soon, the image of the new office was as familiar as a Dilbert cartoon. It was a checkerboard of three-metre-by-three-metre (ten-foot-by-ten-foot) cubicles. Three padded walls, two metres (six feet) high, framed each cubicle. Inside, a computer terminal sat on a desk. A worker quietly tapped away at a keyboard, seemingly entranced by the glow of a video screen.

Sociologist Shoshana Zuboff visited many such offices soon after they were computerized. She sometimes asked the office workers to draw pictures capturing their job experience before and after computerization. The pictures were strikingly similar. Smiles changed to frowns, mobility became immobility, sociability was transformed into isolation, freedom turned to regimentation. Two of the workers' pictures are shown in Figure 13.1 below. Work automation and standardization emerge from these drawings as profoundly degrading and inhuman processes (Zuboff, 1988).

The image conveyed by these drawings is only one view of the transformation of work in the Information Age. There is another, and it is vastly different. Bill Gates argues that computers reduce our work hours. They make goods and services cheaper by removing many distribution costs of capitalism (think of Indigo.ca reducing the need for bookstores). Computers also allow us to enjoy our leisure time more (Gates with Myhrvold and Rinearson, 1996). This vision is well captured by the arresting cover of *Wired* magazine reprinted as Figure 13.2 on page 366. According to *Wired*, computers liberate us. They allow us to become more mobile and more creative. Computerized work allows our imaginations to leap and our spirits to soar.

TECHNOLOGY BYTES

Before

"Before I was able to get up and hand things to people without having someone say, what are you doing? Now, I feel like I am with my head down, doing my work."

After

"My supervisor is frowning because we shouldn't be talking. I have on the stripes of a convict. It's all true. It feels like a prison in here."

FIGURE 13.1

One View of the Effects of Computers on Work

Shoshana Zuboff asked office workers to draw pictures representing how they felt about their jobs before and after a new computer system was introduced. Here are before and after pictures drawn by two office workers. Notice how even the flower on one worker's desk wilted after the new computer system was introduced.

Source: From Shoshana Zuboff, *In the Age of the Smart Machine: The Future of Work and Power* (Basic Books: New York), 1988, p. 146–47. Copyright © 1988 Basic Books, Inc. Reprinted by permission of Basic Books, a member of Perseus Books, L.L.C.

FIGURE 13.2

Another View of the Effect of Computers on Work

Wired magazine is always on high about the benefits of computer technology.

Source: *Wired,* December 1999/ Photograph by James Porto. Reprinted by permission of Wired, Condé Nast Publications, Inc.

These strikingly different images form the core questions of the sociology of work, our focus in this chapter. Is work a salvation or a curse? Or is it perhaps both at once? Is it more accurate to say that work has become more of a salvation or a curse over time? Or is work a salvation for some and a curse for others?

To answer these questions, we first sketch the evolution of work from pre-agricultural to postindustrial times (for a more detailed account, see Chapter 6, Networks, Groups, Bureaucracies, and Societies). As you will see, we have experienced three work-related revolutions in the past 10 000 years. Each revolution has profoundly altered the way we sustain ourselves and the way we live. Next, we examine how job skills have changed over the past century. We also trace changes in the number and distribution of "good" and "bad" jobs over time and project these changes nearly a decade into the future. We then analyze how people have sought to control work through unions, professional organizations, corporations, and markets. Finally, we place our discussion in a broader context. The growth of large corporations and markets on a global scale has shaped the transformation of work over the past quarter century. Understanding these transformations will help you understand the work-related choices you face both as a member of the labour force and as a citizen.

Three Revolutions

The economy is the institution that organizes the production, distribution, and exchange of goods and services.

The **economy** is the institution that organizes the production, distribution, and exchange of goods and services. Conventionally, analysts divide the economy into three sectors. The *primary* sector includes farming, fishing, logging, and mining. In the *secondary* sector, raw materials are turned into finished goods; manufacturing takes place. Finally, in the *tertiary* sector, services are bought and sold. These services include the work of nurses, teachers, lawyers, hairdressers, computer programmers, and so forth. Often, the three sectors of the economy are called the agricultural, manufacturing, and service sectors. We follow that practice here.

Three truly revolutionary events have taken place in the history of human labour. In each revolution, a different sector of the economy rose to dominance. First came the

Agricultural Revolution, then the Industrial Revolution, and finally the Postindustrial Revolution (Gellner, 1988; Lenski, 1966).

The Development of Agriculture

Nearly all humans lived in nomadic tribes until about 10 000 years ago. Then, people in the fertile valleys of the Middle East, Southeast Asia, and South America began to herd cattle and grow plants by using simple hand tools. Stable human settlements spread in these areas. About 5000 years ago, farmers invented the plow. By attaching plows to large animals, they substantially increased the land under cultivation. **Productivity**—the amount produced for every hour worked—soared.

Although nowadays few people think of Canada as an agricultural nation, in the wheat boom of the late nineteenth century, Canada was a world leader. In addition, the harvesting of fish, fur, and timber were important elements of Canada's primary sector. The Biblical phrase "hewers of wood and drawers of water" was sometimes applied to Canadians and it was apt. In 1900, more than 40 percent of the Canadian paid workforce was employed in agriculture, with a smaller percentage involved in resource extraction, such as cutting timber, mining, or fishing. These commodities are, in the lexicon of Canadian social science, *staples*. The harvesting and extracting of these staples, whether nickel from Sudbury, Ontario, oil from Leduc, Alberta, or cod from Petty Harbour, Newfoundland, propelled early economic development in Canada.

The Development of Modern Industry

International exploration, trade, and commerce stimulated the growth of markets from the fifteenth century on. **Markets** are social relations that regulate the exchange of goods and services. In a market, prices are established by how plentiful goods and services are (supply) and how much they are wanted (demand). About 230 years ago, the steam engine, railroads, and other technological innovations greatly increased the ability of producers to supply markets. This was the era of the Industrial Revolution. Beginning in England, the Industrial Revolution spread to Western Europe, North America, Russia, and Japan within a century, making manufacturing the dominant economic sector.

Although Canada began as a staples economy, a stronger manufacturing sector gradually developed, especially in southern Ontario and Quebec, where such firms as Bombardier, Magna, Nortel, and General Motors Canada compete on a world scale. In

Productivity refers to the amount of goods or services produced for every hour worked.

Markets are social relations that regulate the exchange of goods and services. In a market, the prices of goods and services are established by how plentiful they are (supply) and how much they are wanted (demand).

A Canadian engineering feat, Confederation Bridge is the longest bridge over ice-covered waters in the world (at 12.9 kilometres, or 8 miles), linking Borden-Carleton, Prince Edward Island, and Cape Tormentine, New Brunswick. This historic bridge opened June 1, 1997, bringing a new age of transportation to Atlantic Canada.

other regions, manufacturing is far more fragile and the historic roots of the staples economy remain strong. For example, if you were to visit Leduc, Petty Harbour, or Sudbury, you would see little of the manufacturing focus that characterizes Oshawa, Oakville, or Windsor. Canadian manufacturing strength varies significantly by region (Clement, 1997).

The Development of the Service Sector

Service jobs were rare in pre-agricultural societies and few in agricultural societies because nearly everyone had to do physical work for human societies to survive. As productivity increased, however, service sector jobs proliferated. Only at the beginning of the nineteenth century in Western Europe and North America did productivity increase to the point where a quarter of the labour force could be employed in services. By 1960 more than half the labour force of the highly industrialized countries was providing services. Forty years later, the figure was about 75 percent (see Figure 13.3).

The rapid change in the composition of the labour force during the final decades of the twentieth century was made possible in large part by the computer. The computer automated many manufacturing and office procedures. It created jobs in the service sector as quickly as it eliminated them in manufacturing. Thus, the computer is to the service sector as the steam engine was to manufacturing and the plow was to agriculture. Especially in the areas of financial services and communications, the Canadian service sector has boomed.

The Social Organization of Work

Besides increasing productivity and causing shifts between sectors in employment, the Agricultural, Industrial, and Postindustrial Revolutions altered the way work was socially organized. For one thing, the **division of labour** increased. That is, work tasks became more specialized with each successive revolution. In pre-agrarian societies there were four main jobs: hunting wild animals, gathering edible wild plants, raising children, and tending to the tribe's spiritual needs. In contrast, a postindustrial society, such as Canada's, boasts thousands of different kinds of jobs.

In some cases, increasing the division of labour involves creating new skills (e.g., website design, laser eye surgery). Some new jobs require long periods of study. Foremost among these are the professions, such as medicine, law, and engineering. In other cases, increasing the division of labour involves breaking a complex range of skills into a series of simple routines. For example, a hundred years ago, a butcher's job involved knowing how to dissect an entire cow. Today's meat-packing plant employs large stock scalpers, belly shavers, crotch

> The **division of labour** refers to the specialization of work tasks. The more specialized the work tasks in a society, the greater the division of labour.

FIGURE 13.3

Estimated Distribution of Canadian Labour Force in Goods Production and Services, 1946–2005

Source: Adapted from Crompton and Vickers, 2000; Statistics Canada, 2005h.

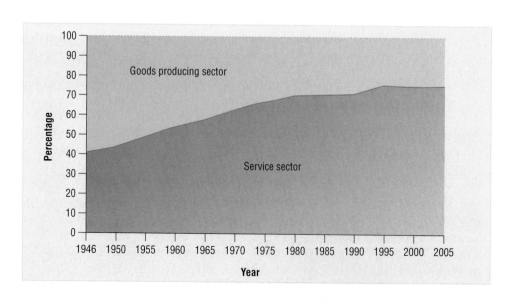

busters, gut snatchers, gut sorters, snout pullers, ear cutters, eyelid removers, stomach washers (also known as belly bumpers), hind leg pullers, front leg toenail pullers, and oxtail washers. A different person performs each routine. None requires much skill.

If the division of labour increased as one work revolution gave way to the next, then social relations among workers also changed. In particular, work relations became more hierarchical. Although work used to be based on cooperation among equals, it now involves superordinates exercising authority and subordinates following commands. Owners oversee executives. Executives oversee middle managers. Middle managers oversee ordinary workers. Increasingly, work hierarchies are organized bureaucratically. That is, clearly defined positions and written goals, rules, and procedures govern the organization of work. Workplaces have grown enormously in size and many Canadians work in large organizations.

"GOOD" VERSUS "BAD" JOBS

PERSONAL ANECDOTE

John Lie once had a job as a factory worker in Honolulu. "The summer after my second year in high school," John recalls, "I decided it was time to earn some money. I had expenses, after all, but only an occasionally successful means of earning money: begging my parents. Scouring the help wanted ads in the local newspaper, I soon realized I wasn't really qualified to do anything in particular. Some friends at school suggested I apply for work at a pineapple-canning factory. So I did.

"At the factory, an elderly man asked me a few questions and hired me. I was elated—but only for a moment. A tour of the factory floor ruined my mood. Row upon row of conveyor belts carried pineapples in various states of disintegration. Supervisors chastened the employees to work faster yet make fewer mistakes. The smell, the noise, and the heat were unbearable. After the tour, the interviewer announced I would get the graveyard shift (11 p.m. to 7 a.m.) at minimum wage.

"The tour and the prospect of working all night finished me off. Now dreading the idea of working in the factory, I wandered over to a mall. I bumped into a friend there. He told me a bookstore was looking for an employee (9 to 5, no pineapple smell, and air conditioned, although still minimum wage). I jumped at the chance. Thus, my career as a factory worker ended before it ever began.

"A dozen years later, just after I got my Ph.D., I landed one of my best jobs ever. I taught for a year in South Korea. However, my salary hardly covered my rent. I needed more work desperately. Through a friend of a friend, I found a second job as a business consultant in a major corporation. I was given a big office with a panoramic view of Seoul and a personal secretary who was both charming and efficient. I wrote a handful of sociological reports that year on how bureaucracies work, how state policies affect workers, how the world economy had changed in the past two decades, and so on. I accompanied the president of the company on trips to the United States. I spent most of my days reading books. I also went for long lunches with colleagues and took off several afternoons a week to teach."

What is the difference between a "good" job and a "bad" job, as these terms are usually understood? As John Lie's anecdote illustrates, bad jobs don't pay much and require the performance of routine tasks under close supervision. Working conditions are unpleasant, sometimes dangerous. Bad jobs require little formal education. In contrast, good jobs often require higher education. They pay well. They are not closely supervised and they encourage workers to be creative in pleasant surroundings. Other distinguishing features of good and bad jobs are not apparent from the anecdote. Good jobs offer secure employment, opportunities for promotion, and other significant benefits. In a bad job, you can easily be fired, you receive few if any fringe benefits, and the prospects for promotion are few (Adams, Betcherman, and Bilson, 1995; Lowe, 2000). Bad jobs are often called "dead-end" jobs.

Most social scientists who discuss today's service revolution tend to have both good and bad jobs in mind. Yet most jobs fall between the two extremes sketched above. They have some mix of good and bad features. What can we say about the overall mix of jobs in Canada? Are there more good jobs than bad jobs? And what does the future hold? Are good jobs or bad jobs likely to become more plentiful? What are your job prospects? These are tough questions, not least because some conditions that influence the mix of good and bad jobs are unpredictable. Nonetheless, social research sheds some light on these issues (Beaudry and Green, 1998; Krahn and Lowe, 1998).

Deskilling refers to the process by which work tasks are broken into simple routines requiring little training to perform. Deskilling is usually accompanied by the use of machinery to replace labour wherever possible and increase management control over workers.

Fordism is a method of industrial management based on assembly-line methods of producing cheap, uniform commodities in high volume.

The Deskilling Thesis

Harry Braverman (1974) proposed one view of the future of work. He argued that owners (capitalists) organize work to maximize profits. One way to increase profits is to break complex tasks into simple routines. This increased division of labour in the workforce has three important consequences. First, machinery can be used to replace workers. Second, given the simplification of work routines, less skilled, cheaper labour can be used. Third, employees can be controlled more directly since less worker discretion and skill is needed to complete each task. As a result, the future of work, as Braverman saw it, involves a **deskilling** trend.

Deskilling can be best understood as a separation between conception and execution in a job. In the 1910s, for example, Henry Ford introduced the assembly line with just this aim in mind. The assembly line enabled Ford to produce affordable cars for a mass market. Workers executed highly specialized, repetitive tasks requiring little skill at a pace set by their supervisors. Automotive designers and managers conceived of the end product and the machinery necessary to build it. The workers merely executed the instructions of their superiors. The term **Fordism** is now often used to refer to mass production, assembly-line work.

Around the same time, Frederick W. Taylor developed the principles of **scientific management**. After analyzing the movements of workers as they did their jobs, Taylor trained them to eliminate unnecessary actions and greatly improve their efficiency. Workers became cogs in a giant machine known as the modern factory.

Many criticisms were lodged against Braverman's deskilling thesis in the 1970s and 1980s. Perhaps the most serious criticism was that he was not so much wrong as irrelevant. That is, even if his characterization of factory work was accurate (and we will see below that in some respects it was not), factory workers represent only a small proportion of the labour force. They represent a smaller proportion with every passing year. In 1974, the year Braverman's book was published, less than a quarter of the Canadian labour force was employed

Charlie Chaplin's 1929 movie *Modern Times* was a humorous critique of the factory of his day. In the movie, Chaplin gets a tic and moves like a machine on the assembly line. He then gets stuck on a conveyor belt and run through a machine. Finally, he is used as a test dummy for a feeding machine. The film thus suggests that workers were being used for the benefit of the machines rather than the machines being used for the benefit of the workers.

in manufacturing. By 2005, the figure had declined to just over 13 percent (Statistics Canada, 2005h).

Science-fiction writer Isaac Asimov's claim that the factory of the future will employ only a man and a dog is clearly an exaggeration. (The man will be there to feed the dog, said Asimov; the dog will be there to keep the man away from the machinery.) It is clear, however, that the manufacturing sector is shrinking and the service sector is expanding. The vital question, according to some of Braverman's critics, is not whether jobs are becoming worse in manufacturing but whether good jobs or bad jobs are growing in services, the sector that accounts for about three-quarters of Canadian jobs today. Put another way, does the deskilling thesis apply to both industrial labour and service work?

Shoshana Zuboff's analysis of office workers, mentioned at the beginning of this chapter, made it appear that Braverman's insights apply beyond the factory walls (Zuboff, 1988; see Lowe, 1987, on the evolution of office work in Canada). Zuboff argues that the computerization of the office in the 1980s involved increased supervision of deskilled work. And she is right, at least in part. The computer did eliminate many jobs and routinize others. It allowed supervisors to monitor every keystroke, thus taking worker control to a new level. Today, employees who consistently fall behind a prescribed work pace or use their computers for personal e-mail, surfing the Web, and other pastimes can easily be identified and then retrained, disciplined, or fired. In the 1980s and 1990s, some analysts feared that good jobs in manufacturing were being replaced by bad jobs in services. From this point of view, the entire labour force was experiencing a downward slide (Bluestone and Harrison, 1982; Rifkin, 1995).

Part-Time Work

The growth of part-time work in Canada has added to concern about the erosion of meaningful, dignified employment. The proportion of part-time workers in the Canadian labour force more than doubled between 1976 and 2000. In 2007, 18.2 percent of all people in the Canadian labour force were part-timers, working fewer than 30 hours a week. Among men, the figure was 11.0 percent, among women, 26.1 percent (Statistics Canada, 2008e).

For two reasons, the expansion of part-time work is not a serious problem in itself. First, some part-time jobs are good jobs in the sense we defined above. Second, some people want to work part time and can afford to do so (Marshall, 2001). For example, some people who want a job also want to devote a large part of their time to family responsibilities. Part-time work affords them that flexibility. Similarly, many high school and university students who work part time are happy to do so. Perhaps you have joined the ranks of part-time retail clerks and fast-food servers to help pay for tuition, a car, a vacation, or a wardrobe.

Although the growth of part-time jobs is not problematic for voluntary part-time workers or people who have good part-time jobs, an increasingly large number of people depend on part-time work for the necessities of full-time living. And the plain fact is that most part-time jobs are bad jobs. Thus, part-time workers make up about two-thirds of the people working at or below minimum wage. Moreover, the fastest-growing category of part-time workers comprises *involuntary* part-timers: According to official statistics, one-third of part-time workers want to be working more hours. And official statistics underestimate the scope of the problem. Surveys show that about one-third of women officially classified as voluntary part-time workers would work more hours if good child care or elder care were available (Duffy, Glenday, and Pupo, 1997).

The downside of part-time work is not only economic, however. Nor is it just a matter of coping with dull routine. If you've ever had a bad part-time job, you know that one of its most difficult aspects involves maintaining your self-respect in the face of low pay, benefits, security, status, and creativity. In the words of Dennis, a McDonald's employee interviewed by sociologist Robin Leidner: "This isn't really a job. . . . It's about as low as you can get. Everybody knows it" (quoted in Leidner, 1993: 182).

And, Dennis might have added, nearly everybody lets you know he or she knows it. Ester Reiter (1991) studied fast-food workers in Toronto, many of whom are teenagers working part time. These workers are trained, Reiter noted, to keep smiling no matter how demanding or rude their customers may be. The trouble is you can only count backward from 100 so many times before feeling utterly humiliated. Anger often boils over.

The difficulty of maintaining your dignity as a fast-food worker is compounded by the high premium most young people place on independence, autonomy, and respect. The problem this creates for teenagers who take jobs in fast-food restaurants is that their constant deference to customers violates the norms of youth culture. Therefore, fast-food workers are typically stigmatized by their peers. They are frequently the brunt of insults and ridicule (Newman, 1999: 97).

Fast-food workers undoubtedly represent an extreme case of the indignity endured by part-timers. However, the problem exists in various guises in many part-time jobs. For instance, if you work as a "temp" in an office, you are more likely than are other office workers to be the victim of sexual harassment (Welsh, 1999). You are especially vulnerable to unwanted advances because you lack power in the office and are considered "fair game."

Scientific management, developed in the 1910s by Frederick W. Taylor, is a system for improving productivity. After analyzing the movements of workers as they did their jobs, Taylor trained them to eliminate unnecessary actions. This technique is also known as Taylorism.

WHERE DO YOU FIT IN?

Thus, the form and depth of degradation may vary from one part-time job to another but, as your own work experience may show, degradation seems to be a universal feature of this type of deskilled work.

A Critique of the Deskilling Thesis

The deskilling thesis undoubtedly captures one important tendency in the history of work, a trend toward the simplification of previously complex jobs. However, it paints an incomplete picture. Such analyses as Braverman's and Zuboff's are too narrowly focused. They analyze specific job categories near the bottom of the occupational hierarchy. Consequently, they do not provide evidence of what is occurring across the entire occupational structure. For instance, Zuboff analyzed lower-level service workers, such as data entry personnel and routine claims processors in a health insurance company. Her research, while helping us understand the bottom range of the service sector, ignores the top.

Taking a broader perspective and examining the entire occupational structure, two lines of argument potentially undermine the deskilling thesis. First, not all jobs are being deskilled. Second, deskilling may be occurring primarily in jobs that are characteristic of the old economy (e.g., assembly-line manufacturing) but not of the new economy (e.g., biotechnology, informatics). In fact, even on Ford's assembly line, not all jobs were deskilled. A new group of workers was required to design the assembly line and the new production machinery. New jobs higher up the skill hierarchy were therefore necessary.

In general, if deskilling has occurred for some jobs, has upskilling or reskilling of other jobs offset this trend or have new high-skilled jobs been introduced? These are not easy questions to answer. How do you measure changes in skill across all jobs in the labour force? For one thing, the meaning of *skill* is itself contentious. As we saw in Chapter 11, Sexuality and Gender, women's work has long been undervalued because the skills women bring to jobs have been devalued (Creese and Began, 1999). Jobs requiring more training and education might be thought of as requiring more skill, but many occupational groups work to inflate the credentials needed for job entry so that the prestige and remuneration of the occupation rises (Rinehart, 2001). Jobs requiring greater skill might be thought of as those generating more income, but here too unions and professional associations work to increase earnings in ways that may be unconnected to skill (see the discussion of unions and professional organizations below).

Although the definition of skill is contentious, this makes research on skills more difficult, not impossible. Research on work requires nuance and sophistication. It should be conducted using multiple methods (such as surveys of the workplace and of earnings, and participant-observation studies of jobs).

One reason social commentators have assumed that deskilling is occurring is because of the rise of the service sector. For example, many jobs in the fast-food business are dead-end jobs. However, although there are many low-paying jobs in services, there are also many high-paying jobs. Moreover, the distribution of income in services is practically the same as in manufacturing. That is, there are just as many high-paid jobs as low-paid jobs in both sectors. On some measures of job quality, such as job security, service jobs are, on average, better than manufacturing jobs (Meisenheimer, 1998). Thus, the decline of the manufacturing sector and the rise of the service sector do not imply a downward slide in the skills of the entire labour force. Indeed, based on evidence from a national survey of Canadians, Clement and Myles (1994: 72) note that "the net result of the shift to services has been to increase the requirements for people to think on the job." Across many kinds of industries, the most rapid growth has been in jobs that require advanced training in information and communication technologies. Growing reliance on computers and related tools is as prominent in services as in other economic sectors (Lavoie, Roy, and Therrin, 2003).

Table 13.1 uses national survey evidence from five countries to examine the skill levels of workers in both the goods-producing and the service sectors. Respondents were asked a series of questions about the requirements of their jobs, such as whether they designed and put into practice important aspects of their work. Skilled jobs were taken to be those

Economic Sector	Country					TABLE 13.1
	Canada	United States	Norway	Sweden	Finland	
Goods-producing sector	26	25	31	23	25	
Service sector	42	38	47	43	46	
Difference between sectors	16	13	16	20	21	

TABLE 13.1

Percentage of Employees in Skilled Jobs by Sector and Country

Source: Clement and Myles, 1994: 7

requiring high levels of both conceptual autonomy and complexity. The results show that, in all countries, jobs in the service sector require higher levels of skill than do jobs in the goods-producing sector. This international evidence is compelling. It undermines the idea of deskilling in the overall workforce since higher skill requirements are reported in the service economy, which is the fastest-growing sector.

Even if we examine the least-skilled service workers—fast-food servers, video store clerks, parking lot attendants, and the like—we find reason to question one aspect of the deskilling thesis. For although these jobs are dull and pay poorly, they are not as much of a dead end as they are frequently made out to be. The least-skilled service workers tend to be under the age of 25 and to hold their jobs only briefly. After working in entry-level jobs for a short time, most men move on to blue-collar jobs and most women move on to clerical jobs. These are not great leaps up the socioeconomic hierarchy, but the fact that they are common suggests that work is not all bleak and hopeless even at the bottom of the service sector (Jacobs, 1993; Myles and Turegun, 1994).

Braverman and Zuboff underestimated the continuing importance of skilled labour in the economy. Assembly lines and computers may deskill many factory and office jobs, but if deskilling is to take place, then some members of the labour force must invent, design, advertise, market, install, repair, and maintain complex machines, including computerized and robotic systems. Most of these people have better jobs than the factory and office workers analyzed by Braverman and Zuboff. Moreover, although technological innovations kill off entire job categories, they also create entire new industries with many good jobs.

Thus, 30 years ago, Santa Clara County in California was best known for its excellent prunes. Today, it has been transformed into Silicon Valley, home to many tens of thousands of electronic engineers, computer programmers, graphic designers, venture capitalists, and so forth. On a smaller scale, Kanata (on the outskirts of Ottawa), Waterloo, and Vancouver are similar success stories. The introduction of new production techniques may even increase a country's competitive position in the world market. This can lead to employment gains at both the low end and the high end of the job hierarchy as consumers abroad rush to purchase relatively low-cost goods.

Our analysis of good and bad jobs raises another question. To what extent, if at all, is the introduction of information technology influencing the nature and quality of work? At the start of the chapter we used the introduction of computers to illustrate the rise of the service sector. What consequence has the introduction of the computer had on the self-reported skills workers use and the income they derive from work?

Recent research suggests that computers may have polarizing effects that magnify pay differences among levels of skill. Computers seem to augment and extend high levels of skill but seem to replace low levels of skills. Those in higher skilled occupations, like design or editing, earn higher wages if they use computers at work. But computer use does not affect wages in low skilled jobs, such as working a cash register. In such jobs, computer use requires little new skill or training and does not command higher earnings. Further, the introduction of computers often reduces demand for such labour. The same studies find that computer use at work increases earnings among the better educated but has no impact on earnings among the less educated. These findings suggest that the introduction of computers tends to enlarge the number and quality of good jobs. However, it does not improve bad jobs and reduces the number of bad jobs that are available (Pabilonia and Zoghi, 2005a, 2005b).

The growing service sector includes routine jobs requiring little training and creative jobs requiring a higher education.

The information technology revolution has transformed work, but there is little systematic evidence that it has degraded work overall. There is significant evidence that gaps are growing between skilled workers who use information technology and those who do not, and between skilled and less skilled workers. So far, information technology appears to be increasing inequalities among work at different skill levels.

The Social Relations of Work

The rise of a more knowledge-intensive economy has had a big impact on the *social relations* of work. The Industrial Revolution began an era of work that might best be described as requiring brute labour and obedience to authority. With the spinning jenny, the assembly line, and the increasing use of machinery in production, more and more work became industrialized, whether with printing presses, welding torches, or sewing machines. Workers were closely supervised in factory settings and an increasing division of labour meant that the skill content of certain jobs eroded.

It is misleading, however, to think that it takes less skill now to produce the goods and services we use than it did in previous centuries. We might have reached this conclusion if we focused on the skills associated with specific jobs or job tasks, but not if we focus on the skills associated with the entire process of providing goods and services. In short, rather than examining discrete parts of a specialized division of labour, it is important to attend to the entire process of producing goods and services. If anything, this process requires more skill because of the complexity of goods and services we now produce.

As Clement and Myles (1994) argue, the skill content of the entire labour process has risen, although much of that skill content now resides in managerial and administrative spheres. After the Industrial Revolution, a managerial revolution evolved, involving the separation of conception and execution. More of the job of conception shifted to the managerial and administrative realm. Before the mass-produced sweater, individual artisans determined the patterns and colours they would use. Now, workers in most textile sweatshops have little discretion over what they produce. Managers choose patterns and colours and they pass along orders to supervisors who direct shop floor production.

The rise of a managerial class that began with the advent of the manufacturing era has intensified in the postindustrial service revolution. Many service sector jobs are knowledge intensive and "postindustrial services employ more skilled managers than firms in goods and distribution" (Clement and Myles, 1994: 80). As well, these managers tend less often to have surveillance and supervision roles, and more often to have real decision-making power. The net result is the rise of a new middle class with greater power to make decisions about what is to be done and how to do it.

The newer social relations of work can be seen perhaps most starkly in Silicon Valley. Some top executives in Silicon Valley earn more than $100 million annually. Even at less lofty levels, there are many thousands of high-paying, creative jobs in the Valley, more than half of them dependent on the high-tech sector (Bjorhus, 2000). Amid all this wealth, however, the electronics assembly factories in Silicon Valley are little better than high-tech sweatshops. Most workers in the electronics factories earn less than 60 percent of the Valley's average wage. They work long hours and are frequently exposed to toxic solvents, acids, and gases. Semiconductor workers suffer industrial illnesses at three times the average rate for other manufacturing jobs. Although the opulent lifestyles of Silicon Valley's millionaires are often featured in the mass media, we must remember that a more accurate picture of the Valley also incorporates those who execute the demands of the knowledge workers and executives. It is not just single jobs that are changing but the full spectrum of jobs that is being transformed.

Figure 13.4 illustrates the changing nature of the Canadian occupational structure. Based on projections by Human Resources Development Canada, the chart shows those areas of the economy, across a set of skill dimensions, that are expected to grow in the next decade. This pattern is consistent with the pattern of growing income inequality discussed in Chapter 8, Social Stratification: Canadian and Global Perspectives. There, you will recall, we noted growing inequality between the top 40 percent of income earners and the remaining 60 percent.

Labour Market Segmentation

The processes described above are taking place in the last of the three stages of labour market development identified by David Gordon and his colleagues (Gordon, Edwards, and Reich, 1982). The period from about 1820 to 1890 was one of *initial proletarianization* in North America. During this period, a large industrial working class replaced craft workers in small workshops. Then, from the end of the nineteenth century until the start of World War II, the labour market entered the phase of *labour homogenization*. Extensive mechanization and deskilling took place during this stage. Finally, the third phase of labour market development is that of **labour market segmentation**. During this stage, which began after

Labour market segmentation is the division of the market for labour into distinct settings. In these settings, work is found in different ways and workers have different characteristics. There is only a slim chance of moving from one setting to another.

Emerging (Growth) Sector	University	College/Technical	High School or Less Than High School
Environment	Biophysicist, agrologist, forest management, environmental engineer	Air quality specialist, environmental technologist, pollution prevention officer, regulations officer	Landfill equipment operator, sylviculture and forestry worker, aquaculture and marine harvest labourer
Biotechnology	Biologist, biophysics, engineering, food science and technology, pharmacy, bioethics	Chemical technician, biological technician, water supply manager, inspector in public and environmental health	Information clerk; reporting, scheduling, and distribution occupations; labourer
Multimedia	Lawyer specializing in protecting intellectual property rights, translator, network architect, information librarian	Animation designer, Web designer, production designer, ideas manager, videographer	Product tester, librarian and information clerk
Aerospace	Aeronautics specialist, aerospace engineer, software engineering, astrophysicist, sales and marketing specialist	Mechanic, aircraft inspector, machinist, tool and die maker, industrial design technologist	Assembler, machining, aircraft electronic assembler

FIGURE 13.4
Sample Occupations in Emerging Sectors

Source: Adapted from Human Resources Development Canada, 2000.

World War II and continues to the present, large business organizations emerged. Thousands of small businesses continue to exist at this stage; however, different kinds of jobs are associated with small businesses than with large business organizations. Good jobs with security and relatively high wages tend to be concentrated in large firms, while smaller businesses cannot afford the same wages and job security provisions. The result is a *segmented* labour market. In these two different settings, workers, and the work they do, have different characteristics:

- The **primary labour market** is made up disproportionately of highly skilled, well-educated workers. They are employed in large corporations that enjoy high levels of capital investment. In the primary labour market, employment is relatively secure, earnings are high, fringe benefits are generous, and opportunities for advancement within the firm are good. Often the work is unionized because workers have the collective ability to exert pressure on their large employer.
- The **secondary labour market** contains a disproportionately large number of women and members of ethnic minority groups, especially recent immigrants. Employees in the secondary labour market tend to be unskilled and lack higher education. They work in small firms with low levels of capital investment. Employment is insecure, earnings are low, fringe benefits are meagre, and mobility prospects are limited. These firms are often subcontracted by large corporations that minimize their risk by off-loading seasonal work (e.g., in logging and oil exploration) and work for which demand is volatile (e.g., in auto parts supply and house construction).

This characterization may seem to advance us only a little beyond our earlier distinction between good jobs and bad jobs. However, proponents of labour market segmentation theory offer fresh insights into two important issues. First, they argue that work is found in different ways in the two labour markets. Second, they point out that social barriers make it difficult for individuals to move from one labour market to the other. To appreciate the significance of these points, it is vital to note that workers do more than just work. They also seek to control their work and prevent outsiders from gaining access to it. Some workers are more successful in this regard than others. Understanding the social roots of their success or failure permits us to see why the primary and secondary labour markets remain distinct. Therefore, we now turn to a discussion of forms of worker control.

Worker Resistance and Management Response

One of the criticisms lodged against Braverman's analysis of factory work is that he inaccurately portrays workers as passive victims of management control. In reality, workers often resist the imposition of task specialization and mechanization by managers. They go on strike, change jobs, fail to show up for work, sabotage production lines, and so forth (Burawoy, 1979; Clawson, 1980; Dunk, 1991).

Eventually, worker resistance causes management to modify its organizational plans. For example, Henry Ford was forced to double wages to induce his workers to accept the monotony, stress, and lack of autonomy associated with assembly-line production. Even so, gaining the cooperation of workers proved difficult. Therefore, beginning in the 1920s, some employers started to treat their employees better and less like cogs in a giant machine. They hoped to improve the work environment and thus make their employees more loyal and productive.

In the 1930s, the **human relations school of management** emerged as a challenge to Frederick W. Taylor's scientific management approach. Originating in studies conducted at the Hawthorne plant of the Western Electric Company near Chicago, the human relations school of management advocated less authoritarian leadership on the shop floor. It encouraged careful selection and training of personnel and greater attention to human needs and employee job satisfaction (see Chapter 5, Social Interaction).

The primary labour market comprises mainly highly skilled or well-educated white males. They are employed in large corporations that enjoy high levels of capital investment. In the primary labour market, employment is secure, earnings are high, and fringe benefits are generous.

The secondary labour market contains a disproportionately large number of women and members of ethnic minorities, particularly recent immigrants. Employees in the secondary labour market tend to be unskilled and lack higher education. They work in small firms that have low levels of capital investment. Employment is insecure, earnings are low, and fringe benefits are meagre.

The human relations school of management emerged in the 1930s as a challenge to Taylor's scientific management approach. It advocated less authoritarian leadership on the shop floor, careful selection and training of personnel, and greater attention to human needs and employee job satisfaction.

In the following decades, owners and managers of big companies in all the rich industrialized countries realized they had to make more concessions to labour if they wanted a loyal and productive workforce. These concessions included not just higher wages but also more decision-making authority about product quality, promotion policies, job design, product innovation, company investments, and so forth. The biggest concessions to labour were made in countries with the most powerful trade union movements, such as Sweden (see Chapter 14, Politics, and Chapter 21, Collective Action and Social Movements). In these countries, large proportions of eligible workers are members of unions (almost 90 percent in Sweden). Moreover, unions are organized in nationwide umbrella organizations that negotiate directly with centralized business organizations and governments over wages and labour policy. At the other extreme is the United States, where less than 12 percent of the workforce are in a union (Olsen, 2002: 134).

Canada is located between these two extremes, although closer to the American than the Swedish model. In Canada in 2007, 4.48 million employees were union members (30.3 percent of the non-agricultural workforce; see Human Resources and Social Development Canada, 2008). Here, there is no centralized, nationwide bargaining among unions, businesses, and governments. Two indicators of the relative inability of Canadian workers to wrest concessions from their employers are given in Figure 13.5 and Figure 13.6 on page 378. Canadians work more hours per week than people in many other rich industrialized countries do. They also have fewer paid vacation days per year. However, Canadian workers are better off than their American counterparts are on these two measures.

In the realm of industry-level decision making, too, Canadian workers lag behind workers in Western Europe and Japan. We can see this if we briefly consider the two main types of decision-making innovations that have been introduced in the factories of the rich industrialized countries since the early 1970s:

1. *Reforms that give workers more authority on the shop floor* include those advanced by the **quality of work life** movement. *Quality circles* originated in Sweden and Japan.

The quality of work life movement originated in Sweden and Japan. It involves small groups of a dozen or so workers and managers collaborating to improve both the quality of goods produced and communication between workers and managers.

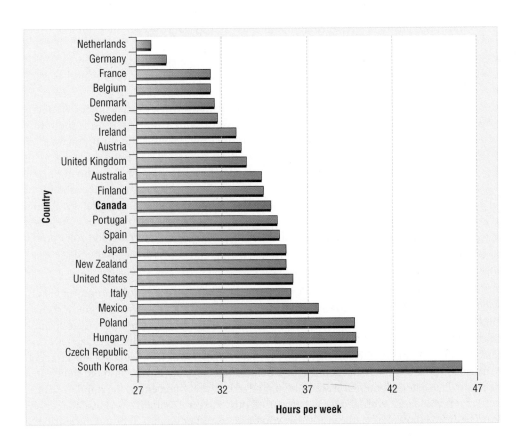

FIGURE 13.5
Average Hours Worked per Week, Selected Countries, 2006

Source: OECD, 2008.

FIGURE 13.6

Average Paid Vacation Days per Year, Selected Countries, 2004

Source: InfoPlease, 2005, "Average Number of Vacation Days Around the World per Year." Retrieved November 21, 2005 (http://www.infoplease.com/ipa/A0922052.html). Reprinted with permission.

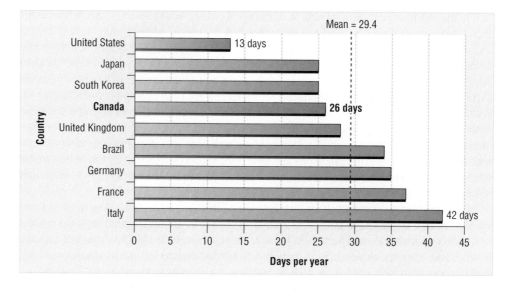

Codetermination is a German system of worker participation that allows workers to help formulate overall business strategy. German workers' councils review and influence management policies on a wide range of issues, including when and where new plants should be built and how capital should be invested in technological innovation.

They involve small groups of a dozen or so workers and managers collaborating to improve both the quality of goods produced and the communication between workers and managers. In some cases, this approach has evolved into a system that results in high productivity gains and worker satisfaction. For example, at Saab's main auto plant in Trolhattan, Sweden, the assembly line was eliminated (Krahn and Lowe, 1998: 239). Robots took over the arduous job of welding. In the welding area, groups of 12 workers program the computers, maintain the robots, ensure quality control, perform administrative tasks, and clean the area. Elsewhere in the plant, autonomous teams build up inventory in "buffer zones" and decide how to use it, thus introducing considerable flexibility into their schedule. All workers are encouraged to take advantage of in-plant opportunities to upgrade their skills. Quality circles have been introduced in some Canadian industries, including automotive and aerospace. However, they are less widespread here than in Western Europe and Japan.

2. *Reforms that allow workers to help formulate overall business strategy* give workers more authority than do quality circles. For example, in much of Western Europe workers are consulted not just on the shop floor but also in the boardroom. In Germany, this system is known as **codetermination**. German workers' councils review and influence management policies on a wide range of issues, including when and where new plants should be built and how capital should be invested in technological innovation. There are a few North American examples of this sort of worker involvement in high-level decision making, mostly in the auto industry. Worker participation programs were widely credited with improving the quality of North American cars and increasing the auto sector's productivity in the 1980s and 1990s, making it competitive again with Japanese carmakers. However, "[w]orker participation programs have had a difficult birth in North America. No broad policy agenda guides their development, and no systematic social theory lights their way" (Hodson and Sullivan, 1995: 449).

Unions have clearly played a key role in increasing worker participation in industrial decision making since the 1920s and especially since the 1970s. To varying degrees, owners and managers of big corporations have conceded authority to workers to create a more stable, loyal, and productive workforce. In Canada, governments too have ceded some workplace authority to unionized workers. Public sector employees who work for government, Crown corporations, public schools, and the health care system are much more likely than their private sector counterparts are to be unionized. Seventy percent of the public sector is unionized compared with about 20 percent of private sector employees. Understandably, workers who enjoy more authority in the workplace, whether unionized or not, have tried to protect the gains they have won. As we will now see, they have thereby contributed to the separation of primary and secondary labour markets.

Unions and Professional Organizations

Unions are organizations of workers that seek to defend and promote their members' interests. By bargaining with employers, unions have succeeded in winning improved working conditions, higher wages, and more worker participation in industrial decision making for their members. One indicator of the power of unions is that the hourly wage gap between unionized and nonunionized full-time workers is about $3, and the hourly wage gap between unionized and nonunionized part-time workers is about $7 (Alberta Federation of Labour, 2005).

In conjunction with employers, unions have also helped develop systems of labour recruitment, training, and promotion. These systems are sometimes called **internal labour markets** because they control pay rates, hiring, and promotions within corporations (Creese, 1999). At the same time, they reduce competition between a firm's workers and external labour supplies.

In an internal labour market, training programs that specify the credentials required for promotion govern advancement through the ranks. Seniority rules specify the length of time a person must serve in a given position before being allowed to move up. These rules also protect senior personnel from layoffs according to the principle of "last hired, first fired." Finally, in internal labour markets, recruitment of new workers is usually limited to entry-level positions. In this way, the intake of new workers is controlled. Senior personnel are assured of promotion and protection from outside competition. For this reason, internal labour markets are sometimes called "labour market shelters."

Labour market shelters operate not only among unionized factory workers but also among professionals, such as doctors, lawyers, and engineers. **Professionals** are people with specialized knowledge acquired through extensive higher education. They enjoy a high degree of work autonomy and usually regulate themselves and enforce standards through professional associations. The Canadian Medical Association is probably the best-known and certainly one of the most powerful professional associations in the country. Professionals exercise authority over clients and subordinates. They operate according to a code of ethics that emphasizes the altruistic nature of their work. Finally, they specify the credentials needed to enter their professions and thus maintain a cap on the supply of new professionals. This reduces competition, ensures high demand for their services, and keeps their earnings high. In this way, the professions act as labour market shelters, much like unions. (For further discussion of professionalization, see Chapter 17, Education.)

Barriers between the Primary and Secondary Labour Markets

We saw above that many workers in the secondary labour market do not enjoy the high pay, job security, and benefit packages shared by workers in the primary labour market, many of whom are members of unions and professional associations. We can now add that these workers find it difficult to exit the "job ghettos" of the secondary labour market, because three social barriers make the primary labour market difficult to penetrate:

1. *Often, there are few entry-level positions in the primary labour market.* One set of circumstances that contributes to the lack of entry-level positions in the primary labour market is corporate "downsizing" and plant shutdowns. These took place on a wide scale in Canada and the United States throughout the 1980s and early 1990s. The lack of entry-level positions is especially acute during periods of economic recession. A recession is usually defined as a period of six months or more during which the economy shrinks and unemployment rises. Canada was in the grip of recession

Unions are organizations of workers that seek to defend and promote their members' interests.

Internal labour markets are social mechanisms for controlling pay rates, hiring, and promotions within corporations while reducing competition between a firm's workers and external labour supplies.

Professionals are people with specialized knowledge acquired through extensive higher education.

about a sixth of the time between 1973 and the present. Big economic forces, such as plant shutdowns and recessions, prevent upward mobility and often result in downward mobility.

2. *Workers often lack informal networks linking them to good job openings.* People frequently find out about job availability through informal networks of friends and acquaintances (Granovetter, 1995). These networks typically consist of people with the same ethnic and racial backgrounds. Recent immigrants, and especially refugees, who comprise a disproportionately large share of workers in the secondary labour market and tend not to be white, are less likely than others to find out about job openings in the primary labour market, where the labour force is disproportionately white. Even within ethnic groups, the difference between getting good work and having none is sometimes a question of having the right connections.

3. *Workers usually lack the required training and certification for jobs in the primary labour market.* What is more, because of their low wages and scarce leisure time, they usually cannot afford to upgrade either their skills or their credentials. Impersonal economic forces, a lack of network ties, and insufficient education often cause people to get stuck, usually permanently, in the secondary labour market.

The Time Crunch and Its Effects

Although the quality of working life is higher in the primary labour market than in the secondary labour market, we must be careful not to exaggerate the differences. Overwork and lack of leisure have become central features of our culture, and this is true in both labour markets. We are experiencing a growing time crunch. All the adults in most Canadian households work full time in the paid labour force and many adolescents work part time. Some people work two jobs to make ends meet. Many managers, truck drivers, and professionals work 10, 12, or more hours a day because of tight deadlines, demands for high productivity, and a trimmed-down workforce.

Over the past 50 years the average number of hours that people spend working at their primary job has remained stable at between 35 and 40 per week. However, if you reflect on the growth of part-time labour discussed earlier, something else must be happening to balance the fewer hours that part-time workers spent at work. The offset comes from a growing number of Canadians working longer hours (Shields, 1999). In 1976, 31 percent of employed Canadian men and 10 percent of employed Canadian women worked more than 40 hours a week. In 2004, 35 percent of men and 16 percent of women worked more than 40 hours a week. Twenty-one percent of men and 8 percent of women worked more than 50 hours a week (Statistics Canada, 2005g). One study showed that such long hours were put in by 38 percent of senior managers, the most overworked job category. Among transport and equipment operators, the second-most-overworked job category, the figure was 27 percent. Among teachers and professors, the sixth-most-overworked job category, the figure was 18 percent (Lowe, 2001: 8, 9). Add to this the heavy demands of family life, especially for women, and you can readily understand why stress, depression, aggression, and substance abuse are on the rise in both the secondary and the primary labour markets. According to one human resources expert:

> People are on the edge, and acting it out in the workplace. They're yelling obscenities at each other, coming into work chronically late, throwing food in the cafeteria, and crying in the hallways. It's not just a matter of acting a little inappropriately any more. No, it's gotten far worse than that. Nice people are having trouble with alcohol, drugs, depression and acting aggressively at work. And these aren't isolated instances—instead, they're a composite picture from chronic work distress, as well as difficulties trying to deal with personal life overload from marital problems, single parenthood, financial worries and the like. The stress is so great that people are snapping. And no one has to tell you that it's getting worse. (Solomon, 1999: 48–49)

Stress is often defined as the feeling of being unable to cope with life's demands given our resources. Work is the leading source of stress throughout the world. In one study of office workers in 16 countries, including Canada, 54 percent of respondents cited work as a current cause of stress in their lives and 29 percent cited money problems—which are also work-related since a job is the main source of income for most people ("Work-Related Stress," 1995). The rate of severe depression is also on the rise. In some countries, including Canada, people born after 1955 are three times more likely to experience serious depression than their grandparents were (Weissman, 1992). According to a World Health Organization study, severe depression is the second leading contributor to "disease burden" (years lived with a disability) in the rich postindustrial countries. It is predicted to rise to the number-one position by 2020 (Vernarec, 2000).

There are three main reasons that leisure is on the decline and the pace of work is becoming more frantic for many people who are employed in the paid labour force (Schor, 1992). First, big corporations are in a position to invest increasingly enormous resources in advertising. As we saw in Chapter 3, Culture, advertising is pushing Canadians to consume goods and services at higher and higher levels all the time. Shopping has become an end in itself for many people, a form of entertainment and, in some cases, a deeply felt "need." They need to work more so that they can earn more to satisfy that need. Second, most corporate executives apparently think it is more profitable to push employees to work more hours rather than hire more workers and pay expensive benefits for new employees. Third, as we have just discussed, most Canadian workers in the private sector are not in a position to demand reduced working hours and more vacation time because few of them are unionized. They lack clout and suffer the consequences in terms of stress, depression, and other work-related ailments.

Bedtime at Yahoo! Inc. In high-tech industries, working on very little sleep is common. Here, David Filo, co-founder of Yahoo!, takes a nap under his desk.

THE PROBLEM OF MARKETS

One conclusion we can draw from the preceding discussion is that the secondary labour market is a relatively **free market**. That is, the supply and demand for labour regulate wage levels and other benefits. If supply is high and demand is low, wages fall. If demand is high and supply is low, wages rise. People who work in the secondary labour market lack much power to interfere in the operation of the forces of supply and demand.

In contrast, the primary labour market is a more **regulated market**. Wage levels and other benefits are not established by the forces of supply and demand alone; workers and professionals are in a position to influence the operation of the primary labour market to their own advantage.

This suggests that the freer the market, the higher the resulting level of social inequality. In fact, in the freest markets, many of the least powerful people are unable to earn enough to subsist. A few of the most powerful people can amass unimaginably large fortunes. That is why the secondary labour market cannot be entirely free. Canadian governments have had to establish a legal minimum wage to prevent the price of unskilled labour from dropping below the point at which people are literally able to make a living (see Box 13.1 on page 382). Similarly, in the historical period that most closely approximates a completely free market for labour—late-eighteenth-century England—starvation became so widespread and the threat of social instability so great the government was forced to establish a system of state-run "poor houses" that provided minimal food and shelter for people without means (Polanyi, 1957).

The question of whether free or regulated markets are better for society lies at the centre of much debate in economics and politics (Kuttner, 1997). For many economic sociologists, however, that question is too abstract. In the first place, regulation is not an either/or issue but a matter of degree. A market may be more or less regulated. No markets

In a free market, prices are determined only by supply and demand.

In a regulated market, various social forces limit the capacity of supply and demand to determine prices.

BOX 13.1
Social Policy: What Do You Think?

Should We Abolish the Minimum Wage?

"Flipping burgers at Mickey D's is no way to make a living," a young man once told John Lie. Having tried his hand at several minimum-wage jobs as a teenager, John knew the young man was right.

In Canada, the provinces and territories set the minimum wage. In 2008 it ranged from $7.60 in Nova Scotia to $8.75 in Ontario, with most provinces and territories around the $8 range. At about $8 an hour, a minimum-wage job may be fine for teenagers, many of whom are supported by their parents. However, it is difficult to live on your own, much less to support a family, on a minimum-wage job, even if you work

full time. This is the problem with the minimum wage: It does not amount to a living wage for many people.

In the 2000s, about half of the Canadians who received minimum wage for their work were adults over the age of 20. Women were overrepresented in this category and many of them were single mothers. Use $8 per hour as the base and calculate the annual income of someone working 52 weeks per year at 40 hours per week. The result: $16 640. This falls below the low-income cutoff for single people living in communities with 30 000 or more people. Welcome to the world of the "working poor." Could you live on $16 640 a year, especially if you had to support a child?

Given the thousands of Canadians who cannot lift them-

selves and their children out of poverty even if they work full time, many scholars and policymakers suggest raising the minimum wage (Goldberg and Green, 1999). Others disagree (Law, 1999). They fear that raising the minimum wage would decrease the number of available jobs. Others disagree in principle with government interference in the economy. Some scholars and policymakers even advocate the abolition of the minimum wage.

What do you think? Should the minimum wage be raised? Should someone working full time be entitled to live above the low-income cutoff? Or should businesses be entitled to hire workers at whatever price the market will bear?

are completely unregulated. For example, various regulations and regulators monitor the Toronto Stock Exchange, the Ontario Securities Commission chief among them. Without some regulation, markets could not function. Second, markets may be regulated by different groups of people with varying degrees of power and different norms and values. Therefore, the costs and benefits of regulation may be socially distributed in many different ways. Sociological analysis can sort out the costs and benefits of different degrees of market regulation for various categories of the population. These, then, are the main insights of economic sociology as applied to the study of markets: (1) The structure of markets varies widely across cultures and historical periods, and (2) the degree and type of regulation depends on how power, norms, and values are distributed among various social groups (Lie, 1992).

The economic sociologist's approach to the study of markets is different from that of the dominant trend in contemporary economics, known as the "neoclassical" school (Becker, 1976; Mankiw, 1998). Instead of focusing on how power, norms, and values shape markets, neoclassical economists argue that free markets maximize economic growth. We can use the minimum wage to illustrate their point. According to neoclassical economists, if the minimum wage is eliminated entirely, everyone will be better off. For example, in a situation where labour is in low demand and high supply, wages will fall. This will increase profits. Higher profits will in turn allow employers to invest more in expanding their businesses. The new investment will create new jobs, and the rising demand for labour will drive wages up. Social inequality may increase but eventually *everyone* will be better off thanks to the operation of the free market.[1]

One difficulty with the neoclassical theory is that, in the real world, resistance to the operation of free markets increases as you move down the social hierarchy from the wealthiest and most powerful members of society to the poorest and least powerful. People at the low end of the social hierarchy usually fight against falling wages. The resulting social instability can disrupt production and investment. The riots in Argentina in late 2001 are an example. A social environment full of strikes, riots, and industrial sabotage is

ACCOUNT OF THE

SALE of a WIFE, by J. NASH,

IN THOMAS-STREET MARKET,

On the 29th of May, 1823.

This day another of those disgraceful scenes which of late have so frequently annoyed the public markets in this country took place in St. Thomas's Market, in this city; a man (if he deserves the name) of the name of John Nash, a drover, residing in Rose-mary-street, appeared there leading his wife in a halter, followed by a great concourse of spectators; when arrived opposite the Bell-yard, he publicly announced his intention of disposing of his better half by Public Auction, and stated that the biddings were then open; it was a long while before any one ventured to speak, at length a young man who thought it a pity to let her remain in the hands of her present owner, generously bid 6d.! In vain did the anxious seller look around for another bidding, no one could be found to advance one penny, and after extolling her qualities, and warranting her sound, and free from vice, he was obliged, rather than keep her, to let her go at that price. The lady appeared quite satisfied, but not so the purchaser, he soon repented of his bargain, and again offered her to sale, when being bid nine-pence, he readily accepted it, and handed the lady to her new purchaser, who, not liking the transfer, made off with her mother, but was soon taken by her purchaser, and claimed as his property, to this she would not consent but by order of a magistrate, who dismissed the case. Nash, the husband, was obliged to make a precipitate retreat from the enraged populace.

Copy of Verses written on the Occasion:

COME all you kind husbands who have scolding wives,
Who thro' living together are tired of your lives,
If you cannot persuade her nor good natur'd make her
Place a rope round her neck & to market pray take her

Should any one bid, when she's offer'd for sale,
Let her go for a trifle lest she should get stale,
If six-pence be offer'd, & that's all can be had,
Let her go for the same rather than keep a lot bad.

Come all jolly neighbours, come dance sing & play,
Away to the wedding where we intend to drink tea;
All the world assembles, the young and the old,
For to see this fair beauty, as we have been told.

Here's success to this couple to keep up the fun,
May bumpers go round at the birth of a son;
Long life to them both, and in peace & content
May their days and their nights for ever be spent.

Shepherd, Printer, No. 6, on the Broad Weir, Bristol.

An unregulated market creates gross inequalities. Here is an account of a wife sold by her husband for nine pence in Britain in 1823. Similar events inspired Thomas Hardy's classic novel *The Mayor of Casterbridge* (1886).

unfavourable to high productivity and new capital investment. That is why the economic system of a society at a given time is a more or less stable set of compromises between advocates and opponents of free markets. Markets are only as free as people are prepared to tolerate, and their degree of tolerance varies historically and among cultures (Berger and Dore, 1996; Doremus, Keller, Pauly, and Reich, 1998).

In the rest of this chapter, we offer several illustrations of how sociologists analyze markets. First, we compare capitalism and communism, the two main types of economic system in the twentieth century. Second, we examine the ability of big corporations to shape Canadian markets today. Finally, we extend our analysis of corporate and free market growth to the global level. We identify advocates and opponents of these developments and sketch the main work-related decisions that face us in the early twenty-first century.

Capitalism, Communism, and Democratic Socialism

Capitalism

Capitalism is the dominant economic system in the world. Private ownership of property and competition in the pursuit of profit characterize capitalist economies.

Corporations are legal entities that can enter into contracts and own property. They are taxed at a lower rate than individuals are and their owners are normally not liable for the corporation's debt or any harm it may cause the public.

The world's dominant economic system today is **capitalism**. Capitalist economies have two distinctive features.

1. *Private ownership of property.* In capitalist economies, individuals and corporations own almost all the means of producing goods and services. Individuals and corporations are therefore free to buy and sell land, natural resources, buildings, manufactured goods, medical services, and just about everything else. Like individuals, **corporations** are legal entities. They can enter contracts and own property. However, corporate ownership has two advantages over individual ownership. First, corporations are taxed at a lower rate than individuals are. Second, the corporation's owners are not normally liable if the corporation harms consumers or goes bankrupt. Instead, the corporation itself is legally responsible for damage and debt (see Box 13.2).

2. *Competition in the pursuit of profit.* The second hallmark of capitalism is that producers, motivated by the prospect of profits, compete to offer consumers desired goods and services at the lowest possible price. A purely capitalist economy is often called a laissez-faire system. *Laissez-faire* is French for "allow to do." In a laissez-faire system, the government does not interfere in the operation of the economy at all; it allows producers and consumers to do what they want. Adam Smith was an eighteenth-century Scottish economist who first outlined the operation of the ideal capitalist economy. According to Smith, everyone benefits from laissez-faire. The most efficient producers make profits while consumers can buy at low prices. If everyone pursues their narrow self-interest, unimpeded by government, the economy will achieve "the greatest good for the greatest number," said Smith (1981 [1776]).

BOX 13.2
Sociology at the Movies

NO. **TAKE** **ROLL**

The Corporation (2003)

Indian farmers have been cultivating the neem tree ever since its valuable medicinal properties first became known 2000 years ago. Various neem extracts kill bacteria, fungi, viruses, and insects, and reduce pain and inflammation. In 1994, W. R. Grace, a large American chemical corporation, patented a fungicide derived from the neem tree. Overnight, a common and naturally occurring life form, the beneficial properties of which had been identified and nurtured by a hundred generations of Indian farmers, became the private property of a multinational corporation. The fungicide derived from the neem tree could still be manufactured and purchased—but only by paying W. R. Grace a fee.

Protestors demonstrate against corporate domination in *The Corporation* (2003).

What is a corporation? How did corporations become so powerful that they can turn nature into private property? Overall, do they do more harm than good? Vancouver filmmakers

Mark Achbar, Jennifer Abbott, and Joel Bakan answer these questions in *The Corporation,* a 2003 documentary that won 26 international film awards, including a Genie for Best

Documentary and the Sundance Film Festival Audience Choice Award.

With an unsettling mixture of humour and alarm, Achbar, Abbott, and Bakan tell the story of a legal entity that started to proliferate only about 150 years ago and now dominates the world. Like individuals, corporations can enter into contracts and buy property. However, corporate ownership has a big advantage over individual ownership. It limits the legal obligations of the owners; they are not normally liable if the corporation harms consumers or goes bankrupt. Instead, the corporation itself is legally responsible for damage and debt. By thus limiting owners' risk, corporations are attractive investment vehicles. That is why they grew quickly.

Governments grant corporations the right to exist, but as corporations have grown, they have come to exercise more and more influence over governments. So, for example, corporations have for many decades impressed upon governments the importance of lowering corporate tax rates to attract business. They have also persistently reminded governments that failure to lower corporate tax rates will result in the relocation of corporations to jurisdictions where governments are more sympathetic to the interests of business. As a result, in Canada and other countries, corporations are taxed at a substantially lower rate than individuals.

From the corporate point of view, limited liability and favourable tax laws are worth the cost to society. After all, corporations provide many useful goods and services, and competition among corporations ensures that prices are kept to a minimum. But business leaders rarely discuss the downside of the corporation. That is where Achbar, Abbott, and Bakan step in.

The Corporation argues that if corporations were people, they would be labelled psychopaths according to the standard psychiatric definition. For example:

- Psychopaths are incapable of maintaining enduring relationships. Likewise, to earn high profits, corporations routinely shut down factories in high-wage, high-tax countries, like Canada, throwing millions of people out of work.
- Psychopaths display callous disregard for the feelings of others. Likewise, to earn high profits, corporations set up factories in poor countries, where women and children work long hours in horrid conditions for meagre wages.
- Psychopaths display reckless disregard for the safety of others. Likewise, to earn high profits, multinational corporations routinely pollute the environment, shirk worker safety regulations, and make unsafe products.
- Psychopaths fail to conform to social norms and behave lawfully. Likewise, to earn high profits, corporations pay many tens of millions of dollars a year in fines for illegal practices, and then turn around and act illegally again if they calculate that the fines are less expensive than complying with the law.

Many people think that just a few bad corporate apples are responsible for such behaviour. They need to see *The Corporation,* which demonstrates that such corporate behaviour is in fact routine.

The Corporation succeeds as a movie because it does not bludgeon or lecture the audience. Instead, it analyzes the history and operation of the corporation in an entertaining and easily digestible way, using cartoons, pop culture, historical footage, and captivating interviews with a wide range of interesting, highly intelligent and amusing people, including corporate leaders and their critics. It succeeds also because it refuses to become dismal. Instead, it concludes on an optimistic note, showing how people from around the world—environmental activists, farmers' groups, consumers' associations, and so on—have succeeded in challenging and limiting the damage done by corporations, forcing them to behave in a more socially responsible way.

A case in point concerns the neem tree patent. In 2005, the Green Party in the European Parliament, the International Federation of Organic Agriculture, and the Research Foundation for Science, Technology and Ecology succeeded in having W. R. Grace's patent for the neem fungicide revoked by the European Patent Office. It was the first time anyone succeeded in having a patent rejected on the grounds of "biopiracy"—corporate theft of traditional agricultural and medical knowledge and practices. Indian farmers celebrated the decision. So should we all.

In reality, no economy is purely laissez-faire. The state had to intervene heavily to create markets in the first place. For example, 500 years ago the idea that land is a commodity that can be bought, sold, and rented on the free market was utterly foreign to the Aboriginal peoples who lived in the territory that is now North America. To turn the land into a marketable commodity, European armies had to force Aboriginal peoples off the land and eventually onto reserves. Governments had to pass laws regulating the ownership, sale, and rent of land. Without the military and legal intervention of government, no market for land would exist.

Today, governments must also intervene in the economy to keep the market working effectively. For instance, governments create and maintain an economic infrastructure (roads, ports, etc.) to make commerce possible. They pass laws governing the minimum wage, occupational health and safety, child labour, and industrial pollution to protect workers and consumers from the excesses of corporations. If very large corporations get into financial trouble, they can expect the government to bail them out on the grounds that their bankruptcy would be devastating to the economy.

Governments also play an influential role in establishing and promoting many leading industries, especially those that require large outlays on research and development. Until the 1960s, the U.S. government covered two-thirds of all research and development costs in the country, and it still covers nearly a third. It developed the foundations of the Internet in the late 1960s. In the late 1980s, it gave $100 million a year to corporations working to improve the quality of the microchip (Reich, 1991). Occasionally, the government even resorts to armed force to ensure the smooth operation of the market, as, for example, when oil supplies are threatened by hostile foreign regimes (Lazonick, 1991).

As these examples of government intervention suggest, we should see Smith's ideal of a laissez-faire economy as just that: an ideal. In the real world, markets are free to varying degrees, but none is or can be entirely free. Which capitalist economies are the most free and which are the least free? The International Institute for Management Development (IMD International) in Switzerland publishes a widely respected annual index of competitiveness. The index is based on the amount of state ownership of industry and many other indicators of market freedom. Figure 13.7 gives the scores for the 10 most and 10 least competitive countries in 2007. The United States tops the list. It is the most competitive economy in the world, with a score of 100. Venezuela ranks 55th, with a score of 30.954. Canada ranks 10th, with a score of 83.824.

Communism

Like laissez-faire capitalism, communism is an ideal. **Communism** is the name Karl Marx gave to the classless society that, he said, is bound to develop out of capitalism. Socialism

Communism is a social and an economic system in which property is owned by public bodies; government planning, not the market, determines production and distribution.

FIGURE 13.7

The World Competitiveness Scoreboard, 2007

Source: IMD International, 2007, "The World Competitiveness Scoreboard 2007." Retrieved May 1, 2008 (http://www.imd.ch/research/publications/wcy/upload/scoreboard.pdf).

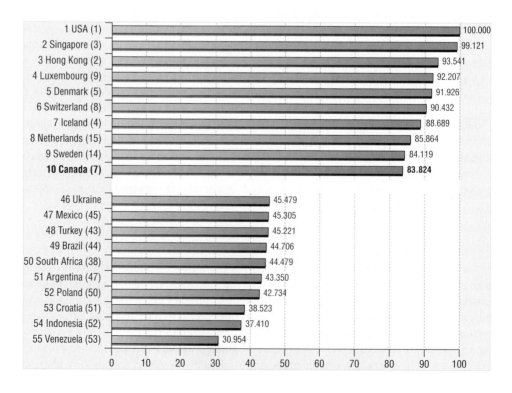

is the name he gave to the transitional phase between capitalism and communism. No country in the world is communist in the pure sense of the term. About two dozen countries in Asia, South America, and Africa consider themselves socialist. They include China, North Korea, Vietnam, and Cuba. As an ideal, communism is an economic system with two distinct features:

1. *Public ownership of property.* Under communism, the state owns almost all the means of producing goods and services. Private corporations do not exist. Individuals are not free to buy and sell goods and services. The aim of public ownership is to ensure that all individuals have equal wealth and equal access to goods and services.
2. *Government planning.* Five-year state plans establish production quotas, prices, and most other aspects of economic activity. Political officials—not forces of supply and demand—design these state plans and determine what is produced, in what quantities, and at what prices. A high level of control of the population is required to implement these rigid state plans. As a result, democratic politics is not allowed to interfere with state activities. Only one political party exists—the Communist Party. Elections are held regularly, but only the Communist Party is allowed to run for office (Zaslavsky and Brym, 1978).

Until recently, the countries of Central and Eastern Europe were single-party, socialist societies. The most powerful of these countries was the Soviet Union, which comprised Russia and 14 other socialist republics. In perhaps the most surprising and sudden change in modern history, the countries of the region started introducing capitalism and holding multi-party elections in the late 1980s and early 1990s.

The collapse of socialism in Central and Eastern Europe was due to several factors. For one thing, the citizens of the region enjoyed few civil rights. For another, their standard of living was only about half as high as that of people in the rich industrialized countries of the West. The gap between East and West grew as the arms race between the Soviet Union and the United States intensified in the 1980s. The standard of living fell as the Soviet Union mobilized its economic resources to try to match the quantity and quality of military goods produced by the United States. Dissatisfaction was widespread and expressed itself in many ways, including strikes and political demonstrations. It grew as television and radio signals beamed from the West made the gap between socialism and capitalism more apparent to the citizenry. Eventually, the communist parties of the region felt they could no longer govern effectively and so began to introduce reforms.

In the 1990s, some Central and East European countries were more successful than others were in introducing elements of capitalism and raising their citizens' standard of living. The Czech Republic was most successful. Russia and most of the rest of the former Soviet Union were least successful. Many factors account for the different success rates, but perhaps the most important is the way different countries introduced reforms. The Czechs introduced both of the key elements of capitalism—private property and competition in the pursuit of profit. The Russians, however, introduced private property without much competition. Specifically, the Russian government first allowed prices to rise to market levels. This made many basic goods too expensive for a large part of the population, which was quickly impoverished. Next, the government sold state-owned property to individuals and corporations. However, the only people who could afford to buy the factories, mines, oil refineries, airlines, and other economic enterprises were organized criminals and former officials of the Communist Party. They alone had access to sufficient capital and insider information about how to make the purchases (Handelman, 1995). The effect was to make Russia's level of socioeconomic inequality among the highest in the world. A crucial element lacking in the Russian reform was competition.

A few giant corporations now control nearly every part of the Russian economy. They tend not to compete against one another. Competition would drive prices down and efficiency up. However, these corporations are so big they can agree among themselves to set prices at levels that are most profitable for them. They thus have little incentive to innovate.

Oligopolies are giant corporations that control part of an economy. They are few in number and tend not to compete against one another. Instead, they can set prices at levels that are most profitable for them.

Moreover, they are so big and rich they have enormous influence over government. When a few corporations are so big they can behave in this way, they are called **oligopolies**.[2] Russia is full of them. The lack of competition in Russia prevented the country from experiencing much economic growth in the 1990s (Brym, 1996a, 1996b, 1996c), although the recent surge in oil prices and demand has helped Russia a great deal because it is a major oil exporter.

Democratic Socialism

Several prosperous and highly industrialized countries in Northwestern Europe, such as Sweden, Denmark, and Norway, are democratic socialist societies. So are France and Germany, albeit to a lesser degree. Such societies have two distinctive features (Olsen, 2002):

1. *Public ownership of certain basic industries.* In democratic socialist countries, the government owns certain basic industries entirely or in part. These industries may include telecommunications, electricity, railways, airlines, and steel. Still, as a proportion of the entire economy, the level of public ownership is not high—far lower than the level of public ownership in socialist societies. The great bulk of property is privately owned, and competition in the pursuit of profit is the main motive for business activity, just as in capitalist societies.

2. *Government intervention in the market.* As the term "democratic socialism" implies, these countries enjoy regular, free, multi-party elections, just like Canada. However, unlike Canada, political parties backed by a strong trade union movement have formed governments in democratic socialist countries for much of the post–World War II period. As many as 90 percent of non-agricultural workers, including white-collar workers, are unionized in democratic socialist countries. (The comparable figure for the United States is 12 percent and for Canada it is 30 percent.) The governments that these unions back intervene strongly in the operation of markets for the benefit of ordinary workers. Taxes are considerably higher than in capitalist countries. Consequently, social services are much more generous. Looking at government expenditure as a percentage of gross domestic product (GDP), the United States government spends only half as much on welfare, unemployment insurance, medical care, child care, worker training, and other social services as Sweden does. Canada spends three-fifths as much as Sweden does. Because of the Swedish government's vigorous role in redistributing income, the gap between rich and poor is much narrower than in the capitalist countries. Moreover, on average, workers earn more, work fewer hours, and enjoy more paid vacation days.

Since the 1980s, the democratic socialist countries have moved in a somewhat more capitalist direction. In particular, they have privatized some previously government-owned industries and services. Still, these countries retain their distinct approach to governments and markets, which is why democratic socialism is sometimes called a "Third Way" between capitalism and socialism.

The Corporation

Oligopolies can constrain innovation in all societies. They can force consumers to pay higher prices. They can exercise excessive influence on governments. However, in Canada and other Western countries, so-called antitrust laws limit their growth. In 1889, Canada first introduced legislation restricting businesses from combining or colluding to control markets. Replaced in 1923 by the Combines Investigation Act, the law allows government to review corporate mergers and acquisitions. Bank mergers have been a recent point of contention in Canada, with several of our largest banks wanting to merge to compete more successfully internationally. Resistance to such mergers is based on concern about job losses and restricted consumer banking choices.

However, the law has been only partly effective in stabilizing the growth of oligopolies. You need look no further than your local gas station to find an example that continues to suggest price competition is not as vigorous as the idea of "antitrust" implies. In the 1970s, Robert Bertrand, then director of the Investigations and Research Branch, Combines Investigation Act, wrote a seven-volume, 1700-page report implying that big oil companies engaged in monopoly practices. In 1981, Bertrand published extracts from the report under the provocative title *Canada's Oil Monopoly: The Story of the $12 Billion Rip-off of Canadian Consumers.*

Canadian banking provides an apt illustration of corporate concentration (although the beer industry, retail gas sales, or the movie theatre industry would provide equally compelling cases). First, there are only 11 domestic banks. Several of them are so small you have likely never heard of them. These include Citizens Bank of Canada and First Nations Bank of Canada. Second, the top four banks, as ranked by the value of their assets, control about 85 percent of all banking assets in the country. Even adding all the credit unions and trust companies in Canada, as well as all the foreign bank subsidiaries, the top four banks still control well over three-quarters of all assets. When Canada Trust was purchased by Toronto Dominion Bank in 2000, this asset concentration increased. Such concentration is a world apart from the early nineteenth century, when most businesses, including banks, were family owned and served only local markets (National Council of Welfare, 1998b; Whittington, 1999).

Recent mergers and acquisitions in the global automotive industry also illustrate corporate concentration. Chrysler and Daimler-Benz merged in a deal worth US$39 billion. Other new partnerships in recent years involved Volkswagen's takeover of Rolls Royce, Ford's takeover of Volvo's car division, and the alliance between Renault and Nissan. Such mergers create enormous organizations.

It is also important to note that a significant effect of Canadian competition law is to encourage big companies to diversify. That is, rather than increasing their share of control in their own industry, corporations often move into new industries, the better to avoid antitrust laws. Big companies that operate in several industries at the same time are called **conglomerates**. For example, Bell Canada Enterprises (BCE) is not just a telephone company. It owns part of CTV, *The Globe and Mail,* and Sympatico, and owns all of Teleglobe and ExpressVu, among other companies. It is a giant conglomerate with more than 50 000 employees and assets of more than $22 billion. BCE is one example of the rapidly expanding conglomerates operating the world over. Big companies are swallowed up by still bigger ones in wave after wave of corporate mergers (Mizruchi, 1982, 1992).

Outright ownership of a company by a second company in another industry is only one way corporations may be linked. **Interlocking directorates** are another. Interlocking directorates are formed when an individual sits on the board of directors of two or more noncompeting companies. (Antitrust laws prevent an individual from sitting on the board of directors of a competitor.) For instance, in 2005 the board of directors of BCE included, among others, the president of Petro-Canada, the chair of the Royal Bank Corporation, and a former president of Canadian National Railway and of the Bombardier Corporation. Such interlocks enable corporations to exchange valuable information and form alliances for their mutual benefit. They also create useful channels of communication to, and influence over, government since some board members of major corporations are likely to be former senior politicians (Carroll, 1986; Marchak, 1991). In 2002, for example, former Prime Minister Brian Mulroney became a member of the board of directors of Quebecor World, the largest commercial print media services company in the world.

Of course, small businesses continue to exist. In Canada, 78 percent of all businesses have fewer than five employees, and 97 percent have fewer than 50 employees (see Table 13.2 on page 390). Small firms, which are a critical feature of the Canadian economy, are particularly important in the service sector. However, compared with large firms, profits in small firms are typically low, and bankruptcies are common. Small firms often use outdated production and marketing techniques. Jobs in small firms frequently have low wages and meagre benefits.

Conglomerates are large corporations that operate in several industries at the same time.

Interlocking directorates are formed when an individual sits on the board of directors of two or more non-competing companies.

TABLE 13.2

Percentage of Employees and Percentage of Firms by Size of Firm, 2003

Source: Adapted from Sri Kanagarajah, 2006, *Business Dynamics in Canada, 2003*. Ottawa: Ministry of Industry, Statistics Canada. Catalogue No. 61-534-XIE. Retrieved November 11, 2008 (http://www.statcan.ca/english/freepub/61-534-XIE/61-534-XIE 200601.pdf).

Size of Firm	Percentage of All Employees	Percentage of All Firms
0–19 Employees	21.45	92.0
20–99 Employees	19.68	6.6
100–499 Employees	15.68	1.1
500+ Employees	43.19	0.2
Total	100.00	100.0

A sizable portion of the Canadian labour force works in large corporations. Specifically, about 4 in 10 workers are employed in firms with more than 500 employees, even though the percentage of such firms is very small (0.2 percent). Canada's largest private sector employer is the Loblaw food chain, owned by George Weston Ltd., with more than 100 000 employees. Onex Corporation, a conglomerate that many people have never heard of, employs more than 80 000 Canadians in diverse firms that include interests in airline catering, electronics manufacturing, sugar refining, and automotive parts.

Globalization

As noted above, in the 1980s and early 1990s Canada was hit by a wave of corporate "downsizing" (Grayson, 1985). Especially in the older manufacturing industries, thousands of blue-collar workers and middle managers were fired. In such places as Cape Breton, Nova Scotia; Ocean Falls, British Columbia; and Ingersoll, Ontario, the consequences were devastating. Unemployment soared. Social problems, such as alcoholism and domestic violence, became acute. Some people blamed government for the plant shutdowns. They said taxes were so high, big corporations could no longer make decent profits. Others blamed the unemployed themselves. They said powerful unions drove up the hourly wage to the point where companies were losing money.

In the 1980s, workers, governments, and corporations got involved as unequal players in the globalization of the world economy. Japan and Germany had fully recovered from the devastation of World War II. With these large and robust industrial economies now firing on all cylinders, American- and Canadian-based multinationals were forced to cut costs and become more efficient to remain competitive. On a scale far larger than ever before, they began to build branch plants in low-wage countries, such as Mexico and China, to take advantage of cheap labour and low taxes. Multinational corporations based in Japan and other highly industrialized countries did the same.

Although multinational corporations could easily move investment capital from one country to the next, workers were rooted in their communities and governments were rooted in their nation-states. Multinationals thus had a big advantage over the other players in the globalization game. They could threaten to move plants unless governments and workers made concessions. They could play one government off another in the bidding war for new plants. And they could pick up and leave when it became clear that relocation would do wonders for their bottom line.

Today, three decades after the globalization game began in earnest, it is easier to identify the winners than the losers. The clear winners are the stockholders of the multinational corporations, whose profits have soared. The losers, at least initially, were blue-collar workers. To cite just one example, in the past two decades General Motors has cut its workforce in Canada and the United States by about one-third in the face of stiff competition from automotive giants in Japan and Germany, in particular.

Even while these cuts were being made, however, some large manufacturers were hiring. For instance, employment at Bombardier grew dramatically, and this Canadian-owned vehicle and aerospace firm is now a world leader. In the service sector, employment soared, as we have seen. Such corporations as Loblaw, Molson Breweries, and the Hudson Bay Company employ tens of thousands of Canadians.

Globalization in the Less Developed Countries

GLOBAL PERSPECTIVE

It is still too soon to tell whether the governments and citizens of the less developed countries will be losers or winners in the globalization game. On the one hand, it is hard to argue with the assessment of the rural Indonesian woman interviewed by Diane Wolf. She prefers the regime of the factory to the tedium of village life. In the village, the woman worked from dawn till dusk doing household chores, taking care of siblings, and feeding the family goat. In the factory, she earns less than $1 a day sewing pockets on men's shirts in a hot factory. Yet because work in the factory is less arduous, pays something, and holds out the hope of even better work for future generations, the woman views it as nothing less than liberating (Wolf, 1992). Many workers in other regions of the world where branch plants of multinationals have sprung up in recent decades feel much the same way. A wage of $3 an hour is excellent pay in Mexico, and workers rush to fill jobs along Mexico's northern border with the United States.

Yet the picture is not all bright. The governments of developing countries attract branch plants by imposing few if any pollution controls on their operations. This has dangerous effects on the environment. Typically, fewer jobs are available than the number of workers who are drawn from the countryside to find work in the branch plants. This results in the growth of urban slums that suffer from high unemployment and unsanitary conditions. High-value components are often imported. Therefore, the branch plants create few good jobs involving design and technical expertise. Finally, some branch plants—particularly clothing and shoe factories in Asia—exploit children and women, requiring them to work long workdays at paltry wages and in unsafe conditions.

Companies, such as Nike and the Gap, have been widely criticized for conditions in their overseas sweatshops. Nike is the market leader in sports footwear. It has been at the forefront of moving production jobs overseas to such places as Indonesia. There, Nike factory workers make about 10 cents an hour. That is why labour costs account for only about 4 percent of the price of a pair of Nike shoes. Workdays in the factories stretch as long as 16 hours. Substandard air quality and excessive exposure to toxic chemicals, such as toluene, are normal. An international campaign aimed at curbing Nike's labour practices has had only a modest impact. For example, in 1999 wages in the Indonesian factories were raised about a penny an hour ("The Nike Campaign," 2000).

Meanwhile, the Gap has invested heavily in the Northern Mariana Islands near Guam. Strictly speaking, the Marianas are not a poor foreign country since they form a U.S. commonwealth territory with a status similar to that of Puerto Rico. But they might as well be. Garment manufacturing is the biggest source of income on the islands and the Gap (which also owns Banana Republic and Old Navy) is the biggest employer. What attracts the Gap to the Marianas are below-minimum-wage rates, duty-free access to American markets, and the right to sew "Made in U.S.A." labels on clothes manufactured there (Bank of Hawaii, 1999). However, work conditions are horrific. Many workers live in guarded dormitories surrounded by barbed wire, preventing their escape. And they work 12 to 18 hours a day without overtime pay. At the very least, cases like the Gap in the Marianas and Nike in Indonesia suggest that the benefits of foreign investment are unlikely to be uniformly valuable for the residents of developing countries in the short term.

The Future of Work and the Economy

Although work and the economy have changed enormously over the years, one thing has remained constant for centuries. Businesses have always looked for ways to cut costs and boost profits. Two of the most effective means they have adopted for accomplishing these goals involve introducing new technologies and organizing the workplace in more efficient ways. Much is uncertain about the future of work and the economy. However, it is a pretty safe bet that businesses will continue to follow these established practices.

Just how these practices will be implemented is less predictable. For example, it is possible to use technology and improved work organization to increase productivity by complementing the abilities of skilled workers. Worldwide, the automotive, aerospace, and

Some people in the rich, industrialized countries oppose the globalization of commerce. Shown here are demonstrators marching the streets of Calgary in June 2002 as part of a protest against the meeting of the G8 economic summit in Kananaskis, Alberta.

computer industries have tended to adopt this approach. They have introduced automation and robots on a wide scale. They constantly upgrade the skills of their workers. And they have proven the benefits of small autonomous work groups for product quality, worker satisfaction, and therefore the bottom line. Conversely, new technology and more efficient work organization can be used to replace workers, deskill jobs, and employ low-cost labour—mainly women and minority group members—on a large scale. Women are entering the labour force at a faster rate than men are. Competition from low-wage industries abroad remains intense. Therefore, the second option is especially tempting in some industries.

Our analysis suggests that each of the scenarios described above will tend to predominate in different industries. As a result, good jobs in the primary sector and bad jobs in the secondary sector are likely to continue. The pressure of competition will continue to prompt innovation and restructuring. However, we have also suggested that workplace struggles have no small bearing on how technologies are implemented and work is organized. To a degree, therefore, the future of work and the economy is up for grabs.

NOTES

1. There is not necessarily a contradiction between one aspect of the sociologist's and the neoclassical economist's approaches to markets. As markets become less regulated, average wealth may grow and the gap between rich and poor may increase at the same time. This is exactly what has been happening in the United States for nearly 30 years. Note also that a less influential school of economic thought known as *institutionalism* is much closer to the sociological perspective on markets than is the neoclassical school.

2. A *monopoly* is a single producer that completely dominates a market.

SUMMARY

1. How and when has work been subject to revolutionary transformations?
   The first work-related revolution began about 10 000 years ago when people established permanent settlements and started herding and farming. The second work-related

revolution began about 230 years ago when various mechanical devices, such as the steam engine, greatly increased the ability of producers to supply markets. The third revolution in work is marked by growth in the provision of various services. It accelerated in the final decades of the twentieth century with the widespread use of the computer.

2. How did the revolutions affect work?
Each revolution in work increased productivity and the division of labour, caused a sectoral shift in employment, and made work relations more hierarchical. However, for the past three decades the degree of hierarchy has been lowered in some industries, resulting in productivity gains and more worker satisfaction.

3. What trends changed work in the twentieth century?
Deskilling and the growth of part-time jobs were two of the main trends in the workplace in the twentieth century. However, skilled labour has remained very important in the economy.

4. What is happening to the numbers of good jobs and bad jobs?
Good jobs have become more plentiful but the number of bad jobs is also growing rapidly. The result is a segmentation of the labour force into primary and secondary labour markets. Various social barriers limit mobility from the secondary to the primary labour market.

5. How have workers responded to deskilling and efforts to increase control over jobs?
Workers have resisted attempts to deskill and control jobs. As a result, business has had to make concessions by giving workers more authority on the shop floor and in formulating overall business strategy. Such concessions have been biggest in countries where workers are more organized and powerful.

6. What groups have fostered internal labour markets and why have they done so?
Unions and professional organizations have established internal labour markets to control pay rates, hiring, and promotions in organizations and reduce competition with external labour supplies.

7. Can markets be classified as free versus regulated?
No. Markets are free or regulated to varying degrees. No market that is purely free or completely regulated could function for long. A purely free market would create unbearable inequalities and a completely regulated market would stagnate.

8. Who or what dominates today's economy?
Corporations are the dominant economic players in the world today. They exercise disproportionate economic and political influence by forming oligopolies, conglomerates, and interlocking directorates.

9. What strategies have corporations followed and how has this affected different groups?
Growing competition among multinational corporations has led big corporations to cut costs by building more and more branch plants in low-wage, low-tax countries. Stockholders have profited from this strategy. However, the benefits for workers in both the industrialized and the less developed countries have been mixed.

KEY TERMS

capitalism (p. 384)

codetermination (p. 378)

communism (p. 386)

conglomerates (p. 389)

corporations (p. 384)

deskilling (p. 370)

division of labour (p. 368)

economy (p. 366)

Fordism (p. 370)

free market (p. 381)

human relations school of
  management (p. 376)

interlocking directorates (p. 389)

internal labour markets (p. 379)

labour market segmentation (p. 375)

markets (p. 367)

oligopolies (p. 388)

primary labour market (p. 376)

productivity (p. 367)

professionals (p. 379)

quality of work life (p. 377)

regulated market (p. 381)

scientific management (p. 371)

secondary labour market (p. 376)

unions (p. 379)

QUESTIONS TO CONSIDER

1. Women are entering the labour force at a faster rate than men are. Members of visible minority ethnic groups are entering the labour force at a faster rate than whites are. What policies must companies adopt if they hope to see women and members of ethnic and racial minority groups achieve workplace equality with white men?

2. The computer is widely regarded as a labour-saving device and has been adopted on a wide scale. Yet, on average, many Canadians work more hours per week now than people in the same occupation did 20 or 30 years ago. How do you explain this paradox?

3. Most of the less developed countries have been eager to see multinational corporations establish branch plants on their soil. What sorts of policies must less developed countries adopt to ensure maximum benefits for their populations from these branch plants? Would it be beneficial if the less developed countries worked out a common approach to this problem rather than competing against each other for branch plants?

WEB RESOURCES

Companion Website for This Book

http://www.compass3e.nelson.com

Begin by clicking on the Student Resources section of the website. Next, select the chapter you are studying from the pull-down menu. From the Student Resources page you have easy access to InfoTrac® College Edition, additional Weblinks, and other resources. The website also has many useful tips to aid you in your study of sociology, including practice tests for each chapter.

InfoTrac® Search Terms

These search terms are provided to assist you in beginning to conduct research on this topic by visiting http://www.infotrac-college.com:

capitalism
deskilling
corporation
free market
communism

Recommended Websites

For information on the Canadian economy, trade, and jobs go to Industry Canada at http://www.ic.gc.ca.

http://www.compass3e.nelson.com

For the unionized workers' perspective, see the Canadian Labour Congress at http://www.clc-ctc.ca.

For research on social and economic justice, see the Canadian Centre for Policy Alternatives at http://www.policyalternatives.ca.

For information to help Canadians successfully participate in the workforce, go to Human Resources and Social Development Canada at http://www.hrsdc.gc.ca/en/home.shtml.

For international information on social justice and human and labour rights, see the International Labour Organization at http://www.ilo.org.

CengageNOW™

http://hed.nelson.com

This online diagnostic tool identifies each student's unique needs with a Pretest that generates a personalized Study Plan for each chapter, helping students focus on concepts they're having the most difficulty mastering. Students then take a Posttest after reading the chapter to measure their understanding of the material. An Instructor Gradebook is available to track and monitor student progress.

CHAPTER

14

Politics

In this chapter, you will learn that

- Political sociologists analyze the distribution of power in society and its consequences for political behaviour and public policy.

- Sociological disputes about the distribution of power often focus on how social structures, and especially class structures, influence political life.

- Some political sociologists analyze how state institutions and laws affect political behaviour and public policy.

- Three waves of democratization have swept the world in the past 180 years.

- Societies become highly democratic only when their citizens win legal protections of their rights and freedoms. This typically occurs when their middle and working classes become large, organized, and prosperous.

- Enduring social inequalities limit democracy even in the richest countries.

INTRODUCTION

Free Trade and Democracy

Just four days before what some people called the most important Canadian election of the twentieth century, the outcome seemed clear. A Gallup poll published November 17, 1988, showed the Liberals with a commanding 43 percent of the popular vote. The Progressive Conservatives (PCs) trailed far behind at 31 percent. The New Democratic Party (NDP) stood at 22 percent.

Then, a mere 100 hours before the first votes were cast, a little-known organization, the Canadian Alliance for Trade and Job Opportunities (CATJO), swung into high gear. With a campaign budget larger than that of the two opposition parties combined, CATJO funded a media blitz promoting the PCs and their free trade policies. A barrage of brochures, newspaper ads, and radio and television commercials supported the idea that Canadian prosperity depended on the removal of all taxes and impediments to trade between Canada and the United States. CATJO argued that if goods and services could be bought and sold across the border without hindrance, and capital invested without restraint, good jobs would proliferate and Canada's future would be assured.

Before the media blitz, an Angus Reid poll disclosed that most Canadians disagreed with CATJO's rosy assessment: 54 percent opposed free trade and 35 percent supported it. A majority of Canadians sensed that free trade might open Canada to harmful competition with giant American companies, thus leading to job losses and deteriorating living standards. Yet the CATJO onslaught succeeded in overcoming some of these fears. Its media campaign hammered the pro-free-trade message into the minds of the Canadian public and drew attention away from the opposition. Then, on election day, the unexpected happened. The PCs won with 43 percent of the popular vote. A mere six weeks later, on January 1, 1989, the Canada–U.S. Free Trade Agreement was implemented. In October 1992, as shown in the photo on this page, officials initialled the North American Free Trade Agreement, bringing Mexico into the free trade zone established in 1989 by Canada and the United States. The agreement went into effect January 1, 1994.

Who backed CATJO? Its sole sponsor was the Business Council on National Issues (BCNI), an organization comprising the chief executive officers of 150 of Canada's leading corporations. These were people with a clear stake in free trade. Their companies stood to benefit from increased business activity between Canada and the United States and unrestricted freedom to invest wherever profits promised to be higher (Richardson, 1996). The degree to which the Canadian people as a whole have benefited from free trade is a matter of ongoing debate.[1]

The 1988 free trade election raises important political questions. Does the victory of the PCs illustrate the operation of government "of the people, by the people, for the people," as Abraham Lincoln defined democracy in his famous speech at Gettysburg in 1863? The election certainly allowed a diverse range of Canadians to express conflicting views. In the end, the people did get the government they elected. This fact suggests that Lincoln's characterization of politics applied as well to Canada in 1988 as it did to the United States in 1863.

However, big business's access to a bulging war chest might lead us to doubt that Lincoln's definition applies. Few groups can act like CATJO and put together $18 million for a media campaign aimed at swaying the hearts and minds of the Canadian people. Should we therefore conclude that (in the words of one wit) Canada is a case of government "of the people, by the lawyers, for the businessmen"?[2]

Mexican, American, and Canadian ministers initial NAFTA in October 1992.

The free trade election of 1988 raises questions that lie at the heart of political sociology. What accounts for the degree to which a political system responds to the demands of all its citizens? As you will see, political sociologists have often answered this question by examining the effects of social structures, especially class structures, on politics. Although this approach contributes much to our understanding of political life, it is insufficient by itself. A fully adequate theory of democracy requires that we also examine how state institutions and laws affect political processes. We elaborate these points in the second section of this chapter.

From the mid-1970s until the early 1990s, a wave of competitive elections swept across many formerly non-democratic countries. Most dramatically, elections were held in the former Soviet Union at the end of this period. Many Western analysts were ecstatic. By the mid-1990s, however, it became clear that their optimism was naive. Often, the new regimes turned out to be feeble and limited democracies. As a result, political sociologists began to reconsider the social preconditions of democracy. We review of some of their work in this chapter's third section. We conclude that genuine democracy is not based just on elections. In addition, large classes of people must win legal protection of their rights and freedoms for democracy to take root and grow. This has not yet happened in most of the world. Finally, in this chapter's fourth section, we discuss some of the ways in which people step outside the rules of normal electoral politics to change society. We focus on two types of "politics by other means": war and terrorism.

Some analysts believe that politics in the rich industrialized countries is less likely to be shaped by class inequality in the future. Others hold that the marriage of home computers and elections will allow citizens to get more involved in politics by voting often and directly on the Internet. Our reading of the evidence is different. In concluding this chapter, we argue that persistent class inequality is the major barrier to the progress of democracy in such countries as Canada.

Before developing these themes, we define some key terms.

What Is Politics? Key Terms

Power is the ability to impose one's will on others.

Authority is legitimate, institutionalized power.

Traditional authority, the norm in tribal and feudal societies, involves rulers inheriting authority through family or clan ties. The right of a family or clan to monopolize leadership is widely believed to derive from the will of a god.

Legal-rational authority is typical of modern societies. It derives from respect for the law. Laws specify how a person can achieve office. People generally believe these laws are rational. If someone achieves office by following these laws, people respect his or her authority.

Charismatic authority is based on belief in the claims of extraordinary individuals that they are inspired by a god or some higher principle.

Politics is a machine that determines "who gets what, when, and how" (Lasswell, 1936). Power fuels the machine. **Power** is the ability to control others, even against their will (Weber, 1947: 152). Having more power than others do gives you the ability to get more valued things sooner. Having less power than others do means you get fewer valued things later. Political sociology's chief task is figuring out how power drives different types of political machines.

The use of power sometimes involves force. For example, one way of operating a system for distributing jobs, money, education, and other valued things is by throwing people who do not agree with the system in jail. In this case, people obey political rules because they are afraid to disobey. More often, however, people agree with the distribution system or at least accept it grudgingly. For instance, most people pay their taxes without much pressure from the Canada Revenue Agency. They pay their parking tickets without serving jail time. They recognize the right of their rulers to control the political machine. When most people basically agree with how the political machine is run, raw power becomes **authority**. Authority is legitimate, institutionalized power. Power is *legitimate* when people regard its use as morally correct or justified. Power is *institutionalized* when the norms and statuses of social organizations govern its use. These norms and statuses define how authority should be used, how individuals can achieve authority, and how much authority is attached to each status in the organization (see Box 14.1).

Max Weber (1947) described three ideal bases on which authority can rest (while stressing that real-world cases often rested on varying mixes of the pure types):

1. **Traditional authority.** Particularly in tribal and feudal societies, rulers inherit authority through family or clan ties. The right of a family or clan to monopolize leadership is widely believed to derive from the will of a god.
2. **Legal-rational authority.** In modern societies, authority derives from respect for the law. Laws specify how a person can achieve office. People generally believe these laws are rational. If someone achieves office by following these laws, his or her authority is respected.

BOX 14.1
Sociology at the Movies

Gangs of New York (2002)

Most nation-states may be imposing structures but there was a time when little was solid, when every nation-state lacked legitimacy in the eyes of many of its citizens, contending groups vied for dominance, violence was widely used to secure power, all was in the balance, and it was uncertain how things would turn out. Martin Scorsese's *Gangs of New York* recounts such a time: New York between the 1840s and the American Civil War.

"The forge of hell" is the way one character describes the city. Elections are rigged, city officials sell their services to the highest bidder, fire fighters loot the buildings they "save," rival police forces brawl in the streets, the poor riot against the draft, Union soldiers force immigrants straight off the boat into uniform, and an audience greets an actor playing Abraham Lincoln with volleys of rotten fruit. At the centre of it all are the mobs of Irish immigrants who battle second- and third- generation "nativists" for political control—the Irish, led by Priest Vallon (Liam Neeson), the nativists led by the vicious William Cutting, widely known as Bill the Butcher (played by Daniel Day-Lewis, who was nominated for a Best Actor Oscar for his performance). With a ferocity unrivalled in the history of cinema, the gangs attack each other on the Lower East Side of Manhattan. When the dust

Amsterdam (Leonardo DiCaprio) leads his men to battle in *Gangs of New York*.

settles, Priest Vallon's young son, Amsterdam (Leonardo DiCaprio), swears to avenge his father's death.

At the level of its individual characters, the film is motivated by Amsterdam's quest. But because Scorsese is blessed with a deep sociological understanding of his subject matter, the individual characters become vehicles for a larger story, the chaotic origins of the American state. In the 1860s, New York was practically destroyed when the poor refused to be drafted to fight in the Civil War. They rioted and looted wealthy neighbourhoods until government ships in the harbour fired their cannons on them and troops marched in to silence them once and for all. The American state

was, in fact, weak well into the 1870s, when it was still common for independent militias funded by wealthy local capitalists to counter labour unrest and riots by the poor (Isaacs, 2002).

In the final scene of *Gangs of New York,* an adult Amsterdam stands in a graveyard with his girlfriend, Jenny Everdeane (Cameron Diaz), remembering the victims of the Draft Riots. The scene fast forwards, and as it does, Amsterdam and Jenny disappear while the tombstones fade and vegetation grows over them. The camera pans up to focus on the familiar skyline of New York, solid and seemingly eternal. Thanks to *Gangs of New York,* however, we remember the frailty of all states and their conflict-ridden origins.

3. **Charismatic authority**. Sometimes, extraordinary and charismatic individuals challenge traditional or legal-rational authority. They claim to be inspired by a god or some higher principle that transcends other forms of authority. Most people believe this claim. One such principle is the idea that all people are created equal. Charismatic figures sometimes emerge during a **political revolution**, an attempt by many people to overthrow existing political institutions and establish new ones. Political revolutions take place when widespread and successful movements of opposition clash with crumbling traditional or legal-rational authority.

A **political revolution** is the overthrow of political institutions by an opposition movement and its replacement by new institutions.

The three faces of authority according to Weber: traditional authority (King Louis XIV of France, circa 1670), charismatic authority (Vladimir Lenin, Bolshevik leader of the Russian Revolution of 1917), and legal-rational authority (Stephen Harper campaigning before the 2008 Canadian federal election).

The **state** consists of the institutions responsible for formulating and carrying out a country's laws and public policies.

Civil society is the private sphere of social life.

Authoritarian states sharply restrict citizen control of the state.

In a **totalitarian** state, citizens lack almost any control of the state.

In a **democracy**, citizens exercise a high degree of control over the state. They do this mainly by choosing representatives in regular, competitive elections.

Politics takes place in all social settings. Such settings include intimate face-to-face relationships, families, and universities. However, political sociology is mainly concerned with institutions that specialize in the exercise of power and authority. Taken together, these institutions form the **state**. The state comprises institutions that formulate and carry out a country's laws and public policies. In performing these functions, the state regulates citizens in **civil society**. Civil society is "made up of areas of social life—the domestic world, the economic sphere, cultural activities and political interaction—which are organized by private or voluntary arrangements between individuals and groups outside the direct control of the state" (Held, 1987: 281; see Figure 14.1).

In turn, citizens in civil society control the state to varying degrees. In an **authoritarian** state, citizen control is sharply restricted. In a **totalitarian** state, it is virtually nonexistent. In a **democracy**, citizens exert a relatively high degree of control over the state. They do this partly by choosing representatives in regular, competitive elections.

In modern democracies, citizens do not control the state directly. They do so through several organizations. **Political parties** compete for control of government in regular elections. They put forward policy alternatives and rally adult citizens to vote. Special interest groups, such as trade unions and business associations, form **lobbies**. They advise politicians about their members' desires. They also remind politicians how much their members' votes, organizing skills, and campaign contributions matter. The **mass media** keep a watchful and critical eye on the state. They keep the public informed about the quality of government. **Public opinion** refers to the values and attitudes of the adult population as a whole. It is expressed mainly in polls and letters to lawmakers, and it gives politicians a reading of citizen preferences. Finally, when

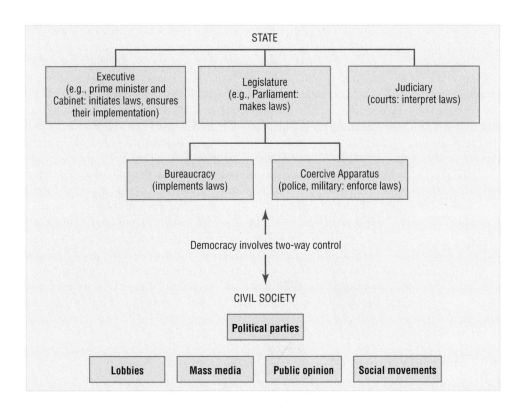

FIGURE 1

The Insti

and Civil

dissatisfaction with normal politics is widespread, protest sometimes takes the form of **social movements**. A social movement is a collective attempt to change all or part of the political or social order. Social movements help to keep governments responsive to the wishes of the citizenry (see Chapter 21, Collective Action and Social Movements).

Bearing these definitions in mind, we now consider the merits and limitations of five sociological theories of democracy.

THEORIES OF DEMOCRACY

Pluralist Theory

In the early 1950s, New Haven, Connecticut, was a city of about 150 000 people. It had seen better times. As in many other American cities, post–World War II prosperity and new roads had allowed much of the white middle class to resettle in the suburbs. This move eroded the city's tax base. It also left much of the downtown to poor residents and members of minority groups. Some parts of New Haven became slums.

Beginning in 1954, Mayor Richard Lee decided to do something about the city's decline. He planned to attract new investment, eliminate downtown slums, and stem the outflow of the white middle class. Urban renewal was a potentially divisive issue. However, according to research conducted at the time, key decisions were made in a highly democratic manner. The city government listened closely to all major groups. It adopted policies that reflected the diverse wants and interests of city residents.

The social scientists who studied New Haven politics in the 1950s followed **pluralist theory** (Dahl, 1961; Polsby, 1959). They argued that the city was highly democratic because power was widely dispersed. They showed that few of the most prestigious families in New Haven were economic leaders in the community. Moreover, neither economic leaders nor the social elite monopolized political decision making. Different groups of people decided various political issues. Some of these people had low status in the community.

Political parties are organizations that compete for control of government. In the process, they give voice to policy alternatives and rally adult citizens to vote.

Lobbies are organizations formed by special interest groups to advise and influence politicians.

The mass media are print, radio, television, and other communication technologies. In a democracy, the mass media help keep the public informed about the quality of government.

Public opinion refers to the values and attitudes of the adult population as a whole.

Social movements are collective attempts to change all or part of the political or social order by means of rioting, petitioning, striking, demonstrating, and establishing lobbies, unions, and political parties.

.uralist theory holds that power is widely dispersed. As a result, no group enjoys disproportionate influence, and decisions are usually reached through negotiation and compromise.

Moreover, power was more widely distributed than in earlier decades. The pluralists concluded that no single group exercised disproportionate power in New Haven.

The pluralists believed that politics worked much the same way in the United States as a whole and in other democracies, such as Canada, too. Democracies, they said, are heterogeneous societies with many competing interests and centres of power. None of these power centres can dominate consistently. The owners of Stelco, for instance, may want tariffs on steel imports to protect the company's Canadian market. Meanwhile, the owners of General Motors Canada may oppose tariffs on steel because they want to keep their company's production costs down. The idea that "industry" speaks with one voice is thus a myth. Competing interests exist even within one industrial group, such as the automobile industry. For instance, a company like Vancouver's Ballard Power, a world leader in the production of electric fuel cells, may favour tougher clean air laws now. A company specializing in the production of internal combustion engines may favour a go-slow approach to such laws. Because there is so much heterogeneity between and within groups, no single group can control political life. Sometimes one category of voters or one set of interest groups wins a political battle, sometimes another. Most often, however, politics involves negotiation and compromise between competing groups. Because no one group is always able to control the political agenda or the outcome of political conflicts, democracy is guaranteed, argued the pluralists.

Elite Theory

Elite theory holds that small groups occupying the command posts of the most influential institutions make the important decisions that profoundly affect all members of society. Moreover, they do so without much regard for elections or public opinion.

Elites are small groups that control the command posts of institutions.

A **ruling class** is a self-conscious, cohesive group of people in elite positions. They act to advance their common interests, and corporate executives lead them.

Elite theorists, C. Wright Mills (1956) chief among them, sharply disagreed with the pluralist argument. According to Mills, **elites** are small groups that occupy the command posts of a society's most influential institutions. In the United States, the country Mills analyzed, these institutions include the 200 to 300 biggest corporations, the executive branch of government, and the military. Mills wrote that the people (nearly all men) who control these institutions make important decisions that profoundly affect all members of society. Moreover, they do so without much regard for elections or public opinion.

Mills showed how the corporate, state, and military elites are connected. People move from one elite group to another during their careers. Their children intermarry. They maintain close social contacts. They tend to be recruited from upper-middle and upper classes. Yet Mills denied that these connections turn the three elites into what Marx called a **ruling class**. A ruling class is a self-conscious and cohesive group of people, led by corporate executives, who act to shore up capitalism. The three elites are relatively independent of one another, Mills insisted. They may see eye to eye on many issues, but each has its own sphere of influence. Conflict among elite groups is frequent (Alford and Friedland, 1985: 199; Mills, 1956: 277).

The Elitist Critique of Pluralism

Most political sociologists today question the pluralist account of democratic politics. That is because research has established the existence of large, persistent, wealth-based inequalities in political influence and political participation.

John Porter's classic work, *The Vertical Mosaic* (1965), was the first in a series of Canadian studies that demonstrate the weaknesses of pluralism and corroborate some aspects of elite theory (Brym, 1989; Clement, 1975; Olsen, 1980). These studies show that a disproportionately large number of people in Canada's political and other elites come from upper-class and upper-middle-class families. For example, about 40 percent of Canadian prime ministers, premiers, and Cabinet ministers were born into the richest 10 percent of families in the country (Olsen, 1980: 129). In their youth, members of Canada's elite are likely to have attended expensive private schools. As adults, they tend to marry the offspring of other elite members and belong to exclusive private clubs. In the course of their careers, they often move from one elite group to another. Arguably, people with this sort of background cannot act dispassionately on behalf of all Canadians, rich and poor. Controversy persists over whether Canada's elites form a ruling class. Porter (1965), noting frequent conflict among elites, argued against the view that a ruling class controls Canada.

His top students disagreed. They argued that the interests of large corporations dominate Canadian political life (Clement, 1975; Olsen, 1980). However, both Porter and his students did agree on one point: Contrary to pluralist claims, Canada's well-to-do consistently exercise disproportionate influence over political life in this country.

Studies of political participation in Canada add weight to the elitist view (Blais, Gidengil, Nadeau, and Nevitte, 1997; Frank, 1992; Mishler, 1979: 88–97). Many surveys show that political involvement decreases with social class (see also Box 14.2). For example, the likelihood of voting falls with a person's class position. The likelihood of phoning or writing a member of Parliament, helping a candidate in an election

---

BOX 14.2
It's Your Choice

Increasing the Participation of Women in Canadian Politics

Just as political participation decreases with social class, so it varies by gender. On the whole, women are less politically active than men. The gender gap in political participation is due to sociological and historical factors. It has been reduced by political pressure and resulting public policy innovations. It can be further reduced by the same means.

By demonstrating, petitioning, and gaining the support of influential liberal-minded men, Canadian women won the right to vote federally in 1917 and in Yukon and all provinces except Quebec by 1925. Quebec fell into line in 1940 and the Northwest Territories only in 1951. Some women have since been elected to Parliament and to provincial and territorial legislatures. As of 2008, about 22 percent of federal members of Parliament and provincial or territorial members of legislative assemblies were women. However, critics emphasize that this level was reached in the later 1990s and subsequently stabilized. Over that same period, slightly fewer women were put forward as candidates by their parties. Many fewer women have been appointed to Cabinet positions both federally and provincially or territorially; and once, for four months (June to October 1993), Canada had a female prime minister (Kim Campbell). As

Kim Campbell, Canada's only female prime minister, June to October 1993

these facts suggest, the more influential the type of political activity, the fewer women we find (Bashevkin, 1993; Equal Voice, 2005).

Active involvement in political life, especially running for office, requires time and money. Women are disadvantaged in this regard. As you saw in Chapter 11 (Sexuality and Gender), women have lower socioeconomic status than men do on average. Women are also saddled with more

domestic responsibilities than men are. These factors prevent many women from running for office. In addition, political parties influence the nomination of candidates for elected office and thus help determine where women run. Most parties tend to assign female candidates to ridings where chances of winning are low (Brodie, 1991).

Public policy analysts note that female political participation can increase if these barriers are removed (Boyd, 2001; Brodie, 1991). For example, laws could be passed that would allow candidates to take unpaid leave from their jobs to contest nominations and elections, set spending limits for nomination and election campaigns, make contributions for nomination campaigns tax deductible, treat child-care and housekeeping costs as reimbursable campaign expenses, and so forth. Additionally, laws could be enacted that make government subsidies to political party campaigns dependent on the proportion of their elected candidates that are women. In such a system, party subsidies would increase with the proportion of women elected, thus creating a powerful disincentive for parties to place most female candidates in ridings where they are likely to lose. Thus, the means to increase the participation of women in politics are available. Whether these means are implemented is your choice.

FIGURE 14.2

Federal Political
Contributors, by Income
and Region, Canada

Note: Data are from 1988.

Source: Adapted from Statistics
Canada, "Voting and contributing:
Political participation in Canada,"
Canadian Social Trends, Catalogue
11-008, Winter 1992, no. 27.

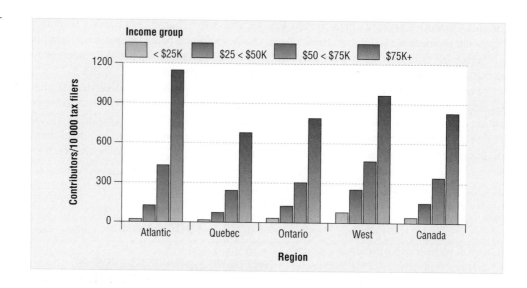

campaign, contributing money to a political party, and running for office declines even
more steeply as we move down the class hierarchy. As intensity of political participation
declines, so does political influence (Eagles, 1993). Consequently, although political
apathy and cynicism are high among Canadians, the poorest Canadians are the most politically apathetic and cynical. They have less interest in politics than the well-to-do and they
are more likely to think that government does not care what they think (see Figures 14.2
and 14.3). As one of the world's leading political sociologists wrote, "The combination of
a low vote and a relative lack of organization among the lower-status groups means that
they will suffer from neglect by the politicians who will be receptive to the wishes of the
more privileged, participating, and organized strata" (Lipset, 1981: 226–27).

Marxist Rejoinders to Elite Theory

Although compelling in some respects, elite theory has its critics, Marxists foremost among
them. Some Marxists, known as "instrumentalists," deny that elites enjoy more or less equal
power. Actually, they say, elites form a ruling class dominated by big business. From their
point of view, the state, for example, is an arm (or "instrument") of the business elite. Big
business gains control of the state in three main ways. First, members of wealthy families
occupy important state positions in highly disproportionate numbers. Second, government

FIGURE 14.3

Political Apathy and
Cynicism, by Annual
Household Income, Canada,
2004

Source: From Blais, Gidengil,
Nevitte, Fournier, and Everitt, 2005;
Canadian Election Study 2004
data set at http://www.ces-eec.
umontreal.ca.

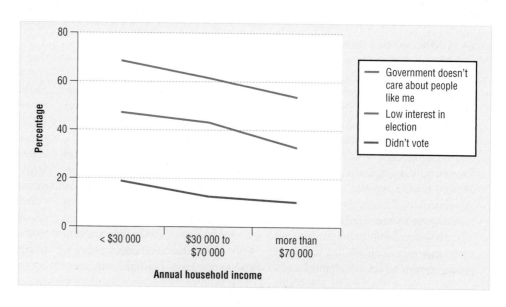

officials rely mainly on the representatives of big business for advice. Third, political parties rely mainly on big business for financial support. According to some Marxists, members of different elites may disagree about specific issues. However, as a result of the three control mechanisms listed above, they always agree about one issue: the need to maintain the health of the capitalist system (Miliband, 1973 [1969]).

A second group of Marxists, known as "structuralists," offers a somewhat different interpretation of why the state in capitalist society is necessarily biased in favour of big business. For the structuralists, it is not so much the *social origins* of high government officials or the *social ties* linking them with big business that encourages the state to act with a pro-capitalist bias. Rather, they argue, the capitalist state acts as an arm of big business because it is constrained to do so by *the nature of the capitalist system itself*. For example, if Canadian government officials take actions that deeply damage capitalist interests, investment would be redirected to countries with regimes that are kinder to company profits. Such a move would cost Canada jobs and prosperity. It would be highly unpopular. The government could easily fall. Fearing this outcome, governments in capitalist societies find their field of action restricted to policies that ensure the well-being of big business. According to the structuralists, it is the very fact that the state is embedded in a capitalist system that forces it to act in this way (Poulantzas, 1975 [1968]).

It follows from both the instrumentalist and the structuralist positions that ordinary citizens, and especially members of the working class, rarely have much influence over state policy. According to Marxists, true democracy can emerge only if members of the working class and their supporters overthrow capitalism and establish a socialist system (see Chapter 13, Work and the Economy).

Power Resource Theory

Both Marxist and elite theories leave some big questions unanswered. For one thing, they pay little attention to how political parties lose office while other political parties get elected. Nor are they much concerned with the effect of one party or another on public policy. In fact, for Marxist and elite theorists, elections are little more than sideshows. They believe that elites or a ruling class always control society, regardless of election outcomes. Therefore, they contend, the victory of one party over another does not deserve much sociological attention because it does not substantially affect the lives of ordinary men and women.

In contrast, many political sociologists today think it matters a great deal which party is in office. After all, the lives of ordinary men and women are hugely affected by whether the governing party supports or opposes free trade, weaker environmental standards, less publicly funded medical care, bigger government subsidies for child care, abortion on demand, and so forth. Elite theorists are correct to claim that power is concentrated disproportionately in the hands of the well-to-do. But we still need a theory that accounts for the successes and failures of different parties and policies in different times and places.

That is where **power resource theory** is helpful. It focuses on how *variations* in the distribution of power affect the fortunes of parties and policies. To understand power resource theory, first consider your own party preference. For many reasons, you may support one political party over another. For instance, your family may have a long tradition of voting for one party. You may have never really questioned this support. Maybe you support a party because you admire the energy, integrity, or track record of its leader. Or you might support a party because you agree with its policies on a range of issues. What factors lead *you* to prefer one party over another?

If a party's policies influence your vote, you are like many Canadians. In fact, Canadian voters cluster in two main policy groups. Voters on the *left* promote extensive government involvement in the economy. Among other things, this means they favour a strong "social safety net" of health and welfare benefits to help the less fortunate members of society. As a result, left-wing policies often lead to less economic inequality.

Power resource theory holds that the distribution of power among major classes partly accounts for the successes and failures of different political parties.

WHERE DO
YOU FIT IN?

In contrast, voters on the *right* favour a reduced role for government in the economy. They want to see a smaller welfare state and emphasize the importance of individual initiative in promoting economic growth. Economic issues aside, leftists and rightists also tend to differ on social or moral issues. Leftists tend to support equal rights for women and racial and sexual minorities. Rightists tend to support more traditional social and moral values.[3]

Figure 14.4 shows one indicator of how left and right sentiments translated into support for Canada's five political parties in 2004. Using data from the 2004 Canadian Election Survey, we first found, for supporters of each political party, the percentage of people who favour tax increases for expanded social programs. This is one indicator of the percentage of people on the left. We then found the percentage of people who support tax cuts for reduced social programs. This is one indicator of the percentage of people on the right. Finally, we subtracted the percentage on the right from the percentage on the left. This difference is what we call the "left-right index." Positive values indicate how far to the left each party's supporters are while negative values record a predominance of supporters of a right agenda. Clearly, there are big differences between parties. Supporters of the Conservatives are farthest to the right. Supporters of the Liberals and of the Bloc are slightly left, while the Greens and the New Democrats draw more support from the left. Do you think of yourself as a supporter of one of these parties? Is your choice related to its policies?

The policies favoured by different parties have different effects on different groups of people. Therefore, different parties tend to be supported by different classes, regions, religious groups, races, and other groups. Do you think the policies of your preferred party favour the class, region, religious group, or race to which you belong? If so, how? If not, why not?

In most Western democracies, one of the main factors that distinguishes political parties is differences in *class* support (Korpi, 1983: 35; Lipset and Rokkan, 1967; Manza, Hout, and Brooks, 1995). But the tendency for people in different classes to vote for different parties varies from one country to the next. In Canada, the tendency is relatively weak.

The strength of the tendency for people in different classes to vote for different parties depends on many factors. One of the most important is how socially organized or cohesive classes are (Brym with Fox, 1989: 57–91; Brym, Gillespie, and Lenton, 1989). For example, an upper class that can create such organizations as the Business Council on National Issues and CATJO, which supported the PCs so effectively in the 1988 free

FIGURE 14.4

How Did Canada's Political Parties Vary from Left to Right in 2004?

Note: The left versus right index is the percentage of each party's supporters who favour enhanced social spending supported by tax increases minus the percentage who favour reduced social spending and tax cuts.

Source: From Blais, Gidengil, Nevitte, Fournier, and Everitt, 2005; Canadian Election Study 2004 data set, at http://www.ces-eec.umontreal.ca.

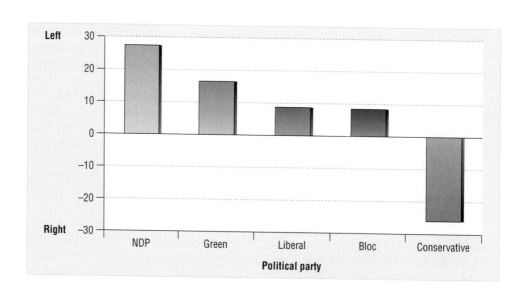

trade election, is more powerful than an upper class that cannot take such action. If an upper class makes such efforts, while a working class fails to organize itself, right-wing candidates have a better chance of winning office. Conservative policies are more likely to become law. Similarly, a working class that can unionize many workers is more powerful than one with few unionized workers. That is because unions often collect money for the party that is more sympathetic to union interests. They also lobby on behalf of their members and try to convince members to vote for the pro-union party. If workers become more unionized, while an upper class fails to organize itself, then left-wing candidates have an improved chance of winning office. Policies that favour lower classes are more likely to become law. This is the main insight of power resource theory. *Organization is a source of power. Change in the distribution of power between major classes partly accounts for the fortunes of different political parties and different laws and policies* (Esping-Andersen, 1990; Korpi, 1983; O'Connor and Olsen, 1998; Shalev, 1983).

You can see how power resource theory works by looking at Table 14.1. This table compares 18 industrialized democracies in the three decades after World War II. It divides the countries into three groups. In group one are such countries as Sweden, where socialist parties usually controlled governments. (Socialist parties are at least as left wing as the NDP in Canada.) In group two are such countries as Australia, where socialist parties sometimes controlled, or shared in the control of, governments. And in group three are such countries as Canada, where socialist parties rarely or never shared in the control of governments. The group averages in column two show that socialist parties are generally more successful in countries where workers are more unionized. The group averages in columns three and four show more economic inequality exists in countries that are weakly unionized and have no socialist governments. In other words, by means of taxes and social policies, socialist governments ensure that the rich earn a smaller percentage of national income and the poor form a smaller percentage of the population. Studies of pensions, medical care, and other state benefits in the rich industrialized democracies reach similar conclusions. In general, where working classes are more organized and powerful, disadvantaged people are economically better off (Lindert, 2004; Myles 1989; O'Connor and Brym, 1988; Olsen and Brym, 1996).

Class is not the only factor that distinguishes political parties. Historically, *religion* has also been an important basis of party differences. For example, in Western European

GLOBAL PERSPECTIVE

	Percentage of Non-agricultural Workforce Unionized	Percentage of Total National Income to Top 10% of Earners	Percentage Poor
Mainly socialist countries (Sweden, Norway)	68.5	21.8	4.3
Partly socialist countries (Austria, Australia, Denmark, Belgium, UK, New Zealand, Finland)	46.6	23.6	7.8
Mainly non-socialist countries (Ireland, West Germany, Netherlands, USA, Japan, Canada, France, Italy, Switzerland)	28.0	28.3	10.8

TABLE 14.1

Some Consequences of Working-Class Power in 18 Rich Industrialized Countries, 1946–1976

Note: "Percentage Poor" is the average percentage of the population living in relative poverty according to OECD standards, with poverty line standardized according to household size.

Source: Korpi, 1983: 40, 196.

In the 2002 election for the French presidency, right-wing candidate Jean-Marie Le Pen placed second. Le Pen's anti-immigrant campaign highlighted the degree to which political cleavages in France are based not just on class but also on race.

State-centred theory holds that the state itself can structure political life, to some degree independently of the way power is distributed between classes and other groups at a given time.

countries with large Catholic populations, such as Switzerland and Belgium, parties are distinguished partly by the religious affiliation of their supporters. In recent decades, *ethnicity and race* have become cleavage factors of major and growing importance in some countries. For example, in the United States, African Americans have overwhelmingly supported the Democratic Party since the 1960s (Brooks and Manza, 1997). Ethnicity has become an increasingly important division in French politics. This is due to heavy Arab immigration from Algeria, Morocco, and Tunisia since the 1950s and growing anti-immigration sentiment among a substantial minority of whites (Veugelers, 1997). *Regional* groups distinguish parties in other countries, such as Canada. In this country, some parties have been particularly attractive to Westerners, others to Québécois. Power resource theory focuses mainly on how the shifting distribution of power between working and upper classes affects electoral success. However, we can also use the theory to analyze the electoral fortunes of parties that attract different religious groups, races, regional groups, and so on.

State-Centred Theory

Democratic politics is a contest among various class, racial, ethnic, religious, and regional groups to control the state for their own advantage. When power is substantially redistributed because of such factors as change in the cohesiveness of these social groups, old ruling parties usually fall and new ones take office.

Note, however, that a winner-take-all strategy would be nothing short of foolish. If winning parties passed laws that benefited only their supporters, they might cause mass outrage and even violent opposition. Yet it would be bad politics to allow opponents to become angry, organized, and resolute. After all, winners want more than just a moment of glory. They want to be able to enjoy the spoils of office over the long haul. To achieve stability, they must give people who lose elections a voice in government. That way, even determined opponents are likely to recognize the government's legitimacy. Pluralists thus make a good point when they say that democratic politics is about accommodation and compromise. They lose sight only of how accommodation and compromise typically give more advantages to some rather than others, as both elite theorists and power resource theorists stress.

There is, however, more to the story of politics than conflict between classes, religious groups, regions, and so forth. Theda Skocpol and others who follow **state-centred theory** show how the state itself can structure political life (Block, 1979; Evans, Rueschemeyer, and Skocpol, 1985; Skocpol, 1979). They regard senior elected officials and state bureaucrats not as agents of economic elites but as major political players in their own right. Moreover, they hold that major political struggles become embodied in the very structure of states. That is, historically important political battles typically end with the passage of new laws and the creation of new political institutions. These laws and institutions go on to influence political life until political conflict becomes serious enough to alter them once again. Until then, the state influences political life *to some degree independently of day-to-day political conflict and the distribution of power at a given point in time.* This argument is a valuable supplement to power resource theory.

To illustrate state-centred theory, recall first that all societies are divided into different classes, religious groups, regions, and so forth. In principle, any one or a combination of these social divisions may be reflected in the policies of different political parties and the social characteristics of party supporters. For example, in some societies, politics is mostly about the attempts of different *classes* to control the state for their own advantage; in other societies, politics is more about the attempts of different *regions* to control the state for their own advantage; and so forth. What then determines which social division—class, region, or another factor—will predominate in political life? State-centred theory provides useful insights into this issue. According to state-centred theory, the state may be organized in such a way as to bias politics toward one social division or another.

Consider the Canadian case. We saw above that different Canadian political parties tend to attract people from different social classes. However, that tendency is weak. Compared with most other democracies, class differences among parties are small in Canada. In contrast, regional differences are comparatively large (Butovsky, 2001; Gidengil, 1992). These large regional differences are evident, for example, in the results of the 2008 federal election (see Figure 14.5).

The results show that, in Quebec, the most popular federal political party is the Bloc Québécois. Although Quebec voters have twice rejected referenda calling for sovereignty, Bloc supporters generally favour holding another referendum in the hope of achieving the separation of Quebec from Canada. The Conservative Party grew from a merger between the Conservative Alliance, which was almost entirely limited to the West, and the remnants of the Progressive Conservatives, mainly from Ontario eastward, excluding Quebec. The former Conservative Alliance members retain a strong belief that the central government neglects Western interests and include those who have advocated separation from Canada as the ultimate remedy.

The Liberals usually win more seats in Ontario than in any other region (although Atlantic Canada strongly supported the Liberals in 2008) but they claim to be the only truly national party in the country. Few Westerners and Québécois see the Liberals that way; they think the Liberals strongly favour central-Canadian interests. The outcome of

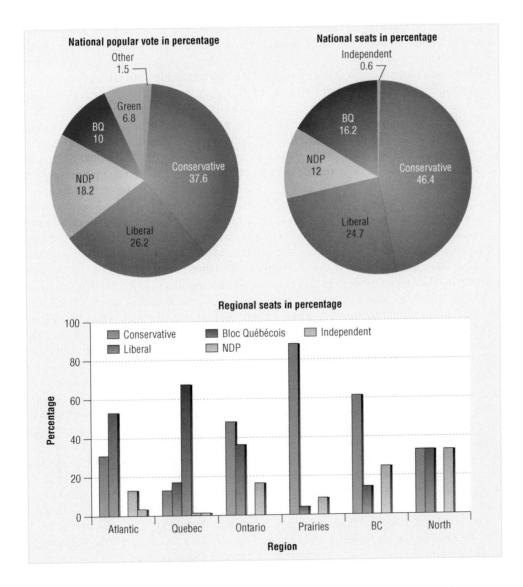

FIGURE 14.5

Results of 2008 Canadian Federal Election

Source: Elections Canada, 2008, "40th General Election." Retrieved October 16, 2008 (http://enr. elections ca). Adapted by Robert Brym.

the 2008 election continues a long national tradition: Politics in Canada focuses on contests among regions seeking to steer state power to their advantage.

Why? What is it that produces such a strong regional bias (and a correspondingly weak class bias) in Canadian political life? The answer lies in the history of Canadian politics and, in particular, in the way that history has structured the laws and policies of the Canadian state. In other words, the explanation for the regional bias of Canadian politics is state-centred.

Before Confederation in 1867, the British North American colonies enjoyed few unifying ties. Vast geographical barriers separated them. No railway or telegraph line linked them. Lower Canada (now Quebec) had become part of British North America by military conquest just a century earlier. It was still divided from the other colonies by religion (Catholic versus Protestant), ethnicity (French versus English), and lingering resentment.

Despite these deep divisions, British North American businessmen tried to forge a union among the colonies in the mid-1860s. They did so because they faced a huge problem that only unification could solve: the loss of their export markets. The British were dismantling the protected market known as the British Empire. The Americans had turned against free trade. To make matters worse, the British North American colonies had accumulated a crippling debt load (mainly through borrowing money to help finance railroad construction), while certain elements in the United States were threatening to expand the border of their country northward. In this context, the business and political leaders of British North America regarded Confederation as a means of creating a new market and an expanded tax base by encouraging mass immigration and promoting economic growth.

To forge a union, however, the Fathers of Confederation had to be careful. For one thing, they had to avoid consulting ordinary citizens for fear of having their plan rejected. They knew the colonies had little in common and that most ordinary citizens had no interest in union. As Canada's first prime minister, John A. Macdonald, wrote in October 1866 to Leonard Tilley, New Brunswick's Father of Confederation: "The [passage of the British North America Act] must be carried out *per saltum* [in one leap], and no echo of it must reverberate through the British provinces till it becomes law. . . . The Act once passed and beyond remedy the people would soon learn to be reconciled to it" (quoted in Ryerson, 1973: 355).

In addition, the Fathers of Confederation also found it necessary to draft a founding document, the British North America (BNA) Act, that played down the deep divisions between the British North American colonies. Most important, the BNA Act left ambiguous the question of how power would be distributed between federal and provincial governments. This vagueness enabled the Fathers of Confederation to forge their union, but it also left the door open to the bickering and bargaining that has characterized federal–provincial/territorial relations ever since 1867. Especially after World War II, the BNA Act (and later the Canadian Constitution) allowed power to continue to drift from the federal to the provincial and territorial governments and thus entrenched regionalism in Canadian political life.

A landmark in the decentralization and regionalization of Canadian politics was reached in 1959. In that year, Quebec and the federal government agreed that a provincial or territorial government not wanting to participate in a federal program could receive federal funds to set up its own parallel program. Thereafter, the provincial and territorial right to opt out of federal programs was widely used not just by Quebec but also by the other provinces and territories, which insisted on having the same rights as Quebec (Bélanger, 2000). Power continued to decentralize and regionalize as the provinces gained more control over taxation, resource revenues, immigration policy, language use, and so on. Canada was a deeply regionally divided society from the start, and the state—through the country's basic laws and policies—entrenched regional divisions. The result was a country in which politics is defined less as a struggle between classes than as a struggle between regions (Brym, 1992).[4] Said differently, from the perspective of state-centred theory, class

	Pluralist	Elite	Marxist	Power-Resource	State-Centred
How is power distributed?	Dispersed	Concentrated	Concentrated	Concentrated	Concentrated
Who are the main power holders?	Various groups	Elites	Ruling class	Upper class	State officials
On what is their power based?	Holding political office	Controlling major institutions	Owning substantial capital	Owning substantial capital	Holding political office
What is the main basis of public policy?	The will of all citizens	The interests of major elites	Capitalist interests	The balance of power among classes, etc.	The influence of state structures
Do lower classes have much influence on politics?	Yes	No	Rarely	Sometimes	Sometimes

TABLE 14.2

Five Sociological Theories of Capitalist Democracy Compared

conflict is given less voice than is regional conflict in Canada because of the way the state structures politics.

In sum, political sociology has made good progress since the 1950s. Each of the field's major schools has made a useful contribution to our appreciation of political life (see Table 14.2). Pluralists teach us that democratic politics is about compromise and the accommodation of all group interests. Elite theorists teach us that, despite accommodation and compromise, power is concentrated in the hands of high-status groups, whose interests the political system serves best. Power resource theorists teach us that, despite the concentration of power in society, substantial shifts in the distribution of power do occur, and they have big effects on voting patterns and public policies. And state-centred theorists teach us that state structures also exert an important effect on politics.

We now turn to an examination of the historical development of democracy, its sociological underpinnings, and its future.

THE FUTURE OF DEMOCRACY

Two Cheers for Russian Democracy

In 1989, the Institute of Sociology of the Russian Academy of Science invited Robert Brym and nine other Canadian sociologists to attend a series of seminars in Moscow. The seminars were designed to acquaint some leading sociologists in the Soviet Union with Western sociology. The country was in the midst of a great thaw. Totalitarianism was melting, leaving democracy in its place. Soviet sociologists had never been free to read and research what they wanted, and they were eager to learn from North American and European scholars (Brym, 1990).

"Or at least so it seemed," says Robert. "One evening about a dozen of us were sitting around comparing the merits of Canadian whisky and Russian vodka. Soon, conversation turned from Crown Royal versus Moskovskaya to Russian politics. 'You must be so excited about what's happening here,' I said to my Russian hosts. 'How long do you think it will be before Russia will have multi-party elections? Do you think Russia will become a liberal democracy, like Canada, or a socialist democracy, like Sweden?'

PERSONAL ANECDOTE

Although luxury businesses, like Versace, do brisk business in Moscow, the streets are filled with homeless people. That is because the richest 10 percent of Russians earn 15 times as much as the poorest 10 percent, making Russia one of the most inegalitarian countries in the world.

"One white-haired Russian sociologist slowly rose to his feet. His colleagues privately called him 'the dinosaur.' It soon became clear why. '*Nikogda*,' he said calmly and deliberately—'never.' '*Nikogda*,' he repeated, his voice rising sharply in pitch, volume, and emphasis. Then, for a full minute he explained that capitalism and democracy were never part of Russia's history, nor could they be expected to take root in Russian soil. 'The Russian people,' he proclaimed, 'do not want a free capitalist society. We know *freedom* means the powerful are free to compete unfairly against the powerless, exploit them, and create social inequality.'

"Everyone else in the room disagreed with the dinosaur's speech, in whole or in part. But not wanting to cause any more upset, we turned the conversation back to lighter topics. After 15 minutes, someone reminded the others that we had to rise early for the next day's seminars. The evening ended, its great questions unanswered."

Today, two decades later, the great questions of Russian politics remain unanswered. And it now seems there was some truth in the dinosaur's speech after all. Russia first held multi-party elections in 1991. Surveys found that most Russians favoured democracy over other types of rule. However, support for democracy soon fell because the economy collapsed (see Chapter 13, Work and the Economy, for details). According to official estimates, nearly 40 percent of the population live below the poverty line (Brym, 1996a, 1996b, 1996c; Gerber and Hout, 1998; Handelman, 1995; Remnick, 1998).

Democratic sentiment weakened as economic conditions worsened (Whitefield and Evans, 1994). In elections held in 1995 and 1996, support for democratic parties plunged as support for communist and extreme right-wing nationalist parties surged (Brym, 1995, 1996d). Nationwide surveys conducted in 38 countries between 1995 and 1997 found that as many as 97 percent of the citizens of some countries viewed democracy as the ideal form of government. Russia ranked last, at a mere 51 percent (Klingemann, 1999). Democracy allowed a few Russians to enrich themselves at the expense of most others. Therefore, many citizens equated democracy not with freedom but with distress.

Russia's political institutions reflect the weakness of Russian democracy. Power is concentrated in the presidency to a much greater degree than in the United States. The Parliament and the judiciary do not act as checks on executive power. Only a small number of Russians belong to political parties. Voting levels are low. Most television stations are tightly state-controlled. Minority ethnic groups are sometimes treated arbitrarily and cruelly.

Clearly, Russian democracy has a long way to go before it can be considered on par with democracy in the West.

The limited success of Russian democracy raises an important question. What social conditions must exist for a country to become fully democratic? We turn to this question next. To gain some perspective, we first consider the three waves of democratization that have swept the world since 1828 (Huntington, 1991: 13–26; see Figure 14.6).

The Three Waves of Democracy

The first wave of democratization began when more than half the white adult males in the United States became eligible to vote in the 1828 presidential election. By 1926, 33 countries enjoyed at least minimally democratic institutions. These countries included most of those in Western Europe, the British dominions (Australia, Canada, and New Zealand), Japan, and four Latin American countries (Argentina, Colombia, Chile, and Uruguay). However, just as an undertow begins when an ocean wave recedes, a democratic reversal occurred between 1922 and 1942. During that period, fascist, communist, and militaristic movements caused two-thirds of the world's democracies to fall under authoritarian or totalitarian rule.

The second wave of democratization swept across a large part of the world between 1943 and 1962. The Allied victory in World War II returned democracy to many of the defeated powers, including West Germany and Japan. The beginning of the end of colonial rule brought democracy to some states in Africa and elsewhere. Some Latin American countries formed limited and unstable democracies. However, even by the late 1950s, the second wave was beginning to exhaust itself. Soon, the world was in the midst of a second democratic reversal. Military dictatorships replaced many democracies in Latin America, Asia, and Africa. One-third of the democracies that existed in 1958 were authoritarian regimes by the mid-1970s.

The third and biggest wave of democratization began in 1974 with the overthrow of military dictatorships in Portugal and Greece. It crested in the early 1990s. In Southern and Eastern Europe, Latin America, Asia, and Africa, a whole series of authoritarian regimes fell. In 1991, Soviet communism collapsed. By 1995, 117 of the world's 191 countries were democratic in the sense that their citizens could choose representatives in regular, competitive elections. That amounts to 61 percent of the world's countries containing nearly 55 percent of the world's population (Diamond, 1996: 26).

The third wave seems less dramatic, however, if we bear in mind that these figures refer to **formal democracies**—countries that hold regular, competitive elections. Many of these countries are not **liberal democracies**. That is, like Russia, they lack the freedoms and constitutional protections that make political participation and competition meaningful. In formal but non-liberal democracies, substantial political power may reside with a military

Formal democracy involves regular, competitive elections.

A liberal democracy is a country whose citizens enjoy regular, competitive elections *and* the freedoms and constitutional protections that make political participation and competition meaningful.

FIGURE 14.6

The Three Waves of Democratization, 1828–1995

Source: Diamond, 1996: 28; Huntington, 1991: 26.

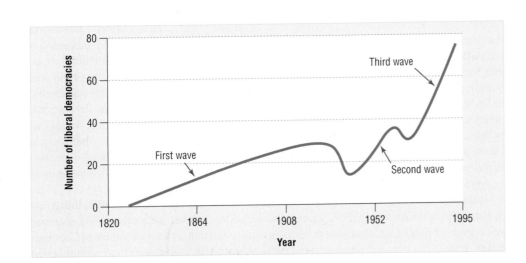

Nigeria celebrates independence from Britain in 1960. In 1993, General Sani Abacha annulled the presidential election, became head of state, and began a reign of brutal civil rights violations. The world's third wave of democratization was drawing to a close.

that is largely unaffected by the party in office. Certain cultural, ethnic, religious, or regional groups may not be allowed to take part in elections. The legislative and judicial branches of government may not constrain the power of the executive branch. Citizens may not enjoy freedom of expression, assembly, and organization. Instead, they may suffer from unjustified detention, exile, terror, and torture. At the end of 1995, 40 percent of the world's countries were liberal democracies, 21 percent were non-liberal democracies, and 39 percent were non-democracies (calculated from Diamond, 1996: 28). The number of liberal democracies in the world fell nearly 2 percent between 1991 and 1995. Some new democracies, including large and regionally influential countries, such as Russia, Nigeria, Turkey, and Pakistan, experienced a decline in freedoms and protections. The third wave was subsiding (U.S. Information Agency, 1998–99).

The Social Preconditions of Democracy

Liberal democracies emerge and endure when countries enjoy considerable economic growth, industrialization, urbanization, the spread of literacy, and a gradual decrease in economic inequality (Huntington, 1991: 39–108; Lipset, 1981: 27–63, 469–76, 1994; Moore, 1967; Rueschemeyer, Stephens, and Stephens, 1992; Zakaria, 1997). Economic development creates middle and working classes that are large, well organized, literate, and well off. When these classes become sufficiently powerful, their demands for civil liberties and the right to vote and run for office have to be recognized. If powerful middle and working classes are not guaranteed political rights, they sweep away kings, queens, landed aristocracies, generals, and authoritarian politicians in revolutionary upsurges. In contrast, democracies do not emerge where middle and working classes are too weak to wrest big political concessions from pre-democratic authorities. In intermediate cases—where, say, a country's military is about as powerful a political force as its middle and working classes—democracy is precarious and often merely formal. The history of unstable democracies is largely a history of internal military takeovers (Germani and Silvert, 1961).

Apart from the socioeconomic conditions noted above, favourable external political and military circumstances help liberal democracy endure. Liberal democracies, even strong ones, such as France, collapse when fascist, communist, and military regimes and empires defeat them. They revive when democratic alliances win world wars and authoritarian empires break up. Less coercive forms of outside political intervention are sometimes effective, too. For example, in the 1970s and 1980s, the European Union helped liberal democracy in Spain, Portugal, and Greece by integrating these countries in the Western European economy and giving them massive economic aid.

In sum, powerful, pro-democratic foreign states and strong, prosperous middle and working classes are liberal democracy's best guarantees. It follows that liberal democracy will spread in the less economically developed countries only if they prosper and enjoy support from the United States and the European Union, the world centres of liberal democracy.

Recognizing the importance of the United States and the European Union in promoting democracy in many parts of the world should not obscure two important facts, however. First, the United States is not always a friend of democracy. For example, between the end of World War II and the collapse of the Soviet Union in 1991, democratic regimes that were sympathetic to the Soviet Union were often destabilized by the United States and replaced by anti-democratic governments. American leaders were willing to export arms and offer other forms of support to anti-democratic forces in Iran, Indonesia, Chile, Nicaragua, Guatemala, and other countries because they believed it was in the United States' political and economic interest to do so (see Chapter 9, Globalization, Inequality, and Development). For similar reasons, the United States supports non-democratic regimes in Saudi Arabia, Kuwait, and elsewhere today. Desire for access to inexpensive oil, copper, and bananas (among other commodities), combined with fear of communist influence, have often outweighed democratic ideals in the United States. Anti-American attitudes in many parts of the world are based on American *opposition* to popular rule.

Second, just because the United States promotes democracy in many parts of the world, we should not assume that liberal democracy has reached its full potential in that country or, for that matter, in any of the other rich postindustrial countries that promote democracy internationally, including Canada. We saw otherwise in our discussion of the limited participation and influence of disadvantaged groups in Canadian politics. It seems fitting, therefore, to conclude this chapter by briefly assessing the future of liberal democracy in Canada.

Some analysts think the home computer will soon increase Canadians' political involvement. They think it will help solve the problem of unequal political participation by bringing more disadvantaged Canadians into the political process. Others think growing affluence means there are fewer disadvantaged Canadians to begin with. This makes economic or material issues less relevant than they used to be. In the next section, we dispute both contentions. We argue that political participation is likely to remain highly unequal in the future. Meanwhile, issues concerning economic inequality are likely to remain important for most people. Liberal democracy can realize its full potential only if both problems—political and economic inequality—are adequately addressed.

Electronic Democracy

On October 20, 1935, the *Washington Post* ran a full-page story featuring the results of the world's first nationwide poll. The story also explained how the new method of measuring public opinion worked. George Gallup was the man behind the poll. In the article, he said that polls allow the people to reclaim their voice: "After one hundred and fifty years we return to the town meeting. This time the whole nation is within the doors" (quoted in London, 1994: 1). Gallup was referring to the lively New England assemblies that used to give citizens a direct say in political affairs. He viewed the poll as a technology that could bring the town hall to the entire adult population of the United States.

Gallup's idea seems naive today. Social scientists have shown that polls allow politicians to mould public opinion, not just reflect it. For example, they can hire public opinion firms that word questions to increase the chance of eliciting preferred responses. Politicians can then publicize the results to serve their own ends (Ginsberg, 1986). From this point of view, polls are little different from other media events that are orchestrated by politicians to sway public opinion.

TECHNOLOGY
BYTES

Recently, however, some people have greeted a new technology with the same enthusiasm that Gallup lavished on polls. Computers linked to the Internet could allow citizens to debate issues and vote on them directly. This could give politicians a clear signal of how public policy should be conducted. Political participation is low and declining (see Figure 14.7). If the trend in voter turnout shown in the figure continues to decline at the 1958–2008 rate, a minority of the voting-age population will vote in a federal election around 2027 (Elections Canada, 2005). Some people think that computers can revive democracy. Public opinion would then become the law of the land (Westen, 1998).

It is a grand vision but flawed. Social scientists have conducted more than a dozen experiments with electronic public meetings. They show that even if the technology needed for such meetings were available to everyone, interest is so limited that no more than a third of the population would participate (Arterton, 1987).

Subsequent experience supports this conclusion. The people most likely to take advantage of electronic democracy are those who have Internet access. They form a privileged and politically involved group. They are not representative of the adult population of Canada or any other country. That is apparent in Tables 14.3 and 14.4. Table 14.3 shows that a digital divide exists in Canada, although it has shrunk in recent years. The worldwide

FIGURE 14.7

Voter Turnout, Canadian Federal Elections, 1958–2008

Source: Elections Canada, 2006, "Report of the Chief Electoral Officer of Canada on the 39th General Election of January 23, 2006"; 2004, "Estimation of Voter Turnout by Age Group at the 38th General Election"; and 2008, "40th General Election. " Retrieved October 16, 2008 (http://enr.elections.ca).

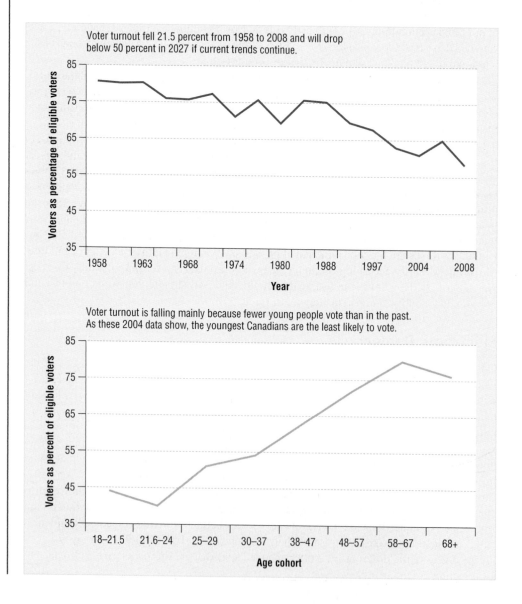

Percentage of Canadian Households with Internet Access

Households in top income quartile	77.7
Households in bottom income quartile	52.3
Households whose head has university degree	83.4
Households whose head lacks high-school diploma	26.5
Households in Canada's 15 largest Census Metropolitan Areas	64.3
Households outside Canada's 15 Largest Census Metropolitan Areas	49.9

TABLE 14.3

The Digital Divide: Social Characteristics of World Wide Web Users, Canada, 2005

Source: Statistics Canada, 2008a.

picture is one of even greater inequality of access. Table 14.4 records the massive overrepresentation on the Internet in 2005 of people from wealthier regions. Far from counteracting class divisions, the pattern of Internet access, for the near future, will magnify them, both in Canada and worldwide.

Postmaterialism and the Dilemma of Canadian Politics

Believers in electronic democracy think the computer will solve the problem of unequal political participation. Those who follow **postmaterialism** believe that economic or material issues are becoming less important in Canadian politics. They argue as follows: Liberal democracies are less stratified than both non-liberal democracies and non-democracies. That is, in liberal democracies, the gap between rich and poor is less extreme and society as a whole is more prosperous. In fact, say the postmaterialists, prosperity and the moderation of stratification have reached a point where they have fundamentally changed political life in Canada. They claim that, as recently as 50 years ago, most people were politically motivated mainly by their economic or material concerns. As a result, parties were distinguished from one another chiefly by the way they attracted voters from different classes. Now, however, many—if not most—Canadians have supposedly had their basic material wants satisfied. Young people, in particular, who grew up in prosperous times, are less concerned with material issues, such as whether their next paycheque can feed and house their family. They are more concerned with postmaterialist issues, such as women's rights, civil rights, and the environment. The postmaterialists conclude that the old left–right political division, based on class differences and material issues, is being replaced. The new left–right political division, they say, is based on age differences and postmaterialist issues (Clark and Lipset, 1991; Clark, Lipset, and Rempel, 1993; Inglehart, 1997).

Postmaterialism is a theory that claims that growing equality and prosperity in the rich industrialized countries have resulted in a shift from class-based politics to value-based politics.

Region	Population	Population as Percentage of World Total	Internet Users as Percentage of World Total	Relative Over- (> 1) or Under- (< 1) representation on Internet Relative to Population
Africa	900 465 411	14.00	1.50	0.11
Asia	3 612 363 162	56.30	34.00	0.60
Europe	730 991 138	11.40	29.20	2.56
Middle East	259 499 772	4.00	2.20	0.55
North America	328 387 059	5.10	24.90	4.88
Latin America/Caribbean	546 917 192	8.50	6.30	0.74
Oceania/Australia	33 443 448	0.50	1.80	3.60

TABLE 14.4

Relative Representation of Different Regions of the World among Persons Accessing the Internet in March 2005

Note: Relative representation is the ratio of Internet usage percentage to population percentage.

Source: From Internet World Stats, 2005, *World Internet Usage and Population Statistics*. Retrieved June 22, 2005 (http://www.internetworldstats.com/stats.htm). Reprinted with permission.

Although Canada is certainly more prosperous and less stratified than the less developed countries of the world, the postmaterialists are wrong to think that affluence is universal in this country, or that inequality is decreasing. These facts were documented at length in Chapter 8, Social Stratification: Canadian and Global Perspectives. Canada has one of the highest poverty rates of the rich industrialized countries, and income equality has not increased in this country for more than three decades. Unemployment and poverty are particularly widespread among youth—the people who, in the post-materialist view, are the most affluent and least concerned with material issues. About two-thirds of single Canadians under the age of 25 live below the low-income cutoff. This suggests that, today, more new voters are poor than at any time since at least 1980, when data on youth poverty were first collected. Under these circumstances, we should not be surprised that bread-and-butter issues remain important to most voters. Canadian public opinion polls repeatedly show that the leading concerns of Canadians are unemployment and related material issues.

And so we arrive at the key dilemma of Canadian politics. Material issues—essentially problems of class inequality—continue to loom large in the minds of most Canadians. However, as we have seen, Canadian politics focuses on regional, not class issues. In other words, there is a disconnect between Canadian priorities and Canadian politics. This probably accounts in part for the declining rate of political participation and the high rates of political cynicism and apathy we have observed, particularly among lower classes (refer back to Figure 14.3 and Figure 14.7). It probably also accounts in large measure for the fact that Canadians are increasingly turning to unconventional means of influencing public policy. In 1980, 24 percent of Canadians said they had joined a boycott, attended an unlawful demonstration, joined an unofficial strike, or occupied a building or a factory at least once. Ten years later, that figure stood at 33 percent. Participation in such unconventional political activities is most common among young, highly educated people (Nevitte, 1996: 75–109). This suggests that the future of Canadian politics may lie outside "normal" politics. We take up the theme of challenges to established power in Chapter 21, Collective Action and Social Movements.

Participating in social movements is not the only way people step outside the rules of normal electoral politics to change society. We conclude our discussion by considering two other types of "politics by other means": war and terrorism.

POLITICS BY OTHER MEANS

Political conflicts can be intense, but much political conflict is bound by rules or normative limits freely accepted by all sides: They accept that some matters are settled, notably boundaries, citizenship, and the basic forms of government. But sometimes these are not settled—sometimes competing bodies seek to impose their favoured basic settlement to the exclusion of alternatives. In the most extreme instances, each side denies legitimacy—the right to rule grounded in shared moral standards—to the opponents and seeks to displace or dislodge them by use of force. Such conflicts often set the boundaries within which later political competition takes place.

War

A war is a violent armed conflict between politically distinct groups who fight to protect or increase their control of territory.

A **war** is a violent armed conflict between politically distinct groups who fight to protect or increase their control of territory. Humanity has spent much of its history preparing for war, fighting it, and recovering from it; war has broken out some 14 000 times between 3600 BCE and the present. It has killed roughly one billion soldiers and two billion civilians, approximately 3 percent of the people born in the last 5600 years. (This is an underestimate because it necessarily ignores armed conflict among people without a recorded history.) Overall, however, and taking a long historical view, wars have become more destructive over time with "improvements" in the technology of human destruction. The twentieth century represents 1.7 percent of the time since the beginning of recorded war history, but it accounts for roughly 3.3 percent of the world's war deaths, military and civilian. Some 100 million people died in wars in the twentieth century (Beer, 1974; Brzezinski, 1993; Haub, 2000).

War is an expensive business, and the United States spends far more than any other country financing it. The United States accounted for about a third of world military expenditures and nearly 30 percent of world arms export agreements in 2005. France ranked second as an exporter (18 percent) and Russia third (17 percent; Grimmett, 2006).

Wars take place between countries (interstate wars) and within countries (civil or societal wars). A special type of interstate war is the colonial war, which involves a colony engaging in armed conflict with an imperial power to gain independence. Figure 14.8 shows the magnitude of armed conflict in the world for each type of war from 1946 to 2002. The magnitude of armed conflict is determined by the total number of combatants and casualties, the size of the area and dislocated populations, and the extent of infrastructure damage for each year the war is active.

You will immediately notice two striking features of the graph. First, after reaching a peak between the mid-1980s and early 1990s, the magnitude of armed conflict in the world dropped sharply. Second, since the mid-1950s, most armed conflict in the world has been societal rather than interstate. Today, countries rarely go to war against each other. They often go to war with themselves as contending political groups fight for state control or seek to break away and form independent states. Don't let the mass media distort your perception of global war. Wars like the ongoing U.S.–Iraq war account for little of the total magnitude of armed conflict, although they loom large in the media. Wars like the recent conflict in the Democratic Republic of Congo account for most of the total magnitude of armed conflict yet are rarely mentioned in the media. Thus, from 2003 to 2007, the U.S.–Iraq war killed roughly 170 000 combatants and civilians. Between 1998 and 2003, deaths caused by the civil war in the Democratic Republic of Congo numbered in the millions (CBC News, 2007; Coghlan et al., 2006; "Iraq Body Count," 2008; "Iraq Coalition Casualty Count," 2008).

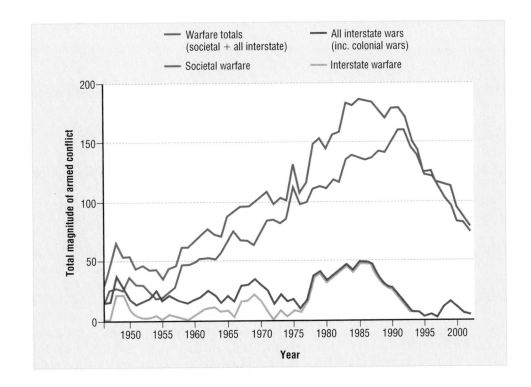

FIGURE 14.8

Global Trends in Violent Conflict, 1946–2002

Note: Data are for 158 countries with populations of at least 500 000 with 500 or more deaths directly related to war between 1946 and 2002.

Source: Monty G. Marshall and Ted Robert Gurr, 2003, *Peace and Conflict*. College Park, MD: CIDCM, University of Maryland. www.cldcm .umd.edu/inscr. Used by permission.

The civil war in the Democratic Republic of Congo (1994–2003) caused millions of deaths.

War risk varies from one country to the next (Figure 14.9), but what factors determine the risk of war on the territory of a given country? Figure 14.10 helps us answer that question by classifying the countries of the world by type of government and level of prosperity. Government types include democracy, autocracy (absolute rule by a single person or party), and "intermediate" forms. Intermediate types of government include some elements of democracy (e.g., regular elections) and some elements of autocracy (e.g., no institutional checks on presidential power). In this graph, a country's gross domestic product per capita (GDPpc) indicates its level of prosperity. The graph divides the world's countries into quarters by GDPpc.

Given our earlier discussion of the social preconditions of democracy, it should come as no surprise that democracy is more common and autocracy less common in prosperous countries. What is particularly interesting about Figure 14.10 is the distribution of countries

FIGURE 14.9

The Risk of War, 2002

Source: Marshall and Gurr, 2003: 4.

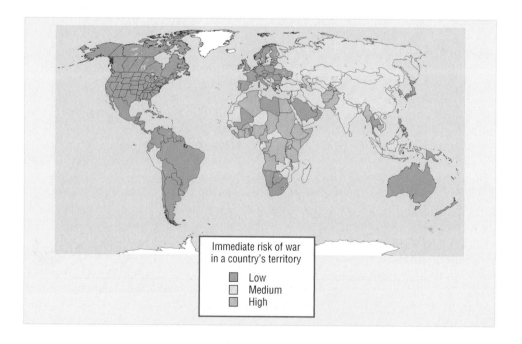

Immediate risk of war in a country's territory

■ Low
□ Medium
■ High

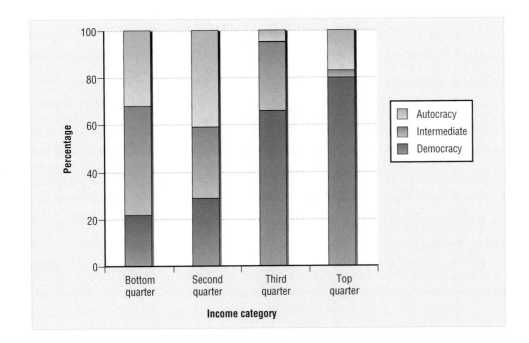

FIGURE 14.10

Type of Government by Income Category

Source: Marshall and Gurr, 2003: 11.

with *intermediate* types of government. Countries with intermediate types of government are at the highest risk of war, especially societal or civil war. A democratic government tends to be stable because it enjoys legitimacy in the eyes of its citizens. An autocratic government tends to be stable because it rules with an iron hand. In contrast, an intermediate type of government is characterized neither by high legitimacy nor by iron rule. It is therefore most prone to collapsing into societal war, with armed political groups fighting each other for state control.

A country's chance of avoiding war on its own territory is high if a country has no recent history of armed conflict, lacks or manages internal groups that want to break away and form their own country, maintains stable and equitable democratic institutions, is well-to-do, and is free of serious external threats. Figure 14.9 assigns a number to each of these factors and adds the numbers for each country to yield a figure that suggests the risk of war breaking out in the territory of each country. Dividing the country scores into three categories (low-, medium-, and high-risk) and assigning different colours to each category allows us to create the world map.

The 34 orange-flagged countries, most in Africa, are at serious risk of war. Examples are Pakistan, Algeria, and Nigeria. The 50 yellow-flagged countries, among them India, China, and Russia, are at moderate risk of war. The 74 green-flagged countries, including most of Western Europe and North and South America, are at low risk of war. Of course, countries that avoid war on their own territory may nonetheless engage in war elsewhere, the United States being the prime example. Since 1850, the United States has intervened militarily in other countries more than once a year on average (Kohn, 1988).

We conclude that economic development and democratization are the two main factors leading to less war in the world today. In a way, this is a deeply disturbing finding. In 2004, the United States allocated about 19 percent of its budget to war (or "defence") spending and only 0.8 percent to international development and humanitarian assistance (U.S. Bureau of the Census, 2004–05: 309). Public opinion polls show that the American public and its leaders regard the promotion of democracy and the improvement of living standards in other countries as the least important of U.S. goals, although, as we learned in Chapter 9, the cost of achieving them would be relatively low (Bardes and Oldendick, 2003: 205; Chapter 9, Table 9.2). It thus seems that Americans prefer to spend very little money promoting higher living standards and democracy in other nations, instead permitting much armed conflict in the world. The United States then spends a great deal of money dealing with the armed conflict.

Terrorism and Related Forms of Political Violence

We can learn much about the sorry predicament of the world today by lingering a moment on the question of why societal warfare has largely replaced interstate warfare since World War II. As usual, historical perspective is useful (Tilly, 2002).

From the rise of the modern state in the seventeenth century until World War II, states increasingly monopolized the means of coercion in society. This had three important consequences. First, as various regional, ethnic, and religious groups came under the control of powerful central states, the number of regional, ethnic, and religious wars declined and interstate warfare became the norm. Second, because states were powerful and monopolized the means of coercion, conflict became more deadly. Third, civilian life was pacified because the job of killing for political reasons was largely restricted to state-controlled armed forces. Thus, even as the death toll from war rose, civilians were largely segregated from large-scale killing. As late as World War I (1914–18), civilians composed only 5 percent of war deaths.

All this changed after World War II (1939–45). Since then, there have been fewer interstate wars and more civil wars, guerrilla wars, massacres, terrorist attacks, and instances of attempted ethnic cleansing and genocide perpetrated by militias, mercenaries, paramilitaries, suicide bombers, and the like. Moreover, large-scale violence has increasingly been visited on civilian rather than on military populations. By the 1990s, civilians composed fully 90 percent of war deaths. The mounting toll of civilian casualties is evident from U.S. Department of State data on casualties from international terrorist attacks (Figure 14.11).[5]

The change in the form of collective violence came about for three main reasons (Tilly, 2002). First, decolonization and separatist movements roughly doubled the number of independent states in the world, and many of these new states, especially in Africa and Asia, were too weak to control their territories effectively. Second, especially during the Cold War (1946–91), the United States, the Soviet Union, Cuba, and China often subsidized and sent arms to domestic opponents of regimes that were aligned against them. Third, the expansion of international trade in contraband provided rebels with new means of support. They took advantage of inexpensive international communication and travel to establish immigrant support communities abroad and export heroin, cocaine, diamonds, dirty money, and so forth. In sum, the structure of opportunities for engaging in collective violence shifted radically after World War II. As a result, the dominant form of collective violence changed from interstate to societal warfare.

From this perspective, and whatever its individual peculiarities, al-Qaeda is a typical creature of contemporary warfare. Al-Qaeda originated in Afghanistan, a notoriously weak

FIGURE 14.11

Casualties from International Terrorist Attacks, 1991–2004, and All Terrorist Attacks, 2005–2006

Note: In 2004, the U.S. Department of State broadened the types of terrorist attacks included in its calculations to include domestic acts of terror. As a result, the post-2004 figuers are considerably higher than the pre-2005 figures.

Source: U.S. Department of State, 1997, 2003: 163, 2004: 178; National Counterterrorism Centre, 2007: 7; Zelikow and Brennan, 2005.

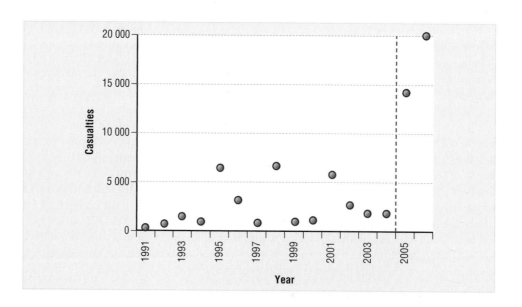

and dependent state. The United States supported al-Qaeda's founders militarily in their struggle against the Soviet occupation of Afghanistan in the 1980s. Al-Qaeda organized international heroin, diamond, and money-laundering operations. It established a network of operatives around the world. All of this was made possible by changes in the structure of opportunities for collective violence after World War II.

International terrorists of the type the U.S. Department of State collects data on typically demand autonomy or independence for some country, population, or region (Pape, 2003). For example, among Al-Qaeda's chief demands are Palestinian statehood and the end of American support for the wealthy regimes in Saudi Arabia, Kuwait, and the Gulf States. Al-Qaeda has turned to terror as a means of achieving these goals because other ways of achieving them are largely closed off. The United States considers support for the oil-rich Arab countries to be in the national interest. It has so far done little to further the cause of Palestinian statehood. Staunch opponents of American policy cannot engage in interstate warfare with the United States because they lack states of their own. At most, they are supported by states that lack the resources to engage in sustained warfare with the United States, including Iran, Syria, and the former regime of Iraq. Because the existing structure of world power closes off other possibilities for achieving political goals, terror emerges as a viable alternative for some desperate people.

NOTES

1. In early 2001, support for free trade had increased to 64 percent of Canadian adults, up from 46 percent in 1991 but down from 70 percent in 1999 (Tuck, 2001).

2. We say businessmen advisedly. Very few women are among Canada's richest people.

3. The clustering of voters on the left and the right does not mean that most Canadians know the difference between left and right in abstract terms or that they can identify specific parties as leftist or rightist. According to one recent poll, almost three-quarters of Canadians do not know, or are fuzzy on, the concept of a political right and left (Cobb, 2002).

4. We emphasize political factors here, but the economic and cultural pull of the United States has also accentuated Canadian regionalism. North–south economic and cultural ties between Canada and the United States are arguably stronger than east–west ties between Canada's regions. For instance, the volume of trade between Canada and the United States is more than twice as large as the volume of trade among Canada's provinces (Statistics Canada, 2001c; Transport Canada, 2001). Similarly, a very large percentage of the most popular television programs, magazines, books, music, and movies in Canada are produced in the United States.

5. Title 22 of the United States Code defines terrorism as "premeditated, politically motivated violence against noncombatant targets [including unarmed or off duty military personnel] by subnational groups or clandestine agents, usually intended to influence an audience" (U.S. Department of State, 2003: 17). However, a broader definition would also include "the use [by states] of indiscriminate violence against civilians in order to achieve military and political goals. Moreover, the label 'terror' is subject to interpretation. What one side in a conflict would call terror might be regarded by the other side as legitimate resistance to occupation, as well as ethnic, religious or national oppression" (Kimmerling, 2003: 73).

SUMMARY

1. What accounts for the level of democracy in a society?
   The level of democracy in a society depends on the distribution of power. When power is concentrated in the hands of few people, society is less democratic.

2. What are the major sociological theories of democratic politics?

   Pluralists correctly note that democratic politics is about negotiation and compromise. However, they fail to appreciate that economically advantaged groups have more power than disadvantaged groups. Elite theorists correctly note that power is concentrated in the hands of advantaged groups. However, they fail to appreciate how variations in the distribution of power influence political behaviour and public policy. Marxists correctly argue that the interests of large business are generally off-limits to challenges. However, they understate the degree to which ordinary citizens, including members of the working class, sometimes influence state policy. Power resource theorists usefully focus on changes in the distribution of power in society and their effects. However, they fail to appreciate what state-centred theorists emphasize—that state institutions and laws also independently affect political behaviour and public policy.

3. What are the social preconditions of democracy?

   Citizens win legal protection of rights and freedoms when their middle and working classes become large, organized, and prosperous; and when powerful, friendly, pro-democratic foreign states support them.

4. What does it mean to say that democracy has developed in waves?

   During three periods, democracy rapidly spread in the world. Then the spurt of democratization slowed or reversed. We may regard each of these periods as a "wave" of democratization. The first wave began when more than half the white adult males in the United States became eligible to vote in the 1828 presidential election. By 1926, 33 countries enjoyed at least minimally democratic institutions. However, between 1922 and 1942, fascist, communist, and militaristic movements caused two-thirds of the world's democracies to fall under authoritarian or totalitarian rule. The second wave of democracy began after World War II, when Allied victory returned democracy to many fascist states, and wars of colonial independence led to the formation of a series of new democracies. Military dictatorships then replaced many of the new democracies; a third of the democracies in 1958 were authoritarian regimes by the mid-1970s. The third wave of democracy began in Portugal in 1974. It had slowed and in some cases reversed by the end of the twentieth century.

5. What is the difference between formal and liberal democracy and why is the distinction important for understanding the third wave of democratization?

   Many new democracies that emerged from the most recent wave of democratization are formal, not liberal democracies. Their citizens enjoy regular, competitive elections (the formal side of democracy) but lack legal protection of rights and freedoms (the liberal side).

6. Do theories of electronic democracy and postmaterialism require a major rethinking of the way Canadian democracy works?

   Believers in electronic democracy and postmaterialism think Canada has reached a new and higher stage of democratic development. However, enduring social inequalities prevent even the most advanced democracies from being fully democratic.

7. What are the main causes of war?

   The risk of war declines with a country's level of prosperity and its level of democratization.

8. How has the nature of the state affected patterns of warfare?

   The rise of the modern state in the seventeenth century led to the monopolization of the means of coercion in society. Once centralized state armies became the major military force in society, interstate warfare became the norm, warfare became more deadly, and few civilians died in war. However, the emergence of many weak states after World War II encouraged the outbreak of societal or civil wars, which are now the norm. Civilian deaths now account for most war deaths. Societal wars gain impetus when hostile outside powers get involved in them and rebels take advantage of increased opportunities to engage in illegal trade and establish support communities abroad. International terrorism has benefited greatly from the combination of weak states, outside support, and new ways of mobilizing resources.

KEY TERMS

authoritarian (p. 400)

authority (p. 398)

charismatic authority (p. 398)

civil society (p. 400)

democracy (p. 400)

elite theory (p. 402)

elites (p. 402)

formal democracy (p. 413)

legal-rational authority (p. 398)

liberal democracy (p. 413)

lobbies (p. 400)

mass media (p. 400)

pluralist theory (p. 401)

political parties (p. 400)

political revolution (p. 399)

postmaterialism (p. 417)

power (p. 398)

power resource theory (p. 405)

public opinion (p. 401)

ruling class (p. 402)

social movements (p. 401)

state (p. 400)

state-centred theory (p. 408)

totalitarian (p. 400)

traditional authority (p. 398)

war (p. 418)

QUESTIONS TO CONSIDER

1. Analyze the 2008 Canadian federal election. What issues distinguished the competing parties or candidates? What categories of the voting population did each party or candidate attract? Why?

2. Younger people are less likely to vote than older people are. How would power resource theory explain this?

3. Do you think Canada will become a more democratic country in the next 25 years? Will a larger percentage of the population vote? Will class inequalities in political participation decline? Will public policy more accurately reflect the interests of the entire population? Why or why not?

WEB RESOURCES

Companion Website for This Book

http://www.compass3e.nelson.com

Begin by clicking on the Student Resources section of the website. Next, select the chapter you are studying from the pull-down menu. From the Student Resources page you have easy access to InfoTrac® College Edition, additional Weblinks, and other resources. The website also has many useful tips to aid you in your study of sociology, including practice tests for each chapter.

InfoTrac® Search Terms

These search terms are provided to assist you in beginning to conduct research on this topic by visiting http://www.infotrac-college.com:

civil society

legitimacy

political party

ruling class

voting

Recommended Websites

For data on Canadian elections, state revenues, debt and expenditures, and employment, visit the Statistics Canada website at http://www40.statcan.ca/z01/cs0002_e.htm.

The most important organization of international governance is the United Nations. For the UN website, go to http://www.un.org.

For data on voter turnout in all democracies from 1945 to the present, go to the website of the International Institute for Democracy and Electoral Assistance at http://www.idea.int.

CengageNOW™

http://hed.nelson.com

This online diagnostic tool identifies each student's unique needs with a Pretest that generates a personalized Study Plan for each chapter, helping students focus on concepts they're having the most difficulty mastering. Students then take a Posttest after reading the chapter to measure their understanding of the material. An Instructor Gradebook is available to track and monitor student progress.

CHAPTER

Families

15

In this chapter, you will learn that

- The traditional "nuclear" family is less common than it used to be. Several new family forms are becoming more prevalent. The frequency of one family form or another varies by class, ethnicity, sexual orientation, and region of the country.

- One of the most important forces underlying the change from the traditional nuclear family is the entry of most women into the paid labour force. Doing paid work increases women's ability to leave unhappy marriages and control whether and when they will have children.

- Marital satisfaction increases as we move up the class structure, in places where divorce laws are liberal, when teenage children leave the home, in families where housework is shared equally, and among spouses who enjoy a satisfying sex life.

- The worst effects of divorce on children can be eliminated if there is no parental conflict and the children's standard of living does not fall after divorce.

- The decline of the traditional nuclear family is sometimes associated with a host of social problems, such as poverty, welfare dependency, and crime. However, policies have been adopted in some countries that reduce these problems.

INTRODUCTION

PERSONAL ANECDOTE

Steven Rytina recalls that when he attended elementary school in an Ohio town of about 13 000 people, the families in his neighbourhood were like the ones in TV sitcoms—just about every household consisted of children, two parents of opposite sexes with fathers in stable jobs and no moms working for pay outside the home. "Although this seemed 'normal,'" says Steven, "I never imagined it was anything like a universal pattern for families. Because although some of the time I belonged to one of these 'standard edition' nuclear households, much of what I experienced as family did not fit that pattern at all.

"Every year at Christmas and Thanksgiving, our unit joined larger units based on my parents' childhood households, alternating between my mother's and father's sides.

My sister and I routinely used ethnic labels to distinguish them. My mother's family was the 'American' one and they lived in Pennsylvania in a neighbourhood much like my own. My father's family was 'Czech' since his parents immigrated from Bohemia (then part of Austria-Hungary) shortly before World War I. By my time, they lived in Queens in New York City.

"There were plenty of differences, including cuisine, social composition, and language. The Pennsylvania branch spoke standard American English but the eastern branch spoke English with Slavic and 'New Yawk' accents and frequently lapsed into Czech, which only my father among us could follow. Our Ohio branch consisted of Mom, Dad, and the kids, but the New York branch shared duplex living quarters with my father's sister and her husband and two children. In Pennsylvania, it was taken for granted that we would all squeeze into the available space at mealtime. That my grandmother was in charge of meal preparation was unquestioned. But in Queens, whether we would all assemble for a given meal was up for grabs, as was who would go to which kitchen to eat or who would prepare what. My sister and I would quietly gather information about strategic supplies, like who was down to the prune pastries we both deemed yucky, and then we'd try to manoeuvre where we ate. But there were minefields as well, since someone was usually on the 'outs' with someone else and, say, not welcome for coffee and only allowed upstairs or downstairs for major meals. As young visitors, my sister and I were largely neutrals but my father usually scoped out the scene and aligned himself accordingly.

"Since I was exposed to this contrasting pattern from the earliest age, I never saw it as anything but as 'natural' as my family unit back in Ohio. I figured the differences existed because the New Yorkers didn't have a lot of money and real estate was far more expensive there. Because the several family units were hardly replicas, it seemed obvious that each of us belonged to more than one family unit: my father to Queens and to Ohio, my mother to Pennsylvania and Ohio, and my sister and I to all three. Whether my father's parents and sister in Queens formed one or two units was debatable. And so from an early age I understood that 'family' is not one household, not one single pattern, and that we do not even belong to the same set of households as the other people in our own families do.

"The differences and discontinuities apparent in my own family serve as reminders that 'family' refers to sequences of multiple households and there is no 'one size fits all' over most individuals' lifetimes. How to understand and appreciate variety and adaptation is one of the great challenges posed by the study of families."

Because families are emotional minefields, few subjects of sociological inquiry generate as much controversy. Much of the debate centres on a single question: Is the family in decline and, if so, what should be done about it? The question is hardly new. John Laing, a Protestant minister in Ontario, wrote in 1878, "We may expect to see further disintegration until the family shall disappear. . . . In all things civil and sacred the tendency of the age is towards individualism . . . its plausible aphorisms and popular usages silently undermining the divine institution of the family" (quoted in Pence and Jacobs, 2001). In 1915, Canadian political economist and humorist Stephen Leacock remarked, "The home has passed, or at least is passing, out of existence. In place of it is the apartment—an incomplete thing, a mere part of something, where children are an intrusion, where hospitality is done through a caterer, and where Christmas is only the twenty-fifth of December" (quoted in Sager, 2000: vii). Such statements, sounding the death of the family, seem more common whenever the family undergoes rapid change and particularly when the divorce rate increases.

Today, when some people speak about "the decline of the family," they are referring to the **nuclear family**. The nuclear family comprises a cohabiting man and woman who maintain a socially approved sexual relationship and have at least one child (Box 15.1).

> A **nuclear family** consists of a cohabiting man and woman who maintain a socially approved sexual relationship and have at least one child.

BOX 15.1
Sociology at the Movies

TAKE   ROLL

Walk the Line (2005)

When legendary country singer Johnny Cash was 12, his older brother was killed in an accident and his father screamed that "God took the wrong son," assuming, unjustly and without evidence, that Johnny was to blame for the boy's death. Burdened by the loss of his beloved brother and his father's constant rejection, Johnny Cash became a deeply troubled adult. Fame didn't help. He drank too much, popped amphetamine pills like they were candy, neglected his children, ruined his first marriage, and did time in prison for trying to smuggle narcotics across the border from Mexico.

Redemption arrives in the form of fellow performer June Carter (Reese Witherspoon, who won the 2005 Best Actress Oscar for the role). Cash (played by Joaquin Phoenix, nominated for the 2005 Best Actor Oscar) pursues her relentlessly for years, eventually resorting to a proposal onstage in the middle of a performance in Toronto, which she accepts.

That moment changes Cash's life. But it is not just June who rescues him with her support and her love. It is the entire Carter family. The Carters display all the grace and generosity one would expect of a royal family, which is just about what they were in the country music scene. At a Thanksgiving dinner attended by the

Joaquin Phoenix and Reese Witherspoon in *Walk the Line*

Carter and Cash families at Johnny's new house, Johnny's father starts in on him with the usual put-downs. "So how do you like it?" Johnny asks his father, referring to the house. "Jack Benny's is bigger," snaps the father. But Mr. Carter springs to Johnny's defence, mildly rebuking Mr. Cash by asking rhetorically, "Oh, have you been to Jack Benny's house?" Johnny is upset enough to leave the meal and Mrs. Carter encourages June to go after him. Later, Johnny's supplier arrives with a fresh bag of pills, but June's parents chase him away with shotguns. They integrate Johnny into their family

as the beloved son he always wanted and needed to be, and he lives with June and their four girls from previous marriages happily ever after.

What is a family? A cohabiting man and woman who maintain a socially approved sexual relationship and have at least one child? By that standard definition, Johnny's parents and their children formed a nuclear family—but a pretty sorry one by any reasonable standard because they failed to provide the emotional support that could have allowed Johnny to thrive and become a happy adult. The Carters were not part of Johnny's family according to the standard definition, but their generosity of spirit led them to treat him like a son anyway. Johnny eventually became part of their extended family because they cared deeply for his welfare. The story of Johnny Cash suggests that the definition of a family as a cohabiting man and woman who maintain a socially approved sexual relationship and have at least one child may be too narrow. Perhaps it is more appropriate to think of a family as a set of intimate social relationships that people create to share resources so as to ensure their welfare and that of their dependants.

What values are implicit in the two definitions of the family offered above? Which definition of family do you prefer? Why?

FIGURE 15.1

Family Types, 1901

Source: Canadian Families Project, 1999.

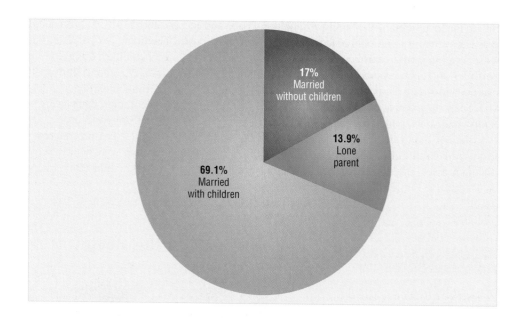

A **traditional nuclear family** is a nuclear family in which the husband works outside the home for money and the wife works without pay in the home.

Others are referring more narrowly to what might be called the **traditional nuclear family**. The traditional nuclear family is a nuclear family in which the wife works in the home without pay while the husband works outside the home for money. This makes him the "primary provider and ultimate authority" (Popenoe, 1988: 1).

In the 1940s and 1950s, many sociologists and much of the Canadian public considered the nuclear family to be the most widespread and ideal family form. However, for reasons we will examine below, fewer than 39 percent of Canadian families in 2006 took the form of the nuclear family (married-couple families with children), compared with more than 69 percent in 1901 (see Figures 15.1 and 15.2). In the second half of the twentieth century, the percentage of women between the ages of 15 and 64 in the paid labour force increased from around 25 percent to 71 percent, close to the percentage for men. In

FIGURE 15.2

Family Types, 2006

Source: Statistics Canada, 2007, "Number of Children at Home (8) and Census Family Structure (7) for the Census Families in Private Households of Canada, Provinces, Territories, Census Metropolitan Areas and Census Agglomerations, 2001 and 2006 Censuses—20% Sample Data." Retrieved January 14, 2008 (http://www12.statcan.ca/ english/census06/data/topics/ RetrieveProductTable.cfm?ALEVEL= 3&APATH=3&CATNO=&DETAIL=1&DIM =&DS=99&FL=0&FREE=0&GAL=0&GC= 99&GK=NA&GRP=1&IPS=&METH=0 &ORDER=1&PID=89016&PTYPE=88971 &RL=0&S=1&ShowAll=No&StartRow=1 &SUB=683&Temporal=2006&Theme=6 8&VID=0&VNAMEE=&VNAMEF=).

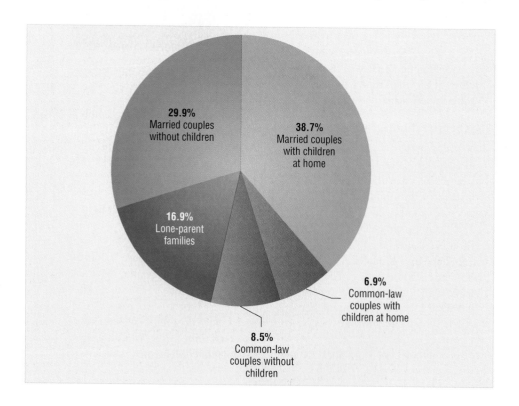

2004, 74 percent of mothers with school-aged children were in the paid labour force, and the percentage was practically the same for women with children under the age of 3 (Statistics Canada, 2006). As a result, only a minority of Canadian adults live in traditional nuclear families today. Many new family forms have become prevalent in recent decades.

Some sociologists, many of them functionalists, view the decreasing prevalence of the married-couple family and the rise of the "working mother" as an unmitigated disaster (Gill, 1997; Popenoe, 1996, 1998). In their view, rising rates of crime, illegal drug use, poverty, and welfare dependency (among other social ills) can be traced to the fact that so many Canadian children are not living in two-parent households with stay-at-home mothers. They call for various legal and cultural reforms to shore up the traditional nuclear family. For instance, they want to make it harder to get a divorce and they want people to place less emphasis on individual happiness at the expense of family responsibility.

Other sociologists, influenced by conflict and feminist theories, disagree with the functionalist assessment (Coontz, 1992; Stacey, 1996). In the first place, they argue that it is inaccurate to talk about *the* family, as if this important social institution assumes or should assume only a single form. They emphasize that families have been structured in many ways and that the diversity of family forms is increasing as people accommodate new social pressures. Second, they argue that changing family forms do not necessarily represent deterioration in the quality of people's lives. In fact, such changes often represent improvement in the way people live. They believe that the decreasing prevalence of the traditional nuclear family and the proliferation of diverse family forms have benefited many men, women, and children, and have not harmed other children as much as the functionalists think. They also believe that various economic and political reforms, such as the creation of an affordable nationwide daycare system, could eliminate most of the negative effects of single-parent households.

This chapter touches on divorce, reproductive choice, cohabitation, single-parent families, and other topics in the sociology of families. However, we have structured the chapter around the debate about the so-called decline of the Canadian family. We first outline the functional theory of the family because the issues raised by functionalism are still a focus of sociological controversy (Mann, Grimes, Kemp, and Jenkins, 1997). Borrowing from the work of conflict theorists and feminists, we next present a critique of functionalism. In particular, we show that the nuclear family became the dominant and ideal family form only under specific social and historical conditions. As the next sections show, once these conditions changed, the nuclear family became less prevalent and a variety of new family forms proliferated. We discuss how these new family forms are structured and how their frequency varies by class, ethnicity, sexual orientation, and region. Although postindustrial families solve some problems, they are hardly an unqualified blessing. The chapter's concluding section therefore considers the kinds of policies that might help alleviate some of the most serious concerns faced by families today. Let us, then, first review the functionalist theory of the family.

FUNCTIONALISM AND THE NUCLEAR IDEAL

Functional Theory

For any society to survive, its members must cooperate economically. They must have babies. And they must raise offspring in an emotionally supportive environment so the offspring can learn the ways of the group and eventually operate as productive adults. Since the 1940s, functionalists have argued that the nuclear family is ideally suited to meet these challenges. In their view, the nuclear family performs five main functions. It provides a basis for regulated sexual activity, economic cooperation, reproduction, socialization, and emotional support (Murdock, 1949: 1–22; Parsons, 1955).

Polygamy expands the nuclear
family "horizontally" by
adding one or more spouses
(usually women) to the
household.

The **extended family** expands
the nuclear family "vertically"
by adding another generation—
one or more of the spouses'
parents—to the household.

Marriage is a socially
approved, presumably long-
term sexual and economic
union between a man and a
woman. It involves reciprocal
rights and obligations
between spouses and between
parents and children.

Functionalists cite the pervasiveness of the nuclear family as evidence of its ability to perform the functions listed above. To be sure, other family forms exist. **Polygamy** expands the nuclear unit "horizontally" by adding one or more spouses (almost always wives) to the household. Polygamy is still legally permitted in many less industrialized countries of Africa and Asia. However, the overwhelming majority of families are monogamous because they cannot afford to support several wives and many children. The **extended family** expands the nuclear family "vertically" by adding another generation—one or more of the spouses' parents—to the household. Extended families used to be common throughout the world. They still are in some places. However, according to the functionalists, the basic building block of the extended family (and of the polygamous family) is the nuclear unit.

George Murdock was a functionalist who conducted a famous study in the 1940s of 250 mainly preliterate societies. Murdock wrote, "Either as the sole prevailing form of the family or as the basic unit from which more complex familial forms are compounded, [the nuclear family] exists as a distinct and strongly functional group in every known society" (Murdock, 1949: 2). Moreover, the nuclear family, Murdock continued, is everywhere based on **marriage**. He defined marriage as a socially approved, presumably long-term, sexual and economic union between a man and a woman. It involves rights and obligations between spouses and between spouses and their children.

Let us consider the five main functions of marriage and the nuclear family in detail:

1. *Sexual regulation.* Imagine a world without an institution that defines the boundaries within which legitimate sexual activity is permitted. Such a world would be disrupted by many people having sex wherever, whenever, and with whomever they pleased. An orderly social life would be difficult. Because marriage provides a legitimate forum for expressing the intense human need for sexual activity, says Murdock, it makes social order possible.

   Sex is not, however, the primary motive for marrying, he continues. After all, sex is readily available outside marriage. Only 54 of Murdock's 250 societies forbade or disapproved of premarital sex between non-relatives. In most of those 250 societies, a married man could legitimately have an extramarital affair with one or more female relatives (Murdock, 1949: 5–6). It is hardly news that premarital and extramarital sex are common in contemporary Canada and other postindustrial societies. Today, Canadians living in Quebec evidence the most liberal sexual attitudes toward premarital and extramarital sex. However, based on current trends, it's been estimated that "by about the year 2010, close to 85 percent of Canadians will approve of nonmarital sex" (Bibby, 1995: 70).

2. *Economic cooperation.* Why then, apart from sex, do people marry? Murdock's answer is this: "By virtue of their primary sex difference, a man and a woman make an exceptionally efficient cooperating unit" (Murdock, 1949: 7). On average, women are physically weaker than men are. Historically, pregnancy and nursing have restricted women in their activities. Therefore, writes Murdock, they can best perform lighter tasks close to home. These tasks include gathering and planting food, carrying water, cooking, making and repairing clothing, making pottery, and caring for children. Because most men possess superior strength, they can specialize in lumbering, mining, quarrying, land clearing, and house building. They can also range farther to hunt, fish, herd, and trade (Murdock, 1937). According to Murdock, this division of labour enables more goods and services to be produced than would otherwise be possible. People marry partly because of this economic fact. In Murdock's words, "Marriage exists only when the economic and the sexual are united into one relationship, and this combination occurs only in marriage" (Murdock, 1949: 8).

3. *Reproduction.* Before the invention of modern contraception, sex often resulted in the birth of a baby. According to Murdock, children are an investment in the future. By the age of six or seven, children in most societies do some chores. Their economic value to the family increases as they mature. When children become adults, they often help support their elderly parents. Thus, in most societies, there is a big economic incentive to having children.

4. *Socialization.* The investment in children can be realized only if adults rear the young to maturity. This involves not only caring for them physically but, as you saw in Chapter 4, Socialization, teaching them language, values, beliefs, skills, religion, and much else. Talcott Parsons (1955: 16) regarded socialization as the "basic and irreducible" function of the family.

5. *Emotional support.* Parsons also noted that the nuclear family universally gives its members love, affection, and companionship. He stressed that, in the nuclear family, it is mainly the mother who is responsible for ensuring the family's emotional well-being. She develops what Parsons calls the primary "expressive" role because she is the one who bears children and nurses them. It falls on the husband to take on the more "instrumental" role of earning a living outside the family (Parsons, 1955: 23). The fact that he is the "primary provider" makes him the ultimate authority.

Foraging Societies

Does functionalism provide an accurate picture of family relations at any point in human history? To assess the adequacy of the theory, let us briefly consider family patterns in the two settings that were apparently foremost in the minds of the functionalists. We first discuss families in preliterate, foraging societies. In such societies, people subsist by hunting animals and gathering wild edible plants. Most of the cases in Murdock's sample are foraging societies. We then discuss families in urban and suburban middle-class Canada in the 1950s. The functionalists whose work we are reviewing lived in such families themselves.

Foraging societies are nomadic groups of 100 or fewer people. As we would expect from Murdock's and Parsons's analyses, a gender division of labour exists among foragers. Most men hunt and most women gather. Women also do most of the child care. However, research on foragers conducted since the 1950s shows that men often tend babies and children in such societies (Leacock, 1981; Lee, 1979; Turnbull, 1961). They often gather food after an unsuccessful hunt. In some foraging societies, women hunt. In short, the gender division of labour is less strict than Murdock and Parsons thought. What is more, the gender division of labour is not associated with large differences in power and authority. Overall, men have few if any privileges that women don't also enjoy. Relative gender equality is based on the fact that women produce up to 80 percent of the food.

There is rough gender equality among the !Kung-San, a foraging society in the Kalahari Desert in Botswana. That is partly because women play such a key economic role in providing food.

Foragers travel in small camps or bands. The band decides by consensus when to send out groups of hunters. When they return from the hunt, they distribute game to all band members based on need. Each hunter does not decide to go hunting based on his or her own nuclear family's needs. Each hunter does not distribute game just to his or her own nuclear family. Contrary to what Murdock wrote, it is the band, not the nuclear family, that is the most efficient social organization for providing everyone with his or her most valuable source of protein.

In foraging societies, children are considered an investment in the future. However, it is not true that people always want more children for purposes of economic security. In fact, too many children are considered a liability. Subsistence is uncertain in foraging societies, and when band members deplete an area of game and edible plants, they move elsewhere. As a result, band members try to keep the ratio of children to productive adults low. In a few cases, such as the pre-twentieth-century Inuit, newborns were occasionally allowed to die if the tribe felt its viability was threatened by having too many mouths to feed.

Life in foraging societies is highly cooperative. For example, women and men care for—and women even breastfeed—each other's children. Despite Parsons's claim that socialization is the "basic and irreducible" function of the nuclear family, it is the band, not the nuclear family, that assumes responsibility for child socialization in foraging societies. Socialization is more a public than a private matter. As a seventeenth-century Innu man from northern Quebec said to a Jesuit priest who was trying to convince him to adopt European ways of raising children, "Thou hast no sense. You French people love only your own children; but we all love all the children of our tribe" (quoted in Leacock, 1981: 50).

In sum, recent research on foraging societies calls into question many of the functionalists' generalizations. In foraging societies, relations between the sexes are quite egalitarian. Children are not viewed just as an investment in the future. Each nuclear unit does not execute the important economic and socialization functions in isolation and in private. On the contrary, cooperative band members execute most economic and socialization functions in public.

Let us now assess the functionalist theory of the family in the light of evidence concerning Canadian middle-class families in the years just after World War II.

The Canadian Middle Class in the 1950s

Functionalists recognized that the economic function of the family was less important after World War II than it had been in earlier times. In their view, the socialization and emotional functions of the family were now most important (Parsons, 1955). Thus, on the nineteenth-century family-owned farm, the wife played an indispensable productive role while the husband was out in the field or on the range. She took responsibility for the garden, the dairy, the poultry, and the management of the household. The children also did crucial chores with considerable economic value. But in the typical urban or suburban nuclear family of the late 1940s and 1950s, noted the functionalists, only one person played the role of breadwinner. That was usually the husband. Children enjoyed more time to engage in the play and leisure-time activities that were now considered necessary for healthy child development. For their part, most women got married, had babies, and stayed home to raise them. Strong normative pressures helped keep women at home. Thus, in the 1950s, sociologist David Riesman called a woman's failure to obey the strict gender division of labour a "quasi-perversion." *Esquire* magazine called women's employment in the paid labour force a "menace." *Life* magazine called it a "disease" (quoted in Coontz, 1992: 32).

As a description of family patterns in the 15 years after World War II, functionalism has its merits. During the Great Depression (1929–39) and after conscription began in 1942 (Oderkirk, 2000: 95), Canadians were forced to postpone marriage (if they married at all) because of widespread poverty, government-imposed austerity, and physical separation. After

Mimi Matte's *Family Outing* (1998): In the 1950s, married women often hid their frustrations with family life.

this long and dreadful ordeal, many Canadians just wanted to settle down, have children, and enjoy the peace, pleasure, and security that family life seemed to offer. Conditions could not have been better for doing just that. The immediate post-war era was one of unparalleled optimism and prosperity. Real per capita income rose, as did the percentage of Canadians who owned their own homes. By the mid-1950s, employment and personal income reached all-time highs. Various services and legislative amendments created during World War II to encourage wives and mothers to join the labour force were rescinded. The expectation was that a return to "normal" meant the resumption of the provider–housewife roles of men and women, respectively (Kingsbury and Scanzoni, 1993).

One result of these combined conditions was a "marriage boom" in Canada (see Figure 15.3). Increasingly, Canadians lived in married-couple families. The proportion of "never married" Canadians decreased and the average age at first marriage dropped from 24.4 years for brides and 27.6 for bridegrooms in 1941, to 23.4 and 26.1 years, respectively, by 1956 (McVey and Kalbach, 1995: 225; see Figure 15.4 on page 436). A second result was a baby boom. During this period Canadian families averaged four children—resulting in proportionally more baby boomers than in the United States, Australia, or New Zealand (Nikiforuk, 1999). And unlike the situation today, married men were much more likely than married women were to be working for pay. For example, in 1951, 90.0 percent of married men but only 11.2 percent of married women were in the paid labour force.

Not all women, of course, could afford to stay out of the workforce. Poor women have often worked both inside and outside the home. However, middle-class women engaged in

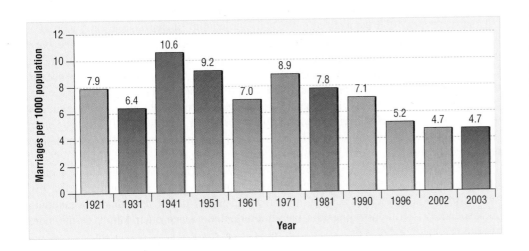

FIGURE 15.3

Marriage Rates, 1921–2003

Source: Adapted from Statistics Canada, "Selected marriage statistics, 1921–1990—Diskette," Catalogue 82-552, October 1, 1992, and *The Daily*, Catalogue 11-001, Thursday, January 29, 1998, available at http://www.statcan.ca/Daily/English/980129/d980129.htm#ART1, and Tuesday, December 21, 2004, available at http://www.statcan.ca/Daily/English/041221/d04122d.htm.

FIGURE 15.4

Average Age at First Marriage

Sources: Adapted from Statistics Canada, "Marriage and Conjugal Life in Canada, 1991," Catalogue 91-534, April 23, 1992; and *The Daily*, Catalogue 11-001, Monday, June 2, 2003. Retrieved July 1, 2004 (http://www.statcan.ca/Daily/English/030602/d030602a.htm).

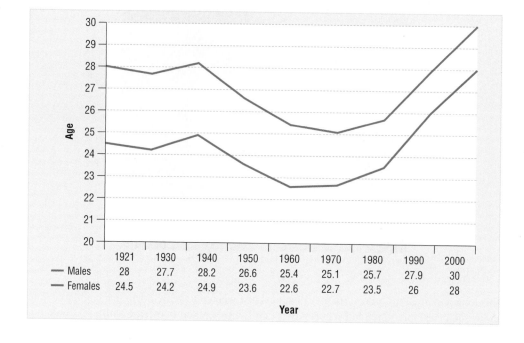

Year	1921	1930	1940	1950	1960	1970	1980	1990	2000
— Males	28	27.7	28.2	26.6	25.4	25.1	25.7	27.9	30
— Females	24.5	24.2	24.9	23.6	22.6	22.7	23.5	26	28

The **divorce rate** is the number of divorces that occur in a year for every 1000 people in the population.

The **marriage rate** is the number of marriages that occur in a year for every 1000 people in the population.

The **total fertility rate** is the average number of children that would be born to a woman over her lifetime if she had the same number of children as women in each age cohort in a given year.

what has been called an "orgy of domesticity" in the post-war years, devoting increasing attention to child rearing and housework. They also became increasingly concerned with the emotional quality of family life as love and companionship became firmly established as the main motivation for marriage (Coontz, 1992: 23–41; Skolnick, 1991: 49–74).

Nevertheless, as sociologist Andrew J. Cherlin meticulously shows for the United States, the immediate post-war period was in many respects a historical aberration (Cherlin, 1992: 6–30). Trends in divorce, marriage, and child-bearing show a gradual *weakening* of the nuclear family from the second half of the nineteenth century until the mid-1940s and continued weakening after the 1950s. Specifically, throughout the nineteenth century, the **divorce rate** rose very slowly. The divorce rate is the number of divorces that occur in a year for every 1000 people in the population. Meanwhile, the **marriage rate** fell. The marriage rate is the number of marriages that occur in a year for every 1000 people in the population. The **total fertility rate** also fell. The total fertility rate is the average number of children that would be born to a woman during her lifetime, assuming she has the same number of children as the average for women in each age cohort. Only the peculiar historical circumstances of the post-war years, noted above, temporarily reversed these trends.

The pattern in Canada was much the same. Immediately following World War II, Canada's marriage and divorce rates both reached unprecedented highs. From a low of 6.4 marriages per 1000 population in 1931, the popularity of marriage peaked with 10.9 marriages per 1000 in 1942 and 1946. It then gradually fell until 1971, when the baby boomers came of marital age, and then began to decline again. Although in 1946 the Canadian divorce rate was three times its prewar level as hasty wartime marriages broke up, the divorce rate declined from that point until the 1960s, when the introduction of more liberal divorce legislation was accompanied by a rising divorce rate. In like fashion, although the fertility rate climbed during the post-war baby boom years, peaking in 1961, this pattern was also reversed (see Figure 15.5). By the early 1960s, the earlier trends in Canada had reasserted themselves.

The functionalists, we may conclude, generalized too hastily from the era they knew best—the period of their own adulthood. Contrary to what they thought, the big picture from the nineteenth century until the present is that of a gradually weakening nuclear family. Let us now consider the conditions that made other family forms more prevalent.

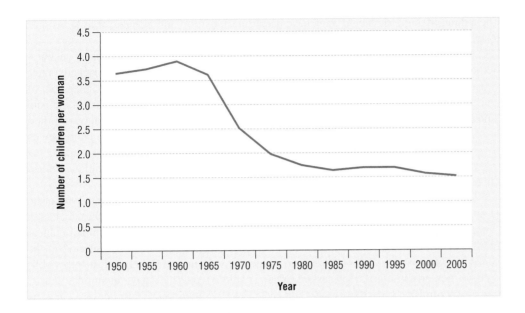

FIGURE 15.5

Total Fertility Rate, Canada, 1950–2005

Note: Values for 2000 and 2005 are projections.

Source: United Nations Statistical Division Common Database.

CONFLICT AND FEMINIST THEORIES

> I hadn't really wanted to marry at all. I wanted to make something of myself, not just give it away. But I knew if I didn't marry I would be sorry. Only freaks didn't. I knew I had to do it quickly, too, while there was still a decent selection of men to choose from. . . . I was twenty. . . .
>
> Though I wanted to be a good wife, from the beginning I found it impossible to subdue my desires. I was in fierce competition with my husband, though Frank, completely absorbed in his own studies, was probably unaware of it. He believed he had married an impulsive girl, even a supergirl, but not a separate, feeling woman. . . . Though we had agreed to study like fury till our money ran out and then take turns getting jobs, at bottom we knew it would be he who would get the degrees and I who would get the jobs. (Shulman, 1997 [1969]: 163, 173)

This quotation, from *Memoirs of an Ex-Prom Queen,* shows a side of family life entirely obscured by the functionalists. As the passage suggests, and as the novel establishes in biting and sometimes depressing detail, post-war families did not always operate like the smoothly functioning, happy, white, middle-class, mother-householder, father-bread-winner household portrayed every week in 1950s TV classics, such as *Leave It to Beaver, Father Knows Best,* and *Ozzie and Harriet* (and revisited in the 1970s sitcom *Happy Days*).

Like the characters in the TV series *Mad Men,* many men and women felt coerced into getting married, trapped in their families, unable to achieve the harmony, security, and emotional satisfaction they had been promised. As a result, the nuclear family was often a site of frustration and conflict. Surveys show that only about a third of working-class couples and two-thirds of middle-class couples were happily married (Bernard, 1972). Wives were less satisfied with marriage than husbands were. They reported higher rates of depression, distress, and feelings of inadequacy. Dissatisfaction seems to have been especially high among those women who, during World War II, had operated cranes in steel mills, greased locomotives, riveted the hulls of ships, worked the assembly lines in munitions factories, planted and harvested crops, and felled Douglas fir trees. They were universally praised for their dedication and industry during the war. Many of them did not want to leave well-paying jobs that gave them gratification and independence. Management fired most of them anyway and downgraded others to lower-paying "women's" jobs to make room for returning soldiers.

The tedium of domestic labour must have been especially difficult for many of these women to accept (Coontz, 1992: 23–41; Skolnick, 1991: 49–74).

Also, many families were simply too poor to participate in the functionalists' celebration of the traditional nuclear unit. Others, because of divorce or widowhood, lacked a male "breadwinner" or "good provider" (Bernard, 1986). For example, in 1951, 11.2 percent of married women and 19.3 percent of divorced and widowed women participated in the paid labour force. Then, as now, some of these women worked as "domestics," allowing their better-off counterparts to escape the drudgery of housework. Others provided child care as live-in or live-out nannies. To a degree not recognized by the functionalists, sustaining the role of the middle-class homemaker sometimes involved lower-class and immigrant women *not* being part of a traditional nuclear family.

Unlike the functionalists, Marxists had long seen the traditional nuclear family as a site of gender conflict and a basis for the perpetuation of social inequality. In the nineteenth century, Marx's friend and co-author, Friedrich Engels, argued that the traditional nuclear family emerged along with inequalities of wealth. Once wealth was concentrated in the hands of a man, wrote Engels, he became concerned about how to transmit it to his children, particularly his sons. How, asked Engels, could a man safely pass on an inheritance? Only by controlling his wife sexually and economically. Economic control ensured that the man's property would not be squandered and would remain his and his alone. Sexual control, in the form of enforced female monogamy, ensured that his property would be transmitted only to *his* offspring. It follows from Engels's analysis that only the elimination of private property and the creation of economic equality—in a word, communism—can bring an end to the traditional nuclear family and mark the arrival of gender equality (Engels, 1970 [1884]: 138–9).

Engels was right to note the long history of male economic and sexual domination in the traditional nuclear family. Early Canadian family law was informed by a vision of the family in which the role of the husband/father was pivotal and in which the labour and services of a wife belonged to her husband as a right. Although a series of legal reforms have altered the formerly harsh position of married women, as recently as a few decades ago a wife could not rent a car, take out a loan, or sign a contract without her husband's permission.

Despite the legally sanctioned domination of wives by husbands under capitalism, Engels was wrong to think that communism would eliminate gender inequality in the family. Gender inequality is as common in societies that call themselves communist as in those that call themselves capitalist. For example, the Soviet Union left "intact the fundamental family structures, authority relations, and socialization patterns crucial to personality formation and sex-role differentiation. Only a genuine sexual revolution [or, as we prefer to call it, a *gender revolution*] could have shattered these patterns and made possible the real emancipation of women" (Lapidus, 1978: 7).

Because gender inequality exists in non-capitalist (including pre-capitalist) societies, most feminists believe that something other than, or in addition to, capitalism accounts for gender inequality. In their view, *patriarchy*—male dominance and norms justifying that dominance—is more deeply rooted in the economic, military, and cultural history of humankind than the classical Marxist account allows (see Chapter 11, Sexuality and Gender). For them, only a "genuine gender revolution" can alter this state of affairs.

Just such a revolution in family structures, authority relations, and socialization patterns picked up steam in Canada and other Western countries about 40 years ago, although its roots extend back to the eighteenth century. The revolution is evident in the rise of romantic love and happiness as bases for marriage, women's increasing control over reproduction through the use of contraceptives, and women's increasing participation in the system of higher education and the paid labour force. We next consider some consequences of the gender revolution for the selection of mates, marital satisfaction, divorce, reproductive choice, housework, and child care. We begin by considering the sociology of mate selection.

POWER AND FAMILIES

Love and Mate Selection

Most Canadians take for granted that marriage ought to be based on love (see Figure 15.6). Our assumption is evident, for example, in the way many popular songs celebrate love as the sole basis of long-term intimacy and marriage. In contrast, most of us view marriage devoid of love as tragic.

Yet in most societies throughout human history, love has had little to do with marriage. Some languages, such as the Chinese dialect spoken in Shanghai, even lack a word for love. Historically and across cultures, marriages were typically arranged by third parties, not by brides and grooms themselves. The selection of marriage partners was based mainly on calculations intended to maximize the prestige, economic benefits, and political advantages accruing to the families from which the bride and groom came. For a family of modest means, a small dowry might be the chief gain from allowing their son to marry a certain woman. For upper-class families, the benefits were typically bigger but no less strategic. In the early years of industrialization, for example, more than one old aristocratic family in economic decline scrambled to have its offspring marry into a family of the upstart bourgeoisie. This does not mean that such marriages were wholly devoid of loving feelings. However, "being in love" was not seen as an essential prerequisite for a successful marital union.

The idea that love should be important in the choice of a marriage partner first gained currency in eighteenth-century England with the rise of liberalism and individualism, philosophies that stressed freedom of the individual over community welfare (Stone, 1977). However, the intimate linkage between love and marriage that we know today emerged only in the early twentieth century, when Hollywood and the advertising industry began to promote self-gratification on a grand scale. For these new spinners of fantasy and desire, an important aspect of self-gratification was heterosexual romance leading to marriage (Rapp and Ross, 1986).

Consider here, for example, the results of a recent study that asked 497 male and 673 female university undergraduates in 10 countries and Hong Kong the following

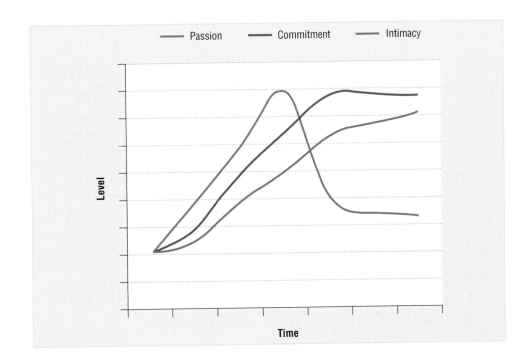

FIGURE 15.6
The Components of Love

According to psychologist Robert Sternberg, love can be built from three components: passion (erotic attraction), intimacy (confiding in others and shared feelings), and commitment (intention to remain in the relationship). In actual relationships, these components may be combined in various ways to produce different kinds of love. The fullest love requires all three components. Research shows that, in long-term relationships, passion peaks fairly quickly and then tapers off. Intimacy rises more gradually but remains at a higher plateau. Commitment develops most gradually but also plateaus at a high level.

Source: Sternberg, 1986.

Clark Gable and Vivien Leigh in *Gone with the Wind* (1939): Hollywood glamorized hetero-sexual, romantic love and solidified the intimate linkage between love and marriage that we know today.

question: "If a man (woman) had all the qualities you desired, would you marry this person if you were not in love with him (her)?" The results (presented in Figure 15.7) suggest that in free-choice cultures, where the value of individualism is highly prized, love has come to be defined as *the* essential basis for marriage. In the United States, a country often considered to be the most individualistic society in the world, only 3.5 percent of the students said they would marry someone whom they were not in love with—even if that person possessed all the qualities they were looking for in a partner (Levine, Sato, Hashimoto, and Verma, 1995).

Still, it would be a big mistake to think that love alone determines mate selection in our society—far from it. Three sets of social forces influence whom you are likely to fall in love with and marry (Kalmijn, 1998: 398–404):

1. *Marriage resources.* Potential spouses bring certain resources with them to the "marriage market." They use these resources to attract mates and compete against rivals.

FIGURE 15.7

Responses to Question: "If a man (woman) had all the other quantities you desired, would you marry this person if you were not in love with him (her)?"

Note: Some percentages do not add to 100 percent because of rounding.

Source: From Robert Levine, Suguru Sato, Tsukasa Hashimoto, and Jyoti Verma, "Love and Marriage in Eleven Cultures," *Journal of Cross-Cultural Psychology 26*, 5(1995): 554–71. Reprinted by permission of Sage Publications.

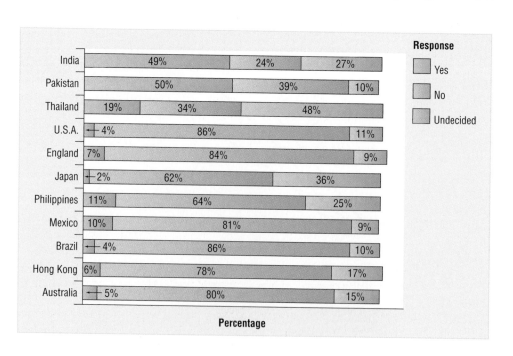

These resources include financial assets, status, values, tastes, and knowledge. Most people want to maximize the financial assets and status they gain from marriage and they want a mate who has similar values, tastes, and knowledge. As a result, whom you fall in love with and choose to marry is determined partly by the assets you bring to the marriage market.

2. *Third parties.* A marriage between people from two different groups may threaten the internal cohesion of one or both groups. Therefore, to varying degrees, families, neighbourhoods, communities, and religious institutions raise young people to identify with the groups they are members of and think of themselves as different from members of other groups. They may also apply sanctions to young people who threaten to marry outside the group. For example, although ethnic intermarriage has become increasingly common in Canada (Kalbach, 2000), parents often encourage their children to marry within their own ethnic group to preserve their unique culture (Kitano and Daniels, 1995). This is especially true among immigrants who come to Canada from more collectivist cultures in which arranged marriages have been the tradition (Dugger, 1996). As a result, whom you fall in love with and choose to marry is determined partly by the influence of third parties.

3. *Demographic and compositional factors.* The probability of marrying inside your group increases with the group's size and geographical concentration. Conversely, if you are a member of a small group or a group that is dispersed geographically, you stand a greater chance of having to choose an appropriate mate from outside your group. There may simply be too few "prospects" in your group from which to choose (Brym, Gillespie, and Gillis, 1985). In addition, the ratio of men to women in a group influences the degree to which members of each sex marry inside or outside the group. For instance, war and imprisonment may eliminate many male group members as potential marriage partners, encouraging female group members to marry outside the group or forgo marriage altogether. Finally, since people usually meet potential spouses in "local marriage markets"—schools, universities and colleges, places of work, neighbourhoods, bars, and clubs—the degree to which these settings are socially segregated also influences mate selection. You are more likely to marry outside your group if local marriage markets are socially heterogeneous. As a result, whom you fall in love with and choose to marry is determined partly by the size, geographical dispersion, and sex ratio of the groups you belong to, and the social composition of the local marriage markets you frequent.

As a result of the operation of these three sets of social forces, the process of falling in love and choosing a mate is far from random. Most of us will select a partner of similar ethnic background, age, and social class. Traditionally, the Protestant, Catholic, Jewish, Muslim, and Hindu religions have encouraged **endogamy**: marrying within your own social group. (The opposite of endogamy is **exogamy**, marrying outside your group.) In the past, social pressures to marry endogamously were more robust than they are today. Nevertheless, although interracial marriage has become more acceptable in Canada (Bibby, 2001: 216), the overwhelming majority of Canadian couples, whether married or living common law, with or without children, are racially homogeneous (Riedmann, Lamanna, and Nelson, 2003: 213).

Endogamy is marrying within your own social group.

Exogamy is marrying outside your own social group.

Marital Satisfaction

Just as mate selection came to depend more on romantic love over the years, so marital stability came to depend more on having a happy rather than merely a useful marriage. This change has occurred because women in Canada and many other societies have become more autonomous, especially over the past half century. One aspect of the gender revolution is that women are freer than ever to leave marriages in which they are unhappy.

One factor that contributed to women's autonomy was the legalization of birth control measures. Since 1969, birth control measures have been legal in Canada. The birth control pill made it easier for women to delay childbirth and have fewer children. A second factor that contributed to women's autonomy was their increased presence in the paid labour force. Although in 1961 only about one in five husband-and-wife families were dual-income families, by 1967 this had increased to just over one in three (Vanier Institute of the Family, 2000: 96). Once women enjoyed a source of income independent of their husbands, they gained the means to decide the course of their own lives to a greater extent than ever before. A married woman with a job outside the home is less tied to her marriage by economic necessity than is a woman who works only at home. If she is deeply dissatisfied with her marriage, she can more easily leave. In addition, beginning in the late 1960s, laws governing divorce were changed to make divorce easier.

If marital stability now depends largely on marital satisfaction, what are the main factors underlying marital satisfaction? The sociological literature emphasizes five sets of forces (Collins and Coltrane, 1991: 394–406, 454–64)

1. *Economic factors.* Money issues are the most frequent subjects of family quarrels, and money issues loom larger when there isn't enough money to satisfy a family's needs and desires. Accordingly, marital satisfaction tends to fall and the divorce rate tends to rise as you move down the socioeconomic hierarchy. The lower the social class and the lower the educational level of the spouses, the more likely it is that financial pressures will make them unhappy and the marriage unstable. Marital dissatisfaction and divorce are also more common among groups with high poverty rates. In contrast, the marital satisfaction of wives and, even more, of husbands generally *increases* when wives enter the paid labour force (Hughes, Galinsky, and Morris, 1992; Lupri and Frideres, 1988). This is mainly because of the beneficial financial effects. However, if *either* spouse spends so much time on the job that he or she neglects the family, marital satisfaction falls.

2. *Divorce laws.* Many surveys show that, on average, married people are happier than unmarried people are. Moreover, when people are free to end unhappy marriages and remarry, the average level of happiness increases among married people. Thus, the level of marital happiness has increased in Canada over the past few decades, especially for wives, partly because it has become easier to get a divorce. For the same reason, in countries where getting a divorce is more difficult (e.g., Italy and Spain), husbands and wives tend to be less happy than in countries where getting a divorce is easier (e.g., Canada and the United States; Stack and Eshleman, 1998).

3. *The family life cycle.* Most divorces occur relatively early in marriage (Clarke, 1995). In Canada, the highest rate of divorce per 1000 population occurs at year five of marriage (with more than 3.5 divorces per 1000 population) and then falls each year thereafter (Ambert, 1998: 5). However, the proportion of divorces for couples married 20 years or more has increased in recent years (Wu and Penning, 1997). Marital satisfaction generally starts high, falls when children are born (especially for wives; Glenn, 1990: 825), reaches a low point when children are in their teenage years, and rises again when children reach adulthood (Rollins and Cannon, 1974).[1] Couples without children and parents whose children have left home (so-called empty-nesters) enjoy the highest level of marital satisfaction. Parents who are just starting families or who have adult children living at home enjoy intermediate levels of marital satisfaction. Marital satisfaction is lowest during the "establishment" years, when children are attending school. Although most people get married at least partly to have children, it turns out that children, and especially teenagers, usually put big emotional and financial strains on families. This results in relatively low marital satisfaction.

4. *Housework and child care.* Marital happiness is higher among couples who perceive an equitable distribution of housework and child care (Rosenbluth, Steil, and Whitcomb, 1998). The further couples are from an equitable sharing of domestic responsibilities, the more tension there is among all family members (Risman and Johnson-Sumerford, 1998). Some research finds that equitable sharing tends to increase with education (Berk, 1985).

5. *Sex.* Having a good sex life is associated with marital satisfaction. Contrary to popular belief, surveys show that sex generally improves during a marriage. Sexual intercourse is also more enjoyable and frequent among happier couples. From these findings, some experts conclude that general marital happiness leads to sexual compatibility (Collins and Coltrane, 1991: 344). However, the reverse may also be true. Good sex may lead to a good marriage. After all, sexual preferences are deeply rooted in our psyches and our earliest experiences. They cannot be altered easily to suit our partners. If spouses are sexually incompatible, they may find it hard to change, even if they communicate well, argue little, and are generally happy on other grounds. Conversely, if a husband and wife are sexually compatible, they may work harder to resolve other problems in the marriage for the sake of preserving their good sex life. Thus, the relationship between marital satisfaction and sexual compatibility is probably reciprocal. Each factor influences the other.

Religion, we note, has little effect on level of marital satisfaction. But religion does influence the divorce rate in a variety of ways. For example, a person may be influenced by biblical teaching that emphasizes the sanctity of marriage and prohibits adultery (Clark, 2000: 113). In addition, religious people are more likely than those who never attend religious services to report that they would remain married "for the sake of the children" and are less likely to view a partner's lack of love and respect or a partner's excessive drinking as grounds for divorce. However, religious people were just as likely as those who did not attend religious services to regard abusive behaviour and infidelity as valid reasons to divorce (Clark, 2000: 110).

Let us now see what happens when low marital satisfaction leads to divorce.

Divorce

Before the turn of the twentieth century, divorce was a complex, drawn-out legal process in Canada. In some provinces, a "parliamentary" divorce was possible. However, this required that a private members' bill pass successfully through two readings in both the House of Commons and the Senate and then be approved by a special divorce committee (Boyd, 1998: 229). As a result, divorce was rare.

Before 1968, adultery was the only grounds for divorce in Canada, except in Nova Scotia, where cruelty was sufficient grounds even before Confederation (Morrison, 1987). The Divorce Act of 1968, the first federal divorce statute, expanded the "fault grounds" under which a divorce could be granted. In addition to adultery, proof that a partner had engaged in prohibited activities, such as mental or physical cruelty, rape, gross addiction to alcohol or other drugs, sodomy, bestiality, and homosexual acts, entitled the petitioner to an immediate divorce. This act also took a first step toward "no-fault" divorce. The dissolution of a marriage was permitted on grounds of unspecified "marital breakdown" if couples had lived "separate and apart" for three years before applying for a divorce and jointly consented to being divorced. In the event that one party did not want to be divorced, the court required that five years pass from the time of the separation before applying for divorce.

With the amendment of Canada's Divorce Act in 1985, only one ground is available for divorce—marital breakdown—but this is defined in three ways: (1) the spouses have lived apart for one year, (2) one of the spouses has committed an act of adultery, or (3) one spouse has treated the other with mental or physical cruelty. Today, a spouse seeking divorce no longer has to prove grounds. Instead, a marriage is legally "dissolved" because the relationship is "irretrievably broken." Following these amendments, the divorce rate reached a historic high in 1987 and has since declined (Statistics Canada, 2000b). The 2003 crude divorce rate of 224 divorces for every 100 000 people was far below its peak in 1987 of 335 divorces per 100 000 people. Based on 2003 divorce rates, projections are that 38.3 percent of marriages will end in divorce within 30 years of marriage (Statistics Canada, 2005c).

Economic Effects

In the first year following divorce, the income of Canadian women declines by about 50 percent, while men's household income decreases by about 25 percent (Finnie, 1993). However, since the majority of children remain with their mothers following divorce, after adjustments for family size the data reveal "a smallish rise in economic well-being for men, versus drops of about 40 percent for women" (Finnie, 1993: 225). After divorce, poverty rates for men rise slightly, from 14 percent to 17 percent, while for women poverty rates leap from 16 percent to 43 percent in the year immediately after divorce. These results paint a picture of divorce in which, on average, women experience steep declines in economic well-being while men enjoy moderate increases. And although there is some recovery for women in the post-divorce years, three full years after the split, they remain well below their pre-divorce levels, as well as below the current economic levels of their ex-husbands (Finnie, 1993: 228).

This pattern occurs because husbands tend to earn more, children typically live with their mothers, and support payments are often inadequate. Although child poverty in Canada is not restricted to single-parent families, a far higher proportion of children of single parents and, in particular, lone-parent mothers live in low-income circumstances (see Figure 15.8). The younger the age of children at the time of divorce or dissolution of a common-law relationship, the more likely they are to be living in a low-income situation (Ambert, 1998: 9).

In the past, Canadian laws regarding the division of marital assets on divorce and the awarding of alimony contributed to women's declining living standards post-divorce. For example, in the early 1970s, Irene Murdock, a farm wife, claimed that her labours over the course of 15 years had earned her a share in the family farm. However, the Supreme Court of Canada ruled that the labours were simply that of an "ordinary farm wife" and did *not* entitle Mrs. Murdock to share in the property that she and her husband had accumulated during their marriage (Steel, 1987: 159).

At present, no federal property law applies throughout Canada. Although all Canadian provinces and territories have laws requiring spouses to share assets in the event of marital breakdown, the precise definition of what constitutes a "family asset" varies and creates inconsistencies across jurisdictions (Dranoff, 2001: 257). In addition, although the

FIGURE 15.8

Incidence (Percentage) Living with Low Income among Canadian Families, 1994–2003

Note: Elderly families are those with heads 65 years of age or older. Couples without children, two-parent, and lone-parent families are under age 65.

Source: Adapted from Statistics Canada, "Income in Canada," 2003, Catalogue 75-202. Retrieved May 12, 2005 (http://www.statcan.ca/english/freepub/75-202-XIE/75-202-XIE2003000.pdf).

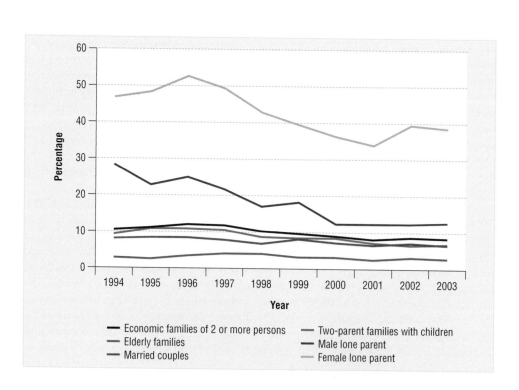

monetary value of tangible "family assets" (e.g., money in the bank, a house) can be calculated and shared, the valuable "new property" (Glendon, 1981) in today's society is the earning power of a professional degree, highly paid employment, work experience, a skilled trade, or other "human capital." On divorce, the wife *may* get an equal share of tangible property, but that does not usually result in her beginning post-divorce life on an equal footing with her former husband—especially if she retains physical custody of the couple's children.

Child support involves money paid by the non-custodial parent to the custodial parent for the purpose of supporting the children of a separated marital, cohabiting, or sexual relationship. Under the Divorce Act, either parent may be ordered to pay child support. However, because mothers retain custody in most cases—and because women are more likely to be economically disadvantaged in employment—the vast majority of those ordered to pay child support are fathers.

Every jurisdiction in Canada requires parents to support their children following separation or divorce. In 1997, the federal government introduced standardized guidelines, based on the income of the non-custodial parent only and the number of children involved, to establish the amount of mandatory payment for child-support orders granted from May 1, 1997, onward under the Divorce Act. Although the intent of these guidelines is to provide more consistency across support orders, slight variations are permitted between jurisdictions to reflect differences in cost of living. Judges may also increase support payments (e.g., to accommodate child care or medical costs) or decrease these payments (e.g., in joint custody cases where the non-custodial parent is responsible for a child at least 40 percent of the time).

Court orders in themselves, however, do not always guarantee that child support will be paid. In practice, orders for child and spousal support have often been difficult to enforce, and there have been high default rates. All Canadian provinces and territories now have their own programs to protect against nonpayment of child support. However, despite the increasing adoption of public enforcement strategies, the problem of "deadbeat parents" in Canada remains significant, with more than $2 billion owed in child support (FAD, 2000).

Some analysts argue that the principal reason for nonpayment of child support is the unemployment or underemployment of the non-custodial parent (Meyer and Bartfield, 1996). If this is correct, "coercive child-support collection policies, such as automatic wage withholding, will have only limited success" and solving the problem "will be the old and unglamorous one, of solving un- and underemployment, both for the fathers and the mothers" (Braver, Fitzpatrick, and Bay, 1991: 184–85). Others recommend that Canada adopt the model of guaranteed child support used in France and Sweden. In these countries, the government gives the custodial parent the full amount awarded in child support, even though this amount may not have been received from the non-custodial parent. The government assumes responsibility for collecting the money from the parent who failed to provide it (Salt, 1991).

Emotional Effects

Although divorce enables spouses to leave unhappy marriages, questions have been raised about the emotional consequences of divorce for children, particularly in the long term. Some scholars claim that divorcing parents are simply trading the well-being of their children for their own happiness. What does research say about this issue?

Research shows that children of divorced parents tend to develop behavioural problems and do less well in school than children in intact families. They are more likely to engage in delinquent acts and to abuse drugs and alcohol. They often experience an emotional crisis, particularly in the first two years after divorce. What is more, when children of divorced parents become adults, they are less likely than children of non-divorced parents are to be happy. They are more likely to suffer health problems, depend on welfare, earn low incomes, and experience divorce themselves. In one study, almost half the children of divorced parents entered adulthood as worried, underachieving, self-deprecating, and sometimes angry

Child support involves money paid by the non-custodial parent to the custodial parent for the purpose of supporting the children of a separated marital, cohabiting, or sexual relationship.

young men and women (Wallerstein, Lewis, and Blakeslee, 2000). Clearly, divorce can have serious, long-term, negative consequences for children.

However, much of the research that seems to establish a link between divorce and long-term negative consequences for children is based on families who seek psychological counselling. Such families are a small and unrepresentative minority. By definition, they have more serious emotional problems than the large majority, who do not need psychological counselling after divorce. We must be careful not to generalize from such studies. Another problem with much of this research is that some analysts fail to ask whether factors other than divorce might be responsible for the long-term distress experienced by many children of divorced parents.

Researchers who rely on representative samples and examine the separate effects of many factors on children's well-being provide the best evidence on the consequences of divorce for children. For example, a re-analysis of 92 relevant studies showed that, on average, the overall effect of divorce on children's well-being is not strong and is declining over time (Amato and Keith, 1991). This research also found that three factors account for much of the distress among children of divorce:

1. *A high level of parental conflict.* A high level of parental conflict creates long-term distress among children. Divorce without parental conflict does children much less harm. In fact, children in divorced families have a higher level of well-being on average than do children in high-conflict, *intact* families. The effect of parental conflict on the long-term well-being of children is substantially greater than the effect of the next two factors.
2. *A decline in living standards.* By itself, the economic disadvantage experienced by most children in divorced families exerts a small impact on their well-being. Nonetheless, it is clear that children of divorce who do not experience a decline in living standards suffer less harm.
3. *The absence of a parent.* Children of divorce usually lose a parent as a role model and a source of emotional support, practical help, and supervision. By itself, this factor also has a small effect on children's well-being, even if the child has continued contact with the non-custodial parent. According to the National Children's Survey, following parental separation about one-third of children have very little contact with their non-custodial fathers (i.e., either irregular visits or no visits at all). Children born of common-law unions are even less likely to see their fathers than are children born to married parents.

Subsequent studies confirm many of these generalizations and add an important observation. Many of the behavioural and adjustment problems experienced by children of divorce existed before the divorce took place. We cannot therefore attribute them to the divorce itself (Stewart, Copeland, Chester, Malley, and Barenbaum, 1997).

In sum, claiming that divorcing parents selfishly trade the well-being of their children for their own happiness is an exaggeration. Although the heightened risk of poverty is real, high levels of parental conflict can also have serious negative consequences for children, even when they enter adulthood. In such high-conflict situations, divorce can benefit children. By itself, the absence of a parent has a small negative effect on children's well-being. But this effect is becoming smaller over time, perhaps in part because divorce is so common, it no longer has a stigma.

Reproductive Choice

We have seen that the power women gained from working in the paid labour force put them in a position to leave a marriage if it made them deeply unhappy. Another aspect of the gender revolution women are experiencing is that they are increasingly able to decide what happens in the marriage if they stay. For example, women now have more say over whether they will have children and, if so, when they will have them and how many they will have.

A high level of parental conflict creates long-term distress among children. Divorce without parental conflict does children much less harm. Children in divorced families have a higher level of well-being on average than do children in high-conflict, intact families.

Children are increasingly expensive to raise. Even a decade ago, "parents could expect to spend close to $154,000 on rearing a child to age 18. . . . Boys cost $154,367 while girls were a bargain at $153,458" (Vanier Institute of the Family, 2000: 136). In 2004, the cost of raising a child in Manitoba to the age of 18 was about $167 000 (Canadian Council on Social Development, 2007). Children no longer give the family economic benefits, as they did, say, on the family farm. Most women want to work in the paid labour force, many of them to pursue a career. As a result, most women decide to have fewer children, to have them further apart, and to have them starting at an older age. Some decide to have none at all (Dalphonse, 1997). In recent years, various organizations for child-free couples have emerged, such as No Kidding, launched by a Canadian with chapters in several Canadian provinces and abroad.

Women's reproductive decisions are carried out by means of contraception and abortion. Under section 179c of Canada's Revised Statutes of 1892, a woman who sought or succeeded in inducing her own abortion—as well as anyone who assisted her—committed a criminal offence. Until 1988, the Canadian Criminal Code defined any attempt to induce an abortion by any means as a crime for which the maximum penalty was life imprisonment or, if the woman herself was convicted, two years.

Laws prohibiting abortion established during the nineteenth century stood almost unchallenged until the 1960s, when an abortion reform movement, spearheaded by Canadian physician Dr. Henry Morgentaler, urged the repeal of abortion laws that, in his words, "compelled the unwilling to bear the unwanted" (in Dranoff, 2001: 16). The first such change occurred with the 1969 amendment that allowed for "therapeutic abortion" *if* performed by a physician in an accredited hospital and *if* a three-member committee certified that the continuation of the pregnancy would likely endanger the health of the mother. After this amendment, both the number and the rate of therapeutic abortions rose significantly. They then began to drop and stabilize beginning in 1983, and then rise substantially in 1988. In that year, the Supreme Court of Canada struck down the law on abortion on the grounds that it contravened a woman's right to control her own reproductive life and, as such, contravened her constitutionally protected guarantees to security of her person (under the equality rights provision of the Canadian Charter of Rights and Freedoms). The Supreme Court also unanimously determined that the civil law in Quebec, the Quebec Charter, and the common law do not protect fetal life or interests.

In 1989, in the case of *Tremblay v. Daigle,* the Supreme Court of Canada ruled that a fetus is not a person in law and that a father of a fetus has no legal right of veto over a woman's decision about the fetus she is carrying. In 1993, the Supreme Court of Canada struck down legislation that banned abortion clinics. By 1995, abortion clinics outside hospitals operated in all Canadian provinces except Prince Edward Island and Saskatchewan.

In 2002, 105 154 women obtained therapeutic abortions in Canada. Women in their 20s accounted for slightly over half (52 percent) of all those who obtained abortions in 2002 (Statistics Canada, 2005f). However, on a global scale, abortion rates in Canada are low at 10.3 per 1000 women aged 15 to 44. In comparison, the rate in the United States is 21 per 1000 women; in Cuba, 57; in Bulgaria, 77; in Vietnam, 84; in the Russian Federation, 119; and in Romania, 172 (Health Canada, 1999a).

Public opinion on the acceptability of abortion is mixed in Canada, although most Canadians agree that abortion should be "legal only under certain [undefined] circumstances" (Tun, 2000).

Attitudes toward abortion vary by age, with Canadian teens more likely than Canadian adults to approve of the availability of legal abortion for any reason (55 versus 43 percent, respectively; Bibby, 2001: 250–51). "Generation Xers," and adult baby boomer parents who participated in the sexual revolution of the 1960s, show a slightly higher approval of abortion on demand (46 percent and 44 percent, respectively) than the previous generation (36 percent). However, 90 percent of adults and 84 percent of teens support the availability of legal abortion when rape is involved.

Right-to-life versus pro-choice activists have been clashing since the 1970s. Right-to-life activists object to the decriminalization of abortion; pro-choice activists want the current situation preserved. Both groups have tried to influence public opinion and lawmakers to achieve their aims. A few extreme right-to-life activists (almost all men) have resorted to violence (Gegax and Clemetson, 1998).

WHERE DO
YOU FIT IN?

What are your views on abortion? Do you think your opinions are influenced by your social characteristics (income, education, occupation, religiosity, etc.)? In thinking about this issue, you will find it useful to know that right-to-life activists tend to be homemakers living in religious, middle-income families. They argue that life begins at conception. Therefore, they say, abortion destroys human life and is morally indefensible. They advocate adoption instead of abortion. In their opinion, the pro-choice option is selfish, expressing greater concern for career advancement and sexual pleasure than for moral responsibility (Erwin, 1988).

In contrast, pro-choice activists tend to be women pursuing their own careers. They are more highly educated, less religious, and better off financially than right-to-life activists are. They argue that every woman has the right to choose what happens to her own body and that bearing an unwanted child can harm not only a woman's career but the child, too. For example, unwanted children are more likely to be neglected or abused. They are also more likely to get in trouble with the law because of inadequate adult supervision and discipline. Furthermore, according to pro-choice activists, religious doctrines claiming that life begins at conception are arbitrary. So, what is your view? And to what degree is it influenced by your social characteristics?

As sociologists Randall Collins and Scott Coltrane (1995) note, it seems likely that the criminalization of abortion would return us to the situation that existed in the 1960s. Specifically, they claim that, on a per capita basis, roughly as many abortions took place then as now. But because they were illegal, abortions were expensive, hard to obtain, and posed more dangers to women's health. They conclude that if abortion were criminalized, poor women and their unwanted children would suffer most.

Reproductive Technologies

For most women, exercising reproductive choice means being able to prevent pregnancy and birth by means of contraception and abortion. For some women, however, it means *facilitating* pregnancy and birth by means of reproductive technologies. As many as 15 percent of couples are infertile. With a declining number of so-called desirable children (i.e., healthy, white newborns) available for adoption, and a persistent and strong desire by most people to have biologically related children, demand is strong for techniques to help infertile couples, some lesbian couples, and some single women have babies.

There are four main reproductive technologies. In *artificial insemination,* a donor's sperm is inserted in a woman's vaginal canal or uterus during ovulation. In *surrogate motherhood,* a donor's sperm is used to artificially inseminate a woman who has signed a contract to surrender the child at birth in exchange for a fee. In *in vitro fertilization,* eggs are surgically removed from a woman and joined with sperm in a culture dish, and an embryo is then transferred to the woman's uterus. Finally, various *screening techniques* are used on sperm and fetuses to increase the chance of giving birth to a baby of the desired sex and end pregnancies deemed medically problematic.

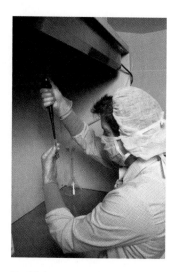

Fertilizing an egg in vitro

These procedures raise several sociological and ethical issues. We mention two here (Achilles, 1993). The first problem is discrimination. Most reproductive technologies are expensive. Surrogate mothers charge $10 000 or more to carry a child. In vitro fertilization (IVF) fees are in the range of $25 000, and only Ontario's health insurance plan covers IVF (and then only in limited circumstances). Obviously, poor and middle-income earners who happen to be infertile cannot afford these procedures. In addition, according to the report of the Royal Commission on New Reproductive Technologies (1993), there is a strong tendency for members of the medical profession to deny single women and lesbian couples access to reproductive technologies. The medical community

TECHNOLOGY
BYTES

discriminates not just against those of modest means but also against those wanting to rear children in non-traditional families.

A second problem introduced by reproductive technologies is that they render the terms *mother* and *father* obsolete, or at least vague. Is the mother the person who donates the egg, carries the child in her uterus, or raises the child? Is the father the person who donates the sperm or raises the child? As these questions suggest, a child conceived through a combination of reproductive technologies and raised by a heterosexual couple could have as many as three mothers and two fathers! This is not just a terminological problem. If it were, we could just introduce new distinctions, such as *egg mother, uterine mother,* and *social mother,* to reflect the new reality. The real problem is social and legal. The question of who has what rights and obligations to the child, and what rights and obligations the child has vis-à-vis each parent, is unclear. This lack of clarity has already caused anguished court battles over child custody (Franklin and Ragone, 1999).

Public debate on a wide scale is needed to decide who will control reproductive technologies and to what ends. On the one hand, reproductive technologies may bring the greatest joy to infertile people. They may also prevent the birth and suffering of children with chronic, progressive, and fatal diseases. On the other hand, reproductive technologies may continue to benefit mainly the well-to-do, reinforce traditional family forms that are no longer appropriate for many people, and cause endless legal wrangling and heartache.

Housework, Child Care, and Senior Care

As we have seen, women's increased participation in the paid labour force, their increased participation in the system of higher education, and their increased control over reproduction transformed several areas of family life. Despite this far-ranging gender revolution, one domain remains resistant to change: housework, child care, and senior care. This fact was first documented in detail by sociologist Arlie Hochschild. She showed that even women who work full time in the paid labour force usually begin a "second shift" when they return home. There, they prepare meals, help with homework, do laundry, and so forth (Hochschild with Machung, 1989).

To be sure, change has occurred as men take a more active role in the day-to-day running of the household. In 2005, Canadian men did nearly 37 percent of the housework and child care (Figure 15.9). But this figure does not reveal the whole picture. Men tend to do low-stress chores that can often wait a day or a week. These jobs include mowing the lawn, repairing the car, and painting the fence. They also play with their children more than they used to. In contrast, women tend to do higher-stress chores that cannot

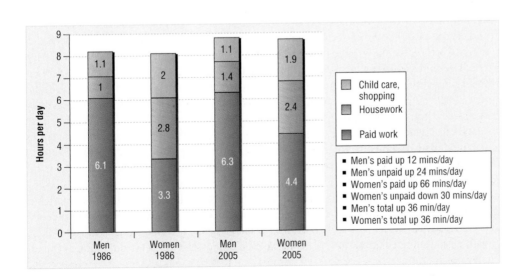

FIGURE 15.9

Hours Spent Doing Unpaid Housework, by Gender, Canada, 1986 and 2005

Source: Statistics Canada, 2005d.

wait. These jobs include getting kids dressed and out the door to school every day, preparing dinner and cleaning up after it is served, washing and ironing clothes, and the like (Harvey, Marshall, and Frederick, 1991).

Two main factors shrink the gender gap in housework, child care, and senior care. First, the smaller the difference between the husband's and the wife's earnings, the more equal the division of household labour. Apparently, women are routinely able to translate earning power into domestic influence. Put bluntly, their increased financial status enables them to get their husbands to do more around the house. In addition, women who earn relatively high incomes are also able to use some of their money to pay outsiders to do domestic work.

Attitude is the second factor that shrinks the gap in domestic labour. The more that a husband and wife agree there *should* be equality in the household division of labour, the more equality there is. Seeing eye to eye on this issue is often linked to both spouses having a postsecondary education (Greenstein, 1996). Thus, if there is going to be greater equality between men and women in doing household chores, two things have to happen. There must be greater equality between men and women in the paid labour force and broader cultural acceptance of the need for gender equality.

Equality and Spouse Abuse

Above we noted that more egalitarian couples are generally more happily married. Said differently, marital satisfaction increases as the statuses of husband and wife approach equality. Does it follow that higher levels of gender equality also result in lower rates of spouse abuse? As we will now see, it does.

The General Social Survey (GSS), based on a large, representative nationwide sample, investigated the experiences of both women and men in relation to violence by current and previous spouses and common-law partners. A person was defined as having a current relationship if he or she was married, living common law, or had a same-sex partner.

Respondents were asked if, "in the past 5 years, your spouse/partner has (1) threatened to hit you with a fist or anything else that could have hurt you, (2) thrown anything at you that could have hurt you, (3) pushed, grabbed, or shoved you in a way that could have hurt you, (4) slapped you, (5) kicked, bit, or hit you with a fist, (6) hit you with something that could have hurt you, (7) beaten you, (8) choked you, (9) used or threatened to use a gun or knife on you, or (10) forced you into any unwanted sexual activity by threatening you, holding you down, or hurting you in some way." Although the survey included questions about emotional abuse, the findings we present here do not.

The survey results suggest that many Canadian women *and* men experience violence in their marriages or common-law relationships. Some 7 percent of Canadians who were in a marital or cohabiting relationship had experienced some form of violence at the hands of their partner over the past five years (Bunge, 2000: 11). However, although the five-year rates of violence were similar for women (8 percent) and men (7 percent), women were more likely to experience severe forms of violence. Specifically, women were three times as likely to suffer an injury, five times as likely to receive medical attention, and five times as likely to report that the violence they had experienced caused them to fear for their lives (Bunge, 2000: 11). Compared with men, women were more likely to report being beaten, choked, or threatened with a gun or knife, or having these weapons used against them. Women were also more likely than men were to report multiple incidents of spousal violence. Compared with women, men were more likely to report being slapped, having something thrown at them, or being kicked, bit, or hit (Bunge, 2000: 12).

The data reveal that women and men from all income and educational levels experience spousal violence. But in general, younger people face the greatest risk of experiencing spousal violence, with the highest rates reported by young women under the age of 25 (5 percent). Men aged 25 to 34 also reported higher rates of violence from partners (4 percent) than did those who were older (1 percent).

Consistent with earlier studies conducted in both Canada and the United States (Kong, 1997; U.S. Department of Justice, 1998), the risk of being a victim of spousal violence was higher for both women and men living in common-law unions (4 percent) than in legal marriages (1 percent). Individuals living in common-law relationships also experience a higher level of lethal spousal violence (Hotton, 2001). This is particularly true for Aboriginal peoples. Aboriginal women in common-law relationships experience homicide rates that are almost eight times as high as those in legal marriages are (111.0 per million and 13.9 per million, respectively). The rate of spousal homicide among Aboriginal men in common-law relationships is almost six times as great as that of Aboriginal men living with legal spouses (60.7 per million and 10.5 per million, respectively; Johnson and Hotton, 2001: 31; see Figure 15.10).

Research suggests that men who abuse their partners may be attempting to compensate for general feelings of powerlessness or inadequacy in their jobs, marriages, or both. This form of family violence has been termed *patriarchal terrorism* (Johnson, 1995). As Chapter 11, Sexuality and Gender, notes, cultural images of take-charge, aggressive masculinity may encourage some men to use physical expressions of power in an attempt to compensate for their perceived lack of occupational success, prestige, or satisfaction (Anderson, 1997). The men most likely to abuse women are between 18 and 30 years old, unemployed, users of illicit drugs or abusers of alcohol, and high-school dropouts. They are more likely than other men are to have witnessed their mothers being abused, to have been abused themselves as children, and to believe that male domination is justified. Those who lack legitimate means of attaining personal or social power may resort to violence in an attempt to gain or regain feelings of personal power (Gelles, 1994, 1997; Pyke, 1997; Ronfeldt, Kimerling, and Arias, 1998; Smith, 1990).

Women also face a heightened risk of homicide following a marital separation (Johnson and Hotton, 2001: 33). Recognition that the most dangerous time for a victim of intimate violence is after leaving a violent relationship helped fuel the 1993 passage of Bill C-126, which made "criminal harassment" a criminal offence. This law is directed against "stalking." In 1999, 5382 incidents of criminal harassment were reported to police in Canada, up 32 percent from 1996 (Greeno, 2000). Consistent with earlier research (Kong, 1997), women were the victims in 75 percent of reported cases. In most of these cases, the woman knew the stalker and, in many instances, had been involved with him in a previous relationship. Although women were most likely to be stalked by an ex-husband, boyfriend, or current husband, 44 percent of male victims were stalked by a casual acquaintance; few male victims of criminal harassment were stalked by an ex-wife or girlfriend. In addition, from 1997 to 1999 there were nine stalking-related

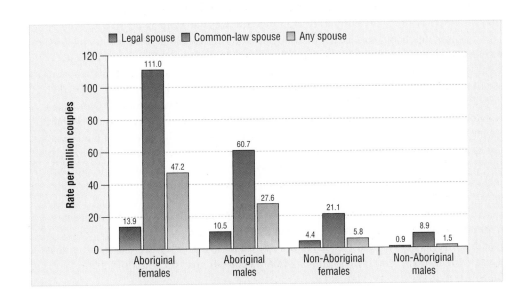

FIGURE 15.10

Aboriginal Women in Common-Law Relationships Have Highest Rates of Spousal Homicide

Source: Adapted from Statistics Canada, 2001, *Family Violence in Canada: A Statistical Profile,* Catalogue No. 85-224. Retrieved June 28, 2001 (http://www.statcan. ca/english/freepub/85-224-XIE/ 0000185-224-XIE.pdf).

homicides reported, each involving a woman who had been stalked by a former partner (Greeno, 2000).

We have seen that male domination in both childhood socialization and current family organization increases the likelihood of wife abuse. Some researchers argue that exposing children to violence results in adults who are more likely to use violence (see Box 15.2). In addition, high levels of wife assault are associated with gender inequality

---

BOX 15.2
It's Your Choice

Is Spanking Ever Appropriate?

On July 4, 2001, child welfare workers took seven children, aged 6 to 14, from their home in southern Ontario amid concerns that they were being spanked with paddles by their fundamentalist Christian parents. The children's parents, members of the Church of God, admitted that they used paddles to discipline their children. However, they noted that doing so was consistent with the teachings of their religion. A media statement released by the Church of God noted the group's belief that "the Word of God advocates corporal punishment under certain circumstances" (Church of God, 2001). According to the group's spiritual adviser, Daniel Layne, "The whole issue is spanking and discipline, and how we see in modern times that when parents don't discipline their children it leads to all kinds of social problems. . . . Switching is used as a last resort, but the Scriptures clearly call for it and we won't give it up" (quoted in Clairborne, 2001).

The children were returned to their home on July 26, after their parents agreed to abstain from the use of corporal punishment while the case was before the courts. Children's Aid Society (CAS) workers were given unannounced access to the children in their homes and at school and allowed to discuss alternative methods of child discipline with the parents. However, more than 100 members of the Church of God fled Canada over fears that authorities would attempt to seize their children. In January 2002, the Ontario

Court of Appeal found in favour of the children's parents and upheld the right of parents, teachers, and persons standing in place of parents to physically discipline their young charges (McCarten, 2002).

In stark contrast to such countries as Austria, Cyprus, Denmark, Finland, Italy, Norway, and Sweden, where the use of corporal punishment against children is prohibited by law, Canadian law has, since 1892, allowed parents to use corporal punishment as a form of child discipline. However, not all Canadians agree with the decision of the Ontario Court of Appeal in the Church of God case—or with the decisions rendered in other Canadian courtrooms. For example, one of the leading decisions used by our courts to interpret this section of the Criminal Code specifies that "the mere fact that the children disciplined suffered contusions and bruises is not in itself proof of exercise of undue force."

Is spanking ever appropriate? Experts themselves have conflicting opinions about this issue. Sociologist Murray Straus (1994) advises parents never to hit children of any age under any circumstances. Considerable evidence suggests that children who are spanked by their parents (including those who are otherwise loving) are more likely to cheat, lie, bully, be intentionally cruel to others, disobey in school, and misbehave in various ways (Stormshak, Bierman, McMahon, and Lengua, 2000; Straus, 1996; Straus and Mouradian, 1998; Straus and Stewart, 1999; Straus, Sugerman, and Giles-Sims, 1997).

Research also links being spanked to depression and suicide in childhood, alcohol and/or drug abuse in adolescence, and, during adulthood, a heightened likelihood of abusing one's own children and/or engaging in spousal violence (Garvey, 1999; Straus and Kantor, 1994; Turner and Finkelhor, 1996). Spanking apparently teaches children that it is acceptable to hit someone and that those who love you may hit you with impunity. This message confuses love and violence—and sets the stage for subsequent abusive acts directed against intimate partners (Straus and Yodanis, 1996).

In contrast, other researchers contend that Straus and others may be overstating and oversimplifying the situation (Gilbert, 1997). One review of the literature on non-abusive and customary physical punishment by parents reports that the observed consequences of such punishment vary by method employed, the child's personality, subcultural factors, and so forth (Larzelere, 2000). Some studies find that non-abusive spanking as an occasional backup form of child discipline had such beneficial outcomes as reduced noncompliance and fighting among two- to six-year-olds.

What do you think? Do you agree with the decision of the Ontario Court of Appeal in the Church of God case? Is corporal punishment an appropriate form of child discipline? Is corporal punishment child abuse? Should parents spank their children? Should Canada repeal the law that allows corporal punishment? Is spanking a training ground for violence against intimate partners later in life?

in the larger society. For example, an American sociologist constructed a measure of wife assault for each American state by using data from a national survey (Straus, 1994). The measure shows the percentage of couples in each state in which the wife was physically assaulted by her partner during the 12 months preceding the survey. He then used government data to measure gender inequality in each state. His measure of gender inequality taps the economic, educational, political, and legal status of women. He found that as gender equality increases—as women and men become more equal in the larger society—wife assault declines. The conclusion we must draw from this research is clear: The incidence of wife assault is highest where early socialization experiences predispose men to behave aggressively toward women, where norms justify the domination of women, and where a big power imbalance between men and women exists.

Summing up, we can say that conflict theorists and feminists have performed a valuable sociological service by emphasizing the importance of power relations in structuring family life. A substantial body of research shows that the gender revolution of the past 40 years has influenced the way we select mates, our reasons for being satisfied or dissatisfied with marriage, our propensity to divorce, the reproductive choices women make, the distribution of housework and child care, variations in the rate of wife abuse—in short, all aspects of family life. As you will now learn, the gender revolution has also created a greater diversity of family forms.

FAMILY DIVERSITY

Sexual Orientation

Modifications in the Canadian census alert us to some of the changes that have occurred with respect to family structures. For example, the 1981 census was the first to report on common-law marriages. The 2001 census was the first to include questions that recognized same-sex partners in cohabiting relationships. It also recognized that some Canadian children are being raised in same-sex households. The 2006 census asked married Canadians the sex of their spouse. It thereby acknowledged that the passage of Bill C-38 in July 2005 made Canada the fourth country (after the Netherlands, Spain, and Belgium) to legalize same-sex marriage.

Research shows that most gays and lesbians, like most heterosexuals, want a long-term, intimate relationship with one other adult (Kurdek, 1995). In fact, in Denmark, where homosexual couples can register partnerships under the law, the divorce rate for registered homosexual couples is lower than for heterosexual married couples (Ontario Consultants on Religious Tolerance, 2000).

However, many people believe that children brought up in homosexual families will develop a confused sexual identity, exhibit a tendency to become homosexuals themselves, and suffer discrimination from children and adults in the "straight" community. There is little research in this area and much of the research that exists is based on small, unrepresentative samples. Nevertheless, the findings are consistent. They suggest that children who grow up in homosexual families are much like children who grow up in heterosexual families. For example, a 14-year study assessed 25 young adults who were the offspring of lesbian families and 21 young adults who were the offspring of heterosexual families (Tasker and Golombok, 1997). It found that the two groups were equally well adjusted and displayed little difference in sexual orientation. Two respondents from the lesbian families considered themselves lesbians, while all of the respondents from the heterosexual families considered themselves heterosexual.

Homosexual and heterosexual families do differ in some respects. Lesbian couples with children record higher satisfaction with their partnerships than lesbian couples without children do. In contrast, among heterosexual couples, it is couples without children who record higher marital satisfaction (Koepke, Hare, and Moran, 1992).

In 2002, in a precedent-setting move hailed by gay-rights activists as the first of its kind in the world, full parental rights were extended to homosexual couples in Quebec. In addition, same-sex couples were granted the same status and obligations as heterosexual married couples when they entered into a civil union. Here, lesbians react as the Quebec legislature passes the law.

On average, the partners of lesbian mothers spend more time caring for children than do the husbands of heterosexual mothers. Since children usually benefit from adult attention, this must be considered a plus. Finally, homosexual couples tend to be more egalitarian than heterosexual couples, sharing most decision making and household duties equally (Rosenbluth, 1997). That is because they tend to consciously reject traditional marriage patterns. The fact that they have the same gender socialization and earn about the same income also encourages equality (Kurdek, 1998; Reimann, 1997). In sum, available research suggests that raising children in lesbian families has no apparent negative consequences for the children. Indeed, there may be some benefits for all family members.

At the same time, homosexual families are not immune from abuse and violence. Although research on violence in gay and lesbian relationships is sparse, some studies suggest that violence between same-sex partners occurs at approximately the same rate as it does in heterosexual relationships (Chesley, MacAulay, and Ristock, 1991). Some of the dynamics involved are similar to those that mark violence in heterosexual relationships (Kurdek, 1998). For example, drug or alcohol abuse is often involved. In both cases, the abusive individual is typically jealous and possessive, and uses violence or its threat to control his or her partner (Renzetti, 1992). At the same time, there are some differences (Obejas, 1994). For example, one study found that although heterosexual men who abuse their partners often insist that it is their "right" to do so, lesbians who are abusive do not. As a result, lesbians who batter their partners are more likely to seek treatment voluntarily than are their heterosexual male counterparts. Moreover, although it may be supposed that "butch/femme" roles or the woman's physical size influences the likelihood of being an abuser or a victim, this is not the case.

Cohabitation

The past half century has witnessed a dramatic rise in rates of cohabitation (unmarried couples who live together). Among Canadian women born from 1931 to 1940, first unions overwhelmingly took the form of legally registered marriage and the rare exceptions were nearly universally disapproved. But among those who have recently come of age, a majority formed first partnerships without marrying (see Figure 15.11). Although sharp differences by age persist, cohabitation at some point in life has become widespread. Although only 8 percent of the population is currently cohabiting, the percentage of cohabiting unions (also called common-law unions) grew from 6 percent to 14 percent between 1981 and 2001.

People who disapprove of cohabitation often do so because they oppose premarital sex. Often, they cite religious grounds for their opposition. In recent decades, however, the force of religious sanction has weakened. The sexual revolution and growing individualism have allowed people to pursue intimate relationships outside marriage if they so choose. Meanwhile, because women have pursued higher education and entered the paid labour force in increasing numbers, their roles are not as closely tied to marriage as they once were. These cultural and economic factors have all increased the rate of cohabitation.

Factors favourable to cohabitation include youth, previous divorce or separation, Quebec residence, Canadian birth, absence of religious affiliation, pregnancy or partner's pregnancy, and non-student status (Wu, 2000). Although cohabitation is now a common form for first unions among the young, for older Canadians, who formed first unions when cohabitation was less common (and more widely disapproved), cohabitation has more often served as a prelude or alternative to remarriage (Le Bourdais, Neill, and Turcott, 2000). But among people in their 30s, cohabitation is twice as likely for those forming second or subsequent unions and is six times as frequent if the initial union, now dissolved, was a cohabitation. Thus, cohabitation is an option that exists alongside marriage, serving some as a prelude, others as a bridge, and still others as a long-term family form.

Cohabiters' unions are markedly less stable than traditional families. One analysis showed that by the 10th year, only 10 percent of first marriages dissolved but slightly more than 50 percent of first cohabitations did. (About three in four of these surviving unions became marriages).

The decision to cohabit reflects an overall orientation—marriage is re-evaluated as an option, not a necessity. Marriage is then set apart from the decision to form a sexual union. In turn, sexual unions become acceptable even when duration is uncertain or relatively short. Although many who adopt this more flexible orientation will eventually marry, and whether married or not remain in unions for long periods, the emergence of such outlooks favours sexual unions of shorter duration. This leads to serial partnerships formed one after another. The overall result is a relaxation of the binding force implicit in marriage.

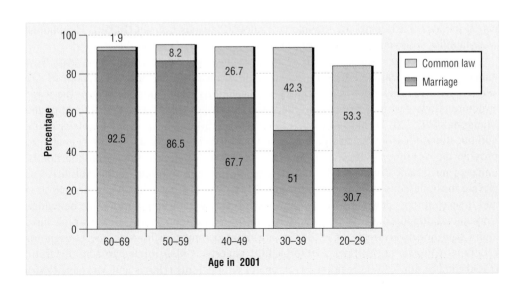

FIGURE 15.11

Probability of Women Experiencing a Marriage or a Common-Law Union as a First Union, Canada, 2001

Source: Adapted from Statistics Canada, 2001, "Canada e-Book," Catalogue 11-404. Retrieved May 26, 2003 (http://142.206.72.67/02/02d_graph/02d_graph_001b_1e.htm).

Divorce is responsible for the majority of lone-parent families in Canada today. Female-headed lone-parent families are far more common than male-headed lone-parent families.

Lone-Parent Families and Poverty

Single-Mother Families

In 2006, 16.9 percent of all Canadian families were headed by a lone parent. During the first half of the twentieth century, lone-parent families generally resulted from the death of one parent (Oderkirk and Lochhead, 1992). However, solo parenting today is most commonly the product of marital dissolution, after which child custody is typically granted to mothers. The vast majority of lone-parent families are headed by women. Compared with lone-parent fathers, lone-parent mothers are more likely to be younger and less well educated, have lower earnings and less income, and be responsible for younger children (Oderkirk and Lochhead, 1992). In 2003, the average income for lone-parent families headed by women was $32 500. By comparison, the average income for two-parent families was $85 600 and for male-led, single-parent families was $54 700 (Statistics Canada, 2005e).

Poverty is far more prevalent among female-headed single-parent households than among other types of family structures. In 2003, 38 percent of families headed by single-parent mothers lived below the low-income cutoff (Statistics Canada, 2005e). The poorest were families with young single-parent mothers.

It is still unclear "whether family structure is the cause or the victim of poverty. How many males disappear because they cannot support the children they have fathered? Are single-parent families poor because they are headed by a woman, or because the wage structure allows few mothers to earn their way out of poverty?" (Levitan, Mangum, and Mangum, 1998: 28). What is clear is that raising children in poverty involves doing without things that other Canadians take for granted. Poor parents are often unable to provide their children with the opportunity to live in relatively safe neighbourhoods, undergo necessary dental work, and participate in such extracurricular activities as private music lessons (Canning and Strong, 1998). Parents' capacity to care for children and their children's developmental outcomes is better at each step up the income ladder. Low social support, family dysfunction, and parental depression, all of which have significant negative effects on children, are more common in low-income households (National Council of Welfare, 1999b). Child poverty is also related to school failure (Fields and Smith, 1998), negative involvement with parents (Harris and Marmer, 1996), stunted growth, reduced cognitive abilities, limited emotional development (Mayer, 1997), and a higher likelihood of dropping out of school (Duncan, Yeung, Brooks-Gunn, and Smith, 1998).

Zero-Child Families

In Canada, what we prefer to call "zero-child families" are increasingly common. Our admittedly clumsy term seems necessary because the alternatives are so value laden: A "childless family" implies that a family without children lacks something it should have, while the more recent "child-free family" suggests that a family without a child is unencumbered and that a child is therefore a burden. To maintain neutrality, we resort to clumsiness.

Roughly a fifth of women between the ages of 40 and 44 had never given birth (Lamanna and Riedmann, 2003: 369). To explain this fact we must first recognize that not having a child may be the result of circumstances beyond a couple's control. For example, one or both partners may be infertile, and evidence suggests that infertility is a growing issue because of chemical pollutants in the air and water. It seems that not having a child is more often a matter of choice, however, and the main reasons for the increasing prevalence of zero-child families are the rising cost of raising a child and the growth of attractive alternatives.

Just how expensive are children? As noted earlier in 2004, it cost about $167 000 raise a child to age 18 (Canadian Council on Social Development, 2007). Add the cost of college or university and that is a lot of money that could be spent on investments, the couple's own education, and other desirable things. Mothers bear most of the cost of lost economic opportunities. Usually, they are the ones whose careers are disrupted when they decide to stay home to raise children and who lose income and pension benefits in the process. Couples also incur non-economic costs when they have a child, the most important of which is stress. The birth of a child requires that couples do more work in the home, give up free time and time alone together, develop an efficient daily routine, and divide responsibilities. All this adds sources of disagreement and tension to daily life.

Alternative attractions decrease the desire of some couples to have a child. People with high income, high education, and professional and managerial occupations are most likely to have zero-child families. Such people tend to place an especially high value on mobility, careers, and leisure-time pursuits. Usually, they are neither frustrated nor unhappy that they do not have a child. Despite their tendency to feel negatively stereotyped as "selfish," they tend to be more satisfied with their marriage than couples with a child (Lamanna and Riedmann, 2003: 380).

FAMILY POLICY

Having discussed several aspects of the decline of the traditional nuclear family and the proliferation of diverse family forms, we can now return to the big question posed at the beginning of this chapter: Is the decline of the nuclear family a bad thing for society? Said differently, do two-parent families—particularly those with stay-at-home moms—provide the kind of discipline, role models, help, and middle-class lifestyle that children need to stay out of trouble with the law and grow up to become well-adjusted, productive members of society? Conversely, are family forms other than the traditional nuclear family the main source of teenage crime, poverty, welfare dependency, and other social ills?

The answer suggested by research is clear: yes and no (Houseknecht and Sastry, 1996; Popenoe, 1996; Sandqvist and Andersson, 1992). Yes, the decline of the traditional nuclear family can be a source of many social problems. No, it doesn't have to be that way.

GLOBAL PERSPECTIVE

The United States is a good example of how social problems can emerge from the decline of the nuclear family. Sweden is a good example of how such problems can be averted. These two cases represent two models that Canadians should consider when thinking about our own family policies. The top panel of Table 15.1 shows that *on most indicators of nuclear family decline, Sweden leads the United States.* In Sweden, a smaller percentage of people get married. People usually get married at a later age than in the United States. The proportion of births outside of marriage is twice as high as in the United States. A much larger proportion of Swedish than of American women with children under the age of three work in the paid labour force.

The bottom panel of Table 15.1 shows that *on most measures of children's well-being, Sweden also leads the United States.* Thus, in Sweden, children enjoy higher average reading test scores than in the United States. The poverty rate in two-parent families is only one-fifth the American rate, while the poverty rate in single-parent families is only one-eleventh as high. The rate of infant abuse is one-eleventh the American rate. The rate of juvenile drug offences is less than half as high. Sweden does have a higher rate of juvenile delinquency than the United States. However, the lead is slight and concerns only minor offences. Overall, then, the decline of the traditional nuclear family has gone further in Sweden than in the United States, but children are much better off on average. How is this possible?

One explanation is that Sweden has something the United States lacks: a substantial family-support policy. When a child is born in Sweden, a parent is entitled to 360 days of parental leave at 80 percent of his or her salary and an additional 90 days at a flat rate. Fathers can take an additional 10 days of leave with pay when the baby is born. Parents are entitled to free consultations at "well-baby clinics." Like all citizens of Sweden, they receive free health care from the state-run system. Temporary parental benefits are

TABLE 15.1

The "Decline" of the Nuclear Family and the Well-Being of Children: The United States and Sweden Compared

Source: Adapted from Houseknecht and Sastry, 1996.

Indicators of Nuclear Family "Decline"	United States	Sweden	#1 "Decline"
Median age at first marriage			
Men	26.5	29.4	Sweden
Women	24.4	27.1	Sweden
Percentage of 45–49 population never married			
Men	5.7	15.4	Sweden
Women	5.1	9.1	Sweden
Non-marital birth rate	25.7	50.9	Sweden
One-parent households with children < 15			
as % of all households with children < 15	25.0	18.0	U.S.A
Percentage of mothers in labour force with			
children < 3	51.0	84.0	Sweden
Total fertility rate	2.0	2.0	Tie
Average household size	2.7	2.2	Sweden

Indicators of Nuclear Family "Decline"	United States	Sweden	#1 "Well Being"
Mean reading performance score at 14	5.14	5.29	Sweden
Percentage of children in poverty			
Single-mother households	59.5	5.2	Sweden
Two-parent households	11.1	2.2	Sweden
Death rate of infants from abuse	9.8	0.9	Sweden
Suicide rate for children 15–19			
(per 100 000)	11.1	6.2	Sweden
Juvenile delinquency rate (per 100 000)	11.6	12.0	U.S.A
Juvenile drug offence rate (per 100 000)	558.0	241.0	Sweden

Painting class in a state-subsidized daycare facility in Stockholm, Sweden

available for parents with a sick child under the age of 12. One parent can take up to 60 days off work per sick child per year at 80 percent of his or her salary. All parents can send their children to heavily government-subsidized, high-quality daycare. Finally, Sweden offers its citizens generous direct cash payments based on the number of children in each family.[2]

Among industrialized countries, the United States stands at the other extreme. Since the Family and Medical Leave Act was passed in 1993, a parent is entitled to 12 weeks of *unpaid* parental leave. About 44 million citizens have no health care coverage. Health care is at a low standard for many millions more. There is no system of state daycare and no direct cash payments to families based on the number of children they have. The value of the dependant deduction on income tax has fallen by nearly 50 percent in current dollars since the 1940s. Thus, when an unwed Swedish woman has a baby, she knows she can rely on state institutions to maintain her standard of living and help give her child an enriching social and educational environment. When an unwed American woman has a baby, she is pretty much on her own. She is more likely than not to sink into poverty, with all the negative consequences that has for her and her child.

Canada is midway between these two extremes. Parental leave allowances in Canada fall short of many European countries but are more generous than those in the United States or United Kingdom (OECD, 2001). The federal Liberal Party proposed a national system of subsidized daycare during the 2004 electoral campaign. By June 2005 initial agreements with four provinces were in place and others were under negotiation. However, the agreements were cancelled in 2006 by the newly elected Tory government. Only Quebec maintains a daycare system that approaches the standards of Western Europe.

In Canada, three criticisms are commonly raised against generous family-support policies. First, some people say they encourage long-term dependence on welfare, illegitimate births, and the breakup of two-parent families. However, research shows that the divorce rate and the rate of births to unmarried mothers are not higher when welfare payments are more generous (Albelda and Tilly, 1997; Ruggles, 1997; Sweezy and Tiefenthaler, 1996).

A second criticism of generous family-support policies focuses on child care. Some critics say that non-family child care is bad for children under the age of three. In their view, only parents can provide the love, interaction, and intellectual stimulation infants and toddlers need for proper social, cognitive, and moral development. However, when studies compare family care and daycare involving a strong curriculum, a stimulating environment, plenty of caregiver warmth, low turnover of well-trained staff, and a low ratio of caregivers to children, they find that daycare has no negative consequences for children over the age of one (Clarke-Stewart, Gruber, and Fitzgerald, 1994). A study of more than 6000 children found that a mother's employment outside the home does have a small negative effect on the child's self-esteem, later academic achievement, language development, and compliance. However, this effect was apparent only if the mother returned to work within a few weeks or months of giving birth. Moreover, the negative effects usually disappeared by the time the child reached the age of five (Harvey, 1999). Research also shows that daycare has some benefits, notably enhancing a child's ability to make friends. The benefits of high-quality daycare are even more evident in low-income families, which often cannot provide the kind of stimulating environment offered by high-quality daycare.

The third criticism lodged against generous family-support policies is that they are expensive and have to be paid for by high taxes. This is true. Swedes, for example, are more highly taxed than are the citizens of any other country. They have made the political decision to pay high taxes, partly to avoid the social problems and associated costs that sometimes emerge when the traditional nuclear family is replaced with other family forms and no institutions are available to help family members in need. The Swedish experience teaches us, then, that there is a clear trade-off between expensive family-support policies and low taxes. It is impossible to have both, and the degree to which any country favours one or the other is a political choice.

NOTES

1. Research comparing marriages with and without children consistently finds marital happiness to be higher in unions without children (Glenn and McLanahan, 1982; Houseknecht, 1987; Somers, 1993). However, at least one analysis concludes that most of the difference in marital happiness between parents and non-parents is not due to a decline in marital happiness after the arrival of a child or children but to the fact that unhappy parents tend to stay married while unhappy non-parents are more likely to divorce. In consequence, when parents and non-parents are compared in cross-sample studies, still-married non-parents appear happier as a group (White, Booth, and Edwards, 1986).

2. We are grateful to Gregg Olsen, Department of Sociology, University of Manitoba, for this information.

SUMMARY

1. What is the traditional nuclear family, and how prevalent is it compared with other family forms?
   The traditional nuclear family consists of a father-provider, mother-homemaker, and at least one child. Today, only slightly more than one in eight Canadian households are traditional nuclear families. Many different family forms have proliferated in recent decades, including cohabiting couples (with or without children), same-sex couples (with or without children), and single-parent families. The frequency of these forms varies by class, sexual orientation, and other factors.

2. What is the functionalist theory of the family, and how accurate is it?
   The functionalist theory holds that the nuclear family is a distinct and universal family form because it performs five important functions in society: sexual regulation, economic cooperation, reproduction, socialization, and emotional support. The theory is most accurate in depicting families in Canada and other Western societies in the two decades after World War II. Families today and in other historical periods depart from the functional model in important respects.

3. What are the emphases of Marxist and feminist theories of families?
   Marxists stress how families are tied to the system of capitalist ownership. They argue that only the elimination of capitalism can end gender inequality in families. Feminists note that gender inequality existed before capitalism and in communist societies. They stress how the patriarchal division of power and patriarchal norms reproduce gender inequality.

4. What consequences does the entry of women into the paid labour force have?
   Among other changes the entry of women into the paid labour force increases their power to leave unhappy marriages and control whether and when to have children.

5. What accounts for variations in marital satisfaction?
   Marital satisfaction is lower at the bottom of the class structure, in places where divorce laws are strict, when children reach their teenage years, in families where housework is not shared equally, and among couples who do not have a good sexual relationship.

6. Under what circumstances are the effects of divorce on children worst?
   The effects of divorce on children are worst if there is a high level of parental conflict and the children's standard of living drops.

7. Does growing up in a homosexual household have any known negative effects on children?
   Children who grow up in homosexual families are much like children who grow up in heterosexual families.

8. Are various social problems a result of the decline of the traditional nuclear family?
   People sometimes blame the decline of the traditional nuclear family for increasing poverty, welfare dependence, and crime. However, some countries have adopted policies that largely prevent these problems. Therefore, the social problems are in a sense a political choice.

KEY TERMS

child support (p. 445)

divorce rate (p. 436)

endogamy (p. 441)

exogamy (p. 441)

extended family (p. 432)

marriage (p. 432)

marriage rate (p. 436)

nuclear family (p. 429)

polygamy (p. 432)

total fertility rate (p. 436)

traditional nuclear
   family (p. 430)

QUESTIONS TO CONSIDER

1. Do you agree with the functionalist view that the traditional nuclear family is the ideal family form for Canada today? Why or why not?

2. Ask your grandparents and parents how many people lived in their household when they were your age. Ask them to identify the role of each household member (mother, brother, sister, grandfather, boarder, etc.) and to describe the work done by each member inside and outside the household. Compare the size, composition, and division of labour of your household with that of your grandparents and parents. How have the size, composition, and division of labour of the household changed over three generations? Why have these changes occurred?

WEB RESOURCES

Companion Website for This Book

http://www.compass3e.nelson.com

Begin by clicking on the Student Resources section of the website. Next, select the chapter you are studying from the pull-down menu. From the Student Resources page you have easy access to InfoTrac® College Edition, additional Weblinks, and other resources. The website also has many useful tips to aid you in your study of sociology, including practice tests for each chapter.

InfoTrac® Search Terms

These search terms are provided to assist you in beginning to conduct research on this topic by visiting http://www.infotrac-college.com:
divorce
extended family
family values
marriage
nuclear family

Recommended Websites

"Marriage and Family Processes" at http://www.trinity.edu/~mkearl/family.html contains a wide range of valuable resources on family sociology.

"Kinship and Social Organization" at http://www.umanitoba.ca/faculties/arts/anthropology/kintitle.html is an online interactive tutorial that teaches you about variations in patterns of descent, marriage, and residence by using five case studies.

Visit these sites for statistics and information on

•   families (The Vanier Institute of the Family, http://www.vifamily.ca)

•   lone-parent families (Parents Without Partners, http://www.parentswithoutpartners.org)

•   family violence (the National Clearinghouse on Family Violence, http://www.pha-caspc. gc.ca/ncfv-cnivf/familyviolence/)

•   sexual behaviour (Human Sexuality: An Encyclopedia, http://www2.hu-berlin.de/sexology/GESUND/ARCHIV/SEN/INDEX.HTM)

•   same-sex marriage (Ontario Consultants on Religious Tolerance, http://www.religioustolerance.org/hom_marr.htm)

http://www.compass3e.nelson.com

CengageNOW™

http://hed.nelson.com

This online diagnostic tool identifies each student's unique needs with a Pretest that generates a personalized Study Plan for each chapter, helping students focus on concepts they're having the most difficulty mastering. Students then take a Posttest after reading the chapter to measure their understanding of the material. An Instructor Gradebook is available to track and monitor student progress.

CHAPTER

16

Religion

In this chapter, you will learn that

- The structure of society and a person's place in it influence his or her religious beliefs and practices.

- Under some circumstances, religion creates societal cohesion, while under other circumstances it promotes social conflict and social change. When religion creates societal cohesion, it also reinforces social inequality.

- Religion governs fewer aspects of most people's lives today than in the past. However, a religious revival has taken place in various parts of the world in recent decades and many people still adhere strongly to religious beliefs and practices.

- Diverse possibilities for religious participation compete in modern societies. For example, although most people are becoming more secularized, many people are becoming more religious.

- Historical information suggests that the major world religions were movements of moral and social improvement that arose in times of great adversity and were led by charismatic figures. As they consolidated, they became more conservative.

- People are more religious if they were brought up in a religious family, if they reside in regions where religion is highly authoritative, and when they are very young and very old.

RELIGION AND SOCIETY

Robert Brym started writing the first draft of this chapter just after returning from a funeral. "Roy was a fitness nut," says Robert, "and cycling was his sport. One perfect summer day, he was out training with his team. I wouldn't be surprised if the sunshine and vigorous exercise turned his thoughts to his good fortune. At 41, he was a senior executive in a medium-sized mutual funds firm. His boss, who treated him like a son, was grooming him for the presidency of the company. Roy had three vivacious children, ranging in age from 1 to 10, and a beautiful, generous, and highly intelligent wife. He was active in community volunteer work and everyone who knew him admired him. But on this particular summer day, he suddenly didn't feel well. He dropped back from the pack and then suffered a massive heart attack. Within minutes, he was dead.

PERSONAL
ANECDOTE

"During *shiva*, the ritual week of mourning following the death of a Jew, hundreds of people gathered in the family's home and on their front lawn. I had never felt such anguish before. When we heard the steady, slow, clear voice of Roy's 10-year-old son solemnly intoning the mourner's prayer, we all wept. And we asked ourselves and one another the inevitable question: Why?"

In 1902, the great psychologist William James observed that this question lies at the root of all religious belief. Religion is the common human response to the fact that we all stand at the edge of an abyss. It helps us cope with the terrifying fact that we must die (James, 1976 [1902]: 116). It offers us immortality, the promise of better times to come, and the security of benevolent spirits who look over us. It provides meaning and purpose in a world that might otherwise seem cruel and senseless.

The motivation for religion may be psychological, as James argued. However, the content and intensity of our religious beliefs, and the form and frequency of our religious practices, are influenced by the structure of society and our place in it. In other words, the religious impulse takes literally thousands of forms. It is the task of the sociologist of religion to account for this variation. Why does one religion predominate here, another there? Why is religious belief more fervent at one time than at another? Under what circumstances does religion act as a source of social stability and under what circumstances does it act as a force for social change? Are we becoming more or less religious? These are all questions that have occupied the sociologist of religion, and we touch on all of them here. Note that we will not have anything to say about the truth of religion in general or the value of any religious belief or practice in particular. These are questions of faith, not science. They lie outside the province of sociology.

The cover of *Time* magazine once proclaimed, "God is dead." As a sociological observation, the assertion is preposterous. In a nationwide Canadian survey in 2000, 81 percent of adults and 71 percent of teenagers agreed with the statement "God or a higher power cares about you." Forty-six percent of adults and 36 percent of teens said they had felt the presence of God or a higher power (Bibby, 2001: 252). By these measures (and by other measures we will examine below), God is still very much alive in Canada. Yet although spirituality is evidently strong, participation in formal religious observance is less frequent than in the past. In Canada, in 1946, two out of every three adults attended worship services every week. In 2001 the figure was just over one in five (Clark, 2003).

The scope of religious authority has also declined in Canada and many other parts of the world. That is, religion governs fewer aspects of life than it used to. Some Canadians still look to religion to deal with all of life's problems. But more and more Canadians expect that religion can help them deal with only a restricted range of spiritual issues. Other institutions—medicine, psychiatry, criminal justice, education, and so forth—have grown in importance as the scope of religious authority has declined.

Although a smaller proportion of the public is active in organized religions now than in the past, many people remain involved. Among the latter, growing evidence suggests that the level of participation in religious services and practices is on the rise. Relatively intense, demanding fundamentalist and conservative religious traditions are gaining strength as more liberal traditions become less appealing. Is this a sign of an overall revival of religion? It is too early to tell. But you will see that viewing the field of religion as a kind of market comprising "sellers" and "buyers" of religious services allows us to understand how and why an overall pattern of decline can be observed alongside growing religious intensity among a large minority of Canadians.

Before we address the issues noted above, let us see how the founding fathers of sociology and some important contemporary innovators in the field have treated the problem of religion in society.

THEORETICAL APPROACHES TO THE SOCIOLOGY OF RELIGION

Durkheim, Functionalism, and the Problem of Order

WHERE DO YOU FIT IN?

Canadian economist Colin Jones once said that hockey is Canada's "national religion" (*The Ring*, 2000). Do you agree with that opinion? Before making up your mind, consider the following facts. In February 2002, more than three million Canadians gathered in front of their TVs to watch the Canadian men's hockey team begin their pursuit of a gold medal at the Winter Olympic games. During the 1998 Winter Olympics, the Canada–Czech Republic game drew more than 2.5 million viewers—even though the broadcast started at 3:30 a.m. And, of course, when Canada's hockey team came from behind to defeat the Soviets in 1972, the nation virtually came to a stop (Kernaghan, 2002). It is also clear that few events attract the attention and enthusiasm of Canadians as much as the annual Stanley Cup finals (*Canadian Global Almanac 2002*, 2001: 627).

Apart from drawing a huge audience, the Stanley Cup playoffs generate a sense of what Durkheim would have called "collective effervescence." That is, the Stanley Cup excites us by making us feel part of something larger than we are: the Montreal Canadiens, the Edmonton Oilers, the Toronto Maple Leafs, the Vancouver Canucks, the Calgary Flames, the Ottawa Senators, the institution of Canadian hockey, the spirit of Canada itself. For many hours each year, hockey enthusiasts transcend their everyday lives and experience intense enjoyment by sharing the sentiments and values of a larger collective. In their fervour, they banish thoughts of their own mortality. They gain a glimpse of eternity as they immerse themselves in institutions that will outlast them and athletic feats that people will remember for generations to come.

So do you think the Stanley Cup playoffs are a religious event? There is no god of the Stanley Cup (although the nickname of Canadian hockey legend Wayne Gretzky—The Great One—suggests that he transcended the status of a mere mortal). Nonetheless, the Stanley Cup playoffs meet Durkheim's definition of a religious experience. Durkheim said that when people live together, they come to share common sentiments and values. These common sentiments and values form a **collective conscience** that is larger than any individual's. On occasion, we experience the collective conscience directly. This causes us to distinguish the secular, everyday world of the **profane** from the religious, transcendent world of the **sacred**. We designate certain objects as symbolizing the sacred. Durkheim called these objects **totems**. We invent certain public practices to connect us with the sacred. Durkheim referred to these practices as **rituals**. The effect (or function) of rituals and of religion as a whole is to reinforce social solidarity, said Durkheim.

Durkheim would have found support for his theory in research showing that, in Quebec from 1951 to 1992, the early ousting of the Montreal Canadiens from the Stanley Cup playoffs was associated with an increased tendency for young men to commit suicide during the hockey series (Trovato, 1998). Similarly, in the United States, the suicide rate dips during

The **collective conscience** comprises the common sentiments and values that people share as a result of living together.

The **profane** refers to the secular, everyday world.

The **sacred** refers to the religious, transcendent world.

Totems are objects that symbolize the sacred.

Rituals in Durkheim's usage are public practices designed to connect people to the sacred.

From a Durkheimian point of view, the Stanley Cup playoffs can be considered a religious ritual.

the two days preceding football's Super Bowl Sunday and on Super Bowl Sunday itself, as well as on the final day of the baseball World Series (Curtis, Loy, and Karnilowicz, 1986). These patterns are consistent with Durkheim's theory of suicide, which predicts a lower suicide rate when social solidarity increases and a higher suicide rate when social solidarity decreases (see Chapter 1, A Sociological Compass).

Durkheim would consider the Stanley Cup and the team insignia to be totems. The insignia represent groups we identify with. The trophy signifies the qualities that professional hockey stands for: competitiveness, sportsmanship, excellence, and the value of teamwork. The hockey games themselves are public rituals enacted according to strict rules and conventions. We suspend our everyday lives as we watch the ritual being enacted. The ritual heightens our experience of belonging to certain groups, increases our respect for certain institutions, and strengthens our belief in certain ideas. These groups, institutions, and ideas all transcend us. Thus, the Stanley Cup playoffs may fairly be regarded as a sacred event in Durkheim's terms. They cement society in the way Durkheim said all religions do (Durkheim, 1976 [1915]). Do you agree with this Durkheimian interpretation of the Stanley Cup playoffs? Why or why not? Do you see any parallels between the Durkheimian analysis of the Stanley Cup playoffs and sports in your community or university?

Marx, Conflict, and Religion as a Prop for Inequality

Durkheim's theory of religion is a functionalist account that offers useful insights into the role of religion in society. Yet conflict theorists have lodged two main criticisms against it. First, it overemphasizes religion's role in maintaining social cohesion. In reality, religion often incites social conflict. Second, when religion does increase social cohesion, it often reinforces social inequality. Durkheim ignored that issue, too.

Consider first the role of religion in maintaining inequality. It was Marx who first stressed how religion often tranquilizes the underprivileged into accepting their lot in life. According to Marx, religion diminishes class conflict; he called religion "the opium of the people" (Marx, 1970 [1843]: 131).

Evidence for Marx's interpretation may be drawn from many times and places. In medieval and early modern Europe, Christianity promoted the view that the Almighty ordains social inequality. In the words of an Anglican verse that was removed from the hymnal only in the 1920s:

> The rich man at his castle,
> The poor man at his gate.
> God made them high or lowly
> And ordered their estate.

Nor were Western Christians alone in justifying social hierarchy on religious grounds. In Russian and other Slavic languages, the words for rich (*bogati*) and God (*bog*) have the same root. This suggests that wealth is God-given and perhaps even that it makes the wealthy godlike. The Hindu scriptures say that the highest caste sprang from the lips of the supreme creator, the next highest caste from his shoulders, the next highest from his thighs, and the lowest, "polluted" caste from his feet. And the Koran, the holy book of Islam, suggests that social inequality is due to the will of Allah (Ossowski, 1963: 19–20).

In Canada today, most people do not think of social hierarchy in such rigid terms—quite the opposite. Most people celebrate the alleged *absence* of social hierarchy. This is part of what sociologist Robert Bellah calls **civil religion**, a set of quasi-religious beliefs and practices that binds the population together and justifies its way of life (Bellah, 1975).[1] When we think of Canada as a land of opportunity, a meritocracy in which everyone (regardless of race, creed, colour, or gender) can achieve success, we are giving voice to Canada's civil religion. The national anthem, the maple leaf, and great public events, such as the Stanley Cup, help make us feel at ease with our way of life. Paradoxically, however, our civil religion may also help divert attention from the many inequalities that persist in Canadian society. Strong belief in the existence of equal opportunity, for instance, may lead people to overlook the lack of opportunity that remains in our society (see Chapter 8, Social Stratification: Canadian and Global Perspectives). In this manner, our civil religion functions much like the Anglican verse cited above, although its content is markedly different.

We can also find plenty of examples to illustrate religion's role in promoting conflict. For example, it is worth remembering the important role played in the creation of our medicare system and our social welfare network by the "radical Christianity" of the early twentieth-century Social Gospel movement. The Social Gospel emphasized that Christians should be as concerned with improving the here-and-now as with life in the hereafter. The efforts of Tommy Douglas, a Baptist minister, the leader of the Co-operative Commonwealth Federation (precursor of the New Democratic Party), and the "father of medicare," exemplify the Social Gospel concern with social justice issues. More recently, a challenge to the status quo is evident in the policy pronouncements of the Social Affairs Commission of the Canadian Conference of Catholic Archbishops. This group has called on the Canadian government to give preferential treatment to "the poor, the afflicted and the oppressed" and recognize that "labour, not capital, must be given priority in the development of an economy based on justice" (Dawson, 1993: 323). Similarly, the United Church of Canada has ignited conflict by declaring that "all persons, regardless of their sexual orientation, are welcome to become full members of the church and are eligible for ordination as ministers" (in Dawson, 1993: 323). These cases illustrate how religion can sometimes promote conflict and change.

In sum, religion can maintain social order under some circumstances, as Durkheim said. When it does so, however, it often reinforces social inequality, as Marx argued. Moreover, under other circumstances religion can promote social conflict.

Weber, Social Change, and Symbolic Interaction

If Durkheim highlighted the way religion contributes to social order, Max Weber stressed the way religion can contribute to social change. Weber captured the core of his argument in a memorable image: If history is like a train, pushed along its tracks by economic and

A **civil religion** is a set of quasi-religious beliefs and practices that bind a population together and justify its way of life.

Tommy Douglas (1904–86) was a Baptist minister from Saskatchewan whose religious ideals encouraged him to become leader of the left-wing Co-operative Commonwealth Federation and the "father of medicare" in Canada.

political interests, then religious ideas are like railroad switches, determining exactly which tracks the train will follow (Weber, 1946: 280).

Weber's most famous illustration of his thesis is his short book *The Protestant Ethic and the Spirit of Capitalism.* Like Marx, Weber was interested in explaining the rise of modern capitalism. Again like Marx, he was prepared to recognize the "fundamental importance of the economic factor" in his explanation (Weber, 1958 [1904–1905]: 26). But Weber was also bent on proving the one-sidedness of any *exclusively* economic interpretation. He did so by offering what we would today call a symbolic interactionist interpretation of religion (see Chapter 1, A Sociological Compass). True, the term "symbolic interactionism" was not introduced in sociology until more than half a century after Weber wrote *The Protestant Ethic.* Yet Weber's focus on the worldly significance of the *meanings* people attach to religious ideas makes him a forerunner of the symbolic interactionist tradition.

Weber made his case by first noting that the economic conditions Marx said were necessary for capitalist development existed in Catholic France during the reign of Louis XIV. Yet the wealth generated in France by international trade and commerce tended to be consumed by war and the luxurious lifestyle of the aristocracy rather than invested in the growth of capitalist enterprise. For Weber, what prompted vigorous capitalist development in non-Catholic Europe and North America was a combination of (1) favourable economic conditions, such as those discussed by Marx, and (2) the spread of certain moral values by the Protestant reformers of the sixteenth century and their followers.

For specifically religious reasons, wrote Weber, followers of the Protestant theologian John Calvin stressed the need to engage in intense worldly activity and to display industry, punctuality, and frugality in their everyday life. In the view of men like John Wesley and Benjamin Franklin, people could reduce their religious doubts and ensure a state of grace by working diligently and living simply. Many Protestants took up this idea. Weber called it the Protestant ethic (Weber, 1958 [1904–1905]: 183).

According to Weber, the Protestant ethic had wholly unexpected economic consequences. Where it took root, and where economic conditions were favourable, early capitalist enterprise grew most robustly. Weber made his case even more persuasive by comparing Protestant Western Europe and North America with India and China. In Weber's view, Protestantism was constructed on the foundation of two relatively rational religions: Judaism and Christianity. These religions were rational in two senses. First, their followers abstained from magic. Second, they engaged in legalistic interpretation of the holy writ. In contrast, said Weber, Buddhism in India and Confucianism in China had strong magical and otherworldly components. According to Weber, this hindered worldly success in competition and capital accumulation. As a result, capitalism developed slowly in Asia (Weber, 1963 [1922]).

In application, two problems have confronted Weber's argument. First, the correlation between the Protestant ethic and the strength of capitalist development is weaker than Weber thought. In some places, Catholicism has coexisted with vigorous capitalist growth and Protestantism with relative economic stagnation (Samuelsson, 1961 [1957]).

Second, Weber's followers have not always applied the Protestant ethic thesis as carefully as Weber did. For example, since the 1960s, the economies of Taiwan, South Korea, Hong Kong, and Singapore have grown quickly. Some scholars argue that Confucianism in East Asia acted much like Protestantism in nineteenth-century Europe, invigorating rapid economic growth by virtue of its strong work ethic (Lie, 1998). This argument ignores the fact that Weber himself regarded Confucianism as a brake on economic growth in Asia. In addition, it plays down the economic and political forces that stimulated economic development in the region. This is just the kind of one-sided explanation that Weber warned against (see Chapter 20, Population and Urbanization).

Despite these problems, Weber's treatment of the religious factor underlying social change is a useful corrective to Durkheim's (and Marx's) emphasis on religion as a source of social stability. Along with Durkheim's work, Weber's contribution stands as one of the most important insights into the influence of religion on society.

Feminism and Religious Leadership

Most of today's religious traditions were shaped in agricultural societies that subordinated women to their husbands and fathers. In general, religious doctrines reinforced patriarchy. Consider the following scriptural examples of the subordination of women:

- Corinthians in the New Testament emphasizes that "women should keep silence in the churches. For they are not permitted to speak, but should be subordinate, as even the law says. If there is anything they desire to know, let them ask their husbands at home. For it is shameful for a woman to speak in church."
- The Sidur, the Jewish prayer book, includes this morning prayer: "Blessed are you, Lord our God, King of the Universe, who did not make me a woman."
- The Koran, the holy book of Islam, contains a Book of Women in which it is written that "righteous women are devoutly obedient. . . . As to those women on whose part you fear disloyalty and ill-conduct, admonish them, refuse to share their beds, beat them."

Today, feminist criticism of gender discrimination has led many people, including many religious individuals, to challenge patriarchal religious doctrines and promote gender equality in positions of religious leadership. True, some important religious traditions (Roman Catholicism, Eastern Orthodoxy, Islam, the orthodox and conservative branches of Judaism, and Mormonism) remain committed to the exclusion of women from clerical roles. Some of the more conservative traditions have met challenges to patriarchy with severe sanctions, including excommunication. But other traditions have been more reform-minded.

The ordination of women occurred sporadically among Protestant North Americans in the nineteenth century. In 1936, the first woman was ordained by the United Church in Canada, while the first Presbyterian female ordination took place in 1967. The Anglicans followed in 1976 (Ontario Consultants on Religious Tolerance, 2006). In the more liberal branches of Judaism, female rabbis have been ordained since the 1970s.

In Canada, the proportion of female clergy grew 61 percent from 1991 to 2001 (Statistics Canada, 2005k). This rapid change is all the more dramatic because the feminization of religious leadership has occurred only within certain religious traditions. Among Episcopalians in the United States, female and male ordinations were about equally common by the mid-1990s (Crew, 2002). In many seminaries, females make up an increasing proportion of students—two-thirds and up for the United Church of Canada in 2002 (Kaasa, 2002). In the meantime, shortages of male candidates for priestly vocations are apparent, notably among Roman Catholics. Do such changes foretell a fundamental reorientation of religious vocations? Will clerics become more oriented to values like service and less to judgmental authority as women become more numerous in clerical positions? At least some sociologists suggest that such "feminization" is already underway. But contrasts between religious sectors are probably more likely than any sort of uniform change (Nesbitt, 1997).

THE RISE, DECLINE, AND PARTIAL REVIVAL OF RELIGION

Secularization

In 1651, British political philosopher Thomas Hobbes described life as "poore, nasty, brutish, and short" (Hobbes, 1968 [1651]: 150). His description fit the recent past. The standard of living in medieval and early modern Europe was abysmally low. On average, a person lived only about 35 years. The forces of nature and human affairs seemed entirely unpredictable. In this context, magic was popular. It offered easy answers to mysterious, painful, and capricious events.

As material conditions improved, popular belief in magic, astrology, and witchcraft gradually lost ground (Thomas, 1971). Christianity substantially replaced them. The better

The persecution of witches in the early modern era was partly an effort to eliminate competition and establish a Christian monopoly over spiritual life. *Burning of Witches by Inquisition in a German Marketplace.* After a drawing by H. Grobert.

and more predictable times made Europeans more open to the teachings of organized religion. In addition, the Church campaigned vigorously to stamp out opposing belief systems and practices. The persecution of witches in this era was partly an effort to eliminate competition and establish a Christian monopoly over spiritual life.

The Church succeeded in its efforts. In medieval and early modern Europe, Christianity became a powerful presence in religious affairs, music, art, architecture, literature, and philosophy. Popes and saints were the rock musicians and movie stars of their day. The Church was the centre of life in both its spiritual and its worldly dimensions. Church authority was supreme in marriage, education, morality, economic affairs, politics, and so forth. European countries proclaimed official state religions. They persecuted members of religious minorities.

In contrast, a few hundred years later, Max Weber remarked on how the world had become thoroughly "disenchanted." By the turn of the twentieth century, he said, scientific and other forms of rationalism were replacing religious authority. His observations formed the basis of what came to be known as the **secularization thesis**, undoubtedly the most widely accepted argument in the sociology of religion until the 1990s. According to the secularization thesis, religious institutions, actions, and consciousness are unlikely to disappear, but they are certainly on the decline worldwide (Tschannen, 1991).

The **secularization thesis** says that religious institutions, actions, and consciousness are on the decline worldwide.

Religious Revival

Despite the consensus about secularization that was still evident in the 1980s, many sociologists modified their judgments in the 1990s. There were two reasons for this. First, accumulated survey evidence showed that religion was not in an advanced state of decay. Actually, in many places, including Canada, it was in fairly good health.

In fact, both the history and the national identity of Canada are indelibly imprinted with the mark of religion. In the words of Reginald Bibby, Canada's leading sociologist of religion, "If one thinks of the past, it is impossible to imagine Quebec with no Roman Catholics, Ontario with no Anglicans or Presbyterians, the Prairies with no evangelical Protestants, and British Columbia and the Atlantic region without the Church of England" (Bibby, 1993: 25). The 1982 Canadian Charter of Rights and Freedoms asserts that our country is founded on principles that recognize the supremacy of God.

FIGURE 16.1

Religious Affiliations,
Canada, 1871–2001

Sources: 1871–1971 from Statistics
Canada, 1999a; 1981 from Ontario
Consultants on Religious Tolerance,
2005; 1991 and 2001 from Statistics
Canada, 2003c.

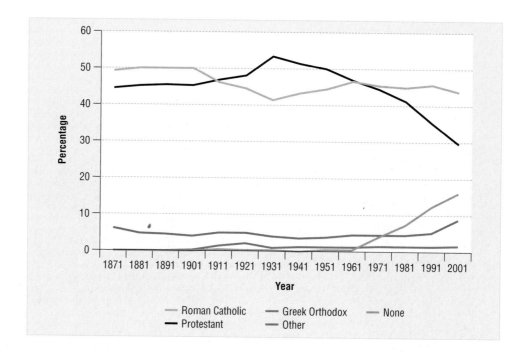

True, religion in Canada has been profoundly altered by social change since World War II. Since the 1970s, confidence in religious leaders has plummeted (Bibby, 2002: 58). Participation levels have fallen. When compared with their grandparents and parents, Canadian teens are now far less likely to say that they were highly involved in religious groups as children (Bibby, 2001: 274). The number of Canadians reporting that they had "no religious affiliation" grew steadily from 0.5 percent in 1961 to 16.2 percent in 2001 (see Figure 16.1). However, "demise is relative; organizationally, religion continues to be a significant force with a significant following in Canada" (Bibby, 2001: 114). Religion and spirituality remain of considerable interest to a sizable number of both young and old Canadians (see Table 16.1).

The second circumstance that has caused many sociologists to revise their judgment about the secularization thesis is the revival of religious fundamentalism. Since the 1960s, fundamentalist religious organizations have rapidly increased their membership, especially among Protestants (Finke and Starke, 1992). **Fundamentalists** interpret their scriptures literally, seek to establish a direct, personal relationship with the higher being(s) they worship, and are relatively intolerant of non-fundamentalists (Hunter, 1991). Fundamentalists often support conservative social and political issues (Bruce, 1988; see Box 16.1).

During the same period, religious movements became dominant forces outside North America too. Hindu nationalists formed the government in India. Jewish fundamentalists were always important players in Israeli political life, often holding the balance of power in Israeli governments, but they have become even more influential in recent years. A revival of Muslim fundamentalism began in Iran in the 1970s. Led by the Muslim cleric the Ayatollah Khomeini, it was a movement of opposition to the repressive, American-backed regime

Fundamentalists interpret their scriptures literally, seek to establish a direct, personal relationship with the higher being(s) they worship, and are relatively intolerant of non-fundamentalists.

TABLE 16.1

Religious Involvement in
Canada (in percent)

Source: Bibby, 2006: 205.

	1975	2005
Pray privately weekly or more often	37	45
Believe in God or a higher power	86	82
Identify with a religion	96	84
Attend monthly services	41	34
Attend weekly services	31	25

BOX 16.1
Sociology at the Movies

TAKE   ROLL

Harry Potter and the Order of the Phoenix (2007)

Harry Potter and the Order of the Phoenix is the fifth movie in the highly popular series about a magical world of witches and wizards. The hero, Harry Potter (played by Daniel Radcliffe) is orphaned at the age of one when the most evil wizard of all, Lord Voldemort, murders Harry's parents and tries to kill Harry. Harry goes to live with his unwelcoming relatives, the Dursleys, who house him in a closet under their stairs. Shortly before his 11th birthday, Harry's life is turned upside down. He learns that his dead parents were wizards and so is he. He is summoned by a blizzard of letters to Hogwarts School of Witchcraft and Wizardry. The school, housed in a 1000-year-old castle and headed by the renowned Professor Dumbledore, provides select students with a seven-year program of instruction.

Harry Potter and the Order of the Phoenix follows the story of Harry and his friends Ron Weasley and Hermione Granger in their fifth year at Hogwarts. There they confront the grim possibility that archvillain Voldemort has returned to wreak havoc on the world. Authorities in the Ministry of Magic and at Hogwarts think that Harry's worries are misplaced, so he finds it necessary to join a secretive group of wizards (the Order of the Phoenix) dedicated to fighting Voldemort. Obstacles remain. Harry's teacher, Dolores Umbridge, is an agent of the Ministry of Truth and High Inquisitor of Hogwarts. She refuses to teach Harry and his classmates how to perform Defense Against the Dark Arts spells. As a result, Harry and his friends must meet secretly to learn and practise the spells on their own. Voldemort is now invading Harry's mind with bizarre and threat-

Harry Potter and the Order of the Phoenix (2007)

ening dreams. The scar that remained on Harry's forehead when Voldemort killed his parents burns whenever Voldemort experiences a powerful emotion. These events signal the impending battle against Voldemort and his Death Eaters, who are narrowly defeated thanks to the defensive skills that Harry and his friends have perfected. But Voldemort escapes, thus leading us ever onward to the two remaining Harry Potter films.

All entries in the Harry Potter series have been enormously successful at the box office. Children are prominent in the lineups, many of them outfitted as if for Halloween. Some of them come to the movies on organized school field trips after studying the Harry Potter books at school.

Although most people viewed the Harry Potter series as harmless, others saw things differently. They denounced both the films and the books on which they are based as "demonic." Many of them were conservative Protestants who

claimed that the books glorify witchcraft, make "evil look innocent," and subtly draw "children into an unhealthy interest in a darker world that is occultic and dangerous to physical, psychological and spiritual well-being" (Shaw, 2001). Two years before he became Pope Benedict XVI, Cardinal Ratzinger wrote a letter of support to a Bavarian sociologist who had written a book critical of the Potter phenomenon. The future pope told her, "It is good that you are throwing light on Harry Potter, because these are subtle seductions that work imperceptibly, and because of that deeply, and erode Christianity in the soul before it can even grow properly" (Associated Press, 2005b). The controversy about the Potter series eased somewhat as some conservative Christian commentators claimed to find Christian themes in the movies and the books ("Finding God," 2005). But the controversy had been great enough to place J. K. Rowling, author of the Harry Potter books, fourth on the American

Library Association's list of Top Ten Challenged Authors 1990–2004 (American Library Association, 2005).

Do you agree with efforts to ban the Harry Potter books and condemn the movies? In general, do you think that religious organizations should be able to get schools to ban books and movies? If so, do you draw the line at some types of influence? Would it be acceptable if a white religious organi-zation got a predominantly white school to ban the works of Toni Morrison and Maya Angelou because they say derogatory things about whites? Would it be acceptable if a Jewish religious organization got a predominantly Jewish school to ban Shakespeare's *The Merchant of Venice* because it portrays Jews in an unflat-tering way? Would it be acceptable if a religious organization strongly influ-enced by feminism convinced students in an all-girls school to ban the works of Ernest Hemingway ("too sexist") or if an anti-feminist religious organiza-tion convinced students in an all-boys school to ban the writings of Margaret Atwood ("too anti-male")? In general, should religious organizations be allowed to influence schools to censor, or should censoring by religious organizations be banned?

of Shah Reza Pahlavi, which fell in 1979. Muslim fundamentalism then swept much of the Middle East, Africa, and parts of Asia. In Iran, Afghanistan, and Sudan, Muslim fundamentalists took power. Other predominantly Muslim countries' governments have begun to introduce elements of Islamic religious law (*shari'a*), either from conviction or as a precaution against restive populations. Religious fundamentalism has thus become a worldwide political phenomenon. In not a few cases it has taken extreme forms and involved violence as a means of establishing fundamentalist ideas and institutions (Juergensmeyer, 2000). These developments amount to a religious revival that was quite unexpected in, say, 1970.

The Revised Secularization Thesis

The developments reviewed above led some sociologists to revise the secularization thesis in the 1990s. The revisionists acknowledge that religion has become increasingly influential in the lives of some individuals and groups over the past 30 years. They insist, however, that the scope of religious authority has continued to decline in most people's lives. That is, for most people, religion has less and less to say about education, family issues, politics, and economic affairs even though it may continue to be an important source of spiritual belief and practice. In this sense, secularization continues (Chaves, 1994; Yamane, 1997).

According to the **revised secularization thesis**, in most countries, worldly institutions have broken off (or differentiated) from the institution of religion over time. One such worldly institution is the education system. Religious bodies used to run schools and insti-tutions of higher learning that are now run almost exclusively by non-religious authorities. Moreover, like other specialized institutions that separated from the institution of religion, the educational system is generally concerned with worldly affairs rather than with spiritual matters. Similarly, laws are enacted that confine religious standards to issues that are private and personal (see Box 16.2).

The overall effect of the differentiation of secular institutions has been to make religion applicable only to the spiritual part of most people's lives. Because the scope of religious authority has been restricted, people look to religion for moral guidance in everyday life less often than they used to. Moreover, most people have turned religion into a personal and pri-vate matter rather than one imposed by a powerful, authoritative institution. Said differently, people feel increasingly free to combine beliefs and practices from various sources and traditions to suit their own tastes. As supermodel Cindy Crawford said in a *Redbook* interview in 1992, "I'm religious but in my own personal way. I always say that I have a Cindy Crawford religion—It's my own" (quoted in Yamane, 1997: 116). No statement could more adequately capture the decline of religion as an authoritative institution suffusing all aspects of life.

The **revised secularization thesis** holds that worldly institutions break off from the institution of religion over time. As a result, religion governs an ever-smaller part of most people's lives and becomes largely a matter of personal choice.

BOX 16.2
It's Your Choice

Should Family Law Allow for Arbitration Based on Different Religious Traditions?

In Ontario, a 1991 law authorized the use of religious rules to govern legal decisions. Members of various religious groups were allowed to settle disputes by agreeing to binding arbitration that would conform to religious precepts. Issues that could be settled included divorce, child custody, and matters of inheritance. Under this allowance, disputes were settled by appeals to diverse legal traditions, including those of Aboriginals, Catholics, Mennonites, Jehovah's Witnesses, and Jews.

Controversy erupted over whether Islamic law, or *shari'a*, should be similarly treated. Some within the Islamic community were strongly opposed. Homa Arjomand, a refugee immigrant

to Canada from Iran, organized an international campaign against the creation of *shari'a* courts in Canada (International Campaign, 2005). However, proponents pointed to a clear issue of equity—if Christians and Jews were allowed to practise their traditions, why could Muslims not do so as well?

A former Ontario Attorney General and feminist activist, Marion Boyd, was commissioned to report on the matter. In the balance were conflicting ideals of multiculturalism and women's rights. Boyd's report of December 20, 2004, attempted to strike a balance. She supported the principle of extending family arbitration rights to Muslims but within strict limits defined by a list of 46 safeguards. Supporters included the rabbi who headed the Toronto *beth din* (court). But with headlines like "Will Canada introduce *shari'a* law?" echoing worldwide, critics con-

tinued to raise alarms about Canada becoming the first Western nation to formally recognize legal standards widely regarded as unjust to women (Trevelyan, 2004).

Ontario Premier Dalton McGuinty took a decisive stand on the symbolic date of September 11, 2005. He announced his intention to introduce legislation to abolish all family law arbitration based on religious traditions. "There will be one law for all Ontarians," he said (Freeze and Howlett, 2005).

What do you think? Should a society committed to multiculturalism allow people to practise their own traditions in resolving family disputes? Should individuals who assent of their own free will not be permitted to use such means? Or should the government use the power of law only when the rules apply to all citizens without exceptions?

The Market Model

To understand how a religious revival among some people can take place in the midst of an overall decline in religious participation, sociologists sometimes think of religion as a market. The market model characterizes religious organizations as *suppliers* of services. For example, religious organizations provide counselling and pastoral care. Religious professionals organize opportunities for social participation, including dinners, youth activities, men's groups, women's groups, mixed groups, lectures, discussions, and singing and other performing groups. These services are in *demand* by people who desire religious activities. According to the market model, religious denominations are similar to product brands. They offer different "flavours" of religious experience. Congregations are local suppliers of a given brand. Denominations compete to establish congregations while congregations compete to attract local followings (Barna, 2002; Bibby, 2002, 2004).

As Table 16.2 on page 476 illustrates, religious variety is reflected in differing mixes of innovation and tradition in worship. In Canada, conservative or fundamentalist Protestants are least likely to hold services that are traditional in content. The weekly attendance rate for conservative Protestants is rising and was already much higher in 1990 than the comparable rate for other groups. Among Roman Catholics outside Quebec, traditional services are especially popular, and weekly attendance is relatively high too, although declining weekly attendance has been evident for decades. Mainline Protestants are most likely to favour services that feature a blend of traditional and contemporary elements but attendance at weekly services has been low since 1990. These results illustrate how diverse religious approaches coexist but undergo changes in fortune as people's tastes shift.

TABLE 16.2

Major Religious Categories by Type of Worship Service and Members Who Attended Weekly (in percent)

Note: Mainline Protestants include Anglican, Lutheran, Presbyterian, and United. Conservative Protestants include Baptists and evangelical denominations. RC refers to Roman Catholic. Types of worship service do not add up to 100 percent because respondents who answered "both in separate services" and "unsure" have been omitted.

Sources: Reginald W. Bibby, 2002, *Restless God: The Renaissance of Religion in Canada* (Toronto, ON: Stoddart), p. 73; and Reginald W. Bibby, 2004, *Restless Churches: How Canada's Churches Can Contribute to the Emerging Religious Renaissance* (Ottawa, ON: Novalis), p. 107. Reprinted with permission.

	Type of Worship Service, 2000			Percentage Attending Services Once a Week+	
	Contemporary	Blend	Traditional	1990	2000
Mainline Protestant	3	56	29	14	15
Conservative Protestant	21	45	17	49	58
RC outside Quebec	4	36	47	37	32
RC in Quebec	10	50	33	28	20
All	8	45	36	24	21

The market model raises the question of what motivates people to participate in religion. Some sociologists have highlighted otherworldly or supernatural rewards. Others have advanced the possibility that religious participation is a way of staking claims to superior status or social prestige.

Two of the earliest proponents of the market model, Rodney Stark and William Bainbridge (1987, 1997), assigned a central role to supernatural beliefs. They argued that religions promise rewards based on supernatural assumptions in exchange for particular types of behaviour now. A central implication of Stark and Bainbridge's argument is that religious participation is particularly attractive to poor people. They argue that wealthy people enjoy real, material benefits and therefore have less need and desire for supernatural promises that might never bear fruit. However, Randall Collins (1993) questions whether religions are limited to offering supernatural rewards. He suggests that participation in religious organizations can also have direct and tangible benefits, such as providing friendly associations and access to pooled resources. Consequently, religions may appeal to everyone, regardless of class position. To make his case, Collins points to many historical examples of upper-class people giving up material rewards for religious vocations. He notes that many religions create high-status rewards and identify people who are closest to sacred ideals, often singling out individuals who are the most learned and of exemplary conduct. Finally, people with the most wealth and political power often gain highly favourable, public endorsement by cooperating with religious organizations. For all these reasons, religion may appeal to the rich just as much as it appeals to the poor.

In sum, the market model has two main strengths:

1. It clarifies the social bases of heterogeneity and change in religious life. Religious observance in North America today is a highly decentralized, largely unregulated, "industry." Although believers generally demand significant continuity with their family experiences, they enjoy wide latitude to innovate. Meanwhile, congregations are free to specialize and adopt different religious strategies. For example, a congregation targeting older, wealthier clients might repeat traditional rituals to nearly empty pews, tolerating lax attendance from families who are unlikely to switch allegiance late in life. A congregation targeting a younger, less wealthy clientele might encourage a high rate of attendance by offering livelier services and more extravagant promises of supernatural rewards. The religious industry is not uniform, and unending competition flourishes among congregations and denominations.

2. The market model also draws attention to the potential advantages of diversification. It is often assumed that the existence of an official or state religion, such as Christianity in the Roman Empire or Islam in contemporary Iran, is the best guarantee of religiosity. However, the market model emphasizes that a system of religious diversity can also be a source of strength because it allows individuals to "shop around" for a religious organization that corresponds to their particular "tastes." In fact, a state monopoly on religion may limit the degree to which individual tastes can be satisfied, while the coexistence

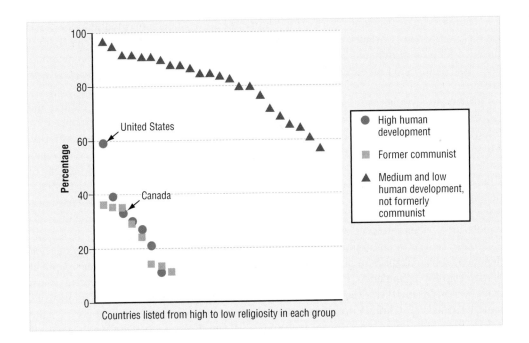

FIGURE 16.2

Percentage of People Who Think Religion Is Very Important, 44 Countries, 2002

This figure is derived from a survey of 38 000 people in 44 countries. (Poland is a former communist country and the UN ranks it 37th in its list of 53 countries in the "high human development" group. It is classified here as a former communist country.)

Sources: Pew Research Center, 2002; United Nations, 2002.

of competing religious traditions can strengthen the entire religious "industry." This may help explain why the United States, a country with one of the longest traditions of banning state support for particular religions, has an exceptionally high rate of religious participation for a highly industrialized country (see Figure 16.2). In contrast, at least some regions in which state and religion remained entwined until quite recently, such as Quebec, have experienced some of the sharpest dropoffs in participation in religious organizations.

RELIGION IN CANADA AND THE WORLD

Church, Sect, and Cult

Sociologists generally divide religious groups into just three types: churches, sects, and cults (Stark and Bainbridge, 1979; Troeltsch, 1931 [1923]; see Table 16.3). In the sociological sense of the term, a **church** is any bureaucratic religious organization that has accommodated itself to mainstream society and culture. As a result, it may endure for many hundreds, if not thousands, of years. The bureaucratic nature of a church is evident in the formal training of its leaders, its strict hierarchy of roles, and its clearly drawn rules and regulations. Its integration into mainstream society is evident in its teachings, which are generally abstract and do not challenge worldly authority. In addition, churches integrate themselves into the mainstream by recruiting members from all classes of society.

A church is a bureaucratic religious organization that has accommodated itself to mainstream society and culture.

TABLE 16.3

Church, Sect, and Cult Compared

Source: Statistics Canada, 2005, "Overview: Canada Still Predominantly Roman Catholic and Protestant." Retrieved November 28, 2005 (http://www12.statcan.ca/english/census01/Products/Analytic/companion/rel/canada.cfm#growth).

	Church	Sect	Cult
Integration into society	High	Medium	low
Bureaucratization	High	Low	Low
Longevity	High	Low	Low
Leaders	Formally trained	Charismatic	Charismatic
Class base	Mixed	Low	Various but segregated

Ecclesia are state-supported churches.

Churches take two main forms. First are **ecclesia** or state-supported churches. For example, Christianity became the state religion in the Roman Empire in 392 CE and Islam is the state religion in Iran and Sudan today.[2] State religions impose advantages on members and disadvantages on non-members. Tolerance of other religions is low in societies with ecclesia.

Alternatively, churches may be pluralistic, allowing diversity within the church and expressing tolerance of non-members. Pluralism allows churches to increase their appeal by allowing various streams of belief and practice to coexist under their overarching authority. These subgroups are called **denominations**. In 2001 (the latest year for which census data are available as of this writing), the major Protestant denominations in Canada were United Church, Anglican, Baptist, Lutheran, Presbyterian, and Pentecostal. The major Catholic denominations were Roman Catholic and Ukrainian Catholic. The major Jewish denominations were Orthodox, Conservative, Reform, and Reconstructionist. Many of these denominations are divided into even smaller groups.

Denominations are the various streams of belief and practice that some churches allow to coexist under their over-arching authority.

Table 16.4 shows the percentage of Canadians who belonged to the major religions and denominations in Canada in 2001. Roman Catholics remained the largest religious group at 43 percent of the population. Protestants were the second-largest group at 29 percent, down from 36 percent in 1991. Despite the common perception that recent waves of immigrants have lessened the Christian domination of Canada, little, in fact, has changed. Of the 1.8 million immigrants who arrived between 1991 and 2001, 15 percent were Muslims, 7 percent identified as Hindus, while Buddhists and Sikhs accounted for 5 percent each. Although Muslims more than doubled in number, the rise in proportion was from about 1 percent to 2 percent (Statistics Canada, 2003c). This parallels earlier findings that immigrants from Asian and other developing countries are mainly Christians (Statistics Canada, 1998a). In 1991, one in three Asian immigrants identified with Protestantism or Roman Catholicism, while most Latin American immigrants were Roman Catholics (Bibby, 1993: 24). Only among African immigrants did the number of non-Christians exceed the number of Christians.

TABLE 16.4

Religious Adherence, Canada, 2001 (in percent)

Source: Statistics Canada, 2005, "Overview: Canada Still Predominantly Roman Catholic and Protestant." Retrieved November 28, 2005 (http://www.12statca.ca/english/census01/Products/Analytic/companion/rel/Canada.cfm#growth).

	Number	Percentage
Catholic	12 936 910	43.65
Roman Catholic	12 793 125	43.16
Ukrainian Catholic	126 200	0.43
Other Catholic	17 585	0.06
Protestant	8 654 850	29.20
United Church	2 839 125	9.58
Anglican	2 035 500	6.87
Baptist	729 475	2.46
Lutheran	606 590	2.05
Presbyterian	409 830	1.38
Pentecostal	369 480	1.24
Other Protestant	1 664 850	5.62
Christian Orthodox	479 620	1.62
Christian, n.i.e	780 450	2.63
Muslim	579 640	1.96
Jewish	329 995	1.11
Buddhist	300 345	1.01
Hindu	297 200	1.00
Sikh	278 410	0.94
Eastern religions	37 545	0.13
Other, para-religious	63 975	0.22
No religious affiliation	4 900 095	16.53
Total	29 639 035	100.00

Sects often form by breaking away from churches because of disagreement about church doctrine. Sometimes, sect members choose to separate themselves geographically, as the Hutterites do in their some 350 colonies in Canada, mostly in the Western provinces. However, even in urban settings, strictly enforced rules concerning dress, diet, prayer, and intimate contact with outsiders can separate sect members from the larger society. Hasidic Jews in Montreal and Toronto prove the viability of this isolation strategy. Sects are less integrated into society and less bureaucratized than churches. They are often led by **charismatic** leaders, men and women who claim to be inspired by supernatural powers and whose followers believe them to be so inspired. These leaders tend to be relatively intolerant of religious opinions other than their own. They tend to recruit like-minded members mainly from lower classes and marginal groups. Worship in sects tends to be highly emotional and based less on abstract principles than on immediate personal experience (Stark, 1985: 314). Many sects are short-lived, but those that do persist tend to bureaucratize and turn into churches. If religious organizations are to enjoy a long life, they require rules, regulations, and a clearly defined hierarchy of roles.

Cults are small groups of people deeply committed to a religious vision that rejects mainstream culture and society. Cults are generally led by charismatic individuals. They tend to be class-segregated groups. That is, a cult tends to recruit members from only one segment of the stratification system: high, middle, or low. For example, many North American cults today recruit nearly all their members from among the university educated. Some of these cults seek converts almost exclusively on university and college campuses (Kosmin, 1991). Because they propose a radically new way of life, cults tend to recruit few members and soon disappear. There are, however, exceptions—and some extremely important ones at that. Jesus and Muhammad were both charismatic leaders of cults. They were so compelling that they and their teachings were able to inspire a large number of followers, including rulers of states. Their cults were thus transformed into churches.

Major World Religions

There are five major world religions: Judaism, Christianity, Islam, Hinduism, and Buddhism (see Figure 16.3 on page 480). They are *major* in the sense that they have had a big impact on world history and, aside from Judaism, continue to have hundreds of millions of adherents. They are *world* religions in the sense that their adherents live in many countries.

Sects usually form by breaking away from churches because of disagreement about church doctrine. Sects are less integrated into society and less bureaucratized than churches.

Charismatic authority is based on belief in the claims of extraordinary individuals that they are inspired by a god or some higher principle.

Cults are small groups of people deeply committed to a religious vision that rejects mainstream culture and society.

Even in urban settings, strictly enforced rules concerning dress, diet, prayer, and intimate contact with outsiders can separate sect members from the larger society.

FIGURE 16.3

The World's Predominant Religions

This map shows the predominant religion in each of the world's countries, defined as the religion to which more than 50 percent of a country's population adheres.

Source: Adherents.com, 2001.

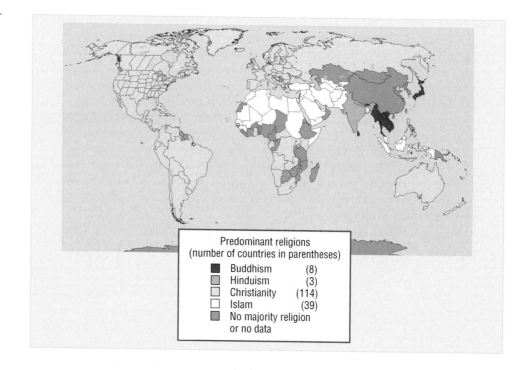

Predominant religions
(number of countries in parentheses)

■	Buddhism	(8)
▨	Hinduism	(3)
▢	Christianity	(114)
▢	Islam	(39)
▨	No majority religion or no data	

Just more than a quarter of the world's population (1.9 billion people) are Christian. Christianity is the predominant religion in 114 countries and is most widespread in North and South America, Europe, Oceania (Australia, New Zealand, etc.), and southern Africa. The second-most-widespread religion in the world is Islam. Muslims compose less than a fifth of the world's population (1.2 billion people). Islam is the predominant religion in 39 countries in the Middle East, central and northern Africa, and parts of Asia. Hinduism is the world's third-largest religion. Although only three countries are predominantly Hindu, one of them is India, so just over 11 percent of the world's population adheres to Hinduism (762 million people). The fourth major world religion is Buddhism, the predominant religion in eight Asian countries. About 5 percent of the world's population are Buddhists (354 million people).[3] Although numerically small on a world scale, Judaism must also be included in any list of major world religions because Christianity and Islam have their roots in Judaism. There are 14 million Jews in the world and Judaism is the predominant religion only in Israel.

Other religions have many adherents too. For example, some scholars consider Confucianism a major world religion. Certainly, Confucianism has had a tremendous impact on East Asian societies, and we still find East Asians who claim to be Confucian, especially in Singapore. Furthermore, some Confucian rituals, such as ancestor worship, resemble religious practice. However, we believe Confucianism is best seen as a worldview or a philosophy of life (Ivanhoe, 2000). Few East Asians regard Confucianism as a religion.

The five major world religions have much in common. First, with the exception of Hinduism, charismatic leaders helped to turn them into world religions. Second, and again with the exception of Hinduism, all five major world religions had egalitarian and emancipatory messages at their origins. That is, they claimed to stand for equality and freedom. Third, over time, the charismatic leadership of the world religions became routinized. The **routinization of charisma** is Weber's term for the transformation of divine enlightenment into a permanent feature of everyday life. It involves turning religious inspiration into a stable social institution with defined roles, such as interpreters of the divine message, teachers, dues-paying laypeople, and so forth. The routinization of charisma often involves the weakening of the ideals of freedom and equality. Under some conditions it gives way to their opposite: repression and inequality.

The routinization of charisma is Weber's term for the transformation of divine enlightenment into a permanent feature of everyday life.

Judaism

According to the Bible, the first Jew was Abraham, who lived nearly 4000 years ago in ancient Mesopotamia, now Iraq (Gottwald, 1979; Roth, 1961). Abraham's unique contribution was to assert that there is only one God; before Abraham, people believed in many gods. The Bible says that God promised Abraham abundant offspring and, for his descendants, a land of their own.

Abraham's great-grandson, Joseph, was sold by his brothers into slavery in Egypt. There, Joseph became a trusted adviser of the Pharaoh. However, a later Pharaoh enslaved the Jews, and about 400 years after Joseph's arrival in Egypt the prophet Moses led them out of bondage. The emancipation of the Jews from slavery still stands as a defining moment in the history of Judaism. It has inspired generations of Jews and non-Jews to believe that God sanctions freedom and equality. Practising Jews celebrate the emancipation annually during Passover, which has become one of the most important Jewish festivals.

The Bible says that after 40 years of wandering in the desert, during which time Moses received the Ten Commandments, the Jews arrived in Canaan, the land that God had promised Abraham. (Modern-day Israel and ancient Canaan occupy roughly the same territory.) Thereafter, Judaism spread throughout the Middle East and established itself as a major religion during Roman rule. Increased persecution in the Roman period led the religious leaders (rabbis) to settle in Galilee. There, between the second and the sixth centuries CE, Judaism assumed its contemporary form, characterized by the centrality of the rabbis and the Torah (the five books of Moses, known to Christians as the first five books of the Old Testament).

The central teachings of Judaism rest above all on belief in one God, Yahweh. However, many commentators argue that the core of Judaism lies less in belief than in the performance of the 613 divine commandments or *mitzvot* mentioned in the Torah. The mitzvoth include prescriptions for justice, righteousness, and observance: rest and pray on the Sabbath, honour the old and the wise, do not wrong a stranger in buying or selling, do not seek revenge or hold a grudge, do not eat the meat of animals with hooves, and so on. Temples or synagogues are common places of worship for Jews, but they are not essential. Worship can take place wherever there is an assembly of 10 adult Jewish males (or females in the more liberal branches of Judaism).

Like some other Middle Eastern peoples, the Jews were involved in international trade long before the birth of Christ. They therefore settled in many places outside the area that is now Israel. However, after the Romans destroyed the Jewish temple in Jerusalem in 70 CE, the Jews dispersed even more widely to the far reaches of Europe, Asia, and North Africa, forming what became known as the Diaspora ("dispersion"). Jews retained their identity in the Diaspora because in pre-modern times they specialized in mercantile activities that separated them from peasants and landowners, because they tended to be strictly observant, and because they were periodically persecuted, mainly by Christians. (In general, Muslims were more tolerant of Jews until recently.) In 1948, Israel was returned to Jewish sovereignty.

There are roughly 5.5 million Jews in North America—about the same number as in Israel. The considerable diversity among Jews in North America derives from disagreements that began nearly 400 years ago. In seventeenth-century Eastern Europe, ecstatic and mystical sects of Hasidim broke away from the staid and bookish Judaism of the time. Today in Toronto and Montreal we can still see Hasidic Jews dressed in their characteristic black robes and broad-brimmed hats (ironically, the garb of seventeenth-century Polish noblemen). In nineteenth-century Germany, the Reform movement also broke with traditional Jewish practice. Influenced by Lutheranism, Reform Judaism was a liberal movement that involved a loosening of strict rules of religious observance, prayer in the German language, the integration of men and women in worship, services that followed the kind of decorum associated with Protestant worship, and the introduction of choirs and organs to enhance prayer. The Reform movement transplanted itself to North America with the immigration of German Jews. Orthodox Judaism emerged as a reaction against the liberalizing tendencies of the Reform movement. It involved a return to traditional observance, including strict adherence to dietary rules, the segregation of men and women in prayer, and so forth. Conservative Judaism crystallized in Britain and the United States in the nineteenth century as an attempt to reconcile what its practitioners regard as the positive elements in Orthodoxy with the dynamism of Reform. Finally, Reconstructionist Judaism is a smaller, twentieth-century American offshoot of Conservatism, known chiefly for its liberalism, social activism, and gender-egalitarianism.

Christianity

Observant Jews believe that God promised them a Messiah, a redeemer whose arrival would signal the beginning of an era of eternal peace, prosperity, and righteousness. Jews believe the Messiah has not yet arrived. Christians believe he has. In the Christian view, the Messiah is Jesus (Brown, 1996; McManners, 1990).

Jesus was a poor Jew and his early followers were all Jewish. Yet he criticized the Judaism of his time for its external conformity to tradition and ritual at the expense of developing a true relationship to God as demanded by the prophets. Believe in God and love him; love your neighbour—these are the two main lessons of Jesus. What made his teaching novel was his demand that people match outward performance with inner conviction. Thus, it was not enough not to murder; a person could not even hate. Nor was it enough not to commit adultery; a person could not even lust after a neighbour's wife (Matt. 5: 21–28).

These lessons made Jesus anti-authoritarian and even revolutionary. Criticizing ritual by rote put Jesus at odds with the established Judaism of his time. Admonishing people to love their neighbours impressed on them the need to emancipate slaves and women. It also challenged people to recognize the essential equality of the beggar and the wealthy merchant in the eyes of God. Roman authorities could hardly be happy with such teachings because they attracted the poor and the dispossessed and they were a direct challenge to the legitimacy of the Roman Empire, built as it was on slavery and privilege. Little wonder that the Romans persecuted Jesus and his followers, eventually executing him by crucifixion, a cruel and painful death reserved for slaves and the worst criminals. Christians interpret the death of Jesus as atonement for the sins of humanity.

For at least a century after Jesus's death, the Christians formed a minor Jewish sect. Aided by 12 of Jesus's main followers, the apostles, Christianity gained adherents largely from within the Jewish community. However, because they encountered opposition from Judaism, the Christians soon began to preach their message to non-Jews. This required that they redefine Jesus's message as a correction and fulfillment of Greek and Roman philosophy. This helped Christianity spread, but even as it did, the Roman Empire continued to persecute Christians. Many heresies and schisms also beset the Christians in these first centuries after the death of Jesus. There thus arose the need for stable, recognized leadership and set, recognized holy texts. The clerical rank of bishop and the canon date from this period. They were the routinization of Jesus's charisma in practice.

In 312 CE, the Roman emperor Constantine I the Great converted to Christianity. He soon turned Christianity into a state religion. It then spread rapidly throughout Europe. By allying itself first with the Roman Empire and then with other earthly powers—European royalty and the landowning class—the Church became the dominant institution, religious or secular, in Europe until the sixteenth century. It also contributed to gender inequality insofar as women played a marginal role in its affairs. Just as Judaism had been transformed from an emancipatory religion into one that could be criticized by Jesus for ritualistic staleness, so Christianity was transformed from a revolutionary force into a pillar of the existing order.

In the sixteenth century, Martin Luther, a German priest, challenged the Christian establishment by seeking to establish a more personal relationship between the faithful and God. At the time, ordinary people were illiterate, and they had to rely on priests to hear the holy word and interpret it for them. However, by insisting that Christians come to know God themselves, as Jesus demanded, Luther called into question the whole Church hierarchy. His protests and his ideas quickly captured the imagination of half of Europe and led to the split of Christianity into the two major branches that persist to this day: Catholicism and Protestantism.

This is by no means the only division within Christianity. In the Middle Ages, Christianity split into Western and Eastern halves, the former centred in Rome, the latter in Constantinople (now Istanbul, Turkey). Various Orthodox churches today derive from the Eastern tradition. Protestantism has been especially prone to splintering because it emphasizes the individual's relationship to God rather than to a central authority. Today, there are hundreds of different Protestant churches.

Christians retained the Jewish Bible as the Old Testament, adding the Gospels and letters of the apostles as the New Testament. The Bible is the most important text for Christians. Especially for Protestants, reading the New Testament is an important part of what it means to be a Christian. Traditionally, the most important holiday for Christians was Easter but increasingly Christians have celebrated Christmas, which became especially popular in the nineteenth century.

Christianity remains the dominant religion in the West. Because of its successful missionary efforts, it can be found almost everywhere in the world. Yet Christianity remains a truly heterogeneous religion. Some Christians are fundamentalist and conservative, others are mainstream and more liberal, while still others are socialist and even revolutionary. Some support feminists and homosexuals, while others regard them as abominations. Its success is due in part to its ability to encompass diverse and even contradictory currents.

Islam

Christianity emerged in a society dominated by Roman conquerors, a society in which ordinary people were burdened by heavy taxes and temple levies. Several military revolts against the Romans took place in this period, and some scholars view Jesus's message as a religious response to the oppressive social conditions of his time.

Islam originated more than 600 years later in the city of Mecca in what is now Saudi Arabia. It, too, can be seen as a religious response to a society in crisis. Mecca was a rich trading centre, and the powerful merchants of that city had become greedy, overbearing, and corrupt. The merchants ignored the traditional moral code that originated with the surrounding nomadic tribes (the Bedouin). The Bedouin themselves were heavily indebted to the merchants and became so poor that some of them were sold into slavery. On a larger canvas, many people in Arabia thought that the Persian and Roman Empires, which dominated the Middle East, might soon fall, heralding the end of the world (Rodinson, 1996).

Into this crisis stepped Muhammad, who claimed to have visions from God (Hodgson, 1974; Lapidus, 2002). His teachings were later written down in the Koran. Certain episodes and personalities that appear in the holy books of Judaism and Christianity also appear in the Koran; Muslims recognize both Moses and Jesus as prophets, for example. The central belief of Islam is that there is one true God, Allah, and that the words of his prophet, Muhammad, must be followed. Islam also emphasizes important teachings of Christianity, such as egalitarianism and universal love. Even more than the Bible for Judaism and Christianity, however, the Koran is important for devout Muslims because they believe it is the direct word of God.

Like Judaism with its Talmudic commentaries on the Bible, Islam stresses the significance of *hadith* (traditions), a corpus of anecdotes and commentaries about Muhammad. Like rabbis in Judaism and priests in Catholicism, *ulamas* (scholars) maintain religious authority in Islam. Unlike Christianity, however, Islam has never had a central Church. Although any place can become a site of prayer and learning, mosques are the traditional places of worship.

People who profess Islam have five core duties. At least once in their life they must recite the Muslim creed aloud, correctly, with full understanding, and with heartfelt belief. (The creed is "There is no god but Allah and Muhammad is his prophet.") Five times a day they must worship in a religious service. They must fast from sunrise to sunset every day during the ninth month of the lunar calendar (Ramadan). They must give to the poor. And at least once in their life they must make a pilgrimage to the holy city of Mecca.

By the time of his death, Muhammad had founded an empire, and a dispute broke out over how his followers could identify his successor (the *khalifa,* or caliph in English). One group claimed that the caliphate should be an elected office occupied by a member of a certain Meccan tribe. These were the Sunni Muslims. A second group claimed that the caliph should be the direct descendant of Muhammad. These were the Shia Muslims. Today, the great majority of Muslims are Sunni, while the Shia are concentrated in Iran and southern Iraq (see Figure 16.4). The Shia are generally more conservative and fundamentalist than the Sunni.

Islam spread rapidly after Muhammad's death, replacing Christianity in much of the Middle East, Africa, and parts of southern Europe. It ushered in a great cultural flowering and an era of considerable religious tolerance by the standards of the time. Significantly, the Jews flourished in Muslim Spain and North Africa at the very time they were being persecuted and expelled from Christian Europe.

Only a few sects developed out of Islam. The most noteworthy was Wahhabism, an extreme fundamentalist movement that originated in the eighteenth century in what is now Saudi Arabia. Its founder, Muhammad Ibn Abd al-Wahhab, upheld ritual over intentions, opposed reverence of the dead, and demanded that prayer and honours be extended only to Allah and not to Muhammad or the saints. He opposed all music and all books other than the Koran, and favoured the extermination of anyone who disagreed with him, especially if they happened to be Shia. Characteristically, in 1801 Wahhabis stormed the Iraqi city of Karbala, wrecked and looted the sacred tomb of Muhammad's grandson, Hussein, and slaughtered thousands of the city's Shia residents.

Wahhabism might be ignored as a minor fanatical sect if it were not for one important historical fact. In 1747, al-Wahhab made a pact with Muhammad ibn Sa'ud whereby ibn Sa'ud became the political ruler of the Arabian peninsula and al-Wahhab its religious authority. In effect, Wahhabism became the state religion of what is now Saudi Arabia. This extreme form of fundamentalism continues to flourish in Saudi Arabia today, where its tenets are taught in the Saudi school system. It is not coincidental that nearly all of the suicide bombers who attacked the United States on September 11, 2001, were Saudi citizens, as is Osama bin Laden himself, and that Saudi money finances schools throughout the Muslim world that propagate anti-Western ideas (Schwartz, 2003).

Hinduism

Hinduism is the dominant religion of India but it has no single founder and no books that are thought to be inspired by God. Its major texts are epic poems, such as the *Bhagavad-Gita*, the *Mahabharata*, and the *Ramayana*. Like Judaism, Hinduism originated nearly 4000 years ago, so we have little sense of the social context in which it first emerged (Flood, 1996). What is clear is that its otherworldliness and mystical tendencies make it very different from the three main Western religions.

Hindus believe in reincarnation, a cycle of birth, death, and rebirth. Only the body dies according to Hindu belief. The soul returns in a new form after death. The form in which it

FIGURE 16.4

Distribution of Sunni and Shia Muslims

Source: University of Texas, 2003.

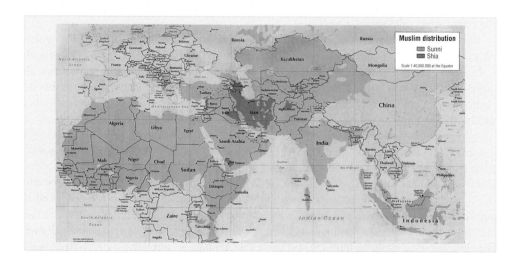

returns depends on how a person lives his or her life. Hindus believe that people who live in a way that is appropriate to their position in society will live better future lives. In rare cases, a person reaches a stage of spiritual perfection (*nirvana*) that allows the soul to escape the cycle of birth and rebirth, and reunite with God. In contrast, people who do not live in a way that is appropriate to their position in society will supposedly live an inferior life when they are reincarnated. In the worst case, evildoers are expected to be reincarnated as non-humans. This way of thinking helped to create a caste system, a rigid, religiously sanctioned class hierarchy. Vertical social mobility was nearly impossible because, according to Hindu belief, striving to move out of your station in life is inappropriate and ensures reincarnation in a lower life form.

There are many gods in the Hindu tradition, although all of them are thought to be aspects of the one true God. This too makes Hinduism different from the Western religions. A final difference between Hinduism and the Western religions is its propensity to assimilate rather than exclude other religious beliefs and practices. Traditionally, Jews, Christians, and Muslims tended to reject non-believers unless they converted. God tells Moses on Mount Sinai, "You shall have no other gods before me." In contrast, in the *Bhagavad-Gita*, Krishna says that "whatever god a man worships, it is I who answer the prayer." This attitude of acceptance helped Hinduism absorb many of the ancient religions of the peoples of the Indian subcontinent. It also explains why there are such wide regional and class variations in Hindu beliefs and practices; Hinduism as it is practised bears the stamp of many other religions.

Buddhism

By about 600 BCE, Hinduism had developed into a system of rituals and sacrifices that was widely considered a burden. For example, a person could escape the consequences of committing inappropriate or evil acts but only by having priests perform a series of mechanical rituals. In a sense, Gautama Buddha was to Hinduism what Jesus was to Judaism. Like Jesus in Palestine 600 years later, Buddha objected to the stale ritualism of the established religion and sought to achieve a direct relationship with God (Gombrich, 1996; Lopez, 2001; Robinson and Johnson, 1997). He rejected Hindu ideas of caste and reincarnation and offered a new way for everyone to achieve spiritual enlightenment. Rather than justifying inequality, he promised the possibility of salvation to people of low status and women, who were traditionally marginalized by Hinduism.

Buddha based his method of salvation on what he called the Four Noble Truths: (1) Life is suffering. There are moments of joy, but poverty, violence, and other sources of sorrow overshadow them. (2) All suffering derives from desire. We suffer when we fail to achieve what we want. (3) Suffering ceases by eliminating desire. If we can train ourselves not to lust, not to be greedy, not to crave pleasure, not even to desire material comforts, we will not suffer. (4) We can eliminate desire by behaving morally, focusing intently on our feelings and thoughts, meditating, and achieving wisdom. Nirvana can be achieved by "blowing out" the futile passions of existence.

Buddhism does not presume the existence of one true God. Rather, it holds out the possibility of everyone becoming a god of sorts. Similarly, it does not have a central church or text, such as the Bible. Not surprisingly, then, Buddhism is notable for its diversity of beliefs and practices. Numerous schools and scriptures make up the Buddhist tradition. Many Westerners are familiar with Zen Buddhism, especially influential in East Asia, which emphasizes the possibility of enlightenment through meditation.

Buddhism spread rapidly across Asia after India's ruler adopted it as his own religion in the third century BCE. He sent missionaries to convert people in Tibet, Cambodia (Kampuchea), Nepal, Sri Lanka (formerly Ceylon), Myanmar (formerly Burma), China, Korea, and Japan. Ironically, the influence of Buddhism in the land of its birth started to die out after the fifth century CE and is negligible in India today. In India, as we have seen, Hinduism predominates. One of the reasons for the popularity of Buddhism in East and Southeast Asia is that Buddhism is able to coexist with local religious practices. Unlike Western religions, Buddhism does not insist on holding a monopoly on religious truth.

Gautama Buddha (about 563–480 BCE)

The Cycle of World Religions

Little historical evidence helps us understand the social conditions that gave rise to the first world religions, Judaism and Hinduism. We are on safer ground when it comes to understanding the rise of Buddhism, Christianity, and Islam. Insofar as we dare to make sociological generalizations about thousands of years of complex religious development spanning many cultures and virtually the entire globe, we can venture four conclusions. First, new world religions are founded by charismatic personalities in times of great trouble. The impulse to find a better world is encouraged by adversity in this one. Second, the founding of new religions is typically animated by the desire for freedom and equality, always in the afterlife and often in this one. Third, the routinization of charisma typically makes religion less responsive to the needs of ordinary people, and it often supports injustices. For this reason, and also because there is no lack of adversity in the world, movements of religious reform and revival are always evident, and they often spill over into politics. For example, the Catholic Church played a critically important role in undermining communism in Poland in the 1970s and the 1980s, and Catholic "liberation theology" animated the successful fight against right-wing governments in Latin America in the same period (Kepel, 1994 [1991]; Segundo, 1976 [1975]; Smith, 1991). It is for this reason, too, that we venture a fourth, speculative conclusion, namely that new world religions could well emerge in the future.

Religiosity

We have reviewed the major classical theories of religion and society, the modern debate about secularization, the major types of religious organizations, and the major world religions. It is now time to conclude our discussion by considering some social factors that determine how important religion is to people; that is, their **religiosity**.

Religiosity refers to how important religion is to people.

We can measure religiosity in various ways. Strength of belief, emotional attachment to a religion, knowledge about a religion, frequency of performing rituals, and frequency of applying religious principles in daily life all indicate how religious a person is (Glock, 1962). Ideally, we ought to examine many measures to get a fully rounded and reliable picture of the social distribution of religiosity. For simplicity's sake, however, we focus on just two measures here: whether people attend religious services at least weekly and whether they regard their level of involvement in religious activities at various points in their life as having been high, moderate, low, or none.

Figure 16.5 focuses on the second measure for Canada in 2000. A fascinating pattern emerges from data. The Canadians most heavily involved in religious activities are preteens and seniors. As a result, involvement forms a U-shaped curve, falling among teenagers and young adults and then beginning to rise steadily after the age of 24. How can we explain this pattern? Preteens have little say over whether they attend Sunday school, Hebrew school, confirmation classes, and the like. Their parents may even drop them off at special religious children's services. For many preteens, religious involvement is high because it is something that is required of them, even if their parents do not always follow suit. Meanwhile, elderly people have more time and need for religion. Because they are not usually in school, employed in the paid labour force, or busy raising a family, they have more opportunity than younger people do to go to church, synagogue, mosque, or temple. Moreover, because seniors are generally closer to illness and death than are younger people, they are more likely to require the solace of religion. To a degree, then, involvement in religious activities is a life-cycle issue. Children are relatively actively involved in religious activities because they are required to be, and the seniors are relatively actively involved because they feel greater need for religious involvement and are in a position to act on that need.

But there is another issue at stake here, too. Different age groups live through different times, and today's older people reached maturity when religion was a more authoritative force in society. A person's current religious involvement depends partly on whether he or she grew up in more religious times. Thus, although young people are likely to become more religiously involved as they age, they are unlikely ever to become as involved as seniors are

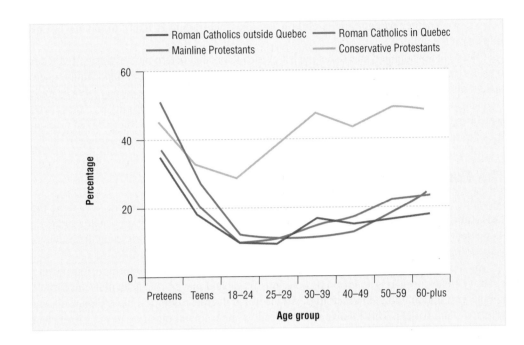

FIGURE 16.5
Religious Involvement over Time by Group

Source: Bibby, 2001: 275.

today. This implies that "fewer young can be expected to . . . 'return to church,' since fewer were ever active in the first place" (Bibby, 2001: 274–75).

Adding weight to our historical argument is research showing that the likelihood of attending religious services at least weekly (our second measure of religiosity) depends on the region of the country in which a person lives. In particular, Canadians who live in the Atlantic provinces are more likely than other Canadians are to attend church weekly (Bibby, 1995: 126). New Brunswick, Nova Scotia, Prince Edward Island, and Newfoundland and Labrador are Canada's poorest and least industrialized provinces, and traditional religion is still quite deeply entrenched there. Religion is a more authoritative force in Atlantic Canada than elsewhere in the country because the region is less modern than the other provinces.

Finally, we note that people whose parents attended religious services frequently are more likely to do so themselves (Jones, 2000). That is because religiosity is partly a *learned*

Religiosity is partly a learned behaviour. Whether parents give a child a religious upbringing is likely to have a lasting impact on the child.

behaviour. Whether parents give a child a religious upbringing is likely to have a lasting impact on the child.

We have not supplied an exhaustive list of the factors that determine religiosity. Even our brief overview, however, suggests that religiosity depends on obligation, opportunity, need, and learning. The people who are most religiously involved and attend religious services most frequently are those who must, those who were taught to be religious as children, those who were brought up in religiously authoritative environments, those who need organized religion most because of their advanced age, and those who have the most time to go to services.

The Future of Religion

A significant religious revival is taking place in Canada and other countries today. At the same time, secularization seems to be a long-term trend. Significantly, in Canada in 2001, 43 percent of adults reported that they did not attend a single worship service in the previous year, compared with only 26 percent in 1986 (Statistics Canada, 2003c).

In the twenty-first century, gradual secularization will likely continue, but strong contrary trends are likely to crop up in various times and places. A substantial minority of people will undoubtedly continue to desire deep involvement with religious organizations, practices, and beliefs. This involvement will allow them to add meaning to their lives, and especially to important events associated with celebration and mourning throughout the life cycle. The fact that today's religious revival was quite unexpected just a few decades ago should warn us against being overly bold in our forecasts. It seems to us, however, that the two contradictory social processes of secularization and revival are likely to persist for some time to come, resulting in a more religiously polarized world.

NOTES

1. Bellah's analysis is based in the United States, where civil religion is stronger than in Canada.

2. CE stands for "common era" and is now commonly preferred over the ethnocentric AD, which stands for *anno Domini* (Latin for "the year of our Lord"). BCE stands for "before the common era."

3. Sikhism is the world's sixth major organized religion. It has 20 million adherents in the state of Punjab in India. (Calculations in this section are based on a world population of 6.7 billion people.)

SUMMARY

1. What was Durkheim's theory of religion and what are the main criticisms that have been lodged against it?
   Durkheim argued that the main function of religion is to increase social cohesion by providing ritualized opportunities for people to experience the collective conscience. Critics note that Durkheim ignored the ways religion can incite social conflict and reinforce social inequality.

2. What was Weber's theory of religion and what are the main criticisms that have been lodged against it?
   Weber argued that religion acts like a railroad switch, determining the tracks along which history will be pushed by the force of political and economic interest. Protestantism, for example, invigorated capitalist development. Critics note that the correlation between economic development and the predominance of Protestantism is

not as strong as Weber thought. They also note that some of Weber's followers offer one-sided explanations of the role of religion in economic development, which Weber warned against.

3. How has feminism contributed to the debate about the role of religion in society?
   Feminists have emphasized the patriarchal nature of all major world religions and promoted gender equality in doctrinal matters and the recruitment of personnel to priestly positions. Although some religions and denominations have resisted gender equality, others have embraced it.

4. What is the secularization thesis and what are the main criticisms that have been lodged against it?
   The secularization thesis holds that religious institutions, actions, and consciousness are on the decline worldwide. Critics of the secularization thesis point out that there has been a religious revival in North America and elsewhere over the past three decades or so. They also note that survey and other evidence shows that religion in North America and elsewhere is resilient.

5. What is the revised secularization thesis?
   The revised secularization thesis recognizes the religious revival and the resilience of religion but still maintains that the scope of religious authority has declined over time. The revisionists say that religion is increasingly restricted to the realm of the spiritual; it governs fewer aspects of people's lives and is more a matter of personal choice than it used to be.

6. What is the market model of religious life?
   The market model of religious life characterizes religious organizations as suppliers of services that are in demand by people who desire religious activities. Accordingly, denominations compete in religious markets to establish congregations while congregations compete to attract local followings. As a result of this competition, religious choices are diverse and changing, and an overall tendency toward secularization may coexist with an intensification of religious practice on the part of a substantial minority of people.

7. What do the main world religions have in common?
   The main world religions are founded by charismatic personalities in times of great trouble. The founding of new religions is typically animated by the desire for freedom and equality, always in the afterlife, and often in this one. The routinization of charisma typically makes religion less responsive to the needs of ordinary people and it often supports injustices. Therefore, the need for religious reform and revival—and the need for new religions—is likely to persist.

8. What determines an individual's religiosity?
   An individual's religiosity is determined by such factors as socialization (whether he or she was brought up in a religious family), the authoritativeness of religion in his or her area of residence (residing in a region where religion is authoritative increases the individual's religiosity), and the individual's age (high religiosity is associated with the very young and the elderly).

KEY TERMS

charismatic authority (p. 479)

church (p. 477)

civil religion (p. 468)

collective conscience (p. 466)

cults (p. 479)

denominations (p. 478)

ecclesia (p. 478)

fundamentalists (p. 472)

profane (p. 466)

religiosity (p. 486)

revised secularization
     thesis (p. 474)

rituals (p. 466)

routinization of charisma (p. 480)

sacred (p. 466)

sects (p. 479)

secularization thesis (p. 471)

totems (p. 466)

QUESTIONS TO CONSIDER

1. Does the sociological study of religion undermine religious faith, make religious faith stronger, or have no necessary implications for religious faith? On what do you base your opinion? What does your opinion imply about the connection between religion and science in general?

2. What influence did religion have on politics in the 2008 Canadian federal election? How influential was the religious right in setting the agenda advanced by the Conservative Party? How was this influence, perceived and actual, used by other parties to try to attract support? Search engines at http://www.politicswatch.com and http://www.journalismnet.com/canada/politics.htm may be helpful in gathering information on this topic.

WEB RESOURCES

Companion Website for This Book

http://www.compass3e.nelson.com

Begin by clicking on the Student Resources section of the website. Next, select the chapter you are studying from the pull-down menu. From the Student Resources page you have easy access to InfoTrac® College Edition, additional Weblinks, and other resources. The website also has many useful tips to aid you in your study of sociology, including practice tests for each chapter.

InfoTrac® Search Terms

These search terms are provided to assist you in beginning to conduct research on this topic by visiting http://www.infotrac-college.com:

cult
secularization
fundamentalism

Recommended Websites

Library and Archives Canada maintains an index to information about religion in Canada at http://www.collectionscanada.ca/caninfo/ep02.htm. Many of the listed items are access points that lead to collections and research centres that focus on religious matters.

Ontario Consultants on Religious Tolerance runs an excellent website that provides basic, unbiased information on dozens of religions, religious tolerance and intolerance, religion and science, abortion and religion, and so forth. Visit the site at http://www.religioustolerance.org.

CengageNOW™

CENGAGENOW™

http://hed.nelson.com

This online diagnostic tool identifies each student's unique needs with a Pretest that generates a personalized Study Plan for each chapter, helping students focus on concepts they're having the most difficulty mastering. Students then take a Posttest after reading the chapter to measure their understanding of the material. An Instructor Gradebook is available to track and monitor student progress.

17

Education

In this chapter you will learn that

- A complete system of schools, from elementary to post-graduate, is the prerequisite of industrial society and is found in all rich societies. Consequently, national wealth and national education levels are strongly related.

- School systems carry out two tasks: homogenizing and sorting. Students are made similar by indoctrination into a common cultural system but are also steered and selected into different socioeconomic classes.

- Mass education, once established, brings about nearly universal literacy and numeracy. Mass education inducts large populations into the linguistic and cultural uniformity that provides the basis for modern nationalism.

- Functionalists believe that education fosters meritocracy. Conflict theorists argue that the high cost of education favours the wealthy and that schools inevitably favour students whose parents are highly educated.

- Inside schools, inequalities are reproduced by a hidden curriculum that values middle-class manners and attitudes, by testing and tracking that segregate students by class background, and by self-fulfilling prophecies of poor performance by lower-class students.

- Females recently have begun to exceed males in years of completed schooling. However, men remain more likely to complete programs that most often lead to high pay.

THE RIOT IN ST. LÉONARD

On the night of September 10, 1969, a confrontation that had long been brewing in the Montreal suburb of St. Léonard boiled over. A march organized by the French unilinguist *Ligue pour l'intégration scolaire* paraded through a predominantly Italian neighbourhood. Despite pleas for calm from leaders on both sides, many people turned out to march while others, hostile to the marchers' cause, showed up to line the route. Scuffles broke out and a full-scale brawl ensued. Roughly a thousand people participated. Police read the Riot Act and made about 50 arrests.

The violence was widely deplored by commentators of all political persuasions, but today the St. Léonard riot is recognized as a turning point in Quebec history. It ultimately culminated in Bill 101, which makes French the language of public administration, imposes French language tests for admission to the professions, requires most businesses with more than 50 employees to operate mainly in French, and requires collective agreements to be drafted in French. Bill 101 also ensured that in Quebec children of immigrants would be required to receive primary and secondary schooling in French.

A year before the street violence erupted, the language of instruction in public schools had emerged as a hotly contested issue. Political commentators raised concerns that French was in demographic decline and that francophones were at risk of becoming a minority in the province's biggest city, Montreal. They noted that in 1963, the St. Léonard school board had responded to an influx of new residents of Italian descent by establishing the option of bilingual education. Soon, more than 90 percent of children with neither an English nor a French background ("allophones") were enrolling in the bilingual track and, of those, 85 percent continued to English secondary schools. The public school system was contributing heavily to the Anglicization of the city.

In 1968, the St. Léonard school board eliminated bilingual programs, setting off a cycle of protests and counter-protests. Allophone parents, mainly of Italian descent and forming 30 percent of the community, withdrew children from the public schools and organized their own "basement schools" in English. Meanwhile, francophone unilinguists mobilized and were able to dominate school board elections and win a referendum requiring a unilingual school system. Elites tried but failed to find a middle ground. Ultimately, in 1976, the Parti Québécois won their first election, Bill 101 was enacted, and immigrants' children were restricted to French schools by law.

Opinions on the wisdom and fairness of Bill 101 still vary, to say the least. But it is hardly surprising that sharp political controversy focused on schooling in Quebec in the 1960s and 1970s. Schools are hugely important institutions. Schools teach students a common culture that forms a framework for social life. Schools shape work, politics, and much else. Moreover, which children have access to which schools is the starting point for sorting children into adult jobs and social classes. Not surprisingly, therefore, fierce conflicts, even riotous outbursts, often arise in educational institutions and around such issues as who can or must go to what kinds of schools and what will be taught there.

What makes schooling important and sometimes controversial is that schools are where societies endow future generations with the key capacities of communication, coordination, and economic productivity. Schools must accomplish two main tasks: homogenizing and sorting. Schools create homogeneity out of diversity by instructing all students using a uniform curriculum, and they sort students into paths that terminate in different social classes. Homogeneity is achieved by enforcing common standards—language, for example—that serve as a cultural common denominator. Sorting favours students who develop the greatest facility in the common culture while confining those of lesser skills to subordinate work roles and lower ranks in the class structure.

Homogenizing and sorting are organized at primary, secondary, and postsecondary levels, and, within those levels, in public and private institutions, the latter of which involve varying degrees of religious instruction. Individuals typically move in a regulated way from one educational site to the next. Curricula are adapted to what has been taught earlier, often in other places, and to prepare students for subsequent studies.

To fully understand education, we must grasp its implications for other facets of social organization. For example, mass schooling is a relatively recent development that is closely tied to industrialism and to maintaining a modern, productive economy. But industrialism needs interchangeable workers who can move among ever-changing, technically sophisticated production facilities. Potential workers have to be culturally homogenized so they have similar outlooks and a common language, but some of them have to be identified as able and willing to receive specialized training to carry out technically demanding tasks.

Although the number of years people devote to education has steadily risen, more education is easier to obtain if you are born in a rich country and into a prosperous family. In turn, more education ensures better treatment in labour markets, such as lower rates of unemployment and higher earnings. Thus, education turns students into citizens by giving them a common outlook but it also reproduces the class structure and the structure of global inequality.

MASS EDUCATION: AN OVERVIEW

By the time you finished high school, you had spent nearly 13 000 hours in a classroom. This fact alone suggests that the education system has displaced organized religion as the main purveyor of formal knowledge. It also suggests that the education system is second in importance only to the family as an agent of socialization (see Chapter 4, Socialization).

Three hundred years ago, only a small minority of people learned to read and write. A century ago most people in the world never attended school. As late as 1950, only about 10 percent of the world's countries boasted systems of compulsory mass education (Meyer, Ramirez, and Soysal, 1992). Even today, more than half the people in developing nations are illiterate. In India alone, more than 400 million people cannot read or write and nearly 35 million children do not attend school (*Hindustan Times,* 1999).

In contrast, in Canada, just over 16 000 elementary and secondary schools employ nearly 276 000 teachers, who educate 5.6 million children. (Elementary schools are primary schools, high schools are secondary schools, and colleges and universities are postsecondary institutions.) In 2005–06, university enrolment stood at 1.05 million students (Statistics Canada, 2008g). The proportion of people between the ages of 25 and 64 with a college or university degree is higher in Canada than in any other country at 48 percent (Japan is in second place at 40 percent, the United States third at 39 percent; Statistics Canada, 2008c). Enrolment rates are more than 95 percent for five-year-olds and remain at about that level through the mandatory schooling age of 16 years. More than half of 19-year-olds are enrolled in college or university (Statistics Canada, 2003b). Clearly, in Canada education is a way of life.

Universal mass education is a recent phenomenon and is limited to relatively wealthy countries (see Figure 17.1). Around 1900, Canada and the United States were the first countries in history to approach universal educational participation by young people. Societies that today are highly advanced in terms of economy and technology, such as Japan, Italy, and England, lagged far behind.

For most of history, families were chiefly responsible for socializing the young and training them to perform adult roles. Thus, in preindustrial Europe, the vast majority of children learned to work as adults by observing and helping their elders in the largely agricultural economy. Only a small urban minority had much use for skills like reading and arithmetic. They were typically trained in religious institutions. In fact, before the rise of

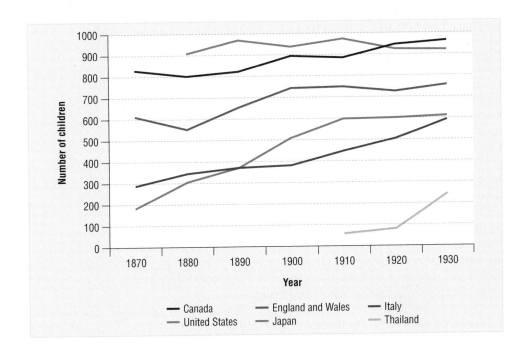

FIGURE 17.1

Elementary School Enrolments per 1000 Children Aged 5–14 for Various Countries, 1870–1930

Source: Peter H. Lindert, *Growing Public: Social Spending and Economic Growth since the Eighteenth Century* (Cambridge, UK, New York: 2004), pp. 91–93. Reprinted with the permission of Cambridge University Press.

Protestantism, priests held a virtual monopoly on literacy. The Catholic Church's authority depended on the *in*ability of ordinary people to read the Bible. It even went so far as to persecute people who made the Bible available in local languages, such as English. (The standard King James Bible is based mainly on the translation by William Tyndale, who was burned at the stake for his efforts in 1536.)

Uniform Socialization

Creating systems of education that had sufficient resources to include all children was a social change of breathtaking scope. Training in families had been decentralized, unorganized, and uneven in quality. Religious training was never widely available and tended to set people apart from the surrounding community. Replacing these forms of instruction with a centralized and rationalized system created strong pressures toward uniformity and standardization. Diversity among families, regions, and religious traditions gradually gave way to homogenized indoctrination into a common culture.

Canada was something of an exception because, in the nineteenth century, the provinces recognized separate school systems for Catholics and Protestants. Today, however, postsecondary institutions make no such distinction in admissions or curricula. Lack of recognition of distinct religious tracks by postsecondary institutions was among the key pressures that forced secondary schools to cover the same topics in the same fashion to prepare their students for more advanced training. Students today can travel hundreds and even thousands of kilometres for higher education and experience no more discontinuity than those who attend the nearest school.

Surrendering children to state control was not universally popular, especially at first. Some students preferred skipping class to sitting in school, and special police (truant officers) were charged with tracking down absentees, who were then punished. Effective mass education was achieved only through laws that made attendance compulsory. All Canadian provinces and territories now require parents to ensure their children are educated up to a certain age. Although more than 5 percent of families send children to private schools and about 1 in 200 children is home-schooled, some 94 percent of families surrender their children to public schooling (Statistics Canada, 2001b). Even today, some children resist the forced drill of cultural ideals that are at odds with their other experiences, but they are in a small minority.

Rising Levels of Education

Making education available to everyone, whether they like it or not, was only a starting point. The amount of education that people receive has risen steadily, and this trend shows no sign of abating. In 1951, fewer than 1 in 50 Canadians had completed a university degree. Completing university allowed a person entry into a narrow elite. Today, nearly 1 in 4 Canadians between the ages of 25 and 64 has a university degree, and postsecondary credentials have been broadened to include trade certificates and college diplomas. In 50 years, a rarity became common (Table 17.1).

In 2002, about 85 percent of Canadian children under the age of six had parents who hoped their children would undertake education beyond high school. About 62 percent had parents who hoped their children would attend university (Shipley, Ouellette, and Cartwright, 2003). The tempering of hopes as children age presumably reflects growing recognition of certain barriers—financial, motivational, and academic performance—that limit how far some students can go. Although overall hopes err on the side of optimism, they are not that far in excess of what ultimately happens. Postsecondary training is increasingly widespread, and the reason for this popularity is apparent: Education is the most visible option for improving employment opportunities.

Sociologists distinguish *educational attainment* from *educational achievement*. **Educational achievement** is the learning or skill that an individual acquires and at least in principle it is what grades reflect. **Educational attainment** is the number of years of schooling completed or, for higher levels, certificates and degrees earned. Some people drop out of programs after gaining admission. Others fail to continue by not pursuing additional programs after completing earlier ones. Who continues schooling and who does not raises important issues that we address below. In principle, selection might depend only on individual educational achievements. In practice, non-academic factors, including family background, play a large role in determining who completes an advanced education.

Individual Advantages and Disadvantages

Higher educational attainment is effective for securing more employment and higher earnings. Figure 17.2 illustrates how education level influenced rates of unemployment in Canada in 2006. Lower rates of unemployment were associated with more education. Unemployment rates for those who did not finish high school were more than twice the level faced by holders of a bachelor's degree.

Education also enhances earnings prospects. As Figure 17.3 shows, the odds of earning high pay steadily improve as educational attainment increases. In the highest income category, $100 000 and up, more than 58 percent of people had completed university. In the lowest income category, $20 000 and less, 26 percent had not finished high school while only 15 percent had a university degree. High-school dropouts are most often found among the lowest earners, and they become steadily rarer among higher earnings levels. University graduates show the opposite pattern. The pattern is far from rigid—people with every level of education are found at each level of earnings. But more education and better earnings tend to go together.

Educational achievement is the actual learning of valuable skills and knowledge.

Educational attainment is the number of years of schooling successfully completed or, for higher learning, the degrees or certificates earned.

TABLE 17.1

Population Aged 25–64, by Highest Level of Educational Attainment, Canada, 2006 (in percent)

* Does not equal 100.0 because of rounding.

Source: Statistics Canada, 2008, "Highest Level of Educational Attainment for the Population Aged 25 to 64, Percentage Distribution (2006) for Both Sexes, for Canada, Provinces and Territories—20% Sample Data." Retrieved March 4, 2008 (http://www12.statcan.ca/english/census06/data/highlights/education/pages/Page.cfm?Lang=E&Geo=PR&Code=01&Table=1&Data=Dist&Sex=1&StartRec=1&Sort=2&Display=Page).

No certificate, diploma, or degree	15.4
High school certificate or equivalent	23.9
Apprenticeship or trades certificate or diploma	12.4
College, CEGEP, or other non-university certificate or diploma	20.3
University certificate or diploma below the bachelor's level	5.0
University certificate, diploma or degree at bachelor's level or above	22.9
Total population age 25–64	99.9*

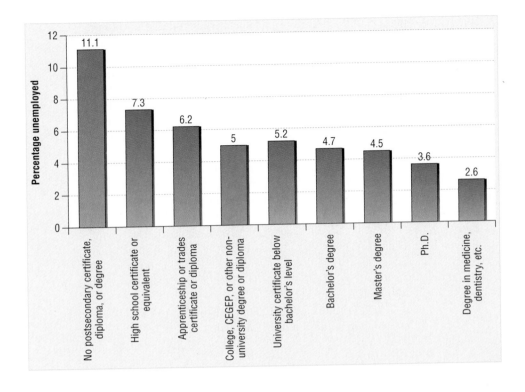

FIGURE 17.2

Unemployment Rate by Highest Level of Education Completed, Canada, 2006 (in percent)

Source: Statistics Canada, 2007, "Labour Force Activity (8), Highest Certificate, Diploma or Degree (14), Location of Study (29), Major Field of Study—Classification of Instructional Programs, 2000 (14), Age Groups (10A) and Sex (3) for the Population 15 Years and Over of Canada, Provinces, Territories, Census Metropolitan Areas and Census Agglomerations, 2006 Census—20% Sample Data." Retrieved March 4, 2008 (http://www12.statcan.ca/english/census06/data/topics/RetrieveProductTable.cfm?Temporal=2006&PID=93715&GID=837928&METH=1&APATH=3&PTYPE=88971&THEME=75&AID=&FREE=0&FOCUS=&VID=0&GC=99&GK=NA&RL=0&d1=0&d2=0&d3=0&d4=0).

In the next section, we examine how mass education arose. We will see that it is a form of collective wealth that serves as a basis for future wealth. We then examine theories that connect the rise of mass education to industrialization, arguing that education provides a basis for collective and individual wealth and motivates widespread loyalty to culture and society. We will see how education reproduces class inequality. We conclude by reviewing a series of recent developments and future challenges for Canada's system of mass schooling.

The Rise of Mass Schooling

What accounts for the spread of mass schooling? Sociologists usually highlight four factors: the development of the printing press that led to inexpensive book production, the Protestant Reformation, the spread of democracy, and industrialism. Let us consider each of these factors in turn.

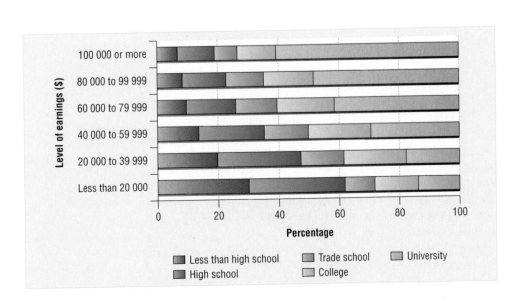

FIGURE 17.3

Earnings by Amount of Education, Canada, 2001

Source: Adapted from Statistics Canada, 2001, "2001 Census: Analysis Series, Earnings of Canadians: Making a Living in the New Economy," Catalogue 96F0030XIE2001013. Retrieved March 11, 2003 (http://www12.statcan.ca/english/census01/products/analytic/companion/earn/canada.cfm).

First, the printing press: In 1436, Johann Gutenberg introduced the printing press with moveable type to Europe. (Comparable devices had been introduced in China 300 years earlier.) The effect was revolutionary. Books had been expensive when scribes were the only source of new copies. The new printing presses led to a dramatic fall in price and an explosion in numbers. Many of the new printed books were in the vernacular—languages used every day by common folk—and not in the Latin that only scholars understood. Literacy spread beyond elite circles, first in cities and eventually into rural areas, as inexpensive books fostered demand for schools to teach children the useful art of reading (Eisenstein, 1983).

Second, Protestantism: The Catholic Church relied on priests to convey dogma to believers. The education of priests was a primary motivation for the foundation of European universities in the Middles Ages. However, in the early sixteenth century, Martin Luther, a German monk, began to criticize the Catholic Church. Protestantism grew out of his criticisms. The Protestants believed that the Bible alone, and not Church doctrine, should guide Christians. They expected Christians to have more direct contact with the word of God than was allowed by the Catholic Church. Accordingly, Protestants needed to be able to read the scriptures for themselves. The rise of Protestantism was thus a spur to popular literacy.

Third, democracy: The rise of political democracy led to free education for all children. Where local populations acquired the democratic means to tax themselves, tax-supported schools arose. Hence, France, which established universal manhood suffrage in 1848 (giving all men the right to vote), expanded education before England, where the right to vote did not spread widely until a few decades later. Similarly, on this side of the Atlantic, nearly universal white male suffrage led to local tax-based funding of a public school system (Lindert, 2004: 107). The earliest such systems were in Upper Canada and the northern United States in about 1870. By 1900, Canada and the United States were the first countries in the world in which enrolment rates for all children aged 5 to 14 exceeded 90 percent. Another first: at least in elementary education, girls were enrolled at almost the same rate as boys were.

Mass Schooling and National Wealth

The fourth and most important reason for the rise of mass schooling was industrialization. Mass education was widely recognized as an absolute necessity for creating an industrial economy.

The Industrial Revolution began in England in the 1780s. Germany and the United States soon sought to catch up to England, and by the turn of the twentieth century, they had surpassed it. Observers noted that both Germany and the United States had school systems that offered places to nearly all young people. Literacy and numeracy were extended to nearly the entire population. Of course, what counted as literacy in those days would not impress us today; historians assess literacy by counting the rate at which people signed marriage registers or similar documents with a name and not merely an X or another mark. However, as the number of people achieving such minimal performance rose, so did the number of people with much higher levels of literacy. Germany had the finest universities in the world. They were particularly famous for scientific research. Although much of the German university system was involved in pure research, some branches, like chemistry, contributed directly to creating new industries. German achievements were widely admired, and German universities were directly copied, first in the United States, and then throughout the world.

Eventually, it was universally acknowledged that the first step to achieving a highly productive economy is to create an education system that is large enough to create a mass labour force and rich enough to train and employ an elite group of researchers able to work at the cutting edge of modern science. Democratic countries led the way, but communist countries, like the former U.S.S.R., also invested heavily in education in an effort to foster economic development.

Today it is widely acknowledged that investment in education is an important step in achieving great national wealth. But the connection between education and wealth is by no means automatic, as Table 17.2 shows. In Table 17.2, countries are grouped by the number of years of education each child born in 2000 can expect to receive. The range is from fewer than 5 years in Chad to more than 17 years in Sweden. Within each group, the country with the lowest, median, and highest gross domestic product per capita (GDPpc) is shown. For example, 20 countries are expected to provide children with 9 or 10 years of education, ranging from Zimbabwe (GDPpc = $190) to Saudi Arabia (GDPpc = $8561), with India representing the group median (GDPpc = $555).

Median GDPpc (column 3) increases steadily with the number of years of education children are expected to receive. This demonstrates that greater amounts of education are associated with greater national wealth. Note, however, that *within* each group of countries, wide differences in wealth exist. Thus, among the countries with the *lowest* GDPpc in each group (column 5), and among countries with the *highest* GDPpc in each group (column 7), GDPpc does *not* increase steadily with the number of years of education children are expected to receive. This suggests that there are exceptions to the general pattern of education generating wealth. Some resource-rich countries, like Saudi Arabia, which has the world's biggest petroleum reserves, have high income but a modest level of education. Some Latin American countries, like Brazil, are not well off economically but manage to achieve a high level of education. We conclude that, in general, education helps to generate wealth but it is by no means the only determining factor.

Education is not only a *source* of wealth; it is also a *product* of wealth. After all, education is expensive. Raising education levels for entire populations requires overcoming a vicious cycle: A significant fraction of a country's population must invest a great deal of money and time to become educated before there are enough teachers to instruct nearly everyone. All this money and time must somehow be saved from the pressures of producing enough to supply necessities, like food and shelter. What is true for individuals is also true for societies: Education enhances the ability to generate earnings and wealth, but educational accumulation is greatly facilitated by earlier accumulation of wealth.

Within each group of countries . . .

1. Expected Years of Education	2. Median Country	3. GDP/ Capita	4. Lowest Country	5. GDP/ Capita	6. Highest Country	7. GDP/ Capita	8. Number of Countries
5 or less	Chad	$290	Burundi	$86	Djibouti	$886	12
6 to 8	Yemen	$484	Rwanda	$185	Nauru	$3 465	15
9 or 10	India	$555	Zimbabwe	$190	Saudi Arabia	$8 561	20
11	Albania	$1 915	Uganda	$242	United Arab Emirates	$22 130	20
12	Bulgaria	$2 533	Paraguay	$1 001	Mexico	$5 945	21
13	Russian Federation	$3 026	Kyrgyzstan	$372	Qatar	$34 685	17
14	Seychelles	$8 814	Bolivia	$878	Luxembourg	$57 379	11
15	Czech Republic	$8 834	Brazil	$2 700	Bermuda	$51 911	15
16	Israel	$18 101	Argentina	$3 375	Switzerland	$43 486	14
17+	Sweden	$33 925	Netherlands	$13 261	Norway	$48 881	11

TABLE 17.2

Gross Domestic Product Per Capita (U.S. dollars) and Average Years of Education for Children Born in 2000

Note: The median country in each group has an equal number of other countries above and below it in GDPpc.

Source: From United Nations, United Nations Statistics Division, 2005, "Social Indicators." Retrieved from http://unstats.un.org/unsd/demographic/products/socind. Reprinted with permission. The United Nations is the author of the original material.

THE FUNCTIONS OF EDUCATION

Schools concentrate young people into a small number of places for extended periods of time. This has unintended consequences, such as encouraging the growth of a separate youth culture.

Assortative mating occurs when marriage partners are selected so that spouses are similar on various criteria of social rank.

The **logic of industrialism** is a specification by functionalists of requirements that social institutions must satisfy before industrialism can be achieved, such as an education system big enough to teach many people a common cultural standard and rich enough to provide specialized scientific and technical training.

The functions that have been attributed to education are numerous and highly varied. We first indicate the range of possibilities and then focus on the close connection between schooling and economic activity.

Unintended Functions

Schools do not merely carry out training; they also concentrate young people into a small number of places. In the earlier years, the law requires attendance. In more advanced programs, economic incentives and family pressures keep many in schools. Unintended consequences arise from segregating people by age and forcing them to spend much of their time together.

For example, schools encourage the development of a separate youth culture that often conflicts with parents' values (Coleman, 1961). Typically, peer rankings in schools don't favour academic success; instead, they reward athletes and students popular with the opposite sex. For some, this works out fine, but a significant number of people experience school as alienating because they are seen as being low on peer rankings.

At higher levels, educational institutions bring potential mates together, thus serving as a "marriage market." This situation facilitates **assortative mating**—choosing a mate who is similar to oneself on various ranking criteria. Since many students postpone final mate selection until they finish school, many marry people who have similar academic qualifications, such as graduate degrees in the same discipline. More generally, since school continuation is highly selective on family background, marriage choices confined to classmates tend to ensure that marrying pairs are also classmates who share social origins and destinations (Rytina, Blau, Blum, and Schwartz, 1988).

Schools also perform a useful custodial service by keeping children under close surveillance for much of the day and freeing parents to work in the paid labour force. Universities and colleges, by keeping young people temporarily out of the full-time paid labour force, restrict job competition and support wage levels (Bowles and Gintis, 1976). Finally, because they can encourage critical, independent thinking, educational institutions sometimes become "schools of dissent" that challenge authoritarian regimes and promote social change (Brower, 1975; Freire, 1972).

The Logic of Industrialism

Many of the functions of mass education have been tied to a functionalist **logic of industrialism**. The functionalist logic of industrialism spells out requirements that social institutions must satisfy to make industrialism possible. The characteristics of institutions in preindustrial, traditional societies varied widely. But functionalists argue that industrialism causes convergence—industrialism presumably dictates that social institutions develop according to a common pattern.

Notably, functionalists claim that industrialism requires the widespread application of science and technology in the economy. Science and technology are dynamic. Therefore, work conditions constantly change. Industrialization requires "an educational system functionally related to the skills and professions imperative to its technology" (Kerr, Dunlop, Harbison, and Myers, 1960: 36).

If mastering increasingly complex technologies requires increased specialist education, the flexibility needed to adapt to change requires increased general education. To respond to both kinds of pressure, schools had to expand in two directions, devoting more time to non-specialist training and then still further time to specialist training. Such expanded demand on children's time inevitably reduced the role of families in shaping children for specific careers. The family's diminished role was supplanted by schools that instruct students in new curricula that are continually readjusted to the occupational world.

Note that homogenization is intensified when the minimum level of education required across the entire population ratchets up. Sorting is intensified as more people participate in longer programs of specialized training. We now continue our exploration of these two processes, first focusing on the enhancement of solidarity and cohesion that mass education brings about, and then looking more closely at how sorting works.

Cultural Homogeneity, Solidarity, and Nationalism

Durkheim emphasized that, for the young, schooling creates cultural uniformity and social solidarity. Human beings, he said, are torn between egoistic needs and moral impulses. Like religion in an earlier era, educational institutions must ensure that the moral side predominates. By instilling a sense of authority, discipline, and morality in children, schools make society cohesive (Durkheim, 1956, 1961 [1925]).

Contemporary sociologists have acknowledged Durkheim's argument and broadened it. They point to a variety of manifest or intended functions performed by schools. Canadian schools try to teach the young to view their nation with pride, respect the law of the land, think of democracy as the best form of government, and value capitalism (Callahan, 1962). Schools also transmit knowledge and culture from generation to generation, fostering a common cultural identity in the process. In recent decades, that common identity has been based on respect for the cultural diversity of Canadian society.

Ernest Gellner (1983) proposed that mass education was the basis for modern **nationalism**—sentiments emphasizing the view that humanity is divided into a limited number of populations defined by common culture, territory, and continuity within the kin group. Is anything like this central to your outlook? A distinction may be useful between awareness of nationalism and embrace of nationalism. Nearly all of us today are able to discuss ourselves and others in vocabularies of national identity. It is hardly possible to be unaware of nationalities and their importance to many. But people differ in the degree to which they embrace or disdain such outlooks. Within most of us is the basic training required to participate in one (or a few) national identities to the exclusion of nearly all others. We differ in how central such participation is to our thinking and actions.

Nationalism refers to sentiments emphasizing, or even favouring, the view that humanity is divided into a limited number of populations defined by common culture, territory, and continuity within the kin group.

Pressures toward Cultural Uniformity

Creating a supply of people able to carry out industrial work together required creating schools that taught to a common standard. It was a tremendous accomplishment to staff such schools—a critical mass of potential teachers had to be brought to the required homogeneity in outlook and skills. Language was a central challenge. In most of the world, minor and not so minor variations in dialect existed over even small distances. Specific conventions of grammar, spelling, and pronunciation had to be singled out and designated as correct. And if lower-level teachers were to pass them on, these rules first had to be imposed on teacher-candidates and certification centres. This required a demanding and expensive arrangement of selection and judgment in which a privileged few were recruited to elite institutions, socialized to the higher standard, and then sent back to peripheral zones to impose it on students. By such means, the language conventions at such university centres as Oxford and the Sorbonne were established as the ideal to which all students had to conform.

Cultural Solidarity

Much or all that a person was, as a worker or a political participant or a communicator, became vested in one culture. Conversely, these same skills were foreign to, and even disdained by, other cultures. A person's own culture inspired deep feeling as the basis for personal identity, sometimes in spite of the fact that the culture was defined by a state and was not that of the person's ancestors. To partake of a culture was to share with others a membership within common boundaries—others with whom a person could, in fact, readily communicate or work with or play alongside, even though most were strangers. The possibility of a relationship gave rise to **imagined communities**—sentiments of solidarity and identification with those who share cultural capacities. This often blossomed into loyalty to the providers and defenders of such cultures.

Usually, such loyalties fixed on states, for only states could afford the enormous expense of mass education. This was not left to chance. Most states provided their classrooms with flags and rituals and patriotic songs and stories, along with adults who supplied enthusiastic leadership.

Nor was participation a matter of choice. Although education is welcomed as a benefit by many families, it is legally required. Upper Canada not only led the world in providing universal education but also in requiring it. In 1871, Ontario pioneered compulsory education by fining parents whose children aged 7 to 12 did not attend school for at least four months each year. Since then, all provinces and territories have gradually tightened such requirements; most now require 16 years as the minimum school-leaving age. Research shows that tightening requirements had the desired effect of increasing the number of years children spent in school. It further shows that individuals who stay in school longer earn more and are unemployed less often (Oreopoulos, 2005). Thus, there are benefits that soften the reality that, for some, schooling is neither desired nor chosen but is a burden imposed by the power of the state.

Mass education is one of the principal institutions that set industrial societies apart from their less wealthy predecessors and contemporaries. Individuals often value education as their ticket into the lifestyles such societies allow and into the cultural riches they offer. But the unprecedented intensity of wars in the twentieth century reveals that the citizens created by mass education systems are all too willing to kill and die for those same societies. When wars started, the educated young were among the most enthusiastic combatants and schools were fertile recruiting grounds. The cohesion and civility fostered by education comes with a challenging counterpart—the creation of sharp, clear differences that can have tragic consequences.

SORTING INTO CLASSES AND HIERARCHIES: CONFLICT PERSPECTIVES

Functionalists and conflict theorists agree that education is a prelude to inequalities in work and manner of living. But they differ sharply on whether mass education results in class assignments that are just.

Functionalists argue that educational institutions are central to defining and implementing the rules and channels by which people are sorted among jobs. Placement based on family status presumably gives way to placement based on education. Family influence over occupation is a form of *ascription*—outcomes assigned to circumstances and traits for which individuals have no responsibility. Occupation obtained via education is seen as a form of *achievement*—outcomes assigned in proportion to individual success in satisfying job-relevant tests of capacity. Functionalists anticipated that education would continue to expand, increasing occupational mobility and swinging the balance against ascription and in favour of achievement (Kerr et al., 1960).

Functionalist accounts emphasize that differences in school outcomes are properly regarded as achievements. A common stock of technical and scientific knowledge has to be transmitted and, if possible, enhanced. At least in principle, public provision of education provides equal access for all young people. It is inevitable that some are quicker at absorbing the material than others are, because of variable mixes of innate ability, motivation, and effort. Each capacity is considered laudable in individuals; that is, they are thought to be merits that morally justify rewards. Competition to see who will get the most desired education (and the good jobs it ensures) therefore brings about a **meritocracy**—a social hierarchy in which rank

Imagined communities are sentiments of solidarity and identification with people who share particular cultural attributes.

Meritocracy is a social hierarchy in which rank corresponds to individual capacities fairly tested against a common standard.

is allocated by tests of individual capacity. In a meritocracy, children born to lower-ranked families can count on upward mobility in exact proportion to their ability to perform well in academic competition. Another, sterner test is that in a true meritocracy, children who are lazier or less intelligent than their parents have to fall to the rank they deserve.

The functionalist argument contains a hidden assumption. Educational attainment is by definition an achievement. But attainment is not regulated solely or strictly by tests of individual merit. Conflict theorists challenge such claims by identifying countervailing factors, and we will survey several of them. In a later section, we also examine how features prominent in secondary and primary schooling tend to preserve class ranks. But we begin by first examining how higher education and advanced degrees are inherently forms of privilege less accessible to those with lower-class backgrounds.

We review three potent challenges to meritocratic interpretations. First, economic barriers filter on the basis of ability to pay. Second, many jobs require academic credentials that are questionable as job skills but are effective at excluding the less advantaged from privileged professions. Third, schooling reproduces differences in "cultural capital" and thus preserves class differences.

Economic Barriers to Higher Education

In principle, it seems possible to create an education system that conforms to functionalist claims. In such a system, performance in academic contests would be the sole criterion for inclusion in higher levels of training. But although many programs do screen for academic performance, almost none is able to admit only the qualified and to supply all who do qualify with funding to meet all expenses. Only a tiny minority is fully funded solely on academic grounds. In a far larger number of cases, higher education in Canada requires students and their families to shoulder significant financial burdens. Tuition fees are rising. On average, Canadian full-time undergraduates paid $4524 in tuition fees in 2007–08, up from $3064 in 1998–99 and $1185 in 1988–89. During the 1990s, undergraduate tuition increased at an annual average rate of nearly 10 percent, and since 2000 it has increased at an annual average rate of nearly 4 percent (Statistics Canada, 2007e). And tuition is only part of the cost of a year at school, particularly for those who leave home to pursue their studies.

Social class origin strongly affects how much education people attain (Goldthorpe and Breen, 1997). In the recent past, this fact was hardly surprising, for few people were able to attend colleges or university. But many countries have greatly expanded postsecondary education, Canada among them. This expansion has lessened class effects but it has not eliminated them.

How does family income affect postsecondary participation rates? The picture is mixed. About a third of Canadians between the ages of 18 and 24 attend *college,* and the rate is highest for families in the middle-income range. Such relatively open access to one form of postsecondary education is a policy success; access to postsecondary education is much less restricted by family income in Canada than it is in the United States (Frenette, 2005). However, inequality remains substantial, especially with respect to university attendance. About half of Canadians between the ages of 18 and 24 whose annual family income is $100 000 or more attend university, but the figure falls to about a fifth for those whose annual family income is less than $25 000 (Drolet, 2005: 30)

Credentialism and Professionalization

Schooling is thus an asset that richer families obtain in greater quantity for their children. Sociologist Frank Parkin (1979) pointed out that education can be used as a means of **social exclusion**—setting up a boundary so that certain social opportunities and positions are restricted to members of one group. Exclusion is achieved when training is required and that training uses up scarce time or money. For such purposes, it is not actually important whether schooling leads to useful knowledge or genuine skill. Exclusion can be enhanced if the skill acquired is esoteric and readily exhibited to mark insiders from outsiders, such as the acquisition of a vocabulary of technical jargon.

Social exclusion is achieved by creating barriers that restrict certain opportunities or positions to members of one group to the exclusion of others.

For example, university-trained medical doctors were unable to deliver health benefits before the scientific advances of the late nineteenth century. But they could set themselves apart from competitors, such as the barbers who commonly did surgery, by naming body parts and health conditions in terminology derived from classical Greek. Such fancy talk had no curative value but it provided clear social distinction for those able to afford study at a university that taught dead languages.

Schooling as a means of exclusion is enhanced by what Randall Collins (1979) calls **credential inflation**. Over time, qualifying for specific jobs requires an ever-increasing collection of degrees and certificates. A century ago, for example, many professors, even at the most prestigious universities, did not hold a doctoral degree. Today, most professors have Ph.D.s. The numbers of people who hold advanced degrees and certificates has been growing rapidly in Canada. For example, in 2006, 142 180 Canadians held Ph.D.s., up 30 percent in just five years (Statistics Canada, 2008c: 9). People with more credentials are positioned to crowd out those with fewer, and more employers enjoy the option of filling positions with such applicants.

Credential inflation occurs in part because the technical knowledge required for jobs has increased. For example, because aircraft engines and avionics systems are more complex than they were, say, 75 years ago, working as an airplane mechanic today requires more technical expertise. Certification ensures that the airplane mechanic can meet the high technical demands of the job. As Collins (1979) points out, however, in many jobs there is often a poor fit between credentials and specific responsibilities. On-the-job training, not a diploma or a degree, often gives people the skills they need to get the job done. Yet, according to Collins, credential inflation takes place partly because employers find it a convenient sorting mechanism. For example, an employer may assume that a university graduate has certain manners, attitudes, and tastes that will be useful in a high-profile managerial position. The effect is to exclude from such positions people from less-advantaged families and groups while favouring individuals from families and groups with the advantages that facilitate education. At least indirectly, such exclusion adds to inheritance of advantage.

Credential inflation is also fuelled by **professionalization**, which occurs when members of an occupation insist that people earn certain credentials to enter the occupation. Professionalization ensures that standards are maintained. It also keeps earnings high. After all, if "too many" people enter a given profession, the cost of services offered by that profession is bound to fall. This helps explain why, on average, physicians and lawyers earn more than university professors who have Ph.D.s. The Canadian Medical Association, for example, is a powerful organization that regulates and effectively limits entry into the medical professions (see Chapter 19, Health and Medicine). Canadian professors have never been in a position to form such powerful organizations.

Because professionalization promotes high standards and high earnings, it has spread widely. Even some clowns now consider themselves professionals. Thus, there is a World Clown Association (WCA) that has turned rubber noses and big shoes into a serious business. At its eighteenth annual conference, the WCA held seminars on a wide variety of subjects, including character development, on-target marketing, incredible bubbles, and simple but impressive balloons (Prittie, 2000). Sociologist David K. Brown tells the story of a friend who had been a successful plumber for more than 20 years but tired of the routine and decided to become a clown (Brown, 1995: xvii). His friend quickly found that becoming a clown is not just a matter of buying a costume and acting silly. First, he had to enter the Intensive Summer Clown Training Institute at a local college. The Institute awarded him a certificate signifying his competence as a clown. Based on his performance at the Institute, the prestigious Ringling Brothers Clown School in Florida invited him to enrol. Even a clown, it seems, needs credentials these days, and a really good clown can dream of going on to clown graduate school.

Cultural Capital

French sociologist Pierre Bourdieu wrote extensively about the role of education in maintaining social inequalities. His central theme grew out of an analogy with the theories of Karl Marx. Marx had emphasized the role of economic capital—ownership of the

Credential inflation occurs when it takes ever more certificates or degrees to qualify for a particular job.

Professionalization occurs to the degree that certain levels and types of schooling are established as criteria for gaining access to an occupation.

Because professionalization promotes high standards and high earnings, it has spread widely. Even some clowns now consider themselves professionals.

physical means of producing wealth—in sustaining inequality. Bourdieu argued that education was central to the creation and transmission of **cultural capital**—learning and skills that ensured superior positions in productive activity (Bourdieu, 1998b; Bourdieu and Passeron, 1979)

Cultural capital is scarce, and therefore valuable, because it is expensive and difficult to acquire. Bourdieu emphasized that learning involves discipline or what he termed **pedagogic violence**—the application by teachers of punishments intended to discourage any deviation from the dominant culture. Teachers routinely insist that there is one "correct" way to speak or to spell or to do arithmetic. The rules are intricate and individuals have to learn to follow them without pause for reflection or judgment. Such learning involves long periods of disciplinary pressure.

Violence is a loaded word. It reminds us that for some students, schooling is painful, as they are forced to try activities at which they are doomed to fail. There is almost endless reiteration of hierarchy—of differential success at the assigned tasks. Success and failure are often put on public display. Students learn a double message: All are forced to accept the truth or correctness of what the teachers convey, but some are clearly shown to be better than others are at mastering this material. Derogatory terms like "teacher's pet" remind us that enforced competition and evaluation sometimes stirs up resentment. But in the end, the teachers tend to prevail. Essentially all students who remain in school for any length of time will internalize most of what their teachers expound.

For Bourdieu, much of what schools teach is how to evaluate. They help establish cultural markers; taste in books, music, food, and clothing thus come to reflect how much schooling a person has had. For example, the books a person can discuss signals his or her place in the class structure. Much of this may seem irrelevant to technical domains, like engineering, but such irrelevant erudition may signal employers or co-workers whether someone has been to the finest schools or not.

Although all students are pressured to internalize the same cultural standard, they do not approach the task as equals. The cultural standard designated as correct or proper in schools matches what families practise at home *to varying degrees*. If your parents are university professors, from your earliest babbling you will be imitating the speech patterns of the dominant cultural group. Different degrees of overlap with the ideal ensure a gradation. Families from less advantaged countries or regions enjoy the least overlap. If your parents are from rural Newfoundland or Bangladesh, the English they speak is likely to be corrected in schools in Toronto or Vancouver. Children from such families will have to struggle more to meet the standards teachers insist on.

When teachers evaluate performance, they inevitably reward students who are close to the standards of the dominant culture. Although some students from all backgrounds succeed, a student's stock of cultural capital—of disciplined familiarity with the dominant culture—will influence how hard or easy success is. More advantaged children will find rewards easier to achieve. Children from families with less cultural capital will be punished more and will tend to experience school as less pleasant.

A key portion of Bourdieu's argument is readily confirmed—educational attainment is strongly enhanced by growing up in a family with parents who were highly educated. Taxpayer support enriches institutions that assist families in preserving advantage. Table 17.3 shows how strongly rates of postsecondary education are influenced by parents' education.

Cultural capital is the stock of learning and skills that increases the chance of securing a superior job.

Pedagogic violence is Bourdieu's term for the application by teachers of punishments intended to discourage any deviation from the dominant culture.

TABLE 17.3

Rates of Participation in Postsecondary Education by Highest Level of Parental Education for Canadians Aged 18–25, 2001

Source: Adapted from Marie Drolet, 2005, "Participation in Postsecondary Education in Canada: Has the Role of Parental Income and Education Changed over the 1990s?" Statistics Canada, Catalogue 11F0019MIE, Analytical Studies Branch research paper series, No. 243. Retrieved May 27, 2006 (http://www.statcan.ca/english/research/11F0019MIE/11F0019MIE2005243.pdf).

Parental Education	Participation rate in . . .	
	College	University
University	31.5	49.6
Postsecondary certificate or diploma	40.4	27.8
High school or less	35.9	16.6

THE PROCESS OF REPRODUCING INEQUALITY: THE CONTRIBUTION OF SYMBOLIC INTERACTIONISM

Many Canadians believe we enjoy equal access to basic schooling. They think schools identify and sort students based only on merit. They regard the education system as an avenue of upward mobility. From this point of view, the best and the brightest are bound to succeed, whatever their economic, ethnic, racial, linguistic, or religious background. The school system is meritocracy in action.

Although some sociologists agree with this functionalist assessment, they are in a minority (Bell, 1973). Most sociologists find the conflict perspective on education more credible. In their view, the benefits of education are unequally distributed and tend to favour the **reproduction of the existing stratification system** (Jencks et al., 1972).

We have already seen how schools help to reproduce the existing system of gender inequality (Chapter 11, Sexuality and Gender). We have also seen that chances for university participation depend on class background. Other factors matter as well. Students with better grades are more likely to advance to further education. Parental encouragement plays a role, as does support from peers and teachers. But research consistently finds that such social supports are linked to class and thus are part of how class advantage is transmitted. Furthermore, indicators of class position, such as family income or parental education, contribute to educational attainment over and above the influence of academic performance or social encouragement (Lambert, Zeman, Allen, and Bussière, 2004).

Why are schools less than successful in overcoming class differences? Symbolic interactionists emphasize three social mechanisms that operate within the school system to reproduce inequality: the hidden curriculum, testing and tracking, and self-fulfilling prophecies.

> **The** reproduction of the existing stratification system **refers to processes ensuring that children will continue in a rank or class similar to or identical to that of their parents.**

The Hidden Curriculum

In addition to academic and vocational subjects, students learn a **hidden curriculum** in school (Snyder, 1971; see also Chapter 4, Socialization). The hidden curriculum teaches obedience to authority and conformity to cultural norms. For example, from kindergarten to university, students are systematically taught to accept the curricula, routines, and grading systems imposed on them by teachers and professors. They are punished when they fail to do so (Gracey, 2001). Moreover, to the extent that a middle-class measuring rod is used to evaluate students, those from lower classes find themselves disadvantaged (Cohen, 1955). The middle-class measuring rod applies specific standards—fashionable attire, "proper" speech, deferred gratification, compliance—to judge competency in the student role. Those who do not meet this standard may be labelled "bad students."

The hidden curriculum also influences the content of classroom lessons. For example, the development of the education system in Ontario proceeded from the assumption that education would be an effective way to teach working-class children that their interests are identical to those of upper-class children. With memories of the failed Rebellion of 1837 in Upper Canada still fresh in his mind, the chief architect of the Ontario school system, Egerton Ryerson, set out to create a system in which young adults would be loyal to the Crown. As two sociologists note, "Ryerson's objective was social control, and he charged the schools with the responsibility of inculcating the beliefs and attitudes of mind that would accomplish it" (Curtis and Lambert, 1994: 12).

Staying in school requires accepting the terms of the hidden curriculum. Continuation in school is strongly influenced by feelings of positive involvement. Researchers at Statistics Canada explored this phenomenon by developing measures of academic and social involvement. Social involvement included not feeling like an outsider and believing that people cared what a student said. Academic involvement consisted of liking teachers, not skipping classes,

> **The** hidden curriculum **in school teaches obedience to authority and conformity to cultural norms.**

and regarding class content as "not useless." Chances of continuing to higher education were as much as doubled for those who reported social acceptance or positive attitudes toward the formal organization, authority, and procedures of the school (Lambert et al., 2004).

Testing and Tracking

Most schools in Canada are composed of children from various socioeconomic, racial, and ethnic backgrounds. Testing and tracking maintain social inequality in these schools. IQ tests sort students, who are then channelled into high-ability (enriched), middle-ability, and low-ability (special needs) classrooms based on test scores. Often, the results are classrooms that are stratified by socioeconomic status, race, and ethnicity, much like the larger society (Samuda, Crawford, Philip, and Tinglen, 1980).

For example, one study that examined the assessments made of the "academic potential" of 400 Western Canadian students enrolled in an English-as-a-second-language program found that the tests used were frequently culturally biased. However, the psychologists who conducted the assessments were more likely to view the child from a minority group, rather than the tests, as "deficient" (Cummins, 1994). In addition, for more than a decade concern has been expressed over the streaming of black students in Ontario into low-level academic and vocational programs. According to research conducted by the Toronto Board of Education, although 1 in 5 black students was enrolled in a basic program, the comparable figures for white students was 1 in 10 and for Asians was 1 in 33 (Henry, Tator, Mattis, and Rees, 2000: 239).

Nobody denies that students vary in their abilities and that high-ability students require special challenges to reach their full potential. Nor does anyone deny that the underprivileged tend to score low on IQ tests. The controversial question is whether IQ is mainly genetic or social in origin. If IQ is genetic in origin, then it cannot be changed, so improving the quality of schooling for the underprivileged is arguably a waste of money (Herrnstein and Murray, 1994). If IQ is social in origin, IQ tests and tracking only reinforce social differences that could otherwise be reduced by changing the social circumstances of students.

Most sociologists believe that IQ reflects social standing in great part. That is because all that IQ tests can ever measure is acquired proficiency with a cultural system. How much exposure a person has had to whatever is counted as proper or correct will play a large role—even the most able Canadian children would perform abysmally if tested in Mongolian. IQ test results turn on a combination of two factors: (1) how effectively an individual absorbs what his or her environment offers, and (2) how closely his or her environment reflects what the test includes.

Most sociologists believe that members of underprivileged groups tend to score low on IQ tests because they do not have the training and the cultural background needed to score high (Fischer et al., 1996). To support their argument, they point to cases in which changing social circumstances result in changes in IQ scores. For instance, in the first decades of the twentieth century, most Jewish immigrants to North America tested well below average on IQ tests. This was sometimes used as an argument against Jewish immigration (Gould, 1996; Steinberg, 1989). Today, most North American Jews test above average in IQ. Since the genetic makeup of Jews has not changed in the past century, why the change in IQ scores? Sociologists point to upward mobility. During the twentieth century, most Jewish immigrants worked hard and moved up the stratification system. As their fortunes improved, they made sure their children had the skills and the cultural resources needed to do well in school. Average IQ scores rose as the social standing of Jews improved.

Canada was one of the first countries in the world to link its student body to the Internet. By 1997, almost all Canadian schools had Internet access through the SchoolNet electronic network.

Another illustration involves the "Flynn effect," named after the political scientist James R. Flynn, who first pointed it out. Flynn showed that average IQ scores increase over time on every major test, in every age range and in every industrialized country (Neisser, 1997: 2). Increases of as much as 21 points in only 30 years were observed. Typical improvements in test performance observed over time were large. For example, the differences between children and their grandparents were far greater than differences observed across race and class divides in contemporary societies. This evidence suggests that IQ tests do not provide a fixed measuring rod that captures innate abilities or, for that matter, any sort of trait fixed by genetic endowment (Flynn, 1987).

The evolutionary theorist Stephen J. Gould (1996) underscored the fallacy of attributing differences to genetic factors when groups live in different environments. The fallacy remains even if we can otherwise show that the factor in question is inherited (within stable environments). Height provides an example. Children's height is strongly influenced by the height of their parents. Asian and European populations differ greatly in height. But the contribution of environment to this difference is revealed by the rapid increase in stature that occurs when nutrition improves. Historical records show that Europeans were also much shorter before their societies obtained reliable food supplies. The comparative giants that live in Europe today are almost wholly descended from shorter people but are indistinguishable in genetic endowment.

Consider this equally dramatic illustration of how changing environments can alter characteristics that some falsely insist are innate. In the United States, the 300 black and Latino students in grade 8 at the Hostos-Lincoln Academy of Science in the South Bronx were all written off as probable dropouts by their counsellors. Yet most seniors in the school now take honours and university-level classes. Eighty percent of them go to university, well above the national U.S. average. The reason? The City of New York designated Hostos-Lincoln as a special school in 1987. It is small, well equipped, attentive to individual students, and demanding. It stresses team teaching and a safe, family-like environment. Is Hostos-Lincoln an exception? No. A study of 820 high schools shows that where similar programs are introduced, students from grades 8 to 12 achieve 30 percent higher scores in math and 24 percent higher scores in reading compared with students in traditional schools (Hancock, 1994). Investing more in the education of the underprivileged can produce results (Schiff and Lewontin, 1986; see Box 17.1).

BOX 17.1
It's Your Choice

Is School Enough?

Sociologists began to understand how little schools could do on their own to encourage upward mobility and end poverty in the 1960s, when sociologist James Coleman and his colleagues conducted a monumental study of academic performance (Coleman, Campbell, Hobson, McPartland, Mood, Weinfeld, and York, 1966). What they found was that differences in the quality of schools—

measured by assessment of such factors as school facilities and curriculum—accounted at most for about a third of the variation in students' academic performance. At least two-thirds of the variation in academic performance was due to inequalities imposed on children by their homes, neighbourhoods, and peers. Forty years later, little research contradicts Coleman's finding.

Various social commentators have argued that if we are to improve the suc-

cess of disadvantaged students, we must develop policies that are aimed at improving the social environment of young, disadvantaged children *before* they enter the formal education system (Hertzman, 2000). Compensatory education programs for preschool children were largely developed in the United States and attempt to meet the needs of children who are socially and economically disadvantaged. In Canada, such programs have also been aimed at "children with special needs" and "at-risk children"—those who, because of one or more factors in their background, are believed to face a heightened risk of poor academic performance or social adjustment. Although the traditional focus of early childhood education has been on children's social and emotional development, at least some of these compensatory education programs focus on children's intellectual development.

The 1996–97 National Longitudinal Survey of Children and Youth (NLSCY) found that household income was clearly associated with school; in fact, it was an important indicator of developmental maturity and future success at school (Doherty, 1997). In addition, as family income decreases, the likelihood that children will experience a host of other problems that will negatively influence their school performance increases. For example, poor health, hyperactivity, and delayed vocabulary development are all higher among children in low-income families than among children in middle- and higher-income families (Ross, 1998). Children who score low on school readiness are also more likely to have mothers with low levels of education and to be living in neighbourhoods that their mothers characterize as unsafe or as lacking in social cohesiveness (Health Canada, 1999b: 79).

It has been suggested that early developmental programs can decrease the chances of developmental problems in children and enhance their school performance. For example, Headstart programs are based on the belief that to assist children, the entire family must be helped. Evaluations of Headstart programs in Canada report such benefits as "more students completing school and with better grades; fewer young people needing mental health services; fewer parents abusing alcohol with concurrent reductions of alcohol's impact on children; a reduction in family violence; fewer students

with preventable disabilities; and reduced demand for medical services" (Government of Canada, 2001). In Edmonton, for example, Headstart programs have existed for 25 years. These programs focus on preschool children aged three to five in low-income families, as well as the parents or other adults involved in raising these children. The programs are designed to respond to the needs of the community in which they are located. Among the forms of parental support provided are access to food banks, nutrition programs, literacy programs, parental support groups, and parenting courses. Promoting child readiness for school is also a key element of these programs.

Headstart programs have been identified as particularly important in increasing the educational success of Aboriginal students. To this end, the federal government announced in 1998 that it would provide permanent funding for the Aboriginal Headstart programs that already existed in Canada, as well as additional funds for the establishment of new Headstart programs on reserves. However, it is estimated that existing programs reach only about 5 percent of the Aboriginal children who could potentially benefit from their availability (George, 1998).

Admittedly, the costs of providing early childhood intervention programs are not insignificant. For example, in 1998 Health Canada spent approximately $22.5 million a year on Headstart programs that served approximately 4000 northern and urban Aboriginal children. It was estimated that to reach the entire target audience would require spending 10 to 20 times that amount. However, the investments we make in the critical early years of a child's life benefit not only Canada's children but our economy as well. Indeed, one Canadian study reports that "every dollar spent in early intervention can save seven dollars in future expenditures in health and social spending" (Health Canada, 1999b: 88).

Do you believe that early childhood intervention programs are useful in improving the educational success of children? If not, why not? If so, do you feel that attendance in these programs should be compulsory? Should parents who refuse to send their children to such programs be penalized for their decision? What background factors do you feel should be used to select children and their families for inclusion in such programs?

Steven Rytina writes, "I had an accidental opportunity to see what so-called ability tracking looked like from 'the other side.' In grade 9, my school had seven ability tracks. Two years before, when these had become controversial, the administration had shuffled the labels, but everyone knew which was which before the first week of school was over. By some mishap later explained to me, two other students, and our dismayed parents as a 'computer mistake,' for grade 9 speech class we were not given our usual A-track assignment but had to join the bottom or G-track, generally known as 'the dummies.' The class was a zoo. The assigned teacher typically sauntered in 20 minutes late, was not always sober, and made almost no effort to control the proceedings. People made loud, rude noises, threw things, and wandered about more or less at will. This wasn't all bad, because I was allowed to wangle frequent absences by using flimsy excuses. But what was particularly striking was how any effort was discouraged. Our assignments were speeches. Many kids made informal announcements all the time and enjoyed the attention. But instead of urging students to take their turn, the way we were called on made it apparent that we weren't really supposed to do it. A few did respond to roll call at first, but gradually it became clear that only the three misfits would reliably come forward and give our three-minute presentations.

"The unfairness of the standard treatment appalled me. When tracking had become controversial a few years earlier, defenders had spoken of benefits to all from adjusting curricula to fit capacities. But there was no curriculum in G-track. It was a holding tank where students were denied any encouragement or even any opportunity to try. I did not question that abilities differed or that different programs for better students were justified. What was not justified was the use of 'difference' as an excuse to provide the less able with nothing but an utter waste of their time."

Self-Fulfilling Prophecies

A third social mechanism that operates in schools to reproduce inequality is the self-fulfilling prophecy. A self-fulfilling prophecy is an expectation that helps to cause what it predicts. In a classic study, Ray Rist (1970) revealed how a self-fulfilling prophecy can influence a person's life chances. He found that after just eight days of observing students in a kindergarten classroom, and without giving a formal intelligence test, the teacher felt she could confidently assign the children to one of three tables. Students she designated "fast learners" were assigned to Table 1, closest to her own desk. Students she judged to be "slow learners" were assigned to Table 3, at the back of the class. Students she judged to be "average" were seated at Table 2, in the middle of the classroom. On what basis did she make these distinctions? Probing the issue, Rist found that the key variable distinguishing the students was social class. Children at Table 1 were overwhelmingly middle class, while those assigned to Tables 2 and 3 were more likely to come from poorer homes. The assignment of these children was consequential because the children at Table 1 received more attention, were treated better, and, as the year progressed, came to see themselves as superior to the other children. In contrast, the other students, who tended to be ignored by the teacher and were referred to by the Table 1 children as "dumb," did not fare well. The following year, the grade 1 teacher took notice of what the children had accomplished during kindergarten. Not surprisingly, the children who had been placed at Table 1 were assigned once again to places in the classroom that marked them as superior students.

These findings suggest that, rather than valuing all students equally and treating them all as children with good prospects, teachers may suspect that disadvantaged students and students who are minority group members are intellectually inferior. In turn, these students may come to feel rejected by teachers, other classmates, and the curriculum. Students from minority groups may also be disadvantaged by overt racism and discrimination. In response, students presumed to be inferior and marginalized in the classroom often cluster together out of resentment and in defiance of authority. Some of them will eventually reject academic achievement as a goal. Discipline problems, ranging from apathy to disruptive and illegal behaviour, can result. Consistent with this argument, Aboriginal and black students in Canada have higher-than-average school dropout rates (Livingstone, 1999: 743; see also Toronto Board of

Education, 1993). In contrast, research shows that challenging lower-class students and those from minority groups, giving them emotional support and encouragement, giving greater recognition in the curriculum to the accomplishments of the groups from which they originate, creating an environment in which they can relax and achieve—all these strategies explode the self-fulfilling prophecy and improve academic performance (Steele, 1992; see Box 17.2).

BOX 17.2
Sociology at the Movies
TAKE   ROLL

The Great Debaters (2007)

The Civil War (1861–65) outlawed slavery in the United States, but legal and violent resistance against black rights persisted for more than a century. In 1866, for example, an amendment to the Texas Constitution stipulated that all taxes paid by blacks had to be used to maintain black schools, and that it was the duty of the legislature to "encourage colored schools" ("Jim Crow Laws: Texas," 2008). In this segregationist atmosphere, the Methodist Church founded Wiley College in the northeast corner of Texas in 1873 "for the purpose of allowing Negro youth the opportunity to pursue higher learning in the arts, sciences and other professions" (Wiley College, 2007).

In 1923, Melvin B. Tolson was hired as a professor of speech and English at Wiley. He proceeded to build up its debating team to the point where they challenged and beat the mighty University of Southern California for the 1935 national debating championship. The victory shocked and scandalized much of the country's white population even as it instilled pride in African Americans, provided them with a shining model of academic achievement, and motivated black youth to strive to new heights. No self-fulfilling prophecy condemning black students to academic mediocrity operated at Wiley. To the contrary, Tolson worked his students hard, demanded excellence, and expected the best from them. Supported by the black community, they rose to his challenge.

English professor Melvin B. Tolson led the Wiley College debate team to a national championship against the University of Southern California (portrayed as Harvard in *The Great Debaters*) in 1935.

The Great Debaters shows why the 1935 victory was anything but easy. Tolson (played by Denzel Washington) is harassed by the local sheriff, who brands him a troublemaker for trying to unionize local black and white sharecroppers. On one out-of-town road trip, Tolson and his debating team come across a white mob that has just lynched a black man and set his body on fire. They barely escape with their lives. The pervasive racism of the times might discourage and immobilize lesser men, but it steels Tolson and his debaters, who feel compelled to show the world what blacks are capable of achieving even in the most inhospitable circumstances.

Historically, black colleges have played an important role in educating the black middle class in the United States, but since the 1960s blacks have been able to enrol in integrated colleges and universities, so many black colleges have fallen on hard times. Wiley itself was in deep financial trouble until *The Great Debaters* sparked new enrolments and endowments (Beil, 2007).

The successes of historically black colleges raise an important policy issue that is being debated in Canada's big cities today. Can segregated black public schools benefit black youth and should they be funded out of general tax revenue? Critics of separate black public schools argue that Canadian multiculturalism seeks to teach tolerance and respect for all cultures, and that separate public schools for any minority group would therefore be a step backward. Arguably, however, integrated public schools are still the home of self-fulfilling prophecies that make it difficult for black students to excel. Their curricula do little if anything to instil pride in the achievements of the black community. As a result, some black public school students dangerously identify academic excellence with "acting white," thus helping to condemn themselves to mediocre academic achievement and restricted social mobility. From this point of view, the achievements of historically black colleges like Wiley should be taken as a model of what is possible when black students are academically challenged and nourished in a non-threatening environment.

In sum, schools reproduce the stratification system because of the hidden curriculum, IQ testing and tracking, and the self-fulfilling prophecy that disadvantaged and minority students are bound to do poorly. These social mechanisms increase the chance that those who are socially marginal and already disadvantaged will, in fact, earn low grades and wind up with jobs closer to the bottom than to the top of the occupational structure.

PROSPECTS AND CHALLENGES FOR EDUCATION IN CANADA

Gender Differences: A Feminist Perspective

Canada is becoming an education society; with every passing decade, Canadians spend more time in school. And with every passing decade, women's level of education increases relative to men's. In 2006, there were about 20 percent more Canadian women over the age of 14 with at least a bachelor's degree than there were men with the same level of educational attainment. Women still lag behind men in medicine and dentistry, and among people with master's degrees and Ph.D.s, but they are catching up (Table 17.4).

However, as feminists note, these figures mask the ways in which greater female participation in postsecondary education still conforms to traditional gender divisions. Figure 17.4 shows the distribution of university degrees by gender and academic field in Canada in 2006. Women outnumbered men overall, but men predominate in business and management, architecture and engineering, physical and life sciences, math, computer and life sciences, and agricultural and related sciences. Differences between women and men are narrowing, but a strong tendency still exists for women to be concentrated in less scientifically oriented fields that pay less, notably education.

Participation and Aboriginal Background

Barriers to education other than gender remain substantial. For example, Canadians with Aboriginal backgrounds lag behind other Canadians in obtaining education. Less than 4 in 10 had postsecondary credentials in 2001—15 percent fewer than the proportion among all

TABLE 17.4

Highest University Degree Obtained, for Population Age 15+, by Sex, Canada, 2006

Source: Statistics Canada, 2007, "Highest Certificate, Diploma or Degree (14), Age Groups (10A) and Sex (3) for the Population 15 Years and Over of Canada, Provinces, Territories, Census Metropolitan Areas and Census Agglomerations, 2006 Census—20% Sample Data." Retrieved March 4, 2008 (http://www12.statcan.ca/english/census06/data/topics/RetrieveProductTable.cfm?Temporal=2006&PID=93609&GID=837928&METH=1&APATH=3&PTYPE=88971&THEME=75&AID=FREE=0&FOCUS=&VID=0&GC=99&GK=NA&RL=0&d1=1).

	Women	Men	Ratio of Women to Men
Bachelor's degree	1 603 040	1 378 425	1.2
University certificate or diploma above bachelor level	269 480	224 060	1.2
Degree in medicine, dentistry, etc.	54 705	82 145	0.7
Master's degree	402 910	464 065	0.9
Ph.D.	55 850	121 090	0.5

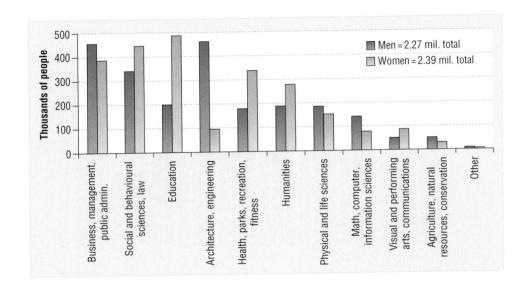

FIGURE 17.4

University Degrees by Field of Study and Gender, Canada, 2006 (in '000s)

Source: Statistics Canada, 2007, "Major Field of Study—Classification of Instructional Programs, 2000 (13), Highest Postsecondary Certificate, Diploma or Degree (12), Age Groups (10A) and Sex (3) for the Population 15 Years and Over with Postsecondary Studies." Retrieved March 4, 2008 (http://www12.statcan.ca/english/census06/data/topics/ListProducts.cfm?Temporal=2006&APATH=3&THEME=75&FREE=0&GRP=1).

working-age Canadians. Despite the increase over the five years from 1996 to 2001 in the numbers of Aboriginal people with university qualifications, anything like equal participation remains a long way off (Statistics Canada, 2003a, 2003b: 45).

Funding and Access

Funding for higher education continues to spark controversy. As we saw earlier, tuition fees have increased dramatically in recent decades. By 2002–03, the median outlay for a year of university studies in Canada was $11 200, compared with $9300 for a year at college and $4550 for a year at CEGEP (*Collège d'enseignement général et professionnel*/College of General and Vocational Education). Living away from home was expensive, adding $4400 to the expenditures for a year at university or at college. Students funded their expenses from various sources, with 77 percent drawing on income from their own employment. Sixty percent received a median of $2000 as a non-repayable transfer from parents or a spouse or partner, while only 36 percent received scholarships or bursaries (median value, $1600). Some 26 percent of full-time students received government loans, and an additional 14 percent took out private loans. The median amount of loans was $5000 (Barr-Telford, Cartwright, Prasil, and Shimmons, 2003).

What are the effects of increases in tuition and other expenses? Several studies indicate that although the initial rise in fees increased differences in educational continuation by family income, these differences returned to earlier levels after the first shocks wore off (Corak, Lipps, and Zhao, 2003; Drolet, 2005). However, as we saw earlier, earlier differences were hardly negligible.

International Competition

Although access to higher education remains uneven, the Canadian accomplishment in education is impressive when compared with that of other countries. Figure 17.5 on page 514 shows rankings of countries in the rate of education for working-age adults in 2002. Canada had the highest percentage of adults with postsecondary education. But the challenge remains. Several other countries have a higher rate of university graduation. And relative latecomers, like South Korea, are making up ground by providing today's youth with many more years in school than earlier generations received. Canada's century-long place at the head of the class may give way before too long to such a newcomer.

In the 1990s, widespread doubts were raised about the quality of Canada's education system. Suspicions grew that students were not applying themselves, that they were not learning enough, and that curricula and requirements had become lax. Critics were in for a surprise. The Organisation for Economic Co-operation and Development (OECD) organized a Programme

FIGURE 17.5

Rates of Postsecondary
Participation among the
Current Labour Force as
Measured by the OECD,
Various Countries, 2002

Source: OECD, 2004b.

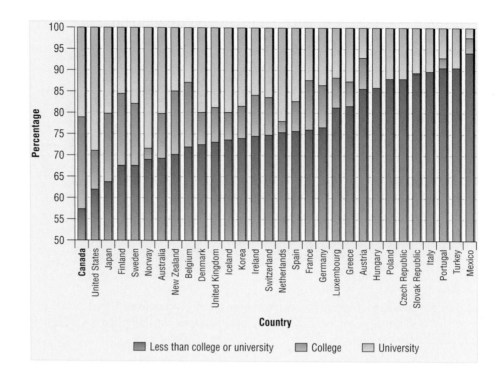

for International Student Assessment (PISA) to assess the academic performance of 15-year-olds. Thirty-one countries were included and great care was taken to ensure that comparisons would be valid. When the first results came in, in 2001, Canadian students placed second in reading, sixth in mathematics, and fifth in science. These results placed Canada among a select group of countries that performed well on all three measures. "Only Finland performed significantly better than Canada in reading, only Korea and Japan performed significantly better than Canada in mathematics and only Korea, Japan and Finland performed significantly better in science" (Bussière, Cartwright, Crocker, Ma, Oderkirk, and Zhang, 2001: 15). In 2003, PISA organized a second comparison among 41 countries focusing on mathematics. Again, Canadian 15-year-olds did very well. Only two countries, Hong Kong and Finland, had significantly better results on the combined mathematics scale (Bussière, Cartwright, Knighton, and Rogers, 2003). By any standard, this was a remarkable showing of which all Canadians should be proud.

SUMMARY

1. What kind of societies provide education for all and specialized training for large minorities?
   Societies that have achieved industrialism, and the wealth industrialism brings, provide complete systems of schooling that take in nearly all children and allow many of them to remain in school for many years.

2. What manifest functions are performed by school systems?
   Schools homogenize future citizens by indoctrination into a common culture. Schools also sort and steer students to different class positions as adults.

3. What latent functions are carried out by schools?
   Latent functions include the creation of a youth culture, a marriage market, a custodial and surveillance system for children, a means of maintaining wage levels by keeping college and university students temporarily out of the job market, and occasionally a "school of dissent" that opposes authorities.

4. What factors account for the rise of mass, compulsory education?

The spread of mass, compulsory education was encouraged by the Protestant Reformation, democratic revolutions, the modern state, and industrialization.

5. What role does education play in the accumulation of national wealth?

Education is a form of wealth. The amount of education that different societies are able to supply for their future citizens corresponds closely with national income levels. Although nearly all countries have systems of mass, compulsory education, illiteracy is still widespread in poor countries, especially in sub-Saharan Africa.

6. What are some results of education that functionalists anticipate?

Functionalists argue that education was critical for achieving industrialism. They also argue that education ensures meritocracy.

7. What are some of the consequences of education that have been identified by conflict theorists?

Conflict theorists argue that education intensifies nationalism. They also argue that success at school is easier for children of privilege and thus tends to perpetuate privilege.

8. What is credential inflation and how is it related to professionalization?

Credential inflation (the need for more certification and diplomas to qualify for a given job) has been fuelled by the increasing technical requirements of many jobs. It has also been encouraged by the ability of people in certain occupations to exercise control over their occupations (professionalization). Credential inflation is thus a means of excluding people from the professions to maintain high standards and income levels.

9. What is cultural capital and how does it influence schooling?

Parents who are advantaged are more likely to have acquired larger stocks of scarce, valued skills—that is, cultural capital. In turn, their children find it easier to win rewards at school by repeating what is familiar from their home life. Children from less advantaged families may have to unlearn family practices, such as vocabulary, grammar, or pronunciation, that are stigmatized as culturally inferior. This makes schooling less pleasant, which in turn is a major factor in the decision to forgo further education.

10. What are some interaction processes in school that tend to reinforce class differences among students?

Positive and negative expectations by teachers result in self-fulfilling prophecies that favour students from privileged backgrounds and discourage students from less privileged origins. A hidden curriculum encourages teachers to reward conformity to middle-class values and standards.

11. What do feminists say about the fact that women are more numerous than men among university graduates?

Feminist scholars point out that the rising levels of female participation in postsecondary and graduate training are largely confined to a narrow range of academic fields and thereby tend to perpetuate occupational segregation by gender.

12. What do standardized tests measure and what are their effects?

Standardized tests are supposed to measure innate ability (IQ tests) or mathematical and reasoning abilities related to performance in college or university. To some extent, they do. Thus, to a degree, they help to sort students by ability and aid in the creation of a meritocracy. However, they also measure students' preparedness to learn and thrive in school, and preparedness is strongly related to background factors, such as a family's class position. Therefore, standardized tests also help to reproduce existing social inequalities.

KEY TERMS

assortative mating (p. 500)

credential inflation (p. 504)

cultural capital (p. 505)

educational achievement (p. 496)

educational attainment (p. 496)

hidden curriculum (p. 506)

imagined communities (p. 502)

logic of industrialism (p. 500)

meritocracy (p. 502)

nationalism (p. 501)

pedagogic violence (p. 505)

professionalization (p. 504)

reproduction of the existing
stratification system (p. 506)

social exclusion (p. 503)

QUESTIONS TO CONSIDER

1. In your opinion, how meritocratic were the schools you attended? Did the most talented students tend to perform best? Did material advantages and parental support help the best students? Did material disadvantages and lack of parental support hinder the achievements of weaker students?

2. How would you try to solve the problem of unequal access to higher education? Should tuition payments be lowered across the board, on the basis of family need, or to reward academic success? Would universal subsidies for some costs, like fees, but not others, like books and living expenses, favour all equally or provide more benefits to those who have more resources to devote to education?

3. Did you feel that either boys or girls were favoured academically in the schools you attended? If so, who benefited, if anyone? Is your perception consistent with the evidence reviewed in the chapter? Do you think gender discrimination takes place in schools? If so, what might be done?

WEB RESOURCES

Companion Website for This Book

http://www.compass3e.nelson.com

Begin by clicking on the Student Resources section of the website. Next, select the chapter you are studying from the pull-down menu. From the Student Resources page you have easy access to InfoTrac® College Edition, additional Weblinks, and other resources. The website also has many useful tips to aid you in your study of sociology, including practice tests for each chapter.

InfoTrac® Search Terms

These search terms are provided to assist you in beginning to conduct research on this topic by visiting http://www.infotrac-college.com:

educational achievement

educational attainment

globalization

multiculturalism

Recommended Websites

Links to research papers on a wide variety of topics related to education may be found at the website of the Council of Ministers of Education, Canada, at http://www.cmec.ca.

Statistics Canada's website at http://www.statcan.ca offers much relevant statistical material.

Material that compares Canada with other nations or that focuses on other nations can be accessed at the Organisation for Economic Co-operation and Development website, http://www.oecd.org/home by searching for "education," "literacy," and other keywords.

UNESCO maintains an informative website at http://www.unesco.org. It is full of revealing documents and startling statistics on international and comparative education and literacy.

CengageNOW™

http://hed.nelson.com

This online diagnostic tool identifies each student's unique needs with a Pretest that generates a personalized Study Plan for each chapter, helping students focus on concepts they're having the most difficulty mastering. Students then take a Posttest after reading the chapter to measure their understanding of the material. An Instructor Gradebook is available to track and monitor student progress.

CHAPTER

18

The Mass Media

In this chapter, you will learn that

- Movies, television, and other mass media sometimes blur the distinction between reality and fantasy.

- The mass media are products of the nineteenth and especially the twentieth centuries.

- Historically, the growth of the mass media is rooted in the rise of Protestantism, democracy, and capitalism.

- The mass media make society more cohesive.

- The mass media foster social inequality.

- Although the mass media are influential, audiences filter, interpret, resist, and even reject media messages if they are inconsistent with their beliefs and experiences.

- The mass media misrepresent women and members of racial minorities in important ways.

- The interaction between producers and consumers of media messages is most evident on the Internet.

THE SIGNIFICANCE OF THE MASS MEDIA

Illusion Becomes Reality

The turn of the twenty-first century was thick with movies about the blurred line separating reality from fantasy. *The Truman Show* (1998) gave us Jim Carrey as an insurance agent who discovers that everyone in his life is an actor. He is the unwitting subject of a television program that airs 24 hours a day. In *The Matrix* (1999), Keanu Reeves plays Neo, who finds that his identity and his life are illusions. Like everyone else in the world, Neo is hardwired to a giant computer that uses humans as an energy source. The computer supplies people with nutrients to keep them alive and simulated realities to keep them happy.

The most disturbing movie in this genre, however, is *American Psycho* (2000), directed by Canadian Mary Harron. Based on a novel that was banned in some parts of North America when it was first published in 1991, the movie is the story of Patrick Bateman, Wall Street yuppie by day, cold and meticulous serial killer by night. Unfortunately, the public outcry over the horrifying murder scenes virtually drowned out the book's important sociological point. *American Psycho* is really about how people become victims of the mass media and consumerism. Bateman, the serial murderer, says he is "used to imagining everything happening the way it occurs in movies." When he kisses his lover, he experiences "the 70 mm image of her lips parting and the subsequent murmur of 'I want you' in Dolby sound" (Ellis, 1991: 265). In Bateman's mind, his 14 murder victims are mere props in a movie in which he is the star. He feels no more empathy for them than an actor would for any other stage object. The mass media have so completely emptied him of genuine emotion he even has trouble remembering his victims' names. At the same time, however, the mass media have so successfully infused him with consumer values he can describe his victims' apparel in great detail—styles, brand names, stores where they bought their clothes, even prices. Thus, in *American Psycho,* killer and killed are both victims of consumerism and the mass media.

In different ways, these movies suggest that the fantasy worlds created by the mass media are increasingly the only realities we know, and they are every bit as pervasive and influential as religion was 500 or 600 years ago. Do you think this is an exaggeration dreamed up by filmmakers and novelists? If so, consider that the average Canadian spends more than three hours a day watching television, three hours listening to the radio, just under an hour reading magazines and books, and more than an hour reading newspapers (Moscovitch, 1998). Add to this the number of hours Canadians spend going to the movies, using the Internet, listening to CDs, and playing video games, and it is clear that we spend close to 40 percent of our time interacting with the mass media—more than we do sleeping, working, or going to school. You might want to keep a tally of your activities for a couple of days to find out how you fit into this pattern of activity. Ask yourself, too, what you get out of your interactions with the mass media. Where do you get your ideas about how to dress, how to style your hair, and what music to listen to? Where do your hopes, aspirations, and dreams come from? If you're like most people, much of your reality is media generated. Canadian media guru Marshall McLuhan, who coined the term *global village* in the early 1960s, said the media are extensions of the human body and mind (McLuhan, 1964). More than four decades later, it is perhaps equally valid to claim that the human body and mind are extensions of the mass media (Baudrillard, 1983, 1988; Bourdieu, 1998a).

**WHERE DO
YOU FIT IN?**

What Are the Mass Media?

The term **mass media** refers to print, radio, television, and other communication technologies. Often, *mass media* and *mass communication* are used interchangeably to refer to the transmission of information from one person or group to another. The word *mass* implies that the media reach many people. The word *media* signifies that communication does not take place directly through face-to-face interaction. Instead, technology intervenes or mediates in transmitting messages from senders to receivers. Furthermore, communication

Canadian media guru Marshall McLuhan said the media are extensions of the human body and mind.

The mass media are print, radio, television, and other communication technologies. The word *mass* implies that the media reach many people. The word *media* signifies that communication does not take place directly through face-to-face interaction.

via the mass media is usually one-way, or at least one-sided. There are few senders (or producers) and many receivers (or audience members). Thus, most newspapers print a few readers' letters in each edition, but journalists and advertisers write virtually everything else. Ordinary people may appear on the Oprah Winfrey show or even delight in a slice of fame on *Survivor*. However, producers choose the guests and create the program content. Similarly, a handful of people may visit your personal website, but more than 100 million people visit Yahoo.com every month (Nielsen/NetRatings, 2002).

Usually, then, members of the audience cannot exert much influence on the mass media. They can choose only to tune in or tune out. And even tuning out is difficult because it excludes us from the styles, news, gossip, and entertainment most people depend on to grease the wheels of social interaction. Few people want to be cultural misfits. However, this does not mean that people are always passive consumers of the mass media. As noted below, we filter, interpret, and resist what we see and hear if it contradicts our experiences and beliefs. Even so, in the interaction between audiences and media sources, the media sources usually dominate.

To appreciate fully the impact of the mass media on life today, we need to trace their historical development. That is the first task we set ourselves in the following discussion. We then critically review theories of the mass media's effects on social life. As you will see, each of these theories contributes to our appreciation of media effects. Finally, we assess developments on the media frontier formed by the Internet, television, and other mass media. We show that, to a degree, the new media frontier blurs the distinction between producer and consumer and has the potential to make the mass media somewhat more democratic for those who can afford access.

The Rise of the Mass Media

It may be difficult for you to imagine a world without the mass media. Yet, as Table 18.1 shows, most of the mass media are recent inventions. The first developed systems of writing appeared only about 5500 years ago in Egypt and Mesopotamia (now southern Iraq). The print media became truly a mass phenomenon only in the nineteenth century. The inexpensive daily newspaper, costing a penny, first appeared in the United States in the 1830s. At that time, long-distance communication required physical transportation. To spread the news, you needed a horse, a railroad, or a ship. The slow speed of communication was costly. For instance, the last military engagement between Britain and the United States in the War of 1812–14 was the Battle of New Orleans. It took place 15 days *after* a peace treaty was signed. The good news did not reach the troops near the mouth of the Mississippi until they had suffered 2100 casualties, including 320 dead.

The newspaper was the dominant mass medium even as late as 1950 (Schudson, 1991; Smith, 1980). However, change was in the air in 1844, when Samuel Morse sent the first telegraphic signal (Pred, 1973). From that time on, long-distance communication no longer required physical transportation. The transformative power of the new medium was soon evident. For example, until 1883, hundreds of local time zones existed in North America. The correct time was determined by local solar time and was typically maintained by a clock in a church steeple or a respected jeweller's shop window. Virtually instant communication by telegraph made it possible to coordinate time and establish just six time zones in Canada. Railroad companies spearheaded the move to standardize time. A Canadian civil and railway engineer, Sir Sandford Fleming, was the driving force behind the adoption of standard time in North America and worldwide (Blaise, 2001).

Most of the electronic media are creatures of the twentieth century. The first commercial television broadcasts date from the 1920s. The U.S. Department of Defense established ARPANET in 1969. It was designed as a system of communication between computers that would automatically find alternative transmission routes if one or more nodes in the network broke down because of, say, nuclear attack. ARPANET begat the Internet, which in turn begat the hyperlinked system of texts, images, and sounds known as the World Wide Web around 1991. Today, more than one billion people worldwide use the Web. It was a quick trip—a mere 140 years separate the Pony Express from the home videoconference.

Year (CE)	Media Development
1450	Movable metal type used in Germany, leading to the Gutenberg Bible
1702	First daily newspaper, London's *Daily Courant*
1833	First mass-circulation newspaper, *New York Sun*
1837	Louis Daguerre invents a practical method of photography in France
1844	Samuel Morse sends the first telegraph message between Washington and Baltimore
1875	Alexander Graham Bell sends the first telephone message
1877	Thomas Edison develops the first phonograph
1895	Motion pictures are invented
1901	Italian inventor Guglielmo Marconi transmits the first transatlantic wireless message from England to St. John's, Newfoundland
1906	First radio voice transmission
1920	First regularly scheduled radio broadcast, Pittsburgh
1925	78 rpm record chosen as a standard
1928	First commercial TV broadcast in United States; Canada follows in 1931
1949	Network TV begins in the United States
1952	VCR invented
1961	First cable television, San Diego
1969	First four nodes of the United States Department of Defense's ARPANET (precursor of the Internet) set up at Stanford University; University of California, Los Angeles; University of California, Santa Barbara; and the University of Utah
1975	First microcomputer marketed
1983	Cellphone invented
1989	World Wide Web conceived by Tim Berners-Lee at the European Laboratory for Particle Physics in Switzerland

TABLE 18.1

The Development of the Mass Media

Sources: Berners-Lee, 1999; Croteau and Hoynes, 1997: 9–10; "The Silent Boom," 1998.

Causes of Media Growth

The rise of the mass media can be explained by three main factors: one religious, one political, and one economic:

1. *The Protestant Reformation.* In the sixteenth century, Catholic people relied on priests to tell them what was in the Bible. In 1517, however, Martin Luther protested certain practices of the Church. Among other things, he wanted people to develop a more personal relationship with the Bible. Within 40 years, Luther's new form of Christianity, known as Protestantism, was established in half of Europe. Suddenly, millions of people were being encouraged to read. The Bible became the first mass media product in the West and by far the best-selling book.

   Technological improvements in papermaking and printing made the diffusion of the Bible and other books possible (Febvre and Martin, 1976 [1958]). The most significant landmark was Johann Gutenberg's invention of the printing press. In the 50 years after Gutenberg produced his monumental Bible in 1455, more books were produced than in the previous 1000 years. The printed book enabled the widespread diffusion and exchange of ideas. It contributed to the Renaissance (a scholarly and artistic revival that began in Italy around 1300 and spread to all of Europe by 1600) and to the rise of modern science (Johns, 1998).

   A remarkable feature of the book is its durability. Many electronic storage media became obsolete just a few years after being introduced. For instance, eight-track tapes are icons of the 1970s and 5.25-inch floppy disks are icons of the early 1980s. They are barely remembered today. In contrast, books are still being published today, 550 years after Gutenberg published his Bible. Approximately 10 000 books are published in Canada each year (Association of Canadian Publishers, 2002).

The newspaper was the dominant mass medium even as late as 1950.

2. *Democratic movements.* A second force that promoted the growth of the mass media was political democracy. From the eighteenth century on, the citizens of France, the United States, and other countries demanded and achieved representation in government. At the same time, they wanted to become literate and gain access to previously restricted centres of learning. Democratic governments, in turn, depended on an

One of the most famous photographs in Canadian history is the driving of the last spike of the Canadian Pacific Railway (CPR) on November 7, 1885, at Craigellachie, British Columbia. The man holding the hammer is Donald Smith, who financed much of the construction of the CPR. The taller man standing behind him to his right in the stovepipe hat is Sir Sandford Fleming, the mastermind behind standard time. The railroads spearheaded the introduction of standard time, which could be coordinated thanks to the introduction of the telegraph.

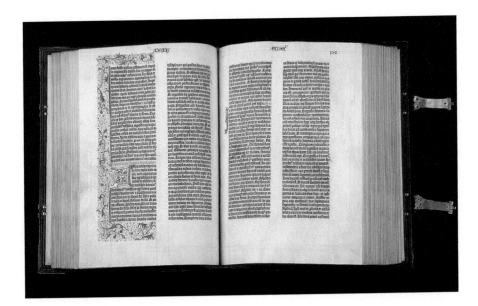

informed citizenry and therefore encouraged popular literacy and the growth of a free press (Habermas, 1989).

Today, the mass media, and especially TV, mould our entire outlook on politics. TV's influence first became evident in the 1960 U.S. presidential election. That was the year of the first televised presidential debate—between John F. Kennedy and Richard Nixon. One of the four reporters who asked questions during the debate later recalled: "The people who watched the debate on their television sets apparently thought Kennedy came off better than Nixon. Those who heard the debate on radio thought Nixon was superior to Kennedy" (quoted in "The Candidates Debate," 1998). Kennedy smiled. Nixon perspired. Kennedy relaxed. Nixon fidgeted. The election was close, and most analysts believe that Kennedy got the edge simply because 70 million viewers thought he looked better on TV. Television was thus beginning to redefine the very nature of politics.

Soon, Canadian politicians were hiring "image consultants." Usually their advice led to the desired results. Sometimes, however, copying American media techniques could backfire. For instance, in recent decades Americans have often used "negative advertising" to trash political opponents, frequently on personal grounds. The Progressive Conservative Party of Canada briefly adopted this approach in the 1993 federal election campaign. It released two ads in English Canada that drew attention to Jean Chrétien's facial paralysis. The ads enraged many Canadians, who thought them grossly unfair. Support for the Conservative Party dropped sharply. Widely expected to win between 25 and 60 seats in the election, the PCs wound up with just 2 seats, partly because of the negative ads (Romanow, de Repentigny, Cunningham, Soderlund, and Hildebrandt, 1999).

The 1993 anti-Chrétien ads and the 1960 Kennedy–Nixon debate suggest that television has oversimplified politics. Some analysts say that politics has been reduced to a series of more or less well-managed images, catchy slogans, and ever-shorter uninterrupted comments or "sound bites." From this point of view, candidates are marketed for high office like Kellogg's sells breakfast cereal, and a politician's stage presence is more important than his or her policies in determining success at the polls.

3. *Capitalist industrialization.* The third major force that stimulated the growth of the mass media was capitalist industrialization. Modern industries required a literate and numerate workforce. They also needed rapid means of communication to do business efficiently. Moreover, the mass media turned out to be a major source of profit in their own right.

The sources of the mass media are deeply embedded in the religious, political, and economic needs of our society. Moreover, the mass media are among the most important institutions in our society today. How, then, do sociologists explain the effects of the mass media on society? To answer this question, we now summarize the relevant sociological theories.

THEORIES OF MEDIA EFFECTS

Functionalism

As societies develop, they become larger and more complex. The number of institutions and roles proliferate. Because of the sheer scale of society, face-to-face interaction becomes less viable as a means of communication. As a result, the need increases for new means of coordinating the operation of the various parts of society. For example, people in New Brunswick must have at least a general sense of what is happening in Alberta, and they need to share certain basic values with Albertans if they are going to feel they are citizens of the same country. The mass media do an important job in this regard. The nineteenth-century German philosopher Georg Hegel once said that the daily ritual of reading the newspaper unites the secular world, just as the ritual of daily prayer once united the Christian world. Stated more generally, his point is valid. The nationwide distribution of newspapers, magazines, movies, and television shows cements the large, socially diverse, and geographically far-flung population of Canada. In a fundamental sense, the nation is an imagined community, and the mass media make it possible for us to imagine it (Anderson, 1991).

Thus, the mass media perform an important function by *coordinating* the operation of industrial and postindustrial societies. But, according to functionalist theorists, their significance does not stop there (Wright, 1975). In addition, the mass media are also important agents of *socialization*. Families have relinquished their formerly nearly exclusive right to transmit norms, values, and culture. The mass media have stepped into the breach. They

Canadians now spend nearly 40 percent of their time interacting with the mass media.

reinforce shared ideals of democracy, competition, justice, and so forth (see Chapter 4, Socialization).

A third function of the mass media involves *social control*. That is, the mass media help to ensure conformity. For example, news broadcasts, TV dramas, and "docutainment" programs, such as *COPS*, pay much attention to crime, and they regularly sing the praises of heroes who apprehend and convict criminals. By exposing deviants and showcasing law enforcement officials and model citizens, the mass media reinforce ideas about what kinds of people deserve punishment and what kinds of people deserve rewards. In this way, they reproduce the moral order. Some people think the *Jerry Springer* show is outlandish, and in a way it is. From a sociological point of view, however, it is also a deeply conservative program, for when television audiences become upset about marital infidelities and other outrages, they are reinforcing some of the most traditional norms of North American society and thus serving as agents of social control. As Nobel Prize–winning author Saul Bellow wrote, "a scandal [is] after all a sort of service to the community" (Bellow, 1964: 18).

The mass media's fourth and final function is to provide *entertainment*. Television, movies, magazines, and so forth give us pleasure, relaxation, and momentary escape from the tension and tedium of everyday life. How often have you come home after a long and frustrating day at college, university, or work, picked up the remote control, channel surfed, concluded that there's nothing really worth watching, but settled for a sitcom or some other form of easily digestible entertainment? It is precisely because some products of the mass media require little effort on the part of the audience that they are important. They relieve stress. Moreover, they do so in a way that doesn't threaten the social order. Without such escapes, who knows how our daily tensions and frustrations might express themselves?

Conflict Theory

Clearly, functionalism offers valuable insights into the operation of the mass media. However, conflict theorists have criticized the functional approach for paying insufficient attention to the social inequality fostered by the mass media. Specifically, conflict theorists say functionalism exaggerates the degree to which the mass media serve the interests of the entire society. They contend that some people benefit from the mass media more than others. In particular, the mass media favour the interests of dominant classes and political groups (Gitlin, 1983; Herman and Chomsky, 1988; Horkheimer and Adorno, 1986 [1944]; Iyengar, 1991).

Conflict theorists maintain that there are two ways in which dominant classes and political groups benefit disproportionately from the mass media. First, the mass media broadcast beliefs, values, and ideas that create widespread acceptance of the basic structure of society, including its injustices and inequalities. Second, ownership of the mass media is highly concentrated in the hands of a small number of people and is highly profitable for them. Thus, the mass media are a source of economic inequality. Let us consider these issues in more detail.

Media Ownership

For decades, most of the Canadian mass media have been owned by fewer than a dozen families: the Siftons, the Thomsons, the Bassetts, the Southams, the Irvings, the Honderiches, the Blacks, and, more recently, the Aspers, the Shaws, the Rogerses, and the Péladeaus. There are just six multimedia giants in the country, with combined annual revenue of about $16.5 billion in 2007.[1] In order of size (as measured by annual revenue), they are as follows:

1. *CTVglobemedia Inc.* Owned mainly by BCE and Toronto's Thomson Corporation, CTVglobemedia controls the CTV television network, *The Globe and Mail*, CFCF (the biggest English-language television station in Montreal), CKY (Manitoba's biggest TV station), *Report on Business* TV, TSN (The Sports Network), and so on. Revenue in fiscal 2004: $4.3 billion.

2. *Rogers Communications Inc.* Controlled by the Rogers family and based in Toronto, Rogers is one of the country's largest cable TV and broadband Internet service providers. It controls The Shopping Channel, CFMT (a multicultural television station in Toronto), Sportsnet, the Toronto Blue Jays, dozens of radio stations, scores of consumer and business magazines (including *Maclean's, Flare,* and *Canadian Business*), and so on. Revenue in fiscal 2007: $3.9 billion.

3. *CanWest Global Communications Corp.* Controlled by the Asper family of Winnipeg, CanWest Global owns the Global Television Network (comprising 11 stations across Canada), 3 independent television stations (CH TV Hamilton, CH TV Vancouver, and CH TV Montreal), the *National Post,* 10 major urban English-language daily newspapers (Montreal's *The Gazette, Ottawa Citizen, The Windsor Star,* Regina's *Leader-Post,* Saskatoon's *The Star Phoenix, Calgary Herald, Edmonton Journal, The Vancouver Sun,* Victoria's *Times-Colonist,* Vancouver's *The Province*), and so on. Revenue in fiscal 2007: $2.9 billion.

4. *Shaw Communications Inc.* Controlled by the Shaw family of Calgary, Shaw Communications is another of the country's largest cable TV and broadband Internet service providers. It also owns 49 radio stations and television specialty stations, including YTV, CMT, and Premium Pay TV Services. Revenue in fiscal 2005: $2.8 billion.

5. *CBC/Radio Canada.* The fifth-largest multimedia giant in Canada is the only one that is publicly owned. Its most important assets are an English-language television network, a French-language television network, and four commercial-free radio networks. Revenue in fiscal 2006–07: $1.6 billion, 56 percent of which is a federal government grant and the balance of which comes from advertising, program sales, and so on (see Box 18.1).

6. Quebecor Inc. Controlled by the Péladeau family of Montreal, Quebecor publishes 28 daily newspapers including *Le journal de Montréal, Le journal de Québec, the Ottawa Sun,* the *Toronto Sun,* the *London Free Press,* the *Winnipeg Sun,* the *Edmonton Sun,* the *Calgary Sun,* and the *Kingston Whig-Standard*). It also owns the largest cable TV provider in Quebec, Quebec's largest private TV network (TVA), Canoe.ca, and so on. Revenue in fiscal 2007: $1.0 billion.

About 90 percent of the mass media in Canada are privately owned. Over time, concentration of the privately owned media has increased. That is, fewer and fewer people control Canada's mass media with every passing decade. Moreover, it is not just the *degree* of media concentration that has changed. The *form* of media concentration began to shift in the 1990s, too. Until the 1990s, media concentration involved mainly "horizontal integration." A small number of firms tried to control as much production as possible in their particular fields (newspapers, radio, television, etc.). In the 1990s, however, "vertical integration" became much more widespread. Media firms sought to control production and distribution in *many* fields. They became media "conglomerates." Today, a media conglomerate may own any combination of television networks, stations, and production facilities; magazines, newspapers, and book publishers; cable channels and cable systems; video store chains; sports teams; Web portals; and software companies. A media conglomerate can create content and deliver it in a variety of forms. For instance, Rogers Communications Inc. owns the Toronto Blue Jays, creates sports entertainment, broadcasts it on its television stations, carries the signal to viewers' homes via its cable system, and spins off Blue Jays merchandise that it can sell at Rogers Video stores.

In the United States, the biggest media players include AOL/Time Warner, Disney, Viacom, and News Corporation. Other international giant media conglomerates include Bertelsmann (Germany), Sony (Japan), and Vivendi (France). You can appreciate the scale of control we're talking about if we simply list some of the better-known companies owned by AOL/Time Warner, the biggest media conglomerate: America Online; Netscape; Amazon.com; Time-Life Books; Book-of-the-Month Club; Warner Books; Little, Brown and Company; HBO; CNN; Warner Bros.; Castle Rock Entertainment;

BOX 18.1
Social Policy: What Do You Think?

Should Canada's Broadcasters Be Subject to More Government Regulation?

The use of the air . . . that lies over the . . . land of Canada is a natural resource over which we have complete jurisdiction. . . . I cannot think that any government would be warranted in leaving the air to private exploitation and not reserving it for . . . the use of the people. Without [complete government control of broadcasting from Canadian sources, radio] can never become the agency by which national consciousness may be fostered and national unity . . . strengthened.

—Prime Minister R. B. Bennett, House of Commons, May 18, 1932 (quoted in Competition Bureau, 2002)

What was self-evident to Prime Minister Bennett more than 70 years ago is a matter of controversy today. Some Canadians, like Bennett, still argue for strict government control of the mass media. Like Bennett, they believe that the mass media should be used to strengthen Canadian culture. Others want a more or less free market in which the great bulk of programming is American in origin or, failing that, American in style. Here we review the state of government regulation of Canadian broadcasting and ask you to decide whether you approve of the status quo or think that more or less government regulation is needed.

The Canadian Radio-television and Telecommunications Commission (CRTC) was established by an act of Parliament in 1968 as an independent agency responsible for regulating Canada's broadcasting and telecommunications systems. Its self-described mandate is to promote Canadian culture and economic competitiveness:

Our mandate is to ensure that programming in the Canadian broadcasting system reflects Canadian creativity and talent, our linguistic duality, our multicultural diversity, the special place of aboriginal people within our society and our social values. At the same time, we must ensure that Canadians have access to reasonably priced, high-quality, varied and innovative communications services that are competitive nationally as well as internationally. ("The CRTC's Mandate," 2002)

In practice, promoting Canadian culture means ensuring that 35 percent of the popular music played on English-language commercial radio stations between 6 a.m. and 6 p.m., Monday through Friday, is Canadian. Regulations for "ethnic" and French-language stations are somewhat different. Privately owned television stations must achieve a yearly Canadian content level of 60 percent between 6 a.m. and midnight and 50 percent between 6 p.m. and midnight. Canadian content rules for the CBC are slightly more demanding.

"Canadian" means that the producer of the program is Canadian, key creative personnel are Canadian, and 75 percent of service costs and postproduction lab costs are paid to Canadians.

As a result of these regulations, about half of TV broadcasts in English Canada and 65 percent of popular music broadcasts are *American*. Moreover, many American TV and radio stations are widely available in Canada via cable, satellite, or the airwaves. (Roughly 75 percent of Canadian households subscribe to cable, and another 20 percent use satellite services; estimated from "Presentation by Canada's Cable Companies," 2002; Statistics Canada, 2002a, 2002e). It seems reasonable to conclude that at least three-quarters of the TV and popular music to which Canadians have access is American.

Bearing the above facts in mind, do you think the Canadian government does enough or too much to ensure the preservation and enrichment of Canadian culture through the broadcast industry? Should the government be in the business of protecting Canadian culture at all? Should it allow free-market forces to shape the structure and content of Canadian broadcasting? Would a free-market approach to broadcasting enable Canadians to get what they really want, or would it allow powerful American broadcasters to completely dominate the marketplace and virtually eliminate Canadian content?

Time; *Fortune*; *Life*; *Sports Illustrated*; *Money*; *People*; *Entertainment Weekly*; Warner Brothers Records; Elektra; the Atlanta Braves; the Atlanta Hawks; the Atlanta Thrashers; and the Goodwill Games.

Media Bias

Does the concentration of the mass media in fewer and fewer hands deprive the public of independent sources of information, limit the diversity of opinion, and encourage the

The Asper family of Winnipeg owns CanWest Global Communications Corp., the third-biggest media conglomerate in Canada. In 2001 and 2002, David Asper, shown here, and his late father Izzy came under widespread criticism for controlling editorial content in their newspapers.

public to accept their society as it is? Conflict theorists think so. They argue that when a few conglomerates dominate the production of news in particular, they squeeze out alternative points of view.

For example, at the end of 2001, CanWest's owners, the Asper family, declared that editorials published in their newspapers should not contradict editorials written in their head office. The Aspers were strong supporters of the Liberal Party, staunchly pro-Israel, and in favour of increased military spending, increased protection of property rights, and an elected Senate. In 2002, two reporters for Halifax's *The Daily News* had their columns "killed" when they criticized the Asper policy. They were then asked if they wanted to continue to work for the paper. They said no. A reporter for *The Windsor Star* had his column killed for the same reason. An Aboriginal columnist for Regina's *Leader-Post* and Saskatoon's *StarPhoenix* had a column killed when he expressed sympathy for stateless Palestinians. Yet another reporter was fired from the *Ottawa Citizen* after unearthing scandalous details about possible corruption involving Prime Minister Jean Chrétien. When reporters at the Montreal *Gazette* and the Saskatoon *StarPhoenix* protested the Aspers' attempts to control editorial policy, CanWest imposed a gag order on all reporters working for the organization, saying it would suspend journalists who publicly objected to its editorial policy. In March 2002, the gag order was extended to all Global TV employees. Then, in June 2002, Russell Mills, the long-time publisher of the *Ottawa Citizen,* was fired because of what the Aspers regarded as too much anti-Chrétien opinion on the editorial page. CanWest's actions are a form of corporate censorship, and they have been roundly criticized by the Newspaper Guild of Canada, the *Washington Post,* and the International Federation of Journalists, among other organizations (Canada NewsWire, 2002; International Federation of Journalists, 2002; Sallot, 2002; Siddiqui, 2002; Worthington, 2002).

CanWest is an extreme case. Such direct and open interference with editorial policy is not common in liberal democracies such as Canada (but see Box 18.2). However, according to Edward Herman and Noam Chomsky (1988), several other, more subtle mechanisms help to bias the news in a way that supports powerful corporate interests and political groups. These biasing mechanisms include advertising, sourcing, and flak:

- *Advertising.* Most of the revenue earned by television stations, radio stations, newspapers, and magazines comes from advertising by large corporations. According to Herman and Chomsky, these corporations routinely seek to influence the news so it will reflect well on them. In one American survey, 93 percent of newspaper editors said advertisers have tried to influence their news reports. Thirty-seven percent of newspaper editors admitted to being influenced by advertisers (Bagdikian, 1997). In addition, big advertisers may influence the news even without overtly trying to influence news carriers. For fear of losing business, news carriers may soften stories that big advertisers might find offensive.

- *Sourcing.* Studies of news-gathering show that most news agencies rely heavily for information on press releases, news conferences, and interviews organized by large corporations and government agencies. These sources routinely slant information to reflect favourably on their policies and preferences. Unofficial news sources are consulted less often. Moreover, unofficial sources tend to be used only to provide reactions and minority viewpoints that are secondary to the official story.

- *Flak.* Governments and big corporations routinely attack journalists who depart from official and corporate points of view. For example, Brian Ross, the leading investigative reporter for *20/20,* prepared a segment about Disney World in 1998. Ross claimed that Disney was so lax in doing background checks on employees that it had hired pedophiles. ABC killed the story before airtime. ABC is owned by Disney (McChesney, 1999). Similarly, tobacco companies have systematically tried to discredit media reports that cigarettes cause cancer. In a notorious case, the respected public affairs show *60 Minutes* refused to broadcast a damaging interview with a former Philip Morris executive because CBS was threatened with legal action by the tobacco company. (This incident is the subject of the Oscar-nominated movie *The Insider,* released in 1999.)

On the whole, the conflict theorists' arguments are compelling. We do not, however, find them completely convincing (Gans, 1979). After all, if 37 percent of newspaper editors have been influenced by advertisers, 63 percent have not. News agencies may rely heavily

---

BOX 18.2
Sociology at the Movies

TAKE | ROLL

The Fog of War (2003)

The Fog of War surveys the life of Robert McNamara, U.S. Secretary of Defense during the Kennedy and Johnson administrations and an architect of the Vietnam War. The film's format—a single talking head plus period film clips, photos, and audio tapes—might seem a recipe for tedium. Instead, master filmmaker Errol Morris presents us with a compelling work that won the 2003 Oscar for best documentary, a film that, if taken seriously by enough people, could change the world.

McNamara does what many people want but too few accomplish. He learns from the mistakes that he and others made or nearly made. That enables him to clear away some of the "fog of war," the muddled thinking that accompanies all armed conflict.

A lesson McNamara learned from his involvement in the 1962 Cuban missile crisis is that you win most and lose least if you empathize with your enemy. He tells the story of how Tommy Thompson, former U.S. ambassador to Moscow, locked horns with President Kennedy. Kennedy believed that negotiating with the Soviets to remove their missiles from Cuba was futile. He was prepared to start a nuclear war. Thompson, however, knew the Soviet president personally and understood that he would back down from his belligerent position if presented with an option that would allow him to remove the missiles from Cuba and still say to his

Robert McNamara (right), with Vice-President Hubert Humphrey (left) and President Lyndon Johnson (centre)

hard-line generals that he had won the confrontation with the United States. "The important thing for [him]," Thompson argued, "is to be able to say, 'I saved Cuba; I stopped the invasion.'" Thompson convinced Kennedy. Negotiations began and nuclear war was averted. "That's what I call empathy," McNamara observes "We must try to put ourselves inside [the enemy's] skin and look at us through their eyes."

Empathy, McNamara acknowledges, was absent a few years later when the United States began carpet bombing and deploying hundreds of thousands of troops in Vietnam. The U.S. administration thought the war would prevent Vietnam from falling under Chinese communist rule. It didn't appreciate that Vietnam had been a colony of China for a thousand years and of France for

nearly a century and was now engaged in a bitter struggle for independence that the United States seemed eager to prevent. It was a costly misunderstanding. The American administration failed to appreciate the nationalist motives of the Vietnamese and underestimated their resolve. Fifty-eight thousand Americans and two million Vietnamese died in the war.

Some analysts argue that the American mass media contributed to the fog of war by obstructing the development of empathy with the enemies of the United States. (Remember, empathy does not mean having warm and fuzzy feelings about an enemy but understanding things from the enemy's perspective so we can design policies that enable us to win most and lose least.) Some representatives of the American mass media are aware of their failings in this regard. Thus, once it became evident in 2004 that Iraq lacked weapons of mass destruction and had few or no ties with Osama bin Laden, and that the Iraqi insurgency against the United States was determined and widespread, representatives of several major American newspapers and television networks virtually apologized to the public for not subjecting the administration's case for war with Iraq to sufficient scrutiny ("*The Times* and Iraq," 2004). Even after these admissions, media self-censorship was widespread according to some analysts. Some media outlets, notably Fox News, failed to present balanced coverage as a matter of editorial policy, while some journalists spoke in muted tones for fear of losing their assignments (Massing, 2004).

Arguably, therefore, Americans have an imprecise picture of the situation on the ground in Iraq. They know little about the true impact of the war on civilians, the extent of popular support for the insurgency, the population's attitudes toward the American military presence, and other crucial matters. In *The Fog of War,* Robert McNamara argues that willingness to re-examine the reasoning is an essential element of successful warfare. Arguably, however, media-imposed limits make it difficult for the American public to develop informed opinion about what to do to maximize their gains and minimize their losses in Iraq.

on government and corporate sources, but this does not stop them from routinely biting the hand that offers to feed them and evading flak shot their way. The daily newspaper is full of examples of mainstream journalistic opposition to government and corporate viewpoints. Even mainstream news sources, although owned by media conglomerates, do not always act like the lap dogs of the powerful (Hall, 1980).

Still, conflict theorists make a valid point if they restrict their argument to how the mass media support core societal values. In their defence of core values, the mass media *are* virtually unanimous. For example, the mass media enthusiastically support democracy and capitalism. We cannot think of a single instance of a major Canadian news outlet advocating a fascist government or a socialist economy in Canada.

Similarly, the mass media virtually unanimously endorse consumerism as a way of life. As discussed in Chapter 3, Culture, consumerism is the tendency to define ourselves in terms of the goods and services we purchase. Endorsement of consumerism is evident in the fact that advertising fills the mass media and is its lifeblood. In 2003, advertising spending in Canada totalled $5.1 billion, nearly half the $10.4 billion spent on Canada's universities and degree-granting institutions (Statistics Canada, 2004d, 2005a). We are exposed to a staggering number of ads each day; in fact, some estimates place the number in the thousands. Companies pay filmmakers to use their brand-name products conspicuously in their movies. In some magazines, ads figure so prominently a reader must search for the articles.

It is only when the mass media deal with news stories that touch on less central values that we can witness a diversity of media opinion. *Specific* government and corporate policies are often the subject of heated debate in the mass media.[2] Thus, despite the indisputable concentration of media ownership, the mass media are diverse and often contentious on specific issues that do not touch on core values (see Figure 18.1).

Interpretive Approaches

The view that the mass media powerfully influence a passive public is common, not least among functionalists and conflict theorists. Many people believe that violence on TV causes violence in real life, pornography on the magazine stands leads to immoral sexual behaviour, and adolescents are more likely to start smoking cigarettes when they see popular movie stars lighting up.

Functionalists and conflict theorists share this top-down, deterministic view; members of both schools of thought stress how the mass media bridge social differences and reinforce society's core values. True, the two schools of thought differ in that functionalists regard core values as serving everyone's interests while conflict theorists regard them as favouring

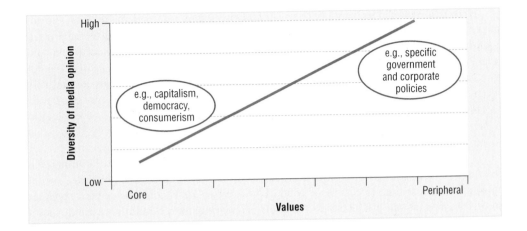

FIGURE 18.1
The Relationship between
Centrality of Values and
Diversity of Media Opinion

the interests of the rich and powerful. By focusing so tightly on core values, however, both approaches understate the degree to which audience members interpret media messages in different ways. The signal contribution of symbolic interactionist and related approaches is that they highlight the importance of such interpretive acts.

Just how much influence do the mass media actually exert over audiences? The question is mired in controversy, but it seems that the top-down, deterministic view is one-sided. You may recall our discussion of media violence in Chapter 2, How Sociologists Do Research. There we found that most experimental research on the subject is plagued by a validity problem. Simply stated, experiments on media violence may not be measuring what they say they are measuring. The sociological consensus seems to be that TV violence influences only a small percentage of viewers to commit acts of violence in the real world.

There are other reasons for questioning the strength of media effects. For instance, researchers have known for half a century that people do not change their attitudes and behaviours just because the media tell them to do so. That is because the link between persuasive media messages and actual behaviour is indirect. A **two-step flow of communication** takes place (Katz, 1957; Schiller, 1989; Schudson, 1995). In step 1, respected people of high status evaluate media messages. They are the opinion leaders of a neighbourhood or a community, people who are usually more highly educated, well-to-do, or politically powerful than others in their circle are. Because of their high status, they exercise considerable independence of judgment. In step 2, opinion leaders *may* influence the attitudes and behaviours of others. In this way, opinion leaders filter media messages. The two-step flow of communication limits media effects. If people are influenced to vote for certain candidates, buy certain products, or smoke cigarettes, it is less because the media tell them to and more because opinion leaders suggest they should.

Yet another persuasive argument that leads us to question the effects of the mass media comes from interpretive sociologists, such as symbolic interactionists and interdisciplinary **cultural studies** experts. They use in-depth interviewing and participant observation to study how people actually interpret media messages.

British sociologist Stuart Hall (1980), one of the foremost proponents of this approach, emphasizes that people are not empty vessels into which the mass media pour a defined assortment of beliefs, values, and ideas. Rather, audience members take an active role in consuming the products of the mass media. They filter and interpret mass media messages in the context of their own interests, experiences, and values. Thus, in Hall's view, any adequate analysis of the mass media needs to take into account both the production and the consumption of media products. First, he says, we need to study the meanings intended by the producers. Then we need to study how audiences consume or evaluate media products. Intended and received meanings may diverge; audience members may interpret media messages in ways other than those intended by the producers (Hall, 1980; Seiter, 1999).

The **two-step flow of communication** between mass media and audience members involves (1) respected people of high status and independent judgment evaluating media messages, and (2) other members of the community being influenced to varying degrees by these opinion leaders. Because of the two-step flow of communication, opinion leaders filter media messages.

Cultural studies is an increasingly popular interdisciplinary area of research. In research on the mass media, it focuses not just on the cultural meanings producers try to transmit but also on the way audiences filter and interpret mass media messages in the context of their own interests, experiences, and values.

PERSONAL
ANECDOTE

Here is a personal example of the way audiences may interpret media messages in unexpected ways: When John Lie's parents were preparing to emigrate to the United States in the late 1960s, his mother watched many American movies and television shows. One of her favourite TV programs was *My Three Sons,* a sitcom about three boys living with their father and grandfather. From the show she learned that boys wash dishes and vacuum the house in the United States. When the Lie family emigrated to Hawaii, John and his brother—but not his sister—had to wash dishes every night. When John complained, his mother reassured him that "in America, only boys wash dishes."

Even children's television viewing turns out to be complex when viewed through an interpretive lens. Research shows that young children distinguish "make-believe" media violence from real-life violence (Hodge and Tripp, 1986). That is one reason why watching of *South Park* has not produced a nation of *South Park* clones. Similarly, research shows differences in the way working-class and middle-class women relate to TV. Working-class women tend to evaluate TV programs in terms of how realistic they are more than middle-class women do. This critical attitude reduces their ability to identify strongly with many characters, personalities, and storylines. For instance, working-class women know from their own experience that families often don't work the way they are shown on TV. They view the idealized, middle-class nuclear family depicted in many television shows with a mixture of nostalgia and skepticism (Press, 1991). Age also affects how we relate to television. Senior viewers tend to be selective and focused in their television viewing. In contrast, people who grew up with cable TV and a remote control often engage in channel surfing, conversation, eating, and housework, zoning in and out of programs in anything but an absorbed fashion (Press, 1991). The idea that such viewers are sponges, passively soaking up the values embedded in TV programs and then mechanically acting on them, is inaccurate.

Feminist Approaches

Finally, let us consider feminist approaches to the study of mass media effects. In the 1970s, feminist researchers focused on the representation—more accurately, the misrepresentation—of women in the mass media. They found that in TV dramas, women tended to be cast as homemakers, as secretaries, and in other subordinate roles, while men tended to be cast as professionals and authority figures. Women usually appeared in domestic settings, men in public settings. Advertising targeted women only as purchasers of household products and appliances. Furthermore, researchers discovered that the news rarely mentioned issues of importance for many women, such as wage discrimination in the paid labour force, sexual harassment and abuse, child-care problems, and so on. News reports sometimes trivialized or denounced the women's movement. Newsworthy issues (the economy, party politics, international affairs, and crime) were associated with men, and men were much more likely than women were to be used as news sources and to deliver the news (Watkins and Emerson, 2000: 152–53).

Most of this early feminist research assumed that audiences are passive. Analysts argued that the mass media portray women in stereotypical fashion; audience members recognize and accept the stereotypes as normal and even natural; and the mass media thereby reinforce existing gender inequalities. However, in the 1980s and 1990s, feminist researchers criticized this simple formula. Influenced by cultural studies, they realized that audience members selectively interpret media messages and sometimes even contest them.

A good example of this subtler and less deterministic approach is a study by Andrea Press and Elizabeth Cole (1999) of audience reaction to abortion as portrayed on TV shows. Over a four-year period, Press and Cole conducted 34 discussion groups involving 108 women. The women watched three TV programs focusing on abortion and then discussed their own attitudes and their reactions to the shows. The programs were pro-choice and dealt with women who chose abortion to avoid poverty.

Press and Cole found complex, ambivalent, and sometimes contradictory attitudes toward abortion among audience members. However, four distinct clusters of opinion emerged:

1. *Pro-life women from all social classes* form the most homogeneous group. They think abortion is never justified. On principle, they reject the mass media's justifications for abortion.

2. *Pro-choice working-class women who think of themselves as members of the working class* adopt a pro-choice stand as a survival strategy, not on principle. They do not condone abortion, but they fear that laws restricting abortion would be applied prejudicially against women of their class. Therefore, they oppose any such restrictions. At the same time, they reject the TV message that financial hardship justifies abortion.

3. *Pro-choice working-class women who aspire to middle-class status* distance themselves from the "reckless" members of their own class who sought abortions on the TV shows. They tolerate abortion for such people but they reject it for themselves and for other "responsible" women.

4. *Pro-choice middle-class women* believe that only an individual woman's feelings can determine whether abortion is right or wrong in her own case. Many pro-choice middle-class women have deep reservations about abortion, and many of them reject it as an option for themselves. However, they staunchly defend the right of all women, especially the kind of women portrayed in the TV shows they watched, to choose abortion.

One of the most striking aspects of Press and Cole's findings is that, for different reasons, three of the four categories of audience members (categories 1, 2, and 3) are highly skeptical of TV portrayals of the abortion issue. Their class position and attitudes act as filters influencing how they react to TV shows and how they view the abortion issue. Moreover, three of the four categories of audience members (categories 2, 3, and 4) reject the simple pro-choice versus pro-life dichotomy often portrayed by the mass media. Many pro-choice women express ambivalence about abortion and even reject it as an option for themselves. We must conclude that real women are typically more complicated than the stereotypes promoted in the mass media, and that women in the audience typically know that.

In recent years, some feminists have focused on the capacity of the mass media to reproduce and change the system of racial inequality in North American society. In the work of these scholars, the twin issues of female misrepresentation and active audience interpretation reappear, this time with a racial twist. On the one hand, they find that certain stereotypical images of women of colour recur in the mass media. Women of African heritage, for example, often appear in the role of the welfare mother, the highly sexualized Jezebel, and the mammy. On the other hand, they recognize that some mass media, especially independent filmmaking and popular music, have enabled women of colour to challenge these stereotypes. The music and videos of Erykah Badu, Missy "Misdemeanor" Elliott, and Lauryn Hill are especially noteworthy in this regard. These artists write and produce their own music. They often direct their own videos. Their work is a running critical commentary on real-world issues confronting young black women. Thus, in terms of both production and content, their work breaks down the established roles and images of black women in North America (Watkins and Emerson, 2000: 159–56).

Still, stereotypes persist. A 2004 study of North American prime-time TV characters found that men predominated in police, military, professional and criminal roles while women predominated in lower-status occupational roles and in the role of homemaker. Five percent of roles played by whites were criminal, compared to 10 percent for blacks, 15 percent for Latinos and Asians, and an incredible 46 percent for Middle Easterners (Figure 18.2 on page 534).

The way in which the mass media treat women and members of various minority groups has for the most part improved over time. We have come a long way since the 1950s, when virtually the only blacks on TV were men who played butlers and buffoons. Research

Missy "Misdemeanor" Elliott writes and produces her own music. She often directs her own videos. Her work is a running critical commentary on real-world issues confronting young black women. Thus, in terms of both production and content, her work breaks down the established roles and images of black women in America.

FIGURE 18.2

Occupations in Prime-Time TV by Gender and Race, 2003–2004

Source: *Fall Colors,* 2004: 4, 17.

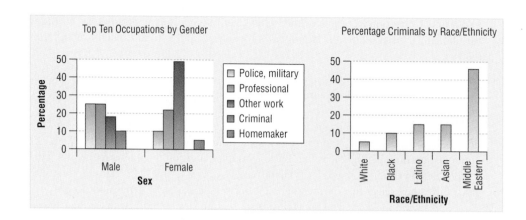

FIGURE 18.2

Occupations in Prime-Time TV by Gender and Race, 2003–2004

Source: *Fall Colors,* 2004: 4, 17.

suggests that the mass media still have a long way to go before they cease reinforcing traditional stereotypes in North America (Dines and Humez, 1995). But research also suggests that audiences and artists are hardly passive vehicles of these stereotypes, instead struggling to diversify the way the mass media characterize them.

Summing Up

We conclude that each of the theoretical approaches reviewed earlier contributes to our understanding of how the mass media influence us (see Table 18.2):

- *Functionalism* usefully identifies the main social effects of the mass media: coordination, socialization, social control, and entertainment. By performing these functions, the mass media help make social order possible.
- *Conflict theory* offers an important qualification. As vast moneymaking machines controlled by a small group of increasingly wealthy people, the mass media contribute to economic inequality and to maintaining the core values of a stratified social order.
- *Interpretive approaches* offer a second qualification. They remind us that audience members are people, not programmable robots. We filter, interpret, resist, and sometimes reject media messages according to our own interests and values. A full sociological appreciation of the mass media is obliged to recognize the interaction between producers and consumers of media messages.
- *Feminist approaches* offer a third qualification. They highlight the misrepresentation of women and members of racial minorities in the mass media. They also emphasize the ways in which women and members of racial minorities have successfully challenged these misrepresentations and sought to diversify the characterization of race and gender by the mass media.

TABLE 18.2

Theories of Mass Media Effects

Theory	Mass Media Effects
Functionalism	Coordination, socialization, social control, entertainment—all of which make social order possible
Conflict theory	The reinforcement of economic inequality and the core values of a stratified society
Interpretive approaches	Because audiences filter, interpret, resist, and sometimes reject media messages, the effects of the mass media are ambiguous and can never be assumed
Feminist approaches	Gender and racial stereotypes in the mass media perpetuate gender and racial inequalities, although resistance and innovation result in change

DOMINATION AND RESISTANCE ON THE INTERNET

We have emphasized the interaction that normally takes place between the mass media and its audiences. To drive the point home, we now offer an in-depth analysis of domination and resistance on the Internet. As you will see, the Internet provides fresh opportunities for media conglomerates to restrict access to paying customers and accumulate vast wealth. Simultaneously, however, the Internet gives consumers new creative capabilities, partially blurring the distinction between producer and consumer. The Internet, we conclude, has the potential to make the mass media more democratic—at least for those who can afford access.

To develop this idea, let us first consider the forces that restrict Internet access and augment the power of media conglomerates. We then discuss some countertrends.

Access

The Internet requires an expensive infrastructure of personal computers, servers, and routers; an elaborate network of fibre-optic, copper-twist, and coaxial cables; and many other components. This infrastructure has to be paid for, primarily by individual users. As a result, access is not open to everyone—far from it. In Canada, for example, households that are richer, better educated, urban, and younger are most likely to enjoy Internet access (see Chapter 14, Politics).

Nor is Internet access evenly distributed globally (see Figure 18.3). The United States is the overwhelming leader in terms of getting its population connected. On a per capita basis, Canada ranks second. Globally, the rate of Internet connectivity is much higher in rich countries than in poor countries.

Content

American domination is even more striking when it comes to Internet content. In rough terms, perhaps 60 percent of the servers that provide content on the Internet are in the United

GLOBAL
PERSPECTIVE

FIGURE 18.3

Internet Connectivity and Population Density

Nearly a quarter of a million routers in the world connected local computer networks (such as the computer network of a company or a university) to the Internet in 2001. The top map shows the number of routers per geographical area (1° of latitude by 1° of longitude) in the world. The bottom map shows the number of people per geographical area (1° of latitude by 1° of longitude) in the world. Darker areas indicate higher density. Based on these maps, what can you conclude about the relationship between Internet usage and population density in the highly developed countries and in the world as a whole?

Source: Soon-Hyung Yook, Hawoong Jeong, and Albert-László Barabási, 2001, "Modelling the Internet's Large-Scale Topology," Department of Physics, University of Notre Dame. Reprinted with permission.

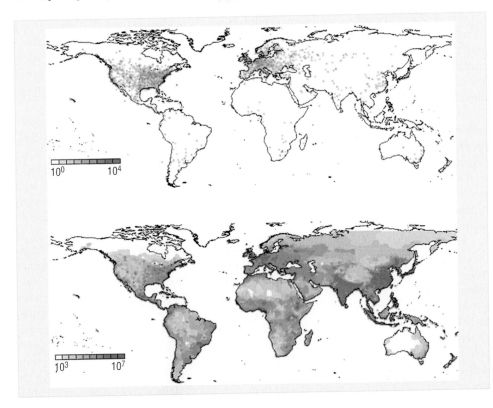

10^0 10^4

10^3 10^7

Media imperialism: watching *Grease* on Enaotai Island in West Papua, New Guinea

Media imperialism is the domination of a mass medium by a single national culture and the undermining of other national cultures.

Media convergence is the blending of the World Wide Web, television, and other communications media as new, hybrid media forms.

States, as are 15 of the 20 most popular search engines (Internet Software Consortium, 2003; "Search Engines," 2002). Some analysts say that American domination of the web is an example of **media imperialism**. Media imperialism is the control of a mass medium by a single national culture and the undermining of other national cultures. France and Canada are perhaps the countries that have spoken out most strongly against the perceived American threat to their national culture and identity. Some French and Canadian media analysts deeply resent the fact that the United States is the world's biggest exporter and smallest importer of mass media products, including web content.

The problem of media imperialism is felt particularly acutely in Canadian broadcasting because the country has a small population (smaller than California's), is close to the United States, and is about 75 percent English speaking. Private broadcasters dominate the Canadian market and rely mainly on American entertainment programming. Moreover, the widespread use of cable and satellite dishes permits most Canadians to receive American programming directly from source (Knight, 1998: 109–10).

According to some media analysts, the Internet not only restricts access and promotes American content, but also increases the power of media conglomerates. That is evident, for example, in the realm of **media convergence**. Media convergence is the blending of the World Wide Web, television, telephone, and other communications media into new, hybrid media forms. Many consumers find a personal computer (PC) too complex to operate and find TV limited in its functionality and entertainment value. Media convergence is intended to appeal mainly to such people. The most visible form of media convergence today is interactive TV.

Interactive TV involves the reception of digital signals via cable, satellite dish, or fibre-optic telephone line. An interactive TV is connected to the Web through a built-in computer and contains a hard drive big enough to record 12 to 30 hours of TV programs. If you have interactive TV in your household, you can instruct it to record the exact blend of programs you want to watch from a long menu of specialty channels. Existing or upcoming features include ordering feature-length movies, using e-mail, holding videoconferences with people in remote locations, visiting websites that offer information on the programs or movies you're watching, shopping for a wide variety of goods, doing your banking, and paying your utility bills—all from the convenience of your couch. The media giants are scrambling for market share. After all, they stand to earn many billions of dollars laying fibre-optic cable, building new media appliances, writing software, creating TV programs, and selling goods and services online.

The control of interactive TV by huge media conglomerates may seem like an old story. In some respects it is. Ownership of every mass medium has become more concentrated over time. Interactive TV seems poised to repeat the pattern more quickly than any other mass medium. Because entry costs are so high, only media giants can get involved.

However, this is a media story with a twist. The big media conglomerates may be able to carve out a new and lucrative niche for themselves by merging the Internet and television. However, they can never fully dominate the Internet. That is because it is the first mass medium that makes it relatively easy for consumers to become producers.

People are not just passive users of the Internet. Instead, they help to create it. For example, the Web boasts millions of personal websites. It contains more than 1500 non-commercial role-playing communities or multiple user dimensions (MUDs), with more than 75 000 registered users ("The MUD Connector," 2008). Second Life, a commercial MUD, claims to have nearly two million "residents" (Second, Life, 2006). In 2007, just three years after it was launched, Facebook boasted more than 21 million registered members. On any given day, two-thirds of them log on for an average of 20 minutes and view 1.6 billion pages, making Facebook the seventh most popular site on the Web (Ellison, Steinfeld, and Lampe, 2007). Tens of thousands of public-access cameras are connected to the Web, opening up a window to the goings-on in people's offices, college dorms, apartments, and frat houses. Many thousands of discussion groups exist on the Web. Each discussion group comprises people who discuss defined subjects by e-mail or in real time. Some discussion groups focus on particle physics. Others are devoted to banjos, lawyer jokes, Russian politics, sadomasochism, and just about every other human activity imaginable. The groups are self-governing bodies with their own rules and norms of "netiquette" (McLaughlin, Osborne, and Smith, 1995; Sudweeks, McLaughlin, and Rafaeli, 1999). Entry costs are relatively low. All you need to join or create a website, a MUD, or a discussion group is your own PC, some free or inexpensive software, and an Internet connection. The media conglomerates have limited control over the communities that are proliferating online.

So we see that we must temper the image of the Internet as a medium that is subject to increasing domination by large conglomerates. There is also a contrary trend. Individual users are making independent, creative contributions to Internet growth. Similarly, the view that the growth of the Web is an example of American media imperialism has not gone unchallenged. Where some media analysts see American media imperialism, others see globalization and postmodernization, social processes we introduced in Chapter 3, Culture. From the latter point of view, all cultures, including that of the United States, are becoming less homogeneous and more fragmented as they borrow elements from one another. Inexpensive international travel and telecommunications make this cultural blending possible. Thus, if you look carefully at the Web, you will see that even U.S. sites adopt content liberally from Latin America, Asia, and elsewhere. Just as international influences can be seen in today's hairstyles, clothing fashions, foods, and popular music, so can the Internet be seen as a site of globalization (Hall, 1992).

Of course, nobody knows exactly how the social forces we have outlined will play themselves out. A phenomenon like Napster emerges, enabling millions of people to share recorded music freely on the Web using a central server. Some analysts point to Napster as evidence of Internet democratization. Then the media conglomerates take Napster to court, forcing it to stop the giveaway on the grounds that it is effectively stealing royalties from musicians and profits from music companies. Some analysts see the court case as evidence of inevitable conglomeration on the Web. Then new Napster-like programs, such as Kazaa, Limewire, and Gnutella emerge (the latter is named after the popular chocolate and hazelnut paste because both spread easily). These programs allow people to share recorded music on the Web *without* a central server, making them virtually impossible to shut down. A group of record companies tried to close Kazaa by taking it to an American court for copyright infringement late in 2002. However, they discovered that the distributor of its software is incorporated in the tiny South Pacific island of Vanuatu. Kazaa is managed from Australia, its servers are in Denmark, its source code is stored in Estonia, its developers live in the Netherlands, and it has 60 million users in 150 countries. It is therefore highly doubtful that a decision on behalf of the record companies could be enforced ("Digital Dilemmas," 2003). And so the tug of war between conglomeration and democratization continues, with no end in sight. As one observer noted, "The recording industry's long-running battle against online music piracy has come to resemble one of those whack-a-mole arcade games, where the player hammers one rubber rodent's head with a mallet only to see another pop up nearby" (Lohr, 2003). One thing is clear, however. The speed of technological innovation and the many possibilities for individual creativity on the Internet make this an exciting era to be involved in the mass media and to study it sociologically.

NOTES

1. The following synopsis is based on the annual reports of the corporations. Revenue reported here for Quebecor does not include printing and related services. Revenue reported here for Rogers does not include wireless telephone services. Throughout, revenue is reported in Canadian dollars unless otherwise specified.

2. Conservatives often criticize the mass media for their allegedly liberal bias. We do not want to enter into this highly charged political debate. It should be noted, however, that the conservative critique of the mass media focuses only on the media's analysis of specific government and corporate policies, not on their analysis of stories relating to core values.

SUMMARY

1. What are the mass media?
   The mass media are means of transmitting information and entertainment from one person or group to another. The communication is typically from a few senders to many receivers. The mass media sometimes blur the line between reality and fantasy.

2. Which historical forces stimulated the growth of the mass media?
   Three main historical forces stimulated the growth of the mass media. The Protestant Reformation of the sixteenth century encouraged people to read the Bible themselves. The democratic movements that began in the late eighteenth century encouraged people to demand literacy. Beginning in the late nineteenth century, capitalist industrialization required rapid means of communication and fostered the mass media as important sources of profit.

3. What are the main theories of mass media effects?
   Functionalism stresses that the mass media act to coordinate society, exercise social control, and socialize and entertain people. Conflict theory stresses that the mass media reinforce social inequality. They do this both by acting as sources of profit for the few people who control media conglomerates and by promoting core values that help legitimize the existing social order. Interpretive approaches to studying the mass media stress that audiences actively filter, interpret, and sometimes even resist and reject media messages according to their interests and values. Feminist approaches concur and also emphasize the degree to which the mass media perpetuate gender and racial stereotypes.

KEY TERMS

cultural studies (p. 531)

mass media (p. 519)

media convergence (p. 536)

media imperialism (p. 536)

two-step flow of communication (p. 531)

QUESTIONS TO CONSIDER

1. Locate webcams in your region or community by searching on http://www. webcamsearch.com. Who has set up these webcams? For what purposes? How might they be used to strengthen ties among family members, friendship networks, special-interest groups, and so forth?

2. Phone TV and radio stations in your community to find out which are locally controlled and which are controlled by large media companies. If there are no locally controlled stations, does this fact have implications for the kind of news coverage and public affairs programming you may be watching? If there are locally controlled stations in your community, do they differ from stations owned by large media companies in terms of programming content, audience size, and audience type? If you can observe such differences, why do they exist?

3. The 1999 movie *Enemy of the State,* starring Will Smith, depicts one drawback of new media technologies: the possibility of intense government surveillance and violation of privacy rights. Do you think new media technologies are unqualified blessings or could they limit our freedom and privacy? If so, how? How could the capacity of new media technologies to limit freedom and privacy be limited?

WEB RESOURCES

Companion Website for This Book

http://www.compass3e.nelson.com

Begin by clicking on the Student Resources section of the website. Next, select the chapter you are studying from the pull-down menu. From the Student Resources page you have easy access to InfoTrac® College Edition, additional Weblinks, and other resources. The website also has many useful tips to aid you in your study of sociology, including practice tests for each chapter.

InfoTrac® Search Terms

These search terms are provided to assist you in beginning to conduct research on this topic by visiting http://www.infotrac-college.com:

cultural studies

media bias

media concentration

media convergence

media imperialism

Recommended Websites

NewsWatch Canada, from Simon Fraser University, "undertakes independent research on the diversity and thoroughness of news coverage in Canada's media, with a focus on identifying blindspots and double-standards." Go to http://www.sfu.ca/cmns/research/ newswatch/intro.html.

http://www.compass3e.nelson.com

The Media Awareness Network at http://www.media-awareness.ca is a Canadian site dedicated to improving the mass media for children by focusing on media education in the home, school, and community.

Media magazine, the journal of the Canadian Association of Journalists, is available online at http://www.caj.ca/mediamag/index.html.

The Media and Communications Studies Site at the University of Wales is one of the best sites on the Web devoted to the mass media. Among other interesting sections, it includes useful theoretical materials and resources on class, gender, and race in the mass media, mainly from a British perspective. Visit it at http://www.aber.ac.uk/media/index.html.

For useful resources on corporate ownership of the mass media and the social and political problems that result from increasingly concentrated media ownership with a primarily American focus, go to the Fairness and Accuracy in Report (FAIR) site at http://www.fair.org/media-woes/corporate.html.

CengageNOW™

http://hed.nelson.com

This online diagnostic tool identifies each student's unique needs with a Pretest that generates a personalized Study Plan for each chapter, helping students focus on concepts they're having the most difficulty mastering. Students then take a Posttest after reading the chapter to measure their understanding of the material. An Instructor Gradebook is available to track and monitor student progress.

CHAPTER

19

Health and Medicine

In this chapter, you will learn that

- Health risks are unevenly distributed in human populations. Men and women, upper and lower classes, rich and poor countries, and privileged and disadvantaged members of racial and ethnic groups are exposed to health risks to varying degrees.

- On several measures of health, Canada ranks among the top countries in the world. Canada's health care system provides access to universal comprehensive coverage for medically necessary in-patient and outpatient physical services. Still, many low-income and moderate-income Canadians have limited or no access to such health services as eye care, dentistry, mental health counselling, and prescription drugs.

- The average health status of Americans is lower than the average health status of people in other rich postindustrial countries, such as Canada. That is partly because the level of social inequality is higher in the United States and partly because the health care system makes it difficult for many people to receive adequate care.

- The dominance of medical science is due to its successful treatments and the way in which doctors excluded competitors and established control over their profession and their clients.

- In some respects, modern medicine is a victim of its own success. For example, the wide availability of antibiotics has led to lax hygiene in hospitals, the spread of drug-resistant germs, and an epidemic of hospital infections leading to death.

- Patient activism, alternative medicine, and holistic medicine promise to improve the quality of health care in Canada and globally.

THE BLACK DEATH

In 1346, rumours reached Europe of a plague sweeping the East. Originating in Asia, the epidemic spread along trade routes to China and Russia. A year later, 12 galleys sailed from southern Russia to Italy. Diseased sailors were on board. Their lymph nodes were terribly swollen and eventually burst, causing a painful death. Anyone who came in contact with the sailors was soon infected. As a result, their ships were driven out of several Italian and French ports in succession. Yet the disease spread relentlessly, again moving along trade routes to Spain, Portugal, and England. Within two years, the Black Death, as it came to be known, killed a third of Europe's population. Six hundred and fifty years later, the plague still ranks as the most devastating catastrophe in human history (Herlihy, 1998; McNeill, 1976; Zinsser, 1935).

Today we know that the cause of the plague was a bacillus that spread from lice to rats to people. It spread so efficiently because many people lived close together in unsanitary conditions. In the middle of the fourteenth century, however, nobody knew anything about germs. Therefore, Pope Clement VI sent a delegation to Europe's leading medical school in Paris to discover the cause of the plague. The learned professors studied the problem. They reported that a particularly unfortunate conjunction of Saturn, Jupiter, and Mars in the sign of Aquarius had occurred in 1345. The resulting hot, humid conditions caused the earth to emit poisonous vapours. To prevent the plague, they said, people should refrain from eating poultry, waterfowl, pork, beef, fish, and olive oil. They should not sleep during the daytime or engage in excessive exercise. Nothing should be cooked in rainwater. Bathing should be avoided at all costs.

We do not know whether the pope followed the professors' advice. We do know he made a practice of sitting between two large fires to breathe pure air. Because the plague bacillus is destroyed by heat, this may have saved his life. Other people were less fortunate. Some rang church bells and fired cannons to drive the plague away. Others burned incense, wore charms, and cast spells. But, other than the pope, the only people to have much luck in avoiding the plague were the well-to-do (who could afford to flee the densely populated cities for remote areas in the countryside) and the Jews (whose religion required that they wash their hands before meals, bathe once a week, and conduct burials soon after death).

Some of the main themes of the sociology of health and medicine are embedded in the story of the Black Death, or at least implied by it. First, recall that some groups were more likely to die of the plague than others were. This is a common pattern. Health risks are almost always unevenly distributed. Women and men, upper and lower classes, rich and poor countries, and privileged and disadvantaged members of racial and ethnic groups are exposed to health risks to varying degrees. This suggests that health is not just a medical issue but also a sociological one. The first task we set ourselves below is to examine the sociological factors that account for the uneven distribution of health in society.

Second, the story of the Black Death suggests that health problems change over time. Epidemics of various types still break out, but there can be no Black Death where sanitation and hygiene prevent the spread of disease. Today we are also able to treat many infectious diseases, such as tuberculosis and pneumonia, with antibiotics. Twentieth-century medical science developed these wonder drugs and many other life-saving therapies. Medical successes allow people to live longer than they used to. **Life expectancy** is the average age at death of the members of a population. Life expectancy in Canada in 1831 was approximately 40 years for men and 42 years for women (Lavoie and Oderkirk, 2000: 3). In contrast, a

Life expectancy is the average age at death of the members of a population.

Canadian girl born in 2005 can hope to live to 83, a boy to 78. Yet, because of increased life expectancy, degenerative conditions, such as cancer and heart disease, have an opportunity to develop in a way that was not possible a century ago (see Table 19.1).

The story of the Black Death raises a third issue, too. We cannot help being struck by the superstition and ignorance surrounding the treatment of the ill in medieval times. Remedies were often herbal but also included earthworms, urine, and animal excrement. People believed it was possible to maintain good health by keeping body fluids in balance. Therefore, cures that released body fluids were common. These included hot baths, laxatives, and diuretics, which increase the flow of urine. If these treatments didn't work, bloodletting was often prescribed. No special qualifications were required to administer medical treatment. Barbers doubled as doctors.

However, the backwardness of medieval medical practice, and the advantages of modern scientific medicine, can easily be exaggerated. For example, medieval doctors stressed the importance of prevention, exercise, a balanced diet, and a congenial environment in maintaining good health. We now know this is sound advice. Conversely, one of the great shortcomings of modern medicine is its emphasis on high-tech cures rather than on preventive and environmental measures. Therefore, in the final section of this chapter, we investigate how

	Deaths per 100 000 Population	Percentage of Deaths	Ratio Male:Female
1901			
1. Tuberculosis	180.8	12.0	–
2. Bronchitis and pneumonia	150.9	10.0	–
3. Affections of the intestines	136.9	9.1	–
4. Senile debility	111.5	7.4	–
5. Congenital debility	106.0	7.0	–
6. Diseases of the heart	84.5	5.6	–
7. Apoplexy and paralysis	67.2	4.4	–
8. Diphtheria and croup	59.7	3.9	–
9. Accidents	51.3	3.4	–
10. Cancer	42.3	2.8	–
11. Influenza	39.7	2.6	–
2004			
1. Major cardiovascular disease	226.2	31.9	1.00
2. Cancer	209.4	29.6	1.13
3. Chronic and acute respiratory diseases other than pneumonia and influenza	31.7	4.4	1.14
4. Accidents	28.1	4.0	1.55
5. Pneumonia and influenza	17.9	2.5	0.82
6. Alzheimer's disease	17.9	2.5	0.41
Other less prevalent causes			
Suicide	11.3	1.6	3.20
Homicide	1.6	0.2	2.56
HIV/Aids	1.3	0.2	4.40
Other	163.4	23.1	–
Total	708.6	100.0	1.04

TABLE 19.1

Leading Causes of Death, Canada, 1901 and 2004

Sources: 1901 data adapted from Dawson, 1906; 2004 data adapted from Statistics Canada, 2007c.

the medical professions gained substantial control over health issues and promoted their own approach to well-being, and how those professions have been challenged in recent years.

HEALTH AND INEQUALITY

Defining and Measuring Health

Health, according to the World Health Organization (WHO), **health** is

> the ability of an individual to achieve his [or her] potential and to respond positively to the challenges of the environment. . . . The basic resources for health are income, shelter and food. Improvement in health requires a secure foundation in these basics, but also information and life skills; a supportive environment, providing opportunities for making health choices among goods, services and facilities; and conditions in the economic, social and physical environments . . . that enhance health. (World Health Organization, 2000)

Health, according to the World Health Organization, is "the ability of an individual to achieve his [or her] potential and to respond positively to the challenges of the environment."

The WHO definition lists in broad terms the main factors that promote good health. However, when it comes to *measuring* the health of a population, sociologists typically examine the negative: rates of illness and death. They reason that healthy populations experience less illness and longer life than unhealthy populations. This is the approach we follow here.

Assuming ideal conditions, how long can a person live? To date, the record is held by Jeanne Louise Calment, a French woman who died in 1997 at the age of 122. (Other people claim to be older, but they lack authenticated birth certificates.)

Calment was an extraordinary individual. She took up fencing at age 85, rode a bicycle until she was 100, gave up smoking at 120, and released a rap CD at 121 (Matalon, 1997). In contrast, only 1 in 100 people in the world's rich countries now lives to be 100. Since 1840 life expectancy in the world's most favoured population has increased at a steady rate of 2.5 years per decade and shows no signs of either accelerating or of approaching some limit. Further increases in the coming century thus seem likely, and if there is an upper limit we don't know what it might be. By 2006, the world's highest life expectancy was 82 years in Japan. By 2050, the upper limit is projected to reach 92 years (Oeppen and Vaupel, 2002).

Unfortunately, conditions are nowhere near ideal. Life expectancy throughout the world is generally less than the 82 years in Japan today. Figure 19.1 shows life expectancy in selected countries. Life expectancy was one to four years shorter in Canada and the other rich postindustrial countries than it was in Japan. But in India, life expectancy was only 64 years. People in the impoverished African country of Swaziland have the world's shortest life expectancy at 33 years, two years lower than life expectancy in Europe in 1600. More than half a billion people in 32 countries—most in sub-Saharan Africa—have a life expectancy less than 50 years (Geohive.com, 2005).

Accounting for the difference between the highest average human life span in the world and life expectancy in a given country is one of the main tasks of the sociologist of health. For example, although the current highest average human life span is 82 years, life expectancy in Canada is 80 years. This implies that, on average, Canadians are being deprived of about two years of life because of avoidable *social* causes ($82 - 80 = 2$). Avoidable social causes deprive the average citizen of Swaziland of 49 years of life ($82 - 33 = 49$). Clearly, social causes have a big—and variable—impact on illness and death. We must therefore discuss them in detail.

The Social Causes of Illness and Death

People get sick and die partly because of natural causes. One person may have a genetic predisposition to cancer. Another may come in contact with a deadly Ebola virus in the environment. However, over and above such natural causes of illness and death, we can single out three types of *social* causes:

In the twenty-first century, the maximum life span may increase because of medical advances. So far, the record for longevity is held by Jeanne Louise Calment, a French woman who died in 1997 at the age of 122.

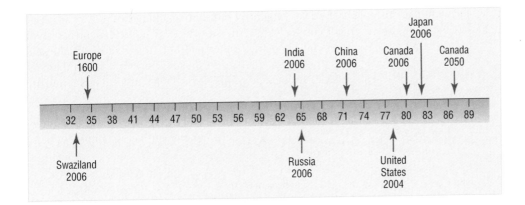

FIGURE 19.1
Life Expectancy, Selected
Countries and Years

Sources: Population Reference
Bureau, 2007; Tuljapurkar, Li,
and Boe, 2000.

1. *Human-environmental factors.* Major health risks arise from how environments are shaped by human activity. Divisions like social class, occupation, and nationality often correspond to sharp differences in the surroundings in which people work and live. Some environments foster good health, while others impose added risks for poor health. For example, the introduction of sour gas wells and logging operations around the reserves of the Lubicon First Nation in Alberta resulted in a dramatic increase in illness. More than one in three members of the Lubicon population suffers from such health problems as tuberculosis, respiratory difficulties, and cancer at rates far above the national average (Barlow and May, 2000: 183). **Environmental racism**, or the tendency for hazardous waste sites and polluting industries to be located near First Nations communities or areas populated by the poor, the politically marginalized, or certain visible minority groups, also contributes to lower levels of health. For example, in the 1980s, the pulp-and-paper industry's mercury poisoning of the English-Wabigoon river system in western Ontario near the Manitoba border led to the virtual destruction of the Grassy Narrows Indians' way of life and means of livelihood (Shkilnyk, 1985). More recently, "patterns of atmospheric cycling have made the North a dumping ground for industrial chemicals that . . . [are] never used there. The chemicals bioaccumulate, delivering a higher level of toxic concentration to each level up the food chain. As a result, the breast milk of Inuit mothers is ten times as contaminated as that of southern Canadian women (Barlow and May, 2000: 184). This situation provides a striking illustration of how human–environmental conditions can cause illness and death (see Chapter 22, Technology and the Global Environment, online at http://www.brym.sociologycompass3.nelson.com).

   Environmental racism is the tendency to heap environmental dangers on the disadvantaged.

2. *Lifestyle factors.* Smoking, excessive use of alcohol and drugs, poor diet, lack of exercise, and social isolation are among the chief lifestyle factors associated with poor health and premature death. For example, smoking is associated with lung cancer, cardiovascular disease, strokes, emphysema, spontaneous abortion, premature birth, and neonatal death. In Canada, about 50 000 deaths a year are caused by smoking and other use of tobacco products. About a fifth of all deaths can be attributed to tobacco use (Makomaski Illing and Kaiserman, 2004). As a cause of early death, smoking far outweighs the combined impact of suicide, homicide and accidents. Social isolation, too, affects a person's chance of becoming ill and dying prematurely. Thus, unmarried people have a greater chance of dying prematurely than do married people. At any age, the death of a spouse increases a person's chance of dying, while remarrying decreases the chance of dying (Helsing, Szklo, and Comstock, 1981). Social isolation is a particularly big problem among older people who retire, lose a spouse and friends, and cannot rely on family members or state institutions for social support. Such people are prone to fall into a state of depression, which contributes to ill health.

3. *Factors related to the public health and health care systems.* The state of a nation's health depends partly on public and private efforts to improve people's well-being and treat their illnesses. The **public health system** comprises government-run programs that ensure access to clean drinking water, basic sewage and sanitation services, and

   The public health system comprises government-run programs that ensure access to clean drinking water, basic sewage and sanitation services, and inoculation against infectious diseases.

The health care system **is composed of a nation's clinics, hospitals, and other facilities for ensuring health and treating illness.**

inoculation against infectious diseases. The absence of a public health system is associated with high rates of disease and low life expectancy. The **health care system** comprises a nation's clinics, hospitals, and other facilities for ensuring health and treating illness. The absence of a system that ensures its citizens access to a minimum standard of health care is also associated with high rates of disease and shorter life expectancy.

Exposure to all three sets of social causes of illness and death listed above is strongly related to country of residence, class, race, and gender. We now consider the impact of these factors, beginning with country of residence.

Country of Residence

HIV/AIDS is the leading cause of death in urban Haiti. Extreme poverty has forced many Haitians to become prostitutes. They cater mainly to tourists from North America and Europe. Some of those tourists carried HIV, the virus that leads to AIDS, and they introduced it into Haiti. The absence of adequate health care and medical facilities in Haiti makes the epidemic's impact all the more devastating (Farmer, 1992).

HIV/AIDS is also the leading cause of death in the poverty-stricken part of Africa south of the Sahara desert. Table 19.2 shows that by 2007, 22.5 million sub-Saharan Africans—5 percent of the adult population—were living with HIV/AIDS. In contrast, 0.6 percent of North American adults and 0.3 percent of Western European adults were living with HIV/AIDS. This means that HIV/AIDS is more than 8 times more common in sub-Saharan Africa than in North America and nearly 17 times more common than in Western Europe. Spending on research and treatment is concentrated overwhelmingly in the rich countries of North America and Western Europe. As the case of HIV/AIDS illustrates, global inequality influences the exposure of people to different health risks.

Prosperity increases health through biomedical advances, such as new medicines and diagnostic tools. In particular, vaccines against infectious diseases have done much to improve health and ensure longer life. However, the creation of a sound public health system was even more important in this regard. If a country can provide its citizens with clean water and a sewage system, epidemics decline in frequency and severity while life expectancy soars.

The industrialized countries started to develop their public health systems in the mid-nineteenth century. Social reformers, concerned citizens, scientists, and doctors joined industrialists and politicians in urging governments to develop health policies that would help create a healthier labour force and citizenry (Bricker and Greenspon, 2001: 178–83; Goubert, 1989 [1986]; McNeill, 1976). But what was possible in North America and Western Europe 150 years ago is not possible in many developing countries today. Most of us take clean water for granted, but more than a sixth of the world's people do not have access to a sanitary water supply (de Villiers, 1999).

Other indicators of health inequality for selected countries are given in Table 19.3. We see that, in general, there is a positive association between national wealth and good health. Canada, the United States, and Japan are rich countries. They spend a substantial part of their wealth on health care. Many physicians and nurses service the populations. As a result, **infant mortality** (the annual number of deaths before the age of one for every 1000 live births) is low. Mexico, which is poorer than Canada, the United States, and Japan, spends a smaller proportion of its wealth on health care. Accordingly, its

GLOBAL
PERSPECTIVE

Infant mortality is the number of deaths before the age of one for every 1000 live births in a population in one year.

A health worker at Nazareth House in Cape Town, South Africa, lavishes care and attention on some of the 41 infected children in her care. Nearly one-fifth of South Africa's adult population is infected with HIV/AIDS.

Beginning of HIV/AIDS Epidemic	People Living with HIV/AIDS	Adult Prevalence (Percentage of Population)	AIDS Deaths, 2007
Late 1970s–Early 1980s			
Sub-Saharan Africa	22 500 000	5.0	1 600 000
Latin America	1 600 000	0.5	58 000
Caribbean	230 000	1.0	11 000
Western Europe	760 000	0.3	12 000
North America	1 300 000	0.6	21 000
Australia and New Zealand	75 000	0.4	1 400
Late 1980s			
North Africa and Middle East	380 000	0.3	25 000
South and Southeast Asia	4 000 000	0.3	270 000
East Asia and Pacific	800 000	0.1	32 000
Early 1990s			
Eastern Europe and Central Asia	1 600 000	0.9	55 000
Total		0.8	2 100 000

TABLE 19.2

A Global View of HIV/AIDS, 2007

Source: United Nations, 2007: 7. The United Nations is the author of the original material.

population is less healthy in a number of respects. The sub-Saharan country of Swaziland is one of the poorest countries in the world. It spends little on health care, has few medical personnel, and suffers from high rates of infant mortality.

Class Inequalities and Health Care

In Canada, despite our system of universal health care, socioeconomic status is related to numerous aspects of health and illness (Raphael, 2004). On average, people with low income die at a younger age than do people with high income. Canadians experience lower rates of sickness, improved health, and longer life expectancies at each step up the income ladder (Health Canada, 1999a, 1999b). A broad range of psychiatric conditions is associated with low socioeconomic status (Williams and Collins, 1999). Poverty is also associated with high rates of tobacco and alcohol consumption, obesity, physical inactivity, and violence (Health Canada, 1999a). But researchers find that "behavioral risk factors [including tobacco use, heavy drinking, and obesity] are rather weak predictors of health status as compared to socioeconomic and demographic measures of which income is a major component" (Raphael, 2004: 10).

Country	Expenditure on Health as Percentage of GDP	Nurses per 1000 Population	Physicians per 1000 Population	Infant Mortality per 1000 Live Births	Deaths per Year Due to HIV/AIDS per 100 000 Population
Japan	7.8	7.79	1.98	3.0	1
Canada	9.8	9.95	2.14	5.0	1
United States	15.4	9.37	2.56	7.0	5
Mexico	6.5	0.90	1.98	22.0	6
Swaziland	4.2	0.20	0.02	150.0	54

TABLE 19.3

Health Indicators, Selected Countries, c. 2007

Source: World Health Organization, 2007.

This pattern may be observed in and between many countries. Longevity and health follow a social gradient. At each successive lower rung in various social hierarchies, we find shorter life expectancies and higher rates of health problems. A social gradient is apparent for cancer, heart disease, accidental injury, and a long list of other conditions. It appears for various social hierarchies including income, education, occupational status, and membership in socially excluded groups (Wilkinson and Marmot, 2003): "It took the poorest fifth of urban Canadians until the mid-1990s to reach the life expectancy experienced by the richest fifth 25 years earlier" (Canadian Institute for Health Information, 2004: 25).

Why does health deteriorate as we move down the class hierarchy? Sociologists have proposed several explanations:

1. *High stress and the inability to cope with it.* People in lower classes experience relatively high stress levels because of their deprived and difficult living conditions (Kessler et al., 1994). Stress has been linked to a variety of physical and mental health problems, including high blood pressure, cancer, chronic fatigue, violence, and substance abuse. Moreover, people higher up in the class structure are often able to turn stress off. They can, for instance, more easily take a few days off work or go on vacation. Many problems are more burdensome when resources like money and influence are not available to address them. Upper-class people can pay others to fix their cars or their offspring's legal mishaps or whatever else may arise. Lower-class families may have to go into debt or simply accept some bad outcomes as unavoidable (Cockerham, 1998; Epstein, 1998; Evans, 1999, Wilkinson and Marmot, 2003). Mishaps aside, lower-class families must endure greater crowding; poorer dwelling quality; working conditions that are more noxious, dangerous, or unpleasant; and longer hours of work to make ends meet.

2. *Differences in the earliest stages of development that have lifelong consequences.* Inequalities at the start of life have strong health consequences for a lifetime (Forrest and Riley, 2004). For example, "poor circumstances during pregnancy can lead to less than optimal fetal development via a chain that may include deficiencies in nutrition during pregnancy, maternal stress, a greater likelihood of maternal smoking and misuse of drugs and alcohol, insufficient exercise and inadequate prenatal care" (Wilkinson and Marmot, 2003: 14). Mothers who have low income or little education are more likely to provide such unfavourable starts to life.

3. *Lack of knowledge.* People who are less educated and who have less exposure to educated advisers tend to have less knowledge about healthy lifestyles. For example, they are less likely to know what constitutes a nutritious diet. This, too, contributes to their propensity to illness. Illness, in turn, makes it more difficult for poor people to escape poverty (Abraham, 1993).

4. *Unequal access to health resources.* A disproportionately large number of poor Canadians live in areas that have inferior medical services. For example, there are fewer hospitals, physicians, and nurses per capita in rural areas than in urban areas. As well, the quality of preventive, diagnostic, and treatment facilities is generally superior in urban areas. Moreover, although access to health care remains largely unrelated to income because of Canada's medicare system, many low- and moderate-income Canadians have limited or no access to eye care, dentistry, mental health counselling, and prescription drugs (Boychuk, 2002; Health Canada, 1999b).

5. *Environmental exposure.* As we saw above, poor people are more likely to be exposed to environmental risks that have a negative impact on their health. There is a striking lack of incinerators, pulp and paper mills, oil refineries, dumpsites, factories, and mines in Westmount (Montreal), Tuxedo (Winnipeg), Rosedale (Toronto), and other wealthy Canadian neighbourhoods (see Chapter 22, Technology and the Global Environment).

Biomedical advances increase life expectancy, but the creation of a sound public health system has even more dramatic effects.

Racial Inequalities in Health Care

Racial disparities in health status are also large. For example, the life expectancy of Status Indians[1] is seven to eight years shorter than that of non-Aboriginal Canadians, and illegal drug use is high among Aboriginal peoples (Canadian Aboriginal News, 2001; Canadian Institute for Health Information, 2004; Scott, 1997). Despite the health risks posed to both the mother and the developing fetus, a national survey found that 76 percent of Inuit women and 54 percent of Indian women smoke during pregnancy, more than two to three times the national average (Canadian Centre on Substance Abuse, 1999).

Such health disparities are partly due to economic differences among racial groups. In addition, researchers have emphasized how racially marginalized groups are subject to negative health outcomes because of the cumulative effects of social exclusion based on race. Researchers have observed these effects for African Americans in the United States, Aboriginal Canadians, and other groups (Galabuzi, 2004; Wilkinson and Marmot, 2003).

How does social exclusion influence health apart from the obvious fact that excluded groups experience higher rates of poverty? In brief, labour market segregation, high unemployment, low occupation status, substandard housing, dangerous or distressed neighbourhoods, homelessness, dangerous worksites, extended hours, multiple jobs, and experience with everyday forms of racism lead to unequal health service utilization and differential health status (Galabuzi, 2004: 3). Even when members of socially excluded groups are employed, they are more likely to continue to live in inferior areas because of racial discrimination in housing, and such areas typically suffer from reduced access to medical services. Those who nevertheless seek medical services often encounter racially based misunderstanding or even hostility. The cumulative result of these and other factors is considerable—27 percent of First Nations members living on reserves report fair or poor health, compared with only 12 percent of other Canadians (Canadian Institute for Health Information, 2004: 81).

Gender Inequalities in Health Care: The Feminist Contribution

Feminist scholars have brought health inequalities based on gender to the attention of the sociological community. In a review of the relevant literature, one researcher concluded that such gender inequalities are substantial (Haas, 1998):

- Gender bias exists in medical research. Public health systems have been slow to address and more likely to neglect women's health issues than men's health issues. Thus, more research has focused on "men's diseases," such as cardiac arrest, than on "women's diseases," such as breast cancer. Similarly, women have been excluded from participating in major health research studies that have examined the relationship between Aspirin use and heart disease; and how cholesterol levels, blood pressure, and smoking affect heart disease (Johnson and Fee, 1997). Medical research is only beginning to explore the fact that women may react differently from men to some illnesses and may require different treatment regimes.
- Gender bias also exists in medical treatment. For example, women undergo fewer kidney transplants, cardiac procedures, and other treatments than men do.
- Because, on average, women live longer than men do, they experience greater lifetime risk of functional disability and chronic illness, and greater need for long-term care. The low status of women in many less developed countries results in their being nutritionally deprived and having less access to medical care than do men. As a result, women in developing countries suffer high rates of mortality and **morbidity** (acute and chronic illness) because of high rates of complication associated with pregnancy and childbirth. About one-quarter to one-half of deaths among women in developing countries are attributed to pregnancy-related complications ("Maternal Mortality," 1998).
- Canadian women face a higher risk than men do of poverty after divorce and of widowhood. Because, as we have seen, poverty contributes to ill health, we could expect improvements in women's economic standing to be reflected in improved health status for women.

In sum, although on average women live longer than men do, gender inequalities have a negative impact on women's health. Women's health is negatively affected by differences between women and men in access to gender-appropriate medical research and treatment, as well as the economic resources needed to secure adequate health care.

Morbidity refers to acute and chronic illness.

Comparative Health Care from Conflict and Functionalist Perspectives

We noted earlier that rich countries spend more on health care than poor countries do, as a result of which their populations enjoy longer life expectancy. We should not infer from this generalization that money always buys good health, however. The United States spends nearly twice as much per person on health care as Japan and nearly 60 percent more than Canada. The United States has 20 percent more doctors per 100 000 people than Canada does and almost 30 percent more than Japan does. Yet the United States has a higher rate of infant mortality and shorter life expectancy than Canada and Japan do. The American case shows that spending more money on health care does not always improve the health of a nation.

What accounts for the American anomaly? Why do Americans spend far more on health care than any other country in the world yet wind up with a population that, on average, is less healthy than the populations of other rich countries?

One reason for the anomaly is that the gap between rich and poor is greater in the United States than in Canada, Japan, Sweden, France, and other rich countries. In general, the higher the level of inequality in a country, the more unhealthy its population is (Wilkinson, 1996). Because, as we saw in Chapter 8, Social Stratification: Canadian and Global Perspectives, the United States contains a higher percentage of poor people than do other rich countries, its average level of health is lower. Moreover, because income inequality has widened in the United States since the early 1970s, health disparities among income groups have grown (Williams and Collins, 1995).

A second reason for the American anomaly is that the cost of health care is unusually high in the United States (Anderson, Reinhardt, Hussey, and Petrosyan, 2003: 89). Physicians, hospitals, pharmaceutical companies, and other providers of health care goods and services are able to charge substantially higher prices in the United States than elsewhere (see Box 19.1). To understand why they are able to do so, we must examine the American health care system from a comparative perspective.

BOX 19.1
Social Policy: What Do You Think?

The High Cost of Prescription Drugs

Americans pay more for prescription drugs than anyone else in the world does. In 2002, prescription drug prices in other rich countries were 37 percent to 53 percent below American prices (see Figure 19.2). Between 1998 and 2002, the price of prescription drugs in the United States increased three times faster than the rate of inflation and faster than any other item in the nation's health care budget. Seniors and people with chronic medical conditions, such as diabetes, feel the burden most acutely because they are the biggest prescription drug users.

Other rich countries keep prescription drug prices down through some form of government regulation. For example, since 1987, Canadian drug companies have not been able to increase prices of brand-name drugs above the inflation rate. New brand-name drugs cannot exceed the highest Canadian price of comparable drugs used to treat the same disease. For new brand-name drugs that are unique and have no competitors, the price must be no higher than the median price for that drug in the United Kingdom, France, Italy, Germany, Sweden, Switzerland, and the United States. If a company breaks the rules, the government requires a price adjustment. If the

government deems that a company has deliberately flouted the law, it imposes a fine (Patent Medicine Prices Review Board, 2002). Not surprisingly, more than one million Americans now regularly buy their brand-name prescription drugs directly from Canadian pharmacies.

American drug manufacturers justify their high prices by claiming they need the money for research and development (R&D). The American public benefits from R&D, they say, while lower drug prices impair R&D in other countries.

Their argument would be more convincing if evidence showed that price curbs actually hurt R&D. However,

FIGURE 19.2

Prescription Drug Costs in Eight Rich Countries

Source: Patent Medicine Prices Review Board Annual Report, 2002: 23.

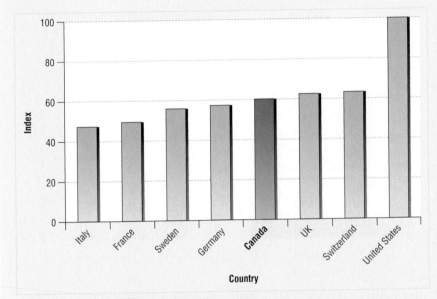

ticals is the most profitable industry by far. In 2001, profit as a percentage of revenue was 18.5 percent—four times higher than that of all other industries combined. We also know that drug companies spend about half as much on advertising and promotions as they do on R&D. This drives up drug prices. Finally, we know that the pharmaceutical industry spends more on lobbying and political campaign contributions than any other U.S. industry. Spending $197 million in 1999–2000, it hired 625 Washington lobbyists, more than one for each member of Congress. Most of the lobbying effort is aimed at influencing members of Congress to maintain a free market in drug prices (Barry, 2002a, 2002b, 2002c).

Why do you think the United States is at the forefront of attempts to maintain a free market in prescription drugs? In countries that regulate prescription drugs, like Canada, are there negative consequences to extending regulation? If so, what are the negative consequences? If not, then how might prescription drugs be further regulated to benefit the population?

in the U.K., where the government regulates prescription drug costs, drug companies spend 20 percent of their sales revenue on R&D. In the United States, the figure is just 12.5 percent. In Canada, expenditure on R&D has increased 1500 percent since the beginning of government regulation (1987–2002). This hardly suggests that price regulation hurts R&D (Barry, 2002c; Patent Medicine Prices Review Board, 2002: 49).

What we can say with confidence is that in the United States, pharmaceu-

You will recall from our discussion in Chapter 1, A Sociological Compass, and elsewhere that conflict theory is concerned mainly with the question of how privileged groups seek to maintain their advantages and subordinate groups seek to increase theirs. As such, conflict theory is an illuminating approach to analyzing the American health care system. We can usefully see health care in the United States as a system of privilege for some and disadvantage for others. It thus contributes to the poor health of less well-to-do Americans.

Consider, for example, that the United States lacks a public system of health insurance that covers the entire population. In the United Kingdom, Sweden, and Denmark, public spending on health care is about 85 percent of the total; in Japan and Germany it is around 80 percent; and in France, Canada, Italy, and Australia it is around 70 percent. The governments of Germany, Italy, Belgium, Denmark, Finland, Greece, Iceland, Luxembourg, Norway, and Spain cover almost all health care costs, including drugs, glasses, dental care, and prostheses. In the United States, only seniors, the poor, and veterans receive medical benefits from the government under the Medicare, Medicaid, and military health care programs. The American government pays about 45 percent of all medical costs out of taxes. Roughly 50 million Americans lack health insurance and another 50 million lack adequate coverage (Anderson et al., 2003; "Health Care Systems," 2001; Schoen, Doty, Collins, and Holmgren, 2005; Starr, 1994). The distinctive feature of the American health care system—substantial private provision—is a very expensive mechanism that leaves many people poorly served. The relatively privileged obtain health services at high prices while the less well-off are effectively priced out (Box 19.2 on page 552).

BOX 19.2
Sociology at the Movies

TAKE   ROLL

Sicko (2007)

Roughly a sixth of Americans have no access to health care and another sixth lack adequate coverage. It would be too easy to tell horror stories about the former, so Michael Moore's *Sicko* does not dwell on them. Instead, his widely acclaimed documentary tells viewers how ordinary Americans who have health care are routinely shocked to discover just how inadequate their coverage is. Here are three cases in point:

- A woman faints on a sidewalk and is taken to the hospital by ambulance, but her insurer bills her for the trip because she didn't have it pre-authorized. "How could I have it pre-authorized when I was unconscious?" she asks.
- When the World Trade Center was attacked in 2001, some brave souls volunteered to help rescue people. Many of them later developed respiratory and other problems but their insurers refused to cover their medical and drug expenses because they voluntarily put themselves at risk.
- A life of hard work enabled Larry and Donna to own their own house and put all six of their children through college. Now retired, and with Larry in poor health, they must sell their house to pay for medical fees not covered by their insurer. They are forced to move into a small

In *Sicko* a doctor explains to an astounded Michael Moore the operation of the British health care system.

room in the home of one of their adult children.

This is what happens when health care becomes a profit-making enterprise. People are forced to visit only the doctors and hospitals designated by their health maintenance organizations (HMOs)—privately owned companies that administer medical treatment in return for a fee paid by individuals, unions, and employers. HMOs give bonuses to claims investigators and doctors for denying claims and avoiding expensive procedures. Fine print denies treatment for medical conditions that existed prior to signing up with an HMO. These mechanisms help to make HMOs profitable, but they lower life expectancy in the United States below

the level of life expectancy in other rich countries.

Moore visits Canada, France, the U.K., and Cuba, and makes the health care systems of these countries seem perfect. They are not. For example, Canadians know all too well that governments and the medical community are working hard (and with some success) to shorten waiting times for elective surgery and diagnostic procedures, increase the availability of expensive imagining equipment, and so on. But whatever the shortcomings of universal medical care, *Sicko* serves as a cautionary tale for those who sing the praises of privatization. As Moore says, "If you want to stay healthy in America, don't get sick."

Private Health Insurance

In the absence of universal provision, health care for Americans turns on private insurance plans. Most people who have private health insurance obtain it through their employers or unions. Good versus bad insurance coverage becomes a class difference—a form of privilege and underprivilege. About 85 percent of employees receive their health coverage through health maintenance organizations (HMOs; Gorman, 1998). HMOs are private corporations. They collect regular payments from employers and employees. When an employee needs medical treatment, an HMO administers it.

Like all corporations, HMOs pursue profit. They employ four main strategies to keep their shareholders happy. Unfortunately, all four strategies lower the average quality of health care in the United States (Kuttner, 1998a, 1998b):

1. Some HMOs avoid covering sick people and people who are likely to get sick. This keeps their costs down. For example, if an HMO can show that you had a medical condition before you came under its care, the HMO won't cover you for that condition.
2. HMOs try to minimize the cost of treating sick people they can't avoid covering. Thus, HMOs have doctor-compensation formulas that reward doctors for withholding treatments that are unprofitable.
3. There have been allegations that some HMOs routinely inflate diagnoses to maximize reimbursements. In 2000, Columbia/HCA, the largest for-profit hospital chain in the United States, agreed to pay the federal government $745 million to settle a federal billing fraud investigation (Galewitz, 2000).
4. HMOs keep overhead charges high. Administrative costs are higher in the private sector of the health care system than in the public sector in almost every country for which data are available. Administrative costs are more than twice as high in the private sector of the American health care system as in the public sector (Figure 19.3).

Despite these drawbacks, running HMOs and other health care institutions, such as hospitals, as for-profit organizations has one big advantage. It is an advantage that functionalists would undoubtedly highlight because they tend to emphasize the contribution of social institutions to the smooth operation of society. Health organizations are so profitable that they can invest enormous sums in research, development, the latest diagnostic equipment, and high salaries to attract many of the best medical researchers and practitioners on the planet. Significantly, for people with adequate coverage, waiting times to see doctors and receive treatment are very short by international standards. Compare the United States with Canada in these respects. In 2003, the United States had twice as many magnetic resonance imaging machines (MRIs) per person as Canada (OECD, 2005). The extended waiting time for non-emergency surgery in Canada has become a hot political issue and it is not unusual for well-to-do Canadians who need elective surgery to travel to the United States and pay for it there. All this suggests that the United States enjoys the best health care system in the world—for those who can afford it.

The main supporters of the current United States health care system are the stockholders of the 1500 private health insurance companies and the physicians and other health professionals who get to work with the latest medical equipment, conduct cutting-edge research, and earn high salaries. Thus, HMOs and the American Medical Association have been at the forefront of attempts to convince Americans that the largely private system of health care serves the public better than any state-run system could.

Still, the American medical system is relatively unpopular. Larger proportions of the American public favour extreme reform than is true in other countries where state provision

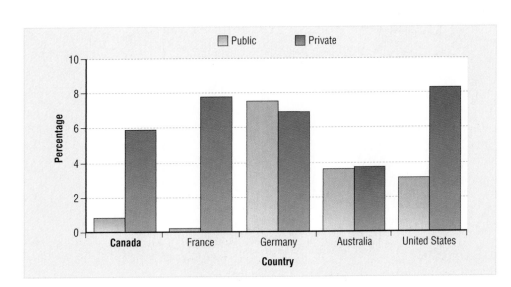

FIGURE 19.3

Administrative Costs as a Percentage of Health Care Spending, Selected Countries

Note: Data are for mid-1990s.

Source: OECD.

plays a much larger role, including Canada and the United Kingdom (Schoen et al., 2004). Americans favouring fundamental change have had limited impact so far, although President Obama's administration promises to change that.

The Canadian Health Care System

In countries with socialized medicine, the government (1) directly controls the financing and organization of health services, (2) directly pays providers, (3) guarantees equal access to health care, and (4) allows some private care for individuals who are willing to pay for their medical expenses.

Canada has a national health insurance system that is sometimes loosely described as **socialized medicine**. Despite differences in how socialized medicine works in such countries as the U.K., Sweden, Germany, and Italy, common to all such systems is the fact that the government (1) directly controls the financing and organization of health services, (2) directly pays providers, (3) guarantees equal access to health care, and (4) allows some private care for individuals who are willing to pay for their medical expenses (Cockerham, 1998). Canada does not have a true system of socialized medicine, however, in that the government does not employ Canadian physicians. Most of Canada's physicians are independent practitioners who are generally paid on a fee-for-service basis and submit claims directly to the provincial or territorial health insurance plan for payment.

Tommy Douglas is widely credited with being Canada's "father of medicare," for which he was voted the greatest Canadian in a nationwide contest held by the Canadian Broadcasting Corporation (CBC) in November 2004. Douglas began his career as a Baptist minister and was strongly influenced by the Christian social gospel, which called for progressive social reform. In 1933, he earned an M.A. in sociology from McMaster University. He led the Co-operative Commonwealth Federation (CCF) to victory in Saskatchewan in 1944, making it the first socialist party to win a North American election. (Subsequently, Douglas helped turn the CCF into the New Democratic Party.) He served as premier of Saskatchewan from 1944 to 1961, introducing many social reforms including universal medical care. This stirred up sharp opposition, including a province-wide physicians' strike, but Saskatchewan's medicare ultimately succeeded and in 1968 it became a model for the whole country (CBC News, 2004a).

Although Canada's health care system is often lauded as among the best in the world, problems exist. We have already noted one source of concern: waiting times for services. Although our health care system is based on the premise that "all citizens will have access to the care they need within a reasonable time period" (Health Canada, 1999b), many people agree that some waits are too long. In 2003, 47.9 percent of Canadians who sought specialist consultation for a new condition were successful in receiving an appointment in one month or less, while nearly one in eight had to wait three months or more. Waiting periods were slightly longer for non-emergency surgery and somewhat shorter for diagnostic tests (see Figure 19.4).

FIGURE 19.4

Waiting Times for Canadians Seeking Health Care Services, 2003

Source: Adapted from Statistics Canada, 2006, "Access to Health Care Services in Canada," Catalogue 82-575, Table 7, January 31, Retrieved November 3, 2008 (http//www.statcan.ca/english/ freepub/82-575-XIE/2006002/ tables/table07.htm).

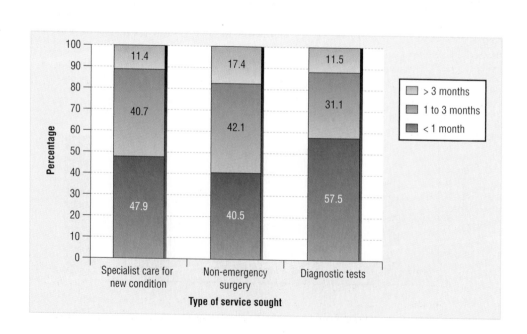

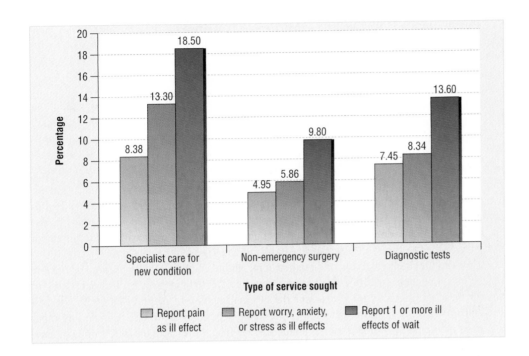

FIGURE 19.5
Reports of Ill Effects of
Waits as Percentages of
Those Seeking Medical
Services, Canada, 2003

Source: Adapted from Statistics
Canada, 2006, "Access to Health
Care Services in Canada," Catalogue
82-575, January 31.

Such waits are often unpleasant. Nearly one person in five who sought specialist care reported ill effects from waiting. More than one in eight complained of anxiety or stress. One in 12 complained of pain. Although those seeking non-emergency surgery reported lower rates of ill effects, 1 in 20 reported pain as a consequence of delay (see Figure 19.5).

The future of health care was a central issue in the 2004 federal election. The Liberals under Paul Martin won a narrow victory on a pledge to shore up the existing system. Two months after the election, Prime Minister Martin had concluded a first ministers' meeting at which $41 billion was added for health care over the next 10 years. On June 9, 2005, the Supreme Court, by a vote of four to three, ruled in favour of a man who had sued the province of Quebec after he was told that the wait for a hip replacement would be more than a year and that he was forbidden from purchasing such service. The Supreme Court ruled that such delays in access amounted to denial of access.

Many commentators believe that the Supreme Court decision opens the door to a two-tier system in which private insurance and provision operate alongside the public system. Implicit in such a system is preferred treatment for those with greater resources. Some individuals and organizations, such as the Canadian Medical Association and elements in the Conservative Party, welcomed the Supreme Court decision, but supporters of equal access were far less enthusiastic. Another possible scenario is that the Supreme Court decision could spur the federal government to inject still more money into the system, thereby cutting wait times and minimizing the perceived need for private provision. It thus remains to be seen how this controversy will play out.

MEDICINE, POWER, AND CULTURE

Symbolic Interaction, Labelling, and the Medicalization of Deviance

You may recall from our discussion of deviance that one of the preoccupations of symbolic interactionism is the labelling process (see Chapter 7, Deviance and Crime). According to symbolic interactionists, deviance results not just from the actions of the deviant but also from the responses of others, who define some actions as deviant and other actions as normal.

The medicalization of deviance is the tendency for medical definitions of deviant behaviour to become more prevalent over time.

Here we may add that the *type* of label applied to a deviant act may vary widely over time and from one society to another, depending on how that act is interpreted. Consider, for instance, the **medicalization of deviance**, which refers to the fact that, over time, "medical definitions of deviant behaviour are becoming more prevalent in . . . societies like our own" (Conrad and Schneider, 1992: 28–29). In an earlier era, much deviant behaviour was labelled "evil." Deviants tended to be chastised, punished, and otherwise socially controlled by members of the clergy, neighbours, family members, and the criminal justice system. Today, however, a person prone to drinking sprees is more likely to be declared an alcoholic and treated in a detoxification centre. A person predisposed to violent rages is more likely to be medicated. A person inclined to overeating is more likely to seek therapy and, in extreme cases, surgery. A heroin addict is more likely to seek the help of a methadone program. As these examples illustrate, what used to be regarded as willful deviance is now often regarded as involuntary deviance. More and more, what used to be defined as "badness" is now defined as "sickness." As our definitions of deviance change, deviance is increasingly coming under the sway of the medical and psychiatric establishments (see Figure 19.6).

How did the medicalization of deviance come about? What social forces are responsible for the growing capacity of medical and psychiatric establishments to control our lives? To answer these questions, we first examine the fascinating case of mental illness. As you will see, our changing definitions of mental illness show perhaps more clearly than any other aspect of medicine how thin a line separates science from politics in the field of health care.

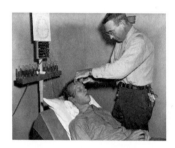

An example of the medicalization of deviance: A lobotomy is performed in a prison in the 1960s to "cure" the inmate of criminality.

FIGURE 19.6
An Example of the Medicalization of Deviance

Five North American surveys conducted in the 1950s and 1960s presented respondents with the boxed anecdote. The graph shows the percentage of respondents who considered the behaviour described in the anecdote evidence of mental illness. Notice the difference between the 1950s and the 1960s. (Nearly 100 percent of the psychiatrists who evaluated the anecdote thought it illustrated "simple schizophrenia.")

Source: Material adapted from table "Results of Studies Using Vignettes in Defining Problem Behavior" from *Deviance and Medicalization: From Badness to Sickness*, Expanded Edition by Peter Conrad and Joseph W. Schneider. Used by permission of Temple University Press. © 1992 by Temple University. All rights reserved.

The Political Sociology of Mental Illness

In 1974, a condition that had been considered a psychiatric disorder for more than a century ceased to be labelled as such by the American Psychiatric Association (APA). Did the condition disappear because it had become rare to the point of extinction? No. Did the discovery of a new wonder drug eradicate the condition virtually overnight? Again, no. In fact, in 1974 the condition was perhaps more widespread and certainly more public than ever before. However, paradoxically, just as the extent of the condition was becoming more widely appreciated, the APA's "bible," the *Diagnostic and Statistical Manual of Mental Disorders (DSM)*, ceased to define it as a psychiatric disorder.

The "condition" we are referring to is homosexuality. In preparing the third edition of the *DSM* for publication, a squabble broke out among psychiatrists over whether homosexuality is in fact a psychiatric disorder. Gay and lesbian activists, who sought to destigmatize homosexuality, were partly responsible for a shift in the views of many psychiatrists on this subject. In the end, the APA decided that homosexuality is not a psychiatric disorder and deleted the entry in the *DSM*. The APA's membership confirmed the decision in 1974.

The controversy over homosexuality was only one of several *political* debates that erupted among psychiatrists in the 1970s and 1980s (Shorter, 1997: 288–327):

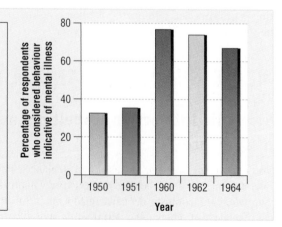

"Now here's a young woman in her twenties, let's call her Betty Smith . . . she has never had a job, and she doesn't seem to want to go out and look for one. She is a very quiet girl, she doesn't talk much to anyone—even her own family, and she acts like she is afraid of people, especially young men her own age. She won't go out with anyone, and whenever someone comes to visit her family, she stays in her own room until they leave. She just stays by herself and daydreams all the time and shows no interest in anything or anybody."

- The *DSM* task force initially decided to eliminate the term "neurosis" on the grounds that its role as a cause of mental disorder had never been proven experimentally. The decision outraged the psychoanalytic community, as "neurosis" is a keystone of its Freudian theories. As a result, psychoanalysts threatened to block publication of the third edition of the *DSM* unless they were appeased. In 1979, the APA's board backed down, placing "neurosis" in parentheses after "disorder." This compromise had nothing to do with science.

- When veterans of the Vietnam War began returning to the United States after 1971, they faced great difficulty re-entering American society. The war was unpopular, so veterans were not universally greeted as heroes. The U.S. economy went into a tailspin in 1973, making jobs difficult to find. And the veterans had suffered high levels of stress during the war itself. Many of them believed their troubles were psychiatric in nature, and soon a nationwide campaign was underway, urging the APA to recognize posttraumatic stress disorder (PTSD) in its manual. Many psychiatrists were reluctant to do so. Nonetheless, PTSD was listed in the third edition of the *DSM*. To be sure, the campaign succeeded partly on the strength of evidence that extreme trauma has psychological (and at times physiological) effects. However, in addition, as one activist later explained, the PTSD campaign succeeded because "[we] were better organized, more politically active, and enjoyed more lucky breaks than [our] opposition" (Chaim Shatan, quoted in Scott, 1990: 308). Again, politics and not just science helped shape the definition of a mental disorder.

- Feminists were unhappy that the 1987 edition of *DSM* contained such listings as self-defeating personality disorder. The *DSM* claimed that this disorder is twice as common among women as it is among men. Feminists countered that the definition is an example of blaming the victim. Under pressure from feminists, the 1994 edition of *DSM* dropped the concept.

Some mental disorders have obvious organic causes, such as chemical imbalances in the brain. These organic causes can often be precisely identified. Often they can be treated with drugs or other therapies. Moreover, experiments can be conducted to verify their existence and establish the effectiveness of one treatment or another. However, the examples listed above show that the definitions of many other mental disorders depend not just on scientific evidence but also on social values and political compromise. As psychologist John Goodman has stated, "No clear line divides the mentally healthy from the mentally unhealthy; and in addition, the definition of mental health is relative and is dependent on cultural context" (Goodman, 1999: 1469).

At the beginning of the twentieth century, just one mental disorder was recognized by the federal government: imbecility/insanity. By 1975, the *DSM* recognized 106 mental disorders. The 1994 edition of the *DSM* lists 297 mental disorders, a remarkable increase of 9.5 percent *per year* over 19 years. As the number of mental disorders has grown, so has the proportion of individuals presumably affected by them. In the mid-nineteenth century, few people were defined as having mental disorders. However, the Canadian Mental Health Association (2001) estimates that one in five Canadians will be affected by a mental illness at some time in their lives. The most common mental disorder, depression, is estimated to affect one in four Canadian women and one in ten Canadian men at some point in their lives (Canadian Psychiatric Association, 2002).

The University of Toronto's Edward Shorter, one of the world's leading historians of psychiatry, notes that in psychiatric practice, definitions of mental disorders are often expanded to include ailments with dubious or unknown biological foundations (e.g., "minor depression" and "borderline schizophrenia"; Shorter, 1997: 228). In addition, as we have seen, the number of conditions labelled as mental disorders increased rapidly during the twentieth century. We suggest four main reasons for expansion in the number and scope of such labels:

1. As we saw in Chapter 13, Work and the Economy, Canadians are now experiencing more stress and depression than ever before, mainly because of the increased demands of work and the growing time crunch. Mental health problems are thus more widespread than they used to be. At the same time, traditional institutions for dealing with mental health problems are less able to cope with them. The weakening authority of the church

and the weakening grip of the family over the individual leave the treatment of mental health problems more open to the medical and psychiatric establishments.

2. **The number of mental disorders has inflated because powerful organizations demand it.** Because public and private organizations find the classification of mental disorders useful, the number of disorders has proliferated. On occasion, the profit motive may be starkly apparent as pharmaceutical companies rush to patent products they claim will cure these conditions. Consider the repackaging of Prozac, the world's most widely prescribed antidepressant, as Serafem, a treatment for women suffering from the newly named premenstrual dysphoric disorder. Prozac represented a pharmaceutical goldmine for Eli Lilly, its manufacturer, accounting for a third of the company's $6.5 billion in annual revenues. However, in 2001, Eli Lilly's patent on Prozac ended, allowing other manufacturers to sell generic versions of this drug at a fraction of the cost. In response, Prozac was quickly renamed and repatented as a treatment for another group of consumers (Bell, 2002: 34).

3. **The cultural context stimulates inflation in the number and scope of mental disorders.** Assailed by the latest bestsellers in the self-help section of our bookstores and lectured by radio "therapists," we may be encouraged to turn our problems into medical and psychological conditions, sometimes without inquiring deeply into the disadvantages of doing so. For example, in 1980 the term *attention deficit disorder* (ADD) was coined to label hyperactive and inattentive schoolchildren, mainly boys. By the mid-1990s, North American doctors were writing more than six million prescriptions a year for Ritalin, an amphetamine-like compound that controls ADD.

   Evidence shows that some children diagnosed with ADD have problems absorbing glucose in the brain or suffer from imbalances in chemicals that help the brain regulate behaviour (Optometrists Network, 2000). Yet the diagnosis of ADD is typically conducted *clinically,* that is, by interviewing and observing children to see whether they exhibit signs of serious inattention, hyperactivity, and impulsivity. This means that many children diagnosed with ADD may have no organic disorder at all. Some cases of ADD may be due to the school system failing to capture children's imagination. Some may involve children acting out because they are deprived of attention at home. Some may involve plain old-fashioned high-spiritedness. A plausible case could be made that Winnie the Pooh suffers from ADD. In fact, this case *was* made by psychiatrists at the Dalhousie University Medical School in Halifax (Shea, Gordon, Hawkins, Kawchuk, and Smith, 2000). However, once hyperactivity and inattentiveness in school are defined as a medical and psychiatric condition, officials routinely prescribe drugs to control the problem and tend to ignore possible social causes.

4. The fourth main reason for inflation in the number and scope of mental disorders is that various professional organizations have promoted them. Consider posttraumatic stress disorder. There is no doubt that PTSD is a real condition and that many veterans suffer from it. However, once the disorder was officially recognized in the 1970s, some therapists trivialized the term, for example, talking about PTSD "in children exposed to movies like *Batman*" (Shorter, 1997: 290). Some psychiatric social workers, psychologists, and psychiatrists may magnify the incidence of such mental disorders because doing so increases their stature and their patient load. Others may do so simply because the condition becomes "trendy." Whatever the motive, overdiagnosis is the result.

The Professionalization of Medicine

The preceding discussion shows that the diagnosis and treatment of some mental disorders is not a completely scientific enterprise. Social and political processes are at least as important as scientific principles in determining how we treat some mental disorders. Various mental health professions compete for patients, as do different schools of thought within professions. Practitioners offer a wide and sometimes confusing array of treatments and therapies. In some cases their effectiveness is debatable, and there is at least some reason to remain skeptical of their ultimate worth.

In the early nineteenth century, the practice of medicine was in an even more chaotic state. Herbalists, faith healers, midwives, druggists, and medical doctors vied to meet the health needs of the public. A century later, the dust had settled. Medical science was victorious. Its first series of breakthroughs involved identifying the bacteria and viruses responsible for various diseases and then developing effective procedures and vaccines to combat them. These and subsequent triumphs in diagnosis and treatment convinced most people of the superiority of medical science over other approaches to health. Medical science worked, or at least it seemed to work more effectively and more often than other therapies.

It would be wrong, however, to think that scientific medicine came to dominate health care only because it produced results. A second, sociological reason for the rise to dominance of scientific medicine is that doctors were able to professionalize. As noted in Chapter 13, Work and the Economy, a profession is an occupation that requires extensive formal education. Professionals regulate their own training and practice. They restrict competition within the profession, mainly by limiting the recruitment of practitioners. They minimize competition with other professions, partly by laying exclusive claim to a field of expertise. Professionals are usually self-employed. They exercise considerable authority over their clients. And they profess to be motivated mainly by the desire to serve their community even though they earn a lot of money in the process. Professionalization, then, is the process by which people gain control and authority over their occupation and their clients. It results in professionals enjoying high occupational prestige and income, and considerable social and political power (Freidson, 1986; Johnson, 1972; Starr, 1982).

The professional organization of Canadian doctors is the Canadian Medical Association (CMA), founded in 1867 by 167 doctors in Quebec City. It quickly set about broadcasting the successes of medical science and criticizing alternative approaches to health as quackery and charlatanism. The CMA was able to have laws passed to restrict medical licences to graduates of approved schools and to ensure that only graduates of those schools could train the next generation of doctors. By restricting entry into the profession, and by specifying what "paramedical" practitioners could and could not do, members of the medical establishment ensured their own status, prestige, and high incomes. For example, midwifery was originally included in the work of the Victorian Order of Nurses, founded in 1897 by the National Council of Women to assist rural women who otherwise lacked access to health care. However, "opposition of the medical establishment in Canada was so great to what it saw as an infringement of its prerogatives that the idea was allowed to die" (Mitchinson, 1993: 396). In short, when medicine became a profession, it also became a monopoly.

The modern hospital is the institutional manifestation of the medical doctors' professional dominance. Until the twentieth century, most doctors operated small clinics and visited patients in their homes. However, the rise of the modern hospital was guaranteed by medicine's scientific turn in the mid-nineteenth century. Expensive equipment for diagnosis and treatment had to be shared by many physicians. This required the centralization of medical facilities in large, bureaucratically run institutions that strongly resist deviations from professional conduct. Practically nonexistent in 1850, hospitals are now widespread. Yet despite their undoubted benefits, economic as well as health related, hospitals and the medicine practised in them are not an unqualified blessing, as you are about to learn.

The Social Limits of Modern Medicine

In early February 2003, a 64-year-old professor of medicine from Guangzhou, the capital of Guangdong Province in southern China, came down with an unidentified respiratory ailment. It did not bother him enough to cancel a planned trip to Hong Kong, so on February 12 he checked into that city's Metropole Hotel. Ironically, as it turned out, the desk clerk assigned him room 911. Other ninth-floor guests included an elderly couple from Toronto and three young women from Singapore. All these people, along with a local resident who visited the hotel during this period, fell ill between February 15 and 27 with the same respiratory ailment as the professor. The professor died on March 4. The Canadian woman returned to Toronto on February 23 and died at her home on March 5. The eventual diagnosis: severe acute respiratory syndrome, or SARS, a new (and in 9 percent of cases, deadly) pneumonia-like illness for which there is no vaccine and no cure.

SARS originated in Guangdong Province. By June 12, 8445 cases of SARS had been identified in 29 countries, and 790 people had died of the disease. Quickly and efficiently, global travel had spread HIV/AIDS, West Nile virus, and now SARS from remote and isolated locales to the world's capitals. The United Nations has labelled Toronto the world's most multicultural city. It has a large Chinese population, mainly from Hong Kong. It is therefore not surprising that, outside of China, Hong Kong, and Taiwan, Toronto became the world's number one SARS hot spot (Abraham, 2003; World Health Organization, 2003).

Once identified as a potential SARS case, a person is quarantined at home for 10 days. However, if people exhibit symptoms of the disease, they go to a poorly ventilated institution where the air is maintained at a constant warm temperature that is ideal for the multiplication of germs. In this institution, many young and older people with weakened immune systems congregate. A steady stream of germs pours in around the clock. Staff members too often fail to follow elementary principles of good hygiene. That institution is a hospital. There, germs spread. Most of the 238 people in Toronto who had SARS as of June 12, 2003, caught it while in the hospital, before stringent isolation and disinfection procedures were imposed.

Our characterization of hospitals as ideal environments for the spread of germs may seem harsh. It is not. Hospitals have become dangerous places in North America. In Canada, about 80 percent of hospitals fall seriously short in preventing patients from getting hospital infections. Some 250 000 patients experience hospital infections every year. If the government classified hospital infections as a cause of death, it would be the fourth-leading cause of death in the country (Zoutman et al., 2003).

The situation has deteriorated largely because we invest disproportionately in expensive, high-tech diagnostic equipment and treatment while we skimp on simple, labour-intensive, time-consuming hygiene. Cleaning staffs are too small and insufficiently trained. Nurses are too few. According to research by the Harvard School of Public Health, these are the kinds of factors correlated with hospital-acquired infections. As one registered nurse says, "When you have less time to save lives, do you take 30 seconds to wash your hands? When you're speeding up you have to cut corners. We don't always wash our hands. I'm not saying it's right, but you've got to deal with reality" (quoted in Berens, 2002a).

It was not always the reality. Until the 1940s, North American hospital workers were obsessed with cleanliness. They had to be. In the era before the widespread use of antibiotics, infection often meant death. In the 1950s, however, the prevention of infections in hospitals became less of a priority because antibiotics became widely available. It was less expensive to wait until a patient got sick and then respond to symptoms by prescribing drugs than to prevent the sickness in the first place. Doctors and nurses have grown lax about hygiene over the past half-century. One American report cites a dozen health care studies showing that about half of doctors and nurses do not disinfect their hands between patients (Berens, 2002a). One small hospital north of Montreal cut serious infections by 80 percent simply by improving hygiene (CBC News, 2004b).

Using antibiotics indiscriminately has its own costs. When living organisms encounter a deadly threat, only the few mutations that are strong enough to resist the threat survive and go on to reproduce. Accordingly, if you use a lot of antibiotics, "super germs" that are resistant to these drugs multiply. This is just what has happened.[2] Penicillin could kill nearly all *Staphylococcus* germs in the 1940s, but by 1982 it was effective in fewer than 10 percent of cases. In the 1970s, doctors turned to the more powerful methicillin, which in 1974 could kill 98 percent of *Staphylococcus* germs. By the mid-1990s, it could kill only about 50 percent. It has thus come about that various strains of drug-resistant germs now cause pneumonia, blood poisoning, tuberculosis, and other infectious diseases. Drug-resistant germs that could formerly survive only in the friendly hospital environment have now adapted to the harsher environment outside the hospital walls. Pharmaceutical companies are racing to create new antibiotics to fight drug-resistant bugs, but germs mutate so quickly our arsenal is shrinking (Berens, 2002b).

The epidemic of infectious diseases caused by slack hospital hygiene and the overuse of antibiotics suggests that social circumstances constrain the success of modern medicine. It is difficult to see how we can solve these problems without enforcing strict rules regarding hospital disinfection.

Meanwhile, many people are growing skeptical of the claims of modern medicine. They are beginning to challenge traditional medicine and explore alternatives that rely less on high technology and drugs and are more sensitive to the need for maintaining balance between humans and their environment in the pursuit of good health. In concluding this chapter, we explore some of these challenges and alternatives.

Recent Challenges to Traditional Medical Science

Patient Activism

By the mid-twentieth century, the dominance of medical science in Canada was virtually complete. Any departure from the dictates of scientific medicine was considered deviant. Thus, when sociologist Talcott Parsons defined the **sick role** in 1951, he first pointed out that illness suspends routine responsibilities and is not deliberate. Then he stressed that people playing the sick role must want to be well and must seek competent help, cooperating with health care practitioners at all times (Parsons, 1951: 428 ff.). Must they? According to Parsons's definition, a competent person suffering from a terminal illness cannot reasonably demand that doctors refrain from using heroic measures to prolong his or her life. And by his definition, a patient cannot reasonably question doctors' orders, no matter how well educated the patient and how debatable the effect of the prescribed treatment. Although Parsons's definition of the sick role may sound plausible to many people born before World War II, it probably sounds authoritarian and utterly foreign to most younger people.

That is because things have changed. The public is more highly educated now than it was in 1951. Many people now have the knowledge, vocabulary, self-confidence, and political organization to participate in their own health care rather than passively accept whatever experts tell them. Research shows that this trend is evident even among older Canadians and lower-income earners. Canadian baby boomers and younger generations are even less likely to follow a doctor's advice uncritically; in fact, only one-third do so (Bricker and Greenspon, 2001: 221). Increasingly, patients are taught to perform simple, routine medical procedures themselves. Many people now use the Internet to seek information about various illnesses and treatments.[3] Increasingly, they are uncomfortable with doctors acting as authoritarian parents and patients acting as dutiful children. Surveys conducted in Canada reveal that 90 percent of Canadians now prefer that their doctor offer many treatment options rather than a single course of action, 86 percent say they usually ask their doctor many questions about procedures, 76 percent say they are more likely to question their doctor now than they were in the past, while about 70 percent claim to always ask their doctor about medicines that are prescribed (Bricker and Greenspon, 2001: 119–220). Doctors now routinely seek patients' informed consent for some procedures rather than deciding what to do on their own. Similarly, most hospitals have established ethics committees, which were unheard of only four decades ago (Rothman, 1991). These are responses to patients wanting a more active role in their own care.

Some recent challenges to the authority of medical science are organized and political. For example, when AIDS activists challenged the stereotype of AIDS as a "gay disease" and demanded more research funding to help find a cure, they changed research and treatment priorities in a way that could never have happened in, say, the 1950s or 1960s (Epstein, 1996). Similarly, when feminists supported the reintroduction of midwifery and argued against medical intervention in routine childbirths, they challenged the wisdom of established medical practice. The previously male-dominated profession of medicine considered the male body the norm and paid relatively little attention to "women's diseases," such as breast cancer, and

Playing the sick role, **according to Talcott Parsons, involves the non-deliberate suspension of routine responsibilities, wanting to be well, seeking competent help, and cooperating with health care practitioners at all times.**

"women's issues," such as reproduction. This, too, is now changing thanks to feminist intervention (Boston Women's Health Book Collective, 1998; Rothman, 1982, 1989; Schiebinger, 1993). And although doctors and the larger society traditionally treated people with disabilities as incompetent children, various movements now seek to empower them (Charlton, 1998; Zola, 1982). As a result, attitudes toward people with disabilities are changing.

Alternative Medicine

Other challenges to the authority of medical science are less organized and less political than those just mentioned. Consider, for example, alternative medicine. In 1994–95, only 15 percent of Canadians used such services (Park, 2005). In 2003, the Canadian Community Health Survey showed that 20 percent of Canadians over the age of 11 used some form of alternative medicine (see Figure 19.7). The most widely used health alternative is chiropractic services, used by just over one in ten Canadians.

In 2003, women were about one-third more likely than men were to use alternative health care. Most users were between the ages of 25 and 65. Use was greatest in British Columbia, Alberta, and Saskatchewan, and lowest in Atlantic Canada and Nunavut. Those with chronic disorders, including back problems and multiple chemical sensitivities, were more likely to consult an alternative health service provider. Income and education influenced choice. Twenty-six percent of the highest income group reported using an alternative, compared with just 13 percent of the lowest income group. Twenty-six percent of postsecondary degree holders used alternatives, while only 16 percent did so among those who did not graduate from high school (Park, 2005).

Despite its growing popularity, many medical doctors were hostile to alternative medicine until recently. They lumped all alternative therapies together and dismissed them as unscientific (Campion, 1993). By the late 1990s, however, a more tolerant attitude was evident in many quarters. For some kinds of ailments, physicians began to recognize the benefits of at least the most popular forms of alternative medicine. For example, a 1998 editorial in the respected *New England Journal of Medicine* admitted that the beneficial effect of chiropractic on low back pain is "no longer in dispute" (Shekelle, 1998). This change in attitude was due in part to new scientific evidence from Canadian research showing that spinal manipulation can be a relatively effective

FIGURE 19.7

Percentage of Canadians Who Used Alternative Health Care, 2003

Source: Adapted from Statistics Canada, 2004, "Health Reports," Catalogue 82-003, Vol. 16, No. 2, March 15, 2005, pages 39–43. Retrieved November 1, 2008 (http://www.statcan.ca/cgibin/downpub/listpub.cgi?catno= 82-003-XIE2004002.

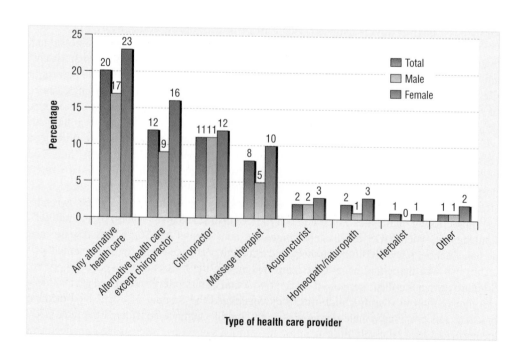

and inexpensive treatment for low back pain (Manga, Angus, and Swan, 1993). At the same time, however, alternative forms of medicine should not be assumed to be entirely risk-free. For example, to date, the majority of Canadian lawsuits against chiropractors have involved claims of muscular skeletal dysfunction, strains and sprains, and rib fractures. In a few cases, more serious injury has occurred, including ruptured vertebral arteries and death (Cohen, 1999: 50).

Nevertheless, the medical profession's grudging acceptance of chiropractic in the treatment of low back pain indicates what we can expect in the uneasy relationship between scientific and alternative medicine in coming decades. Although many, if not most, alternative therapies (such as aromatherapy and foot reflexology) are non-invasive and relatively harmless, doctors will, for the most part, remain skeptical of alternative therapies unless properly conducted experiments demonstrate their beneficial effects.

Holistic Medicine

Medical doctors understand that a positive frame of mind often helps in the treatment of disease. For example, research shows that strong belief in the effectiveness of a cure can by itself improve the condition of about one-third of people suffering from chronic pain or fatigue (Campion, 1993). This is known as the **placebo effect**. Doctors also understand that conditions in the human environment affect people's health. However, despite their appreciation of the effect of mind and environment on the human body, traditional scientific medicine tends to respond to illness by treating disease symptoms as a largely physical and individual problem. Moreover, scientific medicine continues to subdivide into more specialized areas of practice that rely more and more heavily on drugs and high-tech machinery. Most doctors are less concerned with maintaining and improving health by understanding the larger mental and social context within which people become ill.

Traditional Indian and Chinese medicine takes a different approach. India's Ayurvedic medical tradition views individuals in terms of the flow of vital fluids or "humours" and their health in the context of their environment. In this view, maintaining good health requires not only balancing fluids in individuals but also balancing the relationship between individuals and the world around them (Zimmermann, 1987 [1982]). In spite of significant differences, the fundamental outlook is similar in traditional Chinese medicine. Chinese medicine and its remedies, ranging from acupuncture to herbs, seek to restore individuals' internal balance, as well as their relationship to the outside world (Unschuld, 1985). Contemporary **holistic medicine**, the third and final challenge to traditional scientific medicine we will consider, takes an approach similar to these "ethnomedical" traditions. Practitioners of holistic medicine argue that good health requires maintaining a balance between mind and body, and between the individual and the environment.

Most holistic practitioners do not reject scientific medicine. However, they emphasize disease *prevention*. When they treat patients, they take into account the relationship between mind and body and between the individual and his or her social and physical environment. Holistic practitioners thus seek to establish close ties with their patients and treat them in their homes or other relaxed settings. Rather than expecting patients to react to illness by passively allowing a doctor to treat them, they expect patients to take an active role in maintaining their good health. And, recognizing that industrial pollution, work-related stress, poverty, racial and gender inequality, and other social factors contribute heavily to disease, holistic practitioners often become political activists (Hastings, Fadiman, and Gordon, 1980).

In sum, patient activism, alternative medicine, and holistic medicine represent the three biggest challenges to traditional scientific medicine today. Few people think of these challenges as potential replacements for scientific medicine. However, many people believe that, together with traditional scientific approaches, these challenges will help improve the health status of people in Canada and throughout the world in the twenty-first century.

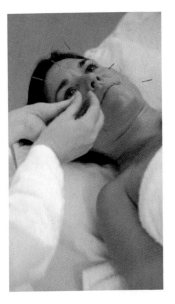

Acupuncture is one of the most widely accepted forms of alternative medicine.

The placebo effect is the positive influence on healing of a strong belief in the effectiveness of a cure.

Holistic medicine emphasizes disease prevention. Holistic practitioners treat disease by taking into account the relationship between mind and body and between the individual and his or her social and physical environment.

NOTES

1. Status Indians are people whose names appear on the Indian Register maintained by the Department of Indian and Northern Affairs.

2. It surely has not helped that antibiotics are routinely added to cattle feed to prevent disease and thereby lower beef production costs. This practice only builds up resistance to antibiotics in humans.

3. There are at least two health-related dangers to using the Internet, however. First, some people may misinterpret information or assume that unreliable sources are reliable. Second, sexual courtship on the Internet may lead to real-world meetings and therefore contribute to the spread of HIV/AIDS and other sexually transmitted diseases.

SUMMARY

1. Are all causes of illness and death biological?
   Ultimately, yes. However, *variations* in illness and death rates are often due to social causes. The social causes of illness and death include human-environmental factors, lifestyle factors, and factors related to the public health and health care systems. All three factors are related to country of residence, class, race, and gender. Specifically, health risks are lower among upper classes, rich countries, and members of privileged racial and ethnic groups than among lower classes, poor countries, and members of disadvantaged racial and ethnic groups. In some respects related to health, men are in a more advantageous position than women are.

2. Does Canada have one of the world's best health systems?
   Canada ranks high on most indicators of population health, but room for improvement remains. There are disparities in health status associated with socioeconomic status, gender, and age. Some racial minority groups, Aboriginal Canadians in particular, remain especially vulnerable to threats in the physical environment, including the dangers of damaging toxins and environmental pollutants.

3. Does the United States have one of the world's best health systems?
   As a rich country, the United States has far better health outcomes than poorer countries. It has outstanding technology and affords some of the best care anywhere to those who can afford it. However, the prices paid for medical services in the United States are considerably higher than elsewhere and substantial numbers of citizens lack adequate insurance yet have no access to public provision. As a result, overall health outcomes are inferior to those achieved elsewhere for considerably less expenditure.

4. How has medicine interacted with conceptions of deviant behaviour?
   Over time, medical definitions of deviance have become more common. The recent history of psychiatry shows that social values and political compromise are at least as important as science in determining the classification of some mental disorders.

5. What are the "social limits of medicine"?
   Shortsighted cost cutting has encouraged the overuse of antibiotics and the neglect of basic hygiene in hospitals, resulting in more hospital-caused infections and the spread of drug-resistant germs.

6. What are the main challenges and alternatives to traditional medicine?
   Several challenges to traditional scientific medicine promise to improve the quality of health care in Canada and worldwide. These include patient activism, alternative medicine, and holistic medicine.

KEY TERMS

environmental racism (p. 545)

health (p. 544)

health care system (p. 546)

holistic medicine (p. 563)

infant mortality (p. 546)

life expectancy (p. 542)

medicalization of deviance (p. 556)

morbidity (p. 549)

placebo effect (p. 563)

public health system (p. 545)

sick role (p. 561)

socialized medicine (p. 554)

QUESTIONS TO CONSIDER

1. Since health resources are scarce, tough decisions have to be made about how they are allocated. For example, drug companies, physicians, hospitals, government research agencies, and other components of the health care system must decide how much to invest in trying to prolong the life of the older people versus how much to invest in improving the health of the poor. What do you think are the main factors that help different components of the health care system decide how to allocate resources between these two goals? Specifically, how important is the profit motive? political pressure? Which components of the health system are most influenced by the profit motive? which by political pressure? If you were in charge of a major hospital or government funding for health research, how would you divide your scarce resources between these two goals? Why? What pressures might be placed on you to act differently from the way you would like to act?

2. Some poor health outcomes stem from individual choices, such as the use of cigarettes, excessive alcohol consumption, and refusal to avoid risk (e.g., driving without a seatbelt). When, if ever, should such factors be taken into account in choosing levels of medical treatment? Should it make a difference whether or not public funding is at issue?

3. Do you believe that patient activism and alternative medicines improve health care or detract from the efforts of scientifically trained physicians and researchers to do the best possible research and administer the best possible treatment? Because patient activists may not be scientifically trained, and because alternative therapies may not be experimentally proven, are there inherent dangers in these challenges to traditional medicine? Conversely, do biases in traditional medicine detract from health care by ignoring the needs of patient activists and the possible benefits of alternative therapies?

WEB RESOURCES

Companion Website for This Book

http://www.compass3e.nelson.com

Begin by clicking on the Student Resources section of the website. Next, select the chapter you are studying from the pull-down menu. From the Student Resources page you have easy access to InfoTrac® College Edition, additional Weblinks, and other resources. The website also has many useful tips to aid you in your study of sociology, including practice tests for each chapter.

InfoTrac® Search Terms

These search terms are provided to assist you in beginning to conduct research on this topic by visiting http://www.infotrac-college.com:

age discrimination
health maintenance organizations
life expectancy
public health

Recommended Websites

Health Canada's website at http://www.hc-sc.gc.ca provides access to information and publications about many health-related issues, including diseases and conditions, consumer product safety, food and nutrition, and the health care system.

The Public Health Agency provides access to a wide range of health information at http://www.phac-aspc.gc.ca. The scope is vast and covers such diverse issues as helping people find information about treatments, international health and development, advice for travellers, and access to statistical materials on health and medicine.

CengageNOW™

http://hed.nelson.com

This online diagnostic tool identifies each student's unique needs with a Pretest that generates a personalized Study Plan for each chapter, helping students focus on concepts they're having the most difficulty mastering. Students then take a Posttest after reading the chapter to measure their understanding of the material. An Instructor Gradebook is available to track and monitor student progress.

Social Change

20   Population and Urbanization

In this chapter, you will learn that

- Many people think that only natural conditions influence human population growth. However, social forces are important influences too.

- In particular, sociologists have focused on two major social determinants of population growth: industrialization and social inequality.

- Industrialization also plays a major role in causing the movement of people from countryside to city.

- Cities are not as anonymous and alienating as many sociologists once believed them to be.

- The spatial and cultural forms of cities depend largely on the level of development of the societies in which they are found.

POPULATION

The City of God

Rio de Janeiro, Brazil, is one of the world's most beautiful cities. Along the warm, blue waters of its bays lie flawless beaches, guarded by four- and five-star hotels and pricey shops. Rising abruptly behind them is a mountain range, partly populated, partly covered by luxuriant tropical forest. The climate seems perpetually balanced between spring and summer. The inner city of Rio is a place of great wealth and beauty, devoted to commerce and the pursuit of leisure.

Rio is also a large city. With a metropolitan population of more than 12 million people in 2002, it is the 18th biggest metropolitan area in the world, larger than Chicago, Paris, and London (Brinkhoff, 2002). Not all of its 12 million inhabitants are well off, however. Brazil is characterized by more inequality of wealth than most other countries in the world. Slums started climbing up the hillsides of Rio about a century ago. Fed by a high birth rate and people migrating from the surrounding countryside in search of a better life, slums, such as the one shown in the photo, are now home to about 20 percent of the city's inhabitants (Jones, 2003).

Some of Rio's slums began as government housing projects designed to segregate the poor from the rich. One such slum, as famous in its own way as the beaches of Copacabana and Ipanema, is Cidade de Deus (the "City of God"). Founded in the 1960s, it had become one of the most lawless and dangerous parts of Rio by the 1980s. It is a place where some families of four live on $50 a month in houses made of cardboard and discarded scraps of tin, a place where roofs leak and rats run freely. For many inhabitants, crime is survival. Drug traffickers wage a daily battle for control of territory, and children as young as six perch in key locations with walkie-talkies to feed information to their bosses on the comings and goings of passersby.

Cidade de Deus is also the name of a brilliant movie released in 2002. Based in part on the true-life story of Paulo Lins, who grew up in a slum and became a novelist, *Cidade de Deus* chronicles the gang wars of the 1970s and 80s. It leaves us with the nearly hopeless message that, in a war without end, each generation of drug traffickers starts younger and is more ruthless than its predecessor.

Paulo Lins escaped Brazil's grinding poverty. So did Luiz Inácio Lula da Silva, Brazil's current president. They are inspiring models of what is possible. They are also depressing reminders that the closely related problems of population growth and urbanization are more serious now than ever. Brazil's 41 million people in 1940 multiplied to about 180 million in 2004. The country is now as urbanized as Canada, with more than three-quarters of its population living in urban areas (estimated from Lahmeyer, 2003; Ministério de Ciência e Tecnologia Brasil, 2002).

This chapter tackles the closely connected problems of population growth and urbanization. We first show that population growth is a process governed less by natural laws than by social forces. We argue that these social forces are not related exclusively to industrialization, as social scientists commonly believed just a few decades ago. Instead, social inequality also plays a major role in shaping population growth.

We next turn to the problem of urbanization. Today, population growth is typically accompanied by the increasing concentration of the world's people in urban centres. As recently as 40 years ago, sociologists typically believed that cities were alienating and anomic (or normless). We argue that this view is an oversimplification. We also outline the social roots of the city's physical and cultural evolution from preindustrial to postindustrial times.

The Population "Explosion"

Twelve thousand years ago there were only about 6 million people in the world. Ten thousand years ago, world population had risen to 250 million, and it increased to some 760 million by 1750. After that, world population skyrocketed. The number of humans reached one billion in 1804 and six billion in 1999. On July 1, 2008, there were an estimated 6.7 billion people in the world (Figure 20.1). Where 1 person stood 12 000 years ago, there are now 1050 people; statistical projections suggest that, by 2100, there will be about 1700 people. Of those 1700, fewer than 250 will be standing in the rich countries of the world. More than 1450 of them will be in the developing countries of South America, Asia, and Africa.

Many analysts project that, after passing the 10 billion mark around 2100, world population will level off. But given the numbers cited previously, is it any wonder that some population analysts say we're now in the midst of a population "explosion"? Explosions are horrifying events. They cause widespread and severe damage. They are fast and unstoppable. And that is exactly the imagery some population analysts, or **demographers**, want to convey (e.g., Ehrlich, 1968; Ehrlich and Ehrlich, 1990; Figure 20.2). They have written many books, articles, and television programs dealing with the population explosion. Images of an overflowing multitude in, say, Bangladesh, Nigeria, or Brazil remain fixed in our minds. Some people are frightened enough to refer to overpopulation as catastrophic. They link it to recurrent famine, brutal ethnic warfare, and other massive and seemingly intractable problems.

If this imagery makes you feel that the world's rich countries must do something about overpopulation, you're not alone. In fact, concern about the population "bomb" is as old as the social sciences. In 1798, Thomas Robert Malthus, a British clergyman of the Anglican faith, proposed a highly influential theory of human population (Malthus (1966 [1798]). As you will soon see, contemporary sociologists have criticized, qualified, and in part rejected his theory. But because much of the sociological study of population is, in effect, a debate with Malthus's ghost, we must confront the man's ideas squarely.

The Malthusian Trap

Malthus's theory rests on two undeniable facts and a questionable assumption. The facts: People must eat, and they are driven by a strong sexual urge. The assumption: Although the food supply increases slowly and arithmetically (1, 2, 3, 4, etc.), population size grows

Demographers are social-scientific analysts of human population.

FIGURE 20.1

World Population, 1750–2150 (in billions, projected)

Sources: Livi-Bacci, 1992: 31; Population Reference Bureau, 2003.

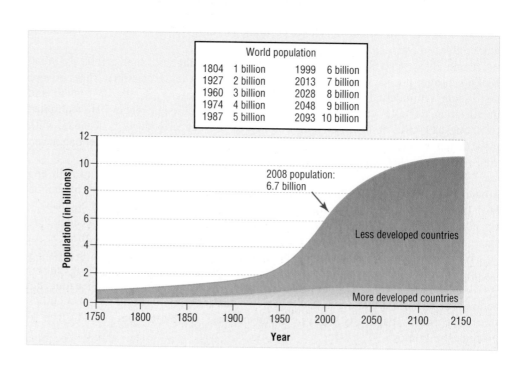

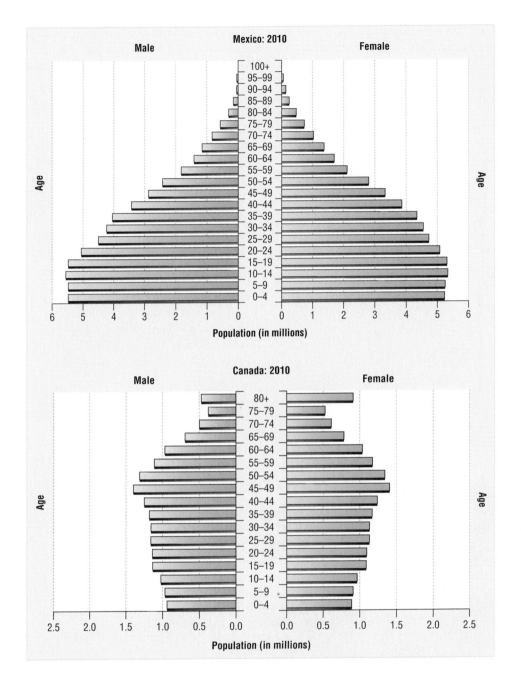

Mexico: 2010

Male · Female

Age

Population (in millions)

Canada: 2010

Male · Female

Age

Population (in millions)

FIGURE 20.2
How Demographers Analyze
Population Changes and
Composition

The main purpose of demography
is to figure out why the size,
geographical distribution, and social
composition of human populations
change over time. The basic equation
of population change is $P2 = P1 + B - D + I - E$, where $P2$ is population
size at a given time, $P1$ is population
size at an earlier time, B is the
number of births in the interval, D is
the number of deaths in the interval,
I is the number of immigrants
arriving in the interval, and E is the
number of emigrants leaving in the
interval. A basic tool for analyzing
the composition of a population is
the "age–sex pyramid," which shows
the number of males and females in
each age cohort of the population at
a given point in time. Age–sex
pyramids for Canada and Mexico are
shown here for 2010. Why do you
think they look so different? Compare
your answer to that of the theory of
the demographic transition, discussed
in this section.

Source: U.S. Census Bureau, 2008.

quickly and geometrically (1, 2, 4, 8, etc.). Based on these ideas, Malthus concluded that
"the superior power of population cannot be checked without producing misery or vice"
(Malthus (1966 [1798]): 217–18). Specifically, only two forces can hold population growth
in check. First are "preventive" measures, such as abortion, infanticide, and prostitution.
Malthus called these "vices" because he morally opposed them and thought everyone else
ought to also. Second are "positive checks," such as war, pestilence, and famine. Malthus
recognized that positive checks create much suffering. Yet he felt they are the only forces
that can be allowed to control population growth. Here, then, is the so-called **Malthusian
trap:** a cycle of population growth followed by an outbreak of war, pestilence, or famine that
keeps population growth in check. Population size might fluctuate, said Malthus, but it has
a natural upper limit that Western Europe has reached.

   Although many people supported Malthus's theory, others reviled him as a misguided
prophet of doom and gloom (Winch, 1987). For example, people who wanted to help the

The **Malthusian trap** refers to
a cycle of population growth
followed by an outbreak of war,
pestilence or famine that keeps
population growth in check.

A "population explosion"? Hong Kong is one of the most densely populated places on earth.

poor disagreed with Malthus. He felt such aid was counterproductive. Welfare, he said, would enable the poor to buy more food. With more food, they would have more children. And having more children would only make them poorer than they already were. Better to leave them alone, said Malthus, and thereby reduce the sum of human suffering in the world.

A Critique of Malthus

Although in some respects compelling, events have cast doubt on several of Malthus's ideas. Specifically:

- Ever since Malthus proposed his theory, technological advances have allowed rapid growth in how much food is produced for each person on the planet. This is the opposite of the slow growth Malthus predicted. For instance, in 1991–93, India produced 23 percent more food per person than it did in 1979–81, and China produced 39 percent more. Moreover, except for Africa south of the Sahara, the largest increases in the food supply are taking place in the developing countries (Sen, 1994).

- If, as Malthus claimed, there is a natural upper limit to population growth, it is unclear what that limit is. Malthus thought the population couldn't grow much larger in late-eighteenth-century Western Europe without "positive checks" coming into play. Yet the Western European population increased from 187 million people in 1801 to 321 million in 1900. It has now stabilized at about half a billion (McNeill, 1990). The Western European case suggests that population growth has an upper limit far higher than that envisaged by Malthus.

- Population growth does not always produce misery. For example, despite its rapid population increase over the past 200 years, Western Europe is one of the most prosperous regions in the world.

- Helping the poor does not generally result in the poor having more children. For example, in Western Europe, social welfare policies (employment insurance, state-funded

Albrecht Dürer's *The Four Horsemen of the Apocalypse* (woodcut, 1498). According to Malthus, only war, pestilence, and famine could keep population growth in check.

medical care, paid maternity leave, pensions, etc.) are the most generous on the planet. Yet the size of the population is quite stable. In fact, as you will learn, some forms of social welfare produce rapid and large *decreases* in population growth, especially in the poor, developing countries.

- Although the human sexual urge is as strong as Malthus thought, people have developed contraceptive devices and techniques to control the consequences of their sexual activity (Szreter, 1996). There is no necessary connection between sexual activity and childbirth.

The developments listed here all point to one conclusion. Malthus's pessimism was overstated. Human ingenuity seems to have enabled us to wriggle free of the Malthusian trap, at least for the time being.

We are not, however, home free. Today there are renewed fears that industrialization and population growth are putting severe strains on the planet's resources. As established by the online chapter that accompanies this book, Chapter 22, Technology and the Global Environment, we must take these fears seriously. It is encouraging to learn that the limits to growth are as much social as natural and therefore avoidable rather than inevitable. However, we will see that our ability to avoid the Malthusian trap in the twenty-first century will require all the ingenuity and self-sacrifice we can muster. For the time being, however, let us consider the second main theory of population growth, the theory of the demographic transition.

Demographic Transition Theory

According to **demographic transition theory**, the main factors underlying population dynamics are industrialization and the growth of modern cultural values (Chesnais, 1992 [1986]; Coale, 1974; Notestein, 1945; see Figure 20.3). The theory is based on the observation that the European population developed in four distinct stages.

The Preindustrial Period

In the first, preindustrial stage of growth, a large proportion of the population died every year from inadequate nutrition, poor hygiene, and uncontrollable disease. In other words, the **crude death rate** was high. The crude death rate is the annual number of deaths (or "mortality") per 1000 people in a population. During this period, the **crude birth rate** was high too. The crude birth rate is the annual number of live births per 1000 people in a population. In the preindustrial era, most people wanted to have as many children as possible. That was partly because relatively few children survived till adulthood. In addition, children were considered a valuable source of agricultural labour and a form of old age security in a society consisting largely of peasants and lacking anything resembling a modern welfare state.

The Early Industrial Period

The second stage of European population growth was the early industrial, or transition, period. At this stage, the crude death rate dropped. People's life expectancy, or average life span, increased because economic growth led to improved nutrition and hygiene. However, the crude birth rate remained high. With people living longer and women having nearly as many babies as in the preindustrial era, the population grew rapidly. Malthus lived during this period of rapid population growth, and that accounts in part for his alarm.

Demographic transition theory explains how changes in fertility and mortality affected population growth from preindustrial to postindustrial times.

The **crude death rate** is the annual number of deaths per 1000 people in a population.

The **crude birth rate** is the annual number of live births per 1000 women in a population.

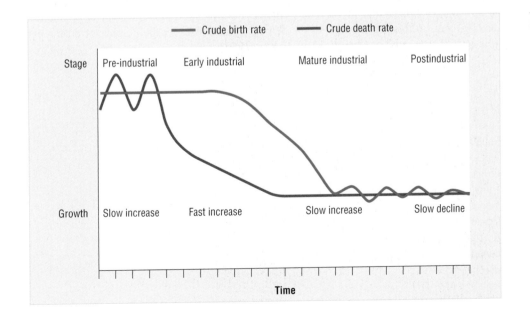

FIGURE 20.3
Democratic Transition Theory

The Mature Industrial Period

The third stage of European population growth was the mature industrial period. At this stage, the crude death rate continued to fall. The crude birth rate fell even more dramatically. The crude birth rate fell because economic growth eventually changed people's traditional beliefs about the value of having many children. Having many children made sense in an agricultural society, where, as we have seen, children were a valuable economic resource. In contrast, children were more of an economic burden in an industrial society. That is because breadwinners worked outside the home for a wage or a salary and children contributed little, if anything, to the economic welfare of the family. Note, however, that the crude birth rate took longer to decline than the crude death rate did. That is because people's values often change more slowly than their technologies do. People can put in a sewer system or a water purification plant to lower the crude death rate faster than they can change their minds about something as fundamental as how many children to have. Eventually, however, the technologies and outlooks that accompany modernity led people to postpone getting married and to use contraceptives and other birth-control methods. As a result, population stabilized during the mature industrial period. This demonstrates the validity of one of the demographer's favourite sayings: "Economic development is the best contraceptive."

The Postindustrial Period

In the last decades of the twentieth century, the total fertility rate continued to fall. (We defined the total fertility rate in Chapter 15, Families, as the average number of children that would be born to a woman over her lifetime if she had the same number of children as women in each age cohort in a given year.) In fact, it fell below the **replacement level** in some countries. The replacement level is the number of children each woman must have on average for population size to remain stable. Ignoring any inflow of settlers from other countries (**immigration, or in-migration**) and any outflow to other countries (**emigration, or out-migration**), the replacement level is 2.1. This means that, on average, each woman must give birth to slightly more than the two children needed to replace her and her mate. Slightly more than two children are required because some children die before they reach reproductive age.

By the 1990s, some Europeans were worrying about declining fertility and its possible effects on population size. As you can see in Table 20.1, Europe as a whole has a fertility rate below the replacement level. In fact, about a third of the world's countries, including Canada, China, and Russia, now have a fertility level below the replacement level, and the number of such countries is growing. Because of the proliferation of low-fertility societies, some scholars suggest that we have now entered a fourth, postindustrial stage of population development. In this fourth stage of the demographic transition, the number of deaths per year exceeds the number of births (Van de Kaa, 1987).

The replacement level is the number of children that each woman must have on average for population size to remain stable, ignoring migration. The replacement level is 2.1.

Immigration, or in-migration, is the inflow of people into one country from one or more other countries and their settlement in the destination country.

Emigration, or out-migration, is the outflow of people from one country and their settlement in one or more other countries.

TABLE 20.1

Total Fertility Rate by Region and Selected Countries, 2007

* Australia, New Zealand, and miscellaneous South Pacific island states
** Canada and the United States only

Source: Population Reference Bureau, 2007.

Africa	5.0
Niger	7.1 (tied for highest in the world)
Latin America/Caribbean	2.5
South America	2.4
Asia	2.4
China	1.6
India	2.9
Mongolia	1.1 (tied for lowest in the world)
Oceania*	2.1
Northern America**	2.0
Canada	1.5
Europe	1.5
Russia	1.3

As outlined earlier, the demographic transition theory provides a rough picture of how industrialization affects population growth. However, research has revealed a number of inconsistencies in the theory. Most of them are due to the theory placing too much emphasis on industrialization as the main force underlying population growth (Coale and Watkins, 1986). For example, demographers have found that reductions in fertility sometimes occur when standards of living stagnate or decline, not just when they improve through industrialization. Thus, in Russia and some developing countries today, declining living standards have led to a deterioration in general health and a subsequent decline in fertility. Because of such findings, many scholars have concluded that an adequate theory of population growth must pay more attention to social factors other than industrialization and, in particular, to the role of social inequality.

Population and Social Inequality

Karl Marx

One of Malthus's staunchest intellectual opponents was Karl Marx. Marx argued that the problem of overpopulation is specific to capitalism (Meek, 1971). In his view, overpopulation is not a problem of too many people; instead, it is a problem of too much poverty. Do away with the exploitation of workers by their employers, said Marx, and poverty will disappear. If a society is rich enough to eliminate poverty, then by definition its population is not too large. By eliminating poverty, we also solve the problem of overpopulation in Marx's view.

Marx's analysis makes it seem that capitalism can never generate enough prosperity to solve the overpopulation problem. He was evidently wrong. Overpopulation is not a serious problem in Canada or the United States or Japan or Germany today.[1] It *is* a problem in most of Africa, where capitalism is weakly developed and the level of social inequality is much higher than in the postindustrial societies. Still, a core idea in Marx's analysis of the overpopulation problem rings true. As some contemporary demographers argue, social inequality is a main cause of overpopulation. In the following, we illustrate this argument by first considering how gender inequality influences population growth. Then we discuss the effects of class inequality on population growth.

Gender Inequality and Overpopulation

The effect of gender inequality on population growth is well illustrated by the case of Kerala, a state in India with more than 30 million people. Kerala had a total fertility rate of 1.8 in 1991, half India's national rate and below the replacement level of 2.1. How did Kerala achieve this remarkable feat? Is it a highly industrialized oasis in the midst of a semi-industrialized country, as we might expect given the arguments of demographic transition theory? To the contrary, Kerala is not highly industrialized. In fact, it is among the poorer Indian states, with a per capita income less than the national average. Then has the government of Kerala strictly enforced a state childbirth policy similar to China's? The Chinese government strongly penalizes families that have more than one child and it allows abortion at 8.5 months. As a result, China had a total fertility rate of just 2.0 in 1992 (Wordsworth, 2000). In Kerala, however, the government keeps out of its citizens' bedrooms. The decision to have children remains a strictly private affair.

The women of Kerala achieved a low total fertility rate because their government systematically raised their status over a period of decades (Franke and Chasin, 1992; Sen, 1994). The government helped to create a realistic alternative to a life of continuous childbearing and child rearing. It helped women understand that they could achieve that alternative if they wanted to. In particular, the government organized successful campaigns and programs to educate women, increase their participation in the paid labour force, and make family planning widely available. These government campaigns and programs resulted in Keralan women enjoying the highest literacy rate, the highest labour force participation rate, and the highest rate of political participation in India. Given their desire for education, work, and political involvement, most Keralan women want small families, so they use contraception to prevent unwanted births. Thus, by lowering the level of gender inequality, the government of Kerala solved its overpopulation problem. In general, where

> women tend to have more power [the society has] low rather than high mortality and fertility. Education and employment, for example, often accord women wider power and influence, which enhance their status. But attending school and working often compete with childbearing and child rearing. Women may choose to have fewer children in order to hold a job or increase their education. (Riley, 1997; Box 20.1)

Class Inequality and Overpopulation

The sex ratio is the ratio of women to men in a geographical area.

Unravelling the Keralan mystery is an instructive exercise. It establishes that population growth depends not just on a society's level of industrialization but also on its level of gender inequality. *Class* inequality influences population growth too. We turn to the South Korean case to illustrate this point.

BOX 20.1
Social Policy: What Do You Think?

How Can We Find 100 Million Missing Women?

World population is expected to grow to about 9.1 billion by 2050. Yet demographers are fairly confident that world population will level off sometime between 2070 and 2100, reaching its peak at more than 10 billion.

Two main factors are causing the rate of world population growth to fall: economic development and the emancipation of women. Agricultural societies need many children to help with farming, but industrial societies require fewer children. Because many countries in the developing world are industrializing, the rate of world population growth is falling apace. The second main factor responsible for the declining growth rate is the improving economic status and education of women. Once women become literate and enter the non-agricultural paid labour force, they quickly recognize the advantages of having few children. The birth rate plummets. In many developing countries, that is just what is happening.

In other developing countries, the position of women is less satisfactory. We can see this by examining the ratio of women to men, or the **sex ratio** (United Nations, 2000).

In Canada in 2000, the sex ratio was about 1.02. That is, there were 102 women for every 100 men. This is about average for a highly developed country. (The sex ratio for Germany was 1.03 and for Japan it was 1.04.) The surplus of women reflects the fact that men are more likely than women to be employed in health-threatening occupations, consume a lot of cigarettes and alcohol, and engage in riskier and more violent behaviour, while women are the hardier sex, biologically speaking.

In the world as a whole, the picture is reversed. There were just 98 women for every 100 men in 2000. In India and China, there were only 94 women for every 100 men. Apart from Asia, North Africa is the region that suffers most from a deficit of women.

What accounts for variation in the sex ratio? According to Amartya Sen (1990, 2001), the sex ratio is low where women have less access to health services, medicine, and adequate nutrition than do men. These factors are associated with high female mortality. Another factor is significant in China, India, and some other Asian countries. In those countries, some parents so strongly prefer sons over daughters that sex-selective abortions contribute to the low sex ratio. Parents who

strongly prefer sons over daughters are inclined to abort female fetuses. In contrast, in highly developed countries women and men have approximately equal access to health services, medicine, and adequate nutrition while sex-selective abortions are rare. Therefore, there are more women than men. By this standard, the world as a whole is "missing" about 5 women for every 100 men (because $103 - 98 = 5$). This works out to about 100 million women missing in 2000 because of sex-selective abortions and unequal access to resources of the most basic sort.

We can "find" many of the missing 100 million women partly by eliminating gender inequalities in access to health services, medicine, and adequate nutrition. Increased female literacy and employment in the paid labour force are the most effective paths to eliminating such gender inequalities. That is because literate women who work in the paid labour force are in a stronger position to demand equal rights and are more likely to be married to men with similar sympathies.

The question of how to eliminate sex-selective abortions is more difficult. Economic factors do not account for variation in the use of sex-selective abortions. In some affluent parts of Asia with high levels of female education and economic participation, sex-selective abortions are common; India's lowest sex ratio—at 79, it is, in fact, the lowest sex ratio in the world—can be found in the wealthy northern states of Punjab and Haryana (Rahman, 2004).[2] In some other parts of Asia with low levels of female education and economic participation, sex-selective abortions are relatively rare. The best explanation for variations in sex-selective abortions seems to be that preference for sons is a strong *cultural* tradition in some parts of Asia. In India, for example, it may not be coincidental that sex-selective abortions are most widespread in the North and the West, where the nationalist and fundamentalist Hindu party, BJP, is most popular. Hindu nationalism and religious fundamentalism may feed into a strong preference for sons over daughters.

This leaves open the question of how, if at all, reformers inside and outside the region might rectify the situation. Cultural and religious traditions do not easily give way to economic forces (Brym et al., 2005). Meanwhile, a strong preference for sons over daughters adds millions to the number of missing women every year.

In 1960 South Korea had a total fertility rate of 6.0. This prompted one American official to remark that "if these Koreans don't stop overbreeding, we may have the choice of supporting them forever, watching them starve to death, or washing our hands of the problem" (quoted in Lie, 1998: 21). Yet by 1989, South Korea's total fertility rate had dropped to a mere 1.6. By 2003 it fell to 1.2. Why? The first chapter in this story involves land reform, not industrialization. The government took land from big landowners and gave it to small farmers. Consequently, small farmers' standard of living improved. This eliminated a major reason for high fertility. Once economic uncertainty decreased, so did the need for child labour and support of elderly parents by adult offspring. Soon, the total fertility rate began to fall. Subsequent declines in the South Korean total fertility rate were due to industrialization, urbanization, and the higher educational attainment of the population. But a decline in class inequality in the countryside first set the process in motion.

The reverse is also true. Increasing social inequality can lead to overpopulation, war, and famine. For example, in the 1960s the governments of El Salvador and Honduras encouraged the expansion of commercial agriculture and the acquisition of large farms by wealthy landowners. The landowners drove peasants off the land. The peasants migrated to the cities. There they hoped to find employment and a better life. Instead, they often found squalor, unemployment, and disease. Suddenly, two countries with a combined population of fewer than five million people had a big "overpopulation" problem. Competition for land increased and contributed to rising tensions. This eventually led to the outbreak of war between El Salvador and Honduras in 1969 (Durham, 1979).

Similarly, economic inequality helps to create famines. As Nobel Prize–winning economist Amartya Sen notes, "Famine is the characteristic of some people not *having* enough food to eat. It is not the characteristic of there not *being* enough food to eat" (Sen, 1981: 1; our emphasis). Sen's distinction is crucial, as his analysis of several famines shows. Sen found that, in some cases, although food supplies did decline, enough food was available to keep the stricken population fed. However, suppliers and speculators took advantage of the short supply. They hoarded grain and increased prices beyond the means of most people. In other cases, there was no decline in food supply at all. Food was simply withheld for political reasons, that is, to subdue a population, or because many people were not considered entitled to receive it by the authorities. For example, in 1932–33, Stalin instigated a famine in Ukraine that killed between 7 million and 10 million people. His purpose: to bring the Ukrainian people to their knees and force them to give up their privately owned farms and join state-owned, collective farms. The source of famine, Sen concludes, is not underproduction or overpopulation but inequality of access to food (Drèze and Sen, 1989). In fact, even when starving people gain access to food, other forms of inequality may kill them. For instance, when food relief agencies delivered three million sacks of grain to prevent famine in Western Sudan in the mid-1980s, tens of thousands of people died anyway because they lacked clean water, decent sanitation, and vaccinations against various diseases (de Waal, 1989). Western aid workers failed to listen carefully to the Sudanese people about their basic medical and sanitary needs, with disastrous results.

Summing Up

A new generation of demographers has begun to explore how class inequality and gender inequality affect population growth (Levine, 1987; Seccombe, 1992; Szreter, 1996). Their studies drive home the point that population growth and its negative consequences do not stem from natural causes alone (as Malthus held). Nor are they only responses to industrialization and modernization (as demographic transition theory suggests). Instead, population growth is influenced by a variety of social causes, social inequality chief among them.

Some undoubtedly well-intentioned Western analysts continue to insist that people in the developing countries should be forced to stop multiplying at all costs. Some observers even suggest diverting scarce resources from education, health, and industrialization into various forms of birth control, including, if necessary, forced sterilization (Riedmann, 1993). They regard the presumed alternatives—poverty, famine, war, ethnic violence, and the growth of huge, filthy cities—as too horrible to contemplate. However, they fail to see how measures that lower social inequality help to control overpopulation and its consequences. Along with industrialization, lower levels of social inequality cause total fertility rates to fall.

URBANIZATION

We have seen that overpopulation remains a troubling problem because of lack of industrialization and too much gender and class inequality in much of the world. We may now add that overpopulation is in substantial measure an *urban* problem. Driven by lack of economic opportunity in the countryside, political unrest, and other factors, many millions of people flock to big cities in the world's poor countries every year. Thus, most of the fastest-growing cities in the world today are in semi-industrialized countries where the factory system is not highly developed. As Table 20.2 shows, in 1900, 9 of the 10 biggest cities in the world were in industrialized Europe and the United States. By 2015, in contrast, 6 of the world's 10 biggest cities will be in Asia, 2 will be in Africa, and 2 will be in Latin America. Only 1 of the 10 biggest cities—Tokyo—will be in a highly industrialized country. Urbanization is, of course, taking place in the world's rich countries too. According to the 2006 census, more than 8 in 10 Canadians now reside in cities, with about 53 percent living in Canada's ten largest metropolitan areas: Toronto, Montreal, Vancouver, Ottawa-Gatineau, Calgary, Edmonton, Quebec City, Winnipeg, Hamilton, and London (Statistics Canada, 2007d). In North America as a whole, urban population is expected to increase to 84 percent of the total population by 2030. In Africa and Asia, however, the urban population is expected to increase much faster to 55 percent by 2030 (United Nations, 1997).

From the Preindustrial to the Industrial City

To a degree, urbanization results from industrialization. As you will learn in the following discussion, many great cities of the world grew up along with the modern factory, which drew hundreds of millions of people out of the countryside and transformed them into urban,

TABLE 20.2

World's 10 Largest Metropolitan Areas, 1900 and 2015, Projected (in Millions)

Sources: Department of Geography, Slippery Rock University, 1997, 2003.

1900		2015	
London, England	6.5	Tokyo, Japan	28.7
New York, United States	4.2	Mumbai (Bombay), India	27.4
Paris, France	3.3	Lagos, Nigeria	24.4
Berlin, Germany	2.4	Shanghai, China	23.4
Chicago, United States	1.7	Jakarta, Indonesia	21.2
Vienna, Austria	1.6	São Paulo, Brazil	20.8
Tokyo, Japan	1.5	Karachi, Pakistan	20.6
Saint Petersburg, Russia	1.4	Beijing, China	19.4
Philadelphia, United States	1.4	Dhaka, Bangladesh	19.0
Manchester, England	1.3	Mexico City, Mexico	18.8

Mexico City during one of its frequent smog alerts. Of the world's 10 biggest cities in 2015, only one—Tokyo—will be in a highly industrialized country. All the others, including Mexico City, will be in developing countries.

industrial workers. Industrialization is not, however, the whole story behind the growth of cities. As we have just seen, the connection between industrialization and urbanization is weak in the world's less developed countries today. Moreover, cities first emerged in Syria, Mesopotamia, and Egypt 5000 or 6000 years ago, long before the growth of the modern factory. These early cities served as centres of religious worship and political administration. Similarly, it was not industry but international trade in spices, gold, cloth, and other precious goods that stimulated the growth of cities in preindustrial Europe and the Middle East. Thus, the correlation between urbanization and industrialization is far from perfect (Bairoch, 1988 [1985]; Jacobs, 1969; Mumford, 1961; Sjöberg, 1960).

Preindustrial cities differed from those that developed in the industrial era in several ways. Preindustrial cities were typically smaller, less densely populated, built within protective walls, and organized around a central square and places of worship. The industrial cities that began to emerge at the end of the eighteenth century were more dynamic and complex social systems. A host of social problems, including poverty, pollution, and crime, accompanied their growth. The complexity, dynamism, and social problems of the industrial city were all evident in Chicago at the turn of the twentieth century. Not surprisingly, therefore, it was at the University of Chicago that modern urban sociology was born.

The Chicago School and the Industrial City

From the 1910s to the 1930s, the members of the **Chicago school** of sociology distinguished themselves by their vividly detailed descriptions and analyses of urban life, backed up by careful in-depth interviews, surveys, and maps showing the distribution of various features of the social landscape, all expressed in plain yet evocative language (Lindner, 1996 [1990]). Three of its leading members, Robert Park, Ernest Burgess, and Roderick McKenzie, proposed a theory of **human ecology** to illuminate the process of urbanization (Park, Burgess, and McKenzie, 1967 [1925]).

The **Chicago school** founded urban sociology in the United States in the first decades of the twentieth century.

Human ecology is a theoretical approach to urban sociology that borrows ideas from biology and ecology to highlight the links between the physical and social dimensions of cities and identify the dynamics and patterns of urban growth.

Carcassone, France, a medieval walled city

Differentiation in the theory of human ecology refers to the process by which urban populations and their activities become more complex and heterogeneous over time.

In the theory of human ecology, **competition** refers to the struggle by different groups for optimal locations in which to reside and set up their businesses.

Ecological succession in the theory of human ecology refers to the process by which a distinct urban group moves from one area to another and a second group comes in to replace the group that has moved out.

Urbanism is a way of life that, according to Louis Wirth, involves increased tolerance but also emotional withdrawal and specialized, impersonal, and self-interested interaction.

Borrowing from biology and ecology, the theory highlights the links between the physical and social dimensions of cities and identifies the dynamics and patterns of urban growth.

The theory of human ecology, as applied to urban settings, holds that cities grow in ever-expanding concentric circles. It is sometimes called the "concentric zone model" of the city. Three social processes animate this growth (Hawley, 1950). **Differentiation** refers to the process by which urban populations and their activities become more complex and heterogeneous over time. For instance, a small town may have a diner, a pizza parlour, and a Chinese restaurant. But if that small town grows into a city, it will likely boast a variety of ethnic restaurants reflecting its more heterogeneous population. Moreover, in a city, members of different ethnic and racial groups and socioeconomic classes may vie with one another for dominance in particular areas. Businesses may also try to push residents out of certain areas to establish commercial zones. When this happens, people are engaging in **competition**, an ongoing struggle by different groups to inhabit optimal locations. Finally, **ecological succession** takes place when a distinct group of people moves from one area to another and another group moves into the old area to replace the first group. For example, a recurrent pattern of ecological succession involves members of the middle class moving to the suburbs, with working class and poor immigrants moving into the inner city. In Chicago in the 1920s, differentiation, competition, and ecological succession resulted in the zonal pattern illustrated by Figure 20.4.

For members of the Chicago school, the city was more than just a collection of socially segregated buildings, places, and people. It also involved a way of life they called **urbanism**. They defined urbanism as "a state of mind, a body of customs[,] . . . traditions, . . . attitudes and sentiments" specifically linked to city dwelling (Park, Burgess, and McKenzie, 1967 [1925]: 1). Louis Wirth (1938) developed this theme. According to Wirth, rural life involves frequent face-to-face interaction among a few people. Most of these people are familiar with one another, share common values and a collective identity, and strongly respect traditional ways of doing things. Urban life, in contrast, involves the absence of community and of close personal relationships. Extensive exposure to many socially different people leads city dwellers to become more tolerant than rural folk are, said Wirth. However, urban dwellers also withdraw emotionally and reduce the intensity of their social interaction with others. In Wirth's view, interaction in cities is therefore superficial, impersonal, and focused on specific goals. People become more individualistic. Weak social control leads to a high incidence of deviance and crime.

After Chicago: A Critique

The Chicago school dominated North American urban sociology for decades and still inspires much interesting research (E. Anderson, 1990; Balakrishnan and Selvanathan, 1990). However, three major criticisms of this approach to understanding city growth have gained credibility over the years.

One criticism focuses on Wirth's characterization of the "urban way of life." Research shows that social isolation, emotional withdrawal, stress, and other problems may be just as common in rural as in urban areas (Crothers, 1979; Webb and Collette, 1977, 1979). After all, in a small community a person may not be able to find anyone with whom to share a particular interest or passion. Moreover, farm work can be every bit as stressful as work on an assembly line. Research conducted in Toronto and other North American cities also shows that urban life is less impersonal, anomic, and devoid of community than the Chicago sociologists made it appear. True, newcomers (of whom there were admittedly many in Chicago in the 1920s) may find city life bewildering if not frightening. Neighbourliness and friendliness to strangers are less common in cities than in small communities (Fischer, 1981). However, even in the largest cities, most residents create social networks and subcultures that serve functions similar to those performed by the small community. Friendship, kinship, ethnic and racial ties, as well as work and leisure relations, form the bases of these urban networks and subcultures (Fischer, 1984 [1976]; Jacobs, 1961; Wellman, 1979). Consider in this context that the United Nations identifies Toronto as the most multicultural city in the world, with more foreign-born than Canadian-born residents. Boasting more than

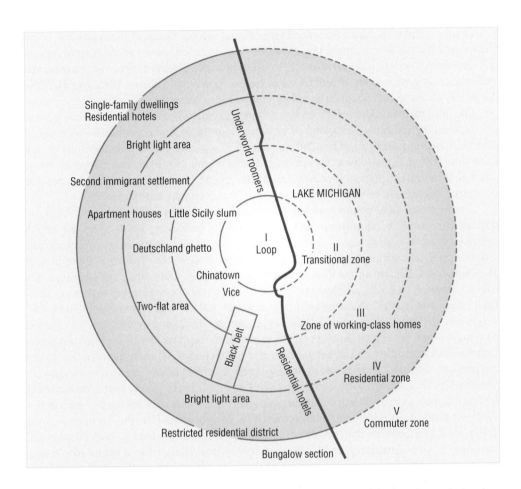

FIGURE 20.4
The Concentric Zone Model of
Chicago, about 1920

Source: From "The Growth of the
City: An Introduction to a Research
Project" Ernest W. Burgess,
pp. 47–62 in *The City* by Robert
E. Park et al. Copyright © 1967
University of Chicago Press. Used
with permission.

60 ethnic communities and 100 spoken languages, "Toronto's multicultural population is a source of community support for people in everyday life" (Geddes, 1997: 91; see also Bricker and Greenspon, 2001). Cities, it turns out, are clusters of many different communities, prompting one sociologist to refer to city dwellers as "urban villagers" (Gans, 1962).

A second problem with the Chicago school's approach concerns the applicability of the concentric zone model to other times and places. Canada, for example, has managed to avoid the American "ghetto" syndrome. In this country we do not find the deep and enduring poverty that characterizes so many central-city neighbourhoods in the United States (Janigan, 2002: 26). True, we have not managed to evade the problem entirely. Although the total metropolitan-area population of Canada grew 6.9 percent between 1990 and 1995, the poor population in those areas grew 33.8 percent. The poor urban population contains a large number of unemployed immigrants who know little English or French, Aboriginal peoples lacking much formal education, and single parents on social assistance (Janigan, 2002: 26). Research also shows that in the last few decades, socioeconomic and ethnic residential segregation has increased in the large cities of Canada. This led one urban sociologist to conclude that "Burgess was generally accurate" in observing that "[t]he socioeconomic status of urbanites increases directly with the distance of their residence from the city centre" (Gillis, 1995: 13.17; see also Kazemipur and Halli, 2000). Still, the core areas of most Canadian cities remain economically vibrant and socially viable, and they boast desirable and expensive housing. We conclude that the concentric zone theory has limited applicability to Canada.

Evidence from preindustrial cities supports the view that the concentric zone model was most applicable to American industrial cities in the first quarter of the twentieth century. In preindustrial cities, slums were more likely to be found on the outskirts. Wealthy districts were more likely to be found in the city core. Commercial and residential buildings were often not segregated (Sjöberg, 1960).

Finally, we note that after the automobile became a major means of transportation, some cities expanded not in concentric circles but in wedge-shaped sectors along natural boundaries and transportation routes (Hoyt, 1939). Others grew up around not one but many nuclei, each attracting similar kinds of activities and groups (Harris and Ullman, 1945; Figure 20.5). All of this serves to cast doubt on the universality of the concentric zone theory.

The third main criticism of the human ecology approach is that it presents urban growth as an almost natural process, slighting its historical, political, and economic foundations in capitalist industrialization. The Chicago sociologists' analysis of competition in the transitional zone came closest to avoiding this problem. However, their discussions of differentiation and ecological succession made the growth of cities seem almost like a force of nature rather than a process rooted in power relations and the urge to profit.

The so-called **new urban sociology**, heavily influenced by conflict theory, sought to correct this problem (Gottdiener and Hutchison, 2000; Zukin, 1980). For new urban sociologists, urban space is not just an arena for the unfolding of social processes like differentiation, competition, and ecological succession. Instead, they see urban space as a set of *commodified* social relations. That is, urban space, like all commodities, can be bought and sold for profit. As a result, political interests and conflicts shape the growth pattern of cities. John Logan and Harvey Molotch (1987), for example, portray cities as machines fuelled by a "growth coalition." This growth coalition comprises investors, politicians, businesses, property owners, real estate developers, urban planners, the mass media, professional sports teams, cultural institutions, labour unions, and universities. All these partners try to get government subsidies and tax breaks to attract investment dollars. Reversing the pattern identified by the Chicago sociologists, this investment has been used to redevelop decaying downtown areas in many North American cities since the 1950s. In Canada, this approach is evident in the development of Harbourfront, a 28.3-hectare (70-acre) property along Toronto's Lake Ontario that mixes recreational, cultural, residential, and commercial elements (Church, Greenberg, and McPhedran, 1997). It is also notable in the re-invigoration of Gastown and the former Expo '86 lands in Vancouver, Quebec City's thriving Lower Town, and the restoration and revitalization of Calgary's downtown area (Janigan, 2002: 25).

According to Logan and Molotch, members of the growth coalition present redevelopment as a public good that benefits everyone. This tends to silence critics, prevent discussion of alternative ideas and plans, and veil the question of who benefits and who does not. In reality, the benefits of redevelopment are often unevenly distributed. Most redevelopments are "pockets of revitalization surrounded by areas of extreme poverty" (Hannigan, 1998a: 53). That is, local residents often enjoy few if any direct benefits from redevelopment. Indirectly, they may suffer when budgets for public schooling, public transportation, and other amenities are cut to help pay for development subsidies and tax breaks. The growth coalition is not all-powerful. Community activism often targets local governments and corporations that seek unrestricted growth. Sometimes activists meet with success (Castells, 1983). Yet for the past 50 years, the growth coalition has managed to reshape the face of North American cities, more or less in its own image.

The new urban sociology emerged in the 1970s and stressed that city growth is a process rooted in power relations and the urge to profit.

FIGURE 20.5

The Peripheral Model of Cities: An Alternative to the Concentric Zone Model

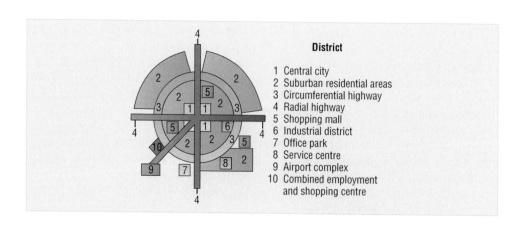

District

1 Central city
2 Suburban residential areas
3 Circumferential highway
4 Radial highway
5 Shopping mall
6 Industrial district
7 Office park
8 Service centre
9 Airport complex
10 Combined employment
   and shopping centre

Africville relocation meeting, Seaview Baptist Church, circa 1962. Halifax's Africville relocation project illustrates how poor urban residents typically have little say over redevelopment plans (Clairmont and Magill, 1999). Africville was settled around 1850 by blacks fleeing slavery in the United States, but it suffered drastic decline after World War I. The Halifax municipal government began to phase Africville out of existence in 1963 against the wishes of its residents. The city promised generous financial compensation and alternative housing, but some residents still refused to move. They were threatened with the expropriation of their property and eventually the community was bulldozed.

The Corporate City

Through the efforts of the growth coalition, the North American industrial city, typified by Chicago in the 1920s, gave way after World War II to the **corporate city**. University of Toronto sociologist John Hannigan defines the corporate city as "a vehicle for capital accumulation—that is, . . . a money-making machine" (Hannigan, 1998b: 345).

In the suburbs, urbanized areas outside the political boundaries of cities, developers built millions of single-family detached homes for the corporate middle class. These homes boasted large backyards and a car or two in every garage. A new way of life developed, which sociologists, appropriately enough, dubbed **suburbanism**. Every bit as distinctive as urbanism, suburbanism organized life mainly around the needs of children. It also involved higher levels of conformity and sociability than did life in the central city (Fava, 1956). Suburbanism became fully entrenched as developers built shopping malls to serve the needs of the suburbanites. This reduced the need to travel to the central city for consumer goods.

The suburbs were at first restricted to the well-to-do. However, following World War II, brisk economic growth and government assistance to veterans put the suburban lifestyle within the reach of middle-class Canadians. Extensive road-building programs, the falling price of automobiles, and the baby boom that began in 1946 also stimulated mushroom-like suburban growth.

The corporate city refers to the growing post–World War II perception and organization of the North American city as a vehicle for capital accumulation.

Suburbanism is a way of life outside city centres that is organized mainly around the needs of children and involves higher levels of conformity and sociability than life in the central city.

TABLE 20.3

The 10 Largest Census Metropolitan Areas in Canada, 1901 and 2006

Sources: Adapted from Kearney and Ray, 1999: 147; Statistics Canada, 2007d.

1901		2006	
CMA	Population	CMA	Population
Montreal	266 826	Toronto	5 113 149
Toronto	207 971	Montreal	3 635 571
Quebec City	68 834	Vancouver	2 116 581
Ottawa	59 902	Ottawa-Gatineau	1 130 761
Hamilton	52 550	Calgary	1 079 310
Winnipeg	42 336	Edmonton	1 034 945
Halifax	40 787	Quebec City	715 515
Saint John	40 711	Winnipeg	694 668
London	37 983	Hamilton	692 911
Vancouver	26 196	London	457 720

A **census metropolitan area (CMA)** includes a large urban area (known as the urban core) along with adjacent urban and rural areas (urban and rural "fringes") that are highly integrated with the urban core.

Edge cities are clusters of malls, offices, and entertainment complexes that arise at the convergence point of major highways.

Gentrification is the process of middle-class people moving into rundown areas of the inner city and restoring them.

FIGURE 20.6

Rural Population, Canada, 2001

Canada's rural population fell below half the total population in 1931. In 2001, it composed just 20.4 percent of the total population. As the accompanying graph indicates, however, there are wide variations in rurality among provinces and territories. The least populous parts of Canada (the north and the Atlantic provinces) are the most rural parts of the country, while the most populous parts (Ontario, Quebec, British Columbia, and Alberta) are the least rural.

In absolute terms, the rural population is decreasing in some parts of Canada but increasing in others. Rural population increase is occurring where individuals can easily commute to cities, where people want to retire, and in the north, where Aboriginal Canadians form a large percentage of the population and their birth rate is high. Rural areas experiencing population decrease are witnessing substantial out-migration of people under the age of 30 and a low birth rate (Bollman, 2000).

Source: Adapted from Statistics Canada, 2001, "Urban-Rural Population as a Proportion of Total Population, Canada, Provinces, Territories and Health Regions, 2001." Retrieved November 11, 2008 (http://www.statcan.ca/english/freepub/82-221-XIE/00503/tables/html/44_01.htm).

Because of the expansion of the suburbs, urban sociologists today often focus their attention not on cities but on **census metropolitan areas (CMAs)**, a term coined by Statistics Canada (Table 20.3). Each CMA includes a large urban area (known as the urban core) along with adjacent urban and rural areas (urban and rural "fringes") that are highly integrated with the urban core. The Statistics Canada definition of a CMA also specifies that it has an urban core population of at least 100 000 at the time of the most recent census.

CMAs also include two recent developments that indicate the continuing decentralization of urban Canada: the growth of rural residential areas within commuting distance of a city (Figure 20.6) and the emergence of **edge cities** where clusters of malls, offices, and entertainment complexes arise, often beside major highways (Garrau, 1991). Edge cities are the "sprawling outer suburbs" of major metropolitan areas (Janigan, 2002: 25). The growth of edge cities in Canada, though less pronounced than in the United States, has been stimulated by many factors. Among the most important are the mounting costs of operating businesses in city cores and the growth of new telecommunication technologies that are changing the location of work. Home offices, mobile employees, and decentralized business locations are all made possible by these technologies.

In the early 1960s, Toronto-based urban critic Jane Jacobs (1961) warned of the dangers of sprawling suburbs and decaying downtowns in *The Death and Life of Great American Cities*. Her forecasts, it seems, proved to be less valid for Canada than for the United States (Box 20.2). The municipal governments of Vancouver, Quebec City, Calgary, and other Canadian cities decided to reinvigorate their downtowns. In addition, deteriorating conditions in many of Canada's central cities were reduced by **gentrification**—a process whereby portions of the inner city are taken over by middle-class or higher-income groups and renovated and upgraded to desirable residential areas (Ley, 1996). Still, some Canadian cities, such as Winnipeg, followed a more American pattern. The downtown core underwent a process of decline as the middle class fled, pulled by the promise of a suburban lifestyle and pushed by such factors as racial animosity and fear of crime.

Some analysts suggest that many of the problems confronting cities are best resolved by amalgamation. They view the creation of "megacities," such as Toronto, now the fifth-largest city in North America, with considerable optimism. They argue that when it comes to

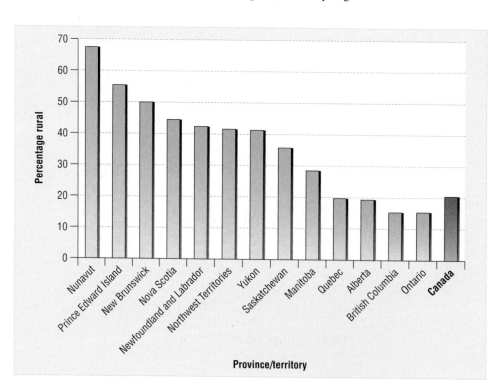

BOX 20.2
Sociology at the Movies

TAKE   ROLL

8 Mile (2002)

8 Mile Road is a depressing stretch of rundown buildings, gas stations, fast-food outlets, and strip malls that separates the rich and poor areas of Detroit, the most racially segregated city in the United States. South of 8 Mile Road, the people are overwhelmingly African American. The people in the suburbs north of 8 Mile Road are overwhelmingly European American.

Jimmy "Rabbit" Smith (Eminem) is a member of the white minority in the poor area. He has left his pregnant girlfriend to move in with his unemployed mother (Kim Basinger), his little sister, and his mother's unemployed boyfriend, with whom he went to high school and whom he hates. They live in a trailer park near 8 Mile Road. Rabbit operates a punch press by day. He is thin and pale. He slouches and keeps a beanie pulled low over his head, as if hiding from the world or keeping it at bay. His close friends think he is a gifted rap artist but his more numerous enemies think a white boy rapping is a travesty. They ridicule Rabbit and call him Elvis. He meets Alex (Brittany Murphy), a beautiful young woman who discerns his talent, but she betrays him. No wonder Rabbit is sullen and angry, reserving his rare smiles for his little sister.

Two rap competitions bracket the movie. In the first session, Rabbit has 45 seconds to out-insult his opponent. Instead, he freezes and is laughed and booed off the stage. In the second session, near the end of the movie, he has 90 seconds to prove his mettle. This time, he succeeds brilliantly.

The lyrics in the second rap session are worth heeding for their

Eminem and Brittany Murphy in *8 Mile*

sociological implications. Rabbit first anticipates the attack of his African-American opponent, Papa Doc, by listing his own deficiencies: I'm a white rapper, I'm a bum, I live in a trailer with my mom, my friend is so dumb he shot himself, my girlfriend betrayed me, and so forth. "Tell these people something they *don't* know about me," Rabbit taunts. After taking the wind out of his opponent's sails, he dissects Papa Doc with the following words:

But I know something about you:
You went to Cranbrook, that's a private school.
What's the matter dawg, you embarrassed?
This guy's a gangster?
His real name's Clarence.
And Clarence lives at home with both parents.
And Clarence's parents have a real good marriage.

Cranbrook is a prep school in Bloomfield Hills, a Detroit suburb north of 8 Mile Road. Clarence, it turns out, is not quite the streetwise

gang member from a single-parent family he makes himself out to be.

Clarence, however, is big news. Between 1970 and 1990, the number of Americans living in high-poverty neighbourhoods (where the poverty rate is 40 percent or higher) doubled. During the economic boom of the 1990s, the process of poverty concentration went into reverse. Two and a half million Americans moved out of high-poverty neighbourhoods and mostly into less impoverished, older, inner-ring suburbs around major metropolitan areas. Nowhere was the reversal more dramatic than in Detroit (Jargowsky, 2003).

The phenomenon represented by Clarence is encouraging yet fraught with danger. On the one hand, poor people are better off if they are widely dispersed rather than spatially concentrated. Spatially concentrated poor people have to deal not only with their own poverty but with a violent environment, low-performing schools, and a lack of positive role models. Thus, the exodus from the inner city is a positive development because it puts poor people in neighbourhoods where poverty is less concentrated. On the other hand, the exodus increases the percentage of poor people in many of the older, inner-ring suburbs around major metropolitan areas. This increase may result in the migration of many of the social ills of the inner city into the inner suburbs. If Clarence's children grow up where he did, they may be less susceptible to the ridicule of an Eminem.

responding to many urban problems—building adequate roads and public transit systems, improving the environment, providing efficient and cost-effective services, and negotiating with provincial or territorial and federal governments—bigger is better.

Although Winnipeg, Halifax, Saint John, Hamilton, and Fort McMurray are among the Canadian cities that have opted for amalgamation, some analysts maintain that "smaller is smarter." Critics argue that amalgamation often *increases* costs (istar, 2001). They also contend that, when compared with larger governmental units, smaller units are more democratic, accountable, and responsive to their citizens; sensitive to local, community, and neighbourhood issues; and capable of responding to local opinion on the types and levels of services desired. Large governments, they claim, are difficult to control, show greater resistance to innovation and government reform, and are more likely to be influenced by special interests and professional advocates, such as lobbyists (Cox, 1997).

The Postmodern City

The postmodern city is a new urban form that is more privatized and socially and culturally fragmented and globalized than the corporate city.

Many of the conditions that plagued the industrial city—poverty, inadequate housing, structural employment—are evident in Canadian cities today. However, since about 1970, a new urban phenomenon has emerged alongside the legacy of old urban forms. This is the **postmodern city** (Hannigan, 1995a). The postmodern city has three main features.

1. The postmodern city is more *privatized* than is the corporate city because access to formerly public spaces is increasingly limited to those who can afford to pay. Privatization is evident in the advertising claims of closed-off "gated communities" that boast of controlled-access front gates and foot patrols on the lookout for intruders. Privatization is also apparent in the construction of gleaming office towers and shopping areas that sometimes replace public urban green spaces. It is evident in pay-for-use public toilets and "patrons-only" washrooms. In the United States, this tendency is even more notable. For example, the private areas of downtown Los Angeles are increasingly intended for exclusive use by middle-class visitors and professionals who work in the information sector, including financial services, the computer industry, telecommunications, entertainment, and so forth.

2. The postmodern city is also more *fragmented* than the corporate city is. That is, it lacks a single way of life, such as urbanism or suburbanism. Instead, a variety of lifestyles and subcultures proliferate in the postmodern city. They are based on race, ethnicity, immigrant status, class, sexual orientation, and so forth.

3. The postmodern city is more *globalized* than is the corporate city. New York, London, and Tokyo epitomize the global city (Sassen, 1991). They are centres of economic and financial decision making. They are also sites of innovation, where new products and fashions originate. They have become the command posts of the globalized economy and its culture.

The processes of privatization, fragmentation, and globalization are evident in the way the postmodern city has come to reflect the priorities of the global entertainment industry. Especially in the 1990s, the city and its outlying districts came to resemble so many Disneyfied "Magic Kingdoms." These Magic Kingdoms are based on capital and technologies from Canada, the United States, Japan, Britain, and elsewhere. There we find the latest entertainment technologies and spectacular thrills to suit nearly every taste. The postmodern city gets its distinctive flavour from its theme parks, restaurants and night-

TECHNOLOGY
BYTES

clubs, waterfront developments, refurbished casinos, giant malls, megaplex cinemas, IMAX theatres, virtual-reality arcades, ride simulators, sports complexes, book and CD megastores, aquariums, and hands-on science "museums." In the postmodern city, nearly everything becomes entertainment or, more accurately, combines entertainment with standard consumer activities. This produces hybrid activities, such as "shoppertainment," "eatertainment," and "edutainment."

John Hannigan has shown how the new venues of high-tech urban entertainment manage to provide excitement—but all within a thoroughly clean, controlled, predictable, and safe environment (Hannigan, 1998a). The new Magic Kingdoms are kept spotless, in excellent repair, and fully temperature- and humidity-controlled. They also provide a sense of security by touting familiar name brands and rigorously excluding anything and anybody that might disrupt the fun. For example, entertainment developments often enforce dress codes, teenager curfews, and rules that ban striking workers and groups espousing social or political causes from their premises. The most effective barriers to potentially disruptive elements, however, are affordability and access. User surveys show that the new forms of urban entertainment tend to attract middle-class and upper-middle-class patrons, especially whites. That is because they are pricey and some are inaccessible by public transit and too expensive for most people to reach by taxi.

Referring to the major role played by the Disney Corporation in developing the new urban entertainment complexes, an architect once said that North American downtowns would be "saved by a mouse" (quoted in Hannigan, 1998a: 193). But do the new forms of entertainment that dot the urban landscape increase the economic well-being of the communities in which they are established? Not much, beyond creating some low-level, dead-end jobs (e.g., security guard, wait staff, janitor). Do they provide ways of meeting new people, seeing old friends and neighbours, and in general improving urban sociability? Not really. You visit a theme park with family or friends, but you generally stick close to your group and rarely have chance encounters with other patrons or bump into acquaintances. Does the high-tech world of globalized urban entertainment enable cities and neighbourhoods to retain and enhance their distinct traditions, architectural styles, and ambience? It would be hard to destroy the distinctiveness of such cities as New York, Montreal, or Vancouver, but many large North American cities are becoming homogenized as they provide the same entertainment services—and the same global brands—as Tokyo, Paris, and Sydney. If the mouse is saving our cities, perhaps he is also gnawing away at something valuable in the process.

NOTES

1. However, because people in the world's rich countries consume so much energy and other resources, they have a substantial negative impact on the global environment. See the online chapter that accompanies this book, Chapter 22, Technology and the Global Environment.

2. This is true not just in some of the more affluent states of India. Sex-selective abortions are also relatively common in well-to-do Singapore, Taiwan, and South Korea. However, the female-to-male sex ratio is rising quickly in South Korea as the preference for boys quickly recedes (Sang-Hun, 2007).

SUMMARY

1. What is the Malthusian theory of population growth? Does it apply today?
   Robert Malthus argued that although food supplies increase slowly, populations grow quickly. Because of these presumed natural laws, only war, pestilence, and famine can

keep human population growth in check. Several developments cast doubt on Malthus's theory. Food production has increased rapidly. The limits to population size are higher than Malthus expected. Some populations are large yet prosperous. Some countries provide generous social welfare and still maintain low population growth rates. The use of contraception is widespread.

2. What is demographic transition theory?

Demographic transition theory holds that the main factors underlying population dynamics are industrialization and the growth of modern cultural values. In the preindustrial era, both crude birth rates and crude death rates were high and population growth was therefore slow. In the first stage of industrialization, crude death rates fell, so population growth was rapid. As industrialization progressed and people's values about having children changed, the crude birth rate fell, resulting in slow growth again. Finally, in the postindustrial era, the crude death rate has risen above the crude birth rate in many societies. As a result, their populations shrink unless in-migration augments their numbers.

3. What factors aside from the level of industrialization affect population growth?

The level of social inequality between women and men, and between classes, affects population dynamics, with lower levels of social inequality typically resulting in lower crude birth rates and therefore lower population growth rates.

4. Is urbanization a function of industrialization?

Much urbanization is associated with the growth of factories. However, religious, political, and commercial needs gave rise to cities in the preindustrial era. Moreover, the fastest-growing cities in the world today are in semi-industrialized countries.

5. What did members of the Chicago school contribute to our understanding of the growth of cities?

The members of the Chicago school famously described and explained the spatial and social dimensions of the industrial city. They developed a theory of human ecology that explained urban growth as the outcome of differentiation, competition, and ecological succession. They described the spatial arrangement of the industrial city as a series of expanding concentric circles. The main business, entertainment, and shopping area stood in the centre, with the class position of residents increasing as they moved from inner to outer rings.

6. What are the main weaknesses of the Chicago school's analysis of cities?

Subsequent research showed that the city is not as anomic as the Chicago sociologists made it appear. Moreover, the concentric zone pattern applies best to the American industrial city in the first quarter of the twentieth century. Preindustrial cities, non-American cities, and contemporary cities do not fit the concentric zone pattern well. Moreover, the new urban sociology criticized the Chicago school for making city growth seem like an almost natural process, playing down the power conflicts and profit motives that prompted the evolution of cities.

7. What are the corporate and postmodern cities?

The corporate city that emerged after World War II was a vehicle for capital accumulation that stimulated the growth of the suburbs and resulted in the decline of inner cities. The postmodern city that took shape in the last decades of the twentieth century is characterized by the increased globalization of culture, fragmentation of lifestyles, and privatization of space.

KEY TERMS

census metropolitan area (CMA) (p. 584)

Chicago school (p. 579)

competition (p. 580)

corporate city (p. 583)

crude birth rate (p. 573)

crude death rate (p. 573)

demographers (p. 570)

demographic transition theory (p. 573)

differentiation (p. 580)

ecological succession (p. 580)

edge cities (p. 584)

emigration (p. 574)

gentrification (p. 584)

human ecology (p. 579)

immigration (p. 574)

in-migration (p. 574)

Malthusian trap (p. 571)

new urban sociology (p. 582)

out-migration (p. 574)

postmodern city (p. 586)

replacement level (p. 574)

sex ratio (p. 576)

suburbanism (p. 583)

urbanism (p. 580)

QUESTIONS TO CONSIDER

1. Do you think rapid global population growth is cause for alarm? If not, why not? If so, what aspects of global population growth are especially worrisome? What should be done about them?

2. Do you think of the city mainly as a place of innovation and tolerance or mainly as a site of crime, prejudice, and anomie? Where does your image of the city come from? your own experience? the mass media? your sociological reading?

WEB RESOURCES

Companion Website for This Book

http://www.compass3e.nelson.com

Begin by clicking on the Student Resources section of the website. Next, select the chapter you are studying from the pull-down menu. From the Student Resources page you have easy access to InfoTrac® College Edition, additional Weblinks, and other resources. The website also has many useful tips to aid you in your study of sociology, including practice tests for each chapter.

InfoTrac® Search Terms

These search terms are provided to assist you in beginning to conduct research on this topic by visiting http://www.infotrac-college.com:

immigration
urbanization
migration
poverty

Recommended Websites

Statistics Canada maintains a data-rich website at http://www.statcan.ca/start.html, including data from recent Canadian censuses (click on "Canadian Statistics") and sociodemographic profiles of many Canadian communities (click on "Community Profiles"). For an animated population pyramid that shows how the age and sex composition of the Canadian population changed during the twentieth century, visit http://www12.statcan.ca/english/census01/products/analytic/companion/age/pyramid.cfm.

Another useful site on demographic trends throughout the world is run by the Population Reference Bureau at http://www.prb.org.

The World Wide Web Library: Demography and Population Studies at http://demography.anu.edu.au/VirtualLibrary offers a comprehensive list of international websites devoted to the social scientific study of population.

For information on all 409 urban areas in the world with a population of more than one million, go to http://www.citypopulation.de.

CengageNOW™

http://hed.nelson.com

This online diagnostic tool identifies each student's unique needs with a Pretest that generates a personalized Study Plan for each chapter, helping students focus on concepts they're having the most difficulty mastering. Students then take a Posttest after reading the chapter to measure their understanding of the material. An Instructor Gradebook is available to track and monitor student progress.

CHAPTER

21

Collective Action and Social Movements

In this chapter, you will learn that

- People sometimes lynch, riot, and engage in other forms of non-routine group action to correct perceived injustices. Such events are rare, short-lived, spontaneous, and often violent. They subvert established institutions and practices. Nevertheless, most non-routine collective action requires social organization, and people who take part in collective action often act in a calculated way.

- Collective action can result in the creation of one or more formal organizations or bureaucracies to direct and further the aims of its members. The institutionalization of protest signifies the establishment of a social movement.

- People are more inclined to rebel against existing conditions when strong social ties bind them to many other people who feel similarly wronged; when they have the time, money, and other resources needed to protest; and when political structures and processes give them opportunities to express discontent.

- For social movements to grow, members must make the activities, goals, and ideology of the movement consistent with the interests, beliefs, and values of potential recruits.

- The history of social movements is a struggle for the acquisition of constantly broadening citizenship rights and opposition to those struggles.

HOW TO SPARK A RIOT

PERSONAL ANECDOTE

Robert Brym almost sparked a small riot once. "It happened in grade 11," says Robert, "shortly after I learned that water combined with sulphur dioxide produces sulphurous acid. The news shocked me. To understand why, you have to know that I lived in Saint John, New Brunswick, about 100 metres downwind of one of the largest pulp-and-paper mills in Canada. Waves of sulphur dioxide billowed from the mill's smokestacks day and night. The town's pervasive rotten-egg smell was a long-standing complaint in the area. But, for me, disgust turned to upset when I realized the fumes were toxic. Suddenly it was clear why many people I knew—especially people living near the mill—woke up in the morning with a kind of 'smoker's cough.' Through the simple act of breathing we were causing the gas to mix with the moisture in our bodies and form an acid that our lungs tried to expunge, with only partial success.

"Twenty years later, I read the results of a medical research report showing that area residents suffered from rates of lung disease, including emphysema and lung cancer, significantly above the North American average. But even in 1968 it was evident my hometown had a serious problem. I therefore hatched a plan. Our high school was about to hold its annual model parliament. The event was notoriously boring, partly because, year in year out, virtually everyone voted for the same party, the Conservatives. But here was an issue, I thought, that could turn things around. A local man, K. C. Irving, owned the pulp and paper mill. *Forbes* magazine ranked him as one of the richest men in the world. I figured that when I told my fellow students what I had discovered, they would quickly demand the closure of the mill until Irving guaranteed a clean operation.

"Was *I* naive. As head of the tiny Liberal Party, I had to address the entire student body during assembly on election day to outline the party platform and rally votes. When I got to the part of my speech that explained why Irving was our enemy, the murmuring in the audience, which had been growing like the sound of a hungry animal about to pounce on its prey, erupted into loud boos. A couple of students rushed the stage. The principal suddenly appeared from the wings and commanded the student body to settle down. He then took me by the arm and informed me that, for my own safety, my speech was finished. So, I discovered on election day, was our high school's Liberal Party. And so, it emerged, was my high-school political career.

"This incident troubled me for many years, partly because of the embarrassment it caused, partly because of the puzzles it presented. Why did I almost spark a small riot? Why didn't my fellow students rebel in the way I thought they would? Why did they continue to support an arrangement that was enriching one man at the cost of a community's health? Couldn't they see the injustice? Other people did. Nineteen sixty-eight was not just the year of my political failure in high school; it was also the year that student riots in France nearly toppled that country's government. In Mexico, the suppression of student strikes by the government left dozens of students dead. In the United States, students at Berkeley, Michigan, and other colleges demonstrated and staged sit-ins with unprecedented vigour. They supported free speech on their campuses, an end to American involvement in the war in Vietnam, increased civil rights for African Americans, and an expanded role for women in public affairs. It was, after all, the 1960s."

The Study of Collective Action and Social Movements

Robert didn't know it at the time, but by asking why students in Paris, Mexico City, and Berkeley rebelled while his fellow high-school students did not, he was raising the main question that animates the study of collective action and social movements. Under what social conditions do people act in unison to change, or resist change to, society? That is the main issue we address in this chapter.

We have divided the chapter into three sections:

Collective action occurs when people act in unison to bring about or resist social, political, and economic change.

1. We first discuss the social conditions leading to the formation of lynch mobs, riots, and other types of non-routine **collective action**. When people engage in collective action,

they act in unison to bring about or resist social, political, and economic change (Schweingruber and McPhail, 1999: 453). Some collective actions are "routine" and others are "non-routine" (Useem, 1998: 219). Routine collective actions tend to be nonviolent and follow established patterns of behaviour in bureaucratic social structures. For instance, when Mothers Against Drunk Driving (MADD) lobbies for tougher laws against driving under the influence of alcohol, when members of a community organize a campaign against abortion or for freedom of reproductive choice, and when workers form a union, they are typically engaging in routine collective action. Sometimes, however, "usual conventions cease to guide social action and people transcend, bypass, or subvert established institutional patterns and structures" (Turner and Killian, 1987: 3). On such occasions, people engage in non-routine collective action, which tends to be short-lived and sometimes violent. They may, for example, form mobs and engage in riots. Until the early 1970s, it was widely believed that people who engage in non-routine collective action lose their individuality and capacity for reason. Mobs and riots were often seen as wild and uncoordinated affairs, more like stampedes of frightened cattle than structured social processes. As you will see, however, sociologists later showed that this portrayal is an exaggeration. It deflects attention from the social organization and inner logic of extraordinary sociological events.[1]

2. We next outline the conditions underlying the formation of **social movements**. To varying degrees, social movements are enduring and bureaucratically organized collective attempts to change (or resist change to) part or all of the social order by petitioning, striking, demonstrating, and establishing lobbies, unions, and political parties. We will see that an adequate explanation of institutionalized protest also requires the introduction of a set of distinctively sociological issues. These concern the distribution of power in society and the framing of political issues in ways that appeal to many people.

3. Finally, we make some observations about the changing character of social movements. We argue that much of the history of social movements is the history of attempts by underprivileged groups to broaden their members' citizenship rights and increase the scope of protest from the local to the national to the global level.

We begin by considering the riot, a well-studied form of non-routine collective action.

> **Social movements are collective attempts to change all or part of the political or social order by means of rioting, petitioning, striking, demonstrating, and establishing pressure groups, unions, and political parties.**

NON-ROUTINE COLLECTIVE ACTION

The Vancouver Riot of 1907

Just after 9 p.m. on September 7, 1907, following a rousing chorus of "Rule Britannia," A. E. Fowler rose to address a crowd of several thousand people outside Vancouver City Hall. Fowler was secretary of the Seattle branch of the Asiatic Exclusion League, an organization of white trade unionists who were trying to convince the American and Canadian governments to keep Chinese, Japanese, Hindus, and Sikhs out of North America. Fowler was a fanatic. He was discharged from the U.S. Army for "unfitness by character and temperament" (quoted in Wynne, 1996). According to rumour, he spent time in the Washington State Asylum at Steilacoom. He certainly knew how to whip up a crowd's emotions. Just two days earlier, he had participated in an anti-Asian riot in Bellingham, Washington, 80 kilometres (50 miles) southeast of Vancouver. He described how 500 white men had invaded the lodgings of more than 1100 Sikh and Hindu mill workers under cover of night, dragged them half-naked from their beds, and beat them. Six of the victims were in hospital. Four hundred were in jail, guarded by police. Seven hundred and fifty had been driven across the U.S.–Canada border.

The Vancouver crowd liked what it heard. They loudly cheered Fowler's impassioned description of the Bellingham violence as they waved little flags inscribed "A white Canada for

Aftermath of the Vancouver
riot, 1907

us." According to one source, Fowler "whipped the crowd into a frenzy" by calling for a "straight-from-the-shoulder blow" against Asian immigration ("Chinese Community," 2001). Suddenly, someone threw a stone. It shattered a window in a nearby Chinese-owned shop. The crowd, its prejudices having been reinforced and inflamed by Fowler, took this as a cue. Its members surged uncontrollably into Vancouver's Chinatown, hurling insults, throwing rocks through windows, and beating and occasionally stabbing any Chinese people who were unable to flee or hide. With Chinatown reduced to a mass of broken glass, the crowd then moved on to the Japanese quarter, a few blocks away. The rioting continued for about three hours.

The next morning's papers in Toronto, Manchester, and London agreed on the main reason for the riot. The Toronto *Globe* said the riot was caused by "a gang of men from Bellingham." The *Manchester Guardian* said it had "proof of the correctness of the theory . . . that the anti-Japanese rioting in Vancouver was due to American agitators" (quoted in Wynne, 1996). In short, according to the papers, the riot resulted less from local social conditions than from the incitement of foreign hoodlums, the half-crazed Fowler foremost among them. Surely, the newspapers suggested, good white Canadian citizens could not be responsible for such an outrage.

Breakdown Theory

Until about 1970, most sociologists believed at least one of three conditions must be met for non-routine collective action, such as the 1907 Vancouver riot, to emerge. First, a group of people—leaders, led, or both—must be socially marginal or poorly integrated in society. Second, their norms must be strained or disrupted. Third, they must lose their capacity to act rationally by getting caught up in the supposedly inherent madness of crowds. Following Charles Tilly and his associates, we may group these three factors together as the **breakdown theory** of collective action. That is because all three factors assume collective action results from the disruption or breakdown of traditional norms, expectations, and patterns of behaviour (Tilly, Tilly, and Tilly, 1975: 4–6). At a more abstract level, breakdown theory may be seen as a variant of functionalism, for it regards collective action as a form of social imbalance that results from various institutions functioning improperly (see Chapter 1, A Sociological Compass). Specifically, most pre-1970 sociologists would have said that the Vancouver riot was caused by one or more of the following factors:

Breakdown theory suggests that social movements emerge when traditional norms and patterns of social organization are disrupted.

1. *The discontent of socially marginal people.* This was the factor Ontario and British newspapers emphasized when they singled out "foreign agitators" as the main cause of the disturbance. According to the papers, the Vancouver rioters were galvanized by people from outside the community; people who had little in common with the solid citizens of Vancouver; people who, nonetheless, were skilled in whipping crowds into a frenzy and getting them to act in extraordinary and violent ways. Breakdown theorists often single out such socially marginal, outside agitators as a principal cause of riots and other forms of collective action.

Sometimes, however, breakdown theorists focus on the social marginality of the led. Often, they say, a large number of the ordinary people who participate in riots, mobs, lynchings, and the like are poorly integrated in society. For example, they may be recent migrants to the area, that is, people who are unsettled and unfamiliar with the peaceable norms and conventions of the community. Pre-1970 sociologists could have made a case for the presence of many such people in Vancouver. The completion of the Canadian Pacific Railway more than two decades earlier and the ongoing construction of other railways had stimulated rapid economic growth and urbanization in British Columbia. Construction, mining, and lumbering were all boom industries. It is at least possible (although it has not been demonstrated empirically) that a large proportion of the rioters in 1907 were poorly integrated newcomers.

2. *The violation of norms* (sometimes called **strain**) is the second factor that pre-1970 sociologists would have stressed in trying to account for the 1907 Vancouver riot (Smelser, 1963: 47–48, 75). Arguably, two norms were violated in Vancouver in 1907, one cultural, the other economic. With rapid economic growth stimulating demand for labour, the number of Asian immigrants in British Columbia grew quickly in the early part of the twentieth century. By 1907, one-quarter of male workers in the province were of Asian origin. Their languages, styles of dress, religions, foods—in short, their entire way of life—offended many residents, who were of British origin. They regarded the Asian immigrants as "a threat to their cultural integrity" (Citizenship and Immigration Canada, 2000). From their point of view, Asian-Canadian cultural practices were violations of fundamental Anglo-Canadian norms.

> **Strain** refers to breakdowns in traditional norms that precede collective action.

A second source of strain may have been the result of rapid economic growth causing British Columbians' material expectations to grow out of line with reality. According to proponents of breakdown theory, it is not grinding poverty, or **absolute deprivation**, that generates riots and other forms of collective action so much as **relative deprivation**. Relative deprivation refers to the growth of an intolerable gap between the social rewards people expect to receive and those they actually receive. Social rewards are widely valued goods, such as money, education, security, prestige, and so forth. Accordingly, people are most likely to engage in collective action when rising expectations (brought on by, say, rapid economic growth and migration) exceed social rewards (sometimes brought on by economic recession or war; Davies, 1969; Gurr, 1970). Neither recession nor war affected Vancouver in 1907. But in that era of heady economic expansion, economic expectations may have risen beyond what society was able to provide. Hence the mounting frustration of Vancouver's workers that left them open to the influence of men like Fowler.

> **Absolute deprivation** is a condition of extreme poverty.

> **Relative deprivation** is an intolerable gap between the social rewards people feel they deserve and the social rewards they expect to receive.

3. *The inherent irrationality of crowd behaviour* is the third factor likely to be stressed in any pre-1970 explanation of the Vancouver riot. Gustave Le Bon, an early French interpreter of crowd behaviour, wrote that an isolated person might be a cultivated individual. In a crowd, however, the individual is transformed into a "barbarian," a "creature acting by instinct" possessing the "spontaneity, violence," and "ferocity" of "primitive beings" (Le Bon, 1969 [1895]: 28). Le Bon argued that this transformation occurs because people lose their individuality and willpower when they join a crowd. Simultaneously, they gain a sense of invincible group power that derives from the crowd's sheer size. Their feeling of invincibility allows them to yield to instincts they would normally hold in check. Moreover, if people remain in a crowd long enough, they enter something like a hypnotic state. This leaves them open to the suggestions of manipulative leaders and ensures that extreme passions spread through the crowd like a contagious disease. (Sociologists call Le Bon's argument the **contagion** theory of crowd behaviour.) For all these reasons, Le Bon held, people in crowds are often able to perform extraordinary and sometimes outrageous acts. "Extraordinary" and "outrageous" are certainly appropriate terms to describe the actions of the citizens of Vancouver in 1907.

> **Contagion** is the process by which extreme passions supposedly spread rapidly through a crowd like a contagious disease.

Assessing Breakdown Theory

Can social marginality, contagion, and strain fully explain what happened in Vancouver in 1907? Can breakdown theory adequately account for collective action in general? The short answer is no. Increasingly since 1970, sociologists have uncovered flaws in all three elements of breakdown theory and proposed alternative frameworks for understanding collective action. To help you appreciate the need for these alternative frameworks, let us reconsider the three elements of breakdown theory in the context of the Vancouver riot.

Social Marginality

Although it is true that Fowler and some of his associates were "outside agitators," the plain fact is that "if there had not been many local people who were deeply concerned about Oriental immigration, no amount of propaganda from the outside would have aroused the crowds" (Wynne, 1996). Moreover, the parade of 7000 to 9000 people who marched to city hall to hear Fowler's incendiary speech was organized locally by Vancouver trade unionists, ex-servicemen, and clergymen: all long-standing pillars of the community. This fits a general pattern. In most cases of collective action, leaders and early joiners tend to be well-integrated members of their communities, not socially marginal outsiders (Brym, 1980; Brym and Economakis, 1994; Economakis and Brym, 1995; Lipset, 1971 [1951]).

Contagion

No evidence suggests that the violence of September 7, 1907, was premeditated. But neither were the day's events spontaneous and unorganized acts of "contagion." A Vancouver branch of the Asiatic Exclusion League had been formed more than a month earlier and held three meetings before September 7. Two hundred people attended its third meeting on August 23. They carefully mapped out the route for the parade ending at city hall. They decided to hire a brass band. They arranged for the manufacture of flags emblazoned with racist slogans. They arranged to mobilize various local organizations to participate in the parade. They decided who would be invited to speak at city hall and what demands would be made of the government. Sophisticated planning went into organizing the day's events.

As the Vancouver example shows, and as much research on riots, crowds, and demonstrations has confirmed, non-routine collective action may be wild and violent but it is usually socially structured. In the first place, non-routine collective action is socially structured by the predispositions that unite crowd members and predate their collective action. Thus, if the Vancouver rioters had not shared racist attitudes, they never would have organized and assembled for the parade and engaged in the riot in the first place (Berk, 1974; Couch, 1968; McPhail, 1991). Second, non-routine collective action is socially structured by ideas and norms that emerge in the crowd itself, such as the idea to throw rocks through the windows of Chinese- and Japanese-owned shops in Vancouver (Turner and Killian, 1987). Third, non-routine collective action is structured by the degree to which different types of participants adhere to emergent and preexisting norms. Leaders, rank-and-file participants, and bystanders adhere to such norms to varying degrees (Zurcher and Snow, 1981). Fourth, pre-existing social relationships among participants structure non-routine collective action. For instance, relatives, friends, and acquaintances are more likely than strangers are to cluster together and interact in riots, crowds, demonstrations, and lynchings (McPhail, 1991; McPhail and Wohlstein, 1983; Weller and Quarantelli, 1973). Thus, non-routine collective action is socially organized in a number of ways, none of which is highlighted by focusing on contagion.

Strain

Contrary to the argument of many breakdown theorists, a large body of post-1970 research shows that, in general, levels of deprivation, whether absolute or relative, are not commonly associated with the frequency or intensity of outbursts of collective action, either in Canada or elsewhere (McPhail, 1994; Torrance, 1986: 115–45). In other words, although feelings of deprivation are undoubtedly common among people who engage in collective action, they are also common among people who do not engage in collective action. Deprivation may therefore be viewed as a necessary, but not a sufficient, condition for collective action. For example, although Asian immigration upset many Anglo-Canadians in Vancouver, the roots of the 1907 riot ran deeper than the violation of their cultural norms. The roots of the riot were embedded in the way the local labour market was organized. Typically, where low-wage workers of one race and high-wage workers of another race compete for the same jobs, racist attitudes develop or are reinforced because high-wage workers resent the presence of low-wage competitors (see Chapter 10, Race and Ethnicity). Conflict almost inevitably results. This happened when African Americans first migrated from the South to northern and western American cities in the early twentieth century. In Chicago, New York, and Los Angeles, the split labour market fuelled deep resentment, animosity, and even anti-black riots on the part of working-class whites (Bonacich, 1972). Similarly, the 1907 Vancouver riot was ultimately the result of the way social life and, in particular, the labour market were organized in the city.

We conclude that non-routine collective action is a two-sided phenomenon. Breakdown theory alerts us to one side. Collective action is partly a reaction to the violation of norms that threatened to *disorganize* traditional social life. But breakdown theory diverts attention from the other side of the phenomenon. Collective action is also a response to the *organization* of social life. And so we arrive at the starting point of post-1970 theories of collective action and social movements. For the past four decades, most students of the subject have recognized that collective action is often not a short-term reaction to disorganization and deprivation. Instead, it is a long-term attempt to correct perceived injustice that requires a sound social-organizational basis.

SOCIAL MOVEMENTS

According to breakdown theory, people typically engage in non-routine collective action soon after social breakdown occurs. In this view, rapid urbanization, industrialization, mass migration, unemployment, and war often lead to a buildup of deprivations or the violation of important norms. Under these conditions, people soon take to the streets.

In reality, however, people often find it difficult to turn their discontent into an enduring social movement. Social movements emerge from collective action only when the discontented succeed in building up a more or less stable membership and organizational base. Once this is accomplished, they typically move from an exclusive focus on short-lived actions, such as demonstrations and riots, to more enduring and routine activities. Such activities include establishing a publicity bureau, founding a newspaper, and running for public office. These and similar endeavours require hiring personnel to work full-time on various movement activities. Thus, the creation of a movement bureaucracy takes time, energy, and money. On these grounds alone, we should not expect social breakdown to result quickly in the formation of a social movement.

Solidarity Theory

Research conducted since 1970 shows that, in fact, social breakdown often does not have the expected short-term effect. That is because several social-structural factors modify the effects of social breakdown on collective action.[2] For example, Charles Tilly and his associates studied collective action in France, Italy, and Germany in the nineteenth and twentieth centuries (Lodhi and Tilly, 1973; Snyder and Tilly, 1972; Tilly, 1979a; Tilly, Tilly, and Tilly, 1975). They systematically read newspapers, government reports, and other sources so they could analyze a representative sample of strikes, demonstrations, and acts of collective violence. (They defined acts of collective violence as events in which groups of people seized or damaged other people or property.) They measured social breakdown by collecting data on rates of urban growth, suicide, major crime, prices, wages, and the value of industrial production. Breakdown theory would be supported if they found that levels of social breakdown rose and fell with rates of collective action. They did not.

As the top half of Table 21.1 shows for France, nearly all the correlations between collective violence and indicators of breakdown are close to zero. This means that acts of collective violence did not increase in the wake of mounting social breakdown, nor did they decrease in periods marked by less breakdown.

Significantly, however, Tilly and his associates found stronger correlations between collective violence and some other variables. You will find them in the bottom half of Table 21.1. These correlations hint at the three fundamental lessons of the **solidarity theory** of social movements, a variant of conflict theory (see Chapter 1, A Sociological Compass) and the most influential approach to the subject since the 1970s:

1. Inspecting Table 21.1, we first observe that collective violence in France increased when the number of union members rose. It decreased when the number of union members fell. Why? Because union organization gave workers more power, and that power increased their capacity to pursue their aims—if necessary, by demonstrating, striking, and engaging in collective violence. We can generalize from the French case as follows: Most collective action is part of a power struggle. The struggle usually intensifies as groups whose members feel disadvantaged become more powerful relative to other groups. How do disadvantaged groups become more powerful? By gaining new members, becoming better organized, and increasing their access to scarce resources, such as money, jobs, and means of communication (Bierstedt, 1974). French unionization is thus only one example of **resource mobilization**, a process by which groups engage in more collective action as their power increases because of their growing size and increasing organizational, material, and other resources (Gamson, 1975; Jenkins, 1983; McCarthy and Zald, 1977; Oberschall, 1973; Tilly, 1978; Zald and McCarthy, 1979).

2. Table 21.1 also shows that there was somewhat more collective violence in France when national elections were held. Again, why? Because elections gave people new political opportunities to protest. In fact, by providing a focus for discontent and a chance to put new representatives with new policies in positions of authority, election campaigns often serve as invitations to engage in collective action. Chances for protest also emerge

Solidarity theory suggests that social movements are social organizations that emerge when potential members can mobilize resources, take advantage of new political opportunities, and avoid high levels of social control by authorities.

Resource mobilization refers to the process by which social movements crystallize because of the increasing organizational, material, and other resources of movement members.

TABLE 21.1

Correlates of Collective Violence, France, 1830–1960

Notes: Correlations can range from −1.0 (indicating a perfect, inversely proportional relationship) to 1.0 (indicating a perfect, directly proportional relationship). A correlation of zero indicates no relationship. The correlation between the major crime and the rate of collective violence is negative, but it should be positive according to breakdown theory. The exact years covered by each correlation vary.

Source: Adapted from Tilly, Tilly, and Tilly, 1975: 81–82.

	Correlation with Frequency of Collective Violence
Breakdown variables	
Number of suicides	.00
Number of major crimes	−.16
Deprivation variables	
Manufactured goods prices	.05
Food prices	.08
Value of industrial production	.10
Real wages	.03
Organizational variable	
Number of union members	.40
Political process variable	
National elections	.17
State repression variable	
Days in jail	−.22

when influential allies offer support, when ruling political alignments become unstable, and when elite groups are divided and come into conflict with one another (Tarrow, 1994: 86–9; Useem, 1998). Said differently, collective action takes place and social movements crystallize not just when disadvantaged groups become more powerful but also when privileged groups and the institutions they control are divided and therefore become weaker. As economist John Kenneth Galbraith once said about the weakness of the Russian ruling class at the time of the 1917 revolution, if someone manages to kick in a rotten door, some credit has to be given to the door. In short, this second important insight of solidarity theory links the timing of collective action and social movement formation to the emergence of new **political opportunities** (McAdam, 1982; Piven and Cloward, 1977; Tarrow, 1994).

3. The third main lesson of solidarity theory is that government reactions to protest influence subsequent protest (see Box 21.1 on page 600). Specifically, governments can try to lower the frequency and intensity of protest by taking various **social control** measures (Oberschall, 1973: 242–83). These measures include making concessions to protesters, co-opting the most troublesome leaders (for example, by appointing them advisers), and violently repressing collective action. The last point explains the modest correlation in Table 21.1 between frequency of collective violence and governments throwing more people into jail for longer periods. In France, more violent protest often resulted in more state repression. However, the correlation is modest because social control measures do not always have the desired effect. For instance, if grievances are very deeply felt, and yielding to protesters' demands greatly increases their hopes, resources, and political opportunities, government concessions may encourage protesters to press their claims further. And although the firm and decisive use of force usually stops protest, using force moderately or inconsistently often backfires. That is because unrest typically intensifies when protesters are led to believe that the government is weak or indecisive (Piven and Cloward, 1977: 27–36; Tilly, Tilly, and Tilly, 1975: 244).

Discussions of strain, deprivation, and contagion dominated analyses of collective action and social movements before 1970. Afterward, analyses of resource mobilization, political opportunities, and social control dominated the field. Let us now make the new ideas more concrete. We do so by analyzing the ups and downs of one of the most important social movements in twentieth-century Canada, the union movement, and its major weapon, the strike.

Political opportunities for collective action and social movement growth occur during election campaigns, when influential allies offer insurgents support, when ruling political alignments become unstable, and when elite groups become divided and conflict with one another.

Social control refers to methods of ensuring conformity and the means by which authorities seek to contain collective action, including co-optation, concessions, and coercion.

Strikes and the Union Movement in Canada

You can appreciate the significance of solidarity theory by considering patterns of strike activity in Canada. When blue-collar and white-collar workers go out on strike, they withhold their labour to extract concessions from employers or governments in the form of higher wages and improved social welfare benefits. How do resource mobilization, political opportunity, and social control influence the willingness of workers to challenge the authority of employers and governments in this way?

Resource Mobilization

Consider first the effect of resource mobilization on the frequency of strikes. Research shows that in Canada between the mid-1940s and the mid-1970s, strike activity was high when (1) unemployment was low, (2) union membership was high, and (3) governments were generous in their provision of social welfare benefits. Low unemployment indicates a strong economy. Workers are inclined to strike when business activity is robust because they know employers and governments can afford to make concessions. (Employers make bigger profits and governments collect more taxes during economic booms.) A high level of unionization is also conducive to more strike activity because unions provide workers

BOX 21.1
It's Your Choice

State Surveillance of Demonstrations

On June 15, 2000, members of the Ontario Coalition Against Poverty (OCAP) organized a demonstration of about 1000 people in front of the provincial legislature at Queen's Park to protest the policies of Mike Harris's Progressive Conservative government toward the poor and homeless. It didn't take long before a violent confrontation developed between protesters and the police. Gary Morton, one of the demonstrators, described the events as follows:

An angry crowd of protesters, most of them wearing clothing to protect them from chemical attack by police, marches across the city to the legislature at Queen's Park. They make noise, bang drums and chant. When they arrive, huge numbers of riot police meet them. . . . [T]he protesters send a delegation to the barricades at the front. Their demand—that they be allowed to address the legislature on homeless issues. The response is that no such thing will be allowed and no representative of the Harris Government will be speaking to them. The delegation informs the crowd of this and they surge forward to [the] barricades. . . . The people at the front grab the barricades and walk backward with them, opening a hole for the crowd to get through. Then all hell breaks loose. Gas smoke rolls and police charge out swinging batons. Some protesters struggle with them and others throw a few things like small water bottles. Horseback cops follow up, riding in from the north to force the crowd back and then swinging back in from the south. Between the horse sweeps the riot cops charge out and then get pushed back in. The police slowly gain ground. People are being picked off and beaten and cops begin to

OCAP versus then Ontario Premier Mike Harris, Toronto, June 15, 2000

charge viciously into the larger body of peaceful protesters. At this point many people, myself included, begin to throw anything they can at the police. Bottles of water, mud and stones from the garden, picket signs. Brutality increases; anarchists tear apart a sidewalk and throw the chunks of stone at police. Horse charges swing in through the grassy area of the park and as the fight continues for some time we get forced out on the road, which we block. . . . The police are now saying that they are going to review their videos frame by frame. (Morton, 2000)

The videos to which Morton refers came from seven cameras police set up to record the demonstration. In addition, police had a still photographer and several plainclothes officers with disposable cameras on duty. Two cameras belonging to Queen's Park security officers were also rolling during the melee. Finally, after the demonstration, the police seized film and videotape of the demonstration from television networks and newspapers (the CBC, CTV, ONtv, Global

Television, *The Globe and Mail*, the *Toronto Star*, and *Sing Tao*).

What effect might police surveillance of demonstrations have on collective action? In the first place, if journalists fear their film and videos might be seized, they may be less likely to produce objective news reports. For example, a journalist might be disinclined to film a demonstrator being beaten by the police knowing that the film could be edited and used to identify and prosecute the demonstrator (Canadian Journalists for Free Expression, 2000). Moreover, according to sociologist Gary Marx, surveillance systems can be "used against those with the 'wrong' political beliefs; against racial, ethnic, or religious minorities; and against those with lifestyles that offend the majority" (quoted in Boal, 1998). One journalist comments: "Social psychologists say that taping political events can affect a participant's self-image, since being surveilled is unconsciously associated with criminality. Ordinary citizens shy away from politics when they see activists subjected to scrutiny. As this footage is splayed across the nightly news, everyone gets the meta-message: hang with dissenters and you'll end up in a police video" (Boal, 1998). In short, police surveillance of demonstrations may limit dissent and the free expression of political opinion.

What do you think? In the interest of maintaining law and order, should the police be entirely free to record demonstrations by using cameras? Should they be allowed to seize film and videos from journalists? Or do such actions infringe the fundamental democratic rights of both the media and the citizenry? As a citizen, it's your choice.

with leadership, strike funds, and coordination. Thus, as resource mobilization principles suggest, strong social ties among workers (as indicated by a high level of unionization) and access to jobs and money (as indicated by a booming economy) increase challenges to authority (as indicated by strikes).[3]

Figure 21.1 shows the pattern of strike activity in Canada between the end of World War II and 2006. It adds substance to the resource mobilization approach. Until 1974, the trend in strike activity was upward. In fact, in the 1970s, Canada was the most strike-prone country in the world. This was a period of growing prosperity, low unemployment, expanding state benefits, and increasing unionization. With access to increasing organizational and material resources, workers challenged authority increasingly more often in the three decades after World War II.

In 1973, however, economic crisis struck. As a result of turmoil in the Middle East, oil prices tripled, and then tripled again at the end of the decade. Inflation increased and unemployment rose. Soon, the government was strapped for funds and had to borrow heavily to maintain social welfare programs. Eventually, the debt burden was so heavy the government felt obliged to cut various social welfare programs. At the same time, federal and provincial and territorial governments introduced laws and regulations limiting the right of some workers to strike and putting a cap on the wage gains that workers could demand. Unionization reached a peak in 1978, stabilized, and then began to decline (see Figure 21.2 on page 602).

Strike action was made even more difficult when Canada signed the free trade deal with the United States and Mexico. It was now possible for some employers to threaten to relocate to the United States or Mexico in the face of protracted strikes. Thus, in the post-1973 climate, the organizational and material resources of workers fell. As a result, strike activity plummeted. In 1974, nearly 16 strikes took place for every 100 000 Canadian non-agricultural workers. By 2006, that number had fallen to just over 1 (Brym, 2008a).

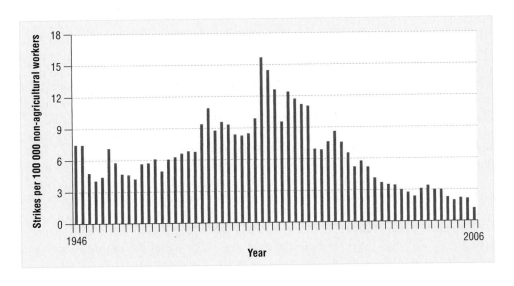

FIGURE 21.1

Weighted Frequency of Strikes, Canada, 1946–2006

Sources: International Labour Organization (2008); Labour Organizations in Canada (1973: xxii-xxiii); 1994–1995 Directory of Labour Organizations in Canada (1995: xiii); 1998 Directory of Labour Organizations in Canada (1998: 15); "Chronological Perspective on Work Stoppage in Canada" (1999, 2001a, 2001b); Strikes and Lockouts in Canada 1968 (1970: 12-13); Strikes and Lockouts in Canada 1985 (1985: 9); Workplace Information Directorate (1996).

FIGURE 21.2

Percentage of Non-agricultural Workers Unionized, Canada and United States, 1925–2005

Sources: *Labour Organizations in Canada 1972*, 1973: xxii–xxiii; 1994–1995 *Directory of Labour Organizations in Canada*, 1995: xiii; *1998 Directory of Labour Organizations in Canada*, 1998: 15; "Union Membership in Canada—2000," 2000; U.S. Bureau of Labor Statistics, 1998, 1999, 2001.

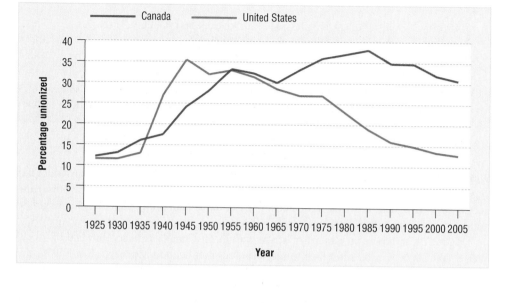

Union density is the number of union members in a given location as a percentage of non-agricultural workers. It measures the organizational power of unions.

Political Opportunities

Comparing Canada and the United States allows us to highlight the effect of *political opportunities* on the health of the union movement. These two cases illustrate that opportunities for union growth are greater when privileged groups and the institutions they control are divided and therefore become weaker. Opportunities for union growth are fewer when privileged groups are socially cohesive and are backed by strong institutions.

The United States and Canada have similar industrial and occupational structures. As the world's two largest trading partners, and linked by a free trade agreement, they are subject to most of the same economic forces. Yet, as Figure 21.2 shows, trends in **union density** (the percentage of the non-agricultural labour force that is unionized) started to diverge in the mid-1960s. In 2006, 12.0 percent of non-agricultural employees in the United States were members of a union. In Canada, the proportion was 30.7 percent. Why?

John F. Kennedy won the closely contested American presidential election of 1960 partly because of the union movement's support. As a result of his victory, government employees were awarded the right to unionize in 1961. Their rights were sharply restricted, however. Striking, bargaining collectively over wages and benefits, and compulsory membership were not allowed. Therefore, public-sector unions did not become a very effective or popular means for furthering employee interests.

The situation in Canada in the early 1960s was different. A new pro-labour political party, the New Democratic Party (NDP), was established in Canada in 1961 with the support of the union movement. The NDP gained enough popularity among voters to be able to exert considerable influence over government policy. In fact, in the mid-1960s, the ruling Liberal Party would have lost office without NDP support. The NDP used its political leverage to convince the government to extend full union rights to public-sector workers, including the right to strike and bargain collectively. Government employees soon joined unions in droves—and to a considerably greater extent than in the United States. Moreover, partly as a result of NDP influence, restrictions on private-sector unionization were eased. Thus, in Canada, union density increased after the mid-1960s because political forces made unions attractive vehicles for furthering workers' interests.

Why, then, has the union movement been more successful in Canada than in the United States since the 1960s? Because in the United States a unified political establishment was able to prevent the union movement from gaining rights that would make it attractive to more workers. Meanwhile, in Canada, a more divided political establishment could not prevent the creation of a legal environment that was favourable to union growth. In both cases, we see how political opportunities affect the growth or decline of social movements.

Social Control

Finally, we turn to the most disruptive and violent strike in Canadian history—the Winnipeg General Strike of 1919—because it illustrates well three features of the use of *social control* on social movements:

1. *If authorities show indecision or weakness, movement partisans often become bolder.* In April 1918, in a smaller general strike, three unions of Winnipeg city employees walked off the job, demanding higher wages. A month later, the strikers and their employers had nearly hammered out a settlement. Just before signing off on the deal, however, the Winnipeg city council added a clause demanding that city workers pledge never to go on strike again. In angry reaction, nearly all city employees walked off the job. The same day, the city council capitulated. The striking workers got almost everything they demanded. After many bitter defeats, this victory convinced Winnipeg's workers they could get what they wanted by participating in a general strike, that is, a strike in which all employees walk off the job. Clearly, the city council's capitulation emboldened the workers (Bercuson, 1974: 7).

2. The second thing the Winnipeg strike teaches us about the use of social control on social movements is that *violence, especially the most extreme forms of violence, is most often initiated by authorities, not movement partisans.* On May 15, 1919, negotiations broke down over building and metalworkers' demands for union recognition and higher wages. They called a general strike. The next morning, the city was paralyzed. Nearly all workers walked off the job. The strike leaders made every effort to keep the streets peaceful. The police, who supported the strike, even agreed to continue working to help maintain law and order. The city council, however, was opposed to having pro-strike police officers on duty. So they fired the entire police force, replacing them with a large group of untrained "special police" who were hostile to the strike. The special police celebrated their first day of service by riding their horses and swinging their batons into a crowd listening to a speech downtown. That was the first act of violence during the Winnipeg General Strike but it was by no means the last. In addition to the special police, a mobile military force of 800 men armed with rifles and machine guns was recruited and trained to deal with the strikers. On the afternoon of Saturday, June 21, that is just what they did. Striking workers had been gathering downtown to hold a parade in defiance of a ban issued by the mayor. They spotted a streetcar driven by a scab (replacement worker), cut the electricity powering it, smashed its windows, slashed its seats, and set the interior on fire. Fifty-four Royal North-West Mounted Police on horses and 36 in trucks were dispatched to break up the crowd. They charged twice. The crowd responded by throwing rocks and bottles. The Mounties then opened fire on the crowd and continued firing for several minutes. One worker was killed and many more were wounded. There is no evidence that workers fired any shots (Bercuson, 1974: 27). As is usually the case when we compare the violence exercised by authorities with the violence exercised by movement partisans, the authorities came out on top (Tilly, Tilly, and Tilly, 1975).

3. Finally, the Winnipeg strike teaches us that *violent repression can still discontent, at least for a time.* That was certainly the case in Winnipeg. Four days after "Bloody Saturday," as June 21 came to be known, the Strike Committee called off the walkout, the strikers having failed to achieve any of their objectives. It took another quarter-century of strikes, many of them bitterly fought, before a larger and more powerful Canadian working class achieved the main demand of the Winnipeg General Strike and won the legal right to form unions.

FRAMING DISCONTENT

As we have seen, solidarity theory helps to explain the emergence of many social movements. Still, the rise of a social movement sometimes takes strict solidarity theorists by surprise. So does the failure of an aggrieved group to press its claims by means of collective

The Winnipeg General Strike of
1919 was the most disruptive
and violent strike in Canadian
history.

Frame alignment is the
process by which individual
interests, beliefs, and values
become congruent and com-
plementary with the activities, goals, and ideology of a
social movement.

action. It seems, therefore, that something lies between (1) the capacity of disadvantaged
people to mobilize resources for collective action and (2) the recruitment of a substantial
number of movement members. That "something" is **frame alignment** (Benford, 1997;
Carroll and Ratner, 1996a, 1996b; Goffman, 1974; Snow, Rochford Jr., Worden, and
Benford, 1986; Valocchi, 1996). Frame alignment is the process by which social movement
leaders make their activities, ideas, and goals congruent with the interests, beliefs, and
values of potential new recruits to their movement—or fail to do so. Thanks to the efforts of
scholars operating mainly in the symbolic interactionist tradition (see Chapter 1,
A Sociological Compass), frame alignment has recently become the subject of sustained
sociological investigation (see Box 21.2).

BOX 21.1
Sociology at the Movies

The Day After Tomorrow
(2004)

Most summers, Hollywood releases a
disaster movie in which a highly
implausible catastrophe serves as the
backdrop for heroism and hope.
Audiences return home momentarily
frightened but ultimately safe in the
knowledge that the chance of any such
cataclysm is vanishingly remote.

The Day After Tomorrow follows
the usual script. The movie opens with a
sequence of bizarre meteorological
events. A section of ice nearly the size
of Prince Edward Island breaks off the
Antarctic ice cap. Snow falls in New
Delhi. Hail the size of grapefruits
pounds Tokyo. Enter Jack Hall (Dennis
Quaid), a scientist whose research suggests an explanation: Sudden climate
change is a very real possibility. The

idea becomes a political football when it
is ridiculed by the vice-president of the
United States, but once torrential rains
and a tidal wave flood New York City,
Hall's theories are vindicated. In a
matter of days, temperatures
plummet—at one point, they fall
10 degrees Fahrenheit a minute to
150 degrees Fahrenheit below the
freezing point (–83 degrees Celsius).
The entire Northern Hemisphere is

plunged into a new ice age. Almost everyone freezes to death in the northern United States, while millions of desperate southerners flee into Mexico.

Although it seems like standard fare, *The Day After Tomorrow* is a Hollywood disaster movie with a difference, for it is based on a three-part idea with considerable scientific support. Part 1 is agreed on by everyone: Since the Industrial Revolution, humans have released increasing quantities of carbon dioxide into the atmosphere as we burn more and more fossil fuels to operate our cars, furnaces, and factories. Part 2 is agreed on by the overwhelming majority of scientists: The accumulation of carbon dioxide allows more solar radiation to enter the atmosphere and less heat to escape. This contributes to global warming. As temperatures rise, more water evaporates and the polar ice caps begin to melt. This causes more rainfall, bigger storms, and more flooding. Part 3 is the most recent and controversial part of the argument: The melting of the polar ice caps may be adding enough fresh water to the oceans to disrupt the flow of the Gulf Stream, the ocean current that carries warm water up the east coast of North America and the west coast of Europe. Computer simulations suggest that decreased salinity could push the Gulf Stream southward, causing average winter temperatures to drop by 10 degrees Fahrenheit (5.6 degrees Celsius) in northeastern Canada, the United States, and other parts of the Northern Hemisphere.

A recent Pentagon study suggests that such climate change could cause

Scene from *The Day After Tomorrow* (2004)

droughts, storms, flooding, border raids, large-scale illegal migration from poor regions, and even war between nuclear powers over scarce food, drink- ing water, and energy (Joyce and Keigwin, 2004; Stipp, 2003). *The Day After Tomorrow* greatly exaggerates the suddenness and magnitude of what scientists mean by abrupt climate change. "Abrupt" can mean centuries to climatologists, and temperature drops of 10 degrees Fahrenheit a minute are pure fantasy. Still, at the movie's core lies an ominous and real possibility.

The Day After Tomorrow also teaches us an important sociological lesson about the framing of issues by social movements and their opponents. Environmental problems do not become social issues spontaneously. They are socially constructed in what might be called a "framing war." Just as Jack Hall and the vice-president spar

over the credibility of Hall's prediction of sudden climate change, so do groups with different interests dispute environmental problems, framing them differently ways so as to win over public opinion.

The Day After Tomorrow became involved in the framing war because in the months leading up to the release of the movie, environmentalists started piggybacking their message on it. They bombarded journalists with e-mails explaining global warming and offering interviews with leading scientists on the subject. Newspapers and magazines around the world subsequently carried stories on the issue. Environmentalists then distributed flyers to moviegoers as they left theatres (Houpt, 2004). In this way, *The Day After Tomorrow* became not just another disaster movie but also part of the framing war around one of the major environmental issues of the day.

Examples of Frame Alignment

Frame alignment can be encouraged in several ways. For example:

1. Social movement leaders can reach out to other organizations that, they believe, contain people who may be sympathetic to their movement's cause. Thus, leaders of an anti-nuclear movement may use the mass media, telephone campaigns, and direct mail to appeal to feminist, anti-racist, and environmental organizations. In doing so, they

assume these organizations are likely to have members who would agree at least in general terms with the anti-nuclear platform.

2. Movement activists can stress popular values that have so far not featured prominently in the thinking of potential recruits. They can also elevate the importance of positive beliefs about the movement and what it stands for. For instance, in trying to win new recruits, movement members might emphasize the seriousness of the social movement's purpose. They might analyze the causes of the problem the movement is trying to solve in a clear and convincing way. Or they might stress the likelihood of the movement's success. By doing so, they can increase the movement's appeal to potential recruits and perhaps win them over to the cause.

3. Social movements can stretch their objectives and activities to win recruits who are not initially sympathetic to the movement's original aims. This may involve a "watering down" of the movement's ideals. Alternatively, movement leaders may decide to take action calculated to appeal to non-sympathizers on grounds that have little or nothing to do with the movement's purpose. When rock, punk, or reggae bands play at nuclear disarmament rallies or gay liberation festivals, it is not necessarily because the music is relevant to the movement's goals. Nor do bands play just because movement members want to be entertained. The purpose is also to attract non-members. Once attracted by the music, however, non-members may make friends and acquaintances in the movement and then be encouraged to attend a more serious-minded meeting.

As we see, then, there are many ways in which social movements can make their ideas more appealing to a larger number of people. However, movements must also confront the fact that their opponents routinely seek to do just the opposite. That is, although movements seek to align their goals, ideas, and activities with the way potential recruits frame issues, their adversaries seek to *disalign* the way issues are framed by movements and potential recruits.

The B.C. Forest Alliance provides a good illustration of this process (Doyle, Elliott, and Tindall, 1997). Launched in British Columbia in 1991, the B.C. Forest Alliance was created and bankrolled by a group of senior forest industry executives and guided by the world's largest public relations firm. Its goal was to counter the province's environmental movement. It did so in two main ways. First, in its TV and print ads, the alliance claimed it represented

The Live 8 concert in Barrie, Ontario, July 2005, featured Bruce Cockburn, Kevin Hearn of the Barenaked Ladies, Neil Young, Gordon Lightfoot, and many other Canadian rock stars. When bands play at protest rallies or festivals, it is not just for entertainment and not just because the music is relevant to a social movement's goals. The bands also attract non-members to the movement. This is one way of framing a social movement's goals to make them appealing to non-members.

the "middle ground" in the debate between forest companies and environmentalists. In practice, the alliance rarely criticized forest companies while it routinely characterized environmentalists as dope-smoking hippies with untenable ideas, such as shutting down the entire forest industry. Actually, very few environmentalists hold such extreme opinions, and research shows that that the middle class in British Columbia broadly supports environmental groups. The second way the alliance sought to counter the environmental movement was by arguing that more environmentalism means fewer jobs. This was a huge oversimplification. Job losses in the forest industry were also caused by the introduction of new technologies in some areas, aging equipment in others, First Nations land claims, and resource depletion through overharvesting and inadequate reforestation.

Muddying the waters in this way is typical of social movement opponents. Frame alignment should therefore be viewed as a conflict-ridden process in which social movement partisans and their opponents use the resources at their disposal to compete for the way in which potential recruits and sympathizers view movement issues.

An Application of Frame Alignment Theory: Back to 1968

Frame alignment theory stresses the strategies employed by movement members to recruit non-members who are like-minded, apathetic, or even initially opposed to the movement's goals. Resource mobilization theory focuses on the broad social-structural conditions that facilitate the emergence of social movements. One theory usefully supplements the other.

The two theories certainly help clarify the 1968 high-school incident described at the beginning of this chapter. In light of our discussion, it seems evident that two main factors prevented Robert Brym from influencing his classmates when he spoke to them about the dangers of industrial pollution from the local pulp-and-paper mill.

First, he lived in a poor and relatively unindustrialized region of Canada where people had few resources they could mobilize on their own behalf. Per capita income and the level of unionization were among the lowest of any state, province, or territory in North America. The unemployment rate was among the highest. In contrast, K. C. Irving, who owned the pulp-and-paper mill, was so powerful that most people in the region could not even conceive of the need to rebel against the conditions of life he created for them. He owned most of the industrial establishments in the province. Every daily newspaper, most of the weeklies, all of the TV stations, and most of the radio stations were his, too. Little wonder people rarely heard a critical word about his operations. Many people believed that Irving could make or break local governments single-handedly. Should we therefore be surprised that mere high-school students refused to take him on? In their reluctance, Robert's fellow students were only mimicking their parents, who, on the whole, were as powerless as Irving was mighty (Brym, 1979).

Second, many of Robert's classmates did not share his sense of injustice. Most of them regarded Irving as the great provider. They thought his pulp-and-paper mill, as well as his myriad other industrial establishments, gave many people jobs. They regarded that fact as more important for their lives and the lives of their families than the pollution problem Robert raised. Frame alignment theory suggests Robert needed to figure out ways to build bridges between their understanding and his. He did not. Therefore, he received an unsympathetic hearing.

Try applying solidarity and frame alignment theories to times when *you* felt a deep sense of injustice against an institution, such as a school, an organization, a company, or a government. Did you do anything about your upset? If not, why not? If so, what did you do? Why were you able to act in the way you did? Did you try to get other people to join you in your action? If not, why not? If so, how did you manage to recruit them? Did you reach the goal you set out to achieve? If not, why not? If so, what enabled you to succeed? If you've never been involved in a collective action to correct a perceived injustice, try analyzing a movie about collective action by using insights gleaned from solidarity and frame alignment theories. Classic movies on this subject include *Norma Rae* (1979), starring Sally Field. Field won the Best Actress Oscar for her performance in this film as a Southern textile

WHERE DO
YOU FIT IN?

worker who joins with a labour organizer to unionize her mill. Another is *Matewan* (1987), a movie about the way employers prevented workers from organizing in the 1920s by fomenting racial and ethnic conflict among them.

THE HISTORY AND FUTURE OF SOCIAL MOVEMENTS

Attempts to synthesize theories of collective action and social movement formation are in their infancy (Diani, 1996; Tarrow, 1994). Still, we can briefly summarize what we have learned about the causes of collective action and social movement formation with the aid of Figure 21.3. Breakdown theory partly answers the question of *why* discontent is sometimes expressed collectively and in non-routine ways. Industrialization, urbanization, mass migration, economic slowdown, and other social changes often cause dislocations that engender feelings of strain, deprivation, and injustice. Solidarity theory focuses on *how* these social changes may eventually facilitate the emergence of social movements. They cause a reorganization of social relations, shifting the balance of power between disadvantaged and privileged groups. Solidarity theory also speaks to the question of *when* collective action erupts and social movements emerge. The opening and closing of political opportunities, as well as the exercise of social control by authorities, helps to shape the timing of collective action. Finally, by analyzing the day-to-day strategies employed to recruit non-members, frame alignment theory directs our attention to the question of *who* is recruited to social movements. All together, then, the theories we have considered provide a comprehensive picture of the why, how, when, and who of collective action and social movements.

Bearing this summary in mind, we can now turn to this chapter's final goal: sketching the prospects of social movements in broad, rapid strokes.

The Past 300 Years

In 1700, social movements were typically small, localized, and violent. In Europe, poor residents of a city might riot against public officials in reaction to a rise in bread prices or taxes.

FIGURE 21.3

Determinants of Collective Action and Social Movement Formation

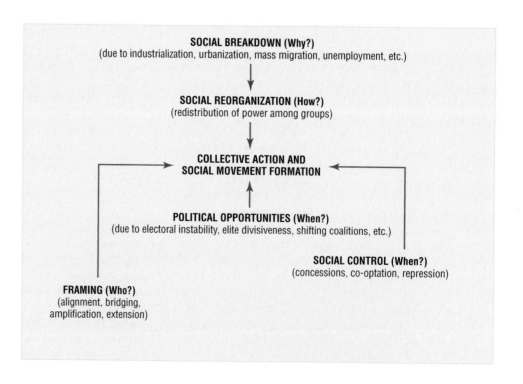

In medieval Europe, social movements were small, localized, and violent. For example, a medieval French historian reported that in 1358, "there were very strange and terrible happenings in several parts of the kingdom. . . . They began when some of the men from the country towns came together in the Beauvais region. They had no leaders and at first they numbered scarcely a hundred. One of them got up and said that the nobility of France . . . were disgracing and betraying the realm, and that it would be a good thing if they were all destroyed. At this they all shouted: 'He's right! He's right! Shame on any man who saves the gentry from being wiped out!' They banded together and went off, without further deliberation and unarmed except for pikes and knives, to the house of a knight who lived near by. They broke in and killed the knight, with his lady and children, big and small, and set fire to the house" (Froissart, 1968 [c. 1365]: 151).

Peasants on an estate might burn their landowner's barns (or their landowner) in response to his demand for a larger share of the crop. However, as the state grew, the form of protest changed. The state started taxing nearly all its citizens at higher and higher rates as government services expanded. It imposed a uniform language and often a common curriculum in a compulsory education system. It drafted most young men for army service. It instilled in its citizens all the ideological trappings of modern nationalism, from anthems to flags to historical myths.

As the state came to encompass most aspects of life, social movements changed in three ways. First, they became national in scope. That is, they typically directed themselves against central governments rather than against local targets. Second, their membership grew. This was partly because potential recruits were now literate and could communicate by using the printed word. In addition, big new social settings—factories, offices, densely populated urban neighbourhoods—could serve as recruitment bases. Third, social movements became less violent. That is, their size and organization often allowed them to bureaucratize, stabilize, and become sufficiently powerful to get their way without frequently resorting to extreme measures (Tilly, 1978, 1979a, 1979b; Tilly, Tilly, and Tilly, 1975).

Social movements often used their power to expand the rights of citizens. We may identify four stages in this process, focusing on Britain and the United States. In Britain, rich property owners fought against the king in the eighteenth century for **civil citizenship**. Civil citizenship is the right to free speech, freedom of religion, and justice before the law. The male middle class and the more prosperous strata of the working class fought against rich property owners in the nineteenth century for **political citizenship**. Political citizenship is the right to vote and run for office. In early twentieth-century Britain, women and poorer workers succeeded in achieving these same rights despite the opposition of well-to-do men in particular. During the remainder of the century, blue-collar and white-collar workers fought against the well-to-do for **social citizenship**. Social citizenship is the right to a certain level of economic security and full participation in social life with the help of the modern welfare state (Marshall, 1965).

Civil citizenship recognizes the right to free speech, freedom of religion, and justice before the law.

Political citizenship recognizes the right to run for office and vote.

Social citizenship recognizes the right to a certain level of economic security and full participation in the social life of the country.

The timing of the struggle for citizenship rights was different in the United States. Universal suffrage for white males was won earlier in the nineteenth century than in Europe. This accounts in part for the greater radicalism of the European working class. It had to engage in a long and bitter struggle for the right to vote, while its American counterpart was already incorporated into the political system (Lipset, 1977). Another important distinguishing feature of the United States concerns African Americans. The 15th Amendment to the Constitution gave them the right to vote in 1870. However, most of them were unable to exercise that right, at least in the South, from the late nineteenth century until the 1960s. That was because of various restrictions on voter registration, including poll taxes and literacy tests. The civil rights movement of the 1960s was in part a struggle over this issue. It helped to create a community that is more politically radical than its white counterpart is.

New Social Movements

So-called **new social movements** emerged in the 1970s (Melucci, 1980, 1995). What is new about new social movements is the breadth of their goals, the kinds of people they attract, and their potential for globalization. Let us consider each of these issues in turn.

Goals

Some new social movements promote the rights not of specific groups but of humanity as a whole to peace, security, and a clean environment. Such movements include the peace movement, the environmental movement, and the human rights movement. Other new social movements, such as the women's movement and the gay rights movement, promote the rights of particular groups that have been excluded from full social participation. Accordingly, gay rights groups have fought for laws that eliminate all forms of discrimination based on sexual orientation. They have also fought for the repeal of laws that discriminate on the basis of sexual orientation, such as anti-sodomy laws and laws that negatively affect parental custody of children (Adam, Duyvendak, and Krouwel, 1999). Since the 1960s, the women's movement has succeeded in getting admission practices altered in professional schools, winning more freedom of reproductive choice for women, and opening up opportunities for women in the political, religious, military, educational, medical, and business systems (Adamson, Briskin, and McPhail, 1988; Box 21.3). The emergence of the peace, environmental, human rights, gay rights, and women's movements marked the beginning of a fourth stage in the history of social movements. This fourth stage involves the promotion of **universal citizenship**, or the extension of citizenship rights to all adult members of society and to society as a whole (Roche, 1995; Turner, 1986: 85–105).

Membership

New social movements are also novel in that they attract a disproportionately large number of highly educated, relatively well-to-do people from the social, educational, and cultural fields. Such people include teachers, professors, journalists, social workers, artists, actors, writers, and student apprentices to these occupations. For several reasons, people in these occupations are more likely to participate in new social movements than are people in other occupations. Their higher education exposes them to radical ideas and makes those ideas appealing. They tend to hold jobs outside the business community, which often opposes their values. And they often become personally involved in the problems of their clients and audiences, sometimes even becoming their advocates (Brint, 1984; Rootes, 1995).

Globalization Potential

Finally, new social movements are new in that they have more potential for globalization than did old social movements.

Until the 1960s, social movements were typically *national* in scope. That is why, for example, the intensity and frequency of urban race riots in the United States in the 1960s did

New social movements became prominent in the 1970s. They attract a disproportionately large number of highly educated people in the social, educational, and cultural fields, and universalize the struggle for citizenship.

Universal citizenship recognizes the right of marginal groups to full citizenship and the rights of humanity as a whole.

GLOBAL PERSPECTIVE

BOX 21.3
The Women's Movement in Canada

The women's movement was the first new social movement. It originated in the late nineteenth century. A century ago, women began to play a smaller role in domestic and farm work and started to enter the paid labour force in significant numbers. Owning more of their own economic resources, they became more independently minded. They began to realize they might free themselves of oppressive authority in the home. They also started to understand that there was nothing inevitable about receiving less pay and working in worse conditions than men with comparable jobs do (Strong-Boag, 1986: 179).

Formulating a program for social change requires such resources as time, money, and education. Not surprisingly, therefore, the "first wave" of the women's movement comprised highly educated professionals. A group of women with just that social profile established the Canadian Woman Suffrage Association in Toronto in 1883. By means of demonstrating, petitioning, and gaining the support of influential liberal-minded men, women won the right to vote federally in 1918, in all provinces and territories but Quebec and the Northwest Territories by 1925, in Quebec in 1940, and in the Northwest Territories by 1951.

Along with the right to vote, women won the right to run for public office. They immediately exercised that right, running mainly on the CCF and Liberal Party tickets. A woman was first elected to provincial or territorial office in Alberta in 1917 and to the federal Parliament in 1921.

In provincial and territorial legislatures and the federal Parliament women sought institutional reform through government action. Specifically, they pursued more equitable pay for women, easier access to higher education, protection from domestic violence, and a fair share of family assets and child support in case of divorce or desertion. Progress was slow on all these fronts. That was partly because women's representation in the country's legislatures remained meagre. Even as late as the 2008 federal election, women composed only 22.1 percent of federal MPs, placing Canada 45th among the world's countries. Moreover, some female MPs were hardly advocates of women's rights (Bashevkin, 1986; "Women in National Parliaments," 2008).

Because of this slow progress, feminists developed a strategy in the 1960s and 1970s that was less oriented toward established political institutions and more oriented toward grassroots action. The new strategy sought to achieve change not just "from above," by means of party politics, but also "from below," by creating a whole network of new organizations, such as study groups, consciousness-raising circles, women's bookstores, rape crisis centres, abortion clinics, and shelters for battered women, and by creating opportunities to publicize the importance of feminist aims such as International Women's Day marches (Adamson, Briskin, and McPhail, 1988).

It was not only slow progress on the established political front that led women to create this network of new organizations. Many "second-wave" feminists were deeply involved in the student movement of the 1960s and 1970s. They were appalled to discover that, despite much rhetoric about liberation and equality, men controlled the student movement and men often refused to allow feminist issues to become part of their agenda. To pursue their aims they felt it was necessary to create new organizations run by women.

Today, then, the women's movement operates at both the grassroots level and within established political organizations to achieve its aims. It contains internal divisions. (See the discussion of liberal, radical, socialist, anti-racist, and postmodern feminism in Chapter 11, Sexuality and Gender.) Notwithstanding these differences, all forms of feminism share a strong desire to see members of a previously marginal group expand their citizenship rights and become full participants in society.

not depend on such local conditions as the degree of black–white inequality in a given city (Spilerman, 1970, 1976). Instead, African Americans came to believe that racial problems were nationwide and capable of solution only by the federal government. Congressional and presidential action (and inaction) on civil rights issues, national TV coverage of race issues, and growing black consciousness and solidarity helped shape this belief (Myers, 1997; Olzak and Shanahan, 1996; Olzak, Shanahan, and McEneaney, 1996).

Many new social movements that gained force in the 1970s increased the scope of protest beyond the national level. For example, members of the peace movement viewed federal laws banning nuclear weapons as necessary. Environmentalists felt the same way about federal laws protecting the environment. However, environmentalists also recognized that

The World Trade Organization (WTO) was set up by the governments of 134 countries in 1994 to encourage and referee global commerce. When the WTO met in Seattle in December 1999, 40 000 opponents of multinational corporations staged protests. Since then, protests have been staged wherever major international trade talks have been held. For example, when the Summit of the Americas took place in Quebec City in April 2001, more than 20 000 protesters took to the streets. They catapulted teddy bears, smoke bombs, and rocks at riot police and at one point breached the chain-link security fence surrounding the summit. Police responded with tear gas, water cannons, rubber bullets, and arrests.

Greenpeace is a highly successful global environmental movement that originated in Vancouver in the mid-1970s and now has offices in 40 countries.

the condition of the Brazilian rain forest affects climactic conditions worldwide. Similarly, peace activists understood that the spread of weapons of mass destruction could destroy all of humanity. Therefore, members of the peace and environmental movements pressed for *international* agreements binding all countries to protect the environment and stop the spread of nuclear weapons. Social movements went global.

Inexpensive international travel and communication facilitated the globalization of social movements. New technologies made it easier for people in various national movements to work with like-minded activists in other countries. In the age of CNN, inexpensive jet transportation, fax machines, websites, and e-mail, it was possible to see the connection between apparently local problems and their global sources. It was also possible to act both locally and globally.

From Greenpeace to al-Qaeda

Consider the case of Greenpeace. Greenpeace is a highly successful environmental movement that originated in Vancouver in the mid-1970s. It now has offices in 40 countries, with its international office in Amsterdam (Greenpeace, 2000). Among many other initiatives, it has mounted a campaign to eliminate the international transportation and dumping of toxic wastes. Its representatives visited local environmental groups in African and other developing countries. They supplied the Africans with organizing kits to help them tie their local concerns to global political efforts. They also published a newsletter to keep activists up to date on legal issues. Thus, Greenpeace coordinated a global campaign that enabled weak environmental organizations in developing countries to act more effectively. Their campaign also raised the costs of continuing the international trade in toxic waste.

Greenpeace is hardly alone in its efforts to go global. In 1953, 110 international social movement organizations spanned the globe. By 1993, there were 631. About a quarter were human rights organizations and about a seventh were environmental organizations. The latter are by far the fastest-growing organizational type (Smith, 1998: 97).

Even old social movements have gone global because of changes in the technology of mobilizing supporters. The anti-Western Muslim fundamentalist al-Qaeda terrorist movement can trace its political and intellectual roots to the formation of the Muslim Brotherhood in Egypt in 1928 (Muslim Brotherhood Movement, 2002). By 2000, Osama bin Laden, the head of al-Qaeda, often used a satellite telephone to communicate with his operatives in as many as 60 countries—until U.S. law enforcement authorities inexplicably revealed they were tapping calls from his base in Afghanistan. Once he learned of these taps, bin Laden increased his use of another, more effective means of global communication: sending messages that are easily encrypted but difficult to decode via the Internet (Kelley, 2001; McCullagh, 2000). Some analysts think such messages were used to help plan and coordinate the complex, virtually simultaneous jet hijackings that resulted in the crash of an airliner in Pennsylvania and the destruction of the World Trade Center and part of the Pentagon on September 11, 2001, killing more than 3000 people.

TECHNOLOGY BYTES

The globalization of social movements can be further illustrated by coming full circle and returning to the anecdote with which we began this chapter. In 1991, Robert Brym visited his hometown. He hadn't been back in years. As he entered the city he vaguely sensed that something was different. "I wasn't able to identify the change until I reached the pulp-and-paper mill," says Robert. "Suddenly, it was obvious. The rotten-egg smell was virtually gone. I discovered that in the 1970s a local woman whose son developed a serious case of asthma took legal action against the mill and eventually won. The mill owner was forced by law to install a 'scrubber' in the main smokestack to remove most of the sulphur dioxide emissions. Soon, the federal government was putting pressure on the mill owner to purify the polluted water that poured out of the plant and into the local river system." Apparently, local citizens and the environmental movement had caused a deep change in the climate of opinion. This influenced the government to force the mill owner to spend millions of dollars to clean up his operation. It took decades, but what was political heresy in 1968 became established practice by 1991. That is because environmental concerns had been amplified by the voice of a movement that had grown to global proportions. In general, as this case illustrates, globalization helps ensure that many new social movements transcend local and national boundaries and promote universalistic goals.

NOTES

1. By the same token, bureaucracies may sometimes use non-routine tactics. The distinction between routine and non-routine collective action is thus a matter of degree, not kind. Note in this connection that mobs, riots, and so on used to be viewed as instances of "collective behaviour." Since the 1990s, however, that term has fallen into disfavour because "behaviour" suggests a relatively low level of consciousness of self and therefore less rationality. Following Weber (1947), "action" denotes greater consciousness of self and therefore more rationality. Crowd action is not as non-routine as was once believed.

2. The broad distinction between breakdown and solidarity theories is due to Tilly, Tilly, and Tilly (1975).

3. Some of these generalizations do not apply to countries with a long tradition of labour government. For example, since World War II Sweden has experienced high levels of unionization and low strike rates. That is because Swedish workers and their representatives are involved in government policymaking. Decisions about wages and benefits tend to be made in negotiations among unions, employer associations, and governments rather than on the picket line.

SUMMARY

1. Common sense and some sociological theory suggest that riots and other forms of collective action are irrational and unstructured actions that take place when people are angry and deprived. Is this view accurate?
   In the short term, deprivation and strain from rapid social change are generally *not* associated with increased collective action and social movement formation. Mobs, riots, and other forms of collective action may be wild and violent but social organization and rationality underlie much crowd behaviour.

2. Which aspects of social organization facilitate rebellion against the status quo?
   People are more inclined to rebel against the status quo when social ties bind them to many other people who feel similarly wronged and when they have the time, money, organization, and other resources needed to protest. In addition, collective action and social movement formation are more likely to occur when political opportunities allow them. Political opportunities emerge through elections, increased support by influential allies, the instability of ruling political alignments, and divisions among elite groups.

3. How do the attempts of authorities to control unrest affect collective action?
   Authorities' attempts to control unrest mainly influence the timing of collective action. They may offer concessions to insurgents, co-opt leaders, and employ coercion.

4. What is "framing"?
   For social movements to grow, members must make the activities, goals, and ideology of the movement congruent with the interests, beliefs, and values of potential new recruits. Doing so is known as *framing*.

5. How have social movements changed in the past three centuries?
   In 1700, social movements were typically small, localized, and violent. By mid-twentieth century, social movements were typically large, national, and less violent. In the late twentieth century, new social movements developed broader goals, recruited more highly educated people, and developed global potential for growth.

6. How is the history of social movements tied to the struggle for the acquisition of citizenship rights?
   The history of social movements is a struggle for the acquisition of constantly broadening citizenship rights. These rights include (1) the right to free speech, religion, and justice before the law (civil citizenship), (2) the right to vote and run for office (political citizenship), (3) the right to a certain level of economic security and full participation in the life of society (social citizenship), and (4) the right of marginal groups to full citizenship and the right of humanity as a whole to peace and security (universal citizenship).

KEY TERMS

absolute deprivation (p. 595)

breakdown theory (p. 594)

civil citizenship (p. 609)

collective action (p. 592)

contagion (p. 595)

frame alignment (p. 604)

new social movements (p. 610)   social control (p. 599)

political citizenship (p. 609)   social movements (p. 593)

political opportunities (p. 599)   solidarity theory (p. 598)

relative deprivation (p. 595)   strain (p. 595)

resource mobilization (p. 598)   union density (p. 602)

social citizenship (p. 609)   universal citizenship (p. 610)

QUESTIONS TO CONSIDER

1. How would you achieve a political goal? Map out a detailed strategy for reaching a clearly defined aim, such as a reduction in income tax or an increase in government funding of universities. Whom would you try to recruit to help you achieve your goal? Why? What collective actions do you think would be most successful? Why? To whose attention would these actions be directed? Why? Write a manifesto that frames your argument in a way that is culturally appealing to potential recruits.

2. Do you think that social movements will be more or less widespread in the twenty-first century than they were in the twentieth century? Why or why not? What kinds of social movements are likely to predominate?

WEB RESOURCES

Companion Website for This Book

http://www.compass3e.nelson.com

Begin by clicking on the Student Resources section of the website. Next, select the chapter you are studying from the pull-down menu. From the Student Resources page you have easy access to InfoTrac® College Edition, additional Weblinks, and other resources. The website also has many useful tips to aid you in your study of sociology, including practice tests for each chapter.

InfoTrac® Search Terms

These search terms are provided to assist you in beginning to conduct research on this topic by visiting http://www.infotrac-college.com:

collective action
frame alignment
relative deprivation
resource mobilization
unions

Recommended Websites

The environmental movement Greenpeace is one of the most successful cases of globalized protest. Its website is at http://www.greenpeace.org.

Since 1910, March 8 has been celebrated as International Women's Day. For information about the demonstrations and other activities that take place around the world (including in Canada) on March 8, go to http://www.internationalwomensday.com.

http://www.compass3e.nelson.com

The Canadian Labour Congress (CLC) is the country's biggest umbrella labour organization, with more than 2.3 million members. To learn about the CLC's current projects, campaigns, and boycotts, visit the CLC website at http://canadianlabour.ca.

CengageNOW™

http://hed.nelson.com

This online diagnostic tool identifies each student's unique needs with a Pretest that generates a personalized Study Plan for each chapter, helping students focus on concepts they're having the most difficulty mastering. Students then take a Posttest after reading the chapter to measure their understanding of the material. An Instructor Gradebook is available to track and monitor student progress.

REFERENCES

ABC Evening News. 1998. April 30.

Abraham, Carolyn. 2003. "Hong Kong Hotel Is Focus of Pneumonia Investigation." *globeandmail.com,* March 20. Retrieved June 16, 2003 (http://globeandmail. workopolis.com/servlet/Content/fasttrack/20030320/UB UGGN?section=Healthcare).

Abraham, Laurie Kaye. 1993. *Mama Might Be Better Off Dead: The Failure of Health Care in Urban America.* Chicago: University of Chicago Press.

Achilles, Rhona. 1993. "Desperately Seeking Babies: New Technologies of Hope and Despair." Pp. 214–29 in Bonnie J. Fox, ed. *Family Patterns, Gender Relations.* Toronto: Oxford University Press.

Adam, Barry, Jan Willem Duyvendak, and Andre Krouwel. 1999. *The Global Emergence of Gay and Lesbian Politics.* Philadelphia: Temple University Press.

Adams, Henry E., Lester W. Wright, Jr., and Bethany A. Lohr. 1998. "Is Homophobia Associated with Homosexual Arousal?" *Journal of Abnormal Psychology* 105: 440–45.

Adams, Michael. 1997. *Sex in the Snow: Canadian Social Values at the End of the Millennium.* Toronto: Penguin.

Adams, R. J., G. Betcherman, and B. Bilson. 1995. *Good Job, Bad Jobs, No Jobs: Tough Choices for Canadian Labor Law.* Toronto: C.D. Howe Institute.

"Adams Mine." 2000. Retrieved October 8, 2000 (http://server1.nt.net/customers/13/tpc/www/ togarbag .htm#Anchor-First-14210).

Adamson, Nancy, Linda Briskin, and Margaret McPhail. 1988. *Feminist Organizing for Change: The Contemporary Women's Movement in Canada.* Toronto: Oxford University Press.

Adherents.com. 2001. "Religion Statistics: Predominant Religions." Retrieved November 30, 2001 (http://www .adherents.com/adh_predom.html).

Adler, Patricia A., and Peter Adler. 1998. *Peer Power: Preadolescent Culture and Identity.* New Brunswick, NJ: Rutgers University Press.

Ahmad, Imad-ad-Dean. 2000. "Female Genital Mutilation: An Islamic Perspective." Retrieved December 1, 2003 (http://www.minaret.org/fgm-pamphlet.htm).

Akin, David. 2002. "Kevin Warwick Is a Borg." *The Globe and Mail* June 1: F7.

Albas, Daniel, and Cheryl Albas. 1989. "Modern Magic: The Case of Examinations." *The Sociological Quarterly* 30: 603–13.

Albelda, Randy, and Chris Tilly. 1997. *Glass Ceilings and Bottomless Pits: Women's Work, Women's Poverty.* Boston, MA: South End Press.

Alberta Federation of Labour. 2005. "Why Join a Union?" Retrieved November 21, 2005 (http://www.afl.org/ need-a-union/why-join.cfm).

Albrow, Martin. 1997. *The Global Age: State and Society Beyond Modernity.* Stanford, CA: Stanford University Press.

Aldrich, Howard E. 1979. *Organizations and Environments.* Englewood Cliffs, NJ: Prentice-Hall.

Alford, Robert R., and Roger Friedland. 1985. *Powers of Theory: Capitalism, the State, and Democracy.* Cambridge, UK: Cambridge University Press.

Allahar, Anton, and James E. Côté. 1994. *Generation on Hold: Coming of Age in the Late Twentieth Century.* Toronto: Stoddart.

Allen, Robert C. 1999. *Education and Technological Revolutions: The Role of the Social Sciences and the Humanities in the Knowledge Based Economy.* Ottawa: Social Sciences and Humanities Research Council of Canada. Retrieved May 8, 2001 (http://www.sshrc .ca/english/resnews/researchresults/allen99.pdf).

Amato, Paul R., and Bruce Keith. 1991. "Parental Divorce and the Well-Being of Children: A Meta-Analysis." *Psychological Bulletin* 110: 26–46.

Ambert, Anne-Marie. 1998. "Divorce: Facts, Figures and Consequences." Vanier Institute of the Family. Retrieved from http://www.vifamily.ca/cft/divorce/divorcer.htm.

American Library Association. 2005. "Top Ten Challenged Authors 1990–2004." Retrieved December 14, 2005 (http://childrensbooks.about.com/gi/dynamic/offsite.htm ?zi=1/XJ&sdn=childrensbooks&zu=http%3A%2F%2F www.ala.org%2Fbbooks%2Ftop100bannedbooks.html).

American Psychological Association. 1998. "Answers to Your Questions About Sexual Orientation and Homosexuality." Retrieved June 14, 2000 (http://www.apa.org/pubinfo/orient.html).

American Society of Plastic Surgeons. 2005. "2000/ 2002/2003/2004 National Plastic Surgery Statistics." Retrieved May 17, 2005 (http://www.plasticsurgery.org/ public_education/loader.cfm?url=/commonspot/ security/getfile.cfm&PageID=16158 (17 May 2005).

American Society of Plastic Surgeons. 2006. "2005 Cosmetic Plastic Surgery Trends." Retreived September 14,

2006 (http://www.plasticsurgery.org/public_education/Statistical-Trends.cfm).

American Sociological Association. 1999. *Code of Ethics and Policies and Procedures of the ASA Committee on Professional Ethics.* Washington, DC.

Anderson, Benedict R. O'G. 1991. *Imagined Communities: Reflections on the Origin and Spread of Nationalism.* London, UK: Verso.

Anderson, Craig, and Brad J. Bushman. 2002. "The Effects of Media Violence on Society." *Science* 295, 5564: 2377–79.

Anderson, Elijah. 1990. *Streetwise: Race, Class, and Change in an Urban Community.* Chicago: University of Chicago Press.

Anderson, Gerald F., Uwe E. Reinhardt, Peter S. Hussey, and Varduhi Petrosyan. 2003. "It's the Prices, Stupid: Why the United States Is So Different from Other Countries." *Health Affairs* 22, 3: 89–105.

Anderson, Kristin L. 1997. "Gender, Status, and Domestic Violence: An Integration of Feminist and Family Violence Approaches." *Journal of Marriage and the Family* 59: 655–59.

Anderson, Michael. 2003. "Reading Violence in Boys' Writing." *Language Arts* 80, 3: 223–31.

Arace, Michael. 2000. "Oft-injured Forward Feels OK." *Columbus Dispatch* 17 September. Retrieved July 22, 2002 (http://www.dispatch.com/news/sports00/sept00/424238.html).

Ariès, Phillipe. 1962 [1960]. *Centuries of Childhood: A Social History of Family Life*, Robert Baldick, trans. New York: Knopf.

———. 1982. *The Hour of Our Death.* New York: Knopf.

Arnett, Jeffrey Jensen. 1995. "Adolescents' Uses of Media for Self-Socialization." *Journal of Youth and Adolescence* 24: 519–33.

Arterton, F. Christopher. 1987. *Teledemocracy: Can Technology Protect Democracy?* Newbury Park, CA: Sage Publications.

Asch, Solomon. 1955. "Opinion and Social Pressure." *Scientific American* July: 31–35.

Asia Pacific Foundation of Canada. 2002. "Generous at Heart, Prudent at Pocket. Foreign Aid and Trade: What Do Canadians Think?" Retrieved May 13, 2006 (http://www.asiapacific.ca/analysis/pubs/listing.cfm?ID_Publication=222).

Associated Press. 2001. "Vancouver Gay Man Beaten to Death: Police Suspect Hate Crime." Retrieved May 12, 2002 (http://www.planetqnews.com/0812/11.shtml).

———. 2005a. "Swiss Vote for Same-Sex Rights." CNN. Retrieved June 12, 2006 (http://www.cnn.com).

———. 2005b. "Writer: Pope Expressed Concern over Harry Potter Books." *USA Today* July 14. Retrieved December 13, 2006 (http://www.usatoday.com/news/world/2005-07-14-pope-potter_x.htm).

Association of Canadian Publishers. 2002. "How to Get Published." Retrieved May 15, 2002 (http://www.publishers.ca/published.html).

Averett, Susan, and Sanders Korenman. 1996. "The Economic Reality of the Beauty Myth." *Journal of Human Resources* 31: 304–30.

Babbie, Earl. 2000. *The Practice of Social Research*, rev. ed. of 9th ed. Belmont, CA: Wadsworth.

Baer, Doug. 1999. "Educational Credentials and the Changing Occupational Structure." Pp. 92–106 in J. Curtis, E. Grabb, and N. Guppy, eds. *Social Inequality in Canada: Patterns, Problems, Policies,* 3rd ed. Scarborough, ON: Prentice Hall Allyn and Bacon Canada.

Bagdikian, Ben H. 1997. *The Media Monopoly,* 5th ed. Boston: Beacon.

Bairoch, Paul. 1988 [1985]. *Cities and Economic Development: From the Dawn of History to the Present*, Christopher Braider, trans. Chicago: University of Chicago Press.

Balakrishnan, T. R., and K. Selvanathan. 1990. "Residential Segregation in Metropolitan Canada." In S. Halli, F. Travato, and L. Driedger, eds. *Ethnic Demography.* Ottawa: Carleton University Press.

Bales, Kevin. 1999. *Disposable People: New Slavery in the Global Economy.* Berkeley, CA: University of California Press.

Bank of Hawaii. 1999. "Commonwealth of the Northern Mariana Islands: Economic Report October." Retrieved June 23, 2000 (http://www.boh.com/econ/pacific/cnmi/1999/cnmi1999.pdf).

Banner, Lois W. 1992. *In Full Flower: Aging Women, Power, and Sexuality.* New York: Knopf.

Bannon, Lisa. 2000. "Why Girls and Boys Get Different Toys." *The Wall Street Journal* February 14: B1, B4.

Baran, Paul A. 1957. *The Political Economy of Growth.* New York: Monthly Review Press.

Barash, David. 1981. *The Whispering Within.* New York: Penguin.

Bardes, Barbara A., and Robert W. Oldendick. 2003. *Public Opinion: Measuring the American Mind.* Belmont, CA: Wadsworth.

Barlow, Maude, and Elizabeth May. 2000. *Frederick Street: Life and Death on Canada's Love Canal.* Toronto: HarperCollins.

Barna, G. 2002. *Grow Your Church from the Outside In: Understanding the Unchurched and How to Reach Them.* Ventura, California: Regal Books.

Barnard, Chester, I. 1938. *The Functions of the Executive.* Cambridge, MA: Harvard University Press.

Barnet, Richard J., and John Cavanagh. 1994. *Global Dreams: Imperial Corporations and the New World Order.* New York: Simon & Schuster.

Bar-On, D. 1999. *The Indescribable and the Undiscussable: Reconstructing Human Discourse after Trauma.* Ithaca, NY: Cornell University Press.

Barr-Telford, Lynn, Fernando Cartwright, Sandrine Prasil, and Kristina Shimmons. 2003. "Access, Persistence, and Financing: First Results from the Postsecondary Education Participation Survey (PEPS)." Ottawa: Statistics Canada. Catalogue No. 81-595-MIE2003007. Retrieved May 27, 2006 (http://www.statcan.ca:8096/bsolc/english/bsolc?catno=81-595-MIE2003007).

Barry, Patricia. 2002a. "Ads, Promotions Drive up Drug Costs." *AARP.* Retrieved June 17, 2003 (http://www.aarp.org/bulletin/departments/2002/medicare/0310_medicare_1.html).

———. 2002b. "Drug Industry Spends Huge Sums Guarding Prices." *AARP.* Retrieved June 17, 2003 (http://www.aarp.org/bulletin/departments/2002/medicare/0510_medicare_1.html).

———. 2002c. "Drug Profits vs. Research." *AARP.* Retrieved June 17, 2003 (http://www.aarp.org/bulletin/departments/2002/medicare/0605_medicare_1.html).

Barth, Fredrik, ed. 1969. *Ethnic Groups and Boundaries: The Social Organization of Cultural Difference.* Boston: Little, Brown.

Bashevkin, Sylvia. 1986. "Independence versus Partisanship: Dilemmas in the Political History of Women in English Canada." Pp. 246–75 in V. Strong-Boag and A. Fellman, eds. *Rethinking Canada: The Promise of Women's History.* Toronto: Copp Clark Pitman.

———. 1993. *Toeing the Line: Women and Party Politics in English Canada,* 2nd ed. Toronto: Oxford University Press.

Baudrillard, Jean. 1983. *Simulations.* New York: Semiotext(e).

———. 1988. *America.* Chris Turner, trans. London: Verso.

Bauman, Zygmunt. 1991. *Modernity and the Holocaust.* Ithaca, NY: Cornell University Press.

Beattie, Karen. 2006. "Adult Correctional Services in Canada, 2004/2005." *Juristat* 26, 5.

Beaudry, P., and D. Green. 1998. *Individual Responses to Changes in the Canadian Labour Market*, Paper Number 9. Ottawa: Industry Canada.

Beaupré, Pascale, Pierre Turcotte, and Anne Milan. 2007. "When Is Junior Moving Out? Transitions from the Parental Home to Independence." *Canadian Social Trends* 82: 9-15. Retrieved March 26, 2007 (http://www.statcan.ca/english/freepub/11-008-XIE/2006002/pdf/11-008-XIE200600292_74.pdf).

Beck, Ulrich. 1992 [1986]. *Risk Society: Towards a New Modernity*, Mark Ritter, trans. London, UK: Sage.

Becker, Ernest. 1973. *The Denial of Death.* New York: Free Press.

Becker, G. 1976. *The Economic Approach to Human Behavior.* Chicago: University of Chicago Press.

———. 1991. *A Treatise on the Family.* Cambridge, MA: Harvard University Press.

Becker, Gaylene. 1980. *Growing Old in Silence.* Berkeley: University of California Press.

Becker, H. S. 1963. *Outsiders: Studies in the Sociology of Deviance.* New York: Free Press.

Beer, Frances A. 1974. *How Much War in History: Definitions, Estimates, Extrapolations and Trends.* Beverly Hills, CA: Sage.

Beil, Laura. 2007. "For Struggling Black Colleges, Hopes of a Big-Screen Revival." *New York Times* December 5. Retrieved December 5, 2007 (wwwnytimes.com).

Bélanger, Claude. 2000. "Readings in Quebec History: Opting Out." Retrieved February 18, 2001 (http://members.nbci.com/history_1/his951/readings/opting.htm).

Bell, Daniel. 1973. *The Coming of Post-Industrial Society: A Venture in Social Forecasting.* New York: Basic Books.

Bell, Gregory Boyd. 2002. "No Strait Jacket Required." *This* January/February: 29.

Bellah, Robert A. 1975. *The Broken Covenant: American Civil Religion in a Time of Trial.* New York: Seabury Press.

Bellow, Saul. 1964. *Herzog.* New York: Fawcett World Library.

Benford, Robert D. 1997. "An Insider's Critique of the Social Movement Framing Perspective." *Sociological Inquiry* 67: 409–39.

Benson, April Lane, ed. 2000. *I Shop, Therefore I Am: Compulsive Buying and the Search for Self.* Northvale, NJ: Jason Aronson Inc.

Bercuson, David. 1974. "The Winnipeg General Strike." Pp. 1–32 in Irving Abella, ed. *On Strike: Six Key Labour Struggles in Canada, 1919–1949.* Toronto: James Lewis & Samuel.

Berens, Michael J. 2002a. "Infection Epidemic Carves Deadly Path." *Chicago Tribune* July 21. Retrieved June 16, 2003 (http://www.chicagotribune.com/news/specials/chi-0207210272jul21.story).

———. 2002b. "Drug-Resistant Germs Adapt, Thrive Beyond Hospital Walls." *Chicago Tribune* June 23. Retrieved June 16, 2003 (http://www.chicagotribune.com/news/specials/chi-0207230231jul23.story).

Berger, Peter L., and Thomas Luckmann. 1966. *The Social Construction of Reality: A Treatise in the Sociology of Knowledge.* Garden City, NY: Doubleday.

Berger, S., and R. Dore, eds. 1996. *National Diversity and Capitalism.* Ithaca, NY: Cornell University Press.

Berk, Richard A. 1974. *Collective Behavior.* Dubuque, IO: Wm. C. Brown.

Berk, Sarah Fenstermaker. 1985. *The Gender Factory: The Apportionment of Work in American Households.* New York: Plenum.

Berkowitz, S. D. 1982. *An Introduction to Structural Analysis: The Network Approach to Social Research.* Toronto: Butterworths.

Bernard, Jessie. 1972. *The Future of Marriage.* New York: World.

———. 1986. "The Good-Provider Role: Its Rise and Fall." Pp. 125–44 in Arlene S. Skolnick and Jerome H. Skolnick, eds. *Family in Transition: Rethinking Marriage, Sexuality, Child Rearing, and Family Organization,* 5th ed. Boston: Little, Brown.

Berners-Lee, Tim. 1999. "Tim Berners-Lee." Retrieved May 2, 2000 (http://www.w3.org/People/Berners-Lee/Overview.html).

Bertrand, Robert J. 1981. *Canada's Oil Monopoly: The Story of the $12 Billion Rip-off of Canadian Consumers.* Toronto: James Lorimer & Company.

Besserer, Sandra. 2002. "Criminal Victimization: An International Perspective: Results of the 2000 International Crime Victimization Survey." *Juristat* 22, 4 (May). Catalogue no. 85-002-XPE.

Besserer, Sandra, Jodi-Anne Brzozowski, Dianne Hendrick, Stacie Ogg, and Catherine Trainor. 1999. A *Profile of Criminal Victimization: Results of the 1999 General Social Survey.* Ottawa: Statistics Canada.

Betcherman, G., and G. Lowe. 1997. *The Future of Work in Canada: A Synthesis Report.* Ottawa: Canadian Policy Research Networks Inc.

Bianchi, Suzanne M., and Daphne Spain. 1996. "Women, Work, and Family in America." *Population Bulletin* 51, 3: 2–48.

Bibby, Reginald W. 1987. *Fragmented Gods: The Poverty and Potential of Religion in Canada.* Toronto: Irwin.

———. 1993. "Secularization and Social Change." Pp. 65–82 in W. E. Hewitt, ed. *The Sociology of Religion: A Canadian Focus.* Toronto: Butterworths.

———. 1995. *The Bibby Report: Social Trends Canadian Style.* Toronto: Stoddart.

———. 2001. *Canada's Teens: Today, Yesterday, and Tomorrow.* Toronto: Stoddart.

———. 2002. *Restless God: The Renaissance of Religion in Canada.* Toronto: Stoddart.

———. 2004. *Restless Churches: How Canada's Churches Can Contribute to the Emerging Religious Renaissance.* Ottawa: Novalis.

———. 2006. *The Boomer Factor: What Canada's Most Famous Generation is Leaving Behind.* Toronto: Bastian.

Biegler, Rebecca S. 1999. "Psychological Interventions Designed to Counter Sexism in Children: Empirical Limitations and Theoretical Foundations." Pp. 129–52 in W. B. Swann, Jr., J. H. Langlois, and L. A. Gilbert, eds. *Sexism and Stereotypes in Modern Society: The*

Gender Science of Janet Taylor Spence. Washington, DC: American Psychological Association.

Bierstedt, Robert. 1963. *The Social Order.* New York: McGraw-Hill.

———. 1974. "An Analysis of Social Power." Pp. 220–41 in *Power and Progress: Essays in Sociological Theory.* New York: McGraw-Hill.

Bissoondath, Neil. 2002. *Selling Illusions: The Cult of Multiculturalism in Canada,* rev. ed. Toronto: Penguin.

Bjorhus, J. 2000. "Gap Between Execs, Rank and File Grows Wider." *San Jose Mercury News* June 18. Retrieved June 20, 2000 (http://www.mercurycenter.com/premium/business/docs/disparity18.htm).

Black, Donald. 1989. *Sociological Justice.* New York: Oxford University Press.

Blais, André, Elisabeth Gidengil, Richard Nadeau, and Neil Nevitte. 1997. "1997 Canadian Election Survey." Retrieved December 1, 1998 (http://prod.library.utoronto.ca/datalib/codebooks/utm/elections/1997).

Blais, André, Elisabeth Gidengil, Neil Nevitte, Patrick Fournier, and Joanna Everitt. 2005. "2004 Canadian Election Study." Retrieved May 26, 2006 (http://www.ces-eec.umontreal.ca/ces.html).

Blaise, Clark. 2001. *Time Lord: The Remarkable Canadian Who Missed His Train and Changed the World.* Toronto: Knopf Canada.

Blau, Peter M. 1963. *The Dynamics of Bureaucracy: A Study of Interpersonal Relationships in Two Government Agencies,* rev. ed. Chicago: University of Chicago Press.

———. 1964. *Exchange and Power in Social Life.* New York: Wiley.

Blauner, R. 1972. *Racial Oppression in America.* New York: Harper & Row.

Block, Fred. 1979. "The Ruling Class Does Not Rule." Pp. 128–40 in R. Quinney, ed. *Capitalist Society.* Homewood, IL: Dorsey Press.

Blossfeld, H., and Y. Shavit, eds. 1993. *Persistant Inequality: Changing Educational Attainment in Thirteen Countries.* Boulder, CO: Westview Press.

Bluestone, B., and B. Harrison. 1982. *The Deindustrialization of America.* New York: Basic Books.

Blum, Deborah. 1997. *Sex on the Brain: The Biological Differences between Men and Women.* New York: Penguin.

Blumberg, Paul. 1989. *The Predatory Society: Deception in the American Marketplace.* New York: Oxford University Press.

Blumer, Herbert. 1969. *Symbolic Interactionism: Perspective and Method.* Englewood Cliffs, NJ: Prentice-Hall.

Boal, Mark. 1998. "Spycam City." *The Village Voice* (September 30–October 6). Retrieved March 26, 2001 (http://www.villagevoice.com/issues/9840/boal.shtml).

Bollman, Ray D. 2000. "Rural and Small Town Canada: An Overview." Statistics Canada and Rural

Secretariat, Agriculture and Agri-Food Canada. Retrieved May 11, 2005 (http://www.statcan.ca/english/freepub/21F0018XIE/21F0018XIE 2001001.htm).

Bonacich, Edna. 1972. "A Theory of Ethnic Antagonism: The Split Labor Market." *American Sociological Review* 37: 547–59.

———. 1973. "A Theory of Middleman Minorities." *American Sociological Review* 38: 583–94.

Bornholt, Laurel. 2001. "Self-Concepts, Usefulness and Behavioural Intentions in the Social Context of Schooling." *Educational Psychology* 21, 1 (March): 67–78.

Bornschier, Volker, and Christopher Chase-Dunn. 1985. *Transnational Corporations and Underdevelopment.* New York: Praeger.

Boston Women's Health Book Collective, ed. 1998. *Our Bodies, Our Selves for the New Century: A Book by and for Women.* New York: Simon & Schuster.

Boswell, A. Ayres, and Joan Z. Spade. 1996. "Fraternities and Collegiate Rape Culture: Why Are Some Fraternities More Dangerous Places for Women?" *Gender and Society* 10: 133–47.

Bouchard, Thomas J., Jr., David T. Lykken, Matthew McGue, Nancy L. Segal, and Auke Tellegen. 1990. "Sources of Human Psychological Differences: The Minnesota Study of Twins Reared Apart." *Science* 250, 4978: 223–26.

Boulding, Elise. 1976. *The Underside of History.* Boulder, CO: Westview.

Bourdieu, Pierre. 1977 [1972]. *Outline of a Theory of Practice,* Richard Nice, trans. Cambridge, UK: Cambridge University Press.

———. 1984 [1979]. *Distinction: A Social Critique of the Judgment of Taste,* R. Nice, trans. Cambridge, MA: Harvard University Press.

———. 1998a. *On Television.* New York: New Press.

———. 1998b. *Practical Reason: On the Theory of Action.* Stanford, CA.: Stanford University Press.

Bourdieu, Pierre, and Jean Claude Passeron. 1979. *The Inheritors: French Students and Their Relation to Culture.* Chicago: University of Chicago Press.

———. 1990. *Reproduction in Education, Society and Culture,* 2nd ed. R. Nice, trans. London: Sage.

Bowles, Samuel, and Herbert Gintis. 1976. *Schooling in Capitalist America: Educational Reform and the Contradictions of Economic Life.* New York: Basic Books.

Boychuk, Gerard W. 2002. "Federal Spending in Health: Why Here? Why Now?" Pp. 121–36 in G. Bruce Doern, ed. *How Ottawa Spends 2002–2003: The Security Aftermath and National Priorities.* Toronto: Oxford University Press.

Boyd, Monica. 1997. "Feminizing Paid Work." *Current Sociology* 45, 2 (April): 49–73.

———. 1999. "Canadian, eh? Ethnic Origin Shifts in the Canadian Census." *Canadian Ethnic Studies* 31, 3: 1–19.

———. 2001. "Gender Inequality." Pp. 178–207 in Robert J. Brym, ed. *New Society: Sociology for the 21st Century,* 3rd ed. Toronto: Harcourt Canada.

———. 2002. "Educational Attainments of Immigrant Offspring: Success or Segmented Assimilation?" *The International Migration Review* 36, 4: 1037–60.

Boyd, Monica, John Goyder, Frank E. Jones, Hugh A. McRoberts, Peter C. Pineo, and John Porter. 1985. *Ascription and Achievement: Studies on Mobility and Status Attainment in Canada.* Ottawa: Carleton University Press.

Boyd, Monica, and Doug Norris. 2001. "Who Are the 'Canadians'? Changing Census Responses, 1986–1996." *Canadian Ethnic Studies* 33, 1: 1–25.

Boyd, Neil. 1998. *Canadian Law: An Introduction.* Toronto: Harcourt Brace Canada.

Bradburn, Norman M., and Seymour Sudman. 1979. *Improving Interview Method and Questionnaire Design.* San Franciso: Jossey-Bass.

Brady, Erik. 2001. "Too Good to Be True?" *USA Today* July 12. Retrieved July 21, 2001 (wysiwyg://14/http://www.usatoday.com/sports/stories/2001-07-12-cover.htm).

Braithwaite, John. 1981. "The Myth of Social Class and Criminality Revisited." *American Sociological Review* 46: 36–57.

———. 1989. *Crime, Shame and Reintegration.* New York: Cambridge University Press.

Brannigan, Augustine. 1984. *Crime, Courts and Corrections.* Toronto: Holt, Rinehart and Winston.

Brannock, K. C., and B. E. Champman. 1990. "Negative Sexual Experiences with Men among Heterosexual Women and Lesbians." *Journal of Homosexuality* 19: 105–10.

Brave, Ralph. 2003. "James Watson Wants to Build a Better Human." *AlterNet* May 29. Retrieved January 19, 2005 (http://www.alternet.org/story/16026).

Braver, Sanford L., Pamela J. Fitzpatrick, and R. Curtis Bay. 1991. "Noncustodial Parent's Report of Child Support Payments." *Family Relations* 40, 2 (April): 180–85.

Braverman, H. 1974. *Labour and Monopoly Capital: The Degradation of Work in the Twentieth Century.* New York: Monthly Review Press.

Brazzini, D. G., W. D. McIntosh, S. M. Smith, S. Cook, and C. Harris. 1997. "The Aging Woman in Popular Film: Underrepresented, Unattractive, Unfriendly, and Unintelligent." *Sex Roles* 36: 531–43.

Brechin, Steven R., and Willett Kempton. 1994. "Global Environmentalism: A Challenge to the Postmaterialism Thesis." *Social Science Quarterly* 75: 245–69.

Breen, Richard, and John Goldthorpe. 1997. "Explaining Educational Differentials." *Rationality and Society* 9: 275–305.

Brennan, Teresa. 2003. *Globalization and Its Terrors: Daily Life in the West.* London: Routledge.

Bricker, Darrell, and Edward Greenspon. 2001. *Searching for Certainty: Inside the New Canadian Mindset.* Toronto: Doubleday Canada.

Brinkhoff, T. 2002. "The Principal Agglomerations of the World." Retrieved August 2, 2003 (http://www.city population.de).

Brint, Stephen. 1984. "New Class and Cumulative Trend Explanations of the Liberal Political Attitudes of Professionals." *American Journal of Sociology* 90: 30–71.

Brodie, Janine. 1991. "Women and the Electoral Process in Canada." Pp. 3–59 in Kathy Megyery, ed. *Women in Canadian Politics: Toward Equity in Representation.* Toronto: Dundurn Press.

Bromley, Julian V. 1982 [1977]. *Present-Day Ethnic Processes in the USSR.* Moscow: Progress Publishers.

Bronowski, J. 1965. *Science and Human Values,* revised ed. New York: Harper & Row.

Brooks, Clem, and Jeff Manza. 1997. "Social Cleavages and Political Alignments: U.S. Presidential Elections, 1960 to 1992." *American Sociological Review* 62: 937–46.

Brower, David. 1975. *Training the Nihilists: Education and Radicalism in Tsarist Russia.* Ithaca, NY: Cornell University Press.

Brown, David K. 1995. *Degrees of Control: A Sociology of Educational Expansion and Occupational Credentialism.* New York: Teachers College Press.

Brown, Laura S. 2000. "Dangerousness, Impotence, Silence, and Invisiblity: Heterosexism in the Construction of Women's Sexuality." Pp. 273–97 in Cheryl Brown Travis and Jacquelyn W. White, eds. *Sexuality, Society, and Feminism: Psychology of Women.* Washington, DC: American Psychological Association.

Brown, Lyn Mikel, and Carol Gilligan. 1992. *Meeting at the Crossroads: Women's Psychology and Girls' Development.* Cambridge, MA: Harvard University Press.

Brown, Peter. 1996. *The Rise of Western Christendom: Triumph and Diversity, A.D. 200–1000.* Oxford: Blackwell.

Brown, P., and R. Rans. 1984. "Material Girl" (recorded by Madonna). On *Like a Virgin* (CD). New York: Sire Records/Warner.

Browne, Kevin D., and Catherine Hamilton-Giachritsis. 2005. "The Influence of Violent Media on Children and Adolescents: A Public-Health Approach." *The Lancet* 365, 9460: 702–10.

Browning, Christopher R. 1992. *Ordinary Men: Reserve Police Battalion 101 and the Final Solution in Poland.* New York: HarperCollins.

Bruce, Steve. 1988. *The Rise and Fall of the New Christian Right: Conservative Protestant Politics in America 1978–1988.* Oxford, UK: Clarendon Press.

Brumberg, Joan Jacobs. 1997. *The Body Project: An Intimate History of American Girls.* New York: Random House.

Brym, Robert J. 1979. "Political Conservatism in Atlantic Canada." Pp. 59–79 in Robert J. Brym and R. James Sacouman, eds. *Underdevelopment and Social Movements in Atlantic Canada.* Toronto: New Hogtown Press.

———. 1980. *Intellectuals and Politics.* London, UK: George Allen and Unwin.

———. 1989. "Canada." Pp. 177–206 in Tom Bottomore and Robert J. Brym, eds. *The Capitalist Class: An International Study.* New York: New York University Press.

———. 1990. "Sociology, *Perestroika,* and Soviet Society." *Canadian Journal of Sociology* 15: 207–15.

———. 1992. "Some Advantages of Canadian Disunity: How Quebec Sovereignty Might Aid Economic Development in English-speaking Canada." *Canadian Review of Sociology and Anthropology* 29: 210–26.

———. 1995. "Voters Quietly Reveal Greater Communist Leanings." *Transition: Events and Issues in the Former Soviet Union and East-Central and Southeastern Europe* 1, 16: 32–35.

———. 1996a. "The Ethic of Self-reliance and the Spirit of Capitalism in Russia." *International Sociology* 11: 409–26.

———. 1996b. "Reevaluating Mass Support for Political and Economic Change in Russia." *Europe-Asia Studies* 48: 751–66.

———. 1996c. "'The Third Rome' and 'The End of History': Notes on Russia's Second Communist Revolution." *Canadian Review of Sociology and Anthropology* 33: 391–406.

———. 1996d. "The Turning Point in the Presidential Campaign." Pp. 44–49 in *The 1996 Presidential Election and Public Opinion.* Moscow: VTsIOM. [In Russian.]

———. 2001. "Jewish Immigrants from the Former Soviet Union in Canada, 1996." *East European Jewish Affairs* 31: 36–43.

———. 2007. "Six Lessons of Suicide Bombers." *Contexts* 6, 4: 40–5.

———. 2008a. "Affluence, Power and Strikes in Canada, 1973–2000." Pp. 55–68 in Edward Grabb and Neil Guppy, eds. *Social Inequality in Canada: Patterns, Problems, Policies,* 6th ed. (Scarborough, ON: Prentice-Hall Canada, 2008).

———. 2008b. *Sociology as a Life or Death Issue.* Toronto: Nelson.

———. 2009. *Canadian Society and the 2006 Census.* Toronto: Nelson.

Brym, Robert J., and Bader Araj. 2006. "Suicide Bombing as Strategy and Interaction: The Case of the Second Intifada," *Social Forces* 84: 1965–82.

Brym, Robert J., and Evel Economakis. 1994. "Peasant or Proletarian? Blacklisted Pskov Workers in St. Petersburg, 1913." *Slavic Review* 53: 120–39.

Brym, Robert J., and Rhonda Lenton. 2001. "Love Online: A Report on Digital Dating in Canada." Toronto: MSN.CA. Retrieved December 20, 2001 (http://www.nelson.com/nelson/harcourt/sociology/newsociety3e/loveonline.pdf).

Brym, Robert J., Michael Gillespie, and A. Ron Gillis. 1985. "Anomie, Opportunity, and the Density of Ethnic Ties: Another View of Jewish Outmarriage in Canada." *Canadian Review of Sociology and Anthropology* 22: 102–12.

Brym, Robert J., Michael Gillespie, and Rhonda L. Lenton. 1989. "Class Power, Class Mobilization, and Class Voting: The Canadian Case." *Canadian Journal of Sociology* 14: 25–44.

Brym, Robert J., with Bonnie J. Fox. 1989. *From Culture to Power: The Sociology of English Canada.* Toronto: Oxford University Press.

Brym, Robert J., with the assistance of Rozalina Ryvkina. 1994. *The Jews of Moscow, Kiev and Minsk: Identity, Antisemitism, Emigration.* New York: New York University Press.

Brym, Robert, Stephanie Chung, Sarah Dulmage, Christian Farahat, Mark Greenberg, Manki Ho, Khadra Housein, Dina Kulik, Matthew Lau, Olivia Maginley, Armen Nercessian, Emilio Reyes Le Blanc, Adrian Sacher, Nadia Sachewsky, Alex Sadovsky, Stephen Singh, Shankar Sivananthan, Nick Toller, Sara Vossoughi, Krista Weger, and Tommy Wu. 2005. "In Faint Praise of the World Bank's Gender Development Policy," *Canadian Journal of Sociology* 30: 95–111.

Brym, Robert J., William Shaffir, and Morton Weinfeld, eds. 1993. *The Jews in Canada.* Toronto: Oxford University Press.

Brzezinski, Zbigniew. 1993. *Out of Control: Global Turmoil on the Eve of the Twenty-first Century.* New York: Scribner.

Bukowski, W., C. Gauze, B. Hoza, and A. Newcomb. 1993. "Differences and Consistency in Relations with Same-Sex and Other-Sex Peers During Early Adolescence." *Developmental Psychology* 29: 255–63.

Bullard, Robert D. 1994. *Dumping in Dixie: Race, Class and Environmental Quality*, 2nd ed. Boulder, CO: Westview Press.

Bunge, Valerie Pottie. 2000. "Spousal Violence." Pp. 11–21 in Statistics Canada. *Family Violence in Canada: A Statistical Profile 2000.* Catalogue no. 85-224-XIE. Ottawa: Minister of Industry.

Burawoy, Michael. 1979. *Manufacturing Consent: Changes in the Labor Process Under Monopoly Capitalism.* Chicago: University of Chicago Press.

Burawoy, Michael, Joseph A. Blum, Sheba George, Zsuszsa Gille, Teresa Gowan, Lynne Haney, Maren Klawiter, Steven H. Lopez, Seán Ó Riain, and Millie Thayer. 2000. *Global Ethnography: Forces, Connections and Imaginations in a Postmodern World.* Berkeley: University of California Press.

Burgess, Ernest. W. 1967 [1925]. "The Growth of the City: An Introduction to a Research Project." Pp. 47–62 in Robert E. Park, Ernest W. Burgess, and Roderick D. McKenzie. *The City.* Chicago: University of Chicago Press.

Burleigh, Michael. 2000. *The Third Reich: A New History.* New York: Hill & Wang.

Burns, Tom, and G. M. Stalker. 1961. *The Management of Innovation.* London, UK: Tavistock.

Bush, Irene R., and Anthony Sainz. 2001. "Competencies at the Intersection of Difference, Tolerance, and Prevention of Hate Crimes." Pp. 205–24 in Mary E. Swigonski and Robin S. Mama, eds. *From Hate Crimes to Human Rights: A Tribute to Matthew Shepard.* New York: Haworth Press.

Buss, David M. 2000. *Dangerous Passion: Why Jealousy Is as Necessary as Love and Sex.* New York: Free Press.

Bussière, Patrick, Fernando Cartwright, Robert Crocker, Xin Ma, Jillian Oderkirk, and Yanhong Zhang. 2001. "Measuring Up: The Performance of Canada's Youth in Reading, Mathematics and Science—OECD PISA Study—First Results for Canadians Aged 15." Ottawa: Statistics Canada. Retrieved May 27, 2006 (http://www.pisa.gc.ca/pisa/81-590-xpe.pdf).

Bussière, Patrick, Fernando Cartwright, Tamara Knighton, with Todd Rogers. 2003. "Measuring Up: Canadian Results of the OECD PISA Study—The Performance of Canada's Youth in Mathematics, Reading, Science and Problem Solving." Ottawa: Statistics Canada. Retrieved May 27, 2006 (http://www.pisa.gc.ca/81-590-xie2004001.pdf).

Butovsky, Jonah. 2001. *The Decline of the New Democrats: The Politics of Postmaterialism or Neoliberalism?* Ph.D. dissertation, Department of Sociology, University of Toronto.

Buxton, L. H. D. 1963. "Races of Mankind." Pp. 864–66 in *Encyclopedia Britannica,* vol. 18. Chicago: Encyclopedia Britannica, Inc.

Callahan, Raymond E. 1962. *Education and the Cult of Efficiency: A Study of the Social Forces That Have Shaped the Administration of the Public Schools.* Chicago: University of Chicago Press.

Campbell, D., and J. Stanley. 1963. *Experimental and Quasi-experimental Designs for Research.* Chicago: Rand McNally.

Campbell, F. A., and C. T. Ramey. 1994. "Effects of Early Intervention on Intellectual and Academic Achievement: A Follow-up Study of Children from Low-income Families." *Child Development* 65: 684–99.

Campbell, Jane, and Mike Oliver. 1996. *Disability Politics: Understanding Our Past, Changing Our Future.* London: Routledge.

Campion, Edward W. 1993. "Why Unconventional Medicine?" *New England Journal of Medicine* 328: 282.

Canada NewsWire. 2001. "Euthanasia Prevention Coalition Responds to Leger Marketing Poll." Retrieved June 15, 2003 (http://www.newswire.ca/releases/July2001/03/c9446.html).

———. 2002. "CanWest Gag Order Now Extends to Global Television Reporters as Company Refuses to Lift Discipline against Regina 10." March 13. Retrieved May 17, 2002 (http://www.newswire.ca/releases/March2002/13/c0319.html).

Canadian Aboriginal News. 2001. "Innu, Health Officials Settle Differences over Treatment for Gas Sniffers." Retrieved June 16, 2006 (http://www.candianaboriginal.com/health/health26b.htm).

Canadian Centre on Substance Abuse. 1999. *Canadian Profile 1999: Alcohol, Tobacco and Other Drugs.* Ottawa: Centre on Substance Abuse and Centre for Addiction and Mental Health.

Canadian Coalition for Nuclear Responsibility. 2000. Retrieved October 8, 2000 (http://www.ccnr.org/#topics).

Canadian Council on Social Development. 2007. "Families: A Canadian Profile." Retrieved November 15, 2008 (http://www.ccsd.ca/factsheets/family).

Canadian Families Project. 1999. *Profiling Canada's Families in 1901.* Victoria: University of Victoria.

Canadian Global Almanac 2000. 1999. Toronto: Macmillan Canada.

Canadian Global Almanac 2002. 2001. Toronto: Macmillan Canada.

Canadian Institute for Health Information. 2004. *Improving the Health of Canadians.* Ottawa: Canadian Institute for Health Information.

Canadian Journalists for Free Expression. 2000. "CJFE Disappointed at Ontario Superior Court Ruling Against Media Freedom." Retrieved March 22, 2001 (http://www.cjfe.org/releases/2000/seizures.html).

Canadian Mental Health Association. 2001. "Depression and Manic Depression." Retrieved June 16, 2006 (http://www.cmha.ca/english/store/mh_pamphlets/mh).

Canadian Psychiatric Association. 2002. "Anxiety, Depression and Manic Depression." Retrieved June 16, 2006 (http://www.cpa-apc.org/MIAW/pamphlets/Anxiety.arp).

Canadian Radio-television and Telecommunications Commission. 2008. "Annual Reports filed by Licensees." Retrieved October 6, 2008 (http://www.crtc.gc.ca/eng/BCASTING/ann_rep/annualrp.htm).

Cancer Care Nova Scotia. n.d. "Cancer Statistics in Nova Scotia: An Overview, 1995–1999." Retrieved January 12, 2008 (http://cancercare.ns.ca/media/documents/CancerinNS_Overview.pdf).

Cancio, A. S., T. D. Evans, and D. J. Maume. 1996. "Reconsidering the Declining Significance of Race: Racial Differences in Early Career Wages." *American Sociological Review* 61: 541–56.

"The Candidates Debate." 1998. MSNBC News. Retrieved May 2, 2000 (http://msnbc.com/onair/msnbc/TimeAndAgain/archive/ken-nix/Default.asp?cp1=1).

Canning, Patricia M., and Charlotte Strong. 1998. *Families Adapting to the Cod Moratorium.* International Sociological Association (ISA).

Cardinal, H. 1977. *The Rebirth of Canada's Indians.* Edmonton: Hurtig Publishers.

Cardoso, Fernando Henrique, and Enzo Faletto. 1979. *Dependency and Development in Latin America,* Marjory Mattingly Urquidi, trans. Berkeley: University of California Press.

Caron, Roger. 1979. *Go-Boy! The True Story of a Life Behind Bars.* London, UK: Arrow Books Limited.

Carpenter, Dave. 2003. "McDonald's High-Tech with Kitchen, Kiosks." Kiosk.com. Retrieved October 23, 2003 (http://www.kiosk.com/articles_detail.php?ident=1856).

Carroll, William. 1986. *Corporate Power and Canadian Capitalism.* Vancouver: University of British Columbia Press.

Carroll, William, and Robert S. Ratner. 1996a. "Master Frames and Counter-Hegemony: Political Sensibilities in Contemporary Social Movements." *Canadian Review of Sociology and Anthropology* 33: 407–35.

———. 1996b. "Master Framing and Cross-Movement Networking in Contemporary Social Movements." *The Sociological Quarterly* 37, 4: 601–25.

Cassidy, B., R. Lord, and N. Mandell. 1998. "Silenced and Forgotten Women: Race, Poverty and Disability." Pp. 26–54 in Nancy Mandell, ed. *Race, Class and Sexuality*, 2nd ed. Scarborough: Prentice-Hall Allyn and Bacon.

Castells, Manuel. 1983. *The City and the Grassroots: A Cross-Cultural Theory of Urban Social Movements.* Berkeley, CA: University of California Press.

Cavalli-Sforza, L. L., P. Menozzi, and A. Piazza. 1994. *The History and Geography of Human Genes.* Princeton, NJ: Princeton University Press.

CBC News. 2001. "Potter Craze Sweeps Theatres across Canada." November 16. Retrieved June 12, 2004 (http://www.cbc.ca/cgi-bin/templates/view.cgi?/news2001/11/16/potter_0011116).

———. 2004a. "The Greatest Canadian." Retrieved April 6, 2006 (http://www.cbc.ca/greatest).

———. 2004b. "Hospital Hygiene Cuts Severe Infections by 80 Per Cent." Retrieved July 27, 2005 (http://www.cbc.ca/story/science/national/2004/01/15/hand_washque04015.html?print).

———. 2005. "Canadians Deeply Split on Same-Sex Marriage, Poll Suggests." Retrieved May 2, 2008 (http://www.cbc.ca/story/canada/national/2005/04/10/gay-marriage-050410.html).

———. 2007. "Casualties in the IRAQ War." Retrieved January 13, 2008 (http://www.cbc.ca/news/background/iraq/casualties.html).

Central Intelligence Agency. 2001. *The World Factbook 2001*. Retrieved June 25, 2002 (http://www.cia.gov/cia/publications/factbook).

———. 2002. *The World Factbook 2002*. Retrieved October 6, 2008. (http://www.faqs.org/docs/factbook/index.html).

———. 2008. *The World Factbook 2008*. Retrieved November 1, 2008 (http://www.cia.gov/library/publications/the-world-factbook/index.html).

Centre for Economic Policy Research. 2002. *Making Sense of Globalization: A Guide to the Economic Issues*. London.

Chambliss, Daniel F. 1996. *Beyond Caring: Hospitals, Nurses, and the Social Organization of Ethics*. Chicago: University of Chicago Press.

Chambliss, William J. 1989. "State-Organized Crime." *Criminology* 27: 183–208.

Chang, Ha-Joon. 2002. Kicking Away the Ladder: Development Strategy in Historical Perspective. London: Anthem Press.

Chard, Jennifer. 2000. "Women in a Visible Minority." Pp. 219–44 in *Women in Canada, 2000: A Gender-Based Statistical Report*. Ottawa: Statistics Canada.

Charlton, James I. 1998. *Nothing about Us without Us: Disability Oppression and Empowerment*. Berkeley, CA: University of California Press.

Chaves, Mark. 1994. "Secularization as Declining Religious Authority." *Social Forces* 72: 749–74.

Cherlin, Andrew J. 1992. *Marriage, Divorce, Remarriage*, rev. ed. Cambridge, MA: Harvard University Press.

Chesley, L., D. MacAulay, and J. L. Ristock. 1991. *Abuse in Lesbian Relationships: A Handbook of Information and Resources*. Toronto: Counselling Centre for Lesbians and Gays.

Chesnais, Jean-Claude. 1992 [1986]. *The Demographic Transition: Stages, Patterns, and Economic Implications*, Elizabeth Kreager and Philip Kreager, trans. Oxford, UK: Clarendon Press.

"Chinese Community." 2001. Retrieved March 15, 2001 (http://www.direct.ca/news/cchi/chin02.shtml).

Chisholm, Patricia. 1996. "The Body Builders: Canadians—Women and Men—Pay the High Price of Beauty." Originally published in *Maclean's* July 8. Retrieved July 20, 2002 (http://www.geocities.com/SunsetStrip/stage/2943/surgery.html).

Chomsky, Noam. 1991. *Deterring Democracy*. London: Verso.

"Chronological Perspective on Work Stoppages in Canada." 1999. Retrieved June 30, 2001 (http://labour.hrdc-drhc.gc.ca/doc/wid-dimt/eng/ws-at/table.cfm).

"Chronological Perspective on Work Stoppages in Canada." 2001a. Retrieved March 22, 2001 (http://labour.hrdc-drhc.gc.ca/doc/wid-dimt/eng/ws-at/table.cfm).

"Chronological Perspective on Work Stoppages in Canada (Work Stoppages Involving One or More Workers), 1976–2000." 2001b. Retrieved March 272, 2001 (http://labour-travail.hrdc-drhc.gc.ca/doc/wid-dimt/eng/ws-at/table.cfm).

Church of God. 2001. Retrieved from http://www.childrentaken.com/mediastatement.html.

Church, Gardner, Kenneth Greenberg, and Marilou McPhedran. 1997. "Toronto: An Urban Alternative." Pp. 93–112 in Robert Geddes, ed. *Cities in Our Future: Growth and Form, Environmental Health and Social Equity*. Washington, DC: Island Press.

Cicourel, Aaron. 1968. *The Social Organization of Juvenile Justice*. New York: Wiley.

Citizenship and Immigration Canada. 2000. "The Vancouver Riot of 1907." Retrieved March 16, 2001 (http://www.cic.gc.ca/english/about/legacy/chap-3a.html).

———. 2004. *Facts and Figures: Immigration Overview, Permanent and Temporary Residents*. Ottawa: Citizenship and Immigration Canada. Retrieved November 30, 2005 (http://www.cic.gc.ca/english/pdf/pub/facts2004.pdf).

Clairborne, William. 2001. "Canadians from Sect Flee to U.S. over Right to Spank." Retrieved November 30, 2005 (http://www.nospank.net/n-i27.htm).

Clairmont, Donald H., and Dennis W. Magill. 1999. *Africville: The Life and Death of a Canadian Black Community*, 3rd ed. Toronto: Canadian Scholars' Press.

Clapp, Jennifer. 1998. "Foreign Direct Investment in Hazardous Industries in Developing Countries: Rethinking the Debate." *Environmental Politics* 7, 4: 92–113.

Clark, S. D. 1968. *The Developing Canadian Community*, 2nd ed. Toronto: University of Toronto Press.

Clark, Terry Nichols, and Seymour Martin Lipset. 1991. "Are Social Classes Dying?" *International Sociology* 6: 397–410.

Clark, Terry Nichols, Seymour Martin Lipset, and Michael Rempel. 1993. "The Declining Political Significance of Class." *International Sociology* 8: 293–316.

Clark, W. 2003. "Pockets of Belief: Religious Attendance Patterns in Canada." *Canadian Social Trends* 68 (Spring): 2–5.

Clark, Warren. 2000. "Religious Observance, Marriage and Family." Pp. 109–14 in *Canadian Social Trends: Volume 3*. Toronto: Thompson Educational Publishing, Inc.

Clarke, Harold D., Jane Jenson, Lawrence LeDuc, and Jon H. Pammett. 1996. *Absent Mandate: Canadian Electoral Politics in an Era of Restructuring*, 3rd ed. Toronto: Gage.

Clarke, Sally. 1995. "Advance Report of Final Divorce Statistics, 1989 and 1990." *Monthly Vital Statistics Report* 43, 9 (Supp., March 22).

Clarke-Stewart, K. Alison, Christian P. Gruber, and Linda May Fitzgerald. 1994. *Children at Home and in Day Care.* Hillsdale, NJ: Lawrence Erlbaum.

Clawson, D. 1980. *Bureaucracy and the Labor Process: The Transformation of U.S. Industry, 1860–1920.* New York: Monthly Review Press.

Clement, W. 1975. *The Canadian Corporate Elite: An Analysis of Economic Power.* Toronto: McClelland & Stewart.

Clement, W., ed. 1997. *Understanding Canada: Building on the New Canadian Political Economy.* Montreal: McGill-Queen's University Press.

Clement, W., and J. Myles. 1994. *Relations of Ruling: Class and Gender in Postindustrial Societies.* Montreal and Kingston: McGill-Queen's University Press.

Clement, W. H. P. 1897. *The History of the Dominion of Canada.* Toronto: William Briggs.

Cleveland, Gordon, and Michael Krashinsky. 1998. *The Benefits and Costs of Good Child Care: The Economic Rationale for Public Investment in Young Children.* Toronto: University of Toronto.

Clinard, Marshall B., and Peter C. Yeager. 1980. *Corporate Crime.* New York: Free Press.

Cloward, Richard A., and Lloyd E. Ohlin. 1960. *Delinquency and Opportunity: A Theory of Delinquent Gangs.* New York: Free Press.

Coale, Ansley J. 1974. "The History of Human Population." *Scientific American* 23, 3: 41–51.

Coale, Ansley J., and Susan C. Watkins, eds. 1986. *The Decline of Fertility in Europe.* Princeton, NJ: Princeton University Press.

Cobb, Chris. 2002. "Canadian Confused by Left and Right." *National Post Online* April 29. Retrieved April 30, 2002 (http://www.nationalpost.com/search/story. html?f=/stories/20020429/63885.html&qs=left%20 right.

Cockerham, William C. 1998. *Medical Sociology,* 7th ed. Upper Saddle River, NJ: Prentice-Hall.

Coghlan, Banjamin, Richard J. Brennan, Pascal Ngoy, David Dofara, Brad Otto, Mark Clements, and Tony Stewart. 2006. "Mortality in the Democratic Republic of Congo: A Nationwide Survey." *The Lancet* 367: 44-51.

Cohen, Albert. 1955. *Delinquent Boys: The Subculture of a Gang.* New York: Free Press.

Cohen, Lynne. 1999. "Suing the Alternative Health-Care Provider." *Canadian Lawyer* November/December: 47–51.

Cohen, Stanley. 1972. *Folk Devils and Moral Panics: The Creation of the Mods and Rockers.* London: MacGibbon and Kee.

Colapinto, John. 1997. "The True Story of John/Joan." *Rolling Stone* December 11: 54–73, 92–97.

———. 2001. *As Nature Made Him: The Boy Who Was Raised as a Girl.* Toronto: HarperCollins.

Cole, Michael. 1995. *Cultural Psychology.* Cambridge, MA: Harvard University Press.

Cole, S., D. Denny, A. E. Eyler, and S. L. Samons. 2000. "Issues of Transgender." Pp. 149–95 in L. T. Szuchman and F. Mascarella, eds. *Psychological Perspectives on Human Sexuality.* New York: John Wiley & Sons.

Coleman, James S. 1961. *The Adolescent Society.* New York: Free Press.

———. 1988. "Social Capital in the Creation of Human Capital." *American Journal of Sociology* 94: 95–120.

———. 1990. *Foundations of Social Theory.* Cambridge, MA: Harvard University Press.

Coleman, James, Ernest Campbell, Carol Hobson, James McPartland, Alexander Mood, Frederic Weinfeld, and Robert York. 1966. *Equality of Educational Opportunity.* Washington, DC: United States Department of Health, Education, and Welfare, Office of Education.

Collins, Randall. 1979. *The Credential Society: An Historical Sociology of Education.* New York: Academic Press.

———. 1982. *Sociological Insight: An Introduction to Non-obvious Sociology.* New York: Oxford University Press.

———. 1993. "Review of *A Theory of Religion* by Rodney Stark and William S. Bainbridge." *Journal for the Scientific Study of Religion* 32, 4: 402–04, 406.

Collins, Randall, and Scott Coltrane. 1991. *Sociology of Marriage and the Family,* 3rd ed. Chicago: Nelson-Hall.

———. 1995. *Sociology of Marriage and the Family,* 4th ed. Chicago: Nelson-Hall.

Commins, Patricia. 1997. "Foreign Sales Prop up McDonald's." *Globe and Mail* August 26: B8.

Competition Bureau. 2002. "Comments of the Commissioner of Competition to the Standing Committee on Canadian Heritage on the Study of the State of the Canadian Broadcasting System." Ottawa: Government of Canada. Retrieved May 19, 2002 (http://strategis.ic.gc.ca/pics/ct/writtensubmission.pdf).

Condry, J., and S. Condry. 1976. "Sex Differences: The Eye of the Beholder." *Child Development* 47: 812–19.

Conley, Dalton. 1999. *Being Black, Living in the Red: Race, Wealth, and Social Policy in America.* Berkeley: University of California Press.

Conrad, Peter, and Joseph W. Schneider. 1992. *Deviance and Medicalization: From Badness to Sickness,* expanded ed. Philadelphia: Temple University Press.

Converse, J. M., and S. Presser. 1986. *Survey Questions: Handcrafting the Standardized Questionnaire.* Newbury Park, CA: Sage.

Conwell, Chic. 1937. *The Professional Thief: By a Professional Thief*, annotated and interpreted by Edwin H. Sutherland. Chicago: University of Chicago Press.

Cooley, Charles Horton. 1902. *Human Nature and the Social Order*. New York: Scribner's.

Coontz, Stephanie. 1992. *The Way We Never Were: American Families and the Nostalgia Trap*. New York: Basic Books.

Coontz, Stephanie, and Peta Henderson. 1986. *Women's Work, Men's Property: The Origins of Gender and Class*. London, UK: Verso.

Corak, Miles, Garth Lipps, and John Zhao. 2003. "Family Income and Participation in Post-secondary Education." Ottawa: Statistics Canada. Catalogue No. 11F0019M2003210. Retrieved May 27, 2006 (http://www.statcan.ca/bsolc/english/bsolc?catno=11F00 19M2003210).

Coser, Rose Laub. 1960. "Laughter among Colleagues: A Study of the Functions of Humor among the Staff of a Mental Hospital." *Psychiatry* 23: 81–95.

Couch, Carl J. 1968. "Collective Behavior: An Examination of Some Stereotypes." *Social Problems* 15: 310–22.

Coupland, Douglas. 1991. *Generation X: Tales for an Accelerated Culture*. New York: St. Martin's Press.

Cox, Wendell. 1997. "Local and Regional Governance in the Greater Toronto Area: A Review of Alternatives." Retrieved from http://www.publicpurpose.com/ tor-demo.htm.

Creedon, Jeremiah. 1998. "God with a Million Faces." *Utne Reader* July–August: 42–8.

Creese, G. 1999. *Contracting Masculinity: Gender, Class, and Race in a White-Collar Union, 1944–1994*. Don Mills, ON: Oxford University Press Canada.

Creese, G., and B. Began. 1999. "Gender at Work: Seeking Solutions for Women's Equality." Pp. 199–211 in J. Curtis, E. Grabb, and N. Guppy, eds. *Social Inequality in Canada,* 3rd ed. Toronto: Prentice-Hall.

Creighton, Sarah, and Catherine Mihto. 2001. "Managing Intersex." *BMJ: British Medical Journal* 323, 7324 (December): 1264–65.

Crew, Louie. 2002. "Female Priests in the Episcopal Church." Retrieved November 12, 2005 (http://newark.rutgers.edu/~lcrew/womenpr.html#upup).

Crick, N. 1997. "Engagement in Gender Normative versus Nonnormative Forms of Aggression: Links to Social-psychological Adjustment." *Developmental Psychology* 33: 610–17.

Crompton, Susan, and Michael Vickers. 2000. "One Hundred Years of Labour Force." *Canadian Social Trends* Summer: 2–6.

Crompton, Susan, Jonathan Ellison, and Kathryn Stevenson. 2002. "Better Things to Do or Dealt out of the Game? Internet Dropouts and Infrequent Users." *Canadian Social Trends* Summer: 2–5.

Croteau, David, and William Hoynes. 1997. *Media/Society: Industries, Images, and Audiences*. Thousand Oaks, CA: Pine Forge Press.

Crothers, Charles. 1979. "On the Myth of Rural Tranquility: Comment on Webb and Collette." *American Journal of Sociology* 84: 429–37.

Crozier, Michel. 1964 [1963]. *The Bureaucratic Phenomenon*. Chicago: University of Chicago Press.

"The CRTC's Mandate." 2002. Retrieved May 15, 2003 (http://www.crtc.gc.ca/eng/BACKGRND/Brochures/B29 903.htm).

Crucefix, Linda. 2003. "Do the Inuit Really Have 200 Words for 'Snow'?" *Ask Us @ U of T*. Retrieved January 22, 2003 (http://www.newsandevents.utoronto .ca/bios/askus3.htm).

Cruikshank, J. 1997. "Negotiating with Narrative: Establishing Cultural Identity at the Yukon International Storytelling Festival." *American Anthropologist* 99: 55–69.

Cummins, Jim. 1994. "Lies We Live By: National Identity and Social Justice." *International Journal of the Sociology of Language* 110: 145–54.

Curran, John. 2000. "Thinner Miss Americas: Study: Some Contestants Undernourished." ABCNEWS.com. Retrieved February 15, 2001 (wysiwyg://7/http:// abcnews.go.com/sections/living/DailyNews/ missamerica000322.htmk).

Curtis, Bruce. 2001. *The Politics of Population: State Formation, Statistics, and the Census of Canada, 1840–1875*. Toronto: University of Toronto Press.

Curtis, James E., and Ronald D. Lambert. 1994. "Ideology and Social Change." Pp. 710–58 in Lorne Tepperman, James E. Curtis, and R. Jack Richardson, eds. *The Social World,* 3rd ed. Toronto: McGraw-Hill.

Curtis, James, John Loy, and Wally Karnilowicz. 1986. "A Comparison of Suicide-Dip Effects of Major Sport Events and Civil Holidays." *Sociology of Sport Journal* 3: 1–14.

CyberPress. 2001. "The Recidivist Roger Caron Stopped Once Again" (translated from the French), October 14. Retrieved October 10, 2002 (http://216.239.37.120/transl).

Dahl, Robert A. 1961. *Who Governs?* New Haven, CT: Yale University Press.

Dalphonse, Sherri. 1997. "Childfree by Choice." *The Washingtonian* 32, 5: 48–57.

Darwin, Charles. 1859. *On the Origin of Species by Means of Natural Selection*. London: John Murray.

———. 1871. *The Descent of Man*. London: John Murray.

Davies, Christine. 1998. *Jokes and Their Relation to Society*. Berlin: Mouton de Gruyter.

Davies, J. B. 1999. "Distribution of Wealth and Economic Inequality." Pp. 138–50 in J. Curtis, E. Grabb, and N. Guppy, eds. *Social Inequality in Canada: Patterns, Problems, Policies,* 3rd ed. Scarborough, ON: Prentice Hall Allyn and Bacon Canada.

Davies, James C. 1969. "Toward a Theory of Revolution." Pp. 85–108 in Barry McLaughlin, ed. *Studies in Social Movements: A Social Psychological Perspective*. New York: Free Press.

Davies, Mark, and Denise B. Kandel. 1981. "Parental and Peer Influences on Adolescents' Educational Plans: Some Further Evidence." *American Journal of Sociology* 87: 363–87.

Davis, Fred. 1992. *Fashion, Culture, and Identity*. Chicago: University of Chicago Press.

Davis, K., and W. E. Moore. 1945. "Some Principles of Stratification." *American Sociological Review* 10: 242–49.

Davis, Lennard J. 1995. *Enforcing Normalcy: Disability, Deafness, and the Body*. London: Verso.

Dawson, C. A. 1936. *Group Settlement: Ethnic Communities in Western Canada*. Toronto: Macmillan Company of Canada Ltd.

Dawson, C. A., and Gettys, W. E. 1929. *An Introduction to Sociology*. New York: Ronald Press.

Dawson, Lorne. 1993. "Religion and Legitimacy." Pp. 311–27 in Peter S. Li and B. Singh Bolaria, eds. *Contemporary Sociology: Critical Perspectives*. Toronto: Copp Clark Pitman.

Dawson, S. E. 1906. "Principal Causes of Death." Table IV. *Fourth Census of Canada, 1901, volume IV*. Ottawa: Library and Archives Canada.

DeFine, Michael Sullivan. 1997. "A History of Governmentally Coerced Sterilization: The Plight of the Native American Woman." Retrieved April 24, 2003 (http://www.geocities.com/CapitolHill/9118/mike2.html).

DeKeseredy, Walter S., and Katherine Kelly. 1993. "The Incidence and Prevalence of Woman Abuse in Canadian University and College Dating Relationships." *Canadian Journal of Sociology* 18: 137–59.

Denzin, Norman K. 1992. *Symbolic Interactionism and Cultural Studies: The Politics of Interpretation*. Oxford, UK: Blackwell.

Department of Geography, Slippery Rock University. 1997. "World's Largest Cities, 1900." Retrieved May 2, 2000 (http://www.sru.edu/depts/artsci/ges/discover/d-6-8.htm).

———. 2003. "World's Largest Urban Agglomerations, 2015." Retrieved August 2, 2006 (http://www1.sru .edu/gge/faculty/hughes/100/100-6/d-6-9b.htm).

Department of Justice, Canada. 1995. "A Review of Firearm Statistics and Regulations in Selected Countries." Retrieved April 29, 2000 (http://www.cfc-ccaf.gc.ca/research/publications/reports/1990%2D95/reports/siter_rpt_en.html).

———. 2004. "Pay Equity: A New Approach to a Fundamental Right." Retrieved May 14, 2006 (http://canada.justice.gc.ca/en/payeqsal/index.html).

Derber, Charles. 1979. *The Pursuit of Attention: Power and Individualism in Everyday Life*. New York: Oxford University Press.

DeSoya, Indra, and John Oneal. 1999. "Boon or Bane? Reassessing the Productivity of Foreign Direct Investment with New Data." *American Sociological Review* 64: 766–782.

DeSteno, David, and Peter Salovey. 2001. "Evolutionary Origins of Sex Differences in Jealousy: Questioning the 'Fitness' of the Model." Pp. 150–56 in W. Gerrod Parrott, ed. *Emotions in Social Psychology: Essential Readings*. Philadelphia: Psychology Press.

de Villiers, Marq. 1999. *Water*. Toronto: Stoddart Publishing.

de Waal, Alexander. 1989. *Famine That Kills: Darfur, Sudan, 1984–1985*. Oxford, UK: Clarendon Press.

Diamond, Larry. 1996. "Is the Third Wave Over?" *Journal of Democracy* 7, 3: 20–37. Retrieved May 1, 2000 (http://muse.jhu.edu/demo/jod/7.3diamond.html).

Diamond, Milton, and H. Keith Sigmundson. 1999. "Sex Reassignment at Birth." Pp. 55–75 in Stephen J. Ceci and Wendy W. Williams, eds. *The Nature–Nurture Debate: The Essential Readings*. Maldan, MA: Blackwell.

Diani, Mario. 1996. "Linking Mobilization Frames and Political Opportunities: Insights from Regional Populism in Italy." *American Sociological Review* 61: 1053–69.

Dibbell, Julian. 1993. "A Rape in Cyberspace." *The Village Voice* December 21: 36–42. Retrieved April 29, 2000 (http://www.levity.com/julian/bungle.html).

Dietz, Tracy L. 1998. "An Examination of Violence and Gender Role Portrayals in Video Games: Implications for Gender Socialization and Aggressive Behavior." *Sex Roles* 38: 425–42.

"Digital Dilemmas." 2003. *The Economist* January 25: 3–26. Retrieved May 29, 2003 (http://www.economist.com/displayStory.cfm?Story_id=1534303).

DiMaggio, Paul, and Walter Powell. 1983. "The Iron Cage Revisited: Institutional Isomorphism and Collective Rationality in Organizational Fields." *American Sociological Review* 48: 147–60.

Dines, Gail, and Jean McMahon Humez. 1995. *Gender, Race, and Class in Media: A Text-Reader*. Thousand Oaks, CA: Sage.

Doberman, J. 1997. *Darwin's Athletes: How Sport Has Damaged Black America and Preserved the Myth of Race*. Boston: Houghton Mifflin.

Doell, R. G. 1995. "Sexuality in the Brain." *Journal of Homosexuality* 29: 345–56.

Doherty, G. 1997. *Zero to Six: The Basis for School Readiness*. Ottawa: Applied Research Branch, Human Resources Development Canada (#R-97-8E).

Dolnick, Edward. 1993. "Deafness as Culture." *The Atlantic Monthly* 272, 3: 37–48.

Donahue, John J., III, and Steven D. Levitt. 2001. "The Impact of Legalized Abortion on Crime." *Quarterly Journal of Economics* 116: 379–420.

Dore, Ronald. 1983. "Goodwill and the Spirit of Market Capitalism." *British Journal of Sociology* 34: 459–82.

Doremus, P. N., W. W. Keller, L. W. Pauly, and S. Reich. 1998. *The Myth of the Global Corporation*. Princeton, NJ: Princeton University Press.

Douglas, Jack D. 1967. *The Social Meanings of Suicide*. Princeton, NJ: Princeton University Press.

Douglas, Susan J. 1994. *Where the Girls Are: Growing Up Female with the Mass Media*. New York: Random House.

Doyle, Aaron, Brian Elliott, and David Tindall. 1997. "Framing the Forests: Corporations, the B.C. Forest Alliance, and the Media." Pp. 240–68 in William Carroll, ed. *Organizing Dissent: Contemporary Social Movements in Theory and Practice*, 2nd ed. Toronto: Garamond Press.

Dranoff, Linda Silver. 2001. *Everyone's Guide to the Law*. Toronto: HarperCollins.

Drèze, Jean, and Amartya Sen. 1989. *Hunger and Public Action*. Oxford, UK: Clarendon Press.

Drolet, Marie. 2005. "Participation in Post-secondary Education in Canada: Has the Role of Parental Education and Income Changed over the 1990s?" Ottawa: Statistics Canada. Retrieved May 27, 2006 (http://www.statcan.ca/cgi-bin/downpub/listpub .cgi?catno=11F0019MIE2005243).

Duffy, A., D. Glenday, and N. Pupo, eds. 1997. *Good Jobs, Bad Jobs, No Jobs: The Transformation of Work in the 21st Century*. Toronto: Harcourt Brace.

Duffy, Jim, Georg Gunther, and Lloyd Walters. 1997. "Gender and Mathematical Problem Solving." *Sex Roles* 37: 477–94.

Dugger, Karen. 1996. "Social Location and Gender-Role Attitudes: A Comparison of Black and White Women." Pp. 32–51 in Esther Ngan-Ling Chow, Doris Wilkinson, and Maxine Baca Zinn, eds. *Race, Class, and Gender*. Newbury Park, CA: Sage.

Duhaime, Lloyd. 1997. "Euthanasia in Canada." Retrieved August 9, 2000 (wysiwyg://17/http://www.duhaime.org/ ca~euth.htm).

Duncan, Greg, W. Jean Yeung, Jeanne Brooks-Gunn, and Judith Smith. 1998. "How Much Does Childhood Poverty Affect the Life Chance of Children?" *American Sociological Review* 63: 402–23.

Dunk, T. 1991. *It's a Working Man's Town: Male Working Class Culture in Northwestern Ontario*. Montreal: McGill-Queen's University Press.

Durham, William H. 1979. *Scarcity and Survival in Central America: Ecological Origins of the Soccer War*. Stanford, CA: Stanford University Press.

Durkheim, Émile. 1951 [1897]. *Suicide: A Study in Sociology*, G. Simpson, ed., J. Spaulding and G. Simpson, trans. New York: Free Press.

———. 1956. *Education and Sociology*, Sherwood D. Fox, trans. New York: Free Press.

———. 1961 [1925]. *Moral Education: A Study in the Theory and Application of the Sociology of Education*, Everett K. Wilson and Herman Schnurer, trans. New York: Free Press.

———. 1973 [1899–1900]. "Two Laws of Penal Evolution." *Economy and Society* 2: 285–308.

———. 1976 [1915]. *The Elementary Forms of the Religious Life*, Joseph Ward Swain, trans. New York: Free Press.

Dutton, Judy. 2000. "Detect His Lies Every Time." *Cosmopolitan* April: 126.

Dyson, Freeman. 1999. *The Sun, the Genome, and the Internet*. New York: Oxford University Press.

Eagles, Munroe. 1993. "Money and Votes in Canada: Campaign Spending and Parliamentary Election Outcomes, 1984 and 1988." *Canadian Public Policy* 19: 432–49.

Eagley, Alice H., and Wendy Wood. 1999. "The Origins of Sex Differences in Human Behaviour: Evolved Dispositions versus Social Roles." *American Psychologist* 54: 408–23.

Earl, Louise. 1999. *Entertainment Services: A Growing Consumer Market*. Ottawa: Statistics Canada. Catalogue no. 63-016-XPB.

Eccles, Jacquelynne S., Robert Roeser, Allan Wigfield, and Carol Freedman-Doen. 1999. "Academic and Motivational Pathways through Middle Childhood." Pp. 287–377 in Lawrence Balter, ed. *Child Psychology*. Philadelphia: Psychology Press.

Eccles, J. S., J. E. Jacobs, and R. D. Harold. 1990. "Gender Role Stereotypes, Expectancy Effects and Parents' Socialization of Gender Differences." *Journal of Social Issues* 46: 183–201.

Economakis, Evel, and Robert J. Brym. 1995. "Marriage and Militance in a Working Class District of St. Petersburg, 1896–1913." *Journal of Family History* 20: 23–43.

Edel, Abraham. 1965. "Social Science and Value: A Study in Interrelations." Pp. 218–38 in Irving Louis Horowitz, ed. *The New Sociology: Essays in Social Science and Social Theory in Honor of C. Wright Mills*. New York: Oxford University Press.

Edmundson, Mark. 2003. "How Teachers Can Stop Cheaters." *New York Times* September 9. Retrieved September 9, 2003 (http://www.nytimes.com).

EGALE. 2001. "Svend Robinson Introduces Bill, EGALE Renews Call for Hate Crimes Protection in Wake of Murder of Gay Man in Vancouver." Press release, November 22. Retrieved February 10, 2002 (http://www.egale.ca/pressrel/011122.htm).

eHarlequin.com. 2000. "About eHarlequin.com." Retrieved May 17, 2000 (http://eharlequin.women.com/harl/ globals/about/00bkrd11.htm).

Ehrlich, Paul R. 1968. *The Population Bomb*. New York: Ballantine.

Ehrlich, Paul R., Gretchen C. Daily, Scott C. Daily, Norman Myers, and James Salzman. 1997. "No Middle

Way on the Environment." *Atlantic Monthly* 280, 6: 98–104. Retrieved October 8, 2000 (http://www.theatlantic.com/issues/97dec/enviro.htm).

Ehrlich, Paul R., and Anne H. Ehrlich. 1990. *The Population Explosion.* New York: Simon & Schuster.

Eichler, Margrit. 1987. *Nonsexist Research Methods.* Boston: Allen & Unwin.

———. 1988a. *Families in Canada Today,* 2nd ed. Toronto: Gage.

———. 1988b. *Nonsexist Research Methods: A Practical Guide.* Boston: Unwin Hyman.

Einstein, Albert. 1954. *Ideas and Opinions,* Carl Seelig, ed., Sonja Bargmann, trans. New York: Crown.

Eisenstadt, S. N. 1956. *From Generation to Generation.* New York: Free Press.

Eisenstein, Elizabeth L. 1983. *The Printing Revolution in Early Modern Europe.* Cambridge/New York: Cambridge University Press.

Eisler, Riane. 1987. *The Chalice and the Blade: Our History, Our Future.* New York: HarperCollins.

Ekman, Paul. 1978. *Facial Action Coding System.* New York: Consulting Psychologists Press.

Elections Canada. 2005. "Estimation of Voter Turnout by Age Group at the 38th General Election." Retrieved June 28, 2006 (http://www.elections.ca/loi/report_e.pdf).

———. 2006. "39th General Election." Retrieved January 24, 2006 (http://enr.elections.ca).

Elias, Norbert. 1985 [1982]. *The Loneliness of the Dying,* Edmund Jephcott, trans. Oxford, UK: Blackwell.

———. 1994 [1939]. *The Civilizing Process,* Edmund Jephcott, trans. Cambridge, MA: Blackwell.

Elliott, H. L. 1995. "Living Vicariously Through Barbie." Retrieved November 19, 1998 (http://ziris.syr.edu/path/public_html/barbie/main.html).

Ellis, Brett Easton. 1991. *American Psycho.* New York: Vintage.

Ellis, Erin Brockovich. 2002. "The Power of One." Retrieved June 30, 2002 (http://www.cincinnati.com/uniquelives/brockovich.html).

Ellison, Nicole B., Charles Steinfeld, and Cliff Lampe. 2007. "The Benefits of Facebook 'Friends:' Social Capital and College Students' Use of Online Social Network Sites." *Journal of Computer-Mediated Communication* 12, 4. Retrieved December 18, 2007 (http://jcmc.indiana.edu/vol12/issue4/ellison.html).

Ellul, Jacques. 1964 [1954]. *The Technological Society,* John Wilkinson, trans. New York: Vintage.

Engels, Frederick. 1970 [1884]. *The Origins of the Family, Private Property and the State,* Eleanor Burke Leacock, ed., Alec West, trans. New York: International Publishers.

England, Charles R. n.d. "A Look at the Indian Health Service Policy of Sterilization, 1972–1976." Retrieved April 23, 2003 (http://www.dickshovel.com/IHSSterPol.html).

England, Paula. 1992. *Comparable Worth: Theories and Evidence.* Hawthorne, NY: Aldine de Gruyter.

Entine, J. 2000. *Taboo: Why Black Athletes Dominate Sports and Why We Are Afraid to Talk about It.* New York: Public Affairs.

Environics Research Group. 1999. *The Focus Canada Report* (March). Toronto.

Epstein, Helen. 1998. "Life and Death on the Social Ladder." *New York Review of Books* 45, 12 (16 July): 26–30.

Epstein, Steven. 1996. *Impure Science: AIDS, Activism, and the Politics of Knowledge.* Berkeley, CA: University of California Press.

Equal Voice. 2005. "The Facts, Ma'am." Retrieved June 12, 2006 (http://www.equalvoice.ca/research.html).

Ericksen, Julia. 1998. "With Enough Cases, Why Do You Need Statistics? Revisiting Kinsey's Methodology." *Journal of Sex Research* 35: 132–40.

Erwin, J. 1988. "R.E.A.L. Women, Anti-Feminism, and the Welfare State." *Resources for Feminist Research* 17, 3 (September): 147–49.

Esping-Andersen, Gøsta. 1990. *The Three Worlds of Welfare Capitalism.* Princeton, NJ: Princeton University Press.

Estrich, Susan. 1987. *Real Rape.* Cambridge, MA: Harvard University Press.

Etcoff, Nancy. 1999. *Survival of the Prettiest: The Science of Beauty.* New York: Anchor Books.

"Ethnic Groups in the World." 2001. *Scientific American.* Retrieved December 4, 2001 (http://www.sciam.com/1998/0998issue/0998numbers.html).

Evans, Peter B., Dietrich Rueschemeyer, and Theda Skocpol. 1985. *Bringing the State Back In.* Cambridge, UK: Cambridge University Press.

Evans, Robert G. 1999. "Social Inequalities in Health." *Horizons* (Policy Research Secretariat, Government of Canada) 2, 3: 6–7.

Everitt, J. 1998. "Public Opinion and Social Movements: The Women's Movement and the Gender Gap in Canada." *Canadian Journal of Political Science* 31: 743–65.

"Face of the Web Study Pegs Global Internet Population at More Than 300 Million." 2000. Retrieved October 2, 2000 (http://www.angusreid.com/media/content/displaypr.?idto_view=1001).

FAD (Families Against Deadbeats). 2000. Retrieved June 14, 2003 (http://www.wantedposters.com).

Fagot, Berly I., Caire S. Rodgers, and Mary D. Leinbach. 2000. "Theories of Gender Socialization." Pp. 65–89 in Thomas Eckes, ed. *The Developmental Social Psychology of Gender.* Mahwah, NJ: Lawrence Erlbaum Associates.

Fall Colors 2003–04: Prime Time Diversity Report. 2004. Oakland CA: Children Now. Retrieved January 14, 2008 (http://publications.childrennow.org/assets/pdf/cmp/fall-colors-03/fall-colors-03-v5.pdf).

Farley, Christopher John. 1998. "Rock Star." *Time* July 20. Retrieved April 9, 2003 (http://www.time.com/time/sampler/article/0,8599,166239,00.html).

Farmer, Paul. 1992. *AIDS and Accusation: Haiti and the Geography of Blame.* Berkeley, CA: University of California Press.

Farrell, Colin. n.d. "The Canadian Prison Strap." Retrieved May 12, 2006 (http://www.corpun.com/canada2.html).

Fattah, Ezzat A. 1991. *Understanding Criminal Victimization: An Introduction to Theoretical Victimology.* Scarborough, ON: Prentice Hall.

Faulkner, Anne H., and Kevin Cranston. 1998. "Correlates of Same-Sex Sexual Behavior in a Random Sample of Massachusetts High School Students." *Journal of Public Health* 88, February: 262–66.

Fava, Sylvia Fleis. 1956. "Suburbanism as a Way of Life." *American Sociological Review* 21: 34–37.

Fearon, E. R. 1997. "Human Cancer Syndrome: Clues to the Origin and Nature of Cancer." *Science* 278: 1043–50.

Febvre, Lucien, and Henri-Jean Martin. 1976 [1958]. *The Coming of the Book: The Impact of Printing 1450–1800,* David Gerard, trans. London: NLB.

Fedorowycz, Orest. 1999. "Homicide in Canada, 1998." *Juristat* 19, 10 (October). Canadian Centre for Justice Statistics. Cat. 85-002-XIE.

Feeley, Malcolm M., and Jonathan Simon. 1992. "The New Penology: Notes on the Emerging Strategy of Corrections and its Implications." *Criminology* 30: 449–74.

Fekete, John. 1994. *Moral Panics: Biopolitics Rising.* Toronto: Robert Davies.

Felson, Richard B. 1996. "Mass Media Effects on Violent Behavior." *Annual Review of Sociology* 22: 103–28.

Fernandez-Dols, Jose-Miguel, Flor Sanchez, Pilar Carrera, and Maria-Angeles Ruiz-Belda. 1997. "Are Spontaneous Expressions and Emotions Linked? An Experimental Test of Coherence." *Journal of Nonverbal Behavior* 21: 163–77.

Fields, Jason, and Kristin Smith. 1998. "Poverty, Family Structure, and Child Well-Being." Population Division. Washington, DC: U.S. Bureau of Census.

Figart, Deborah M., and June Lapidus. 1996. "The Impact of Comparable Worth on Earnings Inequality." *Work and Occupations* 23: 297–318.

"Finding God in Harry Potter." 2005. *The Christian Post* 16 July. Retrieved December 14, 2005 (http://www.christianpost.com/article/education/895/section/finding.god.in.harry.potter/1.htm).

Finke, Roger, and Rodney Starke. 1992. *The Churching of America, 1776–1990: Winners and Losers in Our Religious Economy.* New Brunswick, NJ: Rutgers University Press.

Finnie, Ross. 1993. "Women, Men and the Economic Consequences of Divorce: Evidence from Canadian Longitudinal Data." *Canadian Review of Sociology and Anthropology* 30, 2: 205–41.

Firebaugh, Glenn, and Frank D. Beck. 1994. "Does Economic Growth Benefit the Masses? Growth, Dependence and Welfare in the Third World." *American Journal of Sociology* 59: 631–53.

Fischer, Claude S. 1981. "The Public and Private Worlds of City Life." *American Sociological Review* 46: 306–16.

———. 1984 [1976]. *The Urban Experience,* 2nd ed. New York: Harcourt Brace Jovanovich.

Fischer, Claude S., Michael Hout, Martín Sánchez Jankowski, Samuel R. Lucas, Ann Swidler, and Kim Voss. 1996. *Inequality by Design: Cracking the Bell Curve Myth.* Princeton, NJ: Princeton University Press.

Fisher, John. 1999. *A Report on Lesbian, Gay and Bisexual Youth.* Ottawa: EGALE.

Flood, Gavin D. 1996. *An Introduction to Hinduism.* Cambridge: Cambridge University Press.

Floud, Roderick, Kenneth Wachter, and Annabel Gregory. 1990. *Height, Health and History: Nutritional Status in the United Kingdom, 1750–1980.* Cambridge: Cambridge University Press.

Flowers, Paul, and Katie Buston. 2001. "'I Was Terrified of Being Different': Exploring Gay Men's Accounts of Growing-Up in a Heterosexist Society." *Journal of Adolescence, Special Issue: Gay, Lesbian, and Bisexual Youth* 24, 1 (February): 51–65.

Flynn, James R. 1987. "Massive IQ Gains in 14 Nations: What IQ Tests Really Measure." *Psychological Bulletin* 101: 171–91.

Forrest, C. B., and A. W. Riley. 2004. "Childhood Origins of Adult Health: A Basis for Life-Course Health Policy." *Health Affairs* 23, 5: 155–64.

Förster, M., and M. Pellizzari. 2000. *Trends and Driving Factors in Income Distribution and Poverty in the OECD Area.* Labour Market and Social Policy Occasional Papers No. 42. Paris: OECD.

Foucault, Michel. 1977. *Discipline and Punish: The Birth of the Prison,* Alan Sheridan, trans. New York: Pantheon.

Francis, D. 1992. *The Imaginary Indian: The Image of the Indian in Canadian Culture.* Vancouver, BC: Arsenal Pulp Press.

Franco, Zeno, and Philip Zimbardo. 2006–07. "The Banality of Heroism." *Greater Good* 3, 2: 33–4. Retrieved January 3, 2008 (http://greatergood.berkeley.edu/greatergood/archive/2006fallwinter/francozimbardo.html).

Frank, Jeffrey. 1992. "Voting and Contributing: Political Participation in Canada." *Canadian Social Trends* 27: 2–6.

Frank Porter Graham Child Development Center. 1999. "Early Learning, Later Success: The Abecedarian Study." Retrieved August 10, 2000 (http://www.fpg.unc.edu/~abc/abcedarianWeb/index.htm).

Frank, Robert H. 1988. *Passions within Reason: The Strategic Role of the Emotions.* New York: Norton.

Frank, Thomas, and Matt Weiland, eds. 1997. *Commodify Your Dissent: Salvos from the Baffler.* New York: W. W. Norton.

Franke, Richard H., and James D. Kaul. 1978. "The Hawthorne Experiments: First Statistical Interpretation." *American Sociological Review* 43: 623–43.

Franke, Richard W., and Barbara H. Chasin. 1992. *Kerala: Development through Radical Reform.* San Francisco: Institute for Food and Development Policy.

Frankel, Glenn. 1996. "U.S. Aided Cigarette Firms in Conquests Across Asia." *Washington Post* November 17: A01. Retrieved February 8, 2003 (http://www .washingtonpost.com/wp-srv/national/longterm/tobacco/ stories/asia.htm).

Franklin, Karen. 1998. "Psychosocial Motivations of Hate Crime Perpetrators." Paper presented at the annual meetings of the American Psychological Association (San Francisco: 16 August).

Franklin, Sara, and Helen Ragone, eds. 1999. *Reproducing Reproduction.* Philadelphia: University of Pennsylvania Press.

Freedman, Jonathan L. 2002. *Media Violence and Its Effect on Aggression: Assessing the Scientific Evidence.* Toronto: University of Toronto Press.

Freeze, Colin, and Karen Howlett. 2005. "McGuinty Government Rules out Use of Sharia Law." *Globe and Mail.* Retrieved December 8, 2005 (http://www .theglobeandmail.com/servlet/story/RTGAM.20050912 .wxsharia12/BNStory/National).

Freidson, Eliot. 1986. *Professional Powers: A Study of the Institutionalization of Formal Knowledge.* Chicago: University of Chicago Press.

Freire, Paolo. 1972. *The Pedagogy of the Oppressed.* New York: Herder and Herder.

French, Howard W. 2001. "The Japanese, It Seems, Are Outgrowing Japan." *New York Times* February 1: 4A.

Frenette, Marc. 2005. "Is Post-secondary Access More Equitable in Canada or in the United States?" Ottawa: Statistics Canada. Retrieved May 27, 2006 (http://www.statcan.ca/cgi-bin/downpub/listpub.cgi? catno=11F0019MIE2005244).

Freud, Sigmund. 1962 [1930]. *Civilization and Its Discontents,* James Strachey, trans. New York: W. W. Norton.

———. 1973 [1915–17]. *Introductory Lectures on Psychoanalysis,* James Strachey, trans., James Strachey and Angela Richards, eds. Harmondsworth, UK: Penguin.

———. 1977 [1905]. *On Sexuality,* James Strachey, trans., Angela Richards, comp., and ed. Harmondsworth, UK: Penguin.

Freudenburg, William R. 1997. "Contamination, Corrosion and the Social Order: An Overview." *Current Sociology* 45, 3: 19–39.

Fried, Martha Nemes, and Morton H. Fried. 1980. *Transitions: Four Rituals in Eight Cultures.* New York: W. W. Norton.

Friedenberg, Edgar Z. 1959. *The Vanishing Adolescent.* Boston: Beacon Press.

Friedkin, Noah E. 1998. *A Structural Theory of Social Influence.* Cambridge: Cambridge University Press.

Fröbel, Folker, Jürgen Heinrichs, and Otto Kreyre. 1980. *The New International Division of Labour: Structural Unemployment in Industrialised Countries and Industrialisation in Developing Countries.* Pete Burgess, trans. Cambridge: Cambridge University Press.

Froissart, Jean. 1968 [c. 1365]. *Chronicles,* selected and translated by Geoffrey Brereton. Harmondsworth, UK: Penguin.

Gabor, Thomas. 1994. *Everybody Does It: Crime by the Public.* Toronto: University of Toronto Press.

Gado, Mark. 2003. "A Cry in the Night: The Kitty Genovese Murder." *Court TV's Crime Library.* Retrieved July 23, 2003 (http://www.crimelibrary.com/serial_killers/ predators/kitty_genovese/1.html).

Gaines, Donna. 1990. *Teenage Wasteland: Suburbia's Dead End Kids.* New York: Pantheon.

Galabuzi, G.-E. 2004. *Social Inclusion as a Determinant of Health.* Ottawa: Public Health Agency of Canada. Retrieved July 2, 2005 (http://www.phac-aspc.gc.ca/ ph-sp/phdd/overview_implications/03_inclusion.html).

Galewitz, Phil. 2000. "Firm Settles Fraud Case: Hospital Chain Columbia/HCA to pay $745 Million." *ABCNEWS .com* May 18. Retrieved June 12, 2003 (http://abcnews .go.com/sections/business/DailyNews/columbiahca_ 990518.html).

Gallup Organization. 2000. "Gallup Poll Topics: A–Z." Retrieved July 25, 2002 (http://www.gallup.com/ poll/indicators/indhomosexual.asp).

Galper, Joseph. 1998. "Schooling for Society." *American Demographics* 20, 3: 33–34.

Galt, Virginia. 2006. " 'Working Retired' in Demand as Work Force Ages." *Globe and Mail* February 4: B11.

Gambetta, Diego, ed. 1988. *Trust: Making and Breaking Cooperative Relations.* Oxford, UK: Blackwell.

Gamson, William A. 1975. *The Strategy of Social Protest.* Homewood, IL: Dorsey Press.

Gamson, William A., Bruce Fireman, and Steven Rytina. 1982. *Encounters with Unjust Authority.* Homewood, IL: Dorsey Press.

Gans, Herbert. 1962. *The Urban Villagers: Group and Class in the Life of Italian-Americans.* New York: Free Press.

———. 1979. *Deciding What's News: A Study of CBS Evening News, NBC Nightly News, Newsweek and Time.* New York: Pantheon.

———. 1991. "Symbolic Ethnicity: The Future of Ethnic Groups and Cultures in America." Pp. 430–43 in Norman R. Yetman, ed. *Majority and Minority: The*

Dynamics of Race and Ethnicity in American Life, 5th ed. Boston, MA: Allyn and Bacon.

Garfinkel, Harold. 1967. *Studies in Ethnomethodology.* Englewood Cliffs, NJ: Prentice-Hall.

Garfinkel, Simson. 2000. *Database Nation: The Death of Privacy in the 21st Century.* Cambridge, MA: O'Reilly and Associates.

Garkawe, Sam. 1995. "The Impact of the Doctrine of Cultural Relativism on the Australian Legal System." *E Law* 2, 1. Retrieved May 10, 2000 (http://www .murdoch.edu.au/elaw/issues/v2n1/garkawe.txt).

Garland, David. 1990. *Punishment and Modern Society: A Study in Social Theory.* Chicago: University of Chicago Press.

Garner, David M. 1997. "The 1997 Body Image Survey Results." *Psychology Today* 30, 1: 30–44.

Garrau, Joel. 1991. *Edge City: Life on the New Frontier.* New York: Doubleday.

Garson, Barbara. 2001. *Money Makes the World Go Around.* New York: Viking.

Garvey, Christine Ann. 1999. "The Intergenerational Transmission of Discipline." *Dissertation Abstracts International, Section A: The Sciences and Engineering* 60, 3-B (September): 1027.

Gaskell, Jane, Arlene McLaren, and Myra Novogrodsky. 1995. "What's Worth Knowing? Defining the Feminist Curriculum." Pp. 100–18 in E. D. Nelson and B. W. Robinson, eds. *Gender in the 1990s: Images, Realities, and Issues.* Scarborough: Nelson Canada.

Gates, W., with N. Myhrvold and P. Rinearson. 1996. *The Road Ahead.* New York: Penguin.

Gauvain, Mary, Beverly I. Fagot, Craig Leve, and Kate Kavanagh. 2002. "Instruction by Mothers and Fathers During Problem Solving with Their Young Children." *Journal of Family Psychology* 6, 1 (March): 81–90.

Gebhard, Paul H., and Alan B. Johnson, 1979. *The Kinsey Data: Marginal Tabulations of the 1938–1963 Interviews Conducted by the Institute for Sex Research.* Philadelphia: W. B. Saunders.

Geddes, Robert, ed. 1997. *Cities in Our Future: Growth and Form, Environmental Health and Social Equity.* Washington, DC: Island Press.

Geertz, Clifford. 1973. *The Interpretation of Cultures: Selected Essays.* New York: Basic Books.

Gegax, T. Trent, and Lynette Clemetson. 1998. "The Abortion Wars Come Home." *Newsweek* November 9: 34–35.

Gelbspan, Ross. 1999. "Trading Away Our Chances to End Global Warming." *Boston Globe* May 16: E2.

Gelles, Richard J. 1994. "Ten Risk Factors." *Newsweek* July 4: 29.

———. 1997. *Intimate Violence in Families,* 3rd ed. Thousand Oaks, CA: Sage.

Gellner, E. 1983. *Nations and Nationalism.* Ithaca: Cornell University Press.

———. 1988. *Plough, Sword and Book: The Structure of Human History.* Chicago: University of Chicago Press.

Geohive.com. 2005. "The Demographical Status of the World's Population." Retrieved June 26, 2005 (http://www.geohive.com/global/geo.php?xml=world& xsl=pop_data).

George, Jane. 1998. "Kuujjuaq Daycare Thrives on Federal Head Start Program." *Nunatsiaq News* October 29. Retrieved September 4, 2000 (http://www.nunatsiaq .com/archives/nunavut981031/nvt81030_13.html).

Gerber, Theodore P., and Michael Hout. 1998. "More Shock than Therapy: Market Transition, Employment, and Income in Russia, 1991–1995." *American Journal of Sociology* 104: 1–50.

Germani, Gino, and Kalman Silvert. 1961. "Politics, Social Structure and Military Intervention in Latin America." *European Journal of Sociology* 11: 62–81.

Gerschenkron, Alexander. 1962. *Economic Backwardness in Historical Perspective: A Book of Essays.* Cambridge, MA: Harvard University Press.

Ghalam, Nancy Z. 1997. "Attitudes Towards Women, Work and Family." *Canadian Social Trends* 46: 13–7.

Giddens, Anthony. 1990. *Sociology: A Brief But Critical Introduction,* 3rd ed. New York: Harcourt Brace Jovanovich.

Gidengil, Elisabeth. 1992. "Canada Votes: A Quarter Century of Canadian National Election Studies." *Canadian Journal of Political Science* 25: 219–48.

Gilbert, Susan. 1997. "2 Spanking Studies Indicate Parents Should Be Cautious." *New York Times* August 20.

Gill, Richard T. 1997. *Posterity Lost: Progress, Ideology, and the Decline of the American Family.* London, UK: Rowman & Littlefield Publishers.

Gille, Zsuzsa, and Seán Ó Riain. 2002. "Global Ethnography." *Annual Review of Sociology* 28: 271–95.

Gilligan, Carol. 1982. *In a Different Voice: Psychological Theory and Women's Development.* Cambridge, MA: Harvard University Press.

Gilligan, Carol, Nona P. Lyons, and Trudy J. Hanmer, eds. 1990. *Making Connections: The Relational Worlds of Adolescent Girls at Emma Willard School.* Cambridge, MA: Harvard University Press.

Gillis, A. R. 1995. "Urbanization." Pp. 13.1–13.35 in Robert J. Brym, ed. *New Society Brief Edition: Sociology for the 21st Century.* Toronto: Harcourt Brace.

Gillis, John R. 1981. *Youth and History: Tradition and Change in European Age Relations, 1770–Present,* expanded student ed. New York: Academic Press.

Gilman, S. L. 1991. *The Jew's Body.* New York: Routledge.

Gilpin, Robert. 2001. *Global Political Economy: Understanding the International Economic Order.* Princeton, NJ: Princeton University Press.

Gimbutas, Marija. 1982. *Goddesses and Gods of Old Europe.* Berkeley and Los Angeles: University of California Press.

Ginsberg, Benjamin. 1986. *The Captive Public: How Mass Opinion Promotes State Power.* New York: Basic Books.

Gitlin, Todd. 1983. *Inside Prime Time.* New York: Pantheon.

Glaser, Barney, and Anselm Straus. 1967. *The Discovery of Grounded Theory.* Chicago: Aldine.

Glazer, Nathan. 1997. *We Are All Multiculturalists Now.* Cambridge, MA: Harvard University Press.

Glendon, Mary Ann. 1981. *The New Family and the New Property.* Toronto: Butterworths.

Glenn, Norval D. 1990. "Quantitative Research on Marital Quality in the 1980s: A Critical Review." *Journal of Marriage and the Family* 52 (November): 818–31.

Glenn, Norval D., and Sara McLanahan. 1982. "Children and Marital Happiness: A Further Specification of the Relationship." *Journal of Marriage and the Family* 44: 63–72.

Global Reach. 2001. "Global Internet Statistics (by Language)." Retrieved September 23, 2001 (http://www. glreach.com/globstats/index.php3).

———. 2004. "Global Internet Statistics (by Language)." Retrieved January 27, 2005 (http://www. glreach.com/globstats).

Glock, Charles Y. 1962. "On the Study of Religious Commitment." *Religious Education* 62, 4: 98–110.

Goddard Institute for Space Studies. 2008. "Global Temperature Anomalies in .01 C, base period: 1951-1980." Retrieved January 12, 2008 (http://data.giss.nasa .gov/gistemp/tabledata/GLB.Ts.txt).

Goffman, Erving. 1959. *The Presentation of Self in Everyday Life.* Garden City, NY: Anchor.

———. 1961. *Asylums: Essays on the Social Situation of Mental Patients and Other Inmates.* Garden City, NY: Anchor Books.

———. 1963. *Stigma: Notes on the Management of Spoiled Identity.* Englewood Cliffs, NJ: Prentice-Hall.

———. 1971. *Relations in Public: Microstudies of the Public Order.* New York: Basic Books.

———. 1974. *Frame Analysis.* Cambridge, MA: Harvard University Press.

"Going Native: Dinner Parties." 2003. Retrieved February 3, 2003 (http://www.geocities.com/robainsley2/ eikoku/1.html).

Goldberg, M., and D. Green. 1999. *Raising the Floor: The Social and Economic Benefits of Minimum Wages in Canada.* Vancouver: Canadian Center for Policy Alternatives.

Goldie, Terry. 2001. *In a Queer Country: Gay & Lesbian Studies in the Canadian Context.* Vancouver: Arsenal Pulp Press.

Goldstein, Jay E. 1978. "The Prestige of Canadian Ethnic Groups: Some New Evidence." *Canadian Ethnic Studies* 10: 84–95.

Goldthorpe, J. H., and Richard Breen. 1997. "The Integration of Sociological Research and Theory." *Rationality and Society* 9: 405–26.

Goll, David. 2002. "True Priority of Office Ethics Clouded by Scandals." *East Bay Business Times* August 19. Retrieved January 13, 2003 (http://eastbay.bizjournals .com/eastbay/stories/2002/08/19/smallb3.html).

Gombrich, Richard Francis. 1996. *How Buddhism Began: The Conditioned Genesis of the Early Teachings.* London: Athlone.

Goode, Erich, and Nachman Ben-Yehuda. 1994. *Moral Panics: The Social Construction of Deviance.* Cambridge, MA: Blackwell.

Goodman, John T. 1999. "Mental Health." Pp. 1468–69 in James H. Marsh, ed. *The Canadian Encyclopedia: Year 2000 Edition.* Toronto: McClelland & Stewart.

Gordon, D. M., R. Edwards, and M. Reich. 1982. *Segmented Work, Divided Workers: The Historical Transformation of Labor in the United States.* New York: Cambridge University Press.

Gordon, Linda. 1990. *Woman's Body, Woman's Right: Birth Control in America,* rev. ed. Harmondsworth, UK: Penguin.

Gordon, Sarah. 1984. *Hitler, Germans, and the Jewish Question.* Princeton, NJ: Princeton University Press.

Gorman, Christine. 1997. "A Boy without a Penis." *Time* March 24: 83.

———. 1998. "Playing the HMO Game." *Time* 152, 2 (July 13). Retrieved May 2, 2000 (http://www.time.com/ time/magazine/1998/dom/980713/cover1.html).

Gortmaker, S. L., A. Must, J. M. Perrin, A. M. Sobol, and W. H. Dietz. 1993. "Social and Economic Consequence of Overweight in Adolescence and Young Adulthood." *New England Journal of Medicine* 329, 14: September 30: 1008–12.

Gottdiener, Mark, and Ray Hutchison. 2000. *The New Urban Sociology,* 2nd ed. Boston: McGraw-Hill.

Gottfredson, Michael, and Travis Hirschi. 1990. *A General Theory of Crime.* Stanford, CA: Stanford University Press.

Gottwald, Norman K. 1979. *The Tribes of Yahweh: A Sociology of the Religion of Liberated Israel, 1250–1050 B.C.E.* Maryknoll, NY: Orbis.

Goubert, Jean-Pierre. 1989 [1986]. *The Conquest of Water,* Andrew Wilson, trans. Princeton, NJ: Princeton University Press.

Gould, Stephen Jay. 1988. "Kropotkin Was No Crackpot." *Natural History* 97, 7: 12–18.

———. 1996. *The Mismeasure of Man,* rev. ed. New York: W. W. Norton.

Gould, S. J., and R. C. Lewontin. 1979. "The Spandrels of San Marco and the Panglossian Paradigm: A Critique of the Adaptationist Programme." *Proceedings of the Royal Society of London, Series B, Biological Sciences* 205, 1161, September 21: 581–98.

Government of Canada. 2001. "Early Intervention Programs." Retrieved February 14, 2003 (http://www.crime-prevention.org/english/ publications/youth/mobilize/early_e.html).

Gracey, Harry L. 2001. "Learning the Student Role: Kindergarten as Academic Boot Camp." Pp. 364–76 In James M. Henslin, ed. *Down to Earth Sociology: Introductory Readings,* 11th ed. New York: Free Press.

Graff, Harvey J. 1995. *Conflicting Paths: Growing Up in America.* Cambridge, MA: Harvard University Press.

Granovetter, Mark. 1973. "The Strength of Weak Ties." *American Sociological Review* 78: 1360–80.

———. 1995. *Getting a Job: A Study of Contacts and Careers.* Chicago: University of Chicago Press.

Grayson, P. 1985. *Corporate Strategies and Plant Closures: The SKF Experience.* Toronto: Our Times.

Greenhill, Pauline. 2001. "Can You See the Difference: Queerying the Nation, Ethnicity, Festival, and Culture in Winnipeg." Pp. 103–21 in Terry Goldie, ed. *In a Queer Country: Gay & Lesbian Studies in the Canadian Context.* Vancouver: Arsenal Pulp Press.

Greeno, Cherri. 2000. "Stalking Rate." *KW Record* December 1: A1, A2.

Greenpeace. 2000. "Greenpeace Contacts Worldwide." Retrieved May 2, 2001 (http://adam.greenpeace .org/information.shtml).

Greenstein, Theodore N. 1996. "Husbands' Participation in Domestic Labor: Interactive Effects of Wives' and Husbands' Gender Ideologies." *Journal of Marriage and the Family* 58: 585–95.

Grescoe, P. 1996. *The Merchants of Venus: Inside Harlequin and the Empire of Romance.* Vancouver: Raincoast.

Griffiths, C. T., and J. C. Yerbury. 1995. "Understanding Aboriginal Crime and Criminality: A Case Study." Pp. 383–98 in M. A. Jackson and C. T. Griffiths, eds. *Canadian Criminology: Perspectives on Crime and Criminality,* 2nd ed. Toronto: Harcourt, Brace Canada.

Grimmett, Richard F. 2006. "Conventional Arms Transfers to Developing Nations, 1998–2005." Congressional Research Service. Retrieved January 12, 2008 (http://www.fas.org/sgp/crs/weapons/RL33696.pdf).

Grindstaff, Laura. 1997. "Producing Trash, Class, and the Money Shot: A Behind-the-Scenes Account of Daytime TV Talk Shows." Pp. 164–202 in James Lull and Stephen Hinerman, eds. *Media Scandals: Morality and Desire in the Popular Culture Marketplace.* Cambridge, UK: Polity Press.

Griswold, Wendy. 1992. "The Sociology of Culture: Four Good Arguments (and One Bad One)." *Acta Sociologica* 35: 322–28.

Groce, Nora Ellen. 1985. *Everyone Here Spoke Sign Language: Hereditary Deafness on Martha's Vineyard.* Cambridge, MA: Harvard University Press.

Guillén, Mauro F. 2001. "Is Globalization Civilizing, Destructive or Feeble? A Critique of Five Key Debates in the Social-Science Literature." *Annual Review of Sociology* 27: 235–60. Retrieved February 6, 2003 (http://knowledge.wharton.upenn.edu/PDFs/938.pdf).

Gundersen, Edna, Bill Keveney, and Ann Oldenburg. 2002. "'The Osbournes' Find a Home in America's Living Rooms." *USA Today* April 19: 1A–2A.

Guppy, Neil, James Curtis, and Edward Grabb. 1999. "Age-Based Inequalities in Canadian Society." Pp. 246–57 in James Curtis, Edward Grabb, and Neil Guppy, eds. *Social Inequality in Canada: Patterns, Problems, Policies,* 3rd ed. Scarborough, ON: Prentice Hall Allyn and Bacon.

Guppy, N., and S. Davies. 1998. *Education in Canada: Recent Trends and Future Challenges.* Ottawa: Ministry of Industry.

Guppy, Neil, and R. Alan Hedley. 1993. *Opportunities in Sociology.* Montreal: Canadian Sociology and Anthropology Association.

Gurr, Ted Robert. 1970. *Why Men Rebel.* Princeton, NJ: Princeton University Press.

Haas, Jack, and William Shaffir. 1987. *Becoming Doctors: The Adoption of a Cloak of Competence.* Greenwich, CT: JAI Press.

Haas, Jennifer. 1998. "The Cost of Being a Woman." *New England Journal of Medicine* 338: 1694–95.

Habermas, Jürgen. 1989. *The Structural Transformation of the Public Sphere,* Thomas Burger, trans. Cambridge, MA: MIT Press.

Hacker, Andrew. 1997. *Money: Who Has How Much and Why.* New York: Scribner.

Hagan, John. 1989. *Structuralist Criminology.* New Brunswick, NJ: Rutgers University Press.

———. 1994. *Crime and Disrepute.* Thousand Oaks, CA: Pine Forge Press.

———. 2000. "White-Collar and Corporate Crime." Pp. 459–82 in Rick Linden, ed. *Criminology: A Canadian Perspective,* 4th ed. Toronto: Harcourt Canada.

Hagan, John, John Simpson, and A. R. Gillis. 1987. "Class in the Household: A Power-Control Theory of Gender and Delinquency." *American Journal of Sociology* 92: 788–816.

Haines, Herbert H. 1996. *Against Capital Punishment: The Anti–Death Penalty Movement in America, 1972–1994.* New York: Oxford University Press.

Hajdu, David. 2005. "Guns and Poses." *New York Times* March 11. Retrieved March 11, 2005 (http://www.nytimes.com).

Hall, Edward. 1959. *The Silent Language.* New York: Doubleday.

———. 1966. *The Hidden Dimension.* New York: Doubleday.

Hall, Stuart. 1980. "Encoding/Decoding." Pp. 128–38 in Stuart Hall, Dorothy Hobson, Andrew Lowe, and Paul Willis, eds. *Culture, Media, Language: Working Papers in Cultural Studies, 1972–79.* London: Hutchinson.

———. 1992. "The Question of Cultural Identity." Pp. 274–313 in Stuart Hall, David Held, and Tim

McGrew, eds. *Modernity and its Futures.* Cambridge, UK: Polity and Open University Press.

Hamachek, D. 1995. "Self-Concept and School Achievement: Interaction Dynamics and a Tool for Assessing the Self-Concept Component." *Journal of Counseling and Development* 73: 419–25.

Hamer, D., P. F. Copeland, S. Hu, V. I. Magnuson, N. Hu, and A. M. I. Pattatucci. 1993. "A Linkage Between DNA Markers on the X Chromosome and Male Sexual Orientation." *Science* 261: 321–27.

Hamilton, Roberta. 1996. *Gendering the Vertical Mosaic: Feminist Perspectives on Canadian Society.* Toronto: Copp-Clark.

Hampton, J., ed. 1998. *Internally Displaced People: A Global Survey.* London: Earthscan.

Hancock, Graham. 1989. *Lords of Poverty: The Power, Prestige, and Corruption of the International Aid Business.* New York: Atlantic Monthly Press.

Hancock, Lynnell. 1994. "In Defiance of Darwin: How a Public School in the Bronx Turns Dropouts into Scholars." *Newsweek* October 24: 61.

Handelman, Stephen. 1995. *Comrade Criminal: Russia's New Mafiya.* New Haven, CT: Yale University Press.

Handy, Bruce. 2002. "Glamour with Altitude." *Vanity Fair* October: 214–28.

Haney, Craig, W. Curtis Banks, and Philip G. Zimbardo. 1973. "Interpersonal Dynamics in a Simulated Prison." *International Journal of Criminology and Penology* 1: 69–97.

Hanke, Robert. 1998. "'Yo Quiero Mi MTV!' Making Music Television for Latin America." Pp. 219–45 in Thomas Swiss, Andrew Herman, and John M. Sloop, eds. *Mapping the Beat: Popular Music and Contemporary Theory.* Oxford, UK: Blackwell.

Hannigan, John. 1995a. "The Postmodern City: A New Urbanization?" *Current Sociology* 43, 1: 151–217.

———. 1995b. *Environmental Sociology: A Social Constructionist Perspective.* London: Routledge.

———. 1998a. *Fantasy City: Pleasure and Profit in the Postmodern Metropolis.* New York: Routledge.

———. 1998b. "Urbanization." Pp. 337–59 in Robert J. Brym, ed. *New Society: Sociology for the 21st Century,* 2nd ed. Toronto: Harcourt Brace Canada.

Hannon, Roseann, David S. Hall, Todd Kuntz, Van Laar, and Jennifer Williams. 1995. "Dating Characteristics Leading to Unwanted vs. Wanted Sexual Behavior." *Sex Roles* 33: 767–83.

Hao, Xiaoming. 1994. "Television Viewing among American Adults in the 1990s." *Journal of Broadcasting and Electronic Media* 38: 353–60.

Harding, David J., Cybelle Fox, and Jal D. Mehta. 2002. "Studying Rare Events through Qualitative Case Studies: Lessons from a Study of Rampage School Shootings." *Sociological Methods and Research* 31, 2: 174–217.

Harris, Chauncy D., and Edward L. Ullman. 1945. "The Nature of Cities." *Annals of the American Academy of Political and Social Science* 242: 7–17.

Harris, Kathleen, and Jeremy Marmer. 1996. "Poverty, Parental Involvement and Adolescent Well-Being." *Journal of Family Issues* 17, 5: 614–40.

Harris, Marvin. 1974. *Cows, Pigs, Wars and Witches: The Riddles of Culture.* New York: Random House.

Harrison, Bennett. 1994. *Lean and Mean: The Changing Landscape of Corporate Power in the Age of Flexibility.* New York: Basic Books.

Hartnagel, Timothy F. 2000. "Correlates of Criminal Behaviour." Pp. 94–136 in Rick Linden, ed. *Criminology: A Canadian Perspective,* 4th ed. Toronto: Harcourt Canada.

Harvey, Andrew S., Katherine Marshall, and Judith A. Frederick. 1991. *Where Does the Time Go?* Ottawa: Statistics Canada.

Harvey, Elizabeth. 1999. "Short-term and Long-term Effects of Early Parental Employment on Children of the National Longitudinal Survey of Youth." *Developmental Psychology* 35: 445–49.

Hastings, Arthur C., James Fadiman, and James C. Gordon, eds. 1980. *Health for the Whole Person: The Complete Guide to Holistic Medicine.* Boulder, CO: Westview Press.

Hawley, Amos. 1950. *Human Ecology: A Theory of Community Structure.* New York: Ronald Press.

Häyry, Matti, and Tuija Lehto. 1998. "Genetic Engineering and the Risk of Harm." Paper presented at the 20th World Congress of Philosophy. Boston. Retrieved January 17, 2005 (http://www.bu.edu/wcp/Papers/Bioe/BioeHay2.htm).

Haythornthwaite, Caroline, and Barry Wellman. 2002. "The Internet in Everyday Life: An Introduction." Pp. 3–41 in B. Wellman and C. Haythornthwaite, eds. *The Internet in Everyday Life.* Oxford: Blackwell.

Health Canada. 1999a. "Toward a Healthy Future: Second Report on the Health of Canadians." Prepared by the Federal, Provincial, and Territorial Advisory Committee on Population Health for the Meeting of Ministers of Health, Charlottetown, PEI. September. Retrieved December 25, 1999 (http://www.hc-sc.gc.ca).

———. 1999b. "Statistical Report on the Health of Canadians." Retrieved December 25, 1999 (http://www.hc-sc.gc.ca/hppb/phdd/report/state/englover.html).

———. 2004. "Aboriginal Health: The Government of Canada's Role in Aboriginal Health Care." Retrieved May 17, 2006 (http://www.hc-sc.gc.ca/hcs-sss/delivery-prestation/fptcollab/2004-fmm-rpm/fs-if_02_e.html).

Health Canada. n.d. "Canadian Cancer Statistics, 2003." Retrieved January 12, 2008 (http://www.cancer.ca/vgn/images/portal/cit_776/61/38/56158640niw_stats_en.pdf).

"Health Care Systems: An International Comparison." 2001. Ottawa: Strategic Policy and Research, Intergovernmental

Affairs. Retrieved June 13, 2003 (http://www.pnrec.org/2001papers/DaigneaultLajoie.pdf).

Hechter, M. 1974. *Internal Colonialism: The Celtic Fringe in British National Development, 1536–1966.* Berkeley, CA: University of California Press.

Hechter, Michael. 1987. *Principles of Group Solidarity.* Berkeley, CA: University of California Press.

Held, David. 1987. *Models of Democracy.* Stanford, CA: Stanford University Press.

Helsing, Knud J., Moyses Szklo, and George W. Comstock. 1981. "Factors Associated with Mortality after Widowhood." *American Journal of Public Health* 71: 802–09.

Henry, Frances, Carol Tator, Winston Mattis, and Tim Rees. 2000. *The Colour of Democracy: Racism in Canadian Society,* 2nd ed. Toronto: Harcourt Brace Canada.

Henry, Frances, et al. 2001. "The Victimization of Racial Minorities in Canada." Pp. 145–60 in Robert J. Brym, ed. *Society in Question: Sociological Readings for the 21st Century.* Toronto: Harcourt Canada.

Herdt, Gilbert. 2001. "Social Change, Sexual Diversity, and Tolerance for Bisexuality in the United States." Pp. 267–83 in Anthony R. D'Augelli and Charlotte J. Patterson, eds. *Lesbian, Gay, and Bisexual Identities and Youth: Psychological Perspectives.* New York: Oxford University Press.

Herlihy, David. 1998. *The Black Death and the Transformation of the West.* Cambridge, MA: Harvard University Press.

Herman, Edward S., and Noam Chomsky. 1988. *Manufacturing Consent: The Political Economy of the Mass Media.* New York: Pantheon.

Herman, Edward S., and Gerry O'Sullivan. 1989. *The "Terrorism" Industry: The Experts and Institutions That Shape Our View of Terror.* New York: Pantheon.

Herrnstein, Richard J., and Charles Murray. 1994. *The Bell Curve: Intelligence and Class Structure in American Life.* New York: Free Press.

Hersch, Patricia. 1998. *A Tribe Apart: A Journey into the Heart of American Adolescence.* New York: Ballantine Books.

Hertzman, Clyde. 2000. "The Case for Early Childhood Development Strategy." *Isuma: Canadian Journal of Policy Research* 1, 2: 11–18.

Hesse-Biber, Sharlene. 1996. *Am I Thin Enough Yet? The Cult of Thinness and the Commercialization of Identity.* New York: Oxford University Press.

Hesse-Biber, Sharlene, and Gregg Lee Carter. 2000. *Working Women in America: Split Dreams.* New York: Oxford University Press.

Hindustan Times. 1999. "40% Men and 60% Women Illiterate in India." September 19. Retrieved July 15, 2000 (http://www.hindutimes.com).

Hirschi, Travis. 1969. *Causes of Delinquency.* Berkeley, CA: University of California Press.

Hirschi, Travis, and Hanan C. Selvin. 1972. "Principles of Causal Analysis." Pp. 126–47 in Paul F. Lazarsfeld, Ann K. Pasanella, and Morris Rosenberg, eds. *Continuities in the Language of Social Research.* New York: Free Press.

Hirschman, Albert O. 1970. *Exit, Voice, and Loyalty: Responses to Decline in Firms, Organizations, and States.* Cambridge, MA: Harvard University Press.

Hirst, Paul, and Grahame Thompson. 1999. *Globalization in Question: The International Economy and the Possibilities of Governance,* 2nd ed. London: Polity.

Hobbes, Thomas. 1968 [1651]). *Leviathan.* Middlesex, UK: Penguin.

Hobsbawm, Eric. 1994. *Age of Extremes: The Short Twentieth Century, 1914–1991.* London: Abacus.

Hochberg, Fred P. 2002. "American Capitalism's Other Side." *New York Times* July 25. Retrieved July 25, 2002 (http://www.nytimes.com).

Hochschild, Arlie Russell. 1973. *The Unexpected Community: Portrait of an Old Age Subculture.* Berkeley, CA: University of California Press.

———. 1979. "Emotion Work, Feeling Rules, and Social Structure." *American Journal of Sociology* 85: 551–75.

———. 1983. *The Managed Heart: Commercialization of Human Feeling.* Berkeley: University of California Press.

Hochschild, Arlie Russell, with Anne Machung. 1989. *The Second Shift: Working Parents and the Revolution at Home.* New York: Viking.

Hodge, Robert, and David Tripp. 1986. *Children and Television: A Semiotic Approach.* Cambridge, UK: Polity.

Hodgson, Marshall G. S. 1974. *The Venture of Islam: Conscience and History in a World Civilization,* 3 vols. Chicago: University of Chicago Press.

Hodson, R., and T. Sullivan. 1995. *The Social Organization of Work,* 2nd ed. Belmont CA: Wadsworth.

Hoggart, Richard. 1958. *The Uses of Literacy.* Harmondsworth, UK: Penguin.

Homans, George Caspar. 1950. *The Human Group.* New York: Harcourt, Brace.

———. 1961. *Social Behavior: Its Elementary Forms.* New York: Harcourt, Brace and World.

"Homosexuality and Bisexuality." 2000. Report #5 to the *Toronto Sun* on the Third Annual Sun/COMPAS Sex Survey. Retrieved August 9, 2002 (http://www.compas.ca/html/archivesdocument.asp?compasSection=Sun+Media+Sex+Poll&GO=GO&compasID=61).

hooks, bell. 1984. *Feminist Theory: From Margin to Center.* Boston: South End Press.

Hoover, Robert N. 2000. "Cancer—Nature, Nurture, or Both." *New England Journal of Medicine* 343, 2. Retrieved July 16, 2000 (http://www.nejm.org/content/2000/0343/0002/0135.asp).

Hopkins, Terence K., and Immanuel Wallerstein. 1986. "Commodity Chains in the World Economy Prior to 1800." *Review* 10: 157–70.

Horkheimer, Max, and Theodor W. Adorno. 1986 [1944]. *Dialectic of Enlightenment,* John Cumming, trans. London: Verso.

Hotton, Tina. 2001. "Spousal Violence After Marital Separation." *Juristat* 21, 7. Catalogue no. 85-002. Ottawa: Canadian Centre for Justice Statistics.

Houpt, Simon. 2004. "Pass the Popcorn, Save the World." *The Globe and Mail* May 29: R1, R13.

Houseknecht, Sharon K. 1987. "Voluntary Childlessness." Pp. 369–418 in Marvin B. Sussman and Suzanne K. Steinmetz, eds. *Handbook of Marriage and the Family.* New York: Putnam.

Houseknecht, Sharon K., and Jaya Sastry. 1996. "Family 'Decline' and Child Well-Being: A Comparative Assessment." *Journal of Marriage and the Family* 58: 726–39.

Howell, S. E., and C. L. Day. 2000. "Complexities of the Gender Gap." *Journal of Politics* 62: 858–75.

Hoyt, Homer. 1939. *The Structure and Growth of Residential Neighborhoods in American Cities.* Washington, DC: Federal Housing Authority.

Hughes, Diane, Ellen Galinsky, and Anne Morris. 1992. "The Effects of Job Characteristics on Marital Quality: Specifying Linking Mechanisms." *Journal of Marriage and the Family* 54, 1 (February): 31–42.

Hughes, Everett C. 1943. *French Canada in Transition.* Chicago: University of Chicago Press.

Hughes, Fergus P. 1995. *Children, Play and Development,* 2nd ed. Boston: Allyn and Bacon.

Hughes, H. Stuart. 1967. *Consciousness and Society: The Reorientation of European Social Thought, 1890–1930.* London: Macgibbon and Kee.

Human Resources and Social Development Canada. 2008. "Union Membership in Canada — 2007." Retrieved May 2, 2008 (http://www.hrsdc.gc.ca/en/lp/wid/union_membership.shtml).

Human Resources Development Canada. 2000. "Job Futures 2000." Retrieved June 2001 (http://jobfutures.ca/doc/jf/emerging/emerging.shtml#sample).

Human Rights Watch. 1995. *The Human Rights Watch Global Report on Women's Human Rights.* New York: Human Rights Watch.

Humphreys, L. 1975. *Tearoom Trade: Impersonal Sex in Public Places.* Chicago: Aldine de Gruyter.

Hunter, James Davison. 1991. *Culture Wars: The Struggle to Define America.* New York: Basic Books.

Huntington, Samuel. 1991. *The Third Wave: Democratization in the Late Twentieth Century.* Norman, OK: University of Oklahoma Press.

Hussein, Lula J. 1995. "Report on the Ottawa Consultations on Female Genital Mutilation." Retrieved July 12, 2000 (http://www.129.128.19.162.docs/fgmdoj.html).

Ignatieff, Michael. 2000. *The Rights Revolution.* Toronto: Anansi.

Ignatiev, N. 1995. *How the Irish Became White.* New York: Routledge.

IMD International. 2007. "The World Competitiveness Scoreboard 2007." Retrieved May 1, 2008 (http://www.imd.ch/research/publications/wcy/upload/scoreboard.pdf).

Inglehart, Ronald. 1997. *Modernization and Postmodernization: Cultural, Economic, and Political Change in 43 Societies.* Princeton, NJ: Princeton University Press.

Ingram, Gordon Brent. 2001. "Redesigning Wreck: Beach Meets Forest as Location of Male Homoerotic Culture in Placemaking in Pacific Canada." Pp. 188–208 in Terry Goldie, ed. *In a Queer Country: Gay & Lesbian Studies in the Canadian Context.* Vancouver: Arsenal Pulp Press.

Inkeles, Alex, and David H. Smith. 1976. *Becoming Modern: Individual Change in Six Developing Countries.* Cambridge, MA: Harvard University Press.

Intergovernmental Panel on Climate Change. 2007. Retrieved May 2, 2007 (http://www.ipcc.ch).

International Campaign Against Shari'a Court in Canada. 2005. "Homepage." Retrieved December 8, 2005 (http://www.nosharia.com).

International Federation of Journalists. 2002. "IFJ Condemns Attack on Canadian Journalists: 'Ugly and Intolerant' Vision of Modern Media." March 14. Retrieved May 17, 2002 (http://www.ifj.org/publications/press/pr/315.html).

International Labour Organization. 2008. "Yearly Data." Retrieved January 9, 2008 (http://laborsta.ilo.org).

International Lesbian and Gay Association. 2008. "LGBTI Rights in the World." Retrieved May 2, 2008 (http://www.ilga.org/map/LGBTI_rights.jpg).

International Society of Aesthetic Plastic Surgeons. 2005. "What, Why, Who, When, Where and How—Some Highlights and Facts." Retrieved May 17, 2005 (http://www.isaps.org/Stats2003Res.asp).

Internet Movie Database. 2003. Retrieved March 13, 2003 (http://us.imdb.com).

Internet Software Consortium. 2003. "Internet Domain Survey Host Count." Retrieved February 6, 2003 (http://www.isc.org/ds/hosts.html).

———. 2007 "ISC Internet Domain Survey." Retrieved December 19, 2007 (http://www.isc.org/index.pl).

"Internet Usage Statistics." Retrieved January 4, 2008 (http://www.internetworldstats.com/stats.htm).

Internet World Statistics. 2007. "Internet World Users by Language." Retrieved December 17, 2007 (http://www.internetworldstats.com/stats7.htm).

"Iraq Body Count." 2008. Retrieved January 12, 2008 (http://www.iraqbodycount.org).

"Iraq Coalition Casualty Count." 2008. Retrieved January 12, 2008 (http://icasualties.org/oif).

Iraq Family Health Survey Study Group. 2008. "Violence-Related Mortality in Iraq from 2002 to 2006." *New*

England Journal of Medicine January 9. Retrieved January 16, 2008 (http://content.nejm.org/cgi/content/full/NEJMsa0707782).

Isaacs, Larry. 2002. "To Counter 'The Very Devil' and More: The Making of Independent Capitalist Militias in the Gilded Age." *American Journal of Sociology* 108: 353–405.

istar. 2001. "Why Small Is Smarter." Retrieved June 12, 2004 (http://home.istar.ca/~gskarzn/go/SMALL.HTM).

Ivanhoe, P. J. 2000. *Confucian Moral Self-Cultivation,* 2nd ed. Indianapolis, IN: Hackett.

Iyengar, Shanto. 1991. *Is Anyone Responsible? How Television Frames Political Issues.* Chicago: University of Chicago Press.

Jackson, Carolyn, and Ian David Smith. 2000. "Poles Apart? An Exploration of Single-Sex and Mixed-Sex Educational Environments in Australia and England." *Educational Studies* 26, 4 (December): 409–22.

Jacobs, J. A. 1993. "Careers in the U.S. Service Economy." Pp. 195–224 in G. Esping-Anderson, ed. *Changing Classes: Stratification and Mobility in Postindustrial Societies.* London, UK: Sage.

Jacobs, Jane. 1961. *The Death and Life of Great American Cities.* New York: Random House.

———. 1969. *The Economy of Cities.* New York: Random House.

James, Harold. 2001. *The End of Globalization: Lessons from the Great Depression.* Cambridge, MA: Harvard University Press.

James, William. 1976 [1902]. *The Varieties of Religious Experience: A Study in Human Nature.* New York: Collier Books.

Janigan, Mary. 2002. "Saving Our Cities." *Maclean's* 3 June: 22–27.

Janis, Irving. 1972. *Victims of Groupthink.* Boston: Houghton Mifflin.

Jargowsky, Paul A. 2003. *Stunning Progress, Hidden Problems: The Dramatic Decline of Concentrated Poverty in the 1990s.* Washington, DC: Center on Urban and Metropolitan Policy, The Brookings Institution. Retrieved August 5, 2003 (http://www.brookings.edu/dybdocroot/es/urban/publications/jargowskypoverty.pdf).

Jencks, Christopher, Marshall Smith, Henry Acland, Mary Jo Bane, David Cohen, Herbert Gintis, Barbara Heyns, and Stephan Michelson. 1972. *Inequality: A Reassessment of the Effect of Family and Schooling in America.* New York: Basic Books.

Jenkins, J. Craig. 1983. "Resource Mobilization Theory and the Study of Social Movements." *Annual Review of Sociology* 9: 527–53.

Jensen, Margaret Ann. 1984. *Love's Sweet Return. The Harlequin Story.* Toronto: Women's Press.

"Jim Crow Laws: Texas." 2008. Retrieved March 7, 2008 (http://www.jimcrowhistory.org/scripts/jimcrow/insidesouth.cgi?state=Texas).

Johansen, Bruce E. 1998. "Sterilization of Native American Women." Retrieved April 24, 2003 (http://www.ratical.org/ratville/sterilize.html).

John Howard Society. 1999a. *Check & Balance: The Facts about Facts.* Toronto: The John Howard Society of Ontario.

———. 1999b. *Fact Sheet: Population Trends and Crime.* Toronto: John Howard Society of Ontario.

Johns, Adrian. 1998. *The Nature of the Book: Print and Knowledge in the Making.* Chicago: University of Chicago Press.

Johnson, Chalmers. 2000. *Blowback: The Costs and Consequences of American Empire.* New York: Metropolitan Books.

Johnson, Holly. 2006. "Measuring Violence against Women: Statistical Trends, 2006." Ottawa: Statistics Canada. Retrieved May 2, 2008 (http://www.statcan.ca/english/research/85-570-XIE/85-570-XIE2006001.pdf).

Johnson, Holly, and Tina Hotton. 2001. "Spousal Violence." Pp. 26–41 in Statistics Canada. *Family Violence in Canada: A Statistical Profile 2001.* Ottawa: Minister of Industry. Catalogue no. 85-224-XIE.

Johnson, Michael P. 1995. "Patriarchal Terrorism and Common Couple Violence: Two Forms of Violence Against Women." *Journal of Marriage and the Family* 57, 2 (May): 283–94.

Johnson, S. 2004. "Adult Correctional Services in Canada, 2002/03." *Juristat: Canadian Centre for Justice Statistics* 24, 10: 16. Retrieved May 8, 2005 (http://www.statcan.ca/bsolc/english/bsolc?catno=85-002-X20040108409).

Johnson, Terence J. 1972. *Professions and Power.* London: Macmillan.

Johnson, Tracy L., and Elizabeth Fee. 1997. "Women's Health Research: An Introduction." Pp. 3–26 in Florence P. Haseltine and Beverly Greenberg Jacobson, eds. *Women's Health Research: A Medical and Policy Primer.* Washington, DC: Health Press International.

Jones, Frank. 2000. "Are Children Going to Religious Services?" Pp. 202–05 in *Canadian Social Trends* 3. Toronto: Thompson Educational Publishing.

Jones, Laura. 1997. "Global Warming Is All the Rage These Days . . . Which Enrages Many Doubting Scientists." The Fraser Institute. Retrieved May 5, 2002 (http://oldfraser.lexi.net/media/media_releases/1997/19971201a.html).

Jones, Patrice M. 2003. "Drug Lords Do What Officials Don't—Control Brazil's Slums." *Chicago Tribune* February 2. Retrieved August 5, 2003 (http://www.il-rs.com.br/ilingles/informative/marco_2003/informative_drugs.htm).

Joy, Bill. 2000. "Why the Future Doesn't Need Us." *Wired* 8, 4. Retrieved November 4, 2003 (http://wired.com/wired/archive/8.04/joy_pr.html).

Joyce, Terrence, and Lloyd Keigwin. 2004. "Abrupt Climate Change: Are We on the Brink of a New Little Ice Age?" Ocean and Climate Change Institute, Woods Hole Oceanographic Institution. Retrieved ⟨http://www.whoi.edu/institutes/occi/currenttopics/abruptclimate_joyce_keigwin.html⟩.

Juergensmeyer, Mark. 2000. *Terror in the Mind of God: The Global Rise of Religious Violence.* Berkeley, CA: University of California Press.

Kaasa, Kristin. 2002. "This Is Women's Work, and It's About Time." *United Church Observer* (July–August). Retrieved November 12, 2005 ⟨http://www.ucobserver.org/archives/julyaug02_ministry.htm⟩.

Kalbach, M. A., and W. E. Kalbach. 1998. "Becoming Canadian: Problems of an Emerging Identity." *Canadian Ethnic Studies* 31, 2: 1–17.

Kalbach, Madeline A. 2000. "Ethnicity and the Altar." Pp. 111–21 in Madeline A. Kalbach and Warren E. Kalbach, eds. *Perspectives on Ethnicity in Canada: A Reader.* Toronto: Harcourt Canada.

Kalmijn, Matthijs. 1998. "Intermarriage and Homogamy: Causes, Patterns, Trends." *Annual Review of Sociology* 24: 395–421.

Kanter, Rosabeth Moss. 1977. *Men and Women of the Corporation.* New York: Basic Books.

———. 1989. *When Giants Learn to Dance: Mastering the Challenges of Strategy, Management, and Careers in the 1990s.* New York: Simon and Schuster.

Karklins, Rasma. 1986. *Ethnic Relations in the USSR: The Perspective from Below.* London: Unwin Hyman.

Karl, Thomas R., and Kevin E. Trenberth. 1999. "The Human Impact on Climate." *Scientific American* 281, 6 (September): 100–05.

Karp, David A., and William C. Yoels. 1976. "The College Classroom: Some Observations on the Meaning of Student Participation." *Sociology and Social Research* 60: 421–39.

Karraker, Katherine Hildebrandt, Dena Ann Vogel, and Margaret Ann Lake. 1995. "Parents' Gender-Stereotyped Perceptions of Newborns: The Eye of the Beholder Revisited." *Sex Roles* 33, 9–10 (November): 687–701.

Katz, Elihu. 1957. "The Two-Step Flow of Communication: An Up-to-Date Report on an Hypothesis." *Public Opinion Quarterly* 21: 61–78.

Kay, Fiona, and John Hagan. 1998. "Raising the Bar: The Gender Stratification of Law Firm Capitalization." *American Sociological Review* 63: 728–43.

Kazemipur, Abdolmohammad, and Shiva S. Halli. 2000. *The New Poverty: Ethnic Groups and Ghetto Neighbourhoods.* Toronto: Thompson Educational Publishing, Inc.

———. 2001. "The Changing Colour of Poverty in Canada." *Canadian Review of Sociology and Anthropology* 38, 2: 217–38.

Kearney, Mark, and Randy Ray. 1999. *The Great Canadian Book of Lists.* Toronto: Dundurn Group.

Keister, Lisa A. 2000. *Wealth in America: Trends in Wealth Inequality.* Cambridge: Cambridge University Press.

Keister, Lisa A., and Stephanie Moller. 2000. "Wealth Inequality in the United States." *Annual Review of Sociology* 26: 63–81.

Kelley, Jack. 2001. "Terror Groups Hide behind Web Encryption." *USA Today* June 19. Retrieved September 13, 2001 ⟨http://www.usatoday.com/life/cyber/tech/2001-02-05-binladen.htm⟩.

Kemper, T. D. 1978. *A Social Interactional Theory of Emotion.* New York: Wiley.

———. 1987. "How Many Emotions Are There? Wedding the Social and Autonomic Components." *American Journal of Sociology* 93: 263–89.

Kennedy, Paul. 1993. *Preparing for the Twenty-First Century.* New York: HarperCollins.

Kepel, Gilles. 1994 [1991]. *The Revenge of God: The Resurgence of Islam, Christianity and Judaism in the Modern World,* Alan Braley, trans. University Park, PA: Pennsylvania State University Press.

Kerig, Patricia K., Philip A. Cowan, and Carolyn Pape Cowan. 1993. "Marital Quality and Gender Differences in Parent–Child Interaction." *Developmental Psychology* 29: 931–39.

Kernaghan, John. 2002. "A Hockey-Obsessed Nation Holds Its Breath." *Hamilton Spectator* February 16. Retrieved June 14, 2003 ⟨http://www.hamiltonspectator.com/reports/534665.html⟩.

Kerr, Clark, John T. Dunlop, Frederick H. Harbison, and Charles A. Myers. 1960. *Industrialism and Industrial Man: The Problems of Labor and Management in Economic Growth.* New York: Oxford University Press.

Kessler, Ronald C., Katherine A. McGonagle, Shanyang Zhao, Christopher B. Nelson, Michael Hughes, Suzann Eshleman, Hans Ulrich Wittchen, and Kenneth S. Kendler. 1994. "Life-time and 12-Month Prevalence of DSM-III-R Psychiatric Disorders in the United States." *Archives of General Psychiatry* 51: 8–19.

Kevles, Daniel J. 1999. "Cancer: What Do They Know?" *New York Review of Books* 46, 14: 14–21.

Kimmerling, Baruch. 2003. *Politicide: Ariel Sharon's War against the Palestinians.* London: Verso.

King, Martin Luther. 1967. *Conscience for Change.* Toronto: CBC Learning Systems.

Kingsbury, Nancy, and John Scanzoni. 1993. "Structural-Functionalism." Pp. 195–217 in Pauline G. Boss, William J. Doherty, Ralph LaRossa, Walter R. Schumm, and Suzanne K. Steinmetz, eds. *Sourcebook of Family Theories and Methods: A Contextual Approach.* New York: Plenum.

Kingston, Peter. 1997. "Top of the Class." *The Guardian* October 21: 2.

Kinsey, Alfred C., Wardell B. Pomeroy, and Clyde E. Martin. 1948. *Sexual Behavior in the Human Male.* Philadelphia: W. B. Saunders.

Kinsey, Alfred C., Wardell B. Pomeroy, Clyde E. Martin, and Paul H. Gebhard. 1953. *Sexual Behavior in the Human Female.* Philadelphia: W. B. Saunders.

Kitano, Harry, and Roger Daniels. 1995. *Asian Americans: Emerging Minorities,* 2nd ed. Englewood Cliffs, NJ: Prentice-Hall.

Kleege, Georgina. 1999. *Sight Unseen.* New Haven, CT: Yale University Press.

Klein, Naomi. 2000. *No Logo: Taking Aim at the Brand Bullies.* New York: HarperCollins.

Kling, Kristen C., Janet Shibley Hyde, Carolin J. Showers, and Brenda N. Buswell. 1999. "Gender Differences in Self-Esteem: A Meta-Analysis." *Psychological Bulletin* 125, 4: 470–500.

Klingemann, Hans-Dieter. 1999. "Mapping Political Support in the 1990s: A Global Analysis." In Pippa Norris, ed. *Critical Citizens: Global Support for Democratic Governance.* Oxford, UK: Oxford University Press. Retrieved October 20, 2001 (http://ksgwww.harvard.edu/people/pnorris/Chapter_2.htm).

Klockars, Carl B. 1974. *The Professional Fence.* New York: Free Press.

Knight, Graham. 1998. "The Mass Media." Pp. 103–27 in Robert J. Brym, ed. *New Society: Sociology for the 21st Century,* 2nd ed. Toronto: Harcourt Brace Canada.

Koepke, Leslie, Jan Hare, and Patricia B. Moran. 1992. "Relationship Quality in a Sample of Lesbian Couples with Children and Child-Free Lesbian Couples." *Family Relations* 41: 224–29.

Kohlberg, Lawrence. 1981. *The Psychology of Moral Development: The Nature and Validity of Moral Stages.* New York: Harper and Row.

Kohn, Alfie. 1988. "Make Love, Not War." *Psychology Today* 22, 6: 35–38.

Kolko, Gabriel. 2002. *Another Century of War?* New York: New Press.

Kong, Rebecca. 1997. "Criminal Harassment in Canada." *Canadian Social Trends* 45 (Autumn): 29–33.

Kopun, Francine. 2006. "Older, Single Women Cast off Cat-Food Cliché." *Toronto Star* March 11: A01.

Korpi, Walter. 1983. *The Democratic Class Struggle.* London: Routledge and Kegan Paul.

Kosmin, Barry A. 1991. *Research Report of the National Survey of Religious Identification.* New York: CUNY Graduate Center.

Krahn, Harvey, and Graham S. Lowe, eds. 1998. *Work, Industry, and Canadian Society,* 3rd ed. Scarborough: Nelson.

Kropotkin, Petr. 1908. *Mutual Aid: A Factor of Evolution,* revised ed. London: W. Heinemann.

Kübler-Ross, Elisabeth. 1969. *On Death and Dying.* New York: Macmillan.

Kuhn, Thomas. 1970 [1962]. *The Structure of Scientific Revolutions,* 2nd ed. Chicago: University of Chicago Press.

Kurdek, Lawrence A. 1995. "Assessing Multiple Determinants of Relationship Commitment in Cohabiting Gay, Cohabiting Lesbian, Cohabiting Heterosexual, and Married Heterosexual Couples." *Family Relations* 44: 261–66.

———. 1998. "Relationship Outcomes and Their Predictors: Longitudinal Evidence from Heterosexual Married, Gay Cohabiting and Lesbian Cohabiting Couples." *Journal of Marriage and the Family* 60, 3: 553–68.

Kurtz, Howard. 1997. "U.S. Television News Distorts Reality of Homicide Rates." *Edmonton Journal* August 13: A5.

Kurzweil, Ray. 1999. *The Age of Spiritual Machines: When Computers Exceed Human Intelligence.* New York: Viking Penguin.

Kuttner, Robert. 1997. "The Limits of Markets." *The American Prospect* 31: 28–34. Retrieved April 30, 2000 (http://www.prospect.org/archives/31/31kuttfs.html).

———. 1998a. "In this For-Profit Age, Preventive Medicine Means Avoiding Audits." *Boston Globe* March 22: E7.

———. 1998b. "Toward Universal Coverage." *The Washington Post* July 14: A15.

La Prairie, Carol. 1996. *Examining Aboriginal Corrections in Canada.* Ottawa: Supply and Services Canada.

Labour Organizations in Canada 1972. 1973. Ottawa: Economics and Research Branch, Canada Department of Labour. Cat. No. L2-2-1972.

LaFeber, Walter. 1993. *Inevitable Revolutions: The United States in Central America,* 2nd ed. New York: W. W. Norton.

———. 1999. *Michael Jordan and the New Global Capitalism.* New York: W. W. Norton.

Lahmeyer, Jan. 2003. "Brazil: Historical Demographical Data of the Whole Country." Retrieved August 5, 2003 (http://www.library.uu.nl/wesp/populstat/Americas/brazilc.htm).

Lamanna, Mary Ann and Agnes Riedmann. 2003. *Marriages and Families: Making Choices in a Diverse Society,* 8th ed. Belmont CA: Wadsworth.

Lambert, M., Klarka Zeman, Mary Allen, and Patrick Bussière. 2004. "Who Pursues Postsecondary Education, Who Leaves and Why: Results from the Youth in Transition Survey." Ottawa, Statistics Canada. Retrieved May 27, 2006 (http://www.statcan.ca/cgi-bin/downpub/listpub.cgi?catno=81-595-MIE2004026).

Lane, Harlan. 1992. *The Mask of Benevolence: Disabling the Deaf Community.* New York: Alfred A. Knopf.

Lapidus, Gail Warshofsky. 1978. *Women in Soviet Society: Equality, Development, and Social Change.* Berkeley, CA: University of California Press.

Lapidus, Ira M. 2002. *A History of Islamic Societies,* 2nd ed. Cambridge: Cambridge University Press.

Larzelere, Robert E. 2000. "Child Outcomes of Nonabusive and Customary Physical Punishment by Parents: An

Updated Literature Review." *Clinical Child & Family Psychology Review* 3, 4 (December): 199–221.

Laslett, Peter. 1991. *A Fresh Map of Life: The Emergence of the Third Age,* reprinted ed. Cambridge, MA: Harvard University Press.

Lasswell, Harold. 1936. *Politics: Who Gets What, When and How.* New York: McGraw-Hill.

Laumann, Edward O., John H. Gagnon, Robert T. Michael, and Stuart Michaels. 1994. *The Social Organization of Sexuality: Sexual Practices in the United States.* Chicago: University of Chicago Press.

Lavoie, M., Richard Roy, and Pierre Therrien. 2003. "A Growing Trend Towards Knowledge Work in Canada." *Research Policy* 32, 5: 827–44.

Lavoie, Yolande, and Jillian Oderkirk. 2000. "Social Consequences of Demographic Change." Pp. 2–5 in *Canadian Social Trends,* Volume 3. Toronto: Thompson Educational Publishing, Inc.

Law, M. T. 1999. "The Economics of Minimum Wage Laws." *Public Policy Sources* 14. Retrieved May 29, 2000 (http://www.fraserinstitute.ca/publications/ pps/14).

Laxer, Gordon. 1989. *Open for Business: The Roots of Foreign Ownership in Canada.* Toronto: Oxford University Press.

Lazare, Daniel. 1999. "Your Constitution Is Killing You: A Reconsideration of the Right to Bear Arms." *Harper's* 299, 1793 (October): 57–65.

Lazonick, William. 1991. *Business Organization and the Myth of the Market Economy.* Cambridge: Cambridge University Press.

Leacock, Eleanor Burke. 1981. *Myths of Male Dominance: Collected Articles on Women Cross-Culturally.* New York: Monthly Review Press.

Le Bon, Gustave. 1969 [1895]. *The Crowd: A Study of the Popular Mind.* New York: Ballantine Books.

Le Bourdais, C., Ghyslaine Neill, and Pierre Turcott. 2000. "The Changing Face of Conjugal Relationships." *Canadian Social Trends* (Spring): 14–17.

Lee, Richard B. 1979. *The !Kung San: Men, Women and Work in a Foraging Society.* Cambridge, UK: Cambridge University Press.

Lefkowitz, Bernard. 1997a. *Our Guys: The Glen Ridge Rape and the Secret Life of the Perfect Suburb.* Berkeley, CA: University of California Press.

———. 1997b. "Boys Town: Did Glen Ridge Raise Its Sons to Be Rapists?" *Salon* August 13. Retrieved March 20, 2003 (http://www.salon.com/aug97/mothers/guys970813.html).

Lehoczky, Etelka. 2003. "Stewardess Chic." *Chicago Tribune* Online Edition April 2. Retrieved April 6, 2003 (http://www.chicagotribune.com/shopping/ chi-0304020338apr02,0,3507596.story?coll= chi- shopping-hed).

Leidner, Robin. 1993. *Fast Food, Fast Talk: Service Work and the Routinization of Everyday Life.* Berkeley, CA: University of California Press.

Lenski, G. 1966. *Power and Privilege: A Theory of Social Stratification.* New York: McGraw Hill.

Lenski, G., P. Nolan, and J. Lenski. 1995. *Human Societies: An Introduction to Macrosociology,* 7th ed. New York: McGraw-Hill.

Lerner, Gerda. 1986. *The Creation of Patriarchy.* New York: Oxford University Press.

Lever, J. 1994. "The 1994 Advocate Survey of Sexuality and Relationships: The Men." *Advocate* August 23: 16–24.

Levine, David. 1987. *Reproducing Families: The Political Economy of English Population History.* Cambridge, UK: Cambridge University Press.

Levine, R. A., and D. T. Campbell. 1972. *Ethnocentrism: Theories of Conflict, Ethnic Attitudes, and Group Behavior.* New York: Wiley.

Levine, Robert, Suguru Sato, Tsukasa Hashimoto, and Jyoti Verma. 1995. "Love and Marriage in Eleven Cultures." *Journal of Cross-Cultural Psychology* 26, 5: 554–71.

Levitan, S. A., Garth L. Mangum, and Stephen L. Mangum. 1998. *Programs in Aid of the Poor,* 7th ed. Baltimore: Johns Hopkins University Press.

Levy, Frank. 1998. *The New Dollars and Dreams: American Incomes and Economic Change.* New York: Russell Sage Foundation.

Lewontin, R. C. 1991. *Biology as Ideology: The Doctrine of DNA.* New York: HarperCollins.

Ley, David. 1996. *The New Middle Class and the Remaking of the Central City.* Oxford, UK: Oxford University Press.

Li, P. 1995. "Racial Supremacism under Social Democracy." *Canadian Ethnic Studies* 27, 1: 1–17.

Li, Peter. 1998. *The Chinese in Canada,* 2nd ed. Toronto: Oxford University Press.

———. 2000. "Earning Disparities between Immigrants and Native-Born Canadians." *Canadian Review of Sociology and Anthropology* 37, 3: 289–311.

Lian, J. Z., and D. R. Matthews. 1998. "Does the Vertical Mosaic Still Exist? Ethnicity and Income in Canada, 1991." *Canadian Review of Sociology and Anthropology* 35: 461–81.

Lichtenstein, Paul, Niels V. Holm, Pia K. Verkasalo, Anastasia Iliadou, Jaakko Kaprio, Markku Koskenvuo, Eero Pukkala, Axel Skytthe, and Kari Hemminki. 2000. "Environment and Heritable Factors in the Causation of Cancer—Analyses of Cohorts of Twins from Sweden, Denmark, and Finland." *New England Journal of Medicine* 343, 2: Retrieved July 12, 2001 (http:// content.nejm.org/cgi/content/short/343/2/78).

Lie, John. 1992. "The Concept of Mode of Exchange." *American Sociological Review* 57: 508–23.

———. 1998. *Han Unbound: The Political Economy of South Korea.* Stanford, CA: Stanford University Press.

———. 2001. *Multiethnic Japan.* Cambridge, MA: Harvard University Press.

Liebow, Elliot. 1967. *Tally's Corner: A Study of Negro Street-Corner Men.* Boston: Little, Brown.

Light, I. 1991. "Immigrant and Ethnic Enterprise in North America." Pp. 307–18 in N. R. Yetman, ed. *Majority and Minority: The Dynamics of Race and Ethnicity in American Life,* 5th ed. Boston: Allyn and Bacon.

Lightfoot-Klein, Hanny, Cheryl Chase, Tim Hammond, and Ronald Goldman. 2000. "Genital Surgery on Children Below the Age of Consent." Pp. 440–79 in Lenore T. Szuchman and Frank Muscarella, eds. *Psychological Perspectives on Human Sexuality.* New York: John Wiley & Sons.

Lindert, Peter H. 2004. *Growing Public: Social Spending and Economic Growth Since the Eighteenth Century.* New York: Cambridge.

Lindner, Rolf. 1996 [1990]. *The Reportage of Urban Culture: Robert Park and the Chicago School,* Adrian Morris, trans. Cambridge, UK: Cambridge University Press.

Lips, Hilary M. 1999. *A New Psychology of Women: Gender, Culture and Ethnicity.* Mountain View, CA: Mayfield Publishing Company.

Lipset, Seymour Martin. 1963. "Value Differences, Absolute or Relative: The English-Speaking Democracies." Pp. 248–73 in *The First New Nation: The United States in Historical Perspective.* New York: Basic Books.

———. 1971. *Agrarian Socialism: The Cooperative Commonwealth Federation in Saskatchewan,* revised ed. Berkeley, CA: University of California Press.

———. 1977. "Why No Socialism in the United States?" Pp. 31–363 in Seweryn Bialer and Sophia Sluzar, eds. *Sources of Contemporary Radicalism.* Boulder, CO: Westview Press.

———. 1981. *Political Man: The Social Bases of Politics,* 2nd ed. Baltimore: Johns Hopkins University Press.

———. 1994. "The Social Requisites of Democracy Revisited." *American Sociological Review* 59: 1–22.

Lipset, Seymour Martin, and Stein Rokkan. 1967. "Cleavage Structures, Party Systems, and Voter Alignments: An Introduction." Pp. 1–64 in Seymour Martin Lipset and Stein Rokkan, eds. *Party Systems and Voter Alignments: Cross-National Perspectives.* New York: Free Press.

Lipset, Seymour Martin, Martin A. Trow, and James S. Coleman. 1956. *Union Democracy: The Internal Politics of the International Typographical Union.* Glencoe, IL: Free Press.

Lisak, David. 1992. "Sexual Aggression, Masculinity, and Fathers." *Signs* 16: 238–62.

Livernash, Robert, and Eric Rodenburg. 1998. "Population Change, Resources, and the Environment." *Population Bulletin* 53, 1. Retrieved October 8, 2000 (http://www.prb.org/pubs/population_bulletin/bu53-1.htm).

Livi-Bacci, Massimo. 1992. *A Concise History of World Population.* Cambridge, MA: Blackwell.

Livingstone, D. W. 1999. *The Education-Jobs Gap: Underemployment or Economic Democracy.* Toronto: Garamond Press.

Lock, Margaret. 1993. *Encounters with Aging: Mythologies of Menopause in Japan and North America.* Berkeley, CA: University of California Press.

Lodhi, Abdul Qaiyum, and Charles Tilly. 1973. "Urbanization, Crime, and Collective Violence in 19th Century France." *American Journal of Sociology* 79: 296–318.

Lofland, John, and Lyn H. Lofland. 1995. *Analyzing Social Settings: A Guide to Qualitative Observation and Analysis,* 3rd ed. Belmont, CA: Wadsworth.

Lofland, L. H. 1985. "The Social Shaping of Emotion: Grief in Historical Perspective." *Symbolic Interaction* 8: 171–90.

Logan, John R., and Harvey L. Molotch. 1987. *Urban Fortunes: The Political Economy of Place.* Berkeley, CA: University of California Press.

Logan, Ron. 2001. "Crime Statistics in Canada, 2000." *Juristat* 21, 8 (July). Catalogue no. 85-002-XPE.

Lohr, Steve. 2003. "Whatever Will Be Will Be Free on the Internet." *New York Times* September 14.

London, Scott. 1994. "Electronic Democracy—A Literature Survey." Retrieved August 15, 1998 (http:///www.west.net/~insight/london/ed.htm).

Long, Elizabeth. 1997. *From Sociology to Cultural Studies.* Malden, MA: Blackwell.

Lonmo, Charlene. 2001. "Adult Correctional Services in Canada, 1999–2000." *Juristat* 21, 5 (July). Catalogue no. 85-002-XPE.

Lopez, Donald S. 2001. *The Story of Buddhism: A Concise Guide to Its History and Teachings.* San Francisco: Harper.

Lowe, G. S. 1987. *Women in the Administrative Revolution: The Feminization of Clerical Work.* Toronto: University of Toronto Press.

———. 2000. *The Quality of Work: A People-Centred Agenda.* Don Mills, ON: Oxford University Press.

———. 2001. "Quality of Work—Quality of Life." Keynote talk at the Work/Life Balance and Employee Wellness Strategies Conference, Edmonton. 14 May. Retrieved August 25, 2003 (http://www.cprn.com/work/files/pzqwq_e.pdf).

Lowman, John, Robert T. Menzies, and Ted S. Palys. 1987. *Transcarceration: Essays in the Sociology of Social Control.* Aldershot, ON: Gower.

Lupri, Eugen, and James Frideres. 1988. "Marital Satisfaction over the Life Cycle." Pp 436–48 in Lorne Tepperman and James Curtis, eds. *Readings in Sociology: An Introduction.* Toronto: McGraw-Hill Ryerson.

Lurie, A. 1981. *The Language of Clothes.* New York: Random House.

Lyon, David, and Elia Zureik, eds. 1996. *Computers, Surveillance, and Privacy.* Minneapolis: University of Minnesota Press.

MacKinnon, Catharine A. 1979. *Sexual Harassment of Working Women.* New Haven, CT: Yale University Press.

Maclean's. 2002. "Acceptable but Not Equal." 3 June: 12.

MacLennan, Hugh. 1945. *Two Solitudes.* Toronto: Collins.

"Mad about Hockey: Superstitions." 2002. Retrieved June 2, 2002 (http://www.mcg.org/societe/hockey/pages/aasuperstitions_2.html).

Magro, Albert M. 1997. "Why Barbie Is Perceived as Beautiful." *Perceptual & Motor Skills* 85, 1 (August): 363–74.

Makomaski Illing, E. M., and M. J. Kaiserman. 2004. "Mortality Attributable to Tobacco Use in Canada and Its Regions, 1998." *Canadian Journal of Public Health* 95: 38–44.

Malthus, Thomas Robert. 1966 [1798]. *An Essay on the Principle of Population,* J. R. Bodnar, ed. London: Macmillan.

Manga, Pran, Douglas E. Angus, and William R. Swan. 1993. "Effective Management of Low Back Pain: It's Time to Accept the Evidence." *Journal of the Canadian Chiropractic Association* 37: 221–29.

Mankiw, N. G. 1998. *Principles of Macroeconomics.* Fort Worth, TX: The Dryden Press.

Mann, Susan A., Michael D. Grimes, Alice Abel Kemp, and Pamela J. Jenkins. 1997. "Paradigm Shifts in Family Sociology? Evidence from Three Decades of Family Textbooks." *Journal of Family Issues* 18: 315–49.

Mannheim, Karl. 1952. "The Problem of Generations." Pp. 276–320 in *Essays on the Sociology of Knowledge,* Paul Kecskemeti, ed. New York: Oxford University Press.

Manza, Jeff, Michael Hout, and Clem Brooks. 1995. "Class Voting in Capitalist Democracies since World War II: Dealignment, Realignment, or Trendless Fluctuation?" *Annual Review of Sociology* 21: 137–62.

Marchak, M. P. 1991. *The Integrated Circus: The New Right and the Restructuring of Global Markets.* Montreal: McGill-Queen's University Press.

Markowitz, Fran. 1993. *A Community in Spite of Itself: Soviet Jewish Émigrés in New York.* Washington, DC: Smithsonian Institute Press.

Marshall, Katherine. 2001. "Part-Time by Choice." *Perspectives on Labour and Income* 13, 1: 20–27. Retrieved June 3, 20093 (http://dsp-psd.pwgsc.gc.ca/dsp-psd/Pilot/Statcan/75-001-XIE/75-001-XIE.html).

Marshall, Monty G., and Ted Robert Gurr. 2003. "Peace and Conflict 2003." College Park: Department of Government and Politics, University of Maryland. Retrieved June 3, 2003 (http://www.cidcm.umd.edu/inscr/PC03print.pdf).

Marshall, S. L. A. 1947. *Men Against Fire: The Problem of Battle Command in Future War.* New York: Morrow.

Marshall, T. H. 1965. "Citizenship and Social Class." Pp. 71–134 in T. H. Marshall, ed. *Class, Citizenship, and Social Development: Essays by T. H. Marshall.* Garden City, NY: Anchor.

Martin, Carol Lynn. 1999. "A Developmental Perspective on Gender Effects and Gender Concepts." Pp. 45–74 in William B. Swann, Jr., Judith H. Langlois, and Lucia Albino Gilbert, eds. *Sexism and Stereotypes in Modern Science: The Gender Science of Janet Taylor Spence.* Washington, DC: American Psychological Association.

Marx, Karl. 1904 [1859]. *A Contribution to the Critique of Political Economy,* N. Stone, trans. Chicago: Charles H. Kerr.

———. 1970 [1843]. *Critique of Hegel's "Philosophy of Right,"* Annette Jolin and Joseph O'Malley, trans. Cambridge, MA: Harvard University Press.

Marx, Karl, and Friedrich Engels. 1972 [1848]. "Manifesto of the Communist Party." Pp. 331–62 in R. Tucker, ed. *The Marx-Engels Reader.* New York: Norton.

Massing, Michael. 2004. "Iraq, the Press and the Election." *New York Review of Books* 51, 20. Retrieved December 31, 2004 (http://www.nybooks.com/articles/17633).

Masters, William, Virginia E. Johnson, and Robert C. Kolodny. 1992. *Human Sexuality,* 4th ed. New York: HarperCollins.

———. 1994. *On Sex and Human Loving.* New York: HarperCollins.

Matalon, Jean-Marc. 1997. "Jeanne Calment, World's Oldest Person, Dead at 122." *The Shawnee News-Star* August 5. Retrieved May 2, 2000 (http://www.news-star.com/stories/080597/life1.html).

"Maternal Mortality: A Preventable Tragedy." 1998. *Popline* 20: 4.

Matsueda, Ross L. 1988. "The Current State of Differential Association Theory." *Crime and Delinquency* 34: 277–306.

———. 1992. "Reflected Appraisals, Parental Labeling, and Delinquency: Specifying a Symbolic Interactionist Theory." *American Journal of Sociology* 97: 1577–611.

Mayer, J. P. 1944. *Max Weber and German Politics.* London: Faber and Faber.

Mayer, Susan E. 1997. *What Money Can't Buy: Family Income and Children's Life Chances.* Cambridge, MA: Harvard University Press.

McAdam, Doug. 1982. *Political Process and the Development of Black Insurgency, 1930–1970.* Chicago: University of Chicago Press.

McCarten, James. 2002. "Child Spanking Law Upheld by Ontario Court: Child's Rights Group Ponders Taking Case to Supreme Court." Retrieved July 15, 2003 (http://www.oacas.org/Whatsnew/newsstories/jan02news/spankinglawupheld.pdf).

McCarthy, John D., and Mayer N. Zald. 1977. "Resource Mobilization and Social Movements: A Partial Theory." *American Journal of Sociology* 82: 1212–41.

McChesney, Robert W. 1999. "Oligopoly: The Big Media Game Has Fewer and Fewer Players." *The Progressive* November: 20–24. Retrieved August 7, 2000 (http://www.progressive.org/mcc1199.htm).

McClelland, W. R. 1931. "Precautions for Workers in the Treating of Radium Ores." *Investigations in Ore Dressing and Metallurgy.* Ottawa: Bureau of Mines. Retrieved October 8, 2000 (http://www.ccnr.org/radium_warning.html).

McConaghy, Nathaniel. 1999. "Unresolved Issues in Scientific Sexology." *Archives of Sexual Behavior* 28, 4: 285–318.

McCormick, Chris, ed. 1999. *The Westray Chronicles: A Case Study in Corporate Crime.* Halifax: Fernwood.

McCrum, Robert, William Cran, and Robert MacNeil. 1992. *The Story of English,* new and rev. ed. London: Faber and Faber.

McCullagh, Declan. 2000. "Bin Laden: Steganography Master?" *Wired* February 7. Retrieved September 13, 2001 (http://www.wired.com/news/print/0.1294.41658.00.html1).

McCulloch, Robert. 2003. "Height and Income." Retrieved April 22, 2003 (http://gsbwww.uchicago.edu/fac/robert.mcculloch/research/BusinessStatistics/robHw/SimpleLinearRegression/q11.html).

McDonald's Corporation. 1999. "McDonald's Nutrition Facts." Retrieved August 16, 1999 (http://www.mcdonalds.com/food/nutrition/index.html9).

———. 2005. "Poutine-large." Retrieved December 1, 2005 (http://www.mcdonalds.ca/en/food/ingredient.aspx?menuid=262).

McGinn, Anne Platt. 1998. "Promoting Sustainable Fisheries." Pp. 59–78 in Lester R. Brown, Christopher Flavin, Hilary French et al. *State of the World 1998.* New York: Norton.

McLaren, A. 1990. *Our Own Master Race: Eugenics in Canada, 1885–1945.* Toronto: McClelland & Stewart.

McLaughlin, Margaret L., Kerry K. Osborne, and Christine B. Smith. 1995. "Standards of Conduct on Usenet." Pp. 90–111 in Steven G. Jones, ed. *CyberSociety.* Thousand Oaks, CA: Sage.

McLuhan, Marshall. 1964. *Understanding Media: The Extensions of Man.* New York: McGraw-Hill.

McMahon, Maeve W. 1992. *The Persistent Prison? Rethinking Decarceration and Penal Reform.* Toronto: University of Toronto Press.

McManners, John, ed. 1990. *Oxford Illustrated History of Christianity.* Oxford: Oxford University Press.

McNeill, William H. 1976. *Plagues and Peoples.* Garden City, NY: Anchor Press.

———. 1990. *Population and Politics since 1750.* Charlottesville, WV: University Press of Virginia.

McPhail, Clark. 1991. *The Myth of the Madding Crowd.* New York: Aldine de Gruyter.

———. 1994. "The Dark Side of Purpose: Individual and Collective Violence in Riots." *The Sociological Quarterly* 35: 1–32.

McPhail, Clark, and Ronald T. Wohlstein. 1983. "Individual and Collective Behaviors within Gatherings, Demonstrations, and Riots." *Annual Review of Sociology* 9: 579–600.

McRoberts, Kenneth. 1988. *Quebec: Social Change and Political Crisis*, 3rd ed. Toronto: McClelland & Stewart.

McTeer, Maureen A. 1999. *Tough Choices: Living and Dying in the 21st Century.* Toronto: Irwin Law.

McVey, Wayne W., Jr., and Warren E. Kalbach. 1995. *Canadian Population.* Scarborough, ON: Nelson.

Mead, G. H. 1934. *Mind, Self and Society.* Chicago: University of Chicago Press.

Medawar, Peter. 1996. *The Strange Case of the Spotted Mice and Other Classic Essays on Science.* New York: Oxford University Press.

Meek, Ronald L., ed. 1971. *Marx and Engels on the Population Bomb: Selections from the Writings of Marx and Engels Dealing with the Theories of Thomas Robert Malthus.* Dorothea L. Meek and Ronald L. Meek, trans. Berkeley, CA: Ramparts Press.

Meisenheimer II, Joseph R. 1998. "The Service Industry in the 'Good' versus 'Bad' Jobs Debate." *Monthly Labor Review* 121, 2: 22–47.

Melucci, Alberto. 1980. "The New Social Movements: A Theoretical Approach." *Social Science Information* 19: 199–226.

———. 1995. "The New Social Movements Revisited: Reflections on a Sociological Misunderstanding." Pp. 107–19 in Louis Maheu, ed. *Social Classes and Social Movements: The Future of Collective Action.* London, UK: Sage.

Menzies, C. R. 1999. "First Nations, Inequality and the Legacy of Colonialism." Pp. 236–44 in J. Curtis, E. Grabb, and N. Guppy, eds. *Social Inequality in Canada*, 3rd ed. Scarborough, ON: Prentice Hall Allyn and Bacon Canada Inc.

Merton, Robert K. 1938. "Social Structure and Anomie." *American Sociological Review* 3: 672–82.

———. 1968 [1949]. *Social Theory and Social Structure.* New York: Free Press.

Messerschmidt, J. W. 1993. *Masculinities and Crime: Critique and Reconceptualization of Theory.* Lanham, MD: Roman and Littlefield.

Messner, Michael. 1995. "Boyhood, Organized Sports, and the Construction of Masculinities." Pp. 102–14 in Michael S. Kimmel and Michael A. Messner. *Men's Lives*, 3rd ed. Boston: Allyn and Bacon.

———. 2000. "Barbie Girls versus Sea Monsters: Children Constructing Gender." *Gender & Society, Special Issue* 14, 6 (December): 765–84.

Meyer, David R., and Judi Bartfield. 1996. "Compliance with Child Support Orders in Divorce Cases." *Journal of Marriage and the Family* 58, 1: 201–12.

Meyer, John W., Francisco O. Ramirez, and Yasemin Nuhoglu Soysal. 1992. "World Expansion of Mass Education, 1870–1980." *Sociology of Education* 65: 128–49.

Meyer, John W., and W. Richard Scott. 1983. *Organizational Environments: Ritual and Rationality*. Beverly Hills, CA: Sage.

Meyer, Thomas. 1984. "'Date Rape': A Serious Campus Problem that Few Talk About." *Chronicle of Higher Education* 5 December: 1, 12.

Michael, Robert T., John H. Gagnon, Edward O. Laumann, and Gina Kolata. 1994. *Sex in America: A Definitive Survey*. Boston: Little, Brown and Company.

Michels, Robert. 1949 [1911]. *Political Parties: A Sociological Study of the Oligarchical Tendencies of Modern Democracy*, E., and C. Paul, trans. New York: Free Press.

Milanovic, Branko. 2005. *World Apart: Measuring International and Global Inequality*. Princeton, NJ: Princeton University Press.

Milem, Jeffrey F. 1998. "Attitude Change in College Students: Examining the Effect of College Peer Groups and Faculty Normative Groups." *The Journal of Higher Education* 69: 117–140.

Miles, R. 1989. *Racism*. London: Routledge.

Milgram, Stanley. 1974. *Obedience to Authority: An Experimental View*. New York: Harper.

Miliband, Ralph. 1973 [1969]. *The State in Capitalist Society*. London: Fontana.

Miller, George A. 2001. "Ambiguous Words." KurzweilAI.net. Retrieved December 18, 2007 (http://www.kurzweilai.net/meme/frame.html?main=/articles/art0186.html).

Miller, Ted R. and Mark A. Cohen. 1997. "Costs of gunshot and cut/stab wounds in the United States, with some Canadian comparisons." *Accident Analysis and Prevention* (29) 329-41.

Mills, C. Wright. 1956. *The Power Elite*. New York: Oxford University Press.

———. 1959. *The Sociological Imagination*. New York: Oxford University Press.

Ministério de Ciência e Tecnologia Brasil. 2002. "Brazil Urban Population." Retrieved August 5, 2003 (http://www.mct.gov.br/clima/ingles/comunic_old/res7_1_1.htm).

Minkel, J. R. 2002. "A Way with Words." *Scientific American* 25 March. Retrieved January 21, 2003 (http://www.mit.edu/~lera/sciam).

Minois, George. 1989 [1987]. *History of Old Age: From Antiquity to the Renaissance,* Sarah Hanbury Tenison, trans. Chicago: University of Chicago Press.

Mishler, William. 1979. *Political Participation in Canada*. Toronto: Macmillan of Canada.

Mitchinson, Wendy. 1993. "The Medical Treatment of Women." Pp. 391–421 in Sandra Burt, Lorraine Code, and Lindsay Dorney, eds. *Changing Patterns: Women in Canada*, 2nd ed. Toronto: McClelland & Stewart.

Mittelman, James H. 2000. *The Globalization Syndrome: Transformation and Resistance*. Princeton, NJ: Princeton University Press.

Mizruchi, M. S. 1982. *The American Corporate Network, 1904–1974*. Beverly Hills, CA: Sage.

———. 1992. *The Structure of Corporate Political Action: Interfirm Relations and Their Consequences*. Cambridge, MA: Harvard University Press.

Mohr, Johann W., and Keith Spencer. 1999. "Crime." Pp. 587– 89 in James H. Marsh, editor in chief. *The Canadian Encyclopedia*, Year 2000 Edition. Toronto: McClelland & Stewart, Inc.

Molm, Linda D. 1997. *Coercive Power in Social Exchange*. Cambridge, UK: Cambridge University Press.

Money, John, and Anke Ehrhardt. 1972. *Man and Woman, Boy and Girl*. Boston: Little Brown.

Montgomery, M. 1965. "The Six Nations and the Macdonald Franchise." *Ontario History* 57: 13.

Mooney, Linda A., David Knox, Caroline Schacht, and Adie Nelson. 2001. *Understanding Social Problems*. Toronto: Nelson Thomson Learning.

Moorcroft, Lois. 2005. "Newfoundland Women Want Pay Equity Too." *Canadian Dimension* 15 April. On the Word Wide Web at http://www.vivelecanada.ca/article.php/20050415103547880 (6 August 2005).

Moore, Barrington, Jr. 1967. *Social Origins of Dictatorship and Democracy: Lord and Peasant in the Making of the Modern World*. Boston: Beacon.

Morrison, Nancy. 1987. "Separation and Divorce." Pp. 125–43 in M. J. Dymond, ed. *The Canadian Woman's Legal Guide*. Toronto: Doubleday.

Mortimer, Jeylan T., and Roberta G. Simmons. 1978. "Adult Socialization." *Annual Review of Sociology* 4: 421–54.

Morton, Gary. 2000. "Showdown at Queen's Park." Retrieved March 22, 2001 (http://www.tao.ca/earth/toronto/archive/1999/toronto01278.html).

Moscovitch, Arlene. 1998. "Electronic Media and the Family." Vanier Institute of the Family. Retrieved May 14, 2003 (http://www.vifamily.ca/cft/media/media.htm).

"The MUD Connector." 2008. Retrieved February 14, 2008 (http://www.mudconnect.com).

Mumford, Lewis. 1961. *The City in History: Its Origins, Its Transformations, and Its Prospects*. New York: Harcourt, Brace, and World.

Mundell, Helen. 1993. "How the Color Mafia Chooses Your Clothes." *American Demographics* November.

Retrieved May 2, 2000 (http://www.demographics.com/publications/ad/93_ad/9311_ad/ad281.htm).

Murdock, George Peter. 1937. "Comparative Data on the Division of Labor by Sex." *Social Forces* 15: 551–53.

———. 1949. *Social Structure*. New York: Macmillan.

Murnen, Sarah K., Annette Perot, and Don Byrne. 1989. "Coping with Unwanted Sexual Activity: Normative Responses, Situational Determinants and Individual Differences." *Journal of Sex Research* 26: 85–106.

Murphy, Brian, Paul Roberts, and Michael Wolfson. 2007. "A Profile of High-Income Canadians, 1982–2004." Ottawa: Statistics Canada. Retrieved May 1, 2008 (http://www.statcan.ca/english/research/75F0002MIE/75F0002MIE2007006.pdf).

Muslim Brotherhood Movement. 2002. Homepage. Retrieved May 7, 2001 (http://www.ummah.org.uk/ikhwan).

Myerhoff, Barbara. 1978. *Number Our Days*. New York: Dutton.

Myers, Daniel J. 1997. "Racial Rioting in the 1960s: An Event History Analysis of Local Conditions." *American Sociological Review* 62: 94–112.

Myles, John. 1989. *Old Age in the Welfare State: The Political Economy of Public Pensions*, 2nd ed. Lawrence, KA: University Press of Kansas.

Myles, John, and Adnan Turegun. 1994. "Comparative Studies in Class Structure." *Annual Review of Sociology* 20: 103–24.

Nagle, Matt. 2001. "Gay Man Murdered in Vancouver's Stanley Park." *Seattle Gay News* November 23. Retrieved May 10, 2003 (http://www.sgn.org/2001/11/23).

Nakhaie, M. R. 1997. "Vertical Mosaic among the Elites: The New Imagery Revisited." *Canadian Review of Sociology and Anthropology* 34, 1: 1–24.

National Basketball Association. 2000. "New York Knicks History." Retrieved May 29, 2000 (http://nba.com/knicks/00400499.html#2).

National Council of Welfare. 1998a. "Profiles of Welfare: Myths and Realities: A Report by the National Council of Welfare." Retrieved March 13, 2000 (http://www.ncwnbes.net/htmdocument/reportprowelfare.repprowelfare.htm).

———. 1998b. *Banking and Poor People: Talk Is Cheap*. Ottawa: The Council.

———. 1999a. *A New Poverty Line: Yes, No or Maybe?* Ottawa: Ministry of Public Works.

———. 1999b. "Children First: A Pre-Budget Report by the National Council of Welfare." Retrieved March 13, 2000 (http://www.ncwcnbes.net.htmdocument/reportchildfirst.htm).

———. 2004. *Poverty Profile 2001*. Ottawa: Ministry of Public Works.

National Counterterrorism Center. 2007. "Annex of Statistical Information." Retrieved January 12, 2008 (http://www.state.gov/documents/organization/83396.pdf).

National Opinion Research Center. 2004. *General Social Survey, 1972–2002*. Chicago: University of Chicago. Machine readable file.

Neisser, Ulric. 1997. "Rising Scores on Intelligence Tests." *American Scientist* 85, 5: 440–47.

Nelson, Adie, and Barrie W. Robinson. 2002. *Gender in Canada*, 2nd ed. Toronto: Prentice Hall.

Nesbitt, Paula D. 1997. *Feminization of the Clergy in America: Occupational and Organizational Perspectives*. New York: Oxford University Press.

Neugarten, Bernice. 1974. "Age Groups in American Society and the Rise of the Young Old." *Annals of the American Academy of Political and Social Science* 415: 187–98.

Nevitte, Neil. 1996. *The Decline of Deference*. Peterborough, ON: Broadview Press.

Newcomb, Theodore M. 1943. *Personality and Social Change: Attitude Formation in a Student Community*. New York: Holt, Rinehart & Winston.

Newman, K. 1999. *No Shame in My Game: The Working Poor in the Inner City*. New York: Knopf and the Russell Sage Foundation.

"New York Crime Rates." 2007. Retrieved January 10, 2008 (http://www.disastercenter.com/crime/nycrime.htm).

Nicolaiedis, Nicos. 1998. "Pierre Marty's 'Doll' and Today's Barbies." *Revue française de psychanalyse, Special Issue: Psychosomatique et pulsionnalité* 62, 5 (Nov–Dec): 1579–81.

Nie, Norman H., Sidney Verba, and John R. Petrocik. 1979 [1976]. *The Changing American Voter*, rev. ed. Cambridge, MA: Harvard University Press.

Nielsen/NetRatings. 2002. "Google Gains Four Million Unique Audience Members in May, According to Nielsen/NetRatings' Global Index." Retrieved December 9, 2005 (http://www.nielsen-netratings.com/pr/pr_020701_global.pdf).

"The Nike Campaign." 2000. Retrieved June 23, 2000 (http://www.web.net/~msn/3nike.htm).

Nikiforuk, Andrew. 1998. "Echoes of the Atomic Age: Cancer Kills Fourteen Aboriginal Uranium Workers." *Calgary Herald* March 14: A1, A4. Retrieved October 8, 2000 (http://www.ccnr.org/deline_deaths.html).

———. 1999. "A Question of Style." *Time* 31 May: 58–59.

1994–1995 Directory of Labour Organizations in Canada. 1995. Ottawa: Minister of Supply and Services Canada. Cat. No. L2-2-1995.

1998 Directory of Labour Organizations in Canada. 1998. Ottawa: Workplace Information Directorate.

Nisbett, Richard E., Kaiping Peng, Incheol Choi, and Ara Norenzayan. 2001. "Culture and Systems of Thought:

Holistic versus Analytic Cognition." *Psychological Review* 108: 291–310.

Nolen, Stephanie. 1999. "Gender: The Third Way." *Globe and Mail* September 25: D1, D4.

Norton, Kevin I., Timothy S. Olds, Scott Olive, and Stephen Dank. 1996. "Ken and Barbie at Life Size." *Sex Roles* 34, 3–4 (February): 287–94.

Notestein, F. W. 1945. "Population—The Long View." Pp. 36–57 in T. W. Schultz, ed. *Food for the World*. Chicago: University of Chicago Press.

Novak, Mark. 1997. *Aging and Society: A Canadian Perspective*, 3rd ed. Scarborough, ON: Nelson.

Nowak, Martin A., Robert M. May, and Karl Sigmund. 1995. "The Arithmetics of Mutual Help." *Scientific American* 272, 6: 76–81.

Nowell, Amy, and Larry V. Hedges. 1998. "Trends in Gender Differences in Academic Achievement from 1960 to 1994: An Analysis of Differences in Mean, Variance, and Extreme Scores." *Sex Roles* 39: 21–43.

Nuland, Sherwin B. 1993. *How We Die: Reflections on Life's Final Chapter*. New York: Vintage.

O'Connor, Julia S., and Robert J. Brym. 1988. "Public Welfare Expenditure in OECD Countries: Towards a Reconciliation of Inconsistent Findings." *British Journal of Sociology* 39: 47–68.

O'Connor, Julia S., and Gregg M. Olsen, eds. 1998. *Power Resources Theory and the Welfare State: A Critical Approach*. Toronto: University of Toronto Press.

O'Malley, Martin, and Amina Ali. 2001. "Sticks, Stones and Bullies." CBC.ca. Retrieved June 23, 2002 (http://cbc.ca/national/news/bully).

O'Neil, Dennis. 2004. "Patterns of Subsistence: Classification of Cultures Based on the Sources and Techniques of Acquiring Food and other Necessities." Retrieved January 12, 2005 (http://anthro.palomar.edu/subsistence).

Oates, Joyce Carol. 1999. "The Mystery of JonBenét Ramsey." *New York Review of Books* 24 (June): 31–37.

Obejas, Achy. 1994. "Women Who Batter Women." *Ms.* September/October: 53.

Oberschall, Anthony. 1973. *Social Conflict and Social Movements*. Englewood Cliffs, NJ: Prentice-Hall.

Oderkirk, Jillian. 2000. "Marriage in Canada: Changing Beliefs and Behaviours, 1600–1990." *Canadian Social Trends* 3: 93–98. Toronto: Thompson Educational Publishing, Inc.

Oderkirk, Jillian, and Clarence Lochhead. 1992. "Lone Parenthood: Gender Differences." *Canadian Social Trends* 27, Spring: 16–19.

OECD (Organisation for Economic Co-operation and Development). 2001. "Knowledge and Skills for Life: First Results from PISA 2000." Retrieved December 5,

2001 (http://www.pisa.oecd.org/knowledge/summary/g.htm).

———. 2004a. "Early Childhood Education and Care Policy: Canada Country Note." Retrieved May 14, 2009 (http://www.oecd.org/dataoecd/42/34/33850725.pdf).

———. 2004b. "Education at a Glance 2004—Tables." Retrieved May 27, 2006 (http://www.oecd.org/dataoecd/52/41/33668656.xls).

———. 2005. "Official Development Assistance Increases Further—but 2006 Targets Still a Challenge." Retrieved December 1, 2005 (http://www.oecd.org/document/3/0,2340,en_2649_201185_34700611_1_1_1_1,00.html).

———. 2007. "Aid Statistics, Donor Aid Charts." Retrieved December 20, 2007 (http://www.oecd.org/countrylist/0,3349,en_2649_34447_1783495_1_1_1_1,00.html).

———. 2008. "Average Annual Hours Actually Worked per Worker." Retrieved May 1, 2008 (http://stats.oecd.org/wbos/Index.aspx?DatasetCode=ANHRS).

Oeppen, Jim, and James W. Vaupel. 2002. "Demography: Enhanced: Broken Limits to Life Expectancy." *Science* 296: 1029–31.

Ogmundson, R., and J. McLaughlin. 1992. "Trends in the Ethnic Origins of Canadian Elites: The Decline of the BRITS?" *The Canadian Review of Sociology and Anthropology* 29: 227–42.

Oliver, Melvin L., and Thomas M. Shapiro. 1995. *Black Wealth/White Wealth: A New Perspective on Racial Inequality*. New York: Routledge.

Oliver, Mike. 1996. *Understanding Disability: From Theory to Practice*. Basingstoke, UK: Macmillan.

Olsen, Dennis. 1980. *The State Elite*. Toronto: McClelland & Stewart.

Olsen, Gregg M. 2002. *The Politics of the Welfare State: Canada, Sweden, and the United States*. Don Mills, ON: Oxford University Press Canada.

Olzak, Susan, and Suzanne Shanahan. 1996. "Deprivation and Race Riots: An Extension of Spilerman's Analysis." *Social Forces* 74: 931–62.

Olzak, Susan, Suzanne Shanahan, and Elizabeth H. McEneaney. 1996. "Poverty, Segregation, and Race Riots: 1960 to 1993." *American Sociological Review* 61: 590–614.

Omega Foundation. 1998. "An Appraisal of the Technologies of Political Control: Summary and Options Report for the European Parliament." Retrieved April 29, 2000 (http://home.icdc.com/~paulwolf/eu_stoa_2.htm).

Omi, M., and H. Winant. 1986. *Racial Formation in the United States*. New York: Routledge.

Ontario Consultants on Religious Tolerance. 2000. "Homosexual (Same-Sex) Marriages." Retrieved August 20, 2000 (http://www.religioustolerance.org/hom_marr.htm).

———. 2005. "Information about Religion in Canada." Retrieved November 14, 2005 (http://www.religioustolerance.org/can_rel.htm).

———. 2006. "Women as Clergy: When Some Faiths Started to Ordain Women." Retrieved November 22, 2005 (http://www.religioustolerance.org/femclrg13.htm).

Optometrists Network. 2000. "Attention Deficit Disorder." Retrieved August 14, 2000 (http://www.add-adhd.org/ADHD_attention-deficit.html).

Oreopoulos, Philip. 2005. "Canadian Compulsory School Laws and Their Impact on Educational Attainment and Future Earnings." Ottawa: Statistics Canada. Retrieved May 27, 2006 (http://www.statcan.ca/english/research/11F0019MIE/11F0019MIE2005251.pdf).

Organization of African Unity. 2000. *Rwanda: The Preventable Genocide.* Retrieved January 15, 2005 (http://www.visiontv.ca/RememberRwanda/Report.pdf).

Ornstein, Michael D. 1998. "Survey Research." *Current Sociology* 46, 4: 1–87.

Ossowski, Stanislaw. 1963. *Class Structure in the Social Consciousness*, S. Patterson, trans. London: Routledge and Kegan Paul.

Ouimet, M. 2002. "Explaining the American and Canadian Crime 'Drop' in the 1990s." *Canadian Journal of Criminology* 44, 1: 33–50.

Owen, Michelle K. 2001. "'Family' as a Site of Contestation: Queering the Normal or Normalizing the Queer?" Pp. 86–102 in Terry Goldie, ed. *In a Queer Country: Gay and Lesbian Studies in the Canadian Context.* Vancouver: Arsenal Pulp Press.

Pabilonia, Sabrina Wulff, and Cindy Zoghi. 2005a. "Returning to the Returns to Computer Use." BLS Working Paper 377. Washington DC: U.S. Department of Labor, Bureau of Labor Statistics.

———. 2005b. "Who Gains from Computer Use?" *Perspectives on Labor and Income* 6, 7: 5–11.

Pacey, Arnold. 1983. *The Culture of Technology.* Cambridge, MA: MIT Press.

Pammett, Jon H. 1997. "Getting Ahead Around the World." Pp. 67–86 in Alan Frizzell and Jon H. Pammett, eds. *Social Inequality in Canada.* Ottawa: Carleton University Press.

Pape, Robert A. 2003 "The Strategic Logic of Suicide Terrorism." *American Political Science Review* 97: 343–61.

———. 2005. *Dying to Win: The Strategic Logic of Suicide Terrorism.* New York: Random House.

Park, Jungwee. 2005. "Use of Alternative Health Care." *Health Reports* 16, 2: 39–43.

Park, Robert. E. 1950 [1914]. *Race and Culture.* New York: Free Press.

Park, Robert Ezra, Ernest W. Burgess, and Roderick D. McKenzie. 1967 [1925]. *The City.* Chicago: University of Chicago Press.

Parke, Ross D. 2001. "Paternal Involvement in Infancy: The Role of Maternal and Paternal Attitudes." *Journal of Family Psychology* 15, 4 (December): 555–58.

———. 2002. "Parenting in the New Millennium: Prospects, Promises and Pitfalls." Pp. 65–93 in James P. McHale and Wendy S. Grolnick, eds. *Retrospect and Prospect in the Psychological Study of Families.* Mahwah, NJ: Lawrence Erlbaum Associates, Inc.

Parkin, F. 1979. *Marxism and Class Theory.* New York: Columbia University Press.

Parshall, Gerald. 1998. "Brotherhood of the Bomb." *US News and World Report* 125, 7 (17–24 August): 64–68.

Parsons, Talcott. 1942. "Age and Sex in the Social Structure of the United States." *American Sociological Review* 7: 604–16.

———. 1951. *The Social System.* New York: Free Press.

———. 1955. "The American Family: Its Relation to Personality and to the Social Structure." Pp. 3–33 in Talcott Parsons and Robert F. Bales, eds. *Family, Socialization and Interaction Process.* New York: Free Press.

Pascual, Brian. 2002. "Avril Lavigne Hates Britney Spears." *ChartAttack* April 19. Retrieved January 15, 2003 (http://teenmusic.about.com/gi/dynamic/offsite.htm?site=http%3A%2F%2Fwww.chartattack.com%2Fdamn%2F2002%2F04%2F1901.cfm).

Patent Medicine Prices Review Board. 2002. "Annual Report." Retrieved June 17, 2003 (http://www.pmprb-cepmb.gc.ca/CMFiles/ar-2002e21IRA-6162003-196.pdf).

Pence, Leah, and Monique Jacobs. 2001. "Tracking the Elusive Traditional Family." *UVic KnowlEDGE* 2, 9. Retrieved June 12, 2006 (http://communications.uvic.ca/edge/v2n09_17sep01.pdf).

Pendakur, K., and R. Pendakur. 1998. "The Colour of Money: Earnings Differentials among Ethnic Groups in Canada." *Canadian Journal of Economics* 31: 518–48.

Pendakur, R. 2000. *Immigrants and the Labour Force: Policy, Regulation and Impact.* Montreal: McGill-Queen's University Press.

Peritz, Ingrid. 1999. "Birth Rate in Quebec Lowest Since 1908." *Globe and Mail* October 4: A1.

Perks, Thomas A. 2005. *Height as a Factor in Social Inequality: Analyses Based on Five Canadian National Surveys.* Ph.D. dissertation, Department of Sociology, University of Waterloo.

Perrow, Charles B. 1984. *Normal Accidents.* New York: Basic Books.

Perry-Castañeda Library Map Collection. 2000. "Comparative Soviet Nationalities by Republic." Retrieved November 12, 2000 (http://www.lib.utexas.edu/Libs/PCL/Map_collection/commonwealth/USSR_NatRep_89.jpg).

Peterson, Peter. 1997. "Will America Grow Up Before It Grows Old?" P. 70 in Harold A. Widdison, ed. *Social Problems: Annual Editions.* Guilford, CN: Dushkin.

Pew Research Center for the People and the Press. 2002. "Among Wealthy Nations U.S. Stands Alone in its Embrace of Religion." Retrieved May 3, 2003 (http://people-press.org/reports/display .php3?ReportID_167).

Piaget, Jean, and Bärbel Inhelder. 1969. *The Psychology of the Child*, Helen Weaver, trans. New York: Basic Books.

Pillard, Richard C., and J. Michael Bailey. 1998. "Human Sexuality Has a Heritable Component." *Human Biology* 70, April: 347–65.

Pineo, P. C., and J. Porter. 1985. "Ethnic Origin and Occupational Attainment." In M. Boyd, J. Goyder, F. E. Jones, H. A. McRoberts, P. C. Pineo, and J. Porter, eds. *Ascription and Achievement: Studies in Mobility and Status Attainment*. Ottawa: Carleton University Press.

Pinker, Steven. 1994. *The Language Instinct*. New York: Morrow.

———. 2001. "Talk of Genetics and Vice Versa." *Nature* 413, 6855, 4 October: 465–66.

———. 2002. *The Blank Slate: The Modern Denial of Human Nature*. New York: Viking.

Piven, Frances Fox, and Richard A. Cloward. 1977. *Poor People's Movements: Why They Succeed, How They Fail*. New York: Vintage.

Plummer, Kenneth. 1995. *Telling Sexual Stories: Power, Change and Social Worlds*. London, UK: Routledge.

Podolny, Joel M., and Karen L. Page. 1998. "Network Forms of Organization." *Annual Review of Sociology* 24: 57–76.

Polanyi, K. 1957. *The Great Transformation: The Political and Economic Origins of Our Time*. Boston: Beacon.

Polsby, Nelson W. 1959. "Three Problems in the Analysis of Community Power." *American Sociological Review* 24: 796–803.

Pool, Robert. 1997. *Beyond Engineering: How Society Shapes Technology*. New York: Oxford University Press.

"Poor Palliative Care Encourages Euthanasia." 2001. March 19. Retrieved June 15, 2003 (http://www.savemedicare .com/n19ma01a.htm).

Popenoe, David. 1988. *Disturbing the Nest: Family Change and Decline in Modern Societies*. New York: Aldine de Gruyter.

———. 1996. *Life without Father: Compelling New Evidence that Fatherhood and Marriage Are Indispensable for the Good of Children and Society*. New York: Martin Kessler Books.

———. 1998. "The Decline of Marriage and Fatherhood." Pp. 312–19 in John J. Macionis and Nicole V. Benokraitis, eds. *Seeing Ourselves: Classic, Contemporary and Cross-Cultural Readings in Sociology*, 4th ed. Upper Saddle River, NJ: Prentice Hall.

Population Reference Bureau. 2003. "Human Population: Fundamentals of Growth." Retrieved August 2, 2003 (http://www.prb.org/Content/NavigationMenu/PRB/ Educators/Human_Population/Population_Growth/ Population_Growth.htm).

———. 2007. "2007 World Population Data Sheet." Retrieved January 13, 2008 (http://www.prb.org/ pdf07/07WPDS_Eng.pdf).

Porter, John. 1965. *The Vertical Mosaic: An Analysis of Social Class and Power in Canada*. Toronto: University of Toronto Press.

———. 1979. *The Measure of Canadian Society: Education, Equality, and Opportunity*. Toronto: Gage.

Portes, Alejandro. 1996. "Global Villagers: The Rise of Transnational Communities." *The American Prospect* 25: 74–77. Retrieved April 29, 2000 (http://www .prospect.org/archives/25/25port.html).

Portes, A., and R. D. Manning. 1991. "The Immigrant Enclave: Theory and Empirical Examples." Pp. 319–32 in N. R. Yetman, ed. *Majority and Minority: The Dynamics of Race and Ethnicity in American Life*, 5th ed. Boston: Allyn and Bacon.

Postel, Sandra. 1994. "Carrying Capacity: Earth's Bottom Line." Pp. 3–21 in Linda Starke, ed. *State of the World 1994*. New York: Norton.

Postman, Neil. 1982. *The Disappearance of Childhood*. New York: Delacorte.

———. 1992. *Technopoly: The Surrender of Culture to Technology*. New York: Vintage.

Poulantzas, Nicos. 1975 [1968]. *Political Power and Social Classes*, T. O'Hagan, trans. London: New Left Books.

Pred, Allan R. 1973. *Urban Growth and the Circulation of Information*. Cambridge, MA: Harvard University Press.

"Presentation by Canada's Cable Companies to the Standing Committee on Canadian Heritage, February 19, 2002." 2002. Retrieved May 20, 2002 (http://www.ccta.ca/ english/publications/speeches-presentations/2002/ppt/ e-02-19.ppt).

Press, Andrea. 1991. *Women Watching Television: Gender, Class and Generation in the American Television Experience*. Philadelphia: University of Pennsylvania Press.

Press, Andrea L., and Elizabeth R. Cole. 1999. *Speaking of Abortion: Television and Authority in the Lives of Women*. Chicago: University of Chicago Press.

Priestly, Mark. 2001. "Introduction: The Global Context of Disability." Pp. 3–25 in Mark Priestly, ed. *Disability and the Life Course: Global Perspectives*, Cambridge: Cambridge University Press.

Prigerson, Holly Gwen. 1992. "Socialization to Dying: Social Determinants of Death Acknowledgement and Treatment among Terminally Ill Geriatric Patients." *Journal of Health and Social Behavior* 33: 378–95.

Prittie, Jennifer. 2000. "The Serious Business of Rubber Noses and Big Shoes." *National Post* March 29: A1–A2.

Proctor, Robert N. 1988. *Racial Hygiene: Medicine under the Nazis*. Cambridge, MA: Harvard University Press.

Province of Nova Scotia. 2008. "Counties of Nova Scotia." Retrieved January 12, 2008 (http://www.gov.ns.ca/snsmr/muns/info/mapping/counties.asp).

Provine, Robert R. 2000. *Laughter: A Scientific Investigation*. New York: Penguin.

Pyke, Karen D. 1997. "Class-Based Masculinities: The Interdependence of Gender, Class, and Interpersonal Power." *Gender and Society* 10: 527–49.

Raag, Tarja, and Christine L. Rackliff. 1998. "Preschoolers' Awareness of Social Expectations of Gender: Relationships to Toy Choices." *Sex Roles* 38: 685–700.

Rahman, Shaikh Azizur. 2004. "Where the Girls Aren't." *Globe and Mail* October 16: F2.

Raphael, D. 2004. *Social Determinants of Health: Canadian Perspectives*. Toronto: Canadian Scholars' Press.

Rapp, R., and E. Ross. 1986. "The 1920s: Feminism, Consumerism and Political Backlash in the U.S." Pp. 52–62 in J. Friedlander, B. Cook, A. Kessler-Harris, and C. Smith-Rosenberg, eds. *Women in Culture and Politics*. Bloomington, IN: Indiana University Press.

Reich, Robert B. 1991. *The Work of Nations: Preparing Ourselves for 21st-Century Capitalism*. New York: Knopf.

Reiman, Jeffrey H. 2003. *The Rich Get Richer and the Poor Get Prison: Ideology, Class, and Criminal Justice*, 7th ed. Boston: Allyn & Bacon.

Reimann, Renate. 1997. "Does Biology Matter? Lesbian Couples' Transition to Parenthood and Their Division of Labor." *Qualitative Sociology* 20, 2: 153–85.

Reiter, Ester. 1991. *Making Fast Food: From the Frying Pan into the Fryer*. Montreal: McGill-Queen's University Press.

Reitz, Jeffrey. 2007. "Tapping Immigrants' Skills." Pp. 130-40 in Robert J. Brym, ed. *Society in Question: Sociological Readings for the 21st Century*, 5th ed. Toronto: Nelson.

Reitz, Jeffrey G., and Raymond Breton. 1994. *The Illusion of Difference: Realities of Ethnicity in Canada and the United States*. Toronto: C.D. Howe Institute.

Remennick, Larissa I. 1998. "The Cancer Problem in the Context of Modernity: Sociology, Demography, Politics." *Current Sociology* 46, 1: 1–150.

Remnick, David. 1998. "How Russia Is Ruled." *New York Review of Books* 45, 6: 10–15.

Renzetti, Claire M. 1992. *Violent Betrayal: Partner Abuse in Lesbian Relationships*. Newbury Park, CA: Sage.

Richardson, J. 1832. *Wacousta; Or the Prophecy: A Tale of the Canadas*. London, UK: Cadell.

Richardson, R. Jack. 1996. "Canada and Free Trade: Why Did It Happen?" Pp. 200–09 in Robert J. Brym, ed. *Society in Question*. Toronto: Harcourt Brace Canada.

Richer, Stephen. 1990. *Boys and Girls Apart: Children's Play in Canada and Poland*. Ottawa: Carleton University Press.

Richler, Mordecai. 1959. *The Apprenticeship of Duddy Kravitz*. Don Mills ON: A. Deutsch.

Ridgeway, Cecilia L. 1983. *The Dynamics of Small Groups*. New York: St. Martin's Press.

Riedmann, Agnes. 1993. *Science That Colonizes: A Critique of Fertility Studies in Africa*. Philadelphia: Temple University Press.

Riedmann, Agnes, Mary Ann Lamanna, and Adie Nelson. 2003. *Marriages and Families,* 1st Canadian ed. Toronto: Nelson.

Rifkin, Jeremy. *1995. The End of Work.* New York: Jeremy P. Tarcher/Putnam.

———. 1998. *The Biotech Century: Harnessing the Gene and Remaking the World*. New York: Jeremy P. Tarcher/Putnam.

Riley, Matilda White, Anne Foner, and Joan Waring. 1988. "Sociology of Age." Pp. 243–90 in Neil Smelser, ed. *Handbook of Sociology*. Newbury Park, CA: Sage.

Riley, Nancy. 1997. "Gender, Power, and Population Change." *Population Bulletin* 52, 1. Retrieved August 25, 2000 (http://www.prb.org/pubs/population_bulletin/bu52-1.htm).

Rinehart, J. W. 2001. *The Tyranny of Work: Alienation and the Labour Process*, 4th ed. Toronto: Harcourt Brace.

The Ring (University of Victoria's community newspaper). 2000. "Comment." February 4. Retrieved March 15, 2001 (http://www.communications.uvic.ca/Ring/00feb04/cover.html).

Risman, B. J., and D. Johnson-Sumerford. 1998. "Doing It Fairly: A Study of Postgender Marriages." *Journal of Marriage and the Family* 60: 23–40.

Rist, Ray. 1970. "Student Social Class and Teacher Expectations: The Self-Fulfilling Prophecy in Ghetto Education." *Harvard Educational Review* 40, 3 (August): 411–51.

Ritzer, George. 1993. *The McDonaldization of Society*. Thousand Oaks, CA: Pine Forge Press.

———. 1996. "The McDonalidzation Thesis: Is Expansion Inevitable?" *International Sociology* 11: 291–307.

Robbins, Liz. 2005. "Nash Displays Polished Look: On the Court, of Course." *New York Times* January 19. Retrieved January 19, 2005 (http://www.nytimes.com).

Roberts, C. G. D. 1915. *A History of Canada for High Schools and Academics*. Toronto: Macmillan.

Roberts, D. F. 1995. "The Pervasiveness of Plasticity." Pp.1–17 in *Human Variability and Plasticity*, C. G. N. Mascie-Taylor and Barry Bogin, eds. Cambridge: Cambridge University Press.

Roberts, Julian, and Thomas Gabor. 1990. "Race and Crime: A Critique." *Canadian Journal of Criminology* 92, 2 (April): 291–313.

Robertson, Ian. 1987. *Sociology,* 3rd ed. New York: Worth Publishing.

Robertson, Roland. 1992. *Globalization: Social Theory and Global Culture*. Newbury Park, CA: Sage.

Robinson, John P., and Suzanne Bianchi. 1997. "The Children's Hours." *American Demographics* December: 20–24.

Robinson, Paul. 2004. "Youth Court Statistics, 2002–03." *Juristat,* 24, 2. Statistics Canada Catalogue No. 85-002.

Robinson, Richard H., and Willard L. Johnson. 1997. *The Buddhist Religion: A Historical Introduction,* 4th ed. Belmont, CA: Wadsworth.

Roche, Maurice. 1995. "Rethinking Citizenship and Social Movements: Themes in Contemporary Sociology and Neoconservative Ideology." Pp. 186–219 in Louis Maheu, ed. *Social Classes and Social Movements: The Future of Collective Action.* London, UK: Sage.

Rodinson, Maxime. 1996. *Muhammad,* 2nd ed. Anne Carter, trans. London: Penguin.

Roediger, D. R. 1991. *The Wages of Whiteness: Race and the Making of the American Working Class.* London: Verso.

Roethlisberger, Fritz J., and William J. Dickson. 1939. *Management and the Worker.* Cambridge, MA: Harvard University Press.

Rogan, Mary. 2001. "An Epidemic of Gas Sniffing Decimates Arctic Indian Tribe." *New York Times on the Web.* Retrieved March 4 (http://www.uwec.edu/ Academic/ Curric/majstos/p390/Articles/030301gas-sniffing-Indians.htm (4 March).

Rogers, Everett M. 1995. *Diffusion of Innovations*, 4th ed. New York: Free Press.

Rogers, Jackie Krasas, and Kevin D. Henson. 1997. " 'Hey, Why Don't You Wear a Shorter Skirt?' Structural Vulnerability and the Organization of Sexual Harassment in Temporary Clerical Employment." *Gender and Society* 11: 215–37.

Rollins, Boyd C., and Kenneth L. Cannon. 1974. "Marital Satisfaction over the Family Life Cycle." *Journal of Marriage and the Family* 36: 271–84.

Romaniuc, A. 1984. "Fertility in Canada: From Baby-boom to Baby-bust." *Current Demographic Analysis.* Ottawa: Statistics Canada.

Romanow, Walter I., Michel de Repentigny, Stanley B. Cunningham, Walter C. Soderlund, and Kai Hildebrandt, eds. 1999. *Television Advertising in Canadian Elections: The Attack Mode, 1993.* Waterloo, ON: Wilfrid Laurier Press.

Ron, James. 2007. Personal communication. Norman Paterson School of International Affairs, Carleton University, Ottawa. December 20.

Ronfeldt, Heidi M., Rachel Kimerling, and Ilena Arias. 1998. "Satisfaction with Relationship Power and the Perpetuation of Dating Violence." *Journal of Marriage and the Family* 60: 70–78.

Rootes, Chris. 1995. "A New Class? The Higher Educated and the New Politics." Pp. 220–35 in Louis Maheu, ed. *Social Classes and Social Movements: The Future of Collective Action.* London, UK: Sage.

Rose, Michael S. 2001. "The Facts Behind the Massacre." Catholic World News 17 October. Retrieved January 15, 2005 (http:///www.cwnews.com/news/viewstory .cfm?recnum=20654).

Rosenberg, Janet, Harry Perlstadt, and William Phillips. 1997. "Now That We Are Here: Discrimination, Disparagement and Harassment at Work and the Experience of Women Lawyers." Pp. 247–59 in Dana Dunn, ed. *Workplace/ Women's Place.* Los Angeles: Roxbury.

Rosenbluth, Susan C. 1997. "Is Sexual Orientation a Matter of Choice?" *Psychology of Women Quarterly* 21: 595–610.

Rosenbluth, Susan C., Janice M. Steil, and Juliet H. Whitcomb. 1998. "Marital Equality: What Does It Mean?" *Journal of Family Issues* 19, 3: 227–44.

Rosenthal, Robert, and Lenore Jacobson. 1968. *Pygmalion in the Classroom: Teacher Expectation and Pupils' Intellectual Development.* New York: Holt, Rinehart, and Winston.

Rosin, Hanna, and Richard Morin. 1999. "In One Area, Americans Still Draw a Line on Acceptability." *Washington Post,* National Weekly Edition, 16, 11 (11 January): 8.

Ross, D., P. Roberts, and K. Scott. 2000. "Family Income and Child Well-Being." *Isuma, Canadian Journal of Policy Research* 1, 2 (Autumn): 51–56.

Ross, David. 1998. "Rethinking Child Poverty." *Insight, Perception* 22, 1: 9–11.

Rostow, W. W. 1960. *The Stages of Economic Growth: A Non-Communist Manifesto.* New York: Cambridge University Press.

Roth, Cecil. 1961. *A History of the Jews.* New York: Schocken.

Rothman, Barbara Katz. 1982. *In Labor: Women and Power in the Birthplace.* New York: W. W. Norton.

———. 1989. *Recreating Motherhood: Ideology and Technology in a Patriarchal Society.* New York: W. W. Norton.

Rothman, David J. 1991. *Strangers at the Bedside: A History of How Law and Bioethics Transformed Medical Decision Making.* New York: Basic Books.

———. 1998. "The International Organ Traffic." *New York Review of Books* 45, 5: 14–17.

Rothman, D. J., E. Rose, T. Awaya, B. Cohen, A. Daar, S. L. Dzemeshkevich, C. J. Lee, R. Munro, H. Reyes, S. M. Rothman, K. F. Schoen, N. Scheper-Hughes, Z. Shapira, and H. Smit. 1997. "The Bellagio Task Force Report on Transplantation, Bodily Integrity, and the International Traffic in Organs." Retrieved December 8, 2000 (http://www.icrc.org/web/eng/siteeng0.nsf/htmlall/ 57jnyk?opendocument).

Royal Commission on New Reproductive Technologies. 1993. *Proceed with Caution: Final Report of the Royal*

Commission on New Reproductive Technologies. Ottawa: Canadian Communications Groups.

Rubin, J. Z., F. J. Provenzano, and Z. Lurra. 1974. "The Eye of the Beholder." *American Journal of Orthopsychiatry* 44: 512–19.

Rueschemeyer, Dietrich, Evelyne Huber Stephens, and John Stephens. 1992. *Capitalist Development and Democracy.* Chicago: University of Chicago Press.

Ruggles, Steven. 1997. *Prolonged Connections: The Rise of the Extended Family in 19th-century England and America.* Madison, WI: University of Wisconsin Press.

Rural Advancement Foundation International. 1999. "The Gene Giants." Retrieved May 2, 2000 (http://www.rafi .org/web/allpub-one.shtml?dfl=allpub.db&tfl=allpub-one-frag.ptml&operation=display&ro1=recNo&rf1=34&rt1= 34&usebrs=true).

Rushton, J. P. 1995. *Race, Evolution and Behaviour: A Life History Perspective.* New Brunswick, NJ: Transaction Publishers.

Russett, Cynthia Eagle. 1966. *The Concept of Equilibrium in American Social Thought.* New Haven, CT: Yale University Press.

Ryan, Kathryn M., and Jeanne Kanjorski. 1998. "The Enjoyment of Sexist Humor, Rape Attitudes, and Relationship Aggression in College Students." *Sex Roles* 38: 743–56.

Ryerson, Stanley. 1973. *Unequal Union: Roots of Crisis in the Canadas, 1815–1873,* 2nd ed. Toronto: Progress.

Rytina, Steven, Peter M. Blau, Terry Blum, and Joseph Schwartz. 1988. "Inequality and Intermarriage: A Paradox of Motive and Constraint." *Social Forces* 66: 645–75.

Sager, Eric W. 2000. "Canada's Families—An Historian's Perspective." Pp. vii–xi in Vanier Institute of the Family. *Profiling Canada's Families II.* Nepean, ON: Vanier Institute of the Family.

Sahlins, Marshall D. 1972. *Stone Age Economics.* Chicago: Aldine.

Sallot, Jeff. 2002. "Mills Flouted Principle, CanWest Says." *Globe and Mail* June 21: A4.

Salt, Robert. 1991. "Child Support in Context: Comments on Rettig, Christensen, and Dahl." *Family Relations* 40, 2 (April): 175–78.

Sampson, Robert. 1997. "The Embeddedness of Child and Adolescent Development: A Community-Level Perspective on Urban Violence." Pp. 31–77 in Joan McCord, ed. *Violence and Childhood in the Inner City.* Cambridge, UK: Cambridge University Press.

Sampson, Robert, and John H. Laub. 1993. *Crime in the Making: Pathways and Turning Points through Life.* Cambridge, MA: Harvard University Press.

Samson, Colin, James Wilson, and Jonathan Mazower. 1999. *Canada's Tibet: The Killing of the Innu.* London UK: Survival. Retrieved May 1, 2001 (http://www.survival .org.uk/pdf/Innu%20report.pdf).

Samuda, R. J., D. Crawford, C. Philip, and W. Tinglen. 1980. *Testing, Assessment, and Counselling of Minority Students: Current Methods in Ontario.* Toronto: Ontario Ministry of Education.

Samuelsson, Kurt. 1961 [1957]. *Religion and Economic Action,* E. French, trans. Stockholm: Scandinavian University Books.

Sandqvist, Karin, and Bengt-Erik Andersson. 1992. "Thriving Families in the Swedish Welfare State." *Public Interest* 109: 114–16.

Sang-Hun, Choe. 2007. "Where Boys Were Kings, a Shift Towards Baby Girls." *New York Times* December 23. Retrieved December 23, 2007 (www.nytimes.com).

Sarlo, C. 2001. *Measuring Poverty in Canada.* Vancouver: The Fraser Institute.

Sartre, J. 1965 [1948]. *Anti-Semite and Jew,* G. J. Becker, trans. New York: Schocken.

Sassen, Saskia. 1991. *The Global City: New York, London, Tokyo.* Princeton, NJ: Princeton University Press.

Sauve, Roger. 2002. "Job, Family and Stress among Husbands, Wives and Lone-Parents 15–64 from 1990 to 2000." Retrieved July 15, 2003 (http://www.vifamily .ca/cft/connect.htm).

Saxton, Lloyd. 1990. *The Individual, Marriage, and the Family,* 9th ed. Belmont, CA: Wadsworth.

Scarr, Sandra, and Richard A. Weinberg. 1978. "The Influence of 'Family Background' on Intellectual Attainment." *American Sociological Review* 43: 674–92.

Schiebinger, Londa L. 1993. *Nature's Body: Gender in the Making of Modern Science.* Boston: Beacon Press.

Schiff, Michel, and Richard Lewontin. 1986. *Education and Class: The Irrelevance of IQ Genetic Studies.* Oxford, UK: Clarendon Press.

Schiller, Herbert I. 1989. *Culture Inc.: The Corporate Takeover of Public Expression.* New York: Oxford University Press.

Schippers, Mimi. 2002. *Rockin' Out of the Box: Gender Maneuvering in Alternative Hard Rock.* New Brunswick, NJ: Rutgers University Press.

Schlesinger, Arthur. 1991. *The Disuniting of America: Reflections on a Multicultural Society.* New York: W. W. Norton.

Schneider, Margaret, and Susan Phillips. 1997. "A Qualitative Study of Sexual Harassment of Female Doctors by Patients." *Social Science and Medicine* 45: 669–76.

Schoen, Cathy, Michelle M. Doty, Sara R. Collins, Alyssa L. Holmgren. 2005. "Insured But Not Protected: How Many Adults Are Underinsured?" *Health Affairs Web Supplement* W5. 289, 1. Retrieved July 2, 2005 (http://content.healthaffairs.org/cgi/reprint/hlthaff.w5 .289v1).

Schor, Juliet B. 1992. *The Overworked American: The Unexpected Decline of Leisure.* New York: Basic Books.

———. 1999. *The Overspent American: Why We Want What We Don't Need*. New York: Harper.

Schroeder, K. A., L. L. Blood, and D. Maluso. 1993. "Gender Differences and Similarities Between Male and Female Undergraduate Students Regarding Expectations for Career and Family Roles." *College Student Journal* 27: 237–49.

Schudson, Michael. 1991. "National News Culture and the Rise of the Informational Citizen." Pp. 265–82 in Alan Wolfe, ed. *America at Century's End*. Berkeley, CA: University of California Press.

———. 1995. *The Power of News*. Cambridge, MA: Harvard University Press.

Schuettler, Darren. 2002. "Earth Summit Bogs Down in Bitter Trade Debate." *Yahoo! Canada News* 28 August. Retrieved February 12, 2002 (http://ca.news.yahoo.com/020828/5/olia.html).

Schwartz, James. 1999. "Oh My Darwin! Who's the Fittest Evolutionary Thinker of Them All?" *Lingua Franca* 9, 8. Retrieved January 20, 2003 (http://www.mit.edu/~pinker/darwin_wars.html).

Schwartz, Stephen. 2003. *The Two Faces of Islam: The House of Sa'ud from Tradition to Terror*. New York: Doubleday.

Schweingruber, David, and Clark McPhail. 1999. "A Method for Systematically Observing and Recording Collective Action." *Sociological Methods and Research* 27: 451–98,

Scott, Janny. 1998. "Manners and Civil Society." *Journal* 2, 3. Retrieved April 12, 2003 (http://www.civnet.org/journal/issue7/ftjscott.htm).

Scott, K. 1997. "Indigenous Canadians." Pp. 133–64 in D. McKenzie, R. Williams, and E. Single, eds. *Canadian Profile: Alcohol, Tobacco and Other Drugs, 1997*. Ottawa: Canadian Centre on Substance Abuse.

Scott, Sarah. 2000. "The Deepest Cut of All." Retrieved June 15, 2003 (http://www.chatelaine.com/read/news+views/fgm.html).

Scott, Shirley Lynn. 2003. "The Death of James Bulger." *Court TV's Crime Library*. Retrieved July 23, 2003 (http://www.crimelibrary.com/notorious_murders/young/bulger/1.html?sect=10).

Scott, Wilbur J. 1990. "PTSD in DSM-III: A Case in the Politics of Diagnosis and Disease." *Social Problems* 37: 294–310.

Scully, Diana. 1990. *Understanding Sexual Violence: A Study of Convicted Rapists*. Boston: Unwin Hyman.

"Search Engines of All Countries in All Languages as of August 27, 2002." 2002. WebMasterAid.com. Retrieved May 25, 2003 (http://webmasteraid.com/cgi-bin/d.cgi).

Seccombe, Wally. 1992. *A Millennium of Family Change: Feudalism to Capitalism in Northwestern Europe*. London: Verso.

Second Life. 2006. "I'll See Your Million . . . and Raise You a Million." Retrieved January 14, 2008 (http://blog.secondlife.com/2006/12/14/ill-see-your-million-and-double-that).

Segundo, Juan Luis, S. J. 1976 [1975]. *The Liberation of Theology*, John Drury, trans. Maryknoll, NY: Orbis.

Seiter, Ellen. 1999. *Television and New Media Audiences*. Oxford, UK: Clarendon Press.

Sen, Amartya. 1981. *Poverty and Famines: An Essay on Entitlement and Deprivation*. Oxford, UK: Clarendon Press.

———. 1990. "More than 100 Million Women are Missing." *New York Review of Books* 20 December: 61–66.

———. 1994. "Population: Delusion and Reality." *New York Review of Books* 41, 15: 62–71.

———. 2001. "Many Faces of Gender Inequality." *The Frontline* 9 November. Retrieved August 5, 2003 (http://www.ksg.harvard.edu/gei/Text/Sen-Pubs/Sen_many_faces_of_gender_inequality.pdf).

Senn, Charlene Y., Serge Desmarais, Norine Veryberg, and Eileen Wood. 2000. "Predicting Coercive Sexual Behavior Across the Lifespan in a Random Sample of Canadian Men." *Journal of Social and Personal Relationships* 17, 1 (February): 95–113.

The Sentencing Project. 2006. "New Incarceration Figures." Retrieved March 30, 2007 (http://www.sentencingproject.org/Admin%5CDocuments%5Cpublications%5Cinc_newfigures.pdf).

Sewell, William H. 1958. "Infant Training and the Personality of the Child." *American Journal of Sociology* 64: 150–59.

Shain, A. 1995. "Employment of People with Disabilities." *Canadian Social Trends* 38: 8–13.

Shakur, Sanyika (a.k.a. Monster Kody Scott). 1993. *Monster: The Autobiography of an L.A. Gang Member*. New York: Penguin.

Shalev, Michael. 1983. "Class Politics and the Western Welfare State." Pp. 27–50 in S. E. Spiro and E. Yuchtman-Yaar, eds. *Evaluating the Welfare State: Social and Political Perspectives*. New York: Academic Press.

Shanker, Stuart. 2002. "The Generativist-Interactionist Debate over Specific Language Impairment: Psycholinguistics at a Crossroad." *American Journal of Psychology* 115: 415–50.

Shapiro, Joseph P. 1993. *No Pity: People with Disabilities Forging a New Civil Rights Movement*. New York: Times Books.

Shattuck, Roger. 1980. *The Forbidden Experiment: The Story of the Wild Boy of Aveyron*. New York: Farrar, Straus, and Giroux.

Shaw, Karen. 2001. "Harry Potter Books: My Concerns." Retrieved June 15, 2003 (http://www.reachouttrust.org/regulars/articles/occult/hpotter2.htm).

Shaw, Martin. 2000. *Theory of the Global State: Globality as Unfinished Revolution*. Cambridge: Cambridge University Press.

Shea, Sarah E., Kevin Gordon, Ann Hawkins, Janet Kawchuk, and Donna Smith. 2000. "Pathology in the Hundred Acre Wood: A Neurodevelopmental Perspective on A. A. Milne." *Canadian Medical Association Journal* 163, 12: 1557–59. Retrieved December 12, 2000 (http://www.cma.ca/cmaj/vol-163/issue-12/ 1557.htm).

Shekelle, Paul G. 1998. "What Role for Chiropractic in Health Care?" *New England Journal of Medicine* 339: 1074–75.

Sherif, M., L. J. Harvey, B. J. White, W. R. Hood, and C. W. Sherif. 1988 [1961]. *The Robber's Cave Experiment: Intergroup Conflict and Cooperation.* Middletown, CT: Wesleyan University Press.

Sherrill, Robert. 1997. "A Year in Corporate Crime." *The Nation* 7 April: 11–20.

Shields, M. 1999. "Long Working Hours and Health." *Health Reports* 11, 2: 33–48.

Shipley, Lisa, Sylvie Ouellette, and Fernando Cartwright. 2003. *Planning and Preparation: First Results from the Survey of Approaches to Educational Planning (SAEP) 2002.* Ottawa: Statistics Canada. Catalogue No. 81-595-MIE2003010. Retrieved May 27, 2006 (http://www.statcan.ca/english/research/81-595-MIE/81-595-MIE2003010.pdf).

Shkilnyk, Anastasia. 1985. *A Poison Stronger than Love: The Destruction of an Ojibway Community.* New Haven, CT: Yale University Press.

"Short Guys Finish Last." 1995–96. *The Economist* December 23 –January 5: 19–22.

Short, James F., Jr., and Fred L. Strodtbeck. 1965. *Group Process and Gang Delinquency.* Chicago: University of Chicago Press.

Shorter, Edward. 1997. *A History of Psychiatry: From the Era of the Asylum to the Age of Prozac.* New York: John Wiley and Sons.

Shulman, Alix Kates. 1997 [1969]. *Memoirs of an Ex-Prom Queen.* New York: Penguin.

Siddiqui, Haroon. 2002. "CanWest Censorship Is Shameful." *The Star.com* March 10. Retrieved May 17, 2002 (http://www.thestar.com/NASApp/cs/ContentServer?pagename=thestar/Layout/Article_Type1&c=Article&cid=1015585330473&call_page=TS_Opinion&call_pageid=96825).

Signorielli, Nancy. 1998. "Reflections of Girls in the Media: A Content Analysis Across Six Media: Overview." Retrieved July 15, 2000 (http://childrennow.org/media/mc97/ReflectSummary.html).

Silberman, Steve. 2000. "Talking to Strangers." *Wired* 8, 5: 225–33, 288–96. Retrieved May 23, 2002 (http://www.wired.com/wired/archive/8.05/translation.html).

"The Silent Boom." 1998. *Fortune* 7 July: 170–71.

Silver, Warren. 2007. "Crime Statistics in Canada, 2006." *Juristat* 27, 5.

Simmel, Georg. 1950. *The Sociology of Georg Simmel*, Kurt H. Wolff, trans. and ed. New York: Free Press.

Simon, Jonathan. 1993. *Poor Discipline: Parole and the Social Control of the Underclass, 1890–1990.* Chicago: University of Chicago Press.

Sissing, T. W. 1996. "The Black Community in the History of Québec and Canada." Retrieved June 14, 2003 (http://www.qesnrecit.qc.ca/mpages/title.htm).

Sjöberg, Gideon. 1960. *The Preindustrial City: Past and Present.* New York: Free Press.

Skinner, B. F. 1953. *Science and Human Behavior.* New York: Macmillan.

Skocpol, Theda. 1979. *States and Revolutions: A Comparative Analysis of France, Russia, and China.* Cambridge, UK: Cambridge University Press.

Skolnick, Arlene. 1991. *Embattled Paradise: The American Family in an Age of Uncertainty.* New York: Basic Books.

Smeeding, Timothy M. 2004. "Public Policy and Economic Inequality: The United States in Comparative Perspective." Working Paper No. 367. Syracuse NY: Maxwell School of Citizenship and Public Affairs, Syracuse University. Retrieved January 30, 2005 (http://www.lisproject.org/publictions/LISwps/367.pdf).

Smeenk, Brian P. 1993. "Canada's Pay Equity Experiments—Pay Equity Legislations—Going Global." *HR Magazine* September. Retrieved August 6, 2005 (http://www.findarticles.com/p/articles/mi_m3495/is_n9v38/ai_14530609).

Smelser, Neil. 1963. *Theory of Collective Behavior.* New York: Free Press.

Smith, Adam. 1981 [1776]. *An Inquiry into the Nature and Causes of the Wealth of Nations*, vols. 1 and 2. Indianapolis, IN: Liberty Press.

Smith, Anthony. 1980. *Goodbye Gutenberg: The Newspaper Revolution of the 1980s.* New York: Oxford University Press.

Smith, Christian. 1991. *The Emergence of Liberation Theology: Radical Religion and Social Movement Theory.* Chicago: University of Chicago Press.

Smith, Jackie. 1998. "Global Civil Society? Transnational Social Movement Organizations and Social Capital." *American Behavioral Scientist* 42: 93–107.

Smith, Michael. 1990. "Patriarchal Ideology and Wife Beating: A Test of a Feminist Hypothesis." *Violence and Victims* 5: 257–73.

Smith, Tom W. 1992. "A Methodological Analysis of the Sexual Behavior Questions on the GSS." *Journal of Official Statistics* 8: 309–25.

Snider, Laureen. 1999. "White-Collar Crime." Pp. 2504 in James H. Marsh, editor in chief. *The Canadian Encyclopedia, Year 2000 Edition.* Toronto: McClelland & Stewart Inc.

Snow, David A., E. Burke Rochford Jr., Steven K. Worden, and Robert D. Benford. 1986. "Frame Alignment Processes, Micromobilization, and Movement Participation." *American Sociological Review* 51: 464–81.

Snyder, Benson R. 1971. *The Hidden Curriculum.* New York: Alfred A. Knopf.

Snyder, David, and Charles Tilly. 1972. "Hardship and Collective Violence in France, 1830–1960." *American Sociological Review* 37: 520–32.

Solomon, Charlene Marmer. 1999. "Stressed to the Limit." *Workforce* 78, 9: 48–54.

Somers, Marsha D. 1993. "A Comparison of Voluntarily Childfree Adults and Parents." *Journal of Marriage and the Family* 55, 3 (August): 643–50.

Sorenson, Elaine. 1994. *Comparable Worth: Is It a Worthy Policy?* Princeton, NJ: Princeton University Press.

Spencer, Herbert. 1975 [1897–1906]. *The Principles of Sociology,* 3rd ed. Westport, CT: Greenwood Press.

Spilerman, Seymour. 1970. "The Causes of Racial Disturbances: A Comparison of Alternative Explanations." *American Sociological Review* 35: 627–49.

———. 1976. "Structural Characteristics of Cities and the Severity of Racial Disorders." *American Sociological Review* 41: 771–93.

———. 2000. "Wealth and Stratification Processes." *Annual Review of Sociology* 26: 497–524.

Spillman, Lyn, ed. 2002. *Cultural Sociology.* Malden, MA: Blackwell.

Spitz, René A. 1945. "Hospitalism: An Inquiry into the Genesis of Psychiatric Conditions in Early Childhood." Pp. 53–74 in *The Psychoanalytic Study of the Child,* vol. 1. New York: International Universities Press.

———. 1962. "Autoerotism Re-examined: The Role of Early Sexual Behavior Patterns in Personality Formation." Pp. 283–315 in *The Psychoanalytic Study of the Child,* vol. 17. New York: International Universities Press.

Spitzer, Steven. 1980. "Toward a Marxian Theory of Deviance." Pp. 175–91 in Delos H. Kelly, ed. *Criminal Behavior: Readings in Criminology.* New York: St. Martin's Press.

Srinivas, M. N. 1952. *Religion and Society among the Coorgs of South India.* Oxford, UK: Oxford University Press.

Stacey, Judith. 1996. *Brave New Families: Stories of Domestic Upheaval in Late Twentieth Century America.* New York: Basic Books.

Stack, Carol. 1974. *All Our Kin: Strategies for Survival in a Black Community.* New York: Harper.

Stack, Stephen, and J. Ross Eshleman. 1998. "Marital Status and Happiness: A 17-Nation Study." *Journal of Marriage and the Family* 60: 527–36.

Stark, Rodney. 1985. *Sociology.* Belmont, CA: Wadsworth.

Stark, Rodney, and William Sims Bainbridge. 1979. "Of Churches, Sects, and Cults: Preliminary Concepts for a Theory of Religious Movements." *Journal for the Scientific Study of Religion* 18: 117–31.

———. 1987. *A Theory of Religion.* New York: P. Lang.

———. 1997. *Religion, Deviance, and Social Control.* New York: Routledge.

Starr, Paul. 1982. *The Social Transformation of American Medicine.* New York: Basic Books.

———. 1994. *The Logic of Health Care Reform: Why and How the President's Plan Will Work,* rev. ed. New York: Penguin.

Statistics Canada. 1998a. *Canada Yearbook 1999.* Ottawa: Minister of Industry.

———. 1998b. "1996 Census: Labour Force Activity, Occupation and Industry, Place of Work, Mode of Transportation to Work, Unpaid Work." *The Daily* March 17. Retrieved May 26, 2006 (http://www.statcan.ca/Daily/English/980317/d980317.htm).

———. 1999a. "Principal Religious Denominations of the Population, Census Dates, 1871 to 1971. Series A 164–184." *Historical Statistics of Canada.* Ottawa: Ministry of Industry. Catalogue No. 11-516-XIE. Retrieved October 15, 2005 (http://www.statcan.ca/english/freepub/11-516-XIE/sectiona/A164_184.csv).

———. 1999b. "Low-Income Measures, Low Income After Tax Cut-offs and Low Income After Tax Measure." Retrieved November 14, 2008 (http://www.statcan.ca/english/freepub/13F0019X1B/13F0019X1B1997000.pdf).

———.2000a. *Canada at a Glance.* Ottawa: Ministry of Industry. Catalogue No. 12-581-XPE.

———. 2000b. "Divorces, 1998." *The Daily* 28 September. Retrieved May 26, 2006 (http://www.statcan.ca/Daily/English/000928/d000926.htm).

———. 2000c. "Household Environmental Practices." Retrieved October 7, 2000 (http://www.statcan.ca/english/Pgdb/Land/Environment/envir01a.htm).

———. 2000d. "Population." Retrieved October 7, 2000 (http://www.statcan.ca/english/Pgdb/People/Population/demo02.htm).

———. 2000e. "Population by Aboriginal Group, 1996 Census." Retrieved October 7, 2000 (http://www.statcan.ca/english/Pgdb/People/Population/demo39a.htm).

———. 2001d. "Television Viewing: Fall 1999." *The Daily* January 25. Retrieved July 23, 2002 (http://www.statcan.ca/Daily/English/010125/d010125a.htm).

———. 2001a. "Family Units, Including Employer-Sponsored Registered Pension Plans, by Net Worth Group and Age, 1999." *Survey of Financial Security.* Ottawa: Minister of Industry. Retrieved May 13, 2006 (http://www40.statcan.ca/l01/cst01/famil96a.htm?sdi=net%20worth).

———. 2001b. "Trends in the Use of Private Education." *The Daily* July 4. Retrieved May 26, 2006 (http://www.statcan.ca/Daily/English/010704/d010704b.htm).

———. 2001c. "Imports and Exports of Goods on a Balance-of-Payments Basis." Retrieved February 17, 2001 (http://www.statcan.ca/english/Pgdb/Economy/International/gblec02a.htm).

———. 2002a. "Cable Television Industry." Retrieved May 20, 2002 (http://www.statcan.ca/english/Pgdb/People/Culture/arts11.htm).

———. 2002b. "Canadian Community Health Survey: A First Look." Retrieved May 16, 2005 (http://www.statcan.ca/Daily/English/020508/d020508a.htm).

———. 2002c. "Highlights for: Greater Napanee (Town), Ontario." Retrieved January 15, 2003 (http://www12.statcan.ca/english/profil01/CP01/Details/Page.cfm?Lang=E&Geo1=CSD&Code1=3511021&Geo2=PR&Code2=35&Data=Count&SearchText=Napanee&SearchType=Begins&SearchPR=01&B1=All&GeoLevel=&GeoCode=3511021).

———. 2002d. "National Longitudinal Survey of Children and Youth: Childhood Obesity." Retrieved May 16, 2005 (http://www.statcan.ca/Daily/English/021018/d021018b.htm).

———. 2002e. "Population, Occupied Private Dwellings, Private Households, Collective Dwellings, Population in Collective Dwellings, and Average Number of Persons per Private Household, 1961–1996 Censuses, Canada." Retrieved May 20, 2002 (http://www.statcan.ca/english/Pgdb/People/Families/famil66.htm).

———. 2003a. "Education in Canada: Raising the Standard." *2001 Census Analysis Series.* Retrieved May 26, 2006 (http://www12.statcan.ca/english/census01/Products/Analytic/companion/educ/contents.cfm).

———. 2003b. *Education Indicators in Canada: Report of the Pan-Canadian Education Indicators Program 2003,* p. 249. Ottawa: Statistics Canada. Retrieved May 26, 2006 (http://www.statcan.ca/english/freepub/81-582-XIE/2003001/pdf/81-582-XIE03001.pdf).

———. 2003c. "Religions in Canada." *2001 Census Analysis Series.* Retrieved November 28, 2005 (http://www12.statcan.ca/english/census01/Products/Analytic/companion/rel/canada.cfm).

———. 2004a. *The Canadian Labour Market at a Glance.* Ottawa: Ministry of Industry. Catalogue No. 71-222-XIE. Retrieved May 26, 2006 (http://www.statcan.ca/english/freepub/71-222-XIE/71-222-XIE2004000.htm).

———. 2004b. "Causes of Death, Chapter XX, 2002." Retrieved April 22, 2005 (http://www.statcan.ca/english/freepub/84-208-XIE/2002/tables/table20.pdf), 52–53.

———. 2004c. "Marriages, 2002." *The Daily* December 21. Retrieved May 26, 2006 (http://www.statcan.ca/Daily/English/041221/d041221d.htm).

———. 2004d. "University Finances." *The Daily* August 19. Retrieved December 9, 2005 (http://www4.statcan.ca/survey/2005WES_InviteE/proceed.cgi?loc=http://www.statcan.ca/english/dai-quo).

———. 2005a. "Annual Survey of Advertising and Related Services." *The Daily* April 15. Retrieved December 9, 2005 (http://www.statcan.ca/Daily/English/050415/d050415b.htm).

———. 2005b. "Child Care, 1994/95 and 2000/01." *The Daily* February 7. Retrieved March 114, 2006 (http://www.statcan.ca/Daily/English/050207/d050207b.htm).

———. 2005c. "Divorces." *The Daily* March 9. Retrieved June 12, 2006 (http://www.statcan.ca/Daily/English/050309/d050309b.htm).

———. 2005d. "General Social Survey: Paid and Unpaid Work." July 19. Retrieved January 15, 2008 (http://www.statcan.ca/Daily/English/060719/d060719b.htm).

———. 2005e. *Income in Canada 2003.* Ottawa: Ministry of Industry. Catalogue No. 75-202-XIE. Retrieved May 13, 2006 (http://www.statcan.ca/english/freepub/75-202-XIE/75-202-XIE2001000.pdf).

———. 2005f. "Induced Abortions, 2002." *The Daily* February 11. Retrieved May 26, 2006 (http://www.statcan.ca/Daily/English/050211/d050211a.htm).

———. 2005g. "Labour Force Survey Estimates by Actual Hours Worked, Main or All Jobs, Sex and Age Group, Annual." Table 282-0018. Retrieved May 26, 2006 (http://cansim2.statcan.ca/cgi-win/CNSMCGI.EXE?LANG=E&SDDSLOC=//www.statcan.ca/english/sdds/*.htm&ROOTDIR=CII/&RESULTTEMPLATE=CII/CII_PICK&ARRAY_PICK=1&ARRAYID=2820018).

———. 2005h. "Latest Release from the Labour Force Survey." Retrieved November 21, 2005 (http://www.statcan.ca/english/Subjects/Labour/LFS/lfs-en.htm).

———. 2005i. "Population by Religion, by Provinces and Territories (2001 Census)." Retrieved May 1, 2005 (http://www.statcan.ca/english/Pgdb/demo30a.htm).

———. 2005j. "University Enrolments, by Registration Status, Program Level and Classification of Instructional Programs (CIP), Annual." Table 477-0011. Retrieved Jul6 26, 2005 (http://cansim2.statcan.ca/cgi-win/CNSMCGI.EXE?LANG=E&SDDSLOC=//www.statcan.ca/english/sdds/*.htm&ROOTDIR=CII/&RESULTTEMPLATE=CII/CII_PICK&ARRAYPICK=1&ARRAYID=4770011).

———. 2005k. "Occupation—1991 Standard Occupational Classification (Historical), Age Groups and Sex for Labour Force 15 Years and Over, for Canada, Provinces, Territories, Census Metropolitan Areas and Census Agglomerations, 1991 to 2001 Censuses—20% Sample Data." Retrieved November 28, 2005 (http://www12.statcan.ca/english/census01/products/standard/themes/RetrieveProductTable.cfm?Temporal=2001&PID=60367&GID=431515&METH=1&APATH=3&PTYPE=55440&THEME=46&AID=0&FREE=0&FOCUS=0&VID=0&GC=0&GK=0&SC=1&SR=1&RL=0&CPP=99&RPP=9999&D1=1&D2=0&D3=0&D4=0&D5=0&D6=0&d1=1&d2=0).

———. 2006. *Women in Canada, 5 Edition: A Gender-based Statistical Report.* Retrieved January 14, 2008 (http://www.statcan.ca/english/freepub/89-503-XIE/0010589-503-XIE.pdf).

———. 2007a. "Age and Sex Highlight Tables, 2006 Census." Retrieved January 11, 2008 (http://www12.statcan.ca/english/census06/data/highlights/agesex/Index.cfm).

———. 2007b. "Immigration in Canada: A Portrait of the Foreign-born Population, 2006 Census: Immigration: Driver of Population Growth." Retrieved January 3, 2008 (http://www12.statcan.ca/english/census06/analysis/immcit/foreign_born.cfm).

———. 2007c. "Mortality, Summary List of Causes." Retrieved January 16, 2008 (http://www.statcan.ca/english/freepub/84F0209XIE/84F0209XIE2004000.pdf).

———. 2007d. "Population and Dwelling Count Highlight Tables, 2006 Census." Retrieved January 13, 2008 (http://www12.statcan.ca/english/census06/data/popdwell/Tables.cfm).

———. 2007e. "University Tuition Fees, 2007/2007." *The Daily* October 18. Retrieved March 6, 2008 (http://www.statcan.ca/Daily/English/071018/d071018b.htm).

———. 2008a. "Canadian Internet Use Survey." CANSIM, Tables 3580125, 3580126, and 3580130. Retrieved January 12, 2008 (http://dc1.chass.utoronto.ca.myaccess.library.utoronto.ca/cgi-bin/cansimdim/c2_arraysBrowse.pl).

———. 2008b. "Distribution of Total Income, by Economic Family Type, 2005 Constant Dollars, Annual." CANSIM, Table 202-0401. Retrieved January 12, 2008 (http://cansim2.statcan.ca/cgi-win/cnsmcgi.exe?Lang=E&RootDir=CII/&ResultTemplate=CII/CII_&Array_Pick=1&ArrayId=2020401).

———. 2008c. "Educational Portrait of Canada, 2006 Census." Retrieved March 6, 2008 (http://www12.statcan.ca/english/census06/analysis/education/pdf/97-560-XIE2006001.pdf).

———. 2008d. "Ethnic Origins, 2006 Counts, for Canada, Provinces and Territories—20% Sample Data." Retrieved April 5, 2008 (http://www12.statcan.ca/english/census06/data/highlights/ethnic/pages/Page.cfm?Lang=E&Geo=PR&Code=01&Data=Count&Table=2&StartRec=1&Sort=3&Display=All&CSD Filter=5000).

———. 2008e. "Full-Time and Part-Time Employment by Sex and Age Group." Retrieved May 2, 2008 (http://www40.statcan.ca/l01/cst01/labor12.htm).

———. 2008f. "Visible Minority Groups, Percentage Distribution (2006), for Canada, Provinces and Territories—20% Sample Data." Retrieved April 5, 2008 (http://www12.statcan.ca/english/census06/data/highlights/ethnic/pages/Page.cfm?Lang=E&Geo=PR&Code=01&Table=1&Data=Dist&StartRec=1&Sort=2&Display=Page).

———. 2008g. "University enrolment 2005/2006." *The Daily* 7 February 2008. On the World Wide Web at http://www.statcan.ca/Daily/English/080207/d080207a.htm (accessed 6 March 2008).

———. n.d.. "More Seniors Living with a Spouse, More Living Alone and Fewer Living in Health Care Institutions." Retrieved January 11, 2008 (http://www12.statcan.ca/english/census01/products/analytic/companion/fam/canada.cfm#seniors).

Stearns, Carol Zisowitz, and Peter N. Stearns. 1985. "Emotionology: Clarifying the History of Emotions and Emotional Standards." *American Historical Review* 90: 813–36.

———. 1986. *Anger: The Struggle for Emotional Control in America's History.* Chicago: University of Chicago Press.

Steckel, Richard H. 1995. "Stature and the Standard of Living." *Journal of Economic Literature* 33: 1903–1940.

Steel, Freda M. 1987. "Alimony and Maintenance Orders." Pp. 155–67 in Sheilah L. Martin and Kathleen E. Mahoney, eds. *Equality and Judicial Neutrality.* Toronto: Carswell.

Steele, Claude M. 1992. "Race and the Schooling of Black Americans." *The Atlantic Monthly* April. Retrieved May 2, 2000 (http://www.theatlantic.com/unbound/flashbks/blacked/steele.htm).

Steinberg, Stephen. 1989. *The Ethnic Myth: Race, Ethnicity, and Class in America*, updated ed. Boston: Beacon Press.

Steinem, Gloria. 1994. *Moving Beyond Words.* New York: Simon & Schuster.

Stenger, Richard. 2003. "NASA Chief Blasted over Shuttle Memos." Retrieved March 6, 2003 (http://www.cnn.com/2003/TECH/space/02/27/sprj.colu.memo/index.htm).

The Sterilization of Leilani Muir. 1996. Montreal: National Film Board. (video).

Sternberg, Robert J. 1986. "A Triangular Theory of Love." *Psychological Review* 93: 119–35.

———. 1998. *In Search of the Human Mind*, 2nd ed. Fort Worth, TX: Harcourt Brace.

Steward, Gillian. 1999. "Politicians and the Shrinking Soundbite." *Media Spring.* Retrieved May 29, 2002 (http://www.caj.ca/mediamag/spring99/media99_11.html).

Stewart, Abigail, Anne P. Copeland, Nia Lane Chester, Janet E. Malley, and Nicole B. Barenbaum. 1997. *Separating Together: How Divorce Transforms Families.* New York: The Guilford Press.

Stiglitz, Joseph E. 2002. *Globalization and Its Discontents.* New York: W. W. Norton.

Stiker, Henri-Jacques. 1999 [1982]. *A History of Disability*, William Sayers, trans. Ann Arbor: University of Michigan Press.

Stipp, David. 2003. "The Pentagon's Weather Nightmare." *Fortune* 26 January. Retrieved May 29, 2004 (http://paxhumana.info/article.php3?id_article=400).

Stone, Lawrence. 1977. *The Family, Sex and Marriage in England, 1500–1800.* New York: Harper and Row.

Stopford, John M., and Susan Strange. 1991. *Rival States, Rival Firms: Competition for World Market Shares*. Cambridge: Cambridge University Press.

Stormshak, Elizabeth A., Karen L. Bierman, Robert J. McMahon, and Liliana J. Lengua. 2000. "Parenting Practices and Child Disruptive Behavior Problems in Early Elementary School." *Journal of Clinical Child Psychology* 29, 1 (March): 17–29.

Stotsky, Sandra. 1999. *Losing Our Language: How Multicultural Classroom Instruction Is Undermining Our Children's Ability to Read, Write, and Reason*. New York: Free Press.

Stouffer, Samuel A., Edward A. Suchman, Leland C. De Vinney, Shirley A. Star, and Robin M. Williams, Jr. 1949. *The American Soldier*, 4 vols. Princeton, NJ: Princeton University Press.

Straus, Murray A. 1994. *Beating the Devil Out of Them: Corporal Punishment in American Families*. New York: Lexington Books.

———. 1996. "Presentation: Spanking and the Making of a Violent Society." *Pediatrics* 98: 837–49.

Straus, Murray A., and Glenda Kaufman Kantor. 1994. "Corporal Punishment of Adolescents by Parents: A Risk Factor in the Epidemiology of Depression, Suicide, Alcohol Abuse, Child Abuse, and Wife Beating." *Adolescence* 29, 115: 543–56.

Straus, Murray A., and Vera E. Mouradian. 1998. "Impulsive Corporal Punishment by Mothers and Antisocial Behavior and Impulsiveness of Children." *Behavioral Science & the Law* 16, 3: 353–62.

Straus, Murray A., and Julie H. Stewart. 1999. "Corporal Punishment by American Parents: National Data on Prevalence, Chronicity, Severity, and Duration in Relation to Child and Family Characteristics." *Clinical Child & Family Psychology Review* 2, 2 (June): 55–70.

Straus, Murray A., David B. Sugerman, and Jean Giles-Sims. 1997. "Spanking by Parents and Subsequent Antisocial Behavior of Children." *Archives of Pediatrics & Adolescent Medicine* 151, 8: 761–73.

Straus, Murray A., and Carrie L. Yodanis. 1996. "Corporal Punishment in Adolescence and Physical Assaults on Spouses Later in Life: What Accounts for the Link?" *Journal of Marriage and the Family* 58, 4: 825–924.

Strauss, Anselm L. 1993. *Continual Permutations of Action*. New York: Aldine de Gruyter.

Stretesky, Paul, and Michael J. Hogan. 1998. "Environmental Justice: An Analysis of Superfund Sites in Florida." *Social Problems* 45: 268–87.

Strikes and Lockouts in Canada 1968. 1970. Ottawa: Economic and Research Branch, Canada Department of Labour. Cat. No. L2-1/1968.

Strikes and Lockouts in Canada 1985. 1985. Ottawa: Minister of Supply and Services Canada. Cat. No. L160-2999/85B.

Strong-Boag, Veronica. 1986. "Ever a Crusader: Nellie McClung, First-Wave Feminist." Pp. 178–90 in V. Strong-Boag and A. Fellman, eds. *Rethinking Canada: The Promise of Women's History*. Toronto: Copp Clark Pitman.

Subrahmanyam, Kaveri, and Patricia M. Greenfield. 1998. "Computer Games for Girls: What Makes Them Play?" Pp. 46–71 in Justine Cassell and Henry Jenkins, eds. *From Barbie to Mortal Kombat: Gender and Computer Games*. Cambridge, MA: MIT Press.

Sudweeks, Fay, Margaret McLaughlin, and Sheizaf Rafaeli, eds. 1999. *Network and Netplay: Virtual Groups on the Internet*. Menlo Park, CA: AAAI Press.

Sullivan, Mercer L. 2002. "Exploring Layers: Extended Case Method as a Tool for Multilevel Analysis of School Violence." *Sociological Methods and Research* 31, 2: 255–85.

Sumner, William Graham. 1940 [1907]. *Folkways*. Boston: Ginn.

"A Survey of Human Rights Law." 1998. *The Economist* December 5.

Sutherland, Edwin H. 1939. *Principles of Criminology*. Philadelphia: Lippincott.

———. 1949. *White Collar Crime*. New York: Dryden.

Suttles, G. D. 1968. *The Social Order of the Slum: Ethnicity and Territory in the Inner City*. Chicago: University of Chicago Press.

Sweezy, Kate, and Jill Tiefenthaler. 1996. "Do State-Level Variables Affect Divorce Rates?" *Review of Social Economy* 54: 47–65.

Swiss Re. 2005 "Sigma Natural Catastrophes and Man-Made Disasters in 2004." Retrieved March 2, 2005 (http://www.swissre.com).

———. 2007. "Natural Catastrophes and Man-Made Disasters in 2006." Retrieved April 30, 2007 (http://www.swissre.com/INTERNET/pwswpspr.nsf/fmBookMarkFrameSet?ReadForm&BM=http://www.swissre.com/INTERNET/pwswpspr.nsf/vwAllByIDKeyLu/SBAR-59FDAE).

Sykes, Gresham, and David Matza. 1957. "Techniques of Neutralization: A Theory of Delinquency." *American Sociological Review* 22: 664–70.

Sylwester, Kevin. 2002. "Democracy and Changes in Income Inequality." *International Journal of Business and Economics* 1: 167–78.

Szasz, Andrew, and Michael Meuser. 1997. "Environmental Inequalities: Literature Review and Proposals for New Directions in Research and Theory." *Current Sociology* 45, 3: 99–120.

Szreter, Simon. 1996. *Fertility, Class and Gender in Britain, 1860–1940*. Cambridge, UK: Cambridge University Press.

Tajfel, Henri. 1981. *Human Groups and Social Categories: Studies in Social Psychology*. Cambridge, UK: Cambridge University Press.

Tannen, Deborah. 1990. *You Just Don't Understand Me: Women and Men in Conversation*. New York: William Morrow.

———. 1994a. *Talking from 9 to 5: How Women's and Men's Conversational Styles Affect Who Gets Heard, Who Gets Credit, and What Gets Done at Work*. New York: William Morrow.

———. 1994b. *Gender and Discourse*. New York: Oxford University Press.

Tarrow, Sidney. 1994. *Power in Movement: Social Movements, Collective Action and Politics*. Cambridge, UK: Cambridge University Press.

Tasker, Fiona L., and Susan Golombok. 1997. *Growing Up in a Lesbian Family: Effects on Child Development*. New York: The Guilford Press.

Tavris, C. 1992. *The Mismeasure of Woman*. New York: Simon & Schuster.

Tec, Nechama. 1986. *When Light Pierced the Darkness: Christian Rescue of Jews in Nazi-Occupied Poland*. New York: Oxford University Press.

Terry, Jennifer, and Jacqueline Urla, eds. 1995. *Deviant Bodies: Critical Perspectives on Difference in Science and Popular Culture*. Bloomington: Indiana University Press.

Thoits, Peggy A. 1989. "The Sociology of Emotions." *Annual Review of Sociology* 15: 317–42.

Thomas, Keith. 1971. *Religion and the Decline of Magic*. London: Weidenfeld and Nicholson.

Thomas, Mikhail. 2002. "Adult Criminal Court Statistics, 2000–01." *Juristat* 22, 2. Statistics Canada Catalogue no. 85-002-XPE.

———. 2004. "Adult Criminal Court Statistics, 2003–04." *Juristat* 24, 12. Statistics Canada Catalogue no. 85-002-XPE.

Thomas, W. I., and F. Znaniecki. 1958 [1918–20]. *The Polish Peasant in Europe and America: Monograph of an Immigrant Group*, 2nd ed. (2 vols.). New York: Dover Publications.

Thomas, William Isaac. 1966 [1931]. "The Relation of Research to the Social Process." Pp. 289–305 in Morris Janowitz, ed. *W.I. Thomas on Social Organization and Social Personality*. Chicago: University of Chicago Press.

Thompson, E. P. 1967. "Time, Work Discipline, and Industrial Capitalism." *Past and Present* 38: 59–67.

———. 1968. *The Making of the English Working Class*. Harmondsworth, UK: Penguin.

Thompson, Kenneth, ed. 1975. *Auguste Comte: The Foundation of Sociology*, New York: Wiley.

Thorne, Barrie. 1993. *Gender Play: Girls and Boys in School*. New Brunswick, NJ: Rutgers University Press.

Throng. 2007. "Canada's Ratings Race Officially a Dead Heat. . . ." Retrieved January 10, 2008 (http://www .tvthrong.ca/general/canadas-ratings-race-officially-a-dead-heat).

Tilly, Charles. 1978. *From Mobilization to Revolution*. Reading, MA: Addison-Wesley.

———. 1979a. "Collective Violence in European Perspective." Pp. 83–118 in H. Graham and T. Gurr, eds.

Violence in America: Historical and Comparative Perspective, 2nd ed. Beverly Hills: Sage.

———. 1979b. "Repertoires of Contention in America and Britain, 1750–1830." Pp. 126–55 in Mayer N. Zald and John D. McCarthy, eds. *The Dynamics of Social Movements: Resource Mobilization, Social Control, and Tactics*. Cambridge, MA: Winthrop Publishers.

———. 2002. "Violence, Terror, and Politics as Usual." Unpublished paper, Department of Sociology, Columbia University.

Tilly, Charles, Louise Tilly, and Richard Tilly. 1975. *The Rebellious Century, 1830–1930*. Cambridge, MA: Harvard University Press.

"The *Times* and Iraq." 2004. *New York Times* May 26. Retrieved January 3, 2005 (http://www.nytimes.com).

Tkacik, Maureen. 2002. "The Return of Grunge." *Wall Street Journal* December 11: B1, B10.

Toffler, Alvin. 1990. *Powershift: Knowledge, Wealth, and Violence at the Edge of the 21st Century*. New York: Bantam.

Tong, Rosemarie. 1989. *Feminist Thought: A Comprehensive Introduction*. Boulder, CO: Westview.

Tönnies, Ferdinand. 1988 [1887]. *Community and Society (Gemeinschaft and Gesselschaft)*. New Brunswick, NJ: Transaction.

Tonry, Michael. 1995. *Malign Neglect: Race, Crime, and Punishment in America*. New York: Oxford University Press.

Tooby, John, and Leda Cosmides. 1992. "The Psychological Foundations of Culture." Pp. 19–136 in Jerome Barkow, Lea Cosmides, and John Tooby, eds. *The Adapted Mind: Evolutionary Psychology and the Generation of Culture*. New York: Oxford University Press.

"Top 20 Countries with the Highest Number of Internet Users." 2005. Retrieved February 13, 2005 (http://www.internetworldstats.com/top20.htm).

Toronto Board of Education. 1993. *The 1991 Every Secondary Student Survey. Part II: Detailed Profiles of Toronto's Secondary School Students*. Toronto: Toronto Board of Education Research Services.

Torpey, J. 2001. "Making Whole What Has Been Smashed: Reflections on Reparations." *The Journal of Modern History* 73: 333–58.

Torrance, Judy M. 1986. *Public Violence in Canada*. Toronto: University of Toronto Press.

Tovee, M. J., S. M. Mason, J. L. Emery, S. E. McClusky, and E. M. Cohen-Tovee. 1997. "Supermodels: Stick Insects or Hourglasses?" *Lancet* 350: 1474–75.

Transport Canada. 2001. "Interprovincial Trade." Retrieved February 17, 2002 (http://www.tc.gc.ca/pol/en/report/ Truck_Corridors/Ch6E_HTM.htm).

Travers, Jeffrey, and Stanley Milgram. 1969. "An Experimental Study of the Small World Problem." *Sociometry* 32: 425–43.

Trevelyan, Laura. 2004. "Will Canada Introduce Sharia Law?" BBC News. Retrieved December 8, 2005 (http://news.bbc.co.uk/2/hi/programmes/fromour_own_correspondent/3599264.stm).

Troeltsch, Ernst. 1931 [1923]. *The Social Teaching of the Christian Churches*, Olive Wyon, trans. 2 vols. London, UK: George Allen and Unwin.

Trovato, Frank. 1998. "The Stanley Cup of Hockey and Suicide in Quebec, 1951–1992." *Social Forces* 77, 1 (September): 105–27.

Tschannen, Olivier. 1991. "The Secularization Paradigm: A Systematization." *Journal for the Scientific Study of Religion* 30: 395–415.

Tsutsui, William M. 1998. *Manufacturing Ideology: Scientific Management in Twentieth-Century Japan*. Princeton, NJ: Princeton University Press.

Tufts, Jennifer. 2000. "Public Attitudes Toward the Criminal Justice System." *Juristat* 20, 12 (December). Catalogue no. 85-002-XPE.

Tuljapurkar, Shripad, Nan Li, and Carl Boe. 2000. "A Universal Pattern of Mortality Decline in the G7 Countries." *Nature* 405: 789–92.

Tumin, M. 1953. "Some Principles of Stratification: A Critical Analysis." *American Sociological Review* 18: 387–94.

Tun, Paul. 2000. "Polls Show Canadians Not Settled on Abortion." *The Interim* August. Retrieved June 14, 2002 (http://www.lifesite.net/interim/2000/aug/09pollsshow.html).

Turkel, Ann Ruth. 1998. "All About Barbie: Distortions of a Transitional Object." *Journal of the American Academy of Psychoanalysis* 26, 1 (Spring): 165–77.

Turkle, Sherry. 1995. *Life on the Screen: Identity in the Age of the Internet*. New York: Simon & Schuster.

Turnbull, Colin M. 1961. *The Forest People*. New York: Doubleday.

Turner, Bryan S. 1986. *Citizenship and Capitalism: The Debate over Reformism*. London, UK: Allen and Unwin.

———. 1996. *The Body and Society: Explorations in Social Theory*, 2nd ed. London: Sage.

Turner, Heather A., and David Finkelhor. 1996. "Corporal Punishment as a Stressor among Youth." *Journal of Marriage and the Family* 58, 1: 155–66.

Turner, Ralph H., and Lewis M. Killian. 1987. *Collective Behavior*, 3rd ed. Englewood Cliffs, NJ: Prentice-Hall.

Twenge, Jean M. 1997. "Changes in Masculine and Feminine Traits over Time: A Meta-analysis." *Sex Roles* 36: 305–25.

U.S. Bureau of Labor Statistics. 1998. "Union Members Summary." Retrieved January 2, 2001 (http://stats.bls.gov/news.release/union2.nws.htm).

———. 1999. "Union Members Summary." Retrieved March 17, 2001 (http://stats.bls.gov/news.release/union2.nws.htm).

———. 2001. "Union Members Summary." Retrieved March 21, 2001 (http://stats.bls.gov/news.release/union2.nws.htm).

———. 2008. "Access to Historical Data for Union Membership." Retrieved January 9, 2008 (http://www.bls.gov/webapps/legacy/cpslutab1.htm).

U.S. Bureau of the Census. 2004–05. "Statistical Abstract of the United States 2004–2005." Retrieved April 3, 2005 (http://www.census.gov/prod/www/statistical-abstract-04.html).

———. 2008. "International Data Base." Retrieved January 14, 2008 (http://www.census.gov/ipc/www/idb/pyramids.html).

U.S. Department of Commerce. 1998. "Statistical Abstract of the United States: 1998." Retrieved October 8, 2000 (http://www.census.gov/prod/3/98pubs/98statab/sasec1.pdf).

U.S. Department of Commerce, National Oceanic and Atmospheric Administration. 2008. "Trends in Atmospheric Carbon Dioxide — Mauna Loa." Retrieved January 12, 2008 (http://www.esrl.noaa.gov/gmd/ccgg/trends).

U.S. Department of Justice. 1998. *Stalking and Domestic Violence: The Third Annual Report to Congress under the Violence Against Women Act*. Washington, DC: Violence Against Women Grants Office.

U.S. Department of State. 1997. "1996 Patterns of Global Terrorism Report." Retrieved June 3, 2008 (http://www.state.gov/www/global/terrorism/1996Report/1996index.html#table).

———. 2003. "Patterns of International Terrorism 2002." Retrieved June 3, 2003 (http://www.state.gov/s/ct/rls/pgtrpt/2002/pdf/ (3 June 2003).

———. 2004. "Patterns of Global Terrorism 2003." Retrieved June 2, 2006 (http://www.mipt.org/pdf/2003PoGT.pdf)

U.S. Environmental Protection Agency, Office of Air Quality Planning and Standards. 2000. "National Air Pollutant Emission Trends, 1900–1998." Retrieved August 3, 2000 (http://www.epa.gov/ttn/chief/trends98/emtrnd.html).

U.S. Information Agency. 1998–99. *The People Have Spoken: Global Views of Democracy*, 2 vols. Washington, DC: Office of Research and Media Reaction.

UNAIDS. 2007. "Aids Epidemic Update 2007." Retrieved January 12, 2008 (http://data.unaids.org/pub/EPISlides/2007/2007_epiupdate_en.pdf).

Ungar, Sheldon. 1992. "The Rise and (Relative) Decline of Global Warming as a Social Problem." *Sociological Quarterly* 33: 483–501.

———. 1995. "Social Scares and Global Warming: Beyond the Rio Convention." *Society and Natural Resources* 8: 443–56.

———. 1998. "Bringing the Issue Back In: Comparing the Marketability of the Ozone Hole and Global Warming." *Social Problems* 45: 510–27.

———. 1999. "Is Strange Weather in the Air? A Study of U.S. National Network News Coverage of Extreme Weather Events." *Climatic Change* 41: 133–50.

"Union Membership in Canada—2000." 2000. *Workplace Gazette: An Industrial Relations Quarterly* 3, 3: 68–75.

Union of International Associations. 2001. "International Organizations by Year and Type, 1909–1999 (Table 2)." *Yearbook of International Organizations*. Retrieved February 14, 2006 (http://www.uia.org/statistics/organizations/ytb299.php).

Union of International Associations. 2007. "Number of international organizations in this edition by type (2005/2006)." Retrieved December 19, 2007 (http://www.uia.be/en/stats).

United Airlines. 2003. "Flight Attendant History." Retrieved April 6, 2003 9http://www.ual.com/page/article/0,1360,3191,00.html).

United Nations. 1994. *Human Development Report 1994*. New York: Oxford University Press.

———. 1997. "Percentage of Population Living in Urban Areas in 1996 and 2030." Retrieved May 2, 2000 (http://www.undp.org/popin/wdtrends/ura/uracht1.htm).

———. 1998a. "Universal Declaration of Human Rights." Retrieved January 25, 2003 (http://www.un.org/Overview/rights.html).

———. 1998b. "World Population Growth from Year 0 to 2050." Retrieved July 3, 1999 (http://www.popin.org/pop1998/4.htm).

———. 2000. "Indicators on Income and Economic Activity." Retrieved April 28, 2000 (http://www.un.org/Depts/unsd/social/inc-eco.htm).

———. 2002. "Human Development Report 2002." New York: Oxford University Press. Retrieved April 16, 2003 (http://hdr.undp.org/reports/global/2002/en).

———. 2004a. "Human Development Report 2004." Retrieved February 1, 2005 (http://hdr.undp.org/reports/global/2004).

———. 2004b. "UNAIDS 2004 Report on the Global AIDS Epidemic 2004 (PDF version)." Retrieved June 26, 2005 (http://www.unaids.org/bangkok2004/report_pdf.html).

———. 2005. "Human Development Indicators." Retrieved April 25, 2005 (http://hdr.undp.org/reports/global/2005/pdf/HDR05_HDI.pdf).

———. 2007. "AIDS Epidemnic Update 07." Geneva. Retrieved January 16, 2008 (http://data.unaids.org/pub/EPISlides/2007/2007_epiupdate_en.pdf).

United Nations Conference on Trade and Development. 2007. *World Investment Report 2007*. Geneva. Retrieved December 19, 2007 (http://www.unctad.org/en/docs/wir2007p1_en.pdf).

United Nations Educational, Scientific and Cultural Organization. 2001. "World Culture Report 2000—Cultural Trade and Communications Trends: International Tourism." Retrieved February 6, 2003 (http://www.unesco.org/culture/worldreport/html_eng/stat2/table18.pdf).

United Nations World Tourism Organization. 2007a. "International Tourist Arrivals." Retrieved December 19, 2007 (http://unwto.org/facts/eng/pdf/historical/ITA_1950_2005.pdf).

———. 2007b. *Tourism Highlights 2007 Edition*. Madrid. Retrieved December 19, 2007 (http://unwto.org/facts/eng/pdf/highlights/highlights_07_eng_hr.pdf).

University of Texas. 2003. "Muslim Distribution." Perry-Castañeda Library Map Collection Retrieved May 7, 2003 (http://www.lib.utexas.edu/maps/world_maps/muslim_distribution.jpg).

University of Virginia. 2003. "The Oracle of Bacon at Virginia." Retrieved March 13, 2003 (http://www.cs.virginia.edu/oracle).

Unschuld, Paul. 1985. *Medicine in China*. Berkeley, CA: University of California Press.

Useem, Bert. 1998. "Breakdown Theories of Collective Action." *Annual Review of Sociology* 24: 215–38.

Valocchi, Steve. 1996. "The Emergence of the Integrationist Ideology in the Civil Rights Movement." *Social Problems* 43: 116–30.

Van de Kaa, Dirk. 1987. "Europe's Second Demographic Transition." *Population Bulletin* 42, 1: 1–58.

Van der Laan, Luc J. W., Christopher Lockey, Bradley C. Griffeth, Francine S. Frasier, Carolyn A. Wilson, David E. Onions, Bernhard J. Hering, Zhifeng Long, Edward Otto, Bruce E. Torbett, and Daniel R. Salomon. 2000. "Infection by Porcine Endogenous Retrovirus After Islet Xenotransplantation in SCID Mice." *Nature* 407: 501–04. Retrieved August 15, 2001 (http://www.nature.com/cgi-taf/DynaPage.taf?file=/nature/journal/v407/n6800/full/407501a0_fs.html).

Vanier Institute of the Family. 2000. *Profiling Canada's Families II*. Nepean, ON: Vanier Institute of the Family.

Veblen, T. 1899. "The Theory of the Leisure Class." Retrieved April 29, 2000 (http://socserv2.socsci.mcmaster.ca/~econ/ugcm/3ll3/veblen/leisure/index.html).

Vernarec, E. 2000. "Depression in the Work Force: Seeing the Cost in a Fuller Light." *Business and Health* 18, 4: 48–55.

Veugelers, John. 1997. "Social Cleavage and the Revival of Far Right Parties: The Case of France's National Front." *Acta Sociologica* 40: 31–49.

Vygotsky, Lev S. 1987. *The Collected Works of L. S. Vygotsky*, vol. 1, N. Minick, trans. New York: Plenum.

Wade, Robert, and Martin Wolf. 2002. "Are Global Poverty and Inequality Getting Worse?" *Prospect* March: 16–21.

Wald, Matthew L., and John Schwartz. 2003. "Alerts Were Lacking, NASA Shuttle Manager Says." *New York Times* July 23. Retrieved July 23, 2003 (http://www.nytimes.com).

Waldfogel, Jane. 1997. "The Effect of Children on Women's Wages." *American Sociological Review* 62: 209–17.

Wallace, James, and Jim Erickson. 1992. *Hard Drive: Bill Gates and the Making of the Microsoft Empire*. New York: John Wiley.

Wallace, M. 2004. "Crime Statistics in Canada, 2003." *Juristat: Canadian Centre for Justice Statistics* 24, 6 (July). Retrieved May 8, 2005 (http://dsp-psd.pwgsc.gc.ca/Collection-R/Statcan/85-002-XIE/0060485-002-XIE.pdf).

Wallerstein, Immanuel. 1974–89. *The Modern World-System*, 3 vols. New York: Academic Press.

Wallerstein, Judith S., Julia Lewis, and Sandra Blakeslee. 2000. *The Unexpected Legacy of Divorce: A 25 Year Landmark Study*. New York: Hyperion.

Wallich, P., and M. Mukerjee. 1996. "Regulating the Body Business." *Scientific American* 274, 3 (March): 12–3.

Wanner, R. 1999. "Expansion and Ascription: Trends in Educational Opportunity in Canada, 1920–1994." *Canadian Review of Sociology and Anthropology* 36 (August): 409–42.

Wasserman, Stanley, and Katherine Faust. 1994. *Social Network Analysis: Methods and Applications*. Cambridge: Cambridge University Press.

Watkins, S. Craig, and Rana A. Emerson. 2000. "Feminist Media Criticism and Feminist Media Practices." *Annals of the American Academy of Political and Social Science* 571: 151–66.

Watson, James D. 1968. *The Double Helix: A Personal Account of the Discovery of the Structure of DNA*. New York: Atheneum.

———. 2000. *A Passion for DNA: Genes, Genomes, and Society*. Cold Spring Harbor, NY: Cold Spring Harbor Laboratory Press.

Watson, James L., ed. 1997. *Golden Arches East: McDonald's in East Asia*. Stanford, CA: Stanford University Press.

Watts, Duncan J. 2003. *Six Degrees: The Science of a Connected Age*. New York: W. W. Norton.

Webb, Eugene J., Donald T. Campbell, Richard D. Schwartz, and Lee Sechrest. 1966. *Unobtrusive Measures: Nonreactive Research in the Social Sciences*. Chicago: Rand McNally.

Webb, Stephen D., and John Collette. 1977. "Rural–Urban Differences in the Use of Stress-Alleviating Drugs." *American Journal of Sociology* 83: 700–07.

———. 1979. "Reply to Comment on Rural–Urban Differences in the Use of Stress-Alleviating Drugs." *American Journal of Sociology* 84: 1446–52.

Weber, Max. 1946. *From Max Weber: Essays in Sociology*, rev. ed., H. Gerth and C. W. Mills, eds., and trans. New York: Oxford University Press.

———. 1947. *The Theory of Social and Economic Organization*, T. Parsons, ed., A. M. Henderson and T. Parsons, trans. New York: Free Press.

———. 1958 [1904–05]. *The Protestant Ethic and the Spirit of Capitalism*. New York: Scribner.

———. 1963 [1922]. *The Sociology of Religion*, Ephraim Fischoff, trans. Boston: Beacon Press.

———. 1964 [1949]. "'Objectivity' in Social Science and Social Policy." Pp. 49–112 in Edward A. Shils and Henry A. Finch, trans., and eds. *The Methodology of the Social Sciences*. New York: Free Press of Glencoe.

———. 1978. *Economy and Society*, Guenther Roth and Claus Wittich, eds. Berkeley, CA: University of California Press.

Weeks, Jeffrey. 2000. *Making Sexual History*. Cambridge, UK: Polity Press.

Weis, Joseph G. 1987. "Class and Crime." Pp. 71–90 in Michael Gottfredson and Travis Hirschi, eds. *Positive Criminology*. Beverly Hills, CA: Sage.

Weisbrot, Mark, and Dean Baker. 2002. "The Relative Impact of Trade Liberalization on Developing Countries." Center for Economic and Policy Research, 11 June. Washington, DC. Retrieved February 10, 2003 (http://www.cepr.net/relative_impact_of_trade_liberal.htm).

Weisbrot, Mark, Dean Baker, Egor Kraev, and Judy Chen. 2001. "The Scorecard on Globalization, 1980–2000." Center for Economic and Policy Research. Washington, DC. Retrieved February 10, 2003 (http://www.cepr.net/globalization/scorecard_on_globalization.htm).

Weissman, M. 1992. "The Changing Rate of Major Depression: Cross-National Comparisons." *Journal of the American Medical Association* 268, 21: 3098–105.

Welch, Michael. 1997. "Violence Against Women by Professional Football Players: A Gender Analysis of Hypermasculinity, Positional Status, Narcissism, and Entitlement." *Journal of Sport and Social Issues* 21: 392–411.

Weller, Jack M., and E. L. Quarantelli. 1973. "Neglected Characteristics of Collective Behavior." *American Journal of Sociology* 79: 665–85.

Wellman, Barry. 1979. "The Community Question: The Intimate Networks of East Yorkers." *American Journal of Sociology* 84: 201–31.

Wellman, Barry, and Stephen Berkowitz, eds. 1997. *Social Structures: A Network Approach*, updated ed. Greenwich, CT: JAI Press.

Wellman, Barry, Peter J. Carrington, and Alan Hall. 1997. "Networks as Personal Communities." Pp.130–184 in Barry Wellman and S. D. Berkowitz, eds. *Social Structures: A Network Approach*, updated ed. Greenwich, CT: JAI Press.

Wellman, Barry, Janet Salaff, Dimitrina Dimitrova, Laura Garton, Milena Gulia, and Caroline Haythornthwaite. 1996. "Computer Networks as Social Networks: Collaborative Work, Telework, and Virtual Community." *Annual Review of Sociology* 22: 213–38.

Wells, H. G. 1927. "The Country of the Blind." Pp. 123–46 in *Selected Short Stories*. Harmondsworth, UK: Penguin. Retrieved April 24, 2003 (http://www.fantasticfiction.co.uk/etexts/y3800.htm).

Welsh, Sandy. 1999. "Gender and Sexual Harassment." *Annual Review of Sociology* 25: 169–90.

West, Candace, and Don Zimmerman. 1987. "Doing Gender." *Gender and Society* 1: 125–51.

Westen, Tracy. 1998. "Can Technology Save Democracy?" *National Civic Review* 87: 47–56.

Wetzel, Janice Wood. 2001. "Human Rights in the 20th Century: Weren't Gays and Lesbians Human?" Pp. 15–31 in Mary E. Swigonski and Robin S. Mama, eds. *From Hate Crimes to Human Rights: A Tribute to Matthew Shepard.* New York: Haworth Press.

Wheeler, Stanton. 1961. "Socialization in Correctional Communities." *American Sociological Review* 26: 697–712.

Whitaker, Reg. 1987. *Double Standard.* Toronto: Lester and Orpen Dennys.

White, Lynn K., Alan Booth, and John N. Edwards. 1986. "Children and Marital Happiness." *Journal of Families Issues* 7, 2: 131–47.

Whitefield, S., and G. Evans. 1994. "The Russian Election of 1993: Public Opinion and the Transition Experience." *Post-Soviet Affairs* 10: 38–60.

Whittington, L. 1999. *The Banks: The Ongoing Battle for Control of Canada's Richest Business.* Toronto: Stoddart.

Whorf, Benjamin Lee. 1956. *Language, Thought, and Reality,* John B. Carroll, ed. Cambridge, MA: MIT Press.

"Why Britney Spears Matters." 2001. *The Laughing Medusa.* Retrieved April 18, 2006 (http://www.gwu.edu/ ~medusa/2001/britney.html).

Whyte, W. F. 1981 [1943]. *Street Corner Society: The Social Structure of an Italian Slum,* 3rd ed. Chicago: University of Chicago Press.

Wilder, D. A. 1990. "Some Determinants of the Persuasive Power of Ingroups and Outgroups: Organization of Information and Attribution of Independence." *Journal of Personality and Social Psychology* 59: 1202–213.

Wilensky, Harold L. 1967. *Organizational Intelligence: Knowledge and Policy in Government and Industry.* New York: Basic Books.

———. 1997. "Social Science and the Public Agenda: Reflections on the Relation of Knowledge to Policy in the United States and Abroad." *Journal of Health Politics, Policy and Law* 22: 1241–65.

Wiley College. 2007 "History of Wiley College." Retrieved March 7, 2008 (http://www.wileyc.edu/wly_content/ departments/administrative/history.php).

Wilkinson, Richard G. 1996. *Unhealthy Societies: The Afflictions of Inequality.* London: Routledge.

Wilkinson, Richard, and Michael Marmot, eds. 2003. *Social Determinants of Health: The Solid Facts.* Copenhagen: World Health Organization Regional Office for Europe.

Willardt, Kenneth. 2000. "The Gaze He'll Go Gaga For." *Cosmopolitan* April: 232–37.

Williams, David R., and Chiquita Collins. 1995. "U.S. Socioeconomic and Racial Differences in Health: Patterns and Explanations." *Annual Review of Sociology* 21: 349–86.

———. 1999. "U.S. Socioeconomic and Racial Differences in Health: Patterns, and Explanations." Pp. 349–76 in Kathy Charmaz and Debora A. Paterniti, eds. *Health, Illness, and Healing: Society, Social Context, and Self.* Los Angeles: Roxbury Publishing Co.

Willis, Paul. 1984 [1977]. *Learning to Labour: How Working-Class Kids Get Working-Class Jobs.* New York: Columbia University Press.

Wilson, Brian. 2002. "The Canadian Rave Scene and Five Theses on Youth Resistance." *Canadian Journal of Sociology* 27: 373–412.

Wilson, Edward O. 1975. *Sociobiology: The New Synthesis.* Cambridge, MA: Belknap Press of the Harvard University Press.

Winch, Donald. 1987. *Malthus.* Oxford, UK: Oxford University Press.

Winton, R. 2005. "L.A. Home Turf for Hundreds of Neighborhood Criminal Groups. Los Angeles Community Policing." Retrieved May 13, 2005 (http://www.lacp.org/2005-Articles-Main/ LAGangsInNeighborhoods.html).

Wired. 1999. December.

Wirth, Louis. 1938. "Urbanism as a Way of Life." *American Journal of Sociology* 44: 1–24.

Wolf, D. L. 1992. *Factory Daughters: Gender, Household Dynamics, and Rural Industrialization in Java.* Berkeley, CA: University of California Press.

Wolf, Naomi. 1997. *Promiscuities: The Secret Struggle for Womanhood.* New York: Vintage.

Wolff, Edward N. 1996. *Top Heavy: The Increasing Inequality of Wealth in America and What Can Be Done About It,* expanded ed. New York: New Press.

"Woman Soldier in Abuse Spotlight." 2004. *BBC News World Edition* May 7. Retrieved March 3, 2005 (http://news.bbc.co.uk/2/hi/americas/3691753.stm).

"Women in National Parliaments." 2008. Retrieved November 1, 2008 (http://www.ipu.org/wmn-e/ classif.htm).

Wong, L., and M. Ng. 1998. "Chinese Immigrant Entrepreneurs in Vancouver: A Case Study of Ethnic Business Development." *Canadian Ethnic Studies* 30: 64–85.

Wood, Julia. 1999. *Everyday Encounters: An Introduction to Interpersonal Communication,* 2nd ed. Belmont, CA: Wadsworth.

Wood, W., F. Y. Wong, and J. G. Chachere. 1991. "Effects of Media Violence on Viewers' Aggression in Unconstrained Social Interaction." *Psychological Bulletin* 109: 371–83.

Woodbury, Anthony. 2003. "Endangered Languages." Linguistic Society of America. Retrieved July 19, 2003 (http://www.lsadc.org/web2/endangeredlgs.htm).

Woodrow Federal Reserve Bank of Minneapolis. 2000. "What's a Dollar Worth?" Retrieved October 8, 2000 (http://woodrow.mpls.frb.fed.us/economy/calc/cpihome.html).

Wordsworth, Araminta. 2000. "Family Planning Officials Drown Baby in Rice Paddy." *National Post* August 25: A10.

Workplace Information Directorate. 1996. *Special Tabulation of Strikes Statistics for 1986–95*. Ottawa: Human Resources Development Canada.

"Work-Related Stress: A Condition Felt 'Round the World.'" 1995. *HR Focus* 72, 4 (April): 17.

World Bank. 1999. "GNP Per Capita 1997, Atlas Method and PPP." Retrieved July 10, 1999 (http://www.worldbank.org/data/databytopic/GNPPC97.pdf).

World Conservation Union. 2004. "Species Extinction." Retrieved January 12, 2008 (http://www.iucn.org/themes/Ssc/red_list_2004/Extinction_media_brief_2004.pdf).

World Health Organization. 2000. "WHO Terminology Information System." Retrieved May 2, 2000 (http://www.who.int/terminology/ter/wt001.html#health).

———. 2001. "Female Genital Mutilation." Retrieved January 20, 2003 (http://www.who.int/frh-whd/FGM).

———. 2003. "Cumulative Number of Reported Probable Cases." Retrieved June 16, 2003 (http://www.who.int/csr/sars/country/2003_06_16/en).

———. 2007. "Core Health Indicators." Retrieved January 16, 2008 (http://www.who.int/whosis/database/core/core_select.cfm).

———. 2008. "Health Topic Page." Retrieved January 13, 2008 (http://www.who.int/infobase/report.aspx?rid=112&ind=BMI&goButton=Go).

World Values Survey. 2003. Machine readable data set. Ann Arbor, MI: Inter-University Consortium for Political and Social Research.

Worthington, Peter. 2002. "Aspers Get Press in U.S.: Washington Post Weighs in on 'Free-Speech' Debate." *Toronto Sun* January 28. Retrieved May 17, 2002 (http://www.friendscb.org/articles/TorontoSun/torsun020128.htm).

Wright, Charles Robert. 1975. *Mass Communication: A Sociological Perspective*. New York: Random House.

Wu, Zheng. 2000. *Cohabitation: An Alternative Form of Family Living*. Don Mills, ON: Oxford University Press.

Wu, Zheng, and Margaret J. Penning. 1997. "Marital Instability after Midlife." *Journal of Family Issues* 18, 5: 459–78.

Wynne, Robert E. 1996. "American Labor Leaders and the Vancouver Anti-Oriental Riot." *Pacific Northwest Quarterly* 86: 172–79. Retrieved March 15, 2001 (http://www.vcn.bc.ca/acww/html/body_riot.html).

X, Malcolm. 1965. *The Autobiography of Malcolm X*. New York: Grove.

Yamane, David. 1997. "Secularization on Trial: In Defense of a Neosecularization Paradigm." *Journal for the Scientific Study of Religion* 36: 109–22.

Yancey, W. L, E. P. Ericksen, and G. H. Leon. 1979. "Emergent Ethnicity: A Review and Reformulation." *American Sociological Review* 41: 391–403.

Yates, Gayle Graham, ed. 1985. *Harriet Martineau on Women*. New Brunswick, NJ: Rutgers University Press.

Yook, Soon-Hyung, Hawoong Jeong, and Albert-László Barabási. 2001. "Modeling the Internet's Large-Scale Topology." Department of Physics, University of Notre Dame. Retrieved May 23, 2003 (http://arxiv.org/PS_cache/cond-mat/pdf/0107/0107417pdf).

York, Geoffrey. 2006. "Asian Trade Bloc Would Rival NAFTA, EU." *Globe and Mail* August 24: B1, B8.

Zakaria, Fareed. 1997. "The Rise of Illiberal Democracy." *Foreign Affairs* 76, 6: 22–43.

Zald, Meyer N., and John D. McCarthy. 1979. *The Dynamics of Social Movements*. Cambridge, MA: Winthrop.

Zaslavsky, Victor, and Robert J. Brym. 1978. "The Functions of Elections in the USSR." *Soviet Studies* 30: 62–71.

———. 1983. *Soviet Jewish Emigration and Soviet Nationality Policy*. London: Macmillan.

Zelikow, Philip, and John Brennan. 2005 "Remarks on Release of 'Country Reports on Terrorism' for 2004." U.S. Department of State. Retrieved January 12, 2008 (http://www.state.gov/s/ct/rls/rm/45279.htm).

Zijderveld, Anton C. 1983. "The Sociology of Humour and Laughter." *Current Sociology* 31, 3: 1–59.

Zimbardo, Philip G. 1972. "Pathology of Imprisonment." *Society* 9, 6: 4–8.

Zimmermann, Francis. 1987 [1982]. *The Jungle and the Aroma of Meats: An Ecological Theme in Hindu Medicine*, Janet Lloyd, trans. Berkeley, CA: University of California Press.

Zimring, Franklin E., and Gordon Hawkins. 1995. *Incapacitation: Penal Confinement and the Restraint of Crime*. New York: Oxford University Press.

Zinsser, Hans. 1935. *Rats, Lice and History*. Boston: Little, Brown.

Zola, Irving Kenneth. 1982. *Missing Pieces: A Chronicle of Living with a Disability*. Philadelphia: Temple University Press.

Zoutman, D. E., B. D. Ford, E. Bryce, M. Gourdeau, G. Hebert, E. Henderson, S. Paton, Canadian Hospital Epidemiology Committee, Canadian Nosocomial Infection Surveillance Program, Health Canada. 2003. "The State of Infection Surveillance and Control in Canadian Acute Care Hospitals." *American Journal of Infection Control* 31, 5: 266–73.

Zuboff, S. 1988. *In the Age of the Smart Machine: The Future of Work and Power*. New York: Basic Books.

Zukin, Sharon. 1980. "A Decade of the New Urban Sociology." *Theory and Society* 9: 539–74.

Zurcher, Louis A., and David A. Snow. 1981. "Collective Behavior and Social Movements." Pp. 447–82 in Morris Rosenberg and Ralph Turner, eds. *Social Psychology: Sociological Perspectives*. New York: Basic Books.

Credits and Acknowledgments

Page v (top): Courtesy Robert J. Brym; **Page v (middle):** Courtesy John Lie; **Page v (bottom):** Courtesy Steve Rytina.

Part Opener

Pages 1, 67, 179, 363, 567: José Luis Gutiérrez/iStockphoto.

Chapter Opener

Pages 2, 33, 68, 99, 125, 150, 180, 212, 247, 274, 305, 340, 364, 396, 427, 464, 492, 518, 541, 568, 591, 22–1: José Luis Gutiérrez/iStockphoto.

Chapter 1

Page 3: Lisa M. Ripperton; **Page 5:** Courtesy of A.C. Fine Art, Nova Scotia. Photographer: James Chambers; **Page 7:** Photos.com; **Page 8:** CP Picture Archive/Ryan Remiorz; **Page 11:** 20th Century Fox/Dreamworks/The Kobal Collection; **Page 12:** Robert Fludd, Ultriusque Cosmi Maioris Scilicet et Minoris Metaphysica, Physica Atqve Technica Historia. 1617–19. (Oppenheim, Germany. Johan-Theodori de Bry.) (Black and white print of the chain of being). By permission of the Houghton Library, Harvard University.; **Page 13:** Paul Almasy/Corbis; **Page 14 (top):** Musee du Louvre, Paris/Giraudon, Paris/SuperStock; **Page 14 (bottom):** The Detroit Institute of Arts, USA/Gift of Edsel B. Ford/The Bridgeman Art Library; **Page 16:** Photo Courtesy of Ed Clark; **Page 18:** Carleton University Archives; **Page 19:** American Sociological Association; **Page 20:** Margrit Eichler; **Page 22 (right):** David Bergman/Corbis; **Page 22 (left):** Reuters NewMedia Inc./Corbis.

Chapter 2

Page 34: M.C. Escher's "Relativity" © 2008 The M.C. Escher Company-Holland. All rights reserved. www.mcescher.com; **Page 35:** Blood letting, from 'ractatus de Pestilencia' (vellum), Albik, M. (15th century)/Private Collection, Archives Charmet/The Bridgeman Art Library; **Page 36:** Bettmann/Corbis; **Page 37:** Courtesy of Carol Wainio, London, Ontario, Canada; **Page 45:** Index Stock/James Frank; **Page 47:** Getty Images/Stockbyte Silver; **Page 48:** CP Picture Archive/Ken Frayer; **Page 50:** Antonio Rosario/The Image Bank/Getty Images; **Page 51:** Bob Marshak/The Everett Collection; **Page 53:** Index Stock/Brad Bartholomew; **Page 57:** Courtesy of Tom Campbell; **Page 60:** Ken Regan/TWENTIETH CENTURY FOX/Bureau L.A.Collections/Corbis.

Chapter 3

Page 69: CP Picture Archive/Ron Frehm; **Page 70:** Index Stock/Frank Chmura; **Page 73:** *The National Post*, Toronto, Canada, 2000. Gary Clement; **Page 76:** TM & © 20th Century Fox. All rights reserved.

Courtesy Everett Collection; **Page 78:** Rob Elliott/AFP/Getty Images; **Page 79:** CP PHOTO/*Toronto Star*—Ron Bull; **Page 83:** Courtesy of Kelloggs; **Page 87:** StockXpert; **Page 90 (bottom):** SuperStock; **Page 91:** © INTERFOTO Pressebildagentur/Alamy; **Page 92:** Bill Aron/PhotoEdit Inc.; **Page 94 (top):** CP Picture Archive/Nick Ut; **Page 94 (bottom):** Jonathan Twingley.

Chapter 4

Page 100: Mary Evans Picture Library; **Page 101:** Corbis/Magma; **Page 103:** Index Stock/Key Color; **Page 105:** Piotr Sikora/Photonica/Getty Images; **Page 107:** Courtesy of Carol Gilligan. Photo by Jerry Bauer; **Page 108:** Spencer Grant/PhotoEdit; **Page 109:** Photos.com; **Page 113:** © ANNEBICQUE BERNARD/CORBIS SYGMA; **Page 114:** Jonathan Blair/Corbis; **Page 115:** CP Picture Archive/Tony Gutierrez; **Page 119:** © New Line/courtesy Everett Collection; **Page 121:** CP Picture Archive/Mike Ridewood.

Chapter 5

Page 126: Jonathan Blair/Corbis; **Page 128:** The Everett Collection; **Page 131:** AP Photo/Katina Revels; **Page 132:** D. Le Strat/Sygma/Corbis; **Page 134:** SuperStock; **Page 138:** Castle Rock/Fortis/The Kobal Collection; **Page 141:** Dreamstime; **Page 142 (five images):** Courtesy of Robert J. Brym; **Page 147:** Charles & Josette Lenars/Corbis.

Chapter 6

Page 151: AFP/Getty Images; **Page 152:** The Everett Collection; **Page 155:** Getty Images; **Page 156:** Reuters NewMedia Inc./Corbis; **Page 157:** The Everett Collection; **Page 160:** Brian Leng/Corbis; **Page 162:** CP PHOTO/Adrian Wyld; **Page 163:** JPL/NASA; **Page 167:** © Photodisc/SuperStock; **Page 171:** © Corel; **Page 172:** Ms 65/1284 f.6v June: haymaking (vellum) (for facsimile copy see 65831), Limbourg Brothers (fl.1400-1416)/Musee Conde, Chantilly, France, Giraudon/The Bridgeman Art Library International; **Page 174:** Digital Art/Corbis; **Page 175:** CP PHOTO/Ryan Remiorz.

Chapter 7

Page 181: The Everett Collection; **Page 181:** CP Picture Archive/Frank Gunn; **Page 183:** ©WarnerBros/EverettCollection; **Page 185:** National Library of Medicine, Washington, DC; **Page 186:** CP Picture Archive/Chuck Stoody; **Page 187:** Weegee (Arthur Fellig)/ICP/Getty Images; **Page 196:** The Everett Collection; **Page 199:** Craig Blankenhorn/© HBO/Courtesy Everett Collection; **Page 203:** New York Public Library; **Page 204:** CP Picture Archive/Fred Chartrand; **Page 206:** CP PHOTO/Frank Gunn.

Chapter 8

Page 213: Christie's Images/Corbis; **Page 216:** Photos.com; **Page 217:** CP Picture Archive/Tibor Kolley; **Page 228 (both):** *Saturday Night.* June 3, 2000. "The War Next Door." Page 48. Story and Photographs by Ami Vitale; **Page 236 (left):** Agriculture and Agri-Food Canada; **Page 236 (right):** BSIP Agency/Index Stock Imagery; **Page 238 (left):** Lorne Bridgeman; **Page 238 (right):** CP Picture Archive/Stan Behal; **Page 240:** ©Walt Disney/Courtesy Everett Collection.

Chapter 9

Page 248 (top): Jeremy Horne/Getty Images; **Page 248 (bottom left):** Chuck Savage/Corbis; **Page 248 (bottom right):** Ariel Skelley/Corbis; **Page 253:** John Van Hasselt/Corbis Sygma; **Page 259:** Photo by Miro Cernetig, *Globe & Mail,* Toronto, Canada; **Page 263:** Weidenfeld and Nicolson Archives; **Page 265:** Brand X Pictures/Jupiter Images; **Page 270:** © Warner Bros./Everett Collection.

Chapter 10

Page 275: CP Picture Archive/Frank Gunn; **Page 276:** Source; Samuel Morton's Crania Americana (1839); **Page 278:** © Lions Gate/courtesy Everett Collection; **Page 279:** CP Picture Archive/Andrew Vaughan; **Page 286:** National Archives of Canada/C-030939; **Page 287:** Bettmann/Corbis; **Page 289 (both):** Saskatchewan Archives Board, R-82239[1] and R-82239[2]; **Page 292:** *Upper Canada Gazette,* February 10, 1806; **Page 293:** ©Eyewire/Getty Images; **Page 294:** National Archives of Canada/C149236; **Page 295:** Courtesy of the Pier 21 Society; **Page 296:** Canadian Pacific Airline/National Archives of Canada/C-45080.

Chapter 11

Page 306: CP PHOTO/Winnipeg Free Press; **Page 310:** M. ou Me. Desjeux, Bernard/CORBIS; **Page 312 (bottom):** CP Photo Archive/AP Photo/Jim Mone; **Page 314:** Myrleen Cate/Index Stock; **Page 316 (top left & right):** Courtesy of the White Rock Beverage Company; **Page 316 (bottom):** Lou Chardonnay/Corbis; **Page 320:** © Focus Films/Everett Collection; **Page 321:** CP Picture Archive/David Lucas; **Page 330:** Courtesy of the Canadian Federation of Students; **Page 335:** CP Picture Archive/Jonathan Hayward.

Chapter 12

Page 341: ©FXNetworks/Courtesy Everett Collection; **Page 344:** Bridgeman Art Library, London/SuperStock; **Page 346:** Sinibaldi/Corbis; **Page 347:** Lightscapes Photography, Inc./Corbis; **Page 349:** 20th Century Fox/Conundrument/The Kobal Collection/Watson, Glenn; **Page 351:** Erica Lansner/Getty Images; **Page 356:** ©Corel; **Page 359:** CP Photo Archive/Chuck Stoody.

Chapter 13

Page 366: *Wired.* December 1999. Photograph by James Porto. Reprinted by permission of Wired, Condé Nast Publications, Inc.; **Page 367:** CP Picture Archive/Andrew Vaughn; **Page 370:** The Everett Collection; **Page 374 (left):** Lanny Ziering/Jupiter Images; **Page 374 (right):** LWA- JDC/CORBIS; **Page 381:** Meri Simon. From "Getting a Life Offline," Jeff Bliss. *Financial Post.* June 29, 2000. C3. © San Jose Mercury News; **Page 384:** Courtesy Big Picture Media Corporation; **Page 392:** CP Picture Archive/Jeff McIntosh.

Chapter 14

Page 397: George Bush Presidential Library; **Page 399:** Miramax/Courtesy Everett Collection; **Page 400 (top left):** Archive Iconografico, S.S./Corbis; **Page 400 (bottom left):** SuperStock; Page 400 (right): THE CANADIAN PRESS/Tom Hanson; **Page 403:** CP Picture Archive/Tom Hanson; **Page 408:** CP Picture Archive/Michel Euler; **Page 412:** Peter Turnley/CORBIS; **Page 414:** William Vanderson/Hulton Archive/Getty Images; **Page 420:** Jon Jones/Sygma/Corbis.

Chapter 15

Page 428: ShutterStock/Losevsky Pavel; **Page 429:** 20th Century Fox/Courtesy Everett Collection; **Page 433:** PeterJohnson/Corbis; **Page 435:** Courtesy of the artist and Bau-Xi Gallery, Toronto ON, Canada; **Page 440:** The Everett Collection; **Page 446:** SuperStock; **Page 448:** Jacques M. Chenet/Corbis; **Page 454:** CP Picture Archive/Clement Allard; **Page 456:** ©Photodisc; **Page 460:** Jonathan Blair/Corbis.

Chapter 16

Page 465: Stockbyte/Getty; **Page 467:** CP Photo/Jeff McIntosh; **Page 468:** CP PHOTO/*Globe and Mail*/Boris Spremo; **Page 471:** ©Bettmann/Corbis/Magma; **Page 473:** ©Warner Bros./courtesy Everett Collection; **Page 479:** ©Bill Varie/Corbis/Magma; **Page 485:** The Lowe Art Museum, The University of Miami/SuperStock; **Page 487:** Omni Photo Communications Inc./Index Stock.

Chapter 17

Page 493: Brian Summers/First Light; **Page 500:** CP Picture Archive/Jacques Boissinot; **Page 504:** ©Eyewire/Getty Images; **Page 507:** PhotoDisk/Getty Images; **Page 509:** Courtesy Native Child Family Services of Toronto; **Page 511:** Everett Collection.

Chapter 18

Page 519 (top): The Everett Collection; **Page 519 (bottom):** Bettmann/CORBIS; **Page 522 (top):** Vintage Images/Jupiter Images; **Page 522 (bottom):** CP Picture Archive/National Archives; **Page 523:** The Pierpont Morgan Library/Art Resources, New York; **Page 524:** Reed Kaestner/Corbis/Magma; **Page 528:** CP Photo/*Saskatoon Star Phoenix*—Greg Pender; **Page 529:** Sony Pictures Classics/Courtesy Everett Collection; **Page 533:** The Everett Collection; **Page 536:** Associated Press, Melbourne Age/AP/Wide World Photos.

Chapter 19

Page 542: Museo del Prado, Madrid, Spain/Giraudon, Paris/SuperStock; **Page 544:** CP Picture Archive/Associated Press AP; **Page 546:** Mike Hutchings/Reuters/Corbis; **Page 548:** Mark Richards/PhotoEdit; **Page 552:** © Lions Gate/Courtesy Everett Collection; **Page 556:** Ted Streshinsky/Corbis/Magma; **Page 563:** Francisco Cruz/SuperStock.

Chapter 20

Page 569: Donald Kelin/SuperStock; **Page 572 (top):** The Purcell Group/Corbis; **Page 572 (bottom):** Scala/Art Resource, NY; **Page 579 (top):** Murry Sill/Index Stock Imagery; **Page 579 (bottom):** © Jupiter Images/Agence Images/Alamy; **Page 583:** Bob Brooks/Nova Scotia Archives and Records Management; **Page 585:** The Everett Collection.

Chapter 21

Page 592: Jacob Yuri Wackerhausen/Shutterstock; **Page 594:** Rare Books and Special Collections, University of British Columbia Library, Photo XXXVI-17; **Page 600:** CP Picture Archive/Maclean's Photo/Phill Snel; **Page 604:** National Archives of Canada/PA163001;

Page 605: 20th Century Fox/Courtesy Everett Collection; **Page 606:** CP Photo/Adrian Wyld; **Page 609:** Bibliotheque Nationale de France; **Page 612 (top):** CP Photo/Ryan Remiorz; **Page 612 (bottom):** CP PHOTO/Frank Gunn.

Chapter 22

Page 22–2 (top): Everett/CPL Archives; **Page 22–2 (bottom):** Bettmann/Corbis; **Page 22–3:** The Everett Collection; **Page 22–4:** *Ottawa Citizen*/Grant Collins; **Page 22–5:** Gary Braasch/Corbis; **Page 22–7:** U.S. Army Photos; **Page 22–9:** SuperStock; **Page 22–13:** The Everett Collection; **Page 22–17:** CP Picture Archive/Ray Fahey; **Page 22–19:** Balkis Press/ABACAPRESS.COM; **Page 22–22:** CALVIN AND HOBBES © 1990 Watterson. Dist. By UNIVERSAL PRESS SYNDICATE. Reprinted with permission. All rights reserved.

INDEX